Springer Proceedings in Business and Economics

Springer Proceedings in Business and Economics brings the most current research presented at conferences and workshops to a global readership. The series features volumes (in electronic and print formats) of selected contributions from conferences in all areas of economics, business, management, and finance. In addition to an overall evaluation by the publisher of the topical interest, scientific quality, and timeliness of each volume, each contribution is refereed to standards comparable to those of leading journals, resulting in authoritative contributions to the respective fields. Springer's production and distribution infrastructure ensures rapid publication and wide circulation of the latest developments in the most compelling and promising areas of research today.

The editorial development of volumes may be managed using Springer Nature's innovative EquinOCS, a proven online conference proceedings submission, management and review system. This system is designed to ensure an efficient timeline for your publication, making Springer Proceedings in Business and Economics the premier series to publish your workshop or conference volume.

This book series is indexed in SCOPUS.

Tankiso Moloi
Editor

Impacting Society Positively Through Technology in Accounting and Business Processes

Proceedings of the 5th International Conference of Accounting and Business iCAB, Sun City 2024

Volume I

Springer

Editor
Tankiso Moloi
University of Johannesburg
Johannesburg, South Africa

ISSN 2198-7246 ISSN 2198-7254 (electronic)
Springer Proceedings in Business and Economics
ISBN 978-3-031-84887-2 ISBN 978-3-031-84885-8 (eBook)
https://doi.org/10.1007/978-3-031-84885-8

This Springer imprint is published by the registered company Springer Nature Switzerland AG
The registered company address is: Gewerbestrasse 11, 6330 Cham, Switzerland

Letter from the Editor

Dear *i*CAB 2024 Delegate,

I greet all of you from Johannesburg. As the editor, it is my deepest gratitude to present to you, the conference delegates, the 2024 International Conference of Accounting, and Business conference proceedings.

For the first time in history, *i*CAB was held at Sun City. We successfully delivered the 2024 iteration of the iCAB conference. The papers presented in these proceedings have passed through a stringent peer review process, and I am confident that it is only quality papers included in these proceedings. Our review policy is a **double-blind review process,** and this was stringently applied.

We look forward to having you and your colleagues at the 2024 conference in Cape Town, South Africa.

Tankiso Moloi

Peer Review Statement

Our review policy is a **double-blind review process,** and this was stringently applied. Our process is that the full-length manuscript is anonymised and sent to two or more independent reviewers. The peer reviewers are never disclosed to the authors as anonymity in the review process is crucial as it enables reviewers to freely express their opinions. Sometimes, there are two conflicting reports, and if this is the case, a third independent reviewer is commissioned.

Once the process is complete, anonymous reports are shared with the author. They are asked to respond to the reviews detailing how they will improve the manuscript and what suggestions from the reviewers they accept or reject. In this regard, the approval of the manuscript is subject to a developmental editing process, after which re-submitting to one or both reviewers may be required.

International Steering Committee

Prof T. Moloi	University of Johannesburg, South Africa
Prof Z. Blabler	Salem, State University, United States of America
Prof A. Salman	American University in the Emirates, United Arab Emirates
Prof M. Mangena	University of Nottingham, United Kingdom
Prof S. Romprasert	Srinakharinwirot University, Thailand
Dr. D. Kiriman	University of Texas at El Paso, United States of America
Prof A. Hess	Pontificia Universidade Catolica de Sao Paulo, Brazil
Prof R. Salawu	Obafemi Awolowo University, Nigeria
Prof B. Marx	University of Johannesburg, South Africa
Prof M. Adelowotan	University of Johannesburg, South Africa
Prof B. George	Alcorn State University, United States of America
Prof C. Campos	Pontificia Universidade Catolica de Sao Paulo, Brazil
Dr. B. Shima	Canadian Institute of Technology, Albania
Prof O. R. Uwuigbe	Covenant University, Nigeria
Prof M. Sibanda	University of KwaZulu Natal, South Africa
Prof A. Sibindi	University of South Africa, South Africa
Prof O. Olugbara,	Durban University of Technology, South Africa
Dr. M. Olarewaju,	Coventry University, United Kingdom
Prof M. Mohd Ali	Universiti Teknologi MARA, Malaysia
Prof Youqin Pan	University of Johannesburg, South Africa
Dr. Lethiwe Nzama-Sithole	University of Johannesburg, South Africa
Prof Reon Matemane	University of Pretoria
Prof Sezer B. Kahyaoğlu	Kyrgyz-Turkish Manas University, Turkey

List of Reviewers

No.	Reviewer	Affiliation
1	Dr. L. Nzama-Sthole	University of Johannesburg, South Africa
2	Dr. F. Y. Mpofu	University of Johannesburg, South Africa
3	Prof. R. Matemane	University of Pretoria, South Africa
4	Dr. Trust Chireka	Walter Sisulu University, South Africa
5	Dr. L. Grebe	University of South Africa, South Africa
5	Dr. Inneh Godwin	Obafemi Awolowo University, Nigeria
6	Prof Andries. P. Swanepoel	University of South Africa, South Africa
7	Dr. Mufaro Dzingirai	Midlands State University, Zimbabwe
8	Dr. K. N. Motubatse	Tshwane University of Science and Technology
9	Dr. T. Ololade	University of Johannesburg, South Africa
10	Prof. Freddy Munzhelele	University of Venda, South Africa
11	Dr. Lebogang Mospye-Semenya	University of Johannesburg—JBS, South Africa
12	Prof. Ayoola John	Obafemi Awolowo University, Nigeria
13	Dr. Sylvester Senyo Horvey	University of the Witwatersrand, South Africa
14	Prof Herman Albertus Viviers	North-West University, South Africa
15	Prof. Michael Adelowotan	University of Johannesburg, South Africa
16	Dr Modiha Pulane	FNB Independent Researcher, South Africa
17	Dr Adesanmi Adegbayibi	Adekunle Ajasin University, Nigeria
18	Prof Zlatinka N Blaber	Salem State University, USA
19	Dr. Varaidzo Denhere	University of Johannesburg, South Africa
20	Dr. Dolapo Sule	University of Johannesburg, South Africa
21	Prof Sezer B. Kahyaoglu	Kyrgyz-Turkish Manas University, Turkey
22	Dr. Ayanda Sibiya	University of Johannesburg, South Africa
23	Prof Lungile Ntsalaze	University of Johannesburg, South Africa
24	Dr. Letebele Mphahlele	University of Johannesburg, South Africa
25	Prof Tunde Lawal	Bowen University, Nigeria
26	Dr. Gold Kafilah Lola	University of Johannesburg

Contribution of Individual Universities in these Proceedings

Paper No.	Number of authors	Universities	Points contribution
P02-24	Three	University of Johannesburg	0.17
		University of Johannesburg	0.17
		University of Johannesburg	0.17
P03-24	Three	University of Johannesburg	0.17
		University of Johannesburg	0.17
		University of Johannesburg	0.17
P04-24	Two	University of the Witwatersrand	0.25
		University of the Witwatersrand	0.25
P08-24	Two	University of Johannesburg	0.25
		University of Johannesburg	0.25
P09-24	Two	University of Johannesburg	0.25
		University of Johannesburg	0.25
P10-24	Two	University of Johannesburg	0.25
		University of Johannesburg	0.25
P12-24	Three	Accra Technical University	0.17
		Prince Mohammed Bin Fahd University, Saudi Arabia	0.17
		Accra Technical University	0.17
P13-24	Two	Federal College of Education, Technical, Nigeria	0.25
		University of Johannesburg	0.25
P14-24	Four	University of the Witwatersrand	0.125
		University of the Witwatersrand	0.125
		University of the Witwatersrand	0.125
		University of the Witwatersrand	0.125
P15-24	One	University of the Free State	
P16-24	Two	University of Johannesburg	0.25
		University of Johannesburg	0.25
P17-24	One	University of Johannesburg	0.50

Paper No.	Number of authors	Universities	Points contribution
P18-24	Three	University of Johannesburg	0.17
		University of Johannesburg	0.17
		University of Johannesburg	0.17
P19-24	Three	University of Johannesburg	0.17
		University of Johannesburg	0.17
		University of Johannesburg	0.17
P20-24	Three	National School of Government	0.17
		National School of Government	0.17
		National School of Government	0.17
P21-24	Two	University of Free State	0.25
		University of Free State	0.25
P24-24	Two	University of Johannesburg	0.25
		University of Johannesburg	0.25
P25-24	One	Midlands State University	0.50
P28-24	Four	North-West University	0.125
		North-West University	0.125
		North-West University	0.125
		Vaal University of Technology	0.125
P29-24	Three	University of Johannesburg	0.17
		University of Johannesburg	0.17
		University of Johannesburg	0.17
P30-24	Two	University of KwaZulu Natal	0.25
		University of KwaZulu Natal	0.25
P31-24	One	University of Dar-es-Salaam Business School	0.50
P32-24	Three	Cape Peninsula University of Technology	0.17
		Cape Peninsula University of Technology	0.17
		Cape Peninsula University of Technology	0.17
P33-24	One	Adekunle Ajasin University	0.50
P34-24	Two	Adekunle Ajasin University	0.25
		Adekunle Ajasin University	0.25
P35-24	Three	North-West University	0.17
		North-West University	0.17
		North-West University	0.17
P36-24	Three	University of Johannesburg	0.17
		University of Johannesburg	0.17
		University of Johannesburg	0.17
P38-24	One	University of Johannesburg	0.50
P39-24	Two	University of Cape Coast	0.25
		Walter Sisulu University	0.25
P40-24	Two	University of Cape Coast	0.25
		Walter Sisulu University	0.25
P41-24	Two	University of Johannesburg	0.25
		University of Johannesburg	0.25

Paper No.	Number of authors	Universities	Points contribution
P42-24	One	University of Johannesburg	0.50
P43-24	Two	North-West University	0.25
		North-West University	0.25
P44-24		University of Venda	0.50
P45-24	One	University of Pretoria	0.50
P47-24	Three	University of Johannesburg	0.17
		University of Johannesburg	0.17
		University of Johannesburg	0.17
P48-24	Four	North-West University	0.125
		North-West University	0.125
		North-West University	0.125
		Adeleke University	0.125
P49-24	Two	University of the Witwatersrand	0.25
		University of the Witwatersrand	0.25
P50-24	Two	University of the Witwatersrand	0.25
		University of the Witwatersrand	0.25
P51-24	Three	University of the Free State	0.17
		University of the Free State	0.17
		University of the Free State	0.17
P52-24	Two	University of the Witwatersrand	0.25
		University of the Witwatersrand	0.25
P55-24	One	University of Pretoria	0.50
P56-24	One	University of Johannesburg	0.50
P57-24	Two	University of Johannesburg	0.25
		University of Johannesburg	0.25
P59-24	One	University of Johannesburg	0.50
P60-24	Three	University of South Africa	0.17
		University of South Africa	0.17
		University of South Africa	0.17
P61-24	Three	University of Johannesburg	0.17
		University of Johannesburg	0.17
		University of Johannesburg	0.17
P62-24	Two	University of Johannesburg	0.25
		University of Johannesburg	0.25
P63-24	Four	University of Johannesburg	0.125
		University of Johannesburg	0.125
		University of Johannesburg	0.125
		Stellenbosch University	0.125
P65-24	Three	Walter Sisulu University	0.17
		Walter Sisulu University	0.17
		Cape Peninsula University of Technology	0.17
P68-24	Two	Obafemi Awolowo University	0.25
		Obafemi Awolowo University	0.25

Paper No.	Number of authors	Universities	Points contribution
P69-24	Two	University of Johannesburg	0.25
		University of Johannesburg	0.25
P70-24	Three	University of the Free State	0.17
		University of the Free State	0.17
		University of the Free State	0.17
P71-24	Three	University of Johannesburg	0.17
		University of Johannesburg	0.17
		University of Johannesburg	0.17
P72-24	One	University of Johannesburg	0.50
P74-24	Two	University of South Africa	0.25
		University of South Africa	0.25
P75-24	Two	University of South Africa	0.25
		University of South Africa	0.25
P77-24	One	University of Johannesburg	0.50
P78-24	Three	University of Johannesburg	0.17
		University of Johannesburg	0.17
		University of Johannesburg	0.17
P79-24	One	University of Johannesburg	0.50
P80-24	Two	University of Johannesburg	0.25
		University of Johannesburg	0.25
P82-24	One	North-West University	0.50
P83-24	Two	Walter Sisulu University	0.25
		Walter Sisulu University	0.25
P84-24	One	University of Johannesburg	0.50
P85-24	Four	Salem State University, USA	0.125
		Stockton University, USA	0.125
		Millennium Global Business Solutions, USA	0.125
		Millennium Global Business Solutions, USA	0.125
P86-24	One	University of Johannesburg	0.50
TOTAL			**33.00**

Contents of Volume I

Contents of Volume II

An Expert Evaluated Nomination Process for the Board of Directors in South Africa's State-Owned Companies

Hlobo Modi, Moloi Tankiso, and Marx Ben

Abstract The primary challenge facing most of the South Africa's State-Owned Companies (SOCs) is the implementation of an ineffective nomination process used to appoint directors, which often results in the appointment of incompetent executives and boards of directors. As a result, this chapter provides an effective process that can be used by SOCs when appointing directors. This research paper aims to identify an effective nomination process for non-executive directors overseeing SOCs. This study conducted a systematic literature review as well as a two-round Delphi process where experts provided their input on the most effective nomination process for non-executive directors serving on SOCs. The research study has identified the most effective nomination process that can be used when appointing non-executive directors in SOC. The research study's findings suggest an effective nomination process that SOCs can use to select non-executive directors for SOCs. This study contributes to the scant research on corporate governance in SOC, especially on research focusing on the nomination process of non-executive directors, as the majority of research has been concentrated on listed companies.

Keywords Board members · Non-executive directors · Corporate governance · Nomination process · Competencies and qualities · State-Owned Companies

---

H. Modi (✉) · M. Tankiso · M. Ben
University of Johannesburg, Johannesburg, South Africa
e-mail: modih@uj.ac.za; smoloi@uj.ac.za; benm@uj.ac.za

T. Moloi (ed.), *Impacting Society Positively Through Technology in Accounting and Business Processes*, Springer Proceedings in Business and Economics,
https://doi.org/10.1007/978-3-031-84885-8_1

Introduction

South Africa currently has 21 Schedule 2 State-Owned Companies (SOCs), which are public companies regulated by the Companies Act and the subject of this study (Kikeri, 2016). Most of these SOCs were established to stimulate South African economic growth and to create employment. In 2016, the main SOCs in South Africa, Eskom, Transnet, SAA, and Denel, were valued at R908 billion, and these SOCs were considered key strategic assets that must be preserved (DPE Budget Vote, 2016). Furthermore, the CIPC (2017) states that SOCs play a crucial role in job creation with Eskom, Transnet, SAA, Denel, and Safcol employing around 114,000 people in 2018.

Notwithstanding being entrusted with a critical role in developing the South African economy, these SOCs have undermined corporate governance values in recent years, as evidenced by their poor performance (Thomas, 2012). According to the Auditor General's report for 2017–2018, the audits of the South African Airways (SAA), Denel, the South African Nuclear Energy Company, and SA Express were not completed by the statutory deadline because these SOCs failed to demonstrate that they were operating as "going concerns" (Auditor General, 2018).

According to Madumi (2018), the primary governance challenges that SOCs face are incompetence and misconduct among executives and boards of directors. Thabane and Snyman-Van Deventer (2018) concur with Madumi (2018) and attribute SOC weaknesses to ineffective boards of directors, which are typically politically appointed.

To contextualize the governance and performance deficiencies affecting SOCs, during the 2014/2015 financial year, the SABC reported a loss of about R395 million. In the same year, the company witnessed the resignation of the majority of its board members due to political interference in SABC's operational affairs by the Minister (Thabane & Snyman-Van Deventer, 2018).

Similarly, SAA had seven CEOs in less than 4 years. During that same period, the corporation received a bailout of R550 million to cover fuel costs, and it was granted an additional R5 billion guarantee by the shareholders for a restructuring exercise. Other SOCs such as Eskom, Denel, the South African Post Office, and Transnet have also experienced a high turnover of the board and executive management and continued underperformance, necessitating regular bailouts and challenges among their boards and various shareholders (Hill & Bowker, 2015).

This instability created by the high turnover in the executive and board of directors in SOCs calls for the appointment of board members that are primarily from the private sector, with business, professional, and other relevant backgrounds, based on a structured and transparent nominations process. Furthermore, to ensure properly appointed boards, the board nominations process itself has moved to become more transparent and merit based through a properly outlined board nominations policy and procedures (Kikeri, 2018).

These SOCs have recently been plagued by State capture, which is estimated to have cost South Africa R4.9 trillion and missed opportunities (Merten, 2019).

During the State Capture Commission of enquiry, the chairperson of the commission, Justice Raymond Zondo, is quoted saying, "*Quite frankly, processes followed in terms of which people are appointed as board members in SOEs must be reviewed.*"

Subsequently, the commission of inquiry was completed, and the Zondo Commission report issued in 2022 states:

> With regard to the appointment of members of boards of directors of SOEs as well as senior executives, the commission found that this responsibility can no longer be left exclusively in the hands of politicians, as they have miserably failed in their constitutional mandate to lead these institutions successfully. It has been recommended that a body be established that would be entrusted to identify, recruit and select competent people for such appointments in SOEs (Zondo, 2022a, b, c).

On 27 April 2021, President Cyril Ramaphosa admitted at the Commission of Inquiry into State Capture that:

> The parlous condition of state-owned enterprises was the result of a massive system failure in how the boards of SOEs were appointed, some of the (failures) may have been inadvertent, and some may have been purposeful. Some of (the appointments) were hidden and masked (Zondo, 2022a, b, c).

From the above context, it is clear that the fundamental problem confronting SOCs is the incompetent directors who are politically appointed to oversee these institutions. Ambe and Badenhorst-Weiss (2012) and McGregor (2011) found that SOCs are unable to recruit experienced board members, as most qualified candidates with the appropriate skills and knowledge prefer to serve on private sector boards.

This context demonstrates that the current nomination process for selecting the board of directors in SOCs is inadequate and that a comprehensive screening and selection strategy is required to reduce the appointment of incompetent board members. Minichilli et al. (2007) concur and state that the selection of the appropriate board members with the relevant skills in an organisation is essential in order to enhance the effectiveness and performance of the organisation.

Given the problems mentioned above, the main objective of this study is to identify the most suitable nomination process for the board of directors in SOCs and to address the question of what is the most effective nomination process to adopt for identifying suitable directors in SOCs.

Literature Review

The primary theories adopted in this study are agency theory, resource dependency theory, and trait theory, as these theories are associated with the nomination of competent, ethical directors. The agency theory focuses on the relationship between the principals (the business owners) and the agents (represented by the managers). The shareholders appoint agents to manage the company and increase shareholder value (Boshkoska, 2015). Managers generally have excellent knowledge and expertise in the company's day-to-day operations. However, sometimes they act in their own self-interests rather than the shareholders' (owners') interests (Olowosegun & Moloi, 2021; Fama & Jensen, 1983). Managers' need for self-interest undermines trust between shareholders and managers. As a result, shareholders are compelled to appoint a board of directors to oversee and protect their interests (Mensah & Boachie, 2023, Moloi & Marwala, 2020; Fama & Jensen, 1983).

As with the private sector, SOCs are operated by executive managers, while directors have an oversight role. The agency theory is complicated in the SOC environment as the executives and directors do not own the companies. To further exacerbate the problem, the ministers are assigned to serve as the shareholder representative, yet they also do not own the SOCs. The real owners of the SOCs are the citizens of the country. This structure creates a conflict of interest among managers, directors, and shareholders (Thabane & Snyman-Van Deventer, 2018). According to Menozzi and Vannoni (2014), there is a "double-agency" problem caused by conflicts between managers, boards of directors, politicians, and citizens.

In this double-agency phenomenon, neither the executive, the directors, nor even the ministers can be expected to protect the interests of the SOCs with the same dedication as they would have done if the SOCs had been their own companies. What intensifies this double-agency problem is that citizens (who are shareholders) typically do not have the knowledge or institutional ability to monitor and evaluate the performance of directors and ministers (Thabane & Snyman-Van Deventer, 2018). Thabane and Snyman-Van Deventer (2018) further reveal that an agency system of this nature enables ministers (who are supposed to represent the shareholders) to pursue their own interests instead of those of the citizens (Thabane & Snyman-Van Deventer, 2018). Shapiro and Willig (1990) further point out that this double-agency practice tends to create a culture of unnecessary bureaucracy that inevitably frustrates the company's operating system and the accomplishment of SOC objectives.

According to the agency theory, the purpose of the boards is to monitor managers' activities and, more specifically, to use their expertise to advise the company's management (Fama & Jensen, 1983). Accordingly, the agency theory is relevant to this study as it emphasises on appointing competent, ethical board members.

The resource dependence theory of corporate governance is another theory adopted in this study. It holds that directors bring valuable resources to the organisation, notably knowledge, experience, and access to critical external contacts such as suppliers, buyers, and investors (Muhammad et al., 2023; Hillman et al., 2002). Therefore, it is evident that to be able to play their role efficiently, the board of directors needs to be resourceful and bring knowledge, skills, and networks to the companies they serve. This theory applies to this study, which investigates the ideal nomination process to ensure that competent and ethical directors are appointed.

Considering the fundamental role that SOEs play across the world in implementing the government's socio-economic goals, it is critical that these SOEs are efficiently governed by both their management and directors (Molefe, 2006). McLellan (2009) adds that the public expects nothing less than good governance and administration from these SOEs from management.

Over the past few years, the OECD has played a leading role in setting standards for ethical practice in government, particularly in raising awareness of increased accountability and transparency in public sector organisations. The OECD is also leading in efforts to help governments around the world develop sound corporate governance by developing generally accepted good governance principles. In 2015, standards unique to SOEs, although compatible with the general principles, were published by the OECD and adopted by many countries (Jesover & Kirkpatrick, 2005).

Among the different governance practices addressed in the 2015 OECD SOE Guidelines are the SOE Board Principle. The guideline emphasised that the central function of the SOEs' governance is that the board is responsible for ensuring that the SOEs are successful. The board must act as an intermediary between the government as a shareholder, the SOEs, and the executive management. With the recent increase in "commercialisation" of SOEs, most governments have made efforts to professionalise boards of directors and have given the boards a higher degree of autonomy. The following subsection describes the board nomination processes adopted in various countries.

In 2018, the OECD surveyed SOEs' "board nominations processes" in various countries and found that in countries where they had adopted the centralised form of ownership in SOEs, such as Chile, Slovenia, and South Africa, the government minister was responsible for nominating members to SOE boards. However, in countries where they had adopted the decentralised form of ownership, such as Brazil, Estonia, Latvia, and Turkey, the line ministries were more often responsible for nominations and the public finance ministry may appoint one or more representatives to the board (OECD, 2015).

The 2015 OECD guideline on SOE governance suggests that it is good practice for ministerial decisions on board appointments to be subject to consensus by a wider group of ministers, the Cabinet, or the Head of State, which is practised in various countries such as Norway and Sweden. Furthermore, the Guidelines suggest that appointing members of the board should be supported by transparent and consistent methods of nominating candidates to the board and should involve current members of the SOE board and non-government shareholders (OECD, 2015). Different countries are using different board nomination processes, for instance:

- *In Canada*, a formal nomination process requires current SOE boards to establish a board profile to identify potential directors for the appointment. The board of directors liaises with the responsible minister's office and the portfolio department on all appointment-related issues, including advising the government on selection criteria for chairpersons and developing competency profiles and future needs for directors to fill upcoming vacancies.

- The responsible minister and his or her department will then use the board profile and the director profile to guide them in identifying suitable candidates for consideration for appointment to a board of directors (OECD, 2015).
- *In the UK*: The central ownership advisory unit, the shareholder executive (ShEx), and the SOE Chair agree on the mix of skills and experience required on the board, leading to agreement on a strategic plan of public appointments. A

timetable for recruitment is then agreed upon between the SOE, the lead Director in ShEx, and an Independent Assessor (IA).

- An interview panel is established comprising the lead ShEx policy official, the IA, and the SOE Chair. The panel will then reach an agreement on the preferred candidate and submit a panel report with recommendations to Departmental Ministers; once they have agreed on the recommendation, the appointment can be made (OECD, 2015).
- *In France:* There is an established "directors' pool" which includes pre-selected candidates that have already gone through a formal nomination, and the minister would then choose a suitable board candidate from this pool (OECD, 2015).
- *In Israel*: A special committee approves the board's appointment after verifying that the candidates comply with the minimum requirements laid down by the law. In addition, the Government Companies Authority (GCA) is leading the recruitment process for the board members (OECD, 2015).
- *In New Zealand:* The country has adopted a comprehensive approach to board appointments, from soliciting, vetting, and recommending candidates to conduct induction training after an appointment. There is a Crown Ownership Monitoring Unit (COMU) responsible for managing the appointment process by advising the bodies responsible for appointment (i.e. the relevant Minister after approval by a Cabinet Appointments and Honours Committee and confirmation by Cabinet).
- COMU is responsible for developing a longlist and shortlist of candidates (with options) for consideration by the minister after conducting due diligence on preferred candidates (including conflict of interest clearance, background checks), managing the cabinet approval process, and managing the formal appointment process (OECD, 2015).
- *Finland:* Finland stands out with regard to modernising its selection procedures. The ownership agency outsources the development and maintenance of a database of pre-qualified candidates to a recruitment consulting firm (OECD, 2015). The outsourced contract is subject to competitive tender every 4 years. This arrangement offers some advantages over maintaining an internal database as it provides access to the networks and resources of the recruiting firm, which has specialist skills in sourcing candidates for private sector boards, especially international candidates. This process also reduces the risk of political involvement in the selection process and provides a cost-effective, transparent, and consistent process for dealing with applications received from a wide variety of sources. This solidly structured process proved to be beneficial in avoiding some political interference in the appointment process (OECD, 2015).
- *In Norway*: Nominations to the boards of listed SOEs are made via nomination committees made up of representatives from the government and non-government shareholders (OECD, 2015).

Table 1 summarises the nomination processes adopted by the different OECD countries

Based on the above table, it is evident that it is important for a country to have guidelines and regulations that govern how boards are appointed and ensure that

Table 1 Summary of nomination processes adopted in various OECD countries

OECD Country	Nomination process adopted
Canada	• Existing board profiles potential candidate • *Minister appoints the candidates*
United Kingdom	• Shareholder executives (ShEx) profile potential candidates • *Minister appoints the candidates*
France	• There is an established directors' pool • *Minister appoints candidates* from this pool
New Zealand	• Crown Ownership Monitoring Unit (COMU) profiles potential candidates • *Minister appoints the candidates*
Israel	• Government Companies Authority (GCA) profiles potential candidates • *Special nomination committee appoints candidates*
Finland	The *nomination process is outsourced* to an independent recruitment consulting firm
Norway	Nomination is conducted by *nomination committee* with representatives from both government and private sectors

Source: Researcher's Conceptualisation

suitable candidates with the appropriate competencies and value systems are appointed. Namara et al. (2015) add that good governance extends beyond public companies' compliance to universal governance standards to involve the efficient administration of public affairs in a transparent, responsible, and accountable manner (Kanyane & Sausi, 2015).

Contrary to international practice, governance in South Africa's SOEs is complex, involving many stakeholders, including shareholders, policymakers, government ministers, and other stakeholders (Massie et al., 2014). Concerning the SOEs' oversight role, the relevant political minister represents the shareholders and appoints SOE boards along with the SOE CEOs and CFOs.

While the board may recommend candidates for the CEO position, it is entirely up to the ministers to decide who will be the CEO or CFO. Since the board has no real authority over the CEO, but is responsible for overseeing the company managed by the same CEO, such an administrative situation creates confusion. In addition, Rossouw and Reddy (2009) point out that political ties often inform the board and executive management appointments, and Howard and Seth-Purdie (2005) refer to such practices as "political patronage". Minichilli et al. (2007) suggest that it is essential for Ministers to appoint people with the right level of competence and qualities for board positions. However, political agendas are usually at the centre when deciding on board appointments, and the expertise and integrity of the board members are overlooked. In such instances, politicians will pay less attention to selecting the right people to serve the citizens' interests (Kamal, 2010). Similarly, Vagliasindi (2008) points out that such practices result in the board members protecting the ministers' interests and not the interests of all stakeholders, including the citizens.

SOEs must implement sound corporate governance systems, such as appointing a competent board of directors and an executive management team that is honest, transparent, and responsible in their corporate relations, to operate efficiently and maximise social benefits (Williams, 2010). To address these challenges confronting SOCs, South Africa has enacted legislation and corporate governance guidelines outlined below. In South Africa, SOEs are affected by several legislations and guidelines to ensure good corporate governance in these entities. Such legislations include the 1996 South African constitution, the Companies Act of 2008, and the Public Finance Management Act of 1999. Furthermore, there are the 2016 King IV Code of corporate governance, the DPE Protocol on corporate governance, and the Treasury Regulations.

These regulations and guidelines serve as a foundation for the management and oversight of SOEs. However, these multiple legislations are sometimes inconsistent and contradictory, which has a negative impact on the performance of SOEs (Massie et al., 2014). The following section discusses the board appointment process, as explained by the Legislature and corporate governance codes.

Companies Act of 2008

The Companies Act defines an SOE as "an enterprise registered under this Act that is a public entity in Schedule 2 or Schedule 3 of the PFMA" (Massie et al., 2014, p. 123). The Act applies to certain SOEs and not others, while the PFMA regulates all SOEs' governance aspects. The SOEs listed in Schedule 2 are major public companies under the governance of political ministers, and they supply goods and services in accordance with ordinary business practices and are heavily subsidised by public resources. These entities are designated as "SOC Ltd" and are commonly referred to as SOCs, SOEs, parastatals, and public entities. The Companies Act and the PFMA apply concurrently, although Section 5.4 of the Companies Act specifies that the PFMA shall prevail over the Companies Act in the case of contrary rules.

Section 68 of the Companies Act of 2008 states that each company director must be elected by the persons entitled to exercise voting rights in such an election to serve for an indefinite term or a term as set out in the Memorandum of Incorporation. This means the shareholders' election confirms the directors' appointment at the AGM. The section further states that unless the Memorandum of Incorporation of a company provides otherwise, the board may appoint a person who satisfies the requirements for election as a director to fill any vacancy and serve as a director of the company temporarily until the vacancy can be confirmed at the AGM by the shareholders. In the case of SOCs, the Minister represents the shareholder, and therefore, it is the minister that ultimately appoints the board members.

Public Finance Management Act of 1999

The Act aims to ensure transparency, accountability, and effective control of the entities to which the Act relates to the income, expenditure assets, and liabilities. Although the PFMA addresses various matters on board of directors, the act is silent on board nominations. It is therefore also worth noting that the Companies Act of 2008 and the PFMA of 1999 have long since been updated and that there has been a lot of developments in the corporate governance environment that need the Legislature to be revised, particularly since such revisions could close the gaps that have caused some of the South African corporates to fail. These required updates include board composition, board appointment, and board evaluation processes, particularly in state-owned companies. Such considerations make this study relevant as it proposes an effective nomination process that can be used when appointing directors in South African SOCs.

King IV SOE Supplementary of 2016

The King report entails guidelines that can assist governing bodies to practise good corporate governance. The King IV report is not legislative; however, parliament has recommended that all SOCs comply with practices of the King reports. King IV of 2016 has a special supplemental manual that explicitly points out corporate governance principles applicable to SOCs. These guidelines are adhered to by SOCs to ensure sound financial management and efficient service delivery to citizens that will contribute to overall economic growth (van der Nest et al., 2008). Principle 3.2 of King IV requires that the process of selecting and appointing the board members should be transparent and involve existing governing bodies even though the minister makes the final decision.

Although King IV suggests that the relevant political Ministers (elected to represent the shareholders) are responsible for appointing and dismissing the board of directors and the CEO. Rossouw and Reddy (2009) believe that this practice is vulnerable to the recruitment of politically connected individuals (i.e. board members and senior managers). The process is also complicated because the selected applicants are expected to make strategic decisions that the political minister finds desirable. Williams (2010) points out that this practice can undermine the provisions stipulated in the King report to appoint independent board representatives with the right level of competence and critical skills required by the SOCs.

Table 2 Summary of the board nomination and appointment process as stipulated by the Legislature and the guidelines

Applicable Legislature or guideline	Board nomination and appointment Process
Companies Act of Section 68 (2008)	• The *Board Nomination Committee* appoints a board member • The shareholders at the AGM confirm the appointment
PFMA: Section 50 (1999)	• The *Act is silent* on board appointments
King IV (SOE Supplement) (2016)	• *Relevant political ministers* are responsible for appointing board members
Zondo Commission (2022)	• *An independent nomination body that must identify, recruit, and select competent board members*
DPSA Protocol on appointing directors (2009)	• The appointment process should be standardised, objective, clear, understandable, and transparent • *The Nomination Committee* must make recommendations • The *political minister* makes the final decision on the appointed board candidates in consultation with *cabinet ministers*
OECD Guidelines on SOE (2018)	• The board appointments process should be transparent and consistent • The board appointments are subjected to consensus by a wider *group of ministers* • *Existing board members* should be involved in the appointment process

Source: Researcher's Conceptualisation

Protocol on Appointing Directors of 2009

In September 2009, the parliament approved the "Handbook for the appointment of persons to boards of state and state-controlled institutions" published by the Department of Public Service and Administration (DPSA). The Handbook describes the selection process that needs to be followed when appointing the board of directors. The Handbook further requires that the appointment process should be standardised, objective, clear, understandable, and transparent. It also states that the appointment process should be applied consistently in all cases. However, the document is not detailed about the nomination process followed to ensure that competent and ethical directors are appointed (DPSA Handbook, 2009).

Table 2 summarises the nomination process stipulated in the Legislature and various guidelines that South Africa's SOCs must adopt.

From the above discussion and table, it is clear that there is inconsistency and contradiction in legislation and guidelines prescribed for South Africa's SOCs for the processes that need to be followed when nominating directors. Consequently, this suggests the need for an effective nomination process that all SOCs must adopt.

Methodology

Previous studies that investigated the characteristics of directors have used different research methods. For instance, Vandiar (2015) analysed JSE listed company directors and used a qualitative methodology where he first conducted a document analysis and used the results to compile questionnaires. Serretta et al. (2009) investigated core corporate governance dilemmas facing boards, and the investigation was qualitative and used the Delphi technique. This study adopted a similar research approach and used the Delphi technique. The questionnaire used in the Delphi process was prepared using information collected from the review of literature on processes followed when nominating directors.

In the first round of the Delphi process, the questionnaire required experts to confirm whether the nomination processes identified from the literature were required to confirm the identified nomination processes. In the second round, experts were required to rank the nomination processes that were confirmed as being effective from round one. The essential key to a successful Delphi study is selecting a diverse group of experts. Since the results of a Delphi depend on various individuals' perspectives, it is essential to select individuals who are likely to make significant contributions. In most instances, the experts' profile is diverse and includes academics, business, government officials, and others (Okoli & Pawlowski, 2004). Expert selection criteria usually include publications on the researched problem, years of experience in the field, experts' self-evaluation of their experience and knowledge on the topic, and recommendations from relevant institutions (Gordon, 2009).

Therefore, to understand how these directors are screened and selected, it was important to determine from the senior officials in government departments involved in appointing potential directors. It also added significant value to consult with corporate governance experts, including academics specialising in corporate governance and senior officials from the South African Institute of Directors (IoDSA) (Table 3).

This study used purposive sampling to select participants for the Delphi survey. Since the sample is deliberately chosen and depends on the issue being studied, there are no specific guidelines for the numbers to use in studies when using the Delphi survey. In some trials, 15 participants were used, while 60 participants were acceptable in others (Hasson et al., 2000). Needham and de Loë (1990) suggest a sample size of a minimum of 10 (a smaller size does not generate enough ideas) and a maximum of 50 participants. De Villiers et al. (2005) suggest that the sample size depends on whether it is homogenous or heterogeneous. They suggest the following numbers: if they are homogeneous (same discipline), 15–30 participants are ideal, and if they are heterogeneous (from differing disciplines), 5–10 participants per professional group are ideal. Therefore, this study initially targeted 15 participants from different disciplines, both locally and internationally, and managed to have 50 experts participating on the study.

Table 3 List of identified stakeholder groups and experts consulted

Stakeholders	Rationale for inclusion
Academic researchers and lecturers	Academic researchers and lectures on corporate governance and public administration at higher learning institutions were requested to participate in the study as they have valuable knowledge on the subject matter, and they would have researched the subject matter and have in-depth knowledge
Existing or former board members in both public and private sectors	Existing and former board members in both private and public sectors were requested to participate as they had practical experience on what competencies and qualities were expected from them and what selection and evaluation processes were used to determine these attributes. The sector opted for both public and private sectors as both institutions are governed by the Companies Act and King IV and the requirements for competencies and qualities of directors are the same
South African Institute of Directors (IoDSA)	The primary objective of IoDSA is director development, which includes supporting the continual learning and development of aspiring and experienced directors. Therefore, it was ideal to invite the Director Development Team from IoDSA to participate as they understand what board members' competencies and qualities are required
Office of the Auditor General of South Africa (AGSA)	The office of AGSA audits most of South Africa's SOEs. The institution has continuously raised concern on the quality and calibre of board members in SOEs, and on the process of appointing them. Therefore, it added value to the study to have their perception of what they consider to be the necessary competencies and qualities of directors and their view on board members' selection processes
Government officials (Ministers, Chief of Staff, and Departmental Director-General)	Departmental ministers represent the SOE shareholders; therefore, they are responsible for appointing SOE's board of directors. It added value to the study to find out from their representatives what they consider to be the most suitable way to screen board members as well as what competencies and qualities they consider in potential board members

Source: Researcher's Own Conceptualisation

Validity and Reliability

Validity is concerned with whether the study is credible and accurate and evaluating what it is supposed to evaluate. As a result, validating the data and the research instruments is essential. This study used content validity and triangulation to validate the data and instrument. In this study, the data collected were validated through the administration of two rounds of the Delphi questionnaire, where experts involved in the process of appointing and training directors gave input on the nomination process of directors.

The other validation method used in the study is triangulation. According to Zohrabi (2013), to strengthen the validity of the evaluation of data and findings, the researcher should try to collect data through several sources such as document analysis, questionnaires, interviews, and classroom observations. Gathering data through one technique can be questionable, biased, and weak. However, collecting information from a variety of sources and with a variety of techniques can confirm findings.

Therefore, when the same results are achieved from different data collection methods, the data collected are deemed to be valid. In this study, two data collection methods are used: systematic document analysis from the literature review and questionnaires responses from experts in the two rounds of the Delphi process. These were used in triangulation to validate the data.

Lincoln and Guba (1985) suggest that the reliability of the results can be ensured with three techniques: the investigator's position, triangulation, and audit trial. This study adopted the triangulation method for reliability. In triangulation, the researcher uses different procedures such as questionnaires, interviews, and classroom observations to collect data. In addition, this information is obtained through different sources; therefore, collecting varied types of information through different sources enhanced the reliability of the data and the results. This study used systematic document analysis to collect data and two rounds of the Delphi process to confirm the reliability of the data.

Discussion and Findings

Findings from the Systematic Literature Review

The first part of the study focused on the systematic literature review. The reviewed literature was used to identify effective nomination processes for the board of directors in SOCs. During this phase, four suitable nomination processes were identified and presented to experts. The Delphi participating experts were requested to confirm, reject, and suggest the nomination process. During this phase, the experts suggested two other nomination processes to adopt when appointing directors in SOCs. In the next phase, the Delphi participating experts were requested to rank the confirmed nomination processes according to their importance. The outcome of the Delphi processes is shown in Table 4.

Table 4 First round Delphi: Board of directors nomination process

	Nomination process	%
SP1	By an independent nomination committee	65
SP2	Relevant portfolio minister	3
SP3	Portfolio minister in consultation with other cabinet ministers	9
SP4	Relevant portfolio committee and confirmed by the minister	3
SP5	By the public	12
SP6	Other	10

Source: Researcher's Conceptualisation

First Round of the Delphi Process: Confirmation Nomination Process of Directors

The study investigated the effective nomination process for directors in SOCs, and Table 4 outlines the findings from the first round of the Delphi process.

Regarding the nomination process of the directors, 65% of the participants believed that an independent nomination committee should nominate potential board candidates. This also corresponds to the requirements of the Companies Act, the DPSA Protocol on the Appointment of Directors, and the recent Zondo Commission recommendation (2022). In addition, a number of countries, including Norway and Israel, use an independent nominating committee for potential board candidates (OECD, 2015).

In addition to the identified nomination processes, the participants suggested that the nomination process includes qualification verification and probity checks. Participants also believed that interviews for potential directors should be conducted in public (i.e. televised), like what is currently practised when appointing chairpersons for Chapter 9 institutions.

Even though the President appoints Chapter 9 institution chairpersons, the interviews of the shortlisted candidates are conducted by a panel of members of parliament. In recent years, this process has been televised live on national television for the public (Mkhwanazi, 2016). Although these points are valid, they fall outside the scope of this study, which focuses on who should conduct the nomination processes and not how the processes should be conducted.

Second Round of the Delphi Process: Rating of the Nomination Process of Directors

This section presents the results of the rating and ranking of the nomination process of the potential board of directors. In this round, the experts were required to use a 5-point Likert scale: 5 = highly important; 4 = important; 3 = neutral; 2 = less important; and 1 = not important.

The results are presented in Tables 5.

Rating of Board of Directors Nomination Method

Table 5 illustrates that the participants ranked only one of the five identified nomination processes. Furthermore, it is worth highlighting that most of the participating experts regard nomination by an independent nomination committee as highly important and important (i.e. rated 4 and 5). This means that it is very important that an independent nomination committee conducts the nomination of potential directors.

Table 5 Second round: Board of directors nomination process

	Nomination process	1	2	3	4	5	High ranking %	Lower ranking %
SP1	By an independent nomination committee		4%	7%	22%	67%	**89%**	**4%**
SP2	Relevant portfolio minister							
SP3	Portfolio minister in consultation with other cabinet ministers							
SP4	Relevant portfolio committee and confirmed by the minister							
SP5	By the public							

Source: Researcher's Conceptualisation

Summary and Conclusion

In conclusion, having an effective board begins with identifying and appointing suitable board members. As such, careful consideration and nomination must be conducted to ensure each potential board member's suitability before the appointment. Therefore, the processes followed when nominating board members must be considered. This is usually guided by the Legislature or the corporate governance guidelines adopted in the country.

The literature review above shows that although the existing Legislature governing South Africa's State-Owned Companies is dated it is still relevant as the Companies Act and the DPSA protocol on appointing directors, as well as the Zondo Commission recommendations, recommend the use of an independent nomination committee. These legislations and guidelines are aligned to the findings of this study. The primary objective of this study was to determine the most efficient nominating process for the board of directors in South Africa's SOCs. Following a comprehensive literature review and two Delphi processes, an independent nomination committee was found to be the most effective nomination process when appointing SOC board members.

This suggests that the challenge is not with the approved nomination process but rather with the compliance and implementation of these regulations. Consequently, this non-compliance with the regulation has led to the appointment of incompetent board members, as revealed by the Zondo Commission.

Limitations

This study focused on the nomination process of non-executive directors that are charged with governance with a specific focus on SOCs, thus omitting directors in the private sector. Further, the study is also limited to the nomination process of non-executive directors in SOC, and it can be extended to executives in the SOC, such as the Chief Executive Directors, the Chief Financial Officers, and Chief Operations Officers.

Future Research Recommendation

Based on the above results, future research could focus on identifying an effective evaluation process for existing non-executive directors in SOCs. Further, future research could also focus on using information and communications technology (ICT) in screening and nominating potential board candidates. This could assist in mitigating the reputation and financial risk that results from employing incompetent board members and that lack integrity.

References

Ambe, I. M., & Badenhorst-Weiss, J. A. (2012). Procurement challenges in the South African public sector. *Journal of Transport and Supply Chain Management, 6*(1), 242–261.

Auditor General. (2018). *Auditor-general reports an overall deterioration in the audit results of national and provincial government departments and their entities*. Retrieved July 16, 2020, from https://www.agsa.co.za/Portals/0/Reports/PFMA/201718/MR/2018%20PFMA%20 Media%20Release.pdf

Boshkoska, M. (2015). The agency problem: Measures for its overcoming. *International Journal of Business and Management, 10*(1), 204–212.

CIPC. (2017). *The CIPC as the regulator of state-owned companies "Boards of SOCs"*. Retrieved May 27, 2020, from http://www.cipc.co.za/files/6915/2688/9205/PPT_Boards_of_SOCs_

De Villiers, M. R., de Villiers, P. J., & Kent, A. P. (2005). The Delphi technique in health sciences education research. *Med Teach, 27*(7), 639–643.

Fama, E. F., & Jensen, M. C. (1983). Agency problems and residual claims. *Journal of Law and Economics, 26*(1), 327–329.

Gordon, T. J. (2009). The real-time Delphi method. *Futures Research Methodology, 3(1)*, 19–20.

Hasson, F., Keeney, S., & McKenna, H. (2000). Research guidelines for the Delphi survey technique. *Journal of Advanced Nursing, 32*(4), 1008–1015.

Hill, L., & Bowker, J. (2015). *Transnet would consider Blue Train stake sale - Moneyweb, Money web*. Retrieved February 29, 2020, from https://www.moneyweb.co.za/news-fast-news/ transnet-would-consider-blue-train-stake-sale/

Hillman, A. J., Cannella, A. A., & Harris, I. C. (2002). Women and racial minorities in the boardroom: How do directors differ? *Journal of Management, 28*(6), 747–763.

Howard, C., & Seth-Purdie, R. (2005). Governance issues for public sector boards. *Journal of Public Administration, 64*(3), 56–68.

Jesover, F., & Kirkpatrick, G. (2005). The revised OECD principles of corporate governance and their relevance to non-OECD countries. *Corporate Governance: An International Review, 13*(2), 127–136.

Kamal, M. (2010). Dealing with the Principals Dilemma: A proposal for the Governance of Indonesia's State-owned Enterprises. *Lawasia Journal, 1*(1), 155–156.

Kanyane, M. H., & Sausi, K. (2015). Reviewing State-Owned Entities' Governance Landscape in South Africa. *African Journal of Business Ethics, 9*(1), 28–42.

Kikeri, S. (2016). *Republic of South Africa systematic country diagnostic. An incomplete transition: Overcoming the legacy of exclusion in South Africa background note corporate governance in South African State-Owned Enterprises Corporate Governance in South African State*. Retrieved June 12, 2020, from https://juta.co.za/documents/158/9781775822660_NFjqYOn.pdf

Kikeri, S. (2018). *Corporate governance in South African state-owned enterprises.*

Lincoln, Y. S., & Guba, E. G. (1985). *Naturalistic inquiry*. Sage Publications.

Madumi, P. (2018). Are State-Owned Enterprises (SOEs) Catalysts for or Inhibitors of South African Economic Growth? *3rd Annual International Conference on Public Administration and Development Alternatives*. (IPADA).

Massie, K., Collier, D., & Crotty, A. (2014). *Executive salaries in South Africa: Who should have a say on pay*. Jacana Media (Pty) ltd.

McGregor, L. (2011). *Can South African State Owned Companies succeed?* Retrieved March 20, 2020, from https://portal.regenesys.net/course/discussions/editors/kcfinder/upload/files/McGregor%2C%20L.%202015.%20Can%20State%20Owned%20Companies%20succeed.%20USB..pdf

McLellan, J. G. (2009). Applied corporate governance: New challenges in public sector governance. *Keeping Good Companies, 61*(8), 466–467.

Menozzi, A., & Vannoni, D. (2014). Political connections in boards of directors Anna. *Network Industries Quarterly, 16*(3), 8–10.

Mensah, E., & Boachie, C. (2023). Corporate governance mechanisms and earnings management: The moderating role of female directors. *Cogent Business & Management, 10*(1), 2167290.

Merten, M. (2019). *State Capture wipes out third of SA's R4.9-trillion of the GDP.* Retrieved March 6, 2020, from https://www.dailymaverick.co.za/article/2019-03-01-state-capture-wipes-out-third-of-sas-r4-9-trillion-gdp-never-mind-lost-trust-confidence-opportunity/

Minichilli, A., Gabrielsson, J., & Huse, M. (2007). Board evaluations: Making a fit between the purpose and the system. *Corporate Governance: An International Review, 15*(4), 609–622.

Mkhwanazi, M. (2016). *Efficiency and effectiveness of fraud risk management in the Department of Health, eThekwini District-KwaZulu-Natal Province*. Unpublished (doctoral dissertation). University of Kwa-Zulu-Natal.

Molefe, P. (2006). *Overview by the Director-General, An Analysis of the Financial Performance of State-Owned Enterprises*. Retrieved July 7, 2020, from https://www.gov.za/sites/default/files/gcis_document/201409/analysisfinperformancesoe0.pdf

Moloi, T., & Marwala, T. (2020). The agency theory. In *Artificial Intelligence in Economics and Finance Theories*. Springer.

Muhammad, H., Migliori, S., & Mohsni, S. (2023). Corporate governance and firm risk-taking: The moderating role of board gender diversity. *Meditari Accountancy Research, 31*(3), 706–728.

Namara, R. B., Karyeija, G. K., & Mubangizi, B. C. (2015). Network governance and capacity of local governments to deliver LED in Uganda. *Commonwealth Journal of Local Governance, 18*(1), 82–107.

Needham, R. D., & de Loë, R. C. (1990). The policy Delphi: Purpose, structure, and application. *Canadian Geographer/Le Géographe Canadien, 34*(2), 133–142.

OECD. (2015). *OECD Guidelines on Corporate Governance of State-Owned Enterprises*. Retrieved June 20, 2019, from http://www.oecd.org/daf/ca/OECD-Guidelines-Corporate-Governance-SOEs-2015.pdf

Okoli, C., & Pawlowski, S. D. (2004). The Delphi method as a research tool: An example, design considerations and applications. *Information & Management, 42*(1), 15–29.

Olowosegun, O., & Moloi, T. (2021). Corporate governance disclosures in the annual reports of Nigerian banks. *Acta Commercii, 21*(1), 857.

Rossouw, G. J., & Reddy, Y. R. K. (2009). The ethics of corporate governance. *International Journal of Law and Management, 51*(1), 4–9.

Serretta, H., Bendixen, M., & Sutherland, M. (2009). Core corporate governance dilemmas facing boards: A South African perspective. *South African Journal of Economic and Management Sciences, 12*(2), 194–210.

Shapiro, C., & Willig, R. (1990). Economic rationales for the scope of privatization. The political economy of public sector reform and privatization. *Critical Perspectives on the World Economy, 2*(1), 55–87.

Thabane, T., & Snyman-Van Deventer, E. (2018). Pathological corporate governance deficiencies in South Africa's state-owned companies: A critical reflection'. *Potchefstroom Electronic Law Journal, 2*(1), 1–32.

Thomas, A. (2012). Governance at South African state-owned enterprises: What do annual reports and the print media tell us? *Social Responsibility Journal, 8*(4), 448–470.

Vagliasindi, M. (2008). *Governance arrangements for state owned enterprises*. The World Bank Publication.

van der Nest, D. P., Thornhill, C., & de Jager, J. (2008). Audit committees and accountability in the South African public sector. *Journal of Public Administration, 43*(4), 545–558.

Vandiar, T. (2015). *A critical analysis of the capacity of South African non-executive directors: A model for best practice in South Africa*. Unpublished (doctoral) University of Johannesburg.

Williams, D. (2010). State-owned enterprises: End of the road. *Financial Mail, 205*(7), 34–85.

Zohrabi, M. (2013). Mixed method research: Instruments, validity, reliability and reporting findings. *Theory and Practice in Language Studies, 3*(2), 254–262.

Zondo, R. (2022a). *State-Capture-Commission-Report-part-i-vol-1.pdf*. Retrieved February 19, 2022, from https://www.gov.za/sites/default/files/gcis_document/202201/judicial-commission-inquiry-state-capture-reportpart-1.pdf

Zondo, R. (2022b). *State-Capture-Commission-Report-part-i-vol-1.pdf*. Retrieved February 19, 2022, from https://www.gov.za/sites/default/files/gcis_document/202202/part-2vol2-denelreport-state-capture-commission.pdf

Zondo, R. (2022c). *State-Capture-Commission-Report-part-i-vol-1.pdf*. Retrieved February 19, 2022, from https://www.gov.za/sites/default/files/gcis_document/202204/state-capture-commission-report-part-iv-vol-1.pdf

Comparative Analysis of the Proposed South African Solar Tax Incentives with the Solar Tax Incentives in the USA and India

Kirsten Sydow and Mahmood Surty

Abstract Renewable energy is a topical issue in South Africa due to energy constraints and high levels of blackouts. The advent of renewable energy sources, such as solar power, can assist with combating these issues currently being experienced in the country. Tax incentives are a way to increase the adoption of solar power in South Africa. This study aimed to compare the recently implemented solar tax incentives in South Africa to those in developing and developed countries, namely India and the USA, respectively. Due to the expanded solar incentives in South Africa only recently being implemented in 2023, there are no prior studies on this topic. The study was conducted by using a comparative analysis of literature to compare the incentives in each respective country and subsequently provided recommendations for the South African solar tax incentives, based on these findings. South Africa has less beneficial solar tax incentives as opposed to those in India and the USA for individuals and has more stringent qualification requirements. The incentives available to businesses in South Africa are beneficial; however, there are fewer incentives available compared to India and the USA. Improvements can be made to the South African solar tax incentives by expanding the incentives available to both businesses and individuals based on similar legislation in the USA and India. This study provides insights into potential tax incentives that could be adopted to increase the use of solar energy in South Africa.

Keywords Solar tax incentives · Solar power · South African Revenue Service (SARS) · US Internal Revenue Code · Income Tax Act of India · Loadshedding

K. Sydow · M. Surty (✉)
University of the Witwatersrand, Johannesburg, South Africa
e-mail: Mahmood.surty@wits.ac.za

T. Moloi (ed.), *Impacting Society Positively Through Technology in Accounting and Business Processes*, Springer Proceedings in Business and Economics,
https://doi.org/10.1007/978-3-031-84885-8_2

Introduction

The Department of Mineral Resources and Energy explains in the Integrated Resource Plan (IRP) that electricity is a crucial service that is needed to maintain a decent standard of living (Department of Mineral Resources and Energy, 2019, p. 8). The level of nationwide loadshedding in 2022 surpassed 2021 as the highest amount of loadshedding ever recorded (CSIR, 2023, p. 110). Loadshedding refers to planned power outages undertaken to protect the national power grid from collapse due to insufficient power capacity (Walsh et al., 2021). The amount of loadshedding in December 2022 alone was more than any year prior to 2022 (CSIR, 2023, p. 110). The high levels of loadshedding in South Africa are a threat to both businesses and private households (Mabunda, 2021, p. 1).

One of the United Nations' sustainable development goals to be achieved by 2030 is to ensure affordable, reliable, modern, and sustainable energy to all people (United Nations, 2015, p. 4). One of the sub-targets of this goal is to substantially shift the global energy mix toward renewable energy sources (United Nations, 2018, p. 37). Renewable energy sources include, but are not limited to, wind power, solar power, hydropower, and bioenergy (Intergovernmental Panel on Climate Change, 2012: 8). South Africa has managed to achieve lower levels of fossil fuel generated energy in 2021 and 2022. However, this decline was not due to the country increasing its energy generated from renewable energy sources but due to high levels of loadshedding (PwC, 2022, p. 5).

Importance of This Study

There is a significant need for South Africa to increase the adoption of renewable energy sources in order to achieve the United Nations' energy-related goals, as well as to combat the electricity crisis in South Africa (PwC, 2022, p. 5; United Nations, 2015, p. 4). In order to assist in the adoption of renewable energy sources and combat the above problems, the IRP was published in 2019 by the South African Department of Mineral Resources and Energy (Department of Mineral Resources and Energy, 2019, p. 8). One of the aspects of renewable energy sources discussed in the IRP is solar energy (Department of Mineral Resources and Energy, 2019, p. 13). The focus of this study is on solar energy. The reason that solar power was chosen for this study is because South Africa's weather is ideal for solar power generation as there are copious amounts of sunshine in the country (GC Solar Head Office, 2023). Solar energy can be defined as the utilisation of light energy from the sun and its conversion into usable forms of power, such as light or heat (Solar Energy Technologies Office, n.d.). One way this can be done is through photovoltaic (PV) panels which harness the sun's energy and convert it into useful forms (Maka & Alabid, 2022, p. 477).

In early 2023, the South African government proposed further measures to increase the adoption of renewable energy sources, particularly solar energy (Engelbrecht & Hassan, 2024; National Treasury, 2023a, p. 10). These proposed solar tax incentives were first announced in the 2023 budget speech (National Treasury, 2023a, p. 10) and were later drafted in the Taxation Laws Amendment Bill of 2023 (TLA Act of 2023) (National Treasury, 2023b, p. 4). The solar tax incentives that were proposed aim to encourage both individuals and businesses to install solar power infrastructure (National Treasury, 2023a, p. 10).

Due to the implementation of these new solar tax incentives and their topical nature, this study compares the new solar tax incentives to those in other countries to gain valuable insights. This study compares the solar tax incentives in South Africa to those of the USA and India. Recommendations for South African tax incentives, based on the comparative analysis in this study, can be used to inform tax policy and potentially increase the use of solar energy in South Africa.

The research question addressed is: How do the newly proposed solar tax incentives in South Africa compare to the solar tax incentives implemented by the USA and India, and what improvements could be suggested to the South African incentives, based on the US and India's incentives?

In order to answer the research question, it is stratified into the following sub-questions:

1. What are the details of the new solar tax incentives in South Africa?
2. What are the current solar tax incentives in the USA and how do the new solar tax incentives in South Africa compare to these incentives?
3. What are the current solar tax incentives in India and how do the new solar tax incentives in South Africa compare to these incentives?
4. What improvements could be suggested to the South African solar tax incentives, based on the comparative analysis?

Why Solar Tax Incentives Are Important?

An understanding of the solar tax incentives in South Africa and other countries is important because the International Energy Agency (2020: 12) estimates that by 2025, renewable energy sources will surpass coal as the main method of generating electricity, making renewable energy sources a topical issue in the future of electricity generation. South Africa is the world's largest carbon-intensive electricity producer, which emphasises the importance of migrating to renewable energy sources to reduce carbon emissions (United Nations, n.d.).

Extreme levels of loadshedding and the lack of reliable electricity supply in South Africa are the biggest economic constraint the country is facing (Engelbrecht & Hassan, 2024; National Treasury, 2023a, p. 8). Loadshedding leads to a decrease in production which ultimately has a negative effect on the gross domestic product of South Africa (Lenoke, 2017, p. 1). The switch to renewable energy sources, such as solar energy, is important to reduce these negative effects on the economy (Nedbank, 2021). The solar tax incentives which were introduced in South Africa can be seen as a means to encourage the adoption of solar energy to combat the negative effects of loadshedding on the economy and to move toward renewable energy sources to generate electricity (Nedbank, 2021). Understanding these incentives in comparison with similar incentives already introduced in a developed country, such as the USA, and a developing nation, such as India, can provide valuable insight for lawmakers in South Africa to consider.

The scope of this research is limited to a comparative analysis of the South African proposed solar tax incentives with similar solar tax incentives in the USA and India. No other renewable energy tax incentives, such as wind or hydropower tax incentives, were considered. Only solar tax incentives from a normal tax perspective were considered.

For South Africa, the laws that were analysed are the Income Tax Act of 1962 of South Africa (ITA) and the TLA of 2023. For the USA, the laws that were analysed are section 25D, section 48, and section 168 of the US Internal Revenue Code of 1986 (IRC). Furthermore, for the USA, only incentives relating to the USA, overall, were considered. State-level incentives have not been considered. For India, the laws and regulations that were considered are the Income Tax Act of India 1961 (specifically section 32) (Income Tax Act, 1961 of India) and the Rooftop Solar Programme Phase II published by the Ministry of New and Renewable Energy in 2023. Incentives in relation to power generation for the purposes of resale as a power producer are not considered as they are beyond the scope of this study.

Method

The method used in this study is a detailed literature review. Following the literature review, the literature is analysed and synthesised to make recommendations on how tax incentives concerning solar energy in South Africa could be improved. The literature reviewed was based on journal articles, reports, legislation, websites, and discussion papers that focused on solar energy tax incentives in South Africa, the USA, and India. Information was gathered using Google Scholar and the researchers' online and physical Institution's library. Search terms utilised included, but were not limited to solar tax incentives, solar credits, solar rebates, solar energy, SARS solar incentives, loadshedding, and United Nations' energy goals.

The literature review begins by outlining the new South African proposed solar tax incentives according to the TLA Act of 2023 and the ITA for natural persons and businesses. Thereafter, the solar tax incentives in the USA and India are discussed, using the relevant legislation of both countries. A comparative analysis is then conducted between South Africa, the USA, and India. Finally, recommendations are made on how the solar tax incentives of South Africa could be improved, based on the comparative analysis.

The Basis on Which the USA Is Chosen as a Comparative Country

The USA has been ranked second in the world in its solar generation capacity (International Renewable Energy Agency, 2023). It is also a fast-growing industry, with its renewable energy sector doubling in capacity since 2010 (Motyka et al., 2021). The USA has implemented a wealth of solar tax incentives to increase the adoption of solar energy (Solar Technologies Office, 2023a, 2023b). The US solar tax incentives include incentives similar to those of South Africa. These include incentives, such as the Investment Tax Credit, Production Tax Credit, accelerated depreciation allowance, and bonus depreciation allowance (Solar Energy Technologies Office, 2023b). By evaluating the impact of these similar incentives in the US solar energy sector, valuable insights are drawn for similar incentives to be implemented in South Africa. Furthermore, as the USA has a large number of solar tax incentives, the evaluation of these available other solar tax incentives provides suggestions for South Africa for other possible incentives that could be implemented to increase the adoption of solar energy in the country.

The Basis on Which India Is Chosen as a Comparative Country

India is chosen for this comparative analysis due to its status of being a developing country like South Africa (Department of Foreign Affairs and Trade, 2022), as well as the fact that India is one of the fastest-growing developing countries in the renewable energy sector (Kılıç & Kekezoglu, 2022, p. 8). India's commitment to solar energy is emphasised by the publication in 2010 of Jawaharlal Nehru National Solar Mission (JNNSM) which outlines India's goal to be a leader in the solar energy sector (KPMG, 2015, p. 39). India offers solar tax incentives in order to increase the adoption of solar energy, such as its accelerated depreciation allowance (Income Tax Act, 1961, section 32). By comparing India's incentives, valuable insight into the solar tax incentives in a developing country is gained to suggest possible improvements for South Africa's solar tax incentives.

Discussion and Analysis

South African Solar Tax Incentives

This section details the South African solar tax incentives for both individuals and businesses in order to answer sub-question one of the research questions.

What Solar Incentives Are Available to Individuals?

Before the TLA Act of 2023, no solar tax incentives were available to individuals in South Africa (National Treasury, 2023a). The 2023 Budget Speech mentioned that solar tax incentives would now be available to natural persons (individuals) and the details of the proposed tax incentives would then be drafted in the TLA Act of 2023 (National Treasury, 2023b, p. 4).

According to the TLA Act of 2023, the solar tax incentive for individuals was inserted into the ITA as section 6C (Taxation Laws Amendment Act, 2023, paragraph 2). According to section 6C of the ITA, individuals are allowed to deduct a solar tax credit for installed solar photovoltaic (PV) panels, provided certain requirements are met (Taxation Laws Amendment Act, 2023, paragraph 2). The general requirements to claim the tax credit are detailed below.

The solar PV panels need to be new and unused (Taxation Laws Amendment Act, 2023, paragraph 2). The panels can be purchased as a part of a new system or an extension of a current system (National Treasury, 2023b: 1). Each panel must be capable of the generation of 275 watts or more and the solar panels must be brought into use for the first time between 1 March 2023 and 1 March 2024 (Taxation Laws Amendment Act, 2023, paragraph 2). Further requirements are then imposed; the solar panels must be installed in a residence that is used mainly for domestic purposes, the installation must be connected to the distribution board of that residence, and an electrical certificate of compliance must be issued for the installation (Taxation Laws Amendment Act, 2023, paragraph 2). However, there is no ownership requirement in respect of the residence for the solar PV panels (National Treasury, 2023b, p. 2). Taxpayers who are renting their residence can claim the rebate provided that they are the ones who paid for the panels (National Treasury, 2023b, p. 2).

The following are excluded from the incentive: batteries, inverters, diesel generators, and installation costs (National Treasury, 2023b, p. 1). Some documentary requirements are needed in order to claim this rebate (National Treasury, 2023b, p. 2). The taxpayer must provide a VAT invoice with the cost of the solar panels, proof of payment for the panels, and a certificate of compliance detailing that the panels were brought into use in the timeframe allowed by section 6C (National Treasury, 2023b, p. 2).

The tax credit amount is equal to 25% of the actual cost of the solar panels but is limited to R15,000 (Taxation Laws Amendment Act, 2023, paragraph 2). If a taxpayer decides to sell their home with solar PV panels, there will be no recoupment applicable (National Treasury, 2023b, p. 3). However, if the taxpayer sells their solar PV panels within a year of being brought into use (not their home, just the panels themselves), then there will be a clawback of the rebate (National Treasury, 2023b, p. 3).

What Solar Incentives Are Available to Businesses?

Before the new solar tax incentives for businesses were proposed, section 12B of the ITA related to capital allowances for solar assets (solar panels, inverters and related equipment) (Income Tax Act, 1962, Section 12B) was considered. Under section 12B (Income Tax Act, 1962, section 12B), the following capital allowances for solar assets are permitted:

Solar assets exceeding 1 megawatt are allowed a capital allowance over 3 years in the ratio of 50%, 30%, and 20% of the lower of cost or the cash arm's length value of the solar asset, including installation costs (Income Tax Act, 1962, section 12B(2)(a)). The cost is the cost to the taxpayer and includes the cost to acquire, erect, and install the solar assets (Income Tax Act, 1962, section 12B (3)). Additionally, solar assets not exceeding 1 megawatt are allowed a full 100% capital allowance in the year they are purchased (Income Tax Act, 1962, section 12B(2)(b)). This allowance can only be claimed when the solar assets have been brought into use for the first time by the taxpayer (Stiglingh et al., 2020, p. 334). The allowance is not apportioned within a year of assessment, meaning that the allowance can always be claimed in full even if the taxpayer did not hold it for the full year of assessment (Stiglingh et al., 2020, p. 336).

The TLA Act of 2023 allows a more favourable allowance for solar assets in terms of the insertion of section 12BA into the ITA (Taxation Laws Amendment Act, 2023, paragraph 16). The new incentive allows an accelerated allowance and a bonus allowance for solar assets (Taxation Laws Amendment Act, 2023, paragraph 16). According to the amendment, taxpayers will be allowed to deduct 100% of the cost of the solar assets in the year the solar panels are brought into use and a further 25% additionally in that year, provided that the solar assets are brought into use for the first time between 1 March 2023 and 1 March 2025 (Taxation Laws Amendment Act, 2023, paragraph 16). All other requirements and information relating to section 12B apply to this amendment with slight deviations on leased assets (Taxation Laws Amendment Act, 2023, paragraph 16). The cost will still remain as the lower of cost or the cash arm's length value of the solar asset including installation costs (Income Tax Act, 1962, section 12B(2)(a)).

If a business decides to sell the solar assets before 1 March 2026, then 100% of the allowance will need to be recouped under section 8(4) (nA) of the ITA (Income Tax Act, 1962, section 8(4(a)), and the bonus 25% will be recouped under section 12BA of the ITA (Taxation Laws Amendment Act, 2023, paragraph 4).

The above discussion provides insight in order to answer sub-question one of the research questions, namely, the solar tax incentives available to individuals and businesses in South Africa.

US Solar Incentives

This section details the US solar tax incentives for both individuals and businesses in order to answer sub-question two of the research question.

What Solar Incentives Are Available to Individuals?

The Inflation Reduction Act of 2022 recently amended the solar tax incentives available to individuals in the USA (Internal Revenue Service, 2022, p. 1). Individuals have two options in respect of solar tax incentives, which are outlined in section 25C and section 25D of the Internal Revenue Code of 1986 (IRC) (Internal Revenue Code of 1986, section 25C and section 25D). Section 25C is the energy-efficient home improvement credit available to individuals in the USA (Internal Revenue Code of 1986, section 25C). This incentive is not discussed, as this study is limited to solar tax incentives related to solar panels and related equipment.

Section 25D

Section 25D is the residential clean energy property credit available to individuals in the USA (Internal Revenue Code of 1986, section 25D). This tax credit is available to all individuals for various forms of renewable energy if certain requirements are met (Internal Revenue Code of 1986, section 25D(a)). For the purposes of this study, only the parts of section 25D relating to solar energy are discussed. The relevant definitions from section 25D of the IRC are defined below.

Qualified solar water heating property expenditure is defined in section 25D (d)(1) as:

> Expenditure for property to heat water for use in a dwelling unit located in the United States and used as a residence by the taxpayer if at least half of the energy used by such property for such purpose is derived from the sun.

Qualified solar electric property expenditure is defined in section 25D (d)(2) as:

> Expenditure for property which uses solar energy to generate electricity for use in a dwelling unit located in the United States and used as a residence by the taxpayer.

The section 25D credit is available to individuals as a certain percentage of qualifying solar electric property expenditures and qualifying solar water heating property expenditures (Table 1) that have been installed in that year of assessment providing that certain requirements have been met (Internal Revenue Code of 1986, section 25D(a)).

The percentage of expenditure that is allowed is based on the cost of this qualifying expenditure and is dependent on when the solar system was installed (Solar Technologies Office, 2023a). The cost includes the following: solar photovoltaic panels or cells, labour costs for preparation and installation, other equipment

Table 1 Section 25D percentage of expenditure allowed as a tax credit

The year that the solar power system was installed	Percentage applicable
After 31 December 2016 and before 1 January 2020	30
After 31 December 2019 and before 1 January 2022	26
After 31 December 2021 and before 1 January 2033	30
After 31 December 2032 and before 1 January 2034	26
After 31 December 2033 and before 1 January 2035	22
After 31 December 2034	0

Table adapted from Internal Revenue Code of 1986, section 25D (g) and (h)

needed, such as wiring and inverters, sales taxes, and energy storage devices (Solar Technologies Office, 2023a). Roofing costs are not included unless the roof itself is considered solar equipment (Ibric, 2023).

There is no maximum amount that can be claimed (Solar Technologies Office, 2023a). The section 25D credit can only be claimed if certain requirements are met. The individual must be the owner of the solar electricity or water system (Ibric, 2023). This means that the individual must have purchased the solar system for cash or through a financing agreement (Solar Technologies Office, 2023a). If the individual has acquired the solar system through a leasing arrangement, then the individual will not qualify for the tax credit (Lane, 2023).

The individual must have a taxable income (Ibric, 2023). The section 25D credit is a non-refundable credit (Internal Revenue Service, 2022, p. 7). This means that a taxpayer will not be able to receive a refund for any of the credit that exceeds their tax liability for their year of assessment (Internal Revenue Service, 2022: 7). Any portion that is not claimed in the year that the credit arises can be carried forward to the next year of assessment (Internal Revenue Code of 1986, section 25D(c)).

Further requirements include that the solar power system must be installed at the individual's primary or secondary residence (Ibric, 2023) and the residence must be located in the USA (Internal Revenue Code of 1986, section 25D (d)(1)). The solar system does not necessarily need to be installed at an individual's primary residence; it can also be installed at a secondary residence, such as a holiday home located in the USA (Solar Technologies Office, 2023a). The credit cannot be claimed on solar electricity or water systems that are installed on a dwelling that the taxpayer rents out but does not use as a residence themselves (Internal Revenue Service, 2022: 4). If a taxpayer temporarily rents out their primary residence, then the credit can still be claimed (Internal Revenue Service, 2022: 5). Finally, the credit may only be claimed on the original installation of the solar electricity or water system and not subsequently on repairs or modifications (Ibric, 2023).

What Solar Incentives Are Available to Businesses?

There are multiple solar tax incentives available to businesses in the USA. There is the Investment Tax Credit (ITC) which is outlined in section 48 of the IRC and the Production Tax Credit (PTC) which is outlined in section 45 of the IRC (Solar Energy Technologies Office, 2023b). Businesses can qualify for an accelerated depreciation allowance and bonus depreciation allowance if certain requirements are met (Internal Revenue Code of 1986, section 168(e) and section 168(k)).

Section 45X in the IRC explains the Advanced Manufacturing Production Tax Credit (MPTC). For the purposes of this study, section 45X is not discussed as the MPTC relates to a credit for businesses that manufacture the components that go into solar equipment which is not in the scope of this study (Internal Revenue Code of 1986, section 45X).

Accelerated Depreciation Allowance Under Section 168 of the IRC

Businesses that install solar systems may claim an allowance on the solar equipment installed over a 5-year period (Internal Revenue Code of 1986, section 168(e)(B)(vi)(I)) using a half-year convention and the 200% declining-balance basis, according to the modified accelerated cost-recovery system (Solar Energy Technologies Office, 2023b). A half-year convention means that the installed solar equipment will be treated as if it was installed in the middle of the taxable year (Internal Revenue Code of 1986, section 168(d)(4)(A)). Effectively, this means that the allowance (Table 2) will be claimable for 6 years as only half the allowance will be claimed in year one and year six (Solar Energy Technologies Office, 2023b).

Similar to the tax credit available to individuals, the cost or depreciable amount of the allowance includes the costs related to solar photovoltaic panels or cells, labour costs for preparation and installation, other equipment needed, such as wiring and inverters, sales taxes, and energy storage devices (Solar Technologies Office, 2023b). Roofing costs are not included unless the roof itself is considered solar equipment (Ibric, 2023). The accelerated depreciation allowance can only be claimed on an amount that has not yet been deducted (Solar Technologies Office,

Table 2 Depreciation allowance percentages for accelerated depreciation in the USA under section 168 of the US Internal Revenue Code

Year	Depreciation percentage
1	20.00
2	32.00
3	19.20
4	11.52
5	11.52
6	5.76

Table adapted from Department of the Treasury Internal Revenue Service (2022: 69)

2023b). For example, the depreciable amount for the accelerated allowance will be based on the amount after deducting the bonus depreciation and ITC allowance if applicable (Solar Technologies Office, 2023b).

Businesses can qualify for bonus depreciation (Table 3), as described in section 168(k) of the IRC on a solar power system (Internal Revenue Code of 1986, section 168(k)(6)(A)). This bonus allowance can only be claimed once on the date the system is placed into service and it can be claimed on the cost of the solar power system (Internal Revenue Code of 1986, section 168(k)(6)(A)). Placed in service is defined in section 1(179) of the IRC as: "...the time that property is first placed by the taxpayer in a condition or state of readiness and availability for a specifically assigned function...".

ITC and PTC Under Section 45 and 48 of the US Internal Revenue Code

The ITC is outlined in section 48 of the IRC (Internal Revenue Code of 1986, section 48) and the PTC in section 45 of the IRC. These can be claimed by businesses in addition to accelerated and bonus depreciation (Solar Technologies Office, 2023b). However, businesses cannot claim both the ITC and PTC and must choose the credit that is going to be the most beneficial for them (Solar Technologies Office, 2023b). The PTC is a solar tax credit that is based on electricity generation (Solar Technologies Office, 2023b). For this reason, it is beyond the scope of this study and is not discussed further.

The ITC is a tax credit which means it reduces a business's tax liability for a tax year (Solar Technologies Office, 2023b). To qualify for the credit, the solar power system must be located in either the USA or US territories (Solar Technologies Office, 2023b). The ITC can only be claimed once when the solar power system is placed into service (Internal Revenue Code of 1986, section 48(a)(1)). The equipment must be new and unused (Solar Technologies Office, 2023b). Finally, the solar

Table 3 Depreciation allowance percentages for bonus depreciation in the USA under section 168 of the US Internal Revenue Code

Date placed in service	Bonus depreciation percentage
After 27 September 2022 and before 1 January 2023	100
After 31 December 2022 and before 1 January 2024	80
After 31 December 2024 and before 1 January 2025	60
After 31 December 2024 and before 1 January 2026	40
After 31 December 2025 and before 1 January 2027	20

Table adapted from Internal Revenue Code of 1986, section 168(k)(6)(A)

power system cannot be leased to a tax-exempt entity (Solar Technologies Office, 2023b). The ITC is a once-off tax credit based on the cost of the system and does not vary, based on the electricity produced by the system (Solar Technologies Office, 2023b). The amount of the ITC is based on the cost of the solar energy system (Solar Technologies Office, 2023b). The cost includes elements, such as photovoltaic panels, inverters, sales taxes, installation costs, step-up transformers, circuit breakers, and energy storage devices (Solar Technologies Office, 2023b).

The ITC qualifies for bonus credits (Solar Technologies Office, 2023b). The bonus credits that would be available are the domestic content bonus, energy community bonus, and low-income bonus (Internal Revenue Code of 1986, section 48(a)(12), 48(a)(14) and section 45). It must be noted that the ITC credit does affect the section 168 depreciation allowance as the depreciable amount of the solar power system will be reduced by half the ITC that was claimed (Solar Technologies Office, 2023b). For example, if the cost of a solar system is \$100,000 and qualifies for the ITC at a rate of 30%, this means that the depreciable amount will be 85% (100% -1/2(30%)) of the cost which is \$85,000.

In order to determine what percentage will be claimed as a bonus credit for the ITC (Fig. 1), a business needs to determine in what year the solar power system was placed into service (Internal Revenue Code of 1986, section 48(a)(12), 48(a)(14) and section 45). The percentage applicable will vary, depending on the year the solar power system was placed into service and whether bonus requirements were met, based on whether it qualifies for the domestic content bonus, energy community bonus, and low-income bonus (Internal Revenue Code of 1986, section 48(a)(12), 48(a)(14) and section 45).

Summary of Investment Tax Credit (ITC) and Production Tax Credit (PTC) Values Over Time

			Start of Construction						
			2006 to 2019	2020 to 2021	2022	2023 to 2033	The later of 2034 (or two years after applicable year*)	The later of 2035 (or three years after applicable year*)	The later of 2036 (or four years after applicable year*)
ITC	Full rate (if project meets labor requirements*)	Base Credit	30%	26%	30%	30%	22.5%	15%	0%
		Domestic Content Bonus				10%	7.5%	5%	0%
		Energy Community Bonus				10%	7.5%	5%	0%
	Base rate (if project does not meet labor requirements*)	Base Credit	30%	26%	6%	6%	4.5%	3%	0%
		Domestic Content Bonus				2%	1.5%	1%	0%
		Energy Community Bonus				2%	1.5%	1%	0%
	Low-income bonus (1.8 GW/yr cap)	<5 MW projects in LMI communities or Indian land				10%	10%	10%	10%
		Qualified low-income residential building project / Qualified low-income economic benefit project				20%	20%	20%	20%

Fig. 1 Diagram of percentages applicable for the ITC (Image from Solar Technologies Office, 2023b)

The above discussion enables us to gain a richer understanding of sub-question two of the research question, namely, the solar tax incentives available to individuals and businesses in the USA.

India's Solar Tax Incentives

This section details the solar tax incentives for both individuals and businesses in India in order to answer sub-question three of the research question.

What Solar Incentives Are Available to Individuals?

In India, there are no solar tax incentives for individuals that directly affect their taxes. There is, however, a subsidy that assists with the purchase of solar power systems (Ministry of New and Renewable Energy, 2023b). This is discussed below.

On the 30th of July 2022, India launched a programme called the Rooftop Solar Programme Phase II which grants a central financial assistance (CFA) subsidy to resident individuals in India who install a rooftop solar power system (Ministry of New and Renewable Energy, 2023). The subsidy is available for the entire solar power system, including the solar panels and other costs involved (e.g. inverters, generators, and installation costs) (Ministry of New and Renewable Energy, 2023b).

In order to claim the CFA subsidy, there are some requirements that need to be met (Ministry of New and Renewable Energy, 2023b). These requirements include that the solar power system must be registered through the Rooftop Solar Programme portal, the solar power system has to be installed by a vendor that has been registered and approved on the Rooftop Solar Programme portal, and the solar panels must be manufactured in India (Gupta, 2022). It is also important that the individual submits their application on the Rooftop Solar Programme portal and no third party may submit the application on their behalf (Ministry of New and Renewable Energy, n.d.).

The rates for the CFA subsidy are based on the lower of the solar module capacity and the solar inverter capacity (Ministry of New and Renewable Energy, 2023a, p. 2). Further, the CFA rates are also broken down into general category states and special category states (Ministry of New and Renewable Energy, 2023a, p. 2). Special category states are states in India that are in the north-eastern parts of India and those with hilly terrains (Gupta, 2022). Examples of these states are Sikkim, Uttarakhand, and Himachal Pradesh (Gupta, 2022). Special states will receive a more favourable CFA subsidy, compared to the general category states in order to increase solar power uptake in these states (Gupta, 2022) (Table 4).

There are two mechanisms under which the CFA subsidy operates, namely, mechanism 1 and mechanism 2 (Ministry of New and Renewable Energy, 2023b). Under mechanism 1, the CFA subsidy amount will be paid into the bank account of the individual (Ministry of New and Renewable Energy, n.d.). Under mechanism 2,

Table 4 CFA subsidy rates for the 2023 year of assessment

Capacity (lower of solar module capacity and the solar inverter capacity	Subsidy for general category states (in Indian rupees)	Subsidy for special category states (in Indian rupees)
Up to 3 kW	14,588/kW	17,662/kW
Above 3 kW and up to 10 kW	14,588/kW for the first 3 kW and 7294/kW for the remaining kWs	17,662/kW for the first 3 kW and 8831/kW for the remaining kWs
Above 10 kW	94,922 (fixed amount)	114,803 (fixed amount)

Table adapted from Ministry of New and Renewable Energy (2023a, p. 2)

the CFA subsidy will be paid to the vendor who is installing the solar power system, and the individual will only need to pay the balance after the subsidy has been deducted (Ministry of New and Renewable Energy, n.d.). The CFA subsidy is the only incentive available to individuals in India with regard to solar power. The CFA subsidy is available until 31 March 2026 (Gupta, 2022).

What Solar Incentives Are Available to Businesses?

There are two solar tax incentives available to businesses in India. The first incentive allows an accelerated depreciation allowance and is outlined in section 32 of the Income Tax Act 1961 of India (ITA of India) (Income Tax Act 1961 of India, section 32). The second incentive applies to businesses involved in power generation, transmission, and distribution and is outlined in section 80-IA of the ITA of India (Surana, 2023). Due to this incentive relating to power generation, it is out of the scope of this study and is not explored further.

Accelerated Depreciation Allowance Under Section 32 of the ITA of India

The accelerated depreciation for solar power systems in India is outlined in section 32 of the ITA of India (Income Tax Act, 1961 of India, section 32). Under this section, any assets that are used in the generation or generation and distribution of power qualify for a 40% depreciation allowance (Income Tax Act, 1961 of India, section 32(1) Proviso (i)). To claim the 40% depreciation allowance, there are certain requirements that need to be met. These requirements include that the asset must be owned by the business and the asset must be used for trade purposes (Surana, 2023).

Furthermore, power-generating units qualify for a further 20% depreciation under section 32 of the ITA of India (Income Tax Act, 1961 of India, section 32(1) Proviso (iiA)). The further 20% depreciation allowance under section 32 of the ITA of India cannot be claimed if the equipment is not new and unused or if the equipment is installed in any office premises or residential accommodation (Income Tax Act, 1961 of India, section 32(1) Proviso (iiA)).

The cost of the solar system to be depreciated includes the cost of the solar photovoltaic panels, inverter, cables, switches, circuit breakers, mounting structures, and installation costs (Ministry of New and Renewable Energy, 2021: 1). The sum of these amounts will qualify for the depreciation allowance if all the other requirements are met (Ministry of New and Renewable Energy, 2021: 1). There is currently no end date to the application of section 32 of the ITA of India (Gupta, 2022).

The above discussion provides insight into India's solar tax incentives and answers sub-question three of the research question, namely, what solar tax incentives are available to individuals and businesses in India.

Comparative Analysis and Recommendations

An in-depth discussion and comparative analysis is carried out to answer sub-questions two, three, and four of the research question. This enables the researchers to compare the solar incentives in South Africa with those in the USA and India and make recommendations, based on the comparative analysis on the current South African solar tax incentives.

Comparative Analysis and Recommendations for Solar Tax Incentives for Individuals

South Africa and the USA both have a tax credit available to individuals as a solar tax incentive (Taxation Laws Amendment Act, 2023, paragraph 2; Internal Revenue Code of 1986, section 25D). India, however, has taken a different approach and offers their resident individuals a subsidy to incentivise the adoption of solar power and reduce the cost of the solar power system (Ministry of New and Renewable Energy, 2023b). As a recommendation, South Africa could consider creating a subsidy incentive to assist South African individuals in affording the cost of solar power systems. This subsidy could work in a similar way to India's and could be based on the solar module capacity or solar inverter capacity (Ministry of New and Renewable Energy, 2023a, p. 2). South Africa could also consider having different categories of areas with increased subsidies, similar to India's incentive (Gupta, 2022), in order to encourage adoption of solar power in areas where it is needed the most.

The US incentive for individuals includes costs such as inverters, installation, and batteries (Solar Technologies Office, 2023a). These costs are specifically excluded from the South African solar tax incentives for individuals (National Treasury, 2023b, p. 1). An adaptation that could be made to the South African solar tax incentive would be to include the above costs in the incentive in order to remove some of the cost burden on individuals installing solar power systems. South African solar tax incentives, however, apply to all residential use properties whether rented out or not while the US incentives only apply to the primary and secondary residence of the taxpayer (National Treasury, 2023b, p. 1; Internal Revenue Service, 2022, p. 4). The USA also provides solar tax incentives in respect of water heating

(Internal Revenue Code of 1986, section 25D(d)(1). South Africa could consider expanding the solar incentive to include systems such as solar geysers used for water heating.

Another suggestion is to increase the percentage of the cost that can be claimed for the incentive. In South Africa, the incentive percentage is 25% (Taxation Laws Amendment Act, 2023, paragraph 2) while in the USA, the current percentage for solar power systems installed is 30% (Internal Revenue Code of 1986, section 25D (g) and (h)). South Africa could increase the percentage further to remove the burden of the cost from the individual. Furthermore, the USA does not have a maximum amount that can be claimed (Internal Revenue Code of 1986, section 25D), while South Africa has a maximum amount of R15 000 that can be claimed (Taxation Laws Amendment Act, 2023, paragraph 2). A suggestion would be to either increase this limit or take the limit away completely to further encourage the installation of solar power systems by individuals.

A factor to consider is the amount of time for which the incentives are applicable. South Africa's incentive is applicable until 1 March 2024 (Taxation Laws Amendment Act, 2023, paragraph 2), which is shorter than the time that the US and India's solar tax incentives are applicable which stretch to 31 December 2034 and 31 March 2026, respectively (Internal Revenue Code of 1986, section 25D; Gupta, 2022). A recommendation would be to extend the amount of time the incentive is available to incentivise individuals to install solar power systems.

In respect of the ability to carry over the tax credit, the solar tax incentive in South Africa cannot be carried over while in the USA any unused tax credit can be carried forward to a subsequent year (Taxation Laws Amendment Act, 2023, paragraph 2, 6C(1); Internal Revenue Code of 1986, section 25D(c)). Similar to the USA, South Africa could consider allowing taxpayers to carry forward any unused or limited tax credit on solar panels for individuals to the next year of assessment.

The above discussion enables us to gain a richer understanding of sub-questions one, two, three, and four of the research question, namely, the comparative analysis of the solar tax incentives between South Africa, the USA, and India and suggested improvements to the South African solar tax incentives for individuals.

Comparative Analysis and Recommendations for Solar Tax Incentives for Businesses

Depreciation Allowance

Among the countries being compared, South Africa has the highest percentage in relation to the accelerated depreciation solar tax incentive of 100%, plus an additional 25% of the solar assets cost or arm's length value, whichever is lower (Taxation Laws Amendment Act, 2023, section 12BA, paragraph 16). India has a percentage of 40% and thereafter an additional 20% (Income Tax Act, 1961 of India, section 32). The US depreciates over a 5-year period resulting in the highest percentage claimed in a year being 32% (Department of the Treasury Internal Revenue Service, 2022, p. 69).

For South African businesses to be able to claim the accelerated depreciation, the solar assets must be brought into use for the first time between 1 March 2023 and 1 March 2025 (Income Tax Act, section 12B). India and the USA do not have specific timeframes for this similar incentive to be claimed (Internal Revenue Code of 1986, section 168; Income Tax Act 1961 of India, section 32). South Africa could consider extending the time period for the accelerated depreciation as without the extension, the South African deprecation allowance is far lower and dependent on the capacity of the solar assets under the original section 12B allowance of 50%, 30%, and then 20% of the solar assets cost (Income Tax Act, 1962, section 12B).

South Africa, the USA, and India all base the depreciation allowance on the costs of all the solar assets used to generate power such as installation costs, inverters, batteries, and solar panels (Taxation Laws Amendment Act, 2023, paragraph 16, section12BA(4); Solar Technologies Office, 2023b; Ministry of New and Renewable Energy, 2021: 1). It is suggested that South Africa continues to allow the depreciation allowance on the cost of all the solar assets in line with the comparative countries analysed.

In the USA, bonus depreciation can be claimed once the solar power system is installed, and the percentage varies based on when the system is placed into service (Internal Revenue Code, section 168(k)(6)(A)). South Africa could implement a similar system to increase businesses' adoption of solar power systems in a timely manner.

Other Incentives

India currently has a tax incentive for business involved in power generation (Income Tax Act, 1961 of India, section 80-IA). The USA has further incentives, namely, either the ITC credit based on investment in solar assets or a PTC credit, based on the production of solar energy, which a business can choose to claim in addition to the depreciation allowance (Solar Technologies Office, 2023b). Currently, South Africa has no other incentives besides accelerated depreciation available to businesses. It is recommended that South Africa include other incentives for businesses to further incentivise the adoption of solar power systems. In order to design other incentives to be put in place, South Africa can use incentives implemented in the USA and India to gain inspiration. An example of an incentive that could be implemented is one that is similar to the ITC in the USA (Internal Revenue Code of 1986, section 48).

The above discussion enables us to gain a richer understanding of sub-questions one, two, three, and four of the research question, namely, the comparative analysis of the solar tax incentives between South Africa, the USA, and India and suggested improvements to the South African solar tax incentives for businesses.

Conclusion

The objective of this study was to gain an understanding of the newly proposed solar incentives available in South Africa and to compare these incentives to those of a developing and developed country, namely India and the USA. This was carried out by performing a comparative literature review of the relevant legislation of each of the three countries.

In answering the various sub-questions of the research question, it was found that the recently proposed solar tax incentives in South Africa relating to individuals resulted in the solar tax credit of 25% with a limit of R15,000 being introduced up to 29 February 2024 (National Treasury, 2023b: 1). The solar tax incentives in South Africa relating to businesses were amended to include a 100% depreciation allowance with a further bonus depreciation allowance of 25% (Taxation Laws Amendment Act, 2023, paragraph 16).

In the USA, the solar tax incentives for individuals are also in the form of solar tax credits as in South Africa, but have more costs, such as inverters, generators, and installation, included in the incentive (Solar Technologies Office, 2023a). In addition, the US incentive has a higher percentage that can be claimed and is available for a longer period of time than South Africa's incentive (Internal Revenue Code of 1986, section 25D (g) and (h)). The solar tax incentives in the USA available to businesses are an accelerated depreciation allowance of a lower percentage than in South Africa, a bonus depreciation allowance, and the ITC or PTC (Internal Revenue Code of 1986, section 45 and 168).

In India, the solar incentives available to individuals are quite different from those of South Africa. India's incentive is in the form of a subsidy available to individuals to decrease the upfront cost of the solar power system (Ministry of New and Renewable Energy, 2023b). This incentive varies in amount based on the number of kilowatt hours the system produces (Ministry of New and Renewable Energy, 2023a: 2). The solar tax incentives related to businesses in India include an accelerated depreciation allowance percentage based on a lower percentage than that in South Africa (Income Tax Act, 1961 of India, section 32; Taxation Laws Amendment Act, 2023, paragraph 16).

Key findings from this study are that South Africa's solar tax incentives are still in their infancy and can be further developed. The South African incentive related to individuals was found to be the most stringent with the lowest amount being granted to individuals and only based on the cost of the solar panels and not the entire solar system (Taxation Laws Amendment Act, 2023, paragraph 2). Some valuable recommendations can be drawn from this comparative study to improve or expand the South African solar tax incentives. For incentives relating to individuals, some recommendations would be to include other costs in the tax credit, such as the cost of an inverter and installation costs, increase the percentage of the tax credit, increase the limit per individual that can be claimed, consider including another incentive in the form of a subsidy for solar energy adoption, and extend the date to which the incentive is applicable. For incentives relating to businesses, the recently amended allowance to be drafted in the ITA under section 12BA for businesses is an extremely favourable percentage compared to similar incentives in the USA and India and should remain in legislation. The only recommendations would be to include a bonus depreciation (allowance) for bringing solar assets into use and include a further incentive similar to the ITC and PTC in the USA (Internal Revenue Code of 1986, section 48).

Areas of future research include a comparative analysis of the solar tax incentives of South Africa with respect to power production using solar energy, an expansion of the solar tax incentives examined to include state-level incentives in the USA, and a study on the effectiveness of the solar tax incentives in South Africa, the USA, and India.

References

Agency, I. E. (2020). *Renewables. (2020). Analysis and Forecast to 2025*, viewed 26 August 2023 from https://iea.blob.core.windows.net/assets/1a24f1fe-c971-4c25-964a-57d0f31eb97b/Renewables_2020-PDF.pdf

CSIR Energy Centre. (2023). *Statistics of utility-scale power generation in South Africa*, viewed 26 August 2023 from https://www.csir.co.za/sites/default/files/Documents/Statistics%20of%20power%20in%20SA%202022-CSIR-%5BFINAL%5D.pdf

Department of Foreign Affairs and Trade. (2022). *List of developing countries as declared by the Minister for Foreign Affairs*, viewed on 14 September 2023 from https://www.dfat.gov.au/sites/default/files/list-developing-countries.pdf

Department of Mineral Resources and Energy. (2019). *Integrated Resource Plan 2019*, viewed on 14 September 2023 from https://www.energy.gov.za/irp/2019/IRP-2019.pdf

Department of the Treasury Internal Revenue Service. (2022). *Publication 946. How To Depreciate Property*. https://www.irs.gov/pub/irs-pdf/p946.pdf

Engelbrecht, K. J. B., & Hassan, M. (2024). *Solar photovoltaic panels tax rebate: Is the tax rebate the right tax incentive choice for South Africa?* (pp. 201–215). Springer.

GC Solar. (2023). *Top 10 Benefits of Solar Energy for South African Homes*, viewed on 14 September 2023 from https://gcsolar.co.za/top-10-benefits-of-solar-energy-for-south-african-homes/#:~:text=South%20Africa%20is%20known%20for,a%20significant%20amount%20of%20power

Gupta, M. (2022). *Solar Subsidy in India Explained*, Ornate Solar, viewed 4 August 2023 from https://ornatesolar.com/blog/state-wise-solar-subsidies-in-india-2021#:~:text=Solar%20energy%20systems%20with%20a,%E2%82%B994822%20will%20be%20given

Income Tax Act, 1961 of India.

Income Tax Act, 58 of South Africa, 1962.

Intergovernmental Panel on Climate Change. (2012). *Renewable Energy Sources and Climate Change Mitigation*, viewed on 15 September 2023 from https://www.ipcc.ch/site/assets/uploads/2018/03/SRREN_Full_Report-1.pdf

International Renewable Energy Agency. (2023). *Country rankings*, viewed on 25 April 2023 from https://www.irena.org/Data/View-data-by-topic/Capacity-and-Generation/Country Rankings

Internal Revenue Service. (2022). *Frequently asked questions about energy efficient home improvements and residential clean energy property credits*. Retrieved July 20, 2023, from https://www.irs.gov/pub/taxpros/fs-2022-40.pdf

Ibric, J. (2023). *How does the Federal Solar tax credit work?* viewed 28 July 2023 from https://www.solar.com/learn/how-does-federal-solar-tax-credit-work/

Kılıç, U., & Kekezoğlu, B. (2022). A review of solar photovoltaic incentives and policy: Selected countries and Turkey. *Ain Shams Engineering Journal, 13*(5), 101669. https://doi.org/10.1016/j.asej.2021.101669

KPMG. (2015). *Taxes and incentives for renewable energy*, viewed 20 July 2023 from https://assets.kpmg.com/content/dam/kpmg/pdf/2015/09/taxes-and-incentives-2015-web-v2.pdf

Lane, C. (2023). *Complete guide to the 2023 federal solar tax credit*, viewed 28 July 2023 from https://www.solarreviews.com/blog/federal-solar-tax-credit#qualify

Lenoke, M. (2017). *The Impact of the loadshedding on the economic growth of South Africa.* https://repository.nwu.ac.za/bitstream/handle/10394/35217/LENOKE_M.pdf?sequence=1&isAllowed=y

Mabunda, N. E. (2021). Use of photovoltaic energy to minimize the impact of load-shedding in South Africa. In *2021 International Conference on Electrical, Computer and Energy Technologies (ICECET)* (pp. 1–4). IEEE. https://ieeexplore.ieee.org/stamp/stamp.jsp?tp=&arnumber=9698720

Maka, A. O. M., & Alabid, J. M. (2022). Solar energy technology and its roles in sustainable development. *Clean Energy, 6*(3), 476–483. https://doi.org/10.1093/ce/zkac023

Ministry of New and Renewable Energy. (2021). *Benchmark costs for Grid-connected Rooftop Solar Photo-voltaic systems for the financial year 2021–22*, viewed 4 August 2023 from https://mnre.gov.in/img/documents/uploads/file_f-1629353920466.pdf

Ministry of New and Renewable Energy. (n.d.). *National Portal for Rooftop Solar*, viewed 4 August 2023 from https://solarrooftop.gov.in/

Ministry of New and Renewable Energy. (2023a). *Central Financial Assistance (CFA)/ Central Government Subsidy for rooftop solar plant installed by a residential consumer under simplified procedure*, viewed 4 August 2023 from https://solarrooftop.gov.in/pdf/revised_CFA_structure_08052023.pdf

Ministry of New and Renewable Energy. (2023b). *Solar Schemes*, viewed 4 August 2023 from https://mnre.gov.in/solar/schemes

Motyka, M., Pechowski, M., Thomson, J., & Rizzo, C. (2021). *Renewable transition: Separating perception from reality*. Deloitte, viewed 25 April 2023 from https://www2.deloitte.com/us/en/insights/industry/power-and-utilities/us-renewable-energy-transition.html

National Treasury. (2023a). *Budget 2023.* https://www.treasury.gov.za/documents/national%20budget/2023/speech/speech.pdf

National Treasury. (2023b). *Frequently asked questions: Solar panel tax incentive for individuals.* https://www.treasury.gov.za/documents/national%20budget/2023/2023%20budget%20faqs%20-%20solar%20panel%20tax%20incentive.pdf

Nedbank. (2021). *Load-shedding: Time to invest in Solar Power?* viewed 14 September 2023 from https://personal.nedbank.co.za/learn/blog/time-to-invest-in-solar-power.html

PwC. (2022). *Climate change—the socio-economic opportunity*, viewed 25 July 2023 from https://www.pwc.co.za/en/assets/pdf/net-zero-economy-index-2022.pdf

Stiglingh, M., Koekemoer, A. D., van Heerden, L., Wilcocks, J. S., & van der Zwan, P. (2020). *Silke: First touch to tax 2020.* LexisNexis.

Surana, E. (2023). *Section 80IA: Eligibility, Exemption, Applicability, and Deduction for AY 2022-23*, Cleartax, viewed 4 August 2023 from https://cleartax.in/s/section-80ia-income-tax-act

Solar Technologies Office. (2023a). *Homeowner's Guide to the Federal Tax Credit for Solar Photovoltaics,* viewed 17 October 2023 from https://www.energy.gov/eere/solar/homeowners-guide-federal-tax-credit-solar-photovoltaics

Solar Technologies Office. (2023b). *Federal Solar Tax Credits for Businesses,* viewed 26 August 2023 from https://www.energy.gov/eere/solar/federal-solar-tax-credits-businesses

Taxation Laws Amendment Bill of 2023 (South Africa).

The United States Internal Revenue Code of 1986.

United Nations. (2015). *Resolution adopted by the General Assembly on 25 September 2015*, viewed 25 April 2023 from https://www.undp.org/sites/g/files/zskgke326/files/migration/ua/Agenda2030-eng.pdf

United Nations. (2018). *The 2030 Agenda and the Sustainable Development Goals*, viewed 25 April 2023 from https://repositorio.cepal.org/bitstream/handle/11362/40156/S1801140_en.pdf

United Nations. (n.d.). *COP26: Together for our planet*, viewed 23 May 2023 from https://www.un.org/en/climatechange/cop26

Walsh, K., Theron, R., & Reeders, C. (2021). Estimating the economic cost of load shedding in South Africa. *Nova Economics*. https://www.novaeconomics.co.za/be/wp-content/uploads/2023/01/ESSA_The-economic-cost-of-load-shedding_edit2.pdf

Critical Thinking Skills in Accounting: A Bibliometric Analysis

Letebele Mphahlele, Marx Benjamin, and Tankiso Moloi

Abstract The ongoing debate regarding the relative importance of soft skills over technical skills in accounting continues. Amidst the ongoing debate regarding the important soft skills, critical thinking has been identified as one such significant skill. This is particularly relevant due to the ongoing technological advancement and the increasing volume of data for decision-making. This study aimed to analyse research on critical thinking through bibliometric analysis. Techniques for assessing performance measured by the number of publications and impact, indicated by the number of citations, were employed in the analysis. Research in critical thinking in accounting is increasing although at a slow rate. Nonetheless, the most influential sources (journals) and countries producing in this field were identified. The analysis also revealed that most of the publications on critical thinking in accounting are primarily instructional cases and descriptive papers rather than empirical studies. Identifying primary sources and countries contributing the most to research in this field can highlight to educators and researchers the best practices to adopt to foster critical thinking. It is also evident that it is important to prioritise empirical studies in assessing the effectiveness of interventions to foster critical thinking.

Keywords Bibliometric analysis · Critical thinking · Accounting · Journals · Countries

Introduction

The ongoing advancement of technology and the growing interconnectedness of the global economy are continuously reshaping businesses, industries, and the requisite competencies for organisations to operate (Feliciano-Cestero et al., 2023). These

L. Mphahlele (✉) · M. Benjamin · T. Moloi
University of Johannesburg, Johannesburg, South Africa
e-mail: letebelem@uj.ac.za; benm@uj.ac.za; smoloi@uj.ac.za

T. Moloi (ed.), *Impacting Society Positively Through Technology in Accounting and Business Processes*, Springer Proceedings in Business and Economics,
https://doi.org/10.1007/978-3-031-84885-8_3

advancements are leading to a higher generation of data, which in turn require individuals to possess new skills to be able to critically engage with this data (Cooper et al., 2019). Engaging critically with data requires applying problem-solving skills to turn it into information. This information can then be used to draw reasonable conclusions and make better-informed decisions (Cortes & Salvatori, 2019). Technological advancements have also significantly impacted the accounting profession. The primary reason for this impact is because disciplines such as accounting and auditing are knowledge-intensive and heavily dependent on information and knowledge management (Agustí & Orta-Pérez, 2023). Consequently, technological advancements are affecting how accountants obtain, analyse, interpret data and inform business decision-making (Kotb et al., 2019). These identified changes have also raised growing concerns about the readiness of graduates for uncertain future work environments (De Villiers, 2021).

Given the rapid changes in the environment, it is becoming imperative for accounting students to possess soft or non-technical skills rather than just technical expertise (Jaafar, 2018). Various scholars have over the years contended that technical accounting skills are insufficient for the employment of entry-level accounting graduates (Bui & Porter, 2010; Jackling & De Lange, 2009; Kavanagh & Drennan, 2008a). Historically, technical skills have been seen as necessary and sufficient professional success in accounting. This is because accounting, as a discipline, is very technical and requires students to understand accounting transactions and procedures. But the accounting discipline is experiencing a paradigm shift due to the fast-changing environment and the integration of various technological tools. While employers still value technical skills in accounting graduates, these skills are no longer considered sufficient on their own.

In their research where they analysed job advertisements, Tan and Laswad (2018) found that soft skills were the most frequently sought by accounting employers. The shift in the requisite skills has generated an ongoing debate, with scholars indicating the importance of various soft skills for the employability of accounting students or graduates (Bui & Porter, 2010; De Villiers, 2021; Dolce et al., 2019; Jackling & De Lange, 2009; Jackson et al., 2022a; Kavanagh & Drennan, 2008b; Succi & Canovi, 2019; Tsiligiris & Bowyer, 2021). While there is consensus on the importance of soft skills in accounting, scholars are divided on the crucial soft skills for accounting graduates.

Scholars have identified soft skills such as proactivity, initiative, and teamwork as the most sought after (Carvalho & Almeida, 2022) while others identified communication, teamwork, and interpersonal skills as significant attributes sought by employers in the accounting field (Hassall et al., 2001; Jackson, 2014; Succi & Canovi, 2019; Webb & Chaffer, 2016). Some researchers have determined that the significance of soft skills for accountants varies by country. In their study, Hassall et al. (2005) discovered that employers in the UK prioritised problem-solving skills as an important generic skill for management accountants. Conversely, Spanish companies prioritised communication skills. Other scholars have indicated the importance of soft skills and critical thinking skills for accounting students as these skills enable them to interact with innovations brought by emerging technologies. A multinational Delphi panel of 46 experts defines critical thinking as a deliberate, self-regulatory judgement that leads to interpretation, analysis, evaluation, and inference (Facione, 1990). The panel asserts that critical thinking is interrelated with essential cognitive and meta-cognitive skills and strategies including interpretation, analysis, assessment, inference, explanation, and self-regulation. Various other scholars have indicated the importance of critical thinking skills in accounting.

The technological advancements require accounting graduates to possess classic/stable skills and contemporary/innovative skills (Al-Htaybat et al., 2018). Classic skills include problem-solving, information technology analytical abilities, decision-making, and evaluation. Conversely, contemporary skills include the understanding of accounting principles (Al-Htaybat et al., 2018). In exploring the impact of 4IR on future accounting skills, Tsiligiris and Bowyer (2021) found that a combination of critical thinking, communication, and emotional intelligence is important to adapt to the changing roles of accountants. Therefore, based on the findings of several researchers (Brink & Stoel, 2019; Jackson et al., 2022b), it is argued that early career accountants should possess the skills to collect, analyse, and manage high volumes of data. Graduates should possess skills that will enable them to convert data into accurate and valuable information that can be used for decision-making, strategic planning, and guiding clients (Jackson et al., 2022b). Consequently, possessing critical thinking and human interpretation abilities is important for finding innovative solutions through data analysis. These skills are strategic soft skills that can provide a company with inimitable know-how in this era of technological advancement (Visvizi et al., 2022). Critical thinking skills are also regarded as essential for supporting business development and economic growth in the coming years (Visvizi et al., 2022). Therefore, due to the impact of technological advancement on the accounting profession, it is essential to foster critical thinking in accounting education. Nonetheless, despite the recognised importance of critical thinking skills in accounting, there is a lack of research that evaluates the current state of research on critical thinking in accounting. There is also insufficient research on influential and productive countries contributing to this body of knowledge as well as type and themes of the most cited articles.

As such, this chapter aims to explore the current state of research on critical thinking skills in accounting education by systematically identifying the growth rate of research. Furthermore, it aims to systematically identify which countries contributed significantly to research in this area and the type of research has been carried out.

Therefore, this chapter aims to address the following Research Questions (RQ):

- RQ 1: What is the current status of research on critical thinking skills in accounting?
- RQ 2: Which five primary sources are the most influential publishers of critical thinking in accounting?
- RQ 3: Which countries contributed significantly to research on critical thinking skills in accounting?
- RQ 4: What type and theme of articles on critical thinking skills in accounting have received the most citations?

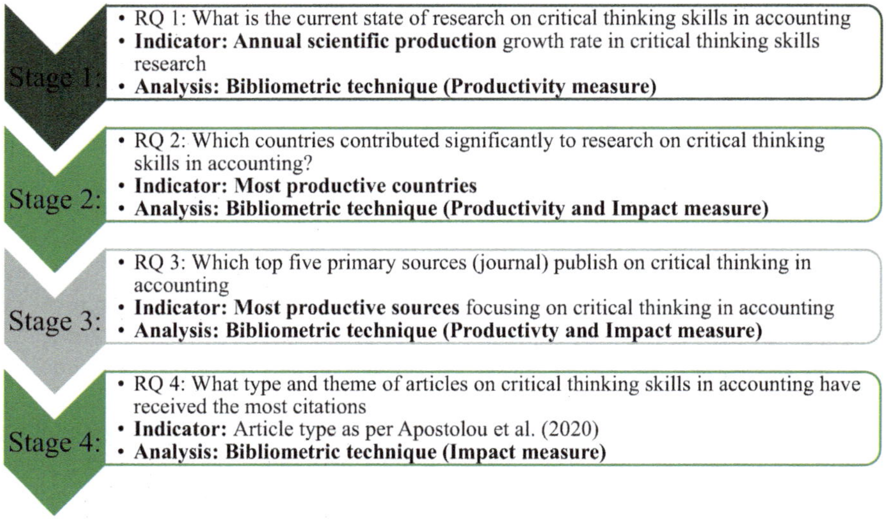

Fig. 1 Stages to answer the research questions

This study employed the bibliometric analysis to address the research questions as presented in Fig. 1. Stage 1 aimed to identify the growth in research on critical thinking skills in accounting. Stage 2 is meant to identify the most productive countries that have significantly contributed to the field of critical thinking. The growth rate in critical thinking research, from stage 1, was used to identify the top five sources (journals) focusing on this area to provide an answer to RQ3, as seen in Stage 3. Lastly, stage 4 aims to address RQ4 by analysing the most cited articles over time to identify the type and main themes of the articles.

Methodology

A bibliometric analysis was conducted to evaluate the performance and longitudinally map scientific publications on "critical thinking" within the field of business, management, and accounting. Bibliometric analysis is suggested as a complementary method to traditional structured literature reviews, as it provides a more objective approach to exploring research trends and performance (Donthu et al., 2021). This systematic literature analysis is often used to examine the evolution of disciplines based on intellectual, social, and conceptual frameworks (Zupic & Čater, 2015). Bibliometry or bibliometric analysis is frequently used to map and analyse the evolution of scientific topics and disciplines (Donthu et al., 2021). Bibliometry employs basic and advanced statistical methods to categorise data on various elements such as citations, author affiliations, keywords, topics, and methods used in published studies within a discipline with the aim of evaluating and tracking its progress (Wamba et al., 2023).

Köseoglu et al. (2016) identified two bibliometric methodologies: evaluative techniques and relational techniques, referred to as performance analysis and science mapping, respectively, by Noyons et al. (1999). Relational techniques focus on understanding the connections and relationships between authors, institutions, journal articles, or concepts. Relational techniques usually include co-citation analysis, keyword co-occurrence analysis, and co-authorship relationships among other measures. Evaluative techniques are methodologies used by the researchers to analyse the performance of publications or contributions by quantifying the output and the impact of the research or journals. Evaluative measures are often categorised into performance measures and impact measures. Performance techniques use a combination of content analysis and metrics to assess factors such as author, institution, country, and journal output over time (Noyons et al., 1999). These techniques measure productivity, which is related to the volume of research produced in a specific field. The alternative evaluative techniques focus on impact measures. Impact measurements are concerned with the extent to which the research is cited or recognised by other scholars in the field. Total citations, citations per academic year, citations per author or journal, and usage log data (average usage rates for journal works) are impact measures (Koseoglu et al., 2016). The average number of citations per manuscript and other indices that include productivity and impact are hybrid measures (Cardoso et al., 2022). This study adopted the evaluative or performance measures shown in Fig. 2 to undertake the bibliometric analysis.

The bibliometric analysis presented in this study was carried out in two phases:

1. Phase 1: Study design, comprising the following steps:
    - Database selection
    - Systematic search process
2. Phase 2: Bibliometric analysis as explained below.

- **Phase 1**

Database selection

The Scopus database was identified as the database to use for this study. Elsevier's (2023) Scopus database includes over 22,600 peer-reviewed journals (including more than 4200 open-access journals). The Scopus database provides detailed information about individual source papers, encompassing many elements such as the title, abstract, keywords, authors, institutional and geographical affiliations, and the references cited in the paper (Jiang et al., 2019).

Systematic search process

The PRISMA (Preferred Reporting Items for Systematic Reviews and Meta-Analyses) was employed in this study to identify the articles included as depicted in Fig. 2. The PRISMA follows a systematic process of identification, screening, eligibility, and inclusion to identify the appropriate literature, which can also be used to carry out a bibliometric analysis. The process allows for transparency, completeness, and reproducibility (Zeng et al., 2024).

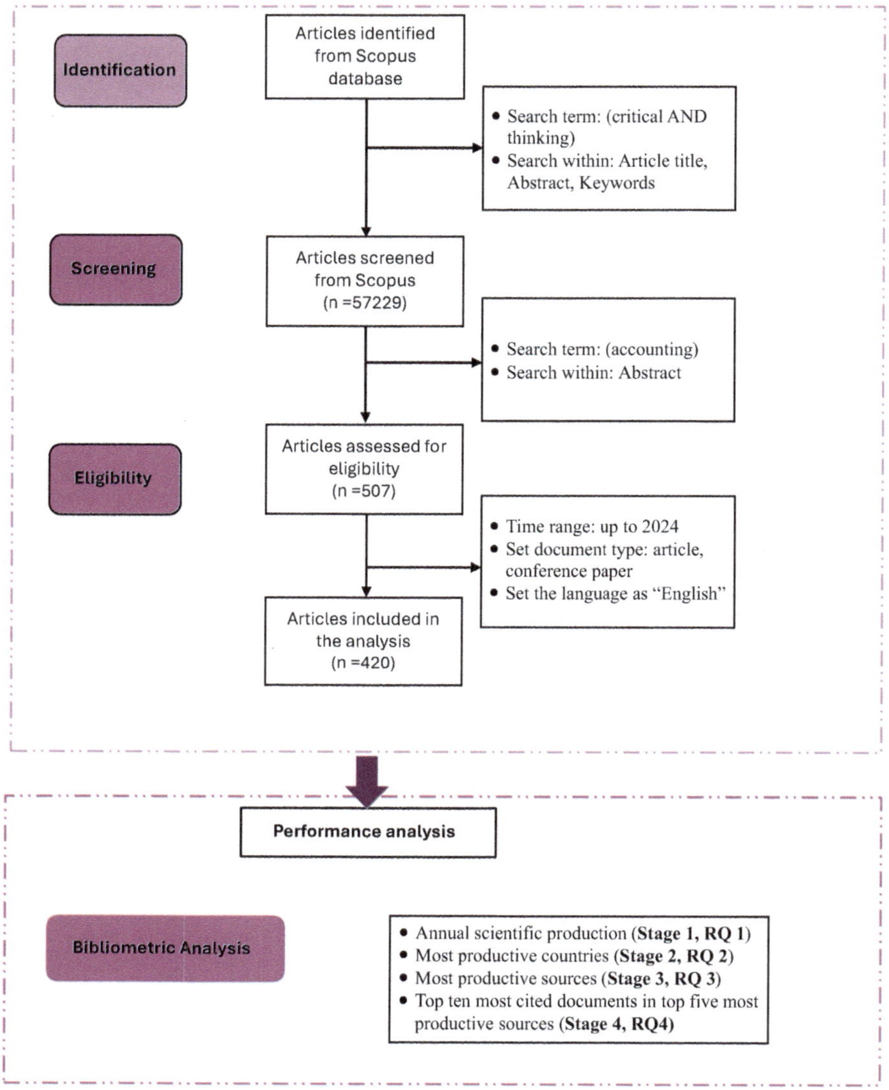

Fig. 2 The PRISMA process of bibliometric data

The search term that was utilised for the identifying articles from the Scopus database was Topic ("critical thinking") in the abstract, title, and keywords and "accounting" in the abstract. While critical thinking is sometimes referred to as "transversal thinking" or "intellectual skills", these phrases could also include various other skills. In their paper, Drummond and Selvaratnam (2009) described intellectual skills as thinking of all types and included language skills, mathematical skills, graphical skills, three-dimensional visualisation skills, information-processing skills, and reasoning skills. On the other hand, transversal skills include other factors such as thinking, communication, and self-management skills among others (Rubene et al., 2024). Furthermore, words such as "generic skills or soft skills" refer to broader non-technical skills that are required by students. Other terms such as "key competencies", "transferable skills", "personal transferable skills", "employability skills", "core skills", "underpinning skills", and "generic attributes" have also been used to describe soft skills (Asonitou & Hassall, 2019; Treleaven & Voola, 2008). Soft skills include a wide range of competencies, such as critical thinking, intellectual curiosity, problem-solving, logical, and independent thought, communication and information management skills, intellectual rigour, creativity and imagination, ethical practice, integrity, and tolerance (Berry & Routon, 2020; Douglas & Gammie, 2019; Jackson et al., 2022b; Tempone et al., 2012). As such, this study focused solely on critical thinking, one of the generic skills, and the search term was streamlined specifically to "critical thinking". The search was conducted from the date of the first publication until June 2024. The search language was set as "English", and the literature type was limited to articles and conference papers. A total of 420 relevant articles were obtained and were used for bibliometric analysis. The study focused mainly on the productivity of articles on the topic of critical thinking assessing the most productive sources, countries, and articles as well as the general type of articles produced and major themes written about.

The papers retrieved from the above systematic search, utilised for the bibliometric analysis, are presented in Table 1.

- **Phase 2: Bibliometric Analysis**

Data core choice

The second phase involved downloading the file to use the open-source statistical tool R. The data collection stage from Scopus allows the creation of a ".bib" file that will be used in the data analysis stage.

Data analysis

Bibliometrics, an R program package, was used as a quantitative tool to identify the developmental trends of critical thinking skills (Gumbo et al., 2023). The extracted ".bib" file containing the collected data was loaded and converted onto the

Table 1 Summary of "critical thinking" and "accounting" from the Scopus database

Description	Results
Main information about data	
Timespan	1969–2024
Annual scientific production growth rate	5.4%
Sources (journals, books, etc.)	225
Documents	420
Authors	977
Authors of single-authored documents	103
Document average age (years)	9.37
Average citations per document	19.43

R-data frame through the biblioshiny tool. The data analysis was then carried out using R's built-in functions. The summary of the papers used in the bibliometric analysis is presented in Table 1.

Results

The summary of the publications extracted from the Scopus database is presented in Table 1. In total, 420 documents published in English and in their final publication stage, were retrieved using the search terms "critical thinking" and "accounting". The documents period was from 1969 to 2024. A total of 977 authors contributed to the literature, as reflected in Table 1.

Table 1 also shows that the average number of citations per document was 19.43, and the average number of authors per document was 0.5. This shows that most authors preferred to collaborate on papers, with single-authored papers making up only 10% of the published papers and conference papers.

- *Annual Scientific Production*

Although the first publication was in 1969, the growth of research on critical thinking in accounting has been slow and gradual as depicted in Fig. 3. This first publication was published in the *Journal of Experiential Education*. The study, conducted by Follman et al. (1969), sought to investigate the interrelationship between scholastic aptitude and achievement tests as well as critical thinking tests and their underlying factorial structure. Since 1969 until 2009, fewer than 10 publications have been produced on the issue. In 2009, the number of publications reached a two-digit figure, with 15 articles produced. Subsequently, it increased to more than 20 papers in 2013 followed by a decline in 2015. Nonetheless, the figure rose to

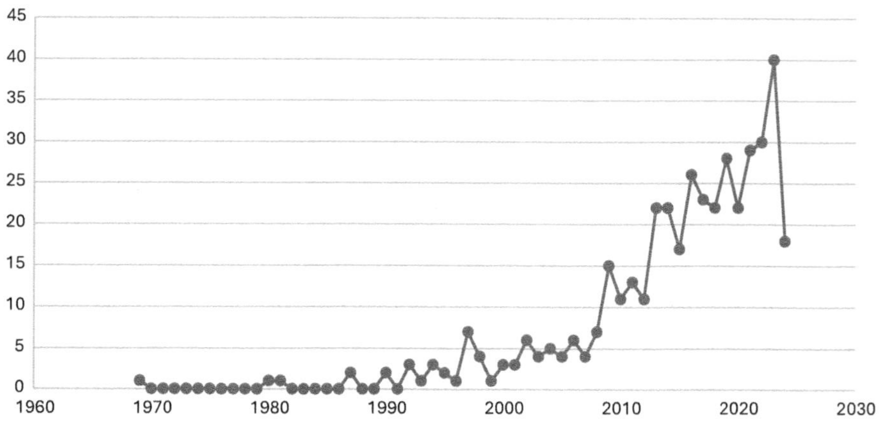

Fig. 3 Annual scientific production

26 in 2016 and has consistently trended upwards since 2021. In 2023, the number of papers on the topic doubled, resulting in 40 papers being published as depicted in Fig. 3.

The publication growth rate has significantly increased in the last decade, approaching 80%. Figure 3 exhibits a decline in 2024, which can be attributed to the timing of data extraction which was on 30 June 2024.

- *The most productive and influential countries*

Table 2 displays countries that are most actively engaged in critical thinking in accounting, based on the total number of publications. The table depicts the number of publications per country (A-E), across different years, starting with the year of their initial publication. The data used for the figure are based on publications in which the country is listed as the primary affiliation of the first author. The figure is based on publications where the country appears as the primary affiliation of the first author. As seen in the figure, the USA has consistently produced the highest number of publications over the years. This can also be attributed to the fact that the two leading accounting journals are in the USA: *Issues in Accounting Education* and *Critical Perspectives on Accounting*. The other two top journals, *Journal of Accounting Education and Accounting* Education, are published in the UK. On the other hand, although the UK began publishing in this area in 1981, its publications have been comparatively lower over the years. Australia, New Zealand, and Canada are among the top five contributors in the field, although they only began publishing on this subject in the early 2000s.

Table 3 depicts the most influential countries. When determining the most influential countries, the total citations were considered, as presented in Table 1. The country of the first author determines the total number of citations. Although the USA has a higher number of publications, the publications from the UK have the highest number of citations. The UK has an average of 51.1 citations per article, while the USA has an average of 12.2 citations. On average, articles from the UK are cited more than three times as often as those from the USA.

Except for Canada and South Africa, which rank among the least influential countries, the selection of language for publications may contribute to the low average citations for other countries. The low average number of citations may also be attributed to the comparatively lower exposure of publications from countries like

Table 2 Countries' scientific production

	(A) UK	(B) USA	(C) Australia	(D) New Zealand	(E) Canada
First publication	1981	1969	2003	2007	2011
<1990	2	2	0	0	0
1990–1999	2	5	0	0	0
2000–2009	8	32	3	3	0
2010–2019	17	90	9	5	9
>2020	9	55	8	6	7
Total cumulative publications	38	184	20	14	16

Table 3 Citation per country, ranked—Top 10 influential countries

Country	TC	Average article citations
UK	868	51.1
USA	477	12.2
Australia	349	29.1
New Zealand	265	37.9
Italy	136	136
Canada	74	18.5
United Arab Emirates	73	36.5
South Africa	66	13.2
Spain	61	15.2
Germany	28	14

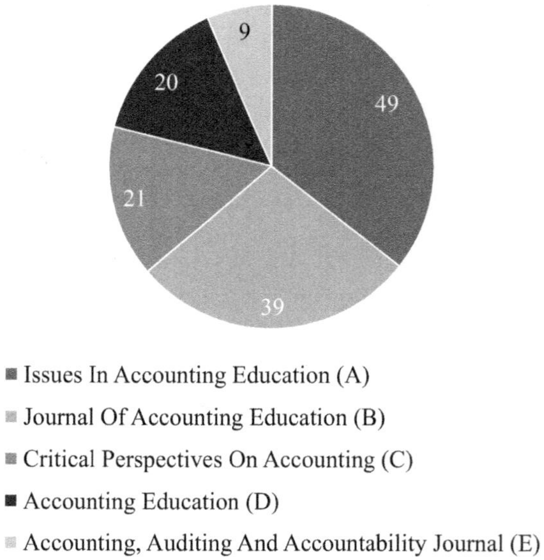

Fig. 4 Primary five productive sources

the United Arab Emirates, South Africa, and Spain compared to countries like the USA, the UK, and Australia (Wamba et al., 2023).

- *Primary five productive sources*

The journals with the greatest number of publications, which are the most productive sources, are ranked based on the total cumulative output in critical thinking. Figure 4 presents the top five most influential journals on critical thinking in accounting. A total of 31 sources were identified, with 21 of these sources only having produced one or two articles each over the years. The top five most producing

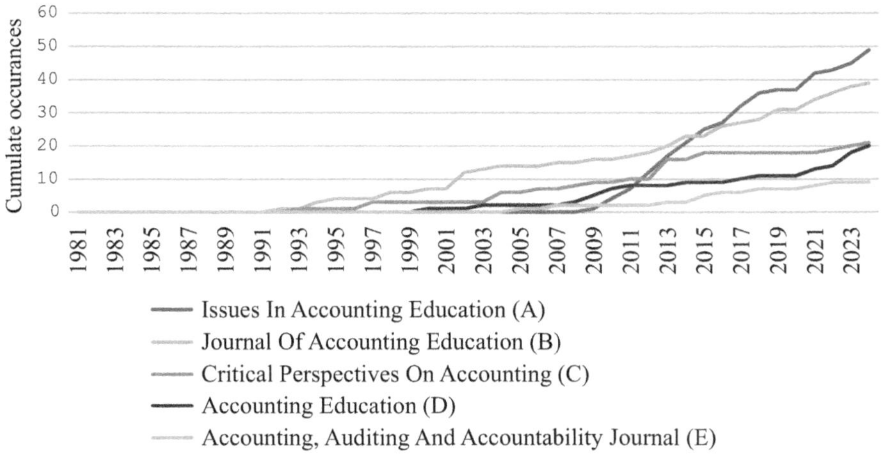

Fig. 5 Top sources of annual growth

journals were *Issues in Accounting Education* (IAE) (A)—49, *Journal of Accounting Education* (JAE) (B)—39, *Critical Perspectives on Accounting* (CPA) (C)—21, *Accounting Education* (AE) (D)—20, and *Accounting, Auditing and Accountability Journal* (AAAJ) (E)—9. The top four journals also represent the leading journals in accounting education, as highlighted by Apostolou et al. (2022) in their systematic literature reviews on accounting education.

Several papers have been published in these top five journals over the years in these sources. The earliest of these publications in these top sources was by Gabriel and Hirsch (1992) in the *Journal of Accounting Education*. The paper examined the challenges associated with implementing an integrated approach for developing critical thinking and communication skills in accounting courses. The research was conducted at the Southern Illinois University at Edwardsville, USA, School of Business, which underwent a comprehensive revision of its undergraduate curriculum. This revision involved modifications to specific courses, including introducing additional requirements such as the inclusion of critical thinking and communication skills. The requirements were implemented through an ongoing collaboration between English and Accounting faculty at the school. Since then, over 190 papers have been produced in these leading journals over the years until 2024.

Although the first article was published in the *Journal of Accounting Education* (JAE) as presented above, the *Issues in Accounting Education* (IAE) journal surpassed the *Journal of Accounting Education* with the cumulative number of publications produced in 2014 to be the leading source on critical thinking, as depicted in Fig. 5.

Issues in Accounting Education publishes research papers aimed to supporting faculty in teaching and addressing significant issues, offering empirical evidence alongside instructional resources and best practices (*Issues in Accounting Education*). Similarly, the *Journal of Accounting Education* focuses on promoting

Table 4 Impact of most productive sources

Source title	SJR	SJR Quartile (Accounting)	H-Index	CiteScore 2023	Country
Accounting, Auditing and Accountability Journal (AAAJ)	1.85	Q1	121	9.5	UK
Critical Perspectives on Accounting (CPA)	1.94	Q1	85	9.4	USA
Accounting Education (AE)	0.91	Q1	51	8	UK
Journal of Accounting Education (JAE)	0.41	Q3	45	4.2	UK
Issues in Accounting Education (IAE)	0.42	Q3	32	2.6	USA

and publishing research on accounting education issues, aiming to improve the quality of accounting education worldwide. In contrast, *Critical Perspectives on Accounting* emphasises broader accounting issues that extend beyond the scope of accounting education, also addressing topics such as social, ecological, and political activity and how they interact with accounting. The production of papers in most of the sources peaked after 2011, as seen in Fig. 5. Figure 5 also illustrates that there has been a steady increase in the number of publications on critical thinking and accounting in all the journals.

While the IAE and JAE are leading in the number of publications on critical thinking, they rank lower than the other journals regarding other impact factor metrics. According to the SCImango Journal Rank (SJR), SJR quartile, H-index, and CiteScore, these two sources rank the lowest. The SJR measures the citations to publications released over a 3-year period. By evaluating the sources of citations, the SJR metric looks at how well-known publications are in the community (Roldan-Valadez et al., 2019). The SJR quartiles, which can be focused on various topics, focused on the accounting field in Table 4 and rank the journals into quartiles. The journals in Q1 form the elite journals within accounting, meaning they have increased visibility and a higher likelihood of frequent citations. The H-index of the journal indicates both the volume of articles published by a journal and the citation impact of those articles, thereby balancing quantity and quality. The CiteScore reflects the average number of citations received by a document in the journal over a 4-year period. Higher metrics indicate a journals' capacity to publish articles that receive extensive citations. Consequently, these metrics will affect the publications in these journals as evidenced by AAAJ and CPA, which hold higher rankings in terms of impact due to their status as top journals with high impact measures such as H-index and CiteScore.

- *The type of most cited publications in the productive journals*

In examining the type and themes of the most frequently cited publications on critical thinking in accounting, the most cited articles were identified as illustrated in Table 5. Table 5 presents the most cited publications from the five most influential

Table 5 Most cited documents in top five sources (2019–2023)

Rank	Title	Year published	Source title	Total citations	Type of article
1	Photography and voice in critical qualitative management research	2005	Accounting, Auditing and Accountability Journal (AAAJ)	174	Descriptive article
2	Wiki art gallery, Inc.: A case for critical thinking	2011	Issues in Accounting Education (IAE)	93	Case
3	Alternative instructional strategies for creative and critical thinking in the accounting curriculum	1998	Journal of Accounting Education (JAE)	86	Instructional resource
4	Knowledge and skills development of accounting graduates: The perceptions of graduates and employers in Ghana	2010	Accounting Education (AE)	70	Descriptive article
5	Student imaginings, cognitive dissonance, and critical thinking	2013	Critical Perspectives in Accounting (CPA)	68	Descriptive article

sources as identified under RQ2. These articles were ranked according to their total citations count. The most cited article appeared in AAAJ over 19 years ago, exemplifying the interdisciplinary studies published in AAAJ. The article aimed to introduce photography, and other visual techniques enhance students' voices in critical accounting and management research. As also seen in Table 5, all the most cited papers in these top five journals were published between 1998 and 2013, more than a decade ago, indicating that their higher citations counts could also be associated with their age relative to more recent publications.

In determining the type of articles that were published, the articles were classified according to the typology established by Apostolou et al. (2022), which encompasses four types of articles: empirical, descriptive, instructional resource, and case. Empirical articles are articles that present conclusions drawn from statistical analysis of data (Apostolou et al., 2020). Empirical articles increase our understanding of the strengths and weaknesses of various instructional strategies and provide action-orientated implications. Descriptive papers, in contrast, provide a detailed account of innovation, present a curriculum model, report student perspectives, present data without statistical testing, or employ qualitative analysis without referencing statistical evaluation (Apostolou et al., 2021). Cases generally present real or hypothetical information alongside questions and activities to facilitate contextual learning of complex subjects. An instructional resource is an article that offers guidance on implementing teaching methodologies, projects, or strategies for teaching technical and soft skills (Apostolou et al., 2022). As depicted in Table 5, the type of articles was a case, a descriptive article, and an instructional resource.

Discussion

The analysis above was based on performance bibliometric analysis enabling the researchers to answer four research questions: (1) the current state of research on critical thinking in accounting (2), primary influential sources on critical thinking research in accounting (3), most productive and influential countries, and (4) the type and themes of research carried out on critical thinking in accounting. The state of research revealed that the most significant increase in publications in this field occurred over the past decade. However, research on critical thinking in accounting is progressing at a slow rate which could be indicative of the lack of importance attributed to this skill.

RQ1 was mainly concerned with the state of research in critical thinking skills within the field of accounting.

The bibliometric analysis showed that the first paper on critical thinking in the accounting field was written in 1969. More than 400 papers have since been published to date (2024) in accounting. Since 1969, there has been an irregular pattern in the number of publications, with constant growth being observed starting in 2021. In 2009, the number of publications reached a two-digit figure, with a total of 15 papers generated. The sudden surge in critical thinking during this period may be attributed to the onset of the Global Financial Crisis in 2008. Researchers indicated that the crisis exposed weaknesses in accounting information (Ravenscroft & Williams, 2021). In the UK, it was suggested that the Big Four audit companies should be prohibited from consulting audits for banks due to their failure to identify issues associated with the financial crisis (Williamson, 2009). The increase in critical thinking research after this could make sense as Asonitou and Hassall (2019) asserted that critical thinking skills enable individuals to analyse complex financial situations to evaluate information, identify risks and opportunities, develop innovative solutions, and make ethical decisions. The authors indicated that critical thinking is important in making informed decisions and promoting financial stability (Asonitou & Hassall, 2019). As such, this could be the reason for the increase in publications on this subject matter after the financial crisis in 2008.

In 2013, the number of publications increased to the 20s followed by a decline in subsequent years. Nevertheless, it rose again to 26 in 2016 and has been consistently above the 20s since then. The increase in 2016 coincides with the World Economic Forum (WEF) future jobs report which indicated that technological advancements were causing shifts in business models, resulting in significant changes to various roles and skills required. The report indicated that the word was in the early stages of a "fourth industrial revolution" (Schwab, 2017), and this era was characterised by interdependent digital technologies with significant advancements in computer power and the capacity to connect devices at a relatively low cost. While Industry 4.0 had its origins earlier, its widespread adoption began to accelerate around 2016, coinciding with the inclusion of critical thinking skills in the WEF's Future of Jobs report from the same year. Also, according to the report, certain roles were expected to be replaced by artificial intelligence and robotic process automation. In the 2020

WEF future jobs report, accountants and auditors were ranked fourth among 20 roles which showed a decline in demand because of technological advancements. Therefore, the growing emphasis on soft skills, such as critical thinking, could be contributing to the increase in accounting research with the aim of enhancing accountants' skill sets to adapt to the evolving demands of the business environment (Jackson et al., 2022a). Critical thinking enables one to analyse information, evaluate evidence, and make informed decisions based on logical reasoning, which is important for problem-solving (Sinnewe et al., 2023). It is a key competency for navigating the challenges of the digital age and adapting to technological advancements (Tsiligiris & Bowyer, 2021). Therefore, the gradual increase in critical thinking research could be supporting earlier research by scholars that indicated that developing critical thinking skills in accounting students to ensure that they are employable is important, especially in the light of advances in technology and digital tools (Kavanagh & Drennan, 2008a; Plant et al., 2019).

The objective of RQ2 was to identify the most influential and productive countries publishing on critical thinking in accounting.

The analysis revealed that developed countries, specifically the USA, UK, and Australia, play a prominent role in research production as evidenced by publication output and citation impact. Legislative requirements may also be influencing the number of publications in some of these countries. The Higher Education Standards Framework (Threshold Standards) 2021, a legislative instrument in Australia, indicates critical thinking as a fundamental learning outcome. Part A, section 1.4 (d) of the legislation states "skills in independent and critical thinking suitable for lifelong learning" (Higher Education Standards Framework (Threshold Standards), 2021, p. 6). The framework is administered by the Tertiary Education Quality and Standards Agency. Consequently, Australian higher education accounting courses must incorporate the development of critical thinking abilities into their curriculum. Similarly, critical thinking is also widely recognised as a vital outcome of higher education in Europe (European Commission, 2012; the USA (Association of American Colleges and Universities, 2015) and Great Britain (The Quality Assurance Agency for Higher Education, 2008). These reforms in tertiary education emphasising critical thinking may have facilitated academic initiatives aimed at aligning the curriculum with the standards set by the higher education groups. Hassall et al. (2005) also found that UK employers prioritised problem-solving as the most sought skill in management accountants. As such, researchers could be increasing the citations of these studies as they are looking for various ways to sufficiently prepare accountants in soft skills for employability as well as aligning to legislative requirements. The increase in the number of publications in the respective countries in 2011 may be attributed to these initiatives.

The impact of publications is assessed by the number of citations per country, as reflected in Table 3. The trend observed showed that although the USA has the most publications, the most cited papers originate from the UK. This trend may be attributed to the two Scopus Q1 sources originating from the UK (JAE, AE). The inclusion of a greater number of journals from a country in indexed and highly ranked journals positively impacts the international prestige in research. Higher ranking journals display greater citation factors than lower-ranking journals (Jamali, 2024). Researchers also believe that a journal's association with a specific country affects perceptions of its quality (Jamali, 2024), which could contribute to higher citations for articles published in these in high-ranking journals. Nevertheless, the overall number of citations may also be influenced by the importance of self-citations. Shehatta and Al-Rubaish (2019) found a strong positive correlation between national self-citation and both total publications and total citations. During their study of the most self-cited countries from 1996 to 2015, China emerged as the leader, with the USA closely behind. The list also featured the UK and Australia. Self-citation has the potential to distort citation-based metrics, such as total citations, average citations per paper, and the percentage of publications that are cited (Shehatta & Al-Rubaish, 2019). Finally, the increased number of citations in the UK may also be attributed to the legislative education reform as presented above, which prioritises critical thinking in that region. As such, the rise in citations could be attributed to researchers and educators aiming to develop students' critical thinking skills to prepare them for their early careers and employability (Jackson et al., 2022b).

RQ3 focused on identifying the five primary most influential sources publishing on critical thinking skills in accounting. The leading sources publishing on critical thinking in accounting are depicted in Fig. 4 *Issues in Accounting Education*. The majority of recent articles in this journal are predominantly cases. Of the 13 papers published in the journal from 2018 and 2023, 11 of the papers were instructional cases. Cases are meant to describe real events and could be developed by the educator for a specified lesson in a class or lecture (Howard & Stout, 2006). In their paper, in which they explain the reasons accounting case or instructional resources papers get rejected for publication, Howard and Stout (2006) note that the increase in case or instructional resource papers is attributed to a call by accounting educators to reconsider their pedagogies. This call aims to emphasise the development of critical knowledge, skills, and attitudes, especially in dealing with uncertainty and enhancing analytical skills. Cases usually include pre-specified educational objectives, supporting evidence demonstrating the successful achievements of these objectives and implementation guidance to facilitate effective use by other accounting educators. The cases suggest that students will develop critical thinking skills as they work through the cases (Gujarathi, 2019; Hux et al., 2022; McGuigan et al., 2021). This may account for the increase in instructional cases as educators can document the lessons delivered in their respective classes or lectures. As such, the research on critical thinking in accounting is more action-orientated towards fostering these skills and places less emphasis on deriving empirical evidence on the effectiveness of these initiatives. Another factor that could be contributing to the number of publications in these sources could be the article processing charge (APC) and the number of days it takes a journal to publish an article. For example, IAE has an average of 95 days from submission to publication time, whereas JAE takes an average of 376 days for submission to acceptance. IAE has 4 issues per year and only charges non-members \$105 for submission fee, whereas JAE charges \$3800 for article publishing charge. Similarly to IAE, more than 60% of the papers published are instructional cases. Other papers published in IAE during this period have been focused on trying to provide a definition for critical thinking and its competencies and strategies to develop critical thinking (Baril et al., 1998; Butler et al., 2019; Kimmel, 1995; Wolcott et al., 2002; Wolcott & Sargent, 2021). Although the third most productive source, the CPA covers various topics in their journal, as indicated in their aim of publishing accounting research that explores the interconnectedness of accounting to allocative, distributive, social, and ecological problems of the modern environment. Of the 21 papers on critical thinking in the journal, only 3 had been published after 2022 with the rest of the papers published before 2016. Similarly, AE also has more than 60% of the articles on critical thinking published pre-2019.

The source with the most empirical studies is AE. Most of the 20 articles published on critical thinking in AE journals are empirical evidence studies that were mostly undertaken with undergraduate accounting students. Like CPA, AAAJ focuses on various investigations of accounting, auditing, and accountability issues and their impacts on policy, practice, and society. As such, the two sources that contribute significantly to accounting education and how to advance accounting education are JAE and AE. However as previously noted, most of the articles on critical thinking in accounting in the primary sources are instructional cases that aim to help accounting educators foster critical thinking in their classes and lectures. There are also some descriptive papers which attempt to define and offer tools that can be used to develop critical thinking skills that are provided for accounting educators. However, there seems to be a lack of empirical studies that provide the effectiveness of these cases in developing critical thinking skills as stated by Wolcott and Sargent (2021). The researchers urged accounting education researchers to use rigorous research methods to generate stronger empirical evidence on how students can acquire critical thinking skills (Wolcott & Sargent, 2021). Empirical articles increase our understanding of the strengths and weaknesses of various instructional strategies and provide action-orientated implications. Therefore, more empirical studies are needed in research towards developing critical thinking skills in accounting.

The objective of RQ4 was to analyse the type and themes of the most cited publications on critical thinking in accounting. The most cited publications in each of the identified top journals were identified. As seen in the results in Table 6, there was no empirical study in these top-cited publications. According to Rebele et al. (1998), who wrote the earliest accounting education literature reviews, nonempirical articles help provide useful information to accounting faculty implementing education technology, those concerned with assessment issues, and those interested in student-related topics. In line with statement, the themes that emerged from the publications and proposed changes were action-orientated, as depicted in Table 6.

The theme that emerged from the top cited articles was the need for accounting education to make changes towards more active learning and student-centred pedagogies to foster critical thinking skills, as reflected in the proposed change column in Table 6. Engaging students in real-world and authentic cases was seen as essential for developing skills (Bonk & Smith, 1998). The authors offered various tools that instructors could use to develop critical thinking and creative skills. They also defined critical thinking as the ability to make sound judgements in complex

Table 6 Themes and proposed changes—most cited publications

Rank	Title	Theme	Proposed change
1	Photography and voice in critical qualitative management research	Pedagogical recommendations	
2	Wiki art gallery, Inc.: A case for critical thinking	Pedagogical recommendations	Incorporate pedagogical initiatives such as case-based learning, allowing students to engage with real-world cases and make judgements and solve problems to foster critical thinking skills
3	Alternative instructional strategies for creative and critical thinking in the accounting curriculum	Pedagogical recommendations	Move from traditional modes of teaching towards active student-centred and consultative models of teaching to develop critical thinking skills
4	Knowledge and skills development of accounting graduates: The perceptions of graduates and employers in Ghana	Curriculum redesign	Include more focus on practical skills relevant to the business environment such as analytical and critical thinking to meet the needs of employers
5	Student imaginings, cognitive dissonance, and critical thinking	Pedagogical recommendations	Introduce pedagogical initiatives that would connect accounting students with broader social and ethical issues to develop their critical thinking skills

real-world situations, based on available evidence and a clearly worked out value system (Bonk & Smith, 1998). Similarly, although they presented a case, Phillips and Mackintosh (2011) defined critical thinking as developing skills that require issue identification, consideration of alternatives, application of relevant knowledge and facts, and tentatively reaching decisions about appropriate course of action. However, this was not the case for the majority of the papers published in these journals, especially the instructional cases. Although the studies aim to foster critical thinking skills, there is never a definition of critical thinking provided. Overall, the themes identified concerning critical thinking in these leading five journals align with the initial paper published by Gabriel and Hirsch (1992) which also aimed to revise an undergraduate curriculum to incorporate the development of critical thinking and communication skills. In their study, Awayiga et al. (2010) investigated important soft skills from the perspective of students and employers. Their research highlighted the importance of also understanding the expectations of the skills expected by employers of new accounting graduates. As such, while there are high-quality instructional resources available in these sources that can be used by accounting educators in fostering critical thinking, there is a need for increased empirical studies as also noted by Wolcott and Sargent (2021), to understand the effectiveness of all these suggested interventions. Therefore, future research could document empirical evidence in using these cases in various regions.

Conclusion

The analysis above was based on performance bibliometric analysis and allowed the researchers to achieve the objective of this study which was to understand the state of critical thinking skills research in accounting. The state of research revealed that the most increase in the number of publications in this field has taken place in the past decade. However, research on critical thinking in accounting is growing at a slow rate. This study has allowed for the understanding of gaps regarding current approaches to fostering critical thinking.

The sources that provide the most research on critical thinking and accounting education are the *Journal of Accounting Education* (JAE) and *Accounting Education* (AE). High-ranking sources in accounting, in ascending order, include *Accounting, Auditing and Accountability Journal* (AAAJ), *Critical Perspectives on Accounting* (CPA), *Accounting Education* (AE), *Journal of Accounting Education* (JAE), and *Issues in Accounting Education* (IAE). Identifying the most influential sources and journals will guide future researchers towards high-quality impactful sources which could help them to identify and refine educational strategies they can adopt to develop critical thinking skills. This information would also allow accounting researchers to be aware of the sources in which they can publish in to make most impact with their research. The disadvantage is that the high-ranking journals take an average of 365 days for an article to be published. Moreover, despite having low citation rankings, JAE and IAE have a high number of publications, particularly recent ones, which could be attributed to their shorter turnaround time. This facilitates researchers to access relevant and current issues in accounting education and research.

The study indicates that the countries that are most influential in fostering critical thinking in accounting include the UK, the USA, Australia, New Zealand, and Canada, with the UK being the country with the most frequently cited publications on this topic. Identifying countries that significantly contribute to enhancing critical thinking in accounting may reveal best practices for accounting researchers and instructors to foster critical thinking skills in their respective regions. These findings could also enable educators to identify potential differences in the fostering and prioritisation of critical thinking in different regions.

Recent publications in critical thinking in accounting primarily consist of instructional cases aimed at helping instructors foster these skills within the discipline. Most of the papers published focus on understanding critical thinking and various techniques to foster and assess critical thinking in accounting. While instructional and descriptive cases are important to sharing research on developing critical thinking, this study also identified that there is still a lack of empirical studies on assessing the effectiveness of the various interventions that are proposed. Researchers in accounting should recognise this trend and pursue empirical studies while implementing the instructional resources. Analysing the themes on publications on fostering critical thinking facilitates the identification of key factors to consider for enhancing the accounting curriculum. Therefore, future studies could also analyse publications in this manner to identify the key factors to consider in fostering critical thinking and other skills.

The limitation of this study is that it mainly focuses on performance measures in analysing state critical thinking research. However, broader generic or non-technical could be considered to identify the top soft skills considered important in the accounting field, especially according to employers. Extending the search to all generic skills could also provide more documents, which will allow for the thorough undertaking of a bibliometric analysis. As a result of the few documents retrieved in this study, the researchers could not undertake other bibliometric techniques such as co-occurrence analysis of keywords, co-citation of tiles, and mapping of the structures' themes. As a result of an increase in the documents, future research could also make use of thematic maps and co-citation analysis to understand the evolution of soft skills in accounting and identify the current soft skills deemed important in this field.

This study also employed only a single database, Scopus. While Scopus was used as it contains the most research publications, a combination of other databases, such as World of Science and Emerald, could be used in future to identify more papers and, hence, expand the results. A systematic literature review on the definition of critical accruing to the current studies could be carried out to provide an aligned definition that could be used in future studies in accounting education. Future research should focus on longitudinal studies to track the development of critical thinking skills over time and across various educational interventions. Additionally, there is a need for studies that explore the impact of these pedagogical approaches on students' professional performance and adaptability in the workplace. Lastly, there is a need for more empirical studies on the development of critical thinking in accounting students, especially concerning assessments of these skills and future research on this should be prioritised.

References

Agustí, M. A., & Orta-Pérez, M. (2023). Big data and artificial intelligence in the fields of accounting and auditing: A bibliometric analysis. *Spanish Journal of Finance and Accounting/Revista Española de Financiación y Contabilidad, 52*(3), 412–438.

Al-Htaybat, K., von Alberti-Alhtaybat, L., & Alhatabat, Z. (2018). Educating digital natives for the future: Accounting educators' evaluation of the accounting curriculum. In *Accounting education* (Vol. 27, pp. 333–357). Routledge.

Apostolou, B., Dorminey, J. W., & Hassell, J. M. (2020). Accounting education literature review (2019). In *Journal of accounting education* (Vol. 51). Elsevier.

Apostolou, B., Dorminey, J. W., & Hassell, J. M. (2021). Accounting education literature review (2020). In *Journal of accounting education* (Vol. 55). Elsevier.

Apostolou, B., Churyk, N. T., Hassell, J. M., & Matuszewski, L. (2022). Accounting education literature review (2022). In *Journal of accounting education* (Vol. 63, pp. 100831). Elsevier.

Asonitou, S., & Hassall, T. (2019). Which skills and competences to develop in accountants in a country in crisis? *International Journal of Management Education, 17*, 100308. https://doi.org/10.1016/j.ijme.2019.100308

Awayiga, J. Y., Onumah, J. M., & Tsamenyi, M. (2010). Knowledge and skills development of accounting graduates: The perceptions of graduates and employers in Ghana. *Accounting Education, 19*(1–2), 139–158. https://doi.org/10.1080/09639280902903523

Baril, C. P., Cunningham, B. M., Fordham, D. R., Gardner, R. L., & Wolcott, S. K. (1998). Critical thinking in the public accounting profession: Aptitudes and attitudes. *Journal of Accounting Education, 16*(3–4), 381–406. https://doi.org/10.1016/s0748-5751(98)00023-2

Berry, R., & Routon, W. (2020). Soft skill change perceptions of accounting majors: Current practitioner views versus their own reality. *Journal of Accounting Education, 53*, 100691.

Bonk, C. J., & Smith, G. S. (1998). Alternative instructional strategies for creative and critical thinking in the accounting curriculum. *Journal of Accounting Education, 16*(2), 261–293. https://doi.org/10.1016/s0748-5751(98)00012-8

Brink, & Stoel. (2019). Analytics knowledge, skills, and abilities for accounting graduates. In *Advances in accounting education: Teaching and curriculum innovations* (pp. 23–43). Emerald Publishing Limited.

Bui, B., & Porter, B. (2010). The expectation-performance gap in accounting education: An exploratory study. In *Accounting education* (Vol. 19, pp. 23–50).

Butler, M. G., Church, K. S., & Spencer, A. W. (2019). Do, reflect, think, apply: Experiential education in accounting. *Journal of Accounting Education, 48*, 12–21. https://doi.org/10.1016/j.jaccedu.2019.05.001

Cardoso, L., Chen, M. M., Araújo, A., de Almeida, G. G. F., Dias, F., & Moutinho, L. (2022). Accessing neuromarketing scientific performance: Research gaps and emerging topics. In *Behavioral Sciences* (Vol. 12).

Carvalho, C., & Almeida, A. C. (2022). The adequacy of accounting education in the development of transversal skills needed to meet market demands. In *Sustainability* (Vol. 14, pp. 5755). Multidisciplinary Digital Publishing Institute.

Cooper, L. A., Holderness, D. K., Sorensen, T. L., & Wood, D. A. (2019). Robotic process automation in public accounting. In *Accounting horizons* (Vol. 33, pp. 15–35). American Accounting Association.

Cortes, G. M., & Salvatori, A. (2019). Delving into the demand side: Changes in workplace specialization and job polarization. In *Labour economics* (Vol. 57, pp. 164–176). Elsevier.

De Villiers, R. (2021). Seven principles to ensure future-ready accounting graduates—A model for future research and practice. In *Meditari accountancy research* (Vol. 29, pp. 1354–1380). Emerald Group Holdings Ltd.

Dolce, V., Emanuel, F., Cisi, M., & Ghislieri, C. (2019). The soft skills of accounting graduates: Perceptions versus expectations. *Accounting Education, 29*, 57–76. https://doi.org/10.1080/09639284.2019.1697937

Donthu, N., Kumar, S., Mukherjee, D., Pandey, N., & Lim, W. M. (2021). How to conduct a bibliometric analysis: An overview and guidelines. *Journal of Business Research, 133*, 285–296.

Douglas, S., & Gammie, E. (2019). An investigation into the development of non-technical skills by undergraduate accounting programmes. In *Accounting education* (Vol. 28, pp. 304–332). Taylor & Francis.

Drummond, H. P., & Selvaratnam, M. (2009). Intellectual skills needed for the effective learning and application of chemical knowledge. *South African Journal of Chemistry, 62*, 179–184.

Facione, P. A. (1990). The California critical thinking skills test- college level. *Technical Report #1*. Experimental Validation and Content Validity.

Feliciano-Cestero, M. M., Ameen, N., Kotabe, M., Paul, J., & Signoret, M. (2023). Is digital transformation threatened? A systematic literature review of the factors influencing firms' digital transformation and internationalization. *Journal of Business Research, 157*, 113546. https://doi.org/10.1016/j.jbusres.2022.113546

Follman, J., Miller, W., & Hernandez, D. (1969). Factor analysis of achievement, scholastic aptitude, and critical thinking subtests. *The Journal of Experimental Education, 38*(1), 48–53. https://doi.org/10.1080/00220973.1969.11011165

Gabriel, S. L., & Hirsch, M. L., Jr. (1992). Critical thinking and communication skills: Integration and implementation issues. *Journal of Accounting Education, 10*(2), 243–270. https://doi.org/10.1016/0748-5751(92)90001-L

Gujarathi, M. R. (2019). Diamond foods, inc.: A comprehensive case in financial analysis and valuation. *Issues in Accounting Education, 34*(1), 13–33. https://doi.org/10.2308/iace-52344

Gumbo, S., Twinomurinzi, H., Bwalya, K., & Wamba, S. F. (2023). Skills provisioning for the fourth industrial revolution: A bibliometric analysis. *Procedia Computer Science, 219*, 924–932. https://doi.org/10.1016/j.procs.2023.01.368

Hassall, T., Joyce, J., Montano, J. L. A., & Anes, J. A. D. (2001). The employers' priorities: Vocational skills and capabilities for management accountants. *Industry and Higher Education, 15*, 421–429. https://doi.org/10.5367/000000001101295920

Hassall, T., Joyce, J., Montaño, J. L. A., & Anes, J. A. D. (2005). Priorities for the development of vocational skills in management accountants: A European perspective. In *Accounting forum* (Vol. 29, pp. 379–394). No longer published by Elsevier.

Howard, T. P., & Stout, D. E. (2006). Reasons accounting case/instructional resource papers are rejected for publication. *Journal of Accounting Education, 24*(1), 1–15. https://doi.org/10.1016/j.jaccedu.2006.04.002

Hux, C., Smith, P. A., & Cefaratti, M. A. (2022). Accounting for revenue recognition in the gig economy: An instructional case. *Issues in Accounting Education, 37*(3), 101–123. https://doi.org/10.2308/ISSUES-2020-040

Issues in Accounting Education. Retrieved 21 August from https://aaahq.org/Research/Journals/Issues-in-Accounting-Education

Jaafar, S. B. (2018). *Are soft skills required for accounting students in future careers?* Available at SSRN 3167595.

Jackling, B., & De Lange, P. (2009). Do accounting graduates' skills meet the expectations of employers? A matter of convergence or divergence. In *Accounting education* (Vol. 18, pp. 369–385).

Jackson, D. (2014). Business graduate performance in oral communication skills and strategies for improvement. In *The international journal of management education* (Vol. 12, pp. 22–34). Elsevier.

Jackson, D., Michelson, G., & Munir, R. (2022a). Developing accountants for the future: New technology, skills, and the role of stakeholders. In *Accounting education* (pp. 1–28). Taylor & Francis.

Jackson, D., Michelson, G., & Munir, R. (2022b). New technology and desired skills of early career accountants. In *Pacific accounting review* (Vol. 34, pp. 548–568). Emerald Publishing.

Jamali, H. R. (2024). Country names in journal titles: Shaping researchers' perception of journals quality. *Scientometrics, 129*(2), 803–823. https://doi.org/10.1007/s11192-023-04904-1

Jiang, Y., Ritchie, B. W., & Benckendorff, P. (2019). Bibliometric visualisation: An application in tourism crisis and disaster management research. *Current Issues in Tourism, 22*, 1925–1957. https://doi.org/10.1080/13683500.2017.1408574

Kavanagh, M., & Drennan. (2008a). What skills and attributes does an accounting graduate need? Evidence from student perceptions and employer expectations. In *Accounting & Finance* (Vol. 48, pp. 279–300).

Kavanagh, M. H., & Drennan, L. (2008b). What skills and attributes does an accounting graduate need? Evidence from student perceptions and employer expectations. In *Accounting and finance* (Vol. 48, pp. 279–300). Wiley.

Kimmel, P. (1995). A framework for incorporating critical thinking into accounting education. *Journal of Accounting Education, 13*(3), 299–318. https://doi.org/10.1016/0748-5751(95)00012-B

Koseoglu, M. A., Rahimi, R., Okumus, F., & Liu, J. (2016). Bibliometric studies in tourism. *Annals of Tourism Research, 61*, 180–198. https://doi.org/10.1016/j.annals.2016.10.006

Köseoglu, M. A., Sehitoglu, Y., Ross, G., & Parnell, J. A. (2016). The evolution of business ethics research in the realm of tourism and hospitality: A bibliometric analysis. *International Journal of Contemporary Hospitality Management, 28*(8), 1598–1621.

Kotb, A., Abdel-Kader, M., Allam, A., Halabi, H., & Franklin, E. (2019). Information technology in the British and Irish undergraduate accounting degrees. In *Accounting education* (Vol. 28, pp. 445–464): Routledge.

McGuigan, N., Ghio, A., & Kern, T. (2021). Designing accounting futures: Exploring ambiguity in accounting classrooms through design futuring. *Issues in Accounting Education, 36*(4), 325–351. https://doi.org/10.2308/ISSUES-2019-508

Noyons, E., Moed, H., & Van Raan, A. (1999). Integrating research performance analysis and science mapping. *Scientometrics, 46*(3), 591–604.

Phillips, F., & Mackintosh, B. (2011). Wiki art gallery, Inc.: A case for critical thinking. *Issues in Accounting Education, 26*(3), 593–608. https://doi.org/10.2308/iace-50038

Plant, K., Barac, K., & Sarens, G. (2019). Preparing work-ready graduates—Skills development lessons learnt from internal audit practice. *Journal of Accounting Education, 48*, 33–47. https://doi.org/10.1016/j.jaccedu.2019.06.001

Ravenscroft, S., & Williams, P. F. (2021). Sustaining discreditable accounting research through ignorance: The mainstream elite's response to the 2008 financial crisis. *Accounting, Organizations and Society, 95*, 101280.

Rebele, J. E., Apostolou, B. A., Buckless, F. A., Hassell, J. M., Paquette, L. R., & Stout, D. E. (1998). Accounting education literature review (1991–1997), part II: Students, educational technology, assessment and faculty issues. *Journal of Accounting Education, 16*(2), 179–245.

Roldan-Valadez, E., Salazar-Ruiz, S. Y., Ibarra-Contreras, R., & Rios, C. (2019). Current concepts on bibliometrics: A brief review about impact factor, Eigenfactor score, CiteScore, SCImago journal rank, source-normalised impact per paper, H-index, and alternative metrics. *Irish Journal of Medical Science (1971 -), 188*(3), 939–951. https://doi.org/10.1007/s11845-018-1936-5

Rubene, Z., Dimdins, G., & Miltuze, A. (2024). Sustainable growth of transversal competencies: Exploring the competence relationships among university students. *Education Sciences, 14*(7), 677. https://www.mdpi.com/2227-7102/14/7/677

Shehatta, I., & Al-Rubaish, A. M. (2019). Impact of country self-citations on bibliometric indicators and ranking of most productive countries. *Scientometrics, 120*(2), 775–791.

Sinnewe, E., Yao, D., & De Zwaan, L. (2023). Developing critical thinking: An examination of contemporary practices in accounting. In *Accounting and finance* (Vol. 63, pp. 403–425). Wiley.

Succi, C., & Canovi, M. (2019). Soft skills to enhance graduate employability: Comparing students and employers' perceptions. In *Studies in higher education* (Vol. 45, pp. 1834–1847). Routledge.

Tan, L. M., & Laswad, F. (2018). Professional skills required of accountants: What do job advertisements tell us? In *Accounting education* (Vol. 27, pp. 403–432). Taylor & Francis.

Tempone, I., Kavanagh, M., Segal, N., Hancock, P., Howieson, B., & Kent, J. (2012). Desirable generic attributes for accounting graduates into the twenty-first century. In *Accounting research journal* (Vol. 25, pp. 41–55). Emerald Group Publishing Limited.

Treleaven, L., & Voola, R. (2008). Integrating the development of graduate attributes through constructive alignment. *Journal of Marketing Education, 30*, 160–173.

Tsiligiris, V., & Bowyer, D. (2021). Exploring the impact of 4IR on skills and personal qualities for future accountants: A proposed conceptual framework for university accounting education. *Accounting Education, 30*, 621–649. https://doi.org/10.1080/09639284.2021.1938616

Visvizi, A., Troisi, O., Grimaldi, M., & Loia, F. (2022). Think human, act digital: Activating data-driven orientation in innovative start-ups. *European Journal of Innovation Management, 25*(6), 452–478.

Wamba, S. F., Gumbo, S., Twinomurinzi, H., Bwalya, K., & Mpinganjira, M. (2023). Digital transformation under Covid-19: A bibliometric study and future research agenda. *Procedia Computer Science, 219*, 271–278. https://doi.org/10.1016/j.procs.2023.01.290

Webb, J., & Chaffer, C. (2016). The expectation performance gap in accounting education: A review of generic skills development in UK accounting degrees. *Accounting Education, 25*, 349–367.

Williamson, M. (2009, 11/23/2009 Nov 23). Auditors attacked over banks Accountancy expert demands shake-up after failures in the lead up to financial crisis. *The Herald*, 24. https://www.proquest.com/newspapers/auditors-attacked-over-banks-accountancy-expert/docview/333119603/se-2?accountid=13425

Wolcott, S. K., & Sargent, M. J. (2021). Critical thinking in accounting education: Status and call to action. *Journal of Accounting Education, 56*, 100731. https://doi.org/10.1016/j.jaccedu.2021.100731

Wolcott, S. K., Baril, C. P., & Cunningham, B. M. (2002). Critical thought on critical thinking research. *Journal of Accounting Education, 20*, 85–103.

Zeng, L., Li, H., Lin, L., Hu, D. J. J., & Liu, H. (2024). ESG standards in China: Bibliometric analysis, development status research, and future research directions. *Sustainability, 16*(16), 7134. https://www.mdpi.com/2071-1050/16/16/7134

Zupic, I., & Čater, T. (2015). Bibliometric methods in management and organization. *Organizational Research Methods, 18*(3), 429–472.

Ownership Structure and Financial Performance of Listed Deposit Money Banks in Nigeria

Adesanmi Timothy Adegbayibi and Michael Olajide Adelowotan

Abstract The low performance of listed deposit money banks has been attributed to poor corporate governance structures, leading to high-risk financial activities driven by the self-interest of managers. In light of this, this study examines the effect of ownership structure on financial performance of listed deposit money banks in Nigeria. An ex post facto research design was adopted for the study, with data obtained from secondary sources such as the annual reports of sampled firms and the Factbook of the Nigerian Exchange Group for a period of 2018–2022. The study population comprised thirteen (13) sampled deposit money banks listed on the Nigerian Exchange Group as of December 31, 2022. The entire listed 13 deposit money banks were selected as a sample size using the census sampling techniques. The data were analyzed using descriptive statistics and panel regression analysis techniques. The study's findings revealed that institutional ownership has a negative and significant effect on the financial performance of listed deposit money banks in Nigeria. Foreign ownership has a positive and significant effect on financial performance of listed deposit money banks in Nigeria, while managerial ownership has a negative and significant effect on financial performance of listed deposit money banks in Nigeria. It is concluded that ownership structures significantly influence the market share of these banks. The study recommends that management should implement a policy allocating a portion of company shares to institutional investors. This could help align institutional interests with those of the business and enhance market stability. Also, government regulators should consider approving broader foreign ownership policies to stimulate performance improvements in their countries. This study has practical policy implications for managers to learn strategies to mitigate agency-related conflicts and optimize financial performance for listed deposit money banks in Nigeria, ultimately fostering sustainable growth and shareholder value.

A. T. Adegbayibi (✉) · M. O. Adelowotan
University of Johannesburg, Johannesburg, South Africa
e-mail: aadegbayibi@uj.ac.za; madelowotan@uj.ac.za

T. Moloi (ed.), *Impacting Society Positively Through Technology in Accounting and Business Processes*, Springer Proceedings in Business and Economics,
https://doi.org/10.1007/978-3-031-84885-8_4

Keywords Institutional ownership · Managerial ownership · Foreign ownership · Financial performance · Market share

Introduction

In today's business environment, where ownership is separated from management, principal-agent problems arise, posing major concerns for corporate governance due to ethical dilemma between principals (owners) and agents (managers). Consequently, economists, the government, and companies have extensively investigated effective corporate governance procedures (Amerta & Soenarino, 2020; Oremu, 2018). The urgency of the issue depends on how well investors or owners can ensure that competent managers, who have been given access to the organization's resources, will operate the business in a manner consistent with the owner's best interests (Igomu, 2020).

The principal objectives of deposit money banks are to generate profit and augment company value, both of which are profoundly dependent on organizational performance. Organizational performance is a measure of how effectively resources are employed to generate profit and enhance value (Amerta & Soenarino, 2020). Some key indicators for measuring an organization's financial performance, such as liquidity, return on assets (ROA), return on equity (ROE), and profitability, serve as essential metrics for transparency and effective risk management. Thus, the success or failure of a business is contingent upon the effectiveness of its organization structure. This implies that evaluating organizational performance is imperative for identifying critical areas in need of improvement and for facilitating the necessary enhancements (Uzun et al., 2018).

Performance is a crucial component for a company's survival and expansion, as it involves the process by which the limited resources available to an organization are effectively and efficiently managed to achieve its predetermined goals for both the short and long term (Kakanda, 2017). Firm performance, as assessed from the start to the end of an accounting period, serves as a crucial indicator of shareholders' wealth (Mustaphar & Othman, 2020). This evaluation not only bolsters investor confidence in anticipating future returns but also reflects the company's proficiency in generating profits. Among the most significant corporate governance challenges is the principle of the agency dilemma, which attracts considerable attention from government entities, company owners, and researchers alike. The structure of a firm benefits significantly from its ownership arrangement, particularly through a diversified shareholder base that enhances management control and, consequently, overall performance (Ogbabo & Elsayed, 2021).

Lack of competent managers, who have been given access to the organization's resources, to operate the business in a manner consistent with the owner's best interests has become worrisome to the investors, policy makers, academia, and stakeholders (Igomu, 2020; Adegbayibi, 2015). The board of directors failed in their oversight function to employ competent managers with essential corporate values and ethical practices that will enhance the integrity of the business environment and improve financial performance. This has eroded public trust and the confidence of investors.

Conflicts of interest stemming from the lack of separation between owners and managers represent a critical issue that significantly impedes the maximization of value for investors (Oluwafunmilayo, 2017). Additionally, the diversity within the ownership structure plays a pivotal role in enhancing the effectiveness of the board, serving as a critical incentive for managers to assume responsibility for firms and uphold exemplary performance. Various factors influence the adoption of ownership arrangements aimed at addressing agency issues, including government policies, cultural and social considerations, cost considerations, and legal requirements, all aimed at fostering mutual trust between shareholders and management (Ogbabo & Elsayed, 2021). Ownership structures that feature large shareholders are inclined to impose greater scrutiny, thereby mitigating the risk of managers exploiting their positions to the detriment of corporate shareholders. This is crucial given the costs associated with concentrated ownership, including the potential for minority shareholder expropriation, which can undermine organizational performance (Lawal et al., 2018). The field of corporate governance highlights that indicators within ownership structure, such as institutional ownership, managerial ownership, and foreign ownership, play a significant role in influencing firm financial performance by addressing principal-agent challenges effectively.

Institutional ownership, defined as the percentage of shares owned by the biggest investors, ensures that the presence of significant financial groups on the market has a positive influence on the overall status of the economy. Institutional investors also access and comprehend a wide range of investment vehicles that individual investors do not have access to. The monitoring of financial markets helps all owners because institutional ownership is seen to promote corporate governance (Adegbayibi, 2015). Similarly, high-quality management ownership guarantees that managerial interests are better aligned with those of shareholders, resulting in improved business performance (Wang & Rowe, 2019). Foreign ownership guarantees that there is a check and balance that prevents senior management from being corrupt at the cost of the investor.

The importance of ownership structures and how they impact organizational performance inspired various studies in the literature on ownership structure and its ability to enhance performance. Numerous empirical studies have investigated the relationship between ownership structure and financial performance in listed deposit money bank in Nigeria. Notably, studies by Abdul et al. (2021), Igomu (2021), Adamu (2020), Alhassan (2019), and Oromu (2018) have explored this area, primarily focusing on return on assets. However, these studies have not comprehensively addressed the effect of ownership structure on other metrics of financial performance. Only a limited number of studies, such as those by Adamu and Haruna (2020) and Amneh et al. (2021), have examined how ownership structure influences market share. This highlights a gap that needs to be addressed. Therefore, this study aims to investigate the effect of ownership structure on financial performance of listed deposit money banks in Nigeria, specifically in terms of market share. This study focused on the period from 2018 to 2022 and specifically analyzed three key indicators of ownership structure: institutional ownership, managerial ownership, and foreign ownership. By doing so, this seeks to contribute to a deeper understanding of how these ownership dynamics impact financial performance of deposit money banks in Nigeria.

The chapter is structured into five separate headings and other subheads; these cover the introductory aspect of the study, the review of the literature to clarify concepts, and interactions between variables in line with previous studies. The third heading is the explanation of data and methods used in the study. The analysis and discussion of findings are explained in the fourth heading, and finally, the conclusion and recommendations are outlined in the fifth heading.

Literature Review

Ownership Structure

Ownership refers to the legal possession and control of property, which can encompass both physical and intangible assets. It involves various rights, collectively known as title, which may be divided and held by different parties. Ownership structure pertains to the internal organization of corporate entities and delineates the rights and obligations of the individuals holding stakes in the firm. In essence, it concerns the distribution of power, responsibilities, rights, and ownership within the organization. The proportion of shares that shareholders own or hold is referred to as the ownership structure that creates individual identity and voting rights for shareholders (Tariq & Naveed, 2016). Ownership structure is significant because management and employee remuneration are primarily a consequence of the company's actions. Chou (2015) asserted that ownership structure pertains to the distribution of equity in terms of votes, capital, and the identity of the equity owners. Similarly, Adegbayibi (2015) describes it as the identification and voting capacity of investors. Lawal et al. (2018) characterized ownership structure in terms of productivity as a combination of concentrated ownership and substantial stockholdings by institutional owners. According to Shehu et al. (2012), a company's cash income is proportional to its shareholdings.

According to the definition provided in the literature, ownership structure is concerned with the holdings of shareholders in a business organization. According to Adegbayibi (2015), ownership structure is the distribution of stock ownership among shareholders. A defined ownership structure aids in the resolution of conflicts between management and shareholders in businesses (Alkurdi et al., 2019). According to Armin et al., joint-stock corporations are less efficient than private enterprises because public company managers may not see other people's resources as seriously as their own assets.

Institutional Ownership

Gugong et al. (2018) postulated that institutional ownership is a large-scale equity holding in a corporation by other institutions. This ownership structure is linked to exceptional financial performance because of improved corporate governance and management. Institutional ownership may help a company's corporate governance. Kenton (2021) asserted that institutional ownership is the percentage of a company's accessible shares held by mutual or pension funds, insurance companies, investment firms, private foundations, endowments, and other big institutions that manage money on others' behalf. Stocks with a high level of institutional ownership are often considered advantageous because large corporations, when purchasing a significant stake in a company's shares, typically employ a team of analysts to conduct comprehensive and costly financial analyses (Almahrog et al., 2018). In the same vein, the reputation of institutional ownership can influence the level of interest exhibited by fund managers and analysts when considering the acquisition of shares (Wang & Rowe, 2019). Moreover, if a business has a track record of consistently selecting high-performing companies, it is likely to motivate fund managers to increase their purchase of stocks or inventories investments in that firm.

There are varieties of difficulties when an institution owns most of a specific security or an institution's resources as most outstanding shares of the securities might be purchased and controlled by entities, including borrowed shares (Sahard et al., 2017). The percentage of shares owned by the biggest investors is referred to as institutional ownership. Thus, institutional ownership is represented by the logarithm of shares owned by a company's shareholders.

Managerial Ownership

Managerial ownership is another strategy for mitigating the impact of agency concerns, where prominent shareholders might make decisions that harm minority investors. Jensen and Meckling postulated that managerial ownership enhances a firm's value by achieving superior financial performance. This type of ownership is referred to as insider ownership (Afang, 2019). It is the percentage of a company's stock owned by its directors and board members. Managers and directors who have a sizable personal fortune based on the firm's worth are more driven to act in the best interests of external shareholders (Badara, 2016; Lin, 2019). Outsider shareholders assess the extent of agency costs imposed by the owner-manager is substantially related to the owner's wealth. Therefore, the lower the expense of assessing such charges, the lower the value of the owner.

Foreign Ownership

Control of a company and natural resource in a nation by persons who are not citizens of that country or by firms whose headquarters are not in the country is referred to as foreign ownership (Bushee & Carter, 2014). That is, a company in which foreigners possess 50% or more of the stock is effectively controlled by foreigners. It is computed by dividing the total number of foreign owners by the total number of shares in issues. The presence of foreign banks in a region enables foreign ownership to exert influence on strategic decisions within the banking industry. Nevertheless, in the case of a financial disaster, foreign ownership via foreign banks' entry into a growing country that alters or precipitates a financial crisis potentially affects the banking system (Lin, 2019).

Financial Performance

Performance is a crucial component for a company's survival and expansion; it involves the process by which the limited resources available to an organization are effectively and efficiently managed to achieve its predetermined goals for both the short and long term (Kakanda, 2017). Firm performance, as assessed from the start to the end of an accounting period, serves as a crucial indicator of shareholders' wealth (Mustaphar & Othman, 2020). This evaluation not only bolsters investor confidence in anticipating future returns but also reflects the company's proficiency in generating profits.

The financial performance of corporations has sparked several arguments and studies involving academics, company management, and a variety of other stakeholders. Analyzing a company's financial performance may require a close examination of several indices/measures such as sales growth, turnover, dividend growth, profitability, asset base, size, capital employed, returns, profits, Tobin's Q, and market share. Connect (2018) opined that a company's success is normally judged in three dimensions: productivity, profitability, and market premium. Productivity is concerned with the input/output mix; market premium is concerned with the market/book value connection (Uzun et al., 2018). In contrast, the profitability dimension focuses on a company's profits maximization.

Theoretical Underpinning

Agency theory underpins this study. Agency theory was propounded by Jensen and Mecklings in 1976, which conceptualizes a contractual relationship in which one or more parties (principals) engage another party (an agent) to perform services on their behalf, relinquishing decision-making authority to the agent. This theoretical framework highlights a contractual relationship between shareholders (principals) and management (agents), where shareholders delegate managerial authority. The theory posits that, in situations where both parties aim to maximize their interests, there is potential for opportunistic behavior by the agent, posing a risk to the principal's objectives. The central focus of agency theory is on the conflicts that arise when the interests of the agent and principal diverge, leading to challenges in understanding the agent's behavior.

Agency theory emphasizes the separation of ownership and control and connects principals and agents. Agency theory is a paradigm used to describe and overcome problems in the interaction between company owners and their agents. Interaction exists between the shareholders known as principles and the company executives (board of directors) to conduct business for a defined objective. The fundamental of agency theory premise is that the actor is likely to be self-centered and motivated to maximize his own benefit. The shareholders (principal) have their own expectations, as do the executives (agents). Because the interests of shareholders vary greatly from those of directors, agency theory is concerned with addressing difficulties that arise because of a conflict of interest between the principal (shareholders) and the agent (executives) (Badara, 2016).

In the context of ownership structure and financial performance, agency theory suggests that firms may face conflicts of interest between top management (agents) and shareholders (principals), resulting in increased agency costs and information asymmetry. To mitigate these issues, Frias-Aceituno et al. propose that firms should enhance information disclosure, addressing the problem of information asymmetry. The implementation of ownership structure can act as a mechanism to establish a balance between the interests of principals and agents, ultimately leading to improved financial performance. Recent studies by Amerta and Soenarino (2020), Afang (2019), and Amneh et al. (2021) have applied agency theory to investigate the relationship between ownership structure and financial performance, emphasizing its role in minimizing information asymmetry and conflicts between shareholders and management. The review of agency theory suggests that ownership structure can reduce conflicts of interest and information asymmetry, contributing to a balance between principals and agents.

This theory is imperative to this study because it emphasized the reason why the management of deposit money banks should place much reliance on its ownership structure. It helps to foster an understanding that the existence of management ownership helps in the minimization of conflict of interest (Ahmed & Wan, 2016). Therefore, management's behavior will be re-shaped positively toward fulfilling the mandate of the shareholders and management will be willing to carry out business activities toward achieving a greater performance.

Empirical Review

Institutional Ownership and Financial Performance

Abdulfatah et al. study the effect of institutional shareholding on the financial performance of Nigerian listed deposit money banks. The study used a correlation research technique. Their findings revealed that institutional ownership has a significant effect on financial performance. Abdul et al. (2021) looked on the ownership structure and financial performance of Nigerian listed insurance companies. The information was gathered and evaluated using 9 years of annual reports and accounts from a sample of manufacturing enterprises. According to the findings of the research, institutional ownership has a favorable and substantial influence on financial performance.

Santoso looked at the ownership structure and financial performance of Indonesian Islamic institutions. The study found that institutional ownership has a positive impact on bank financial performance using multiple linear regression analysis. Yahaya et al. used secondary data from audited reports of Nigerian deposit money banks to examine the effects of institutional ownership structure on financial performance of Nigerian deposit money banks over a 9-year period (2008–2016). It was found out that institutional ownership has a positive and significant impact on financial performance.

Ozer et al. explored how corporate ownership structure affects financial performance. Panel data analysis was performed on models designed to explore the effects of ownership structure on company financial performance and it was observed that institutional ownership had a statistically negative influence on the ROA. Ringim used secondary sources such as annual reports and accounts to study the ownership structure and financial performance of Nigerian conglomerate enterprises over a 6-year period. The data demonstrated that institutional ownership has a negative significant influence on conglomerate company performance.

Managerial Ownership and Financial Performance

Igomu (2020) investigated the ownership structure and financial performance of selected Nigerian banks, using a correlation study approach to assess the link between ownership structures and financial performance of Nigerian listed banks. According to the study, a larger fraction of foreign ownership enhances the performance of selected Nigerian banks. Adamu (2020) explored the association between company performance and ownership structure in Nigeria. The study gathered secondary data on management, foreign, and institutional ownership on return on assets (ROA), return on equity (ROE), and profits per share from 40 selected businesses, revealing that managerial ownership was dominant, while ROA, EPS, and Tobin Q are dominating performance indicators.

Mustapha et al. evaluated the relationship between ownership structure and performance. The study examined the link between ownership structure and financial performance of listed food and beverage enterprises in Nigeria using secondary data on management ownership, employee ownership, private ownership, and return on equity. They discovered that managerial structure had a considerable impact on the financial performance of Nigerian listed food and beverage industries. Okoughenu used a multiple regression technique with ordinary least square estimation to investigate the ownership structure and financial performance of Nigerian listed deposit money banks and discovered that managerial ownership has a positive effect on financial performance.

Abubakar explored the association between ownership structures and financial performance of publicly traded Nigerian construction material manufacturers. The study used multiple regression as an analytical method and looked for fixed and random effects. It was revealed that institutional ownership and management ownership had a considerably favorable influence on the financial performance of Nigerian listed construction material manufacturers. Oluwafunmilayo (2017) used secondary data on management ownership, employee ownership, private ownership, and return on equity to study the ownership structure and financial performance of the Nigerian food and beverage company. Management ownership was determined to have a significant (positive) influence on return on equity.

Arthur (2017) evaluated the association between the Ugandan corporate ownership structure and financial performance. To accommodate for heteroskedasticity and contemporaneous correlation, which might lead to incorrect findings, this research used a fixed effect regression model with a robust standard error option. The study used a panel dataset of 48 companies with 432 observations, which was analyzed using descriptive statistics, correlation matrix, and regression analysis, and it revealed that managerial ownership has a significant positive impact on firm performance with no entrenchment effect at managerial levels above 5%.

Foreign Ownership and Financial Performance

Amneh et al. (2021) evaluated the influence of ownership structure on financial performance in Jordanian listed enterprises using an empirical approach. The multiple regression model and fixed regression effect were employed to examine data in this research, which discovered a positive and substantial association between foreign ownership and financial performance. Alhassan et al. used descriptive statistics, correlation, and multiple regression techniques using panel data to estimate the link between ownership structure and financial performance of publicly listed financial enterprises in Nigeria. According to the findings of the study, foreign ownership structure has a favorable influence on the financial performance of publicly listed financial organizations.

Afang (2019) evaluated the effect of ownership structure on financial performance of Nigerian listed oil and gas businesses. Secondary data were taken from the financial reports and accounts of the study's sample firms, and it was determined that management ownership has a major influence on the financial performance of oil and gas in Nigeria. Gugong et al. (2018) studied the influence of ownership structure on the financial performance of Nigerian listed insurance businesses. Over a 10-year period, the study used panel data from seventeen (17) organizations and discovered a positive significant association between ownership structure and company performance as evaluated by ROA and ROE. Orumo used cross-sectional data from the financial statements of 15 publicly listed commercial banks to analyze the ownership structure and return on assets of commercial banks in Nigeria. A fixed effect model was employed in the study. Foreign ownership was revealed to have a negative connection with the dependent variable, return on investment.

Sahardjanto et al. examined the effect of foreign ownership on financial performance of listed airline firms in Nigeria using quantitative research and purposive sampling techniques. The findings of the study revealed that foreign and government ownership has a positive impact on airline financial performance.

Several studies (Abdul et al., 2021; Igomu, 2021; Adamu, 2020; Alhassan, 2019; Oromu, 2018) have examined the effect of ownership structure and financial performance in deposit money bank. However, these studies were not able to adequately address the area of focus, but their studies consider some financial performance measures such as return on assets, return on equity and return on capital employed. Only a limited number of studies such as Adamu and Haruna (2020) and Amneh et al. (2021) were able to consider market share, and this constitutes a gap to be filled in this study. In light of this, this study examined the effect of ownership structure on financial performance in terms of market share.

Most accounting/finance studies on financial performance (Badara, 2016) were done within the profitability dimension, where performance is primarily assessed by ROA and ROE. As a follow-up to previous research, this study uses market share as a metric of corporate financial success in Nigeria. Market share is a measure of how successfully a business has predicted market trends.

Research Methods

Research Design

This study employed an ex post facto research design. The choice of the design was informed by the ready availability of the data in the annual reports of the selected deposit money bank listed firms on Nigerian Exchange Group Factbook. The data used were collected from secondary source through the annual report and Nigeria Exchange Group FactBook for a period of 2018–2022. The choice of base year 2018 was informed by the recent global economic recession which affected the financial performance of listed deposit money banks in Nigeria. Also, secondary data were employed because data needed on the variables can only be found and assessed in the financial statements of listed deposit money banks.

The population of this study comprised of 13 deposit money banks listed on the Nigerian Exchange Group as of December 31, 2022. The entire 13 deposit money banks were selected as a sample size using the census sampling technique. The model specification was adopted from Elliot (1998) and modified to meet the specific objectives of the study as recently used by Eshleman.

$$FP_{it} = f(OWS) \tag{1}$$

$$FP_{it} = f(INSTOWN, MGOWN, FOWN) \tag{2}$$

$$MKS_{it} = ai + \beta INSTOWN_{it} + \beta 2MGOWN_{it} + \beta 3FOWN_{it} + \varepsilon_{it} \tag{3}$$

where:

FP = financial performance
INSTOWN = institutional ownership
MGOWN = managerial ownership
FO WN = foreign ownership
B1 – $\beta 3$ = coefficient of independent variables
ε_{it} = error terms of firm i and time t.

The independent variable for this study is ownership structure which was proxied by institutional ownership (INSTOWN), managerial ownership (MGOWN), and foreign ownership (FOWN). The dependent variable is financial performance; this was proxied by market share (MKS). Table 1 shows the operational definitions and measurements of the research variables.

Table 1 Measurements of study variables

S/N	Variables	Description	Measurements	Sources
1	Market share	It is the measure of how well companies have been able to predict market dynamics	Percentage of market (in terms of revenue) accounted for by an entity	Adamu and Haruna (2020), Amneh et al. (2021)
2	Institutional ownership structure	It is the amount of share owned by institutions	Natural logarithm of shares owned by institutions	Alhassa and Mamuda (2020)
3	Managerial ownership structure	It is the amount of share owned by managers or directors	Natural logarithm of shares owned by managers or directors	Abdul (2016)
4	Foreign ownership structure	It is the amount of share owned by foreign investors or institutions	Natural logarithm of shares owned by institutions	Abdul (2016)

Source: Authors' Compilation (2023)

Results and Discussion

Descriptive Statistics

The descriptive statistics of variables from deposit money banks in Nigeria is presented in the Table 2. It shows the mean, standard deviation, minimum and maximum values, and normality tests such as skewness and kurtosis for both outcome and predicator variables. The results of the descriptive statistics reported in Table 2 indicate that market capitalization across the firms has an average value of 7.9660, with standard deviation of 0.6989. This suggests a high variation of financial reporting quality across the sampled firms due to the considerable distance from the mean. The minimum market capitalization is 6.6140 and maximum is 9.0590. The data are negatively skewed, with a skewness value of −0.3614 and a normal distribution value of 2.0512.

Similarly, institutional ownership (INSTO) across the firms has an average value of 37.2460 with a standard deviation of 26.7430. This indicates a high variation in institutional ownership across the sampled firms due to the significant distance from the mean. The minimum board independence is 0%, while the maximum is 91%. The data are positively skewed, with a skewness value of 0.2395 with a normal distribution of 2.0772.

In Table 2, foreign ownership (FOW) across the firms is reported to have an average of 0.5384 with standard deviation of 0.5023, indicating significant variation in foreign ownership levels among the firms. Firms are categorized with values of 0 or 1, representing the absence or presence of foreign ownership, respectively. The data for this variable show a negative skewness of −0.1543 and a kurtosis value of 1.0238, indicating a mesokurtic distribution.

Additionally, Table 2 shows that managerial ownership structure has a mean value of 12.7720 with a standard deviation of 19.7252, signifying high variation in managerial ownership structure across the firms. The minimum ownership structure is 0.0620, while the maximum is 101.9760. The data for this variable exhibit a positive skewness of 2.5033 and a kurtosis value of 9.7270.

Table 2 Descriptive statistics

Variables	MKTS	INSTO	FOWN	MGOW
OBS	65	65	65	65
Mean	7.9660	37.2461	0.5384	12.7728
S.D	0.6989	26.7435	0.5023	19.7252
Min	6.6145	0	0	0.0627
Max	9.0590	91	1	101.9769
Skewness	−0.3614	0.2395	−0.1543	2.5033
Kurtosis	2.0512	2.0772	1.0238	9.7272

Source: Authors' computation (2023)

Correlation Matrix

The correlation coefficient represents the linear association or relationship between the dependent and explanatory variables and shows symptoms of multicollinearity. The result in Table 3 shows the relationship between ownership structures and financial performance. The relationship between market share and institutional ownership is negative, having a coefficient of −0.3281. This implies that an increase in the institutional ownership of banks will lead to a decrease in their market share by 32.81%. The relationship is significant at 5% having a *p*-value of 0.0076. Furthermore, the relationship between market share and foreign ownership is positive and insignificant, having a coefficient of 0.0808 and *p*-value of 0.5222. This implies that an increase in foreign ownership will cause an increase in the market share of the deposit money banks by 8%. Likewise, from Table 3, it is shown that the relationship between managerial ownership and market share is negative and significant, having a coefficient of −0.4877 and *p*-value of 0.0000. This implies that with an increase in managerial ownership of the firms, the market share will improve by 48.77%.

From Table 3, it is observed that the relationship between the independent variables does not indicate significant multicollinearity issues, as the coefficients are all less than 0.7. Specifically, the relationship between institutional ownership and foreign ownership is 0.4133, and between institutional ownership and managerial ownership is 0.2197. Furthermore, the relationship between foreign ownership and managerial ownership is positive, with a coefficient of 0.0713.

Multicollinearity Test

Multicollinearity tests are conducted as post-estimation test to validate the assumptions of a regression model. They help determine if there are high correlations among two or more explanatory variables. When such correlations exist, it means that one variable can be linearly predicted from the others with a certain degree of

Table 3 Correlation analysis of study variables

Relationship between ownership structure and market share		
Variables	Coefficients	*P*-value
Market share	1.0000	0.0000
INSTO	−0.3281	0.0076
FOWS	0.0808	0.5222
MOWS	−0.4877	0.0000
INSTO & FOWS	0.4133	0.0006
INSTO & MOWS	0.2197	0.0787
FOWS & MOWS	0.0713	0.5725

Source: Authors' computation (2023)

Table 4 Tolerance and VIF value

Variable Ownership structure	VIF	1/VIF
INSTO	1.26	0.7928
FOWS	1.21	0.8287
MOWS	1.05	0.9512
Mean VIF		1.17

Source: Authors' computation (2023)

Table 5 Test for heteroskedasticity and autocorrelation

	Chi2 (1)	Prob > Chi2	F (1, 12)
Heteroskedasticity test			–
Ho: Constant variance			
Autocorrelation	2.09	0.1484	–
H0: No first-order autocorrelation	–	0.0036	12.996

Source: Authors' computation (2023)

accuracy, indicating an issue of multicollinearity. The variance inflation factor (VIF) value is used to investigate the relationship between the variables themselves. Where the result is not found to be significant, we conclude that there is multicollinearity, because the variance inflation factor and tolerance values are comparatively beyond the established rule of thumb.

Based on the evidence presented in Table 4, it can be concluded that there is no multicollinearity problem for the model. This is because the VIF values for all the variables are less than 10 and the tolerance values for all the variables are greater than 0.10 (rule of thumb). Therefore, the study can rely on regression coefficient to predict the level of impact of independent variables on dependent variables and the outcome of the findings can be considered valid.

Test for Heteroskedasticity and Autocorrelation

A heteroskedasticity test was conducted to check the validity of the homoskedasticity assumption that variance in the residuals is constant, as the absence of homoskedasticity violates the assumption and may lead to a wrong inference. Based on the results in Table 5, the Breusch–Pagan test for heteroskedasticity indicated that heteroskedasticity is not present in the model, as evidenced by a probability value of 0.1484, which exceeds the typical significant level of 0.05. This suggests that the error term does not exhibit systematic changes in variance across the residuals. However, the test for autocorrelation using Wooldridge test for autocorrelation in

Table 6 Unit-root test

	Hadri LM test (unit-root)	
	T-Statistics	*P*-value
Market share	−0.3848	0.6498
Institutional ownership	0.1994	0.4210
Foreign ownership	−4.0311	1.0000
Managerial ownership	1.0331	0.1508

Source: Authors' computation (2023)

panel data yielded a significant result with a *p*-value of 0.0036. This indicates the presence of first-order correlation in the data, implying that there is some level of autocorrelation in the residuals. In summary, while heteroskedasticity is not an issue in the model, there is evidence of autocorrelation in the residuals according to the conducted tests.

Unit-Root Test for Non-stationary Series

To find a suitable model, the stationarity of the time series data was checked using Hadri LM unit-root test for panel unit root and the results were presented in Table 6. The null hypothesis of this test is that all panels are stationary. Given our results, we accept the hypothesis, implying that all panels are stationary, and since the *p*-value is higher than 0.05, we rejected the alternative hypothesis at the 5% level of statistical significance.

The regressed result showing the effect of ownership structure on financial performance of listed deposit money banks in Nigeria after meeting the basis for a best linear unbiased estimate (BLUE) is shown in Table 7. The Hausman specification test produced a *p*-value of 0.0797, which is insignificant at 5%. This implies that the variation across entities is assumed to be fixed with the independent variables included in the model. As a result of this, the result of the fixed effect model was considered suitable for the analysis of the model. More so, the result of heteroskedasticity tests and autocorrelation test in Table 5 shows that there is a problem of auto serial correlation. Hence a panel-corrected linear regression is considered to correct the heteroskedastic and autocorrelation problems identified. The basis of judgment used is the z-statistics and *p*-value.

The result obtained reveals an *R*-square of 0.3413, indicating that the model collectively explains 34.13% of the variation in the dependent variable (market share). The remaining variation is accounted for by the error term, suggesting that there are additional factors not included in this model. The *p*-value of the model 0.0000 shows that the model is statistically significant at 5%. The result further shows that institutional ownership has a z-statistics of −2.98, indicating that institutional ownership has a negative and significant effect on market share, as indicated by the *p*-value of 0.003. The implication is that a level of institutional ownership brings

Table 7 Panel-corrected standard errors regression results

Indep-corrected				
MKTS	Coef.	Std. err.	*z*	*P* > |z|
INSTO	−0.0088	0.0029	−2.98	0.0030
FOWS	0.3490	0.1538	2.27	0.0230
MOWS	−0.0152	0.0036	−4.18	0.0000
__cons	8.3014	0.1288	64.44	0.0000
R-squared = 0.3413	Obs = 65			
Wald chi2 (3) = 33.69	Groups = 13			
Prob > chi2 = 0.0000				
Hausman test				
chi2 (3) = 5.06	Prob > chi2 = 0.0797			

Source: Authors' computation (2023)

stringent rules on the companies' subscription, thereby decreasing their share of the total market in the industry.

The z-statistic for foreign ownership (FOWS) is 2.27, indicating a positive and statistically significant effect of ownership structure at 5% level, as evidenced by a *p*-value of 0.023. This suggests that foreign ownership structures offer substantial potential for companies by providing attributes such as financial discipline, expertise, and diverse perspectives to management. This, in turn, can enhance the confidence of local investors, potentially leading to increased market share indirectly. Conversely, the results also indicate that managerial ownership has a negative and significant effect on financial performance, with a z-statistic of −4.18 and a *p*-value of 0.0000, which is significant at 5% level. The implies that management ownership may lead directors to prioritize preserving their own power and interests, potentially resulting in lower market share. In conclusion, the study finds that ownership structure significantly influences the financial performance of listed deposit money banks in Nigeria.

The results align with the findings of Okoughenu's study, which investigated the ownership structure and financial performance of Nigerian listed deposit money banks and discovered that both foreign ownership and ownership concentration have a positive effect on financial performance. Likewise, Orumo explored ownership concentration, management ownership, and institutional ownership were revealed to have a negative connection with the dependent variable, return on investment, but private ownership and management ownership had a positive relationship. Afang (2019) also submitted that managerial ownership has a major influence on the financial performance of oil and gas in Nigeria. However, the findings contradict the results of Olufunmilayo (2017) who studied ownership structure and financial performance of the Nigerian food and beverage company and inferred that management ownership had a significant (positive) influence on return on equity. The difference may be because of the sector of focus and measure of financial performance.

Conclusion and Recommendations

This study examined the effect of institutional ownership, managerial ownership, and foreign ownership on the financial performance of listed deposit money banks in Nigeria. It concluded that these ownership structures significantly influence the market share of these banks, aligning with agency theory which highlights the potential conflicts between owners (principals) seeking wealth maximization and managers (agents) focusing on profit maximization to secure bonuses and incentives. The findings underscore the importance of addressing agency problems within these institutions to foster market growth. Based on the findings of the study, the following recommendations are made:

1. Management should implement a policy allocating a portion of company shares to institutional investors. This could help align institutional interests with those of the business and enhance market stability.
2. Government regulators should consider approving broader foreign ownership policies to stimulate performance improvements in their countries. Increased foreign investment can bring expertise and capital that benefits the banks and their market positioning.
3. The board of directors should monitor and regulate managerial ownership percentages. High concentrations of managerial ownership have shown a negative correlation with financial performance, suggesting a need for balanced ownership structures that protect investors' interests.

This study has practical policy implications for managers to learn strategies to mitigate agency-related conflicts and optimize financial performance for listed deposit money banks in Nigeria, ultimately fostering sustainable growth and shareholder value. Also, policy makers can clearly observe how different ownership structures affect financial performance.

This study is restricted to listed deposit money banks in Nigeria. More information on ownership structure and financial performance of listed deposit money banks in Nigeria might have been provided if the study covered more period but this study included sample banks actively trading from 2018 to 2022. The result might be different if the period covered is elongated. Also, the current study did not make use of other metrics of financial performance such as Tobin's Q, return on assets, and return on equity. The study only made use of market value as a measure of financial performance.

Further studies may apply metrics of financial performance such as Tobin's Q, return on assets, and return on equity. The study can also be replicated in other sectors of the economy, especially the nonfinancial sector such as the consumer goods sector and manufacturing industry.

References

Adamu, A., & Haruna, J. (2020). Ownership structure and firm performance in Nigeria: A canonical correlation analysis. *Journal of Research in Emerging Markets, 2*(4), 21–32.

Adegbayibi, A. T. (2015). Equity ownership structure and operating performance of non-financial quoted companies in Nigeria. *Journal of Economics and Development Studies, Kaduna State University, Kaduna, 3*(1), 277–301.

Afang, B. (2019). The impact of ownership on building sustainable and responsible businesses. *Journal of the British Academy, 6*(1), 375–403.

Ahmed, A. A. N., & Wan, A. K. (2016). Corporate governance practices, ownership structure, and corporate performance in the GCC countries. *Journal of International Financial Markets, Institutions and Money, 4*(6), 98–110.

Alkurdi, W. K., Al-Shattarat, B. K., & Hamed, R. (2019). Do dividends announcements signal future earnings changes for Jordanian firms? *Journal of Financial Reporting and Accounting, 16*(3), 417–442.

Almahrog, J., Muldoon, J., Liguori, E. W., & Davis, P. E. (2018). Agency theory: Background and epistemology. *Journal of Management History, 22*(4), 437–449.

Amerta, K., & Soenarino, D. (2020). The effect of ownership structure on corporate performance of listed companies in Amman stock exchange: Empirical evidence of Jordan. *International Journal of Managerial Studies and Research, 3*(5), 41–49.

Amneh, A., Amneh, H., Hussam, T., & Mahmoud, E. (2021). Ownership structure's effect on financial performance: An empirical analysis of Jordanian listed firms. *Cogent Business and Management, 8*(1), 1939930. https://doi.org/10.1080/23311999975.2021.1939930

Arthur, B. (2017). Ownership structure and corporate performance: Looking back and looking forward. *Journal of Corporate Finance, 5*(8), 64–67.

Badara, O. (2016). The effect of government ownership, foreign ownership, institutional ownership and audit quality on firm performance of listed companies in Oman. *International Journal of Financial Research, 11*(2), 233–249.

Bushee, A., & Carter, D. (2014). The effects of taxes, agency costs and information asymmetry on earnings management: A comparison of public and private firms. *The Review of Accounting Studies, 4*(3), 299–326.

Chou, B. (2015). Ownership structure and firm performance improvement: Does it matter in the Vietnamese stock market? *A Journal of Applied Economics and Policy, 36*(4), 416–428.

Connect, M. (2018). The impact of ownership structure and dividends on firm's performance: Evidence from manufacturing companies listed on the Amman stock exchange. *Australasian Accounting, Business and Finance Journal, 12*(3), 107–126.

Gugong, C. J., Weldon, R. N., & Gunderson, M. A. (2018). Earnings management through specific accruals and discretionary expenses: Evidence from US agribusiness firms. *Canadian Journal of Agricultural Economics/Revue Canadienne D'agroeconomie, 64*(1), 89–118.

Igomu, S. (2020). The impact of ownership structure and dividends on firm's performance: Evidence from manufacturing companies listed on the Amman stock exchange. *Australasian Accounting, Business and Finance Journal, 12*(3), 107–126.

Kakanda, A. (2017). The relationship between ownership structure, capital structure and performance. *Journal of Accounting, Business and Management, 25*(25), 1–20.

Kenton, H. (2021). The impact of ownership structure on dividend policy of listed firms in Jordan. *Cogent Business and Management, 8*(1), 86–100.

Lawal, A., Hussainey, K., Tahat, Y., & Aladwan, M. (2018). The impact of corporate governance on risk disclosure: Jordanian evidence. *Academy of Accounting and Financial Studies Journal, 23*(1), 71–84.

Lin, B. (2019). Corporate governance and firm performance: The sequel. *International Journal of Managerial Studies and Research, 3*(5), 41–49.

Mustaphar, M., & Othman, Z. (2020). Earnings manipulations in politically influenced firms. *Corporate Ownership and Control, 15*(1), 65–71.

Ogbabo, H., & Elsayed, K. (2021). The mediating effect of financial performance on the relationship between social responsibility and ownership structure. *Future Business Journal, 1*(1–2), 1–12.

Oluwafunmilayo, C. K. (2017). A study of interaction effects of political influences and earnings management on organizational performance. *Asian Economic and Financial Review, 9*(5), 15–25.

Oremu, R. (2018). Do dividends announcements signal future earnings changes for Jordanian firms? *Journal of Financial Reporting and Accounting, 16*(3), 417–442.

Sahard, F., Khairollahi, F., & Alipour, M. (2017). Does ownership structure matter for corporate intellectual capital performance: An empirical test in the Iranian context. *Eurasian Business Review, 7*(1), 67–91.

Shehu, Y., Ali Aribi, Z., & Arun, T. (2012). Earnings management and corporate social responsibility: UK evidence. *Journal of Financial Reporting and Accounting, 16*(2), 311–332.

Tariq, M., & Naveed, H. (2016). The effect of ownership structure on corporate performance of listed companies in Tehran stock exchange: Empirical evidence of Iran. *International Journal of Business and Social Science, 2*(13), 49–55.

Uzun, H., Szewczky, S. H., & Varma, R. (2018). Board composition and corporate fraud. *Financial Analysts Journal, 60*(1), 33–43.

Wang, A., & Rowe, D. (2019). The effects of taxes, agency costs and information asymmetry on earnings management: A comparison of public and private firms. *The Review of Accounting Studies, 4*(3–4), 299–326.

The Impact of Hybrid Working Model on Employee Performance

Ratanang Mathebula and Nyankomo Marwa

Abstract The COVID-19 outbreak has pushed many organizations to implement remote working arrangements to ensure business continuity. The hybrid working model, which incorporates both remote and on-site work, has emerged as a preferred method for many organizations. Yet, little is known about the influence of this paradigm shift on employee performance. The purpose of this research was to explore the impact of the hybrid working model on employee performance in the public sector. Objective of the study is to investigate how the hybrid approach could have affected employee performance by unraveling the understanding of various factors that influence productivity, motivation, and job satisfaction as well as their impact on employees. The study employs a qualitative method research design that includes data collection procedures such as interviews, focus group discussion, and document analysis. The result from this research sheds some light on the dimensions of how the work atmosphere and the support provided by management directly or indirectly affect job performance. Job flexibility and internal drive could also have a direct effect on job performance. While the hybrid working model allows employees more freedom and autonomy; nevertheless, the study discovered several challenges associated with the hybrid working paradigm. In particular, communication and collaboration issues and difficulties separating work and personal life were in the forefront. We conclude that if implemented correctly, the hybrid working model could positively impact employee performance. Organizations must handle the model's challenges while providing staff with the appropriate support and resources to ensure its success. Overall, the findings of this study can help other departments, particularly those in the public sector, adopt and implement the hybrid working model.

Keywords Hybrid work · Telework · Virtual teams · Work–life balance · Job performance · Work from home

R. Mathebula (✉) · N. Marwa
University of Johannesburg, Johannesburg, South Africa
e-mail: nyankomom@uj.ac.za

T. Moloi (ed.), *Impacting Society Positively Through Technology in Accounting and Business Processes*, Springer Proceedings in Business and Economics,
https://doi.org/10.1007/978-3-031-84885-8_5

Introduction

In response to the global outbreak of COVID-19, governments globally were forced to implement lockdown measures to keep the virus from spreading (Hale et al., 2020). How the governments responded globally varied widely; some countries responded quickly and effectively by implementing different measures (Lazarus et al., 2020) such as border closures, conducting contact tracing, and implementing other interventions to limit the spread of the virus by strengthening healthcare systems and addressing the economic impact of these measures. Many other countries were slower to respond or implemented fewer effective measures, leading to more cases and deaths (Hale et al., 2020).

The extent to which the public complies with government orders and prevention pieces of advice thereof can have a considerable impact on the pandemic's trajectory, especially given the skepticism surrounding COVID-19 vaccines and the lack of clear treatments. This emphasizes the importance of understanding the relationship between public trust and compliance with government policies and strategies (Lazarus et al., 2020). Remote working was one of these strategies, which was utilized by a wide range of organizations in both developed and developing countries to protect their employees while also assuring business continuity and limiting potential losses. Although some organizations had previously implemented remote working before the pandemic, most people were not acquainted with this approach (Kniffin et al., 2021).

The pandemic involuntarily compelled private and public organizations to adopt and implement the hybrid working model (Chellam & Divya, 2022). Such adaptation was necessary to address the business's changing needs for the sake of business continuity while ensuring that employees deliver their best performance even under challenging circumstances. To address the changing needs of the workforce and the organization, digital transformation emerged as the preferred means of integrating the traditional office setting with remote work (Chellam & Divya, 2022), Even though the hybrid working model seems to be implemented abruptly across all levels, the model has allowed for greater flexibility in the work location. However, it also could have created challenges such as teamwork and collaborative work performance. Depending on the intensity and dominance of such effects, the overall outcome could lead to a noticeable impact whether negative or positive on overall job performance.

Therefore, the study seeks to unpack whether the net impact on employee performance is positive or negative which remains an empirical question. Hence this research aims to analyze the impact of the hybrid working model on employee performance in the public sector. The study will use department XXX case study to interrogate the employee performance dynamics of the new working model compared to the traditional working model pre-COVID-19.

There are several factors affecting employee performance; the objective is to capture rich and nuanced data that can shed light on employees' views on hybrid working arrangements, including their perceived advantages, challenges, and potential trade-offs.

This study includes five sections: literature review, research design, results, and recommendations.

Literature Review

Theoretical Review

Relevant theoretical literature in this section examines limitations, difficulties, and potential prospects in hybrid work, taking into account key elements like work from home, virtual teams, and work–life balance. Working from home as an alternative to working from the office has taken off as a result of the impact of COVID-19 from March 2020. While there has been significant discussion on the pandemic's impact, the research on how lockdown has affected performance and remote working in the public sector is still in its infancy.

According to Patanjali and Bhatta (2022) medical publications have focused heavily on the pandemic's impact, particularly with the then emergence of new virus variants. That analysis by Patanjali and Bhatta (2022), however, determined that established research journals have given little attention to the effect of hybrid working arrangements on employees (Gigauri, 2020). Even 3 years into the pandemic, or maybe post-pandemic, there are only a few key research articles available that provide an in-depth analysis of the productivity and performance of workers, which could aid in the public sector's seamless adoption of remote working or hybrid work. That gap could have caused some inconsistencies in properly defining the new way of working which has had an impact on how employees perform their duties.

Unique Organizational Limitations and Challenges

As digital transformation has intensified for organizations, remote working necessitates some level of skill and knowledge, and many workers around the world must have the necessary skills to use technologies to perform their jobs remotely (Gigauri, 2020). Given that virtual working was rarely used, all work was done in the office, even most of the financial systems in place in the public sector, particularly used by organization XXX such as the Personal and Salary Administration System (PERSAL), Basic Accounting System (BAS), Financial Management System (FMS), and Logistical Information System (LOGIS) (CHAPTERR44-FINANCIALLMANAGEMENTTISSUES 83 4.4 Financial Systems, n.d.)

The various systems are administered as an independent stand-alone "silo" rather than as a single integrated systems unit. These public sector legacy systems were developed as in-house proprietary solutions over a long period, nearly in an evolutionary approach. These systems can only be accessed from a protected domain within the office and cannot be run remotely. As a result, employees who use these systems as part of their daily tasks may not enjoy, if any, the benefits of remote working.

The pandemic has highlighted the fact that the most in-demand talents for employees are to be skilled in both digital and collaborative work/virtual teams (Gigauri, 2020). Previous reports predicted that the trends toward the outline workforce and platform would increase, presenting reskilling needs from employers and workers (Gigauri, 2020). Organizations should have prepared for this disruption as per their Disaster Recovery Plan (DRP) by introducing and adopting platform-based technologies and developing Business Continuity Plan (BCP) models accordingly.

Previous research revealed that developing technologies such as digital platforms, artificial intelligence, robotics, augmented reality, and blockchain would impact the roles of HR professionals (Parry & Battista, 2019). Employees should gain new skills to boost their productivity and performance to adapt to digital employment (Gigauri, 2020). The findings of the study (Parry & Battista, 2019) indicated that human resource management should assist employees in using modern technologies in the workplace and correctly consider change management for the adoption of these technologies.

Since there are inconsistencies with in-house systems, remote working, and the need for new skills for remote working, as a result, organizations have put in place a suitable structure, such as weekly or monthly rotational work plans, to enable them to conduct business functions both in-house and remotely while maintaining productivity (Mas & Pallais, 2017). Therefore, the swift implementation of remote work has significantly influenced employees' everyday lives and communication with co-workers and family. This has caused various types of depression (Kniffin et al., 2021). In addition, research carried out during the pandemic uncovered various challenges that impacted employee performance and, consequently, productivity.

Key Elements to Hybrid Work: Work from Home, Virtual Teams, and Work–Life Balance

These three components may influence employee performance, namely, work from home (WFH), virtual teamwork (VT), and work–life balance (WLB). The objective is to investigate how the hybrid working model affects employee performance through the recent changes of either working at the office or working from home as this has become the new way of work.

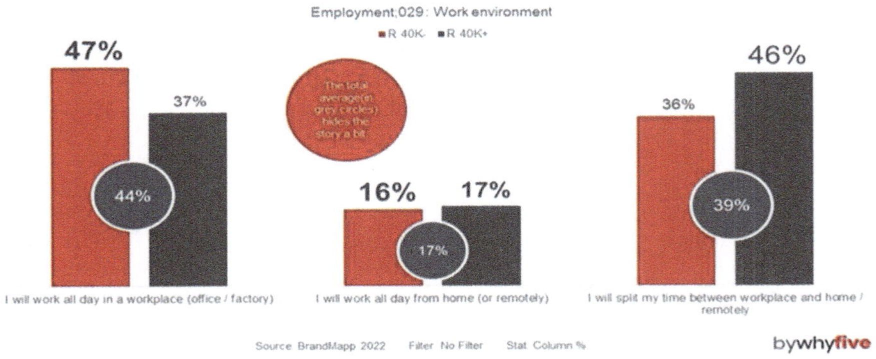

Fig. 1 The response from employees in different categories. Source BrandMapp (2022)

Working From Home (Fig. 1)

The COVID-19 pandemic, according to News24, accelerated remote work trends, transforming work locations and methods. Pre-existing shifts toward remote work, especially in digital sectors, were further propelled by the pandemic's impact. This tendency is not entirely new, as the advancement of networking and communication technologies has long enabled remote work possibilities. Although remote work covers "work from anyplace," studies have shown that certain professions that require less interaction with peers are more productive when they work from home (Allen et al., 2014).

However, the blurring of boundaries between work and personal life, especially in shared living spaces, has been a source of stress and strain for many (Kniffin et al., 2021). In conclusion, this study seeks to provide a comprehensive understanding of the impact of the hybrid working model on employee performance. By examining the theoretical landscape, we explore other factors such as incentives, job satisfaction, and motivation.

Virtual Teamwork

To prevent assuming homogeneity in virtual team traits, it is crucial to acknowledge that the "virtuality of a team" is a complex notion that encompasses factors such as the dispersion of team members and the extent of synchronous and asynchronous electronic communication. Recent studies have resulted in a more nuanced comprehension of virtuality, which is now regarded as a continuous spectrum rather than a simple binary concept (Battisti et al., 2022).

Virtual teams, defined as groups with shared goals that use technology to collaborate across time zones, distances, and organizational boundaries, have become a prevalent approach to structuring flexible and cost-effective operations in modern organizations (Lipnack & Lipnack, 1990). The rise of information and communications technologies (ICTs) has enabled employees to collaborate online with colleagues from their organizations or even different geographic areas. Virtual teamwork involves interactions across major time zones. Some team members may never meet in person but can still form effective teams (Orlikowski, 2002). However, the concept of "virtual" varies across different institutional contexts, making it challenging to define uniformly.

Work–Life Balance

There is research that was conducted at Microsoft, which was based on workplace analytics; the results revealed that workdays were extended as employees working from home signed into work earlier and signed off later while also scheduling time for personal matters (Singer-Velush et al., 2020). This practice is in contravention of the Basic Conditions of Employment Act, 1997, which states, "Schedule 1 establishes procedures for the progressive reduction of the maximum ordinary hours of work to a maximum of 40 ordinary hours of work per week and eight ordinary hours of work per day." Additionally, Regulation 51, which addresses working hours, emphasizes the consideration of employees' needs and circumstances, such as family obligations and transportation arrangements, alongside public service requirements and the department's services delivery improvement plan. Furthermore, it is difficult to manage working hours at home which may harm interactions with family members (Elshaiekh et al., 2019).

The concept of "work–life balance" pertains to how employees perceive their ability to fulfill obligations in the workplace and their personal lives (Linnhoff et al., 2014). This concept extends beyond family life to include various areas of a person's private life. According to boundary theory, even though work and life appear to be separate realms, employees deliberately breach these boundaries, potentially leading to conflicts between their jobs and personal lives. The hybrid working model, as well as improvements in information and communication technology (ICT), has made the line between work and life less rigid by allowing for greater temporal and spatial flexibility in work tasks (Kniffin et al., 2021).

According to Feldman and Gainey (1997), employees opt to telework to achieve a better work–life balance and spend more quality time with their families. As a result, there is a growing demand for teleworking among employees, prompting them to seek job opportunities with organizations that provide teleworking alternatives. To further support that (Patanjali and Bhatta (2022) recently demonstrated that working from home improves the work environment and WLB, thereby improving employee performance.

To summarize, despite increasing awareness of the potential detrimental impact of remote working this area of research is still in its early stages, especially in the public sector (Grant et al., 2013). Having established the possible positive and negative impact of remote working in its stages, let us now look into the empirical framework surrounding the impact of hybrid working models on performance, particularly in the public sector.

The Empirical Framework

In the empirical literature, there is a need for further exploration due to the limited availability of research in the area especially for the public sector. Despite the increasing prevalence of hybrid working models of organizations adopting this flexible work arrangement, especially in the wake of the COVID-19 pandemic (Kokt & Chipunza, 2023), the available research primarily focuses on larger scale organizations and international context and the private sector, the banking industry to be specific, where data accessibility is relatively higher through an online database. Empirical studies examining their effect on employee performance remain scarce.

Existing literature presents mixed insights on the hybrid work model's impact on employee performance. Challenges include resource inadequacy and work–life balance issues, yet some studies suggest remote work enhances performance through improved work–life balance (Kokt & Chipunza, 2023).

By adopting a theoretical lens that encompasses concepts such as work–life balance, job satisfaction, and motivation, the research aims to explore the intricate relationship between these factors and employee performance within the hybrid work context. Through this comprehensive approach, the study aims to contribute to a deeper understanding of the mechanisms through which the hybrid working model influences employee performance.

Key Dominant Theories

The literature suggests that the significance of three dominant theories, namely, self-determination theory (SDT), job demands resources (JD-R) theory, and psychology theory, in understanding employee performance. These theories help to cover the following dimensions: Van Den Broeck et al. (2008) unpack them. Theory one helps to cover this dimension: autonomy, competence, relatedness, target significance, and work–life integration.

Autonomy: this variable helps to the degree of independence, choice, and control that individuals have over their work in the hybrid working model; employees have more autonomy in deciding when and where to work which can impact their motivation and job satisfaction.

Competence: competence relates to the individual sense of capability and effectiveness in performing their work tasks.

Relatedness: this variable refers to the quality of social connections and interactions with others in the workplace. In a hybrid working model, employees may experience changes in their social relationships.

Task significance: refers to the perceived impact or importance of one's work. In a hybrid working model, employees may need to re-evaluate and adjust their understanding of the significance of their work considering the changing dynamics in expectations within a hybrid work environment. Another variable was work–life integration which relates to the extent to which work and personal life domains are integrated harmoniously.

Theory two helps to cover this dimension: job demands, job resources, and work engagement.

Job demands: refer to the physical, psychological, social, or organizational aspects of work that require sustained efforts and can potentially lead to stress or strain. In a hybrid work model, job demands can include factors such as increased workload, blurred boundaries between work and personal life, or challenges in maintaining and managing virtual communication and collaboration (Gordon et al., 2015).

Job resources: these are the physical, psychological, social, or organizational aspects of work that help individuals achieve work goals, reduce job demands, and stimulate growth and development. In a hybrid working model, job resources can include access to necessary technology, supportive leadership, opportunities for skill and development, or a flexible work schedule that promotes work–life balance (Gordon et al., 2015).

Work engagement: refers to the positive, fulfilling, and energized state of mind characterized by dedication, vigor, and absorption in one's work tasks. In a hybrid working model, work engagement can be influenced by the availability of job resources, such as autonomy, social support, and growth opportunities, as well as the management of job demands to maintain a healthy work environment.

And theory three helps to cover this dimension: expectancy theory and procedural justice.

Expectancy theory: this dimension of organizational justice refers to the furnace in the distribution of outcomes rewards and resources in the context of the hybrid working model; it relates to employees' perception of receiving fair incentives or rewards in return for their efforts. When employees feel they are treated fairly in terms of rewards and outcomes, they are more likely to be committed to their work and perform better (Moilanen & Ikäheimo, 2019).

Procedural justice: refers to the fairness of the process and procedures used in decision-making. In a hybrid working model, this dimension relates to the fairness of policies, rules, and practices associated with performance evaluations, promotions, and other organizational procedures. When employees perceive that these processes are fair and transparent, it can enhance their commitment and performance (Moilanen & Ikäheimo, 2019).

However, it is recognized that no single theory can comprehensively explain the complexity of the context. Therefore, the researcher aims to employ a unified framework that incorporates these key theories and supplementary variables, including the hybrid working model, to better understand the factors influencing employee performance.

To present this unified framework, Fig. 2 is proposed as the conceptual framework for employee performance. This framework asserts that the key dominant

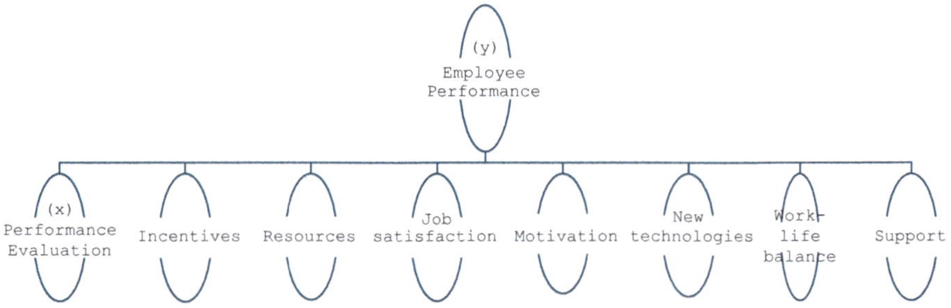

Fig. 2 Conceptual framework for employee performance. Source: Authors' compilation

theories, along with the hybrid working model, directly impact employee performance. By extending the key dominant theories, it is argued that these variables serve as critical links to the performance pathway.

Building upon this foundation, the next phase of this research involves the application of a qualitative methodology to delve deeper into employees' perspectives and actions within the hybrid work context. The following section will outline the research methodology and collection techniques employed to capture the rich experiences and insight of employees, enabling a comprehensive understanding of the factors influencing performance in this evolving work landscape.

Methodology

Research Paradigm

In this study, we employed the interpretive paradigms to comprehend the subjective experiences and perceptions of employees in the context of hybrid work. This qualitative approach utilizes document analysis, interviews, and focus groups to delve into employees' interpretations, experiences, and emotions related to hybrid work, aiming to uncover their meaning and impact on performance (Alhazmi & Kaufmann, 2022).

Research Design

We adopt a qualitative research approach to explore the perceived and observed impact of the COVID-19 pandemic on employees working in hybrid and traditional settings. Our focus spans digitalization, technology adoption, and work–life balance. This research involves open-ended interviews, expert insights as a focus group, and primary data from human resource management.

The data collection occurs in three phases, i.e., historical data on employee performance, pre-, during, and post-COVID-19 from HR records, then interviews with performance managers through focus groups, senior managers in HR, and lastly, interviews with key informants, gauging their perception of hybrid models' impact on employee performance (Chiang et al., 2015).

Strategy

The objective of the study is to explore how the hybrid working model affects employee performance by utilizing performance reviews to evaluate the direct relationship between key variables such as employee performance. The key variables include self-determination theory, job demands resources (JD-R) model, and psychology theory.

Population

The population for this research project consists of one (1) employee from HR, thirteen (13) line managers, and sixteen (16) employees from various business units within the public sector department XXX, specifically employees who have experienced the hybrid working model and the traditional way of working pre-COVID (see Fig. 3, Graph).

In this research, interviews with managers as a key focus group have been selected. Two focus groups with four (4) and another with six (6) managers from different directorates or business units were selected; there were three other managers interviewed separately as they couldn't make it to the groups; this decision was motivated by several reasons that highlight the importance and benefits of including managers in the research process; i.e., minimizing self-reporting biases, managers provide a less biased, objective viewpoint, as they evaluate employee performance across various roles, another factor being the solid and objective performance assessment, meaning managers possess comprehensive data on performance metrics, KPIs, and goal achievements (Bouwens & Van Lent, 2007); lately, managers

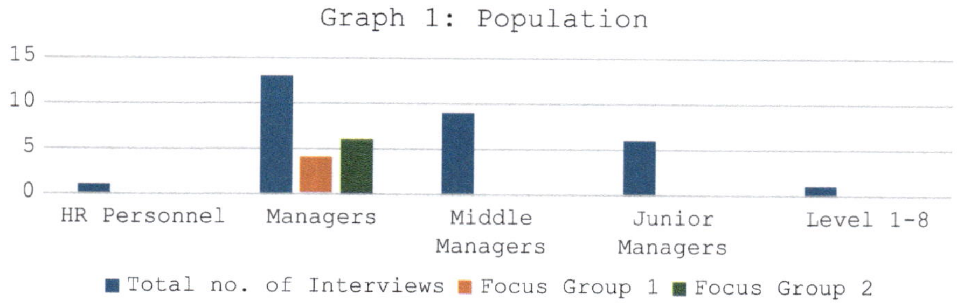

Fig. 3 Population interviewed. Source: Authors' compilation

offer insights into the practical aspects of implementing and maintaining an effective hybrid work environment (Gerrish, 2016).

The study focuses on the South African public sector in Gauteng. A case study approach analyzes the organization XXX, chosen for its unique access to relevant data.

Sample Size

As suggested by Suri (2011), the logic in the power of purposeful sampling lies in selecting information-rich cases for in-depth investigation. A purposive sampling method is utilized to select participants for the study. In this case, employees who have first-hand experience with the hybrid work model will be targeted.

The sample size for this study is determined based on the principle of data saturation, which means that data collection will continue until no new insights or information emerges from the interviews or focus groups (Hennink & Kaiser, 2022).

Data Collection

The analysis of qualitative data is a method that employs inductive reasoning to make sense of and organize the significance extracted from data. This process aims to comprehend and interpret the perspective of the participants as expressed through their spoken or written expressions; furthermore, Thorne (2000) makes a distinction between qualitative and quantitative data analysis in research, with the former focused on explaining how something operates (explanation), while the latter, which this research will employ, emphasizes understanding why it operates in a particular way (interpretation).

In a qualitative study, data analysis is closely intertwined with data collection (Thorne, 2000), while Creswell (2013) underscores that data interpretation is influenced by the researcher's perspective, which may introduce bias. The data collection process involved conducting interviews with various stakeholders within the organizations. All interviews were conducted remotely using Microsoft Teams. These virtual meetings typically ranged in duration from 25 to 60 min.

Primary data from HR were provided through a random selection of employee files that were selected on behalf of the research; the files were provided electronically wherein they were assessed manually (see Fig. 4, Graph).

Thematic analysis and interpretive description are techniques that rely on ongoing comparative analysis to undercover insights into human experiences within their specific context. These methods entail reviewing and organizing data fragments to identify and interpret themes, identifying inconsistencies, and drawing conclusions about the "what" and "why" of the phenomena under study (Thorne, 2000).

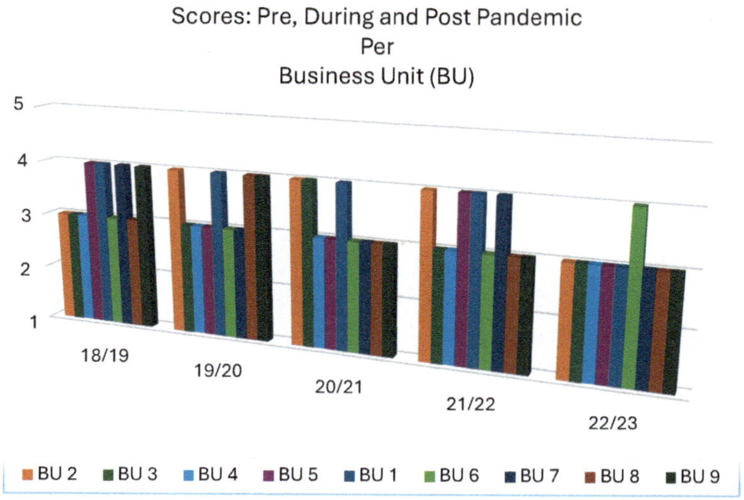

Fig. 4 Scores per business unit. Source: Authors' compilation

The information collected was analyzed using thematic analysis, and the coding and grouping were done manually to identify the emerging common themes. The resulting themes and concerns that arose from this analysis were then contextualized.

Results and Discussions

This chapter explores the analysis of data collected from qualitative research methods like interviews, focus groups, and document analysis, aiming to understand the impact of the hybrid work model on employee performance. It seeks to bridge the gap between existing literature and research findings, addressing discrepancies and exploring various factors influencing productivity, motivation, job satisfaction, and work–life balance.

After in-depth studies of how performance has been impacted by the new way of working, considering the interviews and employee files that consisted of employee contracts and performance appraisals, several concerns emerged as setbacks of the hybrid work model enabling performance optimization. Using a thematic analysis and by manually coding several key indicators and themes emerged, the following ones presented more concerns and opportunities:

All these key indicators and themes include all the opportunities and challenges that directly affect the performance of employees across all levels. The themes that are based on similar key indicators will form a cluster and be narrowed down the following way: *(a) communication, (b) resources, systems, support, and impact on remote work, (c) work–life balance, (d) performance enablers and traditional work, (e) employee performance.*

In the hybrid work model, effective communication, resource availability, VPN access, and management support are crucial for optimal performance. Harmonizing these elements fosters productivity, collaboration, and job satisfaction. Addressing challenges in these areas is essential for a successful hybrid work environment.

Level of Communication

Performance is intricately tied to the realization of goals, but achieving these goals relies heavily on the effectiveness of communication strategies and channels that permeate all organizational tiers. In the context of the hybrid work model, a temporary lapse in communication became evident for a brief period. This transient communication breakdown had the potential to exert a profound influence, both directly and indirectly, on the overall performance of the organization.

During the interview process, most junior managers felt that there was an insufficient level of effective communication which was expressed to be a hindrance to optimally executing duties, as this involves the exchange of information, updates, and instructions between employees, teams, and management. This part created a sense of division as information dissemination was unstructured and one business unit would seem to be more informed than the other.

> I believe that what our department is currently lacking is effective communication, particularly when it comes to timelines. This issue, in my opinion, is a significant challenge within our department. Sometimes, our department experiences communication gaps, especially concerning updates. For instance, if there's a plan for employees to return to the office next week, they should inform us on a specific working day, rather than on WhatsApp over the weekends when some of us are offline. This inconsistency in communication is something that could be improved. In essence, what stands out as a key concern for us is the quality of communication. And, well, that's the primary issue that comes to my mind at the moment.

Successful performance is rooted in the clear and seamless communication of objectives, expectations, and feedback throughout the entire organization. A well-structured communication strategy serves as the connective tissue that binds individuals and teams together, ensuring everyone is aligned with the overarching goals. In the focus group, most of the managers were concerned about teams' collaborations, the gaps in teams' dynamics, and employees now working more in silos and communicating less (Fig. 5).

To ensure that efficient communication strategies are not just established but also sustained, it is imperative to explore the following themes which are resources, systems, and support. These elements are tightly interwoven with communication and facilitate a seamless flow of information and collaboration within an organization.

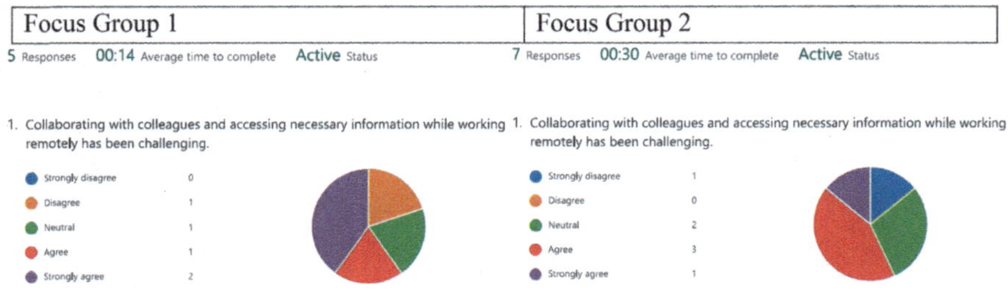

Fig. 5 Group interviews. Source: Forms.office.com

Resources, Systems, and Support

Access to resources, systems, and management support significantly influences remote work performance. Challenges such as VPN restrictions and issues with employee accessibility during remote workdays are noted. Providing adequate tools and resources for remote work is essential to maintain productivity and ensure employee well-being.

> A senior manager emphasized that there is a need for a significant shift in HR practices, "I think more than anything, there a lot of change management that has to take place where we're moving from managing people to managing the outputs and outcomes." She points out that this transition would require a mature system and the development of skills in employee self-awareness and self-management. The aim is for employees to understand their responsibilities and tasks without constant supervision.

Respondents also expressed concerns regarding the consistency of managerial support during the initial implementation of the hybrid work model. There were variations in the level of training provided, while others received awareness sessions or, in certain instances, no support at all. This diversity of experiences highlights the need for a more uniform approach in managing the transition to the hybrid work model.

> We did not receive any training, we adapted as we go, learned Microsoft Teams independently, training issue has been a problem ever since I joined this organization, if there was, I might have missed it due to lack of communication.

Work–Life Balance

In the theoretical literature, work–life balance is often considered a significant factor influencing performance; according to the boundary theory, employees intentionally cross the boundaries between work and personal life, which can create conflicts. This concept, as discussed by Linnhoff et al. (2014), relates to how employees assess their capacity to meet both work and personal obligations, extending beyond family to encompass various aspects of their private lives.

This is crucial for performance, with employees often straddling work and personal boundaries, leading to conflicts. Pre-COVID, 90% rated their balance as good, despite the challenges. Post-pandemic, 99% rated it exceptional, citing reduced commutes and flexible scheduling, enhancing well-being and family relationships.

> Now, as far as balancing with the family, it is exceptional because I'm always at home. There's always a time to engage in whatever matters that I need to engage with, but ensure that by the end of the day, I still deliver, work is not affected but prioritized. So, it was better, but in terms of performance, it did not affect performance. My family got less time from me when I was traveling, even now, they are so happy because I am the present parent. I love being a present parent. It's something that makes you much happier. No need to stress, no need to worry about anything, everything is pashasha.

On the contrary, there are a few individuals who are yearning to return to the conventional work setup. For them, work has infiltrated every aspect of their lives, demanding their attention around the clock. They struggle to establish clear boundaries between work and personal life and find it challenging to disconnect from work, unlike the pre-COVID era. As a consequence, they are grappling with a sense of burnout and perpetual fatigue.

> When I was performing most of my duties, especially those involving strategic planning and interactions with people, it was notably more convenient within the office environment. Now, when working remotely, establishing contact with individuals has become somewhat challenging. This difficulty, in turn, hampers my ability to gather the information I require from people. Moreover, I've noticed a decline in email responsiveness in the past, while in the office, sending an email would be followed by a quick visit to a colleague's office for a direct conversation. This immediate access made communication more efficient.

While employees themselves have expressed how the hybrid work model has positively impacted their work–life balance to a certain degree, managers have provided an overall rating of 3.58 in terms of how they view it (Fig. 6).

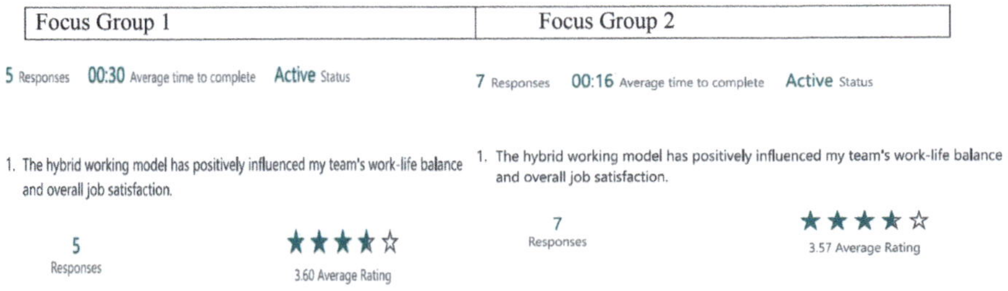

Fig. 6 Group interviews. Source: Forms.office.com

Remote Work and Performance Enablers

The self-determination theory (SDT) from the empirical literature as one of the theories directly relates to the impact of remote work and performance enablers. This theory examines the dynamic relationships between motivation, autonomy, competence, and relatedness in the workplace. It suggests that employees who have a sense of autonomy, competence, and relatedness in their work are more likely to be motivated and engaged, ultimately leading to improved performance (Gagné & Deci, 2005).

Employees noted that remote work flexibility positivity affects motivation and performance by allowing personalized scheduling, fostering autonomy, and competence. However, challenges like load shedding and unstable networks require adaptation and discipline.

> One manager touched on the critical issues of organizational culture in the context of remote work "The cultural aspects of exercising good working ethics, and discipline can start to erode when employees are not physically present in the office. The shared values and behaviors that define a team can become less apparent when team members are dispersed and not within a common environment, affecting the overall culture of the organization."
>
> To counter these challenges, the manager suggested providing employees with the necessary tools for remote work, such as access to a Virtual Private Network (VPN) and crucial connectivity. Additionally, ensuring that all employees have access to a laptop, regardless of their rank, is essential in the hybrid work environment.

The self-determination theory as previously defined emphasizes the significance of personal discipline, the positive impact of flexibility, the challenges posed by factors like load shedding, effective communication, managing distractions, commitment to work, and the growing desire for surveys to evaluate remote work's impact on performance.

Employee Performance

Employee performance as the Y variable relates to the actual study and encompasses all the theories discussed in the empirical literature, i.e., self-determination theory (SDT), job demand resources (JD-R), and psychology theory, wherein this theory suggests that employees who feel they are treated fairly by their employer and receive incentives or rewards in return for their efforts will be more committed to their work and perform better, among others (Moilanen & Ikäheimo, 2019), while the last theory was rarely touched on.

Remarkably, the employees themselves generally do not perceive the hybrid work model as having a negative impact on their performance, even with issues such as access to tools of trade, availability of necessary systems, and the disruptions caused by load shedding, among others.

However, the perspective of management differs; evidence of this narrative was then observed. Stemming from a detailed examination of employee files, the analysis involved the scrutiny of nine employees' records from various business units (see Fig. 4, Graph), which encompasses five (5) financial years that include pre-pandemic, during-pandemic, and post-pandemic periods. Notably, there emerged a consistent pattern of an overall performance score of 3 for all business units in the post-pandemic phase except one (1) business unit.

This pattern could be attributed, in part, to a governmental decision by the previous minister of finance, to phase out performance bonuses for civil servants during the 2021 financial year-end. Hence, it becomes challenging to definitively attribute the rating drop solely to the hybrid work model, particularly when considering that four (4) out of nine (9) business units used to achieve a score of 4 before the bonus phase-out. This situation somewhat aligns with the psychological theories that highlight how employee motivation can wane in the absence of rewards or incentives.

Nevertheless, this analysis is unable to conclusively establish whether a score of 3 indicates a negative impact on performance. To draw such a conclusion, a lower score would have been required, which could have necessitated intervention and enabled a more precise identification of the causes of reduced performance. Only through such an intervention could a definitive link between performance and hybrid work model be established, shedding light on its impact.

Traditional Work

In the theoretical landscape, the theme of traditional work brings several pertinent codes to the forefront, including culture, loss of in-person engagement, and the importance of face-to-face interaction.

Employees generally do acknowledge the importance of traditional work, as it fosters aspects of organizational culture that typically thrive within the physical office environment. Where shared values, norms, and standards shape the workplace atmosphere, these elements often contribute to a sense of identity and unity among employees.

> When working from home, it's nice to be in your zone and doing your work, but you miss that interaction with officials. Having the opportunity for unlimited sharing of information and ideas, which is essential for work, takes time. You have to call someone, and sometimes you feel like you're distracting them. But in the office, these interactions happen spontaneously without being planned. Someone can just walk into your office and share information, facilitating interaction with other units as well. We share our work, and it's all interconnected.
>
> What I miss the most is the face-to-face meetings. Virtual meetings can be challenging, as not everyone attentively listening, and there's less interaction.
>
> Another drawback is the people in virtual meetings may be doing other things, which affects the quality of engagement. So, remote work has its disadvantages in terms of having fruitful engagement.

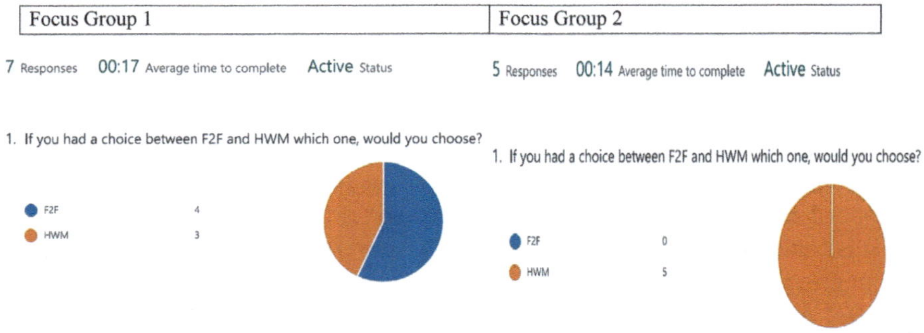

Fig. 7 Group interviews. Source: Forms.office.com

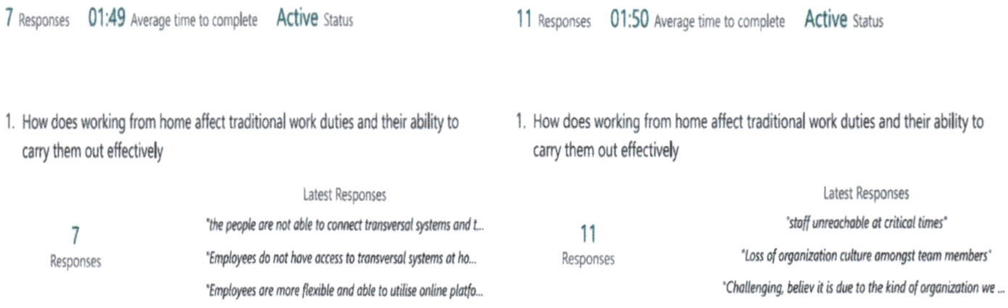

Fig. 8 Individual interviews. Source: Forms.office.com

During the focus group, managers were asked what their current working arrangements are, and all responded rotational/hybrid work model; however when they were asked in the form of a poll, if they prefer that model of face-to-face or the traditional way of working, surprisingly few managers prefer the old way of working. 33.3% of the interviewed managers prefer the old way of working (Fig. 7).

The main reason that was gathered during the focus group was that some employees who report to them are unable to work while at home due to a lack of sufficient resources and most of their duties being system based (Fig. 8).

While it is noteworthy that a minority of managers express reservations about the hybrid work model, their concerns hold validity due to its potential impact on performance and productivity, particularly affecting agility and speed in service delivery.

Nevertheless, most managers acknowledge that the hybrid or rotational work model has had an impact on performance. However, they express a desire for its formal adoption, provided that adequate tools and resources are available for all employees. It is essential to note that a common consensus among all managers is that the hybrid work model may not be suitable for every individual in the current context.

Conclusion and Recommendations

This case study analyzed the impact of the hybrid working model on employee performance in the public sector. We applied dominant theories like self-determination, job demand resources, and psychology theory, along with interviews and using thematic analysis, to gain valuable insights for organizations adapting to the hybrid work environment.

We found that, in the context of the hybrid work model, effective communication emerged as a critical factor for organizational performance. Issues in communication temporarily hindered operations, with many junior managers expressing the need for more open and frequent channels to foster trust and collaboration.

Additionally, access to essential resources, including dealing with challenges like Virtual Private Network systems, played a significant role in maintaining productivity. Work–life balance was positively affected by the hybrid model for many, but some faced difficulties in setting boundaries and suffered burnout.

Employee perspectives on performance positively impacting performance varied slightly from management perspective, potentially due to the performance appraisal score largely remaining on the score of 3 (satisfactory), possibly influenced by incentive changes, although a conclusive link between the two remains uncertain. Furthermore, traditional office settings were valued for their role in fostering organizational culture and enabling in-person engagement.

The dynamic nature of the never-ending evolving world within the fourth industrial revolution, change cannot be ignored, evolution will always take place whether now or later, organization XXX should make room for such, one of the major findings was that remote work may not be suitable for every category of staff and clear administration measures are required to address it.

Conclusively, effective performance management, tailored to each business unit's needs, is vital for efficient public service and service delivery in remote work arrangements. Collaboration with DPSA, NT, and the Department of Communications and Digital Technologies (DCDT) is needed to drive digitization. Ensuring access to essential tools is pivotal for the successful implementation of hybrid work.

Recommendations

Organization XXX should collaborate and benchmark with other stakeholders in the public sector to assess the management of the hybrid work arrangement post-pandemic. These collaborations serve as a foundation for reviewing relevant legislation, regulations, policies, and conditions of service for various categories of occupations and employees. Engaging with the Department of Public Service and Administration (DPSA) is vital in this endeavor.

Organization XXX should strive to balance responsiveness and productivity with work-life balance and employee health and wellness. The head of the department retains legal responsibility for determining workplace requirements and ensuring the full array of public services. Hybrid work arrangements offer benefits such as decongesting workplaces, reducing costs, and increasing meeting departmental needs, However, it is important to note that remote work is not universally applicable, requiring clear organizational policies to define responsibilities, expectations, and availability of resources.

Employees should maintain public service standards and adhere to its rules while working remotely organization XXX should conduct a thorough cost-benefit analysis for implementing hybrid work arrangements in non-service-related functions to identify cost-saving opportunities and recurring expenses. Expanding e-services necessitates reskilling and investing in new skills while optimizing training budgets. Prioritizing HR's role in talent development and culture growth is crucial. Enhanced data utilization, including AI and big data, will improve decision-making organization XXX and the National School of Government (NSG) should implement ongoing training to keep employees informed about hybrid work developments.

The shift to remote work demands changes in organizational culture, systems, and procedures to facilitate goal achievement. Clear guidelines for virtual meetings, communication methods, and turnaround times are essential. Managers and employees should establish formal work schedules for business continuity, ensuring accessibility and service delivery. It is crucial to recognize that remote work does not always mean working from home, employees may operate from different service delivery locations or district offices.

Addressing aspects like working time, tools of trade, office space, and labor matters such as injury on duty while working remotely is crucial, taking a holistic approach to Human Resource Management and Development (HRM&D) while recognizing the HR Value Chain is essential. This will help maximize benefits, by customizing administrative processes, including an internal remote work policy as a legal control measure. Embracing a forward-learning approach aligns with the evolving gig economy and Ama 2000 who are more into flexibility at work.

Limitations of the Study

There are a lot of factors that could positively or negatively affect the adoption of the hybrid working model, some of those factors being, consequence management, this study did look into that area but merely focused on the current status quo. Other factors that have been indicated in the study such as financial systems, corporative technologies in terms of equipping employees in the hybrid paradigm, and financial implications or burdens incurred by employees or employer could add further nuances to the discourse. Hence future research could explore these additional nuances and extend the work beyond a single case study.

References

Alhazmi, A. A., & Kaufmann, A. (2022). Phenomenological qualitative methods applied to the analysis of cross-cultural experience in novel educational social contexts. *Frontiers in Psychology, 13*. https://doi.org/10.3389/fpsyg.2022.785134

Allen, T. D., Cho, E., & Meier, L. L. (2014). WorkFamily boundary dynamics. In *Annual review of organizational psychology and organizational behavior* (Vol. 1, pp. 99–121). Annual reviews Inc. https://doi.org/10.1146/annurev-orgpsych-031413-091330

Battisti, E., Alfiero, S., & Leonidou, E. (2022). Remote working and digital transformation during the COVID-19 pandemic: Economic–financial impacts and psychological drivers for employees. *Journal of Business Research, 150*, 38–50. https://doi.org/10.1016/j.jbusres.2022.06.010

Bouwens, J., & Van Lent, L. (2007). Assessing the performance of business unit managers. *Journal of Accounting Research, 45*(4), 667–697. https://doi.org/10.1111/j.1475-679X.2007.00251.x

CHAPTERR44-FINANCIALLMANAGEMENTTISSUES *83 4.4 Financial Systems*. (n.d.).

Chellam, N., & Divya, D. (2022). A causal study on hybrid model and its impact on employee job performance. *Journal of Pharmaceutical Negative Results, 13*, 866. https://doi.org/10.47750/pnr.2022.13.S09.104

Chiang, I.-C. A., Jhangiani, R. S., & Price, P. C. (2015). Research methods in psychology (2nd Canadian ed.). In *Psychology*.

Elshaiekh, N. E. M., Hassan, Y. A. A., & Abdallah, A. A. A. (2019). The impacts of remote working on workers performance. *ACIT 2018 - 19th international Arab conference on information technology*. https://doi.org/10.1109/ACIT.2018.8672704

Feldman, D. C., & Gainey, T. W. (1997). *PAmERNS of telecommuting and their consequences: Framing the research agenda*.

Gagné, M., & Deci, E. L. (2005). Self-determination theory and work motivation. *Journal of Organizational Behavior, 26*(4), 331–362. https://doi.org/10.1002/job.322

Gerrish, E. (2016). The impact of performance management on performance in public organizations: A meta-analysis. *Public Administration Review, 76*(1), 48–66. https://doi.org/10.1111/puar.12433

Gigauri, I. (2020). Effects of COVID-19 on human resource management from the perspective of digitalization and work-LIFE-balance. *International Journal of Innovative Technologies in Economy, 4*(31). https://doi.org/10.31435/rsglobal_ijite/30092020/7148

Gordon, H. J., Demerouti, E., Bipp, T., & Le Blanc, P. M. (2015). The job demands and resources decision making (JD-R-DM) model. *European Journal of Work and Organizational Psychology, 24*(1), 44–58. https://doi.org/10.1080/1359432X.2013.842901

Grant, C. A., Wallace, L. M., & Spurgeon, P. C. (2013). An exploration of the psychological factors affecting remote e-worker's job effectiveness, well-being and work-life balance. *Employee Relations, 35*(5), 527–546. https://doi.org/10.1108/ER-08-2012-0059

Hale, T., Angrist, N., Kira, B., Petherick, A., Phillips, T., & Webster, S. (2020). *Variation in government responses to COVID-19*. www.bsg.ox.ac.uk/covidtracker

Hennink, M., & Kaiser, B. N. (2022). Sample sizes for saturation in qualitative research: A systematic review of empirical tests. *Social Science and Medicine, 292*, 114523. https://doi.org/10.1016/j.socscimed.2021.114523

Lipnack, J., & Lipnack, J. (1990). *Virtual teams: The new way to work*.

Creswell, J. W. (2013). *Research design_ qualitative, quantitative, and mixed methods approaches*. Sage.

Kniffin, K. M., Narayanan, J., Anseel, F., Antonakis, J., Ashford, S. P., Bakker, A. B., Bamberger, P., Bapuji, H., Bhave, D. P., Choi, V. K., Creary, S. J., Demerouti, E., Flynn, F. J., Gelfand, M. J., Greer, L. L., Johns, G., Kesebir, S., Klein, P. G., Lee, S. Y., van Vugt, M., et al. (2021). COVID-19 and the workplace: Implications, issues, and insights for future research and action. *American Psychologist, 76*(1), 63–77. https://doi.org/10.1037/amp0000716

Kokt, D., & Chipunza, C. (2023). *Remote and hybrid working during crisis: Challenges and implications for employee development in Africa*. https://doi.org/10.5772/intechopen.107023

Lazarus, J. V., Ratzan, S., Palayew, A., Billari, F. C., Binagwaho, A., Kimball, S., Larson, H. J., Melegaro, A., Rabin, K., White, T. M., & El-Mohandes, A. (2020). COVID-SCORE: A global survey to assess public perceptions of government responses to COVID-19 (COVID-SCORE-10). *PLoS One, 15*(10 October). https://doi.org/10.1371/journal.pone.0240011

Linnhoff, S., Smith, K. T., & Smith, L. M. (2014). A comparison of work-life balance perspectives of future business professionals in the USA and Germany. *International Journal of Business and Globalisation, 13*(3), 322–353. https://doi.org/10.1504/IJBG.2014.064679

Mas, A., & Pallais, A. (2017). Valuing alternative work arrangements. *American Economic Review, 107*(12), 3722–3759. https://doi.org/10.1257/aer.20161500

Moilanen, S., & Ikäheimo, S. (2019). Managerial intentions for and employee perceptions of group-based incentives: Social exchange theory-based interpretations. *Journal of Accounting and Organizational Change, 15*(4), 605–625. https://doi.org/10.1108/JAOC-04-2019-0043

Orlikowski, W. J. (2002). Knowing in practice: Enacting a collective capability in distributed organizing. Institute for Operations Research and the Management Sciences.

Parry, E., & Battista, V. (2019). The impact of emerging technologies on work: A review of the evidence and implications for the human resource function. *Emerald Open Research, 1*, 5. https://doi.org/10.12688/emeraldopenres.12907.1

Patanjali, S., & Bhatta, N. M. K. (2022). Work from home during the pandemic: The impact of organizational factors on the productivity of employees in the IT industry. *Vision*. https://doi.org/10.1177/09722629221074137

Singer-Velush, N., Sherman, K., & Anderson, E. (2020). Microsoft analyzed data on its newly remote workforce. *Harvard Business Review*.

Suri, H. (2011). Purposeful sampling in qualitative research synthesis. *Qualitative Research Journal, 11*(2), 63–75. https://doi.org/10.3316/QRJ1102063

Thorne, S. (2000). Data analysis in qualitative research. In *Evidence-based nursing* (Vol. 3, issue 3, pp. 68–70). https://doi.org/10.1136/ebn.3.3.68

Van Den Broeck, A., Vansteenkiste, M., De Witte, H., & Lens, W. (2008). Explaining the relationships between job characteristics, burnout, and engagement: The role of basic psychological need satisfaction. *Work and Stress, 22*(3), 277–294. https://doi.org/10.1080/02678370802393672

Revitalizing Retail: Innovative Strategies for Boosting Employee Morale in the Age of Digital Technology

Baphile Duba and Nyankomo Marwa

Abstract The objective of this chapter is to explore innovative strategies for boosting employee morale in the age of technology in the retail sector. The research highlights key challenges faced by retailers in retaining and motivating employees in the face of technological advancements and ever-changing consumer behaviour. It articulates how technology contributes to low or high employee morale. Herzberg's two-factor theory is a relevant tool for the study as it provides a framework for understanding the factors that influence employee motivation and job satisfaction in the retail industry. A mixed-methods approach involving both qualitative and quantitative research techniques is used. A purposive sampling technique is used to select participants. The data are analysed using descriptive statistics and frequency analysis. The quantitative data gathered from the surveys are analysed using descriptive statistics including mean, standard deviation, and frequency distribution. Thematic analysis was used to examine the qualitative information gathered from the interviews. Gamification, employee recognition, rewards, incentives, and providing access to developmental training sessions on new technologies could encourage employee participation. The right working conditions (such as expertly designed ergonomics) and clear company policies all play a crucial role in fostering employee satisfaction. Other hygiene-related factors, including compensation that is in proportion with employee efforts, job security through carefully drafted contracts or agreements with business partners, or management teams that foster trust and confidence in the organization's overall direction, help build worker loyalty. Workers' engagement may decline if these factors are ignored. By addressing both hygiene factors and motivators, the study provides innovative strategies for boosting employee morale and improving job satisfaction in the age of digital technology. The insights derived from this research could be useful in advising retailers to seek holistic employee engagement strategies that combine interpersonal communica-

B. Duba (✉) · N. Marwa
University of Johannesburg, Johannesburg, South Africa
e-mail: nyankomom@uj.ac.za

T. Moloi (ed.), *Impacting Society Positively Through Technology in Accounting and Business Processes*, Springer Proceedings in Business and Economics,
https://doi.org/10.1007/978-3-031-84885-8_6

tion with digital technology tools while fostering a work environment that can increase employee satisfaction and boost turnover.

Keywords Employee morale · Job satisfaction · Training and development · Incentive and rewards · Employee recognition · Retail

Introduction

As digital technology continues to evolve rapidly across various sectors and industries, unfortunately for retailers, it has introduced unintended disruptions resulting in worrisome impacts on employee morale. This is primarily caused by the rise of e-commerce trends and artificial intelligence which now significantly affect traditional business patterns in physical brick-and-mortar stores (Dhavale, 2019). Consequently, this dynamic marketplace situation brings along significant challenges for workers such as job security, inconsistent working hours, and ever-increasing pressure to meet sales targets (Giri et al., 2019).

The retail industry has undergone a transformation process because of the impact that digital technologies have had on it. These changes affect both the working habits of employees and the purchasing habits of customers. Cashiers and sales associates, for example, are now replaced by self-checkout machines or scanning apps for smartphones. New job categories such as data analysis, data scientists, digital marketing, and more are evolving, because of artificial intelligence (Panori et al., 2021). The current situation has led to a prevailing feeling of job insecurity among retail workers, who are experiencing uncertainty regarding the future direction of their employment prospects within the sector. Furthermore, pressure of meeting sales targets continues to grow as retailers try to sustain competitiveness in the era of digital technology. Particularly when it comes to traditional brick-and-mortar establishments, the retail industry today is characterized by an intense focus on business goals. Retailers are under increasing pressure to succeed as e-commerce has a big impact on consumer preferences and behaviours to guarantee competitive viability in such circumstances; an essential quality for these firms is an unwavering will to defeat digital adversaries.

In recent years, the traditional brick-and-mortar retailers have struggled with severe competition from online businesses; as a result, many stores have closed, leaving many people without jobs (Fihartini et al., 2021). The issues have been made much more difficult by COVID-19, which forced a large decline in foot traffic at physical stores. As a result, the rapid growth of online sales has made things more difficult for traditional shops. Finding practical strategies to raise staff morale considering these circumstances is a major challenge for retailers. Frontline retail employees play a crucial role in providing top-notch customer experiences, and their dissatisfaction or sense of being treated unfairly might eventually harm a retailer's business (Fihartini et al., 2021). The retail sector must make sure to consistently improve employee satisfaction and sense of belonging despite constant shifts.

Retail firms are looking for innovative solutions that integrate motivational strategies with long-term planning considering the impending hurdles. Innovative practices now include putting a high priority on extensive employee development programs that improve workforce capabilities and reinforce a positivity-centred organizational culture, along with hyper-personalized digital experiences made possible by technological innovation and essential for enhancing the customer relationship (Zheng et al., 2015). Successful retailers will surely nurture higher employee satisfaction metrics due to increased levels of engagement, which will ultimately lead to higher performance rates in both sales targets and customer satisfaction surveys.

By exploring cutting-edge strategies that revitalize retail and boost employee morale, this research addresses the current issues that retailers are facing. The main goal of this study is to identify examples of retail stores who successfully adapted to the digital era. All industry leaders, including politicians and other stakeholders looking for insights on how to better their organizations, may gain significantly from the research.

Literature Review

This literature review explores the importance of employee morale in the retail industry and pinpoints creative strategies for revitalizing the industry and boosting employee morale in the age of digital technology. This literature review also examines how technology has transformed processes within retail companies.

Employee morale is a state of employees to feel fulfilled and engaged in their work. It is paramount to maintaining high levels of productivity. This idea is formalized by the term "employee morale", which encapsulates an individual's sense of contentment with their job tasks and the relationship cultivated with their employer (Pattnaik & Jena, 2020). Generally, organizational success depends heavily on strong employee retention rates. High operational levels brought about through a motivated workforce mean that managing employee morale should be prioritized to ensure that the desired outcomes are met.

Leadership has been identified to be one of the most important elements affecting employee morale. Those that inspire and motivate their team members, offer clear guidance and assistance, and foster a great work atmosphere are considered effective leaders (Noor & Ampornstira, 2019). The trust and confidence of employees can be increased by leaders who are approachable, encouraging, and open in their communication, which can boost staff morale. Other factors include communication, the work environment, compensation, and job satisfaction.

Communication is an important element that has an impact on staff morale. Giving clear instructions and feedback is simply one aspect of effective communication; the other is actively listening to the problems and suggestions of the workforce. Employees are more likely to feel engaged and motivated at work when they believe that their thoughts and voices are respected. The work environment that is the state of the workplace has an immense impact on employee morale. Instituting a positive work environment demands providing safety, comfort, and efficiency at the workplace. Employers can boost their employer's spirits by making deliberate efforts in creating an atmosphere of happiness at work. To achieve this goal requires giving employees comfortable workstation arrangements with access to natural light while facilitating opportunities for social interaction (Soetjipto et al., 2021).

Finally, compensation and job satisfaction have been reported to play a significant role in employee morale. Employee morale is greatly influenced by several other important elements, including pay and job satisfaction. Employees are more likely to feel motivated and engaged at work if they believe they are adequately compensated for their labour and have options for professional growth and development (Soetjipto et al., 2021). Employee morale can be raised by employers who offer chances for training and growth, as well as prizes and recognition for exceptional performance.

Morale Theories (Herzberg's Two-Factor Theory Framework)

Frederick Herzberg created Herzberg's two-factor theory of motivation in the 1950s. This theory bases itself on the notion that employee motivation and job satisfaction are influenced by a pair of distinct types of factors (Kim et al., 2022). These are motivators and hygienic factors. Herzberg's two-factor theory is relevant to this study as it focuses on the variables that affect employee motivation and job satisfaction.

The key to ensuring that employees love their work is to create an environment that satisfies some basic requirements. The right working conditions and clear company policies all play a crucial role in fostering employee loyalty. Other hygiene-related factors include compensation that is in proportion with employee efforts, job security through carefully drafted contracts or agreements with business partners, or management teams that foster trust and confidence in the organization's overall direction that help build worker loyalty. Workers' engagement may decline if these factors are ignored. On the other side, motivators are elements that contribute to motivation and job satisfaction. They include things like opportunity for growth and development, recognition, competence, and responsibility. Employees will be motivated and content with their jobs if these conditions exist.

Employee morale plays a crucial role in driving business success, a notion that is especially true for retail firms. However, with new technologies like automation and artificial intelligence affecting work routines, enterprises must prioritize strategies that boost employee morale levels and foster engagement (Nakypbayev, 2022). Positive employee morale is necessary for a successful workplace for several reasons. Its significant impact on productivity and performance indicators is a vital element. When workers are happy in their jobs, they frequently work harder and are more motivated, which leads to improved productivity rates, which in turn raise profitability by increasing customer satisfaction and sales.

Factors Affecting the Employee Morale

There are several factors affecting employee morale. The widely cited factors are job security, training and development, communication, work–life balance, recognition and rewards, and technology (Mallik et al., 2019). Starting with job security, it is a significant element in retailers' efforts to improve the working conditions for their employees because it helps to improve employee well-being and increase work motivation. However, there are worries about the subsequent layoffs that result in feelings of insecurity among individuals affected in areas where technology has replaced manual jobs typically performed by human personnel. Such impacted personnel experience uncertainty because of this continuous sense of vulnerability, which negatively affects their general attitudes towards their jobs (Mallik et al., 2019).

The rising prominence of technology in retail necessitates ongoing learning by its employees. Accordingly, retailers may effectively boost motivation levels amongst staff by providing training opportunities (Mallik et al., 2019). Such developmental initiatives can foster workers' sense of engagement with the brand; furthermore, a strong sense of organizational commitment typically arises from employers who prioritize professional growth among team members. Also, to keep employee morale up in the retail industry requires effective communication. Email and instant messaging are convenient but can result in too much information at once or may not encourage interpersonal interaction. Prioritizing face-to-face conversation and providing consistent feedback would help retailers achieve higher levels of motivation among their workforce while driving business outcomes forward.

Managers must not disregard the impact that neglecting an individual's personal life can bring about, potentially leading to a decrease in employee morale. As research by Dash and Mohanty (2019) suggests, stores that prioritize promoting a healthy work–lifestyle equilibrium and offer leeway in scheduling tend to have highly motivated workers. In the retail industry, maintaining employee morale requires awards and recognition. Through gamification and social recognition initiatives, for example, retailers now have additional chances to reward and acknowledge their staff members. Retailers are more likely to have a motivated and engaged workforce if they prioritize recognition and rewards.

In today's retail industry, harnessing technological advancements carries multiple advantages such as increased productivity levels among employees, greater efficiency, and increasing customer satisfaction. However, one crucial aspect that has not received sufficient attention is the correlation between technology usage and its impact on employee morale within retail settings. The integration of tech facilities can influence job satisfaction levels positively or negatively depending on several factors. One way it positively affects employee motivation is through reducing workload (Krishnan, 2021), for instance, by using automated inventory management systems that simplify inventory planning processes enhancing work efficiency while enabling resource allocation towards other productive tasks like customer service interactions through self-checkout technologies.

However valuable these benefits might be to any organization striving for optimal efficiency and effectiveness within its operations model, certain forms of technological integration carry adverse effects arising from staff perception towards technology use, installing surveillance cameras leading workers to feel under constant observation, or performance tracking software raising anxiety levels among workers caused by undue pressure—ultimately leading to reduced morale levels among such staff members.

Innovative Strategies for Boosting Employee Morale

In the technological age, retailers can use innovative strategies that emphasize employee empowerment and participation to raise staff morale. Giving staff members opportunities for training and development that enables them to pick up new abilities and information is one such strategy (Krishnan, 2021). Increased morale can result from making workers feel more valued and vested in their work.

Another strategy is to establish an environment at work that encourages cooperation and teamwork. This can be accomplished through establishing open lines of communication, valuing employee opinions and suggestions, and fostering an inclusive and diverse culture (Abarantyne et al., 2019). Figure 1 gives a summary of relative frequency of use of the methods and their effectiveness in enhancing morale among employees. It is divided into two sections: The key methods are the financial incentives and the non-financial incentives. Based on this analysis, it is clear that while every manager would like to increase their employees' motivation there is a need to achieve this through financial and non-financial means.

Training and development are one of the best strategies to increase employee morale. The proper use of technology needs to be taught to retail staff. They should also receive training on how to offer first-class customer service. Programs for training and development can make employees feel more appreciated and improve their level of job satisfaction (Leonova et al., 2021).

Programs for employee training and development can also aid in raising productivity. Employees who have received proper training are more effective and productive in their positions. This may result in greater sales, better client satisfaction, and higher company earnings (Leonova et al., 2021). Additionally, training and development initiatives can aid in pinpointing the areas in which staff members require development, allowing for the early intervention of performance-related concerns.

Rewarding employees is crucial for raising employee morale. Retail staff members must feel that their efforts are valued and acknowledged. Retailers can put recognition and incentive programs in place to inspire staff and improve job satisfaction. Offering wages and additional benefits that are competitive to attract and

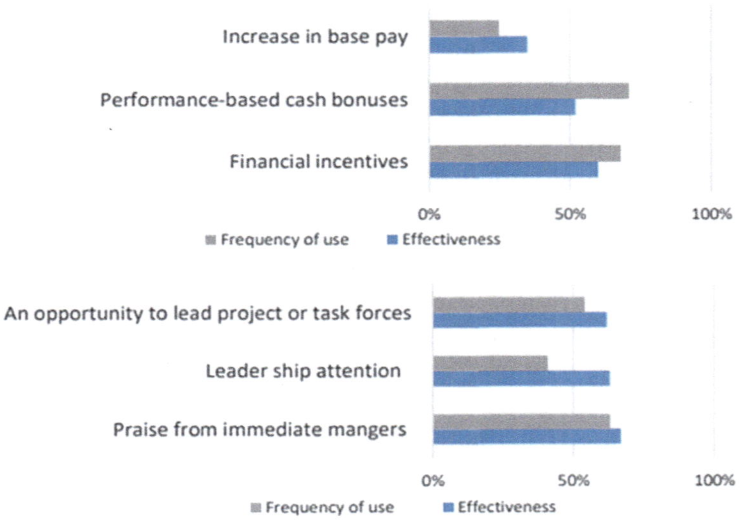

Fig. 1 McKinsey quarterly survey results. Source (adapted from Dewhurst et al., 2009)

keep great employees is key. By demonstrating to workers that their employer values their efforts and is prepared to invest in their well-being, this may assist a lot to raise morale (Ladson, 2019).

Recognition and incentive programs also play a critical role: to effectively recognize and reward employees in the retail industry. Companies can utilize various incentive and recognition programs. Examples of these programs may include:

Employee of the month: Each month employers can designate an "Employee of the Month" to recognize one exceptional performer. They may earn various incentives such as bonuses or prizes like gift cards as rewards for their hard work and valuable contributions. *Sales incentives for e*mployees who surpass sales objectives. The means of compensation may include gift cards, cash bonuses, or other incentives. *The performance-based bonuses* initiative aims to provide rewards to workers who achieve designated performance targets, such as improving customer satisfaction ratings or mitigating customer complaints.

Team-building exercises: Encouraging cooperative dynamics among employees is the aim of this program's incentive system. The offered rewards comprise of enjoyable group outings, appetizing meals, and diverse activities designed specifically to strengthen bonding within teams. Such incentives foster an environment where staff members collaborate effectively towards common goals, making them more motivated and productive in their work duties.

Embracing technology and remaining competitive in the ever-changing business environment. Companies should make use of technological advancements. Businesses may increase productivity, reorganize processes, simplify, and improve employee work environments by embracing technology. Lower stress levels, higher morale, and eventually greater company results can result from this. These coupled with flexible schedules are essential in the retail sector, where workers frequently work long hours and on weekends and holidays. A better work–life balance and job satisfaction are more prevalent in people who have control over their schedules. Increased productivity, improved customer service, and lower turnover rates follow from this (Sapta et al., 2021).

Consistent communication is required in improving employee morale, and to generate good results, communication is essential. Retailers must develop regular channels of communication with staff employees to keep everyone updated on corporate goals, policies, and guidelines. Interactions typically take place in team meetings or privately over email, newsletters, and WhatsApp (Zhang et al., 2022). Giving an employee their role and duties information makes them feel valued as a member of the team, which boosts their motivation and satisfaction with their job.

Open-door policies in creating environments within retail companies that prioritize transparency between employees start by implementing open-door policies which encourage communication channels between management and staff members. These channels provide fluid avenues of communication so it is easier for staff members to express their concerns about challenges they may face. This goes in hand with effective listening. Effective listening is a necessary component of effective communication. Retailers must pay attention to the issues and viewpoints of their employees and take necessary action. Effective listening entails paying attention to what employees are saying, clarifying any points with questions, and correctly reacting. Retailers can demonstrate that they care about their staff by effectively listening.

Team building requires assembling individuals who share the same objectives so they can work collaboratively towards attaining common goals. The core intention behind this exercise is encouraging cooperation and better communication and nurturing productive teamwork among participants. A plethora of activities ranging from basic icebreaker games to intricate problem-solving challenges are incorporated into the process with one singular goal: enhancing community values while promoting crucial group dynamics beneficial for effective collaboration irrespective of difficulty levels or complexity (Khando et al., 2021).

Team-building exercises can aid in removing obstacles and challenges between teammates. Individuals are compelled to talk and collaborate while they are working on a task together. As a result, team members may develop stronger bonds and feel more trusted. Retailers can use a variety of team-building exercises to raise employee satisfaction. Several instances include *Icebreakers*—These quick activities can be utilized to get to know team members better. Games, tests, and other enjoyable activities are some examples of icebreakers. *Problem-solving activities*—These include collaborating to find a solution to a problem. This can be an effective technique to boost teamwork and communication. *Outdoor activities*—Hiking, camping, or team sports are all excellent ways to foster a sense of community and enhance teamwork. *Volunteering*—Participating in volunteer work together can be a brilliant way to forge bonds and increase job satisfaction.

Gamification is the technique of incorporating game mechanics and design features into situations that are not games to engage and inspire individuals to reach their objectives. Gamification has gained popularity as a method of boosting workplace morale in recent years (Benitez et al., 2022). Employers may create a more stimulating and effective work atmosphere by creating games that encourage teamwork, competition, and prizes for achieving specific goals.

Gamification offers several advantages to organizations looking to boost workplace morale. It can first improve staff motivation and engagement. Employees are more likely to be motivated to finish work and reach goals when they are actively playing a game (Benitez et al., 2022). Better job performance and higher productivity may result from this.

Examples of Effective Gamification Techniques

Leaderboards: A well-liked gamification technique, leaderboards can be used to encourage competition among staff. Employers can foster a sense of rivalry and encourage workers to put in more effort to reach their objectives by presenting the top achievers on a leaderboard. *Rewards:* Offering incentives to staff is another well-liked gamification method. Employers can foster a sense of success and inspire staff to work harder by providing prizes for achieving certain goals.

Quests: Setting up a series of tasks or challenges for staff members to complete is part of the quest gamification strategy. Employees can gain points or incentives by finishing these tasks. Employees may feel a sense of success as a result and become more driven to work hard. *Badges:* The use of badges as a gamification method rewards staff members for performing certain tasks or reaching predetermined objectives. This can inspire workers to put in more effort and foster a sense of success.

Technology integration and automating tools. Using technology in the workplace can help improve productivity by streamlining procedures. This can involve using devices like automation tools, communication platforms, and project management software. Retailers might greatly simplify their supply chain cycle by integrating a variety of automation tools, from order processing to inventory management, which also includes essential live customer experience with chat or customer support assistance. For instance, using automated systems could provide effective stock level monitoring and give managers real-time updates (Parker & Grote, 2022).

Platforms for communication and project management. Teams can interact and work in real time using communication platforms, which are computer programs. Platforms for communication can be utilized in the retail sector to enhance communication between staff, vendors, and customers. For instance, a retailer can utilize a messaging app to connect with staff members and enable real-time information sharing and updates (Parker & Grote, 2022). By taking less time and effort to interact with staff members, this can increase productivity. Teams can plan, coordinate, and manage projects with the use of project management software. Project management software can be used in the retail sector to coordinate activities including store openings, product launches, and advertising campaigns (Rotz et al., 2019). For instance, project management software can be used by a retailer to schedule the opening of a new location, allocate responsibilities to team members, and monitor progress. This can ensure that the store opening is finished on schedule and on a reasonable budget.

Benefits of Workplace Technology Integration

Streamlining processes and increased interaction. The use of technology within the workplace has many benefits, one of which is increased process effectiveness. Tools for automation make it easier to handle repetitive jobs, allowing workers to focus their energies on more important tasks. According to a study by Rotz et al. (2019), this method not only lowers errors but also increases manufacturing productivity because robotic programs finish assigned jobs more quickly and precisely than human input. Every business requires effective communication, and technology may help by enhancing communication inside departments, among employees, and even with clients. No matter where they are located, employees can connect in real time using services like Slack, Microsoft Teams, and Zoom. Better results may result from enhancing collaboration and reducing misunderstandings.

Improved project administration. Digital instruments provide a wide range of capabilities that improve task management by utilizing historical data analytics, team collaboration tools, and resource allocation efficiency while monitoring important deadlines so that stakeholders receive timely deliveries, enhancing both implementation process cycles, and lowering the risk of run-away costs associated with stationary or failed initiatives.

Enhanced flexibility. Integrating technological innovations into the workplace might encourage flexibility within businesses. Employees are given the freedom to be productive from any location at any time when remote work choices are available. Such initiatives support enhanced happiness and productivity as well as reduced stress levels, all contributing positively towards an improved work–life balance.

Better management of data. Data is a necessity in any workplace, and technology may improve data management for firms. With the aid of cloud-based storage options like Google Drive and Dropbox, which also ensure data protection and backup, employees may access data from any place. This can boost output while reducing the likelihood of data loss.

Concluding this section, we reiterate that retail revitalization is a tough process that needs a diversified strategy. It entails addressing both customer experience and employee morale. To encourage a sense of loyalty and dedication among employees, retailers must make an investment in the professional development of their staff and establish a favourable work environment. This can be accomplished by offering training and development opportunities, competitive pay packages, and cultivating an environment of recognition and acknowledgement.

Retailers need to use technology and customer data to customize experiences that encourage customer loyalty and repeat business in addition to investing in their employees. To do this, it is necessary to analyse customer data to comprehend their preferences and behaviour before customizing the shopping experience to suit those needs.

Retailers may revitalize their operations and prosper in the digital age by putting these strategies into practice. Through favourable word-of-mouth and Internet evaluations, they can build a following of devoted clients who are eager to frequent their businesses time and time again. The commitment to employee and customer satisfaction, as well as an appetite to adopt innovative technologies and data-driven strategies, is ultimately necessary for revitalizing retail.

Research Methodology

A mixed-methods approach involving both qualitative and quantitative research techniques was used in exploring the theme further. Comprehensive data collection from both primary and secondary sources was a key component for this study. Primary data were collected using Survey instrument administered to Retail Employees and Management Team. Data on employee morale, job satisfaction, and the effect of technology on their work were gathered through the survey. An online questionnaire was created using Google forms and was given to the store managers to share with their employees and distribute the questionnaire link via their work WhatsApp group, for all employees to have access to, which they completed after work and during their lunch break.

The key informant interviews were used to collect qualitative data on innovative strategies for increasing employee morale in the technological era. Structured interviews were held with retail managers and supervisors. Structured interviews were conducted with the store managers and the interviews were recorded for accuracy when analysing data. The interviews consisted mainly of open-ended questions, as they allowed the respondents to fully express their views and experiences, which provided more in-depth data, to help strengthen the study.

Secondary data were collected from peer-reviewed papers on the effect of technology on employee morale in the retail sector from various sources including academic journals, relevant books' secondary data on creative methods for enhancing staff morale, books on employee morale and the retail sector, and online databases on the retail sector and employee morale. The main data repository was sourced from public domain online databases like UJoogle, Google Scholar, and JSTOR.

Target Population and Sample Size

The intention of the study was to collect data from both retail employees and managers by selecting a sample size of 50 employees (cashiers, sales associates, customer service representatives) and 5 managers in Johannesburg. Data were collected in September 2023. The retail employee population in Gauteng is 1,323,000 according to the Quarterly Labour Force Survey (QLFS) which was released in June 2023 by Statistics of South Africa. This means that a sample size of 55 retail employees was a good rule of thumb to ensure that the sample represents the Gauteng retail population. A sample size of 55 has a margin error of 5% at a 95% confidence level.

The formula for calculating the sample size is:

$$n = \left(Z \wedge 2^{*} p^{*} q\right) / \left(d \wedge 2\right)$$

where n is the sample size, Z is the z-score for the desired confidence level (1.96 for 95% confidence), p is the estimated proportion of the population with the characteristic of interest (in this case, the proportion of retail employees who are interested in innovative strategies for boosting employee morale), q is the complement of p (1 - p), and d is the margin of error. The study was interested in a 95% confidence level, so $Z = 1.96$. It was safe to estimate that the proportion of retail employees who are interested in the topic is 0.5, since the topic is not particularly controversial. This means that $p = q = 0.5$. The desired margin of error is 5%.

Therefore,

$$n = \left(1.96 \wedge 2^{*}\, 0.5^{*}\, 0.5\right) / \left(0.05\right) \wedge 2$$

$$n = 52.07$$

We used mall interception study to access the participants. This was most pragmatic and optimal approach due to participant availability and timeliness of data collection. The sample size was not fixed on the size provided, but data were collected until the point of saturation was reached. This is a point where the information that was obtained from the respondents added no value or new insights to the study, and all information received was a repetition of what has been shared by the previous respondents.

The study was conducted in the Johannesburg region. The main retail stores targeted were grocery and the clothing sector. The stores studied were strategically selected based on store performance, employee engagement, managerial support, digital adoption, and location. These stores are brands that have both the grocery and clothing section. The study sites were selected in a sense that they should provide information from the lower Living Standard Measure (LSM) to the higher LSM perspective, to have much more diverse data.

- Woolworths (clothing and grocery) mainly caters for the upper LSM.
- Pick n Pay (clothing and grocery) mainly caters for the middle LSM.
- Shoprite (clothing and grocery) mainly caters for the lower LSM.

Data Analysis

The data were analysed using descriptive statistics and frequency analysis. With the use of frequency analysis and descriptive statistics, important insights on the overall levels of employee morale were obtained. The percentage of retail employees who make use of digital technologies at work, the number of employees who have taken part in digital technology training programs, and the average job satisfaction of retail employees were analysed using descriptive statistics. Frequency analysis was used to determine the most common reasons for employee turnover in the retail industry, the digital technologies that employees use most frequently, and the kinds of digital technology training programs that employees are most interested in.

Results and Discussion

This section presents the findings of our research on the impact of technology on employee morale, creativity and innovation, spirit of belonging and purpose, work–life balance, and learning and development. The chapter also provides recommendations for how retailers can use technology to improve employee morale and productivity (Fig. 2).

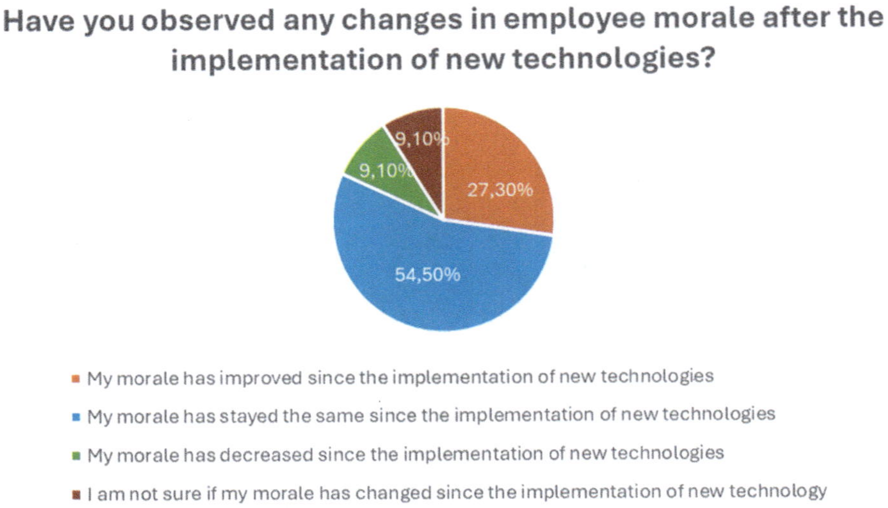

Fig. 2 Technology and employee morale

54.5% of the respondents believed that their morale has remained the same even though new technologies have been introduced. 27.3% believe that their morale levels have improved since the implementation of new technologies. 9.1% believe that there has been a decrease in their morale levels, and the other 9.1% is not sure whether there have been any changes in their morale levels ever since new technologies have been introduced. Overall, the implementation of new technologies in the retail space has had a positive impact on the morale of the employees. Many of the managers have knowledge about new innovative technologies that retail has but a few lack knowledge of how such an innovation can boost employee's morale. Technology can make communication more effective and allow team members to participate in the decision-making process thus leading to production efficiency (Fig. 3).

50% of the respondents believe that their opinions and ideas are appreciated and valued by their superiors. A significant number of 30.6% feel neutral, and 19.4% do not feel like their ideas and opinions are valued by their superiors. The results of this chart are positive and indicate that the management values their staffs' ideas, and when employees feel valued, they are most likely to have increased morale. However, there is a significant number of neutral and respondents who do not feel valued and this means that the management must improve their doings.

When employees feel valued and supported, creativity follows, which is a recipe for innovation and high performance. Managers need to create learning environments that encourage the employees to interact, experiment, and share opinions. Providing access to technology can help fuel creativity and innovation among employees because they have a lot of information that has been gathered for them easily accessible (Fig. 4).

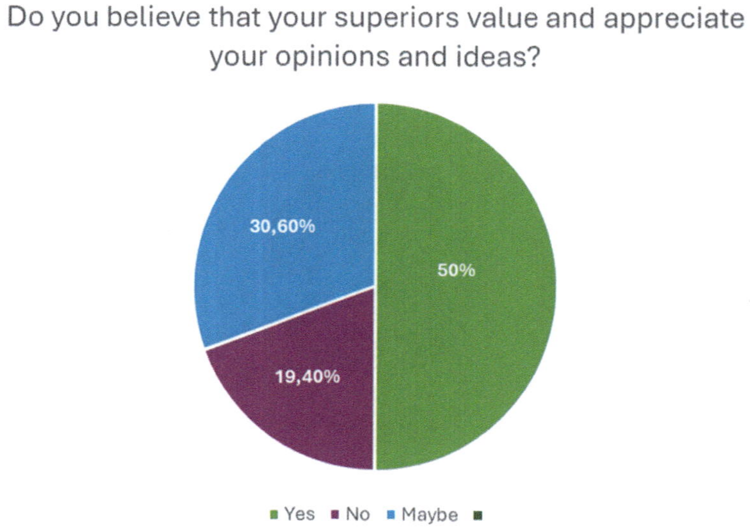

Fig. 3 Creativity and innovation

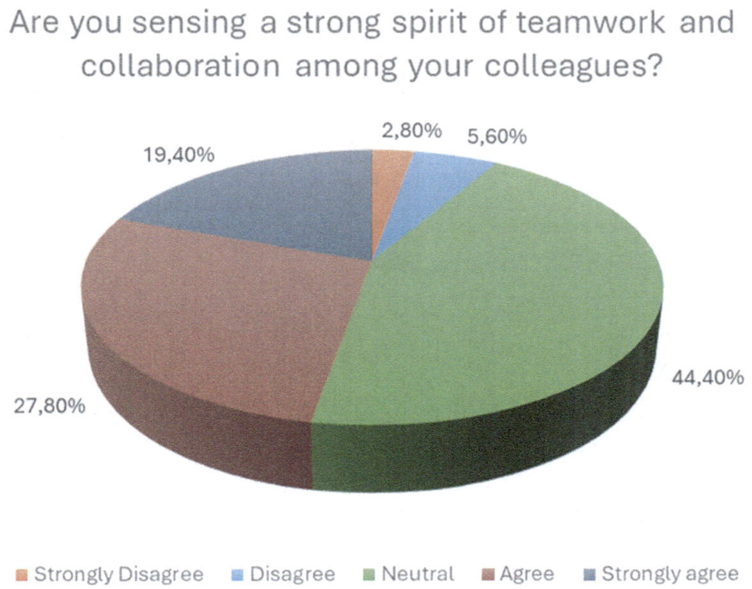

Fig. 4 Spirit of belonging and purpose

44.4% of the respondents feel neutral about the spirit of teamwork and collaboration among their colleagues. 27.8% do agree that there is a spirit of teamwork within their workplaces. 19.4% strongly agree. 5.6% disagree and 2.8% strongly disagree that the spirit of teamwork exists in their workplaces.

The findings of the research indicate that retail enterprises need to make the working environment increasingly more humane. This translates into providing a forum whereby individuals meet one another as friends, appreciate, and embrace them regardless of their cultural backgrounds thus making individuals feel appreciated by the company. This refers to giving the workers a feeling that they have a task and are proud for doing it with integrity.

Providing chances to interact socially with other coworkers away from the workplace makes employees feel appreciated. However, such an approach may assist in development of new contacts and creation of better climate within the workplace. They also desire that their coworkers consider them worthy of some respect and encourage workers to work as team, so that they can support each other and celebrate the achievements at the same time.

It motivates employees when they see that their effort is highly valued. Simple acts by managers like saying a big thank you or giving a high five speak volumes of how much managers appreciate staff. People love working in an organization that offers a good reward system. Managers may make workers proud in the business by giving information on the organization's vision and purpose, and by providing chances for employees to learn (Fig. 5).

62.9% of the respondents believe they have a fair work–life balance. 17.1% of the respondents have a good work–life balance. 14.3% have a poor work–life

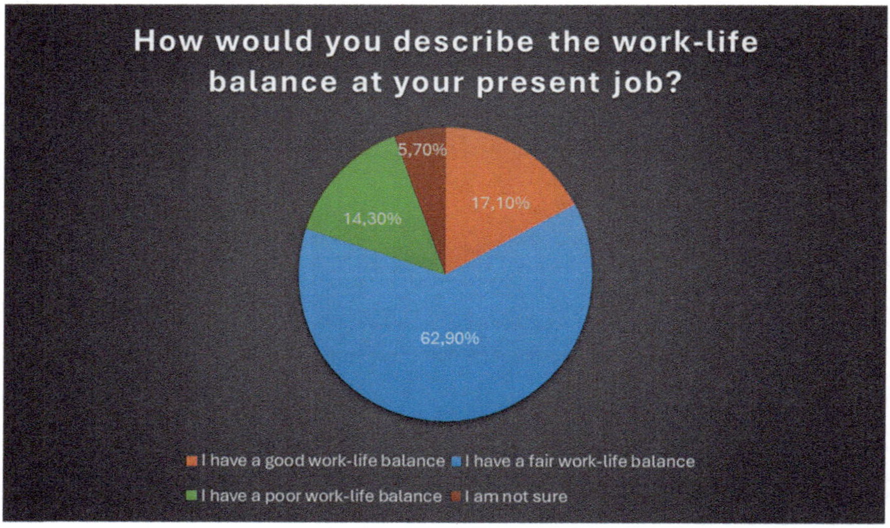

Fig. 5 Work–life balance

balance. 5.7% of the respondents are not sure about their work–life balance levels. This chart shows that many of the respondents are satisfied with their work–life balance, and this is a positive finding. However, there are a significant number of respondents who feel that their work–life balance is poor, and this means that the management should improve and ensure that their staff have a good work–life balance, to enhance their morale.

Work arrangements, like telecommuting and compressed work weeks, are some of the ways that organizations can ensure that their employees get a good work–life balance. For one, employees need to get some sleep during the day. Providing employees with nice restrooms is a good example of motivators. The employee morale of 44.1% of the respondents is high at their place of employment. The other 44.1% of the respondents are neutral about the morale levels at their place of employment. 5.9% indicated a very high morale. 2.9% of the employees feel like there are very low morale levels, while another 2.9% expressed that there is a low morale at their place of employment. A significant number of respondents do not feel like the morale levels are great at work (Fig. 6).

The results indicate that retail companies must build an environment that appreciates employees' contributions and efforts. This, therefore, entails daily appreciation of a worker's efforts and giving rewards for achievements. It also entails offering employees a chance to earn recognition from their colleagues or supervisors. Retail companies should invest in a reward system and recognition by making their workers feel important. It brings about added sales margins and stable and healthy business (Fig. 7).

From the chart above, it shows that 44.4% of the respondents feel that communication lines are very open and transparent between the management and staff. 25%

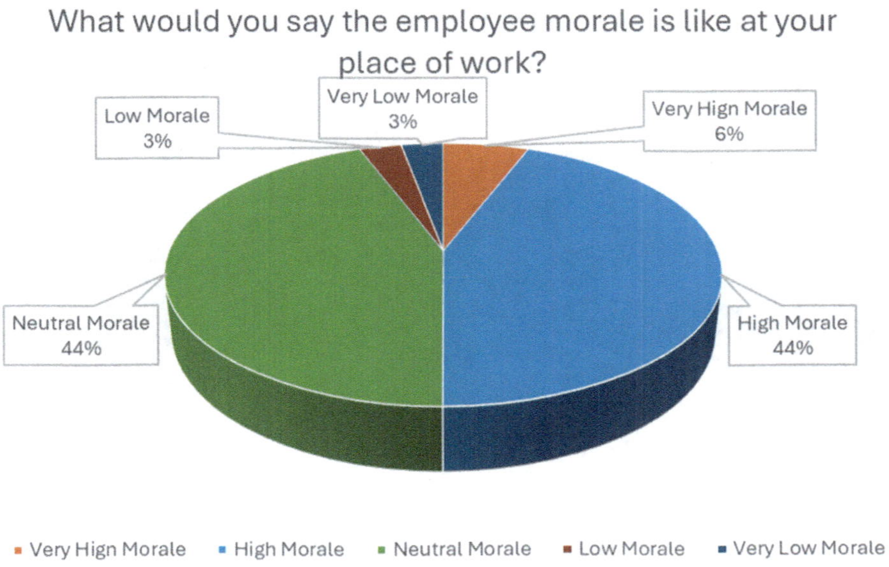

Fig. 6 Boosting morale

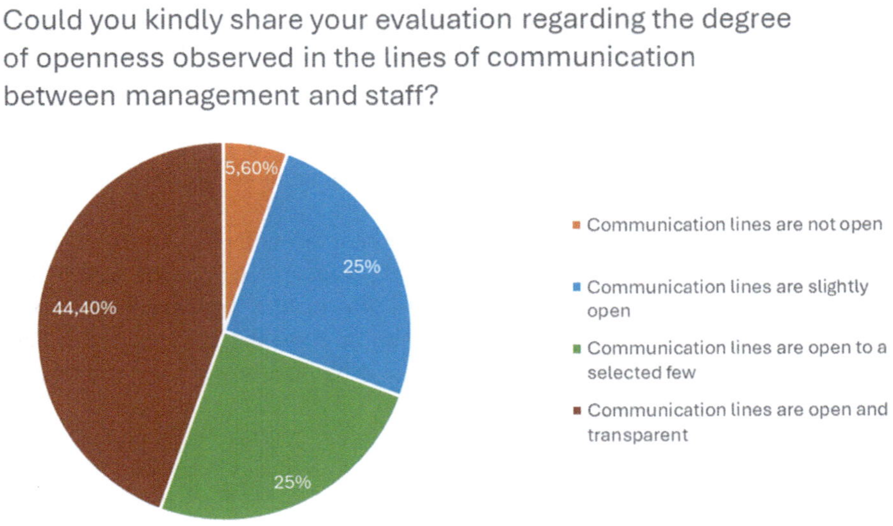

Fig. 7 Communication

feel that communication lines are slightly open. The other 25% feel like the communication lines are only open to a selected few, while 5.6% feel like the communication lines are not open. The research found suggests that there is room for the management to improve their communication channels and openness. The digital age is very fast-paced, and communication must be frequent and in real time (Fig. 8).

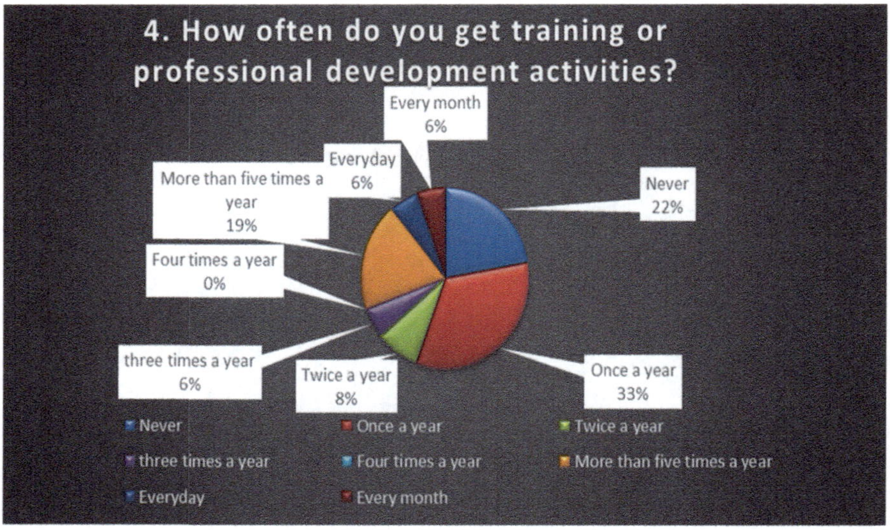

Fig. 8 Learning and development

33% of the respondents mentioned that they receive training once a year. 19% receive training more than 5 times a year, while about 22% of the respondents claimed that they have never received any form of training. 6% of the respondents receive training every month while another 6% of the respondents receive training every day. 8% of the respondents get training two times a year and 6% receive training at least three times a year. These results suggest the need to do a lot of improvements on their training programs and start investing more on the professional development of their staff.

Retailers must also ensure that the new learning technologies they use suit the needs of their employees. Besides, these should be able to harmonize well within their current operational systems as well as IT infrastructure. Training of employees towards using the new technologies should also be considered essential. Retailers can make their business models more sustainable by investing in their employees' learning and development.

The retail industry is dynamic, with newer trends hitting the scene daily. The growing e-commerce trend has been forcing shops to go out of business. This would leave some of the retail employees jobless, thus creating uncertainties that can lead to demoralization among other employees. There are more ethnic minorities as well as millennial and Gen-Z employees who make up the current retail workforce. Retail managers need to be flexible in their methods of managing and developing workers who are generally younger than their older counterparts. The way in which retail workers operate is being affected by technology, which has been growing more important in the retail sector. For instance, several retail merchants use AI for automated roles like service provision and inventory tracking. It may result in some

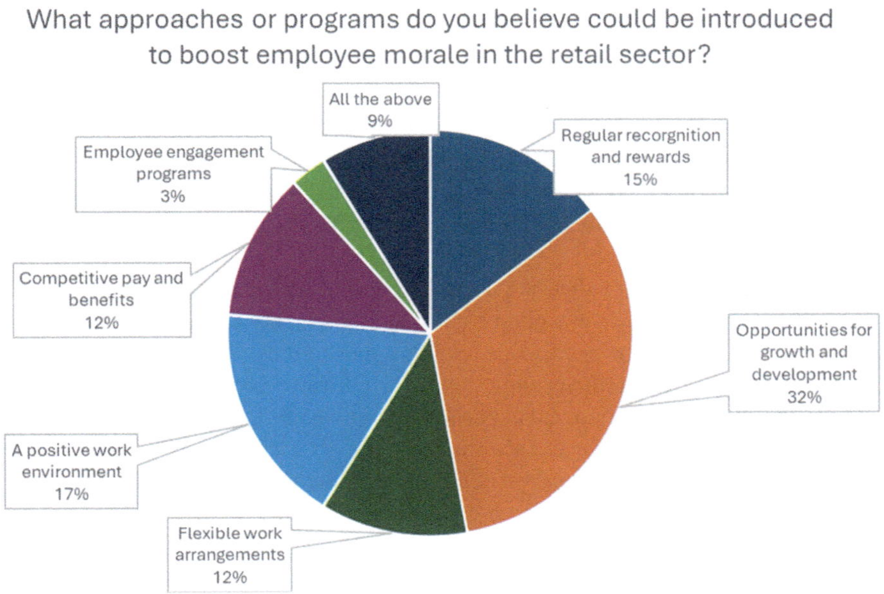

Fig. 9 Approaches to boost employee morale

job elimination; however, it might as well produce new job chances for those retail employees ready to acquire additional training.

As such, retailers need to understand these changing factors and do something to minimize the detrimental effects they have on employee morale. One such possibility is for retailers to establish training and development programs that will enable employees to master new skills and adjust smoothly to this new environment. The management can also make a better and friendly working environment and give employees opportunities for career improvement (Fig. 9).

The pie chart presents the responses of retail employees regarding approaches and programs they would recommend that could increase the morale of retail employees. Employees identified the above approaches and programs as the following results: regular recognition and rewards (14.7%), opportunities for growth and development (32.4%), flexible work arrangements (11.8%), a positive work environment (17.6%), competitive pay and benefits (11.8%), employee engagement programs (2.9%), employee surveys (0%), and all the above (8.8%).

From the research conducted employees identified three main approaches, including regular recognition/rewards, opportunities for growth/development, and flexible work arrangements. All these are important considerations when dealing with staff morale since they help employees feel value in themselves and in control of their work.

Conclusion

Digital technology has brought about a significant transformation in retail. The employee morale among employees has been greatly influenced by this change because of the increased demands, ever-changing customer preferences, and challenges that employees are facing. Retailers can utilize several innovative strategies to boost employee morale and foster a more constructive and effective work environment.

Investing in technology that helps employees and makes their jobs easier is one important strategy. This entails giving staff members access to the most recent technologies and resources as well as providing opportunities for training and professional growth so that employees may pick up innovative skills. Retailers ought to foster a culture of innovation and experimentation where staff members are encouraged to offer their ideas and advance the business.

Putting an emphasis on employee engagement and well-being is another crucial strategy. This entails establishing an environment at work where workers are valued, respected, and given chances for professional advancement. Retailers can also increase morale by fostering a positive work–life balance and providing competitive compensation and benefits. Digital technology has led retail workers to encounter a wide range of difficulties such as high rivalry from Internet traders, long working hours, low salaries, etc. This results in little or no motivation among the employees leading to low morale and employee turnover. Nevertheless, retailers should employ several creative ways that will increase employee morale and develop a better work environment.

Finally, retailers need to ensure that their managers are prepared to boost employees' morale. This includes *giving managers the instruments and materials they require* to mentor, develop, and foster a pleasant work environment for their teams. Retailers may improve employee morale and foster a more successful workplace by executing these innovative strategies.

Recommendations

Retailers should help employees acquire the relevant skills necessary for success in the Digital Age through training in CRM software, social media engagement, and e-commerce. They would feel more respected and empowered, and in turn be able to attend to other customers' needs more productively. Providing updated technologies, comfortable apparel, and good and safe working conditions to employees is vital. Employees will be motivated and contented when they possess the necessary tools that help them achieve more output at work.

There is a need to develop a performance-driven organization with a culture of open communication and feedback and stimulate employees' creativity and make them feel that they are important and valued in an organization by responding promptly and appropriately on their responses as well as giving them room to brainstorm and express opinions on issues that concern the organization. This will make employees realize that they are listened to and their voices matter and will thus impact on the improvement of the company's operations.

There is a need for carefully designed incentive mechanisms like rewarding employees when they do a good job and promoting work–life balance. Such might be a monthly award for an employee of the month, bonuses, and even just simple thanks from their boss. Employees should be appreciated for good performance to motivate them to do more. Managers should provide their employees with flexible schedules, and other measures that ensure a balance between work and their private life. Allowing leisure time is essential for employees as it means happier and more productive staff members of a company.

Use gamification and technology to empower employees. Gamification platforms exist in several varieties which include interactive challenges and incentive programs as well. This will have a positive effect on the morale of workers and could particularly enhance enthusiasm for the employees, especially the younger staff. Employees can have more power in carrying out their duties and technology can help them with their tasks or duties. For instance, mobile devices can help employees to get access to real-time data to carry out their responsibilities. Technology can be used to automate some processes that will make retailers' employees concentrate on more engaging tasks with a direct influence on their customers.

Social media can help the retailers to update about latest company news, showcase employee recognition, and virtually host an event. This may go a long way in fostering feelings of camaraderie as well as belonging among staff members. These recommendations, if implemented by retailers, have the potential to foster a conducive environment and engage workers. Improved morale, productivity, and customer services will consequently be realized.

References

Abarantyne, I., Naidoo, V., & Rugimbana, R. (2019). The impact of psychological contracts on employee engagement at a university of technology. *SA Journal of Human Resource Management, 17*(1), 1–11.

Benitez, J., Ruiz, L., & Popovic, A. (2022). Impact of mobile technology-enabled HR gamification on employee performance: An empirical investigation. *Information & Management, 59*(4), 103647.

Dash, B., & Mohanty, P. K. (2019). The effects of work environment, self-evaluation at workplace and employee morale on employee engagement. *Srusti Management Review, 12*(1), 33–39.

Dewhurst, M., Guthridge, M., & Mohr, E. (2009). Motivating people: Getting beyond money. *McKinsey Quarterly, 1*(4), 12–15.

Dhavale, Y. (2019). Business intelligence in retail industry and E-commerce. *International Journal for Research in Applied Science and Engineering Technology, 7*(5), 58–61. https://doi.org/10.22214/ijraset.2019.5010

Fihartini, Y., Helmi, A., Hassan, M., & Marty Oesman, Y. (2021). Perceived health risk, online retail ethics, and consumer behavior within online shopping during the COVID-19 pandemic. *Innovative Marketing, 17*(3), 17–29. https://doi.org/10.21511/im.17(3).2021.02

Giri, A., Chatterjee, S., Paul, P., & Chakraborty, S. (2019). Determining the impact of artificial intelligence on 'developing marketing strategies' in organized retail sector of West Bengal, India. *International Journal of Engineering and Advanced Technology, 8*(6), 3031–3036. https://doi.org/10.35940/ijeat.f9030.088619

Khando, K., Gao, S., Islam, S. M., & Salman, A. (2021). Enhancing employees' information security awareness in private and public organisations: A systematic literature review. *Computers & Security, 106*, 102267.

Kim, K. K., Park, H. J., & Kim, J. H. (2022). Identification of Herzberg's motivators and hygiene factors for mobile shopping service system based on topic modeling of user reviews. *Informatics and Service Science, 9*(1), 156–176.

Krishnan, L. R. K. (2021). Impact on employee morale and job satisfaction: A case study of Telecom industry network outsourcing. *Journal of the International Academy for Case Studies, 27*(1), 1–8.

Ladson, D. (2019). *Strategies for increasing employee morale and mitigating turnover in the banking industry* (Doctoral dissertation, Walden University).

Leonova, I. S., Pesennikova-Sechenov, E. V., Legky, N. M., Prasolov, V. I., Krutskikh, I. A., & Zayed, N. M. (2021). Strategic analysis of the motivation on employees' productivity: A compensation benefits, training and development perspective. *Academy of Strategic Management Journal, 20*, 1–11.

Mallik, A., Mallik, L., & Keerthi, D. S. (2019). Impact of employee morale on organizational success. *International Journal of Recent Technology and Engineering (IJRTE), 8*(4), 3289–3293.

Nakypbayev, K. (2022). *Impact of training programs on employee job satisfaction, motivation, and turnover on the comparative example of retail branches and franchises.*

Noor, A., & Ampornstira, F. (2019). Effect of leadership on employee morale in higher education. *International Journal of Business and Social Science, 10*(7), 141–144.

Panori, A., Kakderi, C., Komninos, N., Fellnhofer, K., Reid, A., & Mora, L. (2021). Smart systems of innovation for smart places: Challenges in deploying digital platforms for co-creation and data-intelligence. *Land Use Policy, 111*, 104631. https://doi.org/10.1016/j.landusepol.2020.104631

Parker, S. K., & Grote, G. (2022). Automation, algorithms, and beyond: Why work design matters more than ever in a digital world. *Applied Psychology, 71*(4), 1171–1204.

Pattnaik, L., & Jena, L. K. (2020). Mindfulness, remote engagement, and employee morale: Conceptual analysis to address the "new normal". *International Journal of Organizational Analysis, 29*(4), 873–890.

Rotz, S., Gravely, E., Mosby, I., Duncan, E., Finnis, E., Horgan, M., LeBlanc, J., Martin, R., Neufeld, H. T., Nixon, A., & Pant, L. (2019). Automated pastures and the digital divide: How agricultural technologies are shaping labour and rural communities. *Journal of Rural Studies, 68*, 112–122.

Sapta, I., Muafi, M., & Setini, N. M. (2021). The role of technology, organizational culture, and job satisfaction in improving employee performance during the Covid-19 pandemic. *The Journal of Asian Finance, Economics and Business, 8*(1), 495–505.

Soetjipto, N., Priyohadi, N., Sulastri, S., & Riswanto, A. (2021). The effect of company climate, organization citizenship behavior, and transformational leadership on work morale through employee job satisfaction. *Management Science Letters, 11*(4), 1197–1204.

Zhang, C., Khan, I., Dagar, V., Saeed, A., & Zafar, M. W. (2022). Environmental impact of information and communication technology: Unveiling the role of education in developing countries. *Technological Forecasting and Social Change, 178*, 121570.

Zheng, C., Molineux, J., Mirshekary, S., & Scarparo, S. (2015). Developing individual and organizational work-life balance strategies to improve employee health and wellbeing. *Employee Relations, 37*(3), 354–379. https://doi.org/10.1108/er-10-2013-0142

Principal Versus Agent: Are Universities Doing Their Jobs?

Carla Serfontein

Abstract This article considers the principal–agent relationship between top management at universities as agents and the government and students as principals to assess the extent to which the top management of South African universities adhere to the primary objective of their stakeholders. Quantitative data were used first to determine whether universities provided affordable education by focusing on the increases in tuition fees at a sample of publicly funded South African universities from 2010 to 2019 (explicitly excluding the impact of COVID-19). Secondly, an analysis of the enrolments and graduates at the 26 South African public universities for a sample of Classification of Educational Subject Matter Categories (CESMs) was analysed from 2010 to 2021. The findings were then interpreted using the Future of Jobs Survey of 2020 by the World Economic Forum to determine whether universities served the main objective of their primary stakeholders, that is, to deliver affordable, relevant education that will enhance employability. From the analyses performed and literature reviewed in this study, in South Africa, the country with the highest unemployment rate and income inequality in the world, publicly funded universities failed to (a) deliver affordable education, (b) offer relevant education that would adequately prepare graduates for future employment in the changing global business environment; and (c) fulfil their responsibilities as agents of their principals. The information provided in this study could be a starting point for top management at universities to determine a strategy to ensure that they can efficiently act as agents in the best interest of their principals.

Keywords Agency theory · Universities · Employability · Technological disruption · Top management · Public universities

C. Serfontein (✉)
University of the Free State, Bloemfontein, South Africa
e-mail: SerfonteinC@ufs.ac.za

T. Moloi (ed.), *Impacting Society Positively Through Technology in Accounting and Business Processes*, Springer Proceedings in Business and Economics,
https://doi.org/10.1007/978-3-031-84885-8_7

Introduction and Background

Universities are at a crossroads (Serfontein, 2022, p. 14). Technological disruption has changed both how and what universities teach and will continue to do so. The competitive advantage of traditional (face-to-face and on-campus) universities of geographical location and cost seems to be on the decrease, because globally, education is moving towards an online approach (Serfontein, 2022, pp. 99–100). This move to online education means that students can now study at the best institutions in the world at a reduced cost (Collub, 2016, para. 21). In response to this move to online education, enrolments specifically in the United Kingdom and South Africa have declined noticeably since 2019, despite an increase up to the said date (Adams, 2022; Staff Writer, 2023a, para. 1).

In an attempt to adhere to their existing expense structure, universities significantly increased tuition fees above inflation despite the rise in enrolments up to 2019 (Burer & Fethke, 2016, p. 182; Koornhof, 2020, para. 7; Mtshali, 2020, para. 19; Perović & Kosor, 2020, para. 16). Even though most industries have experienced decreased costs and increased efficiency over the last few decades, the increase in tuition fees whilst enrolments increased indicates that universities did not benefit from economies of scale and were subject to significant cost increases (Cooper, 2020, para. 14). Indications point to tuition fee increases stemming from internal inefficiencies, rather than global events.

This study applies the Agency theory to publicly funded universities which could provide a unique approach to assessing higher education's financial performance and efficiency. Already in 2009, Cunningham (2009, p. 444) indicated that universities were facing a principal–agent problem. The primary rationale underlying the statement from Cunningham (2009, p. 444) is the information asymmetry in the decisions of university administrators (top management). Moving forward to 2023, this problem appears to have intensified. In 2016, Huang (2016, p. 1335) pointed out the scarcity of studies applying Agency theory to the higher education sector. The author of this paper did not find a noticeable increase in related studies up to 2023. By focusing on the Agency theory as applicable to publicly funded universities, this paper aims to contribute to filling that gap.

Agency theory studies problems arising from task delegation between principals and agents because of the conflict of interest between the related parties as well as solutions to these problems (Linder & Foss, 2015, p. 344). According to Huang et al., (2016, p. 1334), wherever there is a party (agent) that another party (principal) relies upon to perform the duties of the principal, an agency relationship is present. Part of the focus of the Agency theory is the achievement of efficiency from the principal's perspective in the presence of an agency relationship (Huang et al., 2016, p. 1334).

When considering the role of an agent in a public company, according to Damodaran (2015, pp. 10–11), there should only be one primary objective in corporate finance: to maximize shareholders' value. Whilst the mentioned author acknowledges the fact that some experts are of the opinion that there could be multiple primary objectives, he firmly asserts that having multiple objectives complicates the decision-making process. Although having only one primary objective is more difficult for non-profit organisations, Damodaran (2015, p. 13) maintains a strong position that having multiple objectives complicates the decision-making process.

When applying the Agency theory to universities, the first step is to establish who the principal and the agent are. According to Van Thiel and Smullen (2021, p. 760), when applying this theory to non-profit organisations, a dyadic relationship exists between a political principal and an agent. When examining publicly funded universities, given that the two main income streams of these institutions are subsidies from the government and tuition fees paid by students, it would be reasonable to classify the government and students as the two main principals of publicly funded universities (Editorial, 2022, para. 2). The agent in this scenario is the party responsible for ensuring the objectives of the principal are met, and in the context of universities, this typically refers to the top management of these institutions (Van Thiel & Smullen, 2021, p. 760).

The second step in applying the Agency theory to publicly funded universities is to determine what the primary objective of these universities should be. A traditional university's objectives are typically threefold, that is, teaching, research, and public service as an additional task (Perkins, 1973, pp. 3–12; Etzkowitz et al., 2000, p. 313; Walton & Martin, 2004, p. 11; Bikse et al., 2016, p. 76). These objectives are translated into strategies that encompass variations of "research-led", "research university", "world-leading centre of learning, teaching and research", "research intensive", "internationally distinguished for research" and "student-centred" as their main focus (Staff writer, n.d.-a, para. 1; n.d.-b, para. 1; n.d.-d, para. 1; n.d.-e, para. 1). Depending on the long-term focus of the university, each of these strategic directions could be an objective of the related university. However, since Damodaran suggests focusing on one main objective to apply the Agency theory to an organisation, although it might be open for debate, the author holds the view that providing affordable education to ensure employability should be central to the primary objective of universities (Smit & Serfontein, 2019, p. 1332). This purpose is supported in South Africa, with the highest unemployment rate and income inequality in the world. This high unemployment rate is accentuated by the graduate unemployment rate for the first quarter of 2023 of 10.6%, an increase of 4 percentage points from the first quarter of 2015 and the youth unemployment rate of 51.5% in 2022 (Staff Writer, 2023b, para. 1; Statistics South Africa, 2023, para. 3). The other objectives of traditional universities will not be considered further in this study focusing on the application of Agency theory to universities.

Top management of universities could (and would) prefer to focus on research, industry involvement, community service and international standing, to mention a few alternatives, as part of their multifaceted objectives (Petersen, 2023, para. 10; Staniulyte, 2022, p. 2971). But, given the fact that the top management of universities, as agents, are appointed to act in the interest of the principals, the determination of their primary objective should not solely be at their discretion but a decision involving the two principals, namely students and the government. Considering the above-mentioned income inequality and unemployment, South African youth cannot afford to seek education that is unaffordable or that will not enhance their chances of employment.

Similar to public companies, top management of universities cannot decide WHAT the primary objective of their institutions is but only decide HOW to achieve it. The agents (top management) can, therefore, decide that research, industry involvement and community service, to mention a few, are the secondary objectives (the HOW) of the university but that they should comply with the primary objective (the WHAT) as formulated by the government and students as the principals. Nobody in the academic environment can deny the importance of these secondary objectives of universities, but the question is, to what extent these secondary objectives hurt the primary objective. Whilst it is acknowledged that there will inevitably be some degree of cross-subsidising to fund the various objectives of a university, the precise levels of this cross-subsidising would depend on a variety of factors as well as assessment and planning (Lewis & Pendlebury, 2002, p. 36). For every expense spent on an activity without the corresponding revenue, another activity must forfeit part of its revenue. A critical question to ask is whether these activities (secondary objectives) driven by the top management of many universities are strategically essential for the future sustainability of the institution or driven by ego and status. Regardless, the main issue is that if universities are funding too many (and spending too much on) secondary activities at the expense of their primary objective, namely to provide affordable education to ensure employability, they are creating a substantial Agency problem; thus, the agent is not acting in the best interest of the principal (Espinosa-Méndez et al., 2023, p. 5; Gogineni et al., 2022, p. 1237).

Typically, where there is a principal–agent relationship, a conflict of interest exists between management (agents) and principals, referring to the Agency problem (Damodaran, 2015, p. 12). Management (agents) often want to maximise their own salaries and maximise short-term profits to earn bonuses or grow the company for the wrong reasons, such as status and image, at the expense of the maximisation of shareholders' (principals) value. The principal will have to mitigate these risks by increasing the control and monitoring of the agent or through incentives, which add more costs to the price of hiring an agent (Huang et al., 2016, p. 1335; Van Thiel & Smullen, 2021, pp. 760–761). One of the best ways to mitigate the Agency problem, according to Damodaran (2015, p. 20), is to have predominantly independent directors on the board representing and elected by the stakeholders. Although this aspect is not the specific focus of this research study, it could be valuable for further research to establish how members on university boards are selected and by whom. If this is primarily decided by the top management of the related university, it invalidates the corporate governance of these institutions to ensure that top management addresses the primary objective of the principals.

The main focus and aim of this research article are to assess the extent to which the top management of South African publicly funded universities adhere to the primary objectives of their principals, using the Agency theory as a point of reference. In practical terms, this implies that whatever the top management of a university decides as their secondary objectives, it should not jeopardize or compromise affordable education to enhance employability as part of the primary objectives of the government and students as their principals. The author acknowledges that this approach may spark a heated debate amongst academics about the nature and culture of universities, and rightfully so. However, it is important to note that these broader issues fall beyond the scope of this article. Despite universities being non-profit organisations, it is imperative to recognise that measures of financial efficiency can still be applicable.

Agency Theory

The focus of the literature reviewed is a discussion of the challenges related to the Agency theory, since the Agency theory is already applied to universities in the Introduction and Background to this study (see Sect. "Introduction and Background"). However, to truly understand where the problem with the application of the Agency theory at universities lies, the role of universities must be understood. This role should coincide with the primary purpose of universities, as stated for the purpose of this study, of providing affordable education that should enhance employability.

The Role and Purpose of Publicly Funded Universities

According to the Vice-Chancellor of the University of the Free State, universities are globally regarded as important for the development of economies, societies and individuals. The role that these institutions play in research, dissemination and application of knowledge, and as centres of innovation, is critical in contributing to solving global challenges (Petersen, 2023, para. 3). Universities, though, are quick to defend their independence, wanting full autonomy regarding the modules and programmes they offer, but public service remains one of the main roles of a university. This role is often translated into modules presented purely to fulfil the social responsibility of the university in line with what their immediate community requires (Bikse et al., 2016, p. 76; Etzkowitz et al., 2000, p. 3; Perkins, 1973, pp. 3–12; Walton and Martin, 2004, p. 11).

In a study performed by Serfontein and Smit (2021, pp. 182–183) where the financial viability of modules at a specifically selected publicly funded university in South Africa was investigated, 1769 modules (out of 3689, i.e. 47.9%) did not cover even the direct cost of presenting them. These modules, however, contained only 5.2% of the total enrolments at the related university. The implication of these figures is that if the university decided to close these modules, only 14,867 out of the total 286,832 enrolments at the related university, a negligible number, would be impacted. The question is, would the university, in presenting this high percentage of loss-making modules, indeed serve its community? In contrast, 1391 undergraduate and 461 postgraduate modules (amounting to 46.4%) at the selected university covered not only their direct costs but also all the indirect (other) costs of the institution. The findings from Serfontein and Smit (2021, p. 186) were that these levels of cross-subsidisation would not be acceptable in any organisation and that the universities in similar situations should consider whether these cross-subsidised modules are making any real impact on the need for relevant education that will ensure employability to the community it serves. Employability can be defined as "a set of achievements – skills, understandings and personal attributes – that makes graduates more likely to gain employment and be successful in their chosen occupations, which benefits themselves, the workforce, the community and the economy" (Tsiligiris & Bowyer, 2021, p. 623; Yorke, 2005, p. 8). This definition of employability accentuates that graduates require both technical and soft (emotional) skills to enhance their chances of being employed in the future. Universities, when considering enhancing employability as part of their primary purpose, should have the ability to equip students with the required employability skills. This employability will be explored further in the empirical research of the current study (see Sect. "Employability of Graduates").

The introduction to this study focused both on "What" universities should achieve (their primary purpose) and "How" this primary purpose should be achieved. From the introduction and background of this study (see Sect. "Introduction and Background"), universities, as agents of students and the government, should provide affordable education that will enhance employability. However, when considering the strategies and marketing material of many publicly funded universities in South Africa, it appears as if these universities became more focused on 'How', that is, increasing research, student-centred, etc., than in fact focusing on their primary purpose and, therefore, the research question in this study is whether top management at universities fulfilled their responsibility as agents (Staff writer n.d.-a, para. 1; Staff writer n.d.-b, para. 1; Staff writer n.d.-c, para. 1; Staff writer n.d.-d, para. 1; Staff writer, n.d.-e, para. 1).

The Agency Problem

Wherever there is a party (agent) that another party (principal) relies upon to perform the duties of the principal, an agency relationship is present (Huang et al., 2016, p. 1334). Agency theory focuses on the achievement of efficiency from the principal's perspective in the presence of an agency relationship (Huang et al., 2016, p. 1334).

When considering the possible financial crisis universities are facing, students and the government are the two main principals at these institutions (see Sect. "Introduction and Background"). The student (specifically in South Africa) seeks affordable education that will enhance future employability (and income) and pays tuition fees as part of this pursuit (see the related discussion in Sect. "Introduction and Background"). The government subsidises universities with the objective of equal opportunity for all citizens to be employed and to increase their income potential, decreasing poverty, increasing earnings potential, and therefore increasing economic growth. The students' and the government's pursuits are dependent on the skills provided by academic staff, potentially making them a third principal (Van Thiel & Smullen, 2021, p. 760).

The Agency theory oversees the relationship between principals and agents within an organisation operating on the premise that principals inherently lack trust in agents to fulfil their agreed-upon duties, necessitating additional control and monitoring measures (Van Thiel & Smullen, 2021, p. 758). What this distrust entails is goal divergence, where the agent primarily serves their own goals and not necessarily the goals of the principal (Huang et al., 2016, p. 1335; Van Thiel & Smullen, 2021, p. 759). The principal, therefore, pays the agent to carry out specified tasks, with the assumption that both parties act rationally, that is, in their own self-interest. The different self-interests of the principal and agent cause goal divergence, potentially leading to conflict. This conflict is increased due to information asymmetry, since the agent is usually an expert with substantially more information on what their task involves and how to fulfil this task (Van Thiel & Smullen, 2021, p. 758). This information asymmetry poses a risk to the principal that they will agree to less advantageous circumstances upon hiring the agent, like paying inflated prices or a moral risk in the agent not fulfilling their role to the best of their ability. The distrust and lack of goal congruence between agents (top management at universities for the purpose of this study) and shareholders, that is, principals (the government and students for the purpose of this study), is simplified by stating that agents should, but very often don't, act in the best interest of principals. Agents rather redirect or consume the organisation's resources for their own instead of the principal's benefit. This conflict is referred to as the Agency problem (Espinosa-Méndez et al., 2023, p. 5; Gogineni et al., 2022, p. 1237). The main purpose of this study is to determine whether agents at publicly funded South African universities act in the best interest of their principals, focusing on the affordability and relevance of higher education to enhance employability.

Methodology

Research Method

The empirical research of this study makes use of quantitative data. The quantitative data are used to first determine whether universities provided affordable education by focusing on the increases in tuition fees at South African publicly funded universities. Secondly, an analysis of the enrolments and graduates at the 26 South African publicly funded universities for a sample of Classification of Educational Subject Matter Categories (CESMs) will be analysed. Part of the analysis of the enrolments and graduates is an analysis of the Future of Jobs Survey of 2020 by the World Economic Forum (WEF), as reported by Zahidi (2020), together with literature enhancing the findings in the report. This analysis is to determine what jobs will be more and less in demand to evaluate whether top management at universities acted in line with their primary objective of providing education that will enhance employability. All the data used were secondary data in the public domain, obtained from the PowerHEDA dashboard (Staff Writer, 2023a).

Enrolment Analysis

The analysis of the enrolments in the sampled CESMs was performed using Full-time equivalent enrolments (FTEs). FTEs are defined as "A measurement equal to one student enrolled full time for one academic year" (Staff writer, 2003, p. 1). The author is of the opinion that FTEs are the best measure to consider in analysing enrolments, since they provide a uniform measure for all CESMs without taking the weight added for funding purposes, as is the case with Teaching input/output units into account. FTEs are also used by The South African Department of Higher Education and Training (DHET) (2015, pp. 4–5) as a measure of growth in student enrolments in their calculation of the Block Grant per FTE.

Part of the enrolment analysis of publicly funded universities in South Africa is an analysis of the number of graduates. This analysis used the number of graduates of the 26 publicly funded universities as reported by the Student Headcount Report on the PowerHEDA dashboard (Staff Writer, 2023a). The analysis of the number of graduates was only done in total for the three Categories explained in Sect. "Description of Sample", not for the sampled CESMs.

Description of Sample

The focus of this study is on publicly funded universities in South Africa. Currently, South Africa has 26 publicly funded universities (Universities South Africa, 2018, para. 1). The sample used in this study consisted of all 26 universities, making the sample used representative of 100% of the population. The 26 universities for the purpose of this study were further classified into three groups. Firstly, the 2024 QS World University Rankings were used to determine the top seven South African publicly funded universities (Fraser, 2023b, para. 2). The 2024 QS World University Rankings considered 1500 higher education institutions in 104 locations, highlighting sustainability and employability. The outcome of these rankings is based on more than 17 million academic papers and experts' opinions from around 250,000 academics and employers (Fraser, 2023b, paras. 2–3). The 2024 version of the rankings added three new measurements, that is, sustainability, international research network and employment outcomes. Since employability was flagged as a substantial feature of the study accompanying the said rankings (achieved by increasing the weight of "Employer Reputation Employment Outcomes" as included in the overall score), the researcher is of the opinion that the 2024 QS World University Rankings are a substantial indicator of the top universities achieving the primary objective of universities related to enhancing the employability of graduates (Fraser, 2023b, paras. 4–5).

The remaining 19 universities (26 excluding the top seven) were further split into "other universities" and "technical universities". Technical universities are all universities classified as universities of technology, whilst other universities, for purposes of this study, consist of the 26 publicly funded universities excluding the top seven and technical universities.

What can be considered a further sample is the number of CESMs analysed. CESMs are prescribed by DHET to standardise the classification of higher education institutions' subject matter embedded in their courses or fields of study before submitting their Higher Education Information Management System (HEMIS) annual data returns (Department of Education, 2008, p. 1). DHET prescribes 20 main CESMs listed in Table 1, reduced from 22 CESMs in 1982 (Department of Education, 2008, pp. 2, 4).

Table 1 2008 subject matter categories

CESM Code	Description
01	Agriculture, agricultural operations and related sciences
02	Architecture and the built environment
03	Visual and performing arts
04	Business, economics and management studies
05	Communication, journalism and related studies
06	Computer and information sciences
07	Education
08	Engineering
09	Health professions and related clinical sciences
10	Family ecology and consumer sciences
11	Languages, linguistics and literature
12	Law
13	Life sciences
14	Physical sciences
15	Mathematics and statistics
16	Military sciences
17	Philosophy, religion and theology
18	Psychology
19	Public management and services
20	Social sciences

Source: (Department of Education, 2008, p. 4)

From the 20 CESMs listed in Table 1, four were selected for the purpose of this study. These four CESMs were purposively selected since the primary objective of this study was to determine whether top management at traditional South African universities as agents act in the best interest of their principals (government and students) in terms of offering affordable, relevant education that most likely will enhance employability. The four CESMs sampled for the purpose of this study were:

CESM 06: Computer and Information Sciences

CESM 07: Education

CESM 12: Law

CESM 15: Mathematics and Statistics

The researcher is of the opinion that CESM 06 and CESM 15 should provide graduates with skills aligned with future job requirements in the changing business environment mentioned in the background and introduction to this study (see Sect. "Introduction and Background"). The future job requirements are discussed in more detail in the results in Sect. "Employability of Graduates". Therefore, if universities acted in the best interest of their principals, they should have aimed to boost enrolments, at least in these two CESMs. When considering the opposite, Law (CESM 12) and Education (CESM 07) are subject areas that are not increasing in demand when considering job opportunities. The researcher, therefore, expects universities, when acting in the best interest of their principals, would not prioritise increasing enrolments in these two CESMs. The actual growth in enrolments in the sampled CESMs is discussed in Sect. "Employability of Graduates".

Discussion of Results

The Introduction and Background, and the literature reviewed in this study underscored the notion that, as per Damodaran (2015, p. 3), organisations should focus on a single primary objective. As established through the application of the Agency theory, universities acting in the best interest of their primary stakeholders or principals, that is, the government and students, should provide affordable education that will enhance employability. The main research question this paper aims to answer is whether top management at publicly funded South African universities as agents acted in the best interest of their principals. This main question will be answered by determining firstly how affordable a university education in South Africa is and, secondly, whether universities provide education in scientific areas aligned with the requirements of the 4IR, technological disruption and the changing business environment.

Tuition Fee Increases

In a previous study by Serfontein (2022, p. 240) was found that tuition fees at a sample of 16 (out of 26) South African publicly funded universities increased above the rate of inflation from 2010 to 2019 (specifically excluding the impact of COVID-19). This increase in tuition fees amounted to an average of 10.61% per annum. The total increase above inflation amounted to R138.2 million (or 15.5%) for the sample of 16 universities. When considering affordability for the purpose of this study, the 15.5% increase in tuition fees above inflation must be seen in the light of an increase in the national minimum wage of South Africa from R20 per hour in 2019 (when national minimum wages were first introduced), to R25.42 per hour for 2023, an increase of 27% or an average increase of 6.16% per annum (Heinrich Böll Stiftung, 2023, p. 7; Omarjee, 2019, para. 3). The total revenue above inflation for the related sample amounted to R137.1 million, clearly indicating that tuition fees, not other revenue or subsidies and grants, were increasing above budget from 2010 to 2019 (taking the growth in enrolments over the same period into account), which confirms that the sampled universities used an increase in tuition fees to increase their revenue from 2010 to 2019.

A further finding with a substantial impact with regard to the responsibility of top management at universities as agents of the government and shareholders is that in the same study by Serfontein (2022, p. 240), the increase in tuition fees above inflation was not applicable to the total sample of 16 universities, rendering it unlikely that there could be a common external variable causing the increases. Furthermore, the increase in tuition fees from the findings by Serfontein (2022, p. 216) was primarily to fund the increasing salaries of top management, service and support departments (also referred to as overhead expenses) not directly related to academic personnel, an increase again not uniform for the related sample. These increases, therefore, highlight the role top management at these institutions played in fulfilling their responsibility towards students as one of their primary stakeholders, directly related to the Agency problem. The author is of the opinion that there is little to no justification, from a financial management perspective, substantiating the increases in tuition fees. These increases are purely to the detriment of poor students who need affordable education. Had the increase been to ensure that academic personnel were upskilled for the changing needs of employers and the future work environment of graduates, some form of justification might have been warranted; however, this did not seem to be the case.

The importance of having a single primary objective at public universities to ensure that agents act in the best interest of the stakeholders in providing affordable education to enhance employment (the WHAT) cannot be accentuated enough. The levels of overspending on non-core activities and the cross-subsidising of secondary objectives seen in the increase in other salaries seem to be the main reasons for the unacceptable increase in tuition fees and, thus, the failure to provide affordable education (Serfontein, 2022, p. 216). In the next part of the empirical study, the focus will be on the future of jobs and CESMs with the intent to determine whether

South African public universities are addressing the rapidly changing skills needed to enhance the employability of their graduates.

Employability of Graduates

To determine whether universities did, in fact, contribute to their graduates' ability to be employed in the future, the future job demand and skills required by employers must first be established. From these findings, the enrolments and graduates for a sample of CESMs from 2010 to 2021 will be analysed.

Future of Jobs

When considering the needs of employers and the changing business environment, the mere mention of the 4IR, which includes breakthroughs such as Quantum computing, IoT, Nanotechnology, Blockchain technology, AI, Biotechnology, Neurotechnology and Space technology, in South Africa, raises fear of substantial job losses, specifically when considering the prediction of machines replacing people (De Vries & Kroukamp, 2022, p. 5; Mahlaka, 2020, para. 14). For the purposes of this study, an in-depth understanding of each of these technological breakthroughs is not required. What is indeed crucial to highlight, however, is that these changes present both challenges and opportunities if the response to these changes is effective. This response is intricately linked to education.

One aspect that requires revaluation at universities is the existing curricula. The rationale behind this revaluation is grounded in an estimate that 50% of the knowledge a student in a four-year degree acquires in their first year is outdated by the time of their graduation (Coetzee et al., 2021, pp. 1–2). A further estimate by the WEF (2016, p. 3) is that up to 65% of learners entering primary school today will eventually pursue careers in occupations that do not currently exist. The rate of change in required knowledge may accelerate with the increasing impact of the 4IR. In South Africa, a country plagued by unemployment (32.9% during the first quarter of 2023), any prediction of additional job losses can raise anxiety levels of all parties involved (Statistics South Africa, 2023, para. 3). The only way in which universities can counter the predicted job losses associated with the 4IR is to provide graduates with the skills required to enhance their employability (Tsiligiris & Bowyer, 2021, p. 623; Yorke, 2005, p. 8).

According to the Future of Jobs Survey 2020 by the WEF, as reported by Zahidi (2020, p. 29), approximately 85 million jobs are projected to be displaced due to changes in the labour division between machines and humans. Fortunately, this shift will also create 97 million new roles already aligned with the new labour division, including the use of algorithms. Unfortunately, a crisis is arising where students are trained for jobs that soon might not exist, whereas the skills they obtained should have made them employable (Editorial, 2014, p. 1; Frey & Osborne, 2017, pp. 269–278; RBC, 2018, p. 2). The onus is on universities to provide the right skills for emerging roles to ensure the employability of graduates. Table 2 summarises the demand for various jobs as found in the 2020 Future of Jobs Survey (Zahidi et al., 2020, p. 30).

Table 2 clearly indicates that data analysts and scientists, big data specialists and digital marketing and strategy specialists are the top three jobs that are increasing in demand, whilst data entry clerks, administrative and executive secretaries and accounting, bookkeeping and payroll clerks are the top three jobs that are decreasing in demand. According to Frey and Osborne (2017, p. 255), jobs that are more likely to be automatised are routine intensive with clearly defined procedures for which an algorithm can easily be established. These jobs entail activities that are

Table 2 Future of jobs survey

Increasing demand		Decreasing demand	
1	Data analysts and scientists	1	Data entry clerks
2	AI and machine learning specialists	2	Administrative and executive secretaries
3	Big data specialists	3	Accounting, bookkeeping and payroll clerks
4	Digital marketing and strategy specialists	4	Accountants and auditors
5	Process automation specialists	5	Assembly and factory workers
6	Business development professionals	6	Business services and administration managers
7	Digital transformation specialists	7	Client information and customer service workers
8	Information security analysts	8	General and operations managers
9	Software and applications developers	9	Mechanics and machinery repairers
10	Internet of things specialists	10	Material-recording and stock-keeping clerks
11	Project managers	11	Financial analysts
12	Business services and administration managers	12	Postal service clerks
13	Database and network professionals	13	Sales representatives, wholesale and manufacturing, technology and science products
14	Robotics engineers	14	Relationship managers
15	Strategic advisors	15	Bank tellers and related clerks
16	Management and organisation analysts	16	Door-to-door sales, news and street vendors
17	FinTech engineers	17	Electronics and telecoms installers and repairers
18	Mechanics and machinery repairers	18	Human resources specialists
19	Organisational development specialists	19	Training and development specialists
20	Risk management specialists	20	Construction labourers

Source: (Zahidi et al., 2020, p. 30)

repetitive, methodical and have specified directions (Autor et al. 2003, p. 1283; Jaimovich & Siu, 2012, p. 7).

When considering non-routine tasks, they entail problem-solving, human interaction and adaptability, activities for which an algorithm is not easily achievable (Autor et al. 2003, p. 1283; Jaimovich & Siu, 2012, p. 7). Non-routine tasks typically entail professional and technical work and management. Tasks can also be classified as either cognitive (processing new information) or manual. Occupations consisting of non-routine cognitive tasks include physicians, economists, public relations officers and analysts. Routine cognitive tasks are typically data entry and administration, office support, sales occupations, and mail clerks. Examples of routine manual occupations are "blue-collar" occupations, including mechanics, machine operators and dressmakers. Janitors, bartenders, manicurists and health aids are examples of non-routine, manual occupations (Acemoglu & Autor, 2010, p. 78; Cortes, 2016, p. 78). Routine occupations are also referred to as middle-skills occupations and are at the highest risk of being automated (Acemoglu & Autor, 2010, p. 78; Cortes, 2016, p. 78; Frey & Osborne, 2017, p. 78). University offerings aimed at employing graduates in any middle-skills occupations will decrease in relevance as job offerings at this level decrease (Serfontein, 2019, pp. 41–42).

The next section of this article will evaluate the enrolments at traditional universities in South Africa to establish whether these institutions acted in the best interest of students by improving enrolments in subject areas and adhering to the predicted changes in the job market. This should have been the case if top management at traditional universities acted in accordance with their responsibility as agents of their principals, providing relevant education that would enhance employability.

Enrolment and Graduate Growth at South African Universities

When analysing the effectiveness of enrolment changes in traditional universities, the total enrolment growth should be considered as a benchmark. In this study, FTEs will represent enrolments (see Sect. "Enrolment Analysis"). In Table 3, the total FTEs of the 26 publicly funded universities in South Africa are considered. This table focuses on the growth in FTEs from 2010 to 2021 and also categorises the universities between the traditional universities as identified in the past and technical universities, and specifically highlights the findings from the top seven

Table 3 Growth and composition of FTEs

	FTEs		Growth	Composition	
ALL	2010	2021	2010–21	2010	2021
Universities	*485,567*	*650,139*	*33.9%*	*81.1%*	*82.6%*
Top (7)	207,102	237,812	14.8%	34.6%	30.2%
Other (11)	278,465	412,326	48.1%	46.5%	52.4%
Technical universities (8)	*113,324*	*137,089*	*21.0%*	*18.9%*	*17.4%*
Total	*598,891*	*787,228*	*31.4%*	*100.0%*	*100.0%*

universities as determined by the QS World University Rankings (see Sect. "Description of Sample").

From the results presented in Table 3, the general growth rate in FTEs at South African universities was 31.4% from 2010 to 2021. When considering the three categories presented, the top seven universities experienced a lower growth rate at 14.8%, technical universities at 21.0%, and the most substantial increase in FTEs occurred in other universities not included in the top seven (48.1%). The findings presented in Table 3 support the notion that universities experienced sufficient growth in student numbers (and revenue accordingly) that, in an environment of predominantly fixed and period costs, the increase in revenue should have covered (at least in part) the additional costs to upskill academics in line with the changing skills required of graduates. However, this growth in FTEs, coupled with increases in tuition fees, indicates that the increase in tuition fees highlighted at the beginning of this section was not to the benefit of students. The findings in Table 2 confirm that top management at universities as agents may not have prioritised the best interests of students as principals at a university. When considering the quality of the education provided, the growth and composition of graduates, as indicated in Table 4, is cause for concern.

Focusing on the same categories used in Tables 3 and 4 presents the growth in the number of graduates delivered by the publicly funded universities in South Africa. Focusing on the composition of graduates, the top seven universities contributed the highest percentage of total graduates in 2010 (43.3%). Moving on to 2021, the composition changed substantially, with the top seven now only delivering 33.4% (decreasing by almost 10 percentage points from 2010) of graduates and other universities (excluding technical universities) responsible for 46.5% of total graduates. If the growth rate of graduates from 2010 to 2021 is considered, it is concerning that South Africa's top universities registered only a 17.4% increase over the last decade. In contrast, other universities and technical universities increased their graduate numbers by 91.1% and 55.3%, respectively. When comparing the growth rate in graduates with the growth in FTEs, a few questions require answers. Did the overall standard of university education improve to such an extent that FTEs grew by 31.4%, but graduates grew at over 20 percentage points more (52.1%)? Did the quality of teaching at other universities really improve so considerably that their FTEs grew by 48.1%, but their graduates increased by 91.1%? Are the top seven universities doing something wrong that their rate of increase in graduates (17.4%)

Table 4 Growth and composition of graduates

	Graduates		Growth	Composition	
ALL	2010	2021	2010–21	2010	2021
Universities	*123,123*	*186,352*	*51.4%*	*80.3%*	*79.9%*
Top 7	66,401	77,946	17.4%	43.3%	33.4%
Other	56,722	108,406	91.1%	37.0%	46.5%
Technical universities	*30,204*	*46,905*	*55.3%*	*19.7%*	*20.1%*
Total	*153,327*	*233,257*	*52.1%*	*100.0%*	*100.0%*

is more aligned with the growth in FTEs (14.8%)? In a country with "one of the worst performing education systems in the world", according to Ann Bernstein, Executive Director of the Centre for Development and Enterprise (CDE) (Fraser, 2023a, para. 15), a statement indicative of the ability of students coming out of secondary schooling, it is clear the scholars coming into university is not improving to an extent justifying the increase in graduates.

A further finding from the Serfontein (2022) study is that the expense category that grew at the highest rate from 2010 to 2019 at a sample of South African universities was other personnel salaries, not academic salaries. Hence, the increase in graduates could also not be a result of improving academics. The only logical deduction, therefore, is that the quality of education decreased to ensure an increased number of graduates. To state the impact of the increases in graduates presented in Table 4 in another way, universities are graduating students who might not have the skills required by their future employers. If graduates are decreasing in employability, universities are not fulfilling the employability requirement of their primary objective as agents. The increase in the graduate unemployment rate from 2015 to 2023 by 4 percentage points supports the notion that universities are possibly failing to enhance the employability of graduates (Statistics South Africa, 2023, p. 13). The impact of the increase in graduates might be justified and potentially beneficial if these increases were in modules or Categories (CESMs) that could improve the graduates' future employability status.

The starting point for evaluating how effectively universities increased enrolments in areas that are (or will be) in high demand as a result of the 4IR and the changing business environment is to consider the enrolment growth for the various CESMs. When considering the changes to the global business environment and, more specifically, the 4IR, CESM 06, Computer and Information Sciences and CESM 15, Mathematics and Statistics are examples of two CESMs that are expected to assist students with future employability skills, especially in the light of the jobs rising in demand (see Table 2). Tables 5 and 6 present the growth in FTEs in these CESMs from 2010 to 2021, including how much of the total FTEs are enrolled in these two CESMs.

Tables 5 and 6 present the overall growth in FTEs for the 26 public universities in South Africa from 2010 to 2021 of 31.4%. When considering the growth in FTEs for CESM 06 and CESM 15 from 2010 to 2021 at 20.3% and 20.1%, respectively,

Table 5 CESM 06: Computer and Information Sciences FTE growth and composition

	FTEs		Growth	% All FTEs	
CESM 06—Computer and Information Sciences	2010	2021	2010–21	2010	2021
Universities	*23,939*	*28,795*	*20.3%*	*4.9%*	*4.4%*
Top 7	7256	9270	27.8%	3.5%	3.9%
Other	16,683	19,525	17.0%	6.0%	4.7%
Technical universities	*12,614*	*15,163*	*20.2%*	*11.1%*	*11.1%*
Total	*36,553*	*43,958*	*20.3%*	*6.1%*	*5.6%*
ALL FTEs			*31.4%*		

Table 6 CESM 15: Mathematics and Statistics FTE growth and composition

	FTEs		Growth	% All FTEs	
CESM 15—Mathematics and Statistics	2010	2021	2010–2021	2010	2021
Universities	*21,327*	*25,625*	*20.2%*	*4.4%*	*3.9%*
Top 7	12,482	13,401	7.4%	6.0%	5.6%
Other	8844	12,224	38.2%	3.2%	3.0%
Technical universities	*3693*	*4436*	*20.1%*	*3.3%*	*3.2%*
Total	*25,020*	*30,061*	*20.1%*	*4.2%*	*3.8%*
ALL FTEs			*31.4%*		

Table 7 CESM 07: Education FTE growth and composition

	FTEs		Growth	% All FTEs	
CESM 07—Education	2010	2021	2010–2021	2010	2021
Universities	*74,685*	*109,058*	*46.0%*	*15.4%*	*16.8%*
Top 7	32,328	31,857	−1.5%	15.6%	13.4%
Other	42,357	77,202	82.3%	15.2%	18.7%
Technical universities	*6728*	*15,430*	*129.3%*	*5.9%*	*11.3%*
Total	*81,413*	*124,489*	*52.9%*	*13.6%*	*15.8%*
ALL FTEs			*31.4%*		

Table 8 CESM 12: Law FTE growth and composition

	FTEs		Growth	% All FTEs	
CESM 12—Law	2010	2021	2010–21	2010	2021
Universities	*40,117*	*65,299*	*62.8%*	*8.3%*	*10.0%*
Top 7	13,696	14,208	3.7%	6.6%	6.0%
Other	26,422	51,091	93.4%	9.5%	12.4%
Technical universities	*4951*	*6086*	*22.9%*	*4.4%*	*4.4%*
Total	*45,068*	*71,385*	*58.4%*	*7.5%*	*9.1%*
ALL FTEs			*31.4%*		

it is evident that universities' growth was not within the expected CESMs. Both CESM 06 and CESM 15, therefore, saw decreases in their portion of total university FTEs (0.5% and 0.4%, respectively), with only 5.6%% of total FTEs in CESM 06 and 3.8% in CESM 15 in 2021. A further indicator to take note of is that the top seven universities increased their FTEs in CESM 06 from 2010 to 2021 by 27.8%, whilst other universities (excluding technical universities) had a growth rate of only 17%. For CESM 15, the top seven universities also saw a lower growth from 2010 to 2021 at 7.4% than the overall university FTE growth, whilst other universities and technical universities grew their FTEs by 38.2% and 20.1%, respectively. Where did South African universities' FTE growth come from? As indicated in Tables 7 and 8, it appears that CESM 07: Education and CESM 12: Law were substantial contributors to the growth in FTEs at South African universities, both categories more than 20 percentage points above the overall FTE growth rate.

The growth in FTEs for CESM 07: Education (52.9%) and CESM 12: Law (58.4%) was substantially higher than the total increase in FTEs for the 26 publicly funded South African universities at 31.4% from 2010 to 2021. Compared to CESM 06 and CESM 15, subject fields that should provide the required skills for the jobs increasingly in demand (see Table 2), CESM 07 and CESM 15 are not only growing at a much faster pace but also responsible for a larger portion of the total FTEs. CESM 06 and CESM 15 contained 9.4% of the total FTEs in 2021 (decreasing from 10.3% in 2010), whilst CESM 07 and CESM 12 were responsible for 24.9% of FTEs in 2021 (increasing from 21.1% in 2010). Focusing on the top seven universities as exemplars, these universities decreased their FTEs in Education (CESM 07) from 2010 to 2021 by 1.5% (whilst other universities increased by 82.3%) and grew their FTEs in Law (CESM 15) with only 3.7% compared to other universities at 93.4%.

A possible additional indicator of the lack of strengthening students' ability to be employed is that for 2021, according to the Basic Education Minister, South Africa had 24,556 vacant teaching posts available, but South African universities graduated 41,063 students in Education (indicating a possible oversupply of 167%) (Staff Writer, 2023a, para. 5). For the legal profession, the Law Society of South Africa indicated that there were 29,981 attorneys in South Africa in January 2022 (Staff writer, 2022). Considering that 15,118 legal students graduated in 2021, if all of these graduates must be employed straight out of university, about 50% of the legal workforce will have to be replaced, an unlikely statistic. The substantial difference between the subject fields in which the top seven universities grew their FTEs versus other universities and technical universities should raise some red flags. Shouldn't the 19 other universities and technical universities rather follow the example of the top seven?

From the literature reviewed and results described in this section, South African publicly funded universities failed in many respects: (a) they did not deliver affordable education; (b) they did not offer relevant education that would adequately prepare graduates for future employment in the changing global business environment; and (c) they did not fulfil their responsibilities as agents of their principals namely the government and the students. Top management at South African universities, it seems, did not ensure that these universities achieved their primary objective. What remains uncertain is the sustainability of the current management approach and whether students as principals will continue to enrol in universities managed by agents who do not act in the best interest of their principals. This challenge adds to the already uncertain future of traditional universities, not only in South Africa, but also globally.

Conclusion

Based on the analyses conducted in this study, all indications point to the fact that top management at South African universities as agents did not act in the interest of their primary stakeholders, that is, the government and students, when considering their primary objective as offering affordable education that will enhance employability. This paper considers the tuition fee increases at South African universities from 2010 to 2019 as a possible indicator of affordability and the growth and composition of enrolments and graduates for a sample of CESMs from 2010 to 2021 as indicators for enhancing employability.

The study indicated that tuition fees over the last 10 years (2010–2019) have increased beyond the inflation rate, taking enrolment growth into account, indicating that many universities are not providing affordable education. This trend of increasing tuition fees is not unique to South Africa, but a global phenomenon. The tuition fee trend indicated in this study confirms that top management at universities as principals failed to provide affordable education, taking tuition fee growth as the main indicator.

When shifting the focus to relevant education in pursuit of employability, very little has changed in terms of the scientific areas (CESMs) in which universities enrolled their students in the past decade, regardless of the changing business environment graduates face. On the one hand, a relative decline in FTEs from 2010 to 2021 was observed for computer sciences, statistics and mathematics, all skills required to navigate the 4IR. On the other hand, enrolment growth in law and education, career areas replaceable by AI, seems questionable. The enrolment and graduate trend in the CESMs selected for this study possibly indicates that top management at South African universities is not effectively enhancing the employability of their graduates since enrolments are sought in CESMs for careers that might be redundant in the future.

Top management at universities should face the reality that they have not, according to all indications in this study, acted in the best interest of their primary stakeholders as is required by an agent according to the Agency theory. What top management at universities will do to ensure that they act in the best interest of their primary stakeholders remains to be seen. The researcher is of the opinion that the information provided in this study could be a starting point for universities in this quest, and future research could focus on the strategies required to ensure top management at universities can efficiently act as agents to the government and students. A further option for future research that could substantiate the current study's findings is expanding on the number of CESMs included in the analyses.

Can most traditional universities continue to increase tuition fees whilst demanding increased subsidies from the government? Can these universities continue to ignore the level of cross-subsidising at their institutions and, consequently, ignore their primary objective to meet the needs of the primary target market, affordable education enhancing employability?

References

Acemoglu, D., & Autor, D. (2010). *Skills, tasks and technologies: Implications for employment and earnings. NBER working paper series no. 16082*. National Bureau of Economic Research.

Adams, R. (2022, March 17). Thousands of students drop out of university as pandemic takes its toll. *The Guardian*. https://www.theguardian.com/education/2022/mar/17/thousands-of-students-drop-out-of-university-as-pandemic-takes-its-toll

Autor, D., Levy, F., & Murnane, R. (2003). The skill content of recent technological change: An empirical exploration. *The Quarterly Journal of Economics*, 1279–1333. https://doi.org/10.1162/003355303322552801

Bikse, V., Lusena-Ezera, I., Rivza, B., & Volkova, T. (2016). The transformation of traditional universities into entrepreneurial universities to ensure sustainable higher education. *Journal of Teacher Education for Sustainability, 18*(2), 75–88. https://doi.org/10.1515/jtes-2016-0016

Burer, S., & Fethke, G. (2016). Nearly-efficient tuitions and subsidies in American public higher education. *Economics of Education Review, 55*, 182–197. https://doi.org/10.1016/j.econedurev.2016.09.003

Coetzee, J., Neneh, B., Stemmet, K., Lamprecht, J., Motsitsi, C., & Sereeco, W. (2021). South African universities in a time of increasing disruption. *South African Journal of Economic and Management Sciences, 24*(1), 1–12. https://doi.org/10.4102/sajems.v24i1.3739

Collub, U. (2016). Into the future. *Tesla Forum*. Retrieved September 6, 2021, from https://forums.tesla.com/discussion/66607/an-authors-look-into-the-future

Cooper, P. (2020, August 31). A new study investigates why college tuition is so expensive. *Forbes*. https://www.forbes.com/sites/prestoncooper2/2020/08/31/a--new-study-investigates-why-college-tuition-is-so-expensive/?sh=7e32e27017a0

Cortes, G. M. (2016). Where have the middle-wage workers gone? A study of polarization using panel data. *Journal of Labor Economics, 34*(1), 63–105. https://doi.org/10.1086/682289

Cunningham, B. M. (2009). Faculty: Thy administrator's keeper? Some evidence. *Economics of Education Review, 28*(4), 444–453. https://doi.org/10.1016/j.econedurev.2008.07.005

Damodaran, A. (2015). *Applied corporate finance* (4th ed.). John Wiley & Sons, Inc.

De Vries, M. S., & Kroukamp, H. (2022). Decision-making skills in the fourth industrial revolution. *Teaching Public Administration, 41*(3), 389–407. https://doi.org/10.1177/01447394221119087

Department of Education. (2008). *Classification of educational subject matter*. Retrieved August 31, 2023, from https://www.dhet.gov.za/Management%20and%20Information%20Systems/CESM%20August%202008.pdf

Department of Higher Education and Training (DHET). (2015). *Are we making progress with systemic structural transformation of resourcing, access, success, staffing and researching in higher education: What do the data say*? 2nd National Higher Education Summit, 1. https://www.dhet.gov.za/summit/Docs/2015Docs/Annex3_DHET_Progresswithtransformation_Whatdothedatasay.pdf

Editorial. (2014, June 27). The digital degree—The future of universities. *The Economist*. https://www.economist.com/briefing/2014/06/27/the-digital-degree

Editorial. (2022, November 4). *Tuition revenue jumps as higher education recovers from COVID19*. Statistics South Africa. https://www.statssa.gov.za/?p=15886

Espinosa-Méndez, C., Maquieira, C. P., & Arias, J. T. (2023). The impact of ESG performance on the value of family firms: The moderating role of financial constraints and agency problems. *Sustainability (Switzerland), 15*(7). https://doi.org/10.3390/su15076176

Etzkowitz, H., Webster, A., Gebhardt, C., & Terra, B. R. C. (2000). The future of the university and the university of the future: Evolution of ivory tower to entrepreneurial paradigm. *Research Policy, 29*(2), 313–330. https://doi.org/10.1016/S0048-7333(99)00069-4

Fraser, L. (2023a, May 16). South Africa's massive reading problem. *BusinessTech*. https://businesstech.co.za/news/government/688439/south-africas-massive-reading-problem/

Fraser, L. (2023b, June 29). These are the 11 best universities in South Africa. *BusinessTech*. https://businesstech.co.za/news/lifestyle/699723/these-are-the-11-best-universities-in-south-africa-2/

Frey, C. B., & Osborne, M. A. (2017). The future of employment: How susceptible are jobs to computerisation? *Technological Forecasting and Social Change, 114*, 254–280. https://doi.org/10.1016/j.techfore.2016.08.019

Gogineni, S., Linn, S. C., & Yadav, P. K. (2022). Vertical and horizontal agency problems in private firms: Ownership structure and operating performance. *Journal of Financial and Quantitative Analysis, 57*(4), 1237–1278. https://doi.org/10.1017/S0022109021000363

Heinrich Böll Stiftung. (2023). *Household affordability index*. Retrieved May 8, 2024, from https://za.boell.org/en/2023/03/30/march-2023-household-affordability-index-and-key-data

Huang, I. Y., Raimo, V., & Humfrey, C. (2016). Power and control: Managing agents for international student recruitment in higher education. *Studies in Higher Education, 41*(8), 1333–1354. https://doi.org/10.1080/03075079.2014.968543

Jaimovich, N., & Siu, H. (2012). *The trend is the cycle: Job polarization and jobless recoveries (18334)*. https://doi.org/10.3386/w18334

Koornhof, C. (2020, October 9). Covid-19: The impact on universities and how their business models need to flexible. *News24*. https://www.news24.com/news24/columnists/guestcolumn/opinion-covid-19-the-impact-on-universities-and-how-their-business-models-need-to-flexible-20201009

Lewis, B., & Pendlebury, M. (2002). Surplus or deficit - who cares? Cross-subsidy in colleges of higher education. *Financial Accountability & Management, 18*(1), 25–38. https://doi.org/10.1111/1468-0408.00144

Linder, S., & Foss, N. J. (2015). Agency theory. In *International encyclopedia of the Social & Behavioral Sciences* (2nd ed., pp. 344–350). Elsevier.

Mahlaka, R. (2020, November 12). Embracing the fourth industrial revolution begins with reforming SA's education system. *Daily Maverick*. https://www.dailymaverick.co.za/article/2020-11-12-embracing-the-fourth-industrial-revolution-begins-with-reforming-sas-education-system/

Mtshali, N. (2020, November 12). Three SA vice-chancellors paint a post-COVID picture for universities. *The South African*. https://www.thesouthafrican.com/lifestyle/south-africa-post-covid-universities/

Omarjee, L. (2019, January 1). Everything you need to know about the national minimum wage. *News24*. https://www.news24.com/Fin24/everything-you-need-to-know-about-the-national-minimum-wage-20190101

Perkins, J. A. (1973). *The university as an organisation*. McGraw-Hill Book Company.

Perović, L. M., & Kosor, M. M. (2020). The efficiency of universities in achieving sustainable development goals. *Amfiteatru Economic, 22*(54), 516–532. https://doi.org/10.24818/EA/2020/54/516

Petersen, F. (2023). *Academic freedom and institutional autonomy must not be used to cover up poor governance and lack of accountability at our universities*. University of the Free State. https://www.ufs.ac.za/templates/news-archive-item/campus-news/2023/june/academic-freedom-and-institutional-autonomy-must-not-be-used-to-cover-up-poor-governance-and-lack-of-accountability-at-our-universities

RBC. (2018). *How Canadian Youth can Thrive in the Age of Disruption*. Retrieved May 9, 2024, from https://www.rbc.com/en/future-launch/resource-type/research-insights/humans-wanted-how-canadian-youth-can-thrive-in-the-age-of-disruption/

Serfontein, C. (2019). *Financial viability - costing teaching modules at a South African university*. Master's dissertation. University of the Free State.

Serfontein, C. (2022). *Cost efficiency at South African universities*. Doctoral thesis. University of the Free State.

Serfontein, C., & Smit, A. v. A. (2021). Teaching modules: Levels of cross-subsidising at a south African university. *South African Journal of Higher Education, 35*(6), 169–189. https://doi.org/10.20853/35-6-4130

Smit, A. V. A., & Serfontein, C. (2019). Does the youth have reason to be angry at South African universities? In *International Business Conference*, 1332–1343.
Staff writer. (2003). Full-time equivalent (FTE) calculation. In *Campus compact*. https://compact.org/?s=FTE+calculation
Staff writer. (2022). *Statistics for the attorneys' profession*. Law Society of South Africa. https://www.lssa.org.za/about-us/about-the-attorneys-profession/statistics-for-the-attorneys-profession/
Staff Writer. (2023a). Student Headcount Report. *PowerHEDA*. Retrieved July 28, 2023, from https://www.heda.co.za/powerheda/dashboard.aspx
Staff Writer. (2023b, April 25). *Unemployment, youth total (% of total labor force ages 15–24) (modeled ILO estimate)*. World Bank. https://data.worldbank.org/indicator/SL.UEM.1524.ZS
Staff writer. (n.d.-a). *About Harvard*. Harvard University. Retrieved October 4, 2022, from https://www.harvard.edu/about/
Staff writer. (n.d.-b). *About the University of Oxford*. University of Oxford. Retrieved October 4, 2022, from https://www.ox.ac.uk/about
Staff writer. (n.d.-c). *Vision and goals*. University of the Free State. Retrieved October 4, 2022, from https://www.ufs.ac.za/about-the-ufs/ufs-in-focus/vision-and-goals
Staff writer. (n.d.-d). *Vision and strategy*. Stellenbosch University. Retrieved October 4, 2022, from https://www.sun.ac.za/english/about-us/strategic-documents
Staff writer. (n.d.-e). *Wits University*. Wits University. Retrieved October 4, 2022, from https://www.wits.ac.za/about-wits/
Staniulyte, J. (2022). Towards the entrepreneurial university: The principal-agent problem. *Quality and Quantity, 56*(5), 2971–2988. https://doi.org/10.1007/s11135-021-01246-z
Statistics South Africa. (2023, May 16). *Quarterly Labour Force Survey (QLFS)*, 1st Quarter 2023. https://www.statssa.gov.za/?page_id=1854&PPN=P0211
Tsiligiris, V., & Bowyer, D. (2021). Exploring the impact of 4IR on skills and personal qualities for future accountants: A proposed conceptual framework for university accounting education. *Accounting Education, 30*(6), 621–649. https://doi.org/10.1080/09639284.2021.1938616
Universities South Africa. (2018). *Public universities in South Africa*. Retrieved May 5, 2018, from http://www.usaf.ac.za/public-universities-in-south-africa/
Van Thiel, S., & Smullen, A. (2021). Principals and agents, or principals and stewards? Australian Arm's length agencies' perceptions of Arm's length government instruments. *Public Performance and Management Review, 44*(4), 758–784. https://doi.org/10.1080/15309576.2021.1881803
Walton, J. S., & Martin, M. C. (2004). Corporate universities versus traditional universities: Comparison through published organisation documentation. *Academy of Human Resource Development International Conference (AHRD)*, 10–17. http://files.eric.ed.gov/fulltext/ED491482.pdf
World Economic Forum (WEF). (2016, January 1). *The future of jobs: Employment, skills and workforce strategy for the fourth industrial revolution*. https://doi.org/10.1177/1946756712473437
Yorke, M. (2005). Employability in higher education: What it is—What it is not. In *Learning & Employability* (Vol. 1). The Higher Education Academy. https://doi.org/10.1002/ir.162
Zahidi, S., Ratcheva, V., Hingel, G., & Brown, S. (2020, December). *The future of jobs report 2020*.

An Evaluation of the Challenges Faced by Small and Medium Enterprises (SMEs) in Implementing the International Financial Reporting Standards (IFRSs) in Emerging Markets: Evidence from Ghana

Ibrahim Zubairu, Marim Alenezi, and Husseini Muhammadu

Abstract This research evaluates the challenges encountered by Small and Medium Enterprises (SMEs) in implementing International Financial Reporting Standards (IFRSs) in emerging markets. The study employs a mixed-methods approach, incorporating both quantitative analysis and qualitative exploration, to uncover the multifaceted nature of these challenges. The research begins by reviewing the existing literature to establish a framework for understanding the factors influencing IFRS adoption in the context of SMEs in emerging markets. Subsequently, primary data were collected through surveys, interviews, and case studies from diverse sample of SMEs operating in emerging markets. The survey data quantitatively capture the prevalent challenges faced by SMEs, while qualitative insights from interviews and case studies enrich the understanding of these challenges within the specific contextual nuances of each market. The findings highlight key challenges including limited awareness and understanding of IFRS, financial constraints, complexities in complying with IFRS requirements, shortage of qualified professionals, and cultural and institutional factors unique to emerging markets. Furthermore, the research underscores the varying degrees of impact of these challenges on SMEs of different sizes, sectors, and geographical locations within emerging markets. Drawing on these insights, the study concluded by offering a synthesized set of strategies tailored to address these hurdles, contributing practical recommendations for stakeholders aiming to support IFRS adoption among SMEs in emerging markets.

I. Zubairu (✉) · H. Muhammadu
Accra Technical University, Accra, Ghana

M. Alenezi
Prince Mohammed Bin Fahd University, Al-Khobar, Saudi Arabia
e-mail: malenezi@pmu.edu.sa

T. Moloi (ed.), *Impacting Society Positively Through Technology in Accounting and Business Processes*, Springer Proceedings in Business and Economics,
https://doi.org/10.1007/978-3-031-84885-8_8

Keywords International Financial Reporting Standards (IFRSs) · Small and Medium Enterprises (SMEs) · IFRS adoption · Implementation · Emerging markets

Introduction

The adoption and implementation of International Financial Reporting Standards (IFRSs) have gained significant importance worldwide, including in emerging markets. International Financial Reporting Standards (IFRSs) are a globally recognized set of accounting standards developed by the International Accounting Standards Board (IASB). While larger corporations in emerging markets have been able to navigate the complexities of IFRS implementation, SMEs often encounter unique challenges (Archer & Ghadbane, 2018). This research proposal aims to investigate the specific challenges faced by SMEs in emerging markets when implementing IFRS, with a focus on identifying key barriers and suggesting potential solutions.

IFRS aims to standardize financial reporting practices and enhance the transparency and comparability of financial statements. While the benefits of IFRS adoption are widely recognized, SMEs in emerging markets often face significant challenges in implementing these standards (Nimatiere, 2016).

Pursuant to the Venture Capital Fund 2004 (Act 680), an SME is defined as an industry, project, or economic activity that employs fewer than 100 people and has a total asset base of less than one million dollars in cedi value, (Republic of Ghana, 2004). In addition, over ninety percent (90%) of registered firms in Ghana are SMEs, according to the Registrar General's Department's records. The Social Security and National Insurance Trust (SSNIT) data back up this claim, revealing that ninety percent (90%) of businesses employ fewer than twenty (20) people.

Emerging markets on the other hand refer to economies that are in the process of rapid growth and development, characterized by expanding industrial sectors, increasing trade activities, and improving economic conditions (Archer & Ghadbane, 2018). SMEs play a crucial role in the economic landscape of emerging markets, contributing to job creation, innovation, poverty alleviation, and overall economic growth (Kamotho & Kaudo, 2023). They are often the backbone of these economies, representing a large portion of the business sector. Therefore, improving the financial reporting practices of SMEs becomes vital for fostering economic development and attracting domestic and foreign investments.

The adoption of IFRS in emerging markets is driven by various factors. Firstly, it promotes transparency and comparability, making financial statements more reliable for potential investors, creditors, and other stakeholders. Secondly, it facilitates access to global capital markets, as many multinational corporations and investors prefer to working with IFRS-compliant SMEs. Lastly, it harmonizes accounting practices across borders, reducing information asymmetry, and enhancing the overall credibility of financial reporting. However, due to their limited resources, expertise, and unique operating environments, SMEs encounter specific obstacles when adopting and implementing IFRS.

Addressing these challenges faced by SMEs in implementing IFRS in emerging markets is crucial for their long-term sustainability and growth. Identifying and understanding these obstacles will facilitate the development of tailored strategies, resources, and support mechanisms to enable SMEs to effectively adopt and implement IFRS, leading to improved financial reporting practices and informed decision-making (Gibson & O'Donnel, 2015). Therefore, policymakers, regulators, professional bodies, and other stakeholders must collaborate to provide adequate support, resources, and training to SMEs, enabling them to effectively implement IFRS and reap the benefits of standardized financial reporting practices.

Statement of the Problem

The implementation of IFRS has become a critical agendum for SMEs operating in emerging markets. However, the adoption and effective application of IFRS by SMEs in these contexts are plagued by numerous challenges. According to Hafiku (2017), there is difficulty for user of SMEs financial information to make informed decisions based on full IFRS in their reporting, as the standards were largely not meant for the SMEs. Solanke et al. (2016) indicated that the development of IFRS for SMEs was mainly because of the fundamental theories and guidelines from the IASB framework and full IFRSs with adjustments to account for the SME's specific financial reporting needs and from a cost–benefit perspective. This research aims to comprehensively investigate and evaluate the challenges encountered by SMEs in implementing IFRS within the emerging market landscape, shedding light on the specific obstacles that hinder successful adoption and compliance.

Many SMEs in the emerging markets lack sufficient knowledge and awareness of IFRS requirements, including their purpose, scope, and potential benefits. Furthermore, the complexity of IFRS and its technical language often pose challenges for SME owners, managers, and accountants, leading to a lack of understanding of the standards and their proper application (Rudzani & Charles, 2016). Additionally, SMEs often face resource constraints, including financial limitations, human capital scarcity, and limited technological infrastructure. The adoption and implementation of IFRS require significant investments in terms of training, system upgrades, and professional expertise (Barya, 2017). SMEs need to weigh the costs and benefits associated with implementing IFRS, considering their specific financial capabilities and expected returns.

The regulatory and institutional framework in emerging markets may be less developed or fragmented, leading to inconsistencies and uncertainties regarding the enforcement and interpretation of IFRS. SMEs may encounter challenges in aligning their financial reporting practices with the local regulatory requirements, as well as difficulties in accessing adequate support and guidance from relevant regulatory bodies (Arhin et al., 2017). Furthermore, SMEs face technical complexities and practical difficulties in implementing IFRS. These challenges may include integrating IFRS into existing accounting systems, adapting to new measurement and valuation methods, handling complex financial instruments, and ensuring reliable data collection, verification, and reporting processes (Deloitte, 2017).

By comprehensively analyzing these challenges, this research aims to identify the specific obstacles faced by SMEs in implementing IFRS in emerging markets. The findings will contribute to developing effective strategies, policies, and support mechanisms to address these challenges, ultimately fostering successful IFRS adoption and compliance among SMEs and promoting financial transparency, comparability, and access to capital within emerging economies.

Research Questions

The study seeks to answer the following questions:

(a) What are the key challenges faced by SMEs in emerging markets when adopting and implementing IFRS?
(b) What are the specific financial and nonfinancial benefits that SMEs in emerging markets can derive from adopting and implementing IFRS?
(c) How does the level of accounting and financial reporting expertise within SMEs in emerging markets affect their ability to implement IFRS?
(d) To what extent do regulatory and enforcement mechanisms influence the successful implementation of IFRS by SMEs in emerging markets.

Objectives of the Study

- This research aims to identify the key obstacles and difficulties that SMEs encounter during the adoption and implementation process.
- This study seeks to evaluate the benefits, drawbacks, and overall consequences of adopting IFRS for SMEs.
- This research aims to examine the legal frameworks, institutional support, and government policies related to IFRS adoption, and understanding how they contribute to the challenges faced by SMEs.
- This research intends to identify and highlight best practices and strategies for overcoming the challenges encountered by SMEs in implementing IFRS.
- Based on the findings of the research, the objective is to provide practical recommendations and guidance for the relevant stakeholders.
- The research aims to contribute to the existing body of knowledge on the topic.

Overall, the objectives of this research are to shed light on the challenges faced by SMEs in implementing IFRS in emerging markets, understand their impact, and provide actionable recommendations to enhance the effectiveness of IFRS adoption for SMEs in the municipality.

Literature Review

The International Financial Reporting Standards (IFRSs) are a set of accounting standards developed by the International Accounting Standards Board (IASB) that provide a globally recognized framework for the preparation and presentation of financial statements (IASB, 2016). It aims to enhance transparency, comparability, and reliability of financial reporting across different countries and industries.

Under IFRS, financial statements are prepared using a principle-based approach that focuses on the economic substance of transactions rather than their legal form (IASB, 2020). This approach allows for more flexibility and judgment in applying the standards. The main components of financial statements prepared under IFRS include the statement of financial position (balance sheet), statement of comprehensive income (income statement), statement of changes in equity, and statement of cash flows.

One of the key features of IFRS is the emphasis on fair value measurement. Fair value represents the estimated price that would be received to sell an asset or paid to transfer a liability in an orderly transaction between market participants. This principle promotes transparency and reflects the current market values of assets and liabilities, (Sidhu & Jallow, 2019). IFRS also places significant importance on disclosure requirements. These disclosures help stakeholders understand the financial position, performance, and risks of the company (Archer & Ghadbane, 2018). The development and maintenance of IFRS are carried out by IASB. They follow a rigorous process that involves public consultations, research, and international collaboration to address emerging accounting issues and align with changing business practices.

The adoption of IFRS has gained momentum globally, with over 120 countries currently using or converging with the standards (KPMG, 2021). However, it is important to note that the United States follows its own accounting standards known as Generally Accepted Accounting Principles (GAAP).

Emerging markets play a significant role in the global economy, and their characteristics and importance are particularly relevant in the context of SMEs and financial reporting. Emerging markets are characterized with high economic growth rates compared to developed economies. They often experience significant increase in GDP, industrialization, and urbanization, leading to rising consumer demand and business opportunities. As emerging economies grow, disposable incomes of individuals tend to rise, resulting in an expanding consumer base (World Bank, 2017). This creates new markets and potential consumers for SMEs, providing opportunities for business growth and market penetration. Emerging markets typically have a young and growing population. This demographic advantage translates into a larger workforce, increased productivity, and a potential customer base for SMEs operating in these markets (World Bank, 2017). Many emerging markets are rich in natural resources such as minerals, oil, and gas. This abundance can create opportunities for SMEs involved in sectors such as mining, energy, and related industries.

The importance of emerging markets to SMEs cannot be over emphasized. Emerging markets offer SMEs the opportunity to expand their customer base beyond their domestic markets. By entering these markets, SMEs can tap into growing consumer demand and increase their revenue streams. The agility and flexibility of SMEs enable them to adapt quickly to changing market dynamics, outperform larger competitors, and establish a strong market position, as they offer innovative products or services that meet the unique needs of the markets (Arhin et al., 2017). Emerging markets often offer lower labor and production costs compared to developed economies. SMEs can take advantage of these cost efficiencies to improve their profit margins and competitiveness in the global market.

However, financial reporting in emerging markets presents unique challenges due to variations in regulatory frameworks, accounting standards, and governance practices (Ezeagba, 2017). SMEs operating in emerging markets need to navigate complex regulatory environments and ensure compliance with local accounting and reporting standards. Transparent financial reporting is crucial for building trust among stakeholders and attracting investors. Reliable financial reporting enhances SMEs credibility and improves their chances of accessing capital from local or international investors. Accurate and transparent financial statements provide vital information for investment decision-making, (Pallant, 2017).

In summary, emerging markets offer significant opportunities for SMEs. SMEs must, however, navigate the unique characteristics of these markets and address the challenges associated with financial reporting to thrive in these dynamic environments.

Theoretical Review

In attempt to throw more light and provide understanding on the challenges facing SMEs in adopting and implementing the IFRSs, we reviewed the theoretical literature and explored a number of the theories that could be useful for our study and zeroed on two of them for this research.

Resource Constraints Theory This theory provides the mode for identifying the most important limiting factor that stands in the way of achieving a goal and then systematically improving that constraint until it is no longer the limiting factor (Simist et al., 2014). It focuses on the weakest points which are bottlenecks for the entire entity and try to determine the relationship of these bottlenecks. In the case of this study, lack of financial resources, expertise, and infrastructure required to implement accounting standards like the IFRS for SMEs, considering the fact that SMEs may be constrained with financial, human capital, and technological infrastructure resources to fully adopt the IFRSs and ultimately affect its implementation.

Theory of Planned Behavior (ETPB) The Theory of Planned Behavior brings to bear attitude, subjective norms, and perceived behavioral control as the factors that influence individual's behavioral intentions and actions, which have the potential of ultimately affecting the performance of real behavior (Ajzen, 1991). It provides a framework to understand how attitudes, subjective norms, and perceived behavioral control influence the implementation of IFRSs for SMEs (Ajzen, 1991). Subjective norms look at the extent to which an individual is of the opinion that his or her decision can be influenced by the views of other relevant people. Also, perceived behavioral control explains the level of control (difficulty or opportunity) that a person has regarding his or her capability to be involved in a specific behavior. Therefore, attitudes towards compliance, subjective norms, perceived behavioral control, intentions, and actual behaviors can be addressed through education, stakeholder engagement, resource allocation, support mechanism, regulatory bodies, and gearing SMEs up to successfully adopt and implement the IFRSs meant for them.

Capacity Building Theory In the SMEs adoption and implementation of the IFRSs, the knowledge, skills, and capabilities of the SMEs is critical in their successful implementation. Therefore, Capacity Building Theory which explains the need and capacity in terms of necessary knowledge and skills to understand and apply the principles of IFRS (Labin et al., 2021). This suggests the lack of expertise and resources for training, education, technical assistance, awareness, collaboration, and partnerships required to help SMEs adopt and implement the IFRS can jeopardize its successful implementation. Therefore, investing in capacity building initiatives, policymakers and regulators can support SMEs to unlock their full potential and contribute sustainable growth and prosperity.

Cultural and Institutional Theory The institutional theory has been described as the most useful theory in the evaluation of the adoption of the International Accounting Standards (IASs) and the IFRSs (Mbawuni, 2018). This theory aims to provide a more comprehensive interorganizational framework for understanding the mechanism of organizational behaviors, causes, and effects (Carroll, 2016). It examines how institutions, techniques, norms, and practices establish effective procedures for social behavior by delving into the sturdy and profound aspects of social structures. The various elements in this theory explains how these fundamental ideas are accepted and modified over time as scholars in accountancy have emphasized that, the theory is excellent tool for discussing issues regarding adopting the accounting reporting standards (Sappor et al., 2023). In addition, cultural factors align themselves to the institutional theory factors and affect behaviors that are transferred into the accounting practice. This suggests that cultural attitudes towards financial reporting and disclosure practices may differ across countries and impede the willingness for adoption, looking at cultural attitudes towards transparency, trust and confidence in institutions, professionalism and expertise, enforcement mechanisms, and the perceived relevance of the standards.

Legal and Regulatory Environment Theory This focuses on how the legal and regulatory framework structures can affect the efforts of institutions to achieve their mandatory activities (Lyons, 2014). It provides how legal framework, regulatory oversight, compliance burden, institutional support, and legal enforcement and remedies can be applied to meet the minimum requirement for regulatory compliance. To successfully adopt and implement the IFRS, this theory suggests that the effectiveness of IFRS adoption and compliance by SMEs may be influenced by the legal and regulatory context in which SMEs operate, considering the legal framework, regulatory oversight, institutional support, compliance, enforcements, and remedies. According to Oketch et al. (2020), the legal environments of regulatory agencies are key predictors of their organizational performance, as they influence how the regulatory agencies are created, their mandates, sources of funding, and reporting frameworks. Reporting frameworks include the nature of the relationships between the regulatory agencies and the policymakers, political actors, the legislature, the executive, judicial processes, regulated entities, and the public at large. Addressing the regulatory gaps and promoting a conducive regulatory environment, policymakers and other stakeholders can promote financial transparency, accountability, and investor confidence, fostering sustainable economic growth through vibrant SME sector.

Access to Finance Theory This theory highlights the importance of addressing financial constraints faced by institutions in emerging markets. Access to finance is shifting to embracing the idea of promoting banking services such as credit, savings, and insurance rather than primarily delivering microcredit for SMEs (Karlan & Morduch, 2010). This suggests that limited access to finance may highly likely hinder the capacity to adopt and implement the standards, thereby affecting their financial reporting practices. Access to finance theory looks at the cost of compliance, investor confidence, creditworthiness, access to markets, and once again capacity building. Improving access to finance, reducing borrowing costs, and providing targeted financial support, policymakers and other stakeholders can support SMEs to meet the international accounting standards, enhance their financial reporting practices, and unlock their full growth potential.

Motivation and Challenges for the Adoption of IFRS in Emerging Markets

Adopting IFRS by SMEs in emerging markets is self-motivating. IFRS is widely recognized and adopted globally, providing a common accounting language for businesses (Arhin et al., 2017). By adopting IFRS, SMEs in emerging markets align their financial reporting with international practices, facilitating comparability and transparency. Adopting IFRS can enhance investor confidence in SMEs operating in emerging markets. The use of internationally accepted accounting standards ensures more accurate and reliable financial information, reducing information asymmetry between companies and investors. IFRS adoption can improve SMEs' access to capital and financing options. Investors and lenders often prefer companies that follow globally recognized accounting standards, making it easier to attract investors and secure loans from both domestic and international sources. Abedana et al. (2016) suggest that adopting IFRS necessitates the development of accounting professionals with knowledge and expertise in international standards. This drives the professional growth of accountants and auditors in emerging markets, enhancing their skill and increasing their employability.

Potential benefits of adopting IFRS to SMEs in emerging markets are enormous. IFRS encourages SMEs to produce more accurate and transparent financial statements. Zubairu et al. (2021) posit that accurate and transparent financial statements can enhance the quality and reliability of financial reporting, providing stakeholders with a better understanding of the SMEs' financial performance, position, and risks. They argued that IFRS promotes the use of consistent accounting principles and terminologies, enabling better comparability of financial information across different SMEs within the same industry or region. This facilitates benchmarking and analysis, helping SMEs identify areas for improvement and make informed decisions. Adopting IFRS can attract international investors and potential business partners who are more likely to engage with SMEs that adhere to globally recognized accounting standards (Zubairu, 2010). This can open doors to new collaborations, joint ventures, and expansion opportunities. IFRS requires SMEs to provide comprehensive disclosures about their financial performance and risks. This promotes greater accountability, strengthens corporate governance practices, and helps SMEs to identify and manage risks effectively, leading to improved decision-making (Othman & Ameer, 2014).

Despite the enormous benefits of adopting IFRS, the adoption and implementation of IFRS by SMEs in emerging markets can present several challenges. Many SMEs in emerging markets may have limited knowledge and awareness of the IFRSs as suggested in the Capacity Building Theory. Understanding the principles and requirements of IFRS can be complex and requires significant training and education (Labin et al., 2021). SMEs may struggle to understand the nuances of IFRS, resulting in difficulties in implementation. As the Resource Constraints Theory posits, while the SMEs typically operate with limited financial and human resources, adopting and implementing IFRS often require significant investments in staff training, accounting systems, and infrastructure upgrades (Gray, 2010). SMEs in emerging markets may face financial constraints that make it challenging to allocate resources for these purposes. Implementing IFRS requires a certain level of technical expertise in accounting and financial reporting. SMEs in emerging markets may lack qualified professionals with knowledge of IFRS, making it difficult to interpret and apply the standards correctly. The shortage of skilled accountants and auditors can hinder the effective implementation of IFRS. The regulatory environment in emerging markets may not be fully aligned with IFRS. Local regulations, tax laws, and reporting requirements may differ from IFRS, leading to conflicts and complexities in compliance, (Doupnik & Salter, 2016). SMEs may have to navigate through a dual reporting system, which adds additional burden of compliance. SMEs often have unique characteristics and business models that do not fit well with certain IFRS requirements designed for larger entities (Bhiman & Sidhu, 2013). SMEs may face difficulties in applying certain complex accounting standards, such as fair value measurement, impairment, or hedging. The one-size-fits-all approach of IFRS may not consider the practicality and relevance for SMEs in emerging markets. Emerging markets may lack the necessary institutional support and infrastructure to facilitate the adoption and implementation of IFRS. The absence of a robust framework can make it challenging for SMEs to navigate the IFRS adoption process, Zubairu et al. (2021).

Institutional Factors

Regulatory bodies, government policies, and legal frameworks play a crucial role in the adoption and implementation of IFRS in emerging markets. The legal and regulatory environment theory shapes how legal framework, regulatory oversight, compliance burden, institutional support, legal enforcement, and remedies can be applied to meet the minimum requirement for regulatory compliance (Oketch et al., 2020). In practice, regulatory bodies, such as securities commissions or financial regulators, are responsible for overseeing financial reporting practices and ensuring compliance with accounting standards. They adopt and endorse IFRS as the national accounting standards or work towards convergence with IFRS. They collaborate with IASB to incorporate IFRS into local regulations. They develop rules and regulations that require companies to adopt and implement IFRS in their financial reporting. They establish disclosure requirements, accounting principles, and enforcement mechanisms to maintain transparency and comparability of financial information (GSE, 2022). Regulatory bodies monitor the compliance of companies with IFRS through inspections, audits, and investigations. They may impose penalties for noncompliance, ensuring adherence to reporting standards and boosting investor confidence.

Government policies have a significant impact on the adoption and implementation of IFRS in emerging markets. Governments establish policies that promote the adoption of IFRS, recognizing the benefits of international harmonization in financial reporting. Governments support capacity building initiatives to ensure the availability of skilled professionals who can effectively implement IFRS (Zubairu et al., 2021). This includes investing in training programs, establishing accounting education standards, and supporting professional accounting bodies. Government policies focus on protecting investor interests by implementing IFRS. Enhanced financial reporting transparency and comparability provided by IFRS can attract foreign investments, stimulate economic growth, and foster investor confidence in emerging markets.

Legal frameworks provide the foundation for the adoption and enforcement of IFRS in emerging markets. Governments enact legislation or amend existing company laws to incorporate IFRS requirements. This legal framework mandates the use of IFRS in financial reporting and sets the consequences for noncompliance (Sappor et al., 2023). Legal frameworks establish corporate governance principles that align with IFRS requirements. These principles promote accountability, transparency, and integrity in financial reporting, supporting the adoption of IFRS. The frameworks often define specific disclosure requirements based on IFRS guidelines. They ensure that companies provide relevant and reliable financial information to stakeholders, enabling better decision-making and risk assessment.

Samujh and Dev (2015) indicated that supporting SMEs in transitioning to IFRS involves the active involvement of the accounting profession, educational institutions, and accounting standard-setting bodies. The accounting profession plays a crucial role in supporting SMEs by providing training and education on IFRS. Professional accounting bodies offer courses, seminars, and certification programs to enhance the knowledge and skills of accountants working with SMEs (ICAG, 2021). Accounting professionals assist SMEs in understanding and implementing IFRS requirements. They provide guidance on accounting treatments, financial statement presentation, and disclosure practices specific to SMEs, helping them navigate the complexities of IFRS adoption. Accounting firms offer consultancy services to SMEs, aiding them in the transition to IFRS. They provide expertise in areas such as financial reporting, internal controls, and accounting system implementation, tailored to the specific needs and resources of SMEs.

Educational institutions, including universities and vocational training centers, have a role in developing accounting curricula that incorporate IFRS (Florou et al., 2017). They should ensure that aspiring accountants receive comprehensive education on IFRS principles, standards, and their application to SMEs. Institutions can facilitate practical training opportunities for students to work with SMEs and gain hands-on experience in IFRS implementation. Collaborations between educational institutions and SMEs can bridge the gap between theoretical knowledge and real-world application. Educational institutions can conduct research on the challenges and best practices of SMEs transitioning to IFRS. They can disseminate their findings through publications and conferences, contributing to knowledge base and providing practical insights for SMEs.

Accounting standard-setting bodies recognize unique characteristics and research constraints of SMEs. They develop simplified versions of IFRS, such as the IFRS for SMEs, which are tailored to the needs of SMEs while maintaining the core principles of IFRS. Standard-setting bodies issue implementation guidance, illustrative examples, and explanatory materials specifically addressing the challenges faced by SMEs (IASB, 2018). This support helps SMEs understand and apply IFRS requirements appropriately. Standard-setting bodies encourage SMEs to provide feedback on the practicality and effectiveness of IFRS for SMEs. This feedback is used to evaluate and update the standards, ensuring continuous improvement and alignment with SMEs' needs.

Financial Reporting Practices and Impact on SMEs

The impact of IFRS implementation on the financial reporting quality of SMEs in emerging markets has been the subject of numerous studies; see Kamotho and Kaudo (2023), Hafiku (2017), Sappor et al. (2023), Zubairu et al. (2021), among others. The IFRS adoption in emerging markets aims to improve the comparability of financial statements across countries. SMEs following IFRS can benefit from increased transparency and consistency in reporting, making it easier for investors, creditors, and other stakeholders to assess their financial performance (IASB, 2018). This can lead to improved access to capital and reduced information asymmetry. IFRS implementation often requires SMEs to provide more extensive disclosures, which can contribute to improved financial reporting quality. Enhanced disclosure requirements promote a higher level of transparency, enabling stakeholders to make more informed decisions (Sappor et al., 2023). However, the increased burden of compliance with disclosure requirements can be a challenge for SMEs with limited resources and expertise. IFRS is generally considered more complex than local GAAP in emerging markets (IFRS Foundation, 2017). SMEs may face challenges in understanding and applying the complex accounting standards, potentially leading to errors or misinterpretations. This complexity can be especially burdensome for SMEs with limited financial expertise and resources. IFRS adoption often necessitates a professionalization of accounting practices within SMEs. This includes improving the knowledge and skills of accountants and adopting robust internal control systems. The professionalization process can contribute to higher-quality financial reporting by SMEs, ensuring compliance with the standards and enhancing the reliability of reported financial information (Lazar, 2018).

Vendy and Sucahyati (2022) observed that several SME-specific factors, including size, ownership, structures, and industry sector, can influence the difficulties encountered in the implementation process. The size of an SME can significantly affect its ability to implement IFRS effectively. Smaller SMEs often have limited resources, including financial and human capital. They may lack the necessary expertise or dedicated accounting staff to handle the complexities of IFRS adoption. Larger SMEs may have relatively more resources but might face challenges in coordinating the implementation process across various departments or subsidiaries (Zubairu, 2010).

The ownership structure of an SME can influence IFRS implementation challenges. Family-owned SMEs, for example, may face difficulties in transitioning from traditional accounting practices to the principle-based approach of IFRS. Family dynamics, conflicts of interest, and resistance to change can hamper the implementation process (Albu et al., 2011). In contrast, SMEs with a corporate ownership structure might have a more structured governance system, facilitating smoother IFRS implementation.

The organizational structure of an SME can impact IFRS implementation. Complex organizational structures, such as conglomerates or SMEs with multiple subsidiaries, can face challenges in consolidating financial statements and applying IFRS consistently across all entities (Sautet, 2013). Lack of centralized control, varying accounting practices, and information systems integration can complicate the implementation process. In contrast, SMEs with simpler structures may find it easier to adopt IFRS.

The industry sector in which an SME operates can influence the challenges encountered in implementing IFRS. Different sectors have unique accounting practices, regulations, and specific reporting requirements. SMEs operating in highly regulated sectors, such as financial services or healthcare, may face additional challenges aligning their existing accounting practices with IFRS standards (Albu et al., 2011). Moreover, industry-specific complexities in revenue recognition, inventory valuation, or specialized assets may pose implementation hurdles.

Support Mechanisms

The training programs and educational initiatives should provide SMEs with practical and relevant knowledge about IFRS implementation. The content should be tailored to the specific needs and challenges faced by SMEs, taking into account their size, industry, and level of financial expertise. If the content is generic or not applicable to SMEs, the effectiveness of the program may be limited. Programs and initiatives should be easily accessible to SMEs. This includes factors such as affordability, availability of training materials, delivery formats, and language options. If SMEs face barriers in accessing the programs, such as high costs or limited availability, their effectiveness may be compromised. SMEs require practical guidance on how to implement IFRS in their day-to-day operations. According to Nobes and Zeff (2018), the effectiveness of training programs and educational initiatives can be enhanced by providing real-world examples, case studies, and practical exercises that SMEs can directly apply to their financial reporting processes. It is therefore significant to put many efforts in these areas, because the more practical and applicable the training materials are, the better equipped SMEs will be to navigate the complexities of IFRS implementation. Experienced professionals who have in-depth knowledge of IFRS and understand the challenges faced by SMEs can provide valuable insights and guidance. Their ability to answer questions, address specific concerns, and offer practical advice can greatly enhance the effectiveness of the programs (Zubairu et al., 2021). IFRS implementation can be an ongoing process, and SMEs may require ongoing support even after completing a training program or educational initiative. The availability of post-training resources, such as access to online forums, help desks, or follow-up sessions, can contribute to the overall effectiveness by providing SMEs with opportunities to seek clarification, share experiences, and get further guidance (Daske et al., 2008). It is also crucial to measure the impact of training programs and educational initiatives. This can be done through post-training assessments, surveys, or follow-up evaluations to determine if SMEs have successfully implemented IFRS and whether the training contributed to their understanding and application of the standards.

Accounting firms, consultants, and other professional service providers play a crucial role in assisting SMEs with the adoption of IFRS. Accounting firms, including the Big Four (Deloitte, PwC, EY, and KPMG), as well as smaller local firms, have significant expertise in financial reporting and IFRS. They offer training programs and educational initiatives to help SMEs understand the requirements of IFRS and how to implement them effectively. These programs can cover technical accounting standards, practical examples, and industry-specific guidance. Accounting firms provide SMEs with technical guidance and interpretation of complex accounting standards. They help SMEs navigate the intricacies of IFRS, ensuring proper application and compliance with reporting requirements. They assist SMEs in the conversion process from local GAAP to IFRS. They provide support in mapping existing financial statements to IFRS requirements, adjusting accounting policies, and implementing necessary changes in financial reporting systems (Daske et al., 2008). They perform independent audits of SMEs' financial statements to provide assurance on the compliance of financial reporting with IFRS. These audits ensure that the financial statements present a true and fair view of the SMEs' financial position and performance.

Consultants specializing in accounting and financial reporting can provide valuable assistance to SMEs in IFRS (Deloitte, 2017). They help SMEs assess their readiness for IFRS adoption by conducting gap analysis, evaluating existing processes, and identifying areas requiring improvement. They provide recommendations on the necessary steps and resources to ensure a smooth transition to IFRS. They assist SMEs in managing the IFRS adoption project, including setting up project plans, timelines, and milestones. They coordinate efforts across various departments and stakeholders, ensuring a structured and efficient implementation process. They also offer specialized knowledge and expertise in IFRS to address complex accounting issues faced by SMEs. They provide guidance on specific transactions, accounting treatments, and disclosure requirements, tailoring their advice to the unique needs of the SME (Labin et al., 2021). Consultants support SMEs in managing the organizational and cultural changes associated with IFRS adoption. They help communicate the benefits and challenges of IFRS to stakeholders, develop training programs, and assist in change implementation strategies.

Besides accounting firms and consultants, other professional service providers, such as the law firms, IT consultants, and other valuation experts, can also play a role in assisting SMEs with IFRS adoption. Law firms provide guidance on legal and regulatory implications associated with IFRS adoption. They assist SMEs in understanding the legal requirements and potential impacts on contracts, agreements, and compliance obligations (Islam & Deegan, 2008). IT consultants assist SMEs in adapting their financial reporting systems to accommodate the requirements of IFRS. They ensure that the systems capture the necessary data, generate appropriate reports, and comply with IFRS disclosure requirements. Valuation experts provide assistance in determining fair values of assets, liabilities, and other financial instruments required under IFRS (Iatridis, 2010). They help SMEs with complex valuation methodologies and provide expertise in assessing impairment of assets.

Impact of IFRS on SMEs' Performance and Stakeholder Perspectives

IFRS implementation generally leads to higher-quality financial reporting. SMEs adopting IFRS are required to provide more detailed and standardized financial information, improving the accuracy and reliability of their financial statements (IASB, 2020). This can enhance transparency of SMEs' financial performance, leading to increased trust and confidence from investors, creditors, and other stakeholders. IFRS implementation can improve SMEs' access to capital. Many investors, including both domestic and international ones, prefer to investing in companies that comply with global accounting standards such as IFRS. Adopting IFRS increases the credibility and comparability of SMEs' financial statements, making them more attractive to potential investors and lenders. Improved access to capital can support SMEs' growth, expansion, and competitiveness in emerging markets. According to Hoque (2006) IFRS implementation facilitates cross-border transactions for SMEs operating in emerging markets. With consistent financial reporting standards, SMEs can easily communicate and transact with international partners, investors, and customers. This promotes international business collaborations, joint ventures, and market expansion opportunities, which can enhance SMEs' financial performance and competitiveness on a global scale (Zubairu et al., 2021). IFRS implementation can streamline SMEs' financial operations and processes. It promotes consistency and efficiency in accounting practices, enabling smoother financial reporting, consolidation, and analysis. Standardized financial reporting framework also facilitates the integration of financial information from different business units or subsidiaries, allowing SMEs to make informed strategic decisions and improve operational efficiency (Chui et al., 2015). IFRS emphasizes the recognition and disclosure of financial risks, enabling SMEs to enhance their risk management practices. By implementing IFRS, SMEs gain a more comprehensive understanding of financial risks, such as those related to revenue recognition, financial instruments, and impairment of assets. This enables SMEs to identify, measure, and manage risks effectively, contributing to improved financial performance and long-term competitiveness.

Research Methodology

This study adopted the mixed-methods research approach to evaluate the challenges faced by SMEs in implementing IFRS in emerging markets, where comprehensive and multifaceted approaches were explored. The mixed-methods research approach refers to the type of research in which both quantitative and qualitative research strategies are combined with their associated methods, strategies, languages, or concepts in a single study; see Creswell (2008, 2009), Creswell et al. (2003), and Johnson et al. (2007). This methodology aims to provide a rigorous analysis of the challenges and factors influencing the successful adoption and implementation of

IFRS by SMEs. The combination of quantitative and qualitative methods, along with a diverse sample, will offer valuable insights into the factors influencing successful IFRS adoption by SMEs. The findings will contribute to existing literature, inform policy recommendations, and provide practical strategies to facilitate the effective implementation of IFRS among SMEs, ultimately fostering transparency, comparability, and credibility in financial reporting practices in emerging markets.

Research Design

The mixed-methods research approach adopted in this study is to address the research questions related to challenges faced by SMEs in implementing IFRS in emerging markets where a combination of qualitative and quantitative techniques are applied in data collection and analysis, Bryman and Bell (2003). This approach allows for a comprehensive understanding of the topic by integrating both numerical data and qualitative insights, (Bryaman, 2004). The mixed-methods approach will provide a holistic view of the research topic by combining quantitative data, such as survey response and statistical analysis, with qualitative data, such as interviews and focus groups. This combination allows for a more in-depth exploration of the challenges faced by SMEs in IFRS implementation, capturing both numerical trends and contextual insights. In recent times, Creswell (2009) described mixed-methods research as a research design with philosophical assumptions as well as methods of enquiry with its central premise being that the use of quantitative and qualitative approaches in combination provides a better understanding of research phenomena than either approach alone. The challenges faced by SMEs are multifaceted and influenced by various factors. A mixed-methods approach will allow for a nuanced exploration of these challenges by capturing both objective data and subjective experiences, opinions, and perceptions. Additionally, the mixed-methods approach enables data triangulation. Triangulation enhances the validity and reliability of the findings by cross-verifying information from different sources and perspectives.

By carefully considering access to the target population, the research objectives, available resources, and desired level of representativeness, we have chosen the cluster sampling technique where the population of SMEs is divided into clusters based on geographic proximity, industry, and SME sizes. We will also employ a purposive sampling design where necessary. This technique also involves selecting SMEs based on specific criteria that align with the research objectives.

Data Collection Procedures

The data were collected using structured questionnaires with closed-ended and Likert-scale questions and distributed to SMEs operating in emerging markets. Also, we used surveys to collect quantitative data on the challenges faced by SMEs, the extent of IFRS implementation, and the perceived impact of these challenges. Again, we conducted interviews with SME owners, financial managers, regulatory authorities, and accounting professionals to have an in-depth exploration of their experiences, perspectives, and insights. This was done through either telephone or in person. We also explored the Focus Groups and brought together a group of SME representatives to engage in a guided discussion facilitated by the research team members, Creswll and Creswell (2017). This method provided an interactive platform for participants to share their experiences, exchange ideas, and collectively identified challenges encountered. This helps us to capture group dynamics, consensus, and divergent viewpoints on the challenges. Case Studies were partly used undertake an in-depth examination of selected SMEs that have faced and addressed challenges in implementing IFRS. This will provide detailed and context-specific insights into the challenges, strategies employed, and the outcomes of IFRS implementation efforts. We also carried out Document Analysis and reviewed relevant documents, such as financial statements, regulatory guidelines, policy documents, and academic literature related to IFRS implementation in emerging markets, to obtain valuable information on the challenges, regulatory frameworks, and best practices in IFRS adoption. Finally, Data Triangulation was employed to combine the data from multiple sources to enhance validity and reliability of the findings. This is where we compared and contrasted the data collected through surveys, interviews, focus groups, case studies, and document analysis to cross-validate findings, identify patterns, and develop a comprehensive understanding of the challenges encountered.

Data Analysis Procedures

The data were analyzed descriptively using Statistical Package for Social Sciences (SPSS) for quantitative data and Nvivo for qualitative data. The normal diagnostic test of reliability and validity was conducted on the research instrument. The Quantitative Data Analysis was used in analyzing numerical data collected through surveys or questionnaires, where descriptive statistics were generated through the calculation of measures of central tendency (mean, median, mode) and measures of dispersion (standard deviation, range) to summarize and describe data. A correlation analysis also conducted in determining the strength and direction of relationships between variables using correlation coefficients, Saunders et al. (2019). The Qualitative Data Analysis was used to analyze the nonnumerical data collected through interviews, focus groups, and case studies. Thematic analysis was used in the identification of themes, patterns, and categories within the qualitative data where the coding techniques were applied to assign labels or codes to text segments, and similar codes were grouped into broader themes. Finally content analysis employed to examine the content of documents such as regulatory guidelines or policy documents, to extract relevant information and identify common themes. In the end, the datasets from quantitative and qualitative perspectives were both integrated to gain a comprehensive understanding of the data. This can be achieved through triangulation, which involves comparing and contrasting findings from both data sources. This enriches the interpretation and provides a more comprehensive understanding of the issues.

Validity and Reliability

Validity looks at the extent to which the data collection methods and measures accurately capture what they are intended to measure (Creswll & Creswell, 2017). It ensures that the data collected are relevant, meaningful, and aligned with the research objectives. Our study employed two validity processes, where content validity was used to ensure that the data collection instruments adequately cover the dimensions and concepts related to the topic. This in practice can be enhanced through expert review, pilot testing, and aligning the instruments with existing literature or theoretical frameworks. The construct validity was also used to assess the extent to which the measurement tools accurately measure the underlying constructs or variables of interest (Creswell, 2007). It can be enhanced by using established measurement scales, ensuring clarity in questionnaire items, and conducting factor analysis or confirmatory factor analysis to validate the measurement model.

Reliability on the other hand assesses the consistency and stability of the data collection methods and measures (Beck & Polit, 2017). It ensures that the data collected are replicable and yield consistent results. In this study, we used test–retest reliability to assess the stability of measurements over time by conducting repeated measurement on same participants using correlation coefficients to determine the consistency of responses; in this case, Cronbach's Alpha was used to determine a questionnaire reliability. Beck and Polit (2017) consider the Cronbach's Alpha of 0.70 to 0.90 to be optimally reliable. Also, data collection procedures may be applied in which case, consistent application of standardized procedures during data collection are required to minimize variability and ensure consistency across participants and settings (Table 1).

Table 1 Reliability statistics

Cronbach's Alpha	Number of items
0.765	20

Source: Author's Construct

In conclusion, the methodology employed in this research study has been designed to provide a comprehensive and robust analysis of the study. By utilizing a mixed-methods approach that combines both qualitative and quantitative data collection methods, the research objectives have been effectively addressed.

Results and Discussion

The data extracted from the questionnaires, interviews, and the contents of documents collected were captured in SPSS and Nvivo to aid data analysis to draw conclusions and make recommendations in line with the study objectives, the literature reviewed, and providing answers to the research questions. The outcomes aimed to comprehend the challenges faced by SMEs in emerging markets in the adoption and implementation of IFRS. These approaches allow for a more in-depth exploration of the challenges, capturing both numerical trends and contextual insights. They allow for a nuanced exploration of these challenges by capturing both objective data and subjective experiences, opinions, and perceptions.

Individual and SME Characteristics

Personal Characteristics of Study Participants

A total of 72(100%) participants took part in the current study, out of which 44(61.1%) were males and 28(38.9%) were females. Four (5.6%) were less than 21 years, 44(61.1%) were within the ages of 21–30 years, 18 (25.0%) between the ages of 31 and 40 years, and the remaining 6(8.3%) were aged from 41 to 50 years.

Majority (44.4%) of the participants were designated as Junior staff, 20(27.8%) were Senior staff, 16(22.2%) were Management staff, 2(2.8%) were Contract staff, as well as 2(2.8%) being Founders. Forty-six (63.8%) of the respondents had Bachelor's degree, 12(16.7%) had Master's degree, 10(13.9%) had HND, 2(2.8%) had Doctorate degree, and the remaining 2(2.8%) had Diploma.

Most (61.1%) of respondents had below 5 years of working experience in their current institution or enterprise, 18(25.0%) of them had between 6 and 10 years, 6(8.3%) had 11 to 15 years of experience, whereas 4(5.6%) had more than 15 years of experience. See Table 2 for details.

Table 2 Sociodemographic characteristics of participants

Parameter	Frequency	Percentage (%)
Total	72	100
Gender		
Female	28	38.9
Male	44	61.1
Age group (years)		
Less than 21 years	4	5.6
21–30 years	44	61.1
31–40 years	18	25.0
41–50 years	6	8.3
Designation		
Contract staff	2	2.8
Junior staff	32	44.4
Senior staff	20	27.8
Management staff	16	22.2
Founder	2	2.8
Educational qualification		
Diploma	2	2.8
HND	10	13.9
Bachelor's degree	46	63.8
Master's degree	12	16.7
Doctorate's degree	2	2.8
Years of working experience in your current institution or enterprise		
Below 5 years	44	61.1
6–10 years	18	25.0
11–15 years	6	8.3
16 years and above	4	5.6

Source: Author's Construct

General Information on SMEs

Figure 1 presents the size of SMEs (in terms of employees). More than half (52.8%) of participants attested that their enterprises were microenterprises, 25% were small enterprises, 8.3% were medium-sized enterprises, whereas 13.9% were big-sized enterprises.

Figure 2 presents the years of operation of SMEs. More than half (52.8%) of participants attested that their firms had been in operation for less than 5 years, 25% between 5 and 10 years, 8.3 percent for 11–20 years, whereas 13.9% had been around for between 21 and 30 years.

Table 3 presents SMEs industry of operation and geographical location. Most (36.0%) of the firms provide services (consulting, advertising, etc.), 20(27.8%) were Healthcare and pharmaceuticals enterprises, 10(13.8%) provide financial services and banking. Major part of the enterprises is located at Adentan (19.3%), followed by Accra Central (13.9%), and Newtown (13.9%).

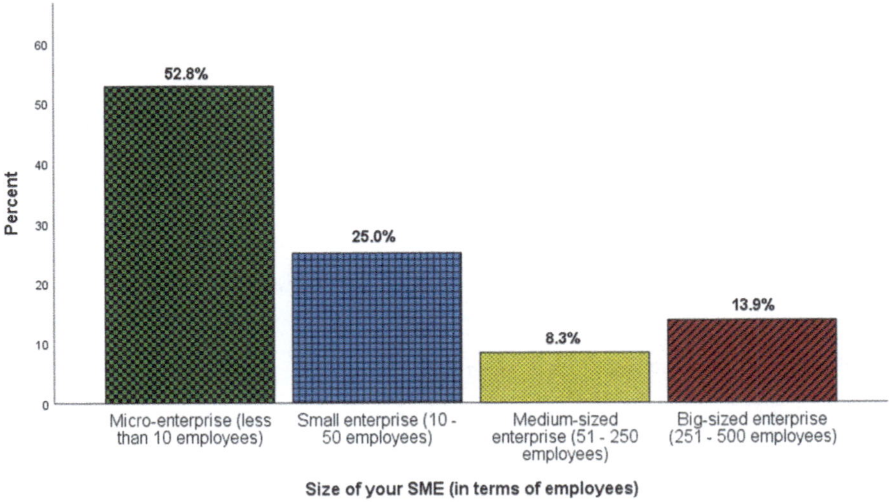

Fig. 1 Size of SMEs (in terms of employees)

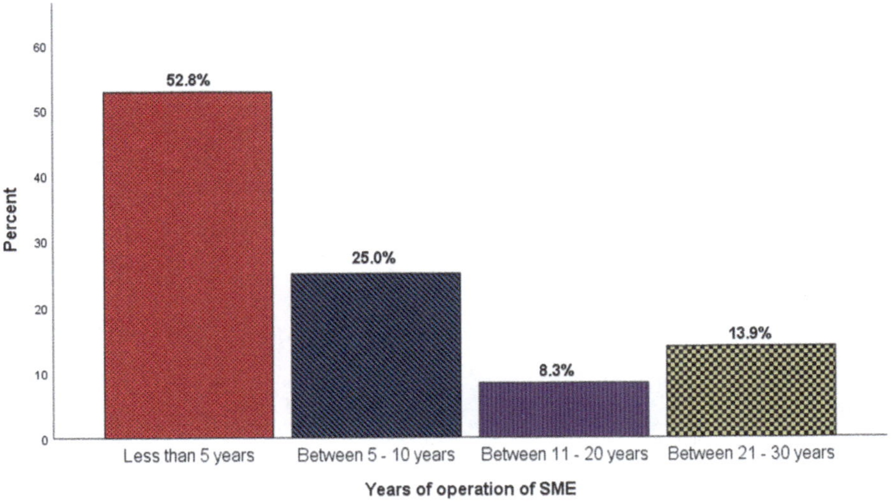

Fig. 2 Years of operation of SMEs

Challenges in IFRS Adoption and Implementation

Table 4 presents the challenges in IFRS adoption and implementation. Majority of the study participants agree that SMEs face financial constraints that hinder effective implementation of IFRS (55.6%), the complexity of IFRS requirements poses significant challenges for SMEs in emerging markets (63.9%), SMEs in emerging markets struggle to access qualified professionals in IFRS implementation (47.2%),

Table 3 SMEs' industry of operation and geographical location

Parameter	Frequency	Percentage (%)
Total	72	100
Industry of SME operation		
Baking	2	2.8
Building finishing	2	2.8
Clothing	2	2.8
Construction	2	2.8
Cosmetics	2	2.8
Estate development	2	2.8
Financial services and banking	10	13.8
Healthcare and pharmaceuticals	20	27.8
Pharmacy council	2	2.8
Services (consulting, advertising, etc.)	26	36.0
Vehicle limited	2	2.8
Geographical location of SME		
Ablekuma	2	2.8
Accra central	10	13.9
Achimota	2	2.8
Adenta	14	19.3
Awoshie	2	2.8
Botwe	6	8.3
Kanda	2	2.8
Kaneshie	2	2.8
Kasoa	2	2.8
Koforidua	4	5.6
Lakeside estates	6	8.3
Lapaz	2	2.8
Madina	4	5.6
Newtown	10	13.8
Old barrier	2	2.8
Ring road west	2	2.8

Source: Author's Construct

cultural and institutional factors in emerging markets create obstacles for SMEs in the adoption and implementation of IFRS (47.2%), limited awareness and understanding of IFRS among SMEs in emerging markets hinder successful implementation (58.3%), and SMEs in emerging markets find it challenging to navigate the legal and regulatory framework related to IFRS adoption (55.6%).

Table 4 Challenges in IFRS adoption and implementation

Parameter	Frequency	Percentage (%)
Total	*72*	*100*
SMEs face financial constraints that hinder effective implementation of IFRS		
Disagree	14	19.4
Undecided	18	25.0
Agree	40	55.6
The complexity of IFRS requirements poses significant challenges for SMEs in emerging markets		
Disagree	12	16.7
Undecided	14	19.4
Agree	46	63.9
SMEs in emerging markets struggle to access qualified professionals in IFRS implementation		
Disagree	18	25.0
Undecided	20	27.8
Agree	34	47.2
Cultural and institutional factors in emerging markets create obstacles for SMEs in the adoption and implementation IFRS		
Disagree	16	22.2
Undecided	22	30.6
Agree	34	47.2
Limited awareness and understanding of IFRS among SMEs in emerging markets hinder successful implementation		
Disagree	10	13.9
Undecided	20	27.8
Agree	42	58.3
SMEs in emerging markets find it challenging to navigate the legal and regulatory framework related to IFRS adoption		
Disagree	10	13.9
Undecided	22	30.6
Agree	40	55.6

Source: Author's Construct

The Impacts and Benefits of IFRS Adoption and Implementation

Table 5 presents the impacts and benefits of IFRS adoption and implementation. More than half (69.4%) of the study participants agree that capacity building initiatives and educational programs are crucial for supporting SMEs in IFRS implementation, and simplification and guidance tailored specifically for SMEs are necessary to facilitate IFRS adoption in emerging markets (61.1%). Close to 65 percent (69.4%) of respondents agreed that the collaboration between accounting professionals and SMEs is essential to overcome the challenges, whereas 13.9% disagreed. 50.0% of the participants agreed that government support and incentives play a crucial role in encouraging SMEs to adopt IFRS, whereas 19.4% thought otherwise.

Table 5 The impacts and benefits of IFRS adoption and implementation

Parameter	Frequency	Percentage (%)
Total	*72*	*100*
Capacity building initiatives and educational programs are crucial for supporting SMEs in IFRS implementation		
Disagree	10	13.9
Undecided	12	16.7
Agree	50	69.4
Simplification and guidance tailored specifically for SMEs are necessary to facilitate IFRS adoption in emerging markets		
Disagree	10	13.9
Undecided	18	25.0
Agree	44	61.1
Collaboration between accounting professionals and SMEs is essential to overcome the challenges		
Disagree	10	13.9
Undecided	12	16.7
Agree	50	69.4
Government support and incentives play a crucial role in encouraging SMEs to adopt IFRS		
Disagree	14	19.4
Undecided	22	30.6
Agree	36	50.0
Collaboration between academia and industry can contribute to enhancing SMEs knowledge and understanding of IFRS		
Disagree	8	11.1
Undecided	12	16.7
Agree	52	72.2
Policy reforms are necessary to create an enabling environment for SMEs in emerging markets to adopt IFRS		
Disagree	10	13.9
Undecided	14	19.4
Agree	48	66.7
Industry associations should play an active role in disseminating information and best practices related to IFRS adoption		
Disagree	8	11.1
Undecided	18	25.0
Agree	46	63.9

Source: Author's Construct

About 72.2 percent of the respondents agreed that collaboration between academia and industry can contribute to enhancing SMEs' knowledge and understanding of IFRS; however, 11.1% disagreed.

Also, 66.7% of participants agreed that the policy reforms are necessary to create an enabling environment for SMEs in emerging markets to adopt IFRS, but 13.9% disagreed. With regard to whether industry associations should play an active role in

Table 6 Strategies and recommendations for implementation of IRFS

Parameter	Frequency	Percentage (%)
Total	72	100
IFRS adoption by SMEs in emerging markets enhances the quality of financial reporting practices		
Disagree	12	16.7
Undecided	16	22.2
Agree	44	61.1
IFRS adoption improves the comparability of financial statements among SMEs in emerging markets		
Disagree	10	13.9
Undecided	10	13.9
Agree	52	72.2
Successful IFRS implementation increases SMEs credibility and enhances trust among stakeholders		
Disagree	12	16.7
Undecided	16	22.2
Agree	44	61.1
Access to capital markets is improved for SMEs in emerging markets that adopt IFRS		
Disagree	10	13.9
Undecided	14	19.4
Agree	48	66.7

The data are presented as frequency and percentage

disseminating information and best practices related to IFRS adoption, 63.9% of respondents agreed, whereas 11.1% disagreed.

Strategies and Recommendations

Table 6 presents the strategies and recommendations for implementation of IFRS. More than 50% (61.1%) of respondents agree that IFRS adoption by SMEs in emerging markets enhances the quality of financial reporting practices; however, 16.7% disagreed. 72.2% of the participants agreed that IFRS adoption improves the comparability of financial statements among SMEs in emerging markets, yet 13.9% disagreed.

Majority (61.1%) of the respondents agreed that successful IFRS implementation increases SMEs credibility and enhances trust among stakeholders; nevertheless, 16.7% disagreed. Also, 66.7% respondents agreed that access to capital markets is improved for SMEs in emerging markets that adopt IFRS; conversely, 13.9% disagreed.

Conclusions

This study concluded based on the research findings inherent in this research, providing highlights on the significance of International Financial Reporting Standards (IFRSs) adoption by Small and Medium Enterprises (SMEs) in emerging markets. A comprehensive review of existing literature was carried out to delve into the factors influencing IFRS adoption by SMEs in emerging markets, exploring prior research on the challenges and opportunities associated with the implementation process, and this highlighted the gaps in the literature that the current study sought to address. The research design and methodology employed was the mixed-methods approach, detailing the use of surveys, interviews, and case studies to gather data from a diverse sample of SMEs operating in different parts of the economies of the emerging markets. The findings of our study were discussed, detailing a comprehensive analysis of the challenges encountered by SMEs during the implementation of IFRS in emerging markets. Examining the challenges faced by SMEs in implementing IFRS within the context of emerging markets. We identified a range of obstacles that hinder the adoption and effective implementation of IFRS by SMEs in these dynamic markets. Our findings underscored several significant challenges, including, but not limited to, very limited awareness and understanding of IFRS, coupled with financial constraints, emerging as primary barriers that SMEs encounter during their IFRS adoption journey.

In examining the existing body of research, a potential research gap emerges (see Kamotho and Kaudo (2023), Hafiku (2017), Sappor et al. (2023), Zubairu et al. (2021), Arhin et al. (2017), and Morrison et al. (2022)). While studies acknowledge the significance of collaboration among stakeholders, there is dearth of comprehensive investigations into the empirical outcomes of collaborative efforts, such as government–industry partnerships and academia–industry collaborations, on the successful IFRS adoption by SMEs in emerging markets. This unexplored area presents an avenue for future research to contribute nuanced insights and practical implications for fostering collaboration that effectively addresses the identified challenges. Finally, our study sheds light on the challenges encountered by SMEs in implementing IFRS in emerging markets. The diverse array of hurdles, ranging from awareness gaps to financial constraints, underscores the need for targeted strategies that leverage collaborative efforts and account for the contextual intricacies unique to these markets. By addressing these challenges, stakeholders can promote transparent financial reporting practices and bolster the growth of SMEs, ultimately contributing to the vibrancy of emerging markets on the global stage.

Recommendations and Policy Implications

With reference to the findings of this study, the following recommendations has been made:

- Regulatory bodies and other relevant stakeholders should develop and promote targeted awareness campaigns and educational programs to enhance the understanding of IFRS among SMEs. These programs can help address the challenge of limited awareness and improve overall adoption and implementation rates.
- The International Accounting Standards Board (IASB) should collaborate with accounting professionals and regulatory bodies to develop simplified and tailored versions of IFRS requirements specifically designed for SMEs in emerging markets. This could facilitate smoother adoption and implementation processes.
- Government should provide financial support and incentives for SMEs to adopt IFRS. This could include grants, subsidies, or tax benefits that help alleviate the financial constraints faced by these businesses during the transition.
- Stakeholders should establish capacity building initiatives that provide hands-on training, workshops, and mentorship opportunities for SMEs. This can help them navigate the complexities of IFRS adoption and implementation effectively.
- Stakeholders should advocate for policy reforms that create a favorable regulatory environment for SMEs to adopt IFRS. This could involve streamlining regulations, reducing bureaucratic hurdles, and providing clear guidelines for compliance.
- Stakeholders should compile case studies of SMEs that have successfully adopted IFRS in emerging markets. These real-world examples can serve as inspiration and provide actionable insights for other SMEs considering adoption.

This study can have a number of policy implications that have been highlighted here for both practitioners and academics as follows:

- *Bridging the Gap in Knowledge*: This research fills an important gap in knowledge. While much research has been conducted on IFRS adoption in developed markets, there is limited understanding of the specific challenges faced by SMEs in emerging markets. This research will contribute to a deeper understanding of the unique obstacles and complexities encountered by SMEs in these markets.
- *Policy Implications*: The findings of this research can have significant policy implications. Governments and regulatory bodies in emerging markets can use the insights gained to design tailored policies, frameworks, and support mechanisms that facilitate the adoption and implementation of IFRS by SMEs. Such policies can contribute to improved financial reporting quality, transparency, and comparability, leading to enhanced investor confidence and economic growth.
- *Empowering SMEs*: SMEs play a crucial role in the economic development of emerging markets. By evaluating the challenges they face in implementing IFRS, this research empowers SMEs by providing them with a better understanding of the potential obstacles and strategies to overcome them.
- *Investor Confidence and Access to Capital*: Accurate and transparent financial reporting is essential for investor confidence. By addressing the challenges faced by SMEs in implementing IFRS, this research contributes to improving the quality and reliability of financial information provided by SMEs in emerging markets. Enhanced financial reporting can increase investor trust, expand access to capital, and encourage domestic and foreign investment in SMEs.

- *Knowledge Sharing and Capacity Building:* The research findings can serve as a valuable resource for academic institutions, professional organizations, and training institutions in emerging markets. The identification of challenges and recommended solutions can inform curriculum development, training programs, and capacity building initiatives aimed at enhancing financial literacy, accounting expertise, and the adoption of IFRS among SMEs.
- *Comparative Analysis and Benchmarking:* The research's comparative analysis of the challenges faced by SMEs across different industries provides insights into the variations and similarities in obstacles. This allows for benchmarking and sharing of best practices among SMEs, enabling policymakers and stakeholders to learn from successful experiences and develop strategies that are tailored to their specific contexts.

Finally, this research study holds significant importance as it addresses the challenges faced by SMEs in implementing IFRS in emerging markets, offering valuable insights for policymakers, SMEs themselves, investors, and other stakeholders. It has the potential to contribute to improved financial reporting practices, investor confidence, access to capital, and overall economic development in these markets.

References

Abedana, V., Omane-Antwi, K., & Oppong, M. (2016). Adoption of IFRS/IAS in Ghana: Impact on quality of corporate financial reporting and related corporate tax burden. *Research Journal of Finance and Accounting, 7*(8), 10–25.

Ajzen, I. (1991). The theory of planned behaviour. *Organizational Behaviour and Human Decision Processes, 50*(2), 179–211. https://doi.org/10.1016/0749-5978(91)90020-T

Albu, N., Albu, C. N., Bunea, S., Calu, D. A., & Gibina, M. M. (2011). A story about IAS/IFRS Implementation in Romania. *Journal of Accounting in Emerging Economies.*

Archer, S., & Ghadbane, A. (2018). An exploration of international financial reporting standard for small and medium-sized entities (IFRS for SMEs) implementation: Evidence from the UK. *Journal of Small Business and Enterprise Development, 25*(2), 201–217.

Arhin, T., Perprem, A., & Huledu, A. (2017). The challenges of adopting and implementing IFRS for SMEs in Ghana. A case of SMEs in the Kumasi Metropolis. *Research Journal's Journal of Accounting*, 1–13.

Barya, H. (2017). *Implementing IFRS for SMEs in Developing Countries*, Afghan Economic Society, Volume 035 Bocheum/Kabul.

Beck, C. T., & Polit, D. F. (2017). *Nursing research: Generating and assessing evidence for nursing practice* (10th ed.). Wolters Kluwer Health. 784p, CrossRef.

Bhiman, A., & Sidhu, B. K. (2013). Financial reporting standards and voluntary disclosures: Analysis of the IFRS adoption process. *Journal of Accounting and Public Policy, 32*(1), 1–31.

Bryman, A. (2004). *Social research methods* (2nd ed.). Oxford University Press.

Bryman, A., & Bell, E. (2003). *Business research methods*. Oxford University Press.

Carroll, C. E. D. (Ed.). (2016). *The sage Encyclopaedia of corporate reputation*. Sage Publication.

Chui, L., Evans, E., & Hassell, J. M. (2015). The impact of international financial reporting standards on small and medium-sized entities: Evidence from New Zealand. *Small Business Economics, 45*(1), 55–77.

Creswell, J. W. (2007). *Qualitative inquiry and research design. Choosing among five approaches* (2nd ed.). Sage Publication Inc.

Creswell, J. W. (2008). *Educational research: Planning, conducting and evaluating quantitative and qualitative research* (3rd ed.). Merrill.

Creswell, J. W. (2009). *Research design: Qualitative, quantitative and mixed methods approaches* (3rd ed.). Sage Publications Inc.

Creswell, J. W., Plano Clark, V. L., Gutmann, M., & Hanson, W. (2003). Advanced mixed methods designs. In A. Tashakkori & C. Teddlie (Eds.), *Handbook of mixed method research in the social and Behavioural sciences* (pp. 209–240). Sage Publications Inc.

Creswll, J. W., & Creswell, J. D. (2017). Research design: Qualitative. In *Quantitative and mixed methods approaches* (5th ed.). Sage Publication.

Daske, H., Hail, L., Leuz, C., & Verdi, R. (2008). Mandatory IFRS reporting around the world: Early evidence on the economic consequences. *Journal of Accounting Research, 46*(5), 1085–1142.

Deloitte Touche Tomatsu. (2017). *IAS Plus*. Available at www.iasplus.com/. Accessed 04.24.

Doupnik, T. S., & Salter, S. B. (2016). *International accounting* (4th ed.). McGraw-Hill Education.

Ezeagba, C. (2017). Financial reporting in SMEs in Nigeria. Challenges and options. *International Journal of Academic Research in Accounting, Finance and Management Sciences, 7*(1), 1–10.

Florou, A., Kosi, U., & Pope, P. F. (2017). Are international accounting standards more credit-relevant than domestic standard? *Accounting and Research, 47*(1), 1–29.

Ghana Stock Exchange GSE. (2022). *Listing rule for small and medium Enterprises in Ghana*. GSE Press.

Gibson, B., & O'Donnel. (2015). Identifying barriers to implementing IFRS for SMEs in a developing economy: A study of Fiji. *Journal of Pacific Rim Psychology, 9*(2), 85–98.

Gray, S. J. (2010). Factors influencing the adoption of international financial reporting standards in developing countries. *The International Journal of Accounting, 45*(1), 1–27.

Hafiku, H. I. (2017). *Constraints of Financing Small and Medium Enterprises in Namibia, Core Collection*. Doctoral Thesis University of Namibia.

Hoque, Z. (2006). An empirical investigation of the implementation of international accounting standards in an emerging economy. *The International Journal of Accounting, 41*(3), 266–288.

IASB. (2016). *Small and medium sized entities*. http://www.ifrs.org/IFRS. Accessed 02.24.

IASB. (2018). *Supporting Material for the IFRS for SMEs*. Retrieved from: http://www.ifrs.org/news-and-events/2024/06-available/(3)(PDF). *The Problem of Training Specialist in IFRS for SMEs*.

IASB. (2020). The Impact of the Adoption of IFRS on the Comparability of Accounting Information. The International Accounting Standards Board (IASB) Research Forum in conjunction with Accounting and Business Research (ABR), 2–3 November 2020.

Iatridis, G. E. (2010). International financial reporting standards and the quality of financial statement information. *International Review of Financial Analysis, 19*(3), 193–204.

IFRS Foundation. (2017). *IFRS Application around the World*, Jurisdictional Profile: Malaysia. http://www.ifrs.org/document. Retrieved: 05.24.

Institute of Chartered Accountants Ghana – ICAG. (2021). *Adopting the International Reporting Standards: A Review for Implementation in Ghana*. ICA Students Journal, Lagos Street, East Legon.

Islam, M. A., & Deegan, C. (2008). Motivations for an organization within a developing country to report social responsibility information: Evidence from Bangladesh. *Accounting, Auditing & Accountability Journal, 21*(6), 850–874.

Johnson, R. B., Onwuegbuzie, A. J., & Turner, J. (2007). Towards a definition of mixed methods research. *Journal of Mixed Methods Research, 1*(12), 112–133.

Kamotho, D. W., & Kaudo, P. K. (2023). The challenges small and medium-sized entities face in adopting and implementing international financial reporting standards for small and medium-sized entities: A case study of Windhoek central Business District. *International Journal of Management Science and Business Administration, 9*(4), 7–20.

Karlan, D., & Morduch, J. (2010). Chapter 71—Access to finance. In O. Roderick & M. Risenzweig (Eds.), *Handbook of development economics* (Vol. 5, pp. 4703–4784). Elsevier.

KPMG. (2021). KPMG's Insights into IFRS 2020/2021. Sweet & Maxwell U.K. ISBN: 9780414079731

Labin, S. N., Duffy, J. L., Meyers, D. C., & Wondersman, A. (2021). A research synthesis of evaluation of capacity building literature. *American Journal of Evaluation, 33*(3). https://doi.org/10.1177/109821011434608

Lazar, A. (2018). International financial reporting standards (IFRS) implementation: Some lessons learned. *Economic Computation and Economic Cybernetics Studies and Research, 52*(1), 103–120.

Lyons, M. (2014). The legal and regulatory environment of the third sector. *Asian Journal of Public Administration, 25*(1), 87–106.

Mbawuni, J. (2018). Perceived Benefits and Challenges of IFRS Adoption in Ghana: Views of Members of Institute of Chartered Accountants, Ghana (ICAG). *International Journal of Financial Research, Sciedu Press, 9*(1), 99–114.

Morrison, L. J., Wilmshurst, T., & Shimeld, S. (2022). "Counting Nature: Some Implications of Quantifying Environmental Issues in Corporate Reports", Meditari Accountancy Research, https://doi.org/10.1108/MEDAR-09-2020-1023

Nimatiere, M. (2016). *An investigation into the challenges faced by small to medium enterprise operators when adopting and implementing IFRS for SMEs in Zimbabwe*. Retrieved 06.24.

Nobes, C., & Zeff, S. A. (2018). A critical perspective on international financial reporting: Old issues and new challenges. *Ababus, 54*(3), 442–477.

Oketch, J. O., Kelika, J. M., & Kinyua, G. M. (2020). The moderating role of the legal environment on the relation between TMT characteristics and Organisational performance in regulatory setting in Kenya. *Journal of Economics and Business, 3*(1) SSRN, http://ssrn.com

Othman, R., & Ameer, R. (2014). Challenges faced by small and medium-sized enterprises (SMEs) in Malaysia: An intellectual capital perspective. *Procedia-Social and Behavioural Sciences, 129*, 389–395.

Pallant, J. (2017). *SPSS survival manual. A step-by-step guide to data analysis using SPSS* (4th ed.). Open University Press.

Republic of Ghana. (2004). *Venture Capital Trust Fund Act, 2004 (Act 680)*. Assembly Press.

Rudzani, S., & Charles, M. D. (2016). An assessment of the challenges of adopting and implementing IFRSS for SMEs in South Africa. *Problems and Perspectives in Management, 14*(2-1), 212–221. https://doi.org/10.21511/ppm.14(2-1).2016.10.

Samujh, H., & Dev, S. S. (2015). Implementing IFRS for SMEs: Challenges for developing economies. *International Journal Managing Sustainability, 4*(3), 39–59.

Sappor, P., Atta, S. F., & Ahmed Seidu Seini, R. (2023). The adoption of IFRS for SMEs in the northern sector of Ghana: A case of structural equation Modelling. *Cogent Business & Management, 10*(1), 2180840. https://doi.org/10.1080/23311975.2023.2180840

Saunders, M. N., Lewis, P., Bristow, A., & Thornhill, A. (2019). *Research methods for business students: Understanding research philosophy and approaches to theory development* (8th ed.). Pearson Education.

Sautet, F. (2013). Local and systemic entrepreneurship: Solving the puzzle of entrepreneurship and economic development. *Entrepreneurship Theory and Practice, 37*(2), 387–402.

Sidhu, B. K., & Jallow, K. (2019). The challenges of implementing international financial reporting standard (IFRS) in emerging economies: Evidence from The Gambia. *Research in International Business and Finance, 47*, 562–571.

Simist, Z. T., Guay, N. S., & Vayvay, O. (2014). *Theory of constraints: A literature review. 10th international strategic management conference*. Procedia. Social Behavioural Sciences (pp. 930–936).

Solanke, A. A., Adinnu, P., & Alhassan, K. A. (2016). Adoption of International Financial Reporting Standard for Small and Medium Enterprises in North Central Nigeria: Implications for Financial Reporting Quality. *International Journal of Sciences: Basic and Applied Research (IJSBAR), 30*(3), 89–101. https://www.gssrr.org/index.php/JournalOfBasicAndApplied/article/view/6456

Vendy, V., & Sucahyati, D. (2022). Issues and Challenges of Adoption of IFRS for SMEs in Malaysia. In *5th International Conference of Economics, Business and Governance Challenges, 2022. NST Proceedings* (pp. 6–12). https://doi.org/10.11594/nstp.2022.2302

World Bank. (2017). *Doing business 2016: Understanding regulations for small and medium-size enterprises*. World Bank Group.

Zubairu, I. (2010). The Effects of Mandatory Adoption of International Financial Reporting Standards (IFRS) on Net Incomes of Listed Companies on Ghana Stock Exchange. In *Conference Proceedings; 3rd Annual Applied Research Conference on Strengthening the Linkage between Theory and Practice*.

Zubairu, I., Dawson, S., & Idrissu, A. J. (2021). Implementation of IFRS in informal sector: An evaluation of the institutional capacity for quality financial reporting. *Journal of Accounting and Auditing, 12*(2), 24–38.

Impact of Money Supply and Exchange Rate on Economic Growth in Nigeria

Azeez Adebanjo Wahab and Michael Olajide Adelowotan

Abstract The study examines the interplay between money supply, exchange rate, and economic growth in Nigeria over a period of 20 years. It sought to evaluate the extent to which the money supply affects gross domestic product and also, to find out the effect of exchange rate on gross domestic product in Nigeria. To achieve these objectives, a model was formulated, and an Autoregressive Distributed Lag (ARDL) Cointegration Technique was used as a method of analysis. The variables used in the study were further subjected to Bounds test and other econometric tests. The data were cointegrated at order 1(1) and order 1(0). The long-run relationship of the underlying variables is detected through the F-statistic (Wald test). The study revealed that exchange rate has positive and significant influence on the economic growth in Nigeria measured with LGDP. The result was not consistent with the negative a priori expectation. Also, the result obtained shows that the relationship between money supply and gross domestic product in Nigeria is positive but insignificant. The study, therefore, recommends that regulators should hand down regulations that control the supplies of money in the circulation and that government should put on policy implementation that will ensure the stability of naira value.

Keywords Money supply · Exchange rate · Gross domestic product · Economic growth · ARDL · Time series

---

A. A. Wahab (✉)
Federal College of Education (Technical), Yaba, Nigeria

M. O. Adelowotan
University of Johannesburg, Johannesburg, South Africa
e-mail: madelowotan@uj.ac.za

T. Moloi (ed.), *Impacting Society Positively Through Technology in Accounting and Business Processes*, Springer Proceedings in Business and Economics,
https://doi.org/10.1007/978-3-031-84885-8_9

Introduction

Background to the Study

Nigeria is the most populous country in Africa and has the largest economy on the continent. It is rich in natural resources, particularly oil, which accounts for a significant portion of government revenue and export earnings (National Bureau of Statistics, 2022). Despite this wealth, Nigeria faces numerous economic challenges, including high unemployment, inflation, and a large informal economy. Nigeria's economy, which depends mostly on imports, is prone to erratic business cycles, stalled growth, and economic turbulence. Common results of this include low productivity, inflation, unemployment, and an imbalance in the balance of payments. The government has managed and controlled the economy in one way or another to maximize the welfare of the people. One way to do this is by implementing monetary policy to ensure that resources are allocated and employed properly (Batrancea et al., 2023). A series of actions referred to as monetary policy are meant to regulate how the economy is financed. In general, these actions are taken by the monetary authorities, in particular the Central Bank, to alter (increase or decrease) the amount of money in the economy, thereby regulating a number of macroeconomic variables like production, investment, consumption, inflation, and even the value of the national currency (Ngouhouo & Nkemgha, 2018). In fact, up until the end of the 1970s, monetary policy was typically utilized as a tool for managing the economy, and it was thus employed for "economic revival" or "contraction" as needed. Since the start of the 1980s, central banks have increased their independence and adopted liberal monetary policies, which are primarily intended to maintain price stability thereby improve the economic growth of the country (Idan & Badan, 2022; Doran et al., 2018). Two major tools of the monetary policy are the money supply and exchange. The relationship between money supply, exchange rate, and economic growth in Nigeria is complex and influenced by both internal and external factors. Policymakers must consider global economic trends, domestic political stability, and structural issues within the Nigerian economy. Understanding these relationships can help guide effective economic policies to promote sustainable growth.

Money supply refers to the total volume of money circulating in an economy at a given time, which includes cash, coins, and balances held in bank accounts. It is a critical component of a nation's monetary policy. In theory, an increase in the money supply can stimulate economic growth by lowering interest rates and encouraging investment and consumption (Mankiw, 2018). However, if the increase is not managed carefully, it can lead to inflationary pressures, which can have a detrimental impact on the economy (Abdurhman & Dagmawe, 2023).

In Nigeria, the Central Bank has used changes in the money supply to steer economic development. In 2017, the Central Bank of Nigeria (CBN) launched the Anchor Borrowers' Programme (ABP) to provide loans to farmers at a subsidized interest rate. The ABP has been successful in boosting agricultural production and economic growth. Expanding the money supply, often through open market operations and lending facilities, can stimulate economic growth by encouraging lending, investments, and consumer spending. Conversely, contracting the money supply can be a measure to control inflationary pressures. The real impact of money supply management in Nigeria's economic development is evident in its role in mitigating economic challenges. For instance, during the COVID-19 pandemic, the Central Bank's monetary policy measures, including increased money supply, helped to stabilize the economy and stimulate growth (Jackson et al., 2020).

In addition, the management of money supply has been a central focus for the Central Bank of Nigeria (CBN). The CBN aims to balance the growth of money supply with other economic indicators to avoid inflation and promote economic stability (Central Bank of Nigeria (CBN), 2022). However, the relationship between money supply and economic growth in Nigeria has been inconsistent, with periods of both rapid growth and high inflation.

Exchange rates, another critical facet of monetary policy, play a pivotal role in influencing the external value of a country's currency and, by extension, its trade balance and international competitiveness. The exchange rate is the value of one currency for the purpose of conversion to another. It affects international trade, capital flows, and overall economic stability. A stable exchange rate can promote economic growth by providing a predictable environment for investors and reducing the risk associated with international transactions (Krugman & Obstfeld, 2017). Conversely, exchange rate volatility can create uncertainty, discouraging investment and impacting economic growth.

Nigeria's economy is highly dependent on oil exports, which means its exchange rate is influenced by global oil prices (Ogbonna, 2019). This dependency has led to significant fluctuations in the exchange rate, affecting the cost of imports and the competitiveness of exports. The CBN has implemented various policies to stabilize the exchange rate, but challenges persist, especially during periods of global economic instability.

In this changing world, economic growth is crucial since it tells us about the economic health and situation of a nation. Economic growth generally refers to an increase in a nation's ability to produce goods and services from one time period to the next. A growth indicator is the gross domestic product (GDP), which measures the value of all finished goods and services produced inside the nation in a given year.

Any country's economic development determines its future. The nations take many actions to strengthen their economies, yet there are some restrictions that serve as a barrier to economic progress, such as (1) Inequalities: Income distribution determines whether or not economic growth reduces relative poverty. The most vulnerable people in society may not benefit from economic improvement (Bogoviz et al., 2022). (2) Negative externalities: Economic growth may have unfavorable effects on the environment, crime, and traffic congestion, all of which degrade living standards. (3) Environmental concerns: A rise in carbon emissions is a contributing factor to global warming. Economic growth could be advantageous in the short run, but it will be costly in the long run.

While there have been several studies examining the effects of money supply and exchange rate on economic growth, the results are often inconclusive or context-specific. Given Nigeria's unique economic structure and its reliance on oil exports, there is a need for further research to understand the specific dynamics within the Nigerian economy.

The purpose of this study is to investigate the effects of money supply and exchange rate on economic growth in Nigeria. By analyzing historical data and examining trends, this study aims to provide insights into how these factors contribute to Nigeria's economic development and offer recommendations for policymakers.

Statement of the Problem

The relationship between money supply, exchange rate, and economic growth has been a subject of considerable debate among economists and policymakers, especially in developing economies like Nigeria. Nigeria, as one of the largest economies in Africa, has experienced significant fluctuations in its economic indicators, making it a crucial case for examining the dynamics of these variables.

Nigeria's economy is heavily dependent on oil revenues, which are susceptible to global price fluctuations. This dependence has resulted in volatile exchange rates, particularly in the wake of significant oil price shocks. Concurrently, the Central Bank of Nigeria (CBN) has adopted various monetary policies, including adjusting money supply, to influence the economy (Sanusi, 2011). These policy shifts are aimed at controlling inflation, managing exchange rates, and promoting economic growth. However, their effectiveness and impact on the broader economy require a deeper examination.

Despite the central role of money supply and exchange rate in economic policy, there is a lack of consensus on how these variables influence economic growth in Nigeria. Some studies suggest that an increase in money supply can stimulate economic growth by providing more capital for investment and consumption (Friedman, 1968). However, others contend that excessive money supply can lead to inflation, which can undermine economic growth (Keynes, 1936).

Similarly, the exchange rate has a complex relationship with economic growth. A stable exchange rate can promote trade and attract foreign investment, leading to economic growth (Mundell, 1968). Conversely, a volatile exchange rate can discourage investment and trade, leading to economic instability (Dornbusch, 1976). The dual pressures of maintaining a stable exchange rate and managing money supply have placed Nigerian policymakers in a challenging position, with conflicting priorities that can impact the overall economy.

The existing literature on the impact of money supply and exchange rate on economic growth in Nigeria often focuses on isolated aspects of these relationships. There is a need for comprehensive research that examines the interplay between money supply, exchange rate, and economic growth in Nigeria.

Research Objectives

The specific objectives of the study include the following:

1. To evaluate the extent to which the money supply affects gross domestic product in Nigeria.
2. To find out the effect of exchange rate on gross domestic product in Nigeria.

Research Hypothesis

The following null hypothesis were formulated to test the above objectives

HO_1 Money supply has no significant on gross domestic product in Nigeria.
HO_2 Exchange rate has no significant on gross domestic product in Nigeria.

Significances of the Study

The result from the study will be having several contributions. First, the study will serve as a valuable instrument to communicate to the stakeholders such as policymaker, Central Bank of Nigeria, investors, management, creditors, customers, government, general public and others about the impact of money supply vis-a-vis monetary policy on economic growth in Nigeria. Therefore, the result will give them guild when making an informed decision either to the existing stakeholders to increase their investment or not. The Central Bank of Nigeria that holds the key of monetary policy will also benefit from the study on the impact that their policies have on the growth of the economy in the country and know where to adjust or improve the policies for the betterment of the nation.

Finally, the study will serve as a valuable material to potential economic researchers, institutions, and other related researchers who may find it interesting to further their research interest in related area. In addition, the result will provide empirical justification on the existing debate on the body of extant literature.

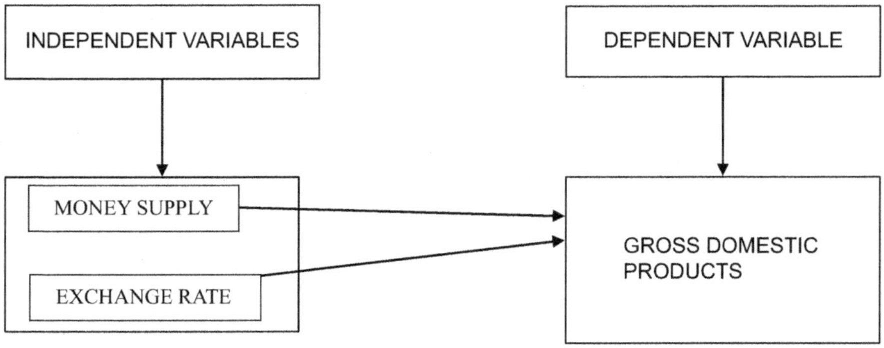

Fig. 1 Conceptualized by the researcher

Literature Review

Conceptual Framework

Based on the gap identified in the body of knowledge, a conceptual framework is presented in diagram as indicated in Fig. 1 showing the influence of the independent variable (money supply, exchange rate, cash reserve ratio, and import of goods and services) on dependent variable (gross domestic product).

The framework shows the direction of relationship between the independent variables and the dependent variable. The independent variable, which is monetary policy, is measured by its determinants such as money supply, exchange rate, inflation rate, and government spending has direct relationship with dependent variable measured by gross domestic product (GDP).

Theoretical Literature Review

In prior studies, a lot of theories on monetary policy have been identified such as Solow-Swan growth model theory, Keynesian Monetary Policy theory, and The Monetarist theory. This study anchors on Monetarist theory.

The Monetarist Theory

Milton Friedman is the leader of the monetarist school of thought. This line of thought is a contemporary adaptation of traditional macroeconomics. They created a more sophisticated and useful variation of the quantity theory of money. Like any school of thought, Friedman highlighted that the availability of money was the main element influencing the health of the economy and that an effective monetary policy was necessary to keep it stable. He also believes that the money supply should increase at a set rate rather than being controlled and altered by the monetary authority(ies) in order to encourage steady growth rates (Igharo et al., 2020). Friedman further asserted that the money supply can be held in a variety of forms, including cash, bonds, stocks, physical assets, and human capital, since it may be required for purposes other than anticipated transactions. Each type of this wealth has a varied yield and a distinct characteristic of its own. In the end, these effects will boost overall money demand and boost output. The monetarists concede that the real GDP level of full employment may not always be reached by the economy. As a result, monetarists contend that in the short run, expansionary monetary policies may raise real GDP by raising aggregate demand. They contend that the quantity theory is still a solid estimate of the relationship between the supply of money, price level, and real GDP in the long run, when the economy is operating at full employment. Additionally, an expansionary monetary policy over the long term has no impact on the level of real GDP; it simply causes inflation.

Empirical Review

Abille and Mpuure (2020) investigated the role of monetary policy as an instrument for growth in the Ghanaian economy. The study was conducted based on yearly data from 1983 to 2017. Economic growth was the regress and in the study, with money supply, inflation, and the lending rate as the repressor. The ARDL Bounds test technique was employed to investigate cointegration among the variables. The results confirmed the presence of cointegration among the variables. The results also showed the money supply as having a significant positive effect on growth in Ghana in the long run but a significant negative effect on growth in the short run. The lending rate, however, was found to have an insignificant negative effect on growth in the long run but a significant positive effect on growth in the short run.

Aliyev et al. (2020) investigated the impact of monetary policy tools on economic growth in Azerbaijan during 2005–2018 using the Vector Error Correction Model (VECM). Also, different cointegration methods, namely, Johansen, DOLS, FMOLS and CCR, were utilized for the robustness test. The outcomes of the different cointegration methods are consistent with one another and confirm the existence of long-run relationships among variables. Furthermore, the estimation results of VECM show that the monetary base and exchange rate have a positive and statistically significant impact on economic growth in the long run, while the discount rate is insignificant. The paper concludes that the monetary base and exchange rate should be promoted by policymakers over other monetary policy tools during monetary policy implementation toward stimulating economic growth.

Nwoko et al. (2016) examined the extent to which the Central Bank of Nigeria Monetary Policies could effectively be used to promote economic growth, covering the period of 1990–2011. The influence of money supply, average price, interest rate, and labor force were tested on gross domestic product using the multiple regression models as the main statistical tool of analysis. Studies show that CBN Monetary Policy measures are effective in regulating both the monetary and real sector aggregates such as employment, prices, level of output, and the rate of economic growth. The study indicates that average price and labor force have significant influence on gross domestic product, while money supply was not significant. Interest rate was negative and statistically significant. The period covered by the study stops at 2011; a lot of events and innovations have taken place since that time up till now.

Igharo et al. (2020) argued that African countries have great potentials to accelerate and sustain economic growth through effective monetary policies due to huge market potentials, growing population, availability of manpower, untapped natural resources, and other growth advantages, provided that effective policies are enacted. The study investigated the effect of monetary policy transmission mechanism and innovation in the banking system on economic growth in Nigeria. Data sourced from the Nigerian Central Bank Statistical Bulletin and World Development Indicators between 1981 and 2015 were engaged. The study adopted a vector autoregression and autoregressive distribution lag approaches for its analysis. The study revealed that, due to the large informal banking sector monetary policies have not been effective, and also supervisory and intermediary financial institutions lack dependence due to frequent government interventions.

In a study conducted on a panel of 133 nations from 1960 to 2018, Yin et al. (2022) explored and rigorously validated the effect of expansionary monetary policy activities on green innovation. Overall, whether in the static or dynamic model, we find that such activities considerably improve the performance of green innovation. It may be difficult for the effects of monetary policy to be effectively communicated to green innovation activities in developing nations due to lower levels of central bank independence and less robust property rights protection. Additionally, strict environmental regulations help to magnify the beneficial effects of the expansionary monetary policy on green innovation, but such a positive moderating effect should be supported by effective national governance (including better control over corruption, increased government efficiency, and a robust legal system). As a result, various policy recommendations are given.

In their study of the effects of monetary policy—including the money supply, repo rate, exchange rate, and inflation—on the economic growth of European Union (EU) nations.

Gap in Research

Based on the empirical studies reviewed, it was observed that differences in findings were indicated by prior studies, and majority of these studies focused on money supply, exchange rate, interest rate, and inflation rate. Many of their findings resulted into controversies. For example, Nwoko et al. (2016), Adegboyo et al. (2021), and

Abille and Mpuure (2020) says money supply has a negative significant on gross domestic product, while Aliyev et al. (2020) and Idowu et al. (2020) agreed that money supply has positive significant effects on gross domestic product of Nigeria. Hence, this led to an inconclusive that needs to be investigated.

Therefore, it is imperative to fill this gap by investigating the effects of money supply and exchange rate on national growth (proxy with growth domestic product) in Nigeria.

Research Methodology

Sample/Data

An ex post facto research design was employed by collecting data from a defined population. This research design leverages historical or past data to analyze and make predictions about future trends. The ex post facto design was chosen, as it allows the researcher to examine the relationship between variables that have already occurred, without the need for manipulation. The population of this study comprises all the major economic policies in Nigeria that drive the economic variables in Nigeria. To choose the study sample for this investigation, the researchers used a purposive sampling strategy. The study is particularly focused on Nigeria, taking into account the distinct elements that influence the country's economic growth. The study could not cover all the economic variables; hence, money supply and exchange rates were taken as the sample of the population of the study. The goal of the study was to provide a thorough understanding of current trends and the effects of money supply and exchange rates on economic growth over a twenty-year period, from 2003 to 2023.

The data for this research work were collected from the Central Bank of Nigeria Statistical Bulletin, Nigeria Bureau of Statistics, and World Bank Statistical Bulletin from the year 2002 to 2023. The Central Bank of Nigeria's Statistical Bulletin and the Nigeria Bureau of Statistics serve as primary sources for monetary policy. To gauge the level of economic growth in Nigeria, we turn to the World Bank Statistical Bulletin.

Research Design

The study used cross-sectional survey design to investigate the relationships that exist between money supply, exchange rate, and economic growth in Nigeria.

Study Area

The study is particularly focused on Nigeria, taking into account the distinct elements that influence the country's economic growth. The study could not cover all the economic policies; hence two variables of the monetary policy (money supply and exchange rate) are taken as the sample of the population of the study. The goal of the study was to provide a thorough understanding of current trends and the effects of the duo of money supply and exchange rate on economic growth over a 20-year period, from 2003 to 2023.

Data Analysis Procedure

Descriptive statistics was used to depict the characteristics of the population. The mean and the variance were calculated using Eview 9 statistical package. This study used Autoregressive Distributed Lag Model (ARDL) where economic growth was regressed against monetary policy.

Model Specification

The goal of multiple linear regression is to estimate the values of the coefficients (β0, β1..., βnβ0, β1..., βn) that best fit the data and allow to make predictions about the impact of the independent variables on the dependent variable. Below is the regression equation in consideration for this dissertation.

This study adopts the model used by Ifurueze and Ezeabasili which is mathematically represented by Eq. (1).

$$\text{GDP} = \text{f}\left(\text{HWCOST,EDCOST,RECCOST,SAFCOST}\right) \quad (1)$$

The above model (1) is modified as follows:

$$\text{GDP} = \text{f}\left(\text{MS,EXTR}\right) \quad (2)$$

Where:

GDP = gross domestic product
MS = money supply
EXTR = exchange rate

The above equation is converted into econometric form as follows:

$$\text{GDP}_{\text{it}} = \beta_0 + \beta_1\text{MS}_{\text{it}} + \beta_2\text{EXTR}_{\text{it}} \quad (3)$$

Transformed with the aid of logarithm into:

$$\log(\mathrm{GDP})_t = \beta_0 + \beta 1\log \mathrm{MSit} + \beta 2\log \mathrm{EXTRit} \quad (4)$$

Where: log(GDP) represents the log of Gross Domestic Product (income) at constant price.

$\log MS_{it}$ represents log of Money Supply.
$\log EXTR_{it}$ represents log of the Exchange Rate.
ε_{it} is the error term/disturbance term.
β_0 is the intercept or constant term.
β_1, β_2, are the estimating parameters of the model and are nonnegative.

Data Presentation and Analysis

Introduction

This chapter focuses on the presentation and interpretation of the methodology applied in this study. The ARDL was used to examine the impact of exchange rate and money supply on the economic growth in Nigeria using time series data from 2003 to 2023.

$$\log(\mathrm{GDP})_t = \beta_0 + \beta 1\log \mathrm{MSit} + \beta 2\log \mathrm{EXTRit} \quad (5)$$

$$\log(\mathrm{GDP})_t = -55.05593 + 23.1155\log \mathrm{MSit} + 1.007291\log \mathrm{EXTRit} \quad (6)$$

Table 1 shows the relationship between the monetary policy and economic growth where economic growth is by proxy gross domestic product in the model. The LGDP represents the dependent variable, and the independent variables are EXTR and MS. The ARDL regression result shows the relationship between money supply and economic growth. The relationship between LGDP and EXTR is positive 23.1155. From the above ARDL regression result, the positive regression result means that 1% increase in EXTR will lead to 23% increase in LGDP. The result therefore corroborated with the assumptions that increase in exchange rate as a proxy for monetary policy would positively affect economic growth (LGDP) in Nigeria.

Also, there is a positive relationship between MS and LGDP of 0.025101 in Nigeria. This means that 1% increase in money supply will lead to 0.03% increase in gross domestic product of the country.

In Table 1 , the R-squared which is the coefficient of determination is 0.560549 indicating that 56% of the independent variables are captured by the dependent variable thereby making the model a good fit. The Durbin-Watson statistics shows

Table 1 ARDL summary of result for model one

Dependent Variable: LGDP				
Method: ARDL				
Variable	Coefficient	Std. error	*t*-statistic	Prob.*
LGDP(−1)	0.057543	0.23461	0.245272	0.8098
EXTR	23.11752	20.47351	1.129143	0.0277
MS	0.025107	0.209157	0.120041	0.9062
C	−55.05593	44.53215	−1.236319	0.02367
FITTED^2	−0.054645	0.169576	−0.322248	0.752
R-squared	0.560549	Mean dependent var		0.561004
Adjusted R-squared	0.372213	S.D. dependent var		2.53448
S.E. Of regression	2.008145	Akaike info criterion		4.493501
Sum squared resid	56.45704	Schwarz criterion		4.841675
Log likelihood	−40.18176	Hannan-Quinn criter.		4.569064
F-statistic	2.976323	Durbin-Watson stat		1.852674
Prob(F-statistic)	0.04343			

Source: Eview 9, output 2024

Table 2 Heteroscedasticity test: Breusch-Pagan-Godfrey

Heteroscedasticity test: Breusch-Pagan-Godfrey			
F-statistic	0.571424	Prob. F(5,15)	0.721
Obs*R-squared	3.359977	Prob. Chi-Square(5)	0.6447
Scaled explained SS	3.897971	Prob. Chi-Square(5)	0.5642

Source: Eview 9, 2024

1.852674 indicating that there is a positive serial correlation and the F-statistic of 0.04343 shows that the model is statistically significant and thus that money supply and exchange rate affect economic growth in Nigeria (Table 2).

Homoscedasticity in regression is an important assumption; if the assumption is violated, you won't be able to use regression analysis. The Breusch-Pagan-Godfrey test is used to test for homoscedasticity. From the result, we can deduce that the Pro. (F-statistics is 0.571424) and the Prob. (Chi-square is 0.6447) indicate that both are not equal to 0, therefore the null hypothesis should therefore be accepted (no heteroscedasticity exists). Heteroscedasticity is mainly due to the presence of outlier in the data. Outlier in heteroscedasticity means that the observations that are either small or large with respect to the other observations are present in the sample. Heteroscedasticity is also caused due to omission of variables from the model.

The Bounds test is used to test for cointegration of the variables, if the variables are integrated in an order of I (1). As seen in Table 3 , the test statistic of the Bounds test of long-run relationship indicates the presence of a long-run relationship among the variables at 5% level of significant, thereby leading to the rejection of the null hypothesis of no long-run relationship and acceptance of the alternative. There are three options for the decision criteria when using the Bounds approach to cointegration: if the F-statistic is greater than the critical value for the upper bound 1(1), then

Table 3 Bounds test

ARDL Bounds Test		
Null hypothesis: No long-run relationships exist		
Test statistic	Value	K
F-statistic	6.696135	4
Critical value bounds		
Significance	I(0)bound	I(1)bound
10%	2.45	3.52
5%	2.86	4.01
2.50%	3.25	4.49
1%	3.74	5.06

Source: Eview 9, 2024

the study can conclude there is long-run relationship. If the F-statistic falls below the critical value for the lower bound 1(0), there is no cointegration, hence no long-run relationship. The test is also considered inconclusive, if the F-statistic falls between the lower bound 1(0) and the upper bound 1(1). Since the F-statistics (6.696135) obtained is greater than the critical value for the upper bound 1(1) at 5% level of significance (6.696135 > 4.01), hence it is concluded that the variables show evidence of long-run relationship.

Test of Hypotheses with ARDL Regression

Hypothesis One Restated

H_0: *Money supply has no significant on gross domestic product in Nigeria.*

Method: ARDL		
Variable	Coefficient	Prob.*
LMS	0.025107	0.9062

Source: Eview 9, output 2024

Decision: This hypothesis is tested based on the results of the ARDL regression. From the results, LMS has a coefficient of 0.025107 and probability value of 0.9062, which implies that the null hypothesis one (H01), which says that money supply has no significant effect on gross domestic product in Nigeria, would be accepted at 5% level. Hence, there is positive insignificant impact of LMS on the economic growth in Nigeria at the 5% level of significance.

Hypothesis Two Restated

HO_2: *Exchange rate has no significant on gross domestic product in Nigeria.*

Method: ARDL		
Variable	Coefficient	Prob.*
LEXTR	23.11752	0.0277

Source: Eview 9, output 2024

Decision: This hypothesis is tested based on the results of the ARDL regression. From the results, LEXTR has coefficient of 23.11752 and probability value of 0.0277, which implies that the null hypothesis two (H02), which says that exchange rate has no significant on gross domestic product in Nigeria, would be rejected at 5% level. Hence, there is positive significant impact of LEXTR on the economic growth in Nigeria at the 5% level of significance.

Discussion and Summary of Major Findings

This section presents the discussion of key findings from the results presented in the previous section as relate to the four objectives of this study. The results are discussed, and the findings are compared with the reports and submissions of previous literature that are related to this study.

The first objective of the study is concerned with the extent to which the money supply affects gross domestic product in Nigeria. The results obtained in relation to the first objective using ARDL regression revealed that the influence of money supply on the economic growth in Nigeria measured with LGDP is positive and insignificant. This implies that when the money supply increases, the GDP tends to increase as well and vice versa. This suggests that there is a tendency for the economy to grow, when there is more money available. However, despite this positive tendency, the effect is not strong enough to be considered. This means that other factors might be playing a larger factor role in influencing GDP. The finding is equally consistent with meaningful or reliable. The reports in many other empirical literatures including the study of Chindengwike (2022) in their study of Nigerian economy. The finding here does not agree with the study by Nwoko et al. (2016) which reported that money supply improves the economic growth in Nigeria.

For the second objective of the study which is to examine the impact of exchange rate on gross domestic product in Nigeria, the outcome of the ARD regression used in achieving the objectives revealed positive and significant influence of exchange rate on the economic growth in Nigeria measured with LGDP. The finding agreed with the submission of the Abille and Mpuure (2020) in which the increase in exchange rate of a country weakens the intrinsic value of money. The result was not consistent with the negative a priori expectation The results could not agree with the findings of some other empirical literature such as that of Igharo et al. (2020) who reported that exchange rate has a negative impact on the economic growth.

Summary, Conclusion, and Recommendations

Summary

This research study empirically examined the link between exchange rate, money supply, and economic growth in Nigeria for a period covering 2003 to 2023 using data obtained from CBN Statistical Bulletin and National Bureau of Statistic. The study used the autoregressive distributed lag model (ARDL). The ARDL was used, because the variables were stationary at different levels of integration.

The results of the analysis were decomposed into two categories of which the first category was based on the descriptive table of the study. The second was the result of the test of hypothesis based on the models. The results of the two hypotheses revealed that

1. There is a positive relationship between money supply and economic growth measured by GDP, and the impact is statistically insignificant.
2. Exchange rate exerts positive influence on the GDP, and the impact is statistically significant. By implication, the results of the ARDL analysis employed in the study indicate that exchange rate plays significant roles in driving the Nigerian economy.

Conclusions

The long-run growth and survival of any nation is hinged on the strategic choices of monetary policies. Hence, this study has examined how money supply and exchange rate affect the economic growth. The results obtained using ARDL analysis revealed that both money supply and exchange rate impact positively on the economic growth in Nigeria, and the impacts are significant. By implication, the ability of money supply and exchange rate to drive the economic growth is not negligible. In addition, the results in respect of the aspects of monetary policy indicate that money supply exerts positive and insignificant influence on the gross domestic products while exchange rate records positive and significant impact on the GDP.

Recommendations

In line with the findings of this study, below are the recommendations:

1. The Nigerian government and the Central Bank of Nigeria (CBN) should focus on improving the mechanisms through which money supply influences economic growth. This can be achieved by:
   (i) Enhance the stability and efficiency of financial institutions to ensure that increases in money supply effectively translate into increased lending and investment in productive sectors.
   (ii) Implement targeted monetary policies that directly support key sectors of the economy such as agriculture, manufacturing, and technology, which can have more immediate and significant impacts on economic growth.
2. Given the significant positive influence of exchange rates on economic growth, policies should aim at stabilizing and optimizing exchange rate management to foster economic stability and growth. This can include:
   (i) Implement policies that reduce volatility in the exchange rate. This can involve maintaining adequate foreign exchange reserves, implementing currency hedging mechanisms, and ensuring a stable macroeconomic environment.
   (ii) Develop and promote policies that enhance the competitiveness of Nigerian exports. This can involve providing incentives for export-oriented industries, reducing bureaucratic hurdles, and improving infrastructure to reduce costs for exporters.
   (iii) Ensure that exchange rate policies do not lead to excessive inflation, which can erode economic growth. This can be managed through a combination of monetary policy adjustments and fiscal discipline.
3. To sustain long-term economic growth, Nigeria should diversify its economy and implement structural reforms that reduce dependency on volatile sectors such as oil and improve the overall economic environment.

Suggestion for Further Research

Further research can be explored to deepen understanding and provide more definitive insights.

1. Investigate the differential impacts of various components of money supply (M1, M2, M3) on economic growth. Different components of money supply may have distinct effects on economic activities. Disaggregating the money supply into its components can help identify which specific elements have more significant and consistent impacts on economic growth.

2. Examine the impact of money supply and exchange rates on different sectors of the economy (e.g., agriculture, manufacturing, services). The effects of monetary and exchange rate policies may vary across sectors. A sectoral analysis can provide insights into which sectors are more sensitive to changes in money supply and exchange rates, thereby guiding more targeted policy interventions.
3. Conduct a comparative analysis of the effects of money supply and exchange rates on economic growth across different countries with similar economic contexts. A cross-country analysis can help identify common patterns and unique factors that influence the relationships between money supply, exchange rates, and economic growth. This can provide broader insights and potentially more robust conclusions.

References

Abdurhman, K. A., & Dagmawe, M. A. (2023). Nexus between inflation, income inequality, and economic growth in Ethiopa. *PLoS One, 18*(11), e0294454. Published Online 2023 Nov. 16.

Abille, A. B., & Mpuure, D. M. N. (2020). Effect of monetary policy on economic growth in Ghana. *Applied Economics Journal, 27*(2), 110–124.

Adegboyo, O. S., Keji, S. A., & Fasina, O. T. (2021). The impact of government policies on Nigeria economic growth (case of fiscal, monetary and trade policies). *Future Business Journal, 7*(1), 1–14.

Adepeju, S. (2018). Government spending on infrastructure and economic growth in Nigeria. *Economic Research-EkonomskaIstraživanja, 31*(1), 997–1014.

Aliyev, J., Mukhtarov, S., Haydarov, K., & Isgandarov, M. (2020). Does monetary policy boost economic growth? The case of small open economy. *Research in World Economy, 11*(3), 216–228.

Batrancea, L. M., Rathnaswamy, M. M., Rus, M. I., & Tulai, H. (2023). Determinants of economic growth for the last half of century: A panel data analysis on 50 countries. *Journal of the Knowledge Economy, 14*(3), 2578–2602.

Bhuiyan, A. G., Sugita, K., Hashimoto, A., & Yamamoto, A. (2012). InGaN solar cells: Present state of the art and important challenges. *IEEE Journal of Photovoltaics, 2*(3), 276–293.

Bogoviz, A. V., Lobova, S. V., & Alekseev, A. N. (2022). Contribution of Enterprise cooperation to the sustainable development of the economy through accelerated modernization and increased corporate responsibility. In *Cooperation and sustainable development* (pp. 1347–1355). Springer International Publishing.

Boivin, J., Kiley, M. T., & Mishkin, F. S. (2010). How has the monetary transmission mechanism evolved over time? In *Handbook of monetary economics* (Vol. 3, pp. 369–422). Elsevier.

Bredin, D., & O'Reilly, G. (2004). An analysis of the transmission mechanism of monetary policy in Ireland. *Applied Economics, 36*(1), 49–58.

CBN. (2021). *Statistical Bulleting, Central Bank Nigeria December*, Vol. 16 Access from: http://www.cenbank.org/OUT/PUBLICATIONS/RE[PRTS/RD/207/STABULL-2021.PDF

Central Bank of Nigeria (CBN). (2022). *Annual Report*. CBN.

Chindengwike, J. (2022). The nexus between money supply and economic development in East Africa countries: An empirical study using ARDL. *Journal of Global Economy, 18*(4), 237–250.

Doran, J., McCarthy, N., & O'Connor, M. (2018). The role of entrepreneurship in stimulating economic growth in developed and developing countries. *Cogent Economics & Finance, 6*(1), 1442093.

Dornbusch, R. (1976). Expectations and exchange rate dynamics. *Journal of Political Economy, 84*(6), 1161–1176.
Ekwezuo, C. S. (2016). *Climate model simulation and projections of precipitation changes over West Africa*. Unpublished M. Sc. thesis, University of Nigeria, Nsukka.
Friedman, M. (1968). The role of monetary policy. *American Economic Review, 58*(1), 1–17.
Huseynli, N. (2022). Econometric analysis of the relationship between tourism revenues, inflation and economic growth: The case of Morocco and South Africa. *African Journal of Hospitality, Tourism and Leisure, 11*(1), 135–146.
Idan, A. M., & Badan, Z. Q. (2022). The influence of monetary policy on the economic growth in European Union countries. *Cuadernos de Economía, 45*(127), 156–162.
Idowu, P., Baba, Y. N., Olufunso, A. O., Aduni, T. O. E., & Joseph, T. E. (2020). How effective is monetary policy in the presence of high informality in Nigeria. *Journal of Accounting, Business and Finance Research, 10*(2), 84–93.
Igharo, A. E., Osabohien, R., Onyemariechi, G. O., & Ibidapo, D. T. (2020). Monetary policy transmission mechanism, innovative banking system and economic growth dynamics in Nigeria. *International Journal of Business Innovation and Research, 21*(1), 1–22.
Jackson, J. K, Weiss, M. A., Schwarzenberg, A. B., Nelson, R. M., Sutter, K. M., & Sutherland, M. D. (2020). *Global Economic Effects of COVID-19.*
Keynes, J. M. (1936). *The general theory of employment, interest, and money*. Macmillan.
Krugman, P., & Obstfeld, M. (2017). *International economics: Theory and Policy_*. Pearson.
Lapčík, O., Klejdus, B., Kokoška, L., Davidová, M., Afandi, K., Kubáň, V., & Hampl, R. (2005). Identification of isoflavones in Acca sellowiana and two Psidium species (Myrtaceae). *Biochemical Systematics and Ecology, 33*(10), 983–992.
Lee, S. K., Dykxhoorn, D. M., Kumar, P., Ranjbar, S., Song, E., Maliszewski, L. E., & Shankar, P. (2005). Lentiviral delivery of short hairpin RNAs protects CD4 T cells from multiple clades and primary isolates of HIV. *Blood, 106*(3), 818–826.
Loayza, N., & Schmidt-Hebbel, K. (2002). *Monetary policy functions and transmission mechanisms: an overview*. Serieson Central Banking, Analysis, and Economic Policies, no. 4.
Mankiw, N. G. (2018). *Principles of economics*. Cengage Learning.
Mengesha, L. G., & Holmes, M. J. (2013). Monetary policy and its transmission mechanisms in Eritrea. *Journal of Policy Modeling, 35*(5), 766–780.
Modugu, K. P., & Dempere, J. (2022). Monetary policies and bank lending in developing countries: Evidence from sub-Sahara Africa. *Journal of Economics and Development, 24*(3), 217–229.
Monamodi, N. E., & Choga, I. (2022). The impact of fiscal and monetary policy on economic growth in southern African custom union: A panel ARDL approach. *International Journal of Economic Policy in Emerging Economies, 15*(1), 86–102.
Mundell, R. (1968). *International economics*. Macmillan.
National Bureau of Statistics. (2022). *Nigeria's economic overview*. NBS.
Ngouhouo, I., & Nkemgha, G. Z. (2018). Inflation and economic growth: A comparative empirical analysis between Cameroon and the Ivory Coast. *International Journal of Economics and Finance, 10*(12), 87–95.
Nwoko, N. M., Ihemeje, J. C., & Anumadu, E. (2016). The impact of monetary policy on the economic growth of Nigeria. *African Research Review, 10*(3), 192–206.
Odelola, B. (2020). *Relationship between economy, education, population, healthcare and prevalence of HIV/AIDS in Nigeria*. Minnesota State University.
Odubuasi, A. C., Ifurueze, M. S., & Ezeabasili, V. N. (2020). *Effect of government expenditure on economic growth in Nigeria.*
Ogbonna, A. (2019). The impact of oil price fluctuations on the Nigerian economy. *Journal of Energy Studies, 13*(2), 65–78.
Okonjo-Iweala, N. (2018). *Fighting corruption is dangerous: The story behind the headlines*. The MIT Press.

Omankhanlen, A. E., Ilori, N., Isibor, A., & Okoye, L. U. (2021). Monetary policies and the achievement of bank profit objective. *Journal of Central Banking Theory and Practice, 10*(2), 201–220.

Orji, A., Ogbuabor, J. E., Ugwu, C. E., Anthony-Orji, O. I., & Nwufo, L. C. (2022). Cash reserve ratio and credit to micro-, small and medium-sized Enterprises in Developing Economies. *Analysis of Transmission Channels Using Nigerian Data. Финансовыйжурнал, 14*(1), 71–88.

Partachi, I., & Mija, S. (2015). Monetary policy–instrument for macroeconomic stabilization. *Procedia Economics and Finance, 20*, 485–493.

Ramlogan, C. (2004). The transmission mechanism of monetary policy: Evidence from the Caribbean. *Journal of Economic Studies, 31*(5), 435–447.

Sanusi, L. S. (2011). Nigeria's Experience with Exchange Rate Policy and Implications for Economic Development. In *Speech Delivered at the Keynote Address at the 25th Anniversary Conference of the Central Bank of Nigeria*.

Srithilat, K., Samatmanivong, T., Lienpaserth, V., Chanthavixay, P., Boundavong, V., & Douangty, V. (2022). The effect of monetary policy on economic growth in Lao PDR. *International Journal of Economics and Financial Issues, 12*(1), 67.

Titiloye, T., & Ishola, V. (2020). *Effect of Fiscal Policy and Monetary Policy on Economic Growth in Nigeria (1989-2018): A Time Series Analysis. Available at SSRN 3706157.*

World Bank. (2021). World bank Data Bank recovered from https://data.worldbank.org/indicator

Yin, H. T., Chang, C. P., & Wang, H. (2022). The impact of monetary policy on green innovation: Global evidence. *Technological and Economic Development of Economy, 28*(6), 1933–1953.

The Tone of Business Model Disclosure: An Analysis of Integrated Reports of Johannesburg Securities Exchange (JSE)-Listed Entities

Phuti Tshepo Moloto, Mahmood Surty, Zakiyyah Varachia, and Irfaan Omarjee

Abstract The business model (BM) disclosures in integrated reports portray how resources provided by stakeholders are utilised to create value. Given the voluntary and unaudited nature of the disclosure, this makes it susceptible to manipulation by management. By employing impression management (IM) techniques, management can shape the information to craft a favourable image. This paper aims to determine whether Johannesburg Securities Exchange (JSE)-listed entities adopt IM strategies by manipulating the tone of the BM disclosure provided in their integrated reports. A quantitative content analysis was utilised, and the BM disclosure section of the Top 100 JSE-listed entities was analysed for the period ending 2018. Each sentence was coded for the tone of the disclosure (positive or non-positive), the type of information (quantitative or qualitative), the period (forward or non-forward) and the content of the information (inputs, business activities and outputs or outcomes). This paper found that a non-positive tone was more dominant in the BM disclosure made by JSE-listed entities, suggesting minimal use of IM techniques. Further, most information was non-forward-looking, indicating that a positive tone and forward-looking information may not be used for IM in BM disclosure. However, most information was qualitative and mainly focused on the resources needed in the value creation process rather than describing the value created for stakeholders (outcomes), allowing management to change narratives to potentially apply IM. The Pearson Chi-square did not indicate a significant association between tone and the time or type of information. However, a significant association was found between tone and the topics' content, which could indicate the use of IM with respect to BM Topics. This paper extends the body of knowledge within a South African context of the use of IM, specifically in BM disclosures of integrated reports.

P. T. Moloto · M. Surty (✉) · Z. Varachia · I. Omarjee
University of the Witwatersrand, Johannesburg, South Africa
e-mail: Mahmood.surty@wits.ac.za; Zakiyyah.varachia@wits.ac.za

T. Moloi (ed.), *Impacting Society Positively Through Technology in Accounting and Business Processes*, Springer Proceedings in Business and Economics,
https://doi.org/10.1007/978-3-031-84885-8_10

Keywords Business model · Corporate governance · Impression management · Integrated reporting

Introduction

A business model is a detailed narrative of how entities generate value over the long-term (PWC, 2016). Business model disclosure is a narrative disclosure primarily based on the six capitals of the International Integrated Reporting Framework (IIRF) (IIRC, 2011). Stakeholders such as investors and lenders provide financial resources to the entities to ensure management has the adequate tools necessary to execute its strategy (Cooper et al., 1994). Business model disclosure is a platform for management to communicate how management plans to utilise resources provided by stakeholders (Zott et al., 2011). In the value creation process, the interests of all stakeholders are of paramount importance and need to be addressed in the business model disclosure (Li et al., 2008). The significance of business model disclosure was further highlighted when reputable professional bodies like the International Accounting and Auditing Standards Board (IASB) stated support of this designated disclosure section (Gutmayer et al., 2022; Melloni et al., 2016). The IASB regards the business model disclosure as a relevant tool that can improve the usefulness of integrated reports (Melloni et al., 2016). Investors also regard business model disclosure as a valuable tool for making informed investment decisions (Athanasakou et al., 2022; Greiner & Ang, 2012).

To add to the increasing prevalence and relevance of business model disclosure, countries such as South Africa decided to mandate the inclusion of business model disclosure in the integrated reports of listed entities (Gutmayer et al., 2022; Sukhari & de Villiers, 2019). However, regulatory bodies and academics have raised some concerns about the quality of the disclosure of business models (Page, 2014). Page (2014) raised the concern that generic, unsupported and biased statements dominate the business model disclosure section. The use of impression management strategies in business model disclosure can be seen as a means to promote the corporate image of an entity and is representative of biased reporting (Melloni et al., 2016).

There is limited research on the manipulation of the tone of the business model disclosure in developing countries (Melloni et al., 2016). The business model concept has attracted much interest from academics and management of entities in the corporate world, who are interested in explaining how an entity can remain sustainable and competitive (PWC, 2016). This paper investigated whether Johannesburg Securities Exchange (JSE)-listed entities adopt impression management strategies by manipulating the tone of the business model disclosure provided in their integrated reports.

This paper aims to contribute to the literature regarding disclosure quality by highlighting possible flaws in the business model disclosure for the benefit of all stakeholders. For example, investors rely heavily on the business model disclosure outlined in the integrated reports in their investment decision-making process

(Melloni et al., 2016). The JSE could benefit from this study as flaws identified in the business model disclosure in integrated reports could indicate a need for change. For example, more rigorous listing requirements could be introduced by the JSE to improve the objectivity and transparency of the business model disclosure. As a result, the stakeholders' exposure to possible manipulation of the business model disclosure could be reduced significantly, and the reputation of the JSE could be maintained. This paper also adds to the existing body of knowledge on narrative disclosures. Studies in this field have primarily focused on other narrative disclosures in the integrated reports, such as the chairman's statement and strategy (Padia & Yasseen, 2011).

The research in this paper is limited to one section of the integrated report, the business model disclosure. The period covered was only the 2018 financial year-end. The findings of this study do not necessarily apply to other narrative disclosures in the integrated report. The sample of this study only consisted of JSE-listed entities, and the findings might not apply to entities in other developing countries.

The paper begins with a review of the prior literature, followed by the method used for the study. The results then follow, and the paper concludes.

Prior Literature and Theoretical Framework

The Business Model and Value Creation

The business model is a key component in integrated reporting (Page, 2014). Prior researchers have struggled to have a set definition of the business model concept (Zott et al., 2011). Zott et al. (2011) reviewed 103 business model publications and found that 37% do not define the concept, whilst 44% explicitly define it by referring to key components making up a business model. However, the dominant definition of the business model concept is that it is a description of how entities create and preserve value over the long-term (Melloni et al., 2016; Szewieczek et al., 2021). Stakeholders need useful information to make informed decisions (Stainbank & Peebles, 2006). The existence of a well-structured business model is one of the ingredients needed for an entity to be successful (Teece, 2010). An entity must be innovative and take advantage of opportunities to ensure consistent success (Teece, 2010). Management that is good at designing a relevant business model understands customer needs and remains up to date with technological developments in order to profit from innovation (Teece, 2010). Entities might have all the necessary resources (i.e. skilled personnel, efficient and effective leadership and advanced technology), but to ensure profitability in the long-term, the business model must be appropriately adapted to the competitive environment (Achtenhagen et al., 2013). Zott et al. (2011) suggest that entities that do not adapt or change their business models over time have greater chances of failure.

A business model must be structured to meet particular customer needs (Teece, 2010). Apart from not adapting the business model regularly, the existence of a mere business model is insufficient to assure competitive advantage as it is often easy for competitors to copy (Teece, 2010). Competitive environments expose entities within a particular sector to lower profit margins (Beynon et al., 2004). Prior research suggests that a business model must consist of attributes that make it difficult to replicate, as that will serve as a constraint for new entrants (Teece, 2010). A business model must be more than just a good, logical way of doing business (Gutmayer et al., 2022; Teece, 2010).

Entities with a good business model are in a position to ensure sustained value creation and significant growth (Achtenhagen et al., 2013). However, the unintended implications of growth might include the inability to control the consumption of resources at the entity's disposal (Achtenhagen et al., 2013). A crisis might unfold instead of creating value for all stakeholders (Achtenhagen et al., 2013). For example, employees might be overworked, and natural resources might be negatively affected. The possible negative repercussions illustrate the importance of an unbiased business model to be communicated to all stakeholders (Melloni et al., 2016). As a result, the business model disclosure was introduced in integrated reporting (IIRC, 2011).

According to the IIRF, the business model disclosure intends to ensure that the value creation process communicated is authentic and brief but comprehensive (IIRC, 2011). The IASB provided a practical guideline on business model disclosure (IASB, 2010). The IASB stepped in due to the unpredictability in the quality of business model disclosure encountered amongst different entities (IASB, 2010). According to the IIRF, the recognition of fundamental business model elements will improve the readability of the business model section (IIRC, 2011). The identified elements also bring an aspect of consistency in terms of business model disclosure (IIRC, 2013). There are four elements in the business model disclosure section found in integrated reports (IIRC, 2013). The business model disclosure is structured to include four elements: inputs, business activities, outputs and outcomes (IIRC, 2013).

The "Inputs" section outlines the use of resources (water, land, capital assets, labour, debt financing and many more), and it is mainly focused on the six capitals on which the entity depends (IIRC, 2013). The six capitals are financial, manufactured, human, intellectual, social and relationship and natural capitals. The "Business activities" section in the integrated report outlines the process and phases involved in converting inputs into finished products to meet customers' needs (Melloni et al., 2016). The "Outputs" section in the integrated report outlines the productivity levels of entities (Melloni et al., 2016). It shows the actual outcome of the inputs put into the production process. The "Outcomes" section outlines the impact of the entity within the internal environment as well as the external environment (IIRC, 2013). An example is disclosure of the impact the operations had on the natural resources and the surrounding community. Management utilises this section to show how the created value is distributed to stakeholders (Melloni et al., 2016). However, management has also been found to be using this section as a marketing tool (Melloni et al., 2016).

Narrative Disclosures

Stakeholders are showing interest in the value provided by narrative disclosures (Clatworthy & Jones, 2006; Hasan, 2020). Davison (2002) also found that stakeholders are broadening the aspects they consider in their investment decision-making process rather than merely inspecting financial statements. The emergence of narrative disclosures has led to an extensive focus change in integrated reporting (IIRC, 2011). The structure of the integrated reports shows that financial statements now usually come at the end (Stanton et al., 2004). Attention is diverted from financial statements and directed towards narrative disclosures (Stanton et al., 2004).

The number of narrative disclosures in the integrated reports is increasing at a higher rate relative to the statutory financial information disclosure (Stanton et al., 2004). Clatworthy and Jones (2006) and Stanton et al. (2004) suggest that there is a possible risk that financial information will not be thoroughly analysed due to the amount of narrative disclosure provided at the beginning of the integrated reports. Narrative disclosures provide context to the numbers in the financial statements, and management can provide justifications to assist stakeholders in predicting future financial performance (Beynon et al., 2004). Impression management is found to occur in less regulated narrative disclosures which focus on interpreting financial outcomes (Brennan et al., 2009; Phesa & Sibanda, 2022).

Impression Management

The concept of impression management was derived from social psychology (Brennan & Merkl-Davies, 2013). Impression management may be defined as deliberately or unintentionally attempting to control the perceptions of human beings (Nichols, 2020; Stanton et al., 2004). Impression management undertaken by management can be seen as part of the legitimacy theory (Ashforth & Gibbs, 1990). Legitimacy theory refers to "a generalised perception or assumption that the actions of an entity are desirable, proper, or appropriate within some socially constructed system of norms, values, beliefs, and definitions" (Suchman, 1995). Prior studies found that some management teams go to extreme lengths to establish their legitimacy through impression management techniques (Ashforth & Gibbs, 1990). Particularly in situations where firms face legitimacy threats, such as corporate scandals, product safety issues or environmental disasters (Brennan & Merkl-Davies, 2013). The preparation of the integrated report presents management with an opportunity to apply impression management strategies (Yasseen et al., 2017). Eventually, management needs to give feedback on the entity's performance and how that has boosted shareholder value and impacted the community in which it operates (Davison, 2002). Powerful management teams tend to be obsessed with control and engage in impression management techniques to control the perceptions of stakeholders (Crowther et al., 2006). Management expects to be evaluated based on decisions taken on behalf of the entity (Brennan et al., 2009). Management that is expected to be judged by stakeholders tends to engage in impression management techniques (Brennan & Merkl-Davies, 2013). As a result, management applies reporting bias in circumstances where the relationship with stakeholders is tense, and there is no room for mistakes (Brennan & Merkl-Davies, 2013).

There is the temptation to solely base the disclosure on matters that put the entity in a favourable light (Stanton et al., 2004). Corporate collapses and major scandals have increased public scrutiny of entities and the performance of management (Merkl-Davies & Brennan, 2007). The increased public scrutiny and higher demands for accountability are factors that add to management's desire to provide corporate disclosures that put the entities in a favourable light (Merkl-Davies et al., 2011). Management of public entities feel responsible for maintaining good investor confidence (Aerts, 2005). Management is incentivised to apply impression management techniques to ensure they remain on the listed exchanges long-term (Aerts, 2005). As a result, management is selective in disclosing narrative information and tends to disclose more positive disclosures and less negative disclosures in their integrated reports (Chotia et al., 2024). Merkl-Davies and Brennan (2007) discuss different forms of impression management strategies used by management to influence the readers' perception. Some of these impression management strategies include the inappropriate use of tone in the integrated reports to conceal negative aspects, taking ownership of good news and shifting responsibility for poor performance to external factors (Merkl-Davies and Brennan, 2007).

When management takes ownership of the positive aspects, this relates to attribution theory (Aerts, 2005). Attribution theory refers to management taking ownership of positive outcomes whilst shifting responsibility for adverse outcomes (Aerts, 2005). Negative outcomes are blamed on external events (Aerts, 2005). Examples of external events include political uncertainty or economic recession (i.e. not within management's control) in the country where operations are based (Aerts, 2005).

Melloni et al. (2016) suggest that tone is used as a manipulation technique in the business model disclosure. Previous studies have attempted to link the tone used in business model disclosure and the financial results of the entity (i.e. performance) (Schleicher & Walker, 2010). Stakeholders expect desirable outcomes at the end of each reporting period (Brennan & Merkl-Davies, 2013). The failure to achieve the targets set by the entity might lead to management attempting to divert attention away from poor performance (Brennan & Merkl-Davies, 2013). In attempting to conceal poor outcomes, tone is found to be a tool that might be used to manipulate the portrayal of a particular image to stakeholders (Clatworthy & Jones, 2003). Previous studies argue that a positive tone in business model disclosure is expected where there is a decline in profitability as management attempts to conceal the bad financial results through narrative disclosures (Clatworthy & Jones, 2003). Melloni et al. (2016) found the tone of business model disclosure to be mainly positive, indicating that impression management is prevalent in business model disclosures. Using prior research, the following research question is formulated:

RQ: Do JSE-listed entities adopt impression management strategies by manipulating the tone (i.e. the use of a more positive tone) of the business model disclosure provided in their integrated reports?

Melloni et al. (2016) tested the relationship between the tone of business model disclosure and disclosure characteristics such as the type of disclosure (qualitative or quantitative), time period of disclosure (forward-looking or non-forward-looking information) and the topic of disclosure (inputs, business activities and outputs or outcomes). Previous studies also show that impression management techniques could be easily applied depending on the disclosure characteristics (Chotia et al., 2024; Dobler et al., 2011). Beattie et al. (2004) suggest that the type of information presented to stakeholders has specific disclosure characteristics. Dobler et al. (2011) found that impression management techniques could be easily applied depending on the disclosure characteristics of the information. Management may easily manipulate the tone when providing information that cannot be corroborated (Bryan, 1997; Cazier et al., 2020; Dobler et al., 2011). For example, qualitative information has been found to be associated with a more positive tone as it is hard to dispute, whereas quantitative information is usually audited and subjected to greater scrutiny (Bryan, 1997). Melloni et al. (2016) found that business model disclosures consist mainly of qualitative information, most of which had a non-positive tone. Furthermore, no significant statistical association was found between business model disclosure tone and the type of information disclosed (Melloni et al., 2016). As a result, this formed the basis for the development of hypothesis 1 (H1):

H1: There is an association between business model disclosure tone and the type of disclosure (qualitative or quantitative).

Forward-looking information has been associated with a more positive tone as it is based on events that have not yet occurred (Bryan, 1997; Mio et al., 2020). Bryan (1997) explains it by stating that information that is not supported by facts and relevant documentation is susceptible to impression management strategies; however, information on past events is easily verifiable and open to fewer opportunities for impression management. Melloni et al. (2016) confirmed the above findings and noted that where information was forward-looking, the business model disclosure was statistically associated with a more positive tone indicative of the use of impression management. This formed the basis for the development of hypothesis 2 (H2):

H2: There is an association between business model disclosure tone and the time period the disclosure relates to (forward-looking information or past information).

In the value creation process, the interests of all stakeholders are of paramount importance and need to be addressed in the business model disclosure (Li et al., 2008). As management is incentivised to disclose information that presents them in the best light to generate investor confidence, entities may engage in impression management in disclosing the different topics of the business model given information asymmetry (Brennan et al., 2009). Melloni et al. (2016) found an association between the topic of disclosure and a positive tone used in business model disclosures regarding outcomes but generally a non-positive tone when disclosing inputs, business activities and outputs. Information which is more easily verifiable tends to be less susceptible to impression management (Bryan, 1997; Cazier et al., 2020), which could indicate why information on inputs, business activities and outputs are not as easy to manipulate as they tend to be more easily verifiable than outcomes of activities. As a result, hypothesis three (H3) is developed:

H3: There is an association between business model disclosure and the type of information disclosed (Inputs, processes and outputs or outcomes).

Methodology

Research Design

A two-level analysis was performed. The method was drawn from similar studies conducted by Melloni et al. (2016) and Beattie et al. (2004). The first phase was a manual content analysis followed by a univariate analysis.

Manual Content Analysis

Business model disclosure consists of sentences, and a manual content analysis was completed as it allows for text compression into fewer content categories based on explicit coding rules (Krippendorff, 2018). The individual sentences in the business model disclosure constitute recording units (Beattie et al., 2004). Consistent with Melloni et al. (2016), each sentence in the business model disclosure was read and coded. Each sentence was coded for the tone of the disclosure (positive or non-positive), the type of information (quantitative or qualitative), the period (forward or non-forward) and the content of the information (inputs, business activities and outputs or outcomes). The "tone" of disclosure can be either positive or non-positive. Consistent with the Clatworthy and Jones (2003) study, positive news for the entity and environment in which it operates implies a positive tone. Therefore, a non-positive tone consists of both neutral and negative news about the entity and the environment in which an entity operates. Quantitative information was coded based on the inclusion of a numerical element in the sentence. Sentences consisting solely of words and no numbers were considered qualitative information. Regarding the "period" category, each sentence was categorised as forward-looking or non-forward-looking information. The headings displayed in the business model disclosure constitute "topics". One topic includes "Inputs, business activities and outputs"; the second topic includes "Outcomes".

Univariate Analysis

A univariate analysis was conducted using the Pearson Chi-square test to determine whether tone is associated with disclosure variables. The tone was the dependent variable. The independent variables were type, period and content of information. If the Pearson Chi-square probability is below the conventionally accepted significance level of 0.05 (i.e. $p < 0.05$), the nominal variables (e.g. "tone" and "type") are statistically associated.

Population, Sample and Data Collection

The population consisted of all entities listed on the JSE. Only integrated reports for the 2018 financial year-end were examined and investigated as part of this exploratory study. However, the researchers only examined the business model disclosure section in the integrated report. The integrated reports of the Top 100 JSE-listed entities were downloaded. The sample size was 88 integrated reports, as 12 integrated reports did not have a specific section designated to business model disclosure. The method followed was a quantitative content analysis. Each integrated report was read to determine if a section was designated for business model disclosure.

Results

Overall Results

A total of 2943 sentences were analysed by the researchers. The results in Table 1 indicate that out of the 2943 sentences analysed, 40.57% have a positive tone, whilst 59.43% have a negative or neutral tone. The results might be attributable to the fact that it is compulsory for JSE-listed entities to provide the business model disclosure. As a result, the management of the entities might feel pressured to improve the quality of their corporate reporting.

Regarding the "type" category, the results illustrate that qualitative information (66.29% Table 1) is dominant in the business model disclosure compared to quantitative information. The results of this study are consistent with those of Melloni et al. (2016), which found that only 25.58% of the sentences have quantitative elements. The results of this paper support the perception that the business model disclosure is dominated by the type of information that is difficult for stakeholders to verify (Beattie et al., 2004). Further analysis revealed that 64.3% of qualitative information was positive. There are more qualitative sentences, and there is a concern that it is difficult for stakeholders to hold management accountable for statements that are not easily verifiable (Beattie et al., 2004).

Table 1 Content analysis results

	Tone		Type		Time		Topic	
Categories	Positive	Non-positive	Quantitative	Qualitative	Forward-looking	Non-forward-looking	Inputs, business activities and outputs	Outcomes
Number of sentences per category	1194	1749	992	1951	165	2778	1607	1336
% per category	40.57	59.43	33.71	66.29	5.61	94.39	54.60	45.40
Number of sentences	2943		2943		2943		2943	

Only 5.61% (Table 1) of the business model disclosure contains forward-looking information. Entities are disclosing more non-forward-looking information (i.e. information based on what has already occurred). The results are consistent with the results of Melloni et al. (2016), namely that only 12.11% of the sentences analysed were forward-looking. Regarding the tone used, a neutral or negative tone is dominant in forward-looking information, as further analysis of the results demonstrates that only 47.3% of the forward-looking sentences have a positive tone. A neutral or negative tone is also used significantly in non-forward-looking statements in the business model disclosure. Of the 2778 non-forward-looking sentences, further analysis 56.5% is attributable to non-positive tone. Hence, the outcome might indicate the restriction on management to apply a positive tone to historical events as they are relatively easily verifiable (Bryan, 1997).

As previously stated in the methodology chapter, the "topics" category deals with two sections in business model disclosure that provide entities with a platform to describe the value creation process and the value generated for stakeholders (IASB, 2010). The results provided in Table 1 indicate that, in terms of the "topics" category, the business model disclosure is spread out as follows: 45.4% of the sentences are in the outcomes category, and the remaining 54.6% are in the inputs, business activities and outputs category. Melloni et al. (2016) also found that only 41.01% of the sentences analysed are under the "outcomes" heading. The results are consistent with Melloni et al. (2016), implying that management focuses more on outlining the resources needed by the entities and the production processes, whilst there is less focus on describing the value created for stakeholders (i.e. outcomes). Further analysis revealed that a positive tone is more dominant in "outcomes", with 64.2% of the positive tone sentences in the "outcomes" category. "Outcomes" are representative of the impact of the business models on an entity itself and the external environment (PWC, 2016). The results of this study imply the existence of the perception that management feels under pressure to disclose outcomes in a positive light.

Univariate Analysis

Relationship Between Tone and Type of Information

Consistent with the results of Melloni et al. (2016), results of the univariate analysis on the relationship between "disclosure tone" and "type of information" show that there is no significant statistical relationship between the former and the latter (Table 2). The Pearson Chi-square value amounted to 3.494 ($p = 0.062$). This indicates no association between the tone and the type of information. H1 is, therefore, rejected. Despite the typical positive connotations associated with qualitative information, which enable management to discuss information optimistically and potentially influence users' perceptions, these results do not align with that expectation.

Relationship Between Tone and Time

Contrary to the results in the study by Melloni et al. (2016), the results of the univariate analysis on the relationship between disclosure tone and its time orientation reveal no association between tone and period of information ($p = 0.073$). H2 is therefore rejected. Although forward-looking information is associated with being more susceptible to manipulation, given that it is non-verifiable, it does not appear that management uses tone and the time orientation of information for impression management purposes. This is consistent with the overall descriptive statistics discussed in Table 3.

Relationship Between Tone and Topic

Consistent with findings by Melloni et al. (2016), the results of the univariate analysis further show that the disclosure tone is associated with the disclosure topic (Table 4). $P = 0.000$ indicates a significant statistical relationship between "tone"

Table 2 Pearson Chi-square Test for the relationship between "Tone" and "Type of information"

	Value	df	Asymptotic significance (2-sided)
Pearson Chi-square	3.494	1	0.062

Table 3 Pearson Chi-square test for the relationship between "Tone" and "Time Orientation"

	Value	df	Asymptotic significance (2-sided)
Pearson Chi-square	3.256	1	0.071

Table 4 Pearson Chi-square test for the relationship between "Tone" and "Topic"

	Value	df	Asymptotic significance (2-sided)
Pearson Chi-square	295.330	1	0.000

and "topic" at the 95% confidence level. H3 is accepted. This may mean that management is using specific disclosure topics as a means to apply impression management.

Conclusion

This paper aimed to determine whether the management of JSE-listed entities adopt impression management strategies by manipulating the tone (i.e. using a more positive tone) of the business model disclosure provided in integrated reports.

Contrary to prior research, the current research results show that a non-positive tone is dominant in the business model of JSE-listed entities. The findings suggest minimal adoption of impression management techniques in the business model disclosure provided in the integrated reports of JSE-listed entities. The results might be attributable to the fact that it is compulsory for JSE-listed entities to provide the business model disclosure. As a result, the management of the entities might feel pressured to improve the quality of their corporate reporting. Further, there is no association between the tone of business model disclosure and the type of information disclosed (qualitative or quantitative), as well as the tone of business model disclosure and the time period of disclosure (forward-looking or past information). However, there is a relationship between the tone of business model disclosure and the topic of information disclosed (inputs, business activities and outputs or outcomes), which could indicate impression management is utilised by management in terms of business model topics.

A limitation of this study is that only integrated reports of the Top 100 JSE-listed entities were analysed and examined for the 2018 financial year. The findings might not be representative of entities in other developing countries. Findings on the use of impression management strategies in the business model disclosure section also do not necessarily entail that they were applied to the entire integrated report.

The findings in this study show interesting areas for future research. A comparison of the quality of the disclosure of business models between entities that voluntarily disclose business models and those that are compelled by regulatory bodies (such as the JSE) could be investigated. This investigation could assist regulatory bodies in other countries determine whether they should follow suit in making business model disclosure compulsory in their respective stock exchanges. Furthermore, the tone of business model disclosure could be analysed over a more extended period of time to determine key trends in business model disclosure and whether the use of impression management in business model disclosure is apparent over an extended period.

References

Achtenhagen, L., Melin, L., & Naldi, L. (2013). Dynamics of business models–strategising, critical capabilities and activities for sustained value creation. *Long Range Planning, 46*(6), 427–442.

Aerts, W. (2005). Picking up the pieces: Impression management in the retrospective attributional framing of accounting outcomes. *Accounting, Organisations and Society, 30*(6), 493–517. https://doi.org/10.1016/j.aos.2004.07.001

Ashforth, B. E., & Gibbs, B. W. (1990). The double-edge of organizational legitimation. *Organisation Science, 1*(2), 177–194. https://doi.org/10.1287/orsc.1.2.177

Athanasakou, V. E., Walker, M., Young, S., Alves, P., El-Haj, M., & Rayson, P. (2022, February 6). *Mandatory annual report descriptions of business model and strategy, investor uncertainty, and disclosure cascade effects. Investor uncertainty, and disclosure cascade effects.*

Beattie, V., McInnes, B., & Fearnley, S. (2004). A methodology for analysing and evaluating narratives in annual reports: A comprehensive descriptive profile and metrics for disclosure quality attributes. *Accounting Forum, 28*(3), 205–236. https://doi.org/10.1016/j.accfor.2004.07.001

Beynon, M. J., Clatworthy, M. A., & Jones, M. J. (2004). The prediction of profitability using accounting narratives: A variable-precision rough set approach. Intelligent Systems in Accounting, Finance & Management. *International Journal, 12*(4), 227–242. https://doi.org/10.1002/isaf.256

Brennan, N. M., Guillamon-Saorin, E., & Pierce, A. (2009). Methodological insights: Impression management: Developing and illustrating a scheme of analysis for narrative disclosures—A methodological note. *Accounting, Auditing & Accountability Journal.*

Brennan, N. M., & Merkl-Davies, D. M. (2013). Accounting narratives and impression management. In *The Routledge companion to accounting communication* (pp. 109–132). Routledge.

Bryan, S. H. (1997). Incremental information content of required disclosures contained in management discussion and analysis. *The Accounting Review, 72*(2), 285–301. http://www.jstor.org/stable/248557

Cazier, R. A., Merkley, K. J., & Treu, J. S. (2020). When are firms sued for qualitative disclosures? Implications of the safe harbor for forward-looking statements. *The Accounting Review, 95*(1), 31–55.

Chotia, A., Surty, M., Yasseen, Y., & Omarjee, F. (2024). The impact of impression management using minimal narrative disclosures in integrated reports on the performance of the top 100 JSE-listed companies. In T. Moloi & B. George (Eds.), *Towards digitally transforming accounting and business processes. ICAB 2023. Springer proceedings in business and economics*. Springer. https://doi.org/10.1007/978-3-031-46177-4_1

Clatworthy, M., & Jones, M. J. (2003). Financial reporting of good news and bad news: Evidence from accounting narratives. *Accounting and Business Research, 33*(3), 171–185.

Clatworthy, M. A., & Jones, M. J. (2006). Differential patterns of textual characteristics and company performance in the chairman's statement. *Accounting, Auditing & Accountability Journal.*

Cooper, A. C., Gimeno-Gascon, F. J., & Woo, C. Y. (1994). Initial human and financial capital as predictors of new venture performance. *Journal of Business Venturing, 9*(5), 371–395. https://doi.org/10.1016/0883-9026(94)90013-2

Crowther, D., Carter, C., & Cooper, S. (2006). The poetics of corporate reporting: Evidence from the UK water industry. *Critical Perspectives on Accounting, 17*(2), 175–201. https://doi.org/10.1016/j.cpa.2003.09.005

Davison, J. (2002). Communication and antithesis in corporate annual reports: A research note. *Accounting, Auditing & Accountability Journal, 15*(4), 594–608. https://doi.org/10.1108/09513570210441431

Dobler, M., Lajili, K., & Zéghal, D. (2011). Attributes of corporate risk disclosure: An international investigation in the manufacturing sector. *Journal of International Accounting Research, 10*(2), 1–22. https://doi.org/10.2308/jiar-10081

Greiner, R., & Ang, S. H. (2012). Biotechnology collaborations: Does business model matter? *Journal of Management & Governance, 16*(3), 377–392. https://doi.org/10.1007/s10997-010-9156-z

Gutmayer, T., Cerbone, D., & Maroun, W. (2022). An evaluation of business model disclosures in integrated reports. *Australian Accounting Review, 32*(2), 220–237.

Hasan, M. M. (2020). Readability of narrative disclosures in 10-K reports: Does managerial ability matter? *European Accounting Review, 29*(1), 147–168.

IASB. (2010). *IFRS practice statements: Management commentary. A framework for presentation.* Retrieved from http://www.ifrs.org/Current-Projects/IASBProjects/Management-Commentary/IFRS

IIRC. (2011). *Towards integrated reporting, communicating value in the 21st century*. http://theiirc.org/wp-content/uploads/2011/09/IR-Discussion-Paper-2011_spreads.pdf

IIRC. (2013). *International Integrated Reporting Committee (IIRC). The Integrated Reporting Framework. II Framework.*

Krippendorff, K. (2018). *Content analysis: An introduction to its methodology*. Sage Publications.

Li, J., Pike, R., & Haniffa, R. (2008). Intellectual capital disclosure and corporate governance structure in UK firms. *Accounting and Business Research, 38*(2), 137–159. https://doi.org/10.1080/00014788.2008.9663326

Melloni, G., Stacchezzini, R., & Lai, A. (2016). The tone of business model disclosure: An impression management analysis of the integrated reports. *Journal of Management & Governance, 20*(2), 295–320. https://doi.org/10.1007/s10997-015-9319-z

Merkl-Davies, D. M., & Brennan, N. M. (2007). Discretionary disclosure strategies in corporate narratives: Incremental information or impression management? *Journal of Accounting Literature, 27*, 116–196.

Merkl-Davies, D. M., Brennan, N. M., & McLeay, S. J. (2011). Impression management and retrospective sense-making in corporate narratives: A social psychology perspective. *Accounting, Auditing & Accountability Journal.*

Mio, C., Marchini, P. L., & Medioli, A. (2020). Forward-looking information in integrated reports: Insights from "best in class". *Corporate Social Responsibility and Environmental Management, 27*(5), 2212–2224.

Nichols, A. L. (2020). Self-presentation theory/impression management. In *The Wiley encyclopedia of personality and individual differences: Models and theories* (pp. 397–400). Wiley.

Padia, N., & Yasseen, Y. (2011). An examination of strategy disclosure in the annual reports of south African listed companies. *South African Journal of Business Management, 42*(3), 27–35. https://doi.org/https://hdl.handle.net/10520/EJC22419

Page, M. (2014). Business models as a basis for regulation of financial reporting. *Journal of Management & Governance, 18*(3), 683–695. https://doi.org/10.1007/s10997-012-9239-0

Phesa, M., & Sibanda, M. (2022). A manifestation of impression management in corporate reporting in jse top 40 listed companies. *Journal of Business and Social Review in Emerging Economies, 8*(4), 669–682.

PWC. (2016). *Reporting your BM: Emerging practices and future trends*. https://www.pwc.co.uk/audit-assurance/assets/pdf/corporate- reporting-business-models.pdf

Schleicher, T., & Walker, M. (2010). Bias in the tone of forward-looking narratives. *Accounting and Business Research, 40*(4), 371–390. https://doi.org/10.1080/00014788.2010.9995318

Stainbank, L., & Peebles, C. (2006). The usefulness of corporate annual reports in South Africa: Perceptions of preparers and users. *Meditari: Research Journal of the School of Accounting Sciences, 14*(1), 69–80. https://doi.org/10.10520/EJC72509

Stanton, P., Stanton, J., & Pires, G. (2004). Impressions of an annual report: An experimental study. *Corporate Communications: An International Journal.*

Suchman, M. C. (1995). Managing legitimacy: Strategic and institutional approaches. *Academy of Management Review, 20*(3), 571–610.

Sukhari, A., & de Villiers, C. (2019). The influence of integrated reporting on business model and strategy disclosures. *Australian Accounting Review, 29*(4), 708–725. https://doi.org/10.1111/auar.12264

Szewieczek, A., Dratwińska-Kania, B., & Ferens, A. (2021). Business model disclosure in the reporting of public companies—An empirical study. *Sustainability, 13*(18), 10088.

Teece, D. J. (2010). Business models, business strategy and innovation. *Long Range Planning, 43*(2), 172–194. https://doi.org/10.1016/j.lrp.2009.07.003

Yasseen, Y., Moola-Yasseen, M., & Padia, N. (2017). A preliminary study into impression management practices in chairman's statements in south African annual reports: An attribution theory perspective. *Communicare: Journal for Communication Sciences in Southern Africa, 36*(1), 47–66. https://hdl.handle.net/10520/EJC-c04f2c909

Zott, C., Amit, R., & Massa, L. (2011). The business model: Recent developments and future research. *Journal of Management, 37*(4), 1019–1042. https://doi.org/10.1177/0149206311406265

An In-Depth Study of the Perceived Fairness in South Africa's VAT System with the Introduction of Automated Assessments

Melinda Dube and Mmatsie Charlotte Mamadi

Abstract Challenges that taxpayers face with Value-Added Tax (VAT) audits are the delay in refunds of VAT, as this is caused by the lengthy and time-consuming audits by the South African Revenue Service (SARS) which then affects the non-payment of their refunds. To try to remedy this issue, SARS then implemented the automated assessments in the VAT. The automated assessment will be issued once the due date for submission of the required documents of the audit has passed. It is therefore critical to understand how fair the automated system is to the taxpayer as the assessments will be based on estimates that SARS has on record, and a request for correction is not allowed in the same period of the submission. The qualitative study aims to explore the fairness of the automated system using the elements of tax fairness which are procedural and distributive. In terms of procedural fairness, the study will focus on the automated assessment process and other aspects of the social process that SARS follows before issuing a VAT automated assessment. Distributive fairness promotes the fairness of outcomes and allocation patterns that were followed. The purpose of this research is to acquire knowledge that can assist tax authorities and policymakers in determining if this system adheres with the theoretical tax framework of fairness. This research also aims to make a valuable contribution to optimise South Africa's VAT system while making sure that new developments in technology are consistent with the principles of fairness and transparency. The study then concluded that the introduction of the VAT automated assessment reflects the elements of fairness and was achieved.

Keywords Automated assessments · Distributive fairness · Procedural fairness · South African Revenue Service · Value-Added Tax

---

M. Dube · M. C. Mamadi (✉)
University of Johannesburg, Johannesburg, South Africa
e-mail: cmamadi@uj.ac.za

T. Moloi (ed.), *Impacting Society Positively Through Technology in Accounting and Business Processes*, Springer Proceedings in Business and Economics,
https://doi.org/10.1007/978-3-031-84885-8_11

Introduction

Value-Added Tax (VAT) according to SARS (2023a) is a crucial element of South Africa's fiscal framework, providing a substantial amount of funding for public services and government operations. The fair administration of VAT is not only essential for revenue collection but also for upholding the principles of equity, transparency, and public trust. Recently, to improve compliance efficiency and modernise tax administration procedures, the SARS has implemented a number of reforms, one of which is the use of VAT automated assessments (SARS, 2023a).

This study thoroughly investigates the perceived elements of fairness of the new VAT automated assessment system's processes in South Africa, particularly considering the system's use of automated assessments. The concept of fairness in the tax system is complex and includes aspects of distributive equity, procedural fairness, accountability, and transparency (Niesiobędzka & Kołodziej, 2020). An important turning point in South Africa's tax administration history, according to Niesiobędzka and Kołodziej (2020), has been the implementation of automated assessments, which offer increased compliance mechanisms, accuracy improvements, and efficiency gains. But even with these technical advances, questions remain of how the introduction of this system was fair to the taxpayers. The purpose of this study is to add to the current discussion on the fairness of the VAT automated assessment by analysing the processes followed by SARS in the implementation of the system.

A brief background of the South African VAT system will be discussed below.

Background of South Africa's VAT System

VAT is an indirect tax on the consumption of goods and services in the economy. Revenue is raised for the government by requiring certain traders (vendors) that carry on an enterprise to register for VAT. According to the budget review (2021), the purpose of the VAT is to generate income for government spending. In South Africa, VAT was first introduced in September 1991 at a rate of 10%. After that, the rate was raised to 14% in 1993. On April first, 2018, it was raised to 15%, and the rate remains the same currently (GTAC, 2018).

VAT is charged on "taxable supplies," which are the supply of goods or services provided by a "vendor" (a person registered with SARS or obliged to register) in the course of, or in support of an enterprise the vendor conducts entirely or partially in South Africa, (PwC, 2023). Vendors are responsible for making sure that taxes are paid on time, returns are filed, and VAT is collected on taxable transactions. Every time a tax period ends, the vendor files a VAT201 return with SARS, in which the amount of input tax paid, along with any other deductions, is deducted from the amount of output tax collected for that particular tax period. The net liability that results is then paid to SARS or claimed as a refund, usually by the 25th day (or the last business day before the 25th should the 25th falls over a weekend or a public holiday) of the first calendar month following the end of the relevant tax period (VAT404, 2021). Vendors who have registered to electronically submit their returns have until the last business day of that calendar month to submit their VAT201 returns and making payment. SARS determines the vendor's VAT liability or refund based on the data included in the VAT201 submission. If vendors have excess input tax claims, they may be eligible for a VAT refund or must pay SARS for any VAT owed (VAT404, 2021) if the output tax exceeds the input tax.

In addition to regular VAT submissions, SARS conducts VAT audits to verify the accuracy and compliance of VAT201 returns submitted by vendors. Many VAT audits occur at random, because they are carried out to identify and discourage non-compliance, such as under-reporting of taxable supplies, inflating input tax claims, and engaging in other types of tax evasion (Barone, 2022). SARS notifies the chosen taxpayers that they have been selected for a VAT audit. The notification contains information about the audit's scope, documentation needs, and procedures. To confirm the accuracy of reported VAT transactions, SARS auditors thoroughly examine the taxpayer's financial records, VAT201 returns, tax invoices, and other pertinent evidence (VAT404, 2021). During a VAT audit, a vendor may be required to submit additional documentation, delays and non-submission of these documents have caused significant interruptions in finalisation and verification of VAT201 returns. To mitigate the problem of non-compliance SARS introduced the automated VAT assessments to enhance tax compliance and streamline the VAT process. Under this method, vendors who do not timely provide the required verification documents will automatically receive assessments from SARS. The introduction of the automated VAT assessment system is explored next.

Introduction of Automated Assessments

According to SARS (2023b), the automated assessment functionality is now available for VAT. If a vendor does not provide the necessary documents that SARS requires or requested for the VAT verification process, SARS may raise an automated assessment in accordance with section 95(1)(c) of the Tax Administration Act No. 28 of 2011 (the TAA).

Please note the following regarding automated assessments:

- *"The details of the automated assessment can be viewed on the notice (VAT217) issued to the vendor,*
- *A request for correction will not be allowed if SARS has raised an automated assessment for VAT in the same period.*
- *If the vendor does not agree with the automated assessment, the required relevant material must be submitted within 40 business days from the date of the (VAT217) notice that was issued.*
- *The vendor can submit the outstanding relevant material* via *eFiling, at a SARS branch or through the SARS Online Query System (SOQS).*

- *The vendor may request for extension if the relevant material cannot be submitted within 40 business days.*
- *If the request for extension is approved, the vendor will have up to the date of extension or five (5) years plus 40 business days to submit the relevant material.*
- *The vendor will be allowed to submit a request for suspension of payment if the automated assessment results in an amount payable for the period stipulated in the VAT217 notice issued.*
- *The vendor will not be allowed to submit a Notice of Objection (NOO) as an automated assessment issued in terms of section 95(1)(c) is not subject to dispute"* (SARS, 2023b).

The VAT self-assessment reforms, among other policy efforts, have had a notable impact on the tax system in South Africa and compliance of taxpayers. In December 2023, SARS introduced the automated VAT system, in the new VAT auto-assessment system if VAT vendors do not timely submit the required verification documents, the new system will automatically issue assessments. Notably, once an automated VAT assessment is issued, corrections will not be permitted for the same VAT period (Mullins, 2023).

This modification has a substantial influence on how VAT providers manage their submissions and handle assessments, underscoring the significance of timely compliance. Given the significance of VAT as a revenue-raising tool, studies investigating VAT compliance and enforcement have become increasingly important. Studies have shown that taxpayers' knowledge of tax laws, fairness, and motivational tendencies all influence tax behaviour and compliance (Mullins, 2023).

Literature Review

The aim of the review of previous literature on the VAT system is to provide an overview of the changes that have occurred throughout time, together with the views and behaviour of the taxpayers who have been subjected to these changes, some of which have been abrupt and some of which have been gradual. A peer review of the literature was done for this study, however the literature was based on the different aspects of VAT.

SA-TIED (2019) focused on assessing the distributional impact of the recent increase in the VAT rate and options for redress through the benefits system.

Nortjie (2010) focused on the reasons of non-clean VAT audits in the municipalities, stressing the fact that their VAT control accounts do not match what is submitted to SARS on the VAT201 returns.

Schoeman et al. (2021) dealt with examining how the change in the VAT rate would affect small business organisations' tax compliance practices.

Smoulders and Naidoo (2013) stressed that SARS had, for the most part, tried to address the tax compliance burdens identified in those studies, according to a comparison of the conclusions and suggestions made in small business tax compliance cost studies conducted in South Africa with initiatives introduced by SARS, as confirmed by interviews with SARS and a South African Institute of Chartered Accountants official.

None of these studies investigated VAT changes regarding the VAT audit (introduction of the automated assessments) from a fairness perspective, therefore this is the gap identified by this study and fairness, as a theoretical underpinning for the study, is addressed extensively below. What follows are the objectives of this study to address fairness as a principle of a good tax system.

Research Objectives

The VAT system in South Africa has seen a dramatic change with the introduction of automated assessments, which has the potential to improve tax compliance, efficiency, and accuracy. However, alongside technological advancements, questions arise regarding the fairness of the VAT processes to the taxpayer since the evaluations will be based on estimations that SARS has on file and because a rectification request cannot be made during the filing period.

The main objective of this study is to determine if the process followed, and the introduction of automated assessments reflect the elements of fairness. To achieve the main objective the following secondary research objectives will be explored:

- Assess if the procedures and the processes followed in the implementation of the introduction of the automated assessment are perceived as fair in the decision-making processes of resolving the non-compliance of VAT audits which leads to non-payouts of VAT refunds.
- Analysing whether there was the need for the introduction of the automated assessment, whether the outcome of this assessment put in place would be fair and the results would be in favour of a fair conclusion for both parties.

Improving tax knowledge and addressing issues of fairness in the VAT processes are crucial for promoting voluntary tax compliance. The theoretical framework for the study, which uses fairness as a conceptual framework, is discussed in depth below. This is the gap that the current study has found.

Theoretical Framework

The principles or canons of taxation were created by Adam Smith in 1776 and were related to the practical aspects of taxation. Fairness, certainty, efficiency, and convenience are the four tax canons that remain acknowledged as masterpieces. The principles of taxation were initially outlined by Adam Smith in his widely read book *The Wealth of Nations* in 1776, even though taxes had been collected for many years prior.

The focus of this study is the principle of fairness from the tax canons above. Fairness is when someone makes a fair decision, they satisfy everyone and offering a workable answer (Vocabulary.com, n.d.). A specific type of moral obligation that emerges when specific conditions are satisfied is explained by the principles of fairness (Boran, 2006).

Wenzel (2003) also refers to a conceptual framework for fairness, which asserts that distributive, procedural, and retributive fairness are the three categories of fairness models in social psychology. Distributive fairness and procedural fairness are the only two categories of fairness models that are the subject of this study. While procedural fairness supports the fairness of decision-making procedures and the other facets of social processes, distributive fairness advances the equity of results and distribution patterns (Tyler & Lind, 1992).

Procedural Fairness

The components of procedural fairness, namely, the impartiality of the process, the credibility of the tax authorities, and the treatment of all parties with respect and decency were crucial for perceived fairness (Tyler & Lind, 1992)

- Impartiality of the process
- Credibility of the tax authorities
- Treatment of respect and decency to all parties

Distributive Fairness

Vermeulen and Coetzee (2006) stated that there are three components under which distributive fairness can be subdivided into being need, equity, and equality.

- Need: There was a *need* for the changes in the VAT systems that arose from the non-compliance of taxpayers to the VAT17 audit at SARS which is causing a delay in the VAT refunds.
- Equity: This focuses on the fairness of an outcome after the automated assessments has been issued.
- Equality: This suggests that the taxpayers and SARS, regardless of their efforts, the results should be in favour of a fair conclusion, which should be the same for both parties.

The aim of this section was to provide the theoretical framework upon which the study is built. The two fairness principles that serve as the foundation for this study's main constructs and the principles of fairness in taxation were articulated in this section. The next section will describe the research plan through the presentation of the research methodology applied.

Methodology

The research methodology section of this study outlines the systematic approach employed to investigate the perceived fairness of the processes and the outcome of the South African VAT system regarding the introduction of the automated assessments. Building upon the defined objectives, this section outlines the research design, data collection methods, analytical techniques, and ethical considerations utilised to address the elements of fairness within the new VAT system.

According to Tenny et al. (2022), qualitative research is a study methodology that aims to investigate and offer more profound understanding of real-world issues. The data gathering in a qualitative study takes place in a natural setting that is sensitive to the people and environments being studied, and data analysis is inductive and establishes patterns (Creswell, 2007). This then suggests that qualitative data can offer information that addresses societal concerns, queries, or issues and benefits humanity (Tracy, 2013). This study which is aimed at understanding the elements of fairness of the VAT automated assessment process was conducted through the documentary analysis approach.

Document analysis is a methodical process for going over and assessing written and digital documents (Bowen, 2009). The documents analysed were the *SARS Guide VAT404*, articles from reputable audit firms, newspaper articles, and scholarly peer reviewed journals. The document analysis assisted with the understanding of the processes and the communication methods followed by SARS to inform the taxpayers about the VAT audits. The document analysis also helped to understand if there was a need for the implementation of the VAT automated assessment system, and if there was a fair outcome for both parties. The analysis of both procedural and distributive analysis was conducted in Sect. "Analysis of the Elements of Fairness" of this study.

Ethical Consideration

Documents were analysed and interpreted with consideration for ethical principles and policies. The data utilised in this study is publicly available, and ethical clearance for the research was granted by the University of Johannesburg's School of Accounting: Ethical clearance code is SAREC20240314/03.

Discussion and Analysis

One of the challenges that businesses have with VAT audits is the non-payment or late payment of VAT refunds, which are a result of the lengthy and tedious audits conducted by SARS, which in turn impacts the non-payment of VAT refunds. SARS then introduced automated assessments in the VAT system to address this problem. The main concern of this study is the implementation process of the automated assessments and whether the outcome reflects the elements of fairness.

Analysis of the Elements of Fairness

According to Mullins (2023), the overview of the automated assessment system is that when the taxpayer is selected for an audit or issued with VAT217 assessment, and they fail to comply then the automated assessment will be issued based on the information that SARS has on record. This could lead to a misrepresentation of the true status of that VAT201 return in question, and the system does not allow correction after the automated assessment has been issued. The automated assessment system is meant to prompt the taxpayers to be compliant to the audit to avoid the possible misrepresentation and that the correct VAT refund could be paid to the taxpayer timeously.

Procedural Fairness Analysis

The elements of the procedural fairness (impartiality of the process, credibility of the authorities, and treatment of respect and decency of all parties) can be assessed. SARS allows 40 business days which is more than a calendar month for the audit response from taxpayers. The process of the automated assessment is a fair treatment of both parties as SARS would have timeously communicated with the taxpayer regarding the audit. SARS will notify the taxpayer regarding the audit through a letter and if a taxpayer is an efiler then the communication will be sent via efiling. SARS' process of communication promotes their credibility and reflects that there is no abuse of power over the taxpayers. This then leads to the fair treatment of respect and decency to both SARS and the taxpayers. All the elements of procedural fairness are upheld.

Distributive Fairness Analysis

The elements of the distributive fairness (need, equity, and equality) can be assessed. Taxpayers in the past have found it challenging to comply with the audit for varied reasons. This led to SARS seeing a need for the automated assessments to be set in motion to motivate the taxpayers to submit the correct supporting documentation required by SARS for the audit. This will lead to the equity element, as it then focuses on the fairness of an outcome after the automated assessments has been put in place. If the taxpayer is not compliant with the audit request, then it is well within

SARS's administrative right, according to section 95(1)(c) of the TAA, to allow the automated assessment to be issued so that their systems can be cleared off the overdue audits. The element of equality suggests that both parties' outcomes, SARS and the taxpayer's, should be a fair conclusion. SARS would have warned the taxpayer and gave them reasonable time to be compliant and failure to do so leads to a system intervention in the form of an automated assessment. As a result, every element of distributive fairness was maintained.

Limitations

Although qualitative research methods provide insightful explanations of complicated phenomena and subjective experiences, it is important to recognise that they have significant limitations. These are some of the limitations that were faced by the researchers of this study:

- Findings in this study of the fairness of the implementation of the automated assessment was exclusively derived from qualitative data which may not have accurately reflected the variety of viewpoints and experiences that South African taxpayers have to offer. Hence, interviews with the relevant affected taxpayers would be required to fully evaluate the genuineness of the elements of fairness and to get the taxpayers' true perceptions of their feelings regarding this innovative technology system.
- Aspects of the VAT administration, such as compliance behaviours, transactional data analysis, or comparative assessments over time were not performed during this study, as they can be achieved using quantitative or mixed methods.

Conclusion and Recommendations

To address the main research objective, the secondary research objectives needed to be analysed and the first secondary research objective was to assess if the procedures and the processes followed in the implementation of the introduction of the automated assessment are perceived as fair in the decision-making processes of resolving the non-compliance of VAT audits which lead to the non-payout of VAT refunds. This was done to evaluate if the elements of the procedural fairness are upheld as the automated assessment system was implemented. The results of this analysis revealed that the impartiality of the process, credibility of the authorities, and the treatment of respect and decency of all parties are upheld as SARS's communication regarding the audit is done timeously and fairly.

The second secondary research objective was to analyse whether there was the need for the introduction of the automated assessment, and whether the outcome of this assessment put in place would be fair and the results would be in favour of a fair conclusion for both parties. The results of this analysis revealed that the need arose because of the non-compliance of the taxpayers to the audit therefore leading to the delay of the VAT refund payouts. The implementation of the automated assessment would attempt to remedy the issue of audit non-compliance and the timeous payouts of VAT refunds. Therefore, it would be a fair conclusion for both parties.

Having addressed all the secondary research objectives, the main objective—to investigate if the process followed and the introduction of automated assessments reflect elements of fairness—was therefore achieved.

To assess the true impact of the implementation of the automated assessment, quantitative research should be undertaken, to assess the perceived elements of fairness from a taxpayer's perspective.

References

Barone, L. (2022). *Common triggers of VAT Audit*. https://sovos.com/blog/vat/common-triggers-of-a-vat-audit/

Boran, I. (2006). Benefits, intentions, and the principle of fairness. *Canadian Journal of Philosophy, 36*(1), 95–115. https://doi.org/10.1353/cjp.2006.0002

Bowen, G. A. (2009). Document analysis as a qualitative research method. *Qualitative Research Journal, 9*(2), 27–40. https://doi.org/10.3316/QRJ0902027

Budget Review. (2021). *Revenue trends and tax proposals*. https://www.treasury.gov.za/documents/national%20budget/2021/review/Chapter%204.pdf

Creswell, J. W. (2007). *Qualitative inquiry & research design. Choosing among five approaches* (2nd ed.). Sage.

GTAC. (2018). *VAT in South Africa*. https://www.gtac.gov.za/wp-content/uploads/2022/02/VAT-in-South-Africa.pdf

Mullins, Z. (2023). *SARS introduces automated VAT assessments*. https://www.fanews.co.za/article/tax/16/tax/1016/sars-introduces-automated-vat-assessments/38588

Niesiobędzka, M., & Kołodziej, S. (2020). The fair process effect in taxation: The roles of procedural fairness, outcome favourability and outcome fairness in the acceptance of tax authority decisions. *Current Psychology, 39*, 246–253. https://link.springer.com/article/10.1007/s12144-017-9762-x#citeas

Nortjie, J.P. (2010). *The importance of VAT compliance*. https://journals.co.za/doi/epdf/10.10520/EJC41848

PWC. (2023). *VAT and indirect taxes in Arica—A Guide 2023—South Africa Overview*. https://www.pwc.co.za/en/publications/vat-in-africa/south-africaoverview.html

SARS. (2023a). *Value-added tax*. https://www.sars.gov.za/types-of-tax/value-added-tax/

SARS. (2023b). *VAT enhancements for estimated assessments*. https://www.sars.gov.za/latest-news/vat-enhancements-for-estimated-assessments/

SA-TIED. (2019). *SA-TIED working paper #30- Modelling VAT in South Africa*. https://satied.wider.unu.edu/sites/default/files/pdf/SATIED_WP30_Gcabo_Moiche_Steyn_Moahlodi_Pirttil%25C3%25A4_Wright_Noble_Barnes_Masekesa_March_2019.pdf

Schoeman, A., Evans, C., & Du Preez, H. (2021). The effect of changes in the value-added tax rate on tax compliance behaviour of small businesses in South Africa: A field experiment. In J. Hasseldine (Ed.), *Advances in taxation* (Vol. 29, pp. 65–88). Emerald Publishing Limited. https://doi.org/10.1108/S1058-749720210000029004

Smoulders, S., & Naidoo, G. (2013). *Addressing the small business tax compliance burden - evidence from South Africa*. https://journals.co.za/doi/abs/10.10520/EJC142883

Tenny, S., Brannan, J. M., & Brannan, G. D. (2022). *Qualitative study*. https://www.ncbi.nlm.nih.gov/books/NBK470395/
Tracy, S. J. (2013). *Qualitative research methods. Selecting evidence, crafting analysis, communicating impact* (1st ed.). Wiley-Blackwell.
Tyler, T., & Lind, E. (1992). A relational model of authority in groups. In M. Zanna (Ed.), *Advances in experimental social psychology* (pp. 115–191). Academic Press.
VAT404. (2021). *Guide for vendors*. https://www.sars.gov.za/wp-content/uploads/Ops/Guides/LAPD-VAT-G02-VAT-404-Guide-for-Vendors.pdf
Vermeulen, L., & Coetzee, M. (2006). Perceptions of the dimensions of the fairness of affirmative action: A pilot study. *South African Journal of Business Management, 37*(3), 53–65.
Vocabulary.com. (n.d.). *Definition: fairness [Online]*. https://www.vocabulary.com/dictionary/
Wenzel, M. (2003). Tax compliance and the psychology of justice: Mapping the field. In V. Braithwaite (Ed.), *Taxing democracy: Understanding tax avoidance and evasion*. Ashgate Publishing. https://doi.org/10.4324/9781315241746

The Impact of an Abrupt Change Caused by COVID-19 on the Taxation of Expatriates in Residence-Based Tax Systems

Charlotte Mamadi

Abstract Many businesses now operate worldwide because of globalization. As a result, human capital is shifting from one tax jurisdiction to another. Understanding the tax rules of different countries is necessary for this movement of human capital. There are some things countries have in common, such as taxing residents on their worldwide income, and the tax exemption on income from a foreign employment. It is possible to compare the tax systems of countries that use residence-based taxation, such as Australia, Ghana, South Africa, and the UK. In 2020, the world experienced COVID-19. Governments were driven to put into effect temporary measures such as restricting both international and domestic travel. Therefore, many expats were forced to remain in their host or home countries. The objective of this research was to explore whether the procedures and measures put in place by the tax authorities adhered to the fairness principles (distributive and procedural) which is the theoretical framework of this study and how the abrupt changes brought by COVID-19 affected the income taxation of expatriates. Prior studies only focused on the changes in the expatriate taxation and not on the elements of fairness when changes are implemented. This is the gap this study will fill. Through the qualitative research methodology, primary and secondary data were used. The study compared different countries using the comparative methodology. The conclusions demonstrate that the procedures and the amendments made are fairer and practical for the countries who implemented them. Future studies may consider the inclusion of more developing countries to conduct quantitative comparative research to evaluate principles of fairness during abrupt changes in the tax laws.

Keywords Australia · Distributive and Procedural fairness · Exempt Foreign Income · Expatriate taxation · Ghana · Residence-based systems · South Africa · The UK

C. Mamadi (✉)
University of Johannesburg, Johannesburg, South Africa
e-mail: cmamadi@uj.ac.za

T. Moloi (ed.), *Impacting Society Positively Through Technology in Accounting and Business Processes*, Springer Proceedings in Business and Economics,
https://doi.org/10.1007/978-3-031-84885-8_12

Introduction

The World Bank (2020) states that countries must collect taxes to create public revenues, which in turn enable investments in human capital, infrastructure, and services for both citizens and businesses. Governments need to strike a balance between objectives such as increasing tax collections and promoting sustainable growth to guarantee a fair and equitable tax system. Kagiri (2022) claims that people are driven to travel farther and quicker over the world by the need for more revenue growth. People relocating across borders helps their businesses grow faster, more profitably, and even more successfully hire and retain employees globally. Usually, these people are called expatriates (or "Expats"). A person who resides or works abroad is known as an expat (McNulty & Brewster, 2016). The Latin terms ex (out of) and patria (fatherland) are the source of the English word "expatriate" (Dictionary.com, 2020).

Mosupye (2013) asserts that human capital is moving between tax jurisdictions and that there are more expatriates than before. This shift is characterized by global mobility. Global mobility is also encouraged by the tax authorities' exemption from taxation or granting of tax credits for income from foreign employment, which is subject to certain requirements in each country (Mosupye, 2013). As per Garbarino's (2022) assertion, the concept of global mobility refers to the ability of skilled persons to relocate to different countries of the world in search of employment opportunities. This illustrates how the business world is changing and making use of global employment, as people are traveling across borders more regularly (Selmer & Lauring, 2015). Although every country has a unique tax system, there are some similarities, claims Mosupye (2013). For instance, countries with residence-based taxation systems may tax residents on their worldwide income, allowing for shared taxation principles. While taxation does play a significant role in expats' decision-making when it comes to accepting international assignments and keeping the benefit of the tax exemption in mind, comprehending domestic tax systems can be complicated for expats at times (Mosupye, 2013).

This study's main objective is to assess the effects of abrupt changes brought about by unforeseen circumstances in this case being the COVID-19 pandemic on the taxation of expatriates' foreign employment income, with a particular focus on determining whether the temporary changes and the procedures used to put them into place, reflect fairness toward the expat community. It will be possible to compare countries with comparable tax structures once the fairness principles have been addressed, for the sake of this study, South Africa (SA), Ghana, the UK, and Australia were chosen. Since these countries are all Commonwealth of Nations members and have residence-based tax systems, the study can therefore compare them using countries with comparable tax structures.

Understanding the similarities and differences between expatriate taxation in each of these residence-based tax countries will be useful for scholars, tax practitioners, and expats. This is especially true considering the large expat populations in the UK and Australia as well as the continent of Africa's rapid economic growth (Mosupye, 2013; World Economic Forum, 2013).

Background

The skilled labor that is imported into countries benefits from expatriate taxes and consequently has a significant impact on the economy. Certain countries encourage the expansion of their expat population by offering income tax exemptions or tax credits based on their income from foreign employment. International travel is essential for expats, in 2020 the world as we knew it changed due to the COVID-19 pandemic, which caused governments to close the domestic and international borders. The taxation of expats' income from foreign employment was unpredictable at the time due to government rulings. A debate over the legitimacy of the government versus the fairness of the temporary changes in tax laws may have arisen because of the aggressive measures taken by governments worldwide to shield their people and companies from the economic harm that COVID-19 brought. Depending on where an expat resides determines which countries tax their income from foreign employment.

Residency, Employment Income and Tax Exemption

Residency

The Organization for Economic Cooperation and Development (OECD, 2019) defines a person as a "resident of a country" if they are subject to taxation in that country under its rules because of their residence, domicile, or any other comparable criteria. This expression, however, does not apply to someone who solely pays taxes in the country where their income is generated. As a result, for the purposes of this study, an expat is a resident in his home country and is subject to taxation on all his worldwide income in countries with resident-based taxation regimes.

Employment Income

According to Article 15 of the OECD Model Tax Convention on Income and on Capital, income from employment is defined as salaries, wages, and other similar remuneration received by a resident of a country in connection with employment. Unless employment is performed in another country, income from employment is only taxable in that country (OECD, 2019).

Tax Exemption

When certain requirements are met, remuneration is exempt from taxation. This is known as a tax exemption. Remember that the movement of expats between their home country and the host country has a big effect on their taxes. Based on these movements, governments can determine which country has taxing authority during each assessment year and if expats are qualified for an exemption from paying taxes on their income from foreign employment (Mosupye, 2013). While the rule of tax exemption is different in the UK and Australia, where a resident is considered a non-tax resident if they are in another country for more than 183 days and are not subject to tax in the UK or Australia on any income they earn from foreign employment, the qualification process for the tax exemption on that foreign employment income had been disrupted in countries such as South Africa and Ghana as a result of the legal restrictions or the global lockdown on international borders brought on by the COVID-19 pandemic.

COVID-19 Pandemic Era Affecting the World

The global spread of COVID-19 in 2020 had an impact on the entire world. On March 11, 2020, the World Health Organization (WHO) proclaimed it to be a pandemic (Savage et al., 2020). The COVID-19 outbreak was designated as a Public Health Emergency of International Concern by March 2020 because of the virus's rapid spread to multiple countries and regions (Bender, 2020). Governments were forced to implement severe restrictions in response to the pandemic, such as banning both domestic and international travel (OECD, 2020). COVID-19 travel limitations prevented many expats from traveling freely, which left them stuck in a place other than their own country or the country in which they were assigned to work (McDermid et al., 2022).

Expatriate Tax Relief in a Global Pandemic

Since the COVID-19 crisis affected the entire world, a worldwide solution was necessary. It was more important than ever to cooperate in the battle against tax evasion, tax avoidance, and illegal financial flows to increase budgetary flexibility. It was also more crucial than ever to work toward a more equitable and fair worldwide taxation of economic activity from an International Monetary Fund perspective (IMF, 2020). It was expected that the response would differ from country to country depending on the severity of the regional virus spread. The most popular remedies included ways to improve financial flow, including postponing tax payments, and acknowledging that people had to spend time in locations other than their usual ones because of the virus (Mazars, 2020). If someone were prohibited from entering or leaving a country, they would fail the "days test" and lose the tax exemption on their income from foreign employment (Visser, 2020).

Fairness Perceptions During Changing Legislation

Wartick (1991) examined how information about the legislative objective of tax law changes was conveyed to determine if this had any impact on people's perceptions of fairness in his study and on how people view these changes. To get ready for a shift in the tax law, taxpayers thought about what would have happened to their finances if the tax laws had not changed. If they felt they would have been worse off, they would experience relative deprivation, and one outcome of this belief was perceived unfairness (Wartick, 1991). People's willingness to obey the law and submit to an authority is strongly influenced by their perceptions of fairness (Farrar et al., 2018).

Objectives

The main research objective for this study is to investigate whether the procedures and policies put in place by the tax authorities of these countries adhere to the principles of fairness, as well as how sudden changes and exceptional circumstances brought about by the COVID-19 pandemic, affected the income taxation of expatriates in the several chosen countries with residence-based tax systems.

Secondary Research Objectives

The secondary research objectives formulated below led the research to achieve the above main research objective for this study:

1. To explore the definition of residency of SA, Ghana, the UK, and Australia to understand the requirements that must be met by an expat to be considered a resident of that country.
2. To explore the income tax treatment of foreign employment income in the selected countries, prior and post to the amendments made during the COVID-19 pandemic, to understand the reasoning behind the temporary amendments and to do a comparison between the above countries of processes that the governments followed through public consultations to see if the distributive and the procedural fairness were reflected or not.

Literature Review

A review of the repository of research on expatriate taxation has been done to fully comprehend the changes that have taken place over time, as well as the attitudes of those who have been subjected to them, some of which have been abrupt, while others have been gradual. The literature that was peer-reviewed for this study focused on various aspects of expatriate taxation.

Residence Status and Expatriates' Taxation

The aim of Mosupye's (2013) study was to improve knowledge about foreign workers' taxes in different African countries. One crucial factor in the taxation of income from foreign employment was residency. Van Wyk (2011) critically examined how South Africans who work abroad are affected by taxes. She focused on double taxation agreements and international tax regulations, particularly those pertaining to Australia.

The Exemption of Foreign Employment Income

Sebashe et al. (2022) assessed whether the foreign employment income tax exemption provided by the Income Tax Act No. 58 of 1962 (the ITA) (section 10(1)(o)(ii)) which limited the exemption to the first 1,25 million ZAR to be exempted rather than the full foreign employment income exemption achieved its goal. Their goal was to ascertain how the adjustments will affect SA expats working in countries with both high- and low-income tax rates, including the UK.

Manenzhe (2023) conducted a global comparison of the income tax exemptions for foreigners granted by SA and Australia. The focus was on whether SA's exemption rules comply with international taxation standards, given the amendments made to section 10(1)(o)(ii). The studies above stressed the value of establishing residence as a foundation for figuring out how expats should be taxed, but they did not go into detail on the cases in which the residence status was unexpectedly interrupted by events beyond the expat's control. None of these studies also examined the changes from a fairness perspective. Fairness as a conceptual basis for the study is covered in detail below as the study's theoretical framework. This is the gap identified by this study.

Theoretical Framework

The main research objective of this study is to determine how the unexpected conditions surrounding the COVID-19 outbreak affected the way in which foreign employment income of expats was taxed in the selected residence-based tax jurisdictions (SA, Ghana, the UK, and Australia). For the study to investigate whether the procedures used by the authorities remedy the COVID-19 disruption, there should be a consistency with the principles of fairness. For this reason, it is critical to comprehend the requirements that must be met for an expat to be considered a resident as well as the tax implications of the income from their foreign employment being exempt from income tax. The theoretical basis for this study is based on the idea of the fairness principles in taxes.

The Principles of Fairness

A particular kind of moral responsibility that arises when specific requirements are met is explained by the fairness principles (Boran, 2006). Kirchler et al. (2008) stated that the slippery slope framework placed a strong emphasis on the idea of perceived fairness. The willingness of individuals to have faith in an authority was influenced by their judgments of fairness (Farrar et al., 2018). The three categories of fairness models in social psychology are distributive, procedural, and retributive, according to a conceptual framework for fairness mentioned by Wenzel (2003). The two types of fairness models that are the focus of this study are distributive and procedural fairness. Distributive fairness promotes the fairness of outcomes, whereas procedural fairness supports the fairness of decision-making processes (Tyler & Lind, 1992).

(a) *Distributive Fairness*

According to Cropanzano and Ambrose (2001), distributive fairness is "the perceived fairness of resources received." When taxpayers wanted to be treated based on their needs, efforts, and merits and felt concerned about the fairness of their results, individual distributive fairness occurred. Three factors can be used to categorize distributive fairness: need, equity, and equality (Vermeulen & Coetzee, 2006). Their research showed that equality and equity are two different concepts. Equity compares and assesses the contributions of various parties to determine how fair a result is.

However, equality disregards those people's contributions in favor of a fair solution that must be applicable to everyone. If a person's tax burden rose from what it was before the involuntary COVID-19 scenario, then tax compliance may decline. The diversion that COVID-19 produced in the tax system made the amendments necessary. The two requirements of equality and equity had to be met when the situation demanded it. Everyone understands that the government must raise money from the people to fulfill its mandate, but that agreement also needs to be upheld and protected from the disruption that the COVID-19 pandemic caused. The rules for equality place more focus on the fair outcome than on the contributions of the parties. Ensuring that the decisions made do not put expats in a worse predicament than they would have under prior to COVID-19 is the primary objective of this study.

(b) *Procedural Fairness*

Procedural fairness, according to Leventhal (1980), refers to the impartiality of the decision-making process that goes into allocating resources. According to Farrar (2015, p. 72), public trust in the tax system and the complexity of the tax laws both have an impact on procedural fairness. The components of procedural fairness, such as the process's impartiality, the tax authorities' credibility, and the treatment of all parties with respect and dignity, were crucial in determining perceived fairness (Tyler & Lind, 1992). A culture of connection and a person's sense of procedural fairness were necessary for building trust (Job et al., 2007).

This illustrated the objective norms upheld by the impartiality principle. The decisions made by the tax authorities gained more legitimacy since all parties were managed with dignity and respect. Due to this situation, the authorities acted quickly and without abuse of power to make decisions that became non-debatable laws. The procedures used by the authorities had to win the trust of the expats for them to view the temporary change of the tax rules as fair.

In conclusion, this study intends to investigate how people perceive the fairness of changes to tax laws and whether knowledge of the legislative rationale behind the change influences people's perceptions of fairness (Wartick, 1991). When tax laws are changed, taxpayers sometimes try to project what their tax position would have been in the absence of the changes. If they believe they would have been worse off, they will experience relative deprivation, and one consequence of feeling unfairly treated is relative deprivation.

The chosen fairness principles used in this study were as follows:

The study investigated whether the tax authorities in each of the four countries had open discussions regarding the temporary amendments to the tax laws with expats. Procedural fairness and its components, that is, the process's impartiality, the tax authorities' credibility, and the treatment of all parties with respect and dignity are utilized to evaluate the procedures that the authorities implemented in this study. The distributive fairness of the results, once the temporary amendments are implemented, is assessed.

Comprehending the meaning of residency and the requirements for the tax exemption of income from foreign employment is crucial for comprehending the temporary amendments to the tax legislation brought about by the sudden disruptions caused by the COVID-19 pandemic.

Definition of Residency and Requirement Tax Exemption of Foreign Employment Income

The objective of this section is to explore the meaning of residency to understand the requirements that must be met for an expat to qualify as a resident and to examine the requirements for tax exemption of income from foreign employment in the selected countries. Secondary research objective 1 and part of secondary research objective 2 will be addressed.

South Africa: Residency

A natural person must either regularly reside in SA or, if they do not, meet every requirement of the physical presence test (PPT) to be considered a resident for income tax purposes in SA. As a result, the individual will meet the requirements set in section (1) of the ITA for "resident" status (SARS, 2018).

The following is the definition of a resident given in section 1 of the ITA:

> Resident' means any natural person who is ordinarily resident in the Republic or not at any time during the year of assessment ordinarily resident in the Republic, if that person was physically present in the Republic for a period exceeding 91 days in aggregate during the year of assessment, as well as for a period exceeding 91 days in aggregate during each of the five years of assessment preceding such year of assessment; and for a period exceeding 915 days in aggregate during such five preceding years of assessment, in which case that person will be a resident with effect from the first day of those relevant years of assessment...(South Africa, 1962).

Ghana: Residency

Section 101(1) of the Act 896 provides a definition of a resident as follows:

> A citizen, other than a citizen who has a permanent home outside of the country and lives in that home for the whole of that year. Present in the country during that year for an aggregate period of one hundred and eighty-three days, or more in any 12-month period that commences or ends during that year.

The UK: Residency

The Statutory Residency Test (SRT) was implemented in April 2013 to provide precise guidelines for determining an individual's tax residency. Three tests are available: the Sufficient Ties Test, the Automatic Overseas Test, and the Automatic UK Test.

The following steps help to understand how the test regarding your residence status under the SRT work:

1. If you have been in the UK for less than 183 days in the tax year (automatic UK test), go to step 2.
2. If you meet any of the automatic overseas tests you will not be resident in the UK for that tax year. If you do not meet any of these tests, go to step 3.
3. If you meet any of the automatic UK tests or the sufficient ties test, you will be a UK resident for that tax year. If you do not meet any of these tests you will not be a UK resident for that tax year (HMRC, 2020).

Australia: Residency

If someone wants to be considered an Australian resident for tax purposes, they must pass a residence test. Subsection 6(1) of the ITA 1936 defines individual residency as follows:

> Resident means a person who resides in Australia and includes a person whose domicile is in Australia, unless the Commissioner is satisfied that the person's permanent place of abode is outside Australia. A person who has been in Australia continuously during more than one-half of the year of income, unless the Commissioner is satisfied that the person's usual place of abode is outside Australia, and that the person does not intend to take up residence in Australia or who is a member of the superannuation scheme established by deed under the Superannuation Act 1990 or an eligible employee for the purposes of the Superannuation Act 1976 (Australia, 1936).

Below is a summary of the different definitions of the above countries to reflect that the days' test is a common theme in all countries' definitions (Fig. 1).

These four countries are quite different from one another as well as remarkably similar. The day's test refers to the criteria that all four countries use to determine whether to tax an expat as a resident. Even if the expats pass the day's test, every country has its own definition and additional standards that distinguish it from the others. For income tax purposes, an individual may be deemed to be an ordinary resident of SA if they choose to make it their permanent home. They would be regarded as UK tax residents, nevertheless, if they work in the country for longer than 183 days. As a result, they might have to pay taxes in SA and the UK in addition to paying taxes on their income worldwide. Since taxpayers are taxed at source in each of these four countries, it is likely that the expat will be subject to double taxation. As a result, the home country will be responsible for resolving any potential double taxation. The laws governing the taxes of income from foreign employment will be covered in the section that follows.

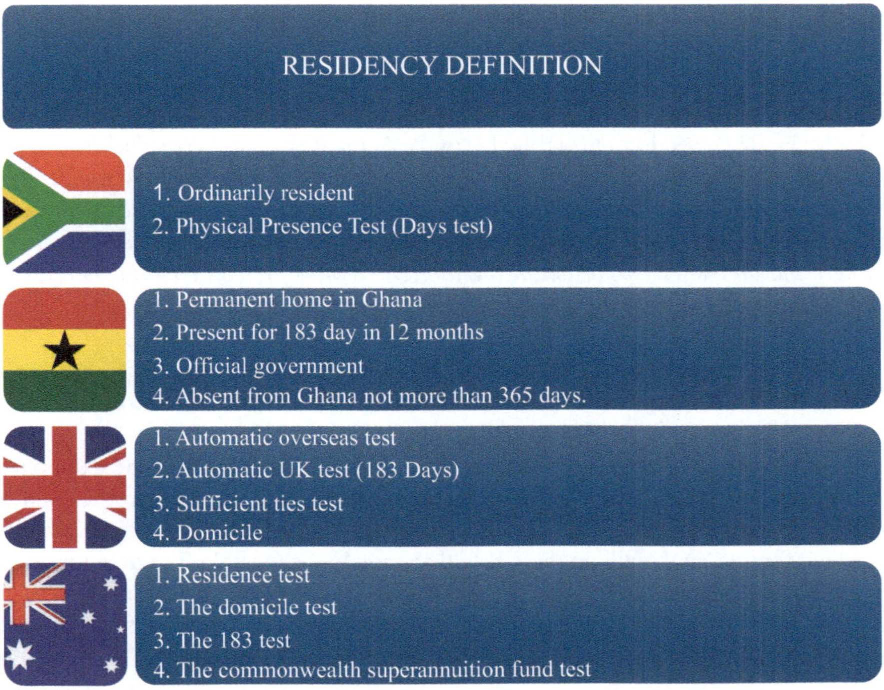

Fig. 1 Residency Definition. *Source*: Author's own diagram

South Africa: Tax Exemption of Foreign Employment Income

While non-residents are only obligated to pay taxes on income earned within the country, South African residents normally pay taxes on their worldwide income. However, a South African resident's income from foreign employment may be excluded from income tax under the South African Income Tax Act. ITA section 10(1)(o)(ii) governs the exemption, which is also known as the foreign employment income exemption. Only when requirements are met may the exemption be applied. Residents of SA are exempt from paying tax on income from foreign employment while it is earned overseas according to the provision. The requirements that must be met to be eligible for the foreign employment income exemption are a person must be a tax resident of SA during any 12-month period and the person is required to render services for a period or periods totaling more than 183 complete days outside of SA. The person must have spent a continuous period of more than 60 full days outside of SA during the previous 12 months. SARS (2021) states that as of March 1, 2020, the first R1,250,000 of income from foreign employment is tax-free.

Ghana: Tax Exemption of Foreign Employment Income

Ghanaian residents are required to pay taxes on their worldwide income, which include any earnings from jobs or businesses they may have during the tax year (KPMG, 2023). Section 111(1) and (2) of the Act 896 provides an explanation of the foreign source of income of a resident as "*the income of a resident person derived from a foreign source is taxable. The income of a resident from employment exercised in a foreign country with a non-resident employer or with a resident employer, where the individual is present in the foreign country for 183 continuous days or more during the year of assessment is exempt from tax*"(Ghana, 2015)

The UK: Tax Exemption/Tax Credit of Foreign Employment Income

The day's test on foreign employment income is not equivalent to the exemption standards that are in place in the UK. A resident of the UK who departs the country for more than 183 days is not considered a tax resident, and they are eligible to receive foreign tax credits in the UK and are solely responsible for paying taxes in their host country.

UK income tax and capital gains tax are applicable to UK residents' worldwide income and gains. Section 790(1) of the Income and Corporation Tax Act 1998 (ICTA) states that UK residents may be eligible to claim credit for foreign taxes paid under the unilateral relief on foreign employment income that is subject to UK taxation. In the event of exceptional circumstances, the number of days spent in the UK may be reduced. According to HMRC (2023), there is a limit of 60 days that can be disregarded in a tax year for exceptional circumstances related to time spent in the UK.

Australia: Tax Exemption/Tax Offset of Foreign Employment Income

Australian residents are obligated to pay taxes on all income, including earnings from foreign employment. Foreign employment income was exempt from taxation until July 1, 2009; after that date, it was only eligible for exemption if the foreign service was closely related to the activities listed below. The overseas services must be provided continuously for 91 days or more to be excluded from income tax (ATO, 2023). A foreign employment income is exempt from tax under (section 23AG of the Income Tax Assessment Act 1936), if you meet *all* four of the conditions which are, *(1)* you are an Australian resident for tax purposes, *(2)* you are engaged in continuous foreign service as an employee for 91 days or more, *(3) your foreign service is* ***directly*** *attributable to any of the following*:

- *Delivery of Australian official development assistance by your employer*
- *Activities of your employer in operating a public fund declared by the Minister to be a developing country relief fund*
- *Activities of your employer in operating a public fund established and maintained to provide monetary relief to people in a developed foreign country impacted by a disaster*
- *Activities of your employer as a prescribed charitable or religious institution*
- *Deployment outside Australia as a member of a disciplined force*

*(4) You are not excluded from exemption by the non-exemption conditions (*ATO, 2023*).*

Reflective Summary

Figure 2 is a summary of the different exemption rules of the above countries, as they were before the COVID-19 pandemic temporary amendments

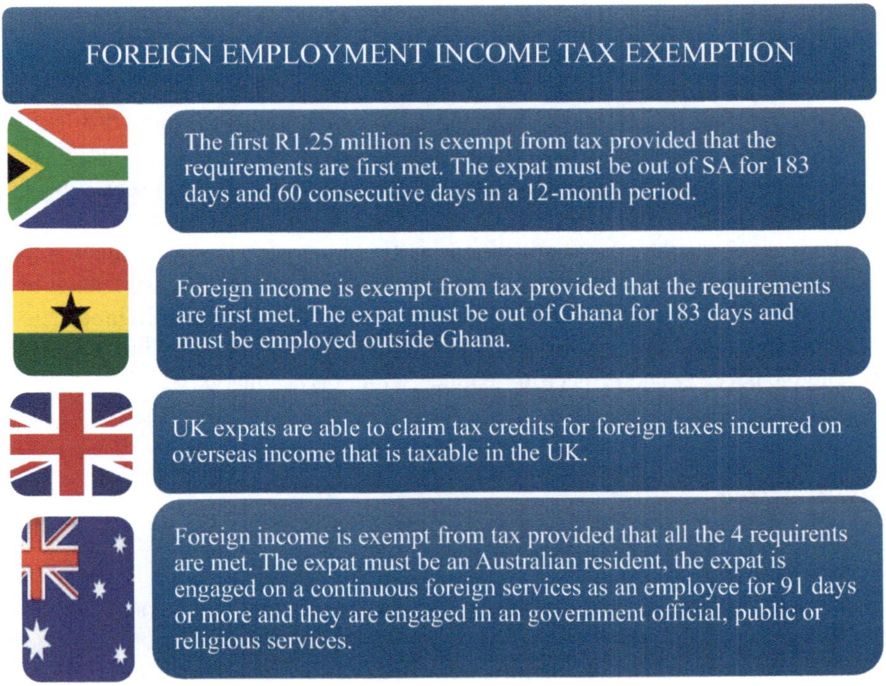

Fig. 2 Summary. *Source*: Author's own diagram

Method

The study's research objectives were approached using a qualitative methodology. The research objectives of this study were accomplished using published papers from professional firms, scholarly literature, and legislative assessments. The amended legislation and the literature analysis allow for a deeper comprehension of the definition of residency and a greater understanding of the requirements for the tax exemption on income from foreign employment. Among the papers that were assessed were official publications that addressed the steps taken by the authorities to inform the public about the temporary changes to the tax laws. The researcher was additionally assisted by these papers to assess the distributive fairness and procedural fairness of these amendments. Our comprehension of how to apply and interpret the temporary amendments to the unique conditions faced by expats because of the COVID-19 pandemic has improved because of these analyses and comprehensions. The comparative method of approach allowed the analysis of the fairness principles of the selected countries.

Discussion

The objective was to assess how well these procedures adhered to the distributive and procedural fairness principles. Two social psychology categories of fairness that were addressed by the conceptual framework for fairness are represented by the distributive and procedural fairness models. The fairness of allocation patterns and results is encouraged by distributive fairness. Three categories comprise distributive fairness: equality, equity, and need. The fairness of decision-making procedures and other elements of social processes is supported by procedural fairness. Three factors make up procedural fairness: the process' impartiality, the tax authorities' credibility, and the decency and respectful treatment of all parties involved.

South Africa

According to National Treasury (2020), during the public hearings held by the joint Standing Committee of Finance (SCoF) to discuss their written comments on these tax measures, representatives from four organizations gave presentations: the South African Institute of Chartered Accountants (SAICA), the South African Institute of Taxation (SAIT), PricewaterhouseCoopers (PwC), and the Congress of South Africa Trade Union (COSATU). SARS and the National Treasury provided the 2020 Draft TALAB to the SCoF.

To account for the effects of the COVID-19 pandemic, a specific exception was provided with respect to one comment which was to "*[c]onsider reducing the number of days that employees had to be outside South Africa to qualify for the tax exemption of foreign remuneration*," which dealt with the tax residence test under *section 10(1)(o)(ii)* of the ITA, which was beyond the purview of the 2020 Draft Tax Law to permit inclusion in the current legislative cycle. The days were reduced from 183 days to 117 days; however, the 60 consecutive days remained unchanged.

Reflection of the Process

The residency test was initially ignored, since it did not present an urgent threat. On the other hand, the number of days that expats needed to satisfy to qualify for an income tax exemption on their income from foreign employment may have been impacted by the travel restriction, which prohibited them from traveling. The Income Tax Act's section *10(1)(o)(ii)* provided a tax exemption; however, this was outside the scope of the 2020 Draft Tax Bills, and an exception was made to account for the impact of the COVID-19 pandemic. This was addressed in the answer document; therefore, the concerns of the stakeholders were addressed.

Analysis of the Procedural Fairness

Since it indicated that all parties' concerns were considered when the final decisions were made, the decision to temporarily amend the tax laws by reducing the number of days from 183 to 117 demonstrated the credibility of the tax authorities. This demonstrated that each party was given due respect and decency. Given this unique circumstance, the authorities made rapid decisions that became non-debatable laws without abusing their authority.

Analysis of the Distributive Fairness

The authorities reduced the 183-day guideline to exclude the 66 inclement lockdown days. As a result, the foreign-employed SA expats were qualified for a tax exemption on their income. A fair outcome is the goal of the equitable component, and this was accomplished by taking the expat's involuntary absence into account. Since the revisions would still allow the expat to be qualified for the exemption and may allow the authorities to continue implementing their administrative procedures, the equality component which tries to give a fair result for all parties was kept in place. Consequently, all components of distributive fairness were upheld.

Ghana

Reflection of the Process

After looking through the Ghanaian tax authority's website, the researcher discovered that no announcements had been made by the Ghanaian authorities about any temporary amendments to the tax exemption of foreign employment income for expats. Due to the closed international borders that prevented Ghanaian expats from traveling like everyone else, they were unable to fulfill the 183-day threshold needed to have their income from foreign employment exempted from tax. This implies that those expats impacted by the travel ban might lose their tax exemption.

Analysis of the Procedural Fairness

Public consultations were not conducted, since there were no changes made to the taxation of expatriates. Consequently, procedural fairness was not upheld in this regard.

Analysis of the Distributive Fairness

Since COVID-19 was a worldwide pandemic, tax laws had to be amended to take its effects into consideration. The equity component, which focuses on the fairness of the outcome, was not supported since COVID-19 was not brought up in the discussion on expatriate taxation. Since the government disregarded the public's concerns, the equity component which concentrates on a fair outcome for both the government and the expats were likewise not sustained. Therefore, none of the conditions for distributive fairness were met.

The UK

The Institute of Chartered Accountants in England and Wales (ICAEW) Tax Faculty, according to TaxGuide (2021), created the TaxGuides to advise tax professionals and businesses on significant changes to tax law and practice. According to TaxGuide (2021), the Tax Faculty has also requested the reduction of the negative effects of the SRT's strict implementation on the remuneration for employees who were prevented from departing the UK because of the COVID-19 pandemic. One of the requests was a change in law to increase the 60-day exceptional circumstances threshold. According to the authorities, since COVID-19 has been deemed an exceptional circumstance, the faculty did not have a compelling case to propose that adjustment.

Reflection of the Process

The HMRC responded to ICAEW by saying that although they understood the issues voiced, they did not believe there was a strong enough reason for amendments. The extraordinary circumstances caused ICAEW to express tremendous frustration. The HMRC said that COVID-19 was just a change that they classified as an extraordinary condition without changing the number of days, and that the 60-day exceptional conditions were implemented by legislation (Accountingweb, 2022).

Analysis of the Procedural Fairness

Although the public was frustrated that they felt the authorities were unable to extend the 60 days of extraordinary circumstances, there was still communication between the people and the government. This demonstrated the authorities' readiness to listen and act, reflected the impartiality element of procedural fairness. Even though the public did not think that the authorities' assessment that COVID-19 was an exceptional occurrence was sufficient, it does demonstrate their reliability. However, the authorities said that the public lacked a convincing case to dispute them. The authorities aided the expats in navigating their tax returns and determining what qualified as an unusual circumstance. This reflected that all parties were treated with respect and decency.

Analysis of the Distributive Fairness

The UK Government chose to bypass the 60-day requirement for extraordinary circumstances and instead add COVID-19 as an exceptional circumstance to the already-existing tax statute rather than passing a new law altogether. The aspect of equality that centers on the fairness of the result was upheld. The administration maintained the equality component, which focuses on a just result for both sides, while taking the public's concerns into account. Nevertheless, their argument was insufficient to support materially altering the law, and the existing legislation sufficed to deal with every problem. The conditions of distributive justice were thus fully met.

Australia

ATO (2020) states that the ATO regularly updated their website with details about the latest legislative actions and the support they were offering in response to the COVID-19 crisis. This includes responses to inquiries from the public on how their tax statuses could be treated considering the potential COVID-19 amendments.

A person would be covered by the fact sheet if they completed their overseas service in response to COVID-19 and had:

- Completed 91 days of continuous foreign service to qualify for the income tax exemption, but it was anticipated that more foreign work would need to be done before returning to Australia
- Completed 91 days of continuous foreign service at the time of your return, but you had not yet started a foreign assignment that would have otherwise qualified for the income tax exemption

Any period of absence from foreign service breaks the continuity of your foreign service, unless the absence:

- Still counts as foreign service
- Does not exceed one-sixth of your total period of foreign service

The one-sixth test can be used to cover absences that would otherwise cause your period of service to no longer qualify as continuous for the purposes of the 91-day requirement.

Reflection of the Process

Unlike SA and the UK, Australia did not engage in an open discourse with the public about the changes brought about by the COVID-19 pandemic. On the other hand, they responded to inquiries from the public on the temporary tax laws that had already been put into effect.

Analysis of the Procedural Fairness

Although there was no open communication between the public and the authorities, the latter established a forum where citizens may voice any concerns they may have had. This demonstrated the authorities' readiness to hear concerns and provide a response, which is a crucial aspect of procedural justice. The fact that the authorities temporarily amended the tax regulations in response to the disturbances brought on by COVID-19 is indicative of their legitimacy. Their readiness to provide a forum for questions and answers does demonstrate that they were aware of the public's concerns about the sudden changes. This illustrates how to treat others with dignity and respect.

Analysis of the Distributive Fairness

The Australian government addressed the need for interim changes to the tax law to comply with the continuous 91-day requirement. An expat's foreign service is interrupted when they are absent; however the norm has been changed to account for the possibility that the COVID-19 pandemic was the reason for their absence. The fact that the remedy in place will result in a fair outcome if the expats are forced to relocate is indicative of the equity component, which argues that the outcome should be equitable. The equality component, which specified that the results should be in favor of a fair conclusion to both the authorities and the expats, is upheld by allowing the absence caused by COVID-19 to be made up for.

Result and Conclusion

The author of the paper investigated how the COVID-19 pandemic affected expatriate taxes in residence-based tax systems of the selected countries. Since COVID-19 was a worldwide pandemic that disrupted tax systems, governments had to follow fair procedures while amending their tax laws to take the pandemic's effects into account. Researching people's perceptions of the fairness of tax law changes and if revealing the purpose of the change affects how people interpret fairness. The two primary areas of examination in this study were distributive fairness (need, equity, and equality) and procedural fairness (process impartiality, authorities' credibility, and treating officials and expats with decency and respect). To understand the rationale behind the temporary amendments, the author had to investigate the definition of residency and the taxation of income from foreign employment in the selected countries, before and after the amendments were made. Additionally, the author had to compare the countries' public consultation processes to determine whether distributive and procedural fairness were reflected.

The author used a qualitative methodology to look at each country's concept of residency, because it is a crucial factor in figuring out where an expat would pay taxes on their income from foreign employment. The study also looked at how the disruptions brought about by the COVID-19 pandemic had influenced the idea of tax exemption on income from foreign work. By using a comparative technique, it was possible to evaluate how each of the four countries managed the unexpected disruptions brought about by the COVID-19 pandemic and determine if the procedures taken to change the tax legislation in each country reflected distributive fairness.

The study investigated procedural fairness by examining the procedures that the authorities used and the public discussions they held in SA, the UK, and Australia. These discussions covered issues of impartiality, credibility, and treating the authorities and expats with a certain amount of decency and respect. The way in which these components were applied was demonstrated by the examination of the public discussions that the authorities conducted in open forums.

The distributive fairness of the temporary amendments to the foreign employment income tax exemptions which addressed the aspects of need, equity, and equality were also examined in this study. SA, the UK, and Australia made temporary amendments to their tax legislation to reflect the use of these elements. Legislation had to be changed because of the COVID-19 pandemic, and the equity part of the bill concentrated on how equitable the results were once the temporary amendments were put into place. Regardless of the authorities' attempts to enact temporary changes, the equality component proposed that the outcome should favor an equitable outcome that benefits both the authorities and expats.

The researcher claims that although the COVID-19 pandemic also had an impact in Ghana, there were no public discussions or temporary amendments implemented there. This indicates that the principles of distributive and procedural fairness were not upheld.

This study is limited to the COVID-19 period. Since temporary amendments had to be made, the focus is solely on the impact that COVID-19 had on the taxation of foreign employment income. Since determining the criteria of fairness was the goal of this study, the taxation of foreign employment income in Ghana remained unchanged.

The results of this study can be expanded upon in future investigations about tax fairness perspectives for expatriate taxation in the event of an abrupt natural disaster. Since international mobility is so important to expatriate taxation, it might be difficult to maintain fairness principles when that mobility abruptly ends owing to unforeseen disasters.

Future studies may consider the inclusion of more developing countries that have similar tax systems to conduct quantitative comparative research to evaluate if principles of fairness are upheld when abruptly changing the tax laws due to natural disasters.

References

Accountingweb. (2022). *HMRC contacts SA clients claiming exceptional days*. https://www.accountingweb.co.uk/any-answers/hmrc-contacts-sa-clients-claiming-exceptional-days

Australia. (1936). *The Income Tax Assessment Act 1936*. http://www.saasso.asn.au/wp-content/uploads/2014/02/Income-Tax-Assessment-Act.pdf

Australian Taxation Office (ATO). (2020). *Early return from foreign service due to Covid-19 foreign employment income*. Australian Taxation Office. https://www.ato.gov.au/law/view/pdf/afs/afs-23ag-covid-19.pdf

Australian Taxation Office (ATO). (2023). *Exempt foreign employment income*. https://www.ato.gov.au/individuals/income-deductions-offsets-and-records/income-you-must-declare/foreign-and-worldwide-income/tax-exempt-income-from-foreign-employment/exempt-income-from-foreign-service/#AustralianOfficialdevelopmentassistance

Bender, L. (2020). *Guidance for Covid-19 prevention and control in schools*. UNICEF. https://www.unicef.org/media/66216/file

Boran, I. (2006). Benefits, intentions, and the principle of fairness. *Canadian Journal of Philosophy, 36*(1), 95–115. https://doi.org/10.1353/cjp.2006.0002

Cropanzano, R., & Ambrose, M. (2001). Procedural and distributive justice are more similar than you think: A monistic perspective and a research agenda. In J. Greenberg & R. Cropanzano (Eds.), *Advances in organization justice* (pp. 119–151). Stanford University Press. https://www.researchgate.net/publication/261358169_Procedural_and_distributive_justice_are_more_similar_than_you_think_A_monistic_perspective_and_a_research_agenda

Dictionary.com. (2020). *Definition: expatriate*. https://www.dictionary.com/browse/expatriate

Farrar, J. (2015). An empirical analysis of taxpayers' fairness preferences from Canada's taxpayer bill of rights. *Journal of Accounting and Taxation, 7*(5), 71–79.

Farrar, J., Massey, D. W., Osecki, E., & Thorne, L. (2018). Tax fairness: Conceptual foundations and empirical measurement. *Journal of Business Ethics, 162*, 487–503. https://doi.org/10.1007/s10551-018-4001-4

Garbarino, C. (2022). Tax treaties and the mobility of workers. *European Business Law Review, 33*(6), 935–956.

Ghana. (2015). *The Income Tax Act 2015, Act 896*. https://pef.org.gh/documents/INCOME%20TAX%20ACT%202015%20(ACT%20896).pdf

His Majesty Revenue & Custom (HMRC). (2020). *Guidance RDR3: Statutory residence test (SRT) notes*. https://www.gov.uk/government/publications/rdr3-statutory-residence-test-srt/guidance-note-for-statutory-residence-test-srt-rdr3#:~:text=The%20test%20allows%20you%20to,relevant%2C%20work%20in%20the%20UK

His Majesty Revenue & Custom (HMRC). (2023). *Residence, domicile and remittance basis manual*. https://www.gov.uk/hmrc-internal-manuals/residence-domicile-and-remittance-basis/rdrm13220

IMF. (2020). *Facing the crisis: The role of tax in dealing with Covid-19*. https://www.imf.org/en/Blogs/Articles/2020/06/16/vc-facing-the-crisis-the-role-of-tax-in-dealing-with-covid-19

Job, J., Stout, A., & Smith, R. (2007). Culture change in three taxation administrations: From command-and-control to responsive regulation. *Law and Policy, 29*(1), 84–101.

Kagiri, R. (2022). *What is global mobility?*. Omnipresent. https://www.omnipresent.com/articles/what-is-global-mobility#:~:text=Global%20mobility%20is%20the%20ability,are%20unique%20benefits%20for%20each

Kirchler, E., Hoelzl, E., & Wahl, I. (2008). Enforced versus voluntary tax compliance: The "slippery slope" framework. *Journal of Economic Psychology, 29*(2), 210–225.

KPMG. (2023). *Ghana: Thinking beyond borders for Ghana*. https://assets.kpmg.com/content/dam/kpmg/xx/pdf/2023/01/TBB-Ghana.pdf

Leventhal, G. S. (1980). What should be done with equity theory? In K. J. Gergen, M. S. Greenberg, & R. H. Willis (Eds.), *Social exchange*. Springer. https://doi.org/10.1007/978-1-4613-3087-5_2

Manenzhe, A. J. (2023). *An international comparison of foreign employment income exemption*. Masters' dissertation. University of Johannesburg. https://hdl.handle.net/10210/504162.

Mazars. (2020). *Expatriate tax relief in a global Pandemic*. https://www.mazars.co.uk/Home/Insights/Covid-19-Insights/Covid-19-International-Client-Support/Expatriate-tax-relief-in-a-global-Pandemic

McDermid, P., Craig, A., Sheel, M., & Seale, H. (2022). How have governments supported citizens stranded abroad due to COVID-19 travel restrictions? A comparative analysis of the financial and health support in eleven countries. *BMC Infectious Diseases, 22*, Article 161. https://doi.org/10.1186/s12879-022-07155-2

McNulty, Y., & Brewster, C. (2016). The concept of business expatriates. In Y. McNulty & J. Selme (Eds.), *Research handbook of expatriates*. Edwards Elgar.

Mosupye, S. (2013). *Expatriate tax in Africa: The taxation of inbound expatriates working in Botswana, Namibia, Nigeria and South Africa* (Masters' Dissertation). University of Pretoria. http://hdl.handle.net/2263/41218

OECD. (2019). *Model tax convention on income and on capital 2017 (full version)*. OECD Publishing. https://read.oecd-ilibrary.org/taxation/model-tax-convention-on-income-and-on-capital-2017-full-version_86783786-en#page2

OECD. (2020). *OECD Secretariat analysis of tax treaties and the impact of the Covid-19 crisis*. https://www.oecd.org/coronavirus/policy-responses/oecd-secretariat-analysis-of-tax-treaties-and-the-impact-of-the-covid-19-crisis-947dcb01/

SARS. (2018). *Resident: Definition in relation to a natural person – Ordinarily Resident. Interpretation Note No.3. Issue 2*. Available from: https://www.sars.gov.za/wp-content/uploads/Legal/Notes/LAPD-IntR-IN-2012-03-Resident-definition-natural-person-ordinarily-resident.pdf

SARS. (2021). *Foreign employment income. Income tax Interpretation Note No.16 issue 4*. https://www.sars.gov.za/wp-content/uploads/Legal/Notes/LAPD-IntR-IN-2012-16-Exemption-Foreign-Employment-Income.pdf

Savage, N., Jain, A., & Ng, S. C. (2020). Impacts of the COVID-19 pandemic on medical students in Australia. *ANZ Journal of Surgery, 90*(7–8), 1244–1245. https://doi.org/10.1111/ans.16103

Sebashe, K., Erasmus, H. L., & Erasmus, M. M. (2022). A case study review and reasonability assessment of foreign employment income tax exemption threshold in section 10(1)(o)(ii) of the Income Tax Act. *South African Journal of Accounting Research, 36*(3), 250–271. https://doi.org/10.1080/10291954.2020.1846860

Selmer, J., & Lauring, J. (2015). Global Mobility. In C. L. Cooper, M. Vodosek, D. N. Hartog, & J. M. McNett (Eds.), *Wiley encyclopedia of management*. Cambridge University Press. https://doi.org/10.1002/9781118785317.weom060212

South Africa. (1962). *The Income Tax Act No. 58 of 1962*. https://sars.mylexisnexis.co.za/#

TaxGuide. (2021). *Covid-19: Displaced expatriate employees: Statutory Residence test and social contributions: Correspondence with FST & HMRC*. https://www.icaew.com/-/media/corporate/files/technical/tax/tax-faculty/taxguides/2021/taxguide-0821-covid-19-displaced-expatriate-employees.ashx

The World Bank. (2020). The global economic outlook during the Covid-19 pandemic. https://www.worldbank.org/en/news/feature/2020/06/08/the-global-economic-outlook-during-the-covid-19-Pandemic-a-changed-world

Tyler, T., & Lind, E. (1992). A relational model of authority in groups. In M. Zanna (Ed.), *Advances in experimental social psychology* (pp. 115–191). Academic Press.

Van Wyk, T.C. (2011). *Critical analysis of the taxation of South African employees working abroad*. [Masters' Dissertation]. University of Pretoria. http://hdl.handle.net/2263/23049

Vermeulen, L., & Coetzee, M. (2006). Perceptions of the dimensions of the fairness of affirmative action: A pilot study. *South African Journal of Business Management, 37*(3), 53–65.

Visser, A. (2020). *Travel bans may affect tax residency status*. https://www.moneyweb.co.za/news/south-africa/travel-bans-may-affect-the-tax-residency-status-of-individuals-and-companies/

Wartick, M. L. (1991). *The effects of knowledge of legislative intent on taxpayer perceptions of fairness*. The Pennsylvania State University.

Wenzel, M. (2003). Tax compliance and the psychology of justice: Mapping the field. In V. Braithwaite (Ed.), *Taxing democracy: Understanding tax avoidance and evasion*. Ashgate Publishing. https://doi.org/10.4324/9781315241746

World Economic Forum. (2013). *Africa is now the world's second fastest growing economy*. Moneyweb. https://www.moneyweb.co.za/moneyweb-world-economic-forum/Africa-is-now-the-worlds-second-fastest-growing-ec

Components of Corporate Strategy Implementation to Ensure a Competitive Advantage

Prisca Kalamba Mbombo, Dirk Rossouw, and Maria Bounds

Abstract The success of corporate strategy implementation has become the focus of many organisations in order for them to sustain a competitive advantage. Strategic management helps organisations to set a vision, a mission and objectives that will enable them to survive and operate within a competitive environment. However, many organisations have experienced little success in the implementation of corporate strategy, mainly because of poor implementation and not because of the strategy itself. Many factors may affect the implementation of corporate strategy within any organisation, such as lack of resources, poor communication and resistance to change. The main objective of this research was to determine how small and medium consulting businesses were implementing corporate strategies to ensure sustainability and growth. To achieve this objective, a qualitative approach was used with the aim of understanding, analysing and evaluating the success of corporate strategy implementation of small and medium consulting businesses. Data were collected by conducting semi-structured interviews with 13 small and medium consulting business owners/managers in the central business district. The empirical findings indicated that corporate strategy implementation, with specific reference to the components of implementation, made a significant contribution to the sustainability, growth and performance of small and medium consulting businesses. Owners/managers of these businesses should ensure that the strategy applied is communicated effectively to the staff members for them to embrace the implementation and understand and adopt the strategy; however, the lack of a strategy implementation can cause the failure of these businesses.

Keywords Strategy implementation · small business and corporate strategy

P. K. Mbombo · D. Rossouw · M. Bounds (✉)
University of Johannesburg, Johannesburg, South Africa
e-mail: drossouw@uj.ac.za; mariab@uj.ac.za

T. Moloi (ed.), *Impacting Society Positively Through Technology in Accounting and Business Processes*, Springer Proceedings in Business and Economics,
https://doi.org/10.1007/978-3-031-84885-8_13

Introduction

The business environment is highly competitive, and organisations have become more future-oriented in order to sustain their competitive advantage. Many organisations have realised that awareness of strategic management is essential (Ehlers & Lazenby, 2022). Researchers (Bateman et al., 2019) confirm that organisations which establish a clear strategy will outperform those organisations which implement numerous strategies that are not well defined.

All levels of management play important and essential roles in organisations when it comes to the implementation of an organisation's strategy (Lazenby, 2022). Middle management are accountable for the strategic decisions and competitive growth that govern the understanding and practice of strategic management and implementation. Any organisation is frequently challenged by several elements such as technology, globalisation and emerging markets. Proactiveness is required to face these challenges, which cannot be resolved by economic interventions alone (Simeone, 2020).

According to Lazenby (2022), an organisation's strategy should form part of its main plan in order to reach its objectives and goals and, additionally, maintain a competitive edge and overcome competition. Therefore, successful implementation needs to be planned carefully so that the strategic goals can be reached. This will result in successful strategies that will allow managers to create, manage and monitor success within organisations. Abosede et al. (2016) state that strategy shapes how an organisation attempts to accomplish its goals and objectives, and it forms part of the strategy management process.

Sharabati and Fuqaha (2014, p. 670) recommend that entrepreneurs and managers should use strategic management to develop their current business performance and maintain their sustainability in a competitive environment that includes larger businesses. An organisation with a clear corporate strategy is more likely to share its goals and objectives with employees, which will make the implementation process easier and increase the organisation's performance and sustainability. Radzi et al. (2017) emphasise that for successful implementation, top management need to understand the strategy, be devoted and provide funds for the development of the strategy as the value of the strategy is recognised throughout its implementation.

Small consulting organisations are faced with severe competition and changes in demands from their customers, whereas big organisations gain major profits from sectors and keep on growing tougher and faster.

Background

The competitive environment within which organisations operate affects the chances of survival and as such is a challenge to the sustainability and growth of any organisation in South Africa. Organisations in South Africa encounter several challenges and are different from those operating in stable environments. Some organisations do not have adequate resources to participate in strong planning and usually end up embracing 'the copy and paste' method of doing business. This then revolves around the factors of strategy implementation within a small organisation and the impact this has on their growth in a fast-changing environment.

This study focuses on the uncertainty of corporate strategy implementation within a consulting organisation and the impact this has on sustainability, growth and maintaining a competitive advantage.

The research question derived from the problem statement is: How do consulting businesses implement corporate strategy to sustain growth and maintain their competitive advantage?

The following additional research question could also be asked: To what extent does strategy implementation impact performance within consulting businesses?

Literature Review

The contributions of various authors and scholars on topics such as corporate strategy by Ansoff (1965); strategy and structure by Chandler (1962); management by objectives (MBO) by Drucker (1954); the nature of managerial work by Mintzberg competitive strategy and competitive advantage (1998) by Porter have added towards the fundamentals of the theory in which organisations are enabled to attain their objectives, mostly entailing gaining profit and competitive advantage over their competitors and reaching their goals.

Concept of Strategic Management

Cyert and March (1963) and Mintzberg and Waters (1985) define strategic management as 'a mixture of various processes to be learnt from and transferred due to the restrictions of the environment and the constrained rationality of human beings that may result in the difference of strategies which is planned and emerges out of the patterns of behaviours'. In addition, Eniola and Ektebang (2014) and Lazenby (2022) define strategic management as a concept that is concerned with making decisions and taking corrective actions to attain the long-term goals and objectives of an organisation.

Porter advises that the essence of formulating competitive strategy is '*relating a company to its environment*'. Porter's important work on competitive strategy as summarised in the infamous '*Forces driving industry competition*' model, lists suppliers and buyers as two of the five basic competitive forces (while potential entrants, substitutes and industry competitors are the three remaining forces). Porter denotes that the goal of competitive strategy for an enterprise is to find a position in the industry where the enterprise can best defend itself against these competitive forces, or where it is able to utilise these forces in its favour. Porter advises that the key to developing strategy is to delve below the surface and analyse the sources of each.

Strategic activity is abridged by Nadler (2004, p. 26) into four types of activity. The board's participation may vary in all the phases of strategic activity. The four types of strategic activities are

- *Strategic thinking*. This is the first stage in strategy development and involves the collection, analysis and discussion of information regarding the nature of competition, the environment of the enterprise and business design choices.
- *Strategic decision-making*. Fundamental decisions in respect of the enterprise portfolio and the business design are core to strategic thinking. This thinking will form part of the platform of the future allocation of restricted resources and capabilities.
- *Strategic planning*. Following the decision-making process, priorities are ascertained, objectives set and resources organised in order to implement the decisions. Typically, this will lead to the formation of a plan and a set of budgets. It must be noted that the plan would typically evolve owing to changes in consequences through changes in the environment and new information being obtained.
- *Strategic execution*. The enterprise will now focus on implementing, monitoring results and undertake corrective actions.

The field of strategic management has evolved rapidly over the years with various areas of interest. Strategic management can be described as a sequence of steps that covers the following tasks (Jones & Hill, 2013):

- Evaluating the external environment in terms of existing opportunities and threats
- Evaluating the internal environment of the organisation in terms of strengths and weaknesses
- Formulating a vision, a mission statement and objectives of the organisation
- Identifying stakeholders
- Formulating strategies that are driven by the strengths and weaknesses of the organisation and the opportunities and threats of the external environment
- Implementing strategies
- Engaging in strategy control in order to evaluate the implementation and to ensure that the objectives are achieved

Sitharam and Hoque (2016) and Chen (2020) maintain that in order for organisations to grow and be sustainable in the competitive business climate, managers must adapt their objectives to align them with the demand of the business environment. A significant number of South African organisations have successfully adapted to align with these paradigms. These managers must develop a strategic plan to compete successfully in the twenty-first-century business environment.

Strategic Levels That Focus on Strategy Implementation

Corporate strategy: This depicts in general the direction of the organisation considering its general outlook towards management and development of its diverse productions and business lines by means of gaining competitive advantage (Hoskisson et al., 2013). *Business strategy:* This level of strategy frequently occurs at the production or business unit level by highlighting the improvement of viability and place of the products or services in a market segment (Rothaermel, 2017).

Functional strategy: This describes the link between corporate and business strategies by optimising the source of production. It relates to the diverse functional aspects of a strategic business unit such as marketing, production and operations, finance and human resources. Managers at functional level formulate these strategies with their groups.

Literature in strategic management has created different links to corporate and business strategy. This difference has frequently been credited as the main core of interest in diverse studies, although the focus of business strategy is to gain a competitive advantage over competitors within the same market of products through the distribution of resources and other decisions. On the other hand, corporate strategy manages the market's demand and the products that an organisation can provide (Rothaermel, 2017).

The growth of any corporate, business and functional strategy needs to take into consideration individuals who are involved in and committed to making sure that the products produced and served to customers are of good quality and match their expectations. To accomplish this, organisations need to connect and train all their human resources before and after the plans and implementation of the strategy (Checco, 2005; Ghosh, 2021). This guarantees that members are keen to operate and turn the strategy implemented into business values.

Corporate Strategy

Furrer (2016) observed that corporate strategy is the overall scope of an organisation and how value is added to different business units of the organisation. It comprises a range of products and services or business units, and how resources are distributed among different sections of the organisation. Corporate strategy is also linked to its customers and shareholders' expectations, and this is clearly revealed in the organisation's mission statement.

Lazenby (2022) indicates that corporate strategy guides the objectives of the organisation and relates them to the resources of the organisation that should be utilised. It is also known as the 'master or the grand' strategy of the organisation which means that it provides a road map of the future of the organisation. Therefore, the growth of a corporate strategy is a process that is very complex as it deals mainly with varieties of business space where the organisation needs to operate, strive, develop, as well as coordinate the business in order to attain its goals and objectives.

Corporate strategy focuses on three core areas (Lynch, 2018):

Strategic analysis involves the analysis of the organisation, its mission and objectives; how value will be generated with its stakeholders; competitor analysis and resource analysis.

- *Strategy development* involves creating several strategies and selecting the most suitable one based on the abilities of the organisation and its environment. This is based on the skills of the organisation and its relationships with suppliers, customers, distributors and government.
- *Strategy implementation* is the awareness of the options. Options can range from the simple (e.g. the same product in the same market) to the more complex (e.g. new products in new markets).

These three core areas give the organisation the credentials to plan and take actions to attain its purpose, find market opportunities and experiment and develop a competitive advantage over time. Moreover, corporate strategy enables the organisation to get answers to its long-term questions such as 'what business are we in or do we want to be in and what do we want to do with this business?' It may be to acquire new businesses to improve, divest business units, plants or product lines or take part in joint ventures with other organisations (Ehlers & Lazenby, 2022).

In the current business environment, it is vitally important for organisations to restructure their strategy implementation as the life cycle of ideas and the selected strategy are reduced owing to the lack of available and accessible data and information. Implementation of the strategy is a vital source of gaining a competitive advantage over competitors with the use of appropriate knowledge (Ungerer et al., 2007). Hrebiniak (2013) states that strategy implementation is an essential element of the strategic management process and can be described as the process that transforms the formulated strategy into a sequence of actions which ensure the successful achievement of the mission, the vision and the goals of the organisation.

Jansson et al. (2017) state that strategy implementation assists organisations in growing and pursuing sustainability within the competitive business environment. Business owners should not only develop their corporate strategies, but also their competencies. David (2023) is of the opinion that strategy implementation in organisations needs strong motivational leadership with sufficient communication as it involves a large group of individuals to take action and apply the strategy across all the functions and management levels.

Hrebiniak (2013) agrees that strategy implementation constantly engages many middle managers as the communication flows across all levels of the organisation; however, this flow of communication might be a challenge as the objectives should be linked to the daily activities within the organisation. Hrebiniak (2013) adds that the more individuals are involved in the process, the bigger the challenge to implement it successfully. Similarly, Nyamwanza and Mavhiki also explain that strategy implementation is a way in which an organisation can expand, use and integrate its structures, culture and control systems to pursue the strategies leading to a competitive edge and improving performance.

Strategic Management Process

The process of strategic management consists of five interrelated and integrated phases, which could mainly be divided into strategic implementation and strategic formulation (David, 2023). This involves how a strategy can be built in order to support the organisation's structure through appropriate, developed policies and plans.

According to Thompson et al. (2016), all five phases are unified, interrelated and important for any organisation to attain its vision and goals through the following: developing and communicating the organisation's strategic vision and its mission; translating the mission into specific long-term objectives; formulating strategies to accomplish the long-term goals and vision; implementing and executing the strategy and monitoring developments, evaluating performance and making corrective adjustments.

The first three phases are part of strategy formulation, which includes analysis, strategy formulation and goal setting. The last two phases constitute implementation, which indicates the structure creation of the internal environment and getting a response from the process. Moreover, every element of the strategic management process requires a judgement on whether to carry on with things as they appear or to generate changes within the organisation.

Business Consultants

Business consultants provide knowledgeable guidance to their customers for remuneration (The Free Dictionary, 2010). These consultants help customers improve their performance by identifying opportunities, problems and formulating plans or strategies to run the business successfully and smoothly (Pleva, 2006).

Already in 1994 Zenger showed that managers of consulting businesses understand and realise that the performance of organisations can be improved by starting consulting businesses in their areas of experience and knowledge, while larger businesses may also use and benefit from their service. This is owing to the competition in the business environment evolving globally; thus, business consultants have become a constant presence in restructuring and bringing change to the corporate environment. Consultancies shape economies by playing a critical role in creating and building values that benefit both public and private industries.

Abosede et al. (2016) point out that the owner is the driver of the business who makes decisions on the implementation of the strategy; thus, the owner should have enough resources to distribute in order for the business to succeed. The sustainability of the organisation depends on the opportunities and threats in the external environment and the weaknesses and strengths in the internal environment. The analysis of these factors will help the organisation to view its competitors and formulate strategies that will enable it to be sustainable and grow in the environment.

Research Methodology

Research methodology can be defined as the general technique of performing or carrying out a research project by the researcher.

Research Philosophy

This research employed the interpretivism or phenomenological paradigm since qualitative research is frequently linked with the interpretivism philosophy. Bryman (2015) describes the latter as 'an epistemology that seeks to find and understand subjective patterns or meaning instead of reaching objective evidence'. It provides qualitative data from a small sample, which generalises theories. Interpretivism seeks to understand occurrences around the world, gives subjective meaning to experiences and relies on the researcher's interpretation of the information gathered instead of making predictions.

Research Approach

This study used an inductive approach as its objectives were to explore and discover corporate strategy implementation among small consulting businesses by relying on available and accessible data to form general patterns. An induction approach can be described as the development of theory from specific to general, resulting in analysis of data collected (Saunders & Lewis, 2012).

Type of Study

Exploratory and descriptive research was applied. Exploratory research is more flexible, creative and objective. It is often used in qualitative research for collecting data and is less linked to a principle (Saunders et al., 2016). Descriptive research was used as it strives to describe individuals and events accurately, locates new data that contradict past data, creates a set of categories, clarifies sequence stages and uses interviews and questionnaires to collect data (Saunders & Lewis, 2012).

Research Strategy

Qualitative research is usually linked with a selection of strategies where the epistemological and the ontological share common characteristic roots (Saunders et al., 2016). For the purpose of this research, a qualitative survey was used as it allowed the researcher to collect data on situations, practices and opinions of respondents during the interviews. Although surveys are used mainly in quantitative research, qualitative surveys were applied in this study as interviews were conducted with management from small consulting businesses around Gauteng.

Population and Sample

The population is a complete and specific group who meet the standards of the research (Zikmund & Babin, 2015). The population consisted of approximately 45 small consulting businesses in the Gauteng metropolitan. The purposively selected sample included 13 small consulting businesses representing the areas of engineering, accounting and management. These businesses had been in existence for 3 years or more. The reason for selecting 13 businesses was that saturation usually occurs after the twelfth interview.

Data Collection and Analysis

An interview is a prominent tool used in collecting data for either qualitative or quantitative research (Bryman et al., 2014, p. 278). Semi-structured interviews with an interview guide were used in this study to collect data. The reasons for using this tool in gathering data are that it is more flexible during the interview, simplifies unclear statements and allows investigation of the topic.

Manually applied content analysis was done to analyse the data from the transcribed interview recordings. Spens and Kovacs (2006) define content analysis as a 'process for objective, logical, consistent study of issued information which is more comprehensive for literature reviews'. Therefore, when the data were being coded, the researcher categorised the data manually using Microsoft Excel to assist and support the development of themes. Suter (2012) indicates that the qualitative analysis of data is mostly time consuming and iterative and focuses on data which need to be reduced, displayed and verified before drawing conclusions. This analysis is therefore suitable for identifying what management should focus on to implement corporate strategy successfully.

Ethical Considerations

Neuman (2011) states that the ethical considerations begin and end with the researcher of the study. These considerations are significant for quantitative and qualitative studies, but more so, in qualitative research since qualitative study methods frequently intrude on the lives of the respondents (Khan, 2014). The quality of the data collection must be directly connected to ethical considerations. Miller and Brewer (2003) state that ethics is about the creation of mutual respect, a win-win relationship where the participants are satisfied to reply truthfully, which validates the results obtained and the community reflects on the conclusions interpreted.

Results and Findings

The themes and the outcome of the study will be reported on according to biographical data, Section A and the questions in Section B.

Section A: Biographical Data

Type of business: Seven of the consulting businesses operated as management consultants, four as engineering consultants and two as accounting consultants. The respondents represented three areas of specialisation, namely accounting, management and engineering, and they all functioned in Gauteng.

Age of business: One of the businesses had been in existence for 21 years or more. Four had been in existence for 16–20 years, followed by three which had been in existence for 11–15 years, two for 6–10 years and three for 0–5 years. None of these businesses had been in existence for less than 3 years. The age of the businesses varied from 3 to 21 years. Neneh (2012) is of the opinion that the age of the businesses and long-term survival are related in sustaining the business.

Position in the business: Eight of the respondents were top management and five were middle management. In view of this brief background on management of the consulting businesses, the following section focuses on the understanding and application of corporate strategy implementation within the businesses.

Section B: Corporate Strategy Implementation

Section B focuses on the corporate strategy implementation of organisations to measure competitive advantage and the viewpoints of the respondents regarding their understanding of the two components of corporate strategy implementation.

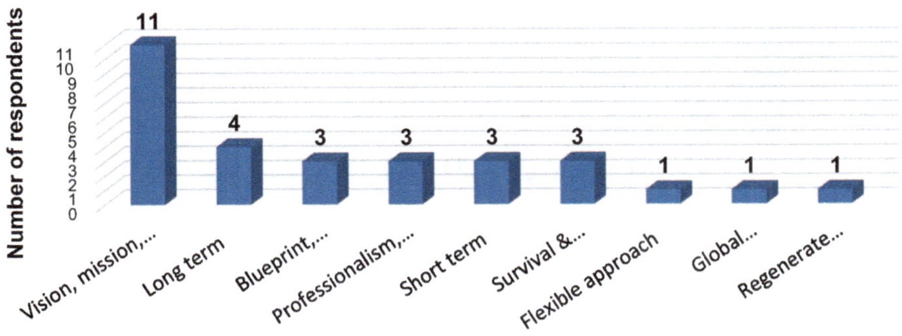

Fig. 1 Understanding: corporate strategy

Understanding of Corporate Strategy

Eleven of the respondents indicated that corporate strategy was about a vision, mission, goals, objectives and giving clear direction. '... *I am saying that corporate strategy is mission, vision and objectives and all of that ...*' and '... *includes the business' goals and objectives ...*' Four respondents mentioned that corporate strategy was long-term oriented. Three respondents mentioned that corporate strategy was 'the blueprint of the business'; 'strategy and processes of the business'; 'professionalism and ethos and values in the business'; 'a short-term objective which affected the success of the business' and 'day-to-day survival instinct and sustainability of the business'. Finally, one respondent indicated that corporate strategy 'was about having flexible approaches; building a global competitive business; and regenerating resources'.

The purpose of this question was to determine whether the management of businesses understood and could describe corporate strategy. It became evident that they had different understandings and perceptions as indicated in Fig. 1.

Based on the above, it is evident that management did not have a clear understanding of corporate strategy as they defined strategy instead of corporate strategy. Furthermore, the respondents' general understanding of corporate strategy seems to differ from the literature.

Components of Strategy Implementation

The following were identified by the respondents as being the components of strategy implementation to ensure a competitive advantage. These are two of the components as listed by Thompson et al. (2016) to implement strategy, such as building the organisation and corporate culture.

Building an organisation with necessary competencies, competitive capabilities and work efforts to support the implementation of the corporate strategy.

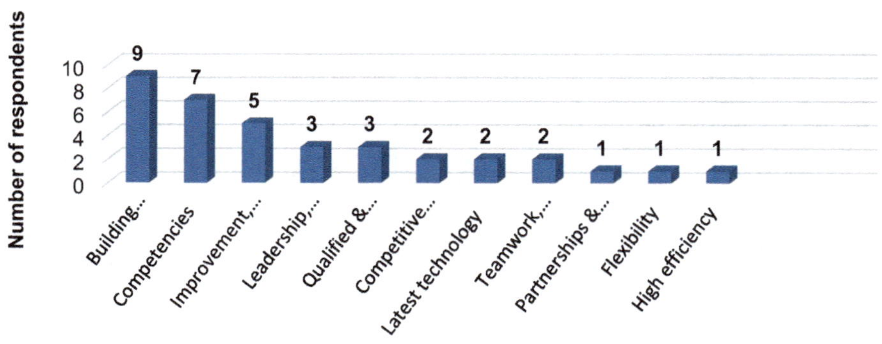

Fig. 2 Building an organisation to ensure competitive advantage

From the findings, the majority (9) of the respondents mentioned building capabilities as the most important for strategy implementation. '... *we build capabilities and competencies, we [are actually able] to meet our own targets*' and '... *part of our strategy is to be able to build capabilities ...*' Seven respondents indicated that competencies are important, while five respondents said that improvement; training and personal objectives are also of importance.

However, three respondents mentioned 'leadership and support'; 'being punctual and professional' and 'employing qualified and experienced staff', respectively. Two respondents referred to 'competitive advantage', 'latest technology and teamwork' and 'knowledge sharing and communication', respectively. Finally, one respondent listed 'partnerships and outsourcing services; flexibility; and high efficiency' as factors that assist in strategy implementation.

The success of corporate strategy implementation is determined by significant capabilities, competencies and work efforts. As illustrated in Fig. 2, most businesses agreed that they had built their businesses with relevant core competencies and capabilities, enabling them to achieve the goals and objectives of the organisation. In addition, the businesses recruited qualified and experienced staff who were willing to work hard through teamwork, sharing of knowledge and communication. Carpenter and Sanders (2009) agree on the importance of building strong, capable and competent businesses.

Management must drive strategy implementation with skilled and experienced employees. They should continue recruiting and retaining skilled employees in order to develop competencies and capabilities that suit the strategy implementation process.

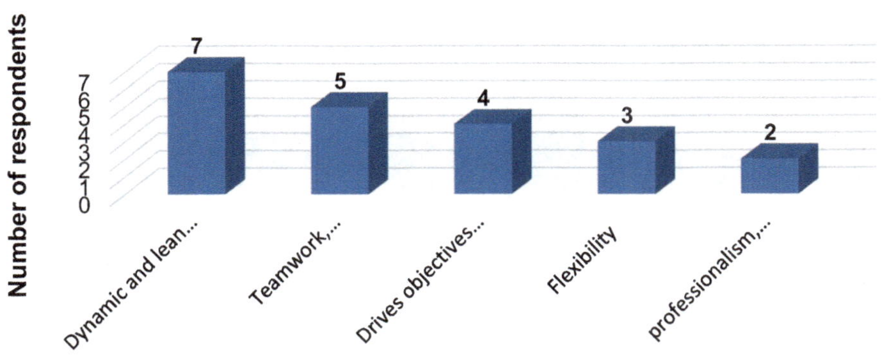

Fig. 3 Corporate culture

Corporate Culture

In support of strategy implementation, more than half of the respondents (7) indicated that a dynamic and lean culture was used to support strategy implementation. '*... yes, performance driven culture with open communication channels which assist employees to be accountable with their actions and decisions ...*' and '*... there is a culture of teamwork, there is a culture of oneness ...*' Five respondents stated that teamwork, communication and knowledge sharing also contributed. Four mentioned that their corporate culture drove the objectives and goals by creating a successful culture among staff. Three believed that flexibility also contributed. Lastly, two respondents said that professionalism, values, beliefs, action, integrity and ethics drove the process of strategy implementation as seen in Fig. 3. It is obvious that corporate culture is crucial for the success of any strategy within the organisation.

This study indicated that corporate culture influences the implementation of strategy within small consulting businesses. A dynamic and lean culture, teamwork, communication and knowledge sharing, a drive towards objectives and goals, flexibility, professionalism, values, beliefs, action, integrity and ethics were mentioned as supporting strategy implementation (Fig. 3). This is in line with the literature, which states that corporate culture promotes values and behaviours that sustain some of the organisation's goals, and is also a tool that affects the performance of employees during the implementation (Wheelen & Hunger, 2012).

Corporate Strategy Implementation on Business Performance

More than half of the respondents (7) mentioned that growth, targets and profits were raised when corporate strategy was implemented effectively. '*... the performance in terms of growth is achieved. The performance in terms of growth is achieved, but the question is, is it easy to achieve those goals...?*' Five respondents pointed out that corporate strategy implementation influenced the direction,

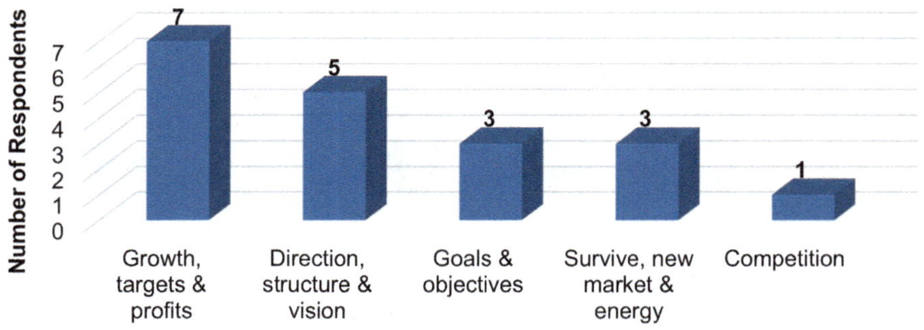

Fig. 4 Impact of corporate strategy implementation on business performance

structure and vision of the business. Three mentioned that strategy implementation assisted in achieving goals and objectives which enabled the business to survive, access new markets and bring energy to the business's performance, respectively. Lastly, one said that it enabled the business to compete in the environment.

From the findings, the business respondents indicated that corporate strategy implementation could influence and increase the performance of the business. The majority mentioned that good implementation enabled a business to grow, meet its targets and increase profits over the years. Other findings were as follows:

- Most did not have strategies that were documented.
- Management valued corporate strategy as an instrument that contributed to the success of their businesses, but they were hesitant of that success within their own businesses.
- Managers were not aware of the difference between strategic management versus corporate strategy.

It is evident that effective strategy implementation would enhance the performance of a business. However, the findings indicate that corporate strategy is not well implemented and should be reviewed by the managers (Fig. 4).

Corporate Strategy Implementation on Sustainability and Growth of Business

Nine respondents believed that corporate strategy implementation impacted the long-term survival and sustainability of the business. '*... have a very great impact on the sustainability as a company ...*' and '*... going to be more sustainable in the future ...*' Eight felt that it sustained and grew the business through market share, profit, productivity and customer satisfaction. Five mentioned that effective corporate strategy implementation was the driving force and guidance that led the business to grow and be sustainable within the competitive business environment. Four were of the opinion that it created a positive impact or improved the image of the

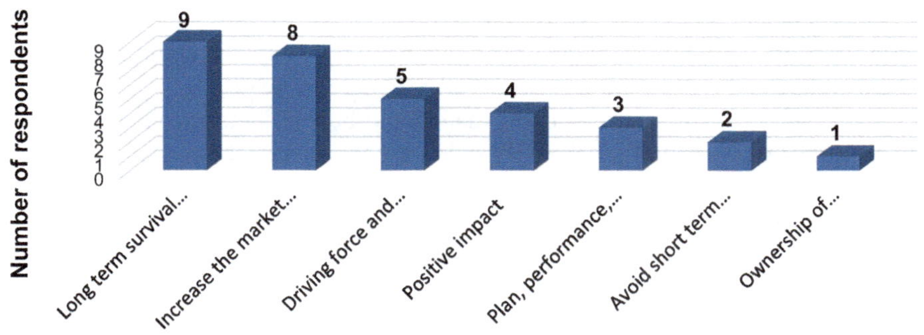

Fig. 5 Corporate strategy implementation on sustainability and growth of business

business within the competitive environment. Three said that it also impacted planning, performance and the objectives and goals of the business. Two said that it helped avoid short-term vision or orientation and one mentioned that it promoted a sense of ownership among employees.

From the findings shown in Fig. 5, many of the managers believed that good implementation of corporate strategy would influence the long-term survival and sustainability of their businesses. This increased their market share, profit, productivity and the satisfaction of customers. From the findings shown in Fig. 5, many of the managers believed that good implementation of corporate strategy would influence the long-term survival and sustainability of their businesses. This increased their market share, profit, productivity and the satisfaction of customers.

The findings showed that although there was an understanding of sustainability and growth among the management, the application of the strategy implementation components to make their businesses grow and be sustainable was lacking.

Limitations

The longitudinal effects of corporate strategy implementation are better observed over a longer period in order to get a better understanding and high-quality data. Therefore, multiple data sources were employed regarding the sustainability and growth of businesses over the past 3 years in order to analyse them.

Managerial Implications and Recommendations

Successful corporate strategy implementation is essential and has managerial implications. The following steps might assist management:

- Management must be able to distinguish between corporate strategy and strategy in order to make decisions and take actions during implementation. This will encourage and ground the success of the corporate strategy.
- Management need to have budgets that should be distributed around the entire department within the business. By doing so, the success of corporate strategy implementation will increase, along with long-term survival and growth.
- Management need to be more conscious of the corporate strategy implementation process and should also allocate enough time to do so. Consulting businesses should improve their corporate strategy implementation skills. This could help to cultivate a culture of corporate strategy implementation among them. They could do this in the following ways:
- Management should ensure that the strategy within the business is communicated effectively to the staff members to embrace the implementation process. Middle management should implement strategy with skilled and experienced employees. Also, they need to ensure that there are sufficient resources to implement corporate strategy.
- Management should also view corporate culture as important to enhance staff members' performance during strategy implementation.

Conclusion

This study has delivered some insights into corporate strategy implementation. All consulting businesses interviewed responded positively and showed evidence and understanding of corporate strategy implementation. However, a lack of differentiating between corporate strategy and strategy is the major reason for not implementing corporate strategy principles and instructions in managing consulting businesses.

The significance of identifying improved strategy formation practices for small and medium enterprises is also recognised through the impact that they have on the South African economy since they contribute up to 60% of the gross domestic product. The findings of this research could benefit small enterprise development centres as well as management consultants who assist small and medium enterprise owners to be more effective.

References

Abosede, A. J., Obasan, K. A., & Alese, O. J. (2016). Strategic management and small enterprises (SMEs) development: A review of literature. *International Review of Management and Business Research, 5*(1), 315–335.

Ansoff, H. I. (1965). *Corporate strategy: An analytic approach to business policy for growth and expansion*. McGraw-Hill.

Bateman, T. S., Snell, S. A., & Konopaske, R. (2019). *Management: Leading and collaborating in a competitive world* (13th ed.). McGraw Hill.

Bryman, A. (2015). *Social research methods* (5th ed.). Oxford University Press.
Bryman, A., Bell, E., Hirschsohn, P., Dos Santos, A., Du Toit, J., Masenge, A., Van Aardt, I., & Wagner, C. (2014). *Research methodology: Business and management contexts*. Oxford University Press.
Carpenter, M. A., & Sanders, W. G. (2009). *Strategic management: A dynamic perspective: Concepts and cases* (2nd ed.). Pearson Prentice Hall.
Chandler, A. D., Jr. (1962). *Strategy and structure: Chapters in the history of the American industrial enterprise*. MIT Press.
Checco, L. (2005). *Branding for success*. Trafford.
Chen, J. (2020). What is influencer marketing: How to develop your strategy. [Online] Available at: https://sproutsocial.com/insights/influencer-marketing/. Accessed: March 2022.
Cyert, R., & March, J. (1963). *A behavioral theory of the firm*. Prentice Hall.
David, F. R. (2023). *Strategic management. Concepts and cases* (18th ed.). Pearson.
Drucker, P. (1954). *The practice of management*. Harper and Row.
Ehlers, T., & Lazenby, K. (2022). *Strategic management: Southern African concepts and cases* (3rd ed.). Van Schaik.
Eniola, A. A., & Ektebang, H. (2014). SME firms performance in Nigeria: Competitive advantage and its impact. *International Journal of Research Studies in Management, 3*(2), 75–86.
Furrer, O. (2016). *Corporate level strategy: Theory and applications* (2nd ed.). Routledge.
Ghosh, P. P. (2021). *Principles and practices of management*. University society Press.
Hoskisson, R. E., Hitt, M. A., Wan, W. P., & Yiu, D. (2013). Theory and research in strategic management: Swings of a pendulum. *Journal of Management, 25*(3), 417–456.
Hrebiniak, L. G. (2013). *Making strategy work: Leading effective executive and change work* (2nd ed.). Pearson Education.
Jansson, J., Nilsson, J., Modig, F., & Vall, G. H. (2017). Commitment to sustainability in small and medium-sized enterprises: The influence of strategic orientations and management values. *Business Strategy and the Environment, 26*(1), 69–83. https://doi.org/10.1002/bse.1901
Jones, G. R., & Hill, C. W. L. (2013). *Theory of strategic management with cases* (10th ed.). South-Western.
Khan, S. N. (2014). Qualitative research method: Grounded theory. *International Journal of Business and Management, 9*(11), 224–233.
Lazenby, K. (2022). *The strategic management process: A South African perspective*. Van Schaik.
Lynch, R. (2018). *Strategic management* (7th ed.). Pearson.
Miller, R. L., & Brewer, J. D. (2003). *A-Z of social research - Dictionary of key social science*. Sage.
Mintzberg, H., & Waters, J. (1985). Of strategies, deliberate and emergent. *Strategic Management Journal, 6*(3), 257–272.
Nadler, D. A. (2004). What's the board's role in strategy development? Engaging the board in corporate strategy. *Strategy & Leadership, 32*(5), 25–33. Available from: EBSCOHost: CINAHL: http://search.global.epnet.com/. Accessed: February 2023
Neneh, B. N. (2012). An exploratory study on entrepreneurial mindset in the small and medium enterprise (SME) sector: A South African perspective on fostering small and medium enterprise (SME) success. *African Journal of Business Management, 6*(9), 3364–3372.
Neuman, W. L. (2011). *Social research methods: Qualitative and quantitative approaches* (7th ed.). Allyn.
Pleva, P. (2006). *Under what conditions should donors promote consulting services in developing countries?* Thesis, Tufts University, Medford, Massachusetts.
Radzi, K. M., Nor, M. N. M., & Ellen, S. M. (2017). The impact of internal factors on small business success: A case of small enterprises under the felda scheme. *Asian Academy of Management Journal, 22*(1), 27–55.
Rothaermel, F. T. (2017). *Strategic management* (3th ed.). McGraw-Hill.
Saunders, M., & Lewis, P. (2012). *Doing research in business & management: An essential guide to planning your project*. Pearson.

Saunders, M., Lewis, P., & Thornhill, A. (2016). *Research methods for business students* (7th ed.). Pearson.

Sharabati, A. A., & Fuqaha, S. (2014). Impact of strategic management on the Jordanian pharmaceuticals manufacturing organisation business performance. *International Review of Management and Business Research, 3*(2), 668–687.

Simeone, L. (2020). Characterizing strategic design processes in relation to definitions of strategy from military, business and management studies. *The Design Journal, 23*(4), 515–534.

Sitharam, S., & Hoque, M. (2016). Factors affecting the performance of small and medium enterprises in KwaZulu-Natal, South Africa. *Problems and Perspectives in Management, 14*(2–2), 277–288.

Spens, K. M., & Kovacs, G. (2006). A content analysis of research approaches in logistics research. *International Journal of Physical Distribution and Logistics Management, 36*(5), 374–390.

Suter, W. N. (2012). *Introduction to educational research: A critical thinking approach* (2nd pure ed.). Sage.

The Free Dictionary. (2010). S.V. 'consulting firm'. Available at: http://www.thefreedictionary.com/consulting+firm

Thompson, A. A., Peteraf, M. A., Gamble, J. E., & Strickland, A. J., III. (2016). *Crafting and executing strategy: The quest for competitive advantage: Concepts and cases* (20th ed.). McGraw-Hill.

Ungerer, M., Pretorius, M., & Herholdt, J. (2007). *Viable business strategies. A systemic people centric approach*. Knowres.

Wheelen, T. L., & Hunger, J. D. (2012). *Essentials of strategic management and business policy toward global sustainability* (13th ed.). Pearson.

Zikmund, W. G., & Babin, B. J. (2015). *Exploring marketing research* (11th ed.). Thompson South-Western.

Xero Software in Accounting Education: Enhancing Digital Acumen and Employability

Mothelesi Charles and Sibanda Julia

Abstract This research investigates the effectiveness of Xero accounting software in enhancing digital acumen and employability within the context of South African accounting education. The study employed a multi-method approach with 839 accounting students; the research investigated how Xero accounting software impacted their digital acumen skills and job readiness. Data was collected through academic performance analysis (quantitative data) and student reflections (qualitative data). This data included students' marks on the Xero assignment's four phases (data migration, processing financial data, importation of financial data and extraction of financial reports). The study's findings offer encouraging preliminary indications that Xero accounting software can contribute to the development of essential digital acumen skills and desirable graduate attributes. While the assignment presented challenges, it demonstrably achieved attainable learning goals and fostered increased student engagement. Additionally, the assignment provided valuable insights into students' strengths and weaknesses for future attention once they have embarked on an employment opportunities search. This paper contributes to our understanding of how Xero accounting software can be utilised to foster meaningful participation and develop students' digital acumen skills to meet the demands of the labour market.

Keywords Accounting students · Continuous assessment · Digital acumen · Graduate attributes · Professional bodies · Xero accounting software

M. Charles (✉) · S. Julia
University of Free State, Bloemfontein, South Africa
e-mail: mothelesioc@ufs.ac.za; sibandaj@ufs.ac.za

T. Moloi (ed.), *Impacting Society Positively Through Technology in Accounting and Business Processes*, Springer Proceedings in Business and Economics,
https://doi.org/10.1007/978-3-031-84885-8_14

Introduction and Background

With the advent of the Fourth Industrial Revolution (4IR), the integration of accounting software applications has become essential. Furthermore, the observable shift over recent years from desktop-based to cloud-based accounting software, accompanied by increased automation, underscores the need for accountants to be proficient in the use of such software (Ghazali et al., 2022). Lim (2013) succinctly defines this accounting software package as programmes tailored to record and manage accounting transactions, encompassing functional modules such as payroll, accounts payable and accounts receivable. This transition within the accounting profession has generated a demand for accountants who possess proficiency in ICT skills (Osmani et al., 2020). In light of this, Osmani et al. (2020) assert that this technological evolution creates competitive pressures within the accounting profession, necessitating that accounting graduates develop soft skills with increasing emphasis on technology proficiency.

This increased emphasis on technology proficiency is attributed to the growing disconnect between future employability skills expected by prospective employers and student perceptions of these skills (Pauceanu et al., 2020). Cele (2022) further emphasises the critical role of accounting technology, particularly accounting software packages, in the preparation of future accounting professionals. Lusher et al. (2012) concurs that using accounting software packages during lectures can enhance student learning outcomes and better equip students for employment in the accounting field.

Given these high demands in the labour market and evolving technologies in the accounting profession, higher education institutions and professional bodies had to reassess whether current assessment models are fit for purpose (Birt et al., 2023). This is attributable to the fact that in the realm of scientific research on higher education, a significant concern has emerged regarding the employability of graduates. This concern arises due to the notable disparities between the skills that university graduates possess and those that employers seek (Pauceanu et al., 2020). This demand has recently intensified even further because of a decrease in job openings for graduates and a shrinking job market (Jackson, 2014).

The South African Institute of Chartered Accountants (SAICA) Competency Framework (2020) posits that the academic programme or syllabus can assist in developing competencies by providing different opportunities to develop and demonstrate these acumens (such as various theories, videos, training sessions and projects). Competencies serve as a bridge between the academic programme and the labour market, ensuring graduates possess the skillsets prospective employers seek (Klemp, 1980). The onus is thus on higher education institutions to produce graduates who possess these enabling competencies (acumens/graduate attributes) to ensure graduates are employable and work-ready (Butler-Adam, 2018; Griesel & Parker, 2009; World Economic Forum (WEF), 2016).

While prior studies have delineated essential skills that should be integrated into graduate education, there is a noticeable gap in the literature, as no or little research has been conducted to systematically identify and consolidate existing knowledge on enabling competencies and acumens (Birt et al., 2023). Although significant changes in accounting education have been discussed for years, universities must take the lead in educating students about the 4IR to prepare them for their future careers (Cele, 2022).

The accountancy profession is undergoing significant transformation in a global landscape characterised by full transparency of transactions and inherent validation mechanisms. Consequently, it is imperative that professional bodies, such as the South African Institute of Professional Accountants (SAIPA) and the South African Institute of Chartered Accountants (SAICA), as well as academic institutions, proactively engage with and adapt to these emerging shifts. Technology is changing the focus of auditors and accountants in business (Hasin et al., 2022). Ultimately, digital disruption will affect the nature of demand and expectations of what an accountant is and does. Accordingly, a teaching strategy, project and assessment styles were introduced, aiming to equip students for the ever-changing world of technology in the last chapter of the module. The researcher used online accounting software (Xero) to address digital acumen skills and to practicalise the theory content to meet real-world expectations.

The COVID-19 disruption also provided an epitome of what we could achieve when we had to come out of our comfort zone (traditional ways of doing things) and acknowledge that technology has evolved so much that it was able to meet our needs during a pandemic. Therefore, technology was used to bridge the gap between theoretical content and the practical expectations envisaged by professional bodies and the university's graduate attributes while still meeting the needs of our students. The university's graduate attributes/acumens serve as a benchmark for evaluating the quality of undergraduate education and preparing students to excel in a rapidly changing and demanding professional environment. These attributes encompass a range of factors, including the cultivation of pertinent skills, competencies, knowledge and attitudes vital for achieving success in diverse workplace environments spanning from local to global contexts (Ncube & Matlala, 2023).

The advancement of skills among graduates in higher education has emerged as a response to the heightened demands placed on industries due to intense global competition and rapid technological progress. According to Mundida (2020), the current accounting software significantly expedites transaction processing, making it significantly faster, easier and more accurate than traditional manual systems. Notably, this aligns with the expectations of prospective employers who have transitioned to the new accounting systems (Boulianne, 2014). Accounting software such as Xero is considered to have the potential to foster these skills and attributes, bridging the gap between a module's theoretical content and real-world expectations.

Xero is a cloud-based accounting software that manages standard accounting transactions, manages expense claims, generates reports, offers invoicing tools and has artificial intelligence-based short-term cash flow forecasts that help owners and accountants make informed business decisions. Xero accounting software may be used to facilitate students' digital acumen skills and to translate the module's theoretical content into real-world expectations. This study, therefore, aims to examine the use of Xero software in accounting education to enhance digital acumen and graduate attributes.

This study, therefore, aims to review the effectiveness of using Xero accounting software in enhancing digital acumen and employability.

The following objectives were therefore identified for the study:

1. To establish the experience of students on utilising the Xero accounting software through data migration, processing, importation and extraction
2. To examine the relationship between student performance on data migration, importation, processing and extraction
3. To determine the impact of software utilisation on accounting students' knowledge acquisition

Literature Review

Industries and professional bodies require accounting graduates who possess digital skills as technology has immensely affected the world in which accountants operate (Muthaiyah et al., 2021). Accounting professional bodies acknowledge the increasing technological demands in the accounting profession and have taken steps to mandate the inclusion of accounting software for undergraduate accounting students aspiring to join one of the professional bodies (Jones et al. (2021). With the significant shift in the accounting profession, which resulted in more than 72% of accounting jobs being automated, the need to train accounting graduates in digital skills to prepare them for the future has become vital in the accounting curriculum (Muthaiyah et al., 2021). Competency-based student learning and assessment have, therefore, become the standard in professional education across various disciplines (Abbasi, 2013). However, critics of contemporary accounting education contend that accounting education is yet to respond to environmental changes and advocate for a paradigm shift in its approach to addressing these changes (Abbasi, 2013; Spraakman et al., 2015). The question, therefore, remains on how higher education and professional bodies may best develop these digital skills in graduates (Pan et al., 2019).

Pan and Seow (2016) maintain that to prepare accounting graduates for digital technology, higher education needs to review current curricula to ensure it includes information systems such as cloud computing. This has become a critical skill for most accounting professionals as most accounting firms make use of a cloud computing system in their daily operations (Mahambo, 2020). Xero accounting software is one of the cloud-based systems that has been adapted by accounting firms and has become highly rated software, one of the top 10 accounting software in the world.

Most graduates usually acquire experience in using accounting software when they serve their articles (3-year training contract) after completing their qualifications. In contrast, only a handful of graduates can acquire the experience when they do vacation work during school holidays. This means that graduates complete their accounting degrees with no real-life experience; meanwhile, employers seek to provide job opportunities to people who are already comfortable with technology (Elaine Gioiosa & Kinkela, 2019). Therefore, higher education institutions have a responsibility to expose students to real-world expectations and develop essential skills, including the use of cloud-based systems. Accordingly, the early introduction to Xero exposes students to some of these required skills. While significant research has been conducted on the need to integrate digital skills into accounting curricula, there is still less known about how digital skills can be taught at higher education institutions. Furthermore, very little research has been conducted on the use of cloud-based accounting software, especially Xero, to develop accounting software skills in graduates. This study, therefore, seeks to evaluate the potential of adapting the Xero accounting software to develop accounting software skills.

Underlying Theory

Johansson et al. (2023) assert that formative assessment (continuous assessment) improves students' knowledge or skills in the subject and is likely to improve student's performance in summative assessments. This is because students' learning benefits from the frequency of assessment. Constructivism, a multifaceted theory originating from philosophy, psychology and cybernetics (Piaget, 2013), provides a comprehensive framework for comprehending knowledge acquisition in the context of accounting education. This theory underscores the active involvement of learners in constructing knowledge through firsthand experiences and social interactions (Brooks & Brooks, 1999). As articulated in 'A Constructivist Model: A Constructivist View of Teaching and Learning', this approach advocates for student-centred learning activities that transcend conventional passive knowledge dissemination methods. In accounting education, constructivism finds practical application through integrating case studies, simulations and group projects. These pedagogical tools enable students to engage with real-world scenarios, fostering the development of critical thinking, problem-solving skills and collaborative abilities. As mentioned, it is apparent that student learning and development of skills required by the labour market will require a change in teaching pedagogies.

Methodology

The participants consist of 839 accounting students who studied (enrolled) for the Information and Digital Environment module at one of the South African universities. A multi-method was employed. In state 1, student marks from the assignment were used. Stage 1 evaluated the students' academic performance for each activity in the assignment. In stage 2, qualitative data was collected through an open-ended questionnaire (students' reflection reports) on the assignment. The feedback from students was recorded and qualitatively analysed to draw themes on student experience with the assignment. Stage 2 aimed to provide an insight into the statistical analysis (stage 1) through students' reflection reports on the assignment.

In total, 965 accounting students were enrolled in the module, and 839 students took part in the Xero assignment, representing a participation rate of 89%. Of the 839 students who participated in the Xero assignment, 60 students completed the questionnaire, representing a response rate of 7%.

Students were required to build commands that automated accounting processes into the system (artificial intelligence), process transactions using the source documents provided and know where to store data. The portfolio of evidence (PoE) file contains the company logo; purchases and payment cycle source documents (customer statement, goods receiving note, purchase invoice and the purchase order); revenue and receipt source documents (delivery note, internal sales order and sales invoice) and the bank statement. Students were expected to interpret information from source documents and process transactions using the Xero accounting system to record transactions using automated commands.

In this study, data was collected and analysed in two stages. Stage 1 evaluated the relationship between continuous assessment and students' academic performance in the assignment. Performance data for 839 students was analysed quantitatively to determine the effectiveness of Xero in aiding students to learn the utilisation of key functions in an accounting software (developing digital acumen). Stage 1 relied on the notion of whether continuous formative assessment enhances student knowledge and skills through repetitive attempts to master learning objectives. Research in the education literature cites adequate empirical evidence showing that continuous assessment results in increased academic performance (Van der Kleij et al., 2015).

Stages	Description
Stage 1	Stage 1 aimed to gauge students' experiences in using Xero accounting software within four phases as follows: *Phase 1*: data migration: this entails registering clients into the Xero accounting system, setting up a chart of accounts, and updating financial data. *Phase 2*: processing financial data: interpretation of purchases and payment cycle source documents (customer statement, goods receiving note, purchase invoice and the purchase order) and revenue and receipt source documents (delivery note, internal sales order and sales invoice) to build commands that automate accounting transactions. *Phase 3*: importation of financial data: importing the bank statement into the system and reconciling it against the processed financial data. *Phase 4*: extraction of financial reports: extractions of meaningful financial reports such as financial statements, inventory reports, trial balances, general ledgers, journal reports, etc.
Stage 2	A questionnaire with three open-ended questions was used to generate central themes (acquiring new factual information, purposeful assessment and needing theoretical preparation).

Data from stage 1 (phases 1–4) were analysed using descriptive statistics depicting the minimum, maximum, mean and standard deviation. In addition, histograms were used to demonstrate the specific performance of participants in the four phases of the project. Furthermore, correlation analysis was employed to compare the relationships among the four phases of the project. Finally, qualitative data from the questionnaire were coded to develop themes used for the study. Students were, therefore, exposed to the following key functions, as depicted in Fig. 1, which are essential in the accounting environment.

Assignment Process

The BCom accounting programme at one of the South African universities underwent a recirculation process of revamping one of its existing modules to meet the abovementioned needs and expectations by introducing the use of an accounting system, Xero. Accordingly, the Xero assignment was created as a personalised case study assignment for students. Each student was given a unique case study in a PDF format as an email attachment and a portfolio of evidence (PoE) of what they could expect from a real-life client in practice. The PoE file contained the company logo, purchases and payment cycle source documents (customer statement, goods receiving note, purchase invoice and purchase order), revenue and receipt source documents (delivery note, internal sales order and sales invoice). Students were expected to interpret the information in the source documents and process the transactions using the Xero accounting system to record transactions using automated commands.

In order to complete the assignment, students were enrolled on the Xero cloud-based accounting system. The university partnered with the industry through Dough Getters Accounting. The academic staff (lecturer) and the students enrolled in the Information and Digital Environment module were enrolled on Xero using the university email address. All participants (students and the lecturer) were required to sign up with their emails and create their unique passwords following the link and prompts in the email they received from Xero.

The assignment was part of a continuous assessment and an unsynchronised formative assessment. Students had a period of 2 weeks to complete and upload the assignment on the learning management system (blackboard). As the assignment was administered on an online system, the lecturer could access all the student's profiles/organisations to track their changes. However, it was unfortunately not practical to track all 839 students; hence, students were given instructions and a rubric of what they were supposed to upload on Blackboard (screenshots of procedures they performed and reports). This was an individual assignment and not group work. A rubric clearly indicating the percentage contribution of each document, the requirement and the number of documents expected per task was provided to the students.

Students were not on campus due to the COVID-19 pandemic, so each student received a unique assignment via email, and a rubric was used to grade the

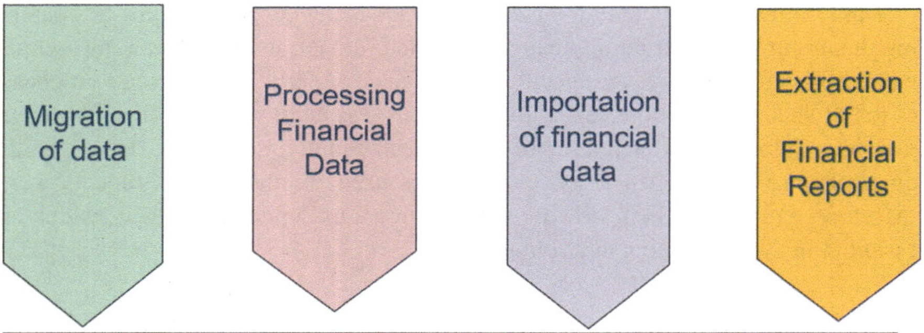

Stages	Description
Stage 1	Stage one aimed to gauge students' experiences in using Xero accounting software ensure within four phases as follows: ***Phase 1***: Data migration: This entails registering clients into the Xero accounting system, setting up a chart of accounts, and updating financial data. ***Phase 2***: Processing Financial Data: Interpretation of purchases and payment cycle source documents (customer statement, goods receiving note, purchase invoice and the purchase order) and revenue and receipt source documents (delivery note, internal sales order and sales invoice) to build commands that automate accounting transactions. ***Phase 3*** : Importation of Financial Data: Importing the bank statement into the system and reconciling it against the processed financial data. ***Phase 4*** : Extraction of Financial Reports: Extractions of meaningful financial reports such as financial statements, inventory reports, trial balances, general ledgers, journal reports, etc.
Stage 2	A questionnaire with three open-ended questions was used to generate central themes (acquiring new factual information, purposeful assessment and needing theoretical preparation).

Fig. 1 The two stages of the assignment

assignment. Because different screenshots of the procedures and reports that students uploaded on Blackboard contributed a specific weighting (mark), so students were given an Excel calculator to confirm their marks' accuracy on Blackboard. As the solution catered for 839 students, the lecturer created one solution with tick marks explaining the different gradings. If the tick was red, it meant that all students were supposed to arrive at the same answer, and a green tick with a hand meant that the steps and/or amounts in the reports were unique for the individual assignment. In such cases, the marker was supposed to use the Excel database to confirm the accuracy of the student's answer.

The assignment bridges the gap between the theoretical content that students covered in the module and brings about real-life expectancy in a quest to stimulate entrepreneurial mindsets and increase our graduates' employability. Worth mentioning is that students had the opportunity of completing the Xero advisor assessments to obtain a Xero advisor certificate that they can use on their CVs when they apply for a job. Moreover, the assignment required students to build a command that automated processes into the system (artificial intelligence) and to know how and where to store data, which developed the student's digital acumen skill.

On the other hand, in the real world of work, people do not work in isolation and, therefore, are assigned to seniors who can assist them. Students were provided with short videos of some of the steps that they were supposed to follow, especially on transactions that one would normally not be able to process if they had never done them before. In the real world of work, we are constantly confronted with new tasks that we have never seen or done before, and this is where we assess the student's cognitive thinking and professional competency envisaged by the professional body. As students could not assist each other, the link to the videos was provided on the assignment to assist students with these new tasks. Dough Getters prepared the videos for the students. A WhatsApp group was created specifically for the assignment so that students could ask the lecturer questions. Frequently asked questions on WhatsApp were collated and discussed with all students during the Blackboard collaboration session (virtual live session) because Blackboard was the approved learning management system of the university.

Students also provided feedback reports on the usage of Xero as a reflection on the assignment. In addition to the assignment, students also had the option of completing the Xero advisor assessments to obtain a Xero advisor certificate that they can use when they embark on an employment opportunity search. The assignment provided students with practical exposure to the efficient and accurate processing of financial transactions within an accounting system and the preparation of financial statements in real-world scenarios, thereby illustrating the accounting cycle in practice.

Findings

In stage 1, student marks from the assignment were used. Stage 1 evaluated the relationship between continuous assessment and students' academic performance in the assignment. In stage 2, qualitative data was collected through an open-ended questionnaire (students' reflection reports) on the assignment. The findings of the study on the two stages are presented as follows:

Stage 1: Quantitative Findings

The project had a total of 100 marks, of which migration weighted 20, importation 10, processing 20 and extraction of financial reports 50; therefore, the descriptive statistics in Table 1 depict the minimum, mean, maximum and standard deviation of student's performance (see Table 2). Histograms 1 to 4 depict the student's performance in each task.

The assignment was evaluated by using a rubric that aimed to evaluate their ability to migrate data from a manual control environment, importation of data, processing of data into an accounting system and exporting of the system-generated reports.

Migration of Data (Phase 1) Table 1 indicates a mean of 17.8284, implying that most of the students could migrate data from source documents into the Xero software. The standard deviation of 4.73540 indicates a low variability from the mean compared to phases 3 and 4.

Processing Financial Data (Phase 2) Table 1 indicates a mean of 5.0608, implying an average number of students could process the financial data using the Xero software. The standard deviation of 4.57083 indicates a low variability from the mean compared to phases 3 and 4.

Importation of Financial Data (Phase 3) Table 1 indicates a mean of 12.3938, implying an above-average number of students were able to import financial data using the Xero software. The standard deviation of 7.43286 indicates a moderate variability from the mean compared to phases 1, 2 and 4.

Extraction of Financial Reports (Phase 4) Table 1 indicates a mean of 25.3063, implying an average number of students were able to extract financial reports from Xero accounting software. The standard deviation of 12.52369 indicates a high variability from the mean compared to phases 1, 2 and 3.

Table 1 Represents the student's overall performance rate across the different phases of the assignment

Descriptive statistics of key variables					
Variable	N	Min	Max	Mean	Std. dev
Migration of data	839	0.00	20.00	17.8284	4.73540
Processing financial data	838	0.00	20.00	12.3938	7.43286
Importation of financial data	839	0.00	10.00	5.0608	4.57083
Extraction of financial reports	839	0.00	47.00	25.3063	12.52369
Valid N (listwise)	838				

Table 2 Link of student's performances on various tasks using the Xero accounting software

Correlations of key variables					
		Migration of data	Importation of financial data	Extraction of financial reports	Processing financial data
Migration of data	Pearson correlation	1	0.098**	0.063	0.012
	Sig. (2-tailed)		0.005	0.067	0.727
	N	839	839	839	838
Importation of financial data	Pearson correlation	0.098**	1	0.238**	0.046
	Sig. (2-tailed)	0.005		<,001	0.180
	N	839	839	839	838
Extraction of financial reports	Pearson correlation	0.063	0.238**	1	0.021
	Sig. (2-tailed)	0.067	<,001		0.545
	N	839	839	839	838
Processing financial data	Pearson correlation	0.012	0.046	0.021	1
	Sig. (2-tailed)	0.727	0.180	0.545	
	N	838	838	838	838

**Correlation is significant at the 0.01 level (2-tailed).

Histogram 1: Migration of Data

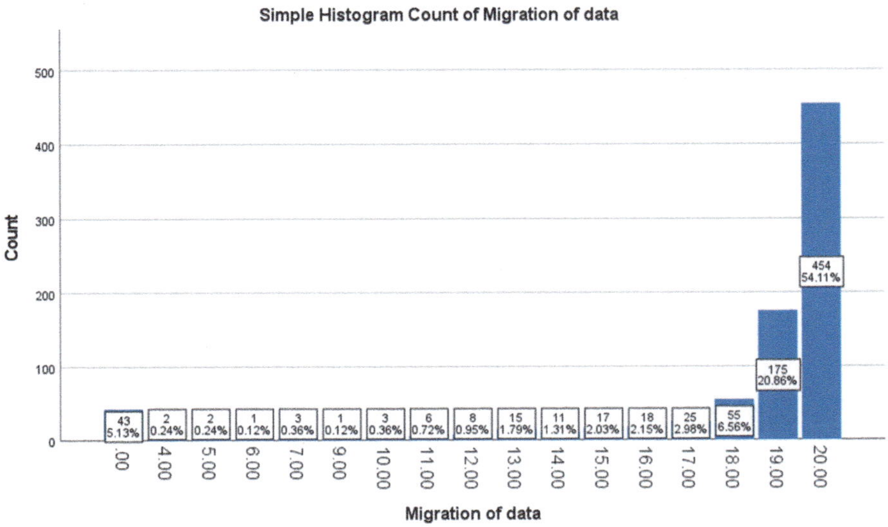

54.11% (454) students achieved 100% on the task. Students were equipped to register their clients into the system, set up their chart of accounts and transfer manual data into the system.

20.86% (175) of the students fell slightly short of scoring 100% on the task.

Histogram 2: Processing Financial Data

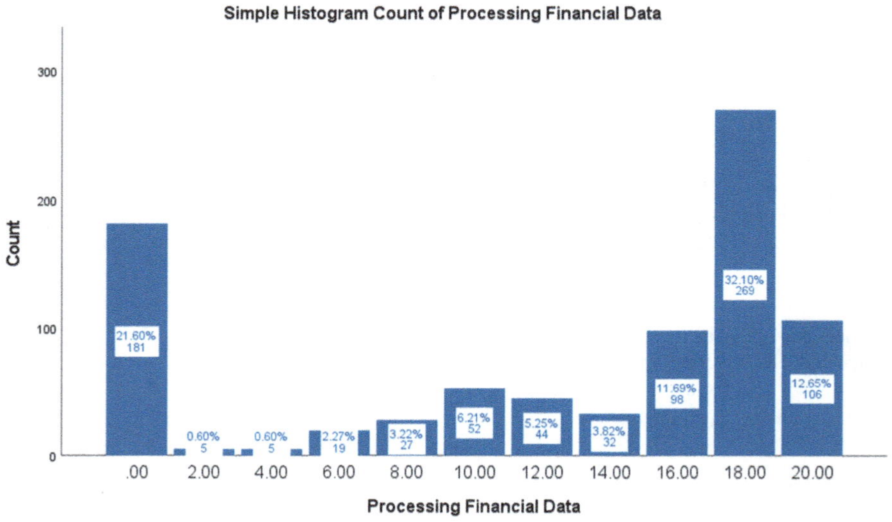

Histogram 2 indicates the student's ability to build commands that automate accounting processes into the system (artificial intelligence), processing accounting transactions and knowledge of where to store the data.

This demonstrates the gap between the student's accounting and auditing knowledge in comparison to their ability to use digital technology skills.

The previous histogram required students to transfer information into the system and did not require interpretation of the data that they imported.

Histogram 3: Extraction of financial reports

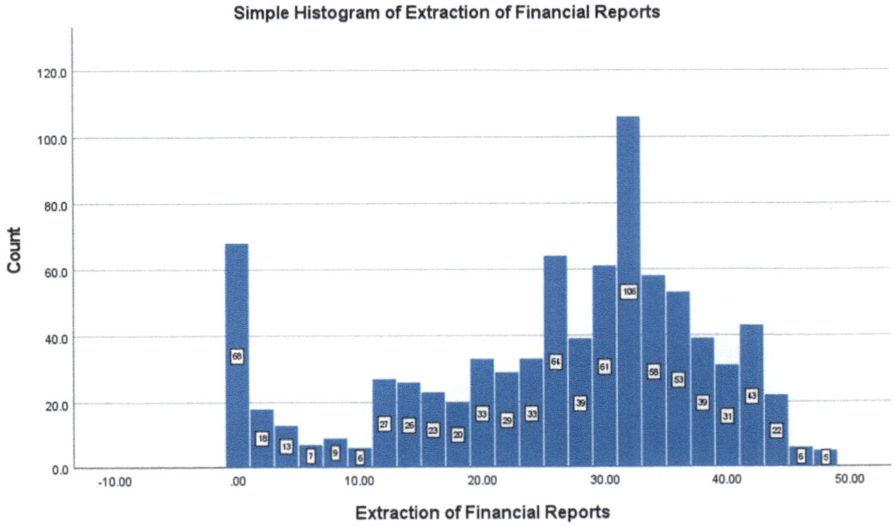

The findings indicate that students were equipped to extract financial reports in the system.

The task relied heavily on financial data processed in the previous histogram. The point where the system processed data was supposed to reconcile with the client's bank activities.

Histogram 4: Importation of financial data

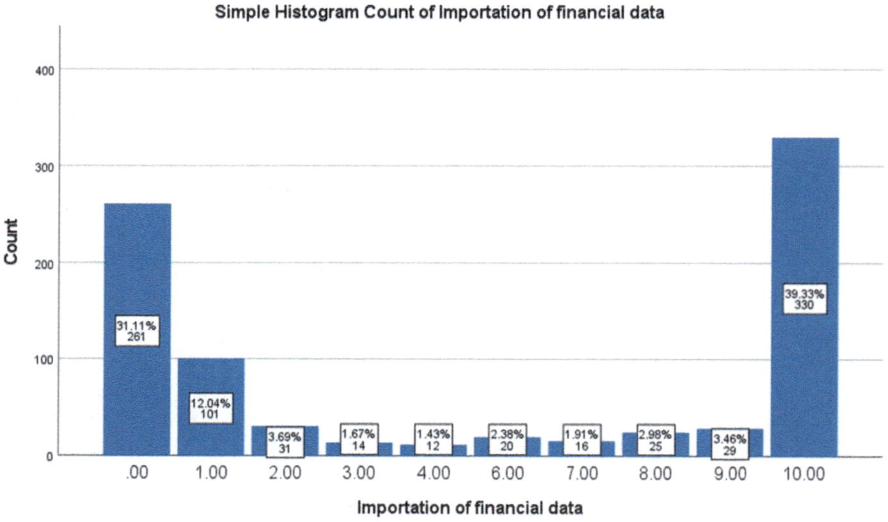

Histogram 4 represents an output of the importation of financial data task that students were expected to execute in the system. The results of this task reveal that 39.33% (330) students obtained a mark of 100% indicating they were well equipped in performing this task. The findings further reveal that the importation of data for processing was challenging with attainable goals and that students had to put in time and effort.

In summary, the quantitative findings for all the tasks indicate that there is a very strong positive correlation between students' performance on migration and importation of financial data, with a coefficient of 0.98. Importation and processing of financial data, migration of data and extraction of financial reports depict moderate correlation with a coefficient of 0.46 and 0.63, respectively. The correlation results for extraction and processing of financial data, as well as the processing of financial data and extraction of financial reports, reflect a weak correlation with a coefficient of 0.021 and 0.238, respectively.

Stage 2: Qualitative Findings

Impact of software utilisation on accounting students' knowledge acquisition. Out of the total participants of 839 who participated in the compulsory stage 1 process of the study, only 60 (7%) students participated in stage 2 of the study as it was not compulsory aim to solicit student feedback. Three central themes (acquiring new factual information, purposeful assessment and needing theoretical preparation) were generated from the open-ended questions that are what the student liked and disliked.

Theme 1: Acquiring New Factual Information

P1: 'The module is really interesting and therefore is a lead to how the accounting practice can be like and its operations. It gives us a very clear introduction to the accounting environment/workplace. The module is also giving an insight of how cautious & informative we should be in the digital environment.'

P2: 'It improved my knowledge and skills, and it opened my mind to most things.'

P3: 'I acquired new information about new software used nowadays and furthered my knowledge about Computer Applications and Technology used.'

Participants were able to acquire new digital skills from the use of the Xero accounting software. The software seemed to have aided the process of bridging the gap between theoretical knowledge and real-world expectations, thereby improving the participants' use of technology in accounting practice. Asserted that educators have to create meaningful learning experiences through the use of digital tools such as apps to facilitate meaningful learning experiences.

Theme 2: Purposeful Assessment

P57: 'All the assessments and activities are more interesting and helping, and they are all related to my career/course.'

P43: 'The Xero section. It was a very good experience to learn about the accounting system that might be useful for me.'

P48: 'Getting to use Xero, which gave me a real accounting experience.'

The participants expressed their views that the assignment exposed them to the processing of accounting processing data. Boulianne (2014) confirmed that the use of accounting software in class prepares students for the workplace and instils important skills. Boulianne (2014) further asserted that curriculum designers should consider integrating accounting software in class as students appear to learn more about accounting through the use of the software.

Theme 3: Needing Theoretical Preparation

P5: 'There was a lot of theory. Although reading is not an issue for me, but I prefer blend of theory and calculations. I feel like more could have been done to prepare us for the Xero Assignment. For example, the lecturer could have processed transactions that deal with the shortage of inventory so that one knows what to expect and how to solve the issue of inventory.'

P19: 'Dig in deeper in terms of covering what students might encounter as challenges so that they know how to tackle them.'

P19: 'First time we were introduced to Xero it was not easy to understand, but as time goes it became my favourite.'

Participants expressed the need for more time for theoretical preparation to enable them to fully engage in the digital accounting software. According to Nkhoma et al. (2017), 'Students' class preparation of basic theoretical concepts makes students more confident to share information and feedback and participate in the practical and problem-solving activities more effectively.'

Discussion

The findings in the study indicated that the majority of the students were able to migrate data while an average number of students were able to process and extract financial data, and an above-average number of students were able to import financial data relating to their experience with the Xero accounting software. The findings further indicate a strong correlation between the migration of data and processing and the importation of financial data. Conversely, the link between the importation and processing of financial data, as well as the migration of data and extraction of financial reports, depicts a moderate correlation. Finally, the extraction and processing of financial data, as well as the processing of financial data and extraction of financial reports, reflect a weak correlation. In summary, participants indicated that they acquired factual information from the Xero accounting software project and were able to acquire skills to use an accounting software.

Conclusion

This chapter contributes to our understanding of how continuous assessment through the use of Xero can be utilised to foster meaningful, participatory and developing student skills to meet the demands of the labour market. Participants expressed the need for more time for theoretical preparation to enable them to fully engage in digital accounting software. According to Nkhoma et al. (2017), 'Students' class preparation of basic theoretical concepts makes students more confident to share information, feedback, and participate in the practical and problem-solving activities more effectively.'

The findings indicate that students specifically mentioned that the assignment assisted them in developing critical thinking skills, problem-solving, ethical reasoning and entrepreneurial mindset and allowed them to take charge of their learning process. Although the Xero assignment was challenging, it had attainable goals.

Students had to put in time and effort; however, they were motivated by an authentic task that adhered to the research-based principles of student engagement. Students performed above expectations with an overall pass rate of 73% and a class average of 61% on the assignment. Even though the assignment might have initially been challenging, most students were motivated by the practical aspect of the assignment to do well. The student's strengths and weaknesses could be identified for future attention. In summary, promising indications were that Xero could aid the development of digital acumen skills and graduate attributes. The Xero assignment was challenging but with attainable goals. Students were motivated by an authentic task that adheres to the research-based principles of student constructivism.

It is recommended that further investigation be conducted to evaluate the impact of Xero on the development of digital acumen and graduate attributes when they have embarked on an employment opportunities journey. It is further recommended that theoretical preparation is required before the implementation of similar projects in the future. In conclusion, the assignment could be an effective steppingstone in aiding students with digital skills at the university level.

References

Abbasi, N. (2013). Competency approach to accounting education: A global view. *Journal of Finance and Accountancy, 13*(1), 1–18.

Birt, J., Safari, M., & de Castro, V. B. (2023). Critical analysis of integration of ICT and data analytics into the accounting curriculum: A multidimensional perspective. *Accounting & Finance, 63*(4), 4037–4063.

Boulianne, E. (2014). Impact of accounting software utilization on students' knowledge acquisition: An important change in accounting education. *Journal of Accounting & Organizational Change, 10*(1), 22–48.

Brooks, J. G., & Brooks, M. G. (1999). *In search of understanding: The case for constructivist classrooms*. ASCD.

Butler-Adam, J. (2018). The fourth industrial revolution and education. *South African Journal of Science, 114*(5–6), 1–1.

Cele, W. (2022). The applicability of accounting information systems for the Financial Accounting curriculum in the Fourth Industrial Revolution era: A case study at the Durban University of Technology (DUT). Doctoral dissertation.

Elaine Gioiosa, M., & Kinkela, K. (2019). Active learning in accounting classes with technology and communication skills: A two-semester study of student perceptions. *Journal of Education for Business, 94*(8), 561–568.

Forum, W. E. (2016). The future of jobs: Employment, skills and workforce strategy for the fourth industrial revolution. *Global Challenge Insight Report*.

Ghazali, A. W., Shafie, N. A., Fernandez, D. F. M. F., & Zolkafli, S. (2022). The integration of ERP in accounting education: Enhancing the experiential learning of accounting information system. *Malaysian Journal of Social Sciences and Humanities (MJSSH), 7*(10), e001819–e001819.

Griesel, H., & Parker, B. (2009). *Graduate attributes: A baseline study on South African graduates from the perspective of employers*. Higher Education South Africa.

Hasin, H., Johari, Y. C., & Jamil, A. (2022). Accountant's digital technologies competencies in the digitalisation era. *International Journal of Academic Research in Business and Social Sciences, 12*(10).

Jackson, D. (2014). Factors influencing job attainment in recent bachelor graduates: Evidence from Australia. *Higher Education, 68*, 135–153.

Johansson, E., Kanapathippillai, S., Khan, A., & Dellaportas, S. (2023). Formative assessment in accounting: Student perceptions and implications of continuous assessment. *Accounting Education, 32*(6), 597–625.

Jones, G., Jones, H., Pensiero, D., & Beattie, C. (2021). Enhancing students' employability skills and experiential learning through integration of Xero software. *ASCILITE Publications*, 121–130.

Klemp Jr, G. O. (1980). The assessment of occupational competence. Final Report: I. Introduction and overview.

Lim, F. P. C. (2013). Impact of information technology on accounting systems. *Asia-Pacific Journal of Multimedia Services Convergent with Art, Humanities, and Sociology, 3*(2), 93–106.

Lusher, A., Huber, M. M., & Valencia, J. M. (2012). Empirical evidence regarding the relationship between the computerized classroom and student performance in introductory accounting. *The Accounting Educators' Journal, 22*.

Mahambo, C. T. (2020). Accounting curriculum in the digital era: Suggestions for preparing Botswana's tertiary accounting graduates. *Research Journal of Finance and Accounting, 11*(16), 15–21.

Mundida, L. (2020). Machine learning and implications for accounting. *Accountancy SA*, 38–39.

Muthaiyah, S., Phang, K., & Sembakutti, S. (2021). Bridging skill gaps and creating future ready accounting and finance graduates: an exploratory study. F1000Research, 10.

Ncube, T. R., & Matlala, M. E. (2023). The role of graduate attributes on student success in the higher institution of learning: A case study of Durban University of Technology, South Africa.

Nkhoma, C., Nkhoma, M., Haq, I. U., & Mai, S. (2017). Enhancing students' learning through early class preparation. In *Proceedings of the 20th informing science and information technology education conference (InSITE 2017)* (pp. 85–95). Informing Science Institute.

Osmani, M., Hindi, N., & Weerakkody, V. (2020). Incorporating information communication technology skills in accounting education. *International Journal of Information and Communication Technology Education (IJICTE), 16*(4), 100–110.

Pan, G., & Seow, P. S. (2016). Preparing accounting graduates for digital revolution: A critical review of information technology competencies and skills development. *Journal of Education for Business, 91*(3), 166–175.

Pan, G., Seow, P. S., Goh, C., & Lee, B. H. Z. (2019). Grooming the next generation of accounting professionals for the age of artificial intelligence.

Pauceanu, A. M., Rabie, N., & Moustafa, A. (2020). Employability under the fourth industrial revolution. *Economics & Sociology, 13*(3), 269.

Piaget, J. (2013). *The construction of reality in the child*. Routledge.

Spraakman, G., O'Grady, W., Askarany, D., & Akroyd, C. (2015). Employers' perceptions of information technology competency requirements for management accounting graduates. *Accounting Education, 24*(5), 403–422.

Van der Kleij, F. M., Feskens, R. C., & Eggen, T. J. (2015). Effects of feedback in a computer-based learning environment on students' learning outcomes: A meta-analysis. *Review of Educational Research, 85*(4), 475–511.

Factors Leading to the Failure of Small, Medium and Micro Enterprises in South Africa

Iyabo Emiloju Akinsolu and Minnette Vermaak

Abstract Many have argued that small, medium and micro enterprises (SMMEs) are the main engines of any economy since they raise living standards, lower rates of poverty and create jobs. This study investigates the factors leading to the failure of SMMEs in South Africa. However, SMMEs face a variety of difficulties, such as how their businesses are run and managed, their business plan, external factors that may have an impact on their operations, how they use information communication technology and the Internet, their management skills and abilities, and how the owners define success. The results of the research demonstrate that the issues SMMEs in South Africa experience are distinct from those that SMMEs in other countries may encounter. The research findings showed which few key elements are thought to play a significant role in the success of SMMEs. The commercial success of SMMEs is facilitated by government policies that support SMMEs in their growth objectives and better communication channels between SMMEs and municipalities. To support this commercial engine of the economy, it is crucial to continue developing an SMME programme and build government policies. The conclusion of this study provides valuable insights that if SMMEs do not apply all seven success factors as specified in the questionnaire, it may lead to their failure as SMMEs in South Africa.

Keywords SMMEs failure and success · South Africa · Business · Government policies · Finances

I. E. Akinsolu · M. Vermaak (✉)
University of Johannesburg, Johannesburg, South Africa
e-mail: mvermaak@uj.ac.za

T. Moloi (ed.), *Impacting Society Positively Through Technology in Accounting and Business Processes*, Springer Proceedings in Business and Economics,
https://doi.org/10.1007/978-3-031-84885-8_15

Introduction and Background to the Study

According to the Small Business Act (102 of 1996) of South Africa, small, medium and micro enterprises (SMMEs) are categorised according to the total number of workers they employ, their yearly revenue, their overall assets (excluding their property), as well as the sub-sector they fall under it. A business categorised as a micro entity is believed to employ no more than five employees and generates an R150 000 annual turnover, which is below the VAT registration limit, and these include informally registered businesses such as tuck shops, household companies and taxi businesses. Very small enterprises employ between 10 and 20 employees, less than 50 for a small business and no more than a hundred employees for a medium enterprise.

SMMEs contribute significantly to employment, social development and the growth of the economy (Rungani & Potgieter, 2018), playing a significant role in the eradication of poverty and unemployment (Bvuma & Marnewick, 2020). The SMMEs sector is recognised as one of the key drivers of growth of many economies globally.

For most SMMEs to prosper or stay in business for a lengthy period, both support and resources are needed from various stakeholders the business comes in contact with (Rungani & Potgieter, 2018). The SMME sector accounts for a large percentage of the country's overall gross domestic product and employment statistics. The small business sector across many parts of the globe is notorious for its inability to grow and for its existence for a short period (Rankhumise & Masilo, 2017).

It may be observed that some SMMEs in South Africa operate without adequate business management expertise and implementation of information communications technologies (ICTs) (Bvuma & Marnewick, 2020). The survival of SMMEs depends on their ability to acquire funding successfully for development and long-term sustainability, even though limited access to funding should not be a hindrance to operating or expanding one's business (Balkenhol & Evans-Klock, 2003). It is believed that it is through support and constant supply of resources that these small businesses can thrive (Rungani & Potgieter, 2018).

Research Problem Statement and Research Question

According to Rankhumise and Masilo (2017), SMMEs still struggle to succeed, and they perform poorly, despite their significant contributions to the economy. Studies Business Partners Limited (2019) and Balkenhol and Evans-Klock (2003) have revealed that small business owners believe that funding accessibility is one of the greatest challenges they encounter at the start or while expanding their small businesses. Many small businesses and entrepreneurs have taken on the responsibility of ensuring that contributions are made from the time they conceptualise their businesses until they are operated daily. This emanates from potential financiers' hesitance to take the risk of entering an unclear market; instead, they fund markets with which they are more familiar (Balkenhol & Evans-Klock, 2003). Most of these financiers tend to target specific industrial sectors, business types and viable locations (Business Partners Limited, 2019).

Several SMMEs thrive for only a few months, with a fortunate few lasting longer than a year or two. Consequently, it is imperative to understand the factors contributing to their failure and develop viable solutions aimed at facilitating their sustained prosperity. It is of paramount significance to acknowledge the vital role played by an in-depth understanding of the requisite strategies in facilitating the success of SMMEs, thereby ensuring that business owners are equipped to efficiently manage thriving enterprises.

The primary question addressed by the study is: What are the factors that lead to the failure of small, medium and micro enterprises in South Africa?

The secondary questions include

- What factors hinder SMMEs from achieving success?
- What measures can be implemented to support small business start-ups and expansions?
- What issues prevent SMMEs from achieving long-term success?
- What are the consequences of small business owners' lack of access to SMME funding and development information?

Conducting this study will empower both current and prospective entrepreneurs by offering insights into the challenges and opportunities inherent in SMME operations. The findings will furnish entrepreneurs with valuable knowledge concerning the potential challenges they may encounter when running an SMME, along with strategies to mitigate these challenges and harness the opportunities. The research outcomes could be instrumental in guiding authorities when formulating SMME policies, thereby facilitating the development and sustainability of SMMEs.

Literature Review

Small, Micro and Medium Enterprises (SMMEs)

In the context of South Africa, small businesses are defined by SMMEs as independent entities that fall under one of four categories: micro, very small, small or medium. These entities can operate within any sector or subsector of the economy. An SMME is further defined under the 2003 and 2004 South African National Small Business Amendment Acts as a unique business entity managed by one or more people that must fulfil certain predetermined requirements. The definition of SMMEs as given by the National Small Business Act of South Africa is shown in Table 1.

Table 1 Definition of SMMEs according to the National Small Business Act of South Africa

Enterprise size	Number of employees	Annual turnover in South African rand	Gross asset, excluding fixed property
Medium	Fewer than 100–200, depending on industry	Less than R4 million to R50m, depending on industry	Less than R2 m to R18 m, depending on industry
Small	Fewer than 50	Less than R2m to R25m, depending on industry	Less than R2m to R4.5m, depending on industry
Very small	Fewer than 10–20, depending on industry	Less than R200,000 to R500,000, depending on industry	Less than R150,000 to R500,000, depending on industry
Micro	Fewer than 5	Less than R150,000	Less than R100,000

In defining SMMEs, it is imperative to differentiate between SMMEs and small, micro and medium businesses. The legislative framework and regulatory oversight of South Africa's small, medium and micro enterprises are established by the National Small Business Act (Noko, 2019). The sector is recognised as a major driver of economic growth across numerous global economies. It accounts for a substantial proportion of the country's overall gross domestic product and employment statistics. Regardless of the significant impact of these small enterprises, most remain inactive, and many face the prospect of liquidation (Pule, 2015). In the South African context, a small- and medium-sized enterprise (SMME) is defined as a company with fewer than 200 employees that meets specific turnover requirements depending on the industry.

SMMEs from an African Perspective

Masocha and Charamba (2014) claim that the majority of small firms in Africa continue to operate primarily through traditional means and have not been able to incorporate digital practices into some or all of their business processes. Due to the enormous volume of items being imported, the majority of these small enterprises face intense rivalry, and some of them operate in an environment with inconsistent, ill-regulated and badly integrated regulations. The scarcity of financial opportunities impedes the potential for these small firms to originate and flourish.

Factors Leading SMMEs to Failure in South Africa

SMMEs encounter a multitude of challenges that can hinder their emergence as well as their medium- and long-term existence. A major hurdle faced by these enterprises is accessing adequate funding. Several financial and lending institutions often view SMMEs as risky and unfamiliar, preferring traditional markets as the favourable option of the two (Rankhumise & Masilo, 2017). Before any business or initiative can be established and efforts be made to ensure that it succeeds, one cannot stress the importance of start-up capital enough (Pule, 2015). Without finances, a significant amount of pressure is felt by the business, and it is therefore more likely to not succeed. The following factors may hinder both entrepreneurs and small businesses from acquiring funding from financial and lending institutions. First, the amount of interest these institutions charge on loans, second, the credit information access by the entrepreneurs, the lack of transparency by these institutions, and lastly, the security, or the lack of, as most of the businesses do not have enough resources to secure the business against the amount of money being offered (Pule, 2015).

The geographical setting of the SMME may also affect their likelihood of accessing possible funding opportunities. Those located farther from industrial or prosperous locations are prone to experience no form of financial investment opportunities from both financial and lending institutions (Bvuma & Marnewick, 2020). Compliance with business regulations and statutory law may be an obstacle for SMMEs as they may require small upcoming enterprises to comply using the same yardstick as the one used when gauging larger corporations. Imposing the same punishment, sanctions and penalties as is done when judging larger enterprises. A significant number of entrepreneurs lack the required entrepreneurial skills, relevant management education or the needed mentorship to enable them to see the business develop, grow and survive (Masocha & Charamba, 2014). Mahambehlala (2019) points out that a significant number of entrepreneurs lack basic education, which places them at a significant disadvantage.

Mismanagement of funds is often one of the issues impeding SMMEs from expanding further and others from operating for a longer period. Funds are often mismanaged when owners divert them for personal interests, primarily because many small businesses' financial statements lack formal auditing (Sitharam & Hoque, 2016). Another notable issue is that SMME owners struggle to identify appropriate methods to finance their enterprises and fail to meet the formal requirements for obtaining financing (Rungani & Potgieter, 2018). Enterprise owners' lack of familiarity with technology and its adoption in the business is among the issues impeding SMMEs from reaching their fullest capability (Sitharam & Hoque, 2016).

Research Methodology

Questionnaire Design

This research study used a seven-structured questionnaire as its measurement tool. A printed, self-administered form called a questionnaire is used to gather data for research projects. The goal of the questionnaire is to gather as much information as possible to identify the factors leading to the failure of small, medium and micro enterprises in South Africa. The Chittithaworn et al. (2011) study in Thailand provided the questionnaire used in this investigation.

Factors leading to the failure of small, medium and micro enterprises in South Africa were identified through seven distinct constructs in the questionnaire. The survey was not administered exactly as it was in Thailand but most of the questions relating to South Africa from the questionnaire were used. There were deviations.

The questionnaire's measuring scale was a five-point Likert scale. To minimise the complexity of the survey for those who responded, a scale was employed. Pearson (2010) states that this measure offers a clear perspective on how participants felt about SMMEs. There was no use of a seven-point Likert scale since Fransman (2014) found that a five-point scale improved both the rate and the number of responses while decreasing respondents' frustration. Respondents to this study were asked to rate their level of company success in 42 questions. The Likert scale, which has five points, was created into strongly agree (1), agree (2), neutral (3), disagree (4) and strongly disagree (5).

Additionally, Chittithaworn et al. (2011) created the survey to investigate the impact of the seven constructs on the failure of SMMEs to succeed in enterprise, which is shown below:

Factors affecting the success of the business (five-point Likert scale)

1. Entrepreneur and SMME characteristics
2. Management knowledge and abilities
3. The way of conducting business and cooperation
4. Business strategy
5. External environment
6. The application of information and communications technologies (ICTs) and Internet usage
7. Perceived success measurement

Questionnaire Instrument

The provided data was analysed using the Statistical Package for the Social Sciences (SPSS) program. In this study, SPSS was used to summarise and analyse the data using the subsequent techniques:

- Descriptive analysis
- Validity and reliability analysis using Cronbach's alpha
- Correlation matrix to identify the relationship between variables

Descriptive Analysis

To analyse the collected data, a descriptive analysis method was applied. Descriptive analysis has the advantages of keeping the researcher close to the data and facilitating an understanding of each variable's distribution (Fransman, 2014). Since Section

A's questions deal with the sample's demographics, descriptive statistics were employed to analyse and summarise the data. The description of the respondents is crucial since it describes the qualities of the sample. The mean and standard deviations of the various concepts were also determined using the descriptive statistical approach.

Validity and Reliability of Constructs

Before data analysis, a collection of data's validity and reliability are crucial. Data that exhibits consistency is considered reliable. The internal stability and consistency of the data were assessed using reliability analysis. This component is required to assess whether the research offers a reliable measurement. According to Chittithaworn et al. (2011), Cronbach's alpha coefficient assesses the interaction between items, while the reliability measure gauges the degree to which items within a set have a positive correlation with each other.

Cronbach's alpha values of less than 0.6 are generally considered poor, those of 0.7–0.8 as worthwhile and those of more than 0.8 as satisfactory, according to Chittithaworn et al. (2011). The data is considered more dependable when its reliability coefficient approaches 1.0. The degree of consistency in findings over time is known as reliability.

Cronbach's Alpha Coefficient: Reliability

The degree to which an instrument's measurements are error-free and produce consistent findings is known as its reliability (Fransman, 2014). If research results can be replicated, they are considered reliable (Collis & Hussey, 2009). Kuder and Richardson (1937:6) created it initially for data that could be scored binary (0 or 1), and Cronbach (1951) later generalised it to take into consideration any scoring scheme.

To evaluate a test's or scale's internal reliability, Cronbach's alpha was created (Tavakol & Dennick, 2011, p. 53). Likert scale questionnaires are a good fit for Cronbach's alpha. The degree of homogeneity and reflection of identical constructs among the measuring instrument items is indicated by Cronbach's alpha (Pallant, 2007). The scale of measurement used by Cronbach's alpha coefficient is split halves. Once calculated, Cronbach's alpha yields a result that ranges from one to zero. Zero denotes no internal dependability while one indicates total internal reliability. High levels of internal reliability are generally indicated by values greater than 0.70 (Bell & Bryman, 2007).

Sample and Data Collection

This section will cover the demographic and sample that were used in the research. The intended audience consists of managers or owners who oversee SMME businesses located within the Gauteng province of South Africa. The SMMEs were contacted through the National Financial Literacy Association (NFLA). An organisation based in South Africa research issues about SMMEs and financial literacy. By offering growth and assistance, they assist SMMEs and cooperatives in expanding and turning into sustainable businesses. SMMEs are registered with the organisation. The survey was carried out by sending out the study questionnaire to their registered SMME clients.

Questionnaire Distribution Strategy and Response Rate

	Distributed number	Total received	Response rate
Through hand	175	116	66%
Through Google Form	75	41	55%
Total	*250*	*157*	*63%*

Similar research was carried out by Chittithaworn et al. (2011) in Thailand. A convenience sample ($N = 250$) was given this questionnaire primarily by hand and through Google Form. Within the boundaries of the Gauteng province, 157 respondents provided the data. 41 responses were obtained through Google Form, while 116 copies were manually obtained by the researcher from the respondents.

Due to the necessity of distributing and gathering questionnaires by hand in order to ensure adequate number of responses, the data collection process took place over the course of 4 months. Both the data's capture and processing came after the data gathering procedure.

The University of Johannesburg's Statistical Consultation Services (Statkon) received the questionnaires once data collecting was finished. Utilising the Statistical Package for the Social Sciences (SPSS), the data was captured, and statistical analysis was performed.

The statistical examination of the data, which was recorded numerically, enabled the formation of facts and the identification of patterns.

Analysis of Results

This section presents and analyses the theoretical and empirical investigation results. Along with the presentation and analysis of the processed data, the statistical processing of the obtained data is covered. In light of the research questions and the objective of determining the factors leading to the failure of small, medium and micro enterprises in South Africa, the results are presented, examined and analysed. The data were analysed and interpreted using statistical techniques such as frequency distribution, factors analysis and percentages.

Demographic, Characteristics and Profile of Respondents

According to the statistics, the majority of respondents were female, between the ages of 26 and 45, with matriculation or a trade certificate being the least degree of education. Some respondents held multiple qualifications. Self-employed individuals or business owners have a minimum of 1–5 years of experience and have at least 1–5 employees. The responses provide a well-aligned representation of the target demographic based on the discussion (Table 2).

Questions B1, B3 and B4 lie between strongly agree and agree according to the mean table, B2 tends towards agree while B5 is between agree and neutral. According to this outcome, business owners largely possess strong administrative, decision-making and communication abilities in addition to strong leadership qualities. The median for B2 shows that half of the respondents strongly agree to agree while the remaining half of the respondents agree to strongly agree. The maximum option picked in B2 is disagreed as shown in Table 3. The median for B5 indicates neutral. This result shows that the entrepreneurial skills characteristic of SMMEs is one of the factors that lead to the success of a business or enterprise. This indicates that, without the entrepreneurial skill and characteristics, a business will fail to survive.

Table 4 shows that most business owners strongly agree with questions B6-B10 indicating their managerial knowledge and competence to operate a business. This section demonstrates that they possess the necessary financial, human and marketing knowledge to run the company and make it survive. From the mean result above, it shows that B6, B8 and B9 tend to agree, while B7 and B10 agreed that this is one of the factors affecting the success of a business.

Table 5 shows that the majority of the business owners are aware of the way their business should be conducted as seen in questions B11–B17. As the owner, they are aware of public and private consultation support which is helpful on all important matters affecting the operation of their business. The majority of the owners are registered with the relevant company registration authority like South African Revenue Services (SARS), Continuous Improvement Programme (CIP), Small Business Corporation (SBC) or Companies and Intellectual Property Commission (CIPC). The mean result shows that the business owners agree with the question, which indicates that the conduct of their businesses and corporations is part of the factors affecting the success of a business.

Sections B18–B22 from Table 6 represent the response of business owner in terms of business strategy. Business owners strongly agree that a business plan was developed to assist them in running their business but agree that all the policies

Table 2 Demographic, characteristics and profile of respondents

	Frequency	Valid percentage
Section A: demographics		
Gender		
Male	76	48.4
Female	78	49.7
Other	3	1.9
Age		
18–25	14	8.9
26–35	54	34.4
36–45	64	40.8
46–55	22	14.0
56 and older	3	1.9
Qualification obtained		
Trade certificate	25	13.2
Matric	46	25.9
Diploma	39	20.6
Degree	37	19.6
Honours degree	35	18.5
PhD	4	2.1
Industry		
Manufacturing, engineering and fabrication	21	13.4
Trade and supply	50	31.8
Transportation	5	3.2
Construction	13	8.3
e-commerce	5	3.2
Training and development	19	12.1
Others	44	28.0
Number of years in business		
Less than 5 years	85	54.1
Between 5 and 10 years	43	27.4
Between 10 and 15 years	17	10.8
More than 15 years	12	7.6
Number of workers the SMMEs employ		
Between 1 and 5	97	61.8
Between 6 and 10	31	19.7
Between 11 and 20	13	8.3
Between 21 and 50	12	7.6
Between 51 and 100	4	2.5

implemented in their business were well-thought and thoroughly planned. The mean result shows that the majority of the business owners agree to their business strategy in running their business and that it is one of the factors affecting the success of their business.

Table 3 Factors affecting the success of the business

Questions	Strongly agree	Agree	Neutral	Disagree	Strongly disagree
B1	54.8%	40.1%	3.2%	0.0%	1.9%
B2	42.7%	33.1%	15.3%	8.9%	0.0%
B3	52.9%	38.2%	2.5%	4.5%	1.9%
B4	53.5%	37.6%	3.2%	5.7%	0.0%
B5	27.4%	22.3%	25.5%	22.3%	2.5%

Table 4 Management knowledge and abilities

Questions	Strongly agree	Agree	Neutral	Disagree	Strongly disagree
B6	38.2%	36.9%	15.3%	9.6%	0.0%
B7	35.7%	23.6%	28.7%	10.8%	1.3%
B8	42.0%	33.8%	18.5%	4.5%	1.3%
B9	40.1%	38.9%	12.7%	6.4%	1.9%
B10	41.4%	27.4%	17.2%	11.5%	2.5%

Table 5 The way of conducting business and cooperation

Question	Strongly agree	Agree	Neutral	Disagree	Strongly disagree
B11	44.6%	29.3%	20.4%	5.7%	0.0%
B12	45.9%	31.2%	8.9%	5.1%	8.9%
B13	36.3%	25.5%	20.4%	15.3%	2.5%
B14	38.9%	31.8%	22.3%	5.7%	1.3%
B15	38.2%	36.3%	14.0%	11.5%	0.0%
B16	38.2%	28.7%	24.2%	7.0%	1.9%
B17	43.3%	31.2%	14.0%	9.6%	1.9%

Table 7 indicates the external environment of a business, in terms of government support, compliance and permit needed for the business to be in operation. The majority of business owners have a reliable business network that is very helpful in running their businesses, they agree that colleagues and friends support their business, and their business complies with all the stipulated statutory small business regulations in South Africa. The mean result shows that most business owners agree that the external environment affects the success of their business while few are neutral, especially when it comes to the government supporting their business.

Most business owners strongly agree that the application of information and communications technologies (ICTs) and Internet usage is one of the elements boosting the prosperity of SMMEs in South Africa as shown in Table 8. This section shows that entrepreneurs are aware of disruptions by the emerging technologies of 4IR, Blockchain and FinTech, most of the owners are interested in learning about them and knowing the impact of this technology on their businesses. The mean result shows that most business owners strongly agree to the use of ICTs in running the operation of their business, and it also contributes to the factors affecting the success of a business as shown in Table 8.

Table 6 Business strategy

Question	Strongly agree	Agree	Neutral	Disagree	Strongly disagree
B18	36.9%	31.8%	19.1%	10.8%	1.3%
B19	26.1%	38.2%	27.4%	5.1%	3.2%
B20	24.8%	42.7%	19.7%	12.7%	0.0%
B21	36.3%	41.4%	13.4%	7.0%	1.9%
B22	29.3%	44.6%	19.1%	5.1%	1.9%

Table 7 External environment

Question	Strongly agree	Agree	Neutral	Disagree	Strongly disagree
B23	41.4%	38.2%	12.7%	4.5%	3.2%
B24	34.4%	49.0%	11.5%	3.2%	1.9%
B25	34.4%	40.8%	12.7%	10.2%	1.9%
B26	10.2%	35.0%	17.8%	14.6%	22.3%
B27	29.3%	18.5%	17.8%	17.2%	17.2%
B28	30.6%	35.0%	17.8%	8.3%	8.3%
B29	36.3%	40.8%	8.9%	6.4%	7.6%

Table 8 The application of information and communications technologies (ICTs) and Internet usage

Question	Strongly agree	Agree	Neutral	Disagree	Strongly disagree
B30	46.5%	29.9%	11.5%	7.0%	5.1%
B31	38.2%	35.7%	11.5%	7.0%	7.6%
B32	34.4%	24.2%	20.4%	13.4%	7.6%
B33	38.2%	29.3%	19.1%	7.6%	5.7%

This section shows that most of the business owners are satisfied with the way their business is operated and are satisfied with the rate at which their business is growing as shown in Table 9. The entrepreneur strongly agrees with the perceived success measurement in this section. The mean result shows that most of the business owners agree to the perceived success measurement as shown in Table 9.

Table 10 shows the overall result of the respondents for all the factors. The result shows that all the factors are proxies for the factors leading to the failure of the small, medium and micro enterprises in South Africa as seen from each result above. A large proportion of the respondents agreed that the factors affecting the success of the business are listed in Section B and success can be perceived with each factor listed in Section C. This implies that, if any of the factors listed are not being utilised, implemented and used in business, it will lead to the failure of the business. For any business to succeed, all the factors in Section B need to be utilised.

Table 9 Perceived success measurement

Question	Strongly agree	Agree	Neutral	Disagree	Strongly disagree
C1	40.1%	26.1%	17.8%	12.7%	3.2%
C2	36.9%	28.0%	19.1%	10.8%	5.1%
C3	40.8%	42.0%	10.2%	2.5%	4.5%
C4	31.8%	26.1%	22.9%	15.3%	3.8%
C5	32.5%	35.0%	19.7%	8.3%	4.5%
C6	31.8%	45.2%	14.6%	3.8%	4.5%
C7	42.7%	45.9%	5.7%	4.5%	1.3%
C8	26.8%	48.4%	17.2%	6.4%	1.3%
C9	32.5%	36.5%	17.8%	8.3%	4.5%

Table 10 Overall descriptive statistics

	N				Std.		
Statistics	Valid	Missing	Mean	Median	deviation	Minimum	Maximum
Entrepreneur and SMME characteristics	157	0	1.8408	1.8000	0.6800	1.00	4.20
Management knowledge and abilities	157	0	2.0025	2.0000	0.8127	1.00	3.60
The way of conducting business and cooperation	157	0	2.0118	2.0000	0.8367	1.00	4.43
Business strategy	157	0	2.1032	2.0000	0.7724	1.00	4.40
External environment	157	0	2.2839	2.1429	0.8188	1.00	4.14
The application of information and communication technologies (ICTs) and Internet usage	157	0	2.1338	2.0000	1.0344	1.00	5.00
Perceived success	157	0	2.0800	2.0000	0.85761	1.00	4.78

Cronbach's Alpha Coefficient: Reliability

According to Bell & Bryman, (2007), the value of Cronbach's alpha can be estimated using the following general rule of thumb:

- More than 0.9 is an indicator of excellent reliability
- More than 0.8 is an indicator of good reliability
- More than 0.7 is an indication of acceptable reliability
- Less than 0.7 results in questionable and unacceptable reliability measures

Six of the factors showed an excellent reliability measurement, one construct in Section B indicated an acceptable degree of dependability and Section C indicated a good reliability measurement, based on the data in Tables 11 and 12 and the rule of thumb indication. This shows that every dimension produced reliable findings, meaning that they can all be replicated with a reasonable chance of getting the same outcomes later on.

Table 11 Cronbach's alpha coefficient for Section B

Factor name	Number of items in the questionnaire	Cronbach's alpha coefficient	Cronbach's alpha rating
Entrepreneur and SMME characteristics	5	0.783	Acceptable
Management knowledge and abilities	5	0.856	Good
The way of conducting business and cooperation	7	0.896	Good
Business strategy	5	0.845	Good
External environment	7	0.823	Good
The application of information and communications technologies (ICTs) and Internet usage	4	0.963	Good

Table 12 Cronbach's alpha coefficient for Section C

Factor name	N of items in the questionnaire	Cronbach's alpha	Cronbach's alpha rating
Perceived business success	9	0.932	Good

First-Order Factor Analysis for Sections B and C

Correlation Matrix for Sections B and C

The instrument used in validating factor analysis is a correlation matrix. For the factor matrix to be conducted, the majority of the items must be greater than 0.3, and if the correlation of most items is less than 0.3, the factor analysis will not be conducted. The research results show that most of the items are above 0.3, which states that the items are highly correlated; therefore, factor analysis can be conducted. This result shows that there is a strong relationship between the factors used in this study.

Rotated Factor Matrix for Sections B and C

The factor transformation matrix describes the specific rotation applied to your factor solution. This matrix is used to compute the rotated factor matrix from the original (unrotated) factor matrix. Smaller off-diagonal elements correspond to smaller rotations. Larger off-diagonal elements correspond to larger rotations. The idea of rotation is to reduce the number of factors on which the variables under investigation have high loadings. Rotation does not change anything but makes the interpretation of the analysis easier.

Table 13 Correlation matrix for Section B

Correlation matrix	Factor 1	Factor 2	Factor 3	Factor 4	Factor 5	Factor 6
Factor 1	1.000	0.699	0.710	0.575	0.724	0.525
Factor 2	0.699	1.000	0.705	0.655	0.573	0.495
Factor 3	0.710	0.705	1.000	0.622	0.540	0.370
Factor 4	0.575	0.655	0.622	1.000	0.536	0.577
Factor 5	0.724	0.573	0.540	0.536	1.000	0.302
Factor 6	0.525	0.495	0.370	0.577	0.302	1.000

Second-Order Factor Analysis for Sections B and C

This is taking the overall six factors and grouping them to see if the factors are more like one another.

Below are the names of the six factors generated by the rotated factor matrix:

Factor 1: measuring performances, competence and support
Factor 2: measuring human resources and innovation
Factor 3: measuring the application of information and communications technologies (ICTs) and Internet usage
Factor 4: measuring business compliances
Factor 5: measuring skills
Factor 6: measuring business registration with the government bodies

Table 13 shows that all the factors are greater than 0.3, which implies that the factor analysis can be conducted.

Summary of the Findings and Conclusion

The study's findings show that the problems small, medium and micro enterprises (SMMEs) in South Africa confront are unique and may vary significantly from those faced by SMMEs in other nations.

In this study, a descriptive research design was adopted. Over the course of 4 months, 157 SMMEs in South Africa answered a total of 250 questionnaires sent by hand and via Google Forms. The study data that was gathered was analysed using the Statistical Package for Social Sciences (SPSS).

Following a thorough examination of the empirical data, it was determined that the seven characteristics were found to be directly correlated with the SMMEs that were chosen and their perceived level of company performance. According to the study, a business's ability to succeed in South Africa is influenced by the elements listed in Section B. The respondents demonstrate that SMMEs need entrepreneurial abilities or traits to succeed in business. It implies that to run their firm an entrepreneur has to possess strong leadership, dependable managerial, decision-making and communication skills. Without these attributes, the company may not function effectively, which could result in its failure.

A business cannot function or survive if it does not have the necessary financial, personnel or marketing resources, as demonstrated by the respondents. The study's conclusions have shown that, as Masocha and Charamba (2014) have shown, one of the major factors determining an SMME's success or failure in South Africa is its management competencies. The owners of SMMEs require education, skill development and training. This will lead to the growth and expansion of the company.

According to respondents, the SMMEs comply with all laws and regulations enforced by the South African government. The majority of the owners of these businesses are registered with the appropriate company registration authority, such as SARS, CIPC, SBC or CIPRO. This suggests that among the elements influencing a business's success are how it runs its business and how well it cooperates.

The results of business strategy for SMMEs in South Africa show that business owners firmly concur that a key factor in their company's success was the business plan, projections and policies that were created to support them. The external environment of business explained the element that the participants did not indicate in their response to government support for their business. One of the main concerns that has to be investigated more thoroughly and given more attention by the government is this one. Additionally, most business owners have a solid support system of friends and family who help them run their companies.

One of the elements that contributes to a successful business is the application of information and communications technologies (ICTs) and Internet usage. Sitharam and Hoque (2016) discussed how SMMEs' inability to use technology prevented them from reaching their full potential. It is impossible to overstate how important technology is to a business; it makes operations easier to manage. Respondents believed that their SMMEs were profitable, growing and providing services to clients in a way they could break even.

Finally, government policies that support small, medium and micro enterprises (SMMEs) in their growth aspirations and improved lines of communication between SMMEs and municipalities help foster the business success of SMMEs. In terms of funding and lending, the government should consider providing more grants to the owners of SMMEs, which would be easier to obtain; moreover, the interest rates and credit information available to SMMEs should be reviewed and addressed.

If SMMEs apply the seven elements listed in the questionnaire, this study's conclusion offers a list of things that must be implemented and adhered to if the SMMEs want to be successful and not be another failing organisation. This will promote the growth and sustainability of small, medium and micro enterprises in the settings if it applies to all SMMEs.

References

Balkenhol, B., & Evans-Klock, C. (2003). Private equity and capitalisation of SMMEs in South Africa: Quo Vadis? *Ebony Consulting International, 34*, 1–27.
Bell, E. & Bryman, A. (2007). The ethics of management research: an exploratory content analysis. *British journal of management, 18*(1), 63–77.
Business Partners Limited. (2019). *South African small, medium, and micro enterprise (SMME) financiers*. Business Partners Limited and the SME Toolkit South Africa.
Bvuma, S., & Marnewick, C. (2020). Sustainable livelihoods of township small, medium and micro enterprises towards growth and development. *Sustainability, 12*(3149), 1–17.
Chittithaworn, C. C., Islam, A., Keawchana, T., & Yusuf, D. H. M. (2011). Factors affecting business success of small & medium enterprises (SMEs) in Thailand. *Journal on Asian Social Science, 7*(5), 180–190.
Collis, J., & Hussey, R. (2009). *Business research: A practical guide for undergraduate and postgraduate students* (3rd ed.). Palgrave Macmillan.
Cronbach, L. J. (1951). Coefficient alpha and the internal structure of tests. *Psychometrika, 16*(3), 297–334.
Fransman, C. (2014). *Assessing perceptions of public servants' trust in leadership*. MBA dissertation, Northwest University.
Kuder, G. F., & Richardson, M. W. (1937). The theory of estimation of test reliability. *Psychmetrika, 2*, 151–160.
Mahambehlala, T. (2019). *Small, medium and micro enterprise development challenges in a post-apartheid South Africa: Lessons learnt*. University of Western Cape.
Masocha, R., & Charamba, M. (2014). Challenges and key success factors of african descent foreign-owned SMES in the Eastern Cape Province of South Africa: A case of selected towns. *Mediterranean Journal of Social Sciences, 5*(04), 59–68.
Noko, I. L. (2019). *SMME funding in South Africa*. Johannesburg.
Pallant, J. (2007). *SPSS survival manual: A step-by-step guide to data analysis using SPSS for windows* (3rd ed.). McGraw Hill Open University Press.
Pearson. (2010). Selecting measuring instruments. http://wps.prenhall.com/chet_airasian_edresearch_8/38/9866/2525943.cw/index.html. Accessed 12 Sept 2023.
Pule, T. M. (2015). *Analysis of success factors for women owned small businesses in Mahikeng, North-West Province*. North-West University.
Rankhumise, E. M., & Masilo, K. H. (2017). The effect of government support on the success of small and medium enterprises: A comparative study between South Africa and China. *Journal of Economics and Behavioural Studies, 9*(6), 166–173.
Rungani, E. C., & Potgieter, M. (2018). The impact of financial support on the success of small, medium and micro enterprises in the Eastern Cape province. *Acta Commercii - Independent Research Journal in the Management Sciences, 18*(1), 1–12.
Sitharam, S., & Hoque, M. (2016). Factors affecting the performance of small and medium enterprises in KwaZulu-Natal, South Africa. *Problems and Perspectives in Management, 14*(2–2), 277–288.
Tavakol, M., & Dennick, R. (2011). Making sense of Cronbach's alpha. *International Journal of Medical Education, 2*, 53.

An Investigation of the Zombie Firms on Zimbabwe Stock Exchange in the Fourth Industrial Revolution

Mufaro Dzingirai

Abstract In a post-COVID-19 era, the issue of underperformance and unproductive firms is gaining momentum in the corporate world. This implies that business resilience, continuity, and transformation are at the center of economic sustenance in the Fourth Industrial Revolution. Interestingly, the COVID-19 pandemic has augmented the adoption of the "new normal" whereby companies migrated to online business supported by the Fourth Industrial Revolution. Even though business resilience, continuity, and transformation are topical issues in both developed and developing countries, it is troublesome to observe that the issue of zombie firms has been largely neglected in the post-COVID-19 epoch, especially in the context of African economies. Therefore, this study aims to investigate the zombie firms on the Zimbabwe Stock Exchange in the current Fourth Industrial Revolution. The results revealed five negative effects of zombie firms, namely, weakening economic status of the country, increasing dumping of foreign products, allocative inefficiency, widening social inequality gap, and fostering zombie lending. These results have strong implications for policymakers when formulating business rehabilitation policies, and for turnaround strategies when conducting corporate rescue as well as for financial institutions when dealing with zombie lending. It is concluded that an in-depth understanding of zombie firms listed on ZSE can assist in promoting economic resilience in Zimbabwe.

Keywords Business Resilience · Zombie Firms · Zombie Lending · Financial Distress Prediction

---

M. Dzingirai (✉)
Midlands State University, Gweru, Zimbabwe
e-mail: dzingiraim@staff.msu.ac.zw

T. Moloi (ed.), *Impacting Society Positively Through Technology in Accounting and Business Processes*, Springer Proceedings in Business and Economics,
https://doi.org/10.1007/978-3-031-84885-8_16

Introduction

In recent years, it is a fact that zombie firms have increased at an unprecedented rate since 1990 (1.5%) to approximately 7% in 2020 owing to unusual market dynamism (Altman et al., 2024). For more than three decades and based on several reported cases of bankruptcy and liquidation of notable companies such as Enron (the United States), WorldCom, Parmalat (Italy), Nortel (Canada), Onetel (Australia), and ZABG (Zimbabwe), a lot of economics, management, and finance scholars appear to be focusing on these zombie firms and their determinants. According to Altman et al. (2024), a zombie firm refers to an insolvent organization that survives with assistance from investors, financial institutions, or the government during turbulent market conditions. With this definition in mind, practitioners, policymakers, media, and academics are increasingly interested in zombie firms, especially in the post-COVID-19 epoch. Noticeably, the emergence of the COVID-19 crisis negatively impacted the continuity and resilience of both small and big organizations that worsened the operational challenges of firms (Altman et al., 2024; Dzingirai, Chagwesha, & Mudzurandende, 2021; Dzingirai & Ndava, 2021; Dzingirai, Tshuma, & Sikomwe, 2021; Mhlanga & Dzingirai, 2024; Nehrebecki, 2023). The distressed firms are struggling to survive without the support from government and financial institutions. The financial support from these institutions to distressed firms leads to zombie lending. Nonetheless, scant attention has been paid to zombie firms in the post-COVID-19 era, especially in African countries.

While there is evidence of the occurrence of zombie firms in developed countries such as the United States, the United Kingdom, and Japan, the understanding of zombie firms as a concept is very limited. Although the research on zombie firms is evolving, evidence from developing countries is scarce in the post-COVID-19 era, which necessitates empirical assessment of zombie firms. This suggests that the research on zombie enterprises is not increasing as it should, meaning that it is an under-researched field with enormous promise for scholars in developing countries. Going forward, in the case of Japan, the real estate sector witnessed an upsurge in zombie firms after the Global Financial Crisis (Campello & Schneider, 2024). This has been a result of Zombie lending whereby Japanese banks were lending to distressed firms. More interestingly, Hong et al. (2021) documented that the COVID-19 pandemic has increased the existence of zombie firms in Japan as these firms are associated with low debt capacity, which hinders the effectiveness of monetary policy. As a result, zombie firms are leading to low employment growth, investment, and growth of productivity. In the same vein, Goto and Wilbur (2019) underscored that Japan experienced a growth in the number of zombie firms in the context of small and medium enterprises (SMEs).

In India, one of the developing economies, Chari et al. (2022) expressed that zombie firms are increasing at an industrial scale indicating a balance sheet problem. In India, about 40% of nonfinancial companies in India are associated with an interest coverage ratio of less than 1 (Chari et al., 2022). This implies that they could not pay their obligations as they came due. More worryingly, the interest coverage ratio in India decreased from 6.92 to 3.38 in 2007 and 2015, respectively. It has been observed that Indian zombie banks emerged owing to forbearance proxies by the central bank (Chari et al., 2022).

Despite the emergence of the Fourth Industrial Revolution (4IR) which is largely associated with improved efficiency and effectiveness owing to the usage of artificial intelligence and robots, it is quite disturbing to observe that zombie firms are dominating the Zimbabwean economy as evidenced by weak balance sheets. In this regard, Nyoni (2024) documented that Zimbabwe is dominated by zombified companies associated with limited cash flows, moribund prospects, and limited market share. These uncompetitive survivors are a grand challenge to productivity growth in the country. In the same vein, the Zimbabwe Mail (2024) documented that zombie firms characterized the Zimbabwean economy due to chaotic growth cycles in the country. Unfortunately, not much is known concerning the zombie firms in developing countries, especially in Zimbabwe, during the post-COVID-19 epoch. To bridge this significant knowledge gap, this study aims to investigate the zombie firms on the Zimbabwe Stock Exchange (ZSE) in the current Fourth Industrial Revolution.

Theoretical Framework

This study aimed at investigating the zombie firms on the Zimbabwe Stock Exchange in the current Fourth Industrial Revolution was underpinned by the Technology Acceptance Model (TAM) as the theoretical lens as discussed below.

Technology Acceptance Model (TAM)

This current study borrows the TAM from the information systems discipline and then applies it to economics and finance fields with a special focus on zombie firms. Accordingly, this study extends the application of TAM to the unique context of zombie firms. With the adoption of TAM, the researcher argued that zombie firms emerged owing to failure to adopt advanced technologies like artificial intelligence and robots in the 4IR, which can boost efficiency and effectiveness. The TAM was proposed by Davis (1986) as a theoretical perspective to understanding how organizations accept technology. More interestingly, Davis (1989) underscored that perceived ease of use, perceived usefulness, and user acceptance are key tenets of TAM. With this in mind, Gonzalez (2024) adopted the TAM in debunking the difference between technology adopters and nonusers of technology. This implies that different organizations have different appetites for technology, which then speaks to why they perform differently in the same operating environment. Put simply, it is widely accepted that the TAM can be employed in predicting user behavior and acceptance of new technology such as intelligent information technology (Noor, 2024; Park et al., 2022). In this respect, the adoption of artificial intelligence and robots by firms can be deeply understood with the aid of the TAM. In the same vein, Saif et al. (2024) underscored that TAM can be applied to understanding advanced technologies that are associated with the 4IR.

Drivers of Zombie Firms in Africa

The drivers of zombie firms worldwide can be categorized into two mutually exclusive groups: internal and external drivers. The internal drivers of zombie firms are company-specific, which implies that they vary from one zombie firm to another depending on the quality of the management team. On the other hand, external drivers refer to unconducive macro-factors and market conditions that threaten the existence of zombie firms. These factors are reported in Table 1.

Historical Development of Zombie Firms in Zimbabwe

The historical development of zombie firms can be traced back to November 14, 1997, which is widely known as the "Black Friday." Black Friday created an unconducive economic environment for companies, especially the manufacturing sector. The skyrocketing of prices was witnessed during the early 2000s. This worrisome development negatively affected the operational viability of many companies in Zimbabwe. Zimbabwe registered a very high inflation rate of 79.6 million percent in November 2008 (Hanke & Kwok, 2009). By early 2009, the Zimbabwean

Table 1 Internal and external drivers of zombie firms

Internal drivers	External drivers
Autocratic leadership	Stiff competition
Adopting red ocean strategy	Technophobia
Bureaucratic organizational structure	Policy inconsistency
High labor turnover	Change in customer preferences and taste
Poor investment and risk management	Zombie lending
Unproductive organizational politics	Tight regulatory framework
Lack of diversity	Political unrest
Lack of innovation	Globalization
Hierarchy culture	Liquidity crisis

Source: Author's compilation.

government officialized the multicurrency regime. Despite the existence of this positive economic development, many manufacturing companies were struggling as they were financially distressed (Dzingirai & Baporikar, 2022a).

In an effort to assist these zombie firms, the Zimbabwean government created the Zimbabwe Asset Management Corporation (ZAMCO) in 2014 whereby the Reserve Bank of Zimbabwe (RBZ) was dealing with the issue of an upsurge in nonperforming loans (NPLs). This development extended the lifespan of zombie firms in Zimbabwe since ZAMCO was the life support for zombification on the Zimbabwe Stock Exchange (Matsika, 2020). According to Guma (2023), "Zamco was set up in 2014 by the Reserve Bank of Zimbabwe (RBZ) to resolve the problem of excess non-performing loans (NPLs) of banking institutions in Zimbabwe through acquiring, restructuring, and disposal of NPLs." The zombie firms that benefited from ZAMCO as uncompetitive survivors include Star Africa Corporation and Cottco Holdings. There are some zombie firms on the Zimbabwe Stock Exchange like General Beltings, Zeco, Border Timbers, and MedTech (Matsika, 2020).

A typical case of a zombie company that benefited from ZAMCO is Turnall Holdings (Matsika, 2020). This is a construction company in Zimbabwe that is struggling to provide construction materials as it faces fierce competition from Chinese companies. Despite the fact that there is a high demand for construction materials in Zimbabwe, Turnall Holdings is facing cutthroat competition when it comes to its concrete piping products. This implies that there is a dire need for mechanization and retooling in an effort to augment competitiveness and efficiencies at Turnal Holdings.

Going forward, with low interest rates during the multicurrency era, zombie firms survived since they were able to borrow from the banks in order to fund their unproductive operations (Magweva, 2023). Moreover, the conversion of US$ debts to Zimbabwean dollars was also life support for zombie firms in Zimbabwe (Matsika, 2020). More interestingly, the upsurge in corporate governance scandals in Zimbabwe has also increased the number of zombie firms in Zimbabwe. Corruption and nepotism are cancerous to the viability of firms, especially during economic turmoil. There are many corruption cases that led to the technical insolvency of many manufacturing companies in Zimbabwe. More recently, the emergence of the unprecedented crisis that is COVID-19 has led exponential increase in zombie firms (Matsika, 2020). COVID-19 negatively affected the operational activities of both small and big companies, which brought about an existential threat.

Research Methodology

This study adopted a descriptive research design in an effort to determine the effects of zombie firms. It is widely accepted that descriptive research can be employed when the researcher is interested in gaining an in-depth understanding of a phenomenon (Saunders et al., 2019). More interestingly, descriptive research design does not apply when the researcher is not interested in manipulating variables but when aiming to provide a picture of a phenomenon in its natural setting (Bell et al., 2022; Creswell & Creswell, 2018). With this in mind, this study targeted zombie firms listed on the Zimbabwe Stock Exchange. In this study, a zombie firm was defined as a company with an interest coverage of less than 1 over 2 years. The interest coverage ratio can be computed by dividing earnings before interest and taxes (EBIT) by interest payments. Secondary data sources from Google Scholar, Web of Science, Scopus database, and organizational sources were used to gather data. Collected data was analyzed using thematic analysis according to the steps suggested by Braun and Clarke (2006). To ensure data quality, error-proof data collection methods and triangulation of data sources were employed in this study.

Results and Discussion

After presenting the research methodology, this section covers the results and discussion. Following data analysis, a myriad of the effects of zombie firms on the Zimbabwean economy emerged. The themes that emerged from this study are captured and discussed as follows.

Theme 1: Weaken Economic Status

It emerged that zombie firms weaken economic status in the sense that zombie firms negatively affect aggregated productivity in the economy. With an understanding that zombie firms are uncompetitive survivors, it is not surprising to observe that they negatively affect capacity utilization. In the Zimbabwean context, capacity utilization exponentially declined owing to the upsurge in zombie firms in the manufacturing sector since 2000. It is within this context that zombie firms accelerated deindustrialization in the Zimbabwean economy whereby Bulawayo, which is widely accepted as the industrial hub in Zimbabwe, was the most negatively affected area (Dzingirai & Baporikar, 2022a; Magidi, 2023; Mbira, 2015; Mlambo, 2017). This is in line with the arguments of Becker and Ivashina (2021) who underscored that bank lending to unviable companies prolongs and deepens economic crises. Moreover, extant literature demonstrated that the presence of zombie firms decreases national aggregated productivity (Amundsen et al., 2023).

Theme 2: Increase Competition and Dumping of Foreign Products

Zombie firms as uncompetitive survivors have increased competition when it comes to limited resources. This implies that the economy associated with a plethora of zombie companies is vulnerable to international competition. The international competition can promote the dumping of products since the local zombie firms struggle to survive. This is true in the Zimbabwean context whereby "China is flooding Africa with its products. This phenomenon is referred to by various scholars and commentators as the "dumping" of cheap manufactured goods on the continent. Use terms such as "zhing-zhongs" in Zimbabwe" (Legodi, 2024). Moreover, Chingono (2021) underscored that "But the Zimbabwean authorities continue to sit back and enjoy the tag "South Africa's supermarket." According to industrialist Busisa Moyo, "Zimbabwe imports 75% of raw materials, finished products, and fuel from South Africa." In this respect, it is clear that the existence of many unproductive firms increases competition and dumping of foreign products into the Zimbabwean market.

Theme 3: Lead to Allocative Inefficiency

Given the fact that many manufacturing companies in Zimbabwe are financially distressed, it is not surprising that zombie lending can lead to allocative inefficiency. For example, "Listed timber producer, Border Timbers Limited, has widened its loss to ZWL$3.2bn in the 12 months to June 30, 2021 from ZWL$487m owing to adverse effects of Covid-19 pandemic. The development means the future of the business operations remain uncertain" (Business Times, 2021). Zombie firms are unproductive survivors that can lead to allocative inefficiency (Becker & Ivashina, 2021). Moreover, Amundsen et al. (2023) expressed that zombie companies impede the reallocation of scarce resources, which constrains the productivity of healthy firms. In the same vein, Rashid et al. (2022) conducted a study in Pakistan and found that zombie companies negatively affected industrial growth owing to high industrial indebtedness.

Theme 4: Widen the Social Inequality Gap

In an attempt to continue to survive the existential threat, zombie firms can engage in a retrenchment strategy. This strategy of downsizing is associated with a decrease in disposable income for the retrenched employees. As such, this widens the social inequality gap in the country. Notably, this can go a long way in straining the social safety nets. For instance, zombie firms can cut employment and investment in the face of a liquidity crisis (Albuquerque & Mao, 2023; Dzingirai & Baporikar, 2022b, 2023).

Theme 5: Lead to Zombie Lending

With an exponential increase in zombie firms, financial institutions can lend money to unproductive firms. This state of affairs implies that limited financial resources are given to unviable firms, which is known as zombie lending. According to Guma (2023), "Zamco was set up in 2014 by the Reserve Bank of Zimbabwe (RBZ) to resolve the problem of excess non-performing loans (NPLs) of banking institutions in Zimbabwe through acquiring, restructuring and disposal of NPLs." This state of affairs promoted zombie lending in Zimbabwe. Notably, Albuquerque and Mao (2023) defined zombie lending as a situation whereby banks are lending to unproductive and inviable firms, which is associated with an increase in nonperforming loans. With this in mind, there are many cases in Zimbabwe whereby many manufacturing firms have been facing loan defaults for the past three decades. This is buttressed by misaligned bank incentives, which support the survival of zombie firms despite the fact that they are insolvent.

Implications of the Study

There is a myriad of theoretical, practical, and policy implications linked to this study on zombie firms within the context of Zimbabwe. Firstly, theoretical implications emanate from extending the applicability of TAM to the unique context of zombie firms. This confirms that the author borrowed the TAM from the field of information systems and argued that zombie firms emerged owing to the failure to adopt advanced technologies like artificial intelligence and robots in the Fourth Industrial Revolution, which can boost efficiency and effectiveness.

Secondly, the results from the current study on zombie firms have several practical implications for the management of zombie firms, financial institutions, and manufacturing firms. In this regard, the management of zombie firms can utilize the findings in this study to advance their understanding of the drivers and effects of zombie firms. This could assist in formulating turnaround strategies for zombie firms in an economic constraint situation. More interestingly, this study helps the managers of financial institutions in dealing with zombie lending. As it emerged that zombie lending promotes zombie firms, strong financial institutions could detect and avoid zombie lending in Zimbabwe. This could assist in channeling limited financial resources toward productive, viable, and healthy firms.

Thirdly, policy implications can be derived from the current study in the sense that this study can help the government of Zimbabwe understand the negative effects of providing financial assistance to zombie firms. Moreover, the RBZ as the policy maker in the financial sector should formulate robust policies to do away with zombie lending in Zimbabwe. Interestingly, the Confederation of Zimbabwe Industries should formulate a policy that supports financial lending to viable and productive firms in Zimbabwe.

Areas for Further Research

This study opened doors for further research related to zombie firms. In this respect, this study focused on Zimbabwe only. Consequently, further research on zombie firms paying particular attention to comparative studies between a developing and developed country is welcomed. This could advance our understanding of zombie firms by taking into account some external factors like the economy, social, and political environment. More interestingly, further research should focus on the role of artificial intelligence in turning around the fortune of zombie firms in Africa.

Conclusion

This study has investigated the effects of zombie firms that are listed on the Zimbabwe Stock Exchange in the current Fourth Industrial Revolution. Given that companies operating in Zimbabwe are confronted with a myriad of challenges, it is common knowledge that the number of unproductive firms is exponentially increasing, especially after the COVID-19 era. As such, the issue of underperformance and unproductive firms is gaining momentum in the corporate world. In spite of the fact that business resilience, continuity, and transformation are topical issues in both developed and developing countries, it is troublesome to observe that the issue of zombie firms has been largely neglected in the post-COVID-19 epoch, especially in the context of African economies. Therefore, this study bridged this research gap by five negative effects of zombie firms in the post-COVID-19 era. These are related to the weakening economic status of the country, dumping of foreign products, allocative inefficiency, widening social inequality gap, and leading to zombie lending. These results have strong implications for policymakers when formulating business rehabilitation policies, and for turnaround strategies when conducting corporate rescue as well as for financial institutions when offering financial support to Zombie firms in Zimbabwe. It is concluded that an in-depth understanding of Zombie firms listed on ZSE can assist in promoting economic resilience in Zimbabwe.

References

Albuquerque, B., & Mao, C. (2023). The Zombie Lending Channel of Monetary Policy. *International Monetary Fund*. https://books.google.co.zw/books?hl=en&lr=&id=VTHYEAAAQBAJ&oi=fnd&pg=PP1&dq=The+Zombie+Lending+Channel+of+Monetary+Policy&ots=wHUfpWxEnF&sig=P8WoGjH91pOgjZBVCvMzQG5hzaA&redir_esc=y#v=onepage&q=The%20Zombie%20Lending%20Channel%20of%20Monetary%20Policy&f=false

Altman, E. I., Dai, R., & Wang, W. (2024). Global zombie companies: Measurements, determinants, and outcomes. *Journal of International Business Studies*, 1–22.

Amundsen, A., Lafrance-Cooke, A., & Danny Leung, D. (2023). *Zombie firms in Canada*. Economic and Social Reports. https://www150.statcan.gc.ca/n1/pub/36-28-0001/2023003/article/00003-eng.htm

Becker, B., & Ivashina, V. (2021). Corporate insolvency rules and zombie lending. *Beyond the pandemic: The future of monetary policy* (p. 32). https://www.ecb.europa.eu/pub/pdf/sintra/ecb.forum_central_banking.202112~3d9f018812.hr.pdf#page=33

Bell, E., Bryman, A., & Harley, B. (2022). *Business research methods*. Oxford University Press.

Braun, V., & Clarke, V. (2006). Using thematic analysis in psychology. *Qualitative Research in Psychology, 3*(2), 77–101.

Business Times. (2021). *Border Timbers loss widens*. https://businesstimes.co.zw/border-timbers-loss-widens-2/

Campello, K. A. M., & Schneider, G. K. K. (2024). *Uncertainty creates Zombie Firms: Implications for industry dynamics and creative destruction*. https://finance.darden.virginia.edu/wp-content/uploads/2023/11/Uncertainty_and_Zombie_Firms-003.pdf

Chari, A., Jain, L., & Kulkarni, N. (2022). The Unholy Trinity: Regulatory forbearance, government-owned banks and zombie firms. *Mimeo*. https://papers.ssrn.com/sol3/papers.cfm?abstract_id=3781322

Creswell, J. W., & Creswell, J. D. (2018). *Research design qualitative, quantitative, and mixed methods approaches*. Sage.

Davis, F. D. (1986). *A technology acceptance model for empirically testing new end-user information systems: Theory and results*. Doctoral dissertation, MIT Sloan School of Management.

Davis, F. D. (1989). Perceived usefulness, perceived ease of use, and user acceptance of information technology. *MIS Quarterly*, 319–340.

Dzingirai, M., & Baporikar, N. (2022a). Trends and patterns in turnaround strategies: A bibliometric perspective and future research agenda. *International Journal of Sociotechnology and Knowledge Development, 14*(1), 1–15.

Dzingirai, M., & Baporikar, N. (2022b). Understanding top management teams' characteristics for effective turnaround management: Evidence from the Zimbabwean manufacturing sector. *International Journal of Sociotechnology and Knowledge Development, 14*(1), 1–14.

Dzingirai, M., & Baporikar, N. (2023). Impact of retrenchment strategy on company performance in the manufacturing sector: A study for Zimbabwe. *FOCUS: Journal of International Business, 10*(1), 44–67.

Dzingirai, M., Chagwesha, M., & Mudzurandende, F. (2021). Challenges and opportunities from COVID-19 vis-à-vis informal cross-border women entrepreneurs scenario in Zimbabwe. In N. Baporikar (Ed.), *Handbook of research on sustaining SMEs and entrepreneurial innovation in the post-COVID-19 era* (pp. 40–59). IGI Global.

Dzingirai, M., & Ndava, R. (2021). Resilient entrepreneurial strategies adopted by Zimbabwean small and medium enterprises during economic crisis. In S. Stephens (Ed.), *Cases on small business economics and development during economic crises* (pp. 119–138). IGI Global.

Dzingirai, M., Tshuma, N., & Sikomwe, S. (2021). Post-pandemic sustainability strategies for Zimbabwean SMEs. In N. Baporikar (Ed.), *Handbook of research on strategies and interventions to mitigate COVID-19 impact on SMEs* (pp. 457–476). IGI Global.

Gonzalez, M. D. R. M. (2024). Technology acceptance in the literature from 2020 to 2024. *Journal of Advance Research in Science and Engineering, 2*(03), 13–18.

Goto, Y., & Wilbur, S. (2019). Unfinished business: Zombie firms among SME in Japan's lost decades. *Japan and the World Economy, 49*, 105–112.

Guma, N. (2023). *MPs probe Kuvimba, Zamco shadowy shareholding set-up*. https://thenewshawks.com/mps-probe-kuvimba-zamco-shadowy-shareholding-set-up/

Hanke, S. H., & Kwok, A. K. (2009). On the measurement of Zimbabwe's hyperinflation. *Cato Journal, 29*, 353.

Hong, M. G. H., Igan, M. D. O., & Lee, D. (2021). Zombies on the brink: Evidence from japan on the reversal of monetary policy effectiveness. *International Monetary Fund*. https://books.google.co.zw/books?hl=en&lr=&id=BrsoEAAAQBAJ&oi=fnd&pg=PA5&dq=Zombies+on+the+Brink:+Evidence+from+Japan+on+the+Reversal+of+Monetary+Policy+Effectiveness&ots=eDbphlpCab&sig=3IMTxm8pfaScQcCxsDDkHML50fs&redir_esc=y#v=onepage&q=Zombies%20on%20the%20Brink%3A%20Evidence%20from%20Japan%20on%20the%20Reversal%20of%20Monetary%20Policy%20Effectiveness&f=false

Magidi, M. (2023). Small towns as research sites: The impacts of deindustrialisation on urban livelihoods in Norton, Zimbabwe. *South African Geographical Journal, 105*(2), 179–199.

Magweva, R. (2023). Multiple currency system and commercial bank deposit mobilisation in Zimbabwe. *African Journal of Business and Economic Research, 18*(1), 35.

Matsika, B. (2020). *The "walking dead" on the ZSE*. https://businesstimes.co.zw/the-walking-dead-on-the-zse/

Mbira, L. (2015). The de-industrialization of Bulawayo manufacturing sector in Zimbabwe: Is the capital vacuum to blame. *International Journal of Economics, Commerce and Management, 3*(3), 1–15.

Mhlanga, D., & Dzingirai, M. (2024). Bibliometric study on organizational resilience: Trends and future research agenda. *International Journal of Corporate Social Responsibility, 9*(1), 9.

Mlambo, A. S. (2017). From an industrial powerhouse to a nation of vendors: Over two decades of economic decline and deindustrialization in Zimbabwe 1990–2015. *Journal of Developing Societies, 33*(1), 99–125.

Nehrebecki, M. (2023). Zombification in Poland in particular during COVID-19 pandemic and low interest rates. *Bank i Kredyt, 54*(2), 153–190.

Noor, N. (2024). Technology acceptance model in halal industries: A systematic literature review and research agenda. *Journal of Islamic Marketing*. (ahead-of-print). https://doi.org/10.1108/JIMA-02-2024-0077

Nyoni, M. (2024). *'Zim littered with zombie firms'*. https://www.newsday.co.zw/business/article/200022133/zim-littered-with-zombie-firms

Park, I., Kim, D., Moon, J., Kim, S., Kang, Y., & Bae, S. (2022). Searching for new technology acceptance model under social context: Analyzing the determinants of acceptance of intelligent information technology in digital transformation and implications for the requisites of digital sustainability. *Sustainability, 14*(1), 579.

Rashid, S., Iqbal Khan, K., Nasir, A., & Rashid, T. (2022). Unveiling living dead: Characteristics and consequences of zombie firms. *Cogent Business and Management, 9*(1), 2121240.

Saif, N., Khan, S. U., Shaheen, I., ALotaibi, F. A., Alnfiai, M. M., & Arif, M. (2024). Chat-GPT; validating technology acceptance model (TAM) in education sector via ubiquitous learning mechanism. *Computers in Human Behavior, 154*, 108097.

Saunders, M. N. K., Lewis, P., & Thornhill, A. (2019). *Research methods for business students* (8th ed.). Person.

The Zimbabwe Mail (2024). *Zimbabwe's Economic Outlook: 'Dogs and Zombie Companies' Dominate Landscape*. https://www.thezimbabwemail.com/economic-analysis/zimbabwes-economic-outlook-dogs-and-zombie-companies-dominate-landscape/

Exploring the Role of Higher Education in Fostering Entrepreneurship Education Among Undergraduate Students in South Africa

Ngozi Blessing Enebe, Calvin Mahlaule, Tlotlo Segotso, and Zanele Sobopha

Abstract The focus of this study is to examine the influence of higher education on the effective delivery of entrepreneurship education in South African universities to foster small business creation after school. In South Africa, fostering entrepreneurship has become a critical endeavor to drive economic growth and innovation. There is an alarming unemployment trajectory, mainly among young people. Higher education institutions serve as incubators for future entrepreneurs, providing a conducive environment for students to acquire essential knowledge, skills, and attitudes that boost their competencies toward self-employment through small businesses and, in turn, promote economic development and growth. Unfortunately, the courses offered in the universities groom students to become employees in the future rather than equipping them to become an employer of labor. This study adopts an Integrative Literature Review (ILR) approach to explore the role of higher education in fostering entrepreneurship education among undergraduate students in South Africa. The ILR methodology allows for the synthesis of existing research, theoretical frameworks, and insights related to the research topic, providing a comprehensive understanding of the complex relationships among variables without collecting new empirical data. Findings suggest that higher education institutions (HEIs) have not paid much attention to their roles in promoting entrepreneurship education among students. The curriculum still teaches students to graduate and seek employment in formal sectors rather than opt in for personal creativity and innovativeness toward business creation. Some of these roles include but not limited to curriculum development, resource allocation, professional development, community engagement, and student support and guidance. The study concludes that higher education offers limited entrepreneurial learning support to undergraduate students and urges

N. B. Enebe (✉) · C. Mahlaule · T. Segotso
North-West University, Potchefstroom, South Africa
e-mail: 36037214@mynwu.ac.za; Calvin.Mahlaule@nwu.ac.za; tlotlo.segotso@nwu.ac.za

Z. Sobopha
Vaal University of Technology, Vanderbijlpark, South Africa
e-mail: zaneles1@vut.ac.za

T. Moloi (ed.), *Impacting Society Positively Through Technology in Accounting and Business Processes*, Springer Proceedings in Business and Economics,
https://doi.org/10.1007/978-3-031-84885-8_17

that high education should among other learning fields prioritize entrepreneurship across disciplines. The study sheds light on the concerted efforts to equip the next generation with the skills needed to drive economic and societal transformation through their roles to increase entrepreneurial endeavors.

Keywords Entrepreneurship education · Small businesses · Undergraduate students · Economic growth · Higher education

Introduction and Background

Higher education institutions (HEIs) are domains for knowledge and skill acquisition and ought to constantly upgrade to meet with business and industry requirements. In addition to the research these institutions provide, the information and skills are generated in the form of graduates with varying talents. According to Nwosu et al. (2023), entrepreneurship is widely acknowledged as a key factor in economic growth, innovation, and job creation. In an age of swift technological progress and intense global rivalry, it is more important than ever to cultivate in students an entrepreneurial mindset and skill set (Rae & Melton, 2017). Educational establishments, especially those offering higher education, are essential in molding and readying the next generation of people for the ever-changing demands of the world. Higher education institutions play a crucial role in molding and developing students' entrepreneurial potential. Ramchander (2019) states that the South African educational system is not raising enough entrepreneurs, which could be due to how EE is designed and delivered. These educational establishments bear the responsibility of establishing a favorable environment that fosters and advances students' entrepreneurial abilities and mindsets. Their roles and responsibilities in promoting entrepreneurship are essential to building an environment that is encouraging and favorable to the development of learners' entrepreneurial attitudes and competencies. The purpose of entrepreneurship education in schools is to equip and develop pupils to be independent contractors. It seeks to inspire prospective business owners and cultivate in people an entrepreneurial mindset (Ahmad et al., 2018).

Majority of individuals believe entrepreneurship is the engine of human growth and the solution to the social and economic problems facing our society. Social vices like unemployment, crime and poverty could be decreased with the rise of entrepreneurship. Empirical evidence suggests that decreasing unemployment necessitates economic expansion, and that the engine of economic expansion is entrepreneurship (Volkman et al., 2009). It is anticipated, according to Uleanya et al. (2018), that curricula in schools will be developed to facilitate the creation of trained labor that will boost the supply of the needed commodities for society's expansion.

The importance of entrepreneurship has long been stressed, especially when talking about economics. Even though they originated in the commercial sector, entrepreneurship and enterprise are subjects that are being considered more and more from an educational perspective, especially in the beginning years of the learner's schooling (Ahmed, 2019). This has led to an increase in the degree of support for policy for entrepreneurship education in countries (O'Connor, 2013; Walter & Block, 2016). Most tertiary institutions are now offering entrepreneurship training programs in anticipation that this will lessen unemployment problems and in the hopes that the skills and knowledge needed for business start-up may be taught. According to Twumasi (2013), graduates of higher education institutions frequently find it difficult to get employment many years after graduation, making the high unemployment rate in rising economies a global issue. The development of vocational and technical skills has been the focus of educational initiatives in many nations, including the United States, Germany, China, and others, in order to facilitate school dropouts'—especially those who have completed their tertiary education—smooth entry into the workforce (Nwachukwu et al., 2021). Regardless of their area of expertise, the aim of entrepreneurship education is to provide graduates with the skills necessary to generate money, regardless of their capacity to secure paid work in any kind of establishment (Fretschner & Weber, 2013).

Employers of labor, meantime, anticipate that HEI graduates will acquire the skills necessary for their various activities (Horn & Moesta, 2019). Organizations in the modern era find it difficult to hire a significant number of graduates for a number of obvious reasons. According to Shava (2021), the reasons can be due to companies' financial difficulties in hiring as many graduates as necessary and graduates' lack of necessary abilities. The incapacity of HEIs to precisely define their graduate qualities is the reason they are not producing the necessary skills (Green et al., 2009; Winberg et al., 2018). These characteristics pertain to the abilities, character traits, and values that graduates—regardless of subject or field of study—should develop in order to succeed in the workforce (Bridgstock, 2009; Smith & Bath, 2006). Graduate qualities should essentially represent student achievements with regard to employability, business, and professional standards of employers (Oraison et al., 2019; Sibanda & Iwu, 2023). Graduates' adoption of entrepreneurial endeavors can also contribute to their employability. Bustamam et al. (2015) highlighted the importance of entrepreneurship education in fostering a culture of entrepreneurship among students, which frequently results in the launch of a business following graduation. Because it has the potential to alleviate unemployment, poverty, and inequality, entrepreneurship has been recognized as a keystone in the discourse on socioeconomic development. Increasing employment and economic growth, particularly in developing nations, can be achieved through entrepreneurship education (Ncube & Zondo, 2018; Waghid, 2019). In order to reduce the nation's rising unemployment rate, higher education in South Africa is crucial in preparing and empowering students to launch side ventures after graduation. To guarantee that all students, regardless of subject, benefit from this, encouraging students to start their own businesses should be ingrained in every aspect of the curriculum. Thus, the objective of this study is to explore the roles of higher education in fostering entrepreneurship education among undergraduate students in South Africa.

Theoretical Framework

Human Capital Theory

Theoretical economists in the Chicago School of Economics, including Theodore Schultz and Gary Becker, primarily constructed the analytical foundation for Human Capital Theory (HCT), which was formally launched in the 1950s (Tan, 2014). According to Garibaldi (2006), human capital refers to the body of information or the intrinsic or learned qualities that a person possesses that contribute to his or her economic production. It is defined as "productive wealth embodied in labour, skills, and knowledge" (OECD, 2001). Fundamentally, HCT contends that education is an investment since it raises people's earnings and productivity. In actuality, this investment is not only vital for people but also essential to a nation's economic development. "The most valuable of all capital is that invested in human beings," as Alfred Marshall (1920) stated (p. 564). According to this economic model and its presumptions about human behavior, people invest in education and training in the hopes of increasing their income in the future in order to optimize their own economic interests (Tan, 2014). This is consistent with the notion that people who want to maximize their own interests are usually the ones who engage in human capital building (Blaug, 1992). That being said, the nonfinancial benefits of education to individuals and society are not often overlooked by human capital economists. The social, cultural, intellectual, and artistic advantages of education are also acknowledged, albeit they are referred to as positive externalities (Tan, 2014). Nonetheless, the instruction and training South African undergraduate students are currently receiving will increase the value of their human capital, enabling them to engage in entrepreneurship both during and after school. Through their participation in entrepreneurship education and training, students will gain information and skills that will enable them to become better employees or small business owners as their capabilities are developed through this process.

Methodology

Research Design

In order to investigate the role of higher education in fostering entrepreneurship education among undergraduate students in South Africa, this study uses an Integrative Literature Review (ILR) methodology. Without gathering empirical data, the ILR technique enables the integration of prior research, theoretical frameworks, and insights pertaining to the study issue, offering a thorough grasp of the intricate interactions among variables (Torraco, 2005).

Literature Search and Selection

A comprehensive review of the literature was done using a number of Internet databases, such as Google Scholar, Scopus, Web of Science, and pertinent academic publications in the fields of entrepreneurial studies and higher education. To guarantee the current and applicability of the material, the search includes peer-reviewed publications, reports, conference proceedings, books, and book chapters that have been published within the last few years.

In order to find pertinent research on entrepreneurship education, higher education, and South African setting, the search technique used keywords and Boolean operators. We used "entrepreneurship education," "higher education," "South Africa," "youth entrepreneurship," and similar variations as our main search phrases.

Inclusion and Exclusion Criteria

A selection of literature that was deemed relevant to the research theme and in line with the study's goals were included. Studies on young entrepreneurship, higher education, and entrepreneurship education were all included in the inclusion criteria. English-language publications were given preference because they were easily readable and accessible.

Studies that do not specifically address the connection between entrepreneurship education, higher education, and youth entrepreneurship were removed from the literature selection.

Ethical Considerations

Since this study is an Integrative Literature Review, ethical approval is not necessary because it does not involve primary data collection from human participants. To maintain academic rigor and credibility, however, ethical considerations will center on citation integrity, respect for intellectual property rights, and open reporting of synthesized literature.

Literature Review

In this review, the focus is on entrepreneurship education in South Africa, entrepreneurship education in higher education and roles of higher education in fostering entrepreneurship education among students.

Overview of Entrepreneurship Education in South Africa

In order to improve people's socioeconomic well-being, entrepreneurship education, according to Omotosho et al. (2022), is the process of cultivating twenty-first-century skills, knowledge, and creative attributes. Curriculum specialists and other education stakeholders in South Africa have been involved in national and international dialogues aimed at fostering entrepreneurship since 1990. One of the most important questions in this regard is whether or if young students could understand the concepts of entrepreneurship, and if they could, how much of them (Davies, 1991) they could understand. In 1991, stakeholders in the South African education system started investigating the feasibility of including entrepreneurship as a curriculum in the near future in order to address these and numerous other concerns. It is important to remember that the several stakeholders in the South African educational system have worked together throughout the years to help the younger students develop an entrepreneurial attitude.

In order to encourage the growth of entrepreneurship-related universities and university students' entrepreneurial endeavors, the Department of Higher Education founded Entrepreneurship Development in Higher Education (EDHE). EDHE is a program with a human focus. The objective is to foster the entrepreneurial skills of academics, managers, and students (Paek et al., 2021). This indicates that the purpose of EDHE is to support students in becoming more economically successful both during and after their higher education. Entrepreneurship can help students make extra money while they are studying and follow the economic activity process more swiftly. After graduation, students may view enterprise as a secondary career path or as their main choice if they are having trouble finding employment. The Statistics South report for 2021 states that there has been a 34.4% increase in unemployment in South Africa (Chodorow-Reich & Coglianese, 2021). This number points to a quicker rate of new venture development and a more aggressive approach to job creation. Numerous youth development initiatives exist in South Africa; however, their effectiveness has been minimal. To effectively address the issue of youth unemployment, a few components of the training that higher education institutions provide to aspiring entrepreneurs need to be improved. Bux and Van Vuuren (2019) agree that entrepreneurship education could be very important in changing young people's perceptions of working for themselves and in providing them with the requisite knowledge to manage an enterprise. Therefore, what really counts during the startup phase is exhibiting the appropriate mentality, and most entrepreneurship schools in South Africa lack this.

Entrepreneurship Education in Higher Education

Higher education establishments are important for a country's development since they are recognized as the guardians of knowledge in society. For this reason, teaching entrepreneurship should not be limited to a certain niche. Higher education institutions have come to this awareness, which has led to a discernible rise in entrepreneurial programs. The trend is continuing, and it will not be long before South Africa has a largely established culture of entrepreneurship. This will provide challenges for both students and academics. Universities are confronting a number of new obstacles in their efforts to create and implement expanding programs in entrepreneurship (Jeyalakshmi & Meenakumari, 2015). In national and international policy, entrepreneurship is becoming more and more important for long-term economic development and for resolving fundamental socioeconomic problems. Employers in both developed and developing nations tend to be small- and medium-sized firms (International Labour Organization, 2020). To increase their citizens' capacity for production, nations all over the world have been putting large sums of money into skills-based training, especially in the higher education sector. The quality of graduates generated in South Africa, however, has not yet reflected the massive investment made in entrepreneurship education and training in higher institutions (Tewari & Ilesanmi, 2020). As a result, graduates' creative and analytical skills fall short of what is needed.

Role of Higher Education in Fostering Entrepreneurship Education Among Students

The HEIs are critical to the promotion of entrepreneurship education among students. Entrepreneurship education has been perceived as a panacea for poor economic growth, youth unemployment, poverty, and vices. It then, however, rests on the shoulders of HEIs to foster the promotion of this discipline through some of the roles that would be discussed below.

Curriculum Development

HEIs are essential to the process of creating curricula that incorporate entrepreneurship studies. This curriculum has to be changed since it continues to instill in undergraduate students the notion to seek for jobs as they graduate, instead of pursuing an innovative and creative career path (Jeyalakshmi & Meenakumari, 2015). SMMEs, however, now represent a sizable portion of the economy. Increasingly, HEIs must reinterpret their place in the South African economy. Therefore, encouraging students to develop stronger entrepreneurial character should be the main goal of HEIs. In addition, higher education institutions (HEIs) ought to make a concerted effort to consider the demands of regional development and to encourage entrepreneurial education programs, not just at the tertiary but also at the elementary school. According to Nieuwenhuizen et al. (2016), the government must fully support these kinds of projects, encourage all levels of holistic education, and assist in the establishment of entrepreneurial endeavors.

Resource Allocation

Resource limitations hinder the activities associated with entrepreneurship education (Sarwar et al., 2021). Therefore, in order for HEIs to create a welcoming environment for entrepreneurship education, efficient resource allocation is essential. According to Bellotti et al. (2012), providing kids with access to state-of-the-art learning materials, maker spaces, and entrepreneurship insights fosters innovative and active participation. Sufficient financial resources allow lecturers and instructors in entrepreneurship to provide their pupils with the necessary instruments, supplies, and tools to fulfill their entrepreneurial goals. Funding for facilities and resources connected to entrepreneurship contributes to the development of a positive learning environment (Wu et al., 2019). HEIs can establish an ecosystem that fosters entrepreneurial aspirations and supports experiential learning by properly allocating their resources.

Professional Development

In the field of entrepreneurial education, the professional development of lecturers is essential. Regular training sessions, workshops, and seminars should be given top priority by HEIs in order to equip entrepreneurship instructors with the knowledge and pedagogical abilities necessary to effectively instruct students in entrepreneurship. Nguyen and Nguyen (2023) assert that enhancing the impact of entrepreneurship education on students' entrepreneurial intents requires professional development. By staying current on industry practices, innovative teaching strategies, and current trends, lecturers are better equipped to deliver engaging and pertinent instruction on entrepreneurship. HEIs should support peer learning and the exchange of best practices in order to further foster collaboration. In the long run, this collaborative environment helps students and empowers instructors by boosting their confidence and ability to teach entrepreneurship. When it comes to training entrepreneurship, professional development programs increase confidence and aptitude (Alakaleek et al., 2023). Zhu et al. (2023) suggest a change in institutional practice from conventional employment to professional growth and development in order to enhance lecturers' entrepreneurship capability.

Community Engagement

In order to inspire students to become entrepreneurs, community participation is crucial, and higher education institutions should be key players in creating these connections. HEIs should partner with nearby businesses, start-ups, and community groups to offer real-world learning opportunities and mentorship programs. Through these interactions, students gain first-hand understanding of real-world business and are able to use their potentials and expertise in practical life circumstances. HEIs, by their community engagement and strong sense of relevance and applicability, can assist in bridging classroom and the real-world experiences. Additionally, community engagement gives students networking opportunities through which they can establish relationships, ask for advice, and obtain resources that can support them in their entrepreneurial endeavors (Hou et al., 2023). HEIs should aggressively incorporate the community in all facets of entrepreneurship education, including industry visits, guest lectures, and internships, in order to offer a thorough and well-rounded learning experience. Weng et al. (2022) claim that this collaboration enables students to build networks that will aid in their entrepreneurial endeavors and gain useful insights into business. Working together with outside partners enhances students' knowledge of practical entrepreneurship and offers networking opportunities (Hou et al., 2023). According to Siqueira et al. (2015), these active learning techniques can help students navigate moral, social, and environmental dilemmas in challenging business situations.

Learner Support and Guidance

HEIs should provide comprehensive support and guidance to interested students who are in entrepreneurship. To assist students in developing their entrepreneurial skills and overcoming obstacles associated with entrepreneurship, mentorship programs, coaching sessions, and counseling services ought to be established. HEIs can help students discover their abilities, investigate opportunities for entrepreneurship, and create workable company plans by offering individualized support and assessment. HEIs can also host pitch competitions, networking events, and entrepreneurial showcases to give students a stage on which to present their ideas, get expert input, and make connections with possible partners or investors. The importance of comprehending and encouraging students' feedback-seeking behavior is emphasized by Liu et al. (2023). HEI-established student support networks can help with this. Personalized supervision and support systems positively impact students' self-efficacy and entrepreneurial objectives (Arpiainen & Kurczewska, 2017; Wu et al., 2019). These support networks help students gain self-assurance and familiarity in the community. Elert et al. (2015) find that participation in the Junior Achievement Company Program increases students' chances of launching a firm in the long run and increases the program graduates' entrepreneurial revenues. According to Ho et al. (2018), students who got entrepreneurship training exhibited significantly higher levels of entrepreneurial efficacy and attentiveness than those who did not.

Conclusion and Recommendations

This study explored the roles and responsibilities of higher education institutions (HEIs) in fostering entrepreneurship among undergraduate students. The study used the Integrative Literature Review (ILR), which examined relevant research that had been published in academic reports, conference proceedings, and peer-reviewed journals. It was discovered that HEIs had a variety of functions in fostering an environment in which entrepreneurship education could take place. These responsibilities include developing curricula, allocating resources, fostering professional growth, participating in the community, and offering support and direction to students. In order to enable students to develop entrepreneurial competencies that would give them the skills to venture into entrepreneurial activities rather than settling with the idea of seeking employment, which the current curriculum emphasizes, the study recommends that HEIs upgrade the entrepreneurship contents in the curriculum. It is essential for lecturers to receive professional development and training in order to expand their knowledge and abilities, stay current on trends and best practices in entrepreneurship education, and be able to offer students meaningful counsel. Furthermore, it is critical to give students networking skills so they may work with local firms and entrepreneurs as well as other community stakeholders. Students may have invaluable opportunity to network with mentors and industry experts as a result of this community participation. Lastly, HEIs may help build an environment that is favorable and supportive of the growth and development of entrepreneurial attitudes and skills. HEIs actively advise and mentor students, which can help aspiring entrepreneurs grow and succeed.

References

Ahmad, S. Z., Abu Bakar, A., & Ahmad, N. (2018). An evaluation of teaching methods of entrepreneurship in hospitality and tourism programs. *The International Journal of Management Education, 4*(1), 232–250.

Ahmed, S. (2019). Including entrepreneurship education into school curriculum: What, why and how. https://www.researchgate.net/publication/337316021.

Alakaleek, W., Harb, Y., Harb, A. A., & Al shishany, A. (2023). The impact of entrepreneurship education: A study of entrepreneurial outcomes. *The International Journal of Management Education, 21*(2), 100800. https://doi.org/10.1016/j.ijme.2023.100800

Arpiainen, R.-L., & Kurczewska, A. (2017). Learning risk-taking and coping with uncertainty through experiential, team-based entrepreneurship education. *Industry and Higher Education, 31*(3), 143–155. https://doi.org/10.1177/0950422217700994

Bellotti, F., Berta, R., De Gloria, A., Lavagnino, E., Dagnino, F., Ott, M., Romero, M., Usart, M., et al. (2012). Designing a course for stimulating entrepreneurship in higher education through serious games. *Procedia Computer Science, 15*, 174–186. https://doi.org/10.1016/j.procs.2012.10.069

Blaug, M. (1992). *The methodology of economics: Or how economists explain*. Cambridge University Press.

Bridgstock, R. (2009). The graduate attributes we've overlooked: Enhancing graduate employability through career management skills. *Higher Education Research & Development, 28*(1), 31–44.

Bustamam, U. S. A., Mutalib, M. A., & Yusof, S. N. M. (2015). Graduate employability through entrepreneurship: A case study at USIM. *Procedia-Social and Behavioral Sciences, 21*(1), 1117–1121.

Bux, S., & Van Vuuren, J. (2019). The effect of entrepreneurship education programmes on the development of self-efficacy, entrepreneurial intention and predictions for entrepreneurial. *Acta Commercii, 19*(2), 1–13.

Chodorow-Reich, G., & Coglianese, J. (2021). Projecting unemployment durations: A factor-flows simulation approach with application to the COVID-19 recession. *Journal of Public Economics, 197*, 104398.

Davies, S. P. (1991). The entrepreneurial capabilities of rural furniture manufacturers in Central Java, Indonesia: A framework and case study. *Entrepreneurship & Regional Development, 3*(3), 253–267.

Elert, N., Andersson, F. W., & Wennberg, K. (2015). The impact of entrepreneurship education in high school on long-term entrepreneurial performance. *Journal of Economic Behavior & Organization, 111*, 209–223. https://doi.org/10.1016/j.jebo.2014.12.020

Fretschner, M., & Weber, S. (2013). Measuring and understanding the effects of entrepreneurial awareness education. *Journal of Small Business Management, 51*(3), 410–428. https://doi.org/10.1111/jsbm.12019

Garibaldi, P. (2006). *Personnel economics in imperfect labour markets*. Oxford Press.

Green, W., Hammer, S., & Star, C. (2009). Facing up to the challenge: Why is it so hard to develop graduate attributes? *Higher Education Research & Development, 28*(1), 17–29. https://doi.org/10.1080/07294360802444339

Ho, M.-H. R., Uy, M. A., Kang, B. N. Y., & Chan, K.-Y. (2018). Impact of entrepreneurship training on entrepreneurial efficacy and alertness among adolescent youth [Original research]. *Frontiers in Education, 3*. https://doi.org/10.3389/feduc.2018.00013

Horn, M. B., & Moesta, B. (2019, October 15). Do colleges truly understand what students want from them? *Harvard Business Review*. https://hbr.org/2019/10/do-colleges-truly-understandwhat-students-want-from-them.

Hou, F., Qi, M.-D., Su, Y., Wu, Y. J., & Tang, J.-Y. (2023). How does university-based entrepreneurship education facilitate the development of entrepreneurial intention? Integrating passion-

and competency-based perspectives. *The International Journal of Management Education, 21*(2), 100798. https://doi.org/10.1016/j.ijme.2023.100798
International Labour Organisation. (2020). COVID-19 crisis and the informal economy: Immediate responses and policy challenges. *ILO Brief.*
Jeyalakshmi, S. S., & Meenakumari, S. (2015). Role of higher education in promoting entrepreneurship. *Shanlax International Journal of Management, 3*(1), 70–77.
Liu, M., Gorgievski, M. J., Zwaga, J., & Paas, F. (2023). Understanding and motivating student feedback seeking: Insights from a lean startup based entrepreneurship program. *The International Journal of Management Education, 21*(2), 100750. https://doi.org/10.1016/j.ijme.2022.100750
Marshall, A. (1920). *Principles of economics* (8th ed.). Macmillan.
Ncube, T. R., & Zondo, R. W. D. (2018). Influence of self-motivation and intrinsic motivational factors for small and medium business growth: A South African case study. *South African Journal of Economic and Management Sciences, 21*(1), e1–e7.
Nguyen, Q. D., & Nguyen, H. T. (2023). Entrepreneurship education and entrepreneurial intention: The mediating role of entrepreneurial capacity. *The International Journal of Management Education, 21*(1), 100730. https://doi.org/10.1016/j.ijme.2022.100730
Nieuwenhuizen, C., Groenewald, D., Davids, J., Rensburg, L. J., & Schachtebeck, C. (2016). Best practice in entrepreneurship education. *Problems and Perspectives in Management, 14*(3), 528–536.
Nwachukwu, P. I., Obisanma, O., Kuromiema, M. I., Ptopregha, M., & Obatola, A. T. (2021). The influence of entrepreneurship education on students' business venturing in tertiary institutions in Nigeria. *International Journal of Research and Innovation in Social Science, 5*(6), 520–532.
Nwosu, L. I., Enwereji, P., Enebe, N. B., & Segotso, T. (2023). Determining the roles of school management teams (SMTs) in fostering entrepreneurship among learners. *International Journal of Learning, Teaching and Educational Research, 22*(9), 478–500.
O'Connor, A. A. (2013). Conceptual framework for entrepreneurship education policy: Meeting government and economic purpose. *J. Bus. Venture., 28*, 546–563.
OECD. (2001). Glossary of statistical terms. Retrieved from http://stats.oecd.org/glossary/detail.asp?ID=1264
Omotosho, A. O., Gamede, B. T., Vezi-Magigaba, M. F., & Ayandibu, A. O. (2022). Is South Africa's entrepreneurship education program successful? A framework for policy and practice. *Journal of Entrepreneurship Education, 25*(4), 1–17.
Oraison, H., Konjarski, L., & Howe, S. (2019). Does university prepare students for employment? Alignment between graduate attributes, accreditation requirements and industry employability criteria. *Journal of Teaching and Learning for Graduate Employability, 10*(1), 173–194.
Paek, C., Guler, I., & Rogan, M. (2021). Are entrepreneurs better start-up investors? In *Academy of management proceedings* (Vol. 2021(1), p. 14205). Academy of Management.
Rae, D., & Melton, D. E. (2017). Developing an entrepreneurial mindset in US engineering education: An international view of the KEEN project. *The Journal of Engineering Entrepreneurship, 7*(3).
Ramchander, M. (2019). Reconceptualising undergraduate entrepreneurship education at traditional South African universities. *Acta Commercii, 19*(2), 1–9.
Sarwar, Z., Khan, M. A., Yang, Z., Khan, A., Haseeb, M., & Sarwar, A. (2021). An investigation of entrepreneurial SMEs' network capability and social capital to accomplish innovativeness: A dynamic capability perspective. *SAGE Open, 11*(3). https://doi.org/10.1177/21582440211036089
Shava, E. (2021). Financial sustainability of NGOs in rural development programmes. *Development in Practice, 31*(3), 393–403.
Sibanda, L., & Iwu, C. G. (2023). Effective interventions for enhancing academic achievements in higher education: Views of entrepreneurship students. *Journal of Research in Higher Education, 7*(1), 70–94.

Siqueira, A. C. O., Ramos, D. P., Kelly, L., Mnisri, K., & Kassouf, P. (2015). Responsible management education: Active learning approaches emphasising sustainability and social entrepreneurship. *International Journal of Innovation and Sustainable Development, 9*(2), 188–202.

Smith, C., & Bath, D. (2006). The role of the learning community in the development of discipline knowledge and generic graduate outcomes. *Higher Education, 51*(2), 259–286.

Tan, E. (2014). Human capital theory: A holistic criticism. *Review of Educational Research, 84*(3), 411–445.

Tewari, D. D., & Ilesanmi, K. D. (2020). Teaching and learning interaction in South Africa's higher education: Some weak links. *Cogent Social Sciences, 6*(1), 1740519.

Torraco, R. J. (2005). Writing integrative literature reviews: Guidelines and examples. *Human Resource Development Review, 4*(3), 43–62.

Twumasi, I. K. (2013). *The challenges of youth unemployment to the church in Ghana: Response of the Methodist Church Kumasi Circuit and Church of God Patasi District*. MSc thesis, Kwame Nkrumah University of Science and Technology Kumasi.

Uleanya, C., Rugbeer, Y., & Martin, D. A. N. (2018). Localizing educational curriculum of tertiary institutions: Approach to sustainable development. *Journal of Entrepreneurship Education, 21*(3), 1–14.

Volkman, C., Wilson, K., Marlotti, S., & Rabuzzi, D. (2009). Educating the next wave of -unlocking entrepreneurial capabilities to meet the global challenges of the 21st century. A report of the global education.

Waghid, Z. (2019). Examining the business education curricula in South Africa: Towards integrating social entrepreneurship. *Education + Training, 4*(1), 332–341.

Walter, S. G., & Block, J. H. (2016). Outcome of entrepreneurship education: An institutional perspective. *Journal of Business Venturing, 31*, 216–233.

Weng, X., Chiu, T. K. F., & Tsang, C. C. (2022). Promoting student creativity and entrepreneurship through real-world problem-based maker education. *Thinking Skills and Creativity, 45*, 101046. https://doi.org/10.1016/j.tsc.2022.101046

Winberg, C., Staak, A., Bester, M., Sabata, S., Scholtz, D., Sebolao, R., Monnapula-Mapesela, M., Ronald, N., Makua, M., Snyman, J., & Machika, P. (2018). In search of graduate attributes: A survey of six flagship programmes. *South African Journal of Higher Education, 32*(1), 233–251. https://doi.org/10.20853/32-1-1642

Wu, Y.-C. J., Wu, T., & Li, Y. (2019). Impact of using classroom response systems on students' entrepreneurship learning experience. *Computers in Human Behavior, 92*, 634–645. https://doi.org/10.1016/j.chb.2017.08.013

Zhu, R., Liu, Z., Zhao, G., Huang, Z., & Yu, Q. (2023). The impact of institutional management on teacher entrepreneurship competency: The mediating role of entrepreneurial behaviour. *The International Journal of Management Education, 21*(2), 100794. https://doi.org/10.1016/j.ijme.2023.100794

Green Accounting Reporting and Firm Value for Southern African Agriculture Firms

Kansilembo Freddy Aliamutu and Msizi Mkhize

Abstract The aim of this research is to investigate the effect of green accounting reporting on firm value in Southern African agriculture firms. The study spanned a 5-year observation period, namely from 2019 to 2023. This study employed control variables, including financial performance, sales growth, leverage, and the size of agricultural firms in Southern Africa. The study conducted the data analysis using a fixed-effect model method for data regression. The results suggest the extent to which green accounting reporting aligns with the global reporting initiative (GRI) guideline has no meaningful impact on the value of agricultural firms. Leverage is the sole variable that affects green accounting reporting. The assessment of green accounting reporting carried out in this research is less flexible than a binary variable; the specific terms required have been established to determine which approach to adopt to identify the green accounting reporting variable. There is no direct correlation between green accounting reporting and firm value. The study revealed that only a limited number of firms in Southern Africa include green accounting in their financial statements. Although green accounting is optional, firms are still hesitant to include it in their annual reports.

Keywords Southern Africa · Green accounting · Financial performance · Leverage

K. F. Aliamutu (✉)
University of KwaZulu Natal, Durban, South Africa

Financial Accounting, University of KwaZulu Natal, Durban, South Africa
e-mail: aliamutuk@ukzn.ac.za

M. Mkhize
University of KwaZulu Natal, Durban, South Africa
e-mail: Mkhizem4@ukzn.ac.za

T. Moloi (ed.), *Impacting Society Positively Through Technology in Accounting and Business Processes*, Springer Proceedings in Business and Economics,
https://doi.org/10.1007/978-3-031-84885-8_18

Introduction

Prior studies have established that market fluctuations can have an impact on the stock values of environmentally conscious or green accounting-implementing firms (Osemene et al., 2021). Implementing green accounting practices has the potential to impact stock prices and improve a firm's overall value and profits. Hence, the introduction of internal environmental costs in the accounting system will help companies make decisions that, in addition to increasing long-term financial performance, will improve the environmental performance and, by introducing themselves as the green industry to the capital market, will increase the shareholder's (Iredele et al., 2020). However, Buallay's (2022) findings indicate that there are no noticeable changes in stock prices before or after the implementation of green accounting.

The response to the challenges of sustainable development is the UN Agenda 2030 adopted in 2015 by the UN member states. It comprises 17 SDGs and 169 interrelated tasks that are, to a large degree, based on the Millenium Development Goals (MDGs) realized in the years 2000–2015 reporting (Nyakuwanika et al., 2021). The Sustainable Development Goals primarily aim to address delicate global issues by integrating green accounting into sustainable development, which focuses on the growth of firms (Khan et al., 2021). From the microeconomic perspective (of a firm), sustainable development means such a strategy of acting that not only satisfies the current needs of the organization and its stakeholders, but also protects, sustains, and reinforces the sources of resources that will be necessary in the future. The disparity in the outcomes of this research is a research gap that scholars are interested in exploring (Attah-Botchwey et al., 2022).

As legislatures, shareholders, and consumers in general become more cognizant of the potential health-related repercussions of a firm's social and ecological efforts on its finances, reports on sustainability and accounting have become increasingly vital for firms. This research has numerous implications to consider (Iredele et al., 2020). To begin with, a limited number of research papers examining green accounting focus on one country and do not provide a comprehensive regional analysis. Using the government's APROPRIATE accreditation rating, the majority of previous studies evaluated the importance of green accounting reporting (Nyakuwanika et al., 2021). Aifuwa (2020) proposed a different method for representing green accounting as a percentage release based on search terms specified in the GRI guidelines. The implementation of the new guideline in Southern Africa toward the end of 2016 called for reporting on green accounting to be subject to environmental-specific reporting, as outlined in GRI 300 Environment Management (Utomo et al., 2020).

This research is motivated by the need to understand the effectiveness of green accounting reporting in enhancing firm values (Khan et al., 2021). Research from various other countries indicates that green accounting reporting not only enhances firm value, but also encourages current and prospective shareholders to purchase the company's stock or aid stakeholders in decision-making (Hatane et al., 2022).

However, previous research has demonstrated that green accounting reporting does not affect the firm's value, as it is voluntary (Faisal et al., 2020). Olaleye and Igbekoyi (2020) stated that when deciding on options, stakeholders rely primarily on the revenues and opinions of the financial statement as opposed to sustainability assessments. As a result, we investigate, in particular, the impact of green accounting records on firm value (Wiredu et al., 2023).

Prior studies on the potential impact of green accounting reporting on financial statements or sustainability documents on firm values have yielded inconclusive results, particularly with regard to environmental friendliness (Qian et al., 2021). Reporting green accounting practices can increase an organization's credibility in the community by demonstrating its commitment to the tripartite bottom line—encompassing social, economic, and environmental dimensions—thereby bolstering shareholder confidence (Chamorro Gonzalez & Herrera Mendoza, 2021). We structure the subsequent sections of the chapter as follows: the second part details the literature review and the formulation of hypotheses. The third part describes the research methodology. The fourth part presents the empirical results. The fifth part serves as the concluding part.

Literature Review

As suggested by the stakeholder theory, the equitable treatment of everyone involved results in a form of cooperation. Alternatively stated, the manner in which a corporation handles its consumers influences the thoughts and conduct of its staff, while the manner in which it handles the societies in which it works influences the thoughts and conduct of its partners and consumers (Van Linh et al., 2022). Stakeholder theory places emphasis on business stakeholders' concerns and interests. Nkwoji (2021) asserts that all stakeholders can access information about the execution of the firm's organizational initiatives and their environmental impact, thereby requiring the firm to disclose all aspects of its operations to these customers. However, legitimacy theory emphasizes how organizations consistently strive to appear to function in accordance with the social expectations and regulations that prevail in that particular location (Aliamutu & Mkhize, 2024).

These reasons suggest that this legitimacy theory might help organizations develop and use ethical and social reporting on their own, which would satisfy social oversight and give them a chance to talk about their goals and precarious survival (Denedo & Egbon, 2021). Legitimacy, within a socially constructed framework encompassing principles, opinions, guidelines, and descriptions, refers to the comprehensive assessment or perspective of a company's legitimate and appropriate conduct. To ensure that the general public continues to recognize the company's right to continue functioning, it is critical that an organization maintains a strong reputation for legitimacy (Aliamutu & Mkhize, 2024b; Dagestani et al., 2022). Reporting green accounting details provides stockholders with a positive indication of the environmental impact of the company's activities. This may entice shareholders to purchase additional shares, thereby contributing to the firm's stock price increase (Maroun & Atkins, 2021).

Moreover, the firm's Efficiency Rating Programme in environmental management will award a certificate known as APPROPRIATE to entities that implement green accounting practices. Shareholders will receive this certification, which will trigger a market reaction characterized by fluctuations in stock prices (Anthony & Morrison-Saunders, 2023). We also utilized literature and theories to support studies on the impact of green accounting on firm value. Stakeholder theory pertains to the concerns and priorities that affect business stakeholders (Anthony & Morrison-Saunders, 2023). In this particular scenario, it is imperative for the organization to set up a substantial merger among CSR and ethics managerial procedures. Consequently, we disseminate information to all stakeholders about how an organization's operations can enhance its reputation in its surrounding environment (Latifah & Soewarno, 2023).

Furthermore, the legitimacy theory can act as a motivator for businesses to establish and implement voluntary social and ecological reporting, enabling them to fulfill their social obligations, achieve their goals, and thrive in an unresolved social environment (Nzama et al., 2022). In addition, implementing green accounting practices can improve an organization's image in the community by demonstrating its commitment to the tripartite bottom line—investor trust, financial, social, and environmental dimensions. Haleem et al.'s (2021) previous study indicated that the firm's stock price surged upon the introduction of green accounting, symbolized by the appropriate certification subcategory. Therefore, a decline in stock price may boost the firm value, suggesting that the implementation of green accounting practices could positively impact the firm value (Crous et al., 2021).

The inclusion of GRI reporting in the sustainability reports provided consumers with an additional lens through which to assess the value of the firm's environmental revelations (Dzomonda & Fatoki, 2020). Nonetheless, research indicates that including green accounting information does not have a significant impact on the firm's valuation. In fact, prospective and current investors place greater reliance on revenues and perspectives contained in annual reports for decision-making purposes, as opposed to environmental reports (Aliamutu & Mkhize, 2024a). The aim of this research is to investigate the effect of green accounting reporting on firm value in Southern African agriculture firms. Therefore, the hypothesis posits that the implementation of green accounting has a significant impact on a business's firm value, consistent with the theory and studies that have previously described a complex outcome. To investigate this hypothesis, the study formulates a research hypothesis that incorporates the following elements:

H1: The implementation of green accounting impacts the firm value.

Table 1 Sample of the study

Sample criteria	Number
The nations	5
Agricultural firms	201
Final financial information	(46)
Final sustainability reports	(30)
Availability content analysis	(43)
Total sample (number of firms)	78
Time frame of investigation (2017–2021)	6
Overall observations (year of firm)	199

Methodology

The financial information is sourced from Capital IQ SnP, while the financial statement and sustainability reports are obtained directly from the websites of the respective listed companies.

The original population the data obtained consists of 1019 firm-year samples. Subsequently, we eliminate companies that do not have comprehensive financial statements, a sustainable report, as well as accessible content analysis (Rahman & Islam, 2023). Consequently, the final dataset for this study consists of 199 firm-year samples spanning from 2019 to 2023. The researchers used imbalanced panel data. Table 1 displays the sample of the study, which consists of an agricultural firm located in Southern Africa.

Measuring of Variables

The research employed the specific terms (not recyclables, ecosystems, pollutants in the air, carbon dioxide emissions, resource plantations, society, sustainability, emissions, environmental expenditure, preserving water, refuse management, natural assets, energy efficiency, and natural resources) to ascertain the reporting of environmentally conscious accounting that adheres to the GRI guideline (Moses & Hopper, 2022). There is a collection of 14 specific terms that have been created based on the GRI 300. The study focuses on the firm value as the dependent variable, which is quantified by applying the Tobins' Q Ratio (Wicaksono & Setiawan, 2022). FV represents the firm's value and indicates how the decisions made by the firm affect its shareholders.

The control variable FINANCIAL PERFORMANCE is assessed using return on assets (ROA), which quantifies the level of financial performance derived from a company's commercial operations (Amahalu, 2020). Sales growth, which is determined by measuring the percentage increase in sales from the year prior to the present year, serves as an indicator of market demand and the amount of competitiveness within the sector for firms (Wirawan et al., 2020). In addition, we account for

LEVERAGE, which refers to the ratio of debt to capital. It quantifies the extent to which a firm's assets are financed by debt and its corresponding responsibilities (Ezenwoke & Tion, 2020). We additionally consider Size, which is determined by the logarithm of the firm's total assets. This metric allows us to categorize the firm's size accurately.

To achieve the goals of this study, we analyze the effects of GREEN ACCOUNTING using robust regression (Ezenwoke & Tion, 2020). Before doing the regression analysis, the data was subjected to a normalization method known as winorizing. The panel data regression models are selected using two approaches. The two models being referred to are the fixed effect model and the random effect model (Ingram et al., 2024). The researchers utilized the Hausman tests to ascertain a suitable model method. This research seeks to implement a regression model as a quantitative tool for data analysis. The statistical data will be collected and analyzed using a dependable methodology. This data could be used to enhance the analysis of firm value. The provided information reveals the regression model employed for testing the hypothesis, which is presented below.

$$TOBQ = a + \beta 1GA + \beta 2ROA + \beta 3SG + \beta 4LEV + \beta 5SIZE + \varepsilon$$

Results and Discussion

Table 2 displays the descriptive statistics of all the variables employed during the research that have been processed so far. The descriptive statistical analysis of the study dependent variable, Firm Value, reveals a minimum value of 0.3456577 and a mean value of 0.8241127. The agricultural firm is valued at 94.6%. If a firm's worth is less than 1, it indicates that its market price is lower than its book price (Saputra et al., 2021). In simple terms, shareholders are not willing to pay a premium for the firm. Regarding our independent variable, the lowest value for green accounting is 0.0000021, whereas the average value is 0.0000657.

This suggests that the agricultural firm's implementation and reporting of green accounting practices are rather limited (Saputra et al., 2021). The reason for this is that the overall rate of keyword reporting is still quite low, and not all companies reveal their sustainability evaluations. In addition, a few of the reports are difficult to read since they are presented as scanned PDF documents. The control variables,

Table 2 Descriptive statistics

Variable	Obs	Mean	SD	Min	Max
FV	199	0.8241127	0.8952965	0.3456577	7.113606
Green A-g	199	0.0000657	0.0000796	0.0000021	0.0002059
FP	199	−0.1218648	0.2787382	−1.664674	0.3601862
Sales Gr-h	199	1.138348	19.66862	−25.85618	344.6593
Lev	199	0.3818412	0.2702132	0.0286144	1.62514
Lnsize	199	2.205558	0.6677192	0.7271588	4.385429

including financial performance, have a minimum value of −1.664674, with a mean value of −0.1218648. The financial performance value is −2.2%, which indicates that it continues to be below the average for the sector of 8%. As a result, the financial performance in the agriculture sectors remains weak. This was attributed to the deficits incurred by 124 out of the 201 enterprises, as well as the uneven duration of the period under consideration. The standard deviation score is 0.2787382, indicating a comparatively low level of variance in financial performance across enterprises. The lowest value of sales growth is −25.85618, while the mean value is 1.138348. Therefore, sales growth of agricultural sectors between 2017 and 2021 is considered very favorable, as it amounts to a 2% increase. The standard deviation value of 19.66862 suggests a significant difference in the sales growth across organizations.

The leverage of agricultural companies exceeds the sector's average of 40%, with a minimum value of 0.0286144 as well as a mean value of 0.3818412, equivalent to 47.5%. The standard deviation value of 0.2702132 suggests that there can be a very small amount of variance in the leverage values across the organizations (Pizzi et al., 2023). The firm's size has a minimum value of 0.7271588 and a mean value of 2.205558, suggesting that agricultural firms tend to be rather modest in size. The size was quantified by measuring the natural logarithm of the total assets. According to decision-making made by agriculture small and medium businesses in South Africa, firms in South Africa are eligible to be classified as large firms if their total assets surpass R 750,001 or if they possess more than 11 assets (Sadovska et al., 2020). On the other hand, firms may be classified as medium or small if their total assets are lower than R 250,000 or if they have lower than 11 assets (Ika et al., 2021).

The standard deviation score of 0.6677192 suggests that there is very little variance in the size of the firms. Table 3 displays the Pearson correlation coefficients for the variables in the sample. The results demonstrate that the data in this research do not violate the assumption of multicollinearity since the correlation values of the variables are not more than or less than ±0.7. These findings indicate a clear negative association between the organization's firm value (TobinQ) and the reporting of green accounting. Furthermore, the dependent variable has a negative association with sales growth, leverage (DAR), and size (LnAssets), in contrast to financial

Table 3 Pearson correlation

Variables	FV	Green accounting	FP	Sales growth	Leverage	Size
FV	1.0000					
Green A-g	−0.0713**	1.0000				
FP	0.1573***	−0.0185	1.0000			
Sales Gr-h	−0.0171***	−0.0635	0.2220***	1.0000		
Lev	−0.2118***	−0.1805***	−0.2213***	−0.0313	1.0000	
Size	−0.1182	0.0764	0.1894	0.0338	0.1522***	1.0000

***Shows significance level at <1%.
**Shows significance level at <5%.
*Shows significance level at <10%.

performance (ROA), which demonstrates a positive relationship. Then, this research conducts tests using the Wald test to assess heteroscedasticity and uses the Wooldridge test to examine autocorrelation. As previously mentioned in Part 2, this study includes just one hypothesis. The objective is to examine the connection between green accounting and firm value (ROA). The findings of the robust regression analysis are examined in Part 4.1, whereas the data did not meet the heteroscedasticity test throughout the traditional assumption test (Büchling & Maroun, 2021). Depending on the Hausman tests, which reveal a probability value of 0.00 under the 0.05 error rate threshold, it can be determined that panel regression testing may be conducted using the fixed-effect model technique.

The Impact of Green Accounting Reporting on the Value of Firms

The outcomes of robust regression are shown in Table 4. Adjusted for both the year and firm variables. The impact of green accounting on firm size (Tobin Q), specifically the reporting of green accounting in agricultural industries in Southern Africa, has a negligible influence on the firm value. The green accounting has a coefficient of −267.1212 and a P-value of 0.296. It exceeds the significance threshold of 0.10. Therefore, H1 is deemed invalid. The revelation of green accounting has no impact on the intrinsic of firm value. The control variable, financial performance, has a coefficient of −0.2476627 and a p-value of 0.410, indicating that it has an insignificant influence on firm value. The p-value is greater than the significance threshold of 0.10. The sales increase has a negligible value, with a coefficient of 0.0022843 and a P-value of 0.826, which is above the significance threshold of 0.10.

The leverage demonstrates a substantial adverse impact, with a correlation coefficient of −3.262162 and a significance level of 0.006 at a 1% threshold. Although size has a coefficient of −0.0111287 and a p-value of 0.814, it does not have a significant influence on business value. The regression analysis of the model reveals that the reporting of green accounting, as measured by the total count of specific terms, is found in GRI guidelines in the financial statement and sustainability reports

Table 4 Robust regression

FV	Coefficient	SE	T	P > [t]	(95% conf. interval)	
Green accounting	−267.1212	282.1748	−1.02	0.296	−708.822	275.5819
FP	−0.2476627	0.171751	−0.95	0.410	−0.91175	0.412422
Sales growth	0.0022843	0.024226	0.09	0.826	−0.03778	0.042164
Lev	−3.262162	0.167587	−2.87	0.007***	−0.85918	−0.21525
Size	−0.0111287	0.227114	−0.08	0.814	−0.56257	0.422

***Shows significance level at <1%.
**Shows significance level at <5%.
*Shows significance level at <10%.

of agriculture firms in Southern Africa, has a negligible impact on firm value. This finding applies specifically to South Africa, Botswana, Namibia, Swaziland, and Mozambique. The insignificance of the business size (Tobin Q) is shown by the independent variables, namely green accounting. This outcome is consistent with other prior research done by Büchling and Maroun (2021) in which the value of the business is not influenced by ESG.

The public reporting additionally includes most of the environmental information relevant to green accounting. In addition, these results contrast with the research conducted by Bebbington et al. (2021), which indicates a considerable impact on the firm's value when businesses adopt or reporting green accounting practices. The outcome obtained by the authors contradicts the assertions made in stakeholder and legitimacy theory. The investor approach argues that the implementation of green accounting will offer shareholders valuable news, thereby enhancing firm value (Adae et al., 2021). Shareholders are further thought to prioritize firms that use sustainable accounting practices. Legitimacy theory posits that the use of green accounting serves as an indication of a firm's dedication to fulfilling its social and environmental obligations.

Nevertheless, this study demonstrates a contradictory outcome regarding the impact of green accounting on firm value. Several firms still neglect to provide details about their initiatives to promote environmental consciousness in their yearly financial statements or sustainability reports (Pangestuti et al., 2022). This might happen since firms had the belief that environmental reporting was discretionary or not obligatory. Since the publication of the GRI Sustainability Reporting requirements in the fourth quarter of 2016, organizations may still need to adjust to these new requirements. It is possible to clarify that the majority of agricultural firms have not yet adopted green accounting practices or provided a comprehensive report in accordance with the Global Reporting Initiative (GRI). Therefore, the adoption or revelation of green accounting has a negligible impact on the firm value. The research's control variables indicate that the financial performance variable, as expressed in ROA, has no impact on the firm's value.

The fluctuation in the business value does not align with the firm's financial performance, regardless of whether it is greater or lower. The relationship between sales growth and company worth is shown to be statistically negligible, suggesting that shifts in sales growth have no impact on firm value. This conclusion aligns with the findings of a study done by Samans and Nelson (2022), which asserts that sales growth has little impact on firm value. The additional independent variable, leverage, demonstrates a significant and adverse impact on the value of the business. The negative impact suggests that a high Debt to Asset Ratio leads to a decline in business value, which in turn might diminish shareholder trust and deter them from adopting substantial risks that may result in significant costs. This fact is substantiated by a study undertaken by Marrone and Oliva (2020), which asserts that the use of leverage has an impact on the valuation of a firm. The last variable, symbolized by Ln Assets, indicates that firm size has no impact on firm value. This might occur due to the firm's insufficient ability to leverage its assets effectively in order to maximize earnings. The size of a firm does not have a direct impact on its value since the size of the firm does not always indicate the quality of its worth in terms of purchase.

Conclusion

The adoption of green accounting, as indicated by the reporting of specific terms following the GRI guidelines, has a negligible impact on the market value of agriculture firms in Southern Africa, specifically in South Africa, Botswana, and Namibia. The aim of this research is to investigate the effect of green accounting reporting on firm value in Southern African agriculture firms. The inclusion of green accounting information in financial statements or sustainability reports will not impact fluctuations in stock prices.

Therefore, this might also imply that an investor may choose not to invest in agricultural sectors due to the firm's reporting of green accounting. In addition, the control factors included in this study, including financial performance (measured by return on assets), sales growth, and firm size (represented by the natural logarithm of assets), did not have any impact on firm value (measured by Tobin's Q). However, the use of leverage had a notable detrimental impact on the overall worth of the organization. Therefore, the primary determinant of a firm's value in this research is leverage. Shareholders prioritize the firm's leverage above its green accounting reporting when making investment decisions. This study also falls in conflict with stakeholder theory and legitimacy theory since it suggests that reporting of green accounting should provide valuable information for investors. Hence, agricultural firms are still reluctant to make an effort to include green accounting in their financial statements.

This study serves as a directive for corporations to increase their awareness of the reporting of green accounting, alongside the GRI guidelines, and to freely include it in their financial statements or separate sustainability reports. This chapter is limited by the modest quantity of observational data, which includes a total of 78 firms. In addition, the research relies on imbalanced panel data due to time restrictions and the challenges in acquiring comprehensive sustainability reports from firms. The reason for this is that several agricultural enterprises in Southern Africa have yet to reveal their sustainability reports. In addition, there are various financial statements and sustainability reports that cannot be analyzed using content analysis tools due to the format of these reports. Based on the aforementioned constraint, researchers may provide the following recommendations: future studies should prolong the duration of observation and incorporate a wider range of companies and sectors in order to achieve more diversified and improved test outcomes.

References

Adae, E. K., Kosiba, J. P. B., Hinson, R. E., Twum, K. K., Newman, N., & Nutsugah, F. F. (2021). *Responsible management in emerging markets: A multisectoral focus*. Springer Nature.

Aifuwa, H. O. (2020). Sustainability reporting and firm performance in developing climes: A review of literature. *Copernican Journal of Finance & Accounting, 9*(1), 9–29.

Aliamutu, K. F., & Mkhize, M. V. (2024). The influence of social responsibility on profitability in the Southern African Banking Industry. *Journal of Accounting Research, Organization and Economics, 7*(1), 111–129.

Aliamutu, K. F., & Mkhize, M. (2024a). Awareness of unpredictability in economic policy, fiscal decentralisation, and innovative approaches for the preservation of the environment in South Africa. *International Journal of Environmental, Sustainability, and Social Science, 5*(1), 91–105.

Aliamutu, K. F., & Mkhize, M. (2024b). The impact of failure to make payment behaviour on the profitability of South African municipal electricity suppliers. *International Journal of Environmental, Sustainability, and Social Science, 5*(3), 435–451.

Amahalu, N. (2020). Effect of environmental cost disclosure on profitability of listed oil and gas firms in Nigeria. *International Journal of Academic Research in Accounting, Finance and Management Sciences, 10*(2), 157–170.

Anthony, S. J., & Morrison-Saunders, A. (2023). Analysing corporate forest disclosure: How does business value biodiversity? *Business Strategy and the Environment, 32*(1), 624–638.

Attah-Botchwey, E., Soku, M. G., & Awadzıe, D. M. (2022). Sustainability reporting and the financial performance of banks in Africa. *Journal of Business Economics and Finance, 11*(1), 43–57.

Bebbington, J., Larrinaga, C., O'Dwyer, B., & Thomson, I. (2021). *Routledge handbook of environmental accounting*. Routledge.

Buallay, A. (2022). Sustainability reporting and agriculture industries' performance: Worldwide evidence. *Journal of Agribusiness in Developing and Emerging Economies, 12*(5), 769–790.

Büchling, M., & Maroun, W. (2021). Accounting for biodiversity and extinction: The case of South African national parks. *Social and Environmental Accountability Journal, 41*(1–2), 66–97.

Chamorro Gonzalez, C., & Herrera Mendoza, K. (2021). Green accounting in Colombia: A case study of the mining sector. *Environment, Development and Sustainability, 23*, 6453–6465.

Crous, C., Owen, J. R., Marais, L., Khanyile, S., & Kemp, D. (2021). Public disclosure of mine closures by listed South African mining companies. *Corporate Social Responsibility and Environmental Management, 28*(3), 1032–1042.

Dagestani, A. A., Qing, L., & Abou Houran, M. (2022). What remains unsolved in sub-African environmental exposure information disclosure: A review. *Journal of Risk and Financial Management, 15*(10), 487.

Denedo, M., & Egbon, O. (2021). Africa, from the past to the present: Moving the critical environmental accounting research on Africa forward. In *Routledge handbook of environmental accounting* (pp. 265–275). Routledge.

Dzomonda, O., & Fatoki, O. (2020). Environmental sustainability commitment and financial performance of firms listed on the Johannesburg Stock Exchange (JSE). *International Journal of Environmental Research and Public Health, 17*(20), 7504.

Ezenwoke, O., & Tion, W. (2020). International financial reporting standards (IFRSs) adoption in Africa: Abibliometric analysis. *Cogent Social Sciences, 6*(1), 1801370.

Faisal, F., Situmorang, L. S., Achmad, T., & Prastiwi, A. (2020). The role of government regulations in enhancing corporate social responsibility disclosure and firm value. *The Journal of Asian Finance, Economics and Business, 7*(8), 509–518.

Haleem, A., Abdul Nazar, M. C., & Mujahid Hilal, M. I. (2021). A systematic review on environmental accounting.

Hatane, S. E., Tarigan, J., Kuanda, E. S., & Cornelius, E. (2022). The contributing factors of intellectual capital disclosures in agriculture and mining sectors of Indonesia and Thailand. *Accounting Research Journal, 35*(2), 196–218.

Ika, S., Akbar, F., Puspitasari, D., Sumbodo, B., & Widagdo, A. (2021). *Corporate social responsibility reporting of agriculture companies: Evidence from Indonesia.* Paper presented at the IOP Conference Series: Earth and Environmental Science.

Ingram, J. C., McKenzie, E. J., Bagstad, K. J., Finisdore, J., van den Berg, R., Fenichel, E., et al. (2024). Leveraging natural capital accounting to support businesses with nature-related risk assessments and disclosures. *Philosophical Transactions of the Royal Society B, 379*(1903), 20220328.

Iredele, O. O., Tankiso, M., & Adelowotan, M. O. (2020). The influence of institutional isomorphism and organisational factors on environmental management accounting practices of listed Nigerian and south African firms. *South African Journal of Accounting Research, 34*(3), 183–204.

Khan, P. A., Johl, S. K., & Akhtar, S. (2021). Firm sustainable development goals and firm financial performance through the lens of green innovation practices and reporting: A proactive approach. *Journal of Risk and Financial Management, 14*(12), 605.

Latifah, S. W., & Soewarno, N. (2023). The environmental accounting strategy and waste management to achieve MSME's sustainability performance. *Cogent Business & Management, 10*(1), 2176444.

Maroun, W., & Atkins, J. (2021). A practical application of accounting for biodiversity: The case of soil health. *Social and Environmental Accountability Journal, 41*(1–2), 37–65.

Marrone, A., & Oliva, L. (2020). The level of integrated reporting alignment with the IIRC framework: Evidence from South Africa. *International Journal of Business and Management, 15*(1), 99–108.

Moses, O., & Hopper, T. (2022). Accounting articles on developing countries in ranked English language journals: A meta-review. *Accounting, Auditing & Accountability Journal, 35*(4), 1035–1060.

Nkwoji, N. (2021). Environmental accounting and profitability of selected quoted oil and gas companies in Nigeria (2012-2017). *Journal of Accounting and Financial Management, 7*(3), 22–39.

Nyakuwanika, M., van der Poll, H. M., & van der Poll, J. A. (2021). A conceptual framework for greener goldmining through environmental management accounting practices (Emaps): The case of Zimbabwe. *Sustainability, 13*(18), 10466.

Nzama, S., Olarewaju, O. M., Arise, O. A., & Ganiyu, I. (2022). Environmental management accounting (EMA) practices and plastic pollution control in selected food and beverage firms. *Cogent Business & Management, 9*(1), 2085368.

Olaleye, A. G., & Igbekoyi, O. E. (2020). Stakeholders' expectations and environmental accounting practices of listed manufacturing firms in Nigeria. *African Journal of Science Policy and Innovation Management, 1*(1), 131–144.

Osemene, O. F., Adinnu, P., Fagbemi, T. O., & Olowookere, J. K. (2021). Corporate governance and environmental accounting reporting in selected quoted African companies. *Global Business Review, 25*, 09721509211010989.

Pangestuti, D. C., Muktiyanto, A., & Geraldina, I. (2022). Role of profitability, business risk, and intellectual capital in increasing firm value. *Journal of Indonesian Economy and Business, 37*(3), 311–338.

Pizzi, S., Principale, S., Fasiello, R., & Imperiale, F. (2023). The institutionalisation of social and environmental accounting practices in Europe. *Journal of Applied Accounting Research, 24*(5), 816–838.

Qian, W., Tilt, C., & Belal, A. (2021). Social and environmental accounting in developing countries: Contextual challenges and insights. *Accounting, Auditing & Accountability Journal, 34*(5), 1021–1050.

Rahman, M. M., & Islam, M. E. (2023). The impact of green accounting on environmental performance: Mediating effects of energy efficiency. *Environmental Science and Pollution Research, 30*(26), 69431–69452.

Sadovska, V., Ekelund Axelson, L., & Mark-Herbert, C. (2020). Reviewing value creation in agriculture—A conceptual analysis and a new framework. *Sustainability, 12*(12), 5021.

Samans, R., & Nelson, J. (2022). *Sustainable enterprise value creation: Implementing stakeholder capitalism through full ESG integration*. Springer Nature.

Saputra, K. A. K., Manurung, D. T., Rachmawati, L., Siskawati, E., & Genta, F. K. (2021). Combining the concept of green accounting with the regulation of prohibition of disposable plastic use. *International Journal of Energy Economics and Policy, 11*(4), 84–90.

Utomo, M. N., Rahayu, S., Kaujan, K., & Irwandi, S. A. (2020). Environmental performance, environmental disclosure, and firm value: Empirical study of non-financial companies at Indonesia Stock Exchange. *Green Finance, 2*(1), 100–113.

Van Linh, N., Hung, D. N., & Binh, T. Q. (2022). Relationship between sustainability reporting and firm's value: Evidence from Vietnam. *Cogent Business & Management, 9*(1), 2082014.

Wicaksono, A. P., & Setiawan, D. (2022). Water disclosure in the agriculture industry: Does stakeholder influence matter? *Journal of Cleaner Production, 337*, 130605.

Wirawan, A. W., Falah, L. J., Kusumadewi, L., Adhariani, D., & Djakman, C. D. (2020). The effect of corporate social responsibility on the firm value with risk management as a moderating variable. *Journal of Asia-Pacific Business, 21*(2), 143–160.

Wiredu, I., Osei Agyemang, A., & Agbadzidah, S. Y. (2023). Does green accounting influences ecological sustainability? Evidence from a developing economy. *Cogent Business & Management, 10*(2), 2240559.

The Environmental Impact of Industrialisation, Productive Capacity, and Governance in the East Africa Community

Elizabeth Joseph

Abstract This study examines the impact of industrialisation, productive capacity index, and governance on CO2 emissions in East Africa from 2002 to 2018. A dataset of five countries—Kenya, Uganda, Tanzania, Burundi, and Rwanda—and Pooled Mean Group Autoregressive Distributed Lag (PMG-ARDL) was used for analysis. Results reveal that, in the long run, industry value added, governance, trade, and population density positively and significantly affected carbon emissions (CO2) per capita. However, the productive capacity index negatively significantly affected carbon emissions per capita. In the short run, the productive capacity index negatively and significantly affected carbon emissions. Variations by country in the short run are observed where industry value added, productive capacity index, governance, and trade significantly negatively affected carbon emissions in Uganda. However, population density in Kenya, Tanzania, Uganda, and Burundi significantly increased carbon emissions in the short run. Only industrialisation had a significant positive effect on carbon emissions in Rwanda. The results imply that industrialisation harms the environment, leading to higher carbon emissions and that poor governance increases the strain on the environment. Moreover, long-run estimation confirms that productive capacity has a significant role in increasing environmental quality. Therefore, emphasis on improving industrialisation across countries should also align with enhancing their governance indicators to strengthen the implementation of policies governing environmental concerns. Thus, policymakers should have an appropriate mix between industrial growth and emission reduction strategies.

Keywords Industrialisation · CO2 emission · Governance · Productive capacity

E. Joseph (✉)
University of Dar-es-Salaam Business School, Dar es Salaam, Tanzania
e-mail: joseph.elizabeth@udsm.ac.tz

T. Moloi (ed.), *Impacting Society Positively Through Technology in Accounting and Business Processes*, Springer Proceedings in Business and Economics,
https://doi.org/10.1007/978-3-031-84885-8_19

Introduction

The rapid growth of fossil energy consumption has resulted in considerable attention towards reducing carbon emissions. Moreover, with economic globalisation and trade liberalisation, exploring the relationship between trade and carbon emission is increasingly critical as foreign trade significantly promotes carbon emissions (Gao et al., 2021; Sun et al., 2022). Therefore, variation in comparative advantages among countries should ensure the optimal allocation of resources to reduce carbon emissions.

Industrialisation growth leading to environmental degradation has been attributed to human activities in various sectors and increasing global fossil fuel consumption such as oil, gas, and coal being key energy sources for industrialisation. According to Sun et al., 2022, the leading cause of emissions is chemical manufacturing in Kenya, while in Tanzania, there is high growth in mining and extraction and a rapid rise in the construction sector. Rural industrialisation has led to the rapid expansion of craft villages and intense market competition in other areas, leading to environmental pollution and resource depletion (Dang & Tran, 2020).

Despite the increase in industrialisation, the role of governance has been instrumental in spearheading the reduction of negative environmental consequences. Governance challenges about the environment include legal documents created to apply to all types of industries, enterprises, and industrial producers; shortage of qualified staff working in the environmental management sector; insufficiency of resources and staff; competing tasks and priorities; and shifting responsibilities to local authorities, especially at the commune level hence leading to a conflict of interest (Dang & Tran, 2020). Moreover, the legal framework needs more legitimacy among craft producers. Therefore, poor regulatory frameworks and implementation mechanisms may adversely affect carbon emissions due to inadequate controls. As a result of immature economies, corruption penetrates the developing economies and eventually causes carbon emissions and pollution (Dash et al., 2020).

Many emerging economies seek to advance through financial development and trade activities. Trade growth has been linked to increased industrialisation due to the growth in manufacturing. However, governance has reduced carbon emissions with higher financial development (Jianguo et al., 2022). Furthermore, institutional quality has moderated the effect of trade on carbon emissions. Growth in trade among countries has been associated with comparative advantages of countries allowing countries to specialise in goods and services they can produce at the lowest opportunity cost, hence increasing efficiency and productivity. For instance, Purwono et al. (2022) found that export expansion occurred in goods with comparative advantage and export specialisation. Therefore, variation in trade patterns among regional partners and countries implies variation in productivity capacities among countries. Productive capacity emanates from a country's productive resources, entrepreneurial capabilities, and production linkages, which determine a country's capacity to produce goods and services and grow and develop (UNCTAD, 2023). Countries are at different levels of development and thus vary in productive capacities and trade. Thus, the impact of trade on carbon emissions has varied across countries (Sun et al., 2019; Gao et al., 2021; Sarkodie et al., 2020).

Globally, emissions from industry declined by 1.7% (IEA, 2022). The global decline was largely driven by a CO2 decrease in China's industry emissions, reflecting a 10% decline in cement production and a 2% decline in steel-making. However, Africa is a minor contributor to global emissions, and it accounts for less than 4% of global energy-related carbon dioxide (CO2) emissions today and has the lowest emissions per capita in the world (IEA, 2023). However, emissions in East Africa have been rising. The combined emissions of Kenya, Tanzania, Ethiopia, and Uganda account for more than 80% of emissions in East Africa (Sun et al., 2022). Therefore, addressing climate change remains paramount. Various efforts have been undertaken to reduce pollution and maintain environmental quality. Being members to the Kyoto Agreement, EAC member states are dedicated to the climate agenda emphasising on pollution reduction. Though the national determined contributions, parties provide information on mitigation targets including emission reduction targets.

Previous literature has served well in understanding the link between industrialisation and governance on carbon emissions (Mahmood et al., 2020; Dash et al., 2020; Ahmed et al., 2022; Sarwar & Alsaggaf, 2021). However, several gaps exist. First, variations exist across countries and regions (Mahmood et al., 2020; Dash et al., 2020). Hence, there is a need to examine carbon emissions across different areas, particularly East African countries (Sun et al., 2022). Second, there is a need to incorporate market-based regulatory or policy variables. Studies have limited governance investigation to include transparency and integrity (Dash et al., 2020), while others use governance effectiveness and regulatory quality (Sarwar & Alsaggaf, 2021). However, governance is broader and constitutes the rule of law, voice, and accountability, considering recipients' perspectives and their impact on implementing laws and regulations. Hence, this study uses a governance index comprising six elements to examine the effect of industrialisation, trading capacity, and governance on CO2 emissions in the East African Community. Moreover, the variation across time reflecting changes in development as countries advance means that examining the short-run and long-run relations is critical. This study applies the Pooled Mean Group ARDL approach which efficiently examines the long-run dynamics by confining long-run equilibrium to become homogeneous across countries and allowing heterogeneity for short-run associations (Asteriou & Hall, 2007). This allows examining countries that have experienced shifts across time given policy changes and developmental initiatives such as industrialisation agenda, hence observing short-run and long-run transitions across countries in East Africa.

This study examined the impact of industrialisation, productive capacity Index, and governance on CO2 emissions in East Africa from 2002 to 2018. The long-run results revealed that, industry value added, governance, trade, and population density positively and significantly affected carbon emissions per capita. However, the productive capacity index negatively significantly affected carbon emissions per capita. The significance of this study is that, it contributes to the empirical literature by investigating the long-run and short-run link between industrialisation, productive capacities and carbon emissions, focusing exclusively on the East Africa region. These countries' emission trends are increasing compared to other developed countries; hence, the need to shift focus to reducing global greenhouse emissions supported by good regulatory frameworks is critical. Furthermore, this study is significant for policy and regulatory players amid emphasis on the growth of industrialisation among economies to foster economic development. Understanding the role of accountability, political stability, government effectiveness, regulatory quality, rule of law, and the control of corruption is crucial for policy implementation as it reflects the extent to which environmental protection is being effectively implemented. Most developing countries do not have strict environmental management guidelines (Ahmed et al., 2022). Moreover, the East Africa region is coupled with population growth challenges, contributing to carbon emissions (Sun et al., 2022). The energy developmental initiatives such as the East Africa Power Pull (EAPP) and the Energy Charter are likely to attract accountable and risk-averse investments (Nyamongo & Nyamongo, 2019). Therefore, there is a need for an appropriate balance between growth objectives and emission reduction objectives.

The rest of the paper is structured as follows: Section 2 discusses the literature review, Sect. 3 examines the methodological approach, Sect. 4 delves into the discussion of the findings, and finally, Sect. 5 gives the conclusions and recommendations.

Theoretical Literature Review

Several theoretical underpinnings elaborate on environmental impact emanating from various factors. These theoretical underpinnings are the Environmental Kuznets Curve (EKC), Stochastic Impacts by Regression on Population, Affluence, and Technology (STIRPAT), and the Pollution Haven Hypothesis (PHH). The Environmental Kuznets curve (EKC) explains the relationship between economic growth and environmental degradation. The EKC explains that increased economic activity harms the environment due to a lack of innovations, creativity, and financial investment.

Accordingly, there is an inverse U-shaped curve between emissions and income. At the beginning of the process of economic development of a society, pollution increases at the start of the economic cycle. This hypothesis explains why there is a positive correlation between income and environmental degradation when a country's income level is low. As pollution levels fall, regulatory institutions become more effective, and people value the environment, which increases the resources available for investment. Once a society reaches an income threshold, demand for environmental quality improvements will increase. This is not only observed concerning income, that is, GDP; other studies have also observed the inverted relationship between the trade of a country and carbon emissions (Sun et al., 2019; Gao et al., 2021).

The Pollution Haven Hypothesis elaborates on the relation between trade and pollution. The PHH elaborates on the trade dynamics and regulatory stringency among countries, such that polluting industries will relocate to jurisdictions with less stringent environmental regulations. Thus, strict environmental regulations in a country force company to relocate to economies with friendly environmental laws (Sun et al., 2019). It has been evidenced in developing countries that higher FDI will achieve lower carbon emissions, provided a strong institutional framework exists (Singhania & Saini, 2021). However, a critique of the PHH argues that it has led to mixed results due to ignoring dynamic factors like technology and market access, which are the most critical determinants of the location of any industry (Gill et al., 2018).

Globalisation concerning trade encompasses trade, composition, scale, and technology effects. Composition reflects that countries should change their production process based on their comparative advantage, scale means that economic growth, mainly due to trade, worsens the environment due to increased economic activity's expansion of energy demand. Technology effects have been linked to the environmental impacts of transferred knowledge and innovative production methods as income and trade expand. Integrating trade and technology establish essential components of countries' productive capacities. This is because productive capacities emphasise interactions among productive resources, entrepreneurial capabilities, and production linkages (UNCTAD, 2023).

Productive resources are factors of production, including different types of productive resources and capital, such as financial and physical capital while entrepreneurial capabilities are the skills, knowledge, and information enterprises have, including entrepreneurship, entrepreneurial, and technological capabilities. Moreover, production linkages are flows among productive units of goods and services, knowledge, technology and information, and productive resources, including human resources. They include exchanges among productive units of different sizes and ownership structures operating in different sectors. A country's combination of productive resources, entrepreneurial capabilities, and production linkages produces distinctive capacities for producing goods and services. These attributes determine the types of goods and services produced, because productive capacities are often activity-specific, as they promote specific products and processes. This can be supported by innovation in research and development. Despite innovation diminishing carbon dioxide emissions for high-income countries, it is not the same for other countries, possibly due to pollution haven (Jiang et al., 2022).

Environmental degradation has largely been associated with the population dynamics of countries. The STIRPAT model asserts that environmental impacts are a function of population, affluence, and technology. Nosheen et al. (2020) established that energy consumption and urbanisation positively impact $CO2$ emissions and output. Moreover, Wen et al. established that population size and urbanisation significantly positively correlated with carbon emissions, aggravating environmental degradation, and hindering sustainable economic development.

Empirical Literature Review

The Impact of Industrialisation and Governance on Carbon Emissions

Ahmed et al. (2022) examined the environmental impact of industrialisation and foreign direct in 55 Asia-Pacific countries from 1995 to 2020. Applying ARDL, results showed that FDI increased methane and CO2 emissions. Moreover, industrialisation positively and significantly impacted the environment, but the impact was moderate. Zafar et al. (2020) also observed the significant positive effect of industrialisation by examining 46 Asian countries divided into five subregion groups from 1991 to 2017. The cointegration test revealed that the variables were cointegrated and verified their long-run relationship. The fully modified ordinary least-squares results concluded that industrialisation positively impacts carbon dioxide emissions in the long run.

Dash et al. (2020) investigated the impact of urbanisation, industrialisation, corruption, human development, energy consumption, and foreign direct investment on carbon dioxide emissions of 61 developing economies in the global south region of Asia, Africa, and Latin America from 1990 to 2015. They found that the effect of corruption on CO2 emissions was heterogeneous and contradictory. Furthermore, FDI predominantly curbs CO2 emissions, pollution, and environmental degradation. Regarding industrialisation, the empirical results revealed that it increases carbon emission rate while incorporating both time- and country-specific effects. Thus, this suggests that industrial-led growth in the region has led to higher carbon emission rates.

Mahmood et al. (2020) investigated the effects of industrialisation and urbanisation on the CO2 emissions per capita in Saudi Arabia using annual data from 1968 to 2014. They found that industrialisation and urbanisation impede the environment, with the inelastic effect of urbanisation and the elastic effect of industrialisation on emissions. There was an asymmetric relationship between industrialisation and emissions, with increasing industrialisation having a more significant environmental impact than decreasing industrialisation.

In their study, Sarwar and Alsaggaf (2021) examined the impact of governance indicators using quantile regression from 1970 to 2018. The study found that both governance effectiveness and regulatory quality led to a reduction in carbon emissions in Saudi Arabia. Similarly, institutions have been found to reduce carbon emissions. This is established by Bayar et al., who examined the impact of institutional development and human capital on CO2 emissions in 11 EU transition economies from 2000 to 2018. Results showed that human capital negatively affected CO2 emissions in Croatia, the Czech Republic, Hungary, and Slovenia and that institutions harmed CO2 emissions in the Czech Republic. However, both institutions and human capital positively affected CO2 emissions in Latvia and Lithuania. The rise in CO2 emissions in Latvia and Lithuania may have resulted from the growth effect of institutions outweighing their environmental effects. The findings further revealed that most countries had not reached their threshold level to experience improvements in ecological quality through institutions. In line with Bayar et al., institutional quality has been examined as a moderating role in reducing carbon emissions. Jianguo et al. (2022) studied 37 OECD nations from 1998 to 2018, and they found that financial development positively affects selected carbon emission dimensions. Furthermore, institutional quality and technology innovation conditioning effects are crucial between economic growth and CO2 emission; hence, technology innovation and institutional quality have a moderating role in reducing CO2 emissions in OECD economies.

Simionescu et al. examined the validation of the Environmental Kuznets curve and the renewable energy Kuznets curve in ten Central and Eastern European countries (Bulgaria, Czech Republic, Estonia, Hungary, Latvia, Lithuania, Poland, Romania, Slovakia, and Slovenia) from 1990 to 2019. The impact of governance in these countries on greenhouse gas emissions was assessed in 2002–2019. Using ARDL, results showed that renewable energy consumption reduced pollution, and labour productivity increased greenhouse gas emissions in the long run. Moreover, domestic credit to the private sector reduced pollution in the long run only from 2002 to 2019. In addition, the rule of law, regulatory quality, and control of corruption contributed to environmental quality in the long run. Furthermore, Gani (2012) examined a cross-section of developing countries using five dimensions of good governance (political stability, government effectiveness, regulatory quality, rule of law, and corruption) and carbon dioxide emissions. Results evidenced that political stability, the rule of law, and control of corruption are negatively and statistically significantly correlated with CO2 emissions per capita. Furthermore, trade openness and the size of the industrial sector are strong correlates of CO2 emissions.

Yu et al. (2024) examined whether industrialisation promoted the emission mitigation agenda in 14 nations in East Africa from 1990 to 2019. Using the cross-sectionally augmented distributed lag estimator and the augmented mean group estimator, results revealed that industrialisation reduced the environmental quality in the region through high CO2 emissions. In addition, financial development, foreign direct investments, urbanisation, and energy consumption were not environmentally friendly in East Africa. Despite investigating East Africa, the study does not consider other aspects, such as the productive capacities of the countries investigated.

The Impact of Trade and Productive Capacities on Carbon Emissions

Sarkodie et al. (2020) examined the global effects of urban sprawl, industrialisation, trade, and economic development on carbon dioxide emissions across 206 countries and territories from 1960 to 2018. They found that increased economic growth, population dynamics, and energy utilisation stimulate global emissions across countries and regions at national, urban and household levels. The triple effect (exploitation of natural resources, production, and consumption) of economic development spurs environmental pollution. The interaction between trade and carbon dioxide emissions is examined by Sun et al. (2019) by integrating economic growth and energy usage in 49 high-emission countries in Belt and Road regions from 1991 to 2014. They found that trade openness had positive and negative impacts on environmental pollution, but this effect varied in different groups of nations. Moreover, results showed a long-run causal effect between trade, economic growth, energy consumption, and environmental pollution in the Belt and Road, Europe, high-income, middle-income, and low-income panels. An inverted U-form relationship exists between trade and carbon emissions. The variation in the effect of trade in different groups of nations is also observed by Gao et al. (2021), who used a spatial econometric and a dynamic panel threshold model to empirically test the spatial effect, non-linear effect, and heterogeneous effect of foreign trade on global carbon emissions. Results showed that carbon emissions in various countries exhibit significant spatial spillover in the overall spatial context. Foreign trade is vital in promoting carbon emissions in local and similar economic areas, but it also has a dual-threshold effect on economic development. Moreover, results also showed significant differences in the impact of foreign trade on carbon emissions in different regions and periods.

Nosheen et al. (2020) examined the impact of energy use and urbanisation on carbon emissions from 1995 to 2018 using the extended STIRPAT model for Asian countries. The results confirmed the presence of long-run cointegration among variables. Furthermore, energy consumption, GDP per capita, and urbanisation directly impact carbon emissions. In contrast, trade openness and domestic credit have an inverse effect on CO2 in the long run. Energy use, domestic credit, and urban population are directly associated with output, whereas trade liberalisation negatively impacts output growth in the long run. The negative impact of trade on CO2 emissions is contrary to Sarkodie et al. (2020), who examined the heterogeneous contribution of immediate and underlying drivers of emissions across 206 countries and territories from 1960 to 2018. Using a dynamic panel estimation, they presented a global accounting of economic policy and debt, population structure, density and urbanisation, and environmental-related aggregate indicators in a carbon emission function. They found that the instantaneous increase in economic development, population dynamics, and energy utilisation stimulate global emissions across countries and territories at national, urban, and household levels. Industrialisation and trade also increased global pollution levels resulting from the impact of carbonised and energy-intensive economic structures in many developing and developed economies.

Regarding the impact of the productive capacity of countries, Oluc et al. (2022) examined the dynamic relationship between carbon dioxide emissions, economic growth, and the productive capacity index for 38 organisations for OECD countries from 2000 to 2018. The pooled mean group-panel autoregressive distributive lag approach confirmed the environmental Kuznets curve hypothesis. Furthermore, findings confirmed that improved productive capacity decreases ecological degradation. These findings are similar to those of Mo and Madni (2023), who examined 52 nations engaged in the Belt and Road Initiative from 2001 to 2022 using OLS, Difference GMM, System GMM, and cross-sectional-ARDL techniques. They found that enhancing productive capacities, foreign direct investment, and institutional quality significantly reduces carbon emissions in the region. At the same time, energy poverty, urbanisation, and economic growth are linked to higher carbon emissions. Moreover, the 'pollution halo effect' is proven, because adopting eco-friendly technologies through foreign corporations reduces carbon emissions.

Literature review indicates that several previous studies have documented a significant relationship between economic growth, energy consumption, urbanisation, population, trade, industrialisation, and carbon emissions. However, two issues are observed; first, limited studies have directed the study of industrialisation and carbon emission in East Africa. In particular, the role of productive capacities remains limited in the investigation of East Africa. Second, most of the studies focusing on governance have left out the role of the rule of law, voice, and accountability, which give perspectives not only from the government but also from the users and recipients of laws and regulations who may have an impact on the practical implementation of these laws and regulations about environmental effects. To account for this gap, the current study examines the impact of the rule of law, voice and accountability, political stability, control of corruption, governance effectiveness, and regulatory quality on carbon emissions for East African community countries. This is accomplished by computing a governance index constructed as an average score across the six governance indicators. Furthermore, the study examines the role of trade, productive capacities, and population dynamics on carbon emissions.

Methodology

Data and Sample

The population comprises eight EAC partner states: Kenya, Uganda, Tanzania, Rwanda, Burundi, Southern Sudan, the Federal Republic of Somalia, and the Democratic Republic of Congo (EAC, 2024). However, DRC, Southern Sudan, and the Federal Republic of Somalia are excluded from the analysis. This is because DRC recently joined the EAC, acceding to the EAC Treaty on 8 April 2022 and becoming a full member on 11 July 2022. Moreover, Southern Sudan joined the EAC on 5 September 2016, and the Federal Republic of Somalia joined the EAC on 15 December 2023. Given the East Africa Industrialization Strategy of 2012–2032 and some recent countries had not joined, the current study focuses on the five countries when the industrialisation strategy began. As a result, the sample comprised five countries. The data are obtained from the World Development Indicators, the World Governance Indicators of the World Bank, and UNCTAD. The sample period ranges from 2002 to 2018. This period is investigated, because it builds on the industrialisation agenda of the nations whose development visions have articulated industrialisation, hence allowing us to examine the transitions from short- and long-run perspectives.

Description of Variables

The description of the variables is summarised in Table 1. The governance measures are obtained from the Worldwide Governance Indicators to assess the quality of governance in countries (Kaufmann et al., 2010). These indicators reflect the vision of these countries' companies, citizens, and experts. They, therefore, indicate governance perspectives from the government, which lays out the policy and regulatory benchmarks, and the citizens and other actors who play a part in implementing such policies and regulations. Government institutions establish priorities for economic agents in terms of environmental resources. As a result, government efficiency in dealing with environmental issues to achieve economic growth plays an important role. Following prior research, the current study investigates population density as people per square km of land. Previous studies have considered variants of population measurement, such as total and urban population (Sarkodie et al., 2020), while

Table 1 Description of variables

Variable	Definition	Symbol	Source
Carbon emission per capita	Carbon emission per capita	CO2	WDI
Industry and construction value added (IVA)	Industry (including construction), value added (current US$)	IVA	WDI, Ahmed et al. (2022)
Governance index	This is an index that comprises the average of Voice and accountability, Political stability, Government effectiveness, Regulatory quality, Rule of law, and Control of corruption (see Appendix 1 for a description of each aspect of governance)	GOVERINDEX	WGI, Gani (2012); Kaufmann et al. (2010)
Trade	Trade as a percentage of GDP is the sum of exports and imports of goods and services measured as a share of gross domestic product	TRADE	WDI, Sun et al. (2019); Mahmood et al. (2020)
Population density	People per sq. km of land area	POPDENSITY	WDI
Productive Industries Capacity Index (PCI)	The productive resources, entrepreneurial capabilities, and production linkages which together determine the capacity of a country to produce goods and services and enable it to grow and develop	PCI	UNCTAD, Oluc et al. (2022)

others use urbanisation as a proxy for modernisation (Nosheen et al., 2020). This study captures the population using population density. This is because population density plays a vital role in harvesting societies, that is, those that depend on agriculture and natural resources, which is the case for most EAC countries. Too high population density decreases the natural endowment per capita but eases infrastructure development, leading to an optimal population density for economic growth (Yegorov, 2015). Moreover, population density is one of the population factors that has been found to impede CO2 emissions in high- and lower-middle-income countries and increase emissions in lower-income nations (Pickson et al., 2024).

Econometric Estimation

The study applied the PMG-ARDL approach, and the econometric estimation of the effect of industrialisation, productive capacities, and governance on carbon dioxide emission is expressed as follows:

$$\Delta CO2_{it} = \varphi E_{i,t-1} + \alpha_0 + \lambda_k \sum_{k=1}^{k} \Delta CO2_{k,t-1} + \lambda_k \sum_{k=1}^{k} \Delta IVA_{k,t-1} + \lambda_k \sum_{k=1}^{k} \Delta GOVERINDEX_{k,t-1}$$
$$+\lambda_k \sum_{k=1}^{k} \Delta TRADE_{k,t-1} + \lambda_k \sum_{k=1}^{k} \Delta PCI_{k,t-1} + \lambda_k \sum_{k=1}^{k} \Delta POPDENSITY_{k,t-1} + \delta_k CO2_{t-1} + \delta_k IVA_{t-1}$$
$$+\delta_k GOVERINDEX_{t-1} + \delta_k TRADE_{t-1} + \delta_k PCI_{t-1} + \delta_k POPDENSITY_{t-1} + \varepsilon_{it}$$

where ε_{it} is the error term, Δ represents the first difference operator of the variables, α is the intercept term, λ and δ are the subsequent long-term and short-term coefficients, respectively, and ε is the error term. $\varphi E_{i,t-1}$ is the error correction coefficient showing speed of adjustment towards equilibrium on the long term and is expected to be negative and statistically significant, confirming the long-run relationship existence. The dependent variable is CO_2 emissions per capita. Five main variables are the independent variables: industry value added (IVA), governance (GOVERINDEX), trade (TRADE), population density (POPDENSITY), and productive capacities (PCI). The Pooled Mean Group auto-regressive distributed lag is used to analyse the unbalanced data. The pooled mean group allows the short-term parameters to differ while imposing equality of the long-term coefficients between groups. Thus, differences between countries concerning the short-run effects on pollution and possible convergence in the long run in EAC countries could be observed.

Findings and Discussion

The descriptive results show that, on average, the level of carbon emissions per capita is 0.132, with a maximum of 0.39. The level of industrialisation is, on average, 19.62, while the maximum is 27.01. Governance is, on average, negative but with a maximum of positive. Thus, while some countries have a poor governance index, there is an indication that some countries have a positive governance quality score. However, the negative skewness and mean governance index show that, on average, EAC countries have poor governance (Table 2).

The correlation matrix in Table 3 reveals that industry value added, productive capacity index, governance index, and trade significantly positively correlate with carbon dioxide emissions per capita. The positive significant correlation indicates that industrialisation, productive capacities, trade, and governance increase carbon emissions per capita. The productive capacity is positively correlated with industrialisation. This could be linked to the productive resources, entrepreneurial capabilities, and production linkages that enhance manufacturing firm production in a country. Governance is positively correlated with industrialisation, meaning that improvement in governance quality improves a nation's industrialisation. This could be attributed to implementing rules, regulations, and strategies that support the development of the industrial sector. For instance, implementing the East African Industrialization Strategy (2012–2032) holds the key to unlocking the region's development potential through structural transformation and diversification of the regional economy. National industrialisation policies and strategies underpin the EAC Industrialization Strategy and draw lessons from best regional and international practices towards diversifying the manufacturing base and strengthening innovation and technology capabilities for structural transformation.

Population density negatively correlates with carbon emissions, industrialisation, productive capacities, governance, and trade. Population density refers to the number of people per square kilometre of land, thus the higher the population density, the less productive land per person on one hand. On the other, it could link to possibility of increased urban land size due to infrastructure development. Thus, raw inputs into manufacturing may be limited due to lower production. Thus, this could reduce trade potential, because the composition of EAC trade is dominated by agricultural commodities and therefore low emissions.

Table 2 Descriptive statistics

Variables	Obs.	Mean	Std. Dev.	Min	Max	p1	p99	Skew.	Kurt.
CO2	85	0.132	0.096	0.02	0.39	0.02	0.39	0.925	2.935
IVA GDP	85	19.623	4.266	10.99	27.01	10.99	27.01	0.114	1.853
PCI	85	22.089	2.057	17.41	25.73	17.41	25.73	−0.205	2.241
GOVERINDEX	85	−0.665	0.349	−1.456	0.021	−1.456	0.021	−0.517	2.906
TRADE	85	41.199	9.401	21.674	64.479	21.674	64.479	0.14	2.587
POPDENSITY	85	208.314	148.86	39.89	498.661	39.89	498.661	0.417	1.636

Table 3 Correlation analysis

Variables	(1)	(2)	(3)	(4)	(5)	(6)
(1) CO2PERCAPITA	1.000					
(2) IVA_GDP	0.267*	1.000				
(3) PCI	0.646*	0.467*	1.000			
(4) GOVERINDEX	0.333*	0.499*	0.723*	1.000		
(5) TRADE	0.406*	0.187	0.329*	0.411*	1.000	
(6) POPDENSITY	−0.681*	−0.626*	−0.235*	−0.175	−0.304*	1.000

*** $p < 0.01$, ** $p < 0.05$, * $p < 0.1$

Table 4 Cross-sectional dependence test

Variable	CD-test	p-value	Corr.	abs(corr.)
CO2	10.440	0.000	0.801	0.801
IVA_GDP	2.650	0.008	0.203	0.542
PCI	12.450	0.000	0.955	0.955
GOVERINDEX	2.730	0.006	0.209	0.380
TRADE	2.410	0.016	0.185	0.448
POPDENSITY	13.030	0.000	0.999	0.999

Notes: Under the null hypothesis of cross-section independence CD ~ N(0,1)

Regression Results

The cross-sectional dependence test in Table 4 revealed the presence of cross-sectional dependence as indicated by the significant p-values. Cross-sectional dependence can substantially complicate statistical inference for a panel data model. Therefore, Hsiao (2014) suggests using the cross-sectional mean augmented approach for controlling the impact of cross-sectional dependency. On one hand, this study uses the PMG-ARDL, because it considers the valid long-run restrictions, it is robust to the outliers and lag orders and allows for differences in the short-run coefficients, error variances, and intercepts (Asteriou & Hall, 2007; Lau et al., 2019). It is, however, limited by the identical long-term coefficients (Pesaran et al., 1999).

On the other hand, given the presence of cross-sectional dependence, this study further applied the group mean error correction approach. It is considered heterogeneous short- and long-run connection, though sensitive to small samples.

Unit Root Test

The Harris–Tzavalis test was used to test for unit root. The null hypothesis tests that panels contain unit roots, while the alternative hypothesis test is that panels are stationary. Results reveal that all the variables had unit root at level variables, as shown by the insignificant p-values in Table 5. However, at the first difference,

Table 5 Harris–Tzavalis unit root test

Variables	At level			At first difference		
	Statistic	z-value	p-value	Statistic	z-value	p-value
CO2	0.358	−2.296	0.011	0.033	−4.870	0.000
IVA_GDP	0.393	−1.969	0.025	−0.213	−7.050	0.000
PCI	0.476	−1.204	0.114	−0.058	−5.674	0.000
GOVERINDEX	0.572	−0.312	0.378	0.007	−5.099	0.000
TRADE	0.669	0.593	0.723	0.029	−4.911	0.000
POPDENSITY	0.932	3.034	0.999	1.035	4.001	1.000

Table 6 Cointegration test

Pedroni test for cointegration		
Ho: No cointegration	Number of panels = 5	
Ha: All panels are cointegrated	Number of periods = 16	
Cointegrating vector: Panel specific		
Panel means: Included.	Kernel: Bartlett	
Time trend: Not included	Lags: 2.00 (Newey-West)	
AR parameter: Panel specific	Augmented lags: 1	
Statistic p-value	Statistic	p-value
Modified Phillips-Perron t	1.7725	0.0382
Phillips-Perron t	−7.4905	0.0000
Augmented Dickey-Fuller t	−6.3441	0.0000

results revealed that all variables were stationary, as reflected by the significant results of the p-value, hence evidence against the null hypothesis, thus concluding that all variables are stationary at the first difference except for population density.

Cointegration Test

The Pedroni test was used because it allows for multiple regressors, for the cointegration vector to vary across different sections of the panel, and also for heterogeneity in the errors across cross-sectional units (Asteriou & Hall, 2007). The results of the Pedroni test for cointegration revealed that the panels are cointegrated, as indicated by the significant p-value in Table 6.

The PMG-ARDL regression estimates in Table 7 show that industrialisation significantly positively affected carbon emissions. This indicates that industrial growth increases carbon emissions, negatively impacting the environment. This implies that as countries increase their industrial activities, they also increase environmental pollution. The positive effect of industrialisation on carbon emission is in line with Mahmood et al. (2020), Ahmed et al. (2022), Zafar et al. (2020), Sarkodie et al. (2020), and Dash et al. (2020). The result supports the Environmental Kuznets Curve, as increased industrial activity increases carbon emissions, increasing

Table 7 The pooled mean group regression

	Pooled Mean Group						
	D.CO2						
	Long-run estimates		Short-run estimates				
			Kenya	Uganda	Tanzania	Rwanda	Burundi
__ec			−0.334**	−1.432***	−0.505*	−0.107*	−0.02
			(−2.69)	(−9.54)	(−2.54)	(−2.32)	(−0.65)
IVA_GDP	0.00838***	D.IVA_GDP	0.01	−0.00428***	−0.01	0.00	0.00
	−7.21		−0.68	(−3.37)	(−1.34)	−1.87	(−0.70)
PCI	−0.0125**	D.PCI	−0.04	−0.0224***	−0.03	0.00	0.00
	(−2.86)		(−1.22)	(−6.66)	(−1.06)	−1.46	(−1.11)
GOVERINDEX	0.127***	D.GOVERINDEX	0.10	−0.0680**	0.02	−0.01	0.00
	−6.09		−1.11	(−2.86)	−0.19	(−1.50)	−0.05
TRADE	0.00123***	D.TRADE	0.00	−0.00123***	0.00	0.00	0.00
	−5.28		(−0.30)	(−5.37)	−0.72	0.00	−1.81
POPDENSITY	0.000577**	D.POPDENSITY	0.170*	0.0118**	0.0879*	0.00	0.00236***
	−3.05		−2.54	−3.27	−2.45	(−1.26)	−3.57
		_cons	−0.18	0.10	0.00	0.01	−0.0223**
			(−1.88)	−1.25	(−0.07)	−1.00	(−3.13)
N	80						

t-statistics in parentheses; $^{*}p < 0.05$, $^{**}p < 0.01$, $^{***}p < 0.001$

pollution. The positive impact of population density on carbon emission support the argument that a higher population density increases intensity in land use, resulting in pollution. This may be due to the possibility of expanding urban land size which increase carbon sources thus increasing carbon emissions. The results align with the STIRPAT model on population increasing pollution. Moreover, the results are similar to those of Sarkodie et al. (2020), who found that increased population dynamics increased carbon emissions.

The positive effect of trade on carbon emissions indicates that higher country trade increases carbon emissions. This aligns with the Pollution Haven Hypothesis and possibly emanates from the low level of governance, which is reflected in the negative skewness in the governance index score. Trade has similarly been established to positively impact emissions in other countries and regions, as Sun et al. (2019) and Gao et al. (2021) observed. Sun et al. (2019) found support for an inverted U-shape relationship, indicating that at first, as trade increases, carbon emissions are also triggered upwards; however, at some point in the future, countries experience decreasing carbon emissions as a result of higher trade. This can partly support the current study findings in the context of developing economies such as East Africa where economies are still striving to ensure that they achieve higher development through higher trading activities. The results are, however, contrary to those of Sarkodie et al. (2020), who found that trade had a positive but non-significant effect on carbon emissions.

The productive capacity index negatively significantly affected carbon emissions. The reducing effect of productive capacity in East Africa is similar to that observed in the BRI (Brazil, Russia and India) by Mo and Madni (2023) and in the OECD by Oluc et al. (2022). Similarly, in the short run, only the productive capacity index negatively and significantly affected carbon emissions. The long-run estimates confirm that productive capacity has a significant role in increasing environmental quality. Therefore, countries must ensure improved productive capacities for a quality environment. Thus, countries must ensure that strategies for productive resources, entrepreneurial capabilities, and production linkages are well set up to facilitate growth and reduce emissions. The LR and SR consistency in results reveals that productive capacity sets the long-term structural transformation of an economy in motion.

Results reveal differences in the short-run and long-run results. The short-run variations in results by country reveal that industry value added, productive capacity index, governance, and trade significantly negatively affected carbon emissions in Uganda. However, population density in Kenya, Tanzania, Uganda, and Burundi increased carbon emissions considerably in the short run. Only industrialisation had a significant positive effect on carbon emissions in Rwanda. The results imply that industrialisation harms the environment, leading to higher carbon emissions, and poor governance increases the strain on the environment.

Further analysis conducted, considering the group mean error correction estimation summarised in Table 8, reveals that only productive capacity significantly reduced carbon emissions, while poor governance increased emissions in the countries. This implies that countries should enhance their productive capacities and improve governance to reduce pollution.

Table 8 Mean group estimation

Mean group estimation error correction form	
	D.CO2
IVA_GDP	−0.0139
	(−1.51)
PCI	−0.0384**
	(−2.69)
GOVERINDEX	0.216*
	−2.13
TRADE	−0.000107
	(−0.07)
POPDENSITY	−0.00382
	(−1.41)
SR	
__ec	−0.870***
	(−4.82)
D.IVA_GDP	0.00526
	−1.02
D.PCI	0.000938
	−0.08
D.GOVERINDEX	−0.0688
	(−1.22)
D.TRADE	0.0000611
	−0.12
D.POPDENSITY	0.304
	−1.65
_cons	0.513***
	−4.63
N	80

t-statistics in parentheses; $*p < 0.05$, $**p < 0.01$, $***p < 0.001$

The SR and LR country estimates in Table 9 show that long-run results reveal non-significant results across Kenya and Tanzania for all variables. However, Uganda evidenced significant positive effect of industrialisation, governance, and trade implying that higher industrialisation, trade, and poor governance increased carbon emissions. However, in the short run, both productive capacity and trade significantly reduced carbon emissions in Uganda, while industrialisation and productive capacity increased carbon emissions in Rwanda.

Table 9 reveals the variation across countries, with Uganda experiencing a significant increase in carbon emissions emanating from industrialisation, trade, and governance. However, productive capacity significantly reduces carbon emissions in the short run for Uganda but increases carbon emissions in Rwanda. These variations indicate that different countries' policies related to trade have various levels of impact on carbon emissions, given the variation in trading volumes.

Table 9 Country mean group estimation with error correction

D.CO2					
Long-run	Kenya	Uganda	Tanzania	Rwanda	Burundi
IVA_GDP	−0.018	0.00841***	0.001	−0.045	−0.015
	(−0.44)	−3.500	−0.030	(−1.49)	(−1.70)
PCI	−0.018	−0.014	−0.062	−0.083	−0.015
	(−0.27)	(−1.49)	(−0.75)	(−1.38)	(−1.18)
GOVERINDEX	0.483	0.133**	0.001	0.433	0.032
	−0.570	−3.080	0.000	−1.270	−0.860
TRADE	−0.006	0.00129**	0.002	0.001	0.00153*
	(−1.23)	−2.640	−0.630	−0.500	−2.010
POPDENSITY	−0.010	0.001	−0.011	0.00114*	0.000
	(−0.66)	−1.530	(−0.48)	−2.110	−0.140
Short run					
___ec	−0.879	−1.406***	−0.894*	−0.268	−0.906
	(−1.60)	(−4.65)	(−2.43)	(−1.64)	(−1.38)
D.IVA_GDP	0.024	−0.004	−0.004	0.00411***	0.00690*
	−0.950	(−1.62)	(−0.48)	−4.740	−2.000
D.PCI	−0.028	−0.0222***	0.036	0.0189***	0.000
	(−0.33)	(−3.30)	−0.620	−7.000	(−0.08)
D.GOVERINDEX	−0.278	−0.069	0.058	−0.0511***	−0.004
	(−0.88)	(−1.46)	−0.350	(−4.03)	(−0.31)
D.TRADE	0.002	−0.00127**	0.000	0.000	−0.001
	−0.360	(−2.75)	(−0.00)	−0.640	(−1.38)
D.POPDENSITY	0.821	0.012	0.685	0.002	0.001
	−1.230	−1.680	−1.380	−1.430	−0.030
_cons	0.576	0.127	0.799	0.601***	0.461*
	−0.860	−0.760	−0.670	−4.450	−2.340
N	80				

t-statistics in parentheses; $^{*}p < 0.05$, $^{**}p < 0.01$, $^{***}p < 0.001$

Conclusion and Recommendations

This study examined the impact of industrialisation, productive capacity Index, and governance index on CO2 emissions in East Africa from 2002 to 2018. A dataset of five countries—Kenya, Uganda, Tanzania, Burundi, and Rwanda—and Pooled Mean Group ARDL was used for analysis. Results revealed that, in the long run, industry value added, trade, governance and population density positively and significantly affected carbon emissions per capita. However, the productive capacity negatively significantly affected carbon emissions per capita. In the short run, it was only the productive capacity index that negatively significantly affected carbon emission. Results also reveal variations by country in the short run, where industry value added, productive capacity index, governance, and trade significantly affected Uganda's carbon emissions. However, in Kenya, Tanzania, Uganda, and Burundi, population density increased considerably carbon emissions in the short run. Only industrialisation had a significant positive effect on carbon emissions in Rwanda. Moreover, long-run estimation confirmed that productive capacity is essential in increasing environmental quality. The long-run mean group estimates consistently supported the results on productive capacity and governance index impact on carbon emissions.

The results imply that industrialisation harms the environment, leading to higher carbon emissions and that poor governance increases the strain on the environment. Long-run estimation confirms that productive capacity has a significant role in raising environmental quality. Therefore, emphasis on improving industrialisation across countries should also go hand in hand with improving their governance indicators to strengthen the implementation of policies governing environmental concerns. This may include enhancing their effectiveness in the quality of policy formulation and implementation and the credibility of the government's commitment to such policies, especially those related to environmental safety. Thus, policymakers should have an appropriate mix between industrial growth and emission reduction strategies. Theoretically, the results confirm the STIRPAT model on the relationship between population and emissions, the Pollution Haven Hypothesis and the Environment Kuznets Curve, indicating that higher trade potential and industrialisation lead to higher pollution.

This study recommends that governments enhance their governance effectiveness in policy implementation. Moreover, regarding trade activities between countries, countries should enhance the incorporation of environmental concerns in their trading agreements. The Kyoto Agreement sets a good foundation towards EAC country's alignment with global environmental goals. Countries should set strategies to enable them to meet their emission reduction targets. Additionally, enhancing productive capacities is crucial as it's a backdrop for future country transformation.

Despite current study highlighting the role of productive capacity in improving environmental quality, it is limited in that only five countries have been examined. Therefore, further investigation of other developing countries is needed to investigate differences across countries. In addition, future studies should examine how productive capacities affect industrialisation, including the moderating role of productive capacities in the relationship between industrialisation and carbon emissions.

References

Ahmed, F., Ali, I., Kousar, S., & Ahmed, S. (2022). The environmental impact of industrialization and foreign direct investment: Empirical evidence from Asia-Pacific region. *Environmental Science and Pollution Research, 29*, 29779–29792. https://doi.org/10.1007/s11356-021-17560-w

Asteriou, D., & Hall, S. G. (2007). *Applied econometrics*. Palgrave Macmillan.

Dang, T. D., & Tran, T. A. (2020). Rural industrialization and environmental governance challenges in the Red River Delta, Vietnam. *Journal of Environment & Development, 29*(4), 420–448. http://us.sagepub.com/en-us/journals-permissions

Dash, D. P., Behera, S. R., Rao, D. T., Sethi, N., & Loganathan, N. (2020). Governance, urbanization, and pollution: A cross country analysis of global south. *Cogent Economics & Finance, 8*(1), 1–24. https://doi.org/10.1080/23322039.2020.1742023

EAC (2024). *EAC partner states*. Accessed at https://www.eac.int/eac-partner-states

Gani, A. (2012). The relationship between good governance and carbon dioxide emissions from developing economies. *Journal of Economic Development, 37*(1), 77–93.

Gao, J., Gao, F., Yin, B., & Zhang, M. (2021). International Trade as a Double-Edged Sword: The Perspective of Carbon Emissions. *Frontiers in Energy Research, 9*. https://doi.org/10.3389/fenrg.2021.764914

Gill, F. L., Viswanathan, K. K., & Karim, M. Z. A. (2018). The critical review of the pollution haven hypothesis. *International Journal of Energy Economics and Policy, 8*(1), 167–174. http://hdl.handle.net/11159/1929

Hsiao, C. (2014). Cross-sectionally dependent panel data. In *Analysis of panel data* (Vol. 9, pp. 327–368). Cambridge University Press. https://doi.org/10.1017/CBO9781139839327.012

IEA. (2022). *CO2 emissions in 2022*. International Energy Agency.

IEA. (2023). *Africa energy outlook 2022*. International Energy Agency. https://iea.blob.core.windows.net/assets/220b2862-33a6-47bd-81e9-00e586f4d384/AfricaEnergyOutlook2022.pdf

Jianguo, D., Ali, K., Alnori, F., & Ullah, S. (2022). The nexus of financial development, technological innovation, institutional quality, and environmental quality: Evidence from OECD economies. *Environmental Science and Pollution Research, 29*, 58179–58200. https://doi.org/10.1007/s11356-022-19763-1

Jiang, W., Cole, M., Sun, J., & Wang, S. (2022). Innovation, carbon emissions and the pollution haven hypothesis: Climate capitalism and global re-interpretations. *Journal of Environmental Management, 307*, 114465. https://doi.org/10.1016/j.jenvman.2022.114465

Kaufmann, D., Kraay, A., & Mastruzzi, M. (2010). *The worldwide governance indicators: Methodology and analytical issues*. World Bank. https://ssrn.com/abstract=1682130

Lau, L. S., Ng, C. F., Cheah, S. P., & Choong, C. K. (2019). Panel data analysis (stationarity, cointegration, and causality). In *Environmental Kuznets Curve (EKC)* (pp. 101–113). Academic Press. https://doi.org/10.1016/B978-0-12-816797-7.00009-6

Mahmood, H., Alkhateeb, T. T. Y., & Furqan, M. (2020). Industrialization, urbanization and CO2 emissions in Saudi Arabia: Asymmetry analysis. *Energy Reports, 6*, 1553–1560. https://doi.org/10.1016/j.egyr.2020.06.004

Mo, Y., & Madni, G. R. (2023). Pollution halo impact in context of productive capacities, energy poverty, urbanization, and institutional quality. *PLoS One, 18*(12), 1–17. https://doi.org/10.1371/journal.pone.0295447

Nosheen, M., Abbasi, M. A., & Iqbal, J. (2020). Analyzing extended STIRPAT model of urbanization and CO2 emissions in Asian countries. *Environmental Science and Pollution Research, 27*, 45911–45924. https://doi.org/10.1007/s11356-020-10276-3

Nyamongo, J., & Nyamongo, L. K. (2019). Energy infrastructure investments in East Africa and the relevance of the energy charter treaty. *Energy Charter Secretariat.*. https://www.energycharter.org/fileadmin/DocumentsMedia/Occasional/Energy_Infrastructure_Investment_in_East_Africa.pdf

Oluc, I., Jebli, M. B., Can, M., Guzel, I., & Brusselaers, J. (2022). The productive capacity and environment: Evidence from OECD countries. *Environmental Science and Pollution Research., 30*, 3453. https://doi.org/10.1007/s11356-022-22341-0

Pesaran, M. H., Shin, Y., & Smith, R. P. (1999). *Pooled mean group estimation of dynamic heterogeneous panels*. 94(446), 621–634. http://www.jstor.org/stable/2670182?origin=JSTOR-pdf

Pickson, R. B., Gui, P., Jian, L., & Boateng, E. (2024). Do population-related factors matter for carbon emissions? Lessons from different income groups of countries. *Urban Climate, 55*, 101934. https://doi.org/10.1016/j.uclim.2024.101934

Purwono, R., Sugiharti, L., Handoyo, R. D., & Esquivias, M. A. (2022). Trade liberalization and comparative advantage: Evidence from Indonesia and Asian trade partners. *Economies, 10*(80), 1–21. https://doi.org/10.3390/economies10040080

Sarkodie, S. A., Owusu, P. A., & Leirvik, T. (2020). Global effect of urban sprawl, industrialization, trade and economic development on carbon dioxide emissions. *Environmental Research Letters, 15*. https://doi.org/10.1088/1748-9326/ab7640

Sarwar, S., & Alsaggaf, M. I. (2021). The role of governance indicators to minimize the carbon emission: A study of Saudi Arabia. *Management of Environmental Quality: An International Journal, 32*(5), 970–988. https://doi.org/10.1108/MEQ-11-2020-0275

Singhania, M., & Saini, N. (2021). Demystifying pollution haven hypothesis: Role of FDI. *Journal of Business Research, 123*, 516–528. https://doi.org/10.1016/j.jbusres.2020.10.007

Sun, H., Clottey, S. A., Geng, Y., Fang, K., & Amissah, J. C. K. (2019). Trade openness and carbon emissions: Evidence from belt and road countries. *Sustainability, 11*. https://doi.org/10.3390/su11092682

Sun, Y., Hao, Q., Cui, C., Shan, Y., Zhao, W., Wang, D., Zhang, Z., & Guan, D. (2022). Emission accounting and drivers in East African countries. *Applied Energy, 312*, 118805. https://doi.org/10.1016/j.apenergy.2022.118805

UNCTAD. (2023). *Productive capacities index for evidence-based policymaking* (TD/B/70/3). United Nations Conference on Trade and Development.

Yegorov, Y. (2015). *Economic role of population density*. https://ideas.repec.org/p/wiw/wiwrsa/ersa15p207.html#:~:text=Economic%20Role%20of%20Population%20Density%201%20Author%20Listed%3A,conference%20papers%20ersa15p207%2C%20European%20Regional%20Science%20Association.%20

Yu, Y., Zhao, J., Musah, M., Owusu-Akomeah, M., Nkyi, J. A., Li, J., Ampong, G. O. A., Kumah, E. A., Cao, S., Xu, Y., Shi, Y., Wang, L., Hui, C., & Li, K. (2024). Does Industrialization promote the emission mitigation agenda of East Africa. A pathway toward environmental sustainability. *Frontiers in Environmental Science, 12*, 1305852. https://doi.org/10.3389/fenvs.2024.1305852

Zafar, A., Ullah, S., Majeed, M. T., & Yasmeen, R. (2020). Environmental pollution in Asian economies: Does the industrialisation matter. *PEC Energy Review., 44*, 227–248.

Value Relevance of Accounting Numbers in Emerging Sub-Saharan Africa Stock Markets: Comparison Between Ghana and Nigeria

Muyiwa Ezekiel Alade

Abstract There is a growing concern regarding how different stock markets respond to diverse accounting information disclosure which is of utmost importance to (foreign) investors and other stock market participants. Thus, the study attempted to investigate and compare value relevance of accounting numbers between Ghana stock exchange and Nigerian Exchange group for an eight-year period from 2015 to 2022. Based on certain selection criteria, secondary data were gathered from annual reports of 19 and 113 listed firms sampled from Ghana and Nigeria stock markets respectively. Descriptive analyses show that share prices at the Ghana stock market are less dispersed compared to that of Nigeria. Ordinary least square regression, Newey–West HAC standard error, and Generalised Method of Moments (GMM) were employed to analyse the data due to the presence of heteroscedasticity, and endogeneity problems. The results show that irrespective of the model, both earnings per share and book value of equity per share jointly explain significant variations in share price of the listed firms in both Ghana and Nigeria stock markets, but more for large firms in both markets and more for financial and non-financial in Ghana and Nigeria, respectively. Furthermore, the accounting information are value relevant in both stock markets, but earnings per share presents positive effect while book value shows antithetic effect at the two markets. Succinctly, the accounting information is more value relevant in the Nigeria exchange group than Ghana stock market, based on the parameters' coefficient and explanatory powers. These results have implications for foreign investors, market regulators and other stock market participants.

Keywords Accounting information · Book value · Earnings · Value relevance · Ghana · Nigeria

---

M. E. Alade (✉)
Adekunle Ajain University, Akungba-Akoko, Nigeria
e-mail: muyiwa.alade@aaua.edu.ng

T. Moloi (ed.), *Impacting Society Positively Through Technology in Accounting and Business Processes*, Springer Proceedings in Business and Economics,
https://doi.org/10.1007/978-3-031-84885-8_20

Introduction

Recently, the trust and reliance of local and foreign investors in stock market performance and development is increasingly becoming of utmost interest to them, especially at the emerging capital markets (Soumaré et al., 2021). Usually, the expectation of a typical investor, particularly at the capital market, is to derive maximum returns on his/her investment. On the other hand, to strengthen the market, and ensure its stable growth and development, several policies are issued and implemented in order to attract more potential investors and sustain existing ones. This corporate-growth-driven move is majorly targeted at attracting more (foreign) direct investment, especially in emerging economies due to market liberalisation according to Song et al. (2003). The fundamental essence is to make the market more attractive to excess unit holders from across the globe. However, different economies have diverse national economic targets which serve as basis for their capital market-based economic policy directives.

Furthermore, development of capital markets depends largely on macroeconomic stability, development of the banking sector of an economy, institutional features, and shareholder shield (Sulaiman, 2023; Yartey & Adjasi, 2007). Also, consistent with the efficient market hypothesis, stock market is seen as developing market when share prices respond to new financial (accounting) and non-financial information upon disclosure or arrival at the market (Chauhan & Kumar, 2019). This depicts ingenuity of the market-driven information upon its arrival, since it has not been traded upon. Besides, the current global business environment, aided by advance technologies, has imprinted its indelible marks on stock market performance and development (Barth et al., 2023). Also, one of the indicators of emerging economy is its ability to reliably attract inflow of capital to enhance its liquidity, driven by trust in its capital market (Njenga et al., 2022).

Specifically, in accounting parlance, relevance or irrelevance of accounting information in explaining changes in the stock market prices has been a subject of empirical debates for decades. This capital market-based aspect of accounting research strives to showcase how investors process available accounting information issued by listed firms to make economic decisions that consequently impact on share price. However, there is a growing concern regarding how different stock markets respond to diverse information disclosure. This is of utmost importance to foreign investors and other market participants in order to guide their investment plans (Chauhan & Kumar, 2019).

Value relevance of accounting information is one of the measures of financial reporting qualities along others such as timeliness, conservatism, earnings persistence and volatility and accrual quality (Barać, 2021). It is a concept that seeks to unveil how accounting information such as book value of equity and earnings per share, according to Ohlson (1995) price model, explain changes in the stock prices. Thus, relevance of accounting information to investors is otherwise referred to as value relevance (Imhanzenobe, 2022).

Several studies such as Badu and Appiah (2018), Almujamed and Alfraih (2019), Almujamed and Alfraih (2019), Badwy (2019), Chen et al. (2020), Bankole and Ukolobi (2020), Rahman and Liu (2021), Mubarika and Handayani (2022), Anchev and Lapanan (2023) Migliavacca (2024) have been conducted to examine value relevance with varying specific focus on sectoral- or country-based listed firms. Other studies such as Adesola et al. (2020), Badwy (2019) Závodný and Procházka (2023) have compared between sectors or countries. Drawing from a review of plethora of extant empirical studies, Mulenga and Bhatia (2018) discovered contradiction in value relevance of different financial accounting metrics across countries and sectors. Whereas, according to Rahman and Liu (2021), though emerging stock markets have the potentials to raise capital for growth and development of economies, the link between changes in share price as a result of accounting information disclosure is not as documented in emerging markets compare to the developed markets such as the United States.

For decades, there have been various scholarly arguments that accounting numbers are losing or have lost their value relevance based on different capital markets development, sectoral, country and cross-countries data, emergence of IFRS, technological advancement, as well as methods of data analysis conducted. Alfraih (2016) ascertained significant decline in the ability of earnings and book value to explain share price, while Čupić et al. (2023) and Kim and Key (2014) noted increased value relevance of the financial data at the Serbian and Korean stock markets, respectively. However, Barth et al. (2023) reported more nuanced rather than declining value relevance of the accounting information based on the United States' listed firms' accounting data. On the contrary, Migliavacca (2024) found out that accounting data are indeed losing its value relevance even upon IFRS adoption as the European-based listed firms' accounting numbers showed that market value is less reliant on the accounting metrics. Although submission of Migliavacca (2024) is at variance with Okezie et al. (2020), Alade (2018) from the Nigeria reporting clime, as well as Mousa and Desoky (2014) from GCC nations, similar declining relevance of the accounting information was gotten by Badu and Appiah (2018) from Ghana reporting environment. This suggests confounding position of relevance and reliability of accounting figures to investors in the markets.

Most of the capital markets in African continent are predominantly emerging, but it has grown from about 5 in 1980s to roughly 30 (Adesina, 2023; Song et al., 2003). Apparently, it is a reflection of investors' trust in the markets and its economic prospects. According to Soumaré et al. (2021), the markets are composed of bond markets and stock exchanges. Although Sulaiman (2023) confirmed that capital markets in ECOWAS region drive economic growth, underdeveloped state of the African stock markets coupled with few listed financial and securities products, impede effective mobilisation of funds for its economic growth (Adesina, 2023). According to Anchev and Lapanan (2023), increase in investors' participation in the stock markets has also reduced relevance of accounting data and their incentives. Thus, intervention move is of essence to upscale the markets' development by building investors' confidence through adequate information disclosure and policies (Njenga et al., 2022). These concerns provide basis to further extend value relevance investigation beyond sectoral or national stock market to cross-countries analysis. Thus, the study made attempt to compare value relevance of basic accounting information between Ghana and Nigerian stock exchanges. Section two presents brief review of related literature followed by sections three and four that showcase data and methods and results and discussion respectively. Section five presents conclusion in line with the findings.

Review of Related Literature and Postulations

Value Relevance of Accounting Information

Value relevance concept is a well-researched measure of financial reporting quality that focuses on investors' reaction to accounting information issued, as well as manner through which it affects capital markets. According to Barać (2021), value relevance construct is an attempt to evaluate decision usefulness of earnings, as it depicts reliability and relevance to stock markets players. It seeks to determine how relevant and reliable accounting metrics drive market value of a listed firm in terms of share price. According to Der et al. (2018), Amir et al. (1993) was the first to use value relevance concept, although seminar paper of Ball and Brown (1968) was the first to provide evidence concerning value relevance of accounting earnings. Thereafter, Ohlson (1995) price model provided very valuable yardstick when attempting to examine pattern in which share price (as a measure of market value) relates to published accounting metrics and other relevant information. It also explains how market participants view accounting data (Dunham & Grandstaff, 2022; Migliavacca, 2024).

A review of literature conducted by Mulenga and Bhatia (2018) showed a plethora of extant empirical studies on value relevance and also discovered contradiction in value relevance of different financial accounting metrics across countries and sectors. For instance, Dunham and Grandstaff (2022) and Damodaran (2024) noted mixed trends in the value relevance of accounting data through review of extant studies. Abdelrahim Ahmad Khader and Shareif Hussein Shanak (2023) observed from the Amman stock market that book value of equity is the most value relevant accounting data consistent with Kaushalya and Kehelwalatenna (2020) based on Colombo stock market data. But, Badu and Appiah (2018) found earnings per share to be of higher value relevance at the Ghana stock exchange in tandem with Mbekomize and Popo (2020) from Botswanan stock exchange accounting figures. These findings are completely different from that of Oyerinde (2011) who discovered that dividend has higher value relevance over earnings and book value, partly in agreement with the finding of Omokhudu and Ibadin (2015) that earnings, dividend and cash flows are more value relevant than book value. In addition, Widianingsih and Setiawan (2021) found out that both earnings and book value are value relevant based on accounting data obtained from 472 listed companies at the

Indonesia stock exchange for a period from 2016 to 2019. However, Migliavacca (2024) recorded that investors depends on other information to determine market price, as relevancy of accounting data is now on diminishing state.

Consistent with signalling theory, and efficient market hypothesis, it is expected that herd behaviour of investors and other capital market participants would be influenced by informative nature of a reporting environment or market. An efficiently or inefficiently disclosed accounting information is capable of conveying diverse signals to investors about the market which could inform their reactions that could impact the market. Thus, since confounding empirical studies exist regarding value relevance of accounting information, the study postulates a null form that:

$H_0$1: Accounting numbers disclosed in Ghana and Nigerian stock markets are not value relevant.

Ghana and Nigeria Reporting Environments and Capital Markets

Both Ghana and Nigeria are Anglophone countries located in the same western region of Africa continent, and also sub-Sahara African nations. The reporting environments are largely influenced by the dictates of their colonial master, and with the use of common laws. Ghana and Nigerian capital markets are emplaced to enhance economic growth and attract direct investment opportunities towards national economic development of the two developing nations. The two markets strive to raise long-term funds towards national and regional economic growth through various capital market-based policies. Another peculiar feature of the two countries is weak nature of business environment, management structures, regulatory framework and financial literacy (Soumaré et al., 2021).

Although the Nigerian exchange group (formerly known as Nigerian stock exchange) has been in existence since 1960, the oldest in West African region and the second largest financial sector in the sub-Saharan Africa, the number of firms listed on the stock market has grown up to as high as 260 but has declined over the years due to the delisting of firms that failed to meet or sustain listing requirements and regulations. The market has premium, alternative, growth and main boards of listed firms. It began operations in 1961 with 19 securities (Okaro, 2002). It has grown from being under-developed to developing market as regulated by Securities and Exchange Commission (SEC), Nigeria. Currently, the Nigerian exchange group has 7 companies on premium board, 4 firms on the alternative security market, 7 companies on the growth board and 132 listed firms on the main board. The market equity capital has grown to ₦55.57 trillion Nigeria Naira. Before convergence to IFRS reporting regime in 2012, accounting information issued in the market were prepared in compliance with local accounting standards called Statement of Accounting Standards (SASs) and International Accounting Standards. All listed firms were encouraged to prepare their financial statements in compliance with IFRS.

On the other hand, Ghana stock exchange market took off in 1990. Since then, the volume of equities traded has grown from 222,000 to as high as 3.816 billion in 2019 and has oscillated to 254 million as at March 2024 (GSE Market report, March 2024); but, the equities market capitalisation has experienced perpetual growth from Gh ₵3.05 million to Gh ₵77,701.17 million. Equity trading on the market has also grown to 31 in the main board and 5 in the alternative market. Ghana was one of the early adopters of IFRS in the sub-Saharan Africa.

Several studies including Omokhudu and Ibadin (2015), Alade et al. (2017), Badu and Appiah (2018), Adesola et al. (2020), Okezie et al. (2020) and Ighosewe (2022) have been conducted to unveil value relevance of diverse accounting figures disclosed in the two markets and at various events such as emergence of Covid-19, adoption of IFRS, global economic or financial crises. These studies have shown different outcomes. Nevertheless, it is of essence to further compare value relevance of the data at different capital markets. Myriads of studies that compare sectoral, multiple capital markets or cross-countries-based value relevance exist, and a few of them were reviewed.

Earlier on, Sami and Zhou (2004) have documented significant difference in the value relevance of accounting metrics between A-share and B-share stock market in China. Further, Ernest and Oscar (2014) investigated whether there is difference in value relevance of accounting information published by banking sector and that of oil and gas listed firms in Nigeria. The study recorded higher value relevance of oil and gas listed firms accounting figures over banking industry listed firms and that earnings per share has higher value relevance above other accounting data. Although Pervan and Bartulović (2014) did not compare value relevance of accounting metrics among South-Eastern European nations, the study documented higher value relevance of book value of equity over earnings per share of the capital markets investigated. Der et al. (2018) compared value relevance of accounting information issued by financial and non-financial listed firms in Ghana stock market and found that non-financial listed firms' accounting information are more value relevant than that of the financial listed firms.

Another comparative study conducted by Adesola et al. (2020) between manufacturing and oil and gas firms in Nigeria shows that accounting numbers disclosed by manufacturing listed firms have higher value relevance over that of the oil and gas listed firms. Also, Badwy (2019) compared value relevance of accounting data between Saudi Arabia and Egyptian listed firms with a submission that although the accounting information are value relevant and that book value of equity is more value relevant to the investors, accounting information disclosed in Saudi Arabia presents higher value relevance than that of Egypt. A quinquennial comparative study between Nigeria and South-Africa conducted by Ighosewe (2022) uncovered higher value relevance of accounting data among listed companies in Nigeria over that of South-Africa, as earnings is more value relevant in the formal but book value in the later.

An empirical investigation into value relevance among four different countries by Závodný and Procházka (2023) revealed that different stock markets present different value relevance of accounting information even under the same reporting economic region. Furthermore, Závodný and Procházka (2023) found that accounting information published in the Hungarian and Czech capital markets are more value relevant than the those issued in Poland capital market, while those of Slovak are not value relevant.

A succinct inference from the above few extant studies is that there are mixed findings regarding value relevance construct at different capital markets. This could be as a result of different accounting bases upon which the accounting information were prepared and regulatory frameworks under which the information were issued. However, drawing from the notion that capital markets are not always informationally perfect as market participants' evaluation is majorly based on available information (Migliavacca, 2024), it would be of tremendous importance to the investors to understand how accounting information is or are value relevant at different capital markets.

According to Soumaré et al. (2021), capital markets in Africa generally have the capability to increase its investors' base through numerous financial endowments of the institutional investors. This can be enhanced when the investors, local or foreign, individual or institutional, could reliably depend on information inter-play in the market. Not only that, but an efficient capital market also plays very attractive role in drawing more investors. All these have the propensity to inform growth and development of the emerging markets, especially in Africa. In addition, quality of a disclosed accounting information reflects its value relevance in the capital market. Since different nations employ diverse policies or implement economic policies differently, perhaps because of the peculiarities of a reporting environment, relevance and reliability power of accounting figures issued under them would be differ too. Therefore, since investors crave to invest their financial resources where it would offer them higher returns, it is very important to examine how value relevant are the accounting information issued in different emerging capital markets. Thus, the study equally hypothesised in a null form as follow;

$H_0$2: Accounting numbers in Ghana stock market are not value relevant than the accounting numbers disclosed in the Nigeria exchange group.

Data and Methods

The study was anchored on quantitative research paradigm. Secondary data sources were explored to gather relevant and required data of the sampled listed firms from their annual financial reports and stock markets. Population comprised all listed 30 and 152 listed companies at the Ghana and Nigerian stock exchanges. The study targeted all listed firms at the two stock markets. However, in order to obtain more efficient coefficients as advanced by Gujarati and Forter (2010), listed firms whose required data were available throughout the period of investigation were sampled leading to 19 and 113 samples, and 152 and 904 firm-year observations from Ghana and Nigeria, respectively. The study covers an 8-year period from 2015 to 2022. These methods and procedures led to emergence of balanced panel data.

According to Widianingsih and Setiawan (2021), Ohlson price model has the capability to predict share prices based on how investors value book value of equity and earnings. Consistent with studies already in existence, Ohlson price model provided basis for analysis carried out. Thus, the study evaluated earnings per share and book value of equity as function of share price in the stock market in same order with Alfraih (2016). Explanatory power and coefficients of the regression model formed bases to establish higher value relevance of the accounting data and at the stock market. The model used is stated thus:

$$SP_{jt} = \beta + \beta_1 EPS_{jt} + \beta_2 BVS_{jt} + \mu_{jt} \tag{1}$$

In which, SP implies stock price of firm *j* at time $t_{(2015-2022)}$ which is the firm's share price at the end of first quarter after the financial year-end, EPS is the earnings per share of the company at the end of a financial year-end of firm *j* at time $t_{(2015-2022)}$, BVS denotes book value of equity per share at the financial year-end of firm *j* at time $t_{(2015-2022)}$, μ becomes the error term, and β is the coefficient estimated.

The data analyses were carried out using combined descriptive and inferential statistics. Descriptive analyses involved the use of mean, deviation from the mean, least and maximum value. Ordinary least square regression, White Heteroscedasticity consistent autocorrelation covariance and Generalised Method of Moments (GMM) were employed to analyse the data due to the presence of heteroscedasticity, autocorrelation and endogeneity problems.

Results and Ensuing Discussion

Descriptive Analysis

Table 1 presents the outcomes of descriptive statistical analysis conducted.

As shown in Table 1, average share price of the listed firms in the Ghana stock exchange for the period considered in this study was ₵3.51 with standard deviation of ₵5.41 suggesting that distribution of the share prices for the period is slightly far from the mean unlike that of Nigeria. The share prices range from the least price of ₵0.02 to maximum ₵35.10. Mean value of earnings per share and book value of equity per share of the firms in Ghana for the period are ₵0.41 and ₵2.16, respectively. Their standard deviation values suggest that the parameters are not significantly widely spread apart from the mean, which suggests that performances of the listed firms do not demonstrate wide departure from one another. This could have been as a result of macroeconomic policies of the country, established profit margin control, and fewer number of the listed firms. The firms' lowest earnings per share and book value are ₵-2.57 and ₵0.00, while the maximum values are ₵4.61 and

Table 1 Descriptive statistics output

	Nigeria			Ghana		
	SP	EPS	BVPS	SP	EPS	BVPS
Mean	23.102	1.456	10.503	3.511	0.414	2.163
Median	2.240	0.180	4.120	1.335	0.170	1.230
Maximum	1985.000	93.240	162.250	35.100	4.610	13.500
Minimum	0.010	−16.160	0.0100	0.020	−2.570	0.000
Std. dev.	121.145	6.469	16.515	5.408	0.871	2.744
Skewness	11.306	7.360	3.198	2.6187	1.783	2.060
Kurtosis	148.207	76.133	17.860	11.499	8.751	6.995
Jarque–Bera	810758.8	208924.9	9825.390	631.234	289.948	208.588
Probability	0.000	0.000	0.000	0.000	0.000	0.000
Sum	20815.08	1311.680	9463.340	533.690	62.990	328.770
Sum Sq. dev.	13,209	37662.62	245462.2	4416.390	114.4503	1136.983
Observations	904	904	904	152	152	152

₵13.50, respectively. The metrics are generally positively skewed and leptokurtic, and the distribution is not normal.

On the flipside, the Nigerian listed firms' average share price for the period stood at ₦23.10 with ₦0.01 being the least share price and ₦1,985 being the highest share price. This depicts widespread of the share prices and a reflection of the level of performance of the firms at the stock market. It also suggests that some of the listed firms are well performing far above others in the market. This is further confirmed with the high standard deviation of ₦121.15 from the mean value. Both earnings per share and book value of equity per share equally depict similar features of the share prices in terms of the link between their mean values, standard deviation, minimum and maximum scores. Succinctly, the earnings per share and book value present average value of ₦1.46 and ₦10.50 with standard deviation of ₦6.47 and ₦16.52, respectively, indicating that the datasets are widely spread unlike those of Ghana listed companies. Their minimum (i.e. -16.16 and 0.01) and maximum (i.e. 93.24 and 162.25) values are reflections of nature of the data's distribution. Just like Ghana listed firms, the parameters are generally positively skewed and highly leptokurtic, and the distribution is not normal. Summarily, the descriptive analysis presents very interesting viewpoint that a large market is most likely to be characterised with dispersed performance measures compare to smaller market.

Correlation Test

Correlations among the parameters under investigation are as shown in Table 2.

Based on the correlation statistical output presented in Table 2, correlations among the variables are positive and significant. However, the correlation is slightly strong between earnings per share and book value of equity among Ghana listed

Table 2 The variables' correlation statistics

	Ghana			Nigeria		
Variables	SP	EPS	BVS	SP	EPS	BVS
SP	1.000000			1.000000		
	-----			-----		
EPS	0.399141	1.000000		0.702390	1.000000	
	0.0000	-----		0.0000	-----	
BVS	0.617216	0.786183	1.000000	0.326668	0.593274	1.000000
	0.0000	0.0000	-----	0.0000	0.0000	-----

firms and between share prices and earnings per share among Nigerian listed firms. This level of correlation was also noted and reported in Alfraih (2016). However, it is believed that the method of regression analysis employed has addressed possible effects of the identified fairly strong association among the variables.

Inferential Analysis

Balanced panel data were obtained and analysed in the study. The nature of the data requires fundamental test with the use of Ordinary Least Square (OLS) regression. The model results show that the data fit the line properly with F-stat of 49.74 and that both earnings and book value per share explained about 39.2% variation in the share price of listed firms in Ghana. The post-estimation tests after the OLS results unveiled absence of multicolinearity, but presence of heteroscedatiscity problem consistent with prior studies such as Alfraih (2016), Tsalavoutas et al. (2012) Alade et al. (2017). This led to the use of Newey–West HAC standard error and covariance in order to address heteroscedatiscity issue in the pooled data in tandem with Alfraih (2016) and Alade (2018). A further post-estimation test for endogeneity was conducted. The test revealed statistically significant value that suggests the presence of endogeneity problem. As a result, Generalised Method of Moments was employed for the analysis in other to obtain most efficient and reliable coefficients. Based on the outcome of Sargan test, instrument in GMM step II was adopted, reported and interpreted. The results are presented in Table 3.

In Ghana stock market financial reporting environment, the results reveal that earnings have positive and statistically significant influence on the share price of listed firms (Coeff = 0.475; $p < 0.01$). Also, the regression results show negative and statistically significant effect of book value of the Ghanaian listed firms on their share prices (Coeff = −0.374; $p < 0.01$). The model was significant, indicating that earnings per share and book value are both value relevant in the Ghana stock market, but antithetic for book value of equity. This implies that earnings per share reported in the Ghana stock exchange is of increasing relevance to the investors leading to increase in the share price of listed stocks in the market, while book value accounting number decreases the share price. The result is in tandem with the one

Table 3 OLS, HAC Robust and GMM Model statistical results

	Ghana			Nigeria		
	OLS	HAC Robust	GMM Model	OLS	HAC Robust	GMM Model
EPS	−1.401* (−2.20)	−1.401 (−1.18)	0.475** {532.00}	14.697** (26.93)	14.698** (3.48)	3.605** (63.97)
BVS	1.566** (7.74)	1.566* (4.30)	−0.374** {−151.7}	−1.019** (−4.77)	−1.019 (−1.37)	−1.382** (−38.79)
_Cons	0.705 (1.59)	0.705* (2.04)	2.518** {8.88}	12.411** (3.64)	12.411* (2.24)	12.671** (6.62)
R-square	0.400	0.400		0.506	0.501	
Adj. R^2	0.392			0.504		
F-stat.	49.74	18.00		459.65	6.82	
Prob > F	0.000	0.000		0.000	0.001	
Root MSE		4.216			85.254	
Wald chi2(3)			5.34e+07			2.36e+06
Prob > chi2			0.000			0.000
Mean VIF	2.62			1.54		
B-P hetero test: Chi2(1), (Prob > chi2)				19577.78 [0.000]		

Note: t-stat in ()parentheses, z-stat in {} parentheses, *p*-value in [] parentheses; *,** symbolise significant at 5% and 1%, respectively

reported by Badu and Appiah (2018) at the Ghana stock exchange and Mbekomize and Popo (2020) from Botswanan stock exchange. However, the finding is not consistent with Abdelrahim Ahmad Khader and Shareif Hussein Shanak (2023) Kaushalya and Kehelwalatenna (2020) and Ighosewe (2022). Therefore, the current study has no ground to accept the null hypothesis but ascertained that accounting numbers issued in the Ghana stock market are value relevant.

The results based on data obtained from the Nigeria reporting environment equally reveal that earnings have positive and statistically significant influence (Coeff = 3.605; $p < 0.01$), while book value has negative and significant influence (Coeff = −1.382; $p < 0.01$) of share prices of listed firms in the market. The model also unveils statistical significance, indicating that the two parameters jointly explain variation in the share prices at the stock exchange market. The results imply that although both earnings and book value are value relevant at the Nigerian stock market, earnings increase while book value decreases share prices of the listed firms. These suggest that earnings determine increasing value attached to the share price in the market, as investors are attracted by it to trade in the stock while book value impounds less attraction. The finding is in consonance with Ighosewe (2022) and Mbekomize and Popo (2020), but it contrasts with the findings of Kaushalya and Kehelwalatenna (2020) and Pervan and Bartulović (2014).

Based on the OLS results, variation in share prices expressed by the joint power of earnings and book value is obviously higher in Nigeria with adjusted R^2 of 50.4% over 39.2% in Ghana. This shows that the two accounting numbers have higher value relevance in the Nigerian exchange group than in the Ghana stock market. This result has signalling implications for potential investors (local and foreign), regulatory bodies and leadership of the listed entities especially in the sub-Saharan developing economics in order to upscale the capital market efficiency. The finding is in similar direction with that of Ighosewe (2022) who found higher value relevance of accounting data among listed companies in Nigeria over that of South-Africa.

To further compare value relevance of accounting metrics at the stock markets of the two countries, additional robust analyses were carried out by comparing between large and small sizes, and between non-financial and financial listed firms. The results are presented in Table 4.

When the Ghanaian listed firms were split into large and small size firms using the firms' total assets, earnings depict downward effect on share price of both large and small size firms and also book value of large firms; only book value of small size firms presents increasing value relevance to investors at the Ghana stock exchange. The data present a distinctive result suggesting that investors evaluate accounting information with regard to the firm size unlike the aggregate results. It further suggests that evaluating data in aggregate may not give similar result when the data are segregated by size or sector. Nevertheless, the OLS regression results reveal higher explanatory influence of the combined accounting data in large firms with roughly 46.6% over small size firms with 32.3%.

On the contrary, the accounting numbers demonstrate a positive effect on share prices of both financial and non-financial listed firms except earnings of financial listed firms that is negative and significant. The result is a pointer that earnings per share impound antithetic effect on share price of both large and small size financial listed firms. This serves as a caution to the investors and other market participants while considering the accounting information to make investment decision in the market but, book value of both financial and non-financial small size listed firms shows increasing value relevance to the market participants. Concisely, accounting numbers of the financial listed firms in Ghana explain more changes in their share prices with about 45.9% than non-financial firms with 27.8%.

At the Nigerian stock market, accounting numbers of large firm size explains very higher variation in share price (adj. R^2 = 51.2%) than small size listed firms (adj. R^2 = 5.8%). Earnings of large and small sizes and non-financial listed firms depict increasing value relevance, while that of financial is negative. Book value of large firm size and non-financial listed firms in Nigeria presents downward effect on their share prices, but positive for small size and financial listed firms. The results imply that investors should thread with caution while trying to invest in financial listed firms in Nigeria. Unlike wide explanatory power between large and small size listed firms in Nigeria, there is an insignificant difference in variation in share price of financial (adj. R^2 = 49.1%) and non-financial (adj. R^2 = 51.0%) listed firms accounted for by the joint accounting numbers examined in the study. Summarily, the accounting numbers have higher value relevance in the Nigerian financial, non-financial and large size listed firms than that of Ghana, but the reverse is the case for small size firms. This also has policy implication for the investors.

Table 4 Sectoral and size robust test

	Ghana				Nigeria			
Variables	Large	Small	Non-Fin.	Fin.	Large	Small	Non-Fin.	Fin.
EPS	−1.943** (−44.34)	−0.349** (−111.15)	0.224** (84.84)	−2.186** (−37.35)	4.344** (157.29)	0.058**(3.49)	3.830** (85.68)	−0.288** (−77.92)
BVS	−0.077** (−3.68)	0.747** 162.73)	0.355** (114.37)	0.064 (1.46)	−1.986** (−77.42)	0.035** (3.49)	−1.686** (−52.26)	0.229** (178.46)
_Cons	5.430** (4.76)	0.104 (1.11)	0.137* (2.23)	6.036** (3.81)	39.060** (7.85)	0.913** (5.68)	20.039** (6.54)	1.131** (5.70)
Mean VIF	3.35	2.67	2.46	3.23	1.52	1.03	1.53	2.98
B-P hetero test: Chi2(1) (Prob > chi2)	79.98 (0.000)	15.86 (0.0001)	24.05 (0.000)	40.70 (0.000)	3999.29 (0.000)	224.54 (0.000)	9571.88 (0.000)	508.03 (0.000)
Wald chi2(3)	45024.37	5.79e+09	4.82e+07	25117.62	1.47e+07	9760.49	3.26e+06	6.34e+07
Prob > chi2	0.000	0.000	0.000	0.000	0.000	0.000	0.000	0.000
OLS R^2	0.478	0.345	0.295	0.476	0.515	0.062	0.512	0.495
OLS Adj. R^2	0.466	0.323	0.278	0.459	0.512	0.058	0.510	0.491

Note: *z-stat* in parentheses; *,** imply significant at 5% and 1%, respectively

Table 5 Yearly regression results

	Ghana				Nigeria			
Years	EPS	BVS	_cons	R^2	EPS	BVS	_cons	R^2
2015	−2.532 (−0.65)	3.723** (3.03)	−0.205 (−0.31)	0.717**	25.344** (5.97)	−1.225* (−2.23)	6.377* (2.03)	0.848**
2016	7.071 (1.92)	−0.151 (−0.12)	0.968 (1.26)	0.756**	2.269 (1.10)	1.682 (1.88)	1.318 (0.34)	0.201*
2017	7.321* (2.26)	−0.297 (−0.31)	0.939 (1.34)	0.740**	11.439* (2.56)	0.302 (0.42)	−2.177 (−0.51)	0.736**
2018	−0.284 (−0.14)	3.515 (2.48)	−0.821 (0.59)	0.694**	20.106** (4.27)	−0.443 (−0.49)	4.597 (0.85)	0.831**
2019	−4.40** (−5.28)	1.875** (8.71)	0.763 (1.18)	0.853**	23.698 (5.90)	−0.508 (−0.66)	2.132 (0.36)	0.855**
2020	−1.797 (−0.28)	1.601 (0.96)	0.048 (0.06)	0.443*	12.316** (4.57)	−0.022 (−0.05)	−0.456 (−0.18)	0.817**
2021	0.172 (0.09)	0.898 (1.64)	−0.340 (−0.48)	0.611*	18.879* (2.51)	−3.109 (−1.59)	24.057 (1.79)	0.645*
2022	−0.912 (−1.12)	1.039* (2.60)	−0.694 (−1.19)	0.692*	13.172 (1.25)	−3.145 (−0.89)	43.154 (1.31)	0.319

Note: *t-stat* in parentheses; *,** imply significant at 5% and 1%, respectively. Standard error was based on robust regression

Trend of the Yearly Cross-Sectional Analysis

Consistent with prior study such as Alfraih (2016), the study carried out yearly regression analysis of the accounting data. The results are presented in Table 5.

The yearly regression results based on robust regression suggest no sufficient fact to establish that the accounting numbers are of increasing or decreasing value relevance over the 8-year IFRS reporting regime period in both Ghana and Nigeria. That is, the variability jointly explained by the data criss-crossed throughout the period, while the accounting data rarely reflect consistent statistical significance or otherwise all through the period under review. However, the accounting numbers declined into the COVID-19 year in the two economies but was more pronounced in Ghana than Nigeria. Thereafter, the results show that investors began to rely more on the accounting data to guide their investment decision at the Ghana stock exchange while the situation remained unchanged in the Nigerian capital market. These results are not consistent with Barth et al. (2023) that found non-declining value relevance based on data from developed economy of the United States and Alfraih (2016) from emerging economy of Kuwait who discovered declining value relevance of the accounting information.

Conclusion

The study made an attempt to extend body of knowledge in the stock market-based accounting research by investigating value relevance of accounting numbers in both Ghana and Nigeria, and also compared value relevance at the main capital markets of the two sub-Sahara West African countries. The results of the quantitative research show that accounting numbers are value relevant in the two capital markets in tandem with extant literature. This connotes that the market participants, particularly the investors, depend on the accounting metrics to make their investment choices in the two developing capital markets. However, earnings per share are more value relevant in the two markets as book value impounds reducing influence on share prices. In addition, the value relevance is more pronounced in the Nigeria than Ghana stock exchange market. This indicates that investors in the Nigerian exchange group value the accounting information more than those in the Ghana stock exchange.

Further robust investigation uncovers different value relevance across sectors and sizes of the firms between the two developing economies. Trend analysis of the yearly cross-sectional enquiry reveals neither declining nor increasing value relevance over the 8-year period covered in the study. Although the period covered was IFRS reporting regime, explanatory power of the accounting numbers reduced significantly as a result of global Covid-19 crisis, but the markets revert thereafter. Generally, the joint influence of the accounting parameters criss-crossed all through the period thereby showcasing the unique finding of the study from African-based developing economies, which is at variance with developed and other emerging economy from the Middle East.

Therefore, the study concludes that earnings are value relevant in both Ghana and Nigeria capital market with higher value in Nigeria. The implication is that investors in the two capital markets need earnings per share (accounting information) to make economic decision that affect share prices in the stock markets. This submission also has implication for the potential investors regarding the choice of capital market, sector and size of the listed firms to invest. Furthermore, it has policy implication for the management of the listed firms on how to ensure that its income statement and statement of financial position are prepared with enhanced cognisance to investor-support (or investor protection) accounting bases, assumptions and methods. It equally has propensity to boost market value of the listed firms at the capital market and also increase opportunity to raise fund for expansion in the long run. Hence, capital market regulators should be spurred by these outcomes to come up with policies capable of making the market more attractive to the investor through conscious effort to ensure accounting information disclosed in the stock market are highly valued by the investors.

References

Abdelrahim Ahmad Khader, O., & Shareif Hussein Shanak, H. (2023). The value relevance of accounting information: Empirical evidence from Jordan. *International Journal of Law and Management, 65*(4), 354–367.

Adesina, A. A. (2023). *Capital markets development trust fund: Creating Africa's future today*. Retrieved on 10 May, 2024.

Adesola, W., Ewa, U., & Edem, N. (2020). Comparative study of value relevance of financial information in the oil and gas and manufacturing sectors in Nigeria. *Research Journal of Finance and Accounting, 11*(12), 28–35.

Alade, M. E. (2018). *Effect of international financial reporting standards adoption on value relevance of accounting information of Nigerian listed firms* (doctoral dissertation).

Alade, M. E., Olweny, T., & Oluoch, O. (2017). Compliance with IFRS and value relevance at the Nigerian stock market. *International Journal of Economics, Commerce and Management, 5*(7), 109–127. http://ijecm.co.uk/

Alfraih, M. M. (2016). Have financial statements lost their relevance? Empirical evidence from the frontier market of Kuwait. *Journal of Advances in Management Research, 13*(2), 225–239. https://doi.org/10.1108/JAMR-06-2015-0043

Almujamed, H. I., & Alfraih, M. M. (2019). Value relevance of earnings and book values in the Qatari stock exchange. *EuroMed Journal of Business, 14*(1), 62–75. https://doi.org/10.1108/EMJB-02-2018-0009

Amir, E., Harris, T. S., & Venuti, E. K. (1993). A comparison of the value-relevance of US versus non-US GAAP accounting measures using form 20-F reconciliations. *Journal of Accounting Research, 31*, 230–264.

Anchev, S., & Lapanan, N. (2023). Stock market participation and accounting information. Available at SSRN 4379045.

Badu, B., & Appiah, K. O. (2018). Value relevance of accounting information: An emerging country perspective. *Journal of Accounting & Organizational Change, 14*(4), 473–491.

Badwy, H. A. E. S. (2019). Value relevance of accounting information: An empirical comparative study on Egyptian and Saudi listed companies. *Alexandria Journal of Accounting Research, 3*(1), 347–405.

Ball, R., & Brown, P. (1968). An empirical evaluation of accounting income numbers. *Journal of Accounting Research, 6*(2), 159–178.

Bankole, K. O., & Ukolobi, I. O. (2020). Value relevance of accounting information and share price in financial service industry. *Research Journal of Finance and Accounting, 11*(8), 140–151.

Barać, Ž. A. (2021, June). Financial reporting quality measurement–approaches, issues and future trends. In *Proceedings of FEB Zagreb international odyssey conference on economics and business, 3(1)* (pp. 1–13). University of Zagreb, Faculty of Economics and Business.

Barth, M. E., Li, K., & McClure, C. G. (2023). Evolution in value relevance of accounting information. *The Accounting Review, 98*(1), 1–28. https://doi.org/10.2308/TAR-2019-0521

Chen, B., Kurt, A. C., & Wang, I. G. (2020). Accounting comparability and the value relevance of earnings and book value. *Journal of Corporate Accounting & Finance, 31*(4), 82–98.

Chauhan, Y., & Kumar, S. B. (2019). The value relevance of nonfinancial disclosure: Evidence from foreign equity investment. *Journal of Multinational Financial Management, 52*, 100595.

Čupić, M., Todorović, M., & Benković, S. (2023). Value relevance of accounting earnings and cash flows in a transition economy: The case of Serbia. *Journal of Accounting in Emerging Economies, 13*(3), 541–565.

Damodaran, A. (2024). *The little book of valuation: How to value a company, pick a stock, and profit*. John Wiley & Sons.

Der, B. A., Masri, M. H., & Abubakari, M. S. (2018). A comparative study of the value relevance of accounting information between financial and non-financial companies listed on the Ghana stock exchange. *Afro-Asian Journal of Finance and Accounting, 8*(3), 271–295.

Dunham, L. M., & Grandstaff, J. L. (2022). The value relevance of earnings, book values, and other accounting information and the role of economic conditions in value relevance: A literature review. *Accounting Perspectives, 21*(2), 237–272.

Ernest, O., & Oscar, M. C. (2014). The comparative study of value relevance of financial information in the Nigeria banking and petroleum sectors. *Journal of Business Studies Quarterly, 6*(1), 42–54.

Eze, C. C., Ezenwa, N., & Chikezie, C. (2020). Effect of the Nigerian Stock Exchange on Economic Growth in Nigeria: Perspectives from Local Investors. Nigerian Journal of Agricultural Economics, 10(1), 18–28.

Gujarati, D. N., & Forter, D. C. (2010). *Essential of econometrics* (4th ed.). McGraw-Hill.

Ighosewe, E. F. (2022). Accounting information and value relevance: A quinquennial comparison of pre-and post-IFRS adoption of listed firms in Nigeria and South Africa. *Modern Economy, 13*(7), 1006–1023.

Imhanzenobe, J. (2022). Value relevance and changes in accounting standards: A review of the IFRS adoption literature. *Cogent Business & Management, 9*(1), 2039057.

Kaushalya, P., & Kehelwalatenna, S. (2020). The impact of IFRS adoption on value relevance of accounting information: The case of Sri Lanka. *International Review of Business Research Papers, 16*(2), 66–86.

Kim, J. Y., & Key, K. G. (2014). Changes in accounting information value relevance and cash flow prediction: Evidence from Korea. *International Journal of Business and Social Science, 5*(9).

Mbekomize, C. J., & Popo, S. (2020). Value relevance of accounting information in the Botswana listed companies. *International Business Research, 13*(5), 1913–9004.

Migliavacca, A. (2024). Value relevance of accounting numbers and sustainability information in Europe: Empirical evidence from nonfinancial companies. *Journal of International Accounting, Auditing and Taxation, 55*, 1–14.

Mousa, G. A., & Desoky, A. M. (2014). The value relevance of international financial reporting standards (IFRS): The case of the GCC countries. *Journal of Accounting, Finance and Economics, 4*(2), 16–28.

Mubarika, N. R., & Handayani, R. S. (2022). Value relevance of accounting information from PSAK 72. *Jurnal Akuntansi dan Keuangan, 24*(1), 1–9.

Mulenga, M. J., & Bhatia, M. (2018). Review of accounting variables affecting stock Price movements. *Amity Business Review, 19*(1), 91–105.

Njenga, G., Machagua, J., & Gachanja, S. (2022). *Capital markets in sub-Saharan Africa* (No. 2022/112). WIDER Working Paper.

Nwanne, T. F. I., & Oleka, C. D. (2015). The Nigerian stock exchange: A bane for sustainable economic development. *European Journal of Business and Social Sciences, 3*(12), 19-27.

Ohlson, J. A. (1995). Earnings, book values, and dividends in equity valuation. *Contemporary Accounting Research, 11*(2), 661–687.

Okaro, S. C. (2002). The Nigerian Stock Exchange and the Challenge of Economic Growth & Development in Nigeria. *The Accountant, 35*(2).

Okezie, B. N., Imoniana, J. O., & Eze, M. G. (2020). Pre and post IFRS and value relevance of accounting information of money deposit banks in Nigeria. *International Journal of Auditing Technology, 4*(3), 177–194.

Omokhudu, O. O., & Ibadin, P. O. (2015). The value relevance of accounting information: Evidence from Nigeria. *Accounting and Finance Research, 4*(3), 1–20.

Oyerinde, D. T. (2011). *Value-relevance of accounting information in the Nigerian stock market*. Covenant University, Ota, Nigeria.

Pervan, I., & Bartulović, M. (2014). Value relevance of accounting information: Evidence from southeastern European countries. *Economic research-Ekonomska istraživanja, 27*(1), 181–190.

Rahman, J. M., & Liu, R. (2021). Value relevance of accounting information and stock price reaction: Empirical evidence from China. *Journal of Accounting and Management Information System, 20*(1), 5–27.

Sami, H., & Zhou, H. (2004). A comparison of value relevance of accounting information in different segments of the Chinese stock market. *The International Journal of Accounting, 39*(4), 403–427.

Song, I., Douthett, E. B., Jr., & Jung, K. (2003). The role of accounting information in stock market liberalization: Evidence from Korea. *Advances in International Accounting, 16*, 67–84.

Soumaré, I., Kanga, D., Tyson, J., & Raga, S. (2021). Capital market development in sub-Saharan Africa: Progress, challenges and innovations. In *Joint FSD Africa and ODI working paper*. Overseas Development Institute.

Sulaiman, L. A. (2023). Capital market development and economic growth of west African countries. *Nigerian Journal of Banking and Financial Issues (NJBFI), 9*(1), 115–125.

Tsalavoutas, I., Andre, P., & Evans, L. (2012). The transition to IFRS and value relevance of financial statement in Greece. *The British Accounting Review, 44*(4), 262–277.

Widianingsih, Y. P. N., & Setiawan, D. (2021, December). Value relevance of accounting information in sustainable finance. In *Conference towards ASEAN chairmanship 2023 (TAC 23 2021)* (pp. 245–250). Atlantis Press.

Yartey, C. A., & Adjasi, C. K. (2007). Stock market development in sub-Saharan Africa: Critical issues and challenges. *IMF Working Paper, No. 07/209*. Available at SSRN: https://ssrn.com/abstract=1012992

Závodný, L., & Procházka, D. (2023). IFRS adoption and value relevance of accounting information in the V4 region. *Economic research-Ekonomska istraživanja, 36*(1), 1–19.

Corporate Environmental Sustainability Reporting and Value Relevance of Listed Financial Service Firms in Nigeria

Wilson Adebayo Adepiti and Muyiwa Ezekiel Alade

Abstract Corporate activities have resulted in depletion of natural resources, environmental pollution and hazard, while reporting such environmental engagements is capable of affecting corporate market values. This study was conducted to examine value relevance of corporate environmental sustainability reporting of listed financial service firms in Nigeria. The study employed ex post facto research design. Data were obtained from secondary sources through published annual reports and sustainability reports of selected firms for the period 2010 to 2020. The population consists of 51 financial service listed firms, while 35 firms were purposively sampled. Data collected were analysed using panel corrected standard error (PCSE) regression. The study revealed that materials, effluents and waste as measures of corporate environmental sustainability reporting are significantly value relevant, while compliance disclosure and energy consumption have no statistically significant effect. The studyconcluded that any improvement in the policy direction of the firms' corporate environmental sustainability reporting will lead to improved corporate value among listed financial service firms. The study recommended that firms should give adequate attention to the projection of their environmental sustainability information in order to promote its value relevance and increase competitive edge.

Keywords Value relevance · Materials · Energy consumption · Effluents and waste · Compliance

W. A. Adepiti · M. E. Alade (✉)
Adekunle Ajasin University, Akungba-Akoko, Nigeria
e-mail: muyiwa.alade@aaua.edu.ng

T. Moloi (ed.), *Impacting Society Positively Through Technology in Accounting and Business Processes*, Springer Proceedings in Business and Economics,
https://doi.org/10.1007/978-3-031-84885-8_21

Introduction

Firms that disclose environmental sustainability performance have the chance of gaining potential benefits, including enhancement of transparency, improving reputation and brand value, motivating employees and supporting the firm's control processes. But, listed financial service firms in Nigeria have encountered decline in value relevance which has been linked with the present global consensus to promote sustainable development goal, among which environmental sustainability is one (Obiora et al., 2022; Ngwakwe, 2008). As a case, deficiency in regulating environmental sustainability reporting practices in Nigeria has led to inadequate disclosure of environmental performances among listed firms in Nigeria. This has had adverse effect on the firms' impending competitive advantage such as patronage, improvement of transparency, improved reputation and trademark-value, employees-motivation, as well as long run effect on share prices of listed firms.

Weak market performance of quoted firms has also been connected to increased corporate activities which has led to damages to the-environment, including depletion of natural resources, environmental pollution and climate change (Obiora et al., 2022; Abdulrahman et al., 2021). Lack of adequate reporting on environmental impacts of firms' activities through the conventional financial reports, on a broader scale, is now posing threats to the goal of sustainable development (Amedu et al., 2019). This has resulted to increasing agitation for improved corporate environmental sustainability reporting capable of contributing to value relevance of the firms.

According to Hassel et al. (2005), Akinlo and Iredele (2014), Olagunju and Ajiboye (2022) and Obiora et al. (2022), environmental sustainability activities disclosure has positive and significant influence on share price with a common conclusion that corporate environmental sustainability reporting is value relevant. On the contrary, Jones et al. (2007), Ngwakwe (2008) and Makori and Jagongo (2013) established negative relationship between market value and environmental sustainability reporting since environmental concerns are considered cost ineffective, thereby creating adverse impact on corporates earnings. These serve as confirmation that confounding submissions exist in literature regarding value relevance of environmental sustainability reporting.

Furthermore, although several studies have been conducted on corporate environmental sustainability practices, existing literature has shown that major focus of these studies has been skewed towards the effect of environmental reporting on financial performance measures. Thus, there is need to examine how this form of sustainability reporting impact corporate market values (value relevance), particularly among financial services sector, which is one of the most vibrant sectors of an economy. Specifically, the study focused on value relevance of corporate environmental sustainability reporting with major attention on four aspects of environmental concerns such as materials, energy consumption, effluent and waste, and compliance in line with Global Reporting Initiatives (GRI). This-study was envisioned to provide empirical evidence that will assist the management, government and other policy makers to enhance value creation potentials of corporate environmental sustainability towards attaining sustainable development goal. Therefore, the study examined the effect of corporate environmental sustainability-reporting on value relevance of listed financial services firms in Nigeria.

This study is structured into five sections, the first part presents introduction which contains background issues. The next section contains conceptual review, theoretical review, empirical review, identified gap and formulation of hypotheses, followed by methods employed in the study. The fourth section showcases the data analysis and discussion of findings. The last section covers concluding remarks and recommendations.

Literature-Review

Value Relevance

Suadiye (2013) described value relevance as a direct dimension of information aids for making decision as it reveals accounting information role of providing investors with essential information for assessment purposes. Halimah et al. (2020) explicate that value relevance can be construed as an arithmetical relationship between accounting data and its effect on company's market value. Value relevance connotes the ability that relevant and reliable financial and non-financial information presented in financial statements reflect market value. Value relevance as a concept is established on relevance and reliability. Thus, the study views value relevance as statistical connection between financial statements information and the influence on changes in the market share price.

In literature, value relevance connotes the capability of disclosed accounting-information through the financial statement to explain information which affects value of stock in the capital market (Amedu et al., 2019). From the investors' viewpoint, relevant information is any information that enhances their decisions about investment in shares and affords a perception on value relevance that describes the presence of a link between firms market share price and financial statement information. This study makes use of market value (share price) as a proxy for value relevance consistent with Ohlson price model.

Studies such as Alade (2018), Cooray et al. (2020) and Echobu et al. (2022) have used Ohlson (1995) price model to express the relationship among the equity market value and two key variables in financial reporting, which are the book value of equity per share which represents figure from statement of financial position and earnings per share which represents figure from statement of financial performance and other comprehensive income. There are various measurements used in previous studies as proxy of market value. These measurements include; Tobin's Q which is described as the proportion of total debt and market capitalization to total assets (Atandal et al., 2021; Govindan et al., 2021; Shaikh, 2022), share price (Nguyen, 2020; Setyahuni & Handayani, 2020; Olagunju & Ajiboye, 2022), among others.

Therefore, the study employed accounting-based valuation model which was developed by Ohlson (1995), where equity market value (share price) is estimated as a function of accounting earnings, book value and other information of which sustainability reporting is among.

Corporate Environmental-Sustainability Reporting

According to Chikwendu et al. (2019), corporate environmental sustainability reporting is concerned with the reporting of firms impacts on the living things and non-living natural resources, including land, air, water and ecosystems. Global Reporting Initiative (GRI), described environmental sustainability reporting as the procedure, whereby firms report environmental impacts of their business performance on the environment. Okoye and Ndum (2020) considered corporate environmental sustainability reporting as the process in which organization discloses to the public concerning environmental impacts of their business actions and environmental prevention strategies embark on to alleviate them by reporting the environmental information linked to those actions.

Based on aforesaid, this study viewed corporate environmental sustainability reporting as reporting approach that ponders on environmental performance of the mutual actions of firms in achieving their primary objectives without endangering the fitness of the impending generations to find long lasting fortune to realize their own needs. This study considered corporate environmental sustainability reporting from the aspects of materials, energy consumption, effluents and waste and compliance which are relevant to the study. There are 13 indicators under these four aspects of corporate environmental sustainability reporting.

Materials reporting indicator describes the reporting entity's contribution to the conservation of the global resource-base and its efforts to decrease the material intensity and increase economy's efficiency. These are expressed goals of the Organisation for Economic Co-operation and Development (OECD) Council and various national sustainability strategies. This indicator seeks to identify the organization's ability to use recycled input materials. Using these materials helps to lessen the demand for virgin material and add to the conservation of the global resource-base and support sustainability development goal. For internal managers and others interested in the financial performance of the firm, substituting recycled materials cancontribute to lowering the overall costs of operation which in turn increase value relevance of firms.

Energy consumption aspect covers the five most important areas of energy usage in the organization: energy usage outside the organization, energy concentration, decrease of energy usage and decreases in energy necessities of services and products. Energy consumption has a direct effect on operational costs and can increase exposure to fluctuations in energy supply and prices. The environmental footprint of an organization is shaped, in part, by its choice of energy sources. Variations in the balance of these sources can indicate the organization's efforts to minimize its environmental impacts. For some organizations, electricity is the only significant form of energy they consume. For other organizations, other energy sources might also be essential, like steam or water generated from a district heating plant or chilled-water plant. Energy may be purchased from sources external to the organization or produced by the organization itself (self-generated). Only energy consumed by entities owned or controlled by the organization is expected to be reported in this indicator.

Effluents and Waste are the amount and quality of the water discharged by the organization which is directly linked to ecological impact and operational costs (International Union for Conservation of Nature-IUCN, 2013). Through gradual enhancement of the quality of water discharged or decreasing capacities, the firm has the ability to decrease its effect on the immediate-environment. If discharged effluents are not properly controlled with active chemical or nutrient-load, it can result to substantial impact on receiving waters. This, in turn, can affect the quality of the water supply available to the organization and its relationship with communities and other water users.

Compliance aspect deals with the financial value of significant penalties and total figure of non-financial fines for not complying with environmental laws and regulations. The level of non-compliance within the organization helps to indicate the ability of directors to confirm that procedures conform to convinced performance parameters. From economic perception, confirming compliance aids in reducing financial risks that arise directly through fines or otherwise through impacts on corporate reputation. Non-compliance in some instances, can result in cleaning-up commitments or other exorbitant environmental liabilities. The stability of the organization's compliance record can also affect its capability to increase operations or gain permits. GRI identify administrative or legal sanctions for non-compliance with environmental laws and regulations, including, as a minimum: voluntary environmental agreements with regulating authorities that are considered binding and developed as a substitute for implementing new regulations.

Environmental Sustainability-Reporting and Value-Relevance

Corporate environmental sustainability reporting can lessen information asymmetry between directors and investors by reporting its good business performance to intensify information transparency and empower investors to incorporate environmental sustainability reporting in valuation of stocks. Prior researches have documented that sustainability reporting is useful for investors in making their investment decisions. Therefore, environmental sustainability reporting has a value relevance, because it can make a difference in decisions making by users of financial statements.

Olagunju and Ajiboye (2022) opine that reporting on environmental sustainability activities influence share price positively and substantially. This study found comprehensive evidence showing that environmental sustainability meaningfully stimulated market value of listed Nigerian non-financial firms. However, presently, non-financial firms quoted in Nigeria presently are not worried about the physical environment in which they meet their objective relating to compliance to the environmental laws and regulations (Okpala & Iredele, 2018).

Obiora et al.'s (2022) findings generally indicate that environmental sustainability reporting has substantial and positive effect on firms' value measured by net assets per share and concluded that environmental sustainability reporting absolutely enhanced value relevance of listed oil and gas companies in Nigeria. The related empirical studies revealed diverse results. Hassel et al. (2005) confirmed that financial analysts found out that environmental information serves as paramount basis for prospective investors to make informed decision. Whereas Ngwakwe (2008) and Jones et al. (2007) established negative relationship between market value and environmental performance, since environmental concerns are considered to be costly, thereby creating adverse impact on value relevance.

Akinlo and Iredele (2014) reported positive relationship connecting between corporate environmental sustainability reporting and market value of Nigerian-quoted firms. Makori and Jagongo (2013) found significant but negative connection between environmental accounting and earnings per share. This finding contradicts the outcomes of Mohammed et al. (2016) and Agbiogwu et al. (2016) who established significant positive relationship between environmental sustainability and earnings per share. Despite the magnitude of demand on reporting of environmenta l sustainability practices, it is not really clear if environmental sustainability is value relevant in Nigeria. Indication from existing studies has, nevertheless, revealed that meanwhile corporate environmental sustainability reporting is voluntary, it has revealed significance in assessing firms' value relevance.

Theoretical Review

Stakeholder Theory

Stakeholder theory was-propounded by Freeman (1984). The main assumption of this theory state that the objective of a firm centred on adding value for not only their shareholders but also their stakeholders (Freeman, 1984). It also assumed that firms' value is imperative feature as how firms go about doing business. Obviously, they must inform stakeholders of those values as to build a sustainable relationship between them. Stakeholder theory has the propensity to drive the link between sustainable practices and firm value (Nguyen, 2020). Stakeholder theory is established on the impression that firms have several groups of stakeholders that need unique information as basis for making informed investment decisions (Freeman, 1984). Stakeholder theory defines stakeholders as any individual or group that can influence or is influenced by the attainment of the firm's objectives.

The-study is hinged on stakeholder's theory, as it believes that when preparing a report about corporate sustainability, the goal is to meet substantial information need of myriads of stakeholders and material aspect. Material aspects are important sustainability dimension impacts that trigger the decisions and assessments of stakeholders. Stakeholder theory is relevant to this study, because the firms are aware that in achieving their primary objective, the stakeholders play significant role in providing the required resources to secure and sustain firm's survival, hence their information need must be accorded priority.

Moreover, the theory has been generally employed in accounting literature as providing strong justification for value relevance of environmental sustainability disclosure (Freeman, 2009; Sarker et al., 2016). Furthermore, stakeholder theory provides means of handling multiple stakeholders with multiple conflicting interests. Moreover, stakeholder theory is relevant to this study, because environmental accounting disclosure is corporate responsibility to the society and the ecosystem, especially in Nigeria where there is no existing regulation that enforces environmental disclosure.

Empirical Review

Myriads of empirical investigations have been done on value relevance of environmental sustainability reporting. Hassel et al. (2005) gave an insight on how environmental performance reflected in market value of firms listed in Sweden. Correlation and regression analyses were performed on environmental performance data obtained from caring companies. The results showed that environmental performance has negative impact on market value. However, Montabon et al. (2007) found entirely different results examining same relationship. Their findings suggested a significant and positive relationship between environmental sustainability performance and firm value. Semenova et al. (2010) investigated value relevance of sustainability information considering the evidence from Sweden listed companies. The study employed residual income estimation model which was tested using data obtained via GES Investment Services opportunity ratings. The study showed a positive and significant influence on value relevance of both environmental performance and social performance at aggregate and sub-aggregated levels. However, the study was limited to listed firms in Sweden.

Makori and Jagongo (2013) examined if there is any significant association between environmental accounting and profitability of selected firms listed in India. Regression analysis was used and found significant negative relationship between environmental accounting and return on capital employed and earnings per share as well as significant positive relationship between environmental accounting and net profit margin and dividend per share. Aggarwal (2013) examined the influence of sustainability disclosures on firms' financial performance of Indian listed firms and used secondary source of data. Regression analyses were run, the results showed positive but insignificant impact of sustainability performance on firms' financial performance. When considered individually, the results showed that environment related performance has significant negative relationship with company's financial performance. This result agrees with that of Makori and Jagongo (2013).

Okpala and Iredele (2018) carried out a study to investigate the effect of corporate social and environmental disclosures on market value of firms listed in Nigeria. The sample size of the study consisted of 84 listed firms in Nigeria. Data were sourced through content from annual reports of sampled firms within the time frame ranging from 2011 to 2016. The result of their findings showed that there exists a significant negative connection between social and environmental reporting and the market value of selected firms in Nigeria. The findings of this study are in conformity with the findings of Makori and Jagongo (2013).

Taliento et al. (2019) examined the relationship between environmental, social, governance information and economic performance. The study considered stocks of a representative sample of European firms listed on similar European directories in Belgium, France, Germany, Italy and Spain for the period 2014–2017. The study adopted descriptive and correlation statistics altogether with Multiple Linear Regression to analyse the data sourced. The study found significant positive relationship between corporate environmental sustainability reporting and market performance.

Olagunju and Ajiboye (2022) examined the effect of environmental disclosure on market value of 72 quoted non-financial firms in Nigeria obtained from firms' annual reports for 2012 to-2020. The study engaged panel regression analysis for data analyses. The outcomes of findings revealed that environmental disclosure has positive and statistical significant influence on both earning per share and share of non-financial listed firms in Nigeria. Obiora et al. (2022) investigated the effect of environmental accounting practice and social responsibility disclosures on firm value of listed oil and gas companies in Nigeria. The results indicated that environmental accounting practices and social sustainability reporting have significant and positive effect on firms' value.

Onyebuenyi and Ofoegbu (2022) examined the impact between environmental sustainability disclosure and financial performance of oil and gas companies listed in three countries: Nigeria, Kenya and Namibia. Panel data collected from fifteen (15) oil and gas listed firms in the three countries for the period 2011–2019 were analysed using Robust Least Square Regression technique. The results of the analyses revealed that environmental sustainability disclosure has significant effect on financial performance of listed oil and gas firms in three countries.

Gap-in Literature

Succinctly, several empirical studies reviewed focused on the effect of corporate environmental sustainability reporting on firm performance without focal consideration on its influence on market based performance measure referred to in the study as value relevance, and specifically among listed financial services firms in Nigeria. It was also established from empirical review that numerous studies using several contexts, scopes, theories and methodologies reported positive significant relationship between sustainability reporting and firm value, while others'found negative and non-existing relationship.

These conflicting findings call for more research to enable convergence in appreciating value relevance of corporate environmental sustainability reporting among listed firms in Nigeria. Despite numerous studies on sustainability reporting, there is still a gap in literature in the area of investigating the value relevance of corporate environmental sustainability reporting especially in financial services sector in Nigeria which is one of the most vibrant sectors that contribute impressively to the gross domestic product of Nigeria economy. Drawing from the findings of majority of the studies reviewed, the gap identified and theoretical background, the following hypothesis was formulated in null form as basis for empirical inference in the study.

Ho1: There is no significant effect of corporate environmental sustainability reporting on value relevance of listed financial service firms in Nigeria.

Data and Methods

The study used ex post facto research design to establish the connection between corporate environmental sustainability reporting and value relevance of listed financial services firms in Nigeria. Data were extracted from secondary sources via published annual reports and sustainability reports made available in their corporate website as-at December 31, 2020 using content analysis. The population of this study consisted of 51 firms listed in financial services sector on NGX. The sample size comprised 35 firms that have been consistently submitting their reports to NGX from 2010 to 2020 were purposively selected using a-number of criteria. The study adapted the model in the study of Amedu et al. (2019) on value relevance of sustainability reporting in Nigerian manufacturing-firms which is stated thus:

$$MV_{i,t} = \beta_{it} + \beta_1 \left(Eco - Sus_{it} \right) + \beta_2 \left(Soc - Sus_{it} \right) + \beta_3 \left(Env - Sus_{it} \right) + \beta_4 \left(\text{Lev}_{it} \right) + \varepsilon_{it}$$

Where:

MV = Market value; Eco-Sus = Economic sustainability; Soc-Sus = Social sustainability;

Env-Sus = Environmental sustainability; Lev = Leverage measured as debt equity ratio.

This study, however, modified the model of Amedu et al. (2019) to examine the effect of corporate sustainability reporting on value relevance of listed financial services firms when all other potential moderating variables are held constant. Thus, the model of this study is as presented in econometric form in Eq. 1.

$$MV_{i,t} = \beta_{it} + \beta_1 \mathrm{Ma}_{it} + \beta_2 EC_{it} + \beta_3 Co_{it} + \beta_4 EW_{it} + \varepsilon_{it} \quad (1)$$

Were:

$MV_{i,t}$ = Market value of firm *i* in time *t*

Ma = Materials

EC = Energy consumption

Co = Compliance

EW = Effluents and Waste

ε_{it} = error-term that represents other independent variables not captured which affect the model

$i_{1, \ldots, 35}$ = Company script

$t_{2010-2020}$ = time

β_0 = Constant parameter

β_{1-4} = Coefficients of variable

ε = Error term

a priori expectation: $\beta_{1-4} > 0$

The data obtained were analysed using descriptive and panel corrected standard error (PCSE) due to identified failed econometric assumptions (Table 1).

Data-Analysis and Discussion of-Findings

Descriptive-Statistics

Table 2 presents the descriptive statistics and as observed, the mean for market-value (MV) measured by share-price stood at 3.523. The standard deviation of 6.822 is very large which specifies the extent of dispersion from the mean and shows that MV of selected firms varies considerably from one firm to another. The maximum and minimum values stood at N48.50 and N0.10, respectively. The Jarque-Bera test of normality indicates the absence of normality in the arrangement for the distribution as the p-value of the Jarque-Bera is less-than 5% significant level. This was supported by the skewness estimate which stood at 3.461 and with kurtosis at 17.389.

Environmental sustainability reporting was measured by using Materials (MA), Effluents and Waste (EW), Energy consumption (EC), Compliance (CO) and revealed that the mean value of MA, EC, CO and EW of the examined firms stood

Table 1 Summary of variables and their measurements

S/N	Variable	Description	Measurement	Sources of measurement
Independent Variable: Environmental Sustainability Reporting (ESR)				
1	Materials (MA)	Inputs used in production processes weight or volume and how it is sourced from renewable sources, reducing material waste, using recycled materials	Dummy of 1 if disclosed otherwise 0	Agu & Amedu (2018); Okoye and Ndum (2020); Amedu et al. (2019).
2	Energy consumption (EC)	Considers the efficient use and consumption of energy as well as energy generated from renewable sources.	Dummy of 1 if disclosed otherwise 0	Amedu et al. (2019); Okoye and Ndum (2020)
3	Compliance (CO)	Monetary value of significant-fines and total number of non-monetary sanctions for non-compliance with environmental laws and Regulations	Dummy of 1 if disclosed otherwise 0	Okoye and Ndum (2020)
4	Effluents and waste (EW)	The water effluents discharged (output or emission), amount of hazardous and non-hazardous waste created (treated effluent before release) and accidental release of hazardous substances	Dummy of 1 if disclosed otherwise 0	Emeka-Nwokeji-&Osisioma; Okoye and Ndum (2020)
Dependent Variable (Value Relevance)				
6	Share price	Share price is a proxy of value-relevance which is the prevailing share price at the end of the third month after financial year-end	Market price per-share as published by NGX at the end of third month after the balance sheet date	Ohlson (1995); Olagunju and Ajiboye (2022)

Source: Authors' compilation (2023)

at 0.146, 0.117, 0.188 and 0.091, respectively. This indicated that firms under investigation disclosed 15% of information on Materials, 11% on Effluents and Waste, 18% on information on Energy consumption and only 9% on Compliance. These outcomes are not unexpected, since the study focused on financial sector that is not into manufacturing activities capable of having huge environmental issues on its environs.

The standard deviation of MA, EW, EC and CO stood at 0.353, 0.322, 0.391 and 0.288, respectively, which is relatively small indicating a small dispersion of the distribution-from the-mean and shows that MA, EW, EC and CO vary considerably from one firm to another. The maximum and minimum values stood at 1_and 0, respectively. The Jarque-Bera test of normality of environmental sustainability measured by Materials (MA), Energy consumption, (EC), Compliance (CO) and

Table 2 Descriptive-statistics

	MV	MA	EW	EC	CO
Mean	3.523	0.146	0.118	0.188	0.091
Median	0.570	0.000-	0.000-	0.000-	0.000-
Maximum-	48.500	1.000	1.000	1.000	1.000
Minimum	0.000	0.000	0.000	0.000	0.000
Std. dev.	6.822	0.353	0.322	0.391	0.288
Skewness	3.461	2.007	2.380	1.601	2.841
Kurtosis	17.389	5.028	6.666	3.564	9.072
Jarque–Bera	4079.221	323.580	577.671	169.194	1106.441
Probability	0.000-	0.000	0.000-	0.000	0.000-
Sum	1352.750	56.000	45.000	72.000	35.000
Sum Sq. dev.	17822.82	47.833	39.727	58.500	31.810
Observations	384	385	385	385	385

Source: Authors' computation (2023)

Table 3 Pearson correlation matrix

	MV	MA	EC	EW	CO
MV	1.000				
MA	0.183**	1.000			
EC	0.192**	0.633**	1.000		
EW	0.037	0.354**	0.613**	1.000	
CO	0.092	0.331**	0.173**	0.222**	1.000

Source: Authors' computation (2023)
** Correlation is-significant at the 0.01 level (2-tailed); * Correlation is significant-at the 0.05 level (2-tailed)

Effluents and Waste (EW) indicate that there is no normality in the arrangement for the distribution as the p-value of the Jarque-Bera is less than 5% significant level. This was supported by the skewness and kurtosis statistics that reveal absence of outliers in the sequence and that the distribution is not normally distributed.

Test-of Variables

Correlation-Matrix for the-Model

Table 3 shows the variables' correlation statistics. Correlation coefficient measures the direction and degree of association between two or more variables. The essence is to depict extent of relationship among the variables in order to establish whether the relationship is too strong or weak since strong relationship among variables suggests the presence of multicollinarity. Based on the results presented in Table 3, it is very obvious that association between the parameters investigated could rather be

Table 4 Variance-inflation-factor test of variables

-Variable	Tolerance	VIF
MA	0.500	2.002
EC	0.309	3.240
EW	0.586	1.708
CO	0.738	1.356

Source: Authors' computation (2023)

described as very weak except for the link between material and energy consumption, and effluent and waste and energy consumption that show relationship around 0.6 which is still below the threshold of 0.8 rule of thumb. Thus, the variables employed in the study are not highly correlated, hence, likelihood of presence of multicollinearity could not be inferred.

The correlations matrix provides preliminary insight into the degree and direction of the relationship between the variables. However, correlations do not necessarily imply functional dependence between variables and hence limited usefulness for causality. Regression analysis is more suitable for this purpose and the results are presented. The variance inflation factor (VIF) test is first presented to recognize the collinearity status of the variables.

A multilinearity between the independent variables, indicates a perfect association. When the independent variables are perfectly associated, the parameters would be undefined. In the case of multicollinearity, the predicted coefficients would be significant standard errors. The VIF test is built to test multicollinearity in this analysis. The VIF explains how often the variance of a regressor calculation was distorted due to collinearity with the other regressors. Essentially, VIFs over 10 are known to be a-cause of alarm. Based on multicollinearity test reported in Table 4, no variables have more than 10 VIF values, and therefore no variables have been found to have-a serious sign of multicollinearity.

Panel Unit-Root-Test

Having described the nature of our data series, the data were further analysed for unit root at individual intercept. The purpose for selecting individual intercept is to confirm that the data will be treated with recognition of differences in the cross-sections; that is, each firm in the panel is treated as different from other firm instead of pooling them together as was presented in the Descriptive Statistics section.

The result of the unit root test as contained in Table 5 shows that all the selected data series are stationary at level, first difference and second difference, as all the null hypotheses of unit root process were rejected given that each series' probability value consistently yield a value less than 5%. It is an evident that all the variables are free from unit root tangle; the Augmented Dickey Fuller (ADF) unit root result with intercept only for instance reveals that all the variables are stationary at first

Table 5 Panel unit-root test [ADF-test with intercept only]

Variable	T-Statistics	*P*-Value	Order of-Integration	Decision
MV	148.007	0.0000	I(0)	Stationary
MA	39.6999	0.0417	I(0)	Stationary
EC	70.7417	0.0000	I(1)	Stationary
EW	50.2871	0.0001	I(1)	Stationary
CO	13.0097	0.0112	I(1)	Stationary

Source: Authors' computation (2023)

difference except for 'MA' which is stationary at level difference. Hence, we accept that there is no unit root in the data series selected for the study based on the result in Table 5 and that the variables are stationary at levels.

Environmental-Sustainability-Reporting and Value-Relevance

Table 6 shows the regression results on how environmental sustainability reporting proxies affect share price of listed financial services firms in Nigeria. All appropriate tests were performed to meet the basis for a Best Linear Unbias Estimate (BLUE) and the findings were presented alongside the regression for interpretation in Table 6. The heteroscedasticity test which was performed to verify the validity of homoscedasticity assumption that variance in the residuals are constant was conducted using Breusch and Pagan-Lagrangian test, and the result shows probability value of 0.0000 which indicate the incidence of heteroscedasticity problem. The study also performed serial correlation test using Woolridge test for autocorrelation in panel data, the results have p-value of 0.0000 which is significant at 1% level. This infers that there is problem of auto correlation.

The Hausman specification test was also conducted, and the result showed *p*-value of 0.5032 which was not significant at 5% level. This implies that the variation in unique features across entities is supposed to be random in the model. Furthermore, Breusch-and Pagan-Lagrangian multiplier test for random effects was-conducted to choose between random effect and pooled OLS and the result favoured the random effect showing probability value of 0.0000. As suggested by Onyebuenyi and Ofoegbu (2022) that in order to correct the problem of autocorrelation and make the results of the regression suitable for interpretation on the basis of best linear unbias estimation, a robust test was conducted. Hence, panel corrected standard error regression was used. The correlation coefficient and probability-value is the basis of judgment used in interpretation of the-results.

Table 6 Environmental sustainability reporting and value relevance

Variable	Fixed effects Model	Random effects-Model	PCSE Model Model
C	3.464 (0.229)**	3.369 (1.041)**	5.945 (0.727)**
CO	−1.720 (1.321)	−1.374 (1.262)	0.626 (1.120)
EC	0.397 (0.838)	0.552 (0.830)	−0.981 (0.895)
EW	−0.612 (0.778)	−0.712 (0.774)	−2.268 (0868)**
MA	1.673 (0.747)*	1.674 (0.743)*	2.227 (0.720)**
R^2	0.0135	0.028	0.1845
Wald chi^2		8.77{0.0671}	16.67{0.0022}
F test	34.73 {0.0000}		
Number of observation	379	379	379
Breusch and-pagan Lagrangian: Chibar2 1032.41{0.0000}			
Modified Wald heteroscedasticity: chi2 1.2e+08{0.0000}			
Hausman fixed random		3.34{0.5032}	
Wooldridge autocorrelation test			128.483{0.0000}

*, ** signify significant at 0.05 and 0.01 level respectively; standard error in parenthesis ( ), *p*-value in { }
Source: Authors' computation (2023)

The R-square test affirms that the explanatory variables in the model is significant, since the probability value stood at 0.0022 which is below 0.05 criterion. This implies that the explanatory variables are capable of explaining the variations on value relevance of listed financial services firms in Nigeria measured in terms of share price. However, the level of variability is low showing R-square value of 18.45% which implies that environmental sustainability reporting practices of listed financial services firms in Nigeria, have low influence on the share price.

Analysis of the panel corrected standard error (PCSE) regression coefficients reveals that the four environmental sustainability parameters, that is, compliance (0.626; $p = 0.576$) has positive but insignificant effect on share price; material (2.227; $p = 0.002$) has positive and significant influence on share price; energy consumption (−0.981; $p = 0.273$) has negative and insignificant influence on share price; effluent and waste (−2.268; $p = 0.009$) present negative but significant influence on share price of listed financial services firms in Nigeria. Succinctly, the results show statistical significance for materials, and effluent and waste while results on compliance and energy consumption revealed statistical insignificance. On the other hand, though the listed firms' reporting on energy consumption and compliance practices have mixed effects on share price, they are not value relevant since the results revealed statistical insignificant outcomes.

Discussion of Findings

Environmental Sustainability Reporting and Value Relevance

Furthermore, the regression outcomes of the effect of environmental sustainability reporting on value relevance of listed financial services firms in Nigeria as presented in Table 6 showed that environmental sustainability reporting measured by Materials (MA), Energy consumption (EC), Compliance (CO) and Effluents and Waste (EW) exhibit both negative and positive as well as significant and insignificant effects on share price. Since the F-statistics returned significant value, therefore, formulated hypothesis that there is no significant effect of corporate environmental sustainability reporting on value relevance of listed financial services firms in Nigeria could not be embraced. Hence, corporate environmental sustainability reporting has significant effect on value relevance of listed financial services firms in Nigeria.

The implication of these findings is that any improvement on firm's policy direction as related to material and effluent and waste disclosure aspect of environmental reporting practices will amount to improvement in the stock market value in terms of share price, attract more economic benefit and solidify relationship with its stakeholders, thereby becoming more value relevant. Thus, both material, and effluent and waste environmental disclosure are value relevant among non-financial listed firms. Furthermore, regarding the other two proxies, the implication is that corporate reporting on energy consumption and compliance have no value relevance to the stock market participants unlike material, and effluent and waste reporting, based on the sector investigated from Nigerian reporting environment. That is, investors derive less value relevance on energy consumption and compliance environmental reporting in the market. The peculiarity of this result might be because of the sector examined as this outcome might not be the same with non-financial manufacturing sector. Thus, these findings should be interpreted with caution.

The results-of this research corroborate with Onyebuenyi and Ofoegbu (2022) and Obiora et al. (2022) studies carried out in Nigeria and contradicted Amedu et al. (2019) who found that environmental sustainability reporting has an insignificant effect on value relevance of listed manufacturing firms in Nigeria. Atandal et al. (2021) examined the effect of sustainability reporting on firm value considering listed deposit money banks in Nigeria. The results of the study showed that environmental sustainability has significant negative relationship with firm value. Okoye and Ndum (2020) examined the effect of sustainability reporting on firm value proxy by economic value added of manufacturing firms listed on the floor of NGX. Findings from the empirical analysis showed that environmental sustainability reporting exerted a significant positive effect on economic value added, of listed manufacturing firms in Nigeria.

Conclusion and Recommendations

This study examines the effect of corporate environmental sustainability reporting on value relevance of listed financial services firms in Nigeria. Based on the results of data analysed, the-study made the following conclusions. First of all, corporate environmental sustainability reporting enhances value relevance of listed financial services firms in Nigeria. This study also indicated that financial rewards of involving in corporate environmental sustainability reporting practices outweigh the associated costs. The study revealed that stakeholders valued firm if they report environmental related issues consistent with some extant literature. This study therefore recommended that firms, financial and non-financial, should embrace environmental sustainability reporting practices designed to achieve respect for natural habitats and ecology, since such practices have the tendency of promoting good corporate image of the firms, thereby increasing firms' value relevance. Also, although no specific law mandating corporate entities in Nigeria, listed firms should prioritize disclosure of environmental information in their annual reports, as they have potential capacity to increase their market value and portray obligation in achieving sustainable development goal.

References

Abdulrahman, B. S., Babangida, M. A., & Mustapha, I. (2021). Sustainability reporting and financial performance of multinational oil and gas firms in Nigeria: The paradox of environmental cost. *International Journal of Innovative Research in Accounting and Sustainability, 6*(1), 1–16.

Aggarwal, P. (2013). Impact of sustainability performance of company on its financial performance: A study of listed Indian firms. *Global Journal Inc., 13*, 61–70.

Agbiogwu, A. A., Ihendinihu, J. U., & Okafor, M. C. (2016). Impact of environmental and social costs on performance of Nigerian manufacturing firms. *International Journal of Economics and Finance, 8*(9), 173–180.

Agu, S. I., & Amedu, J. M. A. (2018). Relevance of sustainability disclosure to profitability of listed pharmaceutical firms in Nigeria. *International Journal of Scientific & Engineering Research, 9*(11), 1195–1202.

Akinlo, O. O., & Iredele, O. O. (2014). Corporate environmental disclosures and market value of quoted companies in Nigeria. *Business and Management Review, 5*(3), 171–184.

Alade, M. E. (2018). *Effect of international financial reporting standards adoption on value relevance of accounting information of Nigerian listed firms* (doctoral dissertation).

Amedu, J. M., Iliemena, R. O., & Umaigba, F. T. (2019). Value relevance of sustainability reporting in Nigerian manufacturing companies. *Journal of Global Accounting, 6*(2), 131–147.

Atandal, F. A., Osemene, F., & Ogundana, H. F. (2021). Sustainability reporting and firm value: Evidence from selected deposit money banks in Nigeria. *Global Journal of Accounting, 7*(1), 47–68.

Chikwendu, O. U., Okafor, G. O., & Jesuwunmi, C. D. A. (2019). Effect of sustainability reporting on Nigerian listed firms' performance. *Canadian Contemporary Research Journal, 1*(1), 96–111.

Cooray, T., Senaratne, S., Gunarathne, A. D. N., Herath, R., & Samudrage, D. (2020). Does integrated reporting enhance the value relevance of information? Evidence from Sri Lanka. *mdpi Sustainability Journal, 12*, 1–25.

Echobu, J., Ekundayo, O. O., & Abu, S. O. (2022). Value relevance of sustainability reporting in the oil and gas sector in Nigeria. *International Journal of Accounting Research, 7*(1), 36–42.

Emeka-Nwokeji, N., & Osisioma, B. C. (2019). Sustainability disclosures and market value of firms in emerging economy: evidence from Nigeria. *European Journal of Accounting, Auditing and Finance Research, 7*(3), 1-19.

Freeman, R. E. (1984). *Strategic management: A stakeholder approach*. Pitman.

Freeman, J. M. (2009). Optimal policies for playing variable wager HILO. *Journal of Operational Research Society, 60*(1), 79–83.

Freeman, R. E., Wicks, A. C., & Parmar, B. (2004). Stakeholder theory and "the corporate objective revisited". *Organization science, 15*(3), 364-369.

Global Reporting Initiative Index (2013). Retrieved from https://documents1.worldbank.org/curated/en/558111467993208712/pdf/100343-WP-GRI-Index-2013-Box393222B-PUBLIC.pdf

Global Reporting Initiative Index (2015). Retrieved from https://documents1.worldbank.org/curated/en/523821467987823156/pdf/100004-WP-PUBLIC-Box393216B-World-Bank-GRI-Index-2015.pdf

Global Reporting Initiative Index (2019). Retrieved from https://documents1.worldbank.org/curated/pt/345091569568201066/pdf/Global-Reporting-Initiative-GRI-Index-2019.pdf

Govindan, K., Kilic, M., Uyar, A., & Karaman, A. S. (2021). Drivers and value-relevance of CSR performance in the logistics sector: A cross-country firm-level investigation. *International Journal of Production Economics, 231*, 1–14.

Halimah, N. P., Irsyanti, A., & Aini, L. R. (2020). The value relevance of sustainability reporting: Comparison between Malaysia and Indonesia stock market. *The Indonesian Journal of Accounting Research, 23*(3), 447–466.

Hassel, L., Nilsson, H., & Nyquist, S. (2005). The value relevance of environmental performance. *European Accounting Review., 14*(1), 41–61.

International Union for Conservation of Nature (IUCN), Red List of Threatened Species, Accessed May 1, 2013., from http://www.iucnredlist.org/

Jones, R. N., Dettmann, P., Park, G., Rogers, M., & White, T. (2007). The relationship between adaptation and mitigation in managing climate change risks: A regional approach. *Mitigation and Adaptation Strategies for Global Change, 12*, 685–712.

Loh, L., Thomas, T., & Wang, Y. (2017). Sustainability reporting and firm value: Evidence from Singapore-Listed Companies, sustainability. *MDPI Open Access Journal, 9 (11)*, 1-12.

Makori, D. M., & Jagongo, A. (2013). Environmental accounting and firm profitability. An empirical analysis of selected firms listed in Bombay stock exchange, India. *International Journal of Humanities and social sciences, 3*(8), 167–179.

Mohammed, N. A., Saheed, Z., & Oladele, O. K. (2016). Corporate social responsibility disclosure and financial performance of listed manufacturing firms in Nigeria. *Research Journal of Finance and Accounting, 7*(4), 47–58.

Montabon, F., Sroufe, R., & Narasimhan, R. (2007). An examination of corporate reporting, environmental management practices and firm performance. *Journal of Operations Management, 25*(5), 998–1014.

Nguyen, T. T. D. (2020). An empirical study on the impact of sustainability reporting on firm value. *Journal of Competitiveness, 12*(3), 119–135.

Ngwakwe, C. (2008). Environmental responsibility and firm performance: Evidence from Nigeria. *International Journal of Social, Behavioral, Educational, Economic, Business and Industrial Engineering, 2*(10), 1055–1062.

Obiora, F., Onuora, J. K. J., & Okoye, O. C. (2022). Environmental accounting practices, social responsibility disclosures and firm value; evidence from listed oil and gas firms in Nigeria. *International Journal of Economics and Business Management, 8*(1), 29–42.

Olagunju, A., & Ajiboye, O. O. (2022). Environmental accounting disclosure and market value of listed non financial firms in Nigeria. *International Journal of Management, Accounting and Economics, 9*(7), 413–430.

Ohlson, J. A. (1995). Earnings, book values, and dividends in equity valuation. *Contemporary Accounting Research, 11*(2), 661–687.

Okoye, E. I., & Ndum, N. B. (2020). Effect of sustainability reporting on economic value added of manufacturing firms listed on Nigeria stock exchange. *Journal of Economics, Management and Trade, 26*(10), 15–33.

Okpala, O. P., & Iredele, O. O. (2018). Corporate social and environmental disclosures and market value of listed firms in Nigeria. *Copernican Journal of Finance & Accounting, 7*(3), 9–28.

Onyebuenyi, F. E., & Ofoegbu, G. N. (2022). Environmental sustainability disclosure and firm performance of quoted oil and gas companies in sub-Saharan Africa countries. *Academy of Accounting and Financial Studies Journal, 26*(1), 1–18.

Sarker, S. H., Alam, A., & Ali, I. (2016). Human resource accounting disclosure practices in Bangladesh. *Australian Journal of Accounting Economics and Finance, 2*(2), 100–113.

Semenova, N., Hassel, L. G., & Nilsson, H. (2010). The value relevance of environmental and social performance: Evidence from Swedish SIX 300 firms. Sustainable investment and corporate governance working papers, sustainable investment research platform, SIRP WP 09-04.

Setyahuni, S. W., & Handayani, R. S. (2020). On the value relevance of information on environmental, social, and governance (ESG): An evidence from Indonesia. *Journal of Critical Reviews, 7*(12), 50–58.

Shaikh, I. (2022). Environmental, social, and governance (Esg) practice and firm performance: An international evidence. *Journal of Business Economics and Management, 23*(2), 218–237.

Suadiye, G. (2013). Value relevance of book value & earnings under the local gaap and IFRS: Evidence from Turkey. *ege akademik review, 12*(3), 301–310.

Sutopo, B., Kot, S., Adiati, A. K., & Ardila, L. N. (2018). Sustainability Reporting and value relevance of financial statements. *Sustainability, 10*(3), 678.

Taliento, M., Favino, C., & Netti, A. (2019). Impact of environmental, social, and governance information on economic performance: Evidence of a corporate 'sustainability advantage' from Europe. *Mdpi Sustainability Journal, 11*, 1738. https://doi.org/10.3390/su11061738

Investigating the Role of Accounting Software in Granting Ease to the Accountants Within Small- and Medium-Sized Enterprises in South Africa

Muhammad Azeem Shaikhnag, Nwosu Lilian Ifunanya, and Calvin Mahlaule

Abstract The main objective of this study is to investigate how accounting software grants ease to the accountant within the Small- and Medium-Sized enterprise (SME) in the retail industry. Accounting software has been employed in several countries throughout the world, with the earliest evidence of unique technological resources. As business processes became more complex, the need for advanced accounting formulas increased to understand the complicated transactions carried out by entities. Accounting consists of several processes which are time-consuming, burdensome, and complex. These hurdles have significantly increased the demand for developing an accounting software system which can assist in resolving these challenges. A qualitative research method, along with a narrative research approach, was adopted to measure how an implemented accounting software system grants ease to the accountant. To reach saturation, the sample size of fifteen accountants employed by different SME owners within the Gauteng province who make use of an accounting software system were interviewed by means of a semi-structured interview schedule. These fifteen accountants who were interviewed were sufficient to reach the point of saturation which allowed the researcher to obtain sufficient information within the study. The findings demonstrated that it is essential for all SME owners to implement an accounting software system. These accounting software systems greatly assist in preparing financial statements to such an extent that it eases the burden of the accountant's complex and time-consuming duties, since all operations are automated. The automation of the accounting processes reduces the actual working hours which the accountant needs to put into preparing the financial statements manually. This study makes significant contributions on the perceptions of the accountants in adopting new accounting software within the context of SMEs in a specific geographical area, enriching the literature on technology adoption in emerging economies. The findings also contribute to the development of best

M. A. Shaikhnag (✉) · N. L. Ifunanya · C. Mahlaule
North-West University, Mahikeng, South Africa
e-mail: Muhammads@vut.ac.za; Lilian.Nwosu@nwu.ac.za; Calvin.Mahlaule@nwu.ac.za

T. Moloi (ed.), *Impacting Society Positively Through Technology in Accounting and Business Processes*, Springer Proceedings in Business and Economics,
https://doi.org/10.1007/978-3-031-84885-8_22

practices for the implementation and utilisation of accounting software in SMEs. The study recommends that SME owners who make use of an accounting software system should provide accountants with adequate training before expecting them to operate accounting software systems effectively and efficiently.

Keywords Accounting · Software · Small- and Medium-Sized enterprises · Ease · Accountants

Introduction

The purpose of this study is to establish how the implementation of accounting software in Small- and Medium-Sized enterprises (SMEs) grants ease to the accountants. This has been escalated by the need of an accounting aid, due to the duties of an accountant becoming time-consuming, complex, and burdensome. Accounting plays a pivotal role in operating a business successfully, and it is critical that all organisations keep their financial information up to date (Chong & Nizam, 2018). Business accounting includes a wide range of activities that constitute the business's financial affairs (Zoho, 2021). Zoho (2021) mentions that accounting for business finances manually can become complex and time-consuming, justifying the rising demand for information technology in accounting. According to Chong and Nizam (2018), accounting consists of several processes which range from simple to complex and sometimes burdensome activities. Complex and burdensome accounting activities may include tracking the business cash flow activities, tracking the payment terms to creditors, managing the payroll, recording large invoices, keeping track of inventory levels, as well as choosing business partners (McLeod, 2023). Chong and Nizam (2018) suggest that business owners need to keep abreast with the novel developments and variations in information technology, so that they maintain accurate and complete accounting, statutory, and inventory records. Accounting software being the "accounting aid" or the information technology needed has since simplified the accounting processes significantly (Zoho, 2021). As a result of this software being implemented, business owners now have more time to focus on other aspects, such as executing their business strategies (Zoho, 2021). Kenton (2021) adds that accounting software is a computer program which assists accountants and bookkeepers to record and report a business's financial activities.

There are several accounting software applications such as Sage, Xero, Quickbooks, Peachtree, SMEASY, and many others which are equipped with diverse features and capabilities available in the business environment which can perform a multiplicity of accounting tasks for organisations (Olufemi et al., 2021). Larger businesses may require implementing a customised software solution which integrates large quantities of information from various departments, but SMEs usually opt for a simple accounting software, off-the-shelf, which is ready to use (Kenton, 2021). Ramklas (2021) indicates that amongst these ready-to-use packages, there are software packages which are the best and most affordable software applications for SMEs to implement within their businesses.

Technology is progressing exponentially and entities around the globe are striving to develop automated software to assist in operating their businesses. Technology is a global necessity for entities from different industries and economies, especially in SMEs. The influence of technological advances contributes to evolving perceptions of manual, global business maps, and even several aspects of economic, social, political, and cultural life. Furthermore, along with the rapid technological developments, companies as well as SMEs continuously require technology to sustain their businesses. Accounting software systems are exponentially becoming a significant business operating tool for SMEs to be efficient, financially organised, and systemically flexible. This study intends to investigate how the implementation of accounting software grants ease to the accountant when performing accounting processes.

Background

Smith (2021) submits that accounting is not just a list of debits and credits, but it is the financial language of business, dating back thousands of years. Accounting has been employed in several countries throughout the world, with the earliest evidence of this unique financial language having evolved from Mesopotamian cultures (Smith, 2021). Mesopotamia, which is a Greek word meaning "between two rivers," is a region in Southwestern Asia where the earliest civilisation developed (Mark, 2018). Research has proven that the Mesopotamians kept the earliest accounting records of goods traded and received with respect to business activities between ancient Egyptians and Babylonians (Smith, 2021). Additionally, Smith (2021) argues that the ancient accounting practices by Mesopotamia were underdeveloped methods which consisted of transactions involving livestock and crops.

As business processes became more complex, the need for advanced accounting formulas increased to understand the complicated transactions carried out by entities in South Africa (Panhalkar, 2020). Panhalkar (2020) explains further that even though such an accounting system was introduced, the older bookkeepers were unable to understand the trends within the scope of accounting. Accounting was then revolutionised by inventing and introducing the double-entry accounting principle (Bellis, 2019). The double-entry principle is a bookkeeping system which debits and credits a single transaction (Bellis, 2019). Furthermore, the double-entry principle is a fundamental aspect to consider when accounting for a business transaction (Johnson, 2019). Panhalkar (2020) explains that businesses became so complex that accounting evolved into a profession on its own and by this time, the double-entry bookkeeping system was not sufficient anymore.

The complexity of accounting for business transactions grew to such an extent that it led to the development of accounting software to simplify the process. Consequently, accounting software systems became a necessity in businesses catering to the rapid growth in complexity of business transactions which were now vulnerable to countless material errors and misstatements (Olufemi et al., 2021). Panhalkar (2020) explains that during the early stages of the implementation of accounting software systems, simple accounting tools were used to record transactions of SMEs, but these simple tools were not enough, since they did not contain memory like a modern-day computer, so personnel were unable to go back to any transactions previously recorded.

The evolution and implementation of accounting software systems in South African SMEs contributed towards significantly assisting the accountants by simplifying all accounting processes within the entity. Such accounting systems are found to help accountants in preparing and analysing financial reports which are much more accurate and reliable.

Problem Statement

Several SMEs in South Africa have implemented accounting software within their organisations, but it remains uncertain whether this has granted ease to the accountants or not (Bellis, 2019). Even though some of the SMEs are convinced that their current accounting software system helps record the flow of the entity's finances as well as examines the financial health of the entity, the problem remains as approximately 53% of SMEs in South Africa fail to implement an accounting software, culminating in them spending more money on correcting errors and paying staff overtime for manually compiling financial statements (Panko, 2018). Due to non-implementation of accounting software by SME owners, scholars have identified major difficulties encountered by SMEs such as incomplete records, financial losses, and inexperienced personnel within the entity (Thottoli, 2020).

This continues to be identified as a problem amongst SMEs, because they fail to adopt the technological resources which serve as assistance towards their accounting departments. Therefore, these SMEs will continue to face financial problems such as wasteful expenditure and inaccurate financial reports. The accounting software systems are designed to strengthen the employee workforce within the accounting departments, and if SMEs continue to not adopt such accounting software systems, then their workforce will not develop. As a result, SMEs will have no development in their accounting software staff which will result in the continuous possibility of wasteful expenditure and inaccurate records due to human error. This study intends to determine the extent to which the accounting software grants ease to the accountant within the SMEs.

Literature Review

Conceptual Review

Accounting plays a vital role in the success or collapse of modern-day SMEs. In the process of keeping track of the financial transactions, businesses are mainly concerned about methods to account for operations, storing records, performing audit procedures, reporting, and analysing financial data, as well as acquiring advice on tax matters (Amanamah et al., 2016). According to Amanamah et al. (2016), every business must keep record of the financial information that recognises its basic, cumbersome, or confusing business operations. SMEs are busy entities, so an accounting software system assists the accountants in producing accurate financial statements.

SMEs are vulnerable to risks and errors which occur at any given time in business operations. For this reason, accounting becomes a fundamental component of running a successful business (Ginting, 2023). Accounting, being a business language, serves all types of businesses and has become integral in running a business (Khanom, 2017). The purpose of accounting is to reconcile and rationalise the functioning of modern industrial societies, and it plays a crucial role in operating a business, in this case, the SMEs (Wickramsainghe et al., 2017). Accounting is the process of recording, classifying, inspecting, and presenting financial transactions in unique ways (Utami & Yulianto, 2019). Accounting provides reports for internal and external users (Salam, 2022). The reports provided to external users are in the form of financial statements clarifying the financial position, profit or loss, and cash flow (Salam, 2022). In tandem, reports are generated and provided to internal users to make managerial decisions (Salam, 2022).

Due to the complexity of accounting transactions in businesses, technology revolutionised and created room for accounting software systems which are now considered significant contributors to the practical usage of accounting software by accountants within the fraternity of SMEs (Thottoli, 2020). Wickramsainghe et al. (2017) narrates that as the business expands, acquires new customers, enters new market areas, and keeps up with the exponential increase in changes in technology, SMEs need to maintain highly accurate and up-to-date accounting, inventory, and statutory records.

Empirical Review

In the current times of globalisation, the evolution of Information Technology (IT) is growing exponentially, and this aids SMEs in developing and experiencing significant growth annually (Utami & Yulianto, 2019). According to Fuscaldo (2023), accounting software helps the accountant to record the flow of the SMEs money, so that the financial position of the entity can be determined. Accounting software packages allow management of the financial departmental activities to be efficient and flexible than previous online facilities (Janrosl & Muda, 2017). Wickramsainghe et al. (2017) argues that in the modern era of computerised, interconnected, and global business environment, accounting software has developed into becoming the "engine of growth" in all business organisations. It can be deduced that accounting software packages have become a vital aspect in all businesses and specifically in SMEs.

In South Africa, during the COVID-19 pandemic, SMEs were affected negatively, compelling them to rethink their business processes and resort to technology to remain sustainable while adapting to transformations in accounting guidelines and procedures (Lutfi et al., 2022). Lutfi et al. (2022) state further that the COVID-19 period was disruptive and it was the biggest challenge in terms of decision-making within an SME. Additionally, SMEs all over the world resorted to the implementation of accounting software systems to address the complex financial operations brought on by the COVID-19 pandemic (Lutfi et al., 2022). Generally, SME firms implement accounting software to improve their competitiveness (Rahman et al., 2017).

Theoretical Framework

Adom et al. (2018) explains that a theoretical framework is a blueprint for a study which is based on a pre-existing theory within a certain area of investigation. This framework guides the researcher to avoid deviations from the research topic. Chukwuere (2021) adds that the theoretical framework of a research project is the brain of the study in analysing and discussing findings, but many researchers still leave this out or misunderstand this vital aspect leaving their research body incomplete.

The Technology Acceptance Model theory is widely used to understand the adoption of information technology and its usage (Julies & Tranos, 2021). According to Harryanto et al. (2018), the theory, developed by Fred Davis in 1986, assumes that when SMEs adopt a technological resource, it is generally determined by their cognitive aims and processes to maximise the usefulness of the implemented technology. A study conducted by Marikyan and Papagiannidis (2022) finds that the aim for TAM was to explicate processes underlying acceptance of information systems to study behavioural patterns of users and provide a sound theoretical understanding for the success gained from the implemented resource of technology. Furthermore, Julies and Tranos (2021) elaborate that TAM's primary determinants are perceived usefulness and perceived ease of use after implementing the automated system within the SMEs.

The usefulness perception is an individual awareness on how a technological system benefits its user within the SMEs (Purnamasari, 2019). Harryanto et al.

(2018) further observe that perceived usefulness is defined as measuring the advantages provided by the technological system to its user. Furthermore, the perception of usefulness gives the user strong conviction that the automated system could improve performance in the SME to such an extent that it reduces the operating expenditure while raising the operating income (Harryanto et al., 2018).

The perceived ease of use factor is the degree to which a technological user presumes that it is simple to operate a particular information system to obtain maximum benefits while operating the SME (Ahmi et al., 2019). The perception of ease of use of a technological resource relates to the user thinking that making use of such an automated system becomes hassle-free and effortless (Ahmi et al., 2019).

One of the components of the TAM theory addresses the area of ease which is expected to be granted by the implemented accounting software system to the accountant. The technological resource is expected to grant ease to the users, and this will contribute to improving the work performed by the accounting workforce. This is ultimately expected to enhance business performance of the SME.

Methodology

Research Approach and Design

A qualitative research approach was used in this study, and this included conducting in-depth interviews with accountants of SMEs in South Africa. According to Defranzo (2019), a qualitative study allows the researcher to collect and analyse non-numerical data to elicit certain concepts, opinions, and experiences of participants, and it also provides the researcher with a dynamic approach to conduct research.

A research design is a set of protocols for collecting, studying, and interpreting data (Boru, 2018). Boru (2018) explains further that the research design is a general plan for attaching conceptual research problems with the applicable and achievable empirical research. In this study, a narrative inquiry design was used to elicit from accountants within the South African SMEs their experiences on the implementation of accounting software within the entities. Questions asked to SME accountants who have implemented accounting software in their entities generated insights as the participants narrated their experiences on whether the accountants were granted ease or not after introducing an accounting software system. The results were studied and compared to determine whether the implementation of accounting software grants ease to its users or not. In this study, narrative inquiry was executed through interviews between the researcher and accountants in the SMEs related to the implementation of accounting software in their entities. These interview questions were developed from the research problem.

Study Population

Specifically in South Africa, the Gauteng province was selected, because it is the centre of entrepreneurship, often referred to as the economic hub of South Africa (Fourie, 2023). Gauteng houses a diverse range of SMEs in various sectors. Fourie (2023) holds that Gauteng has the largest employment rate and business activity compared to anywhere else in the country. Secondly, Chigumadzi (2021) explains that there are approximately 858,000 SMEs operating within the Gauteng province which gave the researcher of this study a wide range of SMEs to select as possible participants.

Sampling and Sample Size

The purposive sampling technique was adopted to identify and select information-rich scenarios related to the area of interest. Information was gathered from participants until the point of saturation was reached. From the 858,000 SMEs in the Gauteng province, a population of 50 SMEs were selected. The researcher arrived at the point of saturation at fifteen participants out of the population of 50 SMEs.

Data Collection Instruments

Data were collected by interviewing fifteen accountants from fifteen different SMEs in the Gauteng province, South Africa. These interviews were conducted by using a semi-structured interview guide.

Interview Guide

An interview guide was used for collecting the qualitative data during the data collection process where individual interviews were conducted to collect data. The interview guide consisted of eleven interview questions for accountants working in SMEs. Interviews were conducted with fifteen accountants in the selected SMEs. The individual interviews were conducted face-to-face, telephonically or through Zoom, depending on the preferences of the participants. Each interview took approximately 30 to 40min to complete, and the questions were structured in accordance with the research objectives (DeJonckheere & Vaughn, 2019). A thematic analysis was adopted to interpret the responses given by the SME participants in these interviews. ATLAS.ti software grounded the thematic analysis generated.

Discussion of the Findings

This study discusses the extent to which the accounting software grants ease to the accountant in improving work efficiency and productivity within the accounting departments of the SMEs. Accounting software systems serve as a resource used to assist accountants to perform their duties which will in return improve business performance. The research findings are discussed below using the responses from participants coded as ***P2*** to ***P8*** and ***P10*** to ***P15*** *(P for participant)*. These participants were from different SMEs in the Gauteng province, South Africa who were all exposed to the operation of an accounting software system. These participants were qualified accountants and had adequate knowledge and training in operating an accounting software system (Table 1).

From the findings, the research participants illustrated how the accounting software system grants ease to the accountant by easing the accountability process, tracking, and monitoring of financial information, recording effect on SME, and so forth. When the accounting software system grants ease to the accountants within the SMEs, this contributes greatly towards promoting efficiently and accurately prepared financial statements.

The following sections discuss the sub-themes in detail.

Reduced Physical Work

Manual accounting processes include the usage of book ledgers and calculators which require countless physical working hours of the accountants which may probably create room for a variety of undetected errors (Jagadeesan, 2019). Furthermore, Jagadeesan (2019) explains that the implementation of an accounting software system reduces the physical working hours put in by the accountant since all the processes are automated. ***P4*** and ***P5*** focused on the physical working hours: ***P4*** stated that, yes, the implementation of this accounting software has reduced physical working hours of the accounting team, since all the information can be inputted into the software and reports automatically get generated. Furthermore, ***P5***said that due to automated reporting and automated accounting processes, the physical working hours of the accounting team have reduced.

Table 1 Theme, sub-themes, and research objective

Research objective	Theme	Sub-themes
The extent to which the accounting software grants ease to the accountant within the SMEs	Effectiveness and relevance to SME	• Reduced physical work • Stock adjustment • Increase accuracy • Informed decision-making • Prepares financial statements

Source: Author's own formulation

When asked whether an accounting software system reduces physical working hours in the SME or not, the responses from ***P6*** and ***P7*** specified the following:

P6 substantiated yes, because there is no manual accounting process involved when using the application. Profit and loss reports are produced in a specific way which extracted from the application. Ultimately, the physical working hours have reduced due to automated accounting processes.

P7 explained that the accounting software that we use is capable of automatically preparing financial reports based on all the accounting aspects, which is then extracted by the accounting team to prepare the financial statements. Thus, their physical working hours have been reduced through the assistance of automated processes.

Keeping track of time is essential to accurately billing clients as well as focusing on other projects. Since manual accounting methods can be time-consuming and prone to errors, modern accounting time sheets have migrated to the online realm and information is stored in live documents which automatically update (Czerwonka, 2023). Furthermore, the implementation of an accounting software system promotes efficient workflow management, automated invoicing, automated data reporting and analysis, accurate billing and automated tracking of inventory, debtors, and creditors, which reduces the physical workload of the accounting team (Czerwonka, 2023).

The accounting system automatically and accurately generates financial reports which are free from any material misstatements. This saves a lot of physical working hours for the employees. A lot of time is also saved, since they do not have to go back and fix errors on the reports.

From the findings, it is evident that an accounting software system significantly reduces the physical work which accountants need to perform, because these are performed by the automated system. Thus, the business avoids spending large amounts of money on physical labour hours which in return reduces business expenditure. This will increase accuracy in the financials of the SMEs, since the implementation of these accounting software systems will grant accountants support while preparing the financial reports which will aid in reducing the possibility of working long hours of work. As such, working long overtime hours could lead to the accountant in making errors or misstatements. However, the accounting software systems will reduce the physical hours that the accountant needs to put in, which will result in the work of the accountant being simplified, since all processes will be automated. As a result, this will improve the accountant's performance and ultimately the performance of the SME.

Stock Adjustments

An accounting software system is capable of tracking inventory levels as well allowing simple stock adjustment operations (Mcleod, 2023). In response to stock adjustments, ***P15*** mentioned the following:

P9 and ***P15*** said yes, in terms of stock adjustments, when the accountants need to do a stock adjustment, it sometimes takes a lot of time which results in additional physical working hours. Also, if the stock adjustment is done incorrectly, the business ends up spending money on inventory which is already in stock. So, in these ways, business expenditure gets affected negatively, because the business may have to spend more in overtime for the accountant's extra hours put in as well as the unnecessary inventory purchased. So, the accounting software system assists the accountant with stock adjustments which does not take up a lot of time.

It can be deduced that an accounting software system is indeed capable of assisting the user in performing stock adjustment operations quicker, resulting in reduced working hours and reduced business expenditure in the SME.

To elaborate on this point further, accounting software systems have an automatic stock counting function where the user enters in the goods received as well as the goods sold. The software then calculates the exact amount of inventory that should be on hand in the entity. This simplifies the duties of the accountant to a large extent, because they do not have to add and subtract inventory items every time purchases or sales transactions occur. Stock adjustment functions can be used to update and correct the quantity and price of the stock on hand. Stock adjustments could also be used for entering new stock, removing damaged or stolen stock as well as fixing data entry errors.

Beyond simple stock adjustments procedures, the implementation of an accounting software system assists in tracking the inventory turnover, as it can automatically calculate and record the cost of goods sold as well as the average inventory levels. With the correct software and features, the users can record and categorise the inventory into specific functions such as purchases, sales, returns, and adjustments. With the aid of an accounting software system, the users can export inventory reports such as inventory valuation, inventory ageing and inventory turnover ratio which helps the accountant to analyse and compare the inventory performance. Users can set a target and safety stock levels, so that they avoid the crisis of running short of stock. This will contribute greatly towards developing the workforce within the accounting department of the SME, since the accounting system will assist the accountants in adjusting stock automatically. This grants significant ease to the accountants as they do not have to manually enter values of trading stock. The system has unique functions in assisting with automated stock adjustments and this contributes towards developing the accountant workforce.

Increase Accuracy

According to Amanamah et al. (2016), an accounting software provides improved accuracy and produces high quality financial reports.

P10 elaborated that the accounting software system actually increased physical working hours of the accountant, since more information had to be entered into the system. However, it has given the business more accuracy in the reports and much more control is maintained in the business. The application also allows us to be more hands-on approach on the business finances.

P4 related that the implementation of an accounting software has not only granted ease to its users but has also significantly increased accuracy to the financial information, such as the financial statements and reports.

To emphasise on these findings further, economies globally have become reliant on an accounting software system to maintain accuracy in their financial reports, and with the sharp rise in technological growth, accuracy becomes the normative expectation (Ismail & Muhammad, 2022). The inference is that accounting software systems promote accuracy in the automatic generation of financial reports which affects business positively. As a result, business expenditure is reduced, since physical maintenance hours are no longer required as the application automatically maintains great accuracy levels.

The accuracy of the financial statements will be improved significantly, since the system assists in preparing accurate results. This will play a huge role in developing the accuracy of the work completed by the accounting staff. As a result, accountants do not have to keep on revisiting financial records to correct errors. This way, their workload becomes easier.

Informed Decision-Making

Beaver (2022) states that an accounting software system provides visibility of more accurate information leading to better and real-time decision-making by management. The response from ***P15*** supports the fact that accounting software systems allow management to make informed and accurate decisions:

P15 stated that firstly, the accounting software comes at a cost to implement. The accountant has more access to the business information which allows for more informed decisions by tracking business expenditure etc. As a result, costs can be managed better.

P4 also mentioned that due to the implementation of an accounting software system, the accuracy of the financial statements improved to such a large extent that it helped managers make excellent decisions within the entity.

Sooza and Burton (2023) explain that decision-making is a crucial part of managing an SME, because if management makes one wrong decision, the entire organisation is at a great risk. Additionally, to make the correct informed decisions for the SME, accurate, accessible, and real-time financial information must be available to the accountant and the best way is through using an accounting software application (Sooza & Burton, 2023).

Implementing an accounting software automatically generates financial reports which assists the accounting team and the management in making budgeting and forecasting decisions. It also assists them in planning exactly how they could wisely utilise the funds available. The strategic planning process of management becomes simplified, since all the financial reports are automatically generated by the system, so all that management needs to do is to study the reports, analyse them, and then make an informed decision. It is clear from these findings that an accounting software system facilitates an SME to make contemporary and accurate decisions.

Accountants being able to make more informed decisions indicates that the accounting software systems assist them in making strong decisions. This contributes towards making the accountants decisions more accurate.

Prepares Financial Statements

This study found that an accounting software system is relevant to SMEs in preparing financial statements. Salam (2022) explains that reports are automatically generated from the accounting software system, and then financial statements are automatically prepared according to those reports. ***P2*** responded by saying yes, the accounting software system has assisted in preparing the financial statements. Additionally, ***P3*** supported this by responding with the following: Of course! The accounting software accurately prepares the income statement and balance sheet. It has assisted our team 99% of time in preparing the financial statements. Finally, ***P4*** reported that yes, the financial records can be drawn from the system which assists the accounting team in preparing detailed and accurate financial statements.

The findings indicate that an accounting software system is highly capable of preparing and producing accurate financial statements automatically. As such, SME owners should investigate the implementation of accounting software to benefit from automated and accurate financial statements, reducing their accountants physical workload, which in return saves the entity from spending excessive amounts on labour hours.

Contribution

This study makes significant contributions to the understanding of how accounting software systems affect the operational efficiency and financial management of SMEs. Firstly, it offers empirical evidence on the perceptions of the accountants in adopting new accounting software within the context of SMEs in a specific geographical area, enriching the literature on technology adoption in emerging economies. The qualitative and narrative approach adopted in this research highlights the nuanced experiences of accountants, providing a deep understanding of the user perspective which is often overlooked in quantitative studies.

Secondly, the findings contribute to the development of best practices for the implementation and utilisation of accounting software in SMEs. The contribution of the study leads to the implementation of an accounting software system which increases accuracy, assists with stock takes, reduces physical work, prepares financial statements, and allows managers to make informed decisions about the entity.

By identifying the specific benefits such as reduced physical working hours and improved accuracy and efficiency in accounting processes, this study underscores the value of technological solutions in enhancing business operations.

Conclusion

The focus of this chapter was to determine the extent to which accounting software systems grants ease to the accountants within an SME. The study established how the accounting software grants ease to the accountants within the SMEs in South Africa by assisting them with preparing financial statements which are accurate, stock adjustments, decision-making through a reduced amount of physical work being put in.

Recommendations

SME owners should provide accountants with adequate training before expecting them to operate accounting software systems effectively and efficiently. SME owners should ensure that they are up to date with software training workshops and insist that accountants attend to gain more knowledge and learn the new developments and updates on accounting software applications. In the training workshops, a great amount of information is covered which then enlightens the accountants on latest changes to the applications. These training workshops will improve the performance of the accountants, since they will know exactly how to operate the accounting software system efficiently.

References

Amanamah, R. B., Morrison, A., & Asiedu, K. (2016). Computerised accounting systems usage by small and medium scale Enterprises in Ghana. *Research Journal of Finance and Accounting, 7*(16), 2222–2847.

Adom, D., Hussein, E. K., & Agyem, J. A. (2018). Theoretical and conceptual framework: Mandatory ingredients of quality research. *International Journal of Scientific Research, 7*(1), 2277–8179.

Ahmi, A., Lanlan, Z., & Popoola, O. M. J. (2019). Perceived ease of use, perceived usefulness, and the usage of computerised accounting systems: A performance of micro and small enterprises. *International Journal of Recent Technology and Engineering, 8*(2), 2277–3878.

Beaver, S. (2022, April 1). *10 Key Accounting software benefits for business*. Retrieved September 12, 2023, from https://www.netsuite.com/portal/resource/articles/accounting/accounting-software-benefits.shtml.

Bellis, M. (2019). History of accounting from ancient time to today. *Journal of the Medieval and Renaissance Revolution of Bookkeeping, 1*(1), 4–12.

Boru, T. (2018). *Research design and methodology*. (Unpublished PhD dissertation). University of South Africa.

Chigumadzi, P. (2021). Domestic tourism to the rescue. *Journal of Small Enterprise Development Agency, 2*(1), 3–9.

Chong, Y., & Nizam, I. (2018). The impact of accounting software on business performance. *International Journal of Information Systems and Engineering, 6*(1), 2289–7615.

Chukwuere, J. E. (2021). Theoretical and conceptual framework: A critical part of information systems research process and writing. *Journal of International Geographical Education, 11*(9), 2679–2681.

Czerwonka, E. (2023, June 14). *Best time tracking software for accountants*. Retrieved September 27, 2023, from https://buddypunch.com/blog/time-tracking-software-for-accountants/.

DeFranzo, S. E. (2019). What's the difference between qualitative and quantitative research? *Journal of Phenomenological Principles, 3*(3), 19–29.

DeJonckheere, M., & Vaughn, L. M. (2019). Semi-structured interviewing in primary care research: A balance of relationship and rigor. *Journal of Family Medicine and Community Health, 7*(2), 4–8.

Fourie, B. (2023, August 15). *SA's employment rate*. Retrieved June 8, 2023, from https://www.iol.co.za/news/sas-unemployment-rate-drops-more-than-150000-people-find-jobs-39fe97dc-7fbd-4874-8d67-7d42a3414a24.

Fuscaldo, D. (2023, March 31). *Accounting software features and benefits*. Retrieved May 5, 2023, from https://www.business.com/articles/features-of-accounting-software/.

Ginting, A. (2023, March 23). *Problems with an online accounting software*. Retrieved May 9, 2023, from https://www.hashmicro.com/blog/minimized-these-four-problems-with-an-online-accounting-software/.

Harryanto, M., Muchrun, M., & Ahmar, A. S. (2018). Application of TAM model to the use of information technology. *International Journal of Engineering & Technology, 7*(2.9), 37–40.

Ismail, A., & Muhammad, Y. (2022). Accounting software. *Journal of Islamic Accounting and Business Research, 14*(7), 62–69.

Jagadeesan, L. (2019). Adoption of computerised accounting systems usage by small and medium scale enterprises. *Journal of Emerging Technologies and Innovative Research, 6*(5), 360–374.

Janrosl, V. S. E., & Muda, I. (2017). Impact of the implementation of the e-accounting system on the internet control system. *Journal of Sumatera Utara, 1*(1), 350–365.

Johnson, R. (2019 January 22). *The importance of double entry principle*. Retrieved February 22, 2022. https://bizfluent.com/info-8691783-importance-doubleentry-bookkeeping.html

Julies, D. B., & Tranos, Z. (2021). A review on TAM framework progression and how the model integrates. *Advances in Science, Technology and Engineering Systems Journal, 6*(3), 137–145.

Kenton, W. (2021, November 18). *Accounting software*. Retrieved November 22, 2021, from https://www.investopedia.com/terms/a/accounting-software.asp.

Khanom, T. (2017). Cloud accounting: A theoretical overview. *Journal of Business and Management, 19*(6), 31–38.

Lutfi, A., Alkelani, S. N., Al-Khasawneh, M. A., Alsshirah, A. F., Alshirah, M. H., Almaiah, M. H., Alrawad, M., Alsyouf, A., Saad, M., & Ibrahim, N. (2022). Influence of digital accounting system usage on SMEs performance: The moderating effect of COVID-19. *Journal on Sustainability, 14*(1), 15048–15050.

Mark, J. J. (2018). Mesopotamia. *World history encyclopaedia* of history (pp. 1-3).

Marikyan, D., & Papagiannidis, S. (2022). *Technology acceptance model: A review*. TheoryHub eBooks. https://open.ncl.ac.uk/theory-library/technology-acceptance-model.pdf

McLeod, K. (2023, July 13). *Managing business finances*. Retrieved November 9, 2023 from https://www.aabrs.com/managing-small-business-finances/

Olufemi, O., Festus, A. F., & Adekunle, A. M. (2021). Accounting software in computerised business environment and quality of corporate reporting. *Journal of Finance and Accounting, 9*(3), 101–110.

Panhalkar, K., (2020, November 9). *How technology has changed the accounting industry*. Retrieved June 15, 2023, from https://technologycounter.com/blog/technology-change-in-accounting-industry/.

Panko, R. (2018, October 1). *Why small businesses lack accounting resources*. Retrieved February 1, 2024, from https://clutch.co/resources/why-small-businesses-lack-accounting-resources/.

Purnamasari, V. (2019). Accounting software for SMEs: Organisational and personal factors based on TAM theory. *Journal of Contemporary Business, Economics and Law, 19*(1), 2289–1560.

Rahman, M. M., Ahammed, M. U., Rouf, A., & Uddin, M. M. (2017). Obstacles and implementation of accounting software system in small medium enterprises (SMEs): Case of South Asian perspective. *International Journal of Science and Business, 1*(1), 7–15.

Ramklas, K. (2021, March 15). *Sage accounting software*. Retrieved November 29, 2021 from https://www.sage.com/africa/accounting-software/?gclid=Cj0KCQiA7oyNBhDiARIsADtGRZaG12bB89XA9Bw7emVkFPpR_f4L7jWES8QbTm3LTHAcjxgB7Prtgx4aAnO6EALw_wcB&gclsrc=aw.ds.

Salam, R. (2022). The effectiveness of accounting information systems. *Journal of economy and Business, 2*(1), 10–18.

Smith, A. (2021). What are the origins of accounting? *Journal of the Evolution of Accounting and Accounting Terminology, 31*(3), 345–355.

Sooza, A., & Burton, G. (2023, September 20). *How accounting software helps your business in decision making*. Retrieved September 27, 2023, from https://www.iplicit.com/blog/how-accounting-software-helps-your-business-decision-making.

Thottoli, M. M. (2020). Knowledge and use of accounting software. *Journal of Industry-University Collaboration, 3*(1), 2–14.

Utami, N., & Yulianto, H. D. (2019). Significant influence of information technology on the use of modern accounting software. *Journal of Materials Science and Engineering, 662*(1), 100–126.

Wickramsainghe, D. M. J., Pemaratha, R. M. M. D., Cooray, N. H. K., & Dissanayake, T. D. S. H. (2017). Impact of accounting software for business performance. *Imperial Journal of Interdisciplinary Research, 3*(5), 2454–1362.

Zoho, B. (2021, March 20). *What is accounting software?* Retrieved November 23, 2021, from https://www.zoho.com/accounting-software/

The Income Tax Deductibility of Expenditure Incurred by Stockbrokers in Earning Exempt Incidental Dividends

Mpho Dibate Christian Lefakane, Riaan Wessels, and Siphamandla Makhaya

Abstract Stockbrokers acquire shares as trading stock rather than as capital assets. They can usually claim a deduction for the cost of buying shares under section11(a) of the Income Tax Act No. 58 of 1962 (hereafter 'the Act'). Where stockbrokers receive incidental dividends while the shares held as trading stock are unsold, section 23(f) of the Act will result in a portion of the expenditure being non-deductible. This study uses a doctrinal research method to evaluate if disallowing stockbroking expenditure under section 23(f) of the Act is justified when stockbroking businesses are primarily engaged in purchasing and selling shares for profit. The study also examines how expenses incurred by stockbrokers in India, which held shares as trading stock, were treated and whether principles from Indian tax court rulings could be adopted in South Africa. It was found that the disallowance of stockbroking expenditure under section 23(f) may not be appropriate given South African stockbrokers' business strategy. Additionally, Indian courts have allowed the full deduction of stockbroking expenses for shares held as trading stock, despite receiving dividends on unsold shares. Subsequently, suggestions were proposed for South African legislation, drawing from the practices observed in India.

Keywords Stockbrokers · Dividends · Expenditure · Section 23(f) · South Africa · India

---

M. D. C. Lefakane · R. Wessels (✉) · S. Makhaya
University of Johannesburg, Johannesburg, South Africa
e-mail: rwessels@uj.ac.za; smakhaya@uj.ac.za

T. Moloi (ed.), *Impacting Society Positively Through Technology in Accounting and Business Processes*, Springer Proceedings in Business and Economics,
https://doi.org/10.1007/978-3-031-84885-8_23

Introduction

Stockbrokers primarily engage in the buying and selling of shares, serving as agents who execute transactions on behalf of clients (Guide to America's Top Stockbrokers, 2007). They also engage in the buying and selling of shares for their own benefit, operating both as a dealer and a broker, commonly known as a 'broker-dealer'. According to section 3(a)(5)(A) of the United States Securities Exchange Act of, 1934, a 'dealer' is defined as someone engaged in the activity of buying and selling securities for their personal benefit. In the role of a dealer, stockbroking entities purchase securities with the expectation of selling them at a profit when their value increases, treating the shares as trading stock (Guide to America's Top Stockbrokers, 2007). In this capacity, they may also earn accidental dividends on shares retained as trading stock.

To be eligible for a deduction, expenses such as the purchase of shares, remuneration for traders, and various operational expenditures (referred to as 'stockbroking expenditure') incurred by stockbroking entities must meet the criteria outlined in the general deduction formula of section 11(a) in conjunction with section 23(g) of the Income Tax Act No. 58 of 1962 (hereafter 'the Act'). Moreover, the Act should not prevent a deduction of stockbroking expenditure under section 23(f).

Section 23(f) of the Act specifies that 'no deduction shall be made in respect of expenses incurred in respect of amount received or accrued which do constitute income'. Income, defined in section 1 of the Act, means 'the amount remaining of gross income after deducting any amounts exempt from normal tax'. Paragraph (k) of the gross income definition includes 'any amount received or accrued by way of a dividend'. However, section10(1)(k) of the Act exempts local dividends received or accrued from normal tax, subject to specific exclusions. Dividends earned by stockbrokers on retained shares are classified as gross income under paragraph (k) of the gross income definition in the Act. However, they are exempt under section 10(1)(k) and, therefore, do not constitute income.

As dividends are exempt from taxes and are not considered part of income, the stockbroking expenses related to the dividends will not be eligible for a deduction according to section 23(f) of the Act. The receipt of dividends on retained trading shares is not derived from actions conducted by the stockbroking businesses that are directly associated with the generation of dividend income.

However, the deduction of stockbroking expenses is not allowed if they are related to dividend income, without considering if there are any costs directly associated with receiving dividend income. Given that the stockbroking businesses earned dividends, it might be inferred that they incurred expenses to generate exempt dividend income.

The research question is whether the apportionment of stockbroking expenditure should be applied according to section 23(f) of the Act when shares held as trading stock earn accidental dividends?

The objectives of the study are to investigate:

1. Whether it is reasonable to disallow stockbroking expenditure under section 23(f) of the Act where stockbroking businesses primarily engage in buying and selling shares for profit.
2. How India treats the expenses related to stockbroking when stockbroking businesses hold shares as trading stock and whether any principles from Indian tax court judgments can be adopted in South Africa.

This study assumes that stockbrokers would not retain shares as trading stock for a period exceeding 3 years. Consequently, the provisions of section 9C are not addressed.

Methodological Approach

The study objectives will be addressed using a qualitative approach. Robinson (2002) characterises qualitative research mainly by its exploratory approach. Exploratory research is defined as a method of acquiring fresh perspectives, posing inquiries, and evaluating a phenomenon from a novel perspective (Robinson, 2002). The study aims to evaluate the potential for using section 23(f) of the Act in a different manner to gain fresh perspectives on its application to stockbroking businesses. The research is conducted using a doctrinal method, which Hutchinson and Duncan (2012) define as systematically explaining the rules that govern a certain legal group or analysing the relationship between rules and regions of complexity. It is performed through a two-part process. Firstly, it is necessary to identify the sources of the law, namely section 23(f) of the Act. Subsequently, the wording within the section of the Act is examined and analysed. The initial step of the process involves ascertaining the objective reality, which refers to a legal statement found in legislation or an established principle of common law. After locating the law, the second phase involves interpreting and analysing it within a particular setting (Hutchinson & Duncan, 2012). The study involves the examination and analysis of section 23(f) of the Act, as well as the evaluation and summarisation of tax court cases in India and South Africa that pertain to the subject matter. The study will concentrate on examining, analysing, and interpreting the legal regulations outlined in section 23(f) of the Act, section 14A of the Indian Income Tax Act, 1961 (43 of 1961), as modified by the Finance Act, 2017 (hereinafter referred to as the 'Indian Act'), in addition to the court decisions that addressed the tax deductibility of stockbroking expenses incurred by stockbrokers that generated income that was exempt from taxation. India was selected the appropriate comparative for this research, because its legislation aligns with section 23(f) of the Act, and there are numerous tax cases that address the deductibility of dividend-earning expenses. Furthermore, both India and South Africa are member countries of the Intergovernmental Organisation (BRICS). These similarities are further discussed in the comparison of Indian and South African Income Tax legislations section.

Literature Review

The Deductibility of Stockbroking Expenditure in South Africa

This research examines whether the expenditure incurred by stockbrokers should qualify for a deduction for income tax purposes. Consequently, it is essential to outline the criteria that must be satisfied for such expenditure to qualify as deductible. This section elucidates the principles underlying the general deduction formula as specified in section 11(a) of the Act, which delineates the expenditure that may be deducted (the positive test), alongside section 23(g), which identifies the expenditure that are non-deductible (the negative test) (CIR v Nemojim (Pty) Ltd., 1983). In adjudicating whether expenditure is deductible for tax purposes, courts have underscored the necessity of interpreting sections11(a) and 23(g) of the Act in conjunction (Port Elizabeth Electric Tramway Co Ltd. v CIR, 1936).

Section 11 of the Act articulates that:

> For the purpose of determining the taxable income derived by any person from carrying on any trade, there shall be allowed as deductions from the income of such person so derived:
>
> (a) expenditure and losses actually incurred in the production of the income, provided such expenditure and losses are not of a capital nature.

Furthermore, section 23 of the Act stipulates that:

> No deductions shall be permitted in respect of the following matters, namely-
>
> (g) any monies, claimed as a deduction from income derived from trade, to the extent to which such monies were not laid out or expanded for the purposes of trade;

A detailed discussion of the components of the general deduction formula as it applies to stockbroking firms follows.

The Preamble: Carrying on Any Trade

The introduction to section 11 of the Act mandates that the taxpayer must carry on a 'trade'. The definition of 'trade' in s1 of the Act encompasses various activities such as a profession, business, occupation, or venture.

According to ITC 1529 (1991), factors indicating that a taxpayer may be conducting a trade include the continuous nature of the taxpayer's activities and the long-term goal of generating profits from the trade. While the definition of 'trade' is meant to be inclusive, encompassing all profitable activities (ITC 770, 1954), it does not cover all revenue-generating activities, such as passive income from sources like dividends or interest (ITC 1275, 1978).

Merely retaining investments acquired during a trade does not necessarily indicate the ongoing conduct of a trade (ITC 1476, 1989). If a taxpayer does not actively engage in trading shares, it may not be considered as conducting a trade (ITC 1476, 1989).

The concept of 'trade' includes conducting a business, and the activities involving the trading of shares by stockbroking firms are deemed to be a business. The activities of stockbroking firms, which involve actively trading shares rather than holding them for investment purposes, demonstrate that they are engaged in a trade. Earning dividends from shares held as trading stock by stockbroking firms does not exclude the trading activities from being considered a trade. The operations of stockbroking firms are continuous, with the long-term motive of selling shares for a profit. These entities take active steps to sell shares held as trading stock at a profit. The activities of stockbroking entities are not geared towards earning passive income; rather, shares held are sold with a profit motive, thereby satisfying the requirement of conducting a trade.

The Positive Test: Section 11(a)

Stockbroking expenses and losses are recognised as being incurred in the relevant year of assessment once an unconditional obligation to settle the expenses arises during that year, as established in Edgars Stores Ltd. v CIR (1988) and Caltex Oil (SA) Ltd. v SIR (1975). The only exception to this rule is when the expenses pertain to variable remuneration under section 7B of the Act, in which case they are deductible upon payment. It is also important that the expenditure must not be of a capital nature. In the case of New Estates Area Ltd. v CIR (1946), it was determined that expenses related to floating capital, such as trading stock, are of a revenue nature, while expenses associated with fixed capital are considered capital in nature. For instance, the costs related to shares held as trading stock, salaries, and other operational expenses of stockbroking entities are considered floating capital, because they are incurred to enable the profitable sale of shares held as trading stock, making them revenue in nature.

In order for expenses to be deductible under section 11(a) of the Act, they must be incurred in the production of income. Expenses accrued by a business must be closely tied to income-generating activities to be considered as incurred in income production, as highlighted in the case of Port Elizabeth Electric Tramway Co Ltd. v CIR (1936). The underlying principle is that revenue is generated through a series of actions, and expenses are a consequence of these actions. Therefore, expenses are deductible provided that they are closely connected to the business and are considered part of the costs of carrying out those actions. Two key questions must be answered affirmatively to qualify for a deduction: (i) whether the expense is related to an income-producing activity and (ii) whether the expense is closely linked to that activity. If the expenditure is incurred in good faith for the purpose of conducting trade aimed at generating income, it will be allowed as a deduction.

It is established that genuine business expenses associated with income-generating activities are deductible, regardless of whether they are essential for the activity or coincidentally related to it, as emphasised by Schreiner JA in CIR v Genn & Co (Pty) Ltd. (1955). In the context of stockbroking expenses, for them to be eligible for a deduction, two key questions need to be answered positively: (i) whether the expenses are related to activities performed to generate income, such as the duties carried out by traders and administrative employees employed by stockbroking firms in the pursuit of profits from share sales and (ii) whether the expenses are closely linked to these income-producing activities. Stockbroking expenses, comprising the costs of employing traders, administrative employees, and other costs, are closely associated with the trading activities of stockbroking entities, thereby meeting the criteria for deduction. Stockbroking expenses are legitimately incurred by these entities for the purpose of trading in shares held as trading stock for profit, thus contributing to income production stemming from the sale of such shares.

The Negative Test: Section 23(g)

Section 23(g) of the Act prohibits the deduction of expenditure that are not incurred for trade-related purposes. The term 'trade' within the context of 'for the purpose of trade' lacks specific qualifications; however, it should be interpreted as pertaining solely to the legitimate commercial activities conducted by the taxpayer. In assessing whether an expenditure was incurred for trade purposes, an analysis of the type of operations conducted, the nature of the expenditure, and the direct or indirect relationship between the outlay and the benefit obtained by the business is imperative (Solaglass Finance Company (Pty) Ltd. v CIR, 1991).

Expenditure related to stockbroking is inherently linked to the activities of selling shares, thereby playing a crucial role in generating profits from the sale of shares held as trading stock. Consequently, the stockbroking expenses accrued meet the criteria for trade as delineated earlier.

In summary, stockbroking expenses may be eligible for deduction under the general deduction formula provided that all aspects of sections 11(a) and 23(g), as elaborated upon above, are duly met.

Application of Section 23(f) of the Act to Expenditure Incurred by Stockbrokers

According to section 23(f) of the Act, costs incurred in connection with amounts received or accrued that do not qualify as income are not eligible for deduction. Stockbrokers retain the shares they acquire as trading stock and have the potential to receive dividends on these unsold shares. The dividends of the stockbroking organisations are secondary to their primary operation of purchasing and selling shares. According to section 23(f) of the Act, stockbrokers must not deduct stock-broking expenses, if they were incurred in earning exempt dividend income. At present, the restriction imposed by section 23(f) applies to expenses undertaken by the entities, regardless of whether they can be directly associated with generating dividend income. The taxpayer carries the burden of proof for presenting evidence that a specific quantity of expenditure can be deducted, as per section 102 of the Tax Administration Act No. 28 of 2011. Therefore, it is the responsibility of the stock-broking organisations to provide evidence that the expenses related to stockbroking are incurred in the generation of taxable income. The following will discuss South African tax court cases that address the handling of stockbroking expenses related to the purchase of shares.

CIR V Nemojim (Pty) Ltd.

In the case of CIR v Nemojim (Pty) Ltd. (1983), the taxpayer in question was engaged in the buying and selling of shares and conducted dividend-stripping operations. The taxpayer acquired stocks in inactive corporations that had, over time, amassed substantial reserves of earnings that could be distributed as dividends. Subsequently, the taxpayer would prompt the corporation to disburse its whole accrued profits in the form of dividends, all of which were received by the taxpayer. Following the company's distribution of dividends to the taxpayer, all the company's shares were sold. The taxpayer received tax-exempt profits from the inactive corporation, in accordance with section 10(1)(k) of the Act. The taxpayer reported the money received from the share sale as part of their gross income and deducted the cost of the shares as an eligible expense. The following question arose: could the taxpayer entirely deduct the purchase price of shares or, was a portion of the cost to be restricted under section 23(f) of the Act? This restriction would be applicable if the cost was not utilised to generate income, but rather to earn dividends that are exempt from taxation.

The court referred to CIR v Genn & Co (Pty) Ltd. (1955) to the principle that when determining whether a taxpayer's expenses can be considered as income-producing expenditures, the primary factors to be considered are: (i) the purpose of the expenditure and (ii) its actual impact. The court also pointed out that the main question was whether there was a sufficiently strong link between the money spent on purchasing the shares and the money received from the dividends.

The deductibility of stockbroking expenses depends on whether the spending is directly related to obtaining money from the selling of shares rather than earning incidental dividends. While using the tests mentioned by the courts, it was found that the stockbroking expenses were not directly related to earning dividends. Instead, these expenses were incurred while making profits from selling shares. Therefore, the taxpayer could not entirely deduce the purchase price of shares, and a portion of the cost needed to be restricted under section 23(f) of the Act.

CIR V Standard Bank of SA Ltd.

In the case of CIR v Standard Bank of SA Ltd. (1985), the bank obtained loans from customers and in return, it provided interest payments on the deposits received, according to the bank's specified conditions. The bank utilised the deposits in diverse ways, generating interest, dividends, and other forms of returns from the funds. The bank's interest collected was included in its gross income and subject to taxation, while the interest incurred was deducted according to section 11(a) of the Act. The bank used a portion of the deposits it received from its clients to purchase redeemable preference shares. The bank then engaged in a limited number of redeemable preference transactions, which were initiated by its established clientele and considered these transactions to be ancillary to its main function of borrowing and lending money. The bank earned dividend income from its investments in redeemable preference shares.

The bank deducted an amount for interest paid on loaned funds for many tax years. The Commissioner disallowed the deduction of a portion of the interest, because the dividend income obtained on redeemable preference shares was considered exempt income according to section 10(1)(k) of the Act. Consequently, a certain amount of the interest paid out to depositors was not deductible, because it was classified as non-deductible expenses unrelated to generating income.

The court referred to the case of CIR v Nemojim (Pty) Ltd. (1983) and stated that when determining whether the funds spent by the taxpayer qualify as expenses incurred in generating income, the primary considerations are the intention behind the expenditure and the actual impact it has. The court added that it is necessary to evaluate the intention behind the spending, its impact, and the degree of correlation between the costs expended and the exempt income received or accrued.

In addition, the court cited the precedent set in the case of CIR v Allied Building Society (1963). The court emphasised that the crucial investigation is around the bank's intention to borrow the funds, for which interest was given to the depositors (CIR v Standard Bank of SA Ltd., 1985). Furthermore, the goal was to ascertain whether the correlation between the acquisition of redeemable preference shares, and interest expenditure was significant enough to substantiate the conclusion that the cost was incurred during the production of the dividends. The court determined that the redeemable preference shares were a small and insignificant part of the bank's overall money lending operations and were secondary to the bank's primary activity. It was additionally mentioned that incidental refers to something that happens by chance or in a subordinate manner in combination with something else. The court determined that the deposits were not specifically increased solely for the purpose of acquiring redeemable preference shares. Consequently, there was not a sufficiently strong connection between raising the deposits and taking up the preference shares. The bank was able to deduct the whole amount of interest given to depositors, because the objective of accepting deposits was not to generate income that was exempt from taxation.

Considering the aforementioned decision, the reception of dividends by stockbroking corporations may be seen as secondary and not significant to their primary activity of selling shares for profit. The stockbroking expenditure is incurred with the aim of generating profits through the selling of shares. In addition, the expenses related to stockbroking are not directly linked to the exempt income obtained. The court's opinion indicates that the applicability of section 23(f) of the Act to the receipt of incidental dividends should not be treated in the same way as a person who plans to invest in shares to earn dividends as their main source of income.

De Beers Holdings (Pty) Ltd. V CIR

The case confirmed that the act of buying and selling shares is a normal part of a stockbroker's operations, as opposed to an investor who simply buys and retains shares (para. 24 and 25). In this case, the dealer acquired shares with the intention of selling them later as part of a profit-making strategy. This set his job apart from that of a stock investor, who buys shares with the goal of holding onto them as a long-term investment and making a profit through dividends.

CIR V Rand Selection Corporation Ltd.

The court determined that in cases where stockbrokers are involved in both holding shares as an investment and trading shares as a means of generating profit, the expenses incurred by the business must be apportioned. The apportionment will aim to limit spending associated with the activities connected to the ownership of shares for investment purposes.

ITC 1589

The court determined that it is not feasible to establish a universal guideline for allocating expenses and emphasised that all factors must be taken into account and a just and rational allocation should be implemented.

Commissioner for the South African Revenue Service V Mobile Telephone Networks Holdings (Pty) Ltd.

In the case of Commissioner for the South African Revenue Service (CSARS) v Mobile Telephone Networks Holdings (Pty) Ltd. (2014), Mobile Telephone Networks Holdings (MTN) was a parent company that owned subsidiary firms. MTN earned interest and dividends from these subsidiaries. MTN paid audit fees and professional consultancy fees for the holding company's operations during the assessment years. The Commissioner raised the assessment for MTN by utilising the ratio of dividend income to total income as a means of allocating the audit fees. The Commissioner dismissed most of the expenses since, during the audited years, an average of 94% of MTN's revenue came in the form of dividend income. The prohibited amount was not considered as a deductible expense for generating income, as specified by section 23(f) of the Act. MTN aimed to prove to the court and Commissioner that the majority of the expenses were not spent in order to generate dividend revenue. This was done by analysing various transactions that were recorded as dividend income compared to those recorded as interest and other income. MTN's contention was that dividends are recorded annually following the announcement by the subsidiary firm, however interest must be recorded on a monthly basis due to the loan's requirement for more regular payments.

The South Gauteng High Court specified that the criterion or standard should be the quantity of work performed rather than the monetary worth of the dividends received. The taxpayer is not required to demonstrate a direct causal relationship, save from the proximity of the connection between the expense and the income.

Upon being appealed to the Supreme Court of Appeal, the judgment cited the case of SIR v Guardian Assurance Holdings (SA) Ltd. (1976), which established that when expenses are incurred for both dual and mixed purposes, courts have approved the principle of apportioning such expenses. In addition, the court cited ITC 1017 (1963), which established that simply stating that minimal time and effort were invested in managing the property company is insufficient. It is necessary to determine the specific amount of time dedicated to the operations in order to make any apportionment, and this apportionment can only be done by comparing different factors. The court determined that apportionment is a factual matter that depends on the specific circumstances of each case. In this particular case, the court concluded that the deduction of the expenditure should be heavily disallowed due to the substantial impact of MTN's equity and dividend operations, which far outweigh its limited revenue-earning operations. In the following section, the principles from court cases will be applied to stockbroking entities.

Application of Court Cases to Expenditure Incurred by Stockbrokers

The disallowances of the spending in the MTN case were mostly influenced by the operations that had a significant impact. Stockbroking businesses primarily engaged in holding shares as trading stock activities to generate taxable income. They only make minimal effort to earn incidental dividends, which are not subject to taxation. Thus, the expense could be considered eligible for a full deduction.

Stockbroking entities do not engage in any activities to earn dividends. Their role is secondary to the main activity of holding shares as trading stock, as established in the CSARS v MTN case. In addition, the earnings of stockbroking entities from incidental dividends are insignificant and inconsequential, just like the court's perception of Standard Bank's earnings from incidental dividends from preference shares as insignificant and inconsequential to the bank's operations. The court

concluded that there was no necessity to allocate the interest earned on deposits that were utilised to acquire preference shares (CIR v Standard Bank of SA).
There is a possible case to suggest that the expenses related to stockbroking, which are incurred while selling shares for a profit and generating taxable revenue, are closely and inherently linked to the income-producing activities of stockbroking businesses. Hence, generating dividend income holds less significance and bears no value in the stockbroking industry. In addition, dividends are acquired without engaging in any labour, hence no expenses may be directly associated with obtaining dividends. Therefore, the expenses paid by stockbroking organisations may be fully deducted, since they are not related to the generation of dividend revenue. The following section outlines Indian tax laws and examines how Indian tax courts handle the expenses incurred by stockbroking businesses.

Indian Tax Statutes

Comparison of Indian and South African Income Tax Legislations

Indian tax legislation contains provisions that bear resemblance to those found in South African tax legislation. These provisions dictate that expenses incurred in generating income that is not subject to assessment ('exempt income' in the context of South Africa) cannot be claimed as a deduction. The similarities between the two regulatory frameworks are expounded upon as follows.

In India, dividends are considered part of the total income, akin to gross income in South Africa, as stipulated in sections 8(a) and (b) of the Indian Act. Subsequently, dividends in India are exempt from income tax liability under sections 10(23F) and 10(23FA) of the Indian Act. Conversely, in South Africa, dividends are encompassed within gross income according to paragraph k of the definition of gross income. Moreover, dividends are exempt from normal tax under section 10(1)(k)(i) of the Act, with certain exceptions. The Indian Act mirrors South African tax provisions by integrating dividends into total income while excluding them from the calculation of taxable income.

Expenses incurred by a taxpayer that are not of a capital nature and are exclusively for business purposes are allowable as deductions in determining taxable income under section 37(1) of the Indian Act. Section 37(1) of the Indian Act shares similarities with section 11(a) of the Act.

Section 14A of the Indian Act prohibits the deduction of expenses related to income that is non-taxable, because it is excluded from total income by section 10 of the Indian Act. Section 14A(1) of the Indian Act parallels section 23(f) of the South African Act in disallowing deductions for expenses incurred in generating income that is not subject to taxation.

The subsequent section delves into various Indian tax court cases that address the interpretation and application of section 14A of the Indian Act in situations where taxpayers engage in share trading and earn dividends from shares held as trading stock.

Indian Court Cases Where Shares Are Held for Investment and Trading

Kolkata DCIT V S.G. Investments and Industries

In the case of Kolkata DCIT v S.G. Investments and Industries (2004), the taxpayer possessed a majority stake in a cluster of companies for investment purposes, while the remaining shares were designated as trading stock intended for resale at a profit within its share-dealing operations. The taxpayer had utilised loan funding in its financial records. By retaining trading shares beyond the specified deadline for dividends, the taxpayer accrued dividends from both the investment and trading stock shares. These dividends were granted exemption under section 10(33) (now section 10(34)) of the Indian Act. The taxpayer sought to claim a deduction for interest on inter-corporate deposits and loans.

The Assessing Officer (AO) rejected the taxpayer's claim for the deduction of expenses, contending that they pertained to income not subject to taxation and invoked the provisions of section 14A of the Indian Act to allocate the expenses. The AO's position was that the dividends previously received by the taxpayer originated from shares held for investment purposes.

The taxpayer contended that no expenses could be allocated for the generation of dividend income. Furthermore, the taxpayer argued that the interest expenditure was linked to its unified business activities, encompassing the trading of shares. The act of earning dividend income could not be delineated as a distinct business activity. The taxpayer also asserted that the reception of dividends could not be construed as the exclusive objective of the business expenditure, thereby rendering the provisions of section 14A of the Indian Act inapplicable.

Ultimately, the court ruled that interest associated with shares held for investment should not be eligible for deduction, while the segment of interest linked to share trading should be deductible.

ACIT, Circle 3(1), New Delhi V M/S Cheminvest Ltd.

In the case of ACIT, Circle 3(1), New Delhi v M/s Cheminvest Ltd. (2007), the taxpayer maintained a portfolio that included both investment shares and trading shares, financed partially through interest-bearing loans. For the trading shares, the proceeds from sales were subject to taxation, and the related expenditure, including interest, was deductible against the income. During the relevant year, the taxpayer did not receive any dividend income from its shares.

The AO contended that section 14A of the Indian Act applied even in the absence of exempt income in the current year, asserting that the deduction limitations were relevant regardless of whether exempt dividends might be earned in the future. Conversely, the taxpayer argued that interest expenses should not be disallowed in a year where no dividend income was received.

The court ruled that any expenditure incurred pertaining to income that does not contribute to the total taxable income must not be deducted, regardless of whether the taxpayer earned any income in that year. Additionally, it was concluded that the actual receipt or earning of income is not a prerequisite for prohibiting the deduction of interest under section 14A of the Indian Act.

Kolkata DCIT Circle-6 V M/S. Kredent Brokerage Services Ltd.

In the legal case Kolkata DCIT Circle-6 v M/s. Kredent Brokerage Services Ltd. (2012), the taxpayer in this case was a stockbroker. They maintained a portfolio consisting of shares held for trading purposes and unlisted shares in held as investments. The taxpayer received dividends on shares held for trading but not on investment shares. The dividend income constituted 10% of the total turnover for the year. In the tax filings, the taxpayer did not claim a tax deduction for expenses related to the tax-exempt dividends derived from the investment shares.

The AO argued that the costs incurred by the taxpayer for acquiring shares were connected to earning dividend income, hence disallowing the deduction claimed against taxable income. The AO disallowed the trading stock under section 14A of the Indian Act. The taxpayer challenged this assessment before the Commissioner of Income Tax (Appeals) [CIT(A)], who ruled that the shares held for trading should be excluded from the application of section 14A as the taxpayer operated as a dealer in shares, with trading securities being its primary activity. The CIT(A) noted that the revenue from the disposal of securities exceeded the dividends received, with dividends representing only a small portion (10%) of the total revenue. The Commissioner of Taxes appealed the CIT(A)'s decision to the tribunal.

In its deliberation, the tribunal referenced the case CCI Ltd. v the JCIT (2011), establishing that if a taxpayer has not incurred expenses directly tied to earning dividends, disallowing notional expenditure against income is unwarranted. The tribunal further stated that where dividends generated from unsold shares held as trading stock are a byproduct of the share-dealing business, the expenses related to acquiring such shares should not be disallowed as deductions against the taxpayer's income.

The tribunal concluded that if shares are not held with the primary purpose of receiving dividend income and dividends are ancillary to the share-dealing business, the prohibition of deduction under section 14A of the Indian Act does not apply. Additionally, the tribunal upheld the CIT(A)'s ruling that disallowance under section 14A does not apply when shares are held for trading purposes.

The tribunal's decision aligns with the notion that stockbrokers maintain shares as trading stock primarily for profit-making purposes. Dividends received by stockbrokers are seen as incidental to the share-dealing business, thus justifying that expenses incurred are directly related to the generation of total income. Therefore, expenses incurred by stockbrokers in trading shares for profit-making should be fully deductible without any apportionment.

The Court Case Where a Taxpayer Only Trades in Shares

Ambit Securities Broking P. Ltd. V the ACIT

In the case of Ambit Securities Broking P. Ltd. v The ACIT (2013), the taxpayer, a share trader, earned dividends on their shares. The Commissioner disallowed the related expenditure, arguing that the dividends constituted income, despite the taxpayer's status as a share trader. The taxpayer contended before the Commissioner that all the shares were classified as trading stock. The court concluded that the provisions of section 14A of the Indian Act were inapplicable to the dividend income derived from shares held as trading stock. Additionally, the court noted that the taxpayer did not retain shares with the primary intention of earning dividend income; such income was secondary to unsold shares, as established in CCI Ltd. v the JCIT (2011). Analysing these Indian tax court rulings reveals that stockbroking firms in India are permitted to claim deductions for expenses incurred in share trading activities, even when exempt dividends are earned from shares held as trading stock.

Conclusion

The study aimed to address two primary objectives, firstly, to evaluate whether the disallowance of stockbroking expenditures under s23(f) of the Act is justified, given that the primary business activity of stockbrokers involves trading in shares for profit. Secondly, the study examined how Indian tax authorities handle stockbroking expenses incurred by entities holding shares for trading purposes. It was also ascertained whether any principles originating from Indian tax court judgments could be implemented in South Africa.

South African courts have determined that an entity's business strategy should be considered when assessing the deductibility of incurred expenditures. The expenditures related to stockbroking activities are closely linked to income-generating operations. The earning of dividends is incidental for stockbrokers, as their principal business is the sale of shares held as trading stock for profit. Therefore, the disallowance of stockbroking expenditures under s23(f) of the Act may not be appropriate when the core business of stockbrokers is the trading in shares for profit.

Section 14A of the Indian Act prohibits the deduction of any expenditure related to income that is exempt from tax under section 10 of the Indian Act. Indian courts have ruled that section 14A does not apply to taxpayers engaged in share trading who hold unsold shares that generate incidental dividend income. However, the courts have differentiated tax treatments for taxpayers based on whether they held shares as trading stock or investments. The study found that Indian courts have permitted the full deduction of stockbroking expenses for shares held as trading stock, even when dividends are received on unsold shares. These principles from Indian tax court judgments could potentially be adopted in South Africa to address the deductibility of stockbroking expenditure.

The study recommends that the limitation imposed by section 23(f) of the Act be reviewed. The South African Institute of Stockbrokers (SAIS) should advocate to SARS and the National Treasury for the inclusion of a proviso stating that section 23(f) should not apply to registered stockbrokers holding shares as trading stock for client sales. This proviso should further specify that the exclusion applies only to shares held unsold for a short duration, thereby preventing the misuse of the amendment for prolonged exempt income generation while claiming full deductions for stockbroking expenses.

If legislative amendment is not feasible, an alternative approach could involve SAIS applying for a binding class ruling from SARS on behalf of licensed stockbroking firms. This ruling should assert that stockbroking expenditure incurred in income production should be fully deductible without limitations, provided the shares are held as trading stock and dividends are incidental to stockbroking activities for a short period. This recommendation might necessitate an amendment to section 10(1)(k) of the Act to disallow the tax exemption for incidental dividends.

The study primarily examined legislation and tax court cases in South Africa and India. Future research could explore other jurisdictions with similar legislative provisions to section 23(f) of the Act, investigating how their tax courts have addressed the deductibility of stockbroking expenditure for shares held as trading stock.

References

ACIT, Circle 3(1), New Delhi v M/s Cheminvest Ltd, ITA No. 4788/Del/2007. (2007). Available from: https://indiankanoon.org/doc/85216823

Ambit Securities Broking P. Ltd v The Additional Commissioner of Income Tax, I.T.A. No. 7856/M/201. (2013). Available from: https://indiankanoon.org/doc/101238369

Caltex Oil (SA) Ltd v SIR, (1) SA 665 (A), 37 SATC 1. (1975).

CCI Ltd v the JCIT, ITA No 359. (2011). Available from: http://itatonline.org/archives/cci-ltd-vs-jcit-karnataka-high-court

CIR v Genn & Co (Pty) Ltd, (3) SA 293 (A), 20 SATC 113. (1955).

CIR v Nemojim (Pty) Ltd, (4) SA 935(A), 45 STC 241. (1983).

CIR v Rand Selection Corporation Ltd, (3) SA 124 A. (1956).

CIR v Standard Bank of South Africa Ltd, (4) SA 485 (A), 47 SATC 179. (1985).
Commissioner for the South African Revenue Service v Mobile Telephone Networks Holdings (Pty) Ltd, (966/12). (2014). *ZASCA, 4.*
De Beers Holdings (Pty) Ltd v CIR, (1) SA 8 (A), 47 SATC 229. (1986).
Edgars Stores Ltd v Commissioner of Inland Revenue, (3) SA 876 (A), 50 SATC 81, Taxpayer 173. (1988).
Guide to America's Top Stockbrokers Consumers' Research Council of America. (2007). 2020. *Consumers' Research Council of America.* Available from: http://www.consumersresearchcncl.org/Stockbrokers/stockbrokers.html#top
Hutchinson, T., & Duncan, N. (2012). *Defining and describing what we do*: Doctrinal legal research. *Deakin Law Review 83, 17*(1), 83–119.
Indian Income Tax Act of 1961 (as amended by the Finance Act of 2017). Available from: http://www.incometaxindia.gov.in/pages/acts/Income Tax-act.aspx
ITC 770. (1954). 19 SATC 216, 216.
ITC 1275. (1978). 40 SATC 197, 197.
ITC 1476. (1989). 52 SATC 141.
ITC 1529. (1991). 54 SATC 252.
ITC 1589. (1993). 57 SATC 153.
Kolkata DCIT, Circle-6 v M/s.Kredent Brokerage Services Ltd, ITA No.806/Kol. (2012). Available from: https://indiankanoon.org/doc/184095710
Kolkata DCIT vs S.G. Investments and Industries, 89 ITD 44 Kol, (2004). 84 TTJ Kol 143. Available from: http://indiankanoon.org/doc/1457564
New States Area Ltd v CIR, AD 610, 14 SATC 155 (1946).
Port Elizabeth Electric Tramway Co Ltd v CIR, CPD 241, 8 SATC 13. (1936).
Robinson, C. (2002). *Real world research* (2nd ed.). Blackwell.
SIR v Guardian Assurance Holdings (SA), (4) SA 522 (A), 38 SATC 11. (1976).
Solaglass Finance Company (Pty) Ltd v CIR, (2) SA 257(A), 53 SATC 1. (1991).
South Africa (Republic). (1962). *Acts, statutes etc. Income Tax Act (Act 58 of 1962 as amended).* Government Printers.
South Africa (Republic). (2011). *Acts, statutes etc. Tax Administration Act (Act No. 28 of 2011 as amended).* Government Printers.
United States Securities Exchange Act of 1934. Available from: https://www.sec.gov/about/laws/sea34.pdf

Financial Analysis in the Context of the Fourth Industrial Revolution: Opportunities and Challenges

Lulama Nhlanhla Ngwenya

Abstract The Fourth Industrial Revolution (4IR) has ushered in a new era of technological advancements, disrupting traditional business models and transforming industries worldwide. This paradigm shift brings both opportunities and challenges for financial analysis as businesses navigate through rapid changes in technology, markets, and consumer behaviour. This study delves into the implications of 4IR on financial analysis, aiming to understand how financial professionals can leverage emerging technologies to enhance decision-making processes. Through a comprehensive review of literature and empirical analysis, this research examines key areas where financial analysis intersects with 4IR, including data analytics, automation, artificial intelligence, and blockchain technologies. One of the primary focuses is on the role of data analytics in financial analysis, exploring how big data and predictive analytics can provide deeper insights into market trends, customer preferences, and risk assessment. Additionally, the study investigates the impact of automation and AI-driven algorithms on financial modelling, risk management, and investment strategies. Furthermore, this research addresses the challenges posed by 4IR, such as data privacy concerns, cybersecurity risks, and the need for upskilling financial professionals to adapt to technological advancements effectively. By analysing case studies and industry best practices, the study proposes strategies for integrating 4IR technologies into financial analysis frameworks, emphasizing the importance of agility, innovation, and ethical considerations. This study contributes to the academic discourse on financial analysis in the 4IR era, offering insights into leveraging technology for informed decision-making and mitigating risks in a rapidly evolving business landscape.

Keywords Financial analysis · Fourth Industrial Revolution · Big data · Innovation · Decision-making · Internet of things · Artificial intelligence · Cybersecurity

L. N. Ngwenya (✉)
University of Johannesburg, Johannesburg, South Africa
e-mail: Ngwenyal@uj.ac.za

T. Moloi (ed.), *Impacting Society Positively Through Technology in Accounting and Business Processes*, Springer Proceedings in Business and Economics,
https://doi.org/10.1007/978-3-031-84885-8_24

Introduction

The Fourth Industrial Revolution (4IR) has sparked a complete transformation in financial analysis, introducing cutting-edge technologies and unprecedented access to data. With the aid of machine learning algorithms and artificial intelligence, analysts now possess the capability to swiftly process vast volumes of financial data with unmatched speed and precision, unearthing valuable patterns and insights previously obscured by noise (Nicoletti et al.,, 2017). Automation has further streamlined repetitive tasks, freeing up analysts to concentrate on higher-level strategic analysis and decision-making. Furthermore, blockchain technology has brought about revolutionary prospects for transparency and security in financial transactions, fundamentally altering how assets are managed and traded (Milosavljevic et al., 2019). The widespread availability of big data has enriched analysts with a plethora of information from diverse sources, facilitating more comprehensive and nuanced assessments of market trends and investment opportunities. In this rapidly evolving landscape, adaptability and technological proficiency have emerged as essential attributes for financial analysts navigating the complexities of modern finance (Müller et al., 2016).

The swift evolution propelled by the escalating availability of data has catalysed advancements in data processing and analysis techniques, challenging traditional analytical approaches heavily reliant on model assumptions. Emerging developments in reinforcement learning (RL) stand at the forefront of this transformation, leveraging vast financial datasets with fewer model assumptions to enhance decision-making in complex financial environments (Dixon & Halperin, 2020). This paradigm shift has significantly altered how companies approach financial analysis on a broad scale.

The Fourth Industrial Revolution (4IR) presents a plethora of benefits to financial analysis, ranging from streamlined data processing to enhanced predictive analytics and personalized financial services. Through the integration of cross-sector data and the automation of routine tasks, 4IR technologies promise increased efficiency, accuracy, and innovation in financial analysis, ultimately benefiting investors, institutions, and the entire financial ecosystem (Baldacci et al., 2019).

In addition to the advancements catalysed by 4IR, big data stands as a pivotal catalyst revolutionizing insights and decision-making across various sectors. The immense volume, variety, and velocity of data empower analysts to unveil previously hidden patterns and correlations, offering profound insights into market trends, customer behaviour, and risk factors. Big data analytics facilitate more precise and timely decision-making by processing and analysing data in real time, enabling financial institutions to respond swiftly to market shifts and emerging opportunities. Moreover, big data enhances risk management by enabling comprehensive identification and assessment of potential risks, thereby bolstering overall portfolio performance and regulatory compliance. Additionally, big data enables the creation of tailored financial products and services, strengthening customer relationships and heightening satisfaction (Moon & Kim, 2020).

The literature review highlights the significant impact of the Fourth Industrial Revolution (4IR) on financial analysis, driven by advancements in big data and information technologies. The following points summarize the key findings:

Technological Innovation and Data: Technological advancements have made vast amounts of data available, positioning data as a crucial commodity in managing automation systems. Financial markets and technological evolution have become closely intertwined, influencing various human activities over the past few decades.

Big Data in Financial Services: Big data is integral to the financial services industry, driving future innovations and encompassing diverse financial businesses such as peer-to-peer lending, crowdfunding, SME finance, wealth management, asset management, trading management, cryptocurrency, money transfers, and mobile payments. These services generate massive amounts of data daily, making effective data management essential.

Decision-Making and Predictive Analysis: Financial analysts increasingly use external and alternative data for better investment decisions. Financial industries leverage big data through predictive analyses and monitor spending patterns to develop comprehensive decision-making models, determining which financial products to offer. The continuous transmission of data among financial companies highlights big data's critical role in the financial services sector.

Applications and Benefits: Big data is pivotal in transforming the financial services sector, particularly in trade and investment, tax reform, fraud detection, risk analysis, and automation. It has improved customer satisfaction and overall banking experiences by overcoming challenges and providing valuable insights. Big data enhances finance by creating transparency, analysing risk, enabling algorithmic trading, leveraging consumer data, and transforming culture.

Economic Analysis and Modelling: Big data significantly influences economic analysis and modelling. Despite its importance, research on big data within financial services is not as extensive as in other financial areas. This study aims to address this gap by providing an in-depth understanding of big data's influence and opportunities in finance.

Novel Contributions: This research presents emerging issues in finance where big data has a significant impact, offering new insights not previously published. It explores big data's influence on financial services from various perspectives, contributing to existing literature and helping readers and researchers gain an integrated concept of big data in finance.

Literature Review

Business Intelligence (BI) encompasses technological tools utilized for collecting, storing, accessing, and analysing data to facilitate informed business decisions, thus enhancing competitiveness by adapting to customer demands and operational changes. The integration of BI with management accounting is crucial, as it enables accountants to shift from mundane tasks to analysing and interpreting data for decision-making. BI's technological aspects include infrastructure, data management, analysis techniques, and information delivery, all aimed at improving managerial decision-making processes. Real-time accounting data facilitated by BI aids in today's fast-paced global economy, enabling managers to make timely decisions. However, the effectiveness of BI relies on concrete procedures and data-driven decision-making by managers.

Accounting Analytics involves utilizing data analytics to interpret data and aid organizations in decision-making. Management accountants need to acquire a new skill set in analytics to extract insights from vast amounts of data and align them with strategic objectives. Analytics directed at big data allows accountants to monitor both structured and unstructured data, leading to the identification of improvement areas. As businesses invest heavily in data collection and analysis, management accountants are expected to possess a deep understanding of data quality, as poor-quality data can lead to forecasting errors.

Big Data encompasses massive volumes of structured and unstructured data, presenting challenges and opportunities for management accountants. Accountants must work with data specialists to comprehend, analyse, and convert big data into actionable information. Systems incorporating big data enable descriptive, predictive, and prescriptive analytics, answering questions about past events, future trends, and optimal solutions. Big data may also drive global convergence in accounting standards and revolutionize financial transaction processing.

The advent of ubiquitous digitalization marks a significant shift in various aspects of life, including work. Industry 4.0 anticipates substantial changes in human resource management and education processes to align with evolving skill requirements. While the technical aspects of the Fourth Industrial Revolution receive significant attention, its social impacts and competency needs are not as widely acknowledged. This revolution is poised to bring about profound societal changes across productive, social, and political spheres. Recognizing the importance of studying the human element in this transformation, particularly its social dimension, is crucial (Markova et al., 2019).

The World Economic Forum predicts potential job losses for millions of workers globally due to increasing automation. While automation may reduce the need for routine tasks, it doesn't necessarily translate to significant unemployment, as advanced technologies aim to augment human capabilities rather than replace them entirely. However, it is essential to understand the implications of new technologies on the future of work, particularly regarding activities at risk of automation. The nature of work and competency requirements are undergoing fundamental changes in Industry 4.0, with a decrease in demand for routine tasks and an increase in demand for highly skilled employees.

Tasks involving managing others are less likely to be automated, emphasizing the importance of continuous training in advanced web-based applications, emotional intelligence, adaptability, leadership, and presentation skills, especially among administrative professionals. As the workforce evolves in response to technological advancements, ongoing education and skill development remain critical for navigating the changing landscape of work.

The integration of artificial intelligence (AI) and big data analytics in decision-making processes ushered in a new era of technological advancements and transformative capabilities across various sectors. However, this burgeoning synergy has also engendered a concomitant rise in ethical dilemmas and considerations. Multifaceted landscape of ethical dilemmas in AI-powered decision-making, with a particular emphasis on the ethical considerations associated with big data-driven decision processes has had an impact on financial analysis (Muniswamaiah et al., 2019).

The literature review highlights the profound impact of big data on financial analysis within the context of the Fourth Industrial Revolution (4IR). Big data permeates various business domains, including business process management, human resources, R&D, business analytics, B2B processes, marketing, sales, industrial manufacturing, operational performance, policymaking, supply chain management, and decision-making.

Key insights and findings include:

Business Process Management and HR: Big data enhances decision-making in business processes and HR through sophisticated analytics techniques—descriptive, predictive, and prescriptive analytics—as noted by Rabhi et al.

Business Analytics: Duan and Xiong (2015), Grover and Kar (2017), Ji et al. (2019), and Pappas et al. (2018) emphasize the importance of big data in business analytics. High-performing organizations leverage analytics more effectively than lower performers, linking business strategy with analytics for better insights. B2B Processes and Sales: Other studies demonstrate the role of big data in B2B relationships and sales growth, improving customer relationship performance and fostering market innovation.

Industrial Manufacturing: Big data analytics (BDA) in manufacturing improves transparency, performance, decision-making, and knowledge. Belhadi et al. identify an overall framework of BDA capabilities in manufacturing, while Cui et al. outline key big data applications essential for smart manufacturing.

Operational Performance: Yadegaridehkordi et al. hypothesize that big data adoption positively affects firm performance, aiding policymakers and businesses in making informed decisions.

Supply Chain Management: Big data significantly influences supply chain management through velocity, variety, and volume, enhancing efficiency, process improvement, cost optimization, and inventory management. Raman et al. develop the Supply Chain Operations Reference (SCOR) model, incorporating big data for financial evaluation and decision support.

Challenges: Integrating big data presents challenges such as storing and processing diverse data types, connecting datasets across sources, and selecting relevant data for analysis. Duan and Xiong (2015) identify these challenges, highlighting the need for innovative storage and processing techniques.

Overall, the literature underscores the transformative potential of big data in financial analysis and various business processes, driven by advanced analytics and technological integration, crucial for thriving in the era of 4IR.

Methodology

This study aims to analyse the scholarly publication output and research trends in the field of financial analysis through a bibliometric research strategy. A bibliometric research strategy involves the use of quantitative methods to analyse scientific literature. This approach leverages statistical and mathematical techniques to evaluate the patterns, trends, and impact of published research within a specific field or across various disciplines. Bibliometric analysis often includes metrics such as citation counts, authorship patterns, publication trends, and journal impact factors.

The strategy is primarily utilized to map the development of research areas, identify influential authors and key papers, and understand collaboration networks among researchers. Techniques such as co-citation analysis, bibliographic coupling, and keyword analysis help uncover relationships and emerging themes in the literature. By providing a comprehensive overview of the research landscape, bibliometric methods assist in identifying gaps in knowledge, directing future research efforts, and informing policy decisions.

Bibliometric research is essential for assessing the performance and influence of researchers, institutions, and journals. It also supports systematic literature reviews by offering an evidence-based approach to understanding the evolution and current state of scientific inquiry. Overall, a bibliometric research strategy is a powerful tool for analysing and interpreting the vast amount of scholarly information available in the digital age. The approach, as outlined by Liang and Liu, employs quantitative techniques to uncover the framework of knowledge in novel research streams. Milosavljevic et al. (2019) propose four key questions to guide the investigation:

1. What is the scholarly publication output development paradigm concerning financial analysis?
2. What is the distribution of insightful literature in terms of conferences and journals?
3. What is the driving force for research between technology and financial analysis?
4. Which geographical region, business entity, or regime is most impactful in financial analysis research?

To address these questions, the study utilizes a corpus base spanning from 2010 to 2022, capturing financial analysis in the context of fourth industrial revolution. The initial search command focused on Boolean phrases related to financial analysis, 4IR, big data, innovation, decision-making resulting in over 11,210 publications. Additional refinements were made to identify papers exploring specific technologies within the financial analysis domain, such as cloud computing, artificial intelligence, big data, Internet of Things, and mobile technology.

Through this process, the sample set was reduced to over 400 publications deemed suitable for further investigation. This comprehensive approach aims to provide insights into the development, distribution, and driving forces behind financial analysis in the context of the Fourth Industrial Revolution research, shedding light on emerging trends and key contributors in this rapidly evolving field.

Results

The study on financial analysis in the context of the Fourth Industrial Revolution (4IR) revealed increased automation in financial analysis processes, reduced manual tasks, and improving accuracy. Evidence of the integration of big data analytics tools and techniques into financial analysis increased deeper insights and more informed decision-making. Advanced technologies like AI and machine learning allowed financial analysts to perform more sophisticated predictive analytics, forecasting trends and risks with higher precision. The adoption of 4IR technologies resulted in improved efficiency in financial analysis processes, leading to cost reductions for organizations. Challenges related to data security and privacy were identified as organizations handled large volumes of sensitive financial data in the 4IR era. Findings regarding the skills gap among financial professionals and the need for training programs to equip them with 4IR-related skills could also emerge from the study.

The ethical implications of AI and automation in financial analysis are multifaceted, encompassing concerns such as job displacement, bias in algorithmic decision-making, and the ethical use of customer data. Transparency and accountability challenges emerged due to the opacity of AI-driven algorithms, necessitating clear guidelines for responsible AI usage. Data privacy and security concerns arose as financial institutions handled sensitive customer information using advanced technologies, prompting questions about data ownership, consent, and cybersecurity. The study concluded that there is a need for enhanced regulatory compliance frameworks and governance structures to address ethical considerations, ensuring adherence to ethical standards and legal requirements (Table 1).

The number of publications on financial analysis and 4IR has increased significantly over the past decade, of the 11,210 publications sample studied was reduced to 400 (Table 2 and 3).

Conclusion

The study on Financial Analysis in the context of the Fourth Industrial Revolution (4IR) revealed a landscape ripe with both opportunities and challenges. The advent of advanced technologies such as AI, big data analytics, and automation presents significant opportunities for increased efficiency, accuracy, and predictive capabilities in financial analysis. However, these opportunities are accompanied by challenges that demand careful navigation. Ethical dilemmas concerning AI and automation, transparency and accountability issues, data privacy and security

Table 1 Number of publications investigated

Year	No of Publications
2013	7
2017	27
2018	68
2019	61
2020	81
2021	68
2022	47
2023	20
2024	20
Total	400

Table 2 Key research clusters

Key Research Clusters		
Cluster	**Keywords**	**Focus area**
1	Big data, machine learning	Data analytics in different companies
2	Blockchain, financial analysis	Blockchain applications in finance
3	Fintech, digital transformation	Impact of digital technologies on financial services
4	Cybersecurity, risk management	Security challenges across different industries in general
5	AI, automation	Automation in financial analysis and reporting

Table 3 Opportunities and challenges

Opportunities and Challenges	
Opportunities	**Challenges**
Enhanced decision-making: Use of AI and big data analytics to improve financial decision-making processes. **Increased efficiency**: Automation of routine financial tasks leading to cost savings and efficiency gains. **Innovation in financial services:** Emergence of new financial products and services through fintech and blockchain technologies.	**Cybersecurity risks**: Increased digitalization poses significant cybersecurity threats. **Regulatory compliance**: Keeping up with evolving regulations in the face of technological advancements. **Data privacy**: Ensuring the privacy and security of sensitive financial data.

concerns, and the need for enhanced regulatory compliance and governance structures highlight the complexity of operating in a 4IR-driven financial environment. Despite these challenges, proactive measures such as developing tailored ethics frameworks, engaging stakeholders, conducting case studies, implementing ethics training programs, and conducting longitudinal studies can pave the way for responsible and ethical practices in financial analysis, ensuring that the potential of 4IR technologies is harnessed effectively and ethically for sustainable financial decision-making.

The Fourth Industrial Revolution (4IR) has dramatically transformed financial analysis through the integration of advanced technologies such as big data, artificial intelligence (AI), and machine learning (ML). These innovations have led to enhanced data availability and management, providing analysts with access to vast amounts of structured and unstructured data from diverse sources. This real-time data analysis enables deeper insights into market trends, consumer behaviour, and economic indicators, facilitating more informed decision-making. Additionally, AI and ML have revolutionized analytical techniques, processing large datasets at unprecedented speeds to uncover hidden patterns and correlations. Predictive analytics powered by these technologies can forecast market movements, assess risk, and optimize investment portfolios with remarkable precision. Furthermore, 4IR technologies have significantly improved risk management, increased transparency, and compliance, ensuring accurate and tamper-proof financial records and fostering trust among market participants and regulators.

Despite these advancements, the 4IR presents several challenges that financial institutions must address to fully harness its potential. Data privacy and security are paramount concerns, as the extensive use of big data in financial analysis involves handling sensitive information that must be protected from unauthorized access and cyberattacks. Integrating new technologies with legacy systems requires substantial investment and infrastructure upgrades, and equipping the workforce with the necessary skills to manage these technologies is essential. Ethical and regulatory considerations are also critical, as AI and ML can lead to biased decision-making if not properly governed. Ensuring fairness, accountability, and transparency in AI-driven analysis is crucial, and regulators must establish clear guidelines for the responsible use of these technologies. Additionally, the complexities and unpredictability of financial markets, including market volatility and geopolitical tensions, necessitate a balanced approach that combines technological advancements with human insights. By addressing these challenges, financial institutions can leverage the transformative power of the 4IR to drive innovation, improve decision-making, and achieve sustainable growth in a dynamic financial landscape.

Suggestions for Further Studies

The study could delve into the specific impact of AI and machine learning algorithms on financial analysis accuracy, efficiency, and decision-making processes. Ethical considerations and implications of using advanced technologies in financial analysis, like algorithmic bias and fairness, should be explored. Regulatory frameworks governing 4IR technologies in financial analysis need scrutiny to identify compliance challenges faced by organizations. Case studies on organizations effectively using 4IR technologies in financial analysis would help extract best practices and lessons learned. Anticipating future trends and emerging technologies, such as blockchain and quantum computing, could further transform financial analysis in the 4IR context. Industry-specific analysis would also be valuable to understand how 4IR impacts financial analysis differently across sectors like banking, healthcare, and manufacturing.

The Fourth Industrial Revolution (4IR) marks an era of unprecedented technological convergence, characterized by advancements in artificial intelligence (AI), robotics, the Internet of Things (IoT), and biotechnology. While these innovations promise significant societal benefits, they also pose profound ethical dilemmas that necessitate in-depth scholarly investigation. Future research should focus on comprehensively examining the ethical implications of 4IR, with particular attention to issues such as data privacy, algorithmic bias, job displacement, and the moral agency of AI. Data privacy concerns are paramount as the IoT and AI systems collect and analyse vast amounts of personal information, often without explicit consent, raising questions about surveillance, data ownership, and the potential misuse of information. A study could explore the development of robust frameworks and policies that balance technological advancement with individual privacy rights, ensuring transparency and accountability in data handling practices.

Algorithmic bias is another critical area requiring thorough exploration. AI systems, often trained on historical data, can perpetuate and even exacerbate existing social biases, leading to discriminatory outcomes in areas such as hiring, law enforcement, and lending. Research should aim to identify the sources and impacts of such biases, proposing methodologies to create more equitable AI systems. This includes examining the role of diverse data sets and inclusive AI development teams in mitigating bias and ensuring fairer outcomes.

The rapid automation driven by 4IR technologies poses significant threats to employment, particularly in sectors reliant on routine tasks. While automation can lead to increased efficiency and new job creation, it can also result in significant job displacement, exacerbating economic inequalities. Future studies should investigate the socio-economic impact of automation, exploring strategies for workforce retraining and upskilling to ensure a just transition. This involves analysing policies that support displaced workers and foster an adaptable labour market resilient to technological shifts.

Moreover, the advent of advanced AI brings forward the ethical question of moral agency and accountability. As AI systems become more autonomous, determining responsibility for their actions becomes increasingly complex. A focused study could delve into the ethical frameworks required to govern AI behaviour, ensuring that these systems align with human values and societal norms. This includes exploring the legal and moral responsibilities of AI developers and users, as well as the potential for creating AI that can make ethical decisions independently.

The integration of biotechnology with digital technologies, another hallmark of 4IR, raises additional ethical concerns. Genetic editing and bio-enhancements, for example, present profound questions about human identity, equity, and the nature of improvement. Future research should consider the long-term societal implications of such technologies, including the potential for exacerbating social inequalities and the ethical limits of human enhancement.

To address these multifaceted ethical issues, an interdisciplinary approach is essential. Collaboration among ethicists, technologists, policymakers, and sociologists can foster a comprehensive understanding of the ethical landscape shaped by 4IR. Additionally, engaging with diverse communities and stakeholders is crucial in ensuring that the perspectives and values of different societal groups are considered.

References

Baldacci, B., Manziuk, I., Mastrolia, T. & Rosenbaum, M. (2019). Market making and incentives design in the presence of a dark pool: A deep reinforcement learning approach. *arXiv preprint arXiv:1912.01129*.

Dixon, M., & Halperin, I. (2020). G-learner and girl: Goal based wealth management with reinforcement learning. *arXiv preprint arXiv:2002.10990*.

Duan, L., & Xiong, Y. (2015). Big data analytics and business analytics. *Journal of Management Analytics, 2*(1), 1–21. https://doi.org/10.1080/23270012.2015.1020891

Ji, W., Yin, S., & Wang, L. (2019). A big data analytics-based machining optimisation approach. *Journal of Intelligent Manufacturing, 30*(3), 1483–1495. https://doi.org/10.1007/s10845-018-1440-9

Markova, P., Prajova, V., Homokyova, M., & Horvathova, M. (2019). In B. Katalinic (Ed.), *Human factor in industry 4.0 in point of view ergonomics in Slovak Republic, proceedings of the 30th DAAAM International Symposium, pp. 0284-0289*. DAAAM International. https://doi.org/10.2507/30th.daaam.proceedings.037

Milosavljevic, M., Joksimovic, N. Z., & Milanovic, N. (2019). Blockchain accounting: Trailblazers' response to a changing paradigm. *Economics of Digital Transformation*, 425–441.

Moon, J., & Kim, J. (2020). Technology predicting the future using data mining techniques. *International Journal of Recent Technology and Engineering, 8*(5), 4204–4208.

Müller, F., Naujoks, H., Singh, H., Schwarz, G., Schwedel, A., & Thomson, K. (2016). *Global digital insurance benchmarking report 2015*. Bain and Company.

Muniswamaiah, M., Agerwala, T. & Tappert, C. (2019). *Big data in cloud computing review and opportunities*. arXiv preprint arXiv:1912.10821.

Nicoletti, B., Nicoletti, & Weis. (2017). *Future of FinTech*. Palgrave.

Pappas, I. O., Mikalef, P., Giannakos, M. N., Krogstie, J., & Lekakos, G. (2018). Big data and business analytics ecosystems: Paving the way towards digital transformation and sustainable societies. *Information Systems and e-Business Management, 16*(3), 479–491. https://doi.org/10.1007/s10257-018-0377-z

Introduction of Electronic Transaction Levy in Ghana: Impact on Mobile Technology Adoption in the Banking Sector

Emmanuel Assifuah-Nunoo and Abor Yeboah

Abstract The paper re-examined the influence of electronic transaction levy on consumer's perception of electronic transaction adoption, particularly, in the banking sector in Ghana, after the tax being pegged at 1% and threshold of Ghc100.00 removed. The study sought to analyze relative advantage, perceived risk, electronic transaction levy (e-levy), perceived ease of use, and perceived usefulness as indicators that affect electronic transaction adoption in the banking sector in Ghana. To obtain this, the study employed quantitative method. Primary data were obtained over a period of 6 months, from 20th January to 25th August 2023, by serving online questionnaires. Using a sample of 648, path analysis was examined by the use of structural equation model (SEM). Perceived ease of use and perceived usefulness nexus; perceived risk and perceived usefulness nexus; perceived usefulness and adoption of mobile banking nexus; and perceived risk and adoption of mobile banking nexus were all revealed to be positive. However, we found a negative relationship between relative advantage and perceived usefulness of mobile banking as well as between e-levy and adoption of mobile banking. The study further revealed that e-levy significantly moderates the relationship between perceived usefulness and adoption of electronic transaction. Findings of the study revealed that negative impact of e-levy on electronic transactions still persists after reform. The study recommends that, if possible, the government should exempt banks from the e-levy to lessen the burden of tax since banks pay income tax. Government should further amend the electronic transaction levy by re-introducing a threshold while maintaining the tax percent at 1%.

E. Assifuah-Nunoo (✉)
Florida Atlantic University, Boca Raton, United States
e-mail: eassifuahnun2024@fau.edu

A. Yeboah
Walter Sisulu University, Mthatha, South Africa
e-mail: ayeboah@wsu.ac.za

T. Moloi (ed.), *Impacting Society Positively Through Technology in Accounting and Business Processes*, Springer Proceedings in Business and Economics,
https://doi.org/10.1007/978-3-031-84885-8_25

Keywords Consumer's perception · e-levy · Mobile banking · Path analysis · Structural equation model

Introduction

The emergence of the COVID-19 spurred a wide adoption and growth of mobile financial services globally (Boamah, 2016; Duho et al., 2022a, 2022b). The imposition of lockdowns by several countries to mitigate the widespread of the disease gave financial institutions options to reach their consumers by technological means of which Ghana was not an exemption. Aside the lockdown, some parts of the world introduced other policies in connection with digital financial services (DFS) or mobile financial services (MFS), which are categorically divided into three, mobile money (MoMo), mobile finance (m-finance), and mobile banking (m-banking), to help reduce the spread of the disease. For instance, the government of Ghana enacted the first digital finance law by decreasing the communications services tax (CST) from 9% to 5% in order to encourage financial inclusion and lessen the burden on the populace (Buruku, 2020). Low-value remittance fees were eliminated, mobile money transaction and wallet size restrictions were eased, know your customer (KYC) was made transferable from SIM registrations to permit remote opening of MoMo accounts, and all interoperable transactions made via the interbank switch were zero-rated (Duho & Kauppinen, 2021).

In environments where social isolation was the norm, MFS provided a way to receive money without going to a bank. A huge portion of the underserved population was accessible to the business, thanks to remote account opening, which increased the subscriber base (Karlan et al., 2021). Consequently, the lockdown led to more use of cash transfer businesses and more growth of DFS or MFS. Mobile Money Interoperability transactions surpassed growth in every other Ghana Interbank Payment and Services System (GhIPSS) platform area (2019–2020); however, majority of mobile money profits were not taxed. This raised a lot of concern in the country and engineered the introduction of a levy on profits made through mobile financial services.

The government of Ghana, therefore, announced the implementation of levy on electronic transactions (hereafter, e-levy) of 1.75% (Minister of Finance, 2021; Ministry of Finance, 2022; Ghana Revenue Authority, 2022; Oni & Gasparri, 2022) just as other countries like Uganda and Nigeria introduced taxes for digital transactions and social media (Boateng et al., 2022). The levy was later reduced to 1.5% and a threshold of GHS 100 (US$16) per day introduced (Boateng et al., 2022). The levy was to cover merchant payments, MoMo payments, bank transfers, and inward remittances where the originator of the transaction would be responsible for paying the fee, with the exception of the inward remittance, which will be the responsibility of the recipients and transactions less than GH¢100 per day (Oni & Gasparri, 2022; Ghana Revenue Authority, 2022).

The intention for the introduction of the levy was to raise money from workers in the informal sector who appeared to be avoiding taxes. This was essential since the informal economy in Ghana had long been accused of having low tax compliance (Okpeyo et al., 2019). The e-levy was estimated to result in a GHS 6.9 billion boost in tax revenues, helping to close the budget deficit and enlarging the tax base from 13% to 16% to encompass workers who fall outside the formal sector (The President of Ghana, 2022; Duho et al., 2022a, 2022b). The government also listed a number of initiatives that the money raised from the e-levy would assist in carrying out. One of them was that it would help Ghana fight its high debt; another was that it would be used to encourage and expand entrepreneurship in Ghana; a third was that it would be used to finance Ghana's infrastructure; and a fourth was that it would give the majority of Ghanaians the chance to pay a quota to the building of the country (Ghana Revenue Authority, 2022; the Minister of Finance, 2022).

Unfortunately, the estimated funds expected to be generated from the e-levy was not actualized. Aside from this, several proposals were put forward to further amend the e-levy policy. Thus, changes were made to the levy in the 2023 budgeting reading which was done in October 2022. The e-levy was moved from 1.5% and pegged at 1%, with the threshold of Ghc100.00 removed. The change was said to commence on the tenth of January 2023.

After the initial passing of e-levy in 2022, researchers performed studies to analyze the view of Ghanaians on the levy, drivers of the approval of e-levy, and the impact of e-levy on continuous adoption of mobile money (Nutassey et al., 2023; Agyeiwaa-Afrane et al., 2023; Mensah et al., 2022; Duho et al., 2022a, 2022b); however, none of the studies on e-levy has looked at the impact of the e-levy on the other aspects of DFS, particularly on mobile banking (wallet to bank account and bank account to wallet). Moreover, studies on mobile banking in Ghana over the years seem to focus mostly on one bank and use perceived credibility, perceived usefulness, perceived financial cost, and perceived ease of use as indicators that impact people's decision to employ mobile banking (Domeher et al., 2014; Cudjoe et al., 2015; Boamah, 2016; Frimpong et al., 2020; Owusu et al., 2021).

Evidently, the focus of the previous studies on e-levy was more on mobile money (phone to phone) rather than other aspects of mobile financial services that also attract the levy (particularly, mobile banking). Moreover, the moderating and mediating role of e-levy on the nexus between consumers' perceived usefulness and adoption of mobile banking has not been researched. In addition to gaps in literature after the initial passing of the e-levy, though the e-levy has been reformed, less study has been found re-examining the impact of e-levy on electronic transactions.

This research assessed consumer's perception of mobile technology adoption in the banking sector in Ghana, analyzing e-levy as one of the indicators that affects mobile banking in Ghana aside relative advantage, perceived ease of use, perceived risk, and perceived usefulness. The originality of this paper stems from the fact that it is the first to examine the impact of e-levy on mobile banking since the introduction of the levy and the first to re-examine consumer's perception of electronic transactions after the levy was last reformed. The study re-examined the perceived usefulness (PU) and adoption of mobile banking nexus, perceived ease of use (PEU) and adoption of mobile banking, perceived risk (PR) and adoption of mobile banking, relative advantage (RA) and adoption of mobile banking and also assessed the moderating role of the e-levy in the nexus between perceived usefulness and adoption of mobile banking. The study further analyzed the mediating effect of perceived usefulness in the perceived ease of use (PEU) and adoption of mobile banking nexus; perceived risk (PR) and adoption of mobile banking nexus; and relative advantage (RA) and adoption of mobile banking nexus.

Literature Review

Theoretical Review

Theories underpinning this research were the theory of planned behavior (Netemeye et al., 1991); technology acceptance model (Davis, 1989); and social psychology theory (Noguera et al., 2014).

Nguena (2019) posits that technology acceptance model (TAM) and theories like planned behavior and reasoned action are relevant theoretical interpretation of the place of technology and innovation such as mobile banking in the current era of life of mankind. The theory of planned behavior posits that the behaviors of people are mostly as a result of different reasons. Most actions seem to be backed by peculiar reasons, and outcomes realized are as a result of such reasons (Netemeye et al., 1991). Charness and Boot (2016) have it that TAM informs that two major components (which are: perceived usefulness and perceived ease of use) affect a person's decision to employ new technology.

Hossain et al. (2020) corroborate that intent to use online transactions is influenced by an individual's viewpoint. This gives an idea that there is high probability that individuals would accept and employ technology when it considered lucid to employ and employable in day to day works. On these, technology in terms of mobile banking has been advertised and has thus risen with haste in both formal and informal sector of some countries, of which Ghana is not an exception. Aligning with this, expectation is at a high rate that many people would employ the use of mobile technology in many sectors (such as the banking sector) since most of these technologies are easy to go by and use.

The social psychology theory explains that in order to assess a citizen's tax payment behavior, individuals should understand how the taxpayer perceives the country by thoughts. This implies that the way a taxpayer considers events in their country influences their payment behavior toward the e-levy (Noguera et al., 2014; Peprah et al., 2016; Haazebroek et al., 2017). As a result, if Ghanaians believe that the e-levy will have a negative impact on their affairs, they will tend to avoid the tax and vice versa.

Empirical Review

Literature seems to be addressing the issue of technology adoption in the banking sector across the globe and the influence of e-levy on electronic transactions. Ideally, the perception of individuals about products informs if an individual would utilize a particular product or not.

Perceived Ease of Use

The rate at which technology product of mobile banking is not too difficult to operate and understand is what defines perceived ease of use (Domeher et al., 2014). It is of the view that individuals patronize the use of modern technology at a lower rate when they perceive it to be challenging to use, for the reason being that they see it to be time and effort demanding. On this, Muchingami (2018) informed that perceive ease of use plays a great role in determining consumer perception. Ghandi et al. (2018) found that structural assurance, perceived usefulness, perceived credibility, and perceived ease of use were factors of behavioral intention and user satisfaction in using mobile banking service. Results of Deshmukh and Sahu (2020), also, revealed that perceived ease of use positively affects the use of mobile banking services. In Ghana, Ekow Kelly and Palaniappan (2022) performed a study on the contribution of government policy and financial security control in Ghana's mobile money services. The study revealed that perceived ease of use has a positive significant impact on intention to use mobile money. The study also revealed a positive relationship between perceived ease of use and perceived usefulness. Until now, no study has been found analyzing the perceived ease of use and perceived usefulness nexus, as well as the perceived ease of use and intention to adopt mobile technology nexus in banking after the e-levy was reformed. Based on this, the study hypothesized that:

H_{1a}: *The association between perceived ease of use and perceived usefulness of mobile banking is positive.*

H_{1b}: *The association between perceived ease of use and intention to adopt mobile technology in banking is positive.*

Perceived Usefulness

Perceived usefulness can be said to play an essential role in determining the costumer's perception of mobile banking (Fonchamnyo, 2013). Safeena et al. (2012) posit that technological (mobile) applications perceived to be of greater value to users are also perceived to be useful. Individuals seem to employ technologies when it is perceived that that will enhance performance of some activity. According to

Domeher et al. (2014), mobile banking is perceived to be useful when it renders the user the comfort in undertaking financial transaction. The study by Deshmukh and Sahu (2020) revealed that variables that positively affect the employability of mobile banking services are effort expectancy, awareness, social influence, performance expectancy, perceived usefulness, facilitating conditions, and perceived ease of use but factors like risk, security, and technical issues negatively influence mobile banking adoption. The finding by Deshmukh and Sahu (2020) seem to be supported by Ghandi et al. (2018), who found that structural assurance, perceived usefulness, perceived credibility, and perceived ease of use were factors of behavioral intention and user satisfaction in using mobile banking service. Nonetheless, in Ghana, perceived usefulness and intention to adopt mobile banking nexus is less researched. Not many studies have been conducted to affirm the positive relationship between perceived usefulness and intention to adopt mobile technology in banking. Moreover, the impact of the e-levy on perceived usefulness has not been studied ever since the e-levy was introduced and later reformed. Based on this, the study hypothesized that:

H_{2a}: *The association between perceived usefulness and intention to adopt mobile technology in banking is positive.*

H_{2b}: *The association between e-levy and perceived usefulness is positive.*

Perceived Risk

Risk is noted to mean uncertainty about a thing that stands to result in either success or failure. Safeena et al. (2012) posit that perceived risk is where a customer believes that some technological product may have a negative influence as a result of some qualities the product exhibits. A deterrent toward the application of mobile banking is regarded as perceived risk (Makongoro, 2014). The perception of suffering loss through the use of mobile banking technology is also said to be perceived risk (Ali & AlSoufi, 2014).

Cost of service, perceived security, usefulness, trust, and accessibility have a relevant influence on attitudes of customers toward electronic banking (Fonchamnyo, 2013; Ghandi et al., 2018). The significance of predictors of intention to use mobile banking, such as social influence, performance expectancy, value, habit, effort expectancy, trust, risk, and hedonic motivation, was tested by Abbas et al. (2018). The study found the predictors of the usage behavior to be significant. Deshmukh and Sahu (2020) revealed that risk, security, and technical issues negatively influence the adoption of mobile technology in banking. After the introduction of the e-levy and its reform, no study has re-examined the perceived risk and adoption of mobile banking nexus in Ghana and the mediating role of perceived usefulness in the nexus between perceived risk and intention to adopt mobile banking in Ghana. Based on this, the study hypothesized that:

H_{3a}: *The association between perceived risk and perceived usefulness of mobile banking is negative.*

H_{3b}: The perceived risk and intention to adopt mobile technology in banking nexus is negative.

Relative Advantage (Time and Cost)

Life is said to be bound by time, making time of high essence. Cost and time play a major role in determining relative advantage (Makongoro, 2014). Makongoro (2014) further posits that relative advantage can be defined to be the benefit a customer expects to attain from the use of mobile banking product. It is obvious of the fact that individuals adopt the use of mobile banking when they realize how much time it saves (Riqueleme & Rios, 2010).

A study by Cudjoe et al. (2015) indicated that people tend to be more willing to employ the use of mobile banking when costs related to such appear to be low. This is affirmed by the results of the study by Deshmukh and Sahu (2020). In Ghana, no study has been found examining the nexus between relative advantage and intention to adopt mobile banking before and after the introduction of e-levy and its reform. Moreover, the mediation role of perceived usefulness in the relationship between relative advantage and intention to adopt mobile technology in banking has not been studied. Based on this, the study hypothesized that:

H_{4a}: The association between relative advantage and perceived usefulness of mobile banking is positive.

H_{4b}: The association between relative advantage and intention to adopt mobile technology in banking is positive.

Electronic Transaction Levy and Intention to Use Mobile Banking

Individuals tend to have negative feeling about tax on financial transactions (World Bank, 2018). Due to this fact, taxation reduces individuals' engagement in financial systems through the use of mobile technology that attracts tax. GSMA (2018) posits that there is a potency in e-levy to incite consumers more toward the use of cash transaction other than electronic transactions. Negative perception of individuals about e-levy decreases electronic transaction activities (Anokye, 2022). Findings by the studies on e-levy after it was introduced revealed that Ghanaians have limited knowledge on e-levy (Nutassey et al., 2023). Other studies also revealed that perception of e-levy reduces the intention to use electronic transactions, particularly, mobile money transactions by phone to phone (Mensah et al., 2022; Akua Anyidoho et al., 2022; Quartey & Nyarko, 2022; Duho et al., 2022a, 2022b; Agyeiwaa-Afrane et al., 2023).

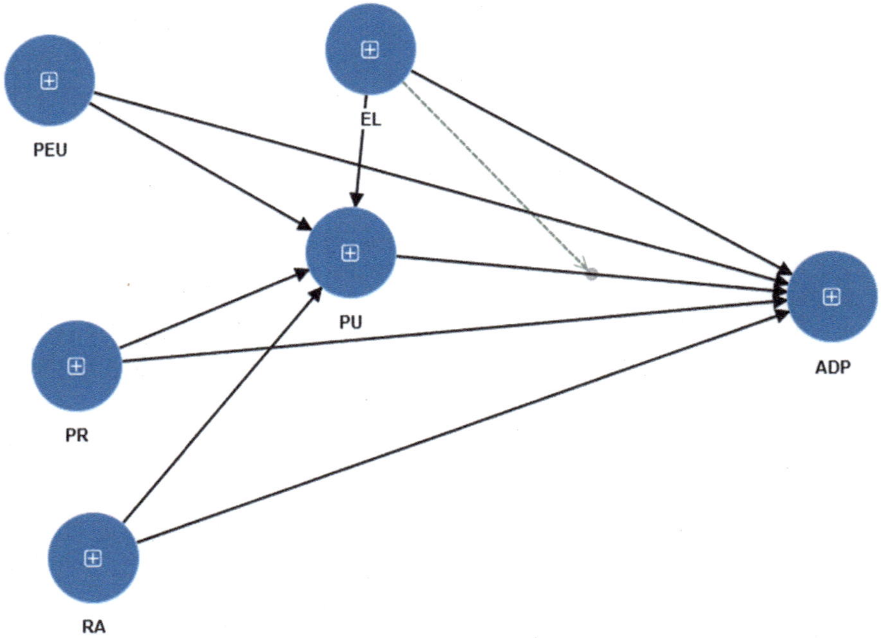

Fig. 1 Structural model

Almost all the studies on e-levy focus only on transactions via mobile money (peer-to-peer) rather than on mobile money-to-bank and bank-to-mobile money (mobile banking). Moreover, all the studies on e-levy so far were conducted when the tax was 1.5% with a threshold of GHS 100.00. After the tax was reformed and reduced from 1.5% to 1% and the threshold removed, no study has re-examined the impact of the new tax level on electronic transactions (Fig. 1). In addition, no study has been found on the moderation role of e-levy on the nexus between perceived usefulness and intention to adopt mobile technology in banking. Based on this, the study hypothesized that:

H_5: The association between e-levy and intention to use mobile banking is positive.
H_6: E-levy moderates the perceived usefulness and intention to adopt mobile technology in banking nexus in Ghana.

Methods

This section presents the sampling procedure, demographics of the respondents, instruments used and their validation, and data analysis.

Sampling Procedure

Since it is impossible to reach the entire population, it is often prudent to resort to samples. Aside from the inability to reach the whole population, working with samples generates accurate results (Saunders et al., 2007). The study adopted the simple random technique to raise the sample's representativeness of the population and to reduce sampling error and sampling variance (Omair, 2014; Singh & Masuku, 2014; Taherdoost, 2016; Etikan & Bala, 2017). A further advantage of simple random technique is that it provides an unbiased and better estimate of the parameters (Acharya et al., 2013).

In view of determining sample size for this study, the study used the sample size determination table by Adam (2020). The sample size determination table of Adam (2020) removes the restriction of the use of Yamane formula for computing sample size of a population. According to sample size determination chart by Adam (2020), minimum sample size of 385 was chosen to satisfy the requirement of 385 minimum samples for a big population greater than 1,000,000 and also for population which is not known.

Demographics of Respondents

A total number of 648 individuals filled the questionnaire. Out of the 648 respondents, 268 representing 41.36% were females and 380 representing 58.64% were males. Out of the 648 persons surveyed, respondents aged up to 20 years were 25 (3.86%), 486 (75%) were aged between 21 and 30 years, 81 (12.5%) were aged between 31 and 40 years, and 42 (6.48%) were aged between 41 and 50. The respondents aged 51 years and above were the least (13, 2.01%) out of the 648 respondents. This implies that males constitute majority of the sample. The majority age was between 21 and 30 years old and above, suggesting that majority of the youths in Ghana are those who mostly use electronic means of transaction. Most of the respondents (n = 550; 84.88%) were found to have education up to tertiary level. Quite an appreciable proportion (n = 80; 12.35%) were found to have schooled up to the Senior Secondary School (SSS) level. However, a few respondents (n = 13; 2.01%) indicated that they ended their education at the Junior High level, whereas those who had ended at the Primary School level were 5 (0.77%).

Out of the 648 respondents, 636 (98.15%) indicated to have bank accounts whereas only 12 (1.85%) did not have a bank account. Most of the respondents (n = 219; 33.80%) have accounts with Ghana Commercial Bank (GCB), followed by Consolidated Bank Ghana (CBG) [n = 135, 20.83%]; First Atlantic Bank (n = 60, 9.26%); Cal Bank (n = 59, 9.10%); ABSA (n = 50, 7.72%), UBA (n = 31, 4.78%); Prudential Bank (n = 30, 4.63%); Investment Bank (n = 25, 3.86%); Access Bank (n = 14, 2.16%); Zenith Bank (n = 13, 2.01%); and Universal Merchant Bank (UMB) [n = 10, 1.54%]. In relation to the 16 regions in Ghana, majority of the respondents were found to be in Greater Accra comprising 184 (28.40%), followed by Ashanti region (n = 97; 14.97%), Eastern region (n = 71; 10.96%), and Central region (n = 52; 8.02%), with the least being from Northern region (n = 10, 1.54%) (Table 1).

Instrument Used and Its Validation

The study adopted closed-ended questionnaire which was shared randomly on social media (Facebook, Instagram, Twitter, and WhatsApp). A 5-point Likert scale was used to score the question items. It was flexible for respondents to participate since the study employed online questionnaire, using google forms. The 648 valid replies were all produced online and included test questions to ensure there was no common method bias (CMB). All question items were "mandatory" so that once a respondent accepted to participate in the survey, he or she could not skip any of the seven pages that made up the instrument.

The questionnaire was analyzed and endorsed to follow ethical standards by the institution where the authors study. Every requirement of the approving authority for ethical clearance was met by the study. Also, only after they had consented were respondents asked to take the survey online. To make sure of this, respondents were personally contacted before they participated in the process, making it completely voluntary. Respondents were informed in the survey's introduction that participating in the exercise was entirely voluntary and that they might stop at any time. The study was conducted between 20th January and 25th March 2023. Over the course of the period of collecting data, the poll garnered 648 replies in total which were all valid and also sufficient for SEM analysis.

Data Analysis

A number of diagnostic tests were run before the regression analysis. Below is a detailed presentation of these. In order to determine the reliability of the measurement model, Cronbach's alpha (CA) (Cronbach, 1951) and composite reliability (CR) statistics were used. The study made sure that all of the factor's CA and CR values were greater than the 0.70 necessary cut-off suggested by Hair et al. (2010). To verify that constructs that are predicted to have no relationship with one another in fact did not, the study employed discriminant validity (DV). The DV of the constructs, according to Hair et al. (2010), is only supported when the "squared correlations below diagonal" do not surpass the average variance extracted of the unobserved constructs. Common method bias (CMB), which refers to the measurement inaccuracies caused by methodological restrictions, was determined not to be a problem in this study.

Table 1 Descriptive statistics of the sample

Variable	N	%
Gender		
Male	380	58.64
Female	268	41.36
Age		
Up to 20	25	3.86
21–30	486	75
31–40	81	12.5
41–50	42	6.48
51 and above	13	2.01
Level of education		
Primary	5	0.77
JHS	13	2.01
SHS	80	12.35
Tertiary	550	84.88
Having bank account		
Yes	636	98.15
No	12	1.85
Number of bank account		
One	234	36.11
Two	284	43.83
More than two	130	20.06
Adoption of mobile banking		
YES	577	89.04
NO	71	10.96
Bank name		
Ghana Commercial Bank	219	33.80
Cal Bank Ltd	59	9.10
Zenith Bank	13	2.01
First Atlantic	60	9.26
Universal Merchant Bank	10	1.54
Prudential Bank	30	4.63
ABSA	50	7.72
Consolidated Bank Ghana	135	20.83
Investment Bank	25	3.86
Access Bank	14	2.16
UBA	31	4.78
Notes: N = 648		
Region of residence	**N**	**%**
Greater Accra	184	28.40
Ashanti	97	14.97
Eastern	71	10.96
Central	52	8.02

(continued)

Table 1 (continued)

Variable	N	%
Bono	15	2.31
Oti	27	4.17
Bono East	16	2.47
Savannah	13	2.01
Western North	25	3.86
Western	30	4.63
Northern	10	1.54
Upper west	19	2.93
Upper East	17	2.62
Ahafo	33	5.09
North East	21	3.24
Volta	18	2.78
N = 648		

Source: Field Survey (2023)

Results

We present the results of the study in the order of measurement model, indicator factor loadings, multicollinearity of indicators, reliability of constructs, validity of constructs, structural model, hypotheses testing, moderation analysis, and mediation analysis.

Measurement Model

The nexus between perceived usefulness, perceived risk, perceived ease of use, relative advantage, e-levy, and adoption of electronic transaction in banking was modelled using the partial least squares structural equation modelling (PLS-SEM) estimator. Version 4 of Smart-PLS was a statistical software program that was utilized to process and analyze the data. The 5000 bootstrap samples used to obtain the regression findings were used to test the hypotheses at a 5% level of significance. PLS-SEM performs a dual analysis by describing the measurement model and analyzing the structural model (Ringle et al., 2015). The assessment of structural models includes evaluation of path coefficients and the relevance of those coefficients.

Indicator Factor Loadings

Factor loadings, which range from −1.0 to 1.0, indicate how much a given factor is correlated with the items in a given correlation matrix. A greater value, expressed in absolute terms, indicates a higher correlation (Pett et al., 2003). Indicators show a

Table 2 Indicator factor loadings, variance inflation factor (VIF), reliability, and validity statistics

Construct	AMT	EL	PEU	PR	PU	RA	VIF	CA	CR	AVE
Adoption of mobile banking								**0.725**	**0.769**	**0.651**
ADP1	0.887						1.939			
ADP2	0.868						1.937			
ADP3	0.642						1.181			
E-levy								**0.911**	**0.964**	**0.729**
EL1		0.78					2.78			
EL2		0.898					5.046			
EL3		0.808					2.86			
EL4		0.921					5.907			
EL5		0.853					3.281			
Perceived ease of use								**0.933**	**0.94**	**0.749**
PEU1			0.867				2.738			
PEU2			0.936				5.925			
PEU3			0.885				3.548			
PEU4			0.847				3.655			
PEU5			0.777				2.56			
PEU6			0.873				3.483			
Perceived risk								**0.76**	**0.786**	**0.51**
PR1				0.552			1.19			
PR2				0.839			1.763			
PR3				0.679			1.791			
PR4				0.753			1.83			
PR5				0.716			1.742			
Perceived usefulness								**0.863**	**0.893**	**0.598**
PU1					0.602		1.491			
PU2					0.805		2.377			
PU3					0.883		3.091			
PU4					0.83		2.311			
PU5					0.683		1.782			
PU6					0.802		2.332			
Relative advantage								**0.83**	**0.877**	**0.599**
RA2						0.873	2.619			
RA3						0.615	1.655			
RA4						0.631	1.539			
RA5						0.9	3.668			
RA6						0.805	2.724			

Notes: CA is Cronbach's alpha, CR is composite reliability, and AVE is average variance extracted
Source: Field Survey (2023)

satisfactory level of reliability when the items have loadings between 0.5 and 0.7 (Hair et al., 2010; Hair et al., 2016). The factor loadings for each indicator used in this investigation, as shown in Table 2, were greater than 0.5 and had a least and a high value of 0.552 and 0.936, respectively, and were significant at $p < 0.005$. In view of that, dependability of the constructs employed in the study was then confirmed. The factor loadings showed that only the RA1 indicator of relative advantage had a factor loading of less than 0.5 and was thus deleted.

Multicollinearity of Indicators

The variance inflation factor (VIF) statistic was used in the study to assess the indicators' collinearity, in line with Fornell and Bookstein (2018). At 5, the criterion for VIF is justified as being conservative but at 10, it is justified as being high. Multicollinearity is deemed to exist when the VIF exceeds the threshold value of 10 high (Alauddin & Nghiemb, 2010; Gomez et al., 2016; Asthana, 2020). Given a threshold of 10, all indicators of this study do not appear to have multicollinearity, according to the indicator VIFs reported in Table 2.

Reliability of Constructs

If an indicator can be replicated in several contexts for the same results and is steady and consistent, it is considered reliable. Latent variable reliability is often established using the Cronbach's alpha (CA) and composite reliability (CR), both of which were used in this study. Table 2 shows the statistics that were generated for the two reliability measurements. The CR statistics were between 0.769 and 0.964, whereas the CA statistics ranged from 0.725 to 0.933. As a result, reliability statistics for both reliability measures were higher than the cut-off point of 0.70 proposed by Hair et al. (2014).

Validity of Constructs

The study performed two tests (discriminant validity and convergent validity) to confirm construct validity. The study made use of the method advocated by Fornell and Larcker (1981), who posit that convergent validity is established when the lowest value of average variance extracted is 0.50, to test for convergent validity. Table 2 presents the convergent validity findings based on the AVE alongside the factor loadings, CR, CA, and VIF. Convergent validity was not a concern in this investigation because all AVE numbers were higher than the suggested cut-off of 0.50. From Table 2, the latent variable AVE statistics ranged from 0.51 to 0.749.

By means of examining the discriminant validity, the study used the Heterotrait-Monotrait (HTMT) ratio, Cross-loadings, and the Fornell and Larcker Criterion. Fornell and Larcker (1981) opine that the correlation with other constructs should be less than the construct's square root of average variance extracted to satisfy the

Table 3 Discriminant validity

Fornell Larcker Criterion: Square root of AVE and indicator correlations						
Construct	AMT	EL	PEU	PR	PU	RA
AMT	**0.807**					
EL	−0.247	**0.854**				
PEU	0.621	0.002	**0.866**			
PR	0.676	−0.099	0.399	**0.714**		
PU	0.714	−0.032	0.745	0.592	**0.773**	
RA	0.537	−0.132	0.691	0.397	0.512	**0.774**
Heterotrait-Monotrait ratio (HTMT)						
Construct	AMT	EL	PEU	PR	PU	RA
AMT						
EL	0.292					
PEU	0.733	0.11				
PR	0.851	0.136	0.455			
PU	0.881	0.16	0.811	0.709		
RA	0.642	0.158	0.788	0.479	0.595	

Notes: Figures in bold represent the square root of AVE for the given construct. Adoption of Mobile Technology (ADP); E-levy (EL); Perceived ease of use (PEU); Perceived Risk (PR); Perceived Usefulness (PU); Relative Advantage (RA)
Source: Field Survey (2023)

Fornell Larcker criterion in a particular model. Results indicated in Table 3 revealed validity among the constructs used in the study. The square root of the average variance extracted for each construct was greater than its co-movement with other constructs.

The estimated linear relations between various constructs in a study serve as the HTMT's foundation for assessing discriminant validity. Conclusions regarding the threshold have not yet been made using this method. For instance, Teo et al. (2008) offered a cut-off point of 0.90 while Kline (2011) advised a cut-off point of 0.85. The HTMT statistics from this study are shown in Table 3. None of the correlations appeared to have exceeded the necessary cut-off of either 0.85 or 0.90, as proposed by Teo et al. (2008) and Kline (2011), respectively, according to the HTMT results in Table 3. Consequently, the HTMT data likewise supported the discriminant validity of the study's constructs.

Structural Model

Following the evaluation of the measurement model, the study analyzed the hypothesized relationship between the variables under study to affirm the suggested hypotheses (Fig. 2).

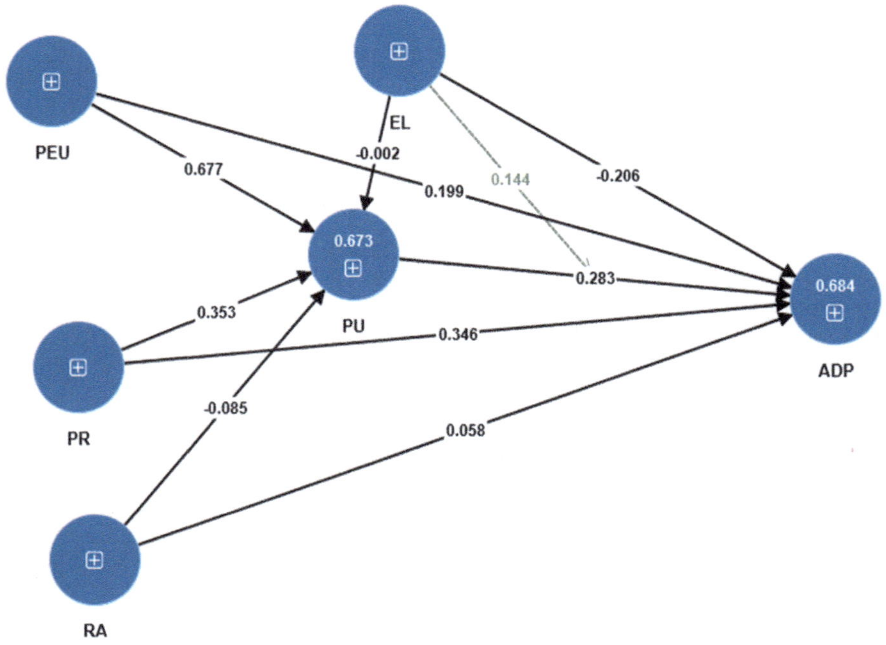

Fig. 2 Path coefficients in regular texts. R-squared values are in white fonts. *Source: SmartPLS Version 4*

Hypotheses Testing

The results obtained from the direct relationships were used as basis for analyzing the hypotheses. Apart from zero, a significant relationship is characterized by a confidence interval. The results are found in Table 4.

H_{1a}: The association between perceived ease of use and perceived usefulness of mobile banking is positive.

H_{1a} assessed if perceived ease of use positively influences perceived usefulness of electronic transaction in banking. The outcome of the study revealed that PEU has a significant positive influence on PU ($\beta = 0.677$; $t = 19.757$; $p < 0.05$). With the sufficient evidence found, the study failed to reject H_{1a}.

H_{1b}: The association between perceived ease of use and adoption of electronic transaction in banking is positive.

H_{1b} analyzed if perceived ease of use positively influences adoption of electronic transaction in banking. The outcome of the study revealed that PEU has a significant positive impact on ADP ($\beta = 0.199$; $t = 4.277$; $p < 0.05$). Hence H_{1b} was maintained based on the sufficient evidence found.

Table 4 Results of direct relationships and hypotheses test

	B	SD	T-stat	P-values	CI	
					2.50%	97.50%
H_{1a}: PEU - > PU	0.677	0.035	19.757	0.000	0.609	0.745
H_{1b}: PEU - > ADP	0.199	0.045	4.277	0.000	0.105	0.28
H_{2a}: PU - > ADP	0.283	0.043	6.712	0.000	0.21	0.381
H_{2b}: EL - > PU	−0.002	0.025	0.223	0.823	−0.052	0.045
H_{3a}: PR - > PU	0.353	0.024	14.618	0.000	0.305	0.399
H_{3b}: PR - > ADP	0.346	0.03	11.446	0.000	0.285	0.403
H_{4a}: RA - > PU	−0.085	0.03	3.221	0.001	−0.15	−0.033
H_{4b}: RA - > ADP	0.058	0.042	1.406	0.16	−0.018	0.145
H_5: EL - > ADP	−0.206	0.024	8.597	0.000	−0.254	−0.16
H_6: EL x PU - > ADP	0.144	0.034	4.195	0.000	0.067	0.203
	R^2	R^2 adjusted				
ADP	0.684	0.681				
PU	0.673	0.671				

Source: Field Survey (2023)

H_{2a}: The association between perceived usefulness and adoption of electronic transaction in banking is positive.

H_{2a} examined if perceived usefulness positively influences adoption of electronic transaction in banking. The outcome of the study revealed that PU has a significant positive influence on ADP ($\beta = 0.283$; $t = 6.712$; $p < 0.05$). The study failed to reject H_{2a} based on the evidence found to support the hypothesis.

H_{2b}: The association between e-levy and perceived usefulness is positive.

H_{2b} assessed if E-levy positively influences perceived usefulness of electronic transaction in banking. The evidence found was not sufficient to maintain the claim that E-levy positively influences perceived usefulness of electronic transaction in banking. The outcome of the study revealed that EL rather has a significant negative impact on PU ($\beta = -0.002$; $t = 0.223$; $p > 0.05$). Hence, the study rejected H_{2b}.

H_{3a}: The association between perceived risk and perceived usefulness of electronic transaction in banking is negative.

H_{3a} assessed if perceived risk positively influences perceived usefulness of electronic transaction in banking. The outcome of the study revealed that PR has a significant positive relationship on PU ($\beta = 0.353$; $t = 14.618$; $p < 0.05$). Having obtained evidence to support H_{3a}, the study failed to reject H_{3a}.

H_{3b}: The association between perceived risk and adoption of electronic transaction in banking is positive.

H_{3b} investigated if perceived risk positively influences adoption of electronic transaction in banking. The outcome of the study revealed that PR has a significant

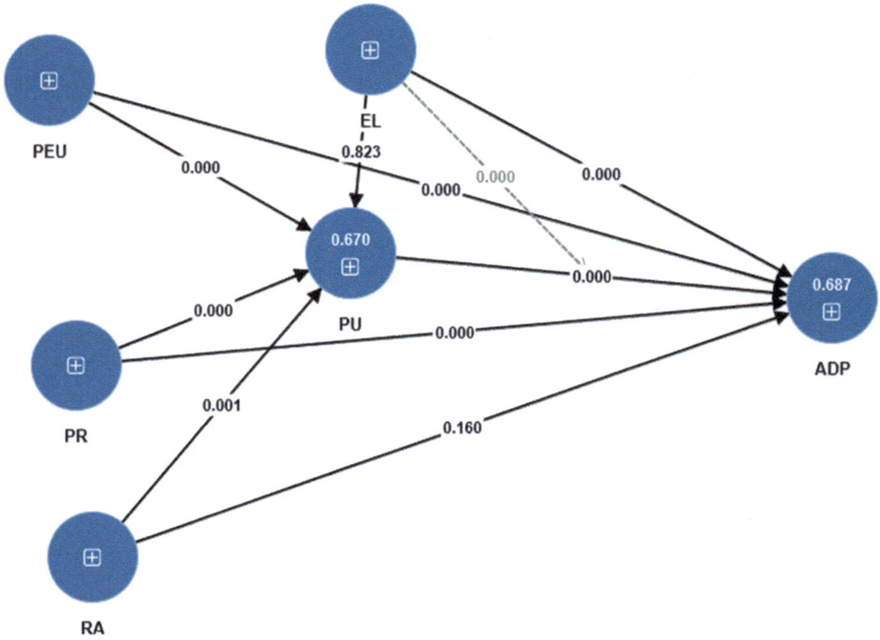

Fig. 3 Structural model, p-values, R-squared. *Notes:* p-values in regular texts

positive relationship on ADP ($\beta = 0.346$; $t = 11.446$; $p < 0.05$). Based on the evidence found to support the hypothesis, H_{3b} was maintained.

H_{4a}: The association between relative advantage and perceived usefulness of electronic transaction in banking is positive.

H_{4a} examined if relative advantage positively influences perceived usefulness of electronic transaction for banking was positive. The outcome of the study showed that RA has a significant positive relationship on PU ($\beta = -0.085$; $t = 3.221$; $p < 0.05$). The study failed to maintain H_{4a} based on the fact that the impact of relative advantage on the perceived usefulness of electronic transaction in banking was negative rather than positive, although significant.

H_{4b}: The association between relative advantage and adoption of electronic transaction in banking is positive.

H_{4b} evaluated if relative advantage positively influences adoption of electronic transaction in banking was positive. The study revealed that the nexus between relative advantage and adoption of electronic transactions in banking is positive, albeit not significant ($\beta = 0.058$; $t = 1.406$; $p > 0.05$). Since the evidence found was not enough to support the hypothesis, the study rejected H_{4b}.

H_5: The association between e-levy and adoption of electronic transaction in banking is negative.

H_5 determined if e-levy negatively influences adoption of electronic transaction for banking. The study found the nexus between e-levy and ADP to be negative and significant ($\beta = -0.206$; $t = 8.597$; $p < 0.05$). With this evidence to support the negative nexus between e-levy and ADP, H_5 was maintained (Fig. 3).

Moderation Analysis

A moderation analysis was conducted to examine the interactive effect of financial literacy on financial planning and financial well-being. The moderation effect strengthens or weakens the relationship between independent variable(s) and dependent variable (s). The results of the study are presented in Fig. 8 and Table 15.

H_6: e-levy moderates the relationship between perceived usefulness and adoption of electronic transaction in banking.

H_6 analyzed if e-levy moderated the PU and ADP nexus. Since e-levy was found to significantly moderate the PU and ADP nexus ($\beta = 0.144$; $t = 4.195$; $p < 0.05$), H_6 was maintained.

Mediation Analysis

From the modelled structure, it was assumed that EL influences ADP through PU. And also, PEU, PR, and RA also influence ADP through PU. Without perceived usefulness, EL, PEU, PR, and RA may not relate to ADP and, hence, provide grounds for exploring the nature of such indirect relations. The study, thus, performed a mediation analysis, and the significant outcomes are summarized in Table 5. Zhao et al. (2010) provide instructions for understanding the results of mediation analysis. Mediation might be partial or complete, in addition to "no mediation." In cases where both the indirect and direct effects are significant, partial mediation is believed to exist whereas when the direct effect is insignificant but only the indirect effect is significant, complete mediation exists.

Table 5 revealed that the total effect of PEU on ADP was significant ($\beta = 0.391$; $t = 10.28$; $p < 0.05$). By introducing PU to mediate the PEU and ADP nexus, effect of PEU on ADP was found significant ($\beta = 0.199$; $t = 4.277$; $p < 0.05$). Moreover, the indirect impact of PEU on ADP via PU was found to be significant ($\beta = 0.192$; $t = 6.196$; $p < 0.05$). This informed that the nexus between PEU and ADP is partially mediated by PU.

The total effect of PR on ADP was found to be significant ($\beta = 0.446$; $t = 19.074$; $p < 0.05$). Having introduced PU as the mediating variable, the effect of PR on ADP was still found to be significant ($\beta = 0.346$; $t = 11.446$; $p < 0.05$). In addition, the indirect impact of PR on ADP through PU was also revealed to be significant

Table 5 Mediation analysis

	Total effect	t-stats	p-values	Direct effect	t-stats	p-values		Indirect Effect	t-stats	p-values
PEU - > ADP	0.391	10.28	0.000	0.199	4.277	0.000	PEU - > PU - > ADP	0.192	6.196	0.000
PR - > ADP	0.446	19.074	0.000	0.346	11.446	0.000	PR - > PU - > ADP	0.1	6.098	0.000
RA - > ADP	0.034	0.692	0.489	0.058	1.406	0.16	RA - > PU - > ADP	−0.001	2.92	0.004
EL - > ADP	−0.207	8.68	0.000	−0.206	8.597	0.000	EL - > PU - > ADP	−0.024	0.224	0.822

Source: Field Survey (2023)

Table 6 Summary of hypotheses and implied mediations

	B	p-values	Comment/Decision
H_{1a}: PEU - > PU	0.677	0.000	Supported
H_{1b}: PEU - > ADP	0.199	0.000	Supported
H_{2a}: PU - > ADP	0.283	0.000	Supported
H_{2b}: EL - > PU	−0.002	0.823	Not supported
H_{3a}: PR - > PU	0.353	0.000	Supported
H_{3b}: PR - > ADP	0.346	0.000	Supported
H_{4a}: RA - > PU	−0.085	0.001	Supported
H_{4b}: RA - > ADP	0.058	0.16	Not supported
H_5: EL - > ADP	−0.206	0.000	Supported
H_6: EL x PU - > ADP	0.144	0.000	Supported
Implied mediations			
RA - > PU - > ADP			Complete mediation
PR - > PU - > ADP			Partial mediation
PEU - > PU - > ADP			Partial mediation
EL - > PU - > ADP			No mediation

Source: Field Survey (2023)

($\beta = 0.1$; $t = 6.098$; $p < 0.05$), suggesting that the PR and ADP nexus is partially mediated by PU.

Table 5 also revealed that although the total effect of RA on ADP was not significant ($\beta = 0.034$; $t = 0.692$; $p > 0.05$), when PU was factored in to mediate the RA and ADP nexus, the effect of RA on ADP was still not significant ($\beta = 0.058$; $t = 1.406$; $p > 0.05$). However, the indirect impact of RA on ADP through PU was found to be significant ($\beta = -0.001$; $t = 2.92$; $p < 0.05$). This indicates that the RA and ADP nexus is completely mediated by PU.

Summary of Hypotheses and Implied Mediations

Summary of the hypotheses and implied mediations are presented in Table 6. The results show that only two of the hypotheses were not supported. Moreover, evidence was found for two partial mediations and one complete mediation in the nexus between PR and ADP; PEU and ADP; and RA and ADP.

Summary of Hypotheses

Discussion

The aim of this paper was to re-examine the impact of electronic transfer levy in Ghana, using evidence from the banking sector after its reform. The findings of the study revealed that e-levy has a negative relationship with perceived usefulness, albeit not significant. Moreover, e-levy was found to have a significant negative influence on the adoption of mobile technology in banking. The intuition is that the tax rate and its threshold negatively motivate customers to adopt the use of mobile technology in banking. This finding of the study follows the finding by Nutassey et al. (2023) that e-levy has a negative impact on the intention to use electronic transactions that attract levy. In the case of the impact of the e-levy on mobile money, all the studies conducted revealed that e-levy has a negative impact on mobile money. The finding of this study suggests that there is a high tendency of customers moving away from the use of mobile technology in banking and resorting back to traditional means of banking and supports that government policy has an influence on consumer's adoption of mobile technology in banking.

Moreover, perceived ease of use was found to be a positive predictor of perceived usefulness and the consumer's intention to adopt mobile technology in banking as confirmed by Sigar (2016), Nguyen (2020), and Hossain et al. (2020). The finding of this study is also consistent with that of Deshmukh and Sahu (2020); Ghandi et al. (2018); and Ekow Kelly and Palaniappan (2022) who revealed that perceived ease of use is one of the factors that influences the adoption of mobile technology in banking. This suggests that the more consumers find it easy to use mobile technology in banking, the more they intend to adopt mobile technology in banking. The relationship between perceived usefulness and adoption of mobile technology in banking was also revealed to be positive and statistically significant. This confirmed the mediating effect of perceived usefulness on the nexus between perceived ease of use and adoption of mobile technology in banking.

In addition, the study found a significant positive impact of perceived risk on perceived usefulness and adoption of mobile technology in banking. Implying that the higher the perceived risk, the more consumers adopt mobile banking. The result also suggests that perceived usefulness mediates the relationship between perceived risk and adoption of mobile technology in banking. This finding of the study, although significant, is contrary to findings of other literatures who found that risk, security, and technical issues negatively influence the adoption of mobile technology in banking (Ghandi et al., 2018; Deshmukh & Sahu, 2020). This calls for more research to be conducted in the Ghanaian context to affirm the finding of our study since it is the first study to look at this relationship after the introduction of the e-levy and its reform.

Furthermore, the nexus between relative advantage and adoption of mobile technology in banking was found to be positive, however, statistically insignificant. This implies that the more consumers realize how much time they save in banking when adopt mobile technology in banking, the more they intend to adopt mobile technology in banking. The finding of the study follows, Makongoro (2014) and Cudjoe et al. (2015), who revealed that relative advantage can be defined to be the benefit a customer expects to attain from the usage of mobile banking product. It is obvious of the fact that individuals adopt the use of mobile banking when they realize how much time it saves. Nonetheless, this finding does not hold as it was found to be insignificant. On the contrary, a statistically significant negative association was found to exist between relative advantage and perceived usefulness. However, although the relationship between relative advantage and adoption was positive, it was insignificant). Relative advantage does not directly influence adoption of mobile technology in banking unless through perceived usefulness.

Following this, factors that influence mobile technology adoption in banking in Ghana include relative advantage, perceived ease of use, e-levy, perceived risk, and perceived usefulness. Perceived usefulness was revealed to mediate perceived ease of use and adoption of mobile banking nexus and perceived risk and adoption of mobile banking nexus in Ghana. e-levy was also revealed to moderate the nexus between perceived usefulness and adoption of mobile banking.

Conclusion

The introduction of the electronic transfer levy caused a spur in the hearts of many concerning the patronage of electronic transactions. Although the introduction of the levy was purposed to generate funds for the country, the expected outcome of funds to be received from the levy seemed not to have been reached at a tax level of 1.5% and threshold of GHS 100.00. This led to the tax being reformed and the tax level changed from 1.5% to 1% and the threshold of Ghs 100.00 removed. Studies have revealed the impact of e-levy on mobile money transactions but the impact on mobile banking is less researched. There is, therefore, the need for the government and policymakers in Ghana to know the influence of the e-levy on mobile banking in the country. This study gives some illumination of the indicators that currently affects the adoption of mobile technology in banking in Ghana by engaging five (5) constructs: perceived ease of use; perceived usefulness; perceived risk; relative advantage; and e-levy. The online survey was conducted to collect data from the masses across the country between the period of 20th January and 25th August, 2023, generating 648 valid responses across all regions in the country. Statistical analysis such as regression, correlation, path and factor analysis were conducted using PLS-SEM with the aid of SmartPLS version 4.

In line with the research hypotheses, the study affirms that there is an association between the predictor variables (perceived ease of use; perceived usefulness; perceived risk; relative advantage; and e-levy) and the response variables (adoption of mobile technology in banking). Secondly, there is a significant negative impact of e-levy on mobile banking in the country. Lastly, the study found e-levy to moderate the nexus between perceived usefulness and adoption of mobile banking but at a minor level. More importantly, perceived usefulness was revealed to completely mediate the nexus between relative advantage and adoption of mobile banking while it partially mediates the nexus between perceived ease of use and the adoption of mobile banking, as well as the nexus between perceived risk and adoption of mobile banking. The study's theoretical and practical ramifications provide relevant policy recommendations for banks hoping to increase customers and increase in wealth by implementing measures to control for the negative impact of e-levy on the adoption of mobile technology in banking.

Although this study comes with novel findings, there are a few flaws that should not be neglected. First, other studies take into consideration many factors that influence the adoption of mobile technology in banking; however, this study did not involve all of such factors. Nonetheless, the study adopted factors that are relevant to meeting the aim of the study, backing the factors with concrete literature. Second, in attempt to attend to software and statistical flaws in terms of processing and analyzing the data obtained, the study performed test for discriminant and convergent validity and also addressed common method variance issues.

Further studies could consider the gender disparity in the perception of electronic transfer levy, impact of level of education and financial know how on perception of electronic transfer levy, and overall impact on financial services that attract the electronic levy.

References

Abbas, K. A., Farah, F. M., & Hasmi, S. J. M. (2018). Mobile-banking adoption: Empirical evidence from the banking sector in Pakistan. *International Journal of Bank Marketing, 36*(7), 1386–1413.

Acharya, A. S., Prakash, A., Saxena, P., & Nigam, A. (2013). Sampling: Why and how of it. *Indian Journal of Medical Specialties, 4*(2), 330–333.

Adam, A. M. (2020). Sample size determination in survey research. *Journal of Scientific Research & Reports, 26*(5), 90–97.

Agyeiwaa-Afrane, A., Agyei-Henaku, K. A., Badu-Prah, C., Srofenyoh, F., Gidiglo, F. K., Amezi, J. K., & Djokoto, J. G. (2023). Drivers of Ghanaians' approval of the electronic levy. *SN Business & Economics, 3*(1), 1–20.

Akua Anyidoho, N., Gallien, M., Rogan, M., & van den Boogaard, V. (2022). Mobile money taxation and informal workers: Evidence from Ghana's E-levy.

Alauddin, M., & Nghiemb, H. S. (2010). Do instructional attributes pose multicollinearity problems? An empirical exploration. *Economic Analysis and Policy, 40*(3), 351–361.

Ali, H., & AlSoufi, A. (2014). Customers' perception of m-banking adoption in Kingdom of Bahrain: An empirical assessment of an extended tam model. *International Journal of Managing Information Technology (IJMIT), 6*(1).

Anokye, K. (2022). E-levy inimical to financial inclusion and digital transformation. Retrieved June 13, 2022, from https://thebftonline.com/2021/12/22/e-levy-inimical-to-financial-inclusionand-digitaltransformation/

Asthana, A. (2020). Multicollinearity. Lucknow. Retrieved from https://www.lkouniv.ac.in/site/writereaddata/siteContent/202003271457478667akash_Multicolliearity.pdf.

Boamah, G. A. (2016). Adoption of E-banking services: Perspective of Ghanaian customers from selected commercial banks in Kumasi (doctoral dissertation).

Boateng, R., Adeniran, A., & Osakwe, S. (2022). Towards A data-driven agenda among indigenous businesses in Africa.

Buruku, B. (2020). Ghana launches world's first digital finance policy amid covid-19. CGAP. https://www.cgap.org/blog/ghana-launches-worlds-first-digital-finance-policy-amid-covid-19

Charness, N., & Boot, W. R. (2016). Technology, gaming, and social networking. In K. W. Schaie & S. L. Willis (Eds.), *Handbook of the psychology of aging* (pp. 389–407). Academic Press.

Cronbach, L. J. (1951). Coefficient alpha and the internal structure of tests. *Psychometrika, 16*(3), 297–334.

Cudjoe, A. G., Anim, P. A., & Nyanyofio, J. G. N. T. (2015). Determinants of mobile banking adoption in the Ghanaian banking industry: A case of access Bank Ghana limited. *Journal of Computer and Communications, 3*, 1–19.

Davis, F. D. (1989). Perceived usefulness, perceived ease of use, and user acceptance of information technology. *MIS Quarterly, 13*(3), 319–340.

Deshmukh, K. G., & Sahu, A. (2020). Mobile banking adoption: A review. *Journal of Critical Review, 7*(2), 860–871.

Domeher, D., Frimpong, J. M., & Appiah, T. (2014). Adoption of financial innovation in the Ghanaian banking industry. *African Review of Economics and Finance, 6*(2), 88–114.

Duho, K. C. T., Abankwah, S. A., Azu, G., Agbozo, D. A., Duho, V. S., & Atigodey, J. S. (2022b). Central Bank digital currency in Ghana, the e-Cedi: Disruptions, opportunities and risks. Dataking Policy Brief, 6.

Duho, K. C. T., & Kauppinen, A. R. (2021). Fiscal relations, class politics, and the election year in Ghana's Covid-19 context. In Society for the advancement of socio-economics (SASE) 33rd annual meeting. Available at SSRN. https://doi.org/10.2139/ssrn.3885997.

Duho, K. C. T., Quansah, D. N., & Atampuri, M. (2022a). Disrupting or enabling the Mobile money sector? Post-COVID insights for Ghana as a developing market. *Post-COVID insights for Ghana as a developing market (July 20, 2022).*

Ekow Kelly, A., & Palaniappan, S. (2022). The contribution of government policy and financial security control in Ghana's mobile money services. *Cogent Social Sciences, 8*(1), 2138105.

Etikan, I., & Bala, K. (2017). Sampling and sampling methods. *Biometrics & Biostatistics International Journal, 5*(6), 00149.

Fonchamnyo, C. D. (2013). Consumers; perception of E-banking adoption in Cameroon: An empirical assessment of as extended TAM. *International Journal of Economics and Finance, 5*(1), 166–176.

Fornell, C., & Bookstein, F. L. (2018). Two structural equation models: LISREL and PLS applied to consumer exit-voice theory. *Journal of Marketing Research, 19*(4), 440–452.

Fornell, C., & Larcker, D. F. (1981). Evaluating structural equation models with unobservable variables and measurement error. *Journal of Marketing Research, 18*(1), 39–50.

Frimpong, K., Shuridah, O., Wilson, A., & Sarpong, F. (2020). A cross-national investigation of trait antecedents of mobile-banking adoption. *Thunderbird International Business Review, 62*(4), 411–424.

Ghana Revenue Authority. (2022). Electronic transfer Levy. Retrieved June 1, 2022, from https://gra.gov.gh/e-levy/on

Ghandi, V. A., Priya, R., & Shaikh, A. (2018). Mobile banking adoption in an emerging economy: An empirical analysis of young Indian consumers. *Benchmarking: An International Journal, 25*(2), 743–762.

Gomez, R. S., Perez, J. G., Martín, M. D. M. L., & García, C. G. (2016). Collinearity diagnostic applied in ridge estimation through the variance inflation factor. *Journal of Applied Statistics, 43*(10), 1831–1849.

Haazebroek, P., Raffone, A., & Hommel, B. (2017). HiTEC: A connectionist model of the interaction between perception and action planning. *Psychological Research, 81*(6), 1085–1109. https://doi.org/10.1007/s00426-016-0803-0

Hair, J. F., Black, W. C., Babin, B. J., & Anderson, R. E. (2010). *Multivariate data analysis: A global perspective* (7th ed.). Pearson Education Inc.

Hair, J. F., Ringle, C. M., & Sarstedt, M. (2014). PLS-SEM: Indeed a silver bullet. *Journal of Marketing Theory and Practice, 19*(2), 139–152.

Hair, J. F., Sarstedt, M., Matthews, L. M., & Ringle, C. M. (2016). Identifying and treating unobserved heterogeneity with FIMIX-PLS: Part I – Method. *European Business Review, 28*(1), 63–76.

Hossain, S. A., Bao, Y., Hasan, N., & Islam, M. F. (2020). Perception and prediction of intention to use online banking systems: An empirical study using extended TAM. *International Journal of Research in Business and Social Science (2147–4478), 9*(1), 112–126. Retrieved June 12, 2022, from https://www.youtube.com/watch?v=u5SWDMPb_UE

Karlan, D., Lowe, M., Osei, R. D., Osei-Akoto, I., Roth, B. N., & Udry, C. (2021). *Cash transfers as COVID-19 relief: Evidence from Ghana*. International Growth Centre. https://www.theigc.org/blog/cash-transfers-as-covid-19-reliefevidence-from-ghana/

Kline, R. B. (2011). Convergence of structural equation modeling and multilevel modeling. In *The SAGE handbook of innovation in social research methods* (pp. 562–589). SAGE Publications Ltd.

Makongoro, G. (2014). *Factors influencing customer adoption of mobile banking services in Tanzania (Doctoral dissertation)*. The Open University of Tanzania.

Mensah, I. K., Mwakapesa, D. S., Mensah, P. A., & Mensah, J. K. (2022, November). The impact of government electronic transaction levy on the continuous adoption of Mobile money transactions in Ghana. In *Proceedings of the 4th Africa-Asia dialogue network (AADN) international conference on advances in business management and electronic commerce research* (pp. 17–23).

Minister of Finance. (2021). Highlights of the 2022 budget and economic policy. Retrieved June 1, 2022, from https://mofep.gov.gh/sites/default/files/budget-statements/2022-BudgetHighlights.pdf

Ministry of Finance. (2022). The national budget. Retrieved June 1, 2022, from https://mofep.gov.gh/publications/budget-statements

Muchingami, L. (2018). An analysis of consumer perception on mobile banking in Botswana. *International Journal of Innovative Research in Science Engineering and Technology, 7*(5), 5801–5805.

Netemeye, R., Ryan Van, M., & A. I. (1991). *The theory of planned behavior*. Organizational Behavior and Human Decision Processes.

Nguena, C. L. (2019). On financial innovation in developing countries: The determinants of mobile banking and financial development in Africa. *Journal of Innovation Economics Management, 2*, 69–94.

Nguyen, O. T. (2020). Factors affecting the intention to use digital banking in Vietnam. *The Journal of Asian Finance, Economics and Business, 7*(3), 303–310. https://doi.org/10.13106/jafeb.2020.vol7.no3.303

Noguera, J. A., Quesada, F. J. M., Tapia, E., & Llàcer, T. (2014). Tax compliance, rational choice, and social influence: An agent-based model. *Revue Française de Sociologie, 55*(4), 765–804.

Nutassey, V., Agyei, S., Frimpong, S., & NoKoe, K. (2023). Introducing electronic transaction levy in Ghana: A possible curse or a blessing? The public's perception. *Cogent Economics & Finance, 11*(1), 2167361.

Okpeyo, E. T., Musah, A., & Gakpetor, E. D. (2019). Determinants of tax compliance in Ghana. *Journal of Applied Accounting and Taxation, 4*(1), 1–14. https://doi.org/10.30871/jaat.v4i1.935

Omair, A. (2014). Sample size estimation and sampling techniques for selecting a representative sample. *Journal of Health Specialties, 2*(4), 142.

Oni, O., & Gasparri, A. (2022, 7 April). Ghana announces electronic Levy: Possible scenarios on the progress of digital financial inclusion. Retrieved from https://www.uncdf.org/article/7408/ghana-electronic-levy [15].

Owusu, G. M. Y., Bekoe, R. A., Addo-Yobo, A. A., & Otieku, J. (2021). Mobile banking adoption among the Ghanaian youth. *Journal of African Business, 22*(3), 339–360.

Peprah, J. A., Mensah, A. O., & Akosah, N. B. (2016). Small and medium sized enterprises (SMEs) accessibility to public procurement: SMEs entity perspective in Ghana. *European Journal of Business and Social Sciences, 4*(11), 25–40.

Pett, M. A., Lackey, N. R., & Sullivan, J. J. (2003). *Making sense of factor analysis: The use of factor analysis for instrument*. Sage Publications Inc.

Quartey, J. D., & Nyarko, L. G. (2022). Economic sustainability of mobile money payments in Ghana: Does a tax on transactions matter? *African Journal of Economic Review, 10*(5), 112–131.

Ringle, C. M., Wende, S., & Becker, J. -M. (2015). SmartPLS 3. Boenningstedt: SmartPLS GmbH. Retrieved from http://www.smartpls.com

Safeena, R., Date, H., Kammani, A., & Hundewale, N. (2012). Technology adoption and Indian consumers: Study on mobile banking. *International Journal of Computer Theory and Engineering, 4*(6), 1020.

Saunders, M., Lewis, P., & Thornhill, A. (2007). Research methods for business students, 4th edition, Prentice Hall.

Sigar, J. F. (2016). The influence of perceived usefulness, perceived ease of use and perceived enjoyment to intention to use electronic money in Manado. *Jurnal EMBA: Jurnal Riset Ekonomi, Manajemen, Bisnis Dan Akuntansi, 4*, 2. https://doi.org/10.35794/emba.4.2.2016.13083

Singh, A. S., & Masuku, M. B. (2014). Sampling techniques & determination of sample size in applied statistics research: An overview. *International Journal of Economics, Commerce and Management, 2*(11), 1–22.

Taherdoost, H. (2016). Sampling methods in research methodology; how to choose a sampling technique for research. *How to choose a sampling technique for research (April 10, 2016).*

Teo, T. S. H., Srivastava, S. C., & Jiang, L. (2008). Trust and electronic government success: An empirical study. *Journal of Management Information Systems, 25*(3), 99–132.

The President of Ghana. (2022). President Nana AkufoAddo defends Ghana's 'not terrible' economy. In An interview at British Broadcasting Corporation-Africa. https://www.youtube.com/watch?v=BO4uTZvTKMo

World Bank. (2018). Financial inclusion is a key enabler to reducing poverty and boosting prosperity, the world bank brief.

Zhao, X., Lynch, J. G., & Chen, Q. (2010). Reconsidering baron and kenny: Myths and truths about mediation analysis. *Journal of Consumer Research, 37*(2), 197–206.

Financial Planning and Financial Well-Being of Informal Sector Workers in Central Region of Ghana: The Moderating and Mediating Role of Financial Literacy

Emmanuel Assifuah-Nunoo and Abor Yeboah

Abstract This research sought to find the nexus between financial literacy (FL) and financial planning (FP), FL and financial well-being (FW), and FP and FW of informal sector workers in Ghana focusing on Cape Coast and Elmina, which are towns noted for their contribution to the economy through informal working activities. The study employed quantitative method, where primary data were obtained by serving questionnaires from January 2024 to April 2024, spanning 4 months. A total of 408 responses were garnered. Path analysis was performed by the use of Partial Least Squares-Structural Equation Modelling (PLS-SEM). From the analysis, the study found a positive significant relationship between FL and FP, FL and FW, and FP and FW of informal sector workers in Cape Coast and Elmina. The study also found that FP mediates the relationship between FL and FW. These imply that if informal sector workers become financially literate and plan more financially, it will help enhance their FW. Consequently, we recommend that policymakers, financial institutions, and the government promote FL and FP of the informal sector workers and also formulate and intensify policies that will directly benefit the underprivileged in society such as the informal sector workers. The study contributes to the attainment of SDGs on poverty reduction and economic inequalities.

Keywords Financial well-being · Financial literacy · Financial planning · Structural equation model · Sustainable development goals

E. Assifuah-Nunoo (✉)
Florida Atlantic University, Boca Raton, United States
e-mail: eassifuahnun2024@fau.edu

A. Yeboah
Walter Sisulu University, Mthatha, South Africa
e-mail: ayeboah@wsu.ac.za

T. Moloi (ed.), *Impacting Society Positively Through Technology in Accounting and Business Processes*, Springer Proceedings in Business and Economics,
https://doi.org/10.1007/978-3-031-84885-8_26

Introduction

Financial well-being is reported to be the condition where an individual is capable of providing for present and on-going needs/responsibilities, is happy with their current income or expenditure, has a safe and sound mind regarding the future in terms of finance, and can also make choices that allow life to be enjoyed (Shams, 2016). However, basic human rights, including financial well-being, seem to be an issue in many parts of the world, especially in developing countries like Ghana. In an attempt to help curb fundamental human right issues, the United Nations (UN), in 2015, adopted seventeen (17) Sustainable Development Goals (hereafter, SDGs) as part of the 2030 Agenda for Sustainable Development. The 17 SDGs are somehow interconnected global goals to provide a framework for addressing the world's most pressing social, economic, and environmental challenges, aimed at achieving a more sustainable and equity future by the year 2030. Notwithstanding, as of now, people in developing economies still seem to be battling with extreme poverty, hunger, economic inequalities, access to basic health, and well-being (Shams, 2016;).

Although financial well-being (hereafter, FW) has caught the attention of researchers in many jurisdictions due to its implications in the lifetime of individuals (Foroudi et al., 2019; Spuhlera & Dew, 2019), the FW of individuals in the informal sector in developing economies is less researched. The informal sector is seen as unregulated economic activities (Hart, 1973) or economic activities that contribute to the officially calculated Gross National Product (GNP) but not registered (Feige, 1990). The sector is sometimes referred to as the market-based production of goods and services, whether legal or illegal, that is not included in the official estimate of the Gross Domestic Product [GDP] (Smith, 2013). Activities in the sector are grouped into two, namely: rural activities and urban activities. The rural activities of the informal sector actually comprise fishing and fishing processing, agro-based processing, and farming, whereas the urban activities of the informal sector comprise construction, services, and manufacturing activities.

The service activities under the urban informal sector include food traders and processors, chemical sellers, night soil carriers, drugstore operators, refuse collectors, funeral undertakers, traditional/herbal healers, attendants in private maternity homes, refrigeration equipment, traditional birth attendants, repairers of watches, radios, mechanical or electrical/electronic equipment, auto mechanics, sprayers, welders, vulcanizers, auto electricians, musicians, graphic designers, photographers, cinema/video operators, performers, film-makers, audio-visual workers, hairdressers, and barbers/private security men. The construction activities, categorized under the urban activity of the informal sector, consist of textile and garments, masons, house-wiring electricians, steel benders, carpenters, and small-scale plumbers, whilst the manufacturing activities consist of food processing, wood processing, and metal works. In Ghana, the informal sector is noted to contribute to about 70% of Ghana's gross domestic product (GDP) (Abor & Quartey, 2010) and eighty percent (80%) of the overall labour force (Hormeku, 1998).

Extant studies reveal that financial well-being has considerable implications at the individual, organizational, and societal levels (Netemeyer et al., 2018; Agyei et al., 2019; Kim, 2019). Kim (2019) opines that increasing the financial well-being of both employees and customers as part of a company's corporate social responsibility strategy is known to frequently help establish a better reputation at the organizational level. Consequently, a company's financial performance and competitive advantage grows further with increased corporate reputation (Foroudi et al., 2019). On societal level, financial well-being is informed to have significant societal ramifications since poor household financial condition frequently causes significant societal problems, especially in developing economies (Netemeyer et al., 2018). Due to the fact that households control a sizable portion of a country's financial resources, it is believed that their financial situation has a considerable impact on the economy as a whole. Spuhlera and Dew (2019) also opined that one's perceived financial well-being plays a significant role in determining their degree of pleasure and quality of life, as well as their psychological health (Netemeyer et al., 2018). Nevertheless, fewer studies have researched the financial well-being of informal sector workers in Ghana, despite their immense contribution to the economy.

Agyei et al. (2019) opined that financial planning (hereafter, FP) is apposite for well-being of individuals in many ways, albeit active employees in the formal sector seem not to give much attention to FP (especially, retirement planning). Hence, some people tend to be surprised at ages of retirement due to the fact that they could not save much towards retirement during the early stages of their working lives (Alkhawaja & Albaity, 2022). The case of informal sector workers, who are associated with illiteracy in developing economies appears to be somewhat worse and under-researched.

According to Adam et al. (2017), although FP is apposite for well-being of individuals, there are other factors that influence FP, which then influences FW of individuals. Arguably, FP and financial literacy (that is, financial knowledge, behaviour, attitude, and skills) are critical indicators of financial capability which influences FW. However, a few researchers have focused on the impact of both financial literacy (hereafter, FL) and FP on FW (e.g., Adam et al., 2017; Agyei et al., 2019; Oquaye et al., 2020). Remund (2010) opined that FL is the means to comprehend the operation of money, means by which one obtains money and how to manage money by spending, saving, or investing. The ability to understand and apply the fundamental principles of finance is non-negotiable (Safari et al., 2021).

According to Lusardi (2008), ignorance about key financial concepts leads to lack of wealth and retirement planning, albeit FL forms part of many essential factors of individual savings and influences the rate at which one makes plans towards retirement. Individuals with good financial knowledge (FK), financial skills (FS), financial attitude (FA), and financial behaviour (FB), which are indicators of FL, seem to plan for retirement and have good FW while lack of literacy in finance and lack of information affect the ability to save and secure a cosy retirement (Adam et al., 2017; Sarpong-Kumankoma, 2021). Unfortunately, majority of people seem to struggle in grasping the concept of finance and how that influences their FP and FW (Adam et al., 2017; Agyei et al., 2019).

Extant research reveals that of all areas of functional literacy (financial literacy, media literacy, cultural literacy, health literacy, emotional literacy, and among others), FL is an important factor in making decision in all aspects of life (Mihalcova et al., 2014). Financially literate individuals are able to set accurate and realistic retirement goals, device strategies, and undertake profitable investment to be able to achieve goals which help them to enjoy good FW (Agyei et al., 2019; Sarpong-Kumankoma, 2021). Based on empirical evidence, the impact of FL on FP and FW cannot be denied. Considering the erratic growth of the global economy, it is prudent for individuals to possess the necessary skills in making good financial decisions (Sarpong-Kumankoma, 2021).

However, the informal sector has received less attention in relation to studies on FL, FP, and FW. Following this, the objectives of the study were set to find the nexus between FL and FP, FL and FW, and FP and FW of informal sector workers in Ghana. What sets this paper apart is its thorough examination, as it takes into account all the various activities encompassed within the informal sector. The paper also uses all the indicators of FL (being FS, FK, FA, and FB), FP (being financial budgeting, savings, investment planning, and retirement planning), and FW (being happiness, ability to meet needs, and safe and sound mind). This paper further distinguishes from other studies by examining the moderating role of FL in the nexus between FP and FW and the mediating role of FP in the nexus between FL and FW of informal sector workers and examining the mediating role of FL in the nexus between education and FP. The study also relooks the nexus between FL and FP of informal sector workers, taking into consideration workers in all activities under the informal sector and all components of FL and FP. In addition, the study examined the nexus between Education and FL, Education and FW, Age and FP, Age and FW, Number of dependents and FP, and Number of Dependents and FW.

The remaining four sections of the paper include a review of relevant theories and works, the methods used, results, discussion, and conclusions in respect of Sections "Literature Review", "Methods", "Results", "Discussion", and "Conclusion".

Literature Review

Theoretical Review

Life-cycle theory (Modigliani & Brumberg, 1954; Friedman, 1957), self-determination theory (Ryan & Deci, 2000), and cognitive-affective processing system by Mischel & Shoda (1995) provide the theoretical foundation for this study.

Modigliani introduced the life-cycle theory in two research articles written in the 1950s (Modigliani & Brumberg, 1954; Friedman, 1957). The theory posits that individuals make well-informed decisions regarding the allocation of funds for expenditures during each stage of their life. The life-cycle model assumes optimization of consumption smoothing, decision-making under certainty, and lifetime utility. In other words, assumptions that people are sagacious, circumspect, and also rightly informed about the various factors which contribute to wealth amassment are the central predictions that the life-cycle theory rests on (Modigliani & Brumberg, 1954; Friedman, 1957). According to the theory, a person saves money when they are young but spends more throughout their prime earning years and refrains from saving money for retirement. The idea goes that people save more money in their middle years so they can continue to consume as much when they retire (Kenton, 2020). The theory was employed to establish the relationship between FP and FW of informal sector workers.

As per the self-determination theory, individuals can experience an enhancement in their overall well-being when their psychological needs for autonomy, connection, efficacy, or competence are fulfilled (Ryan & Deci, 2000). The cognitive-affective processing system by Mischel and Shoda (1995) posits that individuals process information through two systems (that is, cognitive system and affective system). The cognitive system involves rational and deliberate thinking, whereas the affective system involves emotional and intuitive processing. The theory is useful in investigating the moderating effect of FL on the nexus between FP and FW. FL is believed to enhance the cognitive system by increasing an individual's ability to process and understand financial information. FP is also a rational and deliberate process associated with cognitive system. In contrast, FW is related to affective system as it involves emotions such as satisfaction, happiness, and security. Thus, FL moderates the relationship between FP and FW as it enhances the cognitive system which leads to the affective system.

Empirical Review

Financial Literacy and Financial Planning

Among the studies that looked at the relationship between FL and FP, Selvadurai et al. (2018) considered the factors that influence FL and the impact of FL on FP. The study revealed that psychological factors such as goal setting (monetary), early financial exposure, and financial consciousness influence the aged in increasing financial literacy, and, in the long run, influence financial retirement planning.

Safari et al. *(2021) examined the impact of FL on personal retirement planning of public sector workers and found that it* exerts a notable influence on the personal retirement planning of public sector employees. *The finding was corroborated by the findings of Larisa* et al. *(2020), who* revealed that *income, future time perspective, and FL seem to influence people's view towards retirement planning. However, the impact of FL on FW was not addressed. Moreover, the case of informal sector workers was not addressed. The study was just limited to public sector workers.*

Investigating the effect of FL on savings and retirement planning of formal sector workers in Ghana, Sarpong-Kumankoma (2021) revealed that many people have inadequate knowledge in basic financial concepts. The *study further revealed that*

FL positively impacts the chance of saving towards retirement and that the young, the old, women, low-income earners, and the less educated performed worse on FL measures. This study failed to address the influence of FL on FW of informal sector workers. Based on this, the study hypothesized that:

H_1: The association between FL and FP of informal sector workers is positive.

Financial Literacy and Financial Well-Being

FW is a condition where an individual is capable of providing for present and ongoing needs/responsibilities, is happy with their current income or expenditure, has a safe and sound mind regarding the future in terms of finance, and can also select among choices that allow life to be enjoyed (Shams, 2016). Spuhlera and Dew (2019) opined that one's perceived FW plays a significant role in determining their degree of pleasure and quality of life, as well as their psychological health. The impact of FW has been found to extend significantly across individual, organizational, and societal dimensions (Netemeyer et al., 2018).

Enhancing the FW of both employees and customers as part of a company's corporate social responsibility strategy is known to frequently help establish a better reputation at the organizational level (Kim, 2019). On societal level, FW is informed to have significant societal ramifications since poor household financial condition frequently causes significant societal problems (Netemeyer et al., 2018). Due to the fact that households control a sizable portion of a country's financial resources, it is believed that their financial situation has a considerable impact on the economy as a whole.

Talking about studies that considered FL as an influence on FW Taft et al. (2013) found that there is a significant association between FL and FW. Agyei et al. (2019) examined the role that cultural values (Protestantism and Catholicism) played in explaining the FW of small- and medium-sized business (SME) owners in Ghana. The study found that these owners' FL tends to have a positive impact on their FW. A little evidence was discovered to support the claim that culture modifies the association between FL and FW. Additionally, it was revealed that protestant ideology weakens SME Owners' ability to acquire financial riches.

Oquaye et al. (2020), in a study on the effect of financial behaviour, financial self-efficacy (FSE) on FW, revealed that individuals with high level of FSE practice responsible FB and found FB to be a good predictor of FW. Adam et al. (2017) also found that FL positively influences FW of retirees from the formal sector in Cape Coast Metropolis. However, the case of informal sector workers is less known. Based on this, the study hypothesized that:

H_{2a}: The association between FL and FW of informal sector workers is positive.

Moderating Effect of Financial Literacy on Financial Planning and Financial Well-Being Nexus

Bongomin et al. (2017) conducted a study on the relationship between access to finance and growth of SMEs in developing economies, analysing FL as a moderator. The study found that FL positively moderates the relationship between access to finance and the growth of SMEs in developing economies. A study by Ahmad and Shah (2020) revealed that FL moderates the relationship between overconfidence and investment decision-making and also FL moderates overconfidence and investment performance nexus.

Sabir et al. (2019) conducted research that explored the relationship between overconfidence, prior investment experience, and herding behaviour, taking into account the moderating impact of FL. The study revealed that FL has a moderate impact on the relationship between cognitive profile and herding behaviour. However, in a study carried out by Hayat and Anwar (2016), which focused on examining the influence of FL as a moderator in the context of behavioural biases affecting investment decisions, it was revealed that FL had a diminishing effect on herding bias and an enhancing effect on overconfidence bias in investment decision-making. Surprisingly, the moderation effect of FL on the relationship between FP and FW of both formal and informal sector workers in Ghana has received less attention. Based on this, the study hypothesized that:

H_{2b}: FL moderates the nexus between FP and FW of informal sector workers.

Financial Planning and Financial Well-Being

Adam et al. (2017) performed a study to analyse FP-FW nexus of formal sector retirees in Cape Coast Metropolis. The study revealed that FP-FW nexus is significantly positive. Looking at subjective financial knowledge, prudent behaviour, and income, as predictors of FW, Riitsalu and Murakas (2019) revealed that level of income and FB correlate with FW and, also, subjective knowledge has a high association with FW as compared to objective knowledge. There are less studies on the nexus between FP and FW in the context of both formal and informal sectors. Based on this, the study hypothesized that:

H_{3a}: The association between FP and FW of informal sector workers in Cape Coast and Elmina is positive.

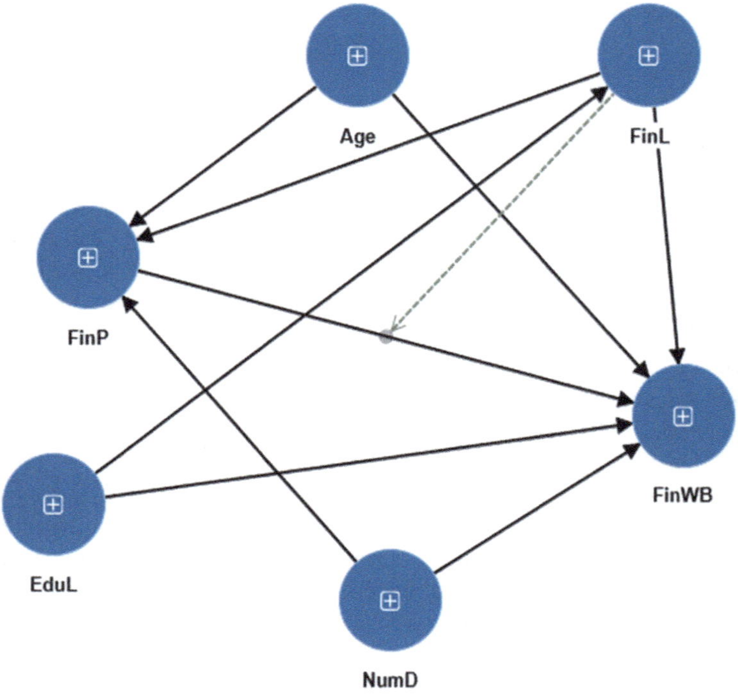

Fig. 1 Structural model. *Source: SmartPLS Version 4*

Mediating Role of Financial Planning in the Nexus Between Financial Literacy and Financial Well-Being

Oquaye et al. (2020) showed that FB mediates FSE and FW nexus, whilst found that financial capability partially mediates FL-FW nexus. However, the mediating role of FL in the FP and FW nexus is less known. Based on this, the study hypothesized that (Fig. 1):

H_{3b}: FP mediates the nexus between FL and FW of informal sector workers.

Methods

This section presents the sampling procedure, demographics of the respondents, instruments used and their validation, and data analysis.

Sampling Procedure

Since it is impossible to reach the entire population, it is prudent to resort to samples. Aside from the inability to reach the whole population, working with samples generates accurate results (Saunders Lewis, & Thornhill, 2007). The study's population comprised informal sector workers (rural and urban) in Cape Coast and Elmina, Ghana. As it is informed that a researcher should be trusted by the population under study and have a personal relationship built (in other words, have a rapport built), be comfortable with the people in the field and, as well, know the activities of the study population, their interests, cultural dynamics (local customs and norms), and among others, the Cape Coast and Elmina towns were chosen as the study area for the study. Moreover, the two towns were chosen on the basis of them being part of Ghana's major cosmopolitan and heterogeneous regions, illustrating diverse religious, cultural, and demographic characteristics (GSS, 2015) and are noted to be historical towns. In addition, the two towns are populated by all varieties of informal sector activities.

The study's population size met the criteria of being "unknown" but still categorized as a large population according to Smith (2013) definition because, at the time of the study, the exact size of the population, although substantial, could not be determined. The study adopted the simple random technique. Simple random sampling helps to raise the sample's representativeness of the unknown total population and to reduce sampling error and sampling variance. A further advantage of simple random technique is that it provides an unbiased and better estimate of the parameters (Omair, 2014; Taherdoost, 2016).

A sample size of 385 was opted for in the study to satisfy the minimum sample size criteria, as specified for a large population exceeding 1,000,000 or for populations with an undisclosed size, according to the sample size determination table provided by Adam (2020). The sample size determination table of Adam (2020) removes the restriction of the use of Yamane formula for computing sample size of a population.

Demographics of Respondents

Although the sample size was set at 385, the study made room for collecting extra responses to enhance the representation of the unknown large population. A total of 408 individuals were served the questionnaire. Out of the 408 respondents, 219 representing 53.68% were females and 189 representing 46.32% were males. This implies that females constitute most of the informal sector workers in Cape Coast and Elmina. The majority age was between 21 and 30 years. This suggests that the youthful population of Ghana's economy who are not employed in the formal sector are found engaging in the informal sector in these two towns. Most of the respondents (n = 153; 37.5%) were found to have education up to Junior Secondary School (JSS) level. In relation to the two main activities under the informal sector, those under the urban activity comprised 273 (66.91%) and those under the rural activity were 135 (33.09%) as shown in Table 1.

Under the rural activity, individuals who were found to be in the fishing and fishing processing were 75 (18.38%); individuals in the agro-based processing were 21 (5.15%); and those in the farming activity were 39 (9.56%). Out of the 408 respondents, 213 (52.21%) were revealed to belong to the services activity under the urban activity of the informal sector; 72 (17.65%) belonged to the manufacturing activity; and 71 (17.40%) belonged to the construction activity.

Instrument Used and Its Validation

The study adopted questionnaire with response options. A 5-point Likert scale was used to score the question items. It was flexible for respondents to participate since the researchers took time to explain the questions on the survey material to the respondents. All question items were "mandatory" so that once a respondent accepted to participate in the survey, he or she could not skip any of the seven pages that made up the instrument. The questionnaire was analysed and endorsed to follow ethical standards by the institution where the corresponding author works. Every requirement of the approving authority for ethical clearance was met by the study. Also, only after they had consented were respondents asked to take the survey.

To make sure of this, respondents were personally contacted before they participated in the process, making it completely voluntary. Respondents were informed in the survey's introduction that participating in the exercise was entirely voluntary and that they might stop at any time. The study was conducted between January 2024 and April 2024. Over the course of the period of collecting data, the poll garnered 408 replies in total which were all valid and also sufficient for Structural Equation Model (SEM) analysis.

Data Analysis

A number of diagnostic tests were run before the regression analysis. Below is a detailed presentation of these. In order to determine the reliability of the measurement model, Cronbach's alpha (CA) and composite reliability (CR) statistics were used. The study made sure that all of the factor's CA and CR values were greater than the 0.70 necessary cut-off suggested by Hair et al. (2010). To verify that constructs that are predicted to have no relationship to one another in fact did not, the study employed discriminant validity (DV). The DV of the constructs, according to Hair et al. (2010), is only supported when the "squared correlations below diagonal" do not surpass the average variance extracted of the unobserved constructs. Common method bias (CMB), which refers to the measurement inaccuracies caused by methodological restriction, was determined not to be a problem in this study.

Table 1 Descriptive statistics of the sample

Variable	N	%
Gender		
Male	189	46.32
Female	219	53.68
Age		
Up to 20	39	9.56
21–30	150	36.76
31–40	90	22.06
41–50	84	20.59
51 and above	45	11.03
Level of education		
Never been to school	54	13.24
Primary	30	7.35
JSS	153	37.5
SSS	99	24.26
Tertiary	72	17.65
Activity of informal sector		
Urban	273	66.91
Rural	135	33.09
Category of rural activity		
Fishing and fishing processing	75	18.38
Agro-based processing	21	5.15
Farming	39	9.56
Category of urban activity		
Service activities	213	52.21
Manufacturing activities	71	17.40
Construction activities	72	17.65
Notes: N = 408		
Item	**N**	**%**
Classification of construction activity		
Masons	33	8.09
Carpenters	30	7.35
Steel benders	12	2.94
Small-scale plumbers	9	2.21
House-wiring electricians	12	2.94
Classification of manufacturing activity		
Food processing	72	17.65
Textile and garments	21	5.15
Wood processing and metal works	39	9.56
Classification of services activity		
Food traders and processors	50	12.25
Seamstress and tailors	39	9.59
Drivers	12	2.94

(continued)

Table 1 (continued)

Variable	N	%
Chemical sellers/drugstore operators	10	2.45
Funeral undertakers	2	0.49
Night soil carriers	3	0.74
Refuse collectors	6	1.47
Traditional/herbal healers	4	0.98
Attendants in private maternity homes	3	0.74
Repairers of watches	6	1.47
Radios, mechanical or electrical/ electronic equipment	3	0.74
Auto mechanics	8	1.96
Sprayers	9	2.21
Welders	9	2.21
Technician	11	2.70
Auto electricians	12	2.94
Graphic designers	4	0.98
Cinema/video operators,	7	1.71
Performers, musicians, and film-makers,	9	2.21
Hairdressers and barbers	34	8.33
Private security men.	6	1.47
Notes: N = 408		

Source: Field Survey (2023)

Results

We present the results of the study in the order of measurement model, indicator factor loadings, multicollinearity of indicators, reliability of constructs, validity of constructs, structural model, hypotheses testing, moderation analysis, and mediation analysis.

Measurement Model

The nexus between FL and FP, FL and FW, FP and FW, and moderation and mediating role of FL on FP-FW nexus of informal sector workers were modelled using the Partial Least Squares-Structural Equation Modelling (PLS-SEM) estimator. The PLS-SEM has the advantage of capturing measurement errors in observed variables and allows the inclusion of unobserved variables measured indirectly by indicator variables (Hair et al., 2014). PLS-SEM comprises two major factors: structural models and measurement models (Ringle et al., 2015). While the former is known to exhibit the relationship that exists between constructs of the study, the latter is

Table 2 Indicator factor loadings, variance inflation factor (VIF), reliability, and validity statistics

Construct	Age	EduL	FinL	FinP	FinWB	NumD	FinL x FinP	VIF	CA	CR	AVE
AGE	1							1			
EDL		1						1			
Financial literacy (FinL)									0.942	0.948	0.755
FINL(FA1)			0.701					3.09			
FINL(FA2)			0.759					3.883			
FINL(FA3)			0.728					4.415			
FINL(FA4)			0.706					3.271			
FINL(FB1)			0.835					1.513			
FINL(FB3)			0.884					1.561			
FINL(FB6)			0.904					2.257			
FINL(FK1)			0.727					2.726			
FINL(FK2)			0.85					3.15			
FINL(FK3)			0.757					3.13			
FINL(FK4)			0.731					4.645			
FINL(FK5)			0.762					4.151			
FINL(FK6)			0.748					3.428			
FINL(FK7)			0.782					2.862			
FINL(FK8)			0.878					3.363			
FINL(FS1)			0.705					3.004			
FINL(FS2)			0.777					4.298			
FINL(FS3)			0.727					4.028			
FINL(FS4)			0.787					3.482			
FINL(FS5)			0.715					3.639			
Financial planning (FinP)									0.859	0.887	0.634
FinP (FBG1)				0.729				1.778			
FinP (FBG2)				0.776				1.666			
FinP (FBG3)				0.797				1.712			
FinP (FBG4)				0.805				2.186			
FinP (IP1)				0.788				2.046			
FinP (IP2)				0.825				2.935			
FinP (IP3)				0.853				2.761			
FinP (IP4)				0.815				2.741			
FinP (RP1)				0.835				2.64			
FinP (RP2)				0.793				2.495			
FinP (RP3)				0.831				2.249			
FinP (S1)				0.744				2.888			
FinP (S2)				0.724				3.457			
FinP (S3)				0.703				2.817			

(continued)

Table 2 (continued)

Construct	Age	EduL	FinL	FinP	FinWB	NumD	FinL x FinP	VIF	CA	CR	AVE
FinP (S4)				0.768				2.981			
Financial Well-being (FinWB)									0.924	0.935	0.57
FinWB (AB1)					0.718			2.157			
FinWB (AB2)					0.818			3.942			
FinWB (AB3)					0.813			4.016			
FinWB (AB4)					0.824			4.346			
FinWB (AB5)					0.698			2.487			
FinWB (H1)					0.885			3.167			
FinWB (H2)					0.931			3.816			
FinWB (H3)					0.864			2.807			
FinWB (SSM1)					0.818			3.678			
FinWB (SSM2)					0.766			3.21			
FinWB (SSM3)					0.777			2.978			
Number of dependents (NUMD)									0.95	0.96	0.827
NUMDP1						0.888		3.127			
NUMDP2						0.939		4.87			
NUMDP3						0.953		7.405			
NUMDP4						0.898		7.517			
NUMDP5						0.867		5.484			
FinL x FinP							1	1			

Notes: CA is Cronbach's alpha; CR is composite reliability; AVE is average variance extracted; Ability to meet needs (AB); Financial Attitude (FA); Financial Behaviour (FB); Financial Budgeting (FBG); Financial Knowledge (FK); Financial Skills (FS); Happiness (H); Investment Planning (IP); Number of dependents (NUMD); Retirement planning (RP); Safe and sound mind (SSM); Savings (S)
Source: Field Survey (2023)

employed for validation of construct and refinement of scale. PLS-SEM was performed using Version 4 of SmartPLS software, not leaving out, assessing the measurement model. The assessment of structural models includes evaluation of path coefficients and the relevance of those coefficients. The 5000 bootstrap samples used to obtain the regression findings were used to test the hypotheses at a 5% level of significance.

Indicator Factor Loadings

Factor loadings, which range from −1.0 to 1.0, indicate how much a given factor is correlated with the items in a given correlation matrix. A greater value, expressed in absolute terms, indicates a higher correlation (Pett et al., 2003). Indicators show a satisfactory level of reliability when the items have loadings between 0.5 and 0.7 (Hair et al., 2016; Hair et al., 2010). The factor loadings for each indicator used in this investigation, as shown in Table 2, were greater than 0.5 and had the smallest and largest value of 0.751 and 0.948, respectively, and were significant at $p < 0.005$. In view of that, dependability of the indicators employed in the study was then confirmed. However, FB2, FB4, and FB5 indicators of financial behaviour had factor loadings of less than 0.5 and thus were deleted.

Multicollinearity of Indicators

The variance inflation factor (VIF) statistic was used in the study to assess the indicators' collinearity, in line with Fornell and Bookstein (2018). At 5, the criterion for VIF is justified as being conservative but at 10, it is justified as being high. Multicollinearity is deemed to exist when the VIF exceeds the threshold value of 10 high (Alauddin & Nghiemb, 2010; Gomez et al., 2016; Asthana, 2020). Given a threshold of 10, all indicators of this study do not appear to have multicollinearity, according to the indicator VIFs reported in Table 2.

Reliability and Validity of Constructs

If an indicator can be replicated in several contexts for the same results and is steady and consistent, it is considered reliable. Latent variable reliability is often established using the Cronbach's alpha (CA) and composite reliability (CR), both of which were used in this study. Table 2 shows the statistics that were generated for the two reliability measurements. The CR statistics were between 0.769 and 0.964, whereas the CA statistics ranged from 0.725 to 0.933. As a result, reliability statistics for both reliability measures were higher than the cut-off point of 0.70 proposed by Hair et al. (2014).

The study performed two tests (discriminant validity and convergent validity) to confirm construct validity. The study utilized the methodology proposed by Fornell and Larcker (1981), which asserts that convergent validity is affirmed when the AVE equals or exceeds 0.50, as a means to evaluate convergent validity. Table 2 presents the convergent validity findings based on the AVE alongside the factor loadings, CR, CA, and VIF. Convergent validity was not a concern in this investigation because all AVE numbers were higher than the suggested cut-off of 0.50. From Table 2, the latent variable AVE statistics ranged from 0.51 to 0.749.

By means of examining the discriminant validity of the constructs, the study used the Heterotrait-Monotrait (HTMT) ratio and the Fornell and Larcker Criterion. Fornell and Larcker (1981) opine that the correlation with other constructs should be less than the construct's square root of average variance extracted to satisfy the Fornell-Larcker criterion in a particular model. Results indicated in Table 3 reveal

Table 3 Discriminant validity

Heterotrait-Monotrait ratio (HTMT)							
Variable	Age	EduL	FinL	FinP	FinWB	NumD	FinL x FinP
Age							
EduL	0.39						
FinL	0.235	0.388					
FinP	0.165	0.388	0.754				
FinWB	0.076	0.085	0.685	0.566			
NumD	0.028	0.158	0.168	0.277	0.139		
FinL x FinP	0.095	0.028	0.098	0.145	0.048	0.206	
Fornell-Larcker criterion: Square root of AVE and indicator correlations							
Variable	Age	EduL	FinL	FinP	FinWB	NumD	
Age	**1**						
EduL	−0.39	**1**					
FinL	−0.226	0.381	**0.726**				
FinP	−0.136	0.332	0.695	**0.621**			
FinWB	0.048	0.046	0.643	0.552	**0.755**		
NumD	−0.014	0.159	0.107	0.158	0.124	**0.909**	

Notes: Figures in bold represent the square root of AVE for the given construct. Educational level (EduL), Financial Well-being (FinWB), Financial Planning (FinP), Number of Dependents (NumD)
Source: Field Survey (2023)

validity among the constructs used in the study. The square root of the average variance extracted for each construct was greater than its co-movement with other constructs. The estimated co-movement between various constructs in a study serves as the HTMT's foundation for assessing discriminant validity. Conclusions regarding the discriminant validity threshold have not yet been made using this method. For instance, Teo et al. (2008) offered a cut-off point of 0.90, while Kline (2011) advised a cut-off point of 0.85. The HTMT statistics from this study are shown in Table 3. None of the correlations appeared to have exceeded the necessary cut-off of either 0.85 or 0.90, as proposed by Teo et al. (2008) and Kline (2011), respectively, according to the HTMT results in Table 3. Consequently, the HTMT data likewise supported the discriminant validity of the study's constructs

Structural Model

Following the evaluation of the measurement model, the study analysed the hypothesized relationship between the variables under study to affirm the suggested hypotheses (Fig. 2).

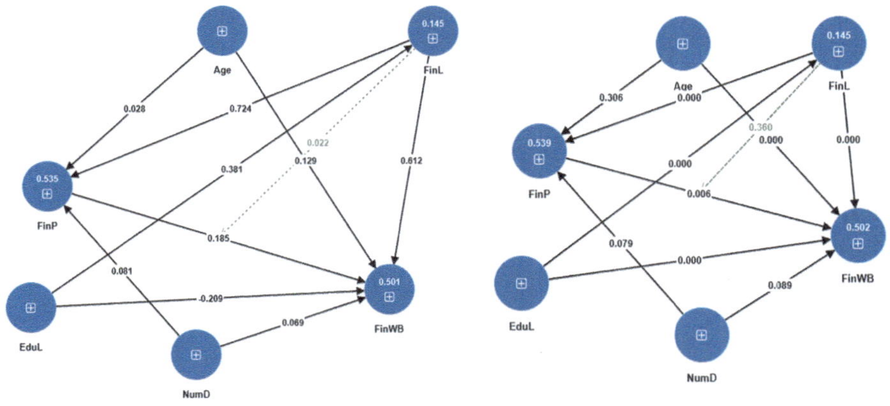

Fig. 2 Path coefficients (left) and p-values (right) in regular texts. R-squared values are in white fonts. *Source: SmartPLS Version 4*

Hypotheses Testing

The results obtained from the direct relationships were used as basis for analysing the hypotheses. The findings presented in this study were derived from an analysis of 5000 bootstrap samples, yielding a two-tailed confidence interval of 95%. Apart from zero, a significant relationship is characterized by a confidence interval. The results are found in Table 4.

H_1: The association between FL and FP is positive.

H_1 assessed if FL positively influences FP of informal sector workers. The outcome of the study revealed that FL has a significant positive impact on FP of informal sector workers in Cape Coast and Elmina ($\beta = 0.749$; $p < 0.05$). With much evidence found to support H_1, the study failed to reject $H_{1.}$

H_{2a}: The association between age and FP is positive.

H_{2a} examined if there is a positive nexus between FL and FW of informal sector workers in Cape Coast and Elmina. The outcome of the study revealed that FL-FW nexus is significantly positive ($\beta = 0.497$; $p < 0.05$). Hence, H_{2a} was maintained based on the sufficient evidence found.

H_{3a}: The association between FP and FW is positive.

H_{3a} assessed to affirm that the nexus between FP and FW is positive among informal sector workers in Cape Coast and Elmina. The outcome of the study revealed that FP has a significant positive influence on FW of informal sector workers in Cape Coast and Elmina ($\beta = 0.211$; $p < 0.05$). The study failed to reject H_3 based on the evidence found.

H_{2b}: FL moderates the relationship between FP and FW.

Table 4 Results of direct relationships and hypotheses test

	Beta	SD	T-stat	P-values	CI	
					2.50%	97.50%
Age - > FinP	0.028	0.033	1.024	**0.306**	−0.031	0.097
Age - > FinWB	0.129	0.034	3.721	0.000	0.06	0.194
EduL - > FinL	0.381	0.044	8.679	0.000	0.29	0.463
EduL - > FinWB	−0.209	0.039	5.425	0.000	−0.291	−0.134
H_1: FinL - > FinP	0.724	0.023	31.835	0.000	0.679	0.769
H_{2a}: FinL - > FinWB	0.612	0.066	9.179	0.000	0.476	0.734
H_{3a}: FinP - > FinWB	0.185	0.069	2.753	0.006	0.054	0.324
NumD - > FinP	0.081	0.042	1.754	**0.079**	−0.009	0.155
NumD - > FinWB	0.069	0.043	1.703	**0.089**	−0.018	0.154
H_{2b}: FinL x FinP - > FinWB	0.022	0.023	0.916	**0.36**	−0.026	0.065
	R-square	R-square adjusted				
FinL	0.145	0.143				
FinP	0.535	0.531				
FinWB	0.501	0.493				

Source: Field Survey (2023)

H_{2b} examined if FL strengthens or weakens the relationship between FP and FW of informal sector workers in Cape Coast and Elmina. The outcome of the study revealed that FL slightly strengthens the nexus between FP and FW of informal sector workers in Cape Coast and Elmina; however, the moderation role is insignificant ($\beta = 0.034$; $p > 0.05$). Since the study did not find sufficient evidence to support the hypothesis, the study rejected H_{2b}.

Mediation Analysis

From the modelled structure, it was assumed that FL influences FW through FP. The structure suggests that without FP, FL may not relate with FW and, hence, provides grounds for a search into the nature of such indirect relations. The study, thus, performed a mediation analysis, and the significant outcomes are summarized in Table 5. Zhao et al. (2010) provide instructions for understanding the results of mediation analysis. Mediation might be partial or complete, in addition to "no mediation". In cases where both the indirect and direct effects are significant, partial mediation is believed to exist whereas when the direct effect is insignificant but only the indirect effect is significant, complete mediation exists.

H_{3b}: FP mediates the nexus between FL and FW.

Table 5 reveals that the total effect of FL on FW was significant ($\beta = 0.749$; $p < 0.05$). Having introduced FP as the mediating variable, the direct effect of FL on FW was still found to be significant ($\beta = 0.749$; $p < 0.05$). In addition, the indirect impact of FL on FW through FP was also revealed to be significant ($\beta = 0.158$; $p < 0.05$), suggesting that FL and FW nexus is partially mediated by FP. With enough evidence to support H_{3b}, the study failed to reject H_{2c}.

Table 5 Mediation analysis

	Total effect	t-stats	p-values	Direct effect	t-stats	p-values		Indirect effect	t-stats	p-values
Age - > FinP	0.028	1.024	0.306	0.028	1.024	**0.306**	Age - > FinP - > FinWB	0.005	0.89	**0.374**
Age - > FinWB	0.134	3.834	0.000	0.129	3.721	0.000	EduL - > FinL - > FinP	0.276	8.105	0.000
EduL - > FinL	0.381	8.679	0.000	0.381	8.679	0.000	EduL - > FinL - > FinP - > FinWB	0.051	2.553	0.011
EduL - > FinWB	0.075	1.269	0.204	−0.209	5.425	0.000	FinL - > FinP - > FinWB	0.134	2.777	0.006
FinL - > FinP	0.724	31.835	0.000	0.724	31.835	0.000	EduL - > FinL - > FinWB	0.233	6.177	0.000
FinL - > FinWB	0.746	20.429	0.000	0.612	9.179	0.000	NumD - > FinP - > FinWB	0.015	1.478	**0.14**
FinP - > FinWB	0.185	2.753	0.006	0.185	2.753	0.006				
NumD - > FinP	0.081	1.754	0.079	0.081	1.754	**0.079**				
NumD - > FinWB	0.084	2.048	0.041	0.069	1.703	**0.089**				
FinL x FinP - > FinWB	0.022	0.916	0.36	0.022	0.916	**0.36**				

Source: Field Survey (2023)

Table 6 Summary of hypotheses and implied mediations

	Beta	p-values	Comment/Decision
Age - > FinP	0.028	**0.306**	Not supported
Age - > FinWB	0.129	0.000	Supported
EduL - > FinL	0.381	0.000	Supported
EduL - > FinWB	−0.209	0.000	Supported
H_1: FinL - > FinP	0.724	0.000	Supported
H_{2a}: FinL - > FinWB	0.612	0.000	Supported
H_{3a}: FinP - > FinWB	0.185	0.006	Supported
NumD - > FinP	0.081	**0.079**	Not supported
NumD - > FinWB	0.069	**0.089**	Not supported
H_{2b}: FinL x FinP - > FinWB	0.022	**0.36**	Not supported
Implied mediations			
Age - > FinP - > FinWB			No mediation
EduL - > FinL - > FinP			Partial mediation
EduL - > FinL - > FinP - > FinWB			Partial mediation
FinL - > FinP - > FinWB			Partial mediation
EduL - > FinL - > FinWB			Partial mediation
NumD - > FinP - > FinWB			No mediation

Source: Field Survey (2023)

Summary of Hypotheses and Implied Mediations

Summary of the hypotheses and implied mediations are presented in Table 6. The results show that only one of the hypotheses (H_{2b}) was not supported. Evidence was found for one partial mediation in the nexus between FL and FW.

Discussion

The aim of this paper was to examine the impact of FL and FP on FW of informal sector workers in Cape Coast and Elmina. The findings of the study revealed that FL positively influences FP of informal sector workers in Cape Coast and Elmina. The study further revealed that both FL and FP positively influence FW of informal sector workers.

The findings of the study imply that FL can enhance the FP of the informal sector workers of both urban and rural activities in the Cape Coast and Elmina. The findings of this study are consistent with prior studies by Selvadurai et al. (2018), Ofori (2021), and Sarpong-Kumankoma (2021), who found that literacy significantly influences FP in a positive way for formal sector workers.

The findings also imply that FP can enhance the FW of the informal sector workers of both urban and rural activities in the Cape Coast and Elmina. The finding of this study is consistent with prior studies by Adam et al. (2017) who found a significant and a positive relationship between FP and the FW of formal sector retirees in the Cape Coast Metropolis. Since this study is the first to analyse the nexus between FP and FW of informal sector workers, the finding of this study requires that other studies are done to verify the positive relationship between FP and FW of informal sector workers of both urban and rural activities.

The study further revealed that FL has a positive impact on FW of informal sector workers in Cape Coast and Elmina; however, FP partially mediates the nexus between FL and FW. This implies that FL can improve the FW of the informal sector workers of both urban and rural activities in Cape Coast and Elmina through FP. Consequently, a higher FL would lead to higher FW of the informal sector workers in Cape Coast and Elmina whereas a lower FL would lead to lower FW. Furthermore, individuals who are financially literate and utilize their knowledge to manage their income and plan for retirement are more likely to enjoy enhanced financial well-being in their retirement phase. This enables them to save and allocate their income in a way that ensures a smoother and more consistent consumption pattern throughout their lifetime, aligning with the principles set forth by the theory.

The finding of this study is consistent with prior studies by who found that FL significantly influences perceived FW. Taft et al. (2013) similarly revealed that higher FL leads to greater FW. Adu-Asare (2018) and Amenuku (2018) also found a positive relationship between FL and FW of cocoa farmers in the Brong-Ahafo region of Ghana and artisanal fishermen in Elmina, respectively.

Oquaye et al. (2020) revealed that FB mediates the relationship between FSE and FW and concluded that well-being impacts positively on happiness. Found that financial capability partially mediates the association between FL and FW; nonetheless, no study seems to have looked at the mediating role of FP in the relationship between FL and FW. This requires that other studies are done to verify the mediating role of FP in the relationship between FL and FW and that of the relationship between number of dependents and FW of informal sector workers.

The study further revealed that FL slightly strengthens the relationship between FP and FW of informal sector workers in Cape Coast and Elmina in a positive way, albeit insignificant. This could be a result of the low level of FL of the informal sector workers in Cape Coast and Elmina and the low level of applying their FL in planning financially. It can be inferred that although the informal sector workers of both urban and rural activities have some level of FL, how their FP correlates with their FW is not strengthened by their level of FL. To support the findings of this study, Mutlu and Özer (2021) found that FL changes the nexus between internal locus of control and FB. A study by Bongomin et al. (2017) revealed that FL positively moderates the relationship between access to finance and growth of SMEs in developing economies. However, Hayat and Anwar (2016) revealed that FL has a negative moderating role in herding bias and positive moderating role of overconfidence bias in investment decision.

Conclusion

The role of FL in enhancing the FP and FW of individuals cannot be downplayed. Although studies reveal the impact of FL on FP, the Ghanaian context is less known as well as the context of informal sector workers in Ghana. The role of FP on FW and the mediating role of FP in the nexus between FL and FW of informal sector workers are less considered by researchers. There is, therefore, the need for the government and policymakers in Ghana to know the influence FL and FP on FW of informal sector workers in the country.

The study provides novel grounds concerning the relationship between FP and FW and the mediating role of FP in the nexus between FL and FW of the informal sector workers in Cape Coast and Elmina. Survey was conducted to collect data from the informal sector workers in Cape Coast and Elmina between the period of January 2024 and April 2024, generating 408 valid responses. Concerning respondent demographic indicators, the outcome revealed that respondents aged *21–30* constituted majority of the informal sector workers in Ghana. Statistical analysis such as path analysis and factor analysis were conducted using PLS-SEM with the aid of SmartPLS version 4. Statistical analysis such as regression, correlation, path and factor analysis were conducted using a structural equation model procedure. Upon assessing the outcome of this research, outcome of this study met the objectives of this research. It was revealed that the association between FL and FP, FL and FW, and FP and FW is positive and significant. The study further found FP to mediate the nexus between FL and FW.

Notwithstanding, there are few flaws that should not be neglected. First, some of the outcomes of this research were found to be consistent with previous studies by other researchers, whereas some were also found to be inconsistent with other studies by some other researchers. Nonetheless, the study adopted factors that are relevant to meeting the aim of the study, backing the factors with concrete literature. Second, in attempt to attend to software and statistical flaws in terms of processing and analysing the data obtained, the study performed test for discriminant and convergent validity and also addressed common method variance issues.

Overall, the study makes contribution to a better understanding of the problem and/or to its solution. The study's theoretical and practical ramifications provide relevant policy recommendations for financial planners and pension trusts firms hoping to increase customers and increase wealth by implementing measures to encourage informal sector workers to sign up for more FP options. Based on the findings, the study recommends that the government and financial institutions try to offer more financial education to the informal sector workers in Cape Coast and Elmina. Since a positive and significant relationship was revealed to exist between FL and FP, more literacy on finance would help the informal sector workers to plan more. This would, overall, give room for financial institutions to create more wealth and contribute to national development. Not only would financial institutions be able to create more wealth, but the informal sector workers would also have better FW which will cushion them to work more to contribute to the economy of the country since the study also revealed that there is a significant positive relationship between FL and FW and FP and FW.

Although the study offers fertile ground for future studies on how FL and FP play an important role in the FW of informal sector workers in the Cape Coast and Elmina, there seem to be other factors that may possibly influence the FW of informal sector workers, aside from FL and FP. Impact of demographic indicators like gender and marital status were not analysed to examine if they could be influencing indicators of the FW of the informal sector workers. Further studies may consider looking at how other demographic indicators (such as gender and marital status), cultural dominance, religious orientation, financial concerns, and among others, influence the FW of informal sector workers or consider expanding this study by adding other regions.

References

Abor, J., & Quartey, P. (2010). Issues in SME development in Ghana and South Africa. *International research journal of finance and economics, 39*(6), 215-228.

Adam, A. M. (2020). Sample size determination in survey research. *Journal of Scientific Research & Reports, 26*(5), 90–97.

Adam, A. M., Frimpong, S., & Boadu, M. O. (2017). Financial literacy and financial planning: Implication for FW of retirees. *Business and Economic Horizons, 13*(2), 224–236. https://doi.org/10.15208/beh.2017.17

Adu-Asare, K. (2018). *Cocoa farming business, financial literacy and social welfare of farmers in Brong-Ahafo region of Ghana (Doctoral dissertation).* University of Cape Coast.

Agyei, S. K., Adam, A. M., & Agyemang, O. S. (2019). Financial literacy, cultural dominance, and financial Well-being of SME owners in Ghana. *Poverty & Public Policy, 11*(3), 222–237.

Ahmad, M., & Shah, S. Z. A. (2020). Overconfidence heuristic-driven bias in investment decision-making and performance: Mediating effects of risk perception and moderating effects of financial literacy. *Journal of Economic and Administrative Sciences, 31*(2), 127–141.

Alauddin, M., & Nghiemb, H. S. (2010). Do instructional attributes pose multicollinearity problems? An empirical exploration. *Economic Analysis and Policy, 40*(3), 351–361.

Alkhawaja, S. O., & Albaity, M. (2022). Retirement saving behavior: evidence from UAE. *Journal of Islamic Marketing, 13*(2), 265–286.

Amenuku, M. A. (2018). *Financial literacy, microfinance, and performance of artisanal fishermen in Elmina fishing community (Doctoral dissertation).* University of Cape Coast.

Asthana, A. (2020). Multicollinearity. Lucknow. Retrieved from https://www.lkouniv.ac.in/site/writereaddata/siteContent/202003271457478667akash_Multicolliearity.pdf

Bongomin, G. O. C., Ntayi, J. M., Munene, J. C., & Malinga, C. A. (2017). The relationship between access to finance and growth of SMEs in developing economies: Financial literacy as a moderator. *Review of International Business and strategy, 15*(2), 177–196.

Fornell, C., & Bookstein, F. L. (2018). Two structural equation models: LISREL and PLS applied to consumer exit-voice theory. *Journal of Marketing Research, 19*(4), 440–452.

Fornell, C., & Larcker, D. F. (1981). Evaluating structural equation models with unobservable variables and measurement error. *Journal of Marketing Research, 18*(1), 39–50.

Foroudi, P., Cuomo, M. T., Foroudi, M. M., Katsikeas, C. S., & Gupta, S. (2019). "Linking identity and heritage with image and a reputation for competition", *Journal of Business Research, 113* (May 2020), pp. 317–325.

Friedman, M. (1957). Introduction to "a theory of the consumption function". In *A theory of the consumption function* (pp. 1–6). Princeton University Press.

Ghana Statistical Service. (2015). 2015 Labour force report. Accessed December 10, 2019, from http://www2.statsghana.gov.gh/docfiles/publications/Labour_Force/LFS%20REPORT_fianl_21-3-17.pdf

Gomez, R. S., Perez, J. G., Martín, M. D. M. L., & García, C. G. (2016). Collinearity diagnostic applied in ridge estimation through the variance in financial literacy action factor. *Journal of Applied Statistics, 43*(10), 1831–1849.

Hair, J. F., Black, W. C., Babin, B. J., & Anderson, R. E. (2010). *Multivariate data analysis: A global perspective* (7th ed.). Pearson Education Inc.

Hair, J. F., Ringle, C. M., & Sarstedt, M. (2014). PLS-SEM: Indeed, a silver bullet. *Journal of Marketing Theory and Practice, 19*(2), 139–152.

Hair, J. F., Sarstedt, M., Matthews, L. M., & Ringle, C. M. (2016). Identifying and treating unobserved heterogeneity with FIMIX-PLS: Part I – Method. *European Business Review, 28*(1), 63–76.

Hart, K. (1973). Informal Income Opportunities and Urban Employment in Ghana. *The Journal of Modern African Studies 11*(1), pp. 61–89

Hayat, A., & Anwar, M. (2016). Impact of behavioral biases on investment decision; moderating role of financial literacy. Moderating Role of Financial Literacy (September 23, 2016).

Hormeku, T. (1998). The transformation and development of the informal sector and the role of trade unions. In Proceedings of the OATUU/ILO/ETUF Seminar on "Trade Unions and the Informal Sector", Cairo, Egypt (pp. 4-6).

Kenton, W. (2020). Life-cycle hypothesis (LCH). https://www.investopedia.com/terms/l/life-cycle-hypothesis.asp

Kim, S. (2019), "The process model of corporate social responsibility (CSR) communication: CSR communication and its relationship with consumers' CSR knowledge, trust, and corporate reputation perception", *Journal of Business Ethics, 154*(4), pp. 1143–1159.

Kline, R. B. (2011). Convergence of structural equation modeling and multilevel modeling. In *The SAGE handbook of innovation in social research methods* (pp. 562–589). SAGE Publications Ltd.

Larisa, E. L., Njo, A., & Wijaya, S. (2020). Female workers' readiness for retirement planning: An evidence from Indonesia. *Journal of Review of Behavioral Finance, 13*(5), 566–583. https://www.emerald.com/insight/1940-5979.htm

Lusardi, A. (2008). Household saving behavior: The role of financial literacy, information, and financial education programs (No. W13824), National Bureau of Economic Research, Cambridge.

Mihalcova, B., Csikosova, A., & Antosova, M. (2014). Financial literacy–the urgent need today. *Procedia-Social and Behavioral Sciences, 109*, 317–321.

Mischel, W., & Shoda, Y. (1995). A cognitive-affective system theory of personality: Reconceptualizing situations, dispositions, dynamics, and invariance in personality structure. *Psychological Review, 102*(2), 246–268.

Modigliani, F., & Brumberg, R. (1954). Utility analysis and the consumption function: An interpretation of cross-section data. *Franco Modigliani, 1*(1), 388–436.

Mutlu, Ü., & Özer, G. (2021). The moderator effect of financial literacy on the relationship between locus of control and financial behaviour. *Kybernetes*.

Netemeyer, R. G., Warmath, D., Fernandes, D., & Lynch, J. G., Jr. (2018). How am I doing? Perceived FW, its potential antecedents, and its relation to overall Well-being. *Journal of Consumer Research, 45*(1), 68–89.

Ofori, E. (2021). FP for retirement of self-employed workers in the Ghanaian economy. *International Journal of Social Economics, 48*(6), 811–825.

Omair, A. (2014). Sample size estimation and sampling techniques for selecting a representative sample. *Journal of Health Specialties, 2*(4), 142.

Oquaye, M., Owusu, G. M. Y., & Bokpin, G. A. (2020). The antecedents and consequence of FW: A survey of parliamentarians in Ghana. *Review of Behavioral Finance, 4*(2), 120–141.

Pett, M. A., Lackey, N. R., & Sullivan, J. J. (2003). *Making sense of factor analysis: The use of factor analysis for instrument*. Sage Publications Inc..

Remund, D. L. (2010). Financial literacy explicated: The case for a clearer definition in an increasingly complex economy. *The Journal of Consumer Affairs, 44*(2), 276–295.

Riitsalu, L., & Murakas, R. (2019). Subjective financial knowledge, prudent behaviour and income: The predictors of FW in Estonia. *International Journal of Bank Marketing, 37*(4), 934–950.

Ringle, C. M., Wende, S., & Becker, J. M. (2015). SmartPLS 3. Boenningstedt: SmartPLS GmbH. Retrieved from http://www.smartpls.com

Ryan, R. M., & Deci, E. L. (2000). Intrinsic and extrinsic motivations: Classic definitions and new directions. *Contemporary Educational Psychology, 25*(1), 54–67.

Sabir, S. A., Mohammad, H. B., & Shahar, H. B. K. (2019). The role of overconfidence and past investment experience in herding behaviour with a moderating effect of financial literacy: evidence from Pakistan stock exchange. *Asian Economic and Financial Review, 9*(4), 480–490.

Safari, K., Njoka, C., & Munkwa, M. G. (2021). Financial literacy and personal retirement planning: A socioeconomic approach. *Journal of Business and Socio-economic Development, 1*(2), 121–134.

Sarpong-Kumankoma, E. (2021). Financial literacy and retirement planning in Ghana. *Journal of Review of Behavioral Finance, 15*(1), 103–118. https://www.emerald.com/insight/1940-5979.htm

Saunders, M., Lewis, P., & Thornhill, A. (2007). *Research methods for business students* (4th ed.). Prentice Hall Singh.

Selvadurai, V., Kenayathulla, H. B., & Siraj, S. (2018). Financial literacy education and retirement planning in Malaysia. *MOJEM: Malaysian Online Journal of Educational Management, 6*(2), 41–66.

Shams, K. (2016). Developments in the measurement of subjective Well-being and poverty: An economic perspective. *Journal of Happiness Studies, 17*(6), 2213–2236.

Smith, S. M. (2013). Determining sample size. *Qualitative Health Research, 10*(1), 1–7.

Spuhlera, B. K., & Dew, J. (2019). Sound financial management and happiness: Economic pressure and relationship satisfaction as mediators. *Journal of Financial Counseling and Planning, 30*(2), 157–174.

Taft, M. K., Hosein, Z. Z., Mehrizi, S. M. T., & Roshan, A. (2013). The relation between financial literacy, financial wellbeing and financial concerns. *International Journal of Business and Management, 8*(11), 63–78.

Taherdoost, H. (2016, April 10). Sampling methods in research methodology; how to choose a sampling technique for research. *How to choose a sampling technique for research.*

Teo, T. S. H., Srivastava, S. C., & Jiang, L. (2008). Trust and electronic government success: An empirical study. *Journal of Management Information Systems, 25*(3), 99–132.

Zhao, X., Lynch, J. G., & Chen, Q. (2010). Reconsidering Baron and Kenny: Myths and truths about mediation analysis. *Journal of Consumer Research, 37*(2), 197–206.

The Impact of Multilingual Tutorials on Second-Year Auditing Students' Participation and Engagement

Munyadziwa Nevhutanda and Melinda Dube

Abstract English is commonly used in academic settings despite being a secondary language for a considerable portion of the student population. Recognising the critical role that language plays in shaping educational experiences in the South African constitution and related legislative tools provides a supportive framework for multilingual education. In support of the framework Auditing and Internal controls lecturers developed multilingual glossaries which were translated into the majority of the South African official languages and also introduced tutorial classes that were conducted in IsiZulu and Sepedi. Therefore, the purpose of this paper is to determine whether these tutorials conducted in indigenous languages for second-year students in auditing had an impact on their level of participation and engagement in the tutorial classes. The study will follow a mixed methodology approach to evaluate the participation and engagement levels of students who attended the multilingual tutorials. Qualitative data will be collected through focus group discussions, which will explore students' experiences and attitude towards attending multilingual tutorials and using the glossaries. Quantitative data would be collected through google forms, which will include questions about students' engagement levels and understanding of Auditing concepts. This will provide numerical data to complement the qualitative insights, obtained from the focus group discussion. The findings from this study will assist universities in recognising the necessity of using translanguaging or code-switching to breach the gap caused by monolingual use of English.

Keywords Class participation · Engagement · Multilingual · Tutorials · Translanguaging

---

M. Nevhutanda (✉) · M. Dube
University of Johannesburg, Johannesburg, South Africa
e-mail: mnevhutanda@uj.ac.za; mdube@unitec.ac.nz

T. Moloi (ed.), *Impacting Society Positively Through Technology in Accounting and Business Processes*, Springer Proceedings in Business and Economics,
https://doi.org/10.1007/978-3-031-84885-8_27

Introduction (Project Description)

Language diversity is a major challenge in the field of higher education, especially in nations where English is the primary language of instruction but is not the first language of many students. South Africa epitomises this dynamic, where English is commonly used in academic settings despite being a secondary language for a considerable portion of the student population. Recognising the critical role that language plays in shaping educational experiences in the South African constitution and related legislative tools provides a supportive framework for multilingual education. South Africa is a country with a diverse population represented by 11 official languages. Section 6 (4) of the Republic of South Africa's Constitution (1996) confers parity of esteem to all the country's official languages. The Constitution further mandates the Pan South African Language Board to promote and create conditions for the development of all official languages of the Republic (Schultz, 2022). The policy framework adapted from the constitution is also meant to highlight the role of higher education in creating and promoting conditions for the development of historically marginalised official South African languages including the Khoi, San, and the South African Sign Language.

In 2020 the Department of Higher Education and Training published a language policy framework for public higher education institutions. These policies are intended to develop and strengthen indigenous languages as languages of scholarship, teaching, and learning and communication in South African universities. There had been a few policies and initiatives developed from Language policy from Higher education in 2002, development of African Languages in Higher Education (MAPALHE) established in 2012, which resulted in the "Report on the Use of African Languages as Mediums of Instruction in Higher Education" (2015). Due to little progress made in exploring African languages in facilitating success in higher education institutions, the Department of Higher Education and Training published a language policy framework for public higher education institutions.

Clause 29 of the Language policy framework for Public Higher Education and Institution states that "Language of Learning and Teaching (LOLT): Recognising the de facto status of English as the language of learning and teaching across South African higher education institutions, this policy calls upon universities to adopt a flexible approach in the implementation of English as the language of learning and teaching. Necessary support must be provided to students for whom English is not their first language or mother tongue, in order to ensure academic success". Language Policy Framework for Public Higher Education Institutions 2020. The multilingual tutorial seeks to achieve this objective and the background of this study follows below, which provides the context and rationale of this research.

Background of the Study

The composition of the student body in higher education has changed with a greater proportion of students from historically marginalised communities enrolled. For many years, the mission of the University of Johannesburg (UJ) has been to give formerly underprivileged students—mostly those from quintile 1 to 3 schools—access to higher education. English is not the first language of these UJ students from these backgrounds; however, the modules are taught and assessed in English.

This study will focus on the Diploma accounting students in UJ. The programme consists of four main modules of the accounting discipline and they are Cost and Financial Management, Taxation, Financial Accounting, and Auditing. The other three modules except auditing primarily teach theories that are based on numbers. In these three modules calculations are used in practice questions, tutorials, and evaluations to explain the theories taught. Additionally, there is some overlap in the terminology and language utilised in these modules. However, Auditing is regarded as the opposite of the other three modules because the theories taught are predominantly written and include very minimal numbers. As a result, the practical questions, tutorials, and assessments are written in English and need that student be familiar with the module's language.

To identify languages suitable to conduct the study, the authors needed to understand the distribution of the 11 official languages in South Africa. According to the BusinessTech (2023) Stats SA in the 2022 census released that isiZulu is the highest spoken language in households at 24.4%, followed by isiXhosa at 16.3%. Collectively these two languages fall under the Nguni category, i.e. they are deemed to be linguistically and culturally correlated. After Afrikaans, the fourth most spoken language in a household in South Africa is Sepedi sa Leboa at 10%. Hence IsiZulu and Sepedi sa Leboa were utilised to advance the development of subject-field multilingual glossaries which are currently for previously marginalised indigenous South African official languages. This falls squarely within the domain of decolonising education.

In South Africa's educational system, English is commonly used as the major language of instruction. This presents a considerable barrier for pupils for whom English is a second language and this is highlighted in the background of this study. Given the complexity of auditing concepts and the importance of active participation and engagement in the learning process, it becomes imperative to explore innovative approaches that can address language barriers and enhance students' comprehension and involvement. This theory is supported by the literature review provided below, which offers information on how linguistic diversity affects academic performance and how well multilingual teaching methods work to create inclusive learning environments.

Literature Review

A study by Chetty (2014) explored how students felt about the idea of introducing IsiZulu as a language of instruction (to improve throughput and increase the number of graduates) and developing policies that allow for this implementation. A survey was conducted, and responses showed mixed feelings surrounding teaching of physics in IsiZulu. Most participants felt that teaching physics or science in general in IsiZulu should be introduced in primary schools and not at university level (Chetty, 2014). Professor Kioko (2015) shares the same sentiments, indicating that using the mother tongue in early education leads to a better understanding of the curriculum content and to a more positive attitude towards school.

This is in line with Section 36 of the Language Policy Framework for Public Higher Education Institutions, which states that the Department, in partnership with relevant government departments, in particular, the Department of Basic Education, should rally support for meaningful multilingual education embracing all indigenous African languages, starting from the school level. Starting learners at school level may be beneficial in developing their basic literacy skills.

Hungwe (2019) study attests to this as the researcher established that due to student's lack of basic literacy skills such as reading with understanding, they assisted students by using paraphrasing strategy together with translingual approach to instruct students on how to read and comprehend text (Hungwe, 2019). Hungwe explored first-year students and encouraged group collaboration in order to enhance deeper comprehension of text using a translingual approach (use of any language students are comfortable using). The results show that when students are afforded the opportunity to freely utilise their mother tongue or any other language at their disposal, they are able to comprehend texts.

According to Bhorat et al. (2012) and Whitelaw et al. (2019) a student who has English as their first language, has a higher chance of completing tertiary education successfully; however, only 10% of students at tertiary institutions in South Africa speak English at home. Students who cannot express themselves due to a lack of initiatives, such as translanguaging, may hinder their participation in the classroom. Due to feeling silenced, this may ultimately impact their academic outcomes (Whitelaw et al., 2019).

Omidire and Ayob (2022) support this view; however, they raised certain enablers and constraints of using learners' home languages as a support strategy to facilitate learning and teaching within multilingual classrooms. They further defined translanguaging as a teaching strategy that can be used at all levels of a person's development, though their study mainly addressed primary school learners. In its simplest sense, multilingualism is defined as a situation where there are many languages operating in a country (Ndiribe & Aboh, 2020). Some of the limitations cited by Omidire and Ayob (2022) include a lack of resources (such as training of teachers, classroom furniture due to overcrowding and study materials). The teacher:learner ratio was also a concern in addition to time constraints—not enough time to teach and translate relevant material—insufficient training, and lack of confidence of teachers to facilitate classes.

In the context of auditing, where English is the dominant language, there is a need to address language barriers for students who are not first-language English speakers. Developing subject-specific multilingual glossaries and adopting trans-languaging strategies such as multilingual tutorials could help bridge this gap, making auditing concepts more accessible to second or third English language speaking students, thereby enhancing their chances of engagement and participation within the tutorial.

Despite the growing recognition of the importance of language diversity in educational settings, there remains a noticeable gap in the literature regarding the specific impact of multilingual tutorials on the participation and engagement of auditing students. While existing research offers valuable insights into the broader implications of multilingual education and instructional strategies across various disciplines, there is a scarcity of studies that focus specifically on auditing education. Fields for which multilingual glossaries have been developed in South Africa include Economics, Statistics, Science, Law, and Psychology. Thus, this study is critical, at least in a South African context given concerns with student participation in class and comprehension of auditing concepts, and ultimately impacting throughput.

Research Objectives

In South Africa, English serves as the primary language of instruction, yet for the majority of students, it functions as a second language, presenting a linguistic challenge that influences their educational experience. In trying address, the challenges encountered by students for whom English is a second language, Auditing and Internal controls lecturers developed multilingual glossaries translated into the majority of the South African official languages and also introduced tutorial classes that were conducted in IsiZulu and Sepedi. To understand the impact that the multilingual tutorial had on the students, this study's main objective is to assess and analyse the influence of multilingual tutorials on the levels of participation and engagement among second-year auditing students, with the aim of understanding how incorporating multilingual tutorial sessions positively impacted the learning experience in the field of auditing. To achieve the main objective the following sub-objectives will be explored:

- Evaluating the effectiveness of multilingual tutorials in promoting increased participation and engagement among second-year auditing students.
- Investigating the potential impact of multilingual tutorials on students' understanding of auditing concepts.

The insights provided in this study will assist in developing effective instructional strategies that can enhance the learning experience for students in the field of auditing. Additionally, the study seeks to identify any potential advantages or challenges associated with the use of multilingual tutorials in this academic context, contributing valuable information to educational practices and curriculum development.

Methodology

This section presents the research methodology that was followed in this study. The study followed a mixed methodology approach to evaluate the participation and engagement levels of students who attended the multilingual tutorials. According to Shorten and Smith (2017), a research methodology known as "mixed methods" allows scientists to gather and examine both quantitative and qualitative data for a single study and it helps in understanding the research problem.

Qualitative research collects the views, behaviours, and experiences of people (Creswell & Poth 2018). Fundamental to qualitative research are open-ended inquiries like "how" and "why", the responses to which are difficult to quantify (Tenny et al., 2022). Therefore, this study collected qualitative data through interviews, which explored students' experiences and attitude towards attending multilingual tutorials and using glossaries. The interviews were designed in a way that both students and tutors participated in focus group discussions. To guarantee that the questions asked at each focus group are consistent, a set of interview questions were produced. According to Prasad and Garcia (2017), the focus group discussion is beneficial especially if the researcher wants to explain an issue at a deeper level than a questionnaire method would.

A quantitative research approach focuses on measuring and analysing variables to produce findings (Creswell & Poth 2018). In order to respond to inquiries about who, how much, what, where, when, how many, and how, it entails the use and analysis of numerical data using particular statistical approaches (Apuke, 2017). Quantitative data can include numerical measurements, counts, or ratings obtained through structured methods such as surveys, experiments, or observations. Quantitative data were also collected through multiple questionnaires, which were distributed to students throughout the project via google forms. The questionnaires included questions about students' engagement levels and their perception of the effectiveness of the multilingual tutorials and glossaries, and these were scaled. Following each tutorial session, students were asked to fill out a questionnaire to reflect on the tutorial and to indicate if there were any improvements in terms of their engagement in class and learning process.

Coding and analysis of the focus group discussion was done using the computer-aided software, Atlas.ti. Atlas.ti is a robust tool for qualitative data analysis, offering extensive capabilities for handling various types of data such as text, audio, and visual content. Researchers can utilise its features for coding and annotating data, enabling them to analyse and interpret their findings effectively (Smit, 2002). Due to the nature of the data collected the researchers specifically utilised sentiments analysis within Atlas.ti. The software automatically processed the transcribed data into quantitative sentiment scores as either positive or negative. The quantitative and qualitative sentiment analysis are used complementarily, ideally the qualitative sentiment analysis provides context by its nature, thereby deepening understanding.

Population

The population of this study refers to the entire group consisting of 497 students registered for AIC22A2 in 2023. All registered students were asked to fill out the project questionnaire, even if they didn't take part in the multilingual tutorials. The objective of this questionnaire was to gather voluntary data, such as demographics and the degree of student participation and glossary usage. Participants were also invited to participate in the multilingual tutorials that were offered in isiZulu and Sepedi. The multilingual tutorials were attended on a voluntary basis, this was dependent on the participant' understanding of those specific languages.

Sample

A non-probability sample was used for the purpose of this study because the aim was to gain insights, generate hypotheses, and understand in depth how the students who participated in the multilingual tutorial benefited. There were eight focus groups for the undergraduate students registered for AIC22A2. Each of the focus group interviews was audio recorded and transcribed and both maintained safely. The student focus groups had a mix of isiZulu and Sepedi speaking students within the group. The interviews outlined the students' experiences of using the glossaries and engaging with the auditing concepts using their preferred languages during the multilingual tutorials. A tutor focus group was also conducted, and it outlined the tutor's experience in facilitating tutorials in either of the two languages, highlighting how students were engaging with the material as well as participating in the tutorial class.

Ethical Considerations

Ethical principles and policies were applied throughout this study. Participants in this study were fully informed about the study's purpose and procedures. Informed consent was obtained from all participants. Participation was entirely voluntary, and participants data are kept anonymised. The study received the ethical clearance approval from the University of Johannesburg's School of Accounting: Ethical clearance Code is SAREC2020070201.

Results

Google Form Results

Google Forms were used to collect data from students who took part in the multilingual sessions. Analysing the data from Google Forms filled out by students who took part in the multilingual tutorials offered important insights into how well this teaching strategy worked. By systematically examining the responses collected through the survey tool, researchers could quantitatively assess various aspects of the students' experiences, including their perceived levels of understanding of auditing concepts, satisfaction with the multilingual tutorial format, and self-reported participation rates during tutorial sessions. Additionally, the data collected via Google Forms could facilitate the identification of patterns and trends in students' feedback, allowing for a comprehensive evaluation of the impact of multilingual tutorials on the learning outcomes and experiences of second-year auditing students.

The Google Forms were created as they provide a flexible and efficient means of gathering data for research. The aim was to obtain understanding of the student's background and how they found multilingual tutorial. Table 1 column one sets out the questions that were created by the researchers and it used to understand the students. Column two sets the type of test if it was a "yes" or "no" or an open-ended question. Lastly, column three indicates the paragraph numbers where the findings and recommended requirements are further discussed.

The reseach results from the responses submitted by the students about the multilingual tutorials are explained in the following paragraphs.

Table 1 Google form feedback on multilingual tutorial—students' response

Google form question	Type of answer expected	Paragraph
Is this the first year of registration for AIC2A?	Yes or no	6.1.1
Select your home language	Either of the 11 official languages	6.1.2
The multilingual tutorial sessions are essential/important for understanding auditing concepts:	1 = Strongly disagree 2 = Disagree 3 = Neither agree nor disagree 4 = Agree 5 = Strongly agree	6.1.3
In your own words, describe your overall experience with the option to attend multilingual tutorials and its impact on your learning.	Open-ended answer	6.1.4
Would you support/oppose multilingual tutorials being made compulsory for all students or for students at risk of not passing auditing?	1 = Strongly oppose 2 = Somewhat oppose 3 = Somewhat favour 4 = Favour 4 = Strongly favour	6.1.5

Research results on Google Forms: Students responses

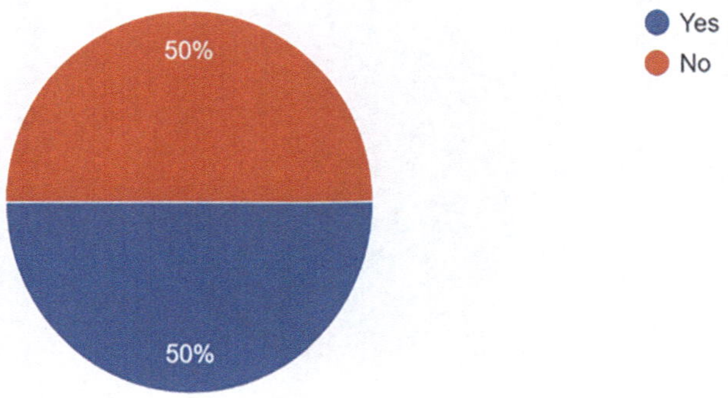

Graph 1 First year of registration for AIC2A

First Year of Registration for AIC2A

Determining whether students who attended the multilingual tutorial were first-timers in auditing is crucial for identifying whether students who are not newcomers to auditing provide a baseline understanding of their prior knowledge and experience with the module. This information helps contextualise their responses to the tutorial and subsequent assessments, allowing researchers to discern the impact of multilingual tutorials on both first-timer and the students repeating the module.

The graph below sets out the percentage of first-timers who registered for Auditing 2 and those that were repeating the module (Graph 1).

The results show that 50% of the students were first-timers and the other 50% were repeating the module. This information assisted the researcher in interpreting the following responses provided by the students because for first-timer students, foundational concepts needed to be emphasised.

Home Language Spoken by the Students

Understanding the home language of students who attended the multilingual tutorial is of paramount importance as the tutorials were offered only in IsiZulu and sePedi (Northern Sotho). Students' home language proficiency can significantly impact their comprehension and participation in tutorial activities.

The graph below sets out the home languages spoken by the students who attended the multilingual tutorial.

In Graph 2 the results indicate that 50% of the students who attended spoke Northern Sotho, while the other 50% is divided equally into isiZulu and Southern Sotho. This is an indication that 75% of students who participated in the multilingual tutorials and completed the Google Form were from the Sepedi group. In

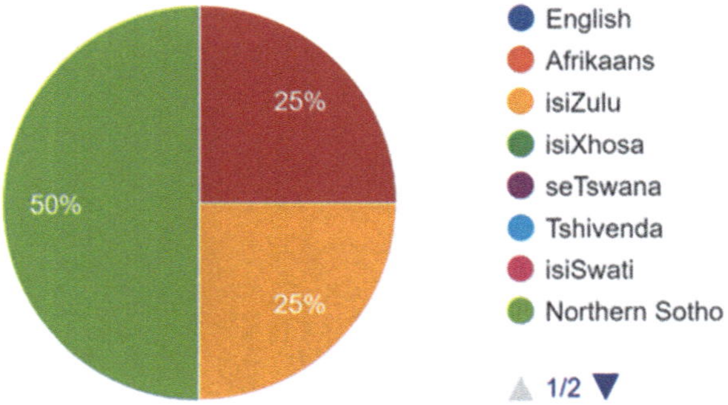

Graph 2 Home language

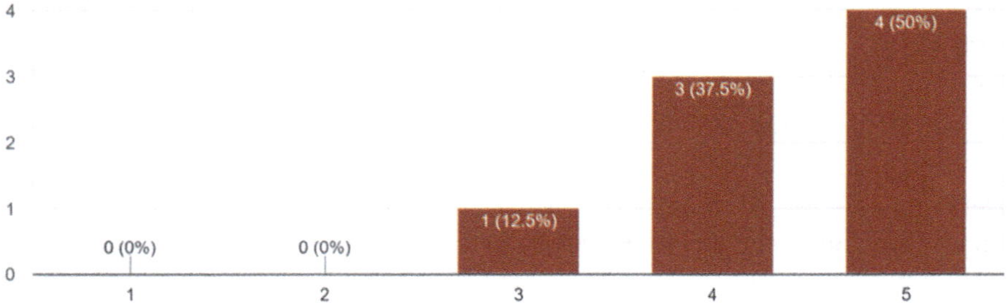

Graph 3 Understanding auditing concepts

understanding and acknowledging students' linguistic diversity, tutors could create an inclusive and supportive learning environment.

The Multilingual Tutorial Sessions Are Important for Understanding Auditing Concepts

Gauging from students whether the multilingual tutorial sessions were important for understanding auditing concepts is crucial because students' perspectives provide valuable insights into the effectiveness of the multilingual tutorial sessions in facilitating their understanding of auditing concepts. By soliciting feedback, we could identify areas of strength and areas needing improvement in the tutorial content, format, and delivery, allowing for continuous refinement of the tutorials to better meet students' learning needs.

Below is the graph that represents the results obtained from the Google Forms on the importance of multilingual tutorials in understanding auditing concepts (Graph 3).

The graph indicates that a majority of the students which is 50% believe that attending the multilingual tutorials helped in understanding the auditing concepts.

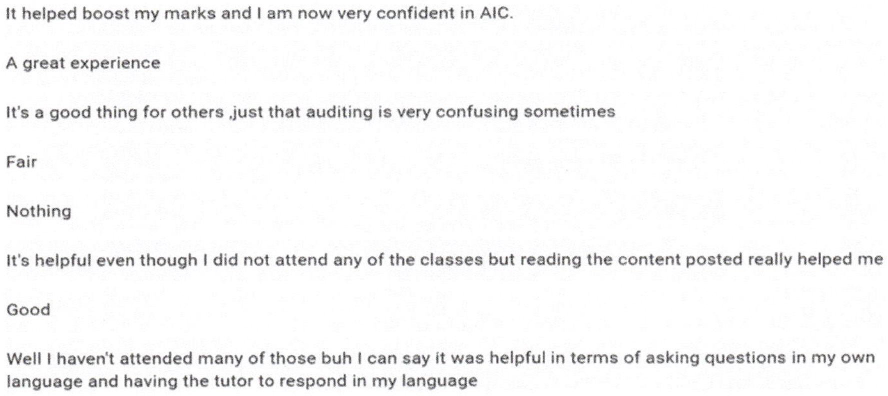
It helped boost my marks and I am now very confident in AIC.

A great experience

It's a good thing for others ,just that auditing is very confusing sometimes

Fair

Nothing

It's helpful even though I did not attend any of the classes but reading the content posted really helped me

Good

Well I haven't attended many of those buh I can say it was helpful in terms of asking questions in my own language and having the tutor to respond in my language

Diagram 1 Positive and negative sentiments of students attending multilingual tutorials. *Source: ATLAS.ti output*

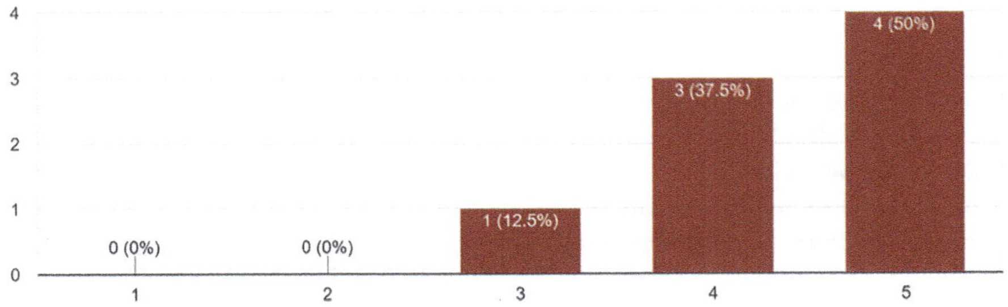

Graph 4 Student's overall experience

Overall Experience of Attending the Multilingual Tutorial

Rich qualitative data that transcend numerical evaluations and predetermined survey responses are provided by students using their own words. It was therefore important to allow students to articulate their experiences and emotions to assist the researchers to gain deeper insights into the distinctions of their learning experiences and the factors that influenced their engagement and satisfaction. The student's emotions and sentiments are further displayed in Diagram 1.

Below is a snippet of the opinions that the students shared on attending the multilingual tutorials (Graph 4).

Some students share the sentiments that the multilingual tutorials were good and helpful in boosting their Auditing marks and confidence in participating in class. Other students felt that the initiative was helpful for others but auditing in general for them is confusing. While others felt that even though they did not manage to attend the classes, having the content in their own language was very helpful.

Graph 5 Sentiments of students attending Multilingual tutorials

Making Multilingual Tutorials Compulsory

Determining the attitudes and preferences of students towards mandatory multilingual tutorials aids in determining the degree of acceptability and buy-in. Positive feedback will indicate that students recognise the value and benefits of multilingual tutorials for their learning experience, increasing the likelihood of active participation and engagement.

The below graph indicates how students felt about making the multilingual tutorial compulsory (Graph 5).

The graph indicates that the students favour making the multilingual tutorials compulsory and this could be an indication that the tutorials had an influence in enhancing students' comprehension, engagement, and academic performance.

Through rigorous analysis of the information gathered from these forms, researchers gained an understanding of the strengths and limitations of the multilingual instructional approach, ultimately informing recommendations for optimising teaching practices and enhancing the overall educational experience in auditing education. Below is the information that was obtained utilising the focus group interviews and the information was analysed using Atlas.ti.

Sentiment Analysis

According to Wankhade et al. (2022), sentiment analysis is significant as it helps companies or organisations to understand their consumers' sentiment towards their brand. The analysis is a form of strategy that is used to enable companies or organisations to examine data about how their customer base feels about a given product or service. The data range from movie review, teaching review, product review, hotel review, and many more (Aung & Myo, 2017). Taboada (2016) states that the importance of sentiment analysis is first to determine whether a text is subjective or not and, if subjective, whether it expresses a positive or negative view.

This section focuses on student satisfaction analysis through sentiment analysis. The students shared their experience in the multilingual tutorial classes and communicated their opinion and attitude through a focus group discussion. The transcribed data were kept in two separate documents, one being the Sepedi discussion and the other IsiZulu discussion. This was crucial as the researchers wanted to get the opinion of both groups. This provided the researchers with crucial insight into whether the students were satisfied and, if necessary, how the programme can improve.

The Sankey diagram below shows the different sentiments of the students who attended the Sepedi tutorial versus the students who attended the IsiZulu classes.

The Sankey diagram above depicts the opinions of students who attended the Sepedi class versus the students who attended the IsiZulu class. Each flow-path was colour coded to show and compare the distribution between the two categories. The green nodes symbolise the positive sentiments, whilst the red symbolise the negative opinion. The width of each line and the flow-path that stems from it are determined by the proportional fraction of the category total. The positive sentiments with a total of 8 quotations have a smaller width compared to the negative sentiments with 14 quotations. The positive category has a thicker connection to Sepedi views and a narrow connection to IsiZulu. This visual indicates that there are more positive feedbacks from the Sepedi group as opposed to IsiZulu group. The same applies with the negative category, more students responded negatively in the IsiZulu group than the Sepedi group. The numbers related to this diagram can be clearly seen in Table 2 below.

The table above quantifies the number of quotations drawn from Atlas that represents students' opinion about the multilingual tutorials, with 75% showing a more positive emotion towards Sepedi classes and 25% showing positive feedback from the IsiZulu class. The negative sentiments are much less for Sepedi class, at 21% and 79% for IsiZulu class. In order to further understand the quantitative data, Atlas.ti generated quotations are presented in Tables 3 and 4 below.

Table 3 above gives a clear view of why the Sepedi group had more students with a positive feeling towards the multilingual tutorial. The common feeling from most

Table 2 Quantified sentiments of students attending multilingual tutorials

	Sepedi_ view Gr = 24 Absolute	Row-relative	IsiZulu_ view Gr = 19 Absolute	Row-relative	Totals Absolute	Row-relative
• Sentiment: Sentiments: Negative Gr = 14	3	21%	11	79%	14	100%
• Sentiment: Sentiments: Positive Gr = 8	6	75%	2	25%	8	100%
Totals	9	41%	13	59%	22	100%

Source: ATLAS.ti output

Table 3 Focus group feedback Sepedi group

Feedback no	Qualitative comment	Sentiments
1	The only issue I have is the time. 45 min for me, we are rushing to finish, it's not enough time.	Negative
2	Most of them are just like they think it is a waste of time. So now everything they don't take it serious, OK, whatever that we learn during the class. Like, last tutorial we did an engagement letter Yes, I did not fully understand. I did understand certain things during the class, but after that session I was comfortable and then I say ohh its doable.	
3	Definitely the same way. So I would like to have both of them. Yeah do not have a preference. I don't prefer Sepedi over English or even English over Sepedi. They are equally beneficial.	
4	You were given an engagement letter with errors and they tell you fix it. You cannot tell the weaknesses in the letter. Right. But whenever it's translating my mother tongue, I tend to get focused and understand.	Positive
5	Personally because I feel comfortable in my Sepedi tutorials I will participate and my tutors are more like my age, my peers, we are a few years apart so I personally speak and engage in those tutorials.	
6	But for me tutorial it's more important and it's working. The information you receive in an English lecture or English tutorial is minimal, in the Sepedi tutorial it is more informative because even with examples given you can easily relate and you understand it more.	
7	I come to the tutorial always, always prepared, even if I don't understand, I'll attend and ask.	
8	I will nail it during the exam. So I think different. How we take our school work is different.	
9	Ohh for me I think for Sepedi it helps polish or clarifies like whatever that we did during English tutorial. So I think it's for Sepedi is important yes for English it's important for all students, it's compulsory. So for Sepedi yes, if I don't understand something that was discussed during English class, I can consult and get clarity in the Sepedi class.	

Source: ATLAS.ti output

students was that the tutorial brought clarity or improved their level of understanding of Auditing concepts that they previously struggled with. With that understanding it made it easier for students to engage. Students indicated that they felt more comfortable when engaging in their mother tongue, that in itself removed any timidness, which ultimately enhanced their learning experience. It is clear from the above table that any negative sentiments from the Sepedi group were related to the duration of the tutorial and the perception that students who did not attend considered the tutorial a waste of time. The negative opinion was not necessarily related to the delivery of the multilingual tutorial.

Table 4 above gives a clear view of why the IsiZulu group had more students with a negative feeling towards the multilingual tutorial. It is clear from that table that there was a mix of IsiZulu, Swati, and Xhosa speaking students attending the IsiZulu class. This made it difficult for the Swati and Xhosa speaking students to

Table 4 Focus group feedback IsiZulu group

Feedback no	Qualitative comment	Sentiments
1	So in my situation the class is in Zulu and I am Swati so when you say, what do you mean by that word in Zulu? You try to explain in English why I am misunderstanding and find it difficult because I am misunderstanding even the English that is being used to explain the term.	Negative
2	It will be good because when he arrives there, he speaks in Zulu. There is this one that I attended for sure it was 70% English and 30% Zulu. You can hear the person that he is used to English as he just defaults back to English when speaking and only speaks in Zulu here and there. And the Zulu is deep because I am used to Kasi Zulu, and when he speaks he puts the deep Zulu and you question what he is really trying to explain. You will also want him to explain in English because he also does not understand my Swati and I also do not understand his Zulu. And when you speak in English you confuse me more. If Xhosa's also got someone who spoke in their language they would understand fully and will be able to communicate so when I attend I will end up not engaging if I am not accommodated in my Swati. I will be difficult to participate because at the end of the day he won't hear me and I also won't hear him.	
3	And some of the words whether in Zulu and Swati they do not mean one and the same thing.	
4	It's something else. If I am sitting with a Xhosa, they will explain to me in their Xhosa and I would not understand and be more confused.	
5	OK for me now. I feel like this, that the Zulu they use in class is deep. And some of us grew up in townships and not necessarily back home in the village. So it is deep so if it can be average so we can fully understand. That would be great.	
6	The Sepedi guys were very active. And then in the Zulu group maybe because there is a mix of Swati's and Xhosa's that with the conversation you could hear something, but now to really engage with the others it's a challenge.	
7	If we are alone we going to speak Kasi, mixing all languages until you understand. I think you can just separate us in our different languages. So that we can speak in our own language, for example isiZulu, Swati and If we do not understand another Swati speaking student can explain. We are used to our language the other one can explain it better for me than the lecture or tutor could do so. And I would feel more comfortable if someone will ask if I heard what the lecture said.	Positive
8	What I can say is learning in Zulu makes a difference compared to when I attended the English because in Zulu there is parts where I understood and I felt comfortable and made it easy to talk. Which made a difference unlike attending the English tutorial and not even understand the example given. For me there has been a difference in some of the things in the Zulu tutorial because I could understand the examples made and made it easy for me to talk but here and there, there has been some language barrier challenges because Zulu we only learnt it here in Joburg through meeting other people, Otherwise we grew up only speaking and understanding Xhosa.	

Source: ATLAS.ti output

engage. Although some words may mean the same thing in these three dialects, the differences that are apparent created much confusion with the Swati and Xhosa speaking students. The results are by no means an indication that the multilingual tutorials are not working, it is a positive feedback that can assist in improving the initiative. This aspect was also addressed under limitations of the study.

Conclusion and Future Studies

The objective of the article was to examine the impact the multilingual tutorial had on student participation and engagement within the IsiZulu and Sepedi classes. Students had differing views, ranging from being taught in their mother tongue enhanced their participation due to feeling more comfortable and confident to engage, to it was hard to participate due to the level at which the class was delivered. Although the multilingual nature of the country is reflected in institutional policies, and more institutions are showing interest in implementing the use of indigenous language in their classroom, a lot of work and training is required. This is to ensure that the institutions meet the needs of students who may prefer to learn in their mother tongue.

The research was context specific. The focus was on second-year students in the accounting discipline. The study focused on the issue of students participating in class without reflecting on whether participation correlates to performance. Future studies can be conducted to explore whether students attending the multilingual tutorials perform better than students who solely rely on the monolingual tutorials.

Limitations

While the study holds promise for enhancing educational practices, it is crucial to acknowledge certain limitations. Even though the tutorial was open to all Auditing 2 students, the multilingual tutorials were only limited to those who could understand either isiZulu or Sepedi. Some students attended the multilingual tutorials, whilst other students interacted with the glossaries; however, not all students who attended or interacted with the glossaries completed the questionnaires or attended the focus group discussions. This was a pilot project, and the focus of the study was on second-year auditing students. Therefore, the study may have overlooked differences in their experiences and the needs of students at different stages of their academic journey.

References

Apuke, O. D. (2017). Quantitative research methods: A synopsis approach. *Arabian Journal of Business and Management Review (Kuwait Chapter), 6*, 40–47. https://doi.org/10.12816/0040336

Aung, K. Z., & Myo, N. N. (2017). Sentiment analysis of students' comment using lexicon-based approach. In *2017 IEEE/ACIS 16th International Conference on Computer and Information Science (ICIS), Wuhan, China, 2017* (pp. 149–154). https://doi.org/10.1109/ICIS.2017.7959985

Bhorat, H., Mayet, N., & Visser, M. (2012). Student graduation, labour market destinations and employment earnings. DPRU Working Paper 12/153. Cape Town: Development Policy Research Unit.

BusinessTechSA. (2023). These are the most spoken languages in South Africa. https://businesstech.co.za/news/lifestyle/724160/these-are-the-most-spoken-languages-in-south-africa/

Chetty, N. (2014). The first-year augmented programme in physics: A trend towards improved student performance. *South African Journal of Science, 110*(1/2), 9. Art. #2012-0096. https://doi.org/10.1590/sajs.2014/20120096

Constitution of the Republic of South Africa [South Africa]. (1996, December 10). https://www.justice.gov.za/legislation/constitution/SAConstitution-web-eng.pdf

Creswell, J. W., & Poth, C. N. (2018). *Qualitative inquiry and research design: Choosing among five approaches*. University of Michigan.

Hungwe, V. (2019). Using a translanguaging approach in teaching paraphrasing to enhance reading comprehension in first-year students. *Reading & Writing – Journal of the Reading Association of South Africa, 10*(1), a216. https://doi.org/10.4102/rw.v10i1.216

Kioko, A. (2015). Why schools should teach young learners in home language. https://www.britishcouncil.org/voices-magazine/why-schools-should-teach-young-learners-home-language

Ndiribe, M. O., & Aboh, S. C. (2020). Multilingualism and marginalisation: A Nigeria diversity approach. *International Journal of Multilingualism, 19*(1), 1–15. https://doi.org/10.1080/14790718.2020.1818752

Ngidi, S. A., & Mncwango, E. M. (2022). University students' perspectives on an English-only language policy in higher education. *The Journal for Transdisciplinary Research in Southern Africa, 18*(1), a1189. https://doi.org/10.4102/td.v18i1.1189

Omidire, F., & Ayob, S. (2022). The utilisation of translanguaging for learning and teaching in multilingual primary classrooms. *Multilingua – Journal of Cross-Cultural and Interlanguage Communication, 41*, 105–129. https://doi.org/10.1515/multi-2020-0072

Prasad, M., & Garcia, C. (2017). How to conduct a successful focus group discussion. https://humansofdata.atlan.com/2017/09/conduct-successful-focus-group-discussion/.

Schultz. (2022). The role of PanSALB in upholding multilingualism in SA's society. https://www.usaf.ac.za/the-role-of-pansalb-in-upholding-multilingualism-in-sas-society/

Shorten, A., & Smith, J. (2017). Mixed methods research: Expanding the evidence base. https://ebn.bmj.com/content/ebnurs/20/3/74.full.pdf

Smit, B. (2002). Atlas. ti for qualitative data analysis. *Perspective in Education, 20*(3), 65–76.

Taboada, M. (2016). Sentiment analysis: An overview from linguistics. *Annual Review of Linguistics, 2*, 325–347. https://doi.org/10.1146/annurev-linguistics-011415-040518

Tenny, S., Brannan, J. M., & Brannan, G. D. (2022). Qualitative study. https://www.ncbi.nlm.nih.gov/books/NBK470395/.

Wankhade, M., Rao, A. C. S., & Kulkarni, C. (2022). A survey on sentiment analysis methods, applications, and challenges. *Artificial Intelligence Review, 55*, 5731–5780. https://doi.org/10.1007/s10462-022-10144-1

Whitelaw, E., Dowling, T., & Filby, S. (2019). Leveraging language: Preliminary evidence from a language-based intervention at the University of Cape Town. *Critical studies in Teaching and Learning, 7*(2), 75–93. https://doi.org/10.14426/cristal.v7i2.223

The Role of Business Ethics in Local Economic Development in South Africa

Crossman Mayavo

Abstract The study explores the interplay between ethical business practices and the socio-economic life of the South African communities and how it can support sustainable development. This abstract provides a succinct overview of the research focus on the significant role that business ethics plays in fostering local economic development within the unique context of South Africa. This is a nation characterised by a diversity of people and shows the socio-economic disparities existing among its citizens and is struggling to achieve sustainable and inclusive economic growth. Against this background, the research delves into the pivotal role that business ethics plays to propel local economic development. Business ethics entails principles and practices that guide any organisation to conduct business affairs responsibly, transparently and committing to society's well-being. The study employs a qualitative method to investigate the challenges of employing ethics in local economic development and engaging with key stakeholders. The expected outcome of this study goes beyond academic insights to inform policymakers, communities, and business on strategies to enhance ethical fabric of local economic development. The study will contribute to the creation of a sustainable economic ecosystems that prioritise the well-being of stakeholders in the communities and advancing the goals of social and economic development. The findings of the study have the possibility of influencing both policy frameworks and corporate practices binding with more equitable and ethical environment in support of the local economic development. The study concluded that ethics have a role to play in ensuring the ethos of local economic development are maintained and achieved for the emancipation of the local citizens in South Africa.

Keywords Ethics · Local economic development · Stakeholders · Sustainable · Economic growth

---

C. Mayavo (✉)
University of Johannesburg, Johannesburg, South Africa
e-mail: cmayavo@uj.ac.za

T. Moloi (ed.), *Impacting Society Positively Through Technology in Accounting and Business Processes*, Springer Proceedings in Business and Economics,
https://doi.org/10.1007/978-3-031-84885-8_28

Introduction

The relationship between ethical business practices and socio-economic growth has become more and more important in the ever-changing world of global trade. This intersection is never more evident than in South Africa's many and complex communities. The ethical conduct of corporate activities is deeply ingrained in South Africa's socio-economic fabric, which is shaped by a convoluted historical past (Ayubi, 2023; Mayer, 2001). The present research endeavours to investigate the intricate relationship between ethical business practices and the socio-economic well-being of South African communities, specifically focusing on Local Economic Development (LED). The nation has begun a journey towards change and inclusivity after emerging from a past marked by colonialism and apartheid (Azi Ayubi, 2023). The role that corporations and businesses play in this journey is crucial, as they are not only profit-driven entities but also players in the larger societal structure and sustainable growth is being driven more and more by ethical business practices, which include social responsibility, accountability, and openness (Bowie, 2017; Dunfee, 1991; Evans, 1991). Communities that are diverse in terms of culture, tradition, and economic pursuits are at the centre of South Africa's socio-economic environment and these communities serve as the testing ground where the effects of corporate actions are most immediately felt. Businesses' decisions and deeds have an impact on the social and economic dynamics of communities anywhere they operate, from urban centres to rural lands (Freeman, 2000).

Furthermore, the notion of Local Economic Development (LED) emphasises how critical it is to support economic expansion and grassroots empowerment, which improves community well-being and advances inclusivity. This study essentially acts as a wake-up call for local municipalities and businesses to understand their position as change agents who can promote inclusive growth and the welfare of South African communities by embracing good ethical practice (Nyberg et al., 2022; Sen, 1993). These may significantly contribute to the social fabric of the country while also promoting economic growth by adopting moral values and putting the needs of all stakeholders first. The need for ethical business practices becomes clear as South Africa negotiates the complexity of the global economy of the twenty-first century. It is not just a moral duty; it is also a strategic necessity for creating a society that is more resilient and egalitarian (Bhorat, et al., 2018; McGranahan, & Turok, 2016; Ngcobo, 2020). In light of this, this study aims to clarify the complex relationship—with a focus on LEDs—between moral business conduct and the socio-economic well-being of South African communities. Through a critical analysis of the ways in which ethical behaviour affects local economies, livelihoods, and social cohesion, this study aims to highlight the transformative potential that results from matching corporate objectives with larger social objectives. The study intends to add to the conversation on sustainable development and ethical business practices in the context of South Africa through empirical analysis and qualitative insights. The next section will be focusing on the objectives of this study, literature review, methodology, results, discussion, implications, and finally conclusion and recommendations.

Objective

The study explores the interplay between ethical business practices and the socio-economic life of the South African communities and how it can support sustainable development.

Literature Review

What Is Business Ethics?

A key component of organisational behaviour is business ethics, which describes the moral standards and ideals that direct decisions and acts in the corporate world. It includes a set of guidelines and rules that control how companies behave morally, striking a balance between the pursuit of profit, social responsibility, and legal requirements (Ferrell et al., 2022; Skooglund & Nichols, 1998). Fundamentally, the goal of business ethics is to make sure that companies behave morally, considering how their decisions will affect different stakeholders such as workers, clients, shareholders, and the general public. Integrity, which includes being truthful, open, and consistent in interactions with both internal and external parties, is one of the cornerstones of business ethics. Integrity cultivates credibility and trust, all of which are necessary for establishing enduring bonds with stakeholders (Enderle, 2018).

Furthermore, justice and fairness are essential components of business ethics, guaranteeing that all people and organisations engaged in commercial dealings are treated equally. Corporate social responsibility (CSR), which is the voluntary consideration of the social and environmental effects of a firm's operations, is another important component of business ethics and this covers programmes aimed at reducing the impact on the environment, fostering community growth, and maintaining human rights norms along the entire supply chain (Bhorat, et al., 2018; Mayer, 2001; McGranahan, & Turok, 2016). A non-negotiable aspect of business ethics is compliance with legal requirements and industry standards, which guarantees that companies follow industry-specific norms and guidelines and operate within the confines of the law.

The Role of Economic Development in LED in South Africa

In South Africa, corporate ethics have a significant impact on stakeholder involvement, sustainable growth, and many facets of business operations. Applying moral principles to corporate operations is especially important in South Africa, a nation with a complicated socio-economic landscape marked by historical injustices and present difficulties (Azi Ayubi, 2023; Crane, & Matten, 2019). First, by encouraging confidence and trust among stakeholders, business ethics help to create a favourable business climate and businesses that uphold strong ethical standards might stand out in South Africa, where problems like corruption and unethical behaviour have historically been common (Ayubi, 2023; Evans, 1991; Freeman, 2000). This commitment strengthens their credibility and reputation, both of which are essential for drawing in capital, creating alliances, and keeping clients. Research conducted highlights the significance of moral leadership and corporate governance in restoring confidence in South Africa's business environment following the end of apartheid (Adegbite, et al., 2016; Brabeck, 1984). Local economic development is embedded in the National Framework for LED (NFLED), which was constituted in 1998 and is still in existence since then. Additionally, the white paper on LED stands as the guiding principle as LED is not part of the constitution of South Africa as explained by the NFLED, but all the structures are part of the municipalities.

In addition to legal compliance, corporate social responsibility (CSR) initiatives that address socio-economic concerns are also included in the field of business ethics in South Africa (Gerged et al., 2024). Initiatives for job creation, skill development programmes, and community development are all included in this. Companies that take part in CSR projects demonstrate their commitment to upholding moral principles and the welfare of stakeholders in addition to fostering regional economic growth (Crane, & Matten, 2019; Hamington, 2011). Furthermore, ethical supply chain management techniques are essential for South Africa's local economic growth. Small businesses and the community can benefit from supply chain practices that uphold labour standards, encourage local sourcing, and ensure equitable treatment of suppliers. Businesses that prioritise ethical sourcing practices help to foster the growth of local industries and promote inclusive economic growth (De Lange et al., 2019).

Additionally, diversity and inclusion in the workforce are critical for South Africa's sustainable economic development, and business ethics play a part in fostering these qualities. Accepting diversity tackles historical injustices, encourages social solidarity, and stimulates innovation and creativity (Adiguzel, 2021; De Lange et al., 2019). Fair employment practices, equal chances, and inclusive workplace rules are given first priority by ethical enterprises, which helps to create a more just society and a skilled labour force. Furthermore, in South Africa, business ethics play a crucial role in the development of local economies by impacting stakeholder interactions, company conduct, and sustainable growth. Businesses can help to create trust, promote socio-economic development, and rectify historical injustices by upholding strong ethical standard and adopting ethical standards is advantageous for companies as well as inclusive growth and the general well-being of South African society (Carrington et al., 2021; Crane & Matten, 2019; Evans, 1991). Additionally, the NFLED's major objectives were as they appear in the framework and only 5 of 10 objectives were provided:

1. To shift towards a more strategic approach to the development of local economies and overcome challenges and failures in respect of instances where municipalities themselves try to manage litany of non-viable projects or start-ups.
2. To support local economies in realising their optimal potentials and making local communities active participants in the economy of the country.
3. To elevate the importance and centrality of effectively functioning local economies in growing the national economy.
4. To wage the national fight against poverty more effectively through local level debates, strategies, and actions.
5. To improve the coordination of economic development planning and implementation across government and between government and non-governmental actors.

The Current State of LED in South Africa

Local Economic Development (LED) in South Africa is currently experiencing both ongoing development and chronic obstacles, and local community well-being, employment possibilities, and economic progress are the main objectives of LED programmes (Bhorat et al., 2018; Chikazunga & Mazibuko, 2018). The success of LED initiatives is impacted by structural limitations, socio-economic inequality, and the legacy of historical injustices, even though South Africa has achieved tremendous progress since the end of apartheid. The high rate of unemployment in South Africa, especially among young people and marginalised communities, is one of the main obstacles facing LED (Den Hond & Moser, 2023; McGranahan, & Turok, 2016; Ngcobo, 2020). Poverty and inequality are made worse by persistently high unemployment rates, which are the result of numerous government actions as well as private sector activities. This emphasises the need for more focused, inclusive, and high-priority LED programmes that prioritise skills development and job creation (Ngcobo, 2020).

Inadequate infrastructure is another barrier to LED in South Africa, especially in rural and peri-urban regions. Limited access to necessities like power, water, and transportation stifles business ventures and blocks avenues for investment. The public and private sectors must work together to address infrastructure shortages, and this includes funding infrastructure development projects and enhancing service delivery (Chikazunga & Mazibuko, 2018). Moreover, equitable LED is hampered by the unequal distribution of opportunities and resources throughout regions. Compared to rural and underdeveloped areas, urban areas—especially metropolitan areas—tend to draw more investment and development potential. This spatial inequality impedes inclusive growth and sustains socio-economic divides and LED initiatives must take a more balanced stance in order to solve this, giving marginalised populations' demands top priority and advancing spatial equity (McGranahan & Turok, 2016).

Notwithstanding these obstacles, LED technology in South Africa has seen some noteworthy achievements and encouraging advancements (Idahosa, 2002; Suhonen et al., 2011). To encourage local economic growth, the government has put in place a number of policy frameworks and initiatives, such as the National growth Plan (NDP) and the Integrated Urban Development Framework (IUDF). These programmes highlight how crucial multi-stakeholder cooperation, creativity, and sustainable development are to the advancement of LED (Bhorat et al., 2018). Additionally, there are chances for inclusive LED in South Africa due to the increased awareness of the informal sector as a vital engine of economic activity. Informal businesses, which are frequently run by marginalised groups like women and young people, help to reduce poverty, create jobs, and strengthen the local economy (Böhm et al., 2022; Rogerson, 2019). Targeted initiatives that support and formalise the informal sector can increase its contribution to LED and foster inclusive economic growth (Rogerson, 2019).

A complex interplay of possibilities and problems characterises the position of LED in South Africa today and even if enduring problems like high unemployment, poor infrastructure, and geographical inequality still present challenges, there have also been encouraging advances and possible paths forward. A comprehensive strategy that incorporates social, economic, and environmental factors and promotes inclusive growth and sustainable development at the local level is needed to address these issues (Carrington et al., 2021; Fatoki & Chiliya, 2012; Johansson & Wickström, 2023).

Business Ethics Vs Sustainable Development

Because business ethics steer corporate behaviour towards ethical and environmentally sound methods, they have a substantial impact on sustainable development. Sustainable development objectives are furthered by ethical business conduct, which extends beyond simple legal compliance and includes a dedication to social and environmental responsibility (Adiguzel, 2021; Grace, 2006). Businesses are encouraged by business ethics to think about how their decisions may affect different stakeholders over the long run, such as the environment, communities, and employees. Businesses can promote sustainable development by reducing negative externalities including pollution, resource depletion, and social inequality through the integration of ethical principles into their decision-making processes (Crane & Matten, 2019).

Furthermore, ethical companies are more likely to implement sustainable business plans that give social justice, resource efficiency, and environmental stewardship first priority. In addition to minimising environmental impact, sustainable practices including the use of renewable energy, trash minimisation, and fair labour practices can boost community resilience and well-being (Brammer, et al., 2012). Furthermore, the promotion of sustainability throughout international value chains is greatly aided by ethical supply chain management techniques. Businesses can reduce social and environmental risks and promote sustainable economic development in supplier communities by guaranteeing fair treatment of workers, transparent sourcing methods, and adherence to environmental standards (Brammer et al., 2012). Additionally, ethical businesses are more likely to put into practice sustainable business plans that prioritise environmental stewardship, resource efficiency, and social justice. Sustainable practices, such as the use of renewable energy, trash reduction, and fair employment standards, can improve community resilience and well-being in addition to limiting their negative effects on the environment (Alvesson, 2002; Den Hond & Moser, 2023; Ngcobo, 2020). Furthermore, ethical supply chain management strategies play a major role in promoting sustainability across global value chains. By ensuring fair treatment of workers, transparent sourcing practices, and adherence to environmental standards, businesses can decrease social and environmental hazards and promote sustainable economic development in supplier communities (Brammer et al., 2012; Clegg et al., 2007; Gerged et al., 2024; Lutge & Uhl, 2021).

Methodology

The study takes the form of a secondary qualitative method (document review) where the data collected from the Auditor General of South Africa's reports were used (Bowen, 2009; Silverman, 2011). The data were collected from the Auditor General's website and further analysed mainly focusing on the municipalities' reports for a period 2021 to 2023. The inclusion criteria were when the audit speak on municipalities (material irregularities) and any report that had nothing to do with material irregularities was not considered in the collection and analysis of the data. In addition, the researchers also focused on areas where principles of business ethics were manipulated such as accountability and transparency, leadership, responsibility, fairness, and integrity including compliance with the law as some key variables centred on. These reports provide a great deal of information concerning the ethical conduct of the municipalities as change agents of the local economic development in local municipalities and the country at large. The documents used to collect data were coded, for example, Integrated Annual Report 2021–2022 was coded as IAR2021–2022 and Integrated Annual Report for 2022–2023 was coded as IAR2022–2023, and finally where the information was taken from the AGSA website, this was coded as WBS2024.

Results and Discussions

The researchers used the Auditor General of South Africa's website to find data and analysed in categories and the results are that the state of business ethics in the local governance are in bad shape. The audit reports have shown that there are many financial regularities, called material irregularities, on the part of local governments, which further affect the lives of local communities. **Material irregularities (irresponsibility)** are defined by the AGSA office as "any non-compliance with or contravention of legislation, fraud, theft, or a breach of fiduciary duties identified during audit performed under the Public Act that resulted in or likely to result in a material financial loss, the misuse or loss of material public sector institution or the general public", this was mainly found procurement and billing and "*we identified 268 MIs, mostly relating to non-compliance with legislation. We estimate the total financial loss of the 194 MIs that involved a material financial loss to be R5,19 billion, with R1,6 billion of that being lost by municipalities that invested in VBS Mutual Bank*" (IAR2021–2022).

The irresponsibility shown and stated in the 2021–2022 continued unabated in the following period (2022–2023). The result stimulates the idea that there is no balance in pursuit of profit and social responsibility as mentioned by Ferrell et al. (2022) and Skooglund and Nichols (1998). It is the responsibility of the local municipalities to make sure that service delivery and local empowerment is done to all community citizens, however, with the current state of affairs, it may be difficult for such a fit to be met. The material irregularities shown in Fig. 1 are costly. Additionally, the study further found that the municipalities are not following due diligence in their procurement processes, which resulted in the municipalities losing a lot of money due to overpriced goods and services, meaning that there was or could have been a deliberate move by the procurement sections within the municipalities.

Lack of Accountability and Transparency

The study further found out that in the 2021–2022 audit report, some municipalities had adverse audit reports' opinion for four consecutive years (financial statements submitted are so unreliable that they cannot be used for decision making or for an oversight), e.g. Emakhazeni Local Municipality in Mpumalanga, Ngaka Modiri Molema District Municipality in North-West. Three municipalities regressed to this category, which are City of Tshwane Metro (Gauteng), uMzinyathi District Municipality (Kwazulu Natal), and Laingsburg Local municipality in Eastern Cape. Furthermore, to prove that business ethics are no longer effective in the local governance development, the 2021–2022 audit report further claimed that "*there is little transparency and accountability on how these municipalities use their funds*" (IAR2021–2022, p. 18). Fig. 1 below shows some statistics of the audit findings for the municipalities.

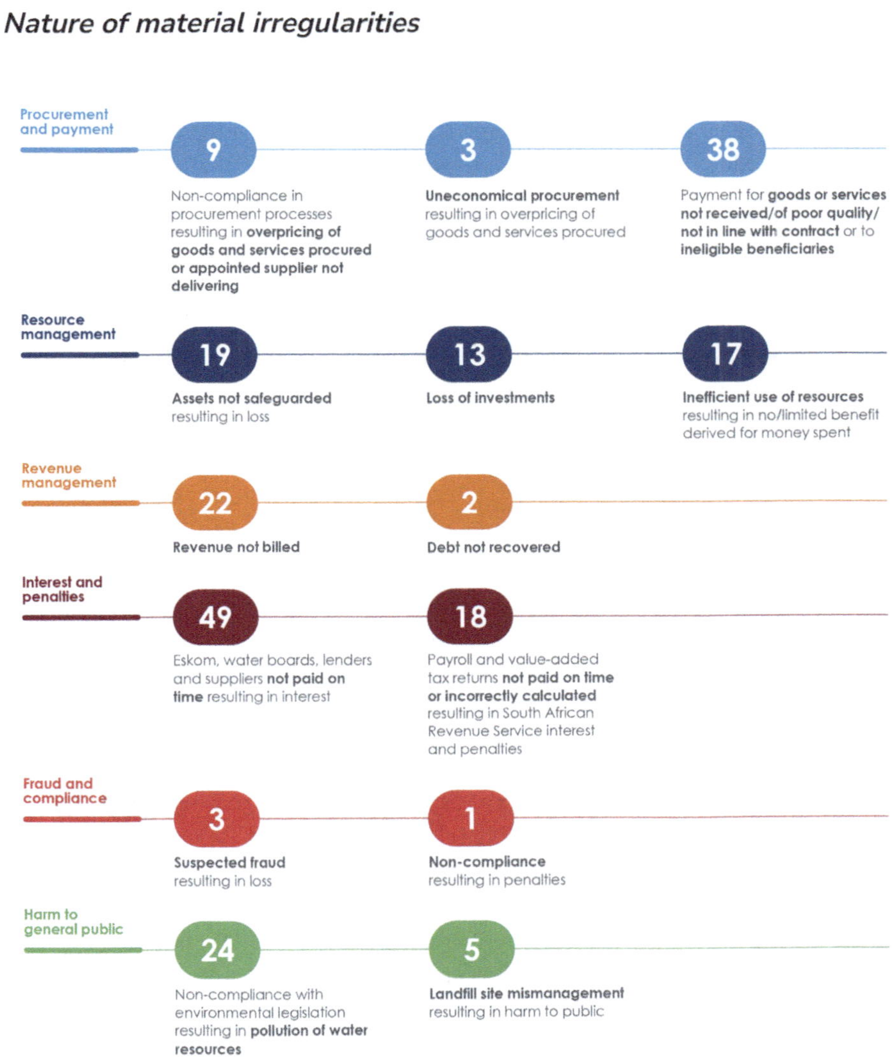

Fig. 1 Nature of financial irregularities in municipalities 2022–2023 Audit report

Accountability and transparency are some of the key pillars of the business ethics and are lacking in the municipalities of South Africa. Lack of such principles obvious has a negative effect on fostering economic growth and community development, according to research done by Crane and Matten (2019). In cases where there is full accountability and transparency, the community maintains confidence, trust, and empowerment through strong ethical standards. This has been the same thing with the years 2022–2023, the municipalities continued in the same trajectory as seen with other municipalities regressing even having done better in the previous year.

Lack of Integrity in Local Municipalities

The study further found that lack of integrity is now a major challenge in the municipality as shown below in Fig. 2 where some authorities did not provide statements as expected and others submitted late which further delayed auditing process.

According to Figs. 2 and 3 municipalities didn't submit their financial statements to the audit team as required by the law, 12 local governments submitted their statement late, which further speaks volume in terms of the integrity and credibility of the same institutions. Additionally, they further pointed out that 1 delayed the audit, unfortunately, it is not clear if the municipality only delayed but audited late. This is against the business ethics where the leadership of these authorities should strengthen the credibility and reputation, moral leadership, and corporate governance (Adegbite et al., 2016; Brabeck, 1984).

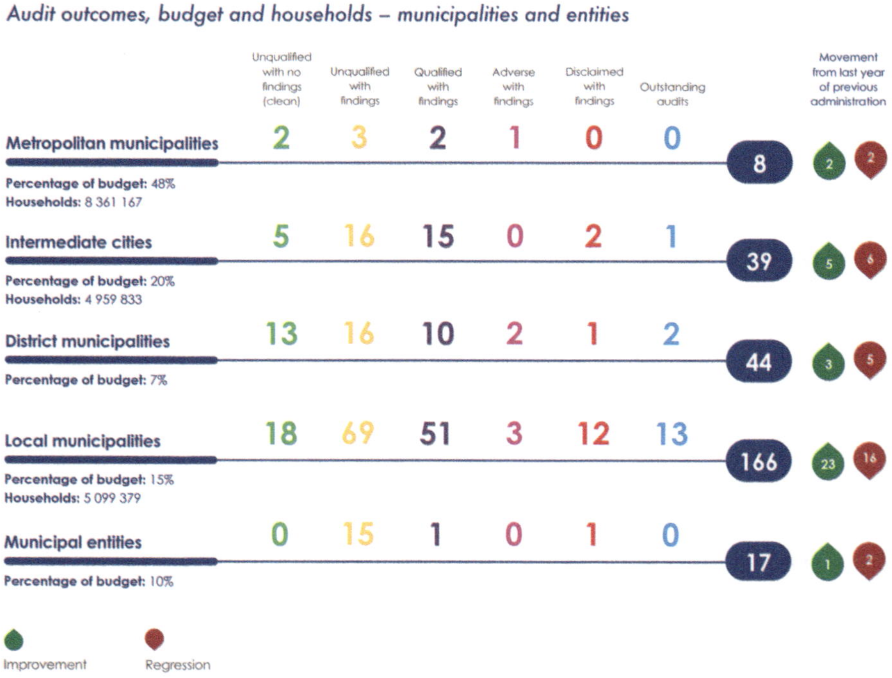

Fig. 2 Audit outcomes for municipalities 2021–2022

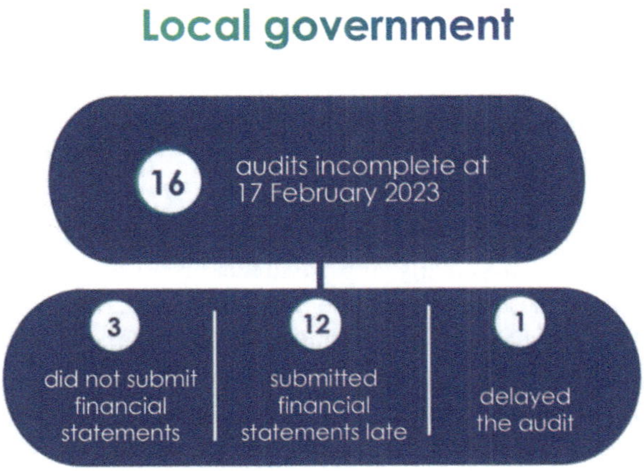

Fig. 3 Local government with outstanding audit results (source: IAR2022–2023)

Non-compliance with Legislation

The results further show that most of the municipalities are not compliant with the requirements of the law. According to **IAR2021–2022,** "*The audit outcomes, along with non-compliance with legislation and the insights from our audits as detailed in this report, reflect the concerning state of financial and performance management in local government. This situation resulted in some municipalities suffering material financial losses, while others caused substantial harm to people because they could not fulfil their mandates and deliver services to the public. For many years, our audits have highlighted that not only are irregularities – and the resulting impact – not prevented from happening; when they do happen, they are not properly dealt with*". Due to failure to comply with the regulations some of the municipalities are in financial trouble according to **WBS2024**, "*The financial position of 70 (29%) of the 241 municipalities where we completed our audits was so dire that they had to disclose significant doubt about their ability to fully operate in future…*" These conditions are not conducive for the municipalities to fulfil the roles and duties of the LED comprehensively since they are in dire need of finances and failure to comply with the legislation which further cast doubt if these can also comply with the legal compliance and industry standards according to Crane and Matten (2019). Justice and fairness are essential ingredients for business ethics and community growth.

Unfair Procurement Practice

The results of the study found that the municipalities are not following sound procurement practices as required by law, causing the government to lose billions of Rands each year. According to WBS2024, "*Local government needs fair and competitive procurement processes to get the best value for its limited funds and to give suppliers fair and equitable access to government business*". The same went on to say that there are poor contract and procurement processes in the local municipalities, which compromise the viability of these municipalities, "*Uncompetitive and unfair procurement processes and inadequate contract management remained widespread. We reported findings (62% of which were material) on uncompetitive and unfair procurement processes at 83% of municipalities, and contract management findings (39% of which were material) at nearly half of all municipalities (47%)*". This clearly shows that there is no ethical business practice in place, as over half of these authorities are found to be deficient in procurement practices and fraud is said to be prevailing so much. The role of these municipalities is being diminished each day and ethically. Furthermore, the promotion of sustainability throughout international value chains is greatly aided by ethical supply chain management techniques. Businesses can reduce social and environmental risks and promote sustainable economic development in supplier communities by guaranteeing fair treatment of workers, transparent sourcing methods, and adherence to environmental standards (Brammer et al., 2012).

Conclusion and Recommendations

The study concluded that there is no legal framework in place besides the white paper of 1998 which speaks about the local economic development embedded in the National Framework of Local Economic Development (NFLED); however, the challenge is in the fact that the constitution does not have such to support the structure hence the researchers concluded that there is a need for alignment between the NFLED and the constitution of South Africa. Furthermore, the authors also concluded that most principles of business ethics are not existing in the municipalities. Additionally, we concluded that the legal framework to deal with the business ethics offenders is not seriously implemented. Furthermore, it must be clear to municipalities that LED is part of their structure as mentioned in the NFLED. Additionally, the researchers concluded that there is no monitoring and evaluation in the municipalities and provincial department because there is no way such negative issues are only picked during Auditor General's office visits. However, the authors recommended the creation of monitoring and evaluation officers in the Municipalities who are responsible for making sure that LED is being supported and business ethics being implemented.

Additionally, the authors recommended that for LED to be taken seriously, there is a need to align the constitution and the NFLED such that LED do not only appear in the NFLED but also in the constitution. Furthermore, the researchers recommended that policy makers may need to be trained to ensure that they take development seriously and tackle any gross negligence. Full restoration of business ethics principles is a must under the current circumstances where most of the municipalities are struggling financially and leaders of integrity should be deployed. This will ensure poverty and inequality reduction and increased well-being of the local communities. An increased oversight role including monitoring and evaluation currently from the audit reports and the study results, it seems like auditor's office is the only one playing such role. Business ethics are missing in the activities of the local economic development. Additionally, one of the LED objectives was "*to support local economies in realising their optimal potential and making local communities active participants in the economy of the country*" and as it stands, the researchers recommend the review of the NFLED to reflect the honest status on the ground since the inception of the framework, as the objectives seem to have been overtaken by events.

Implications

The study's conclusions highlight how important moral business conduct is to promote socio-economic growth in South Africa. Municipalities may help create healthy connections with stakeholders, promote transparency, and establish trust by upholding high ethical standards and in turn, this can foster an atmosphere that is favourable for investment, economic expansion, and the creation of jobs, especially in less privileged and underserved areas. Additionally, the study emphasises how ethical corporate practices can help alleviate socio-economic problems and disparities in South Africa and ethical companies such as municipalities may significantly improve healthcare, education, poverty reduction, and community development by participating in corporate social responsibility (CSR) programmes. This might significantly improve South Africans' quality of life and general well-being, especially for those living in underprivileged areas. Furthermore, the study also highlights how crucial it is to incorporate ethical issues into corporate governance frameworks and business decision-making processes. Businesses can reduce risks, improve reputation of the municipalities, and create long-term sustainability by integrating ethics into their organisational culture and procedures. This helps the municipalities as well as the resilience and competitiveness of the South African economy as a whole since the municipalities are part of the economic growth strategy.

References

Adegbite, E., Rajwani, T., & Amaeshi. (2016). Corporate social responsibility in challenging and non-enabling institutional contexts: Do institutional voids matter? *Journal of Business Ethics, 134*(1), 135–153.

Adiguzel, Z. (2021). Evaluation and importance of business ethics in terms of organizational culture. In M. N. Taskiran & F. Pinarbaşi (Eds.), *Advances in information security, privacy, and ethics* (pp. 248–275). IGI Global. https://doi.org/10.4018/978-1-7998-4117-3.ch014

Alvesson, M. (2002). *Understanding organizational culture*. SAGE Publications Ltd. https://doi.org/10.4135/9781446280072Azi

Ayubi, A. (2023). Apartheid policy in South Africa. *International Journal of Science and Society, 5*(1), 124–131. https://doi.org/10.54783/ijsoc.v5i1.634

Bhorat, H., Cassim, A., & Hirsch, A. (2018). The South African National Development Plan and the economy*:* Can the economy deliver?*, 35*(3), 369–387.

Böhm, S., Carrington, M., Cornelius, N., De Bruin, B., Greenwood, M., Hassan, L., Jain, T., Karam, C., Kourula, A., Romani, L., Riaz, S., & Shaw, D. (2022). Ethics at the Centre of Global and Local Challenges: Thoughts on the future of business ethics. *Journal of Business Ethics, 180*(3), 835–861. https://doi.org/10.1007/s10551-022-05239-2

Bowen, G. A. (2009). Document analysis as a qualitative research method. *Qualitative Research Journal, 9*(2), 27–40. https://doi.org/10.3316/QRJ0902027

Bowie, N. E. (2017). *Business ethics: A Kantian perspective* (2nd ed.). Cambridge University Press. https://doi.org/10.1017/9781316343210

Brabeck, M. (1984). Ethical characteristics of whistle blowers. *Journal of Research in Personality, 18*(1), 41–53. https://doi.org/10.1016/0092-6566(84)90037-0

Brammer, S., Hoejmose, S., & Millington, A. (2012). Managing supply chain ethical risks: Insights from case study research. *Long Range Planning, 45*(1–2), 77–95.

Carrington, M., Chatzidakis, A., Goworek, H., & Shaw, D. (2021). Consumption ethics: A review and analysis of future directions for interdisciplinary research. *Journal of Business Ethics, 168*(2), 215–238. https://doi.org/10.1007/s10551-020-04425-4

Chikazunga, D., & Mazibuko, N. (2018). Spatial planning and local economic development in South Africa: An investigation into spatial planning frameworks. *Journal of Public Administration, 53*(4), 797–813.

Clegg, S., Kornberger, M., & Rhodes, C. (2007). Business ethics as practice. *British Journal of Management, 18*(2), 107–122. https://doi.org/10.1111/j.1467-8551.2006.00493.x

Crane, A., & Matten, D. (2019). *Business ethics: Managing corporate citizenship and sustainability in the age of globalization.* Oxford University Press.

De Lange, W., Visser, W., Pienaar, J., & Smit, E. (2019). Ethical supply chain management practices in the south African manufacturing industry. *Journal of Contemporary Management, 16*(1), 56–76.

Den Hond, F., & Moser, C. (2023). Useful servant or dangerous master? Technology in Business and Society Debates. *Business & Society, 62*(1), 87–116. https://doi.org/10.1177/00076503211068029

Dunfee, T. W. (1991). Business ethics and extant social contracts. *Business Ethics Quarterly, 1*(1), 23–51. https://doi.org/10.2307/3857591

Enderle, G. (2018). How can business ethics strengthen the social cohesion of a society? *Journal of Business Ethics, 150*(3), 619–629. https://doi.org/10.1007/s10551-016-3196-5

Evans, R. (1991). Business ethics and changes in society. *Journal of Business Ethics, 10*(11), 871–876. https://doi.org/10.1007/BF00383705

Fatoki, O., & Chiliya, W. (2012). An investigation into the attitudes toward business ethics and corporate social responsibility by local and immigrant SME owners in South Africa. *Journal of Social Sciences, 32*(1), 13–21. https://doi.org/10.1080/09718923.2012.11893048

Ferrell, O. C., Fraedrich, J., & Ferrell, L. (2022). *Business ethics: Ethical decision making and cases* (13th ed.). South-Western.

Freeman, R. E. (2000). Business ethics at the millennium. *Business Ethics Quarterly, 10*(1), 169–180. https://doi.org/10.2307/3857703

Gerged, A. M., Kehbuma, K. M., & Beddewela, E. S. (2024). Corporate social responsibility disclosure and corporate social irresponsibility in emerging economies: Does institutional quality matter? *Business Ethics, the Environment & Responsibility, beer.12683*, 1–19. https://doi.org/10.1111/beer.12683

Grace, D. (2006). For business ethics. *Australian Journal of Management, 31*(2), 371–380. https://doi.org/10.1177/031289620603100211

Hamington, M. (2011). Care ethics, knowledge management, and the learning organization. In M. Hamington & M. Sander-Staudt (Eds.), *Applying care ethics to business* (Vol. 34, pp. 245–257). Springer. https://doi.org/10.1007/978-90-481-9307-3_13

Idahosa, P. (2002). No title found. *Journal of Business Ethics, 39*(3), 227–246. https://doi.org/10.1023/A:1016546308886

Johansson, J., & Wickström, A. (2023). Constructing a 'different' strength: A feminist exploration of vulnerability, ethical agency and care. *Journal of Business Ethics, 184*(2), 317–331. https://doi.org/10.1007/s10551-022-05121-1

Lutge, C., & Uhl, M. (2021). *Business ethics: An economically informed perspective* (1st ed.). Oxford University Press. https://doi.org/10.1093/oso/9780198864776.001.0001

Mayer, D. (2001). Community, business ethics, and global capitalism. *American Business Law Journal, 38*(2), 215–260. https://doi.org/10.1111/j.1744-1714.2001.tb00289.x

McGranahan, G., & Turok, I. (2016). Urbanization and economic development in South Africa: Meeting the challenges of spatial redistribution. *Development Southern Africa, 33*(2), 155–170.

Ngcobo, N. C. (2020). Unemployment in South Africa: Trends, causes, and policy challenges. *Journal of Economics, Management, and Trade, 26*(3), 75–89.

Nyberg, D., Ferns, G., Vachhani, S., & Wright, C. (2022). Climate change, business, and society: Building relevance in time and space. *Business & Society, 61*(5), 1322–1352. https://doi.org/10.1177/00076503221077452

Rogerson, C. M. (2019). The informal economy in South Africa: Understanding trends, characteristics, and policy responses. *South African Geographical Journal, 101*(1), 1–19.

Sen, A. (1993). Does business ethics make economic sense? In P. M. Minus (Ed.), *The ethics of business in a global economy* (Vol. 4, pp. 53–66). Springer. https://doi.org/10.1007/978-94-015-8165-3_6

Silverman, D. (2011). *Interpreting qualitative data: A guide to the principles of qualitative research* (4th ed.). SAGE.

Skooglund, C. M., & Nichols, S. P. (1998). Friend or foe: A brief examination of the ethics of corporate sponsored research at universities: A response to 'ethics and the funding of research and development at universities' (R. E. Spier). *Science and Engineering Ethics, 4*(3), 385–390. https://doi.org/10.1007/s11948-998-0031-0

Suhonen, R., Stolt, M., Virtanen, H., & Leino-Kilpi, H. (2011). Organizational ethics: A literature review. *Nursing Ethics, 18*(3), 285–303. https://doi.org/10.1177/0969733011401123

Pricing the Cost of Carbon Using Net Emissions Technologies

Kgalalelo Constance Makamela

Abstract Carbon pricing policies are vital in global climate change mitigation efforts by incentivising reductions in greenhouse gas emissions (GHG) linked to fossil fuel use. Equating the price of carbon to the cost of abatement is paramount for the effectiveness of such policies, as affirmed by Pigou's theory of negative externalities. The urgent need to limit global warming to 1.5 °C has resulted in growing recognition of the importance of removing carbon emissions from the atmosphere. Net Emission Technologies (NET) have emerged as instrumental technologies in achieving this target, as found by climate-integrated assessment methods. However, there remains a gap in the literature regarding the cost of carbon abatement through NETs. This study addresses this gap by pricing carbon based on the cost of using NETs. A qualitative review of carbon taxes, NETs, and associated costs estimates that carbon prices between USD 90 (ZAR 1710) and USD 600 (ZAR 11400) per tonne of CO2 are needed to incentivise NET investment. The study highlights that current carbon tax rates, particularly in South Africa, are insufficient to encourage NET adoption. It suggests that revised carbon pricing aligned with global climate targets and increased investment in research and development are necessary to enhance NET scalability and cost-effectiveness. Despite challenges such as scalability, sustainability, and resource competition, NETs such as BECCS are vital for decarbonisation, especially in fossil-fuel-dependent regions like South Africa. Collaborative efforts between governments, industries, and research institutions are essential to accelerate the transition to a low-carbon economy and mitigate climate change impacts.

Keywords Bioenergy with carbon capture and storage · Carbon price · Net emissions technology · Climate change · Direct air capture and storage

K. C. Makamela (✉)
University of Pretoria, Pretoria, South Africa
e-mail: Kgalalelo.Makamela@up.ac.za

T. Moloi (ed.), *Impacting Society Positively Through Technology in Accounting and Business Processes*, Springer Proceedings in Business and Economics,
https://doi.org/10.1007/978-3-031-84885-8_29

Introduction

The world is experiencing an imminent threat of global warming and climate change (Almena et al., 2022; Ginanjar & Mubarrok, 2020; Mikhaylov et al., 2020; Manta et al., 2023; Wolde-Rufael & Mulat-Weldemeskel, 2021). The reality of climate change is irrefutable in contemporary times (Ghazouani et al., 2020). The consequences of persistent reliance on fossil fuels are becoming more evident, as demonstrated by mounting evidence of adverse weather patterns (Okonkwo et al., 2023). Fossil fuel use is the main contributor of the release of greenhouse gases (GHG) (Ghazouani et al., 2020) that attribute to the changes in the Earth's climate (IPCC, 2014). Changes in the Earth's climate causes negative effects such as altered ecosystems and desert land, a rise in the frequency and intensity of extreme weather events, ocean acidification, and the extinction of living things (IPCC, 2014). Several climate-integrated assessment models indicate that in order to reach the 1.5 °C target, the atmospheric carbon dioxide (CO2) concentration must cease its increase by the latter half of this century (Okonkwo et al., 2023). This cessation is crucial for mitigating the risks associated with climate change (Okonkwo et al., 2023). Simply reducing emissions from existing technologies may not be adequate to meet these objectives. To make progress towards these targets, it will be necessary to implement NETs (Almena et al., 2022; Doelman et al., 2020; Forster et al., 2021; Okonkwo et al., 2023; Terlouw et al., 2021). NETs are technologies that can remove CO2, directly or indirectly, from the atmosphere (Daggash et al., 2019). Globally, carbon pricing mechanisms have been central to keeping global warning below 1.5 °C and 2 °C temperature rise since pre-industrial times (Nong et al., 2021; Wolde-Rufael & Mulat-Weldemeskel, 2021). Carbon pricing policies stem from economic theory of negative externalities that aims to internalise the cost of pollutions into goods and services (Halkos & Kitsou, 2018; Heal & Schlenker, 2019; Jaqua & Schaffa, 2022; Wang & Zhang, 2019). Integrating the costs associated with negative environmental effects into product prices reduces consumption and incentivises a shift to more environmentally friendly practices (Dissanayake et al., 2020; Manta et al., 2023; Tan et al., 2022). There has been much criticism, however, over the current carbon tax rates (Baranzini et al., 2017; Boyce, 2018; National Treasury, 2010; OECD, 2023 Rosenbloom et al., 2020; Van der Wolk, 2021). They are argued to be too low to effect any real change in behaviour away from carbon-intensive operations (Baranzini et al., 2017; Boyce, 2018; Rosenbloom et al., 2020; National Treasury, 2010; Van der Wolk, 2021). An effective carbon policy equates the cost of damage to the cost of abatement (OECD, 2010).

The abatement measures will require extensive removal of CO2 from the atmosphere due to the present rate of CO2 emissions nearing 40 gigatonnes of CO2 per year and the delay in global mitigation endeavours (Realmonte et al., 2019). Deep reductions of historical emission in the atmosphere are necessary as a climate mitigation strategy (Bui et al., 2018; Young et al., 2023). NETs encompass various methods such as bioenergy with carbon capture and storage (BECCS), direct air capture and storage (DACS), afforestation, ocean fertilisation, enhanced weathering of minerals, and biochar (Asibor et al., 2022; Daggash et al., 2019; Lehtveer & Emanuelsson, 2021). BECCS and afforestation are often highlighted as the most promising options for achieving negative emissions and have been extensively investigated in Integrated Assessment Model (IAM) studies (Realmonte et al., 2019). However, concerns regarding the sustainability of biological approaches and potential competition with food, water resources, and ecosystems have prompted exploration into alternative methods for carbon sequestration. DACS serves as a complementary technology in this regard (Realmonte et al., 2019). Achieving efficient technology governance for NETs is deemed essential for realising decarbonisation goals effectively (Lehtveer & Emanuelsson, 2021).

The research question for this study is: What is the carbon price range that will incentivise adoption of NETs? This paper adopts a qualitative review approach with the objective of examining the suitability of South Africa's carbon pricing to encourage accelerated adoption of net emissions technology. The study will recommend a carbon price range that will encourage adoption of net emissions technology. The study enhances understanding of carbon pricing through the theoretical foundations of Pigouvian taxes and the economic theory of negative externalities. The paper proceeds as follows: This paper reviews carbon pricing as a mechanism to encourage adoption of net emissions technology. First, a review is conducted on carbon pricing as an instrument of decarbonisation, highlighting the South Africa's carbon policy impediments. Second, a review of net emissions technologies and the related cost of carbon per net emissions technology is conducted. Third, recommendations of the carbon price level that will encourage NET adoption in South Africa.

Literature Review

Globally, environmental taxes and stringent environmental policies have become central instrument to mitigate environmental destruction (Nong et al., 2021; Wolde-Rufael & Mulat-Weldemeskel, 2021). Environmental taxes, particularly carbon taxes, regulate activities with adverse environmental impacts (Kotlán et al., 2021), by imposing financial costs on polluters based on their carbon emissions (Baranzini et al., 2017; Cheng et al., 2021). This increases the cost of goods leading to decreased consumption, impacting the profitability of businesses. This prompts entities to adopt environmentally friendly practices (Dissanayake et al., 2020). Carbon taxes, therefore, incentivise the adoption of sustainable practices and products, aiming to shift behaviour towards eco-friendly technologies and reduce environmental harm (Wolde-Rufael & Mulat-Weldemeskel, 2021). South Africa introduced carbon tax in 2019 as a climate change mitigation strategy (Department of Environment Forestry and Fisheries, 2020). The introductory rate was ZAR 120 (EUR6) and has since increased to ZAR190 (EUR 9.5) per tonne of CO2 in 2024. The carbon tax is applied directly on the total GHG emissions from combustion, fugitive, and industrial process (National Treasury, 2017). The carbon tax applies to Scope 1 CO2 emissions, which are caused by direct fuel combustion, gasification, and non-energy industrial processes (National Treasury, 2013). Transitionary support measures such as tax-free allowances were implemented to minimise the adverse effects on competitiveness of businesses (National Treasury, 2013, 2018). The tax-free emission allowances range from 60% to 90% in South Africa, further reducing the effective carbon price to ZAR 19 (EUR 0.95) to ZAR76 (EUR3.8). This pricing level is substantially lower than the recommended carbon prices to achieve net zero in 2030. The global carbon target-oriented benchmarks a minimum carbon price of EUR 30 (ZAR 600) and mid-range price of EUR 120 (ZAR 2400) as necessary today to achieve net zero by 2030 (OECD, 2023). Nong et al. (2021) found that a ZAR 120 (EUR 6) price for South Africa achieves emission reduction levels between 12.25% and 15.6% that are lower than the decarbonisation target pledged in the Paris Agreement. The capacity of South Africa's carbon tax to shift production and consumption away from carbon-intensive activities has been constrained by these low-carbon prices, excessive free emission allowances, and ongoing subsidy support of fossil fuels (Makamela & Ramfol, 2023). Without new climate policies, South Africa's total CO2 emissions are projected to rise, reaching 622 metric tonnes of CO2 per year by 2050, marking a 23% increase from 2020 levels (Afrane et al., 2024). Pursuing net-zero emissions in South Africa with the deployment of NETs could potentially enable sequestration of 104 to166 mega tonnes of CO2 per year by 2050 (Afrane et al., 2024). This is a significant sequestration level in comparison with the yearly average of 400 metric tonnes of CO2 emitted. The future decarbonisation trajectory requires NETs and the carbon pricing levels should incentivise its adoption. The Pigouvian principle suggests an ideal minimum environmental tax to efficiently decrease GHG (Manta et al., 2023). Investments occur when benefits exceeded the costs (Hanlon & Heitzman, 2010), therefore carbon tax rates need to exceed NET investment costs to incentivise accelerated adoption of these technologies.

Bioenergy with Carbon Capture and Storage

BECCS is the most investigated potential negative emission technology that is increasingly incorporated into future emission scenarios designed to curb global warming to 2 °C (Bui et al., 2018; Desport et al., 2024; Mander et al., 2017; Tanzer et al., 2021). BECCS has the potential to significantly aid in reducing emissions in the latter part of this century, to align with climate targets of 1.5 and 2 °C (Fajardy et al., 2021). Plants are used to absorb carbon dioxide from the atmosphere and subsequently burned to produce energy in a BECCS system. The carbon dioxide from the combustion process is then captured and stored permanently (Bui et al., 2018; Tanzer et al., 2021). The absorption and capture of carbon dioxide enable permanent removal from the atmosphere leading to an overall negative carbon balance (Bui et al., 2018). Figure 1 depicts a BECCS process from biomass harvest to electricity generation:

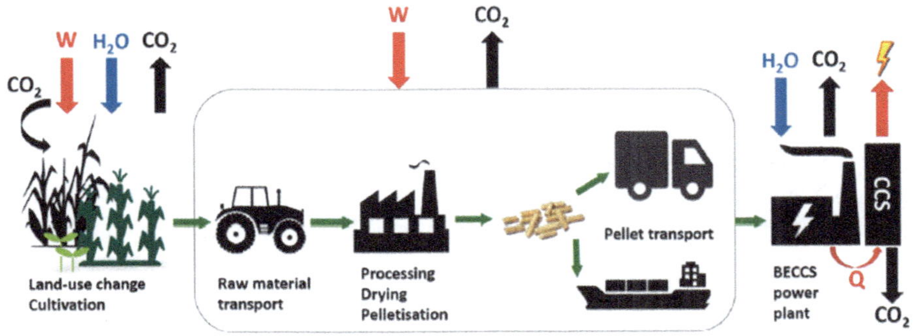

Fig. 1 BEECs power system. Source: Daggash et al. 2019 adapted from (Fajardy et al., 2021)

BECCS is acknowledged as a feasible and immediate strategy to reduce coal use to achieve decarbonisation in the electricity industry (Bui et al., 2018). BEECS provides consistent low-carbon electricity with no intermittent issues that are experienced with renewable energy sources such as wind and solar (Bui et al., 2018). Current technology considerably lowers the carbon prices and worldwide economic costs required to meet stabilisation goals. At carbon prices of approximately USD 240 (ZAR 4560) per tonne of carbon dioxide, BECCS performs well as a backstop technology (Fajardy et al., 2021) with average emissions capture rates of 50–94% (Fasihi et al., 2019).

The widespread adoption of BECCS carries risks to biodiversity, water, and food security due to its high land requirements (Fasihi et al., 2019), primarily due to potential competition with food production and significant needs for fertilisation and irrigation, raising sustainability concerns (Zhang et al., 2020). This risk can be reduced with the use of secondary biomass from urban and industrial wastes, agricultural and forest residues (Zhang et al., 2020). Secondary biomass use has significant potential as an alternative energy source with approximately 1.3 billion tonnes of solid waste currently generated globally from the urban population potentially increasing to 4 billion tonnes by 2100 (Zhang et al., 2020).

Adopting BECCS in South Africa is currently a challenge due to the slow development and implementing progression (Ko et al., 2021). A pilot carbon storage project, assessing geological storage and monitoring for 10,000 to 50,000 tonnes of CO2, was scheduled for completion between 2017 and 2021 (Beck et al., 2017). The road map indicated that they expected commercialisation of CCS in 2025, however, due to the delays the timelines need to be updated. The infancy of technological development of CCU in South Africa restricts the availability of the technology, which hinders the acceleration of BECCS adoption. Globally CCS technology is an emerging technology with 45 metric tonnes of CO2 capturability per year (International Energy Agency, 2023). Carbon capture technology in a BECCS is a crucial decarbonisation strategy requiring further investments in research and development to enhance the scalability and required decarbonisation.

Direct Air Capture and Storage (DACS)

DACS is an emerging technology aimed at removing significant amounts of CO2 from the atmosphere (Terlouw et al., 2021). DACS is poised to effectively remove CO2 from the atmosphere regardless of the origin of CO2 emissions, and its capture devices can be utilised in any geographical setting (Sodiq et al., 2023). DACS involves capturing CO2 from ambient air through a contactor and releasing it in a purer form during regeneration, utilising either high-temperature or low-temperature systems (Terlouw et al., 2021; Lehtveer & Emanuelsson, 2021). The sequestrated CO2 is then injected and permanently stored underground (Terlouw et al., 2021). Figure 2 depicts a DACS process form air capture to geological storage:

DACS reduces mitigation costs and complements other carbon removal methods rather than replacing them (Realmonte et al., 2019). The limited bio-geophysical and techno-economic analysis of feasibility of the GHG removal potential at national level limits accelerated adoption of DACS (Asibor et al., 2022). Scalability also remains a challenge (Realmonte et al., 2019). Initial commercialisation efforts involve small-scale plants using captured carbon for various purposes, including carbonated drinks and synthetic fuel production, with some storing carbon underground (Okonkwo et al., 2023). Scaling up DACS to 1.5 gigatonnes of CO2 per year would necessitate significant production of sorbents and up to 300 exajoules per year of energy input by the year 2100. Assuming DACS can be deployed at such a scale and then discovering it is unavailable could result in a global temperature overshoot of up to 0.8 °C. Therefore, DACS should be developed and implemented alongside, rather than in lieu of, other mitigation options (Realmonte et al., 2019).

Compared to other sequestration options, capturing CO2 directly from the air presents a number of advantages. DACS can address distributed emissions, such as those from transport, aviation, and intensive industrial sectors, together accounting for almost 50% of total emissions (Realmonte et al., 2019). The current cost of CO2 from DACS varies based on literature and ranges from USD 250 (ZAR 4750) to

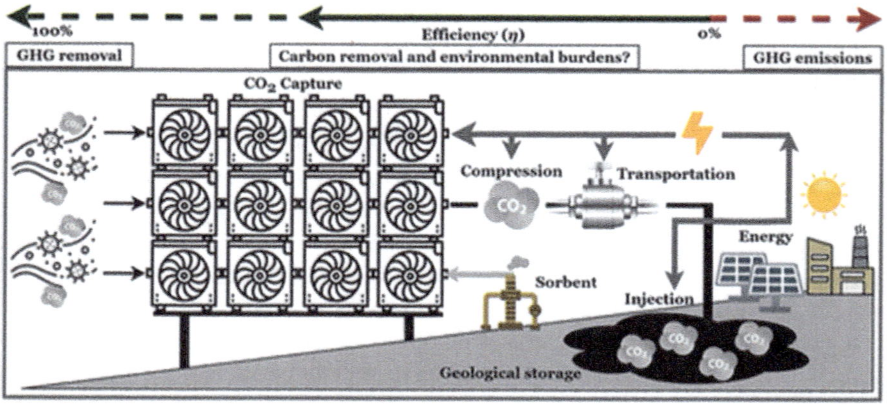

Fig. 2 DACS system. *Source: Terlouw* et al. (2021)

USD 600 (ZAR 11400) depending on the technology (Okonkwo et al., 2023). These are not competitive when compared to CO2 from other sources in the carbon market (Okonkwo et al., 2023).

Afforestation

The practice of growing more forests, or afforestation (Doelman et al., 2020), is acknowledged as a crucial tool for reducing greenhouse gas emissions (Forster et al., 2021). Expanding forests aid in decarbonisation through accelerating photosynthesis with vegetation absorbing CO2 and storing CO2 in ground vegetation (Desport et al., 2024; Doelman et al., 2020). While increasing the amount of forest area increases the amount of carbon stored in terrestrial plants, the effectiveness of this strategy depends on a number of variables, including the climate, the type of tree, management techniques, and product substitution (Forster et al., 2021). Afforestation on agriculturally spared land is highly context dependent. The objectives go beyond cutting emissions, but they also include combating desertification and boosting carbon sequestration in arid areas (Liu et al., 2022).

Large-scale afforestation projects, however, may be vulnerable to aridification since some plantations are located in marginal locations and are densely populated with genetically dubious tree stock, which can have a negative effect on soil and water quality (Liu et al., 2022). Afforestation also threatens biodiversity, water, and food security due to the substantial land requirements (Fasihi et al., 2019). Despite these challenges, afforestation is heralded as a cost-effective and readily implementable solution for climate change mitigation (Doelman et al., 2020). Afforestation has the potential to reduce CO2 emissions by 4.9 gigatonnes annually by 2050 at a cost of USD 200 (ZAR 3800) per tonne of CO2, particularly if done extensively as part of a scenario that aims to keep global warming to 2 °C (Doelman et al., 2020).

Ministry of Water Affairs and Forestry (1997) found land suitable for further afforestation in KwaZulu Natal, Mpumalanga, and the Eastern Cape provinces in South Africa. In efforts to promote sustainability the Department of Trade, Industry and Competition (2020) has earmarked 10,000 hectares of land in the Eastern Cape and KwaZulu Natal for new afforestation projects. Previously afforested land of 85,000 hectares is planned to be restored to full productivity in Western Cape and other unproductive or damaged areas (Department of Trade, Industry and Competition, 2020). Du Preez et al. (2022) transformed a 160-hectare grassland catchment in the Eastern Cape Province into a forest. This afforestation effort resulted in adding 2187 megagrams of carbon to the catchment, with an annual rate of 273 megagrams, or 3.59 megagrams per hectare. Consequently, the forest system sequestered carbon 2.6 times faster than the grassland system according to their findings (Du Preez et al., 2022). These results illustrate the efficacy of the technology and further exploration of scalability of this technology is required to advance the decarbonisation measures in South Africa.

Ocean Fertilisation

The emerging climate change mitigation strategy of ocean fertilisation involves modifying the ocean's pH to enhance its capacity for absorbing and retaining carbon dioxide from the atmosphere (Eisaman et al., 2023). Marine unicellular phytoplankton, responsible for the majority of total primary production, plays a crucial role in this process, contributing significantly to CO2 removal from the atmosphere (Jiang et al., 2024). Phytoplankton biomass absorbs CO2 and converts it into organic matter, then stores the organic carbon in the deep ocean (Jiang et al., 2024). Artificial ocean fertilisation (AOF) aims to stimulate ocean phytoplankton growth to enhance carbon sequestration, but its efficiency is lower than natural fertilisation due to limited nutrient bioavailability and low export rates of AOF-produced biomass to the deep ocean (Babakhani et al., 2022). Babakhani et al. (2022) estimate AOF using iron sulphate costs of approximately USD 0.030–0.300 (ZAR0.57–5.71) per kilogram (kg) of CO2 removed, falling within previously reported ranges of USD 0.008 and 0.450 (ZAR0.152–8.55) and resulting in 2.97 kg CO2 equivalent emissions per kg of iron used (Babakhani et al., 2022).

Ocean fertilisation can lead to eutrophication, anoxia, and changes in pH, affecting oxygen levels, phytoplankton species, and marine life (Lampitt et al., 2008). Global alkalinisation shows promise in effectiveness but lacks technological readiness, with uncertainty in large-scale deployment (Gattuso et al., 2018). Further drawbacks include ocean acidification, heightened production of additional greenhouse gases, uncertain effects on food webs, emergence of harmful algal blooms, and varied impacts on seafloor and upper ocean ecosystems (Fawzy et al., 2020). Altering nutrient balances may have widespread impacts on biological productivity and ecosystem structure, necessitating careful consideration of potential side effects when assessing its use for climate mitigation (Lampitt et al., 2008).

Enhanced Weathering of Minerals

Enhanced weathering, a simple and scalable negative emissions technology, with an estimated carbon dioxide removal potential of multiple gigatonnes per year, has captured the scientific community's attention (Tan & Aviso, 2021). Enhanced weather entails spreading crushed silicate minerals on land and water to remove CO2 from the atmosphere by accelerating the reaction of GHG with alkaline minerals (Power et al., 2023; te Pas et al., 2023). The breakdown of silicate rocks absorbs carbon dioxide, which then forms bicarbonate that is stored permanently underground (Lewis et al., 2021). Enhanced weathering could potentially achieve the removal of more than one gigatonne of CO2 annually, though it will necessitate the availability of gigatonnes of appropriate rock (Power et al., 2023). Tan and Aviso (2021) estimate that applying pulverised basalt on land in Sao Paulo State, Brazil, could remove a range of 1.3 to 2.4 metric tonnes of CO2 per year through accelerated natural weathering reactions with alkaline minerals, CO2, and moisture.

The efficacy of enhanced weathering is influenced by varied factors. The composition and size of silicate minerals affect their dissolution rate, with smaller particles dissolving faster, necessitating fine grinding for timely carbon removal (Tan & Aviso, 2021). Stubbs et al. (2022) find that the mining industry can play a role in adopting enhanced weathering to reduce their net GHG. Mine tailings contain substantial silicate minerals that have the potential to remove substantial CO2 from the air (Bullock et al., 2022). Rocks such as kimberlite, serpentinite, and wollastonite skarns have significant potential to capture CO2 through enhanced rock weathering; however, only a fraction of these rocks is suitable for CO2 removal (Paulo et al., 2021). Paulo et al. (2021) find that the Venetia kimberlites from the Venetia Diamond Mine demonstrated a CO2 storage capacity of 268 to 342 kilograms per tonne. The mineralogical composition primarily influenced CO2 removal, with Venetia Diamond Mine residues achieving CO2 removal rates of negative 870 grams of CO2 per square metre per year, in the presence of labile magnesium (Stubbs et al., 2022).

Enhanced weathering has been found to be cost-competitive compared to other NETs (Vandeginste et al., 2024). Estimates suggest prices of USD 63 (ZAR 1197) per tonne CO2 for dunite and USD 81 (ZAR 1539) to USD 211(ZAR 4009) per ton CO2 for basalt enhanced weathering (Vandeginste et al., 2024). McQueen et al. (2020) project a cost range of between USD 46 and USD 159 (ZAR 874–3021) per ton of CO2 for the continuous capture of CO2 from the atmosphere through calcined magnesite. Their assessment suggests that this method could potentially sequester between 2 and 3 gigatonnes of CO2 annually. Enhanced weathering can capture CO2 without compromising food production (Vandeginste et al., 2024). Enhanced weathering can improve soil pH and fertility, but its efficacy depends on factors like temperature, precipitation, and soil complexity, while concerns about mineral deposition, heavy metal traces, and health impacts from particulate matter emissions could affect public acceptance (Tan & Aviso, 2021).

Biochar

Biochar is recognised as a promising technology to remove GHG (Lefebvre et al., 2021; Wang et al., 2020). Biochar involves the thermal decomposition of organic materials like biomass without oxygen (Anand et al., 2022; Asibor et al., 2022; Terlouw et al., 2021). Carbon dioxide is absorbed from the atmosphere through the process of photosynthesis (Bo et al., 2023; Terlouw et al., 2021). The biomass is harvested and converted into biochar (Terlouw et al., 2021) and applied to the soil for permanent storage of the carbon in the soil (Bo et al., 2023; Wang et al., 2020). The application of biochar to soil enhances soil quality, boosts fertility, and increases water retention, thereby reducing the likelihood of land degradation (Terlouw et al., 2021; Tisserant & Cherubini, 2019). Biochar deployment offers additional advantages such as energy generation from pyrolysis, pollution remediation, and waste management (Asibor et al., 2022). The positive effects of biochar are contingent upon specific factors including the type of biochar, application rate, soil characteristics, climate, and crop variety (Wang et al., 2020).

South African biochar research has focused on the benefits of biochar in wastewater treatment, its impact on soil properties, and its effects on crop growth (Carrier et al., 2012; Dzvene et al., 2019; Nyambo et al., 2020; Späth et al., 2021; Semida et al., 2019). Global studies have found biomass to sequester CO2 at varying levels, depending on the specific crop variety and soil characteristics (Anand et al., 2022; Lefebvre et al., 2021; Tisserant & Cherubini, 2019). Lefebvre et al. (2021) found the conversion of 100% of the available sugarcane bagasse to biochar in São Paulo State to sequestrate between 0.5 and 6.3 metric tons of carbon dioxide equivalent per hectare per year. Anand et al. (2022) found the addition of approximately 212.04 to 44.27 metric tonnes of biochar to soil captures between 78.52 and 376.11 metric tonnes of carbon dioxide equivalent and retention of between 0.46 and 1.66 megatons of soil nutrients in India.

Bo et al. (2023) found the use of biochar in Chinese agricultural fields to raise soil organic carbon levels by 1.9 pentagrams of carbon and decrease methane and nitrous oxide emissions by 25 and 20 megatons of carbon dioxide equivalent per year, respectively. The biochar further increased crop yields by 19% (Bo et al., 2023). A quantitative life-cycle assessment of biochar systems indicates that biochar's impact on climate change varies, ranging from emitting 0.04 tonnes of carbon dioxide equivalent to reducing 1.67 tonnes of carbon dioxide per tonne of feedstock (Tisserant & Cherubini, 2019). By 2050, it is projected that biochar could remove between 0.3 and 2 gigatonnes of CO2 annually, with associated costs ranging from USD 90 to USD 120 (ZAR1710 to 2280) per tonne of CO2 (Fuss et al., 2018). Although there is growing evidence of the benefits of biochar, further research is needed to investigate factors that could diminish its ability to combat climate change and ensure crop productivity (Bo et al., 2023).

Conclusion and Recommendations

The urgency of addressing global warming and climate change is indisputable, as evidenced by the adverse weather patterns. Decarbonisation efforts to limit global warming to 1.5 °C requires large-scale adoption of NETs (Almena et al., 2022; Doelman et al., 2020; Forster et al., 2021; Okonkwo et al., 2023; Terlouw et al., 2021). However, the deployment of NETs at the gigatonne scale is still debatable, and large-scale demonstration projects are limited. While some land-based are ready for large-scale deployment from technical and economical perspectives, they may not remove sufficient CO2 to achieve the climate goals (Terlouw et al., 2021). Concerns about sustainability, competition with food and water resources, scalability, and cost competitiveness remain challenges for many NETs.

Despite the implementation challenges, BECCS remains an important decarbonisation strategy in South Africa. The benefits of energy production have potential to reduce the fossil fuel intensive energy mix in South Africa and aid in reducing the part of the 42% of GHG that stem from fossil fuel electricity generation. However, substantial investment costs hinder the scalability of technologies like afforestation, necessitating policymakers to explore the use of revenue from carbon taxes to accelerate the adoption of NETs. Carbon taxes can serve as a funding mechanism to expedite the adoption of NETs by pooling resources at the government level, leveraging synergistic benefits that are unavailable to individual businesses due to limited resources.

Meaningful behavioural changes away from carbon-intensive activities require policymakers to prioritise the adoption of NETs and implement carbon pricing mechanisms that reflect the true cost of carbon emissions. Current carbon tax rates, particularly in South Africa, are insufficient to incentivise the adoption of NETs. Carbon price estimates to adopt NETs range between USD 90 (ZAR 1710) and USD 600 (ZAR 11400) per tonne of CO2, which significantly exceeds the South African carbon price ZAR 159 (USD 8.37) per tonne of CO2. The current South African carbon price would not incentivise businesses to invest in NETs, due to the implementation costs that exceed the benefits of a carbon tax cost saving.

Revising carbon pricing to align with global climate targets and investing in research and development to enhance the scalability and cost-effectiveness of emerging NETs like DACS and enhanced weathering are crucial steps in accelerating the transition to a low-carbon economy and mitigating the impacts of climate change. Collaborative efforts between governments, industries, and research institutions are essential to address these challenges and pave the way for a sustainable future.

References

Afrane, S., Ampah, J. D., Yusuf, A. A., Jinjuan, Z., Yang, P., Chen, J. L., & Mao, G. (2024). Role of negative emission technologies in South Africa's pathway to net zero emissions by 2050. *Energy for Sustainable Development, 79*, 101401. https://doi.org/10.1016/j.esd.2024.101401

Almena, A., Thornley, P., Chong, K., & Röder, M. (2022). Carbon dioxide removal potential from decentralised bioenergy with carbon capture and storage (BECCS) and the relevance of operational choices. *Biomass and Bioenergy, 159*, 106406. https://doi.org/10.1016/j.biombioe.2022.106406

Anand, A., Kumar, V., & Kaushal, P. (2022). Biochar and its twin benefits: Crop residue management and climate change mitigation in India. *Renewable and Sustainable Energy Reviews, 156*, 111959. https://doi.org/10.1016/j.rser.2021.111959

Asibor, J. O., Clough, P. T., Nabavi, S. A., & Manovic, V. (2022). A country-level assessment of the deployment potential of greenhouse gas removal technologies. *Journal of Environmental Management, 323*, 116211. https://doi.org/10.1016/j.jenvman.2022.116211

Babakhani, P., Phenrat, T., Baalousha, M., Soratana, K., Peacock, C. L., Twining, B. S., & Hochella, M. F., Jr. (2022). Potential use of engineered nanoparticles in ocean fertilization for large-scale atmospheric carbon dioxide removal. *Nature Nanotechnology, 17*(12), 1342–1351. https://doi.org/10.1038/s41565-022-01226-w

Baranzini, A., Van den Bergh, J., Carattini, S., Howarth, R., Padilla, E., & Roca, J. (2017). Seven reasons to use carbon pricing in climate policy. *Wiley Interdisciplinary Reviews: Climate Change, 8*(4), e462. https://doi.org/10.1002/wcc.462

Beck, B., Kulichenko-Lotz, N., & Surridge, T. (2017). World Bank CCS program activities in South Africa–Results and lessons learned. *Energy Procedia, 114*, 5636–5649. https://doi.org/10.1016/j.egypro.2017.03.1702

Bo, X., Zhang, Z., Wang, J., Guo, S., Li, Z., Lin, H., Huang, Y., Han, Z., Kuzyakov, Y., & Zou, J. (2023). Benefits and limitations of biochar for climate-smart agriculture: A review and case study from China. *Biochar, 5*(1), 77. https://doi.org/10.1007/s42773-023-00279-x

Boyce, J. K. (2018). Carbon pricing: Effectiveness and equity. *Ecological Economics, 150*, 52–61. https://doi.org/10.1016/j.ecolecon.2018.03.030

Bui, M., Fajardy, M., & Mac Dowell, N. (2018). Bio-energy with carbon capture and storage (BECCS): Opportunities for performance improvement. *Fuel, 213*, 164–175. https://doi.org/10.1016/j.fuel.2017.10.100

Bullock, L. A., Yang, A., & Darton, R. C. (2022). Kinetics-informed global assessment of mine tailings for CO2 removal. *Science of the Total Environment, 808*, 152111. https://doi.org/10.1016/j.scitotenv.2021.152111

Carrier, M., Hardie, A. G., Uras, Ü., Görgens, J., & Knoetze, J. H. (2012). Production of char from vacuum pyrolysis of south-African sugar cane bagasse and its characterization as activated carbon and biochar. *Journal of Analytical and Applied Pyrolysis, 96*, 24–32. https://doi.org/10.1016/j.jaap.2012.02.016

Cheng, Y., Sinha, A., Ghosh, V., Sengupta, T., & Luo, H. (2021). Carbon tax and energy innovation at crossroads of carbon neutrality: Designing a sustainable decarbonization policy. *Journal of Environmental Management, 294*, 112957. https://doi.org/10.1016/j.jenvman.2021.112957

Daggash, H. A., Heuberger, C. F., & Mac Dowell, N. (2019). The role and value of negative emissions technologies in decarbonising the UK energy system. *International Journal of Greenhouse Gas Control, 81*, 181–198. https://doi.org/10.1016/j.ijggc.2018.12.019

Department of Environment Forestry and Fisheries. (2020). *South Africa's low- emission development strategy 2050*. Department of Environment Forestry and Fisheries.

Department of Trade, Industry and Competition. (2020). *Master plan for the commercial forestry sector in South Africa 2020–2025*. Department of Environment Forestry and Fisheries.

Desport, L., Gurgel, A., Morris, J., Herzog, H., Chen, Y. H. H., Selosse, S., & Paltsev, S. (2024). Deploying direct air capture at scale: How close to reality? *Energy Economics, 129*, 107244. https://doi.org/10.1016/j.eneco.2023.107244

Dissanayake, S., Mahadevan, R., & Asafu-Adjaye, J. (2020). Evaluating the efficiency of carbon emissions policies in a large emitting developing country. *Energy Policy, 136*, 111080. https://doi.org/10.1016/j.enpol.2019.111080

Doelman, J. C., Stehfest, E., van Vuuren, D. P., Tabeau, A., Hof, A. F., Braakhekke, M. C., Gernaat, D. E., van den Berg, M., van Zeist, W. J., Daioglou, V., van Meijl, H., & Lucas, P. L. (2020). Afforestation for climate change mitigation: Potentials, risks and trade-offs. *Global Change Biology, 26*(3), 1576–1591. https://doi.org/10.1111/gcb.14887

Du Preez, C. C., Lebenya, R. M., & van Huyssteen, C. W. (2022). Change in total carbon stocks eight years after afforestation of a sub-humid grassland catchment with Pinus and eucalyptus species. *New Forests, 53*(2), 267–284. https://doi.org/10.1007/s11056-021-09854-1

Dzvene, A. R., Chiduza, C., Mnkeni, P. N., & Peter, P. C. (2019). Characterisation of livestock biochars and their effect on selected soil properties and maize early growth stage in soils of eastern cape province, South Africa. *South African Journal of Plant and Soil, 36*(3), 199–209. https://doi.org/10.17159/wsa/2021.v47.i4.3861

Eisaman, M. D., Geilert, S., Renforth, P., Bastianini, L., Campbell, J., Dale, A. W., Foteinis, S., Grasse, P., Hawrot, O., Löscher, C., Rau, G., & Rønning, J. B. (2023). Assessing the technical aspects of ocean-alkalinity-enhancement approaches. *State of the Planet, 3*, 29. https://doi.org/10.5194/sp-2-oae2023-3-2023

Fajardy, M., Morris, J., Gurgel, A., Herzog, H., Mac Dowell, N., & Paltsev, S. (2021). The economics of bioenergy with carbon capture and storage (BECCS) deployment in a 1.5 C or 2 C world. *Global Environmental Change, 68*, 102262. https://doi.org/10.1016/j.gloenvcha.2021.102262

Fasihi, M., Efimova, O., & Breyer, C. (2019). Techno-economic assessment of CO2 direct air capture plants. *Journal of Cleaner Production, 224*, 957–980. https://doi.org/10.1016/j.jclepro.2019.03.086

Fawzy, S., Osman, A. I., Doran, J., & Rooney, D. W. (2020). Strategies for mitigation of climate change: A review. *Environmental Chemistry Letters, 18*, 2069–2094. https://doi.org/10.1007/s10311-020-01059-w

Forster, E. J., Healey, J. R., Dymond, C., & Styles, D. (2021). Commercial afforestation can deliver effective climate change mitigation under multiple decarbonisation pathways. *Nature Communications, 12*(1), 3831. https://doi.org/10.1038/s41467-021-24084-x

Fuss, S., Lamb, W. F., Callaghan, M. W., Hilaire, J., Creutzig, F., Amann, T., Beringer, T., de Oliveira Garcia, W., Hartmann, J., Khanna, T., Luderer, G., & Minx, J. C. (2018). Negative emissions—Part 2: Costs, potentials and side effects. *Environmental Research Letters, 13*(6), 063002. https://doi.org/10.1088/1748-9326/aabf9f

Gattuso, J. P., Magnan, A. K., Bopp, L., Cheung, W. W., Duarte, C. M., Hinkel, J., Mcleod, E., Micheli, F., Oschlies, A., Williamson, P., Billé, R., & Rau, G. H. (2018). Ocean solutions to address climate change and its effects on marine ecosystems. *Frontiers in Marine Science, 5*, 410554. https://doi.org/10.3389/fmars.2018.00337

Ghazouani, A., Xia, W., Ben Jebli, M., & Shahzad, U. (2020). Exploring the role of carbon taxation policies on CO2 emissions: Contextual evidence from tax implementation and non-implementation European countries. *Sustainability, 12*(20), 8680. https://doi.org/10.46507/jcgpp.v1i1.8

Ginanjar, W. R., & Mubarrok, A. Z. (2020). Civil society and global governance: The indirect participation of extinction rebellion in global governance on climate change. *Journal of Contemporary Governance and Public Policy, 1*(1), 41–52. https://doi.org/10.46507/jcgpp.v1i1.8

Halkos, G. E., & Kitsou, D. C. (2018). Weighted location differential tax in environmental problems. *Environmental Economics and Policy Studies, 20*, 1–15. https://doi.org/10.1007/s10018-016-0179-9

Hanlon, M., & Heitzman, S. (2010). A review of tax research. *Journal of Accounting and Economics, 50*(2–3), 127–178. https://doi.org/10.1016/j.jacceco.2010.09.002

Heal, G., & Schlenker, W. (2019). *Coase, Hotelling and Pigou: The incidence of a carbon tax and CO_2 emissions (No. w26086)*. National Bureau of Economic Research. https://doi.org/10.3386/w26086

Intergovernmental Panel on Climate Change (IPCC). (2014). Climate change 2014: Impacts, adaptation, and vulnerability. Part A: Global and Sectoral aspects. In *Contribution of working group II to the fifth assessment report of the intergovernmental panel on climate change*. Cambridge University Press.

International Energy Agency. (2023). CCUS projects database [online]. Paris International Energy Agency. http://www.iea.org/data-and-statistics/data-product/ccus-projects-database

Jaqua, D., & Schaffa, D. (2022). The case for subsidizing harm: Constrained and costly Pigouvian taxation with multiple externalities. *International Tax and Public Finance, 29*(2), 408–442. https://doi.org/10.1007/s10797-021-09670-5

Jiang, H. B., Hutchins, D. A., Zhang, H. R., Feng, Y. Y., Zhang, R. F., Sun, W. W., Ma, W., Bai, Y., Wells, M., He, D., Jiao, N., & Chai, F. (2024). Complexities of regulating climate by promoting marine primary production with ocean iron fertilization. *Earth-Science Reviews, 249*, 104675. https://doi.org/10.1016/j.earscirev.2024.104675

Ko, Y. C., Zigan, K., & Liu, Y. L. (2021). Carbon capture and storage in South Africa: A technological innovation system with a political economy focus. *Technological Forecasting and Social Change, 166*, 120633. https://doi.org/10.1016/j.techfore.2021.120633

Kotlán, I., Němec, D., Kotlánová, E., Skalka, P., Macek, R., & Machová, Z. (2021). European green deal: Environmental taxation and its sustainability in conditions of high levels of corruption. *Sustainability, 13*(4), 1981. https://doi.org/10.3390/su13041981

Lampitt, R. S., Achterberg, E. P., Anderson, T. R., Hughes, J. A., Iglesias-Rodriguez, M. D., Kelly-Gerreyn, B. A., Lucas, M., Popova, E. E., Sanders, R., Shepherd, J. G., Smythe-Wright, D., & Yool, A. (2008). Ocean fertilization: A potential means of geoengineering? *Philosophical Transactions of the Royal Society A: Mathematical, Physical and Engineering Sciences, 366*(1882), 3919–3945. https://doi.org/10.1098/rsta.2008.0139

Lefebvre, D., Williams, A., Kirk, G. J., Meersmans, J., Sohi, S., Goglio, P., & Smith, P. (2021). An anticipatory life cycle assessment of the use of biochar from sugarcane residues as a greenhouse gas removal technology. *Journal of Cleaner Production, 312*, 127764. https://doi.org/10.1016/j.jclepro.2021.127764

Lehtveer, M., & Emanuelsson, A. (2021). BECCS and DACCS as negative emission providers in an intermittent electricity system: Why levelized cost of carbon may be a misleading measure for policy decisions. *Frontiers in Climate, 3*, 647276. https://doi.org/10.3389/fclim.2021.647276

Lewis, A. L., Sarkar, B., Wade, P., Kemp, S. J., Hodson, M. E., Taylor, L. L., Yeong, K. L., Davies, K., Nelson, P. N., Bird, M. I., Kantola, I. B., & Beerling, D. J. (2021). Effects of mineralogy, chemistry and physical properties of basalts on carbon capture potential and plant-nutrient element release via enhanced weathering. *Applied Geochemistry, 132*, 105023. https://doi.org/10.1016/j.apgeochem.2021.105023

Liu, H., Xu, C., Allen, C. D., Hartmann, H., Wei, X., Yakir, D., Wu, X., & Yu, P. (2022). Nature-based framework for sustainable afforestation in global drylands under changing climate. *Global Change Biology, 28*(7), 2202–2220. https://doi.org/10.1111/gcb.16059

Makamela, K. C., & Ramfol, R. (2023, June). A comparative analysis of South Africa's carbon pricing policy in the power and energy-intensive industries. In *ICABR conference* (pp. 817–834). Springer Nature Switzerland.

Mander, S., Anderson, K., Larkin, A., Gough, C., & Vaughan, N. (2017). The role of bio-energy with carbon capture and storage in meeting the climate mitigation challenge: A whole system perspective. *Energy Procedia, 114*, 6036–6043. https://doi.org/10.1016/j.egypro.2017.03.1739

Manta, A. G., Doran, N. M., Bădîrcea, R. M., Badareu, G., & Țăran, A. M. (2023). Does the implementation of a Pigouvian tax be considered an effective approach to address climate change mitigation? *Economic Analysis and Policy, 80*, 1719–1731. https://doi.org/10.1016/j.eap.2023.11.002

McQueen, N., Kelemen, P., Dipple, G., Renforth, P., & Wilcox, J. (2020). Ambient weathering of magnesium oxide for CO2 removal from air. *Nature Communications, 11*(1), 3299. https://doi.org/10.1038/s41467-020-16510-3

Mikhaylov, A., Moiseev, N., Aleshin, K., & Burkhardt, T. (2020). Global climate change and greenhouse effect. *Entrepreneurship and Sustainability Issues, 7*(4), 2897. https://doi.org/10.9770/jesi.2020.7.4(21)

Ministry Of Water Affairs and Forestry. (1997). *Sustainable forest development in South Africa the policy of the government of National Unity White Paper*. Ministry of Water Affairs and Forestry.

National Treasury. (2010). *Discussion paper for public comment reducing greenhouse gas emissions: The carbon tax option*. National Treasury.

National Treasury. (2013). *Reducing greenhouse gas emissions and facilitating the transition to a green economy*. National Treasury.

National Treasury. (2017). *Explanatory memorandum on the carbon tax bill*. National Treasury.

National Treasury. (2018). *Explanatory memorandum on the carbon tax bill*. National Treasury.

Nong, D., Simshauser, P., & Nguyen, D. B. (2021). Greenhouse gas emissions vs CO2 emissions: Comparative analysis of a global carbon tax. *Applied Energy, 298*, 117223. https://doi.org/10.1016/j.apenergy.2021.117223

Nyambo, P., Chiduza, C., & Araya, T. (2020). Carbon input and maize productivity as influenced by tillage, crop rotation, residue management and biochar in a semiarid region in South Africa. *Agronomy, 10*(5), 705. https://doi.org/10.3390/agronomy10050705

Okonkwo, E. C., AlNouss, A., Shahbaz, M., & Al-Ansari, T. (2023). Developing integrated direct air capture and bioenergy with carbon capture and storage systems: Progress towards 2° C and 1.5° C climate goals. *Energy Conversion and Management, 296*, 117687. https://doi.org/10.1016/j.enconman.2023.117687

Organisation for Economic Co-operation and Development (OECD). (2010). *Taxation, innovation, and the environment*. Organisation for Economic Co-operation and Development.

Organisation for Economic Co-operation and Development (OECD). (2023). *Effective carbon rates 2023: Pricing greenhouse gas emissions through taxes and emissions trading, OECD series on carbon pricing and energy taxation*. OECD Publishing. https://doi.org/10.1787/b84d5b36-en

Paulo, C., Power, I. M., Stubbs, A. R., Wang, B., Zeyen, N., & Wilson, S. (2021). Evaluating feedstocks for carbon dioxide removal by enhanced rock weathering and CO2 mineralization. *Applied Geochemistry, 129*, 104955. https://doi.org/10.1016/j.apgeochem.2021.104955

Power, I. M., Paulo, C., & Rausis, K. (2023). The mining industry's role in enhanced weathering and mineralization for CO2 removal. *Environmental Science & Technology, 58*(1), 43–53. https://doi.org/10.1021/acs.est.3c05081

Realmonte, G., Drouet, L., Gambhir, A., Glynn, J., Hawkes, A., Köberle, A. C., & Tavoni, M. (2019). An inter-model assessment of the role of direct air capture in deep mitigation pathways. *Nature Communications, 10*(1), 3277. https://doi.org/10.1038/s41467-019-10842-5

Rosenbloom, D., Markard, J., Geels, F. W., & Fuenfschilling, L. (2020). Why carbon pricing is not sufficient to mitigate climate change—And how "sustainability transition policy" can help. *Proceedings of the National Academy of Sciences, 117*(16), 8664–8668. https://doi.org/10.1073/pnas.2004093117

Semida, W. M., Beheiry, H. R., Sétamou, M., Simpson, C. R., Abd El-Mageed, T. A., Rady, M. M., & Nelson, S. D. (2019). Biochar implications for sustainable agriculture and environment: A review. *South African Journal of Botany, 127*, 333–347. https://doi.org/10.1016/j.sajb.2019.11.015

Sodiq, A., Abdullatif, Y., Aissa, B., Ostovar, A., Nassar, N., El-Naas, M., & Amhamed, A. (2023). A review on progress made in direct air capture of CO2. *Environmental Technology & Innovation, 29*, 102991. https://doi.org/10.1016/j.eti.2022.102991

Späth, J., Arumugam, P., Lindberg, R. H., Abafe, O. A., Jansson, S., Fick, J., & Buckley, C. A. (2021). Biochar for the removal of detected micropollutants in South African domestic wastewater: A case study from a demonstration-scale decentralised wastewater treatment system in eThekwini. *Water SA, 47*(4), 396–416. https://doi.org/10.1080/02571862.2018.1536930

Stubbs, A. R., Paulo, C., Power, I. M., Wang, B., Zeyen, N., & Wilson, S. (2022). Direct measurement of CO2 drawdown in mine wastes and rock powders: Implications for enhanced rock weathering. *International Journal of Greenhouse Gas Control, 113*, 103554. https://doi.org/10.1016/j.ijggc.2021.103554

Tan, R. R., & Aviso, K. B. (2021). On life-cycle sustainability optimization of enhanced weathering systems. *Journal of Cleaner Production, 289*, 125836. https://doi.org/10.1016/j.jclepro.2021.125836

Tan, Z., Wu, Y., Gu, Y., Liu, T., Wang, W., & Liu, X. (2022). An overview on implementation of environmental tax and related economic instruments in typical countries. *Journal of Cleaner Production, 330*, 129688. https://doi.org/10.1016/j.jclepro.2021.129688

Tanzer, S. E., Blok, K., & Ramirez, A. (2021). Decarbonising industry via BECCS: Promising sectors, challenges, and techno-economic limits of negative emissions. *Current Sustainable/Renewable Energy Reports*, 1–10. https://doi.org/10.1007/s40518-021-00195-3

te Pas, E. E., Hagens, M., & Comans, R. N. (2023). Assessment of the enhanced weathering potential of different silicate minerals to improve soil quality and sequester CO2. *Frontiers in Climate, 4*, 954064. https://doi.org/10.3389/fclim.2022.954064

Terlouw, T., Bauer, C., Rosa, L., & Mazzotti, M. (2021). Life cycle assessment of carbon dioxide removal technologies: A critical review. *Energy & Environmental Science, 14*(4), 1701–1721. https://doi.org/10.1039/D0EE03757E

Tisserant, A., & Cherubini, F. (2019). Potentials, limitations, co-benefits, and trade-offs of biochar applications to soils for climate change mitigation. *Land, 8*(12), 179. https://doi.org/10.3390/land8120179

Vandeginste, V., Lim, C., & Ji, Y. (2024). Exploratory review on environmental aspects of enhanced weathering as a carbon dioxide removal method. *Minerals, 14*(1), 75. https://doi.org/10.3390/min14010075

VanderWolk, J. P. (2021). Carbon tax: The global perspective. *Bulletin for International Taxation, 75*(5), 250–255. https://www.ibfd.org/shop/oecdinternational-carbon-tax-global-perspective

Wang, D., Jiang, P., Zhang, H., & Yuan, W. (2020). Biochar production and applications in agro and forestry systems: A review. *Science of the Total Environment, 723*, 137775. https://doi.org/10.1016/j.scitotenv.2020.137775

Wang, Y. K., & Zhang, X. (2019). Firm's imperfect compliance and pollution emissions: Theory and evidence from South Africa. *Asian Journal of Economics, Business and Accounting, 1*(9), 1–9. https://doi.org/10.9734/ajeba/2019/v11i330129

Wolde-Rufael, Y., & Mulat-Weldemeskel, E. (2021). Do environmental taxes and environmental stringency policies reduce CO2 emissions? Evidence from 7 emerging economies. *Environmental Science and Pollution Research, 28*(18), 22392–22408. https://doi.org/10.1007/s11356-020-11475-8

Young, J., McQueen, N., Charalambous, C., Foteinis, S., Hawrot, O., Ojeda, M., Pilorgé, H., Andresen, J., Psarras, P., Renforth, P., & Garcia, S. (2023). The cost of direct air capture and storage can be reduced via strategic deployment but is unlikely to fall below stated cost targets. *One Earth, 6*(7), 899–917. https://doi.org/10.1016/j.oneear.2023.06.004

Zhang, D., Bui, M., Fajardy, M., Patrizio, P., Kraxner, F., & Mac Dowell, N. (2020). Unlocking the potential of BECCS with indigenous sources of biomass at a national scale. *Sustainable Energy & Fuels, 4*(1), 226–253. https://doi.org/10.1039/C9SE00609E

Determinants of Growth of Companies Listed on the Johannesburg Securities Exchange

Mwambenu Nephtali Tshitadi, Minnette Vermaak, and Darius du Plessis

Abstract This study investigates the determinants of growth of companies listed on the Johannesburg Securities Exchange. The literature on firm growth has identified numerous determinants of growth, demonstrating that growth is a multidimensional and complex phenomenon. The factors identified, however, have often yielded contradictory results regarding their influence, primarily since the operationalisation of growth relies on several approaches in terms of measures or periods retained. This study focuses on firm-specific determinants, which include firm size, firm age, gender diversity, liquidity, leverage, and profitability. The dependent variable, firm growth, was measured using the logarithmic difference in total sales. The data were collected from the INET BFA (IRESS) database and published annual reports. Using panel data of 187 companies listed on the Johannesburg Securities Exchange (JSE) during the period 2009–2018, the fixed-effect results show that firm growth, liquidity, and profitability are negatively correlated with firm growth. The results further reveal that the law of proportionate effect or Gibrat's law is not valid for JSE-listed companies since a positive and significant relationship between firm size and firm growth was found in this research. Moreover, gender diversity and leverage were found to have no significant effect on the growth of JSE-listed companies.

Keywords Determinants of growth · Firm growth · Firm size · Firm age · Gender diversity · Gibrat's law · Leverage · Liquidity · Profitability · Johannesburg Securities Exchange

---

M. N. Tshitadi · M. Vermaak (✉) · D. du Plessis
University of Johannesburg, Johannesburg, South Africa
e-mail: mvermaak@uj.ac.za; dariusdp@uj.ac.za

T. Moloi (ed.), *Impacting Society Positively Through Technology in Accounting and Business Processes*, Springer Proceedings in Business and Economics,
https://doi.org/10.1007/978-3-031-84885-8_30

Introduction

Firm growth has been the primary concern of researchers for many years within the fields of accounting, management, and finance. The 2008 global financial and economic crisis has led researchers and policymakers to become even more interested in understanding and analysing the factors affecting the growth of firms, especially Small and Medium Enterprises (Thu & Xuan, 2023; OECD, 2009; Steinerowska-Streb et al., 2022). Consequently, the objective commonly targeted by researchers has been to create a universal model capable of predicting growth, which would identify, in advance, the entrepreneurial factors, mindset, strategies, and environmental conditions that enhance a company's growth prospects (Baskoro et al., 2022; Janssen, 2011). In this respect, the literature has identified an impressive number of determinants of growth, demonstrating that firm growth is a multidimensional and complex phenomenon (Tunberg & Anderson, 2020).

However, the factors identified have often yielded contradictory results regarding their influence, primarily since the operationalisation of growth relies on several approaches regarding measures or retained periods (Delmar et al., 2003; Janssen, 2009). These factors are numerous, ranging from entrepreneurial aspects, the economic environment, and structure of the industry, to the origins of the firm, financial systems, or the strategy pursued (Vaz, 2021; Lakuma et al., 2019; Arthur-Aidoo et al., 2017). While proposing a comprehensive review of all factors affecting growth is quite challenging, two main classifications are often distinguished: external and internal factors. External factors include the broader environment over which the firm has no control, such as technological advancement, macroeconomic indicators, competition, industry-specific factors, market conditions, and regulatory frameworks (Kyläheiko et al., 2017; Nanda & Panda, 2018; Purwanto & Purwanto, 2020; Rico et al., 2021). Internal factors, on the other hand, encompass the entrepreneur's characteristics, organisational capabilities, financial factors, company size and age, company resources, management quality, and the strategic decisions that drive firm growth (Vučenović et al., 2021; Ilmiyono & Widyowati, 2021; Haruyama & Fujiyama, 2022).

The neoclassical approach first insists that a firm's growth is related to external factors or characteristics of the industry in which the firm operates (Dromby, 2000). The growth trajectory will not be specific to a single firm but will depend on the overall economic environment (Tarillon, 2006; Haschka et al., 2022). This approach is based on the maximising attitude of firms and their managers and on the idea that each firm seeks to minimise its cost function to maximise its profit function. Thus, in a situation of pure and perfect competition, the firm will grow until its long-term marginal cost of production equals the unit selling price of its products (Tarillon, 2006). The company will then have reached its optimal size (Davidsson, 1989).

The theoretical approach based on an explanation of internal growth factors proposes to consider firm-specific factors. Firms are no longer considered passive agents; instead, they become active agents with the ability to shape and influence this environment according to, for example, their interests (Janssen, 2011). Given the above, Tarillon (2006) highlights that each firm may have a specific growth trajectory whose origin and explanatory factors must be investigated. Penrose (1959) was one of the first to consider this question regarding the firm's resources. According to Penrose (1959), the phenomenon of growth is a process based on the endogenous (internal) characteristics of firms and especially on the evolution of the internal resources available to them (Foss, 1998). This approach explains the growth of firms by their characteristics. The emphasis is on the idea that firm growth is caused by a combination of numerous factors related, in particular, to the characteristics of the organisation, its operating constraints, its financial structure, as well as its strategic positioning (Vaz, 2021; Haruyama & Fujiyama, 2022).

Building on this empirical and theoretical foundation, it becomes essential to examine how these internal growth dynamics manifest within specific market contexts. The primary objective of this study is to investigate the determinants of the growth of companies listed on the Johannesburg Securities Exchange. This study approaches the topic of firm growth from the broader perspective of JSE-listed companies, regardless of their size or the sector/industry in which these firms operate.

Literature Review

Definition of Firm Growth

Since the early twentieth century, defining "firm growth" has been a point of contention among corporate finance and management scholars. While no universal definition exists, two perspectives have prevailed: growth as a quantitative outcome and growth as a qualitative internal process (Penrose, 1959; Tunberg, 2017). Quantitative definitions focus on measurable increases in parameters like sales, employees, or production (Hanifzadeh et al., 2018; Delmar et al., 2003; Murathe, 2016). Qualitative definitions emphasise improvements in areas like product quality, goodwill, customer relationships, or market position (Tingler, 2015; Hampton, 2009). Most studies favour the quantitative approach due to its compatibility with economic models prevalent in corporate growth literature (Davidsson et al., 2010). However, acknowledging both perspectives is crucial for comprehensively understanding firm growth.

Theoretical Framework

This study adopts Penrose's (1959) theory of firm growth, which emphasises the crucial role of managerial capabilities and internal resources in driving growth (Nason & Wiklund, 2018). Penrose (1959) diverges from neoclassical theory, which attributes firm growth to the optimisation of resource allocation to achieve an ideal size, typically associated with the minimum point on their cost curve (Neri, 2020). In this view, growth is seen as an increase in production volume resulting from this optimisation process (Penrose, 1959; Neri, 2020). Instead, Penrose (1959) posits that growth is an endogenous process fuelled by the management team's ambition, motivations, and ability to effectively utilise available resources (both physical and human), with firm size being a consequence rather than a target (Arena, 2013).

Penrose (1959) highlights the importance of human resources, particularly senior executives, in planning and directing growth. As firms grow, their organisational structure evolves, leading to greater decentralisation of authority (Kim, 2018; Waeger & Weber, 2019). Penrose (1959) argues that growth stems from the management team's drive to utilise underemployed resources, creating new opportunities and further fuelling expansion. This framework is particularly relevant for investigating the determinants of firm growth through firm-specific characteristics, as it highlights the significance of internal factors like gender diversity, firm size, firm age, liquidity, leverage, and profitability.

Empirical Evidence on the Determinants of Firm Growth

While firm growth is crucial for economic dynamism, research on its determinants yields mixed and sometimes contradictory results, hindering a clear understanding of the factors driving growth. Many factors have been identified within the literature. However, this study explores the impact of six key factors—firm size, age, gender diversity, leverage, liquidity, and profitability—on firm growth, acknowledging the complexities and inconsistencies within the existing literature.

- **Firm size and firm growth**

The growth-size relationship has fuelled considerable debate over time. Gibrat (1931), a pioneer in studying this relationship, proposed the "law of proportionate effect," often referred to as Gibrat's Law. This law posits that a firm's growth is independent of its size and follows a stochastic process (Gibrat, 1931). This implies that all firms, regardless of their current scale, have an equal chance of experiencing a certain growth rate (Bienaymé, 1973). Early studies supported this notion, finding no correlation between size and growth in various contexts, including Malaysian construction (Rasiah et al., 2014), UK firms (Hermelo & Vassolo, 2007), and JSE-listed companies (Bethlehem, 1979).

However, a growing body of evidence challenges this view, suggesting a positive relationship between firm size and growth. Studies on Romanian automotive firms (Albulescu et al., 2021), French new ventures (Cesinger et al., 2018), Australian ICT SMEs (Perényi & Yukhanaev, 2016), Jordan-listed firms (Hamouri et al., 2018), and Croatian manufacturing and hospitality firms (Perić et al., 2020) have rejected Gibrat's Law by finding a positive and statistically significant impact of firm size on firm growth. This indicates that larger firms tend to experience higher growth rates. Therefore, we hypothesise that:

Hypothesis 1: Firm size positively impacts JSE-listed companies' growth.

- **Firm age and firm growth**

Growing literature within the fields of management, finance, and economics indicates that the age of a company is likely to affect its growth dynamics. Coad (2009) suggested that younger and smaller firms tend to grow faster than older ones. While some studies, like Shanmugan and Bhaduri (2002) on Indian companies and Anton (2016), found a positive relationship between age and growth, significant evidence points to a negative correlation. Research on US firms (Evans, 1987; Variyam & Kraybill, 1992) and Japanese manufacturing firms (Yasuda, 2005) revealed that firm growth declines with age. Furthermore, Daunfeldt et al. (2014) showed that high-growth firms tend to be younger, suggesting a negative correlation between a firm's age and growth. Megaravalli and Sampagnaro (2018) also found a negative age-growth relationship, though they noted that younger firms have a higher chance of achieving high growth. Therefore, we propose that:

Hypothesis 2: Firm age has a negative impact on the growth of JSE firms.

- **Gender diversity and firm growth**

Although it is widely believed that companies that actively employ more women in managerial roles improve their performance (Nakagawa, 2015), empirical evidence suggests mixed results. Most studies show that a firm performs better if there is a diversity of gender on the board of directors (Carter et al., 2003; Campbell & Mínguez-Vera, 2008; Julizaerma & Sori, 2012). Using a sample of S&P 1500 firms, Dezso and Ross (2012) found that female representation in top management improves firm performance, but only to the extent that a firm's strategy is focused on innovation.

In contrast, Cooper et al. (1994) found that the gender of the manager or entrepreneur is negatively correlated with the growth of SMEs. Terjesen and Szerb (2008) employed a sample of 25,384 companies from 35 countries and found that the male gender is associated with high-growth expectations and that the female gender negatively affects business growth. The results from the study by Schwab et al. (2016) also show that firm performance decreases as the firm moves from homogeneous (all-male managers) to gender diversity.

Hypothesis 3: There is a positive relationship between gender diversity and the growth of JSE-listed companies.

- **Leverage and firm growth**

A growing body of research has explored the relationship between financial leverage and firm growth. While some studies suggest no significant link (Yasemi & Jalilian, 2014; Mutai, 2014), much evidence points to a positive correlation. For instance, Anton (2016) found a positive relationship between the age and growth of Romanian listed firms. Similarly, Iqbal and Usman (2018) found that financial leverage positively impacts firm performance, but only when debt levels remain below equity levels. Javadi and Alimoradi (2017) also found a positive relationship between leverage and firm growth, suggesting that companies may utilise debt financing to pursue riskier growth opportunities.

Conversely, Lang et al. (1996) found a negative relationship between leverage and growth in European firms, including high-growth firms. Similarly, Dzafic and Polic (2019) and Oliveira and Kayo (2019) observed a negative correlation between leverage and growth over Bosnian and Herzegovinian firms and Brazilian companies, respectively. Despite these contrasting findings, the overall impression is that leverage positively affects firm growth. Thus, we propose the following hypothesis:

Hypothesis 4: Financial leverage has a positive and significant impact on the growth of JSE-listed companies.

- **Liquidity and firm growth**

Waswa et al. (2018) argue that liquidity is one of the key drivers of working capital optimisation, revenue enhancement, and strong financial performance. Companies that prioritise and effectively manage liquidity tend to achieve higher corporate growth, regardless of their specific structural characteristics or financial systems (Waswa et al., 2018). However, the impact of liquidity on firm growth presents conflicting findings in the literature. While some studies suggest a positive relationship, others highlight a negative correlation. For instance, research by Donati (2015), Quader (2017), and Megaravalli and Sampagnaro (2018) suggests a positive relationship between liquidity and growth. These studies posit that a strong liquidity position enables firms to pursue growth opportunities and reduces the risk of default (Megaravalli & Sampagnaro, 2018).

Conversely, Oliveira and Fortunato (2006) found a negative relationship between liquidity and firm growth, implying that liquidity constraints can hinder firm growth, particularly for smaller companies with limited cash flow. Similarly, Waswa et al.'s (2018) study reported a negative relationship between liquidity and firm performance of Kenyan sugar firms. This conflicting evidence regarding the impact of liquidity on firm growth necessitates further investigation. Therefore, this study proposes the following hypothesis:

Hypothesis 5: Liquidity has a negative impact on the growth of JSE-listed companies

- **Profitability and firm growth**

Profitability is another financial ratio that has been linked to firm growth. However, the literature reveals no consensus on whether profitability precedes growth or vice versa. Most studies across different countries and sectors have found positive and significant links between current growth rates and profitability, hypothesising that more profitable firms will experience higher growth rates (Costa & Donner, 2016). For instance, Geroski et al. (1997) reported a positive relationship between profitability and the growth of UK firms, implying that profit creates growth. Similar results were evidenced by Piao et al. (2017) over manufacturing listed companies, Lee (2014) over Korean firms, Costa and Donner (2016) over Swiss Listed companies, and Coban (2014) over Turkish-listed manufacturing firms.

In contrast, Lee's study of Korean firms and Piao et al. (2017), and Lee's (2014) research on Chinese manufacturing firms found a negative relationship between profitability and subsequent firm growth. However, given the preponderance of evidence suggesting a positive relationship between profitability and firm growth, this study proposes the following hypothesis:

Hypothesis 6: Growth of JSE-listed companies is positively related to firm profitability.

While the literature on firm growth is extensive, there is limited research examining the determinants of growth specifically for listed companies from the South African point of view. This study offers a unique contribution by investigating a comprehensive range of internal factors influencing the growth of listed companies in South Africa. It considers not only firm management (gender diversity) and characteristics (size and age) but also focuses on the crucial role of financial ratios—leverage, liquidity, and profitability. This emphasis on financial data stems from the recognition that well-managed finances are a key indicator of firm success and form the basis for critical managerial decisions (Gupta et al., 2023).

Research Methodology

This section discusses the specific research methods used in this study to collect and analyse the data. The definitions, as well as the description of dependent and explanatory variables used for this research, are included.

Population and Sample

The targeted population of this current study consists of all companies listed on the Johannesburg Securities Exchange (JSE), and the study period stretches from 2009 to 2018. The study population initially consisted of 356 listed companies, and the final sample comprised 187 listed firms from various JSE sectors, according to the Industry Classification Benchmark (ICB). Some listed companies did not provide sufficient information for all the variables, especially the figures about total sales; therefore, they were not included in the sample. Other companies, especially newly listed SMEs, were under 10 years of operations, so they were excluded from the sample to get a balanced panel. Additionally, a firm had to remain JSE listed until the 30th of September 2019, the date on which the data were collected, to be included in the analysis. All firms delisted from the JSE before that date were excluded from the sample. An additional requirement was imposed for the remaining firms in the sample, which was that companies must report gender board composition information during the period 2009–2018.

Data Collection Methods

The study used secondary data obtained from the INET BFA (IRESS) database and audited annual reports. Since JSE-listed companies have to publish annual reports as part of standard listing requirements, the study considered audited annual reports as a reliable source of accurate information, including gender diversity and company age, as they contain demographic and career profiles of board members, financial statements, and the establishment date of companies. In the case where the gender of a director was not specified in the annual report of a particular JSE-listed company, a Google search was carried out to determine the gender of a director.

Description of Variables

Dependent Variable

The dependent variable consists of firm growth. Following Coad and Hölzl (2010) and García-Manjóna and Romero-Merino (2012), firm growth is measured in this study by using the log-difference values of total sales at time t and time t-1.

$$Growth_{i,t} = \log\left(\text{Sales}_{i,t}\right) - \log\left(\text{Sales}_{i,t-1}\right) \tag{1}$$

where Growth_{it} is the growth rate of the firm i at time t.

According to Coad and Hölzl (2010), a unique feature of using the log differences over the percentage growth is that the results of the econometric model will be less affected by heteroskedasticity.

Independent Variables

The independent variables used in this study consist of firm age, firm size, gender diversity, and financial ratios (liquidity, profitability, and leverage).

Firm Size

Following Loi and Khan (2012) and Rosa and Musdholifah (2016), firm size (Size_{it}) is proxied in this current research by the natural logarithm of the total company's assets. The reason for choosing the natural logarithm is justified by the fact that the natural logarithm reduces the probability that extreme observations would bias the findings (Loi & Khan, 2012).

$$Size_{it} = \ln\left(assets\right) \tag{2}$$

where Size_{it} is the size of the firm i at time t and ln the natural logarithm.

Firm Age

Empirical evidence reveals that younger firms grow faster than older firms. The information about the age of firms was obtained from audited annual reports. Following Pervan et al. (2017) and Waluyo (2017), the variable age (AGE_{it}) is computed as the number of years since the company was established.

$$Age_{it} = Age\, of\ the\ company\ since\ establishment \qquad (3)$$

where Age_{it} is the age of the firm i at time t.

Gender Diversity

Dutta and Bose (2006) define gender diversity as the presence of women managers on the Board of Directors. Perryman et al. (2016) refer to gender diversity as the degree of representation of female executives in the Top Management Team (TMT). Following Perryman et al. (2016), Baixauli-Soler et al. (2015), and Guetsop (2016), gender diversity ($Gender_{it}$) in this study is measured in terms of the percentage of women directors on the board of directors. In other words, the proportion of women directors over the total number of directors in the board of directors:

$$Gender\ Diversity_{it} = \frac{Number\ of\ female\ Directors\ in\ the\, BOD}{Total\ Directors\ in\ the\, BOD} x100 \qquad (4)$$

Leverage

Leverage is measured in this study using the debt/equity ratio (Wippern, 1966; Loi & Khan, 2012; Rosa & Musdholifah, 2016). The debt/equity was used in this study because information about companies' debts and equity is easily obtainable from financial statements.

$$Leverage_{it} = \frac{Total\ debts}{Total\ equity} \quad (5)$$

where total debts = current liabilities + non-current liabilities.

Liquidity

The majority of studies have used the current ratio to measure liquidity (Loi & Khan, 2012; Ehiedu, 2014; Rosa & Musdholifah, 2016; Demirgüneş, 2016). Given the above, this study uses the current ratio as a measure of liquidity and is calculated using the following formula:

$$Liquidity_{it} = \frac{Current\ Assets}{Current\ Liabilities} \qquad (6)$$

Profitability

Profitability expresses the ability of a firm to generate income from the financial resources it uses (Lee, 2014). Organisations that have high profitability in the long term are particularly preferred and sought since they provide financial security to their shareholders. Scholars have used several ratios to measure profitability: net profit margin (NPM) (Lee, 2014; Rosa & Musdholifah, 2016), EBIT/Total Assets (Razaq & Akinlo, 2017), gross operating profit margin (Coban, 2014). For this study, NPM was used as a predictor of profitability.

$$Profitability_{it} = \frac{Net\ Profits}{Sales} \quad (7)$$

Data Analysis Methods

This study aims to examine the determinants of growth of South Africa's firms listed on the JSE. Panel data regression analysis was applied to this study to achieve this purpose. Panel data has two dimensions: one for cross-sections and the other for time (Leblond & Belley-Ferris, 2004; Frees, 2004). These two dimensions are generally represented by *i* for companies or cross-sections and *t* for the period.

From the hypotheses formulated above, a panel data regression analysis will be run, whereby firm growth is expressed using the following econometric model:

$$\begin{aligned}\text{GROWTH}_{\text{it}} &= \beta_0 + \beta_1\text{SIZE}_{\text{it}} + \beta_2\text{AGE}_{\text{it}} + \beta_3\text{GENDER}_{\text{it}} + \beta_4\text{LEVERAGE}_{\text{it}} \\ &+ \beta_5\text{LIQUIDITY}_{\text{it}} + \beta_6\text{PROFITABILITY}_{\text{it}} + \varepsilon \quad (8)\end{aligned}$$

Results and Findings

This section presents the results of the descriptive statistics, followed by the results of the panel data analysis.

The descriptive statistics in Table 1 above show that the average growth rate of JSE-listed companies from 2009 to 2018 is 0.0369. This means that JSE-listed companies grew at an average rate of 3.69% per year between 2009 and 2018. The results further show that the average age of JSE-listed companies is 46.03, and gender diversity has a mean of 0.176, suggesting that, on average, women hold as low as 17.6% of board seats in a JSE-listed company. These results show the male predominance within the boardroom of JSE-listed companies, in the sense that men hold nearly 83% of board seats. Previous literature found a relatively low percentage of women present on the Board of Directors in South Africa. Soares

Table 1 Descriptive statistics

Variables	Tot. Obs.	Mean	Std. Dev.	Skewness
Growth (log sales)	1870	0.0369	0.1565	−0.04173
Size (ln assets)	1870	22.5811	2.1871	0.08083
Age	1870	46.0294	34.2124	1.09651
Gender diversity (%)	1870	17.6059	12.5024	0.48623
Leverage	1870	1.7301	7.2712	33.4403
Liquidity	1870	1.7610	1.3437	3.45479
Profitability (%)	1870	11.6904	180.3180	−33.8898

Source: Author's own construction

Table 2 Results of the fixed-effects model

Total panel (balanced) observations: 1870				
Dependent variable: Growth				
Variables	Coefficient	Std. error	t-statistic	P-value
Intercept	−1.0982	0.4575	−5.5262	0.0000*
Size	0.0701	0.0245	6.5887	0.0000*
Age	−0.0090	0.0040	−5.1397	0.0000*
Gender diversity	−0.0008	0.0012	−1.5433	0.1229
Leverage	−6.16E-05	0.0013	−0.1091	0.9131
Liquidity	−0.0084	0.0097	−1.9883	0.0469**
Profitability	−0.0002	0.0001	−3.3083	0.0010*
R-squared	0.4928		F-statistic	28.0376
Adjusted R-squared	0.4462		Prob(F-statistic)	0.0000

Source: Author's own construction
** and ** means statistically significant at 1% and 5%, respectively*

et al. (2009) found that women hold 17.1% of board seats in South Africa. The mean value of the variable leverage measured in terms of debt/equity ratio is 1.7, which is higher than 1, suggesting that JSE-listed companies are more leveraged. In other words, JSE-listed companies rely more on debts to finance their growth than on shareholders' funds. The variable liquidity has a mean value of 1.76107. A value of liquidity greater than 1 indicates how good the company's financial health is. The results in Table 1 further show that JSE-listed companies generated, on average, 11.7% net income from 2009–2018. This shows how successful these companies have been during the period under study.

The results of the fixed-effects model reported in Table 2 indicate a negative relationship between firm growth and age (−0.0090), liquidity (−0.0084), and profitability (−0.0002), all significant at the 5% level ($p < 0.05$). Conversely, firm size (0.0701) demonstrates a positive impact on growth ($p < 0.01$). Gender diversity and leverage show no significant relationship with firm growth. The model exhibits a good fit, with an adjusted R-squared of 0.446, suggesting that the explanatory variables explain 44.6% of the variation in firm growth. The F-statistic of 28.04 (significant at 1%) further supports the model's overall significance.

The results from Table 3 below show that we should not account for time differences because the p-value associated with Period F-statistic and period Chi-square accept the null hypothesis at a 5% level. In other words, Period-fixed effects are not statistically significant. Conversely, the results indicate we should reject the null hypothesis of no cross-sectional effects. This means there is strong evidence that firm-specific effects are present, making the fixed-effects model appropriate for cross-sections only (Table 4).

The results of the random-effects model, as reported in Table 4 above, suggest that company age is the only statistically significant variable with a negative impact on corporate growth. All the other explanatory variables are not significant at 5%. The results report an adjusted R-squared of 0.45, which means that the explanatory variable explains 45% of the variation of the dependent variable. The F-statistic of

Table 3 Redundant fixed-effects test

Effects test	Statistic	d.f.	P-value	Null Hypothesis
Cross-section F	33.2377	−186,1668	0.0000*	
Cross-section Chi-square	2896.4727	186	0.0000*	Reject (at 1%)
Period F	1.5663	−91,668	0.1200	
Period Chi-square	15.7377	9	0.0726	Accept (at 5%)

Source: Author's own construction
** and ** means statistically significant at 1% and 5%, respectively*

Table 4 Results of the random-effects model

Total panel (balanced) observations: 1870				
Dependent variable: Growth				
Variables	Coefficient	Std. error	t-statistic	P-value
Intercept	0.1644	0.0926	1.7739	0.0762
Size	−0.0008	0.0040	−0.2030	0.8391
Age	−0.0006	0.0002	−2.7754	0.0056*
Gender diversity	−0.0004	0.0006	−0.6494	0.5162
Leverage	7.57E-06	0.0011	0.0066	0.9947
Liquidity	−0.0101	0.0064	−1.5808	0.1141
Profitability	−0.0002	0.0001	−1.8728	0.0612
R-squared	0.4565		F-statistic	26.8648
Adjusted R-squared	0.4548		Prob(F-statistic)	0.000000

Source: Author's own construction
** and ** means statistically significant at 1% and 5%, respectively*

Table 5 Results of the Hausman test

Test cross-section random effects			
Test Summary	Chi-Sq. Statistic	Chi-Sq. d.f.	p-value
Cross-section random	62.1471	6	0.0000*

Source: Author's own construction
** and ** means statistically significant at 1% and 5%, respectively*

26.04 is also significant at the 1% level, which implies that the model fits the data well.

To determine the most appropriate model for the data—fixed effects or random effects—a Hausman test was conducted, with results presented below (Table 5).

The Hausman test for cross-sectional randomness (Table 5 above) yields a significant Chi-square statistic ($p < 0.01$), leading to the rejection of the null hypothesis. This result confirms the presence of unobserved heterogeneity correlated with the independent variables, making the fixed-effects model the most appropriate model for analysing the study's data.

Discussion and Conclusion

This study aimed to investigate the determinants of growth for companies listed on the Johannesburg Stock Exchange. Firm growth, measured as the log difference in sales, was the dependent variable. Independent variables included size (natural logarithm of total assets), age, gender diversity (percentage of women directors), leverage (debt-to-equity ratio), liquidity (current ratio), and profitability (net profit margin). Data were collected from the INET BFA database and audited annual reports for a sample of 187 JSE-listed companies from 2009 to 2018.

The Hausman test indicated that the fixed-effects model is the best and most appropriate model for the data used in the study, and the results of the fixed-effects model show that firm size is positive and significant at a 1% level. This implies that firm size positively affects firm growth in South Africa. Gibrat's law is thus not valid for JSE-listed firms. These results are in contrast with the findings of Bethlehem (1979) that support Gibrat's law over South African listed companies but are in line with the findings of Heshmati (2001), Bentzen et al. (2012), Daunfeldt et al. (2012), and Hamouri et al. (2018).

The results further demonstrate a statistically significant negative relationship between firm age and growth ($p < 0.01$). Specifically, a one-unit increase in a JSE-listed company's age corresponds to a 0.021 decrease in its growth rate. This negative association aligns with research suggesting that smaller, younger firms experience faster growth than larger, more established ones (Coad, 2009). These findings are consistent with several studies, including Yasuda (2005), Daunfeldt et al. (2014), and Megaravalli and Sampagnaro (2018), which also identified a negative correlation between firm age and growth.

Furthermore, the fixed-effects model results show that the coefficient of gender diversity is negative but insignificant at a 5% level, implying that gender has no significant impact on firm growth. Recently, Peens and Taylor (2017) found that gender diversity does not significantly impact the financial performance of firms listed on the JSE. Similarly, Wachudi and Mboya (2012) and Marinova et al. (2010) also found that female representation in the boardroom does improve firm financial performance. These results are inconsistent with the findings by Carter et al. (2003), Julizaerma and Sori (2012), and Campbell and Mínguez-Vera (2008), who found that gender diversity positively affects corporate growth.

Moreover, the fixed-effects model shows no significant relationship between leverage (measured by the debt-to-equity ratio) and firm growth, consistent with findings from Mutai (2014) and Yasemi and Jalilian (2014). On the other hand, the results indicate that liquidity has a significant and negative effect on firm growth. An increase in the variable liquidity of 1 unit is associated with a decrease in firm growth by 0.019401 units at the 5% significance level. Carpenter and Petersen (2002) found that liquidity inhibits companies' growth. Broome et al. (2011) also found that a higher opening cash balance had a negative impact on firm growth, implying that firms tend to use opening cash to finance internal operations rather than generate higher growth in terms of sales. Waswa et al. (2018) support this result by showing that liquidity negatively affects firm performance.

Furthermore, the fixed-effects model reveals a negative relationship between profitability (measured by net profit margin) and the growth of JSE-listed companies. A one-unit increase in the net profit margin decreases the JSE-listed firm growth by 0.000472. While the negative relationship between profitability and firm growth aligns with findings from Lee (2014) and Piao et al. (2017), it contradicts studies by Jang and Park (2011) and Coban (2014), which identified a positive link between corporate growth and profitability.

Recommendations for Future Research

Future research should explore alternative indicators of firm growth, such as employment, value-added and innovation, to validate the findings of this research and assess the robustness of the results. Additionally, family businesses are a sizeable pillar of the South African economy. About 80% to 90% of South African SMEs are owned and controlled by families (Venter & Farrington, 2009), while 80% of all businesses belong to families (Van der Merwe et al., 2009), and nearly 60% of all the companies listed on the JSE had some family involvement at start-up (Van Buuren, 2007). Given the importance of family firms to the South African economy and their desire for quick and aggressive growth for the next decade, future researchers should investigate the determinants of growth of family businesses listed on the Johannesburg Securities Exchange. This will provide valuable insights into a dominant business model within the South African context.

References

Albulescu, C. T., Tămăşilă, M., & Tăucean, I. M. (2021). The nonlinear relationship between firm size and growth in the automotive industry. *Journal of Industry, Competition and Trade, 21*(3), 445–463. https://doi.org/10.1007/s10842-021-00364-6

Anton, S. G. (2016). The impact of leverage on firm growth: Empirical evidence from Romanian listed firms. *Review of Economics and Business Studies, 9*(2), 147–158.

Arena, L. (2013). *Taille versus croissance de l'entreprise* In: *Édith Penrose et la croissance des entreprises: suivi de Limites à la croissance et à la taille des entreprises d'Édith Penrose* [online]. ENS Éditions: Lyon. Available on the Internet: http://books.openedition.org/enseditions/4177

Arthur-Aidoo, B. M., Aigbavboa, C., & Thwala, W. D. (2017). Evaluating entrepreneurial features of firm's growth using confirmatory factor analysis. *Journal of Economics and Behavioral Studies, 9*(3(J)), 171–179.

Baixauli-Soler, J. S., Belda-Ruiz, M., & Sanchez-Marin, G. (2015). Executive stock options, gender diversity in the top management team and firm risk-taking. *Journal of Business Research, 68*, 451–463.

Baskoro, H., Prabowo, H., Meyliana, M., & Gaol, F. L. (2022). Predicting startup success, a literature review. *International Conference on Information Science and Technology Innovation (ICoSTEC), 1*(1), 123–129. https://doi.org/10.35842/icostec.v1i1.6

Bentzen, J., Madsen, E. S., & Smith, V. (2012). Do firms' growth rates depend on firm size? *Small Business Economics, 39*(4), 937–947.

Bethlehem, G. (1979). Note on growth, profitability and size of firms. *South African Journal of Economics, 47*(2), 130–134.

Bienaymé, A. (1973). Les processus de croissance des entreprises sont-ils déterminés ou indéterminés ? *Revue économique, 24*(2), 216–234.

Broome, T., Robinson, J., & Moore, W. (2011). Liquidity and the firm size-growth nexus in Barbados. *The Annual Review. Seminar Research Department Central Bank of Barbados*, 27–30.

Campbell, K., & Mínguez-Vera, A. (2008). Gender diversity in the boardroom and firm financial performance. *Journal of Business Ethics, 83*, 435–451.

Carpenter, R., & Petersen, B. (2002). Is the growth of small firms constrained by internal finance? *The Review of Economics and Statistics, 84*(2), 298–309.

Carter, D. A., Simkins, B. J., & Simpson, W. G. (2003). Corporate governance, board diversity, and firm value. *Financial Review, 38*, 33–53.

Cesinger, B., Gundolf, K., & Géraudel, M. (2018). Growth intention and sales revenue growth in small business: The mediating effect of firm size growth. *International Journal of Technology Management, 78*(3), 163–181.

Coad, A. (2009). *The growth of firms: A survey of theories and empirical evidence* (New perspectives on the modern corporation series). Edward Elgar Publishing. ISBN 9781848443273.

Coad, A., & Hölzl, W. (2010). *Firm growth: An empirical analysis*. WIFO working papers 361. WIFO.

Coban, S. (2014). The interaction between firm growth and profitability: Evidence from Turkish (listed) manufacturing firms. *The Journal of Knowledge Economy & Knowledge Management, 9*(1), 41–50.

Cooper, A., Gimeno-Gascon, F., & Woo, C. (1994). Initial human and financial capital as predictors of new venture performance. *Journal of Business Venturing, 9*(5), 371–395.

Costa, M., & Donner, N. (2016). *Determinants of firm growth: Empirical evidence from Swiss listed Companie*. Available at SSRN: https://ssrn.com/abstract=2995522

Daunfeldt, S. O., Elert, N., & Johansson, D. (2014). The economic contribution of high-growth firms: Do policy implications depend on the choice of growth indicator? *Journal of Industry, Competition, and Trade, 14*(3), 337–365.

Daunfeldt, S. O., Halvarsson, D., & Johansson, D. (2012). A cautionary note on using the Eurostat OECD definition of high growth firms. The Swedish Retail Institute working papers, No. 65.

Davidsson, P. (1989). Entrepreneurship – And after? A study of growth willingness in small firms. *Journal of Business Venturing, 4*(3), 211–226.

Davidsson, P., Achtenhagen, L., & Naldi, L. (2010). Small firm growth. *Foundations and Trends in Entrepreneurship, 6*(2), 69–166.

Delmar, F., Davidsson, P., & Gartner, W. B. (2003). Arriving at the high-growth firm. *Journal of Business Venturing, 18*(2), 189–216.

Demirgüneş, K. (2016). The effect of liquidity on financial performance: Evidence from Turkish retail industry. *International Journal of Economics and Finance, 8*(4), 63–79.

Dezso, C., & Ross, D. (2012). Does female representation in top management improve firm performance? A panel data investigation. *Strategic Management Journal, 33*(9), 1072–1089.

Donati, C. (2015). Firm growth and liquidity constraints: Evidence from the manufacturing and service sectors in Italy. *Journal of Applied Economics, 48*(20), 1881–1892.

Dromby, F. (2000). Les déterminants de la volonté de croissance chez les dirigeants Français de PME. Proposition d'un modèle intégrant les aspects économiques et sociaux. Proceedings of the congrès de l'association internationale de management stratégique. Montpelier, France.

Dutta, P., & Bose, S. (2006). Gender diversity in the boardroom and financial performance of commercial banks: Evidence from Bangladesh. *The Cost and Management, 34*(6), 70–74.

Dzafic, J., & Polic, N. (2019). The impact of financial leverage on firm growth: Empirical evidence from Bosnia & Herzegovina. *Eurasian Journal of Business and Management, 7*(1), 65–73.

Evans, D. (1987). Tests of alternative theories of firm growth. *Journal of Political Economy, 95*(4), 657–674.

Foss, N. (1998). The resource-based perspective: An assessment and diagnosis of problems. *Scandinavian Journal of Management, 14*(3), 133–149.

Frees, E. (2004). *Longitudinal and panel data*. Cambridge University Press.

García-Manjóna, J. V., & Romero-Merino, M. E. (2012). Research, development, and firm growth. Empirical evidence from European top R&D spending firms. *Research Policy, 41*(6), 1084–1092.

Geroski, P., Machin, S., & Walters, C. (1997). Corporate growth and profitability. *Journal of Industrial Economics, 45*(2), 171–189.

Gibrat, R. (1931). *Les inégalités économiques*. Recueil Sirey.

Guetsop, S. F. A. (2016). Gender diversity in the board of directors and performance of enterprises: A study from Cameroonians experiences. *International Journal of Innovation and Applied Studies, 15*(1), 164–174.

Gupta, M. J., Makwana, C., Naik, S., & Rao, W. R. (2023). *Fundamentals of financial management*. AG PUBLISHING HOUSE (AGPH Books).

Hamouri, B., Al-Rdaydeh, M., & Ghazalat, A. (2018). Effect of financial leverage on firm growth: Empirical evidence from listed firms in Amman stock exchange. *Investment Management and Financial Innovations, 15*(2), 154–164.

Hanifzadeh, F., Talebi, K., & Sajadi, S. M. (2018). The analysis of effect of aspiration to growth of managers for SMEs growth case study: Exporting manufacturing SMEs in Iran. *Journal of Entrepreneurship in Emerging Economies, 10*(2), 277–301.

Haruyama, S., & Fujiyama, K. (2022). A study on the relationship between "managerial decision making" and "factors influencing innovation success" in Japanese niche top firms. *Salud, Ciencia Y Tecnología, 2*(S2), 193. https://doi.org/10.56294/saludcyt2022193

Haschka, R. E., Herwartz, H., Struthmann, P., Tran, V. T., & Walle, Y. M. (2022). The joint effects of financial development and the business environment on firm growth: Evidence from Vietnam. *Journal of Comparative Economics, 50*(2), 486–506.

Ilmiyono, A. F., & Widyowati, M. (2021). The effect of profitability and company size on equity structure of pharmaceutical company listed on IDX period 2012–2017. In *Proceedings of the 1st International Conference on Science and Technology in Administration and Management Information*. ICSTIAM. https://doi.org/10.4108/eai.17-7-2019.2302904

Iqbal, U., & Usman, M. (2018). Impact of financial leverage on firm performance. *SEISENSE Journal of Management, 1*, 70–78. https://doi.org/10.33215/sjom.v1i2.13

Jang, S., & Park, K. (2011). Inter-relationship between firm growth and profitability. *International Journal of Hospitality Management, 30*(4), 1027–1035.

Janssen, F. (2009). Does the environment influence the employment growth of SMEs? *Journal of Small Business & Entrepreneurship, 22*(3), 311–325.

Janssen, F. (2011). *La croissance de l'entreprise : Une obligation pour les PME ?* De Boeck.

Javadi, S. M., & Alimoradi, A. (2017). Relationship between financial leverage and firm growth in the oil and gas industry: Evidence from OPEC. *Petroleum Business Review, 1*(1), 9–21.

Julizaerma, M. K., & Sori, Z. M. (2012). Gender diversity in the boardroom and firm performance of Malaysian public listed companies. *Procedia: Social and Behavioural Sciences, 65*(3), 1077–1085.

Kim, L. (2018). Organizational innovation and structure 1. In *Organizational Innovation* (pp. 35–56). Routledge.

Kyläheiko, K., Puumalainen, K., Pätäri, S., & Jantunen, A. (2017). How do firm-and industry-specific factors affect innovation and financial performance? *International Journal of Technology Intelligence and Planning, 11*(3), 230–251.

Lakuma, C. P., Marty, R., & Muhumuza, F. (2019). Financial inclusion and micro, small, and medium enterprises (MSMES) growth in Uganda. *Journal of Innovation and Entrepreneurship, 8*(1), 15. https://doi.org/10.1186/s13731-019-0110-2

Leblond, S., & Belley-Ferris, F. I. (2004). *Guide d'économétrie Appliquée à l'intention des Étudiants du Cours ECN 3950*. Université de Montréal.

Lee, S. (2014). The relationship between growth and profit: Evidence from firm-level panel data. *Structural Change and Economic Dynamics, 28*(C), 1–11.

Loi, T., & Khan, A. (2012). *Determinants of firm growth: Evidence from Belgian companies. Master's Thesis*. Universiteit Gent.

Megaravalli, A. V., & Sampagnaro, G. (2018). Firm age and liquidity ratio as predictors of firm growth: Evidence from Indian firms. *Journal of Applied Economics Letters, 25*(19), 1373–1375.

Mutai, B. (2014). *The relationship between financial leverage and asset growth of firms listed at the Nairobi securities exchange. Master's thesis*. University of Nairobi.

Nakagawa, Y. (2015). The gender diversity – Firm performance relationship by industry type, working hours, and inclusiveness: An empirical study of Japanese firms. *Journal of Diversity Management, 10*(1), 61–78.

Nanda, S., & Panda, A. K. (2018). The determinants of corporate profitability: An investigation of Indian manufacturing firms. *International Journal of Emerging Markets, 13*(1), 66–86. https://doi.org/10.1108/ijoem-01-2017-0013

Nason, R. S., & Wiklund, J. (2018). An assessment of resource-based theorizing on firm growth and suggestions for the future. *Journal of Management, 44*(1), 32–60.

Neri, S. (2020). The theory of economic growth: A 'Classical' perspective.

OECD. (2009). The impact of the global crisis on SME and entrepreneurship financing and policy responses. Accessed June 18, 2019, from https://www.oecd.org/industry/smes/49316499.pdf

Oliveira, B., & Fortunato, A. (2006). Firm growth and liquidity constraints: A dynamic analysis. *Small Business Economics, 27*(2–3), 139–156.

Oliveira, R. L., & Kayo, E. K. (2019). Leverage and investment opportunities: The effect on high growth firms. *Revista Contabilidade & Finanças, 31*, 302–317.

Penrose, E. (1959). *The theory of the growth of the firm*. Oxford University Press.

Perényi, Á., & Yukhanaev, A. (2016). Testing relationships between firm size and perceptions of growth and profitability: An investigation into the practices of Australian ICT SMEs. *Journal of Management & Organization, 22*(5), 680–701.

Perić, M., Vitezić, V., & Perić Hadžić, A. (2020). Firm size–firm growth relationship during economic crisis. *Ekonomska misao i praksa, 29*(1), 29–53.

Perryman, A. A., Fernando, G. D., & Tripathy, A. (2016). Do gender differences persist? An examination of gender diversity on firm performance, risk, and executive compensation. *Journal of Business Research, 69*(2), 579–586.

Pervan, M., Pervan, I., & Ćurak, M. (2017). The influence of age on firm performance: Evidence from the Croatian food industry. *Journal of Eastern Europe Research in Business and Economics, 2017*(2017), 1–10.

Piao, Z., Zhang, L., Miao, B., & Li, R. (2017). Research of dynamic inter-relationship between firm growth and profitability: A case of manufacturing listed companies. *Revista de la Facultad de Ingeniería U.C.V., 32*(5), 272–281.

Purwanto, E., & Purwanto, A. D. B. (2020). An investigative study on sustainable competitive advantage of manufacture companies in Indonesia. *Business: Theory and Practice, 21*(2), 633–642. https://doi.org/10.3846/btp.2020.12256

Quader, S. M. (2017). Differential effect of liquidity constraints on firm growth. *Review of Financial Economics, 32*(1), 20–29.

Razaq, I. T., & Akinlo, A. E. (2017). Interrelationship between size, growth and profitability of non-financial firms in Nigeria. *European Journal of Business and Management, 9*, 76–86.

Rico, A. J., Gutiérrez-Rangel, H. F., & Galván-Zavala, K. (2021). Systemic review of the context of external financing of msmes in Mexico. *Journal Business Administration and Business Economics Marketing Accounting, 5*(8), 12–22. https://doi.org/10.35429/jbab.2021.8.5.12.22

Rosa, V., & Musdholifah, M. (2016). The effect of leverage, liquidity, profitability, coverage, growth, and firm size with Auditor's reputation as a moderating to bond rating of banking firm. *Jurnal Bisnis & Manajemen, 17*(1), 48–57.

Schwab, A., Werbel, G. D., Hofmann, H., & Henriques, P. L. (2016). Managerial gender diversity and firm performance: An integration of different theoretical perspectives. *Group & Organisation Management, 41*(1), 5–31.

Shanmugan, K. R., & Bhaduri, S. (2002). Size, age and firm growth in the Indian manufacturing sector. *Applied Economics Letters, 9*(9), 607–613.

Soares, R., Carter, N. M., & Combopiano, J. (2009). *Catalyst census: Fortune 500 women board directors*. Catalyst.

Steinerowska-Streb, I., Glod, G., & Steiner, A. (2022). What do we know about small and medium enterprises' survival in a post-global economic crisis context? *Local Economy, 37*(4), 259–278.

Tarillon, C. (2006). (17). Comment soutenir la croissance des start-ups? Une analyse au travers des représentations des dirigeants en matière de croissance et de gouvernance. In *Conference paper: 10ème Congrès de l'Académie de l'Entrepreneuriat et de l'Innovation*.

Terjesen, S., & Szerb, L. (2008). Dice thrown from the beginning? An empirical investigation of determinants of firm-level growth expectations. *Estudios de Economia, 35*(2), 153–178.

Thu, N. T. P., & Xuan, V. N. (2023). Factors affecting the performance of small and medium enterprises regarding the sustainable development goals—The case of foreign direct investment firms in Vietnam. *Economies, 11*(3), 72.

Tingler, S. (2015). *The modes of firm growth and their effects on firm performance-an empirical analysis of the chemical industry. PhD thesis*. Bergische Universität.

Tunberg, M. (2017). *Rethinking small firm growth, while absorbing the processual. Masters Dissertation*. Acta Universitatis Agriculturae Sueciae.

Tunberg, M., & Anderson, A. R. (2020). Growing a small firm; experiences and managing difficult processes. *International Entrepreneurship and Management Journal, 16*(4), 1445–1463.

Van der Merwe, S., Venter, E., & Ellis, S. M. (2009). An exploratory study of some of the determinants of management succession planning in family businesses. *Management Dynamics: Journal of the Southern African Institute for Management Scientists, 18*(4), 2–17.

Variyam, J. N., & Kraybill, D. S. (1992). Empirical evidence on determinants of firm growth. *Economic Letters, 38*(1), 31–36.

Vaz, R. (2021). Firm growth: A review of the empirical literature. *Revista galega de economía: Publicación Interdisciplinar da Facultade de Ciencias Económicas e Empresariais, 30*(2), 74–93.

Venter, E., & Farrington, S. (2009). The nature of family businesses and their importance for economic development.

Vučenović, S., Poljašević, B. Z., & Mišić, I. (2021). Business growth management in republic of srpska. *Acta Economica, 19*(34), 45–64. https://doi.org/10.7251/ace2134045v

Waeger, D., & Weber, K. (2019). Institutional complexity and organizational change: An open polity perspective. *Academy of Management Review, 44*(2), 336–359.

Waluyo, W. (2017). Firm size, firm age, and firm growth on corporate social responsibility in Indonesia: The case of real estate companies. *European Research Studies Journal, 20*(4a), 360–369.

Waswa, C. W., Mukras, M. S., & Oima, D. (2018). Effect of liquidity on financial performance of the sugar industry in Kenya. *International Journal of Education and Research, 6*(6), 29–44.

Wippern, R. F. (1966). Financial structure and the value of the firm. *The Journal of Finance, 21*(4), 615–633.

Yasemi, S., & Jalilian, Z. (2014). Studying financial leverage relation to firm's growth and financial strength in the accepted (listed) companies in Tehran stock exchange in various industries. *Indian Journal of Scientific Research, 3*(1), 355–361.

Yasuda, T. (2005). Firm growth, size, age and behaviour in Japanese manufacturing. *Small Business Economics, 24*, 1–15.

Moderating Role of Audit Tenure in the Relationship Between Audit Fees and Financial Performance: Evidence from the Nigerian Banking Sector

Omobolade Stephen Ogundele, Nwosu Lilian Ifunanya, Mordi Kanayo Innocent, and Shaikhnag Muhammad

Abstract Audit fees and audit tenure are critical factors in the auditing process, particularly in the banking sector where financial performance is closely scrutinized. Investigating how these factors interact with financial performance can provide valuable insights. This study examined the moderating role of audit tenure in the relationship between audit fees and the financial performance of the Deposit Money Banks (DMBs) in Nigeria listed on the Nigeria Exchange Group from 2012 to 2021. The study explored secondary data that is sourced from the audited annual reports and accounts of the selected DMBs. A purposive sampling technique was used to choose 12 DMBs whose stocks were actively traded on the stock market during the sample period and for which necessary information was readily available. In analyzing the data, the study explored multiple regression analysis by using Return on Asset as the dependent variable; Audit Fee as the independent variable; Audit Tenure as the moderating variable, and Firm Size, Firm Age, and Leverage as the control variables. The result showed that the Firm Size and Interaction of Audit Fee and Audit Tenure had a positive and significant effect on financial performance while Audit Fee, Audit Tenure, Firm Age, and Leverage had a negative and significant effect on financial performance. The result concluded that audit tenure, audit fees, and their interactions have a significant effect on the financial performance of

O. S. Ogundele (✉)
Adeleke University, Ede, Osun State, Nigeria
e-mail: ogundele.omobolade@adelekeuniversity.edu.ng

N. L. Ifunanya · S. Muhammad
North-West University, Potchefstroom, South Africa
e-mail: 23012064@nwu.ac.za; Muhammad.Shaikhnag@nwu.ac.za

M. K. Innocent
Obafemi Awolowo University, Ile Ife, Nigeria
e-mail: 23012064@nwu.ac.za; Muhammad.Shaikhnag@nwu.ac.za

T. Moloi (ed.), *Impacting Society Positively Through Technology in Accounting and Business Processes*, Springer Proceedings in Business and Economics,
https://doi.org/10.1007/978-3-031-84885-8_31

the DMB. The study therefore recommended that the Nigerian banking industry should develop strategies for managing audit relationships over the long term while ensuring the effectiveness and integrity of the audit process. This study contributes to the understanding of audit dynamics within the banking sector, highlighting the relationship between audit fees, audit tenure, and financial performance. By demonstrating the moderating effect of audit tenure on this relationship, it emphasizes the importance of long-term audit relationships in enhancing the effectiveness and integrity of the auditing process, providing valuable insights for regulatory bodies and banking institutions alike.

Keywords Audit fees · Audit tenure · Deposit money bank · Financial performance

Introduction

The banking sector in Nigeria has its unique characteristics and challenges, which makes studying it particularly relevant for understanding broader issues in auditing and financial performance within emerging markets. In the dynamic landscape of the Nigerian banking sector, the effect of audit fees in influencing financial performance has been and is still harvesting significant attention (Chinedu & Chidoziem, 2017; Awinbugri & Prince, 2019; Kajola et al., 2022). With the sector's fundamental role in the nation's economic stability, development, and growth, ensuring the effectiveness of auditing processes is essential. An independent audit would improve a company's financial performance by supporting robust internal control, risk management practices, and corporate governance guidelines (Hassan & Farouk, 2014). A key factor is the company's financial performance listed on the capital market, which is also perceived as a medium to attract capital and reduce financing costs of businesses. It is a fact that a firm with very strong financial performance would get a positive reputation among investors.

In addition, the capital market, managers, financial analysts, and investors rely on the audited financial reports of businesses, including banks, to assess the efficiency and performance of such organizations. The profitability of the business will be utilized for measuring the study's financial performance. Several metrics are used to measure profitability, including the Return on Equity (ROE), Return on Assets (ROA), and Price Earnings Ratio (PER) among others. ROA was utilized in this study as the proxy for financial performance. ROA reflects how effectively management is using the company's assets to generate earnings and also Investors often use ROA as one of the metrics to assess the profitability and efficiency of a company.

One key element affecting the relationship between audit fees and a firm's financial performance is audit tenure, which is the number of years that a business has been audited by the same audit firm. Audit Tenure is the number of years that the audit firm has been auditing a specific entity, working in the same entity as an auditor. An auditor may become less independent and probably have his objectivity impaired in providing an audit opinion if they are involved in the audit for an extended period. However, long-term audit engagements can also help accounting firms identify problems with company going concerns and gain a deeper understanding of their financial status. This is also said by (Ruiz-Barbadillo et al., 2004; Januarti, 2019), who contends that extended audit involvement may cause the auditor to lose his objectivity and make it harder for the organization to function as a going concern, or it may help comprehend the situation and identify going concern issues more quickly.

Research findings on the relationship between audit fees and financial performance have been mixed, and different studies have produced conflicting results. Some studies found that the audit fee does have a negative relationship with financial performance (Francis & Ke, 2006; Reynolds & Francis, 2004; Ugwu et al., 2020) while some scholars stated that audit fee has positive effect on financial performance (Moutinho et al., 2012; Ziaee, 2014; Awinbugri & Prince, 2019). Greater audit fees may be linked with enhanced audit quality, characterized by more thorough and rigorous auditing procedures. This can lead to improved financial reporting accuracy, reduced risk of misstatement or fraud, and increased investor confidence in the reliability of financial statements (Hribar et al., 2014). Also, paying higher audit fees can impose a financial burden on companies, especially smaller firms or those operating in highly competitive or economically challenging environments (Naser & Nuseibeh, 2008). Excessive audit fees relative to a firm's financial resources can erode profitability, liquidity, and overall financial performance.

Also, research findings on the relationship between audit tenure and firm financial performance have been mixed, and different studies have produced conflicting results (Adeniyi & Mieseigha, 2013; Oyebamiji, 2022). Some studies suggested that longer audit tenure may lead to better financial performance due to increased auditor–client familiarity and understanding, which could result in more effective audits and improved internal controls. Conversely, others suggested that longer audit tenure may lead to decreased financial performance due to potential independence threats, such as reduced auditor skepticism or the possibility of becoming too close to the client. Despite the relevance of audit fees and financial performance in the Nigerian banking sector, there remains a gap in understanding how audit tenure shapes their relationship. Moreover, the moderating role of the audit tenure in this relationship remains underexplored. Addressing this gap is essential for stakeholders, including regulators, auditors, and banking institutions, to enhance accountability, transparency, and financial stability within the banking industry. Understanding the relationship could help in designing more effective audit practices, policies, and regulations. Nigeria's banking sector has its exceptional features and challenges, which makes its study relevant for a better understanding of auditing and financial reporting within emerging markets.

Literature Review

Conceptual Review

Audit Tenure

Audit tenure is regarded as the length of time an auditing firm has been engaged to audit the financial statements of a particular client. Long-term ties between the client and the auditor might have an impact on the independence and quality of an audit (Qawqzeh et al., 2018). It is an essential aspect of auditor independence and is subject to regulations and guidelines to ensure objectivity and integrity in the audit processes. The audit tenure is the duration an auditing firm serves a client and is a pivotal factor influencing various aspects of the audit process and the relationship between auditors and clients. Research indicates that audit tenure affects the quality of audit, with both positive and negative effects. Longer audit tenure may facilitate a deeper insight and understanding of the client's operations, leading to more effective risk assessment and audit procedures (Francis, 2011). However, extended tenure also raises concerns about auditor objectivity and independence (Martani et al., 2021). Long-term relationships between clients and auditors have been observed to raise the risk of familiarity threats and decrease auditor skepticism (DeFond et al., 2002). Moreover, audit tenure plays a very vital role in shaping the dynamics of auditor–client relationship. Long-term auditors often develop a sense of familiarity and trust with their clients, which can facilitate communication and cooperation. This familiarity may lead to smoother audit processes and potentially more accurate financial statements (Gul et al., 2013).

Audit Fee

An audit fee is regarded as the remuneration paid by a client to the audit firm for conducting an audit of the client's financial statements. It encompasses various components, including fees for audit services, additional services, and expenses incurred all through the auditing process. The determination of audit fees is determined by factors such as the complexity of the client's operations, the scope of the audit engagement, regulatory requirements, and the reputation and expertise of the auditing firm. Research indicates that audit fees play a vital role in shaping the auditor–client relationship and can impact audit quality and the independence of the auditor (Tepalagul & Lin, 2015). Studies have shown that audit fees are positively associated with audit quality, as higher fees may enable auditing firms to allocate more resources and employ more experienced personnel to conduct thorough and effective audits (Hoitash et al., 2007; Choi et al., 2010 & Huang et al., 2016). However, excessively low audit fees may raise concerns about the adequacy of audit procedures and the independence of auditors, as auditors may face pressure to compromise on audit quality in order to maintain profitability (Palmrose, 1986).

Regulatory bodies such as the Public Company Accounting Oversight Board (PCAOB) have emphasized the importance of ensuring that audit fees are commensurate with the degree of effort required to perform a high-quality audit and have implemented rules and guidelines to promote transparency and accountability in the determination of audit fees (PCAOB, 2009). Moreover, audit fees are influenced by factors such as auditor tenure, client size, industry dynamics, and regulatory changes. Long audit tenure and provisions of the non-audit service may impact audit fees and raise concerns about auditor independence and objectivity (Simunic & Stein, 1987). Additionally, clients operating in highly regulated industries or facing complex accounting issues may incur higher audit fees due to the increased degree of audit risk and the need for specialized expertise (Abbott et al., 2006). Understanding the determinants and implications of audit fees is essential for regulators, auditors, and clients to ensure the integrity and effectiveness of the audit process and maintain investor confidence in financial reporting.

Financial Performance

An organization's capacity to generate profits and add value for its stakeholders over a certain time frame is measured by its financial performance. It encompasses numerous financial metrics and indicators that reflect the organization's efficiency, profitability, liquidity, solvency, and overall health (Diana, 2020). These metrics include but are not limited to net income, return on equity (ROE), return on assets (ROA), earnings per share (EPS), profit margins, and cash flow ratios. Analyzing financial performance is crucial for investors, management, creditors, and other stakeholders in assessing the financial health of companies, making informed decisions, and measuring its success in achieving its strategic objectives.

Financial performance analysis provides insights into the strengths and weaknesses of a company, identifies areas for improvement, and helps stakeholders make informed decisions regarding investment, lending, and strategic planning (Boesso et al., 2013). By comparing a company's financial performance with industry benchmarks, historical trends, and competitors' performance, stakeholders can assess its relative position and competitive advantage in the market. Additionally, financial performance analysis is essential for monitoring the effectiveness of management's decisions and corporate governance practices, as well as for evaluating the effect of factors that are external such as technological advancements, regulatory changes, and market trends on the company's financial outcomes. By analyzing financial performance, stakeholders can make informed decisions, identify opportunities for improvement, and monitor the company's progress toward achieving its strategic goals.

Empirical Review

Over the years, there has been a lot of interest in studies on the effect of audit fees on the financial performance of Nigerian banks. Yuniarti (2011), Farouk and Hassan (2014), Ugwu et al. (2020), and Bakr et al. (2023) have carried out studies on the relationship between audit fees and firm financial indicators such as return on equity (ROE) and return on asset (ROA). These studies have found mixed results regarding the impact of audit fees on financial performance. Bakr et al. (2023) report that audit fees had a positive and insignificant relationship with ROA. Some studies, such as Farouk and Hassan (2014) and Yuniarti (2011), suggest a positive association between higher audit fees and improved financial performance indicators like ROE and ROA. Awinbugri and Prince (2019) examined how audit committee meetings and audit fees affected the financial performance of Ghanaian listed banks. They found that both audit committee size and audit fees had a positive effect on financial performance (ROA). Nevertheless, other research, such as that of Ugwu et al. (2020), presents a better view, indicating a complex relationship influenced by factors such as audit quality and corporate governance. Studies by Chinedu and Chidoziem (2017), and Boo and Sharma (2008) found no significant effect of audit fees on financial performance, highlighting the need for further exploration of the dynamics at play.

Studies investigating the effect of audit tenure on the bank's financial performance have yielded diverse findings, reflecting the complexity of this issue across different contexts. For instance, research in Germany by Quick and Schmidt (2018) explored the effect of auditor retention, audit firm rotation, and joint audits on audit quality and perceived auditors' independence among bank directors and institutional investors. They found that longer rotation cycles marginally affected perceptions of audit quality, with implications for regulatory measures aimed at enhancing auditor independence. The favorable relationship between the tenure of an audit firm and the quality of financial reporting has also been noted by Bratten et al. (2019), especially in complex banking environments. In Nigeria, research on the effect of audit tenure on the banks' financial performance has yielded mixed results, reflecting the better nature of this relationship within the local banking landscape. Studies by Adeniyi and Mieseigha (2013) and Oyebamiji (2022) suggested a negative relationship between audit tenure and audit quality, although not statistically significant. Despite this, there is a recognition of the relevance of audit quality in enhancing firm financial performance, as evidenced by the findings of Ogbodo and Akabuogu (2018) regarding the significance of audit firm size and audit committee independence on various financial performance metrics. However, further research is needed to explore the specific mechanisms through which audit tenure influences financial performance in the Nigerian banking sector, taking into account factors such as regulatory frameworks, market competition, and client-specific dynamics.

Theoretical Framework

The theoretical framework underpinning this study is rooted in agency theory and institutional theory, widely utilized perspectives in corporate governance and auditing research. According to Jensen and Meckling (2019), agency theory centers on the principal–agent relationship, in which managers (the agents) make decisions on behalf of shareholders (the principals). When it comes to auditing, shareholders look to auditors to guarantee the dependability and accuracy of the financial information that management has supplied (DeAngelo, 1981). Auditors play a pivotal role as agents in the agency relationship, tasked with independently verifying financial statements to mitigate agency conflicts and ensure the integrity of financial reporting (Abbott et al., 2016). The duration of the auditor–client relationship, known as audit tenure, and the fees charged for audit services, termed audit fees, are key variables that influence the effectiveness of auditors in fulfilling their role as agents (Bratten et al., 2019). Longer audit tenure may compromise auditor independence due to familiarity with the client's operations, potentially leading to reduced skepticism and increased susceptibility to management influence (Abbott et al., 2016). Conversely, higher audit fees may signal a commitment to quality and thoroughness in auditing procedures, thereby enhancing auditor independence and mitigating agency conflicts (Azizkhani et al., 2018).

Drawing on institutional theory; the institutional pressures that encompass regulatory environments, professional norms, and industry practices shape the behavior of banks and auditors alike. Regulatory frameworks, such as those set by the Central Bank of Nigeria, impose standards on auditing practices, while professional norms within the auditing profession influence fee negotiation and audit conduct. Additionally, industry practices regarding audit tenure, fee structures, and financial reporting further mold the interactions between auditors and banks, impacting financial performance metrics. Longer audit tenure may foster trust and deepen relationships between auditors and banks, potentially influencing the negotiation of audit fees and the thoroughness of audit procedures conducted (Chen et al., 2023). Moreover, banks may conform to institutional pressures related to audit tenure, reflecting industry norms and regulatory expectations, thereby influencing the relationship between audit fees and financial performance through processes of institutional isomorphism (Scott, 2013).

Methodology

Research Design

Ex post facto and longitudinal research designs were investigated in this study. The *ex post facto* research is necessary since the firms' audited financial reports have easily available data on variables of interest. Additionally, because the data were panel in nature and covered 12 cross-sectional units between 2012 and 2021, the study used a longitudinal research design.

Population, Sampling Technique, and Sample Size

The article's primary focus was Deposit Money Banks (DMBs) in Nigeria. As of 2021, 14 DMBs that are listed on the Nigerian Exchange Group (NGX) comprise the study's population. The study employed secondary data. Twelve DMBs with stocks that were actively traded on the stock market throughout the sample period and for which relevant data were easily accessible were chosen for this study using a purposive sample technique. The information covered the years 2012 through 2021 and came from the audited financial reports of the selected listed DMBs.

Model Specification, Data Analysis Technique, and Measurement of Variable

The study examines the moderating role of audit tenure in the relationship between audit fees and the financial performance of the Nigerian DMBs listed on the Nigeria Exchange Group from 2012 to 2022. The study explored panel regression analysis as a technique to analyze the data. Panel regression is particularly useful for capturing dynamic relationships and understanding how these variables interact over time within individual banks and for dealing with possible individual heterogeneity. Based on previous studies carried out (Ado et al., 2020; Wahyudi & Sabaruddin, 2023; Ardilawati & Cahyati, 2023) we construct the relationship below,

$$\begin{aligned}&Financial\ Performance =\\&f\left(Audit\ Tenure, Audit\ Fee, Audit\ Fee * Audit\ Tenure, Control\ Variables\right)\end{aligned}$$

$$\begin{aligned}ROA_{it} &= \beta_1 AUT_{it} + \beta_2 AUF_{it} + \beta_3 AUF * AUT_{it} + \beta_4 FSZ_{it}\\&+\beta_5 AGE_{it} + \beta_6 LEV_{it} + \varepsilon_{it\ldots}\end{aligned} \quad (1)$$

The dependent variable is Return on Asset (ROA) which is proxied as profit after tax divided by total assets. The independent variables are Audit Tenure (AUT), Audit Fee (AUF), and Interaction of Audit Fee and Audit Tenure (AUF*AUT). Audit Tenure is proxied as a dummy variable where is computed as "1" is assigned to companies that use an external auditor that has stayed for 3 years and "0" for auditors with less than 3 years of engagement" while Audit fee is measured as audit fee or the amount paid to the auditors that are the Logarithmic transformation of Naira-value remunerated to the auditor for the audit services. The Audit Tenure* Audit fee is measured by the interaction of audit tenure and audit fee. The control variables explored in the study are Leverage, Firm listing Age, and Firm Size. Leverage (LEV) is proxied as the Ratio of Total Debt to Equity, Firm Age (AGE) is measured as the number of years a company is trading in the stock exchange while Firm Size (FSZ) is measured as the natural log of total asset. The a priori expectations for the variables are stated.

A Priori Expectation

Variable	Expected sign	Rationale
Audit Tenure (AUT)	Positive (+)	Longer audit tenure is anticipated to positively influence financial performance (ROA) as auditors become more familiar with the firm's operations and financial intricacies over time, potentially leading to more effective and efficient audits.
Audit Fee (AUF)	Negative (−)	Higher audit fees may be seen as a burden on financial resources, reducing profitability.
Audit Fees and Audit Tenure (AUF*AUT)	Positive (+)	The interaction term is expected to be positive, suggesting that the negative impact of high audit fees on financial performance might be mitigated by longer audit tenure. Over time, auditors can achieve greater efficiencies and provide more value, offsetting the cost.

Results and Discussion

Descriptive Statistics

The variability around the mean Audit Fee (AUF) is captured by a standard deviation of approximately 0.367. The distribution is positively skewed (0.610), indicating a tail toward larger values, and it exhibits leptokurtosis (4.532), indicating heavier tails and a sharper peak compared to a normal distribution. The Jarque–Bera test also confirms significant deviation from normality (Jarque–Bera statistic = 19.180, p-value = 0.000). The Audit Tenure (AUT) variable reflects an average tenure of approximately 0.750, with a median of 1.000, indicating a concentration of observations below this median. The variability around the mean is captured by a standard deviation of around 0.435. The distribution is negatively skewed (−1.155), indicating a tail toward smaller values, and it exhibits leptokurtosis (2.333), suggesting heavier tails and a sharper peak compared to a normal distribution. The Jarque–Bera test confirms significant deviation from normality (Jarque–Bera statistic = 26.000, p-value = 0.000).

The mean age of approximately 27 years indicates the average firm age, while the median of 20 years signifies the middle value, suggesting that the dataset comprises a mix of relatively young and older companies. The range from 8 years to 53

Table 1 Descriptive Statistics

	AUT	AGE	FSZ	LEV	AUF
Mean	0.750	27.250	9.240	6.625	5.477
Median	1.000	20.500	9.240	6.420	5.490
Maximum	1.000	53.000	10.070	13.310	7.070
Minimum	0.000	8.000	8.190	−2.980	4.810
Std. Dev.	0.435	15.370	0.412	2.589	0.367
Skewness	−1.155	0.358	−0.186	−0.907	0.610
Kurtosis	2.333	1.468	2.411	5.927	4.532
Jarque–Bera	26.000	14.300	2.428	57.813	19.180
Probability	0.000	0.001	0.297	0.000	0.000

Authors' computation (2024)

years shows the variability in age among the companies studied. The slightly positively skewed distribution, indicated by a skewness value of 0.36, suggests a slight tail toward older firms, although the distribution is generally symmetrical. The kurtosis value of 1.468 indicates a distribution with moderate peaks and lighter tails compared to the normal distribution, suggesting that the age distribution is less extreme. The descriptive statistics for leverage (LEV) present insights into the financial risk and capital structure of the dataset. The mean and median values of 6.625 and 6.420, respectively, suggest moderate levels of leverage among the firms. The standard deviation of 2.589 indicates moderate dispersion around the mean, while the negative skewness of −0.907 suggests a slight leftward skew in the distribution, indicating more observations with higher leverage. Moreover, the kurtosis value of 5.927 indicates a heavy-tailed distribution, signifying potential outliers or extreme values (Table 1).

Multicollinearity

In the result shown in Table 2, no two independent variables exhibit a strong enough correlation to raise the possibility of multicollinearity in the regression. The strongest correlation, 0.26, is found between AUF and FSZ. Multicollinearity is not anticipated at all because the other correlation coefficients are all less than 0.20. The presence of multicollinearity is often indicated by a correlation coefficient of 0.70 or higher between two variables, which is not the case in our data. The Variance Inflation Factors (VIF) for each variable in the regression model are shown in the table. The degree of multicollinearity between the independent variables is calculated using VIF. Table 3 also includes the Variance Inflation Factor (VIF) test for multicollinearity. Every single VIF coefficient is less than eight. Generally speaking, if the VIF score is less than 10, the degree of multicollinearity may be accepted.

Table 2 Correlation Matrix

Sample: 2012–2021					
Included observations: 120					
Correlation					
Probability	AUF	AUT	AGE	FSZ	LEV
AUF	1.000				
AUT	0.060	1.000			
	0.535	—			
AGE	0.155	−0.043	1.000		
	0.109	0.658	—		
FSZ	0.263	0.105	0.174	1.000	
	0.000	0.281	0.072	—	
LEV	−0.076	−0.155	0.125	−0.156	1.000
	0.433	0.109	0.196	0.107	—

Authors' computation (2024)

Table 3 Variance inflation factors

Sample: 2012–2021		
Included observations: 120		
Variables	Coefficient variance	Centered VIF
AUT	0.127	1.034
AGE	0.000	1.065
AFE	1.033	7.110
LEV	0.000	1.080
AUF	1.547	6.916
C	16.302	NA
		3.441

Authors' computation (2024)

Table 4 Correlated random effects—Hausman test

Test cross-section random effects			
Test summary	Chi-sq. statistic	Chi-sq. d.f.	Prob.
Cross-section random	14.515	6	0.0244

Researchers' computation (2024)

Hausman Test

The appropriateness of fixed effects versus random effects models was evaluated using the Hausman (1978) test. The results of the test, presented in Table 4, demonstrated that the *p*-value was statistically significant ($p < 0.05$). As a result, a fixed effects model was selected for analysis.

Table 5 Regression analysis

Dependent variable: ROA						
Periods included: 10						
Cross-sections included: 12						
Total panel observations: 120						
	Random			Fixed		
Variable	coefficient	t-Statistic	Prob.	coefficient	t-Statistic	Prob.
AUT	−10.721	−2.367	0.020	−11.642	−2.525	0.013
AUF	−3.995	−2.593	0.011	−4.180	−2.249	0.027
AUF*AUT	1.931	2.316	0.023	2.081	2.456	0.016
FSZ	3.541	3.048	0.003	5.026	3.472	0.001
LEV	−0.017	−2.382	0.019	−0.020	−2.736	0.008
AGE	−0.043	−1.902	0.060	−0.195	−2.001	0.048
C	−7.738	−1.167	0.246	−16.236	−1.423	0.158
R-squared	0.184			0.651		
Adjusted R-squared	0.136			0.585		
S.E. of regression	1.215			1.189		
F-statistic	3.797			9.870		
Prob(F-statistic)	0.002			0.000		
Mean dependent var	0.539			1.673		
S.D. dependent var	1.307			1.845		
Sum squared resid	149.137			127.202		
Durbin–Watson stat	2.290			2.573		

Authors' computation (2024)

Regression Analysis

The regression analysis in Table 5 showed that the explanatory variables (Audit Tenure, Audit Fee, Audit Tenure*Audit Fee, & other control variables such as Firm Age, Leverage, and Firm Size) account for 65.1% of the variation in the dependent variable (ROA). This is indicated by the coefficient of determination (R Square) of 0.651 (65.1%) and adjusted R-Square of 0.585 (58.5%). At the 1% significance level, the F-statistic of 9.870 is significant ($p = 0.000$). This validates that the entire model is jointly fitted. As a result, the dependent variable and the explanatory factors have a significant relationship.

In the fixed effects model, the coefficient for audit fee (AUF) is −4.180 with a t-statistic of −2.249 and a p-value of 0.027. The negative coefficient for audit fee suggests that, on average, firms paying higher audit fees tend to have lower financial performance, after accounting for other factors such as firm size, leverage, age, etc. This could imply that higher audit fees might reflect increased costs or challenges faced by the firm, such as regulatory scrutiny, complexity of operations, or the need for additional assurance. Alternatively, it could suggest that firms investing more in audit fees might prioritize compliance and risk management over short-term profitability. The result is in alignment with Krishnan et al. (2011); Moutinho et al. (2012). Also, the findings revealed that Audit Tenure (AUT) and Return on Asset have a negative relationship (*p*-value = 0.013, *t*-value = −2.525, and coefficient = −11.642). This is consistent with the result of Fasua (2023). The significant negative coefficient of Audit Tenure indicates that, within both models, there is a consistent adverse effect of prolonged Auditor Tenure (AUT) on Return on Assets (ROA). This finding is crucial as it suggests that as audit tenure increases, a firm's financial performance tends to deteriorate. One possible interpretation is that over time, auditors may become overly familiar with the client's operations, potentially leading to complacency or reduced rigor in their auditing procedures. This familiarity might hinder their ability to identify emerging risks or areas of concern accurately, ultimately impacting the reliability of financial statements and, consequently, the firm's financial performance. Also, this implies that firms with longer auditor tenure may face challenges in maintaining or improving their profitability over time.

In the fixed effects model, the coefficient for the interaction term (audit fee * audit tenure) is 2.081 with a t-statistic of 2.456 and a *p*-value of 0.016. The interaction term captures the combined effect of audit fee and audit tenure on ROA. It assesses whether the relationship between audit fee and ROA varies depending on the duration of the audit engagement. The positive coefficient for the interaction term suggests that the relationship between audit fee and ROA is moderated by audit tenure. Specifically, as the duration of the audit engagement (audit tenure) increases, the positive impact of audit fees on ROA becomes more pronounced. This implies that the effectiveness or benefits derived from higher audit fees are greater for firms with longer audit tenure. It could indicate that over time, the value added by auditors through higher fees becomes more evident or significant, potentially enhancing the financial reporting quality and thereby positively impacting firm profitability. The results are logical and consistent with expectations based theoretical reasoning. Higher audit fees might initially impact performance negatively, but their effectiveness in improving financial reporting quality and enhance performance becomes more evident over time, particularly for firms with longer audit tenure.

The results indicate that, with coefficient of 5.026, firm size reveals a positive and significant effect with financial performance at 5% level. This result indicates that economies of scale or resource advantages associated with larger firms contribute positively to profitability. Larger firms may benefit from better access to capital, operational efficiencies, and market dominance, leading to higher profitability. It suggests that investors and stakeholders may view larger firms as more stable and financially robust due to their ability to generate higher returns. Findings revealed that Firm Age (AGE) showed a significant and negative effect on Financial Performance of Firms ($c = -2.001$, $p < 0.05$) in the selected DMBs in Nigeria. The negative coefficient for firm age suggests that younger firms tend to have lower Return on Assets (ROA). This result implies that younger firms face challenges or constraints that affect their performance compared to more established firms. Younger firms may have limited resources, market recognition, or operational experience, which could hinder their ability to generate higher returns.

Also, the significant and negative effect for leverage in Table 5 suggests that higher leverage is associated with lower Return on Assets ($c = -0.020$, $p = 0.008$). This result implies that firms with higher levels of debt relative to their equity tend to have lower profitability. Higher leverage indicates higher financial risk and financial leverage, which can lead to increased interest expenses and debt servicing obligations. The result agrees with Akinadewo et al. (2023).

Conclusion and Recommendations

Investigating the moderating role of audit tenure in the relationship between audit fee and financial performance of Nigerian Deposit Money Banks (DMBs) was the objective of the study. We selected 10 DMBs in Nigeria from the 14 banks that serve as the population of the study from the Nigerian Exchange Group utilizing data spanning between 2012 and 2021. The dependent variable is Return on Asset (ROA) while the explanatory variables are Audit Tenure (AUT), Audit Fee (AUF), and Interaction of Audit Fee and Audit Tenure (AUF*AUT). The control variables explored are Leverage, Firm Age, and Firm Size. The result showed that the Firm Size and Interaction of Audit Fee and Audit Tenure had a positive and significant effect on financial performance while Audit Fee, Audit Tenure, Leverage, and Firm Age had a negative and significant effect on financial performance. The result concluded that audit tenure, audit fees, and their interactions had a significant effect on the DMBs financial performance of the

In conclusion, the findings of this study shed light on several crucial factors influencing the financial performance of the selected DMBs in Nigeria. The negative coefficient for audit fees suggests that firms paying higher fees tend to exhibit lower financial performance, possibly due to increased costs or regulatory challenges. Moreover, prolonged auditor tenure is associated with deteriorating financial performance, potentially due to auditor complacency. However, the positive interaction between audit fees and audit tenure indicates that higher fees may enhance financial reporting quality hence financial performance over time, particularly for firms with longer audit engagements. Additionally, firm size shows a positive effect on financial performance, highlighting the benefits of economies of scale and market dominance. Conversely, firm age and leverage display negative effects, indicating that younger firms and those with higher leverage face challenges in generating higher returns. These findings offer valuable insights for stakeholders in understanding and managing the complexities of financial performance within the Nigerian banking sector.

The study recommended that firms should carefully assess the cost–benefit trade-offs associated with audit fees, considering factors such as regulatory requirements, operational complexity, and risk management needs. While higher audit fees may initially impact profitability negatively, they may lead to long-term benefits in terms of enhanced financial reporting quality and improved performance, particularly for firms with longer audit tenure. Also, regulatory authorities should consider the interactive effects of audit fees and audit tenure when formulating audit-related policies and standards. For instance, regulators may explore incentives or guidelines to encourage firms to invest in higher audit fees, especially in situations of prolonged audit engagements.

Limitations and Future Research Directions

The study's reliance on secondary data from audited annual reports limits the analysis to publicly available information, which may not capture all relevant variables affecting financial performance. Future research should consider incorporating primary data through surveys or interviews to gain deeper insights. Additionally, expanding the sample size and including other financial institutions beyond DMBs could provide a more comprehensive understanding of the audit dynamics in the broader financial sector. Future research could also explore similar relationships in different economic environments or sectors to validate and extend these findings. Additionally, examining other moderating factors, such as regulatory changes or technological advancements in auditing, could provide a better understanding of how audit practices impact financial performance.

References

Abbott, L. J., Parker, S., & Peters, G. F. (2006). Earnings management, litigation risk, and asymmetric audit fee responses. *Auditing: A Journal of Practice & Theory, 25*(1), 85–98.

Abbott, L. J., Daugherty, B., Parker, S., & Peters, G. F. (2016). Internal audit quality and financial reporting quality: The joint importance of independence and competence. *Journal of Accounting Research, 54*(1), 3–40.

Adeniyi, S. I., & Mieseigha, E. G. (2013). Audit tenure: An assessment of its effects on audit quality in Nigeria. *International Journal of Academic Research in Accounting, Finance and Management Sciences, 3*(3), 275–283.

Ado, A. B., Rashid, N., Mustapha, U. A., & Ademola, L. S. (2020). The impact of audit quality on the financial performance of listed companies Nigeria. *Journal of Critical Reviews, 7*(9), 37–42.

Akinadewo, I. S., Ogundele, O. S., Odewole, P. O., & Akinadewo, J. O. (2023). Empirical investigation of financial performance determinants: Evidence from deposit money banks in Nigeria. *Res Militaris, 13*(2), 6926–6936.

Ardilawati, S. Y., & Cahyati, A. D. (2023, July). The influence of audit tenure and audit fees on audit quality with audit committee quality as a moderating variable. In *Proceeding of International Conference on Innovations in Social Sciences Education and Engineering* (Vol. 3, p. 114).

Awinbugri, A. E., & Prince, G. (2019). The impact of audit committees' meetings and audit fees on the financial performance of listed banks in Ghana. *International Journal of Research and Innovation in Social Science, 3*(5), 341–346.

Azizkhani, M., Daghani, R., & Shailer, G. (2018). Audit firm tenure and audit quality in a constrained market. *The International Journal of Accounting, 53*(3), 167–182.

Bakr, D. J., Ali, S. H., & Jameel, S. A. (2023). The role of audit fees in improving financial performance: A case study of eight selected commercial banks of Iraqi stock exchange over the period (2006–2020). *Journal of Duhok University, 26*(1), 634–645.

Boesso, G., Kumar, K., & Michelon, G. (2013). Descriptive, instrumental and strategic approaches to corporate social responsibility: Do they drive the financial performance of companies differently? *Accounting, Auditing & Accountability Journal, 26*(3), 399–422.

Boo, E. F., & Sharma, D. (2008). Effect of regulatory oversight on the association between internal governance characteristics and audit fees. *Accounting & Finance, 48*(1), 51–71.

Bratten, B., Causholli, M., & Omer, T. C. (2019). Audit firm tenure, bank complexity, and financial reporting quality. *Contemporary Accounting Research, 36*(1), 295–325.

Chen, L., Xiao, T., & Zhou, J. (2023). Do auditor changes affect the disclosure of critical audit matters? Evidence from China. *Economic Modelling, 122*, 106245.

Chinedu, E. F., & Chidoziem, A. M. F. (2017). Audit firm report and financial performance of money deposit banks in Nigeria. *The Nigerian Accountant Journal*, 25–39.

Choi, J. H., Kim, J. B., & Zang, Y. (2010). Do abnormally high audit fees impair audit quality? *Auditing: A Journal of Practice & Theory, 29*(2), 115–140.

DeAngelo, L. E. (1981). Auditor independence, 'low balling', and disclosure regulation. *Journal of Accounting and Economics, 3*(2), 113–127.

DeFond, M. L., Raghunandan, K., & Subramanyam, K. R. (2002). Do non–audit service fees impair auditor independence? Evidence from going concern audit opinions. *Journal of Accounting Research, 40*(4), 1247–1274.

Diana, H. I. (2020). Indicators for measuring the financial performance of economic\entities. *Ovidius University Annals, Economic Sciences Series, 20*(1), 945–953.

Farouk, M. A., & Hassan, S. U. (2014). Impact of audit quality and financial performance of quoted cement firms in Nigeria. *International Journal of Accounting and Taxation, 2*(2), 1–22.

Fasua, H. K. (2023). Audit quality and firm financial performance. *Contemporary Economy Journal, 8*(4), 33–45.

Francis, J. R. (2011). A framework for understanding and researching audit quality. *Auditing: A Journal of Practice & Theory, 30*(2), 125–152.

Francis, J. R., & Ke, B. (2006). Disclosure of fees paid to auditors and the market valuation of earnings surprises. *Review of Accounting Studies, 11*, 495–523.

Gul, F. A., Wu, D., & Yang, Z. (2013). Do individual auditors affect audit quality? Evidence from archival data. *The Accounting Review, 88*(6), 1993–2023.

Hassan, M. A., & Farouk, S. U. (2014). Impact of audit quality and financial performance of quoted cement firms in Nigeria. *International Journal of Accounting and Taxation, 2*(2), 1–22.

Hausman, J. A. (1978). Specification tests in econometrics. *Econometrica: Journal of the econometric society, 46*, 1251–1271.

Hoitash, R., Markelevich, A., & Barragato, C. A. (2007). Auditor fees and audit quality. *Managerial Auditing Journal, 22*(8), 761–786.

Hribar, P., Kravet, T., & Wilson, R. (2014). A new measure of accounting quality. *Review of Accounting Studies, 19*, 506–538.

Huang, T. C., Chang, H., & Chiou, J. R. (2016). Audit market concentration, audit fees, and audit quality: Evidence from China. *Auditing: A Journal of Practice & Theory, 35*(2), 121–145.

Januarti, I. (2019). Determinants of audit quality: An empirical insight from Indonesia. *International Journal of Scientific & Technology Research, 8*(7), 570–578.

Jensen, M. C., & Meckling, W. H. (2019). Theory of the firm: Managerial behavior, agency costs and ownership structure. In *Corporate governance* (pp. 77–132). Gower.

Kajola, S. O., Olabisi, J., Tonade, A. A., & Agbatogun, T. O. (2022). Determinants of audit fees in Nigerian banks. *Accounting and Taxation Review, 6*(1), 29–45.

Krishnan, J., Krishnan, J., & Song, H. (2011). The effect of Auditing Standard No. 5 on audit fees. *Auditing: A Journal of Practice & Theory, 30*(4), 1–27.

Martani, D., Rahmah, N. A., Fitriany, F., & Anggraita, V. (2021). Impact of audit tenure and audit rotation on the audit quality: Big 4 vs non big 4. *Cogent Economics & Finance, 9*(1), 1901395.

Moutinho, V., Cerqueira, A., & Brandao, E. (2012). *Audit fees and firm performance*. Available at SSRN 2180020.
Naser, K., & Nuseibeh, R. (2008). Determinants of audit fees: Empirical evidence from an emerging economy. *International Journal of Commerce and Management, 17*(3), 239–254.
Ogbodo, O. C., & Akabuogu, N. J. (2018). Effect of audit quality on the financial performance of selected banks in Nigeria. *International Journal of Trend in Scientific Research and Development (IJTSRD), 3*(1), 45–61.
Oyebamiji, O. A. (2022). Audit tenure and financial reporting quality of listed Nigerian deposit money banks (2008-2018). *European Business & Management, 8*(4), 81–88.
Palmrose, Z. V. (1986). Audit fees and auditor size: Further evidence. *Journal of Accounting Research*, 97–110.
PCAOB. (2009). *Auditing Standard No. 9: Audit Planning*. Public Company Accounting Oversight Board.
Qawqzeh, H. K., Endut, W. A., Rashid, N., Johari, R. J., Hamid, N. A., & Rasit, Z. A. (2018). Auditor tenure, audit firm rotation and audit quality: A literature review. *International Journal of Academic Research in Business and Social Sciences, 8*, 12.
Quick, R., & Schmidt, F. (2018). Do audit firm rotation, auditor retention, and joint audits matter? An experimental investigation of bank directors' and institutional investors' perceptions. *Journal of Accounting Literature, 41*(1), 1–21.
Reynolds, J. K., Deis Jr, D. R., & Francis, J. R. (2004). Professional service fees and auditor objectivity. *Auditing: A Journal of Practice & Theory, 23*(1), 29–52.
Ruiz-Barbadillo, E., Gómez-Aguilar, N., De Fuentes-Barberá, C., & García-Benau, M. A. (2004). Audit quality and the going-concern decision-making process: Spanish evidence. *European Accounting Review, 13*(4), 597–620.
Scott, W. R. (2013). *Institutions and organizations: Ideas, interests, and identities*. Sage.
Simunic, D. A., & Stein, M. T. (1987). Product differentiation in auditing: Auditor choice in the market for unseasoned new issues. *(No Title)*.
Tepalagul, N., & Lin, L. (2015). Auditor independence and audit quality: A literature review. *Journal of Accounting, Auditing & Finance, 30*(1), 101–121.
Ugwu, C. C., Aikpitanyi, L. N., & Idemudia, S. (2020). The effect of audit quality on the financial performance of deposit money banks (evidence from Nigeria). *Journal of Economics and Business, 3*(1).
Wahyudi, S., & Sabaruddin, S. (2023). The role of audit quality in moderating audit tenure, audit fees, auditor's reputation and audit committees on the integrity of financial statements. *International Journal of Social Service and Research, 3*(8), 2080–2086.
Yuniarti, R. (2011). Audit firm size, audit fee and audit quality. *Journal of Global Management*.
Ziaee, M. (2014). The effect of audit quality on the performance of listed companies in Tehran Stock Exchange. *International Letters of Social and Humanistic Sciences, 10*, 36–43.

Analysis of Tax Relief Measures as a Result of the COVID-19 Pandemic in South Africa

Elsie Selemela and Asheer Jaywant Ram

Abstract COVID-19 led to numerous business liquidations and employment losses. Governments worldwide had to intervene to support their citizens and keep businesses afloat. It fell to tax administrators to ease the tax burden on taxpayers, all the while facing hardships in respect of tax collection. National Treasury and the South African Revenue Service (SARS) implemented tax relief measures because of COVID-19. Despite this, taxpayers are still experiencing the detrimental effects of COVID-19. It is the government's aim to offer additional help to businesses and individuals who are still facing these hardships and assist in rebuilding businesses. This paper considers the tax measures that were taken by South Africa in comparison to those that were taken by Brazil, Russia, India, China, and South Africa (BRICS) countries to determine the usefulness of these measures in dealing with the effects of COVID-19 on taxes. It is critical to understand these tax relief measures to be ready if a pandemic were to recur in the future. A comparative analysis method is applied using BRICS countries. This is appropriate, as the BRICS group consists of developing countries with mutual economic ties. The findings of this analysis indicate which measures were used, when they were implemented, and how tax policies in the BRICS countries changed while adjusting to COVID-19. It was found that tax policies put in place in South Africa decreased tax collection without any measures in place to boost it. Examining the tax policy amendments made by BRICS nations during COVID-19 assists in identifying areas for improvement.

Keywords BRICS · COVID-19 · Income tax · Tax relief measures

E. Selemela · A. J. Ram (✉)
University of the Witwatersrand, Johannesburg, South Africa
e-mail: Asheer.Ram@wits.ac.za

T. Moloi (ed.), *Impacting Society Positively Through Technology in Accounting and Business Processes*, Springer Proceedings in Business and Economics,
https://doi.org/10.1007/978-3-031-84885-8_32

Introduction

Background and Importance

COVID-19 emerged from China in late 2019 and rapidly spread throughout the globe. To mitigate the risk of infection, countries worldwide implemented national lockdowns despite their economic challenges (Lone & Ahmad, 2020). COVID-19 significantly impacted taxation, and tax authorities had to take steps to survive through it (Sadiq & Krever, 2021). Taxation plays a key role in maintaining access to basic goods and services (IMF, 2020).

The sectors that were mostly affected by the pandemic included retail, hospitality, travel, restaurants, transport, leisure, and other service sectors (Xiang et al., 2021). This resulted in many job losses due to business closures. The decreased economic activity gave rise to unplanned government expenditure, which eroded the tax base (PwC, 2020). Taxes worldwide were mostly affected by these changes, and adjustments to tax systems were made to accommodate them.

The effects of COVID-19 on economies and vulnerability to COVID-19 were different across social groups, while developing countries will experience long-lasting implications (IMF, 2020). Developed countries with sufficient resources also struggled with the effects of COVID-19, so this can only mean that developing countries were bound to suffer even greater and lingering consequences (de Villiers et al., 2020).

South Africa, as a developing country, faced an immediate challenge in responding to the effects of COVID-19. The initial lockdown in South Africa damaged an already fragile economy. This is evident from several problems, including poor service delivery, ongoing load shedding, constant hikes in interest rates after the pandemic, and others (Arndt et al., 2020). COVID-19 negatively impacted society due to the government's increased borrowing and the anticipated significant reduction in tax revenue, which resulted in the public purse being severely constrained (de Villiers et al., 2020).

In light of COVID-19, the Minister of Finance issued several tax adjustment measures (SAICA, 2020). These adjustments were dealt with in the 2020 Disaster Management Tax Relief Act and the 2020 Disaster Management Tax Relief Administration Act. These Acts contain exceptional tax measures intended to aid taxpayers whose financial situation was impacted by COVID-19 and a needed national lockdown (National Treasury, 2022).

To assess the tax measures implemented in South Africa, this research will compare South Africa's measures with those implemented in Brazil, Russia, India, and China as members of the BRICS group. This paper will illustrate the measures taken in the above-mentioned countries individually, refer to the COVID-19 tax ideas stated in the BRICS collaboration, and identify what South Africa could have done better looking at the effects of COVID-19 on the South African economy. The use of the BRICS group is appropriate as it consists of developing countries with mutual economic ties. Comparisons to developed economies like the United States of

America, the United Kingdom, or Australia would not be appropriate in this instance.

Research Questions

The following research questions are considered:

1. Taxes had to accommodate the changes in the economy caused by COVID-19 but what were the effects of these changes?
2. Which principles of the South African income tax, VAT, corporate tax, and personal income tax were adjusted?
3. What was the approach by the other members of the BRICS organisation and what should have been done better by South Africa?
4. Which tax reform measures could be suggested for South Africa, considered against tax reform best practice?

Method

The research is qualitative in nature and a comparative research method is applied. Comparative research involves analysing similarities and differences across different contexts to identify areas for improvement (Indiana University, 2019). Information was collected from journal articles, academic books, case law literature, Organisation for Economic Co-operation and Development (OECD) reports, budget speeches and the Treasury and SARS websites, as they addressed COVID-19 relief measures.

South African Approach

Due to economic damage caused by the lockdown, National Treasury introduced the Disaster Management Tax Relief Act of 2020 and the Disaster Management Tax Relief Administration Act of 2020 as tax relief measures (SARS, 2021). These Acts contain exceptional tax measures introduced to assist taxpayers that experienced cash flow problems during COVID-19.

Disaster Management Tax Relief Act

The Disaster Management Tax Relief Act (2020) was promulgated in South Africa to amend the Employment Tax Incentive Act (2013) and include a new provision for the tax treatment of specific organisations and the ability to donate to those organisations.

Employment Tax Incentive Act

An Employment Tax Incentive was created to encourage employment by reducing the employees' tax payable by an employer (Employment Tax Incentive Act, 2013). During COVID-19, this Act was amended, and the amendments applied for the period 1 May 2020 to 1 July 2020 and 1 August 2021 to 30 November 2021. The amendments were as follows:

- Due to employees working reduced hours to adhere to the lockdown rules, the monthly remuneration definition in Section 1 of the Employment Tax Incentive Act was revised so that the employment tax incentive did not have to be reduced where employees worked fewer than 160 h in 1 month.
- Where an employer did not have a wage regulation measure in place, the requirement that an employee had to be paid a minimum of R2000 per month for the employer to qualify for the tax incentive as per section 7(1) of the Employment Tax Incentive Act was removed.
- The employment tax incentive was claimed for employees not qualifying under the normal Employment Tax Incentive Act provisions. Section 6 of the Employment Tax Incentive Act defines a qualifying employee as someone who is between the ages of 18 and 29. The amendment to this section of the act increased the age limit from 29 to 65 years old.
- The amount of the employment tax incentive changed:

  (a) If an employees' monthly compensation was less than R2000, the amount of employment tax incentive increased by 37.5%.
  (b) If the employees' remuneration was between R2000 and R4500, the amount of employment tax incentive increased by R750.

- The SARS tax refund could be claimed monthly rather than at the end of the period during which the employer must file a return under section 14(3)(a) of the Fourth Schedule to the Income Tax Act. This was implemented to improve the liquidity of compliant employers (Disaster Management Tax Relief Act, 2020).

COVID-19 Disaster Relief Organisations and Donations Tax (Section 18A)

A COVID-19 disaster relief organisation is defined as any corporation, trust, or individual association that has been incorporated, formed, or founded in the Republic of South Africa for the purpose of establishing a disaster relief fund for COVID-19 (Disaster Management Tax Relief Act, 2020).

For the purposes of the Income Tax Act, any COVID-19 disaster relief organisation was deemed to be a public benefit organisation (from 1 April 2020 to 31 September 2020) as defined in section 30(1) of that Act if that COVID-19 disaster relief organisation met the requirements below (Disaster Management Tax Relief Act, 2020) such that it:

(a) carries out public benefit activity as described in paragraph (a) of the definition of 'public benefit activity'; and
(b) the standards set out in section 30(3) of the Act and is approved as a public benefit organisation by the Commissioner, subject to—
    (i) that COVID-19 disaster relief organisation meeting all of the requirements imposed by section 30 of that Act in respect of a public benefit organisation; and
    (ii) any power granted to the Commissioner to revoke the approval of any public benefit organisation under section 30 of that Act.

Disaster Management Tax Relief Administration Act

The Disaster Management Tax Relief Administration Act 14 of 2020 dealt with the deferral of employees' tax, the deferral of provisional tax, the deferral of interim payments by micro and small to medium-sized businesses, and changes in the VAT category of vendors that would have an impact on monthly returns and refunds, as well as the extension of certain time periods. This relief was extended to the 2021 calendar year because COVID-19 was still affecting many firms (Disaster Management Tax Relief Administration Act, 2020).

Qualifying Taxpayer

To qualify for a deferral of employees' tax, the taxpayer had to be a qualifying taxpayer. A qualifying taxpayer is defined in Section 1 of the Disaster Management Tax Relief Administration Act as a corporation, trust, partnership, or individual who is a taxpayer under section 151 of the Tax Administration Act and meets the following requirements (Disaster Management Tax Relief Administration Act, 2020):

- Was carrying on a trade from 1 April 2021 to 1 April 2022 and had a gross income of R100 million or less during that assessment year (Disaster Management Tax Relief Administration Act, 2020); and
- their gross income did not contain more than 20% of their employer's interest, dividends, foreign dividends, royalties, rental from letting fixed property, annuities, and any other remuneration (Disaster Management Tax Relief Administration Act, 2020); and
- did not have any outstanding debt (other than a debt that is being paid off, compromised, suspended, or less than R100) (Disaster Management Tax Relief Administration Act, 2020); and
- did not have any outstanding return, unless alternative arrangements have been made by SARS for rendering such a return (section 256(3) of the Tax Administration).

Tax Deferral of Employees' Tax (PAYE)

A qualifying taxpayer who was registered as an employer (or representative employer as defined in paragraph 2 of the Fourth Schedule to the Income Tax Act) by 25 March 2020 was permitted to pay only 65% of the employees' tax payable under paragraph 2(1) of the Fourth Schedule to the Income Tax Act for amounts deducted or withheld during the period beginning 1 April 2020 and ending 31 August 2020. This relief was reinstated in 2021 to include taxpayers that were registered as employers for the period 1 August 2021 to 31 October 2021 (Disaster Management Tax Relief Administration Act, 2020).

In 2020, when the deferral could be applied, 35% of the employees' tax had to be paid over six equal monthly instalments (Disaster Management Tax Relief Administration Act, 2020). In 2021, the period was reduced to 4 months (Disaster Management Tax Relief Administration Act, 2020). These measures applied to medium-sized firms run by a company, partnership, individual, or trust with a gross income of less than R100 million for the fiscal year ending on or after 1 April 2020, but before 1 April 2021 (Disaster Management Tax Relief Administration Act, 2020). The calculation of gross income should not exceed 20% of income from dividends, interest, overseas dividends, royalties, rent from letting fixed property, annuities, and any compensation from an employer (Disaster Management Tax Relief Administration Act, 2020). When making a reduced payment, the employer must comply with tax law as defined by the Tax Administration Act (Disaster Management Tax Relief Administration Act, 2020).

There were no penalties under paragraph 6 of the Fourth Schedule to the Income Tax Act levied on amounts deferred; no interest under section 89*bis* of the Income Tax Act was charged on amounts deferred; and the amounts due were only subject to penalties under paragraph 6 of the Fourth Schedule to the Income Tax Act and interest under section 89*bis* of the Act if not paid when due and payable (Disaster Management Tax Relief Administration Act, 2020).

Provisional Tax Relief

A qualifying taxpayer who was a provisional taxpayer might have to pay 15% instead of half of the total estimated liability (as determined in accordance with paragraph 17 of the Fourth Schedule) for normal tax in respect of the relevant year of assessment less the total ad valorem tax from 1 April 2020 to 30 September 2020, in respect of provisional tax payable in terms of paragraph 21(1)(a) or 23(a) of the Income Tax Act during the period (Disaster Management Tax Relief Administration Act, 2020) and less:

- any employees' tax deducted by the taxpayer's employer during the fiscal year up to and including the day the provisional tax is due and payable; and
- any tax paid to the government of another nation that qualifies for a rebate under section 6*quat* of the Income Tax Act (Disaster Management Tax Relief Administration Act, 2020).

From the period starting on 1 April 2020 to 31 March 2021, taxpayers were only required to pay 65% of provisional tax payable in terms of paragraph 21(1)(b) or 23(b) of the Fourth Schedule to the Income Tax Act and not the total estimated liability (as finally determined in accordance with paragraph 17 of the Fourth Schedule) for normal tax in respect of the relevant year of assessment less (Disaster Management Tax Relief Administration Act, 2020):

- any amount paid as provisional tax for the year within the 6-month period following the start of the year (Disaster Management Tax Relief Administration Act, 2020);
- any amount paid as provisional tax for the year within 6 months of the year's beginning (Disaster Management Tax Relief Administration Act, 2020); and
- any tax proven to be owing to the government of another nation and eligible for reimbursement under section 6*quat* of the Income Tax Act (Disaster Management Tax Relief Administration Act, 2020).

Deferral of Interim Payments

The interim payments by micro-businesses in terms of paragraph 11(1)(*c*) of the Sixth Schedule to the Income Tax Act were reduced to a rate of 15% payable instead of the normal rate of 50% of the amount of tax so calculated in terms of paragraph 11(1)(*a*) and (*b*). This applied for the period 1 April 2020 to 31 August 2020. During the period 1 September 2020 to 28 February 2021, only 65% of interim payment was due, not an amount equal to the amount of tax determined in accordance with paragraph 11(4)(a) and (b) of the Sixth Schedule (Disaster Management Tax Relief Administration Act, 2020).

Change in Value-Added Tax Category

Vendors who were supposed to file their VAT returns every 2 months under category A or B tax periods were assumed to come under category C and submit monthly, despite anything in the Value-Added Tax Act to the contrary (Disaster Management Tax Relief Administration Act, 2020). For the purposes of section 28 of the Act, a vendor was obliged to file a return with the Commissioner, and the Commissioner determined the tax payable by or rebate due to the vendor for each month that fell within the 2 months that comprised the Category A or Category B tax period (Disaster Management Tax Relief Administration Act, 2020), provided that:

- The tax payable or reimbursement owing to the vendor was calculated using the category C tax period; and
- The vendor filed a return with the commissioner and determined the tax payable or refund due for the month in which the Category A or Category B tax period ends (Disaster Management Tax Relief Administration Act, 2020). This section operated for 4 months in 2020.

Corporate Income Tax

The following steps were announced in the 2020 Budget to keep businesses solvent throughout the pandemic:

- The deduction for net interest expense was restricted to 30% of earnings (Disaster Management Tax Relief Administration Act, 2020).
- The number of assessed losses that could be carried forward was limited to 80% of taxable income (Disaster Management Tax Relief Administration Act, 2020).
- These measures applied from 1 January 2021 to at least 1 January 2022 (Disaster Management Tax Relief Administration Act, 2020).

Extension of Time Periods

In calculating a time period in terms of the Tax Administration Act, certain days were regarded as *dies non*. The ordinary dictionary meaning of the term *dies non* is a day on which no legal business can be conducted, or which does not count for legal purposes (Disaster Management Tax Relief Administration Act, 2020). These days were not considered in calculating the time this Act set aside for certain administrative matters (Disaster Management Tax Relief Administration Act, 2020). The period of lockdown in South Africa was regarded as *dies non*.

The periods to which this applies included:

- The 3-year period for submitting required documentation under sections 49G (1), 50G (1) and 64G (1) of the Income Tax Act. These included refunds of withholding tax on royalties, refunds of withholding tax on interest, dividend refunds for dividends declared and paid by corporations, and tax refunds for dividends paid by regulated intermediaries (Disaster Management Tax Relief Administration Act, 2020).

- The period as per Section 47 of the Tax Administration Act, where a taxpayer had to produce relevant material in person during the lockdown (Disaster Management Tax Relief Administration Act, 2020).
- A notice that SARS would undertake a field audit during the lockdown period (section 48 of the Tax Administration Act) (Disaster Management Tax Relief Administration Act, 2020).
- A notice requiring the taxpayer to appear at an investigation pursuant to Section 53 of the Tax Administration Tax Act (Disaster Management Tax Relief Administration Act, 2020).
- Section 60 of the Tax Administration Act, which required the execution of a search and seizure warrant (Disaster Management Tax Relief Administration Act, 2020).
- The time frames specified in Chapter 7 of the Tax Administration Act for applying for an advanced ruling (Disaster Management Tax Relief Administration Act, 2020).
- The 3-year and 5-year prescription periods for assessment, in terms of section 99(1) of the Tax Administration Act (Disaster Management Tax Relief Administration Act, 2020).
- Section 100 of the Tax Administration Act deals with the finality of assessments, excluding section 100(1)(a)(I)—estimated assessments where no corrected return has been received by SARS from the taxpayer (Disaster Management Tax Relief Administration Act, 2020).
- The time frames for resolving disputes under Tax Administration Act Chapter 9, including the dispute resolution provisions under Section 103 (Disaster Management Tax Relief Administration Act, 2020).
- The extension of time needed to calculate the period for the remittance of penalties under section 215(3) of the Tax Administration Act (Disaster Management Tax Relief Administration Act, 2020).
- The 3-year period that SARS must issue a penalty incorrectly assessed under section 219 of the Tax Administration Act (Disaster Management Tax Relief Administration Act, 2020).
- Section 244(3) of the Tax Administration Act deals with deadlines for paying tax or the submission of information, returns, or documents. In exceptional circumstances, where the taxpayer applied for the extension within 21 business days of the deadline, the time period did not consider the *dies non* rule (Disaster Management Tax Relief Administration Act, 2020).
- The time needed for the election of a public officer under section 246(2)(d) of the Tax Administration Act (Disaster Management Tax Relief Administration Act, 2020).
- The time period in which a taxpayer can respond to SARS's notice that intends to revoke third party access under section 256(6) of the Tax Administration Act

to the taxpayer's compliant status (Disaster Management Tax Relief Administration Act, 2020).

COVID-19 Tax Policies by Other BRICS Members

Overview

BRICS is an international organisation that consists of five countries, namely Brazil, Russia, India, China, and South Africa. All the BRICS nations launched fiscal measures to shield their economies against the impact of COVID-19 (Reserve Bank of India, 2021). The focus of BRICS countries was on macroeconomic policies and the implementation of well-targeted fiscal and monetary interventions on both supply and demand sides in an effort to halt the recession, boost employment, safeguard livelihoods, and stabilise the world economy (Wang, 2020). Different approaches were taken by members of the BRICS organisation to protect their economies during and after COVID-19 (Jiao et al., 2022). Each member nation enacted different tax policies to lessen the pandemic's socioeconomic effects. The measures taken include relaxation of fiscal laws, tax relief, tax reductions and deferments, amongst others (Reserve Bank of India, 2021).

In the meeting held by the Heads of Tax Authorities of the BRICS countries that took place in Moscow, Russia, in 2021, it was stated that the BRICS tax authorities remained committed to taking measures that ensured business continuity while also taking the responsibility to secure tax revenue necessary to provide state support to businesses and individuals (Reserve Bank of India, 2021). This section will consider the tax policies of BRICS countries and compare them to South Africa's tax policies.

Brazil

COVID-19 had a negative impact on the Brazilian economy and the federal government put measures in place to protect individuals, maintain Brazilian employment levels, and reduce the virus's impact on the country's health system (Deloitte, 2020). The federal government of Brazil granted tax advantages to businesses and individuals to support them through the pandemic (Orsolon et al., 2020).

Tax Relief

Within the Brazilian federal revenue, the federal government halted court lawsuit deadlines, procedural deadlines, and administrative procedures. Administrative tax appeals were also suspended. The Brazilian Central Bank introduced a new emergency credit line to allow small- and medium-sized businesses to cover 2 months' worth of labour, tax, and staff salaries at a reduced rate of interest. This line of credit required that the companies maintain their staff and not fire employees during the loan period, up to 2 months after the loan had been paid off. Brazilian companies were allowed to temporarily suspend employment contracts and offer virtual courses or a programme of professional qualifications in lieu of employment for the duration of the suspension period (Deloitte, 2020; Orsolon et al., 2020). Medium and large companies were given an extraordinary settlement programme to pay outstanding tax debts for 81 months, while individuals and small businesses were given 142 months. The federal government also granted a 90-day extension for the validity of tax clearance certificates (Bottino et al., 2020).

Tax Exemptions

Companies and individuals were exempt from tax payments, either in full or in part, for some taxes. The tax on industrialised products used by medical professionals and the import duty rate of medical products used for COVID-19 purposes were reduced to zero (Ministério da Economia, 2020). Companies and individuals whose average income typically corresponds to 3.38% were also exempted from tax on financial operations. Due to this exemption, the aforementioned taxpayers were able to borrow money during the pandemic to pay their employees, repay their taxes, and settle other debts without incurring additional taxes. In addition, there was a reduction of 50% in payroll tax rates for contributions to the autonomous social services for 3 months (Morceiro et al., 2022; Orsolon et al., 2020).

Extension of Deadlines

The federal government also extended deadlines so that there was enough time to comply with tax obligations. Extensions for administrative defence, appeals against decisions rendered in the administrative procedure for recognition of responsibility, nonconformity defence, appeals against decisions made in the Special Tax Amnesty Programme exclusion process, early offers of guarantees in tax execution, requests for Review of Registered Debt (PRDI), and appeals against decisions that were rejected were all extended for a period of 90 days (Bottino et al., 2020).

The municipal governments of Brazil announced a suspension of the date by which administrative defences must be filed, conditions must be met, and the procedure to cancel municipal registrations must be followed. This was extended for 60 days. The tax clearance certificate for tax on services and fees, in effect as of 18

March 2020, that determines the virtual service of tax duty to dispel tax obligation questions was also extended and was now effective for an additional 60 days (Bottino et al., 2020; CMS Law, 2020a).

Russia

The Russian government introduced measures to support businesses and ensure sustainable economic development. Russia amended the tax legislation due to the spread of the virus to help Russian taxpayers that were most affected by the pandemic (Tissot & Kabanova, 2020).

Measures to Support Businesses

The Russian government was authorised to issue legal acts in the domain area of tax, particularly the suspension, abolition, or deferral of the tax in all control measures, the extension of the due dates for filing and paying taxes, and new criteria and processes for additional tax relief measures (Tissot & Kabanova, 2020).

All tax examinations were suspended until 1 May 2020. The deadline for filing annual tax returns was postponed from 31 March 2020 (Morozov, 2020; Noerr, 2020). All taxes, except VAT were deferred for 6 months. This applied to the air transportation sector, airport activities, trucking services, cultural services, leisure and entertainment, fitness activities and sports, travel agencies and tourism-related organisations, hotels, catering, education and non-governmental educational institutions, the organisation of conferences and exhibitions and the provision of domestic services to the population (Nistratov, 2020).

Measures to Support SMEs

Social contribution rates decreased by 15% and this applied to salaries above the minimum monthly salary (Tissot & Kabanova, 2020). Razumovskaia et al. (2020) stated in their thorough analysis that a payment postponement for all taxes excluding VAT, a loan payment deferral, and an insurance premium holiday for 6 months were the most frequently employed ways to promote SMEs.

Tax Measures to Ensure Sustainable Economic Development in Russia

The Russian resolution stated that until 1 June 2020, no new field tax audits were started, and existing field tax audits were not continued. Audits conducted for transfer pricing and currency control purposes must follow similar procedures. Also, on request, taxpayers could take advantage of several deadline extensions for submitting paperwork and information to tax authorities. At this time, penalties for submitting information or papers late to the tax authorities were not applicable (Noerr, 2020; Tissot & Kabanova, 2020).

The Russian government also saw it necessary to introduce measures aimed at boosting their tax collection during COVID-19. Measures taken included a reduced interest rate and the removal of dividends tax under international treaties. This meant that a treaty to avoid double taxation was removed and non-residents were required to pay 15% interest and 15% dividends tax on their income. Interest income earned on deposits from banks situated in Russia was subject to taxation. The tax base would be calculated as the excess of total interest received by the taxpayer during the tax period on all deposits (Dmitrieva, 2020).

New Tax Line of Taxing Interest Earned on Personal Bank Deposits

The law established personal taxation of interest income from bank deposits in Russian banks. The same law repealed a tax break that had previously been in place for interest income derived by people from specific kinds of debt securities (CMS Law, 2020b; Tissot & Kabanova, 2020).

Tax Administration and Payment

The obligation to pay taxes was placed directly on the individual taxpayers by banks because they were not operating in the capacity of tax agents when they paid interest due to individuals. The tax obligation would be paid in accordance with a tax notice issued by the tax authorities no later than the first day of the year following the year in which the taxpayer earned the income. As a result, the first tax payments for the year 2021 must be made by the first day of December 2022. The new regulations exempted the taxation of earnings from escrow accounts and rouble bank deposits with annual interest rates under 1% (CMS Law, 2020b).

Information Sharing and New Responsibilities for Russian Banks

Russian banks were required to provide the country's tax authorities with details on the interest income that was paid to each person within a specific calendar year. By 1 February of the year that followed the ended tax period, this information had to be given in the format specified, which would be further regulated by the Russian tax authorities (CMS Law, 2020b; Tissot & Kabanova, 2020).

The tax rate adjustment for SMEs was a useful policy to implement during times when taxes were stagnant since it would attract taxpayers. The introduction of interest generated on personal bank accounts was also a critical step in increasing the tax base.

India

The Income Tax Department of India took immediate action to amend strict timelines in the Indian Income Tax Act of 1961 (Sharma, 2022). The amendments were as follows:

Direct Tax Measures in the COVID-19 Period

A processing initiative was introduced, which allowed India's Central Board of Direct Taxes to speed up processing income tax returns and therefore grant refunds more rapidly. Individual taxpayers filing income tax returns and non-tax audit cases had until December 2020; and for other cases with the year of assessment ending 2020–2021, the deadline was extended to 31 January 2021 (Sirwalla, 2020). A new dispute resolution process for clearing huge pending tax appeals was introduced from March 2020 to 28 February 2021. India also introduced a taxpayer's charter that entailed duties and responsibilities of the Income Tax Department of India and the taxpayers (Sharma, 2022).

Payroll Tax

Businesses with fewer than 100 employees and up to 90% of workers receiving salaries of up to INR (Indian Rupees) 15,000 a month had to pay up to 12% of basic salaries to the employees' provident fund from March to August 2020. Workers who did not qualify for the above-mentioned support had an extra reduction of 2% in their employees' provident fund (De I'Estoile-Campi, 2020; Sharma, 2022).

Extension of Tax-Compliant Timelines

In India, the government extended the due date for filing original and revised tax returns for the financial year of 2018–2019, which ended on 31 March 2020. This was extended to 30 June 2020. Additionally, from 30 June to 31 July 2020, the deadline for making tax-saving investments for the 2020 fiscal year was extended. This gave the taxpayer additional time to invest in tax-saving tools and file tax relief claims under the various sections of the Indian Income Tax Act (Sharma, 2022; Sirwalla, 2020).

Corporate Income Tax

The filing of returns deadlines for the financial year that started on 1 April 2019 and ended on 30 November 2020 were extended again from 30 September 2020 to the financial year that started on 1 April 2020. No penalty was assessed for late tax payments made between 20 March 2020 and 30 November 2020, and the interest rate for overdue payments was decreased to 0.75% per month (I'Estoile-Campi, 2020).

Tax Deducted at Source and Tax Collection at Source Rate Cuts

The rate of tax deduction at source was reduced by 25% for non-salaried payments made to residents to enhance liquidity in the hands of taxpayers. The rate of tax collection at source was also reduced by 25% to provide taxpayers with more funds (I'Estoile-Campi, 2020; Sharma, 2022).

Issuance of Tax Refunds

To help taxpayers with cash flow issues, the Indian government stated that any delayed income tax refunds up to INR 500,000 would be issued promptly. This measure helped small businesses including sole traders and partnerships, charitable trusts, and non-corporate businesses (Global VAT Compliance, 2020; I'Estoile-Campi, 2020; Sharma, 2022).

China

China released several tax laws to help firms affected by the COVID-19 outbreak with their financial burdens (Zhou, 2022). The following measures were taken by the government of China:

Value-Added Tax

Businesses that produce protective supplies for the COVID-19 epidemic were eligible for a full VAT credit. The transportation of protective materials required for the prevention and management of COVID-19 was not subject to VAT. Certain products were eligible for an increased refund on exports (Crowell, 2020; Lu, 2020).

Enterprise Tax and Donations

Businesses that were severely impacted by COVID-19 were permitted to carry losses from 2020 forward for up to 8 years instead of 5 years. Manufacturing businesses were given a one-time pre-tax deduction for equipment purchases that would increase their ability to provide essential protective products for containing and preventing the pandemic (Lu, 2020).

Furthermore, some cities allowed businesses to defer the payment of social security contributions on behalf of employees for a period of up to 3 months (Chen et al., 2022). Donations made to non-profit organisations, county-level governments, state agencies, or other government entities were fully deductible from enterprise income tax prior to taxes being applied to the full amount of cash and in-kind donations (Crowell, 2020; INS Global, 2020).

Individual Income Tax and Social Security

Individual income tax was not applied to benefits and bonuses for temporary work performed to stop and contain the outbreak of the disease. Individual income tax exemptions were granted for COVID-19 medications and protective equipment provided to individuals through businesses (Crowell, 2020; INS Global, 2020).

Improvements to Consider

Globally, tax administrators have taken measures to support taxpayers by easing the tax burden and supporting businesses and individuals with cash flow problems. To assist taxpayers during COVID-19, the OECD has suggested the measures below:

Enhancing Services and Communication Initiatives

Over time, tax administrators might think about extending their digital communication options. The rising usage of digital services could lessen personal interaction and speed up responses for taxpayers. The SARS website was developed by the South African government as a way to enhance communication services (OECD, 2020). The SARS website primarily aids in the filing of returns. Compared to other BRICS countries, the following initiatives were implemented:

- Brazil: The Internet and the traditional media were the main platforms for Brazilian government communication. To answer taxpayers' questions about personal income taxes via a digital app, a chatbot was created (Abonizio et al., 2023).

- Russia: The COVID-19 web page maintained by the Russian government included relevant details and connections to online remedies.
- India: No measures were listed.
- China: The People's Republic of China also used official websites, hotlines, text messages, as well as online interviews and video demos, to react to inquiries (OECD, 2020).

Deferral of Payments

Tax administrators in South Africa were able to assist taxpayers by postponing payments due in instalments, adjusting advance tax payments downward, or even suspending such payments (SARS, 2021).

Businesses that paid their taxes on time and had annual revenue under R50 million were allowed to defer 20% of their employees' tax obligations and a portion of their provisional corporate income tax payments over 4- and 6-month periods, respectively, without incurring penalties or interest (Disaster Management Tax Relief Administration Act, 2020). It was anticipated that this action would support over 75,000 small- and medium-sized businesses in the countries that implemented it (OECD, 2020). Compared to other BRICS countries, the following measures were taken to defer payments:

- Brazil: No measures were taken in this regard.
- Russia: For a maximum of 5 years, taxes might be deferred, but there were restrictions. Business industries received an extension for filing taxes or paying for filing taxes (Sharma, 2022; Sirwalla, 2020):
  - All taxes (apart from VAT, professional income tax, and taxes withheld by the tax agent) had a 4-month extension if payment was due in April through June second quarter and the first 6 months of 2020; and a 6-month extension if payment was due in March 2020.
  - Taxes paid under the Simplified Tax System, the Unified Agricultural Tax, and Corporate Income Tax that were due in 2019.
  - Tax payments made under the patent tax system that were due in the second quarter of 2020 received a 4-month delay.
  - A 3-month delay was granted to individual entrepreneurs who owed personal income tax in 2019.
  - Advance payments for land, transportation, and property taxes that were due in the first quarter of 2020 had deadline extensions of 30 October 2020 and 30 December 2020, respectively.
- India: No extension measures were implemented.
- China: The contributions made by employers for their employees' endowment insurance, unemployment insurance, and employment accident insurance were temporarily reduced and exempted. The grace period for large companies, small

and medium-sized firms, and micro-enterprises was 3–5 months (Chen et al., 2022).

Audit Policies and Tax Certainty

Tax audits were suspended, and considerations were also given where it might be possible to provide taxpayers with early tax certainty about their tax payments if doing so could free up resources or increase cash flow. Civil litigation in South Africa continued with fewer officials present, and newly scheduled court cases were delayed. SARS, on the other hand, requested that all SARS criminal prosecution matters be postponed, as directed by the Chief Justice (OECD, 2020). The other BRICS countries took the measures below:

- Brazil: The postponement of deadlines and administrative procedures helped taxpayers (Bottino et al., 2020; CMS Law, 2020a). Also, there was no suspension of tax procedures regarding fraud, smuggling, tax crimes, or misbehaviour regarding the effort to mitigate COVID-19 (OECD, 2020).
- Russia: The following compliance activities were suspended until 31 May 2020:
  - Tax audits and currency control audits that were ongoing, and procedural measures to address tax offences
  - Opening fresh tax audits and currency control audits (except for audits that may be deemed invalid by a statute of limitations)
  - Suspension of bank accounts (Nistratov, 2020).
- China: Non-contact audits that were mainly focused on desk audits and big data analyses were applied (OECD, 2020).

Increased Cash Benefits

South Africa can also take guidance from measures implemented by the Central Board of Direct Taxes (CBDT) of the government of India, which is in charge of managing direct taxes in India. The CBDT took quick action to mitigate the effects of declining economic growth as a result of the March 2020 national lockout (Sharma, 2022).

The measures taken include:

- The CBDT launching the 'Jhatpat Processing' effort to expedite the processing of income tax returns (ITRs) and the granting of refunds. By the end of January 2021, around 150,863 crore (crore means 10 million) Rupees in income tax refunds had been distributed to more than 1.18 crore people (Business Today, 2020).

- Extending the due dates of all ITRs filers up to 31 December 2020, for individual and non-tax audit cases and up to 31 January 2021 for other cases for the assessment year 2020–2021.
- Addressing the massive backlog of ongoing direct tax appeals, the government launched the Vivad se Vishwas (From Conflict to Trust) Scheme in March 2020, which was extended until 28 February 2021.
- The introduction of the Income Tax Department's Faceless Assessment Scheme for scrutinising ITRs in an e-mode as part of an endeavour to offer transparent governance was introduced (Sharma, 2022).

Conclusion

Tax collection was impeded by changes in taxes made during COVID-19, especially because there were no means in place to ensure tax collection. Countries must make plans, have a tax reserve, or find a means to stabilise taxes during pandemics in the future if they want to be better prepared. During COVID-19, South Africa was not very effective in keeping taxes stable. This is evident from several problems, including poor service delivery, ongoing load shedding, constant hikes in interest rates after the pandemic, and many others. With the aforementioned being said, it is safe to assume that the measures taken by the South African tax system to combat COVID-19 were taken in haste and that the finances of the country are constrained (Arndt et al., 2020).

The lockdown measures and inability to raise taxes during the period of the pandemic have raised these negative economic effects (Arndt et al., 2020). The effects of the pandemic on demand for South Africa's exports and the rest of the globe are not as large as they were, but they are still beyond normal. South Africa can consider the actions of members of the BRICS organisation, especially since Brazil managed to collect more than normal tax revenues during the pandemic. While South Africa focused on providing critical support to taxpayers who were most vulnerable to COVID-19, it did not have a backup plan to recover the money that was spent. South Africa can also consider the measures that the Russian government implemented to boost tax collection during the pandemic.

Taxing wealth may be a smart way to stabilise the nation's revenue after COVID-19, but it could also encourage tax fraud and financial secrecy. To effectively address these situations, tight measures must be put in place and studies must be conducted.

References

Abonizio, H. Q., Barbon, A. P. A. D. C., Rodrigues, R., Santos, M., Martínez-Vizcaíno, V., Mesas, A. E., & Barbon Junior, S. (2023). How people interact with a chatbot against disinformation and fake news in COVID-19 in Brazil: The CoronaAI case. *International Journal of Medical Informatics, 177*, 1–6. https://doi.org/10.1016/j.ijmedinf.2023.105134

Arndt, C., Davies, R., Gabriel, S., Harris, L., Makrelov, K., Robinson, S., Levy, S., Simbanegavi, W., van Seventer, D., & Anderson, L. (2020). *Covid-19 lockdowns, income distribution, and food security: An analysis for South Africa*. Accessed June 12, 2023, from https://pubmed.ncbi.nlm.nih.gov/32834

Bottino, C. M., Castro, D., & Iecker, M. S. (2020). *COVID-19 tax and customs extraordinary measures in Brazil*. Accessed March 18, 2023, from https://www.mayerbrown.com/en/perspectives-events/publications/2020/03/covid19-medidas-extraordinarias-adotadas-no-ambito-tributario-e-aduaneiro

Business Today. (2020). *CBDT refunds Rs 1,50,863 crore to more than 1.18 crore taxpayers*. Accessed June 7, 2024, from https://www.businesstoday.in/latest/economy-politics/story/cbdt-refunds-over-rs-150863-crore-to-118-crore-taxpayers-282359-2020-12-23

Chen, J., Cheng, Z., Gong, R. K., & Li, J. (2022). Riding out the COVID-19 storm: How government policies affect SMEs in China. *China Economic Review, 75*, 1–23. https://doi.org/10.1016/j.chieco.2022.101831

CMS Law. (2020a). *Law and regulation of Covid-19 tax relief in Brazil*. Accessed June 6, 2024, from https://cms.law/en/int/expert-guides/cms-expert-guide-to-covid-19-tax-relief-measures/brazil

CMS Law. (2020b). *Russia amends tax legislation due to COVID-19 spread*. Accessed May 20, 2023, from https://cms-lawnow.com/en/ealerts/2020/04/russia-amends-tax-legislation-due-to-covid-19-spread

Crowell. (2020). *China Tax policies to address the COVID-19 pandemic*. Accessed March 21, 2023, from https://www.crowell.com/NewsEvents/AlertsNewsletters/all/China-Tax-Policies-to-Address-the-COVID-19-Pandemic

De l'Estoile-Campi, A. (2020). *Law and regulation of COVID-19 tax relief in India*. Accessed March 29, 2023, from https://cms.law/en/int/expert-guides/cms-expert-guide-to-covid-19-tax-relief-measures/india#:~:text=Reduction%20by%2025%20%25%20of%20rates,2,%202020%20to%2031%20March%202021

de Villiers, C., Cerbone, D., & van Zijl, W. (2020). The South African government's response to COVID-19. *Journal of Public Budgeting, Accounting & Financial Management, 3*(5), 797–811. https://doi.org/10.1108/JPBAFM-07-2020-0120

Deloitte. (2020). *COVID-19: Latest tax measures approved by government*. Accessed March 29, 2023, from https://www.taxathand.com/article/13315/Brazil/2020/COVID-19-Latest-tax-measures-approved-by-government

Disaster Management Tax Relief Act 2020. Accessed March 10, 2023, from http://www.saflii.org/za/legis/num_act/dmtra2020l3o2020g43883334.pdf

Disaster Management Tax Relief Administration Act 2020. Accessed March 10, 2023, from https://www.gov.za/sites/default/files/gcis_document/202011/43884gon1189.pdf

Dmitrieva, I. (2020). *COVID-19 – The Russian government's measures to support the Russian economy*. Accessed June 6, 2024, from https://www.whitecase.com/insight-alert/covid-19-russian-governments-measures-support-russian-economy

Employment Tax Incentive Act 2013. Accessed March 10, 2023, from https://www.gov.za/sites/default/files/gcis_document/201409/37185gon1032.pdf

Global VAT Compliance. (2020). *Customs, GST refunds to be released immediately*. https://www.globalvatcompliance.com/globalvatnews/india-covid-19-vat-implications/.

Indiana University. (2019). *Legal Dissertation: Research and Writing Guide*. Accessed January 25, 2024, from https://law.indiana.libguides.com/dissertationguide

INS Global. (2020). *China tax relief policy due to coronavirus*. Accessed June 7, 2024, from https://ins-globalconsulting.com/news-post/china-tax-relief-policy-coronavirus/

International Monetary Fund (IMF). (2020). Tax and Customs Administration Responses. Accessed March 18, 2023, from https://www.imf.org/-/media/Files/Publications/covid19-special-notes/special-series-on-covid-19-tax-and-customs-administrationresponses

Jiao, J., Shi, L., Zhang, Y., Chen, H., Wang, X., Yang, M., Yang, J., Liu, M., & Sun, G. (2022). Core policies disparity response to COVID-19 among BRICS countries. *International Journal for Equity in Health, 21*(9) https://equityhealthj.biomedcentral.com/articles/10.1186/s12939-021-01614-z

Lone, S. A., & Ahmad, A. (2020). COVID-19 pandemic – an African perspective. *Emerging Microbes & Infections, 9*(1), 1300–1308. https://doi.org/10.1080/22221751.2020.1775132

Lu, L. (2020). *China announces tax relief measures to tackle coronavirus disruption.* Accessed June 7, 2024, from https://www.internationaltaxreview.com/article/2a6a544fgrgchygyw99fk/china-announces-tax-relief-measures-to-tackle-coronavirus-disruption

Ministério da Economia. (2020). *Brazil's policy responses to COVID-19.* Accessed June 6, 2024, from https://www.google.com/url?sa=t&source=web&rct=j&opi=89978449&url=https://www.gov.br/economia/pt-br/centrais-de-conteudo/publicacoes/publicacoes-em-outros-idiomas/covid-19/brazil2019s-policy-responses-to-covid-19&ved=2ahUKEwi95%2D%2DH0saGAxUHWUEAHcogFaYQFnoECBAQAQ&usg=AOvVaw3Z_AR07qmwc0tiAWH8wU75

Morceiro, P. C., Tessarin, M. S., & Pereira, H. I. (2022). Macroeconomic policies in response to COVID-19 pandemic in Brazil. *Textos de Economia, 25*(1), 1–23. https://doi.org/10.5007/2175-8085.2022.e89609

Morozov, A. (2020). *COVID 19: Tax measures to support the business in Russia.* Accessed June 6, 2024, from https://www.dejalex.com/wp-content/uploads/2020/05/Articolo_Covid-19-Tax-measures-in-Russia.pdf

National Treasury. (2022). *Chapter 4: Revenue trends and tax proposals.* Accessed June 12, 2023, from https://www.treasury.gov.za/documents/national%20budget/2023/review/Chapter%204.pdf

Nistratov, G. (2020). COVID-19 tax measures Russian federation. *ITSG Global Tax Journal, 3*(2), 77–78. https://www.itsgnetwork.com/itsg/globalTaxJournal.asp?aid=54

Noerr. (2020). *Russian tax support measures due to COVID-19.* Accessed June 6, 2024, from https://www.noerr.com/en/insights/russian-tax-support-measures-due-to-covid-19

Organisation for Economic Cooperation and Development (OECD). (2020). *Developing countries and development co-operation – what is at stake.* Accessed June 14, 2023, from https://www.oecd.org/coronavirus/policy-responses/developing-countries-and-development-co-operation-what-is-at-stake-50e97915/

Orsolon, C., Advogados, D. & Paulo, S. (2020). *Taxation in a pandemic: an overview of Brazilian federal government tax reliefs.* Accessed March 18, 2023, from https://www.ibanet.org/article/05651 2a1-6fee-4936-874e-80b38aa8720e

PricewaterhouseCoopers (PwC). (2020). *COVID-19 will force a major rethink of tax systems.* Accessed March 12, 2023, from https://www.pwc.com/gx/en/services/tax/publications/covid-19-will-force-a-major-rethink-of-tax-systems.html

Razumovskaia, E., Yuzvovich, L., Kniazeva, E., Klimenko, M., & Shelyakin, V. (2020). The effectiveness of Russian government policy to support SMEs in the COVID-19 pandemic. *Journal of Open Innovation: Technology, Market, and Complexity, 6*(4), 1–21. https://doi.org/10.3390/joitmc6040160

Reserve Bank of India. (2021). *Virtual Meeting of BRICS Tax Ministers was held.* Accessed June 13, 2023, from http://www.chinatax.gov.cn/eng/c101269/c5169467/content.html

Sadiq, K., & Krever, R. (2021). Does tax policy fit in the portfolio of COVID-19 responses? *Pacific Accounting Review, 33*(2), 212–220. https://doi.org/10.1108/PAR-08-2020-0119

Sharma, M. (2022). Covid-19 pandemic: Response of the government through public policy mainly direct taxation. *Indian Journal of Public Administration, 68*(2), 219–232. https://doi.org/10.1177/00195561211072422

Sirwalla, P. (2020). *India – COVID-19: Tax relief measures.* Accessed June 6, 2024, from https://kpmg.com/xx/en/home/insights/2020/05/flash-alert-2020-228.html. Accessed 6 June 2024.

South African Institute of Chartered Accountants (SAICA). (2020). *Technical guidance on the COVID-19 tax relief measures and other practical matters*. Accessed March 10, 2023, from https://www.saica.org.za/resources/52818

South African Revenue Service (SARS). (2021). *Tax relief measures*. Accessed June 13, 2023, from https://www.sars.gov.za/media/tax-relief-measures/#:~:text=The%20deferred%20PAYE%20liability%20for,made%20on%207%20December%202021

Tissot, D., & Kabanova M. (2020). *Russia amends tax legislation due to COVID-19 spread*. Accessed March 28, 2023, from https://www.lexology.com/library/detail.aspx?g=2dd2cc44-e889-43a1-8816-1036a2dd471f

Wang, Y. H. (2020). *Deepening BRICS cooperation to combat COVID-19*. Accessed June 16, 2023, from https://www.fmprc.gov.cn/eng/wjdt_665385/zyjh_665391/202004/t20200428_678853.html

Xiang, S., Rasool, S., Hang, Y., Javid, K., Javed, T., & Artene, A. E. (2021). The effect of COVID-19 pandemic on service sector sustainability and growth. *Frontiers in Psychology, 12*, 1–10. https://doi.org/10.3389/fpsyg.2021.633597

Zhou, Q. (2022). *Tax incentives available to businesses impacted by the Shanghai lockdown*. Accessed June 29, 2023, from https://www.china-briefing.com/news/what-tax-incentives-can-businesses-enjoy-under-the-shanghai-lockdown/

GPSR Compliance

The European Union's (EU) General Product Safety Regulation (GPSR) is a set of rules that requires consumer products to be safe and our obligations to ensure this.

If you have any concerns about our products, you can contact us on ProductSafety@springernature.com

In case Publisher is established outside the EU, the EU authorized representative is:

Springer Nature Customer Service Center GmbH
Europaplatz 3
69115 Heidelberg, Germany

Batch number: 10798362

Printed by Printforce, the Netherlands

Springer Proceedings in Business and Economics

Springer Proceedings in Business and Economics brings the most current research presented at conferences and workshops to a global readership. The series features volumes (in electronic and print formats) of selected contributions from conferences in all areas of economics, business, management, and finance. In addition to an overall evaluation by the publisher of the topical interest, scientific quality, and timeliness of each volume, each contribution is refereed to standards comparable to those of leading journals, resulting in authoritative contributions to the respective fields. Springer's production and distribution infrastructure ensures rapid publication and wide circulation of the latest developments in the most compelling and promising areas of research today.

The editorial development of volumes may be managed using Springer Nature's innovative EquinOCS, a proven online conference proceedings submission, management and review system. This system is designed to ensure an efficient timeline for your publication, making Springer Proceedings in Business and Economics the premier series to publish your workshop or conference volume.

This book series is indexed in SCOPUS.

Tankiso Moloi
Editor

Impacting Society Positively Through Technology in Accounting and Business Processes

Proceedings of the 5th International Conference of Accounting and Business iCAB, Sun City 2024

Volume II

Springer

Editor
Tankiso Moloi
University of Johannesburg
Johannesburg, South Africa

ISSN 2198-7246 ISSN 2198-7254 (electronic)
Springer Proceedings in Business and Economics
ISBN 978-3-031-84887-2 ISBN 978-3-031-84885-8 (eBook)
https://doi.org/10.1007/978-3-031-84885-8

This Springer imprint is published by the registered company Springer Nature Switzerland AG
The registered company address is: Gewerbestrasse 11, 6330 Cham, Switzerland

Letter from the Editor

Dear *i*CAB 2024 Delegate,

I greet all of you from Johannesburg. As the editor, it is my deepest gratitude to present to you, the conference delegates, the 2024 International Conference of Accounting, and Business conference proceedings.

For the first time in history, *i*CAB was held at Sun City. We successfully delivered the 2024 iteration of the iCAB conference. The papers presented in these proceedings have passed through a stringent peer review process, and I am confident that it is only quality papers included in these proceedings. Our review policy is a **double-blind review process,** and this was stringently applied.

We look forward to having you and your colleagues at the 2024 conference in Cape Town, South Africa.

Tankiso Moloi

Peer Review Statement

Our review policy is a **double-blind review process,** and this was stringently applied. Our process is that the full-length manuscript is anonymised and sent to two or more independent reviewers. The peer reviewers are never disclosed to the authors as anonymity in the review process is crucial as it enables reviewers to freely express their opinions. Sometimes, there are two conflicting reports, and if this is the case, a third independent reviewer is commissioned.

Once the process is complete, anonymous reports are shared with the author. They are asked to respond to the reviews detailing how they will improve the manuscript and what suggestions from the reviewers they accept or reject. In this regard, the approval of the manuscript is subject to a developmental editing process, after which re-submitting to one or both reviewers may be required.

International Steering Committee

Prof T. Moloi	University of Johannesburg, South Africa
Prof Z. Blabler	Salem, State University, United States of America
Prof A. Salman	American University in the Emirates, United Arab Emirates
Prof M. Mangena	University of Nottingham, United Kingdom
Prof S. Romprasert	Srinakharinwirot University, Thailand
Dr. D. Kiriman	University of Texas at El Paso, United States of America
Prof A. Hess	Pontificia Universidade Catolica de Sao Paulo, Brazil
Prof R. Salawu	Obafemi Awolowo University, Nigeria
Prof B. Marx	University of Johannesburg, South Africa
Prof M. Adelowotan	University of Johannesburg, South Africa
Prof B. George	Alcorn State University, United States of America
Prof C. Campos	Pontificia Universidade Catolica de Sao Paulo, Brazil
Dr. B. Shima	Canadian Institute of Technology, Albania
Prof O. R. Uwuigbe	Covenant University, Nigeria
Prof M. Sibanda	University of KwaZulu Natal, South Africa
Prof A. Sibindi	University of South Africa, South Africa
Prof O. Olugbara,	Durban University of Technology, South Africa
Dr. M. Olarewaju,	Coventry University, United Kingdom
Prof M. Mohd Ali	Universiti Teknologi MARA, Malaysia
Prof Youqin Pan	University of Johannesburg, South Africa
Dr. Lethiwe Nzama-Sithole	University of Johannesburg, South Africa
Prof Reon Matemane	University of Pretoria
Prof Sezer B. Kahyaoğlu	Kyrgyz-Turkish Manas University, Turkey

List of Reviewers

No.	Reviewer	Affiliation
1	Dr. L. Nzama-Sthole	University of Johannesburg, South Africa
2	Dr. F. Y. Mpofu	University of Johannesburg, South Africa
3	Prof. R. Matemane	University of Pretoria, South Africa
4	Dr. Trust Chireka	Walter Sisulu University, South Africa
5	Dr. L. Grebe	University of South Africa, South Africa
5	Dr. Inneh Godwin	Obafemi Awolowo University, Nigeria
6	Prof Andries. P. Swanepoel	University of South Africa, South Africa
7	Dr. Mufaro Dzingirai	Midlands State University, Zimbabwe
8	Dr. K. N. Motubatse	Tshwane University of Science and Technology
9	Dr. T. Ololade	University of Johannesburg, South Africa
10	Prof. Freddy Munzhelele	University of Venda, South Africa
11	Dr. Lebogang Mospye-Semenya	University of Johannesburg—JBS, South Africa
12	Prof. Ayoola John	Obafemi Awolowo University, Nigeria
13	Dr. Sylvester Senyo Horvey	University of the Witwatersrand, South Africa
14	Prof Herman Albertus Viviers	North-West University, South Africa
15	Prof. Michael Adelowotan	University of Johannesburg, South Africa
16	Dr Modiha Pulane	FNB Independent Researcher, South Africa
17	Dr Adesanmi Adegbayibi	Adekunle Ajasin University, Nigeria
18	Prof Zlatinka N Blaber	Salem State University, USA
19	Dr. Varaidzo Denhere	University of Johannesburg, South Africa
20	Dr. Dolapo Sule	University of Johannesburg, South Africa
21	Prof Sezer B. Kahyaoglu	Kyrgyz-Turkish Manas University, Turkey
22	Dr. Ayanda Sibiya	University of Johannesburg, South Africa
23	Prof Lungile Ntsalaze	University of Johannesburg, South Africa
24	Dr. Letebele Mphahlele	University of Johannesburg, South Africa
25	Prof Tunde Lawal	Bowen University, Nigeria
26	Dr. Gold Kafilah Lola	University of Johannesburg

Contribution of Individual Universities in these Proceedings

Paper No.	Number of authors	Universities	Points contribution
P02-24	Three	University of Johannesburg	0.17
		University of Johannesburg	0.17
		University of Johannesburg	0.17
P03-24	Three	University of Johannesburg	0.17
		University of Johannesburg	0.17
		University of Johannesburg	0.17
P04-24	Two	University of the Witwatersrand	0.25
		University of the Witwatersrand	0.25
P08-24	Two	University of Johannesburg	0.25
		University of Johannesburg	0.25
P09-24	Two	University of Johannesburg	0.25
		University of Johannesburg	0.25
P10-24	Two	University of Johannesburg	0.25
		University of Johannesburg	0.25
P12-24	Three	Accra Technical University	0.17
		Prince Mohammed Bin Fahd University, Saudi Arabia	0.17
		Accra Technical University	0.17
P13-24	Two	Federal College of Education, Technical, Nigeria	0.25
		University of Johannesburg	0.25
P14-24	Four	University of the Witwatersrand	0.125
		University of the Witwatersrand	0.125
		University of the Witwatersrand	0.125
		University of the Witwatersrand	0.125
P15-24	One	University of the Free State	
P16-24	Two	University of Johannesburg	0.25
		University of Johannesburg	0.25
P17-24	One	University of Johannesburg	0.50

Paper No.	Number of authors	Universities	Points contribution
P18-24	Three	University of Johannesburg	0.17
		University of Johannesburg	0.17
		University of Johannesburg	0.17
P19-24	Three	University of Johannesburg	0.17
		University of Johannesburg	0.17
		University of Johannesburg	0.17
P20-24	Three	National School of Government	0.17
		National School of Government	0.17
		National School of Government	0.17
P21-24	Two	University of Free State	0.25
		University of Free State	0.25
P24-24	Two	University of Johannesburg	0.25
		University of Johannesburg	0.25
P25-24	One	Midlands State University	0.50
P28-24	Four	North-West University	0.125
		North-West University	0.125
		North-West University	0.125
		Vaal University of Technology	0.125
P29-24	Three	University of Johannesburg	0.17
		University of Johannesburg	0.17
		University of Johannesburg	0.17
P30-24	Two	University of KwaZulu Natal	0.25
		University of KwaZulu Natal	0.25
P31-24	One	University of Dar-es-Salaam Business School	0.50
P32-24	Three	Cape Peninsula University of Technology	0.17
		Cape Peninsula University of Technology	0.17
		Cape Peninsula University of Technology	0.17
P33-24	One	Adekunle Ajasin University	0.50
P34-24	Two	Adekunle Ajasin University	0.25
		Adekunle Ajasin University	0.25
P35-24	Three	North-West University	0.17
		North-West University	0.17
		North-West University	0.17
P36-24	Three	University of Johannesburg	0.17
		University of Johannesburg	0.17
		University of Johannesburg	0.17
P38-24	One	University of Johannesburg	0.50
P39-24	Two	University of Cape Coast	0.25
		Walter Sisulu University	0.25
P40-24	Two	University of Cape Coast	0.25
		Walter Sisulu University	0.25
P41-24	Two	University of Johannesburg	0.25
		University of Johannesburg	0.25

Paper No.	Number of authors	Universities	Points contribution
P42-24	One	University of Johannesburg	0.50
P43-24	Two	North-West University	0.25
		North-West University	0.25
P44-24		University of Venda	0.50
P45-24	One	University of Pretoria	0.50
P47-24	Three	University of Johannesburg	0.17
		University of Johannesburg	0.17
		University of Johannesburg	0.17
P48-24	Four	North-West University	0.125
		North-West University	0.125
		North-West University	0.125
		Adeleke University	0.125
P49-24	Two	University of the Witwatersrand	0.25
		University of the Witwatersrand	0.25
P50-24	Two	University of the Witwatersrand	0.25
		University of the Witwatersrand	0.25
P51-24	Three	University of the Free State	0.17
		University of the Free State	0.17
		University of the Free State	0.17
P52-24	Two	University of the Witwatersrand	0.25
		University of the Witwatersrand	0.25
P55-24	One	University of Pretoria	0.50
P56-24	One	University of Johannesburg	0.50
P57-24	Two	University of Johannesburg	0.25
		University of Johannesburg	0.25
P59-24	One	University of Johannesburg	0.50
P60-24	Three	University of South Africa	0.17
		University of South Africa	0.17
		University of South Africa	0.17
P61-24	Three	University of Johannesburg	0.17
		University of Johannesburg	0.17
		University of Johannesburg	0.17
P62-24	Two	University of Johannesburg	0.25
		University of Johannesburg	0.25
P63-24	Four	University of Johannesburg	0.125
		University of Johannesburg	0.125
		University of Johannesburg	0.125
		Stellenbosch University	0.125
P65-24	Three	Walter Sisulu University	0.17
		Walter Sisulu University	0.17
		Cape Peninsula University of Technology	0.17
P68-24	Two	Obafemi Awolowo University	0.25
		Obafemi Awolowo University	0.25

Paper No.	Number of authors	Universities	Points contribution
P69-24	Two	University of Johannesburg	0.25
		University of Johannesburg	0.25
P70-24	Three	University of the Free State	0.17
		University of the Free State	0.17
		University of the Free State	0.17
P71-24	Three	University of Johannesburg	0.17
		University of Johannesburg	0.17
		University of Johannesburg	0.17
P72-24	One	University of Johannesburg	0.50
P74-24	Two	University of South Africa	0.25
		University of South Africa	0.25
P75-24	Two	University of South Africa	0.25
		University of South Africa	0.25
P77-24	One	University of Johannesburg	0.50
P78-24	Three	University of Johannesburg	0.17
		University of Johannesburg	0.17
		University of Johannesburg	0.17
P79-24	One	University of Johannesburg	0.50
P80-24	Two	University of Johannesburg	0.25
		University of Johannesburg	0.25
P82-24	One	North-West University	0.50
P83-24	Two	Walter Sisulu University	0.25
		Walter Sisulu University	0.25
P84-24	One	University of Johannesburg	0.50
P85-24	Four	Salem State University, USA	0.125
		Stockton University, USA	0.125
		Millennium Global Business Solutions, USA	0.125
		Millennium Global Business Solutions, USA	0.125
P86-24	One	University of Johannesburg	0.50
TOTAL			**33.00**

Contents of Volume II

Contents of Volume I

A Systematic Review of Material Flow Cost Accounting

Hlayiseko Dougmore Sithole, Cosmas M. Ambe, and Marne Van Niekerk

Abstract Existing research suggests that Material Flow Cost Accounting (MFCA) has led to significant environmental and economic advantages, with the private sector dominating MFCA-related research and case studies. The main objective of this study is to enhance the understanding of MFCA implementation through a systematic review of existing literature. The study employed the Preferred Reporting Items for Systematic Reviews and Meta-Analyses (PRISMA) framework to scrutinize articles from peer-reviewed journals. Relevant studies were meticulously selected and evaluated based on specific inclusion and exclusion criteria. The chosen keywords were restricted to "Material Flow Cost Accounting (MFCA)," "material flow cost accounting," and "MFCA," which were then utilized for searches on databases such as Scopus and Google Scholar. An initial keyword search conducted for studies published between 2010 and 2024 resulted in a total of 505 publications. The search focus was refined by selecting articles as the preferred publication type, which led to 348 remaining articles. Further filtering based on subject relevance resulted in the exclusion of 270 articles, leaving 78 records. Non-English publications were excluded, resulting in 72 English language articles for consideration. Additionally, a filter was applied to only include articles related to MFCA/Material flow cost accounting published after 2014, which excluded 54 articles. The decision to use the year 2014 as a cut-off point was made to ensure the relevance and currency of the study. Results highlighted the advantages of incorporating MFCA, including increased transparency in cost management, improved decision-making capabilities, and a boost in environmental sustainability practices. The findings collectively suggest that organizations can benefit significantly from adopting MFCA to optimize their material utilization and lower operational costs. Scholars highlighted the need for further research to explore the long-term effects of incorporating MFCA on sustainability efforts and financial performance across various industries. This highlights the ongoing need to explore and understand the potential

H. D. Sithole (✉) · C. M. Ambe · M. Van Niekerk
University of the Free State, Bloemfontein, South Africa
e-mail: 2019859046@ufs4life.ac.za; ambecm@ufs.ac.za; VanNiekerkMM@ufs.ac.za

T. Moloi (ed.), *Impacting Society Positively Through Technology in Accounting and Business Processes*, Springer Proceedings in Business and Economics,
https://doi.org/10.1007/978-3-031-84885-8_33

long-term benefits of MFCA adoption in different organizational settings. This study presents a research agenda for MFCA tools to support the sustainable growth of municipalities, economies, and societies. Practitioners may find value in this paper by exploring additional areas where MFCA could be applied in their specific sectors and in making decisions about reducing process waste.

Keywords Material flow cost accounting · Public sector · Systematic review

Introduction

The aim of this research is to delve deeper into the implementation of Material Flow Cost Accounting (MFCA) by conducting a thorough examination of existing literature. This study offers a roadmap for the utilization of MFCA tools to bolster the sustainable progress of municipalities, economies, and societies. Professionals in various sectors can derive value from this paper by identifying new areas where MFCA can be implemented to reduce process waste and make informed decisions. MFCA has gained traction as a crucial tool in achieving environmental sustainability objectives by providing organizations with a comprehensive insight into their resource consumption and associated expenses (ISO 14051, 2011, p V), with the private sector dominating MFCA-related research and case studies (Christ & Burritt, 2015; Kokubu & Kitada, 2015; Schmidt, 2015; Dierkes & Siepelmeyer, 2019; Tran & Herzig, 2020; Kitada et al., 2022).

Many organizations are still relying on traditional costing methods, overlooking the inefficiency in production and the detrimental environmental effects. Often, businesses prioritize the results they achieve over the resources they consume as input, and the waste they generate during their operations (Yagi & Kokubu, 2018). Despite the growing awareness of the shortcomings of conventional costing systems, many companies are hesitant to adopt more sustainable practices. The researchers noted that traditional costing methods often fail to account for the full costs of production, leading to inaccurate financial assessments (Arieftiara et al., 2021).

Taking proactive measures to address environmental issues not only benefits the environment but also leads to cost savings and enhanced competitiveness for businesses in the long term (ISO, 2017). The effectiveness of MFCA in quantifying material flow and stock using physical and monetary units is widely acknowledged (Bux & Amicarelli, 2022). Drawing from the findings and gaps in MFCA literature, the research outlines future avenues for MFCA research that include assessing the current rate of MFCA application, identifying factors that influence its implementation through qualitative research, conducting comparative analyses of critical aspects of MFCA application, and exploring the expansion of MFCA practices across various sectors and industries.

The paper is structured as follows: The subsequent section offers a brief overview of MFCA, while third section delineates the methodology employed for conducting the systematic review. Fourth section summarizes the results, which are illustrated in tables accompanied by detailed analysis. Following this, fifth section presents empirical evidence on MFCA applications, sixth section provides recommendations, and seventh section concludes the paper.

MFCA Overview

The International Standards Organisation (ISO) 14051 defines MFCA as a method that traces the flow of stocks of materials within an organization and quantifies the material flows in physical units, and evaluates the cost associated with material flows and energy uses (ISO, 2017). The idea of MFCA originated because of environmental management initiatives in Germany during the late 1980s and early 1990s. Subsequently, it evolved through environmental management accounting projects carried out by the Ministry of Economy, Trade, and Industry in Japan in the 2000s. This development process, as discussed by Kokubu and Kitada (2015) and Wagner (2015), led to the formation of MFCA in its current format. Japan played a crucial role in promoting the standardization of MFCA within the framework of the ISO 14000 family. This led to the international publication of the ISO standards for MFCA, including ISO 14051 in 2011, ISO 14052 in 2017, and ISO 14053 in 2021, according to Nishitani et al. (2022). The standardization efforts by ISO have significantly contributed to the global adoption of MFCA, particularly in Asia. The implementation of MFCA has gained traction in various Asian countries, such as India, Malaysia, Taiwan, Thailand, and Vietnam, during the 2010s. This expansion can be attributed to the growing awareness and acceptance of MFCA practices in the region, as highlighted by Christ and Burritt (2015). The spread of MFCA in Asia was further facilitated by a diffusion project initiated by the Asian Productivity Organization, as mentioned by Yagi and Kokubu (2018).

Methodology

The researcher carefully examined and analyzed various studies relating to the application of MFCA through a systematic review. This process involved three distinct phases: first, planning the review by outlining the scope and objectives. Second, conducting the review by gathering and analyzing the necessary data and information. And lastly, reporting on the findings and conclusions drawn from the review process in a comprehensive manner.

Planning Review

During the planning phase, the researcher developed a review protocol that included keywords, inclusion criteria, and exclusion criteria. The selected keywords were limited to "Material Flow Cost Accounting (MFCA)," "material flow cost accounting," and "MFCA." These keywords were then used to conduct searches on databases like Scopus and Google Scholar. To determine relevant publications, specific inclusion and exclusion criteria were used, as detailed in Table 1.

Conducting the Review

During the selection process, relevant studies were carefully chosen and evaluated based on specific inclusion and exclusion criteria established earlier. Initial keyword search conducted for studies published between 2010 and 2024 yielded a total of 505 publications. The focus was refined by selecting articles as the preferred publication type, resulting in 348 remaining articles. Further filtering based on subject relevance led to the exclusion of 270 articles. The remaining 78 records were narrowed down by excluding non-English publications, leaving only 72 English language articles for consideration. Additionally, a filter was applied to only include articles related to MFCA/Material flow cost accounting published after 2014, resulting in the exclusion of 54 articles. The decision to use the year 2014 as a cut-off point was made to ensure the relevance and currency of the study.

Subsequently, a more detailed review of the abstracts of the remaining 18 records was conducted, leading to the exclusion of one article that did not mention MFCA/Material flow cost accounting in the title or abstract. This left a final total of 17 articles that met all criteria and were included in the analysis.

Table 1 Selection criteria of the systematic review

No	Criteria	Inclusion	Exclusion
1	Publication type	Articles	All other publication types
2	Theme	Material flow cost accounting, MFCA	All other research areas
3	Availability	Full text	N/A
4	Language	English	All other languages
5	Location	Any location	N/A
6	Level	Any level	N/A

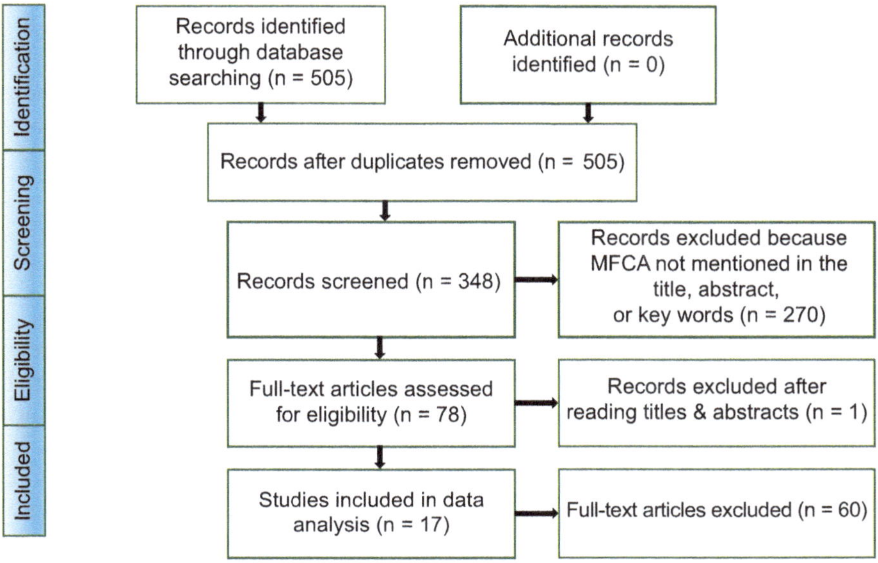

Fig. 1 PRISMA flow diagram, adopted from Tran and Herzig (2020:P5)

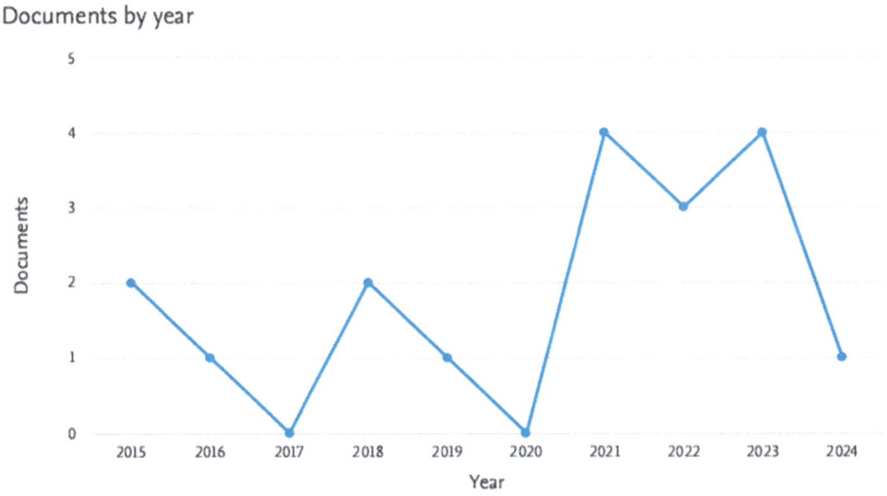

Fig. 2 Studies on MFCA applications from 2014 to 2024

Reporting Results

The systematic review of MFCA literature involved a thorough study selection process to identify relevant articles. The PRISMA diagram was utilized to visually represent the flow of information during the literature search, screening, and selection stages, which resulted in 17 publications found in the review (Fig. 1).

Analysis of the Results

The bibliographic research findings, analyzed by year, type, and author, are shown below. Subsequently, articles are described based on the location and methodology. Finally, the publications' themes are synthesized.

Bibliographic Findings

The analysis revealed 17 publications that were released over a span of 10 years, from 2014 to 2024. Despite the review covering a decade, the total number of publications is relatively low. Figure 2 below illustrates the changes in MFCA publication volume. The number of publications started at two in 2015, then dropped to one in 2016 and zero in 2017. In 2018, there was an increase to two publications per year, followed by a decrease to one in 2019 and zero in 2020. The year 2021 saw a peak of four publications, one of which was excluded from the study due to lacking keywords. In 2022, the number decreased to three before increasing again in 2023 to reach another peak. Currently, there is only one publication in 2024, authored by Christ, Burritt, Tran & Herzig, who also conducted a literature review of MFCA. Their work aims to lay the groundwork for the future development of the material flow cost accounting tool and enhance the understanding of MFCA applications (Christ & Burritt, 2015; Tran & Herzig, 2020).

The review only includes one category of publications, which are journal articles. These articles cover a wide range of disciplines such as Accounting, Auditing, and Accountability. They also delve into topics like International Productivity and Quality Management, Sustainability Science and Management, and Clean Technologies. Additionally, the publications touch on areas like Accounting Education, Environmental Science, and Environmental Management. Furthermore, there are articles related to Resources Policy, Industrial Ecology, and the IBIMA Business Review. The review also features publications on Environmental Engineering and Management, Life Cycle Assessment, and Resources Conservation and Recycling. In addition, there are articles that discuss topics like Risk Governance and Control in Financial Markets and Institutions. Moreover, Environment Development and Sustainability as well as Foundations of Management are also examined in some of the journal articles. Table 2 below illustrates the number of publications per discipline.

The quantity of articles focusing on Material Flow Cost Accounting (MFCA) has progressively grown as time has passed. Out of the total of 17 articles examined and analyzed in this study, each one was released in 2014 or beyond. These studies were carried out within a private sector environment, showcasing a trend in research focus. Interestingly, none of these 17 studies were conducted in a public sector setting, highlighting a potential gap in the existing literature on MFCA.

Table 2 Studies on MFCA applications per discipline from 2014 to 2024

Disciplines	No. of publications
Accounting, Auditing, and Accountability	1
International Productivity and Quality Management	1
Sustainability Science and Management	1
Clean Technologies	1
Accounting Education	1
Environmental Science	1
Environmental Management	2
Resources Policy	1
Industrial Ecology	1
IBIMA Business Review	1
Environmental Engineering and Management	1
Life Cycle Assessment	1
Resources, Conservation, and Recycling	1
Risk Governance and Control in Financial Markets and Institutions	1
Environment Development and Sustainability	1
Foundations of Management	1
Total	17

Background Publications

Table 3 demonstrates that all 17 research articles utilized a qualitative research approach, specifically case studies. This finding indicates a prevailing trend in the field of MFCA research, as qualitative methods are often employed in the initial phases of studying MFCA implementation, given their suitability for exploratory investigations (Tran & Herzig, 2020). When examining the geographical location of MFCA studies, the analysis showcases a diverse range of locations where research has been conducted. Ten countries have been identified where MFCA has been studied, including Germany, South Africa, China, Japan, Australia, France, India, Indonesia, Italy, and Poland. Notably, Germany and South Africa emerged as the primary contributors in terms of the number of publications on MFCA over the last decade (Fig. 3). Table 3, presented below, provides an overview of publications on MFCA implementation categorized by research methodology and location of study focus. This comprehensive analysis offers valuable insights into the global landscape of MFCA research and its application across various sectors.

Themes

Analysis of the literature on the application of Material Flow Cost Accounting (MFCA) has identified two predominant themes that were consistently emerging. The first theme revolved around the numerous advantages associated with the

Table 3 MFCA applications by method and location

No.	Method	Location	Source
1	Case study	Vietnam	Tran et al. (2024). Material flow cost accounting in Vietnam: a multi-level exploration.
2	Case study	Germany	Walls et al. (2023). Material Flow Cost Accounting as a Resource-Saving Tool for Emerging Recycling Technologies.
3	Case study	India	Santoki et al. (2023). Evaluating MFCA-based system framework for performance improvement in ceramic tile manufacturing industry.
4	Case study	South Africa	Nyakuwanika et al. (2023). Validating an environmental management accounting practices framework for the greening of Zimbabwean gold mining
5	Case study	Germany	Tran and Herzig (2023). Blended case-based learning in a sustainability accounting course: An analysis of student perspectives
6	Case study	China	Qu et al. (2022). Application of ABB in environmental management accounting: Incorporating MFCA into the budget process
7	Case study	Japan	Nishitani et al. (2022). Material flow cost accounting (MFCA) for the circular economy: An empirical study of the triadic relationship between MFCA, environmental performance, and the economic performance of Japanese companies
8	Case study	Italy	Bux and Amicarelli (2022). Material flow cost accounting (MFCA) to enhance environmental entrepreneurship in the meat sector: Challenges and opportunities.
9	Case study	China	Zeng et al. (2021). MFCA extension from a life cycle perspective: Methodical refinements and use case
10	Case study	Japan	Walz and Guenther (2021). What effects does material flow cost accounting have for companies? Evidence from a case studies analysis
11	Case study	Indonesia	Arieftiara et al. (2021). Sustainability in health service industry: The implementation of material flow cost accounting (MFCA) as an eco-efficient analysis
12	Case study	Poland	Kluczek (2019). Assessment of manufacturing processes eco-efficiency based on MFA-LCA-MFCA methods
13	Case study	Germany	Rieckhof and Guenther (2018). Integrating life cycle assessment and material flow cost accounting to account for resource productivity and economic-environmental performance
14	Case study	Sri Lanka	Dunuwila et al. (2018). Sustainability of natural rubber processing can be improved: A case study with crepe rubber manufacturing in Sri Lanka
15	Case study	South Africa	Nyide (2016). Material flow cost accounting as a tool for improved resource efficiency in the hotel sector: A case of emerging market.
16	Case study	South Africa	Fakoya (2015). Adopting material flow cost accounting model for improved waste-reduction decisions in a micro-brewery
17	Case study	South Africa	Doorasamy (2015). Theoretical developments in environmental management accounting and the role and importance of MFCA

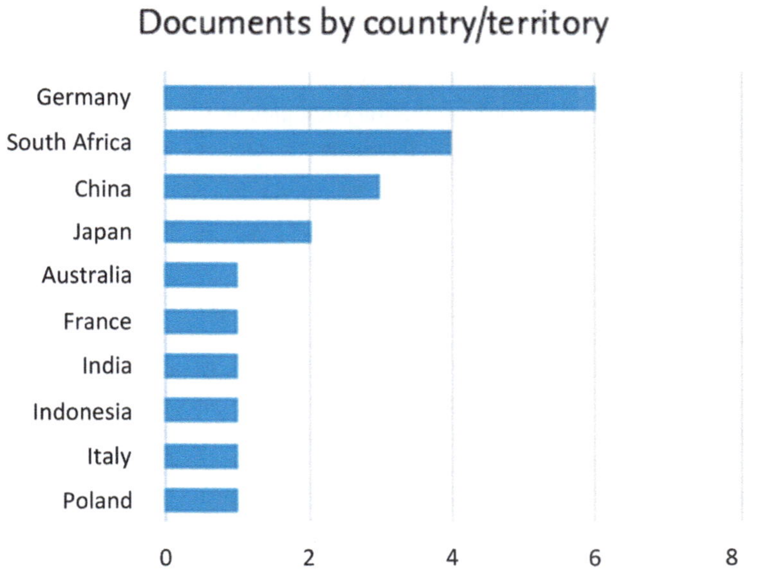

Fig. 3 Publications per country

implementation of MFCA, highlighting its potential benefits for businesses. The second theme delved into the detailed process involved in applying MFCA, shedding light on the various steps and considerations that need to be considered. These overarching themes will be further elaborated upon and discussed in the following sections.

Benefits of MFCA

The concept of Material Flow Cost Accounting (MFCA) has been proven to be an effective tool for businesses in identifying hidden costs, minimizing losses and waste, and reducing environmental impacts. It also provides strategies for companies to address unsustainability issues and transition toward sustainable management and waste reduction practices. Researchers such as Tran et al. (2024) along with Nyakuwanika et al. (2023) have highlighted the benefits of MFCA in reducing material waste, enhancing material and energy efficiency, and assessing the financial viability of firms. Moreover, studies by Santoki et al. (2023), Bux and Amicarelli (2022), and Nishitani et al. (2022) have emphasized the importance of MFCA in improving transparency in material use practices. By developing a material flow model that tracks and quantifies the movement of materials within an organization in both physical and monetary terms, MFCA enables companies to gain insights into their resource consumption patterns.

Furthermore, MFCA can be seamlessly integrated with other management systems to capture comprehensive waste-cost information, thereby supporting informed decision-making on waste reduction, and enabling the evaluation of both environmental and economic performance (Zeng et al., 2021; Fakoya, 2014; Kluczek, 2019; Rieckhof & Guenther, 2018; Dunuwila et al., 2018). This integration enhances the overall effectiveness of waste reduction strategies and facilitates a more holistic approach to sustainable management practices.

Process in Applying MFCA

MFCA is a highly effective tool that has been widely acclaimed for its numerous benefits in various applications. These benefits have been observed through the implementation of MFCA in various contexts. Across the case studies reviewed, there were some minor differences in the way MFCA was implemented, with 17 cases providing detailed insights into how companies have successfully applied this tool in practice. For instance, a study by Dunuwila et al. (2018) focused on the application of MFCA in a crepe manufacturing company. This study meticulously outlined the various stages of the manufacturing process, including rubber latex collection, standardization, coagulation, milling, drying, folding, dry blanket milling, cutting, and packing. By conducting MFCA calculations, the study identified three key areas for improvement related to the reduction of fresh water, chemicals, and electricity usage. Implementation of these improvement options resulted in significant reductions in water and electricity consumption, greenhouse gas emissions, and overall costs for the company.

Furthermore, the process of implementing MFCA is guided by a structured set of five steps outlined by ISO (2011). These steps are crucial for the successful deployment of MFCA within an organization. Firstly, it is essential to engage management and clearly define roles and responsibilities to ensure accountability throughout the process. Secondly, identifying the scope and boundaries of the process and developing a comprehensive material flow model is imperative. Additionally, allocating costs accurately, including material costs, energy costs, system costs, and waste management costs, is crucial for an effective MFCA implementation. Once the data is collected and analyzed, the results need to be interpreted and effectively communicated to stakeholders to drive informed decision-making. Finally, utilizing the insights gained from MFCA results to improve production practices and minimize material losses is essential for continuous improvement within the organization (Huang et al., 2019). In conclusion, the application of MFCA has proven to be a valuable tool for companies seeking to enhance their environmental performance, reduce costs, and optimize resource utilization.

Empirical Evidence on MFCA in Practice

Currently, the empirical evidence on MFCA implementation has mainly focused on action-based projects. This term refers to studies where the primary researchers play an active role in guiding and supporting the development of MFCA within the organizations under study (Christ & Burritt, 2015). This emphasis on action-based projects is not surprising, considering the prevailing trends in the MFCA literature. However, for MFCA to progress further, organizations must be convinced of its benefits and be willing to implement it without relying heavily on academic support.

To determine how organizations can reach this level of conviction and readiness for MFCA implementation, empirical evidence is crucial. There are still many unanswered questions in this area that need to be addressed. Therefore, this section aims to offer an overview of previous research, which has predominantly been focused on case studies. While the intention was to provide a comprehensive summary of current MFCA work, it is important to note a limitation.

The literature reviewed for this paper was limited to studies available in English. It is acknowledged that there may be additional publications on MFCA, particularly in languages like German and Japanese. However, for the purpose of this review, these resources were not included.

Discussion

After a review of the available research, it is evident that most empirical studies have concentrated on action-based case studies rather than survey or interview-based quantitative or qualitative studies specifically focused on MFCA. While Nyakuwanika et al. (2023) attempted to refine and corroborate the framework through interviews within mining companies and validation in a focus group setting, they ultimately chose to utilize case studies in Zimbabwean gold mines. The scarcity of research in this area suggests that the implementation of MFCA may not be as straightforward as indicated in theoretical literature. Furthermore, awareness of material flow cost accounting (MFCA) does not guarantee its implementation within organizations. According to Christ and Burritt (2015), the adoption of environmental accounting tools is often influenced by their level of recognition, with more widely known tools being more commonly used. However, this principle may not necessarily hold true for MFCA, indicating a need for deeper exploration and research to gain a comprehensive understanding of its implementation in practice.

Recommendations

The discussion above highlights various areas where the MFCA literature requires further development and where unanswered questions still exist. Below recommendations can be drawn from the literature presented to address these gaps. Firstly, although the focus on action-based case studies is important, the research methods utilized to investigate MFCA in practice have been notably limited. A broader range of methodological approaches and tools are available to researchers today, yet survey-based research is scarce and the use of statistical analysis beyond basic percentage counts is largely absent.

The current narrow approach severely restricts the generalizability of research findings and may have contributed to the stagnation in the development of MFCA literature. Christ and Burritt (2015) suggest that different research methods, qualitative and quantitative research designs should not be pitted against each other, but rather viewed as complementary tools. By examining MFCA from various research perspectives, a more comprehensive understanding of its current state can be gained, including the identification of barriers and facilitators to its implementation.

Survey-based statistical research has the potential to provide more generalized findings and recommendations for the utilization and advancement of MFCA in diverse contexts. Therefore, it is recommended that researchers in this field explore alternative research methods and processes to supplement existing approaches, leading to a more diverse and thorough comprehension of MFCA as a subject matter.

Conclusion

Research has indicated that the focus of MFCA research has mainly been on laying the foundation for the future development of the material flow cost accounting tool and improving the understanding of its applications (Christ & Burritt, 2015; Tran & Herzig, 2020). Additionally, although using MFCA is often linked to enhancing eco-efficiency, the studies reviewed also point to its significant relevance in strategic decision-making processes within organizations. It has been noted that one of the primary challenges in the application of MFCA, as reported in studies, is the presence of existing accounting systems with limited data availability and inadequate cost allocation methods.

However, this research has also faced certain limitations. The first limitation is related to the databases utilized to search for relevant publications, as it is possible that publications matching the research focus may not have been found due to being stored in other databases. The second limitation pertains to language barriers, as some studies may not have been conducted in English. Based on our findings and the identified gaps in the MFCA literature, we propose avenues for further research.

Firstly, there is a need for quantitative research to gain a better understanding of the current level of MFCA application and to validate the factors that have been shown to impact its implementation through exploratory case study research. Secondly, exploring comparative studies on MFCA application holds promise in enhancing comprehension of the various factors influencing the adoption of innovative accounting methods like MFCA. Thirdly, future research could delve into investigating the process of MFCA application across different sectors and industries. Fourthly, despite the predominance of research on MFCA in the private sector, future studies could extend their examination to cover these industries more comprehensively. In addition to the private sector, there is also a pressing need to further explore MFCA application and diffusion within service industries due to their economic significance and the environmental consequences linked to the activities of the private sector.

References

Arieftiara, D., Theresa, R. M., & Sari, R. (2021). Sustainability in health service industry: The implementation of material flow cost accounting (MFCA) as an eco-efficient analysis. *Journal of Southeast Asian Research, 747009.*

Bux, C., & Amicarelli, V. (2022). Material flow cost accounting (MFCA) to enhance environmental entrepreneurship in the meat sector: Challenges and opportunities. *Journal of Environmental Management, 313*, 115001.

Christ, K. L., & Burritt, R. L. (2015). Material flow cost accounting: A review and agenda for future research. *Journal of Cleaner Production, 108*, 1378–1389.

Dierkes, S., & Siepelmeyer, D. (2019). Production and cost theory-based material flow cost accounting. *Journal of Cleaner Production, 235*, 483–492.

Doorasamy, M. (2015). Theoretical developments in environmental management accounting and the role and importance of MFCA. *Foundations of Management, 7*(1), 37–52.

Dunuwila, P., Rodrigo, V. H. L., & Goto, N. (2018). Sustainability of natural rubber processing can be improved: A case study with crepe rubber manufacturing in Sri Lanka. *Resources, Conservation and Recycling, 133*, 417–427.

Fakoya, M. B. (2014). An adjusted material flow cost accounting framework for process waste-reduction decisions in the South African Brewery industry (Doctoral dissertation, University of South Africa).

Fakoya, M. B. (2015). Adopting material flow cost accounting model for improved waste-reduction decisions in a micro-brewery. *Environment, Development and Sustainability, 17*, 1017–1030.

Huang, S. Y., Chiu, A. A., Chao, P. C. & Wang, N. (2019). The application of Material Flow Cost Accounting in waste reduction. *Sustainability, 11*(5), 1270.

International Organization for Standardization (ISO). (2011). *Environmental Management—Material Flow Cost Accounting—General Framework (ISO 14051:2011)*. ISO.

ISO, International Organisation for Standardisation. (2017). *ISO 14052:2017. Environmental Management—Material Flow Cost Accounting—Guidance for practical implementation in a Supply Chain.*

Kitada, H., Tennojiya, T., Kim, J., & Higashida, A. (2022). Management practice of material flow cost accounting and its discontinuance. *Cleaner Environmental Systems, 6*, 100089.

Kluczek, A. (2019). Assessment of manufacturing processes eco-efficiency based on MFA-LCA-MFCA methods. *Environmental Engineering & Management Journal (EEMJ), 18*(2).

Kokubu, K., & Kitada, H. (2015). Material flow cost accounting and existing management perspectives. *Journal of Cleaner Production, 108*, 1279–1288.

Nishitani, K., Kokubu, K., Wu, Q., Kitada, H., Guenther, E., & Guenther, T. (2022). Material flow cost accounting (MFCA) for the circular economy: An empirical study of the triadic relationship between MFCA, environmental performance, and the economic performance of Japanese companies. *Journal of Environmental Management, 303*, 114219.

Nyakuwanika, M., Van Der Poll, H. M., & Van Der Poll, J. A. (2023). Validating an environmental management accounting practices framework for the greening of Zimbabwean gold mining. *Journal of Sustainability Science and Management, 18*(10), 98–125.

Nyide, C. J. (2016). Material flow cost accounting as a tool for improved resource efficiency in the hotel sector: A case of emerging market. *Risk Governance & Control: Financial Markets & Institutions (Online)*.

Qu, L., Wang, Z., Sun, C., & Yin, L. (2022). Application of ABB in environmental management accounting: Incorporating MFCA into the budget process. *Frontiers in Environmental Science, 10*, 963903.

Rieckhof, R., & Guenther, E. (2018). Integrating life cycle assessment and material flow cost accounting to account for resource productivity and economic-environmental performance. *The International Journal of Life Cycle Assessment, 23*, 1491–1506.

Santoki, H. D., Acharya, G. D., & Acharya, S. G. (2023). Evaluating MFCA-based system framework for performance improvement in ceramic tile manufacturing industry. *International Journal of Productivity and Quality Management, 40*(3), 383–405.

Schmidt, M. (2015). The interpretation and extension of Material Flow Cost Accounting (MFCA) in the context of environmental material flow analysis. *Journal of Cleaner Production, 108*, 1310–1319.

Tran, T. T., & Herzig, C. (2023). Blended case-based learning in a sustainability accounting course: An analysis of student perspectives. *Journal of Accounting Education, 63*, 100842.

Tran, T. T., Burritt, R. L., Herzig, C., & Christ, K. L. (2024). Material flow cost accounting in Vietnam: A multi-level exploration. *Accounting, Auditing & Accountability Journal*.

Tran, T. T., & Herzig, C. (2020). Material flow cost accounting in developing countries: A systematic review. *Sustainability, 12*(13), 5413.

Wagner, B. (2015). A report on the origins of Material Flow Cost Accounting (MFCA) research activities. *Journal of Cleaner Production, 108*, 1255–1261.

Walls, C., Putri, A. R. K., & Beck, G. (2023). Material flow cost accounting as a resource-saving tool for emerging recycling technologies. *Clean Technologies, 5*(2), 652–674.

Walz, M., & Guenther, E. (2021). What effects does material flow cost accounting have for companies?: Evidence from a case studies analysis. *Journal of Industrial Ecology, 25*(3), 593–613.

Yagi, M., & Kokubu, K. (2018). Corporate material flow management in Thailand: The way to material flow cost accounting. *Journal of Cleaner Production, 198*, 763–775.

Zeng, H., Zhou, Z., & Xiao, X. (2021). MFCA extension from a life cycle perspective: Methodical refinements and use case. *Resources Policy, 74*, 101507.

A Comparative Analysis of Wealth Taxation in South Africa and France: Assessing the Viability and Implications for Implementing a Wealth Tax in South Africa

Jessica Edwards and Tsireledzo Ambani Mulaudzi

Abstract This paper investigates the viability and implications of establishing a wealth tax policy in South Africa through a comparative analysis with France. This paper examines the development, adjustments, and outcome of the wealth tax policies in France. The paper considers the justifications for wealth taxes, emphasizing its dual potential in mitigating socioeconomic inequality and strengthening resources for social welfare endeavours. The paper furnishes applicable recommendations to inform South Africa's potential implementation strategies for wealth tax by extrapolating insights from France's wealth tax policies. The research took the form of a comparative analysis which involved the review of relevant existing literature. Wealth taxes can be a potent policy tool for mitigating economic inequality, fostering social equity, and raising funds for social welfare programmes. For the effective implementation of the wealth taxes, revenue collection from wealth tax, and combating tax evasion, South Africa must navigate complex challenges including administrative convolutions, compliance, and behavioural responses. To foster economic growth and retain income-producing assets while promoting a more equitable distribution of resources, a country must maintain a balance between the collection of tax revenue and investment incentives. Based on France's history of wealth tax continuous reassessment and adaptation of wealth tax policies is important to remain responsive to evolving economic conditions and societal objectives.

Keywords Wealth tax · South Africa · France · Tax base · Tax system

J. Edwards · T. A. Mulaudzi (✉)
University of the Witwatersrand, Johannesburg, South Africa
e-mail: 2330817@students.wits.ac.za; tsireledzo.mulaudzi@wits.ac.za

T. Moloi (ed.), *Impacting Society Positively Through Technology in Accounting and Business Processes*, Springer Proceedings in Business and Economics,
https://doi.org/10.1007/978-3-031-84885-8_34

Introduction

A wealth tax is a tax levied on the net value of an individual's or household's assets, which can include cash, real estate, investments, and personal property (Scott, 2022). Wealth tax is commonly levied on high-net-worth individuals or households and is determined by taking a percentage of the total value of the assets. To create a more equitable taxation system a wealth tax is implemented, where those with the most resources contribute more to society. Adversaries of a wealth tax argue that the implementation and enforcement will deter investment and entrepreneurship (Scott, 2022).

A greater emphasis has been placed in recent years on new taxation methods, such as wealth tax. The focus on wealth tax has been sparked by two phenomena in South Africa. First, there is the ongoing and growing need for additional tax revenue to cover the budget deficit, which has been worsened by a protracted period of slow economic growth, rising public debt, and a very small base of individual taxpayers. Second, South Africa is one of the most unequal societies in the world. A wealth tax has emerged as a potential solution to the twin problems of increased tax revenue collection and economic inequality. Even though South Africa has a long history of wealth transfer taxes in the form of estate duty and donations tax, there has never been a tax on an individual's net wealth holdings during their lifetime (Arendse & Stack, 2018).

This study focuses on a comparison of wealth tax between South Africa and France. The concept of wealth tax was first introduced in France in 1982, but it has undergone several changes recently (Dupas, 2020). France has a wealth tax that is more established and has been in place for a longer period. As a result, more comprehensive information regarding the wealth tax is available to conduct the comparison (Dupas, 2020).

The objective of this study is to investigate the viability and implications of establishing a wealth tax policy in South Africa, by providing recommendations based on evidence and insights, as well as what potential modifications may be required to ensure the social and economic context of South Africa is addressed. To identify the factors that influenced the adoption or rejection of wealth taxes, the historical context of wealth taxation in both countries will be analysed. The distinctive features of the proposed wealth tax system in South Africa and France's policies, such as tax rates, thresholds, and assessment systems, will be examined.

Scope and Delimitations

While this research aims to be a comparative analysis of wealth taxation in South Africa and France, the research contains limitations. Rather than proposing policy recommendations, the study will focus on the wealth tax systems and their implications in the countries mentioned above.

Institutional Framework of France as a Comparative Country

The taxation systems in France and South Africa share several similarities. Both countries levy taxes at both the national and subnational levels. Additionally, they both have the presence of Value-Added Tax (VAT) and social security taxes (Neethling, 2023). Moreover, when considering their economic development, South Africa and France are both classified as middle-income nations.

Comparing South Africa to a developed nation like France when considering the implementation of a wealth tax offers several advantages. Developed nations, such as France, have well-established wealth tax policies with a longer history and more comprehensive data on their implementation and impacts. This wealth of data is supported by more effective data collection systems, allowing for more accurate research on the effects of wealth taxes on various economic indicators, wealth distribution, and tax revenue production.

Literature Review

Wealth Tax in South Africa

Historical Context of Wealth Taxes in South Africa

Throughout its history, South Africa has utilized various taxes, such as income tax, value-added tax (VAT), corporate tax, property tax, and capital gains tax, to generate revenue for the government. Even though South Africa has a long history of wealth transfer taxes in the form of estate duty and donations tax, there has never been a tax on an individual's net wealth holdings during their lifetime (Arendse & Stack, 2018).

The National Development Plan (NDP) of South Africa, published in 2012, outlines the country's strategic economic direction for the next two decades with the primary objective of eliminating poverty and inequality by 2030. While the NDP does not explicitly mention wealth taxes, it openly acknowledges the pressing issue of income and wealth disparities, which threaten economic and social stability. The plan anticipates that achieving its goals will require a comprehensive reorganization of the government and economy, leading some economists to speculate that wealth taxes might play a more significant role in this restructuring (Arendse & Stack, 2018).

In 2014, during the delivery of the Budget Speech focused on implementing the NDP, references were made to the government's commitment to reducing poverty and inequality. This fueled speculation about the introduction of higher or new wealth taxes. Subsequently, the government initiated a fiscal consolidation programme, primarily aimed at raising taxes for higher-income individuals and taxing the wealthy more heavily. Over the years, the tax system underwent several modifications, focusing on estate duty, donations tax liabilities, transfer duty on high-value properties, effective capital gains tax rate, dividends tax rate, and estate duty tax base. These changes were implemented to raise the tax burden on the wealthiest individuals (Arendse & Stack, 2018).

Despite these changes, it remains uncertain whether the current tax system should be supplemented by a new wealth tax. While a new wealth tax is hoped to address economic disparities, some concerns must be carefully evaluated. The potential fiscal benefits of the new wealth tax need to be realistically projected and weighed against the risks, notably the impact on the economy's growth potential. Wealth, being highly mobile, provides owners with various options on how to handle and invest it, deciding to introduce wealth taxes is complex. The potential financial or distributive advantages of such taxes may be offset by adverse effects on economic growth (Davis Tax Committe, 2018).

As the nation continues to grapple with economic disparities, the viability and consequences of introducing a wealth tax remain subjects of ongoing discussion and analysis (Davis Tax Committe, 2018; Matobela, 2012).

Reasons for the Absence of a Wealth Tax in South Africa

In 2015, the renowned economist Thomas Piketty reignited the discussion during the Nelson Mandela lecture, proposing a global net wealth tax to reduce inequality in South Africa. While many organizations and experts endorsed Piketty's ideas, some, including the African National Congress (ANC) and economist Dr. Jammine Azar, disagreed, expressing concerns about potential impacts on investment and administrative difficulties (Mofokeng, 2018).

The Davis Tax Committee received submissions from various organizations expressing their views on wealth taxation in South Africa. South African Institute of Chartered Accountants (SAICA) believes that net wealth taxes would be ineffective in addressing inequality and suggests using other policy tools. South African Institute of Taxation (SAIT) raises concerns about the administrative burden on taxpayers and the South African Revenue Service. Concerns have been raised regarding the potential shortfall in revenue generated by the net wealth tax, primarily attributed to substantial expenses related to its collection and compliance. Conversely, there are staunch advocates of wealth taxes who see them as a crucial instrument for addressing wealth inequality, while there are critics who argue that such taxation could disproportionately benefit a specific demographic and inadequately confront the issue of inequality (Arendse & Stack, 2018).

Political and Economic Climate: The current economic challenges, including slow growth and high unemployment rates, deterred policymakers from implementing a new tax that could affect capital formation and investment (Davis Tax Committe, 2018).

Administrative Difficulty: Valuing various types of assets for wealth taxation purposes can be complex and challenging, which has influenced tax authorities' considerations (Chatterjee et al., 2019).

Potential Impact on Investment: Critics argue that wealth taxes could discourage foreign investment and capital inflows, which South Africa aims to attract for economic growth (Chatterjee et al., 2019).

Existing Tax System: South Africa already has a range of taxes in place that generate revenue, and policymakers prefer relying on these existing taxes for funding (Davis Tax Committe, 2018).

Tax Avoidance and Evasion Concerns: Implementing a wealth tax might lead high-net-worth individuals to explore tax avoidance measures to protect their assets, raising concerns about effectiveness and unintended consequences (Chatterjee et al., 2019; Davis Tax Committe, 2018).

Factors Influencing the Adoption of Wealth Taxes in South Africa and France

During the apartheid era (1948–1994), South Africa implemented tax policies that favoured the white minority and disadvantaged the black majority, contributing to economic disparities and the dominance of the ruling elite. After the end of apartheid, the democratic government focused on economic and social reforms to address historical injustices and inequalities. However, wealth taxation was not extensively utilized for wealth redistribution (Arendse & Stack, 2018).

South Africa relies mainly on income tax and capital gains tax to generate revenue from higher-income individuals. The progressive income tax system partially contributes to wealth redistribution, but there are concerns that it may not sufficiently address deep-rooted economic disparities (Arendse & Stack, 2018; Mofokeng, 2018).

The introduction of a specific wealth tax in South Africa has been a topic of debate. Critics raise concerns about potential negative effects on investment, capital flight, and the competitiveness of the economy, which have influenced the government's decisions on wealth taxation (Chatterjee et al., 2019; Mofokeng, 2018).

Wealth Tax in France

Historical Context of Wealth Taxation in France

The concept of wealth taxation in France has roots in the early twentieth century, arising as a response to the country's economic and social challenges, such as post-war reconstruction and efforts to address income inequality. In 1982, under President François Mitterrand's socialist government, the first modern wealth tax known as the "Solidarity Tax on Wealth" (Impôt de Solidarité sur la Fortune, ISF) was introduced. This tax was specifically designed to target the wealthiest individuals in society and applied progressive tax rates based on their net assets. However, in 1986, Jacques Chirac repealed the ISF (Dupas, 2020).

Over the years, France has made several adjustments to its wealth taxation policy, reflecting changes in economic conditions and political ideologies. During periods of economic growth and efforts to attract foreign investment, debates arose regarding the potential impact of the wealth tax on entrepreneurship and capital flight. As a result, the thresholds and tax rates were modified multiple times to strike a balance between generating revenue and providing economic incentives. In 2008, the ISF was reinstated, contributing significantly to the country's revenue (Dupas, 2020; Matobela, 2012).

Challenges and Repeal of the Wealth Tax

Throughout its existence, the French wealth tax encountered significant challenges. Critics contended that the tax hindered investment and capital formation, as it encompassed net assets, including real estate, business assets, and financial holdings. This raised concerns that the tax might discourage affluent individuals from investing in productive ventures or even prompt them to relocate elsewhere, potentially leading to capital flight. Moreover, debates emerged concerning the administrative complexities and compliance costs associated with enforcing the wealth tax (Matobela, 2012; Davis Tax Committe, 2018).

In response to these issues, President Emmanuel Macron's government acted in 2018 and decided to reform the wealth tax. The reform transformed the original tax into the "Real Estate Wealth Tax" (Impôt sur la Fortune Immobilière, IFI). The reformed tax specifically targeted only real estate assets, while excluding financial holdings and business assets from its purview. The primary purpose of this change was to alleviate the burden on wealth invested in productive activities and redirect the tax's focus towards immovable property (Dupas, 2020).

Factors Influencing the Adoption of Wealth Taxes in Respect?

Wealth taxation has a long history in France, dating back to the French Revolution, with periodic reintroduction and abolishment based on economic and political circumstances. In 1982, the French government established the Impôt de Solidarité sur la Fortune (ISF) as a comprehensive wealth tax system to address wealth concentration and promote social solidarity. Over the years, the ISF faced criticism and debates regarding its impact on capital flight and investment. Despite this, the French government maintained the wealth tax as a means of income redistribution. In 2018, President Emmanuel Macron reformed the system, transforming the ISF into the Impôt sur la Fortune Immobilière (IFI), focusing solely on real estate assets to attract investments while still addressing wealth disparities. Ongoing discussions persist in France, with some advocating for a broader wealth tax reintroduction to tackle income inequality more effectively (Dupas, 2020).

The Impact of Wealth Taxation in France

The impact of wealth taxation in France has been a subject of ongoing debate, with proponents highlighting its role in addressing wealth inequality and funding social programmes. However, critics express concerns about its potential negative effects on investment, economic growth, and capital mobility. The decision to repeal the full-scale wealth tax in favour of the Impôt sur la Fortune Immobilière (IFI) marked a shift in France's approach to wealth taxation, acknowledging the challenges faced during its implementation (Dupas, 2020; Mofokeng, 2018).

The benefits of France's former wealth tax (ISF) were subject to debate and had both supporters and critics. Here are some arguments put forward by its proponents:

Redistribution of wealth: One of the primary objectives of the wealth tax was to promote a more equitable distribution of wealth. By imposing a tax on the net wealth of high-net-worth individuals, the government aimed to reduce income inequality and support social cohesion (Mofokeng, 2018).

Funding public services: The revenue generated from the wealth tax could be used to fund various public services, including education, healthcare, infrastructure, and welfare programmes. This would, in turn, benefit the entire population, not just the wealthy (Davis Tax Committe, 2018).

Encouraging investment and entrepreneurship: Proponents argued that the wealth tax could incentivize the wealthy to invest their money in productive assets or businesses, rather than allowing it to accumulate passively. This could lead to increased economic growth and job creation (Davis Tax Committe, 2018).

Mitigating tax evasion: By taxing wealth directly, the wealth tax could potentially reduce tax evasion and avoidance strategies that high-net-worth individuals might employ to minimize their tax liability (Mofokeng, 2018).

However, there were also criticisms of the wealth tax, which led to its replacement with the IFI in 2018. Some arguments against the wealth tax include:

Negative impact on competitiveness: Detractors claimed that the wealth tax might drive wealthy individuals to move their assets and even themselves to countries with more favourable tax regimes, potentially leading to a loss of economic activity and talent (Mofokeng, 2018).

Limited revenue impact: Some critics suggested that the wealth tax might not generate significant revenue compared to the administrative costs and potential negative economic effects it could bring. Currently, wealth taxes contribute only 2% of total revenue in France (Matobela, 2012).

Economic Impact: Opponents contend that a wealth tax may have unfavourable economic effects. High tax rates may deter investment and entrepreneurship and savings, as taxpayers could be penalized for holding certain types of assets, which could result in slower economic expansion and fewer new jobs being created (Mofokeng, 2018; Matobela, 2012).

Potential Wealth Erosion: A wealth tax could cause wealth to slowly erode over time as people continue to pay taxes on their assets even when they don't experience any liquidity events (Davis Tax Committe, 2018).

Design and Administration of Wealth Taxes in France

Taxable Base and Assets Inclusion

The design of wealth taxes revolves around determining the tax base, which comprises the assets subject to taxation. In France, the wealth tax initially included a broad range of assets, such as real estate, financial investments, business assets, and personal property. However, concerns over the impact on entrepreneurship and investment prompted reforms, leading to the IFI, which focused solely on real estate assets (Garbinti et al., 2023).

Tax Thresholds and Progressive Rates

In France, the ISF employed a progressive tax scale, with rates ranging from 0.5% to 1.5% on net assets above certain thresholds meaning that higher levels of wealth are subject to higher tax rates. When revising wealth taxation, France adjusted these thresholds and tax rates multiple times to strike a balance between revenue generation and encouraging investment (Garbinti et al., 2023).

Valuation Methods and Assessments

Determining the valuation methods for various assets can be complex and require robust assessment mechanisms. Real estate assets, for instance, may be valued based on market prices or assessed by relevant authorities. Financial assets may be subject to market values, while business assets might require different valuation methodologies. A well-defined and transparent valuation process is essential to minimize disputes and ensure tax compliance (Dupas, 2020; Garbinti et al., 2023).

Exemptions and Deductions

To address potential unintended consequences and maintain policy coherence, wealth taxes often include exemptions and deductions. For example, some countries exempt certain assets, such as primary residences, from wealth taxation to protect homeowners. France implemented similar exemptions in the IFI, excluding financial assets and business assets (Garbinti et al., 2023).

Administrative Mechanisms and Compliance

Wealth taxes require efficient administrative mechanisms to ensure proper assessment, collection, and enforcement. Effective administration involves gathering accurate financial information, implementing reporting requirements, and addressing tax evasion. Properly enforcing a wealth tax may necessitate cooperation between tax authorities, financial institutions, and relevant regulatory bodies (Dupas, 2020).

Behavioural Implications and Economic Impact

The design of wealth taxes can have significant behavioural implications. Changes in tax rates or asset inclusion may influence investment decisions, asset allocation, and capital mobility. It is essential to assess the potential economic impact of the tax policy on investment, entrepreneurship, and overall economic growth (Garbinti et al., 2023; Dupas, 2020).

Research Methodology

This paper compares the wealth taxes of two countries; this requires a detailed literature review followed by analysis and synthesis of the literature. Using a comparative analysis approach, the study will compare the South African proposed wealth tax to the wealth tax in France. An explanatory study is required to meet the objectives of this paper. A qualitative research method was followed where journal articles, legislation, websites, media articles, discussion papers, and books were reviewed. Data from both countries will be analysed to identify similarities and differences.

Results and Discussion Behavioural Implications and Economic Impact of Wealth Tax

Economic Implications of Wealth Taxation

Impact on Investment Behaviours

Wealth taxation can influence the investment decisions of high-net-worth individuals and businesses. The prospect of having a portion of their accumulated wealth subjected to taxation may alter risk-reward considerations, leading some individuals to reevaluate their investment strategies. Individuals may opt for tax-exempt assets or seek tax-efficient investment vehicles to minimize their tax liabilities. These behaviours could impact the allocation of capital, potentially diverting funds away from productive investments and towards tax-favoured assets (Chatterjee et al., 2019).

Capital Flight and Brain Drain

One of the most significant concerns surrounding wealth taxation is the potential for capital flight and the emigration of wealthy individuals. If the tax burden becomes onerous, affluent individuals may choose to relocate to jurisdictions with more favourable tax policies, leading to a loss of investment and entrepreneurial activity within the country. This phenomenon, often referred to as "brain drain", can result in reduced job creation, limited access to expertise, and a slowdown in economic growth (Neethling, 2023).

Entrepreneurship and Business Formation

High levels of wealth taxation could deter potential entrepreneurs from taking risks and investing in new ventures, particularly in high-risk industries or innovative sectors. Additionally, existing business owners may face challenges in raising capital, as investors may be cautious about investing in ventures subject to wealth taxation. The net effect on entrepreneurship depends on the overall business climate, access to alternative sources of funding, and the government's ability to foster an enabling environment for startups (Neethling, 2023; Chatterjee et al., 2019).

Economic Growth and Investment Incentives

If the tax system disincentivizes investment and hampers economic activities, it may result in reduced GDP growth and slower wealth accumulation over time. On the other hand, if the revenue generated from wealth taxes is effectively channeled into productive investments and social welfare programmes, it may stimulate economic activity and contribute to long-term sustainable growth (Chatterjee et al., 2019).

Revenue Generation and Fiscal Impact

Wealth taxation has the potential to generate significant revenue for the government, especially in countries with high levels of wealth concentration. This additional revenue stream can be used to finance public services, infrastructure projects, and social welfare programmes. However, the extent of revenue generation depends on the design of the tax policy, its impact on asset valuation, and the behaviours of taxpayers in response to the tax (Chatterjee et al., 2019).

Wealth Redistribution and Income Equality

A key objective of wealth taxation is to reduce wealth disparities and promote a more equitable distribution of resources. By taxing the accumulated wealth of the richest individuals, wealth taxation aims to redistribute resources to fund public services and support the less affluent segments of society. The effectiveness of wealth taxation in achieving wealth redistribution depends on its design and the willingness of taxpayers to comply (Scott, 2022).

Compliance Costs and Administrative Complexity

Wealth taxation can introduce administrative complexities and compliance costs for both taxpayers and tax authorities. Wealth taxation can be challenging due to the complexities of valuing diverse assets, the need for accurate reporting, and the risk of tax evasion, which can burden both taxpayers and tax authorities, making it essential to strike a balance in the design to avoid undue burdens while achieving equitable wealth redistribution. The cost of compliance and enforcement should be carefully considered in the design of the tax to avoid unduly burdening taxpayers and the government (Neethling, 2023, p. 1; Scott, 2022, p.1).

Social Implications of Wealth Taxation

Impact on High-Net-Worth Individuals' Behaviours

The implementation of wealth taxation may lead to changes in behaviours among high-net-worth individuals. Some may adapt their financial strategies to minimize tax liabilities, while others may consider emigrating to countries with more favourable tax regimes. Consequently, governments need to carefully assess the potential behavioural responses of high-net-worth individuals and adjust policy accordingly to strike a balance between revenue generation and retaining productive assets and investments within the country (Chatterjee et al., 2019).

Philanthropic Behaviours and Charitable Giving

On one hand, some may view wealth taxation as a form of social responsibility and increase their charitable giving to support causes they care about. Alternatively, others may perceive the tax as already contributing to societal well-being and reduce their voluntary philanthropic efforts. The net effect on charitable giving can depend on cultural norms, individual values, and the perceived impact of government support through wealth taxation (Chatterjee et al., 2019).

Social Cohesion and Perceptions of Fairness

If citizens believe that the tax policy is progressive and ensures that the burden is shared equitably among the wealthiest individuals, it may strengthen trust in the tax system and the government. If the tax is perceived as arbitrary or unfair, it may lead to public discontent and erode social cohesion (Scott, 2022).

Impact on Entrepreneurship and Innovation

While some argue that higher taxes on accumulated wealth might discourage entrepreneurial risk-taking, others contend that such policies can free up resources for social investments, education, and research that foster innovation. The net effect on entrepreneurship and innovation depends on the balance between revenue generation for societal investments and the potential dampening of entrepreneurial drive (Chatterjee et al., 2019).

Wealth Mobility and Social Mobility

Wealth taxation may influence wealth mobility, which refers to the movement of individuals and families up or down the economic ladder. By reallocating resources towards social welfare programmes, wealth taxation can provide opportunities for upward social mobility for those in lower-income brackets. However, the potential impact on wealth mobility depends on how the revenue from wealth taxes is allocated and whether it genuinely supports upward mobility for disadvantaged communities (Chatterjee et al., 2019; Neethling, 2023).

Public Perception and Political Support

Public perception plays a significant role in the success and sustainability of wealth taxation. The way wealth taxes are portrayed in the media and perceived by the public can impact political support for such policies. Public attitudes towards wealth taxation can influence the government's willingness to implement and maintain the tax over the long term (Chatterjee et al., 2019).

Comparative Analysis

Table 1 provides a comparative overview of the implementation reasons for a wealth tax in South Africa and draws parallels with France's historical use of such taxes. Both South Africa and France share common objectives related to taxation and social equity, but they approach them with nuanced differences. South Africa's goal

Table 1 Comparison between South Africa's possible implementation reasons with those with France

Implementation reasons:	
South Africa	France
Restore social justice and stability	Horizontal equity
Simplify tax system	Efficiency
Reduce inequality	Reduction of inequality
Redress the wrongs of the past	Administrative control
Supplement tax revenue	

Table 2 Comparison between the potential problems associated with wealth tax in South Africa as identified by Katz Commission and abolishment reasons of France

South Africa	France
Valuation problems Problems with tracking assets Payment difficulties High compliance and collection costs	Practical difficulties
Negative effect on entrepreneurship Decrease willingness to save by taxpayers. It encourages capital flight	Adverse economic consequences

of restoring social justice and stability is closely tied to addressing historical injustices and creating a more stable societal environment. In contrast, France emphasizes "horizontal equity", focusing on treating individuals in similar situations with fairness within the tax system. South Africa seeks to simplify its tax system to enhance accessibility and comprehension for taxpayers, while France prioritizes tax system efficiency to improve effectiveness and streamline administration. Both nations aim to reduce inequality. Lastly, South Africa seeks to supplement tax revenue, possibly for budgetary needs or targeted programmes, while France emphasizes "administrative control" to enhance the management of the tax system, which indirectly can boost tax revenue. These distinctions reflect the unique priorities and historical contexts of each country's taxation goals (Arendse & Stack, 2018).

Table 2 compares the challenges associated with the Katz Commission's proposed wealth tax in South Africa with those experienced by France who have implemented the tax in the past.

In South Africa, concerns primarily revolve around valuation problems, where accurately assessing individuals, wealth is a complex and contentious endeavour. France, on the other hand, refers to these issues as "practicable difficulties", encompassing not only valuation but also operational challenges in implementing the tax (Davis Tax Committe, 2018).

Additionally, South Africa highlights problems with tracking taxpayers' assets, crucial for effective wealth tax enforcement, while France emphasizes the "negative effect on entrepreneurship", indicating that the tax may discourage entrepreneurial activities and wealth creation. South Africa's mention of "payment difficulties" implies that some taxpayers may struggle to meet their wealth tax obligations, whereas in France, there is a concern about a "decrease in willingness to save by taxpayers", suggesting that individuals might reduce their savings due to the wealth tax burden (Matobela, 2012; Mofokeng, 2018).

Table 3 Comparative summary

Aspect	France	South Africa
Existence of wealth tax	"Solidarity Tax on Wealth" (ISF)	No specific wealth tax
	Renamed "Real Estate Wealth Tax" (IFI) in 2018	Utilizes income tax, capital gains tax, etc.
Tax base and rates	Tax on net assets exceeding a threshold	Tax based on earnings, capital gains, etc.
	Focused on various types of wealth	No specific tax based on net worth
Tax rates and thresholds	Progressive rates based on net worth	Tax rates vary depending on income levels
	IFI thresholds for real estate assets	No specific wealth tax thresholds
Exemptions	Some exemptions for certain business assets	No specific wealth tax exemptions
Enforcement	Rigorous tax enforcement system	Compliance with existing tax laws required
	Penalties and legal actions for non-compliance	Penalties for non-payment of taxes
Economic impact	Concerns about investment and capital flight	Potential focus on investment and growth
	IFI introduced to encourage business investment	
Social and political aspects	Debate on income inequality and social justice	Social and political factors influence policy
	Effectiveness of wealth tax in achieving goals	Prioritization of other tax measures

Furthermore, South Africa anticipates high compliance and collection costs linked to the wealth tax, while France goes further, expressing worries about the tax "encouraging capital flight", as individuals and businesses may move their assets abroad to evade the tax's impact. It is noteworthy that South Africa lacks a direct equivalent concern to France's "adverse economic consequences". This suggests that France may have experienced broader negative economic effects related to their wealth tax, which are not explicitly mentioned as concerns in South Africa's context (Arendse & Stack, 2018) (Table 3).

Analysis

Challenges and Lessons Learned from France's Wealth Tax

1. Administrative Complexity and Compliance:

The wealth tax imposed a significant administrative burden on both taxpayers and tax authorities. The process of assessing and verifying taxpayers' assets was resource-intensive and required substantial paperwork. Complying with the wealth tax requirements was costly for both individuals and businesses. They often had to hire tax experts and spend considerable time and effort to meet their tax obligations. Accurately assessing the value of various assets, such as real estate, financial holdings, and business assets, can be complex and may lead to disputes between taxpayers and tax authorities. Additionally, ensuring compliance and preventing tax evasion in the context of wealth taxation can be resource-intensive for both taxpayers and the government. Learning from France's experiences, South Africa must establish robust administrative mechanisms to streamline tax collection, reporting, and enforcement (Pichet, 2007).

2. Behavioural Responses and Capital Flight:

   One of the most significant challenges was capital flight. High-net-worth individuals and businesses often moved their assets and investments abroad to countries with more favourable tax regimes to avoid the high taxation associated with the French wealth tax. This led to a loss of capital and investments within the country. South Africa must carefully consider the potential for capital flight and adopt measures to balance revenue generation with incentives for productive investment within its borders (Pichet, 2007).

3. Impact on Investment and Economic Growth:

   Critics argued that wealth tax deterred wealth generation, entrepreneurship, and risk-taking. The wealth taxation system in France was believed to deter high-net-worth individuals from investing in French businesses and startups, which led to a decrease in economic growth. The use of tax shelters and incentives for tax evasion were created due to the high tax rates of wealth tax. Some individuals sought to reduce their tax obligation by concealing their assets or with the use of tax planning strategies. Investment behaviour is influenced by the high tax rates on accumulated wealth, leading to the prioritization of tax-efficient assets over productive investments. This could have a negative impact on job creation, entrepreneurship, and overall economic growth. For South Africa to achieve both its economic and social objectives, a balance between generating revenue for social welfare programmes and fostering investment incentives is critical (Davis Tax Committe, 2018; Pichet, 2007).

4. Evaluating Revenue Generation and Social Impact:

   Determining the revenue potential of wealth taxation and evaluating its social impact requires careful analysis. While wealth taxation can contribute to revenue generation, it is essential to assess the net effect on income distribution, poverty alleviation, and the effectiveness of social welfare programmes. Governments must consider whether wealth taxation aligns with broader social policies and effectively addresses income inequality (Chatterjee et al., 2019).

5. Political and Public Support:

In France, there was political controversy regarding wealth tax. Fluctuations in the tax policy were caused due to the continuous discussions about the effectiveness, fairness, and economic impact that wealth tax created. Governments must address public sentiment and effectively communicate the rationale and benefits of wealth taxation for it to be sustainable. Ensure that the tax is perceived as fair and equitable is crucial for gaining public support and maintaining political support over the long term (Pichet, 2007).

Rationale for Wealth Taxation in South Africa

1. Addressing Income Inequality:

Wealth taxation addresses income inequality and wealth concentration within a society. The wealth distribution is highly skewed, with a small percentage of the population holding a disproportionate share of the nation's assets. Wealth tax reduces resources and promotes a more equitable distribution of economic benefit, by levying taxes on accumulated wealth. The inequalities between the wealthy and the economically disadvantaged can be reduced by creating social welfare programmes and initiatives that support the less fortunate, funded by wealth tax revenue (Boadway & Pestieau, 2021).

2. Revenue Generation for Social Welfare Programmes:

Wealth taxation offers a means of generating substantial revenue for the government, enabling increased investments in critical social welfare programmes. This includes funding for education, healthcare, housing, and infrastructure development, which can contribute to improving the overall well-being and quality of life of the population. By focusing on the accumulated wealth of the richest individuals, wealth taxation offers a unique funding source separate from income or consumption-based taxes. This diversifies the government's revenue streams and reduces dependence on regressive taxation methods (Chatalova & Evans, 2013).

3. Promoting Fiscal Sustainability:

By enhancing the tax base and revenue stability, wealth taxation can ensure economic sustainability. Economic changes can have a significant impact on government revenues that rely heavily on income or consumption taxes. As wealth tends to be more susceptible to short-term economic volatility, wealth taxation must be effectively implemented to provide a more stable source of income. Long-term economic sustainability will create the ability of the government to finance public services and investments even during economic downturns (Chatalova & Evans, 2013).

4. Encouraging Social Responsibility of the Wealthy versus the high net worth:

Beyond revenue generation, wealth taxation seeks to encourage the socially responsible behaviours of the wealthy. By imposing a tax on accumulated wealth, the policy signals an expectation that the wealthy should contribute proportionately to the society from which they have benefited. This can foster a sense of social responsibility among the affluent, encouraging charitable activities, investments in community development, and initiatives aimed at addressing social issues. As a result, wealth taxation can act as a mechanism for enhancing social cohesion and a sense of shared responsibility for societal welfare (Chatalova & Evans, 2013; Pichet, 2007).

5. Reducing Tax Avoidance and Evasion:

By taxing wealth holdings directly, rather than relying solely on income taxation, wealth taxes limit opportunities for the wealthy to hide assets or engage in aggressive tax planning. Implementing robust reporting and enforcement mechanisms can improve tax compliance, ensuring a fairer tax system that benefits all segments of the population (Davis Tax Committe, 2018).

6. Symbolic Value and Political Significance:

Wealth tax can signal a commitment to social justice and economic equity, reflecting a government's responsiveness to the needs of its citizens. Introducing wealth taxation can demonstrate the political will to tackle income inequality and address the concerns of the less privileged, enhancing public trust and legitimacy in governance (Chatterjee et al., 2019).

Rationale Against Wealth Taxation in South Africa

1. Economic Impact and Investment Flight:

High tax rates may deter both domestic and foreign investment, resulting in slower economic growth and fewer new jobs being created. Wealthy people may also try to move themselves or their assets to a country with lower taxes, which could result in capital flight (Schnellenbach, 2012).

2. Administrative Difficulty:

Implementing and managing a wealth tax can be challenging; it calls for thorough asset valuations and ongoing oversight. Higher administrative costs for the government and taxpayers could result from this complexity (Matobela, 2012).

3. Impact on Savings and Retirement:

According to critics, a wealth tax may deter people from saving for retirement and planning because it could eventually reduce the value of accumulated assets (Chatterjee et al., 2019).

4. Effects on Capital Formation:

Some contend that a wealth tax could have unintended consequences, such as asset misallocation or decreased capital formation, as people may change their investment choices to lessen the tax impact (Schnellenbach, 2012).

Conclusion

The implementation of wealth taxation in South Africa warrants careful consideration, given its potential economic and social implications. Drawing valuable insights from France's experiences with wealth taxation, this comparative analysis provides essential lessons for South Africa's policymakers.

Wealth taxes can be a powerful policy tool for addressing economic inequality, promoting social fairness, and raising funds for social welfare programmes. Wealth taxes aim to promote a fairer allocation of resources and chances for upward social mobility by targeting the accumulated wealth of the wealthiest individuals.

The design and implementation of wealth taxes are significant to reduce risks and optimize advantages. South Africa must navigate complicated concerns such as administrative complexity, compliance, and behavioural responses, to achieve effective tax collection and combat tax evasion. To promote economic growth and keep productive assets in the country, a balance between tax generation and investment incentives needs to be created. The lessons learned by France demonstrate the importance of constantly analysing and altering wealth taxation policy in response to changing economic conditions and societal objectives.

The successful implementation and long-term viability of wealth taxation is influenced by the public's support and politics. To gain public trust and political support it is critical to ensure that tax policy is regarded as fair, equal, and consistent with broader social policies.

Due to the potential benefits and drawbacks of wealth taxes, South Africa is at a crossroads. South Africa may make considerable progress in addressing income inequality, promoting economic growth, and improving social welfare by establishing a balanced wealth taxation regime. Wealth taxes have the potential to be a key tool in fostering a more inclusive and equal society in South Africa when properly implemented and investigated. Wealth taxes have been suggested to not be a reliable source of tax collection on its own based on global practice. The lessons learned from France will be crucial in ensuring that South Africa's wealth tax system is effective and long lasting. The research's conclusions indicate that implementing a wealth tax in South Africa is not considered feasible.

References

Arendse, J., & Stack, L. (2018). Investigating a new wealth tax in South Africa: Lessons from international experience. *Journal of Economic and Financial Sciences*, 1–12. https://doi.org/10.4102/jef.v11i1.175

Boadway, R., & Pestieau, P. (2021). *An annual wealth tax: Pros and cons*. https://dial.uclouvain.be/pr/boreal/object/boreal%3A254856/datastream/PDF_01/view

Chatalova, N., & Evans, C. (2013). Too rich to rein in? The under-utilised wealth tax base. *eJournal of Tax Research*, 434–452.

Chatterjee, A., Czajka, L., & Gethin, A. (2019). *A wealth tax South Africa*.

Davis Tax Committe. (2018). *Feasibility of a wealth tax in South Africa*.

Dupas, M. (2020). *Wealth tax: France*. Wealth Tax Commision.

Garbinti, B., Goupille-Lebret, J., Muñoz, M., Stantcheva, S., & Zucman, G. (2023). *TAX DESIGN, INFORMATION, AND ELASTICITIES*. National Bureau of Economic Research.

Matobela, C. (2012). *Wealth tax in South Africa: Analysis of proposals for the introduction of an annual tax on personal wealth*.

Mofokeng, M. O. (2018). *Wealth tax: A systematic literature review*.

Neethling, B. (2023, April 14). *Daily Investor*. https://dailyinvestor.com/finance/13420/south-african-wealth-tax-warning/

Pichet, E. (2007). *THE ECONOMIC CONSEQUENCES OF THE FRENCH WEALTH TAX (ISF)*. La Revue de Droit Fiscal.

Schnellenbach, J. (2012). The economics of taxing net wealth: A survey of the issues. *Public Finance and Management*.

Scott, M. P. (2022, November 12). *Investopedia*. https://www.investopedia.com/terms/w/wealth-tax.asp

Addressing Jurisdiction to Tax Challenges Posed by the Digital Economy: A Comparative Analysis of Amount A and Article 12B as Solutions for South Africa

Khodani Sengwane

Abstract South Africa can only tax the business profits of a company if the company is a South African tax resident or the business profits are from a South African source. The determination of South African tax residency or source rules largely require companies to be "physically present" in South Africa. The advent of digital companies that can operate virtually anywhere in the world renders such tax rules inadequate to cover business profits generated by digital companies. The Organisation for Economic Co-operation and Development has proposed Pillar One Amount A (Amount A) as a global solution that provides new tax nexus and profit allocation rules that do not require the physical presence of companies. On the other hand, the United Nations developed a bilateral treaty solution in the form of Article 12B which can be used to allocate taxing rights in respect of income generated from automated digital services. The purpose of this paper was to determine what the best solution would be for South Africa to adopt between Amount A and Article 12B as solutions to address the tax challenges that the digital economy poses to South Africa's jurisdiction to tax business profits of digital companies. The research used a qualitative methodology which involved the review of relevant existing literature and comparison of the design of Amount A and Article 12B rules. This paper argued that both solutions have their advantages and disadvantages. However, compared to each other, Article 12B (subject to a few recommended alterations as discussed in the paper such as setting a de minimis threshold and expanding its scope) is better suited for South Africa to adopt in addressing the tax challenges in the digital economy.

Keywords Digital economy · Jurisdiction to tax · Tax challenges · Tax nexus · Article 12B · Amount A · Pillar One

K. Sengwane (✉)
University of Pretoria, Pretoria, South Africa
e-mail: Khodani.tshidzumba@up.ac.za

T. Moloi (ed.), *Impacting Society Positively Through Technology in Accounting and Business Processes*, Springer Proceedings in Business and Economics,
https://doi.org/10.1007/978-3-031-84885-8_35

Introduction

Jurisdiction to tax refers to the legal and factual authority of a country to levy taxes on a person or on income (Ketchemin, 2002, p. 9). Before a country can levy tax on an amount, it must have the jurisdiction to tax such income, in that, there must be a basis or tax nexus (connection) between the amount and the country or a connection between the person who received the amount and the country (Legwaila et al., 2020, p. 27). South Africa's jurisdiction to tax rules applies a combination of the residency and source bases of taxation (Stiglingh, 2024:26). In terms of the residence basis of taxation, residents are taxed on their worldwide income despite the source of the income because they have an intricate connection to the country (Legwaila et al., 2020, p. 27). In terms of the source basis of taxation, persons are taxed on income that originates from the geographical confines of the country despite the residency of the person (Legwaila et al., 2020, p. 27).

According to section 1 of the Income Tax Act 58 of 1962 (ITA), South Africa can only tax the business profits of a company if the company is a South African tax resident or the business profits are from a South African source. The determination of South African tax residency or source rules largely require companies to be "physically present" in South Africa, for example having the place where key management and commercial decisions are made in South Africa or having a fixed place of business where the business of the company is carried on in the jurisdiction. The advent of digital companies that can operate virtually anywhere in the world without the need for a physical presence in a particular jurisdiction renders such tax rules inadequate to cover business profits generated by digital companies (OECD, 2015:54). This means that businesses can generate substantial economic benefits in South Africa without having a traditional "taxable nexus" in the country (OECD, 2015, p. 98). This challenge is not unique to South Africa but a worldwide issue. The ability for a business to be able to operate in a jurisdiction without any physical presence in such jurisdiction poses a direct tax challenge as profits that a digitalised business derives in a market jurisdiction remains untaxed because there is no tax nexus between the digitalised business and the market jurisdiction (Harpaz, 2021, p. 58).

In response to these challenges, there are several potential solutions that have been proposed to address the tax challenges posed by the digital economy. There are three main potential solutions that have been adopted internationally, namely, a Two-Pillar solution proposed by the OECD to be internationally consented to and implemented by countries; a withholding source tax developed by the United Nations (UN) in the form of a treaty provision, and unilateral measures adopted by different countries imposed on digital services. The focus of this paper is on "Pillar One Amount A" (Amount A), which forms part of the Two-Pillar solution and Article 12B of the UN model tax convention. Amount A aims to establish new tax nexus and profit allocation rules that do not rely on the physical presence of companies (OECD, 2020). Similarly, Article 12B suggests a method for allocating taxing rights concerning income derived from automated digital services (United Nations, 2021).

The objective of this paper is to conduct a comparative analysis of these two solutions to determine the most suitable approach for South Africa to address the jurisdiction to tax challenges posed by the digital economy. The paper sets out the methodology used, mentions the jurisdictions to tax challenges posed by the digital economy, analyses the two solutions (Amount A and Article B), compares the solutions against each other, and reaches a conclusion with recommendations.

Methodology

The paper uses a qualitative methodology, which involves a comprehensive analysis, interpretation, and synthesis of data to gain a deeper understanding of the problem at hand. As described by Jackson et al. (2007, p. 23–24), qualitative research focuses on exploring underlying reasons, opinions, and motivations, providing valuable insights into the subject matter. The research encompasses a critical examination of the UN Model Tax Convention and the OECD Pillar One report, alongside conducting an extensive literature review of authoritative textbooks, reports, peer-reviewed journal articles, policy papers, and pertinent electronic sources related to the topic. The data from the literature review is used to compare the two designs of the solutions specifically looking at their scope, nexus, profit allocation, and implementation. The focus of the study is on the income of companies, and there is no discussion on individuals.

Literature Review

Jurisdiction to Tax Challenges Posed by the Digital Economy

A company is resident in South Africa if it is incorporated in or has its place of effective management (POEM) in South Africa (Section 1 of the Income Tax Act 58 of 1962). The terms "incorporated" and "POEM" are not defined in the ITA. A company incorporated in terms of section 13 read with section 14 of the Companies Act 71 of 2008 is resident in South Africa mainly because its formation and incorporation are in South Africa. This is a formalistic test and does not depend on where the company operates or is managed (Tshidzumba-Sengwane, 2023). It is easy to manipulate the incorporation of the company in the digital economy as there is no requirement for the company to operate in South Africa (Olivier & Honiball, 2011, p. 24). Founders can choose to incorporate companies in low-tax jurisdictions and those companies can operate in other countries like South Africa without a physical presence (Eliffee, 2021:42–43). A company may be incorporated outside South Africa simply to avoid being a South African resident.

POEM has been interpreted as "the place where key management and commercial decisions that are necessary for the conduct of the entity's business are in substance made" (*Oceanic Trust Co Ltd NO v CSARS* unreported case no 22556/09 (WCC) 13 June 2011; South African Revenue Service Interpretation Note 6 (2023); paragraph 24 of the commentary to Article 4(3) of the 2014 OECD MTC). Due to advances in information, communications, and technology (ICT), global travel, and modern business practices, it is no longer necessary for meetings to be conducted in a physical location, meetings can be held virtually, and the participants of the meeting can be spread in various locations (SARS Interpretation Note 6, 2023, p.11). This then makes it hard to determine the POEM as there is no one location where the key management and commercial decisions are being made (Naicker, 2003. p. 3). Companies can also manipulate their POEM by choosing the ideal location to host meetings where key management and commercial decisions are made (Avi-Yonah, 1997, p. 520).

Non-resident companies are those that are not incorporated in South Africa, nor have their POEM in South Africa, or are deemed to be exclusively resident in another country in terms of a double tax treaty (see section 1 of the Income Tax Act 58 of 1962). Non-resident companies are liable for income tax in South Africa if the income they derive is from a South African source (section 1 of the Income Tax Act 58 of 1962). The term "source" is not defined in the ITA, and as such it is left to be interpreted by the courts (Olivier & Honiball, 2011, p. 11). The source of income in South Africa can be determined in terms of statutory provisions and common law principles. The statutory sources provisions are contained in section 9 of the ITA which specifies the source of a number of income streams (mostly passive income) such as royalties, dividends, and interest. For example, section 9(2)(a) of ITA provides that dividends are from a South African source if declared and paid by a South African company.

As legislation trumps common law, if the source of income is specified in section 9, there is no need to consider the common law position. However, the common law will be applicable in cases where the source of income is not dealt with in the legislation. The common principles are established in case law. In the classical case, *CIR v Lever Bros and Another* 1946 AD 411 442, the court held that to determine whether income is from a South African source, it must be established what the originating cause of the income is and then determine the location of the originating cause. In terms of double tax treaty allocation of taxing rights rules, the profits of a non-resident company may be taxed in South Africa if such profits are attributable to a permanent establishment (PE) in South Africa (Article 7(1) of the OECD MTC). Article 5(1) of the OECD MTC provides the general definition of a PE as a fixed place of business through which the business of an enterprise is wholly or partly carried on. In terms of Article 5(3) of the OECD MTC, a building site, construction, or installation project will also give rise to a PE if it lasts more than 12 months. A PE will also exist if there is a dependent agent in another country that acts on behalf of the company and habitually concludes or plays the principal role leading to the conclusion of contracts in the name of the foreign company (Article 5(5) of the OECD MTC).

Determining whether income is from a South African source largely depends on the place where the transaction occurs. "Place" has little meaning in the digital economy as it is hard to ascribe a particular place to transactions that occur online (Oguttu & Van der Merwe, 2005:313–314). This means that determining the place where the funds in respect of which the payment arises or is utilised may be difficult for online transactions (Gutuza, 2010, p. 329). This may result in the payment being sourced outside South Africa because the place where the funds are applied is not conclusively determined to be in South Africa. The PE is impacted by the digital economy as it requires some level of physical presence of an enterprise in a country, whether in the form of a fixed place of business in the country; construction or installation project, or dependent agents operating from the country before a PE can exist. The requirement of physical presence has become outdated in the digital economy and as such the current construct of the PE concept is inadequate to deal with the taxation of income in the digital economy.

OECD Pillar One Amount A as a Solution

Amount A represents a significant step in addressing the jurisdiction to tax challenges posed by the digital economy. It emerged as part of the OECD's efforts to tackle base erosion and profit shifting (BEPS). BEPS refers to schemes that aim to achieve low or zero taxation by moving profits from high-tax jurisdictions where the activities that generate those profits occur, to low-tax jurisdictions or by taking advantage of gaps in the interaction of domestic tax rules, resulting in corporate income that is not subject to taxation (OECD, 2013, p. 14). Amount A rules are contained in the Multilateral Convention to Implement Amount A of Pillar One (Pillar One MLC). Discussion of Amount A below is divided into the scope, nexus, profit allocation, and implementation.

Scope

Amount A proposes new tax nexus and profit allocation rules (OECD, 2020, p. 3). It extends taxing rights to jurisdictions where businesses operate and have a sustained presence *albeit* remotely without a physical presence (OECD, 2020, p. 3). Amount A will only apply to multinational enterprise (MNE) groups with a global turnover above 20 billion euros and profitability above 10% calculated using an averaging mechanism (Article 3(1) of the Pillar One MLC). This is referred to as the "covered group" or "in-scope MNEs". Where a group does not meet the thresholds but one of its segments disclosed in its consolidated financial statements meets the group revenue and profitability tests on a stand-alone basis, the segment will be in scope (Article 3(6) of the Pillar One MLC). Specific industries such as extractives, financial services, defence entities, and business that are only domestic orientated are excluded from the scope of Amount A (Articles 3(4) to 3(8) of the Pillar One MLC).

Amount A only applies to highly profitable MNEs as smaller MNEs may not meet the threshold (Rakotonirina, 2023:3). This means that the jurisdiction to tax challenges in respect of MNEs outside the threshold will remain unaddressed. Harpaz (2021, p. 96) recommends the removal of the global revenue threshold and the application of the new tax nexus based on market thresholds. He argues that the global revenue threshold materially narrows the scope of the proposal that aims to provide a long-term solution to the tax challenges of the digital economy and would only apply to a small set of businesses. He maintains that the global revenue threshold does not show significant and sustained involvement in the economy of a market jurisdiction, but this could be indicated by a market threshold. While the author of this paper agrees with Harpaz, the author acknowledges that the threshold is there to alleviate the administrative compliance burden for tax administrators and smaller MNEs that may not afford to comply with the tax rules. The author accordingly submits that the OECD should consider lowering the threshold.

Nexus and Profit Allocation

A market jurisdiction will be allocated the new taxing right in terms of the in-scope MNEs when such MNEs derive at least 1 million euros (250,000 euros for smaller jurisdictions with GDP lower than 40 billion euros) in revenue from that jurisdiction (Article 8 of the Pillar One MLC; OECD, 2021, p. 1). It should be noted that South Africa's GDP is currently around 346 billion euros (IMF, 2024) and in order for it to have a nexus to the MNE, the MNE must derive at least 1 million euros from South Africa. The purpose of the threshold is to limit the cost of compliance for MNEs (OECD, 2021, p. 1).

According to Article 4(1) of the Pillar One MLC, a market jurisdiction will be able to impose tax on the "Designated Payment Entity of the Covered Group" on the "Amount A Profit" of the Covered Group allocated to it in terms of Article 5 of the Pillar One MLC. The Designated Payment Entity of the Covered Group is defined in Article 2(l) of the Pillar One MLC as the Ultimate Parent Entity, provided that it is a resident of the market jurisdiction, or in all other cases, it will be the Group Entity identified using the rules stipulated in Section 3 of Annex B to the Pillar One MLC. Amount A Profit is the amount determined for a "Covered Group" by subtracting 10% of the Adjusted Revenues of the group from its profit before tax and multiplying it by 25%.

According to Article 5 of the Pillar One MLC, the portion of the Amount A Profit to be allocated to a market jurisdiction is determined by:

(a) multiplying the Amount A Profit of the Covered Group for the reporting period by the revenue of the Covered Group for the reporting period that are sourced to the market jurisdiction, divided by the Adjusted Revenues of the Covered Group for the reporting period and

(b) if the adjusted elimination profit (or loss) of the Covered Group in the market jurisdiction for the reporting period is more than or equal to EUR 50 million, subtracting the marketing and distribution profits safe harbour adjustment from the amount determined under subparagraph (a)

The marketing and distribution profits safe harbour adjustment in a Covered Group shall be the lower of:

- the amount established by multiplying the Amount A Profit of the Covered Group for the reporting period by the revenue of the Covered Group for the reporting period that are sourced to the market jurisdiction, divided by the Adjusted Revenues of the Covered Group for the reporting period and
- the adjusted jurisdictional excess profits of the Covered Group in the Jurisdiction multiplied by the jurisdictional offset percentage (Article 5(2) of the Pillar One MLC)

Article 5(2)(c) of the Pillar One MLC provides that the adjusted jurisdictional excess profits shall be "the higher of zero or the adjusted elimination profit (or loss) for the Covered Group in the Jurisdiction for the Period minus the higher of:

- the Elimination Threshold Return on Depreciation and Payroll of the Covered Group multiplied by the Jurisdictional Depreciation and Payroll of the Covered Group in the Jurisdiction for the Period and
- 3 percent of the Adjusted Revenues of the Covered Group that are sourced under Article 6 to the Jurisdiction for the Period".

Article 5(2)(d) read with Article 5(2)(e) of the Pillar One MLC provides that the jurisdictional offset percentage shall be 90% for "jurisdiction in which the ratio of Jurisdictional Depreciation and Payroll to the Adjusted Revenues sourced to the Jurisdiction under Article 6 is less than 75 per cent of the ratio of the sum of the accounting depreciation and accounting payroll of the Covered Group determined under Annex B Section 5 to the Adjusted Revenues for the Covered Group" and 25% where the Jurisdiction is a Lower Income Jurisdiction and 35% in all other cases.

The portion of Amount A to be allocated to a market jurisdiction will be reduced by the product of:

- the total of Amount A allocated to the market jurisdiction pursuant to Article 5 of the Pillar One MLC and
- the amount obtained from dividing the sum of the Amount A relief amount with respect to which the obligation to provide relief from double taxation is allocated to any relieving jurisdiction under Article 11 by the Amount A relief amount of the Covered Group (Article 4(2) of the Pillar One MLC)

Article 6 of the Pillar One MLC provides the sourcing rules that determine the jurisdictions where the Adjusted Revenues of a Covered group are treated as arising.

There are sourcing rules for different categories of Adjusted Revenues. The specified categories of revenues are:

- finished goods
- digital content
- components
- services (location-specific services, advertising services, online intermediation services, passenger transport services, cargo transport services, customer reward programmes, and other services)
- intangible property (relating to finished goods, components, services, and digital content)
- user data
- immovable property
- government/international organisation grants and
- non-customer revenues (See Paragraph 230 of the Explanatory Statement to Pillar One MLC)

The categories depend on the ordinary or predominant character of the transactions that give rise to the Adjusted Revenues on the basis of their substance and not legal form (Article 6(1)(b) of the Pillar One MLC). Each jurisdiction shall require the Group Entities of a Covered Group to apply a reliable method to determine the sources of all Adjusted Revenues of the Covered Group from each category of transactions in which it engages (Article 6 of the Pillar One MLC). A reliable method refers to the use of reliable information that is available to the MNE and allocation keys specified in the rules.

Article 7 of the Pillar One MLC provides the principles that should be applied to determine the jurisdictions in which the Adjusted Revenues of a Covered Group shall be treated as arising. Article 7 provides, amongst others, that the source of Adjusted Revenues generated from–

(a) the sale of finished goods is the jurisdiction in which the finished goods are delivered to the final customer.
(b) the provision of digital content that is not a component described in (c) is in the jurisdiction where the services is used.
(c) the sale of a component that is designed to be incorporated into a finished product that will be sold is the jurisdiction where the finished product containing the component is delivered to the final customer.
(d) the provision of services depends on the type of service. For example, the source of the provision of online advertising services arises in the jurisdiction in which the viewer of the advertisement is based, whereas the provision of services that are connected to tangible property is sources in the jurisdiction where the tangible property is situated.

Implementation

Amount A taxing right will be implemented using a multilateral convention (MLC) (OECD, 2020:14). The objective is for the MLC to enter into force during 2025 (OECD, 2022:5). The MLC will come into force once it has been ratified by at least 30 countries accounting for at least 60% of the ultimate parent entities (UPEs) of businesses expected to be in scope for Amount A (OECD, 2023a, 2023b:3). The representation of UPEs is determined on a points system reflecting the estimation of the number of very large in-scope multinationals per country. Since the USA has the largest number of in-scope MNEs, it must ratify the multilateral convention for the Amount A rules to take effect (Brauner, 2021). This means that the success of Amount A relies on the USA getting on board. This might be unlikely to happen as it would result in the USA giving away its taxing rights to foreign jurisdictions (Christensen, 2023). While the Biden administration supports Pillar One, it will be difficult to get Congressional approval for the MLC (Christensen, 2023). The USA needs a two-third majority in the Senate to ratify the MLC. The Senate Republicans have made it clear that they want to protect America's sovereignty. Some feel that Amount A would result in a global tax surrender which will allow foreign governments to tax revenue of USA companies. It is also still to be determined what the view of the Congress to be formed after the November 2024 elections will be on Amount A.

The rules will be stand-alone provisions and will not abolish the existing nexus rules. Amount A rules are not a replacement to the existing tax rules but applies in addition to those rules (OECD, 2020:13). However, in order for Amount A to apply there has to be some modification of some rules. For example, the business profits of a company are taxable in the resident country and would only be taxable in the source country if there is a PE. Amount A allocates taxing rights despite the existence of a PE. Articles 5 and 7 would have to be modified in order to allow the allocation of taxing rights to market jurisdiction despite the existence of a PE (Bravo & Dozsa, 2021). Profit allocation in Amount A uses a formulaic approach, and as such the traditional transfer pricing principles will not apply (Bravo & Dozsa, 2021).

Article 38 of the Pillar One MLC read with Article 49(4) provides that countries may not apply digital service taxes (DSTs) and other similar measures listed in "Annex A" as from the first date of the next year that begins on or after the expiration of a period of 6 months from the date on which the Pillar One MLC comes into force for that country. Countries that impose DSTs or similar measures or fail to withdraw a DST or similar measure listed in "Annexure A" shall not be allocated any Amount A Profit or be able to impose tax under any domestic laws implementing the provisions of the Pillar One MLC. According to Article 39(2) of the Pillar One MLC, "DST or similar measure" refers to any taxes imposed by a country and meets the following criteria:

- The application of such tax, or the amount of tax imposed is determined primarily by reference to the location of customers or users or other similar market-based criteria.

- Such tax either applies solely to non-resident business or business that are primarily owned by non-residents, or applies revenue thresholds, exemptions for taxpayers subject to domestic corporate income tax in the country or other scope restrictions that has the effect of making it apply solely to non-residents.
- Does not fall within the ambit of any tax treaties entered into by the country.

The mere fact that a measure is listed in Annexure A does not of itself provide evidence that it meets the criteria set out in Article 39(2) of the Pillar One MLC. In turn, the fact that a measure is not included in Annexure A does not mean such measure does not meet the criteria set out in Article 39(2) of the Pillar One MLC. DST and other similar measure do not include:

- anti-avoidance rules that address artificial structuring to avoid creating a physical taxable presence in a country
- VAT, GST, sales taxes, and other similar taxes on consumption or
- generally applicable taxes imposed in terms of a transaction on a per unit or per transaction basis rather than on an ad valorem basis

Table 1 shows the measures listed in Annexure A to the Pillar One MLC.

Article 12B as a Solution

In 2020, the UN Subcommittee on Tax Challenges related to Digitalisation of the Economy proposed Article 12B of the UN Model Tax Convention (UN MTC) between Developed and Developing Countries (UN MTC) as an additional tax treaty provision to regulate the taxation of income generated from automated digital services (ADS). Article 12B was accordingly included in the 2021 UN MTC (United Nations, 2021). South Africa mostly uses the OECD model tax convention to negotiate its treaties but do also includes some articles from the UN MTC. The discussion of Article 12B is divided into the scope, nexus, profit allocation, and implementation.

Table 1 Measures listed in Annexure A to the Pillar One MLC

Country that implemented the measure	Description of measure
Austria	DST
France	DST
India	Equalisation levy on online advertisement services
India	Equalisation levy on e-commerce
Italy	DST
Spain	DST
Tunisia	DST
Türkiye	DST
United Kingdom	DST

Scope and Nexus

Article 12B grants market jurisdictions taxing rights in respect of the income of an MNE derived from providing ADS to customers located in the market jurisdictions (United Nations, 2021). Paragraph 5 of Article 12B of the UN MTC defines ADS as "any service provided on the internet or another electronic network, in either case requiring minimal human involvement from the service provider". It has not been discussed exactly how minimal human intervention will be measured. Paragraph 6 of Article 12B of the UN MTC sets out an exhaustive list of what constitutes ADS, and it includes online advertising services, online search engines, social media services, cloud computing services, supply of user data, and online teaching activities.

Income from ADS is deemed to arise in a source country if the underlying payments for the income from ADS are made by a resident of the country of source or a non-resident with a PE in the country of source unless the underlying payment is attributable to a PE outside the source country (United Nations, 2021). Accordingly, unlike the traditional jurisdiction to tax rules, Article 12B does not require "physical presence" but creates a nexus where there is ADS.

Profit Allocation

According to Article 12B(2), the income from ADS is generally taxable in the country where the supplier of the ADS is a resident, and it may also be taxable in the source country where the ADS arises. However, if the beneficial owner of the ADS payments resides in the other contracting country, the source country's tax on the ADS income must not exceed a specified maximum percentage of the gross income, as determined through bilateral treaty negotiations. The fact that the percentage to be levied is not set and up to contracting parties to negotiate might result in countries with more bargaining power deciding a rate that suits them best, for example, insisting on a low rate if most of their companies would be providing ADS to the other contracting state (Peeters & Waetens, 2022, p. 268).

Alternatively, the beneficial owner of the income generated from the supply of ADS may request the source country to subject its qualified profits from ADS for the year of assessment concerned with taxation at the source country's tax rate (Article 12B (3) of the UN MTC). Qualified profits are 30% of the amount resulting from applying the profitability ratio of that beneficial owner's ADS business segment (if the beneficial owner does not maintain segmental accounts, the overall profitability ratio of the beneficial owner will be used instead to determine the qualified profits) to the gross annual revenue from ADS derived from the source country (Article 12B (3) of the UN MTC). If the beneficial owner belongs to a multinational group, the profitability ratio to be applied will be that of the group or the ADS segment of the group if available (Article 12B (3) of the UN MTC). Chand and Vilaseca (2021, p. 6) have raised concerns about Article 12B's revenue sourcing rules limiting revenue allocation to developing countries in certain scenarios, such as triangular transactions, where the source of income depends on the location of the payer rather than the consumer of the ADS. For instance, in the case of online advertising, if a company in State S pays for online advertising provided by a company in State R, and the advertising is seen by consumers in State D, the income from the online advertising will only be taxable in States S and R, not in State D. Considering that Article 12B is a bilateral solution and not a multilateral solution, this can lead to abuse by companies structuring their affairs in such a way that payment for ADS comes from a country with no or limited tax on ADS (Peeters & Waetens, 2022, p. 258).

Implementation

Countries can adopt Article 12B by implementing provisions for taxing rights concerning ADS in their domestic law and by amending their treaties to include the provision through negotiations with other contracting states and negotiation to include provision to new treaties (ATAF, 2020). The provision is available to be used in bilateral tax treaties that states negotiate with each other. Bilateral tax treaties are treaties entered into between two contracting parties; for example, comprehensive double tax treaties on income and on capital (Olivier & Honiball, 2011:290). Since double tax treaties do not create taxing rights, domestic provisions allowing for taxing ADS have to be enacted. Countries could use digital services tax laws and other similar measures for this.

The use of a bilateral arrangement limits the possible wide adoption of the provision (Starkov & Jin, 2022, p. 3). For a country with many tax treaties, it might also be a time-consuming and administrative option that requires the use of resources and will also depend on the willingness of the other contracting states to incorporate the article (Peeters & Waetens, 2022, p. 268). Hadzovic (2021:66) notes that it is questionable if jurisdictions with a lot of digital MNEs that offer ADS, for example, the United States of America, would be interested in including Article 12B in their treaties with South Africa as that would mean it shares its taxing rights of such companies with South Africa and financially burden their resident companies.

Article 12B is a form of withholding tax. Withholding taxes are a simple and efficient way for tax administrators to collect taxes imposed on non-residents (Peeters & Waetens, 2022, p. 258). However, a concern is that it is easy for suppliers to pass over the cost of withholding taxes to the consumers by increasing the prices of the ADS to factor in taxes payable (Chand & Vilaseca, 2021:4). It should also be noted that withholding taxes imposed on ADS may be easy to implement in business-to-business ("B2B") models for example, the provision of online advertising but may face challenges in business-to-consumer ("B2C") models as individuals should not be expected to withhold taxes on behalf of the non-resident supplier (Chand & Vilaseca, 2021, p. 3). Chand & Vilaseca (2021, p. 5) give the example of B2C businesses that provide ADS, such as Netflix, Airbnb, Uber, and Amazon. It is submitted that an alternative collective method be considered for B2C transactions (Chand & Vilaseca, 2021, p. 5). The UN Committee suggests alternative mechanisms already adopted in some jurisdictions such as requesting the supplier to file tax returns where the tax obligation has been self-observed or requiring the financial intermediary used by the customer for making payments to withhold the tax (United Nations, 2021). These alternative measures are not without shortcomings and may have to be refined, for example, financial intermediaries may be foreign themselves or not always aware of the underlying transaction.

Findings

Comparative Analysis of Amount A and Article 12B

Amount A is one of the solutions proposed by the OECD to address the challenges the digital economy poses to tax rules, whereas Article 12B is the solution proffered by the UN. It should be noted that the OECD's main objective is to foster economic development and growth for its member countries which are largely developed economies, and the residence countries of many digital companies (Olivier & Honiball, 2011, p. 271). There is a concern about the OECD solutions (Amount A being one of them) largely protecting the interests of the OECD members to further its main objective, rather than the interests of developing countries like South Africa, that is largely a source country where digital companies operate. Unlike the OECD, the UN member states are a mixture of developing and developed countries, including many African countries like South Africa. The UN MTC entails rules that protect the interests of both developing and developed countries while providing more taxing rights to source countries, normally developing countries (United Nations, 2021). The commentary to article 12B of the UN MTC notes that many developing countries have limited administrative tax capacity and require simple and efficient methods to enforce tax imposed on the income of non-residents sourced in developing countries (United Nations, 2021).

The below table provides an overview of the comparison of Amount A and Article 12B in respect of scope, nexus, profit allocation, and implementation. The paper then discusses the comparison points in more detail (Table 2).

Scope

Both Amount A and Article 12B create a tax nexus without requiring "physical presence" of companies in the jurisdiction (OECD, 2020, p. 3). However, Amount A sets specific revenue thresholds for MNEs to fall within its scope, potentially leaving out smaller and medium-sized MNEs, which are vital for South Africa as a developing African country (Rakotonirina, 2023, p. 96). The author submits that what is considered a smaller MNE from a developed country's perspective may differ from that of developing African country like South Africa. It may be crucial for South Africa to

Table 2 Overview comparisons between Amount A and Article 12B

Category	Amount A	Article 12B
Scope	MNE group with a global turnover above 20 billion Euro and profitability above 10%	Provision of ADS
Nexus	MNE derives at least 1 million Euro (250,000 euros for smaller jurisdictions with GDP lower than 40 billion euros) in revenue from that jurisdiction.	Generally taxable in the country where the supplier of the ADS is a resident but may also be taxable in the source country where the ADS arises.
Profit allocation	25% of residual profit to be allocated to market jurisdictions with a nexus using various revenue-based allocation keys.	If the beneficial owner of payments resides in the other contracting country, the source country's tax on the ADS income must not exceed a specified maximum percentage of the gross income.
Implementation	Multilateral convention	Bilateral tax treaty

be able to tax the profits of MNEs that may appear smaller in the perspective of developed countries but be considered large from South Africa's standpoint.

On the other hand, Article 12B does not have a threshold, covering more businesses. It should be noted that the commentary on Article 12B UN MTC provides a default paragraph for countries that would like to include a threshold (based on the size of the taxpayer or revenues generated in the source country) and to exclude payments by individuals for personal use (similar to the exclusion of individuals acquiring services for personal use from the application of Article 12A UN MTC). Although a lack of a threshold may be beneficial in that more business may be covered under the ambit of the rules, Chand and Vilaseca (2021, p. 3) argue that the lack of any entry requirements for Article 12B of the UN MTC may lead to a disproportionate administrative burden for taxpayers and tax administrators as all businesses engaged in ADS will fall within the scope of the article regardless of their global revenue. However, it should be noted that having a threshold will not necessarily reduce entities' administrative burdens as the entities will then have to monitor whether they have met the local threshold in each country they provide ADS and which applies Article 12B (Chand & Vilaseca, 2021, p. 3). The author of this paper submits that as Article 12B is a treaty provision, South Africa as a contracting state could negotiate a suitable threshold that will in the first instance eliminate the administrative burden on smaller MNEs and in the second instance may take into account its interest in taxing certain "small" MNEs that are actually "large" in its eyes.

Amount A has a broader scope than Article 12B, in that Amount A is not limited only to any sector but applies quantitative threshold. However, Lammers (2020) submits that Amount A will not generate substantial revenue for developing countries (which includes South Africa). His findings are based on an analysis of the profits and profit margins of 10 of the world's largest digital companies. In terms of this, he found that developing countries could, on average, expect about

USD100,000 in extra tax revenue per billion in reallocated (residual) profit. This re-allocable profit would further have to be divided among eligible markets based on relevant local sales, meaning that most developing countries would get far less than larger, richer markets (Lammers, 2020).

Article 12B only focuses on ADS and as such does not carter for other digital economy business models and would be limited in addressing South Africa's challenges posed by the digital economy other than ADS. New digital businesses may arise in future and may not be covered if not ADS. Perhaps a closed list should not be used as law constantly playing catchup is not efficient. The digital economy is fast growing, and a solution ring-fencing it might face limitations in the future and may thus not be suitable for a growing and changing digital environment (Hadzovic, 2021, p. 54). The ring-fencing to only ADS also falls short of the principle of neutrality as other digital businesses that may not qualify as ADS will be left out of scope (Chand & Vilaseca, 2021, p. 3). Amount A covering more transactions will be more beneficial in that more revenue will be allocated to market jurisdictions instead of just the income from ADS. The author proposes that should South Africa choose to negotiate Article 12B into its treaties, it should consider broadening its scope.

Nexus

The Amount A nexus rules are restrictive and may exclude smaller economies (ATAF, 2021), whereas the nexus for Article 12B is the payment for the provision of ADS in a market jurisdiction. The main concern with Article 12B is that it focuses on the payment and does not consider circumstances where ADS may arise in market jurisdiction, but payment occurs in a third country to a supplier in a different country (ATAF, 2020). It is recommended that Article 12B's nexus and scope be amended to not only consider payment but also the consumer of the ADS. Article 12B has a less restrictive nexus to Amount A and is accordingly better for South Africa in that its taxing rights will not be hampered by the size of its economy. (See also ATAF, 2020).

Profit Allocation

Amount A rules are more complex than Article 12B in that, amongst others, they have various sourcing rules. Hadzovic (2021) submits that the rules are very complex and may not be easy to enforce and monitor for developing African countries tax administrators that may have low capacity and resources. Implementing Amount A may also result in administrative systems incurring major expenses for training their staff to apply and enforce the rules, which may be a blow for South Africa as an African country with limited financial resources (Rukundo, 2020). Whereas

Article 12B as a withholding tax makes it attractive for South Africa as withholding taxes are easier to implement for tax administrations (Hadzovic, 2021).

Implementation

In terms of implementation, Article 12B is integrated into the UN MTC, offering countries the option to incorporate it into their treaties and domestic laws. For a country like South Africa with about 79 tax treaties, this might be a time-consuming and administrative option that requires the use of resources and will also depend on the willingness of the other contracting states to incorporate the article (Hadzovic, 2021, p. 66). It is specifically questionable if jurisdictions with a lot of digital MNEs that offer ADS, for example, the USA, would be interested in including Article 12B in their treaties with South Africa as that would mean it shares its taxing rights of such companies with South Africa and financially burden their resident companies (Peeters & Waetens, 2022, p. 26; Hadzovic, 2021, p. 66), whereas Amount A will be implemented using an MLC. The author of this paper submits that Amount A being implemented using an MLC is convenient as it eliminates the administrative task of amending treaties individually, however, its effectiveness will depend on the number of countries interested in signing and ratifying the MLC. The author of this paper further submits that the UN should consider using an MLC approach to implement Article 12B to make the process more efficient. If possible, the existing OECD Multilateral Instrument to Implement Tax Treaty Related Measures to Prevent Base Erosion and Profit Shifting could be a useful and efficient tool to use and not have to design one specifically for Article 12B only.

Another consideration to note is that Article 12B requires domestic rules to be enacted that allow for the taxation of ADS. This might be considered as "DSTs and similar measures" under the OECD call to withdraw DSTs and other similar measures. Therefore, countries intending to adopt Amount A in which South Africa has indicated interest might be reluctant to adopt Article 12B. The call to withdraw DSTs and other similar measures seems to have the consequence of the OECD outlawing or rendering Article 12B unadoptable. This is something South Africa will have to consider. Amount A is still taking a long time to be finalised, whereas Article 12B is finalised and included in the 2021 UN MTC and ready to be used. South Africa which has not yet adopted unilateral measures will continue to lose out on tax revenue they could collect from companies in the digital economy if they wait for the finalisation of Amount A (See also ATAF, 2020). Article 38 of the Pillar One MLC requires countries to remove or not enact DSTs or similar measures in order for Amount A to apply to the countries. However, Pillar One does not offer a similar tax like DST for digital services and goods for companies that fall outside the scope of Pillar One. This means that countries may not have an effective measure to tax non-resident countries that do not create a taxable presence using traditional taxing rules.

Conclusion and Recommendations

The research findings highlight that both Amount A and Article 12B exhibit distinct merits and limitations. However, the author of this paper submits that Article 12B, with specific recommended modifications as outlined in this paper, emerges as a more favourable option for adoption by South Africa when compared to Amount A. The primary reasons for this preference are its relative simplicity and the potential for further negotiations among contracting states. The author proposes that, in addressing the tax challenges posed by digital companies, South Africa should carefully consider the adoption of Article 12B as a viable solution due to its advantages in terms of administrative simplicity and enforceability compared to Amount A.

In conclusion, the digital economy presents significant challenges to the current jurisdictional tax rules that require some physical presence to create a tax nexus. Businesses can derive substantial economic benefits from a country without having a traditional taxable presence there, such as a fixed place of business. To address these tax challenges in the digital economy, two sets of solutions have been proposed: Amount A and Article 12B. Amount A introduces new nexus and profit allocation rules for large MNEs based on revenue and profitability thresholds, regardless of physical presence. On the other hand, Article 12B is a double tax treaty rule designed to allocate taxing rights concerning income generated from automated digital services. Both Amount A and Article 12B offer potential solutions for South Africa to tackle the tax challenges in the digital economy, but they come with distinct strengths and weaknesses. This paper asserts that, with some necessary modifications, Article 12B would be a more suitable option for adoption by South Africa than Amount A. The primary reasons supporting this stance are the relative simplicity of Article 12B and its potential for further negotiation by contracting states, making it a more practical and viable choice for the region.

References

Avi-Yonah, R. S. (1997). International taxation of electronic commerce. *Tax Law Review, 52*, 507–556.

African Tax Administration Forum. (2020). *Technical review of the Draft Article 12B United Nation Model Tax Convention*. https://events.ataftax.org/includes/preview.php?file_id=81&language=en_US#:~:text=The%20draft%20Article%2012B%20states,by%20the%20business%27s%20profitability%20ratio

African Tax Administration Forum. (2021). *A new era of international taxation rules – What does this mean for Africa?* https://www.ataftax.org/a-new-era-of-international-taxation-rules-what-does-this-mean-for-africa

Brauner, Y. (2021). *Serenity now! The (not so) inclusive framework and the multilateral instrument*. University of Florida Levin College of Law Legal Studies Research Paper Series No. 22-6 1-44.

Bravo, N., & Dozsa, M. (2021). *A multilateral convention to implement amount a of pillar one Kluwer International Tax Blog*. https://kluwertaxblog.com/2021/12/03/a-multilateral-convention-to-implement-amount-a-of-pillar-one/

Chand, V., & Vilaseca, C. (2021). *The UN proposal on automated digital services: is it in the interest of developing countries?* Kluwer International Tax Blog, Wolters Kluwer. http://kluwertaxblog.com/2021/03/05/the-un-proposal-on-automated-digital-services-is-it-in-the-interest-of-developing-countries/

Christensen, R. C. (2023). *The Show must go on' PHD Skat.* https://phdskat.org/2023/10/17/the-show-must-go-on/

Elliffe, C. (2021). *Taxing the digital economy: Theory, policy and practice.* Cambridge University Press.

Gutuza, T. (2010). Tax and E-commerce: Where is the source? *South African Law Journal*, 328–338.

Hadzovic, E. (2021). *Taxing the digital economy in developing countries.* (Unpublished Master's thesis). Lund University.

Harpaz, A. (2021). Taxation of the digital economy: Adapting a twentieth-century tax system to a twenty-first century economy. *The Yale Journal of International Law, 46*(17), 57–101.

International Monetary Fund. (2024). *South Africa Data set.* https://www.imf.org/external/datamapper/profile/ZAF

Jackson, I. I., Ronald, L., Drummond, D. K., & Camara, S. (2007). What is qualitative research? *Qualitative Research Reports in Communication, 8*(1), 21–28.

Ketchemin, E. P. (2002). *A comparative analysis of the concept of fiscal jurisdiction in income law.* Doctoral dissertation, University of Cape Town.

Lammers, J. (2020). *Can developing countries do better than the unified approach?* https://www.ictd.ac/blog/developing-countries-unified-approach-digital-economy-tax/

Legwaila, T., Oguttu, A. W., Muller, E., Williams, R. C., Louw, C., & Surtees, P. I. (2020). *Tax law: An introduction.* Cape Town Juta & Co..

Naicker, K. (2003). *The taxation of e-commerce: An examination of the impact and challenges posed by electronic commerce on the existing tax regime.* Masters dissertation, University of Natal.

Oguttu, A. W., & Van der Merwe, B. (2005). Electronic commerce: Challenging the income tax base? *SA Merc LJ, 17*, 305–322.

Olivier, L., & Honiball, M. (2011). *International tax: A South African perspective* (5th ed.). Siber Ink.

Organisation for Economic Co-operation and Development. (2013). *Action plan on base erosion and profit shifting.* OECD Publishing. https://doi.org/10.1787/9789264202719-en

Organisation for Economic Co-operation and Development. (2015). *Addressing the tax challenges of the digital economy, action 1 – 2015 final report, OECD/G20 Base Erosion and Profit Shifting Project.* OECD Publishing.

Organisation for Economic Co-operation and Development. (2020). *Tax challenges arising from digitalisation – Report on pillar one blueprint inclusive framework on BEPS, OECD/G20 Base Erosion and Profit Shifting Project.* OECD Publishing.

Organisation for Economic Co-operation and Development. (2022). *Progress Report on Amount A of Pillar One, Two-Pillar Solution to the Tax Challenges of the Digitalisation of the Economy, OECD/G20 Base Erosion and Profit Shifting Project.* OECD Publishing.

Organisation for Economic Co-operation and Development. (2023a). *The multilateral convention to implement Amount A of Pillar One overview.* https://www.oecd.org/tax/beps/multilateral-convention-amount-A-pillar-one-overview.pdf

Organisation for Economic Co-operation and Development. (2023b). *The multilateral convention to implement Amount A of Pillar One.* https://www.oecd.org/tax/beps/multilateral-convention-to-implement-amount-a-of-pillar-one.pdf

Peeters, B., & Waetens, S. (2022). The United Nations response to the digitalisation and globalisation of the economy: The introduction of Article 12B into the UN Model Tax Convention. In J. Korving, N. Kerinc, & F. Souza de Man (Eds.), *Taxes crossing borders' (and tax professors too).* Maastricht University Press.

Rakotonirina, E. (2023). Digital taxation under the OECD Amount A and UN Article 12B mechanisms for market jurisdictions in Africa: A comparative analysis. *South Centre Tax Co-operation Policy Brief* no. 29, pp. 1–12.

Rukundo, S. (2020). *Addressing the challenges of taxation of the digital economy: Lessons for African countries*. ICTD Working Paper 105 (first published by the Institute of Development Studies in January 2020).

South African Revenue Service Interpretation Note 6 (2023/06/30) Issue 3.

Starkov, V., & Jin, A. (2022). A tough call? Comparing tax revenues to be raised by developing countries from Amount A and the UN model treaty article 12B regimes Research Paper 156 South Centre and Coalition for Dialogue on Africa 1–64

Stiglingh, M., Koekemoer, A. D., Van Heerdan, L., Wilcocks, J., & Van Der Zwan, P. (2023). *Silke: South African income tax*. Lexisnexis.

Tshidzumba-Sengwane, K. (2023). South Africa's response to digital economy's direct tax challenges—Part 1. *Obiter Law Journal, 44*(2), 366–382.

United Nations, UN Member States. https://www.un.org/en/about-us/member-states

United Nations Model Double Taxation Convention between developed and developing countries, 2021.

Benefits and Challenges of Utilizing Automation and Artificial Intelligence in Auditing Firms in South Africa

Justine Gomolemo Nkobane

Abstract We are living in a world where automation and artificial intelligence (AI) are being embraced by society at large as well as businesses operating in the public and private sectors. COVID-19 heightened the utilization of automation and AI in auditing procedures. Therefore, the purpose of this study is to investigate and identify the benefits and challenges of automation and AI in auditing faced by the auditing industry in applying AI technologies. Through the systemic review of literature and review of transparency reports of the Big 4 audit firms in South Africa, this study concluded that automation and AI are being utilized in the Big 4 audit firms with the intention to operate efficiently and effectively. The results revealed that the Big 4 audit firms are all using a digital audit methodology for the purpose of servicing clients and as a result are utilizing AI and automation in delivering this service. However, the study further found that the development of AI brings about both opportunities and challenges in auditing firms. The study also highlighted that auditing firms should continue integrating and developing new AI theories and improve the application of big data and cloud computing to continue improving audit quality and efficiency. The study concluded that the automation and use of AI are beneficial in ensuring that audit firms in South Africa improve audit quality and efficiency by ensuring that more focus can be placed on decision-making and reliance can be placed on automation and AI for more routine procedures. In contrast, the use of automation and AI is reducing the dependence on human labor as it gradually improves efficiency, thus resulting in resistance by employees.

Keywords Automation · Artificial intelligence · Audit and Big data

J. G. Nkobane (✉)
University of Johannesburg, Johannesburg, South Africa
e-mail: jgnkobane@uj.ac.za

T. Moloi (ed.), *Impacting Society Positively Through Technology in Accounting and Business Processes*, Springer Proceedings in Business and Economics,
https://doi.org/10.1007/978-3-031-84885-8_36

Introduction

The world we are living in is changing at a rapid pace and to participate South African firms need to continually transform their businesses. Audit firms are undergoing extreme advancements due to changes in data analytics and AI (Agnew, 2016). Automation and AI have gained popularity as it is being used in multiple sectors and across various fields and disciplines. Therefore, auditing is no exception as auditing firms in South Africa must use and manage automation and AI to remain competitive and innovative within their respective sector.

Automation is derived from the word automatic which means self-thinking or self-moving (Lombardi et al., 2015). The word automation was initially popularized in the manufacturing industry. Automation in auditing is currently being used for more repetitive transactional tasks, which allow auditors to use their professional judgement on more complex tasks (Lombardi et al., 2015). AI, on the other hand, is the outcome of successful applications of big data and machine learning technologies to understand the past and predict the future based on enormous data (Yu et al., 2018).

A study was done by Fedyk et al. (2022) where audit partners and national technology leaders were interviewed. Amongst the interviewees there were different experience tenures from 8 to 35 years (Fedyk et al., 2022). The results of the interviews revealed that all firms use technologies, e.g. robotic process automation, data analytics, and AI (Fedyk et al. 2022). Overall responses showed that the Big 4 as well as non-Big 4 audit firms use technology extensively (Fedyk et al. 2022). This shows that in audit firms AI and automation are being utilized therefore the gap that appears is determining whether it is more beneficial or not to continue using automation and AI in auditing firms.

A similar earlier study was done which focused on the application of big data analytics in Financial Auditing in the Big four auditing firms which followed a mixed method approach which indicated that 85% of respondents have experience in incorporating traditional data analytics into auditing, however less than 30% of them have used big data analytics in auditing (Haddara et al., 2018). Rakipi et al. (2021) study found that there was a positive correlation between data analytics use and IAF (International Accreditation Forum) reporting to the audit committee and Chief Audit Executives' ability to build positive relationships with managers. They also found a positive correlation between data analytics use and IAF's involvement in the assurance enterprise risk management, fraud detection, and IT risk audit activities (Rakipi et al., 2021).

Another study done by Ribeiro et al. (2021) indicated that the current 4IR we are experiencing today lives on the fusion of the Internet of Things, intelligent automation, intelligent devices and processes, and cyber-physical systems, where automation is used to improve business processes (Ribeiro et al., 2021). Lastly, a study done by Parker and Appel (2021) showed that the introduction of Robotics Process Automation (RPA) in businesses removed the repetitiveness of tasks for employees and overall productivity of teams increased; it further allows for businesses to rethink their business model and create more value.

This paper is motivated by the need for audit firms to perform quality audits in an efficient and effective manner and them utilizing automation and AI to do so. It was estimated in 2021 that AI will create a market well above $35 billion by 2025 and multiply annual economic growth rates (Schoeman et al., 2021). In South Africa, AI has been embraced by many entities, however plenty of work remains as South Africans like many other developing countries believe that embracing AI will eliminate their jobs and worsen the current income inequalities that exist (Schoeman et al., 2021).

The research question that results from the review of the above literature is that although audit firms in South Africa are embracing automation and AI, there seems to be reservations as well as concerns; this paper seeks to resolve these reservations and concerns.

The objective of the research is to highlight the benefits and understand the challenges of utilizing automation and AI in audit firms in South Africa to allow audit firms to embrace AI and automation more efficiently and reach global standards for utilization of automation and AI.

Literature Review

Automation and AI

Automation and AI have changed the way in which the world operates and specifically the world of business (Ali et al., 2022). Automation is defined by Nof (2009) as the art of making processes or machinery that is self-acting or self-moving. This technology is used to monitor and control the production and delivery of products and services. According to Antonoaie et al. (2017), automation processes are those used by businesses to speed up, analyze processes, and reduce manual labor. Automation is seen as more and more critical in today's times mainly because businesses are required to work through complex issues and improve productivity continuously (Antonoaie et al., 2017).

According to Zhou (2021), AI is defined as a theory, method, technology, and the application system that makes use of a computer or a machine to acquire knowledge or to utilize knowledge to acquire results. The following are some advantages of AI; firstly, AI has no personal biases that a human would have so there would be less motivation for fraud and work efficiency does not decline based on a person being physically tired (Zhou, 2021). In the traditional sense, if overtime labor was required this would cost more, however with AI this will not cost more even if the technology is used after hours when necessary. Another advantage is with the use of AI human error is eliminated because if the AI is programmed appropriately there will be a huge advantage of accuracy and as a result greater efficiency and work output (Zhou, 2021).

Accenture defined AI as different technologies that can be combined in different ways to sense, comprehend, act, and learn as per Fig. 1. Accenture has identified three factors that enable AI to flourish in recent years; the first being quantum leaps in computing power, driven by growth of cloud computing, second being an increase in big data which has in turn increased the annual growth rate as more devices have become connected (Schoeman et al., 2021). Lastly there needs to be a significant investment in research and development (R&D) of basic AI technologies (Schoeman et al., 2021).

Three key trends that have been identified from Accenture's technology division are adaptive workforce, ecosystem power plays, and AI as the UI (Schoeman et al., 2021). Since Covid-19 in March 2020, South African Audit firms were forced to adapt an agile core of workers that were allowed to work from home to complete audits and only meet when necessary and this hybrid work environment continues to take place. The current ecosystem power plays are that more businesses are making use of service providers to perform other non-core functionalities, and these seem to be unlocking strategic growth as well as value chains (Schoeman et al.,

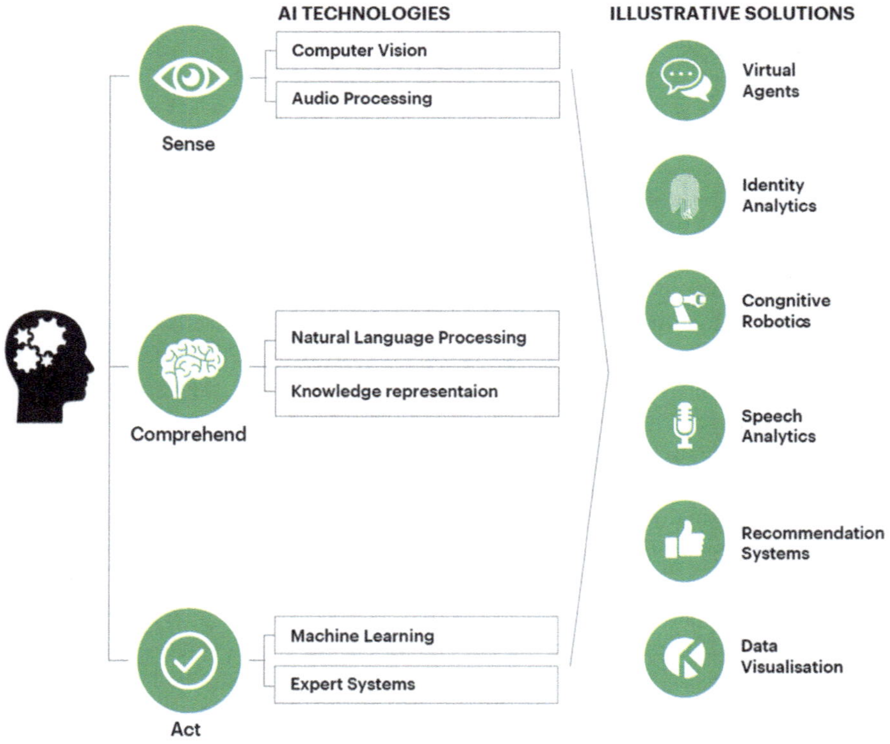

Fig. 1 Emerging AI technologies in South Africa. Source: Accenture's analysis (Schoeman et al., 2021)

Fig. 2 Economic impact of AI in South Africa. Source: Accenture's analysis (Schoeman et al., 2021)

2021). AI is becoming the face of a company's digital brand by ensuring it aligns itself with the needs and wants of customers, employees, etc. Figure 1 illustrates the emerging AI technologies as well as the illustrative solutions currently in South Africa as per Accenture (Schoeman et al., 2021).

AI is expected to have a positive impact on the economy; firstly, it is expected to assist existing labor to be more productive by supporting them with the use of machines. Secondly, it is expected to inspire innovation and creativity. Figure 2 illustrates the economic impact of AI in South Africa as per Accenture's expectations.

Technology development in automation of judgement systems that require human intervention in auditing and accounting is deemed to be more relevant to confront a transformation through RPA (Gotthardt et al., 2020). RPA and AI are two closely knit terms that both have a big impact on accounting and auditing practices (Gotthardt et al., 2020).

Big Data

According to De Mauro et al. (2016), there are various definitions of big data which come from various perspectives and denote the chaotic state of the art, and these are described in literature as a social phenomenon, information assets, data sets, storage technologies, analytical techniques, processes, and infrastructures. De Mauro et al. (2016) opted to analyze the existing definitions of big data to come to a more structured definition which is "Big data is the information asset characterized by such a high volume, velocity and variety to require specific technology and analytical methods for its transformation into value." Big data is used to ease the processing of data by companies and audit firms. In carrying out an audit acquiring large volumes of data is crucial from both an internal and external perspective and this data is normally of a sensitive nature with regard to audits.

Big data and data analytics create multiple opportunities and challenges for the external auditing profession (Balios et al., 2020). Dagilienė and Klovienė (2019) stated in a 2019 article that auditing firms had approximately 3 years of experience in the use of Big Data Analytics (BDA) tools and that the companies that made use of BDA did so because of a global strategy of IT innovations and to ensure quality audits. According to a descriptive qualitative research study done by Handoko et al. (2020), it was revealed that big data has both advantages and disadvantages to audits; the results of the study state that audit firms must be aware of obstacles that result due to big data analytics audits as these will reduce the pace at which big data audits are embraced. The analysis of big data sets, enabled by AI-powered analytics, overcomes the limitations of traditional audit sampling techniques and allows auditors to analyze larger, more diverse datasets (Antonoaie et al., 2017). According to Antonoaie et al. (2017), BDA will assist auditing in various ways firstly by reducing the risk of overlooking material misstatements and enhancing the sufficiency of audit evidence.

AI Technologies Used in Auditing in South Africa

Some studies were done with a focus on how AI is being used in auditing, one of these was Schulenberg (2007) who investigated how AI is being used in auditing through cognitive auditing; cognitive auditing is a computerized process that uses AI in auditing to find errors and issues in financial information. A more recent study was done by Gentner et al. (2018) which showed that AI is being used by auditors in their work field to detect errors faster, find patterns, and assist in making predictions. Ikechukwu and Nwakaego (2015) mentioned that AI is revolutionizing the auditing process and AI-enabled auditing software can now carry out complex audits efficiently and accurately than humans can. Today AI is applied in all accounting and auditing operations which has led to the reduction of the use of human accountants, however along with the progression of technology many jobs and professions are eliminated while others are created (Ali et al., 2022). This shows why AI has become vital in auditing and being applied more and more.

A mixed method study by Haddara et al. (2018) was done which revealed that 80% to 50% of the auditors indicated that there are clear guidelines in their audit firms to adopt more data analytics and big data analytics in the future which indicates that there is a huge future ahead for AI, big data, and other technologies.

South African Institute of Chartered Accountants (SAICA) believes that technology is very important for audit and assurance and specifically automated tools and techniques that are used in performing audit procedures (SAICA, 2021). SAICA (2021) has developed an Accounts Production and Accounting Software Guide for Practitioner which is meant to assist with selecting appropriate software for accounts further demonstrating how SAICA has embraced technology.

Saaleha Akoojee CA (SA) partner at PWC has indicated that although AI and machines can increase the quality of audits it should not replace human auditors as humans benefit from high speed and accuracy with which machines can analyze large data sets and give insights allowing humans hands to perform more complex work that requires judgement and professional skepticism (Akoojee, 2021). Akoojee (2021) further predicted that 30% of corporate audits will be carried out by machine learning and AI platforms by the year 2025. The use of AI now is making the accounting profession easier, more precise, and much more efficient (Ali et al., 2022). According to Antonoaie et al. (2017), a collaboration between auditors and data scientists is vital to create transparent and explainable AI models that align with auditing standards and regulations.

The auditing profession has gone through a lot of scrutiny over the years due to fraudulent financial reporting that was not detected and reported timeously and therefore the auditing profession can benefit from the utilization of machine learning, AI, and other technologies in their audits to gain back the trust of investors and creditors.

Advantages and Disadvantages of Utilizing AI in Auditing

The integration of AI technologies in auditing holds immense potential for transforming the profession (Antonoaie et al., 2017). Auditing systems as well as client accounting systems have moved from the previous paper entries and ledgers to computer-based data formats and systems entries powered with AI to ensure efficiency (Ali et al., 2022). AI technologies are used to integrate both accounting and auditing processes to the business (Ali et al., 2022). In a traditional audit environment from client acceptance to issuing an audit report auditors would rely on their audit experience and professional competence to complete an audit and a lot of time would be spent doing repetitive tasks and basic tasks (Schiefer et al., 2003).

As per Fig. 3 below, the audit work of a traditional audit firm consists of five steps listed below which were mostly manually completed:

Since AI has been utilized in audits various advantages have resulted by using big data, cloud computing, and many other technologies that allow the audit of financial data (Zhou, 2021). AI technologies used in auditing can extract valuable information from big datasets and compare variances in documents and allow for auditors to perform work that requires judgement thus creating more efficiencies (Issa et al., 2016). Big data is defined by De Mauro et al. (2015) as a technological ability to store aggregate, and process data. In simple terms, big data can be defined as the backbone or support for AI. Therefore, in an audit sense, for example, data collection is not limited and data can be collected using intelligence systems, robots, software systems and a wider range of data can be collected, e.g. images, videos, recordings and not just documents and spreadsheets therefore full samples can be tested if beneficial or even larger samples (Chowdhury, 2021). AI can also assist with changing the direction of an audit. AI audits have moved from just the

Fig. 3 Traditional audit workflow chart. Source: Authors illustration, information obtained from the review of literature

prevention, detection, and correction of fraud and error to more value adding services like offering results on how to improve the efficiency within the organization, providing predictive reports and forward-looking audit suggestions to assist management with their duties in future (Zhou, 2016). The limitation of cost–benefit of carrying out an audit is lifted because AI technology can assist with saving time and labor costs while still ensuring that the appropriate audit evidence is obtained.

Like with every good thing in life it brings about new challenges, therefore the use of AI, big data, cloud computing also brings out challenges. The use of AI brings about security risks and manipulation by phishers (Blauth et al., 2022). Another important risk is that the use and reliance on AI needs to be accompanied by professionals who know how to use these systems and tools appropriately and therefore thus creating a need to train professionals as well as university students so that they can utilize these systems appropriately (Blauth et al., 2022). In July of 2017, a discussion was held in South Africa by Accenture as well as the GIBS Business School which identified some concerns which are holding South Africans back from fully embracing AI which included data quality, data privacy, workforce readiness, and re-skilling, as well as potential job loss (Schoeman et al., 2021). As early as 2014, a study by Alex et al. (2014) indicated that Accountants may be at risk of being replaced by AI software systems, which made professionals reluctant to embrace it.

Research Methodology

This research is descriptive and uses secondary data. This study employed a desk review to investigate the challenges and benefits of automation and AI systems in South African auditing firms. A desk review, as defined by Travis (2016), is a form of secondary research that summarizes and collates previously collected data. A systemic review of literature was done to explore the utilization of automation and AI in auditing firms in South Africa today. Data from Google Scholar database and company websites of the Big 4 audit firms were analyzed, thus KPMG, PWC, EY, and Deloitte Transparency reports will be analyzed in detail to identify automation and AI systems used by these companies in carrying out audits.

Data

A systematic review of information is required when there is a huge amount of information available for a given topic, this strategy entails gathering important information in a systematic manner (Aaron, 2008). As a result, company websites of the Big 4 firms were inspected for transparency reports and these were downloaded for 2022 and 2021 and inspected using a keyword search of automation and AI. Secondly, applicable articles and journals on automation and AI in South Africa and globally were inspected. Peer-reviewed studies published during the last 10 years, media stories, reports on benefits and challenges of automation and AI, Internet blogs discussing BDA were among the literature sources we used. Some of the documents consulted are summarized in Fig. 4.

Figure 4 above summarizes the resources used in the research. Peer-reviewed publications published within the last 10 years, press reports, articles, conference proceedings, policy recommendations, and monographs were among the secondary sources we used.

Results

Results from the review of literature highlight that since the COVID-19 lockdown, South African audit firm's employees were forced to adapt a hybrid work environment that allowed them to work from home to complete audits and only meet when necessary. Automation and AI are becoming the face of audit firms by ensuring it aligns itself with the needs and wants of customers, employees, etc. Automation and AI are being used in business and auditing more and more to make processes more efficient and effective. The advantages of AI are that there are no personal biases that a human would have so there would be less motivation for fraud. Work efficiency will not decline based on a person being physically tired when AI is used. AI is expected to have a positive impact on the economy as illustrated in Fig. 2 in the literature review above.

Big data and data analytics generate various opportunities and challenges for external auditors. Big data has both advantages and disadvantages to audits, and for auditors to perform their duties effectively they need to embrace the challenges and work on mitigating the disadvantages. BDA allows for auditors to work with large

Fig. 4 Documents consulted in the systematic literature review. Source: Author's analysis of literature

data sets in a short time frame and allows for full population testing instead of sample testing.

The review of literature further reveals that AI is being used by auditors in their work environment to detect errors faster, find patterns, and assist in making predictions, this is being done to aid with fraud detection as it has been a major issue in recent years. Auditors have also communicated that there are clear guidelines in their audit firms to adopt more data analytics and big data analytics in the future and this is part of their company strategy.

There are various benefits as well as challenges to utilizing and adopting AI in auditing firms. Some of the key benefits are that AI technologies used in audit can extract valuable information from big datasets and compare variances across different documents and allow for auditors to perform work that requires judgement thus creating more efficiencies. The normal limitation of cost–benefit of carrying out an audit is lifted because AI technology can assist with saving time and labor costs while still ensuring that the appropriate audit evidence is obtained. However, like with all things the use of AI brings about some challenges like security risks, reputational damage, and the risk of being attacked by cyber criminals. Other challenges may be additional costs to train staff to use this technology as well as continue training and improving the usage of this technology. Staff members may lose their work moral due to them feeling like the utilization of AI technologies is taking over their work duties and replacing them.

The results from the inspection of the transparency reports of the big 4 audit firms Deloitte, EY, KPMG, and PWC revealed that all these audit firms are embracing digital audits more and they all have a unique platform that they use to perform digital audits (Deloitte, 2021, 2022; EY, 2021, 2022; KPMG, 2021, 2022; PWC, 2021, 2022).

Since the Covid-19 lockdown Deloitte has allowed virtual working and a hybrid work environment as an agile response to this disruption (Deloitte, 2022). Deloitte (2022) has rapidly adjusted to the changing world and audit teams are empowered by advanced tools and technologies and a new data management platform is being utilized which is called Cortex which is built to support data of all sizes. Deloitte (2022) is making use of real-time audit quality. Deloitte Global has released Deloitte Omnia, our next generation cloud-based audit delivery platform, as well as Deloitte Levvia, a tailored solution to support their non-complex audits.

EY was able to respond to the limitations caused by the Covid-19 lockdown as EY South Africa was able to respond rapidly to these changes as it utilized already existing digital systems (EY, 2021). EY (2021) is making use of a digital audit approach which has automated routine tasks and processes, EY Canvas audit program is being used and is aligned to the digital audit methodology. According to EY's Transparency Report the company is continuously developing automations and AI bot technology to drive standardization and consistency (EY, 2021). EY has deployed leading technological tools that enhance the quality and value of our audits, including the EY Canvas online audit platform, EY Helix analytics platform, and EY Atlas research platform.

KPMG CLARA assisted with coping with lockdown restrictions. CLARA provided a platform for sharing the latest technology-enabled data analytics, AI and RPA in audits while remote working was occurring. KPMG (2021) utilizes KPMG CLARA which is a cloud-based audit methodology and technical tool. KPMG CLARA provides a platform for sharing latest technology-enabled data analytics, AI and RPA in audit routines specific to our client industries (KPMG, 2021). As per KPMGs transparency Report KPMG CLARA enables technologies such as AI, block chain and cognitive capabilities. KPMG has implemented a global transition for very small and less complex national audits from e-audit to KPMG Clara (KPMG, 2022).

PWC was also able to adjust to Covid-19 lockdown restrictions with the assistance of their existing digital technology and was able to work remotely. PWC (2022) developed a Real-Time Quality Assurance (RTA) program designed to provide support to engagement teams on audits. PWC also makes use of Aura which is a global audit documentation platform and Halo which is a data auditing tool used to test large volumes of data or to test a population (PWC, 2022).

Table 1 Platforms and tools used to carry our digital audits across the Big 4 firms

Tools/platforms/technologies utilized	Deloitte	EY	KPMG	PWC
Cloud-based audit platform	Deloitte Omnia Deloitte Levvia	EY Canvas	KPMG CLARA	Aura
Documentation analyzing platform	Cortex	EY Helix analytics platform	KPMG CLARA	Halo

Source: Authors illustration of information obtained from the review of literature

Table 1 below shows a summary of the Tools, platforms and technologies utilized. The big four audit firms have chosen to automate audit procedures and processes to reduce the burden on clients and allow teams to focus on areas that require more focus and judgement (Deloitte, 2021, 2022; EY, 2021, 2022; KPMG, 2021, 2022; PWC, 2021, 2022).

Discussion

The results from the review of literature show that AI is being embraced in SA largely because it eliminates human error and promotes the advantage of accuracy and efficiency. Accenture has identified three factors to enable AI growth, firstly growth in computing power, an increase in big data, and significant investment in R&D of AI technologies. Accenture further forecasted that economic growth with AI is much greater than without AI in South Africa as per Fig. 2.

It has been noted that big data analytics is being utilized in South Africa for the past few years and to continue doing so successfully audit firms must be aware of both advantages and disadvantages of its usage.

It has been revealed that AI is revolutionizing the auditing process and AI-enabled auditing software is now able to carry out complex audits efficiently and more accurately.

SAICA has embraced technology, and this can be seen in an accounts production and accounting software guide for practitioners which they developed to assist practitioners which they developed to assist with selecting appropriate software for accounts. An audit partner at PWC has predicted that 30% of corporate audits will be carried out by machine learning and AI platforms by 2025.

The benefits and challenges of the utilization of automation and AI in audit firms in South Africa as per a review of literature is summarized below in Table 2.

The results from the inspection of the transparency reports of the Big 4 Audit firms reveal that all four firms are making use of AI and automation to provide audit and assurance services to clients.

All four firms have their how digital audit methodology that is being used and are utilizing a cloud-based audit platform to carry out audits as well as real-time audit

Table 2 Benefits and challenges of utilizing automation and AI in Audit Firms in South Africa

Benefits	Challenges
AI technologies can extract valuable information from big data sets and compare variances in documents, allowing audits to be performed more efficiently.	Use of AI, big data, and automation brings about new challenges to audits being security risks and possible manipulation by phishers.
Larger samples or entire population testing can be tested when utilizing AI and Big data in audits.	Reliance and use of AI technologies requires professionals who know how to use the systems and tools appropriately.
Different data can be collected using intelligence systems, robots, and software, e.g. images, videos, and recordings	Staff constantly needs to be trained to be able to use AI technologies that are utilized.
AI technologies can assist with saving time costs and labor costs for audit teams.	Some employees believe that embracing AI technologies will result in job losses for them.

Source: Authors review of literature

quality assurance programs to ensure that best quality audits are carried out. EY utilizes EY CANVAS as a cloud-based audit platform, EY client portal as a cloud-based storage of information, and EY HELIX is being utilized as an analytics suite where audit procedures are enabled with data analytics. KPMG has one platform CLARA that is utilized for analyzing documents as well as an auditing platform, whereas all the other firms have different platforms for documentation storing and analyzing. All four firms indicated that covid-19 lockdown accelerated the use of digital audit tools that already existed and remote working.

Conclusion

The development of AI brings about both opportunities and challenges to auditing firms. Auditing firms should continue integrating and developing new AI theories and improve the application of big data and cloud computing to continue improving audit quality and efficiency.

Some of the key benefits of using AI and automation is the efficiency it brings to an audit for example through enabling quicker and bigger extracts of data, tools like variances analysis and comparisons, allowing for the testing of larger samples or entire data sets, and lastly allowing for usage of different data sources for evident such as images, videos and recordings.

The key challenges due to utilizing automation and AI are security risks and manipulation by phishers that need to be managed. Using AI requires trained professionals managing it and training staff members gradually as well to keep up with the changes. Lastly employees buy-in and loss of morale are major challenges.

The following are emerging AI technologies: computer vision, audio processing, natural language processing, machine learning, and expert systems. Future research can be directed toward enabling AI solutions like cognitive robotics (robots that can learn from experiences and the environment), speech analytics (software that recognizes patterns in speech, be able to understand emotions expressed in speech), identity analytics (solutions that assist with defining access to critical data systems based on information from authoritative systems), and data virtualization (an app that is able to retrieve and manipulate data regardless of the format or where it is stored) and audit firms can invest time and resources in these technologies that will improve their audits.

Limitations of the Study

The limitation of the study is that the data utilized is secondary information as per the transparency reports of the Big 4 audits firms as this information is historic. Secondly the information was also limited to a systematic literature review.

Future Research

Future research can be focused on how far in the past few years audit firms have implemented automation and AI relative to other countries globally and this can be done via interview with relevant parties within audit firms.

References

Aaron, L. (2008). Writing a literature review article. *Radiologic Technology, 80*(2), 185–186.

Agnew, H. J. F. T. (2016). Auditing: Pitch battle. *Financial Times, 5*, 2016.

Akoojee, S. (2021). *AI (Artificial Intelligence) in auditing*. Accessed January 15, 2024, from https://www.uj.ac.za/event/ai-artificial-intelligence-in-auditing/

Alex, H., Fogel, K., Wilbank, C., Benard, G., & Serge, M. (2014). *AI, robotics and the future of jobs*. Pew Research Centre.

Ali, S. M., Hasan, Z. J., Hamdan, A., & Al-Mekhlaf, M. (2022, March). Artificial intelligence (AI) in the education of accounting and auditing profession. In *International Conference on Business and Technology* (pp. 656–664). Springer International Publishing.

Antonoaie, V., Irimeş, A., & Chicoş, L. A. (2017). ERP processes automation in corporate environments. In *MATEC Web of Conferences* (Vol. 94, p. 06001). EDP Sciences.

Balios, D., Kotsilaras, P., Eriotis, N., & Vasiliou, D. (2020). Big data, data analytics and external auditing. *Journal of Modern Accounting and Auditing, 16*(5), 211–219.

Blauth, T. F., Gstrein, O. J., & Zwitter, A. (2022). Artificial intelligence crime: An overview of malicious use and abuse of AI. *IEEE Access, 10*, 77110–77122.

Chowdhury, E. K. (2021). Prospects and challenges of using artificial intelligence in the audit process. *The Essentials of Machine Learning in Finance and Accounting*, 139–156.

Dagilienė, L., & Klovienė, L. (2019). Motivation to use big data and big data analytics in external auditing. *Managerial Auditing Journal, 34*(7), 750–782.

De Mauro, A., Greco, M., & Grimaldi, M. (2015, February). What is big data? A consensual definition and a review of key research topics. In *AIP conference proceedings* (Vol. 1644, No. 1, pp. 97–104). American Institute of Physics.

De Mauro, A., Greco, M., & Grimaldi, M. (2016). A formal definition of Big Data based on its essential features. *Library Review, 65*(3), 122–135.

Deloitte and Touche South Africa. (2021). *Audit Regulatory Transparency Report*. Accessed December 8, 2022, from https://www2.deloitte.com/za/en/pages/audit/articles/audit-transparency-report.html

Deloitte and Touche South Africa. (2022). *Audit Regulatory Transparency Report*. Accessed December 8, 2022, from https://www2.deloitte.com/za/en/pages/audit/articles/audit-transparency-report.html

EY South Africa. (2021). *Transparency Report 2021*. Accessed December 7, 2022, from https://www.ey.com/en_za/assurance/south-africa-transparency-report-2021

EY Transparency Report, *EY*, 1, https://www.ey.com/content/dam/ey-unified-site/ey-com/en-gi/documents/ey-transparencyreport-2022.pdf (2022).

Fedyk, A., Hodson, J., Khimich, N., & Fedyk, T. (2022). Is artificial intelligence improving the audit process? *Review of Accounting Studies, 27*(3), 938–985.

Gentner, D., Stelzer, B., Ramosaj, B., & Brecht, L. (2018). Strategic foresight of future b2b customer opportunities through machine learning. *Technology Innovation Management Review, 8*(10), 5–17.

Gotthardt, M., Koivulaakso, D., Paksoy, O., Saramo, C., Martikainen, M., & Lehner, O. (2020). Current state and challenges in the implementation of smart robotic process automation in accounting and auditing. *ACRN Journal of Finance and Risk Perspectives*.

Haddara, M., Su, K. L., Alkayid, K., & Ali, M. (2018). Applications of big data analytics in financial auditing-A study on the big four.

Handoko, B. L., Mulyawan, A. N., Tanuwijaya, J., & Tanciady, F. (2020). Big data in auditing for the future of data driven fraud detection. *International Journal of Innovative Technology and Exploring Engineering, 9*(3), 2902–2907.

Ikechukwu, O. I., & Nwakaego, D. A. (2015). The effect of accounts payable ratio on the financial performance of food and beverages manufacturing companies in Nigeria. *Journal of Research in Business and Management, 3*(9), 15–21.

Issa, H., Sun, T., & Vasarhelyi, M. A. (2016). Research ideas for artificial intelligence in auditing: The formalization of audit and workforce supplementation. *Journal of Emerging Technologies in Accounting, 13*(2), 1–20.

KPMG. (2021). *Transparency Report 2021*. Accessed November 28, 2022, from https://home.kpmg/za/en/home/about/governance/transparency-report.html

KPMG Transparency Report, *KPMG*, KPMG Transparency Report (2022).

Lombardi, D. R., Bloch, R., & Vasarhelyi, M. A. (2015). The current state and future of the audit profession. *Current Issues in Auditing, 9*(1), P10–P16.

Nof, S. Y. (2009). Automation: What it means to us around the world. *Springer Handbook of Automation*, 13–52.

Parker, H., & Appel, S. E. (2021). On the path to artificial intelligence: The effects of a robotics solution in a financial services firm. *South African Journal of Industrial Engineering, 32*(2), 37–47.

PWC South Africa. (2021). *Transparency Report 2021*. Accessed November 28, 2022, from https://www.pwc.co.za/en/about-us/transparency-report.html

PWC South Africa. (2022). *Transparency Report 2022*. Accessed November 28, 2022, from https://www.pwc.co.za/en/about-us/transparency-report.html

Rakipi, R., De Santis, F., & D'Onza, G. (2021). Correlates of the internal audit function's use of data analytics in the big data era: Global evidence. *Journal of International Accounting, Auditing and Taxation, 42*, 100357.

Ribeiro, J., Lima, R., Eckhardt, T., & Paiva, S. (2021). Robotic process automation and artificial intelligence in industry 4.0–a literature review. *Procedia Computer Science, 181*, 51–58.

SAICA. (2021). *ACCOUNTS PRODUCTION AND ACCOUNTING SOFTWARE GUIDE FOR PRACTITIONERS*. Accessed April 10, 2024, from https://saicawebprstorage.blob.core.windows.net/uploads/resources/Software-Guide-for-Practitioners.pdf

Schiefer, J., Jeng, J. J., & Bruckner, R. M. (2003, September). Real-time workflow audit data integration into data warehouse systems. In *ECIS* (pp. 1697–1706).

Schoeman, W., Moore, R., Seedat, Y., & Chen, J. Y. J. (2021). Artificial intelligence: Is South Africa ready?

Schulenberg, J. L. (2007). Analysing police decision-making: Assessing the application of a mixed-method/mixed-model research design. *International Journal of Social Research Methodology, 10*(2), 99–119.

Travis, D. (2016). *Desk research: The what, why and how*. Accessed February 16, 2022, from https://www.userfocus.co.uk/articles/desk-resaerch-the-what-why-and-how.html

Yu, H., Yang, X., Zheng, S., & Sun, C. (2018). Active learning from imbalanced data: A solution of online weighted extreme learning machine. *IEEE Transactions on Neural Networks and Learning Systems, 30*(4), 1088–1103.

Zhou, G. X. (2016). Analysis of the problems that should be paid attention to in the leaving audit of natural resources assets. *Journal of Industry and Technology Forum, 22*, 229–230.

Zhou, G. (2021). Research on the development of CPA audit from the perspective of artificial intelligence. In *E3S Web of Conferences* (Vol. 251, p. 01056). EDP Sciences.

Unveiling the Pivotal Role of Diverse Representation in Audit Committees Across the Corporate Landscape

Natasha Singo and Collins Leke

Abstract This chapter addresses the often overlooked but critical contributions of a diverse group of women within audit committees. Set against the backdrop of the evolving discourse on gender diversity and inclusion in corporate governance, the study explores the nuanced nature of this area of research. This study employs a qualitative research methodology using existing literature. By utilizing empirical data analysis, the study delves into how these diverse women's perspectives and leadership styles impact decision-making processes, financial oversight, and overall corporate governance within audit committees. The results highlight the substantial influence of a diverse group of women in shaping corporate dynamics, providing specific insights derived from a systematic analysis of case studies and empirical data. This study offers valuable contributions to the ongoing dialogue on gender issues and corporate governance, emphasizing the necessity of a more inclusive and diverse approach for the success and sustainability of corporate practices globally. In conclusion, the research advocates for increased recognition and support for a diverse female representation in audit committees, emphasizing the broader benefits of diverse perspectives in fostering robust and sustainable corporate practices. As global corporations aim for greater inclusivity, understanding and acknowledging the pivotal role of a diverse group of women in audit committees become imperative for creating an equitable and effective corporate landscape.

Keywords Diversity · Audit committee · Corporate governance · Representation

N. Singo (✉) · C. Leke
University of Johannesburg, Johannesburg, South Africa
e-mail: nsingo@uj.ac.za; collinsl@uj.ac.za

T. Moloi (ed.), *Impacting Society Positively Through Technology in Accounting and Business Processes*, Springer Proceedings in Business and Economics,
https://doi.org/10.1007/978-3-031-84885-8_37

Introduction

In the realm of corporate governance, the spotlight has increasingly turned towards discussions on gender diversity and inclusion, acknowledging the pivotal roles that diverse perspectives play in shaping organizational dynamics (Al-Shaer & Zaman, 2016; Zalata & Roberts, 2016). While much attention has been rightly directed towards gender diversity on corporate boards, one area that has often been overlooked yet holds immense significance is the representation of diverse women within audit committees (Orazalin & Baydauletov, 2020). This chapter delves into this crucial but underexplored facet of corporate governance, shedding light on the profound impact that diverse women have within audit committees (Rezaee et al., 2003; Ud Din et al., 2021).

Against the backdrop of evolving discourse on gender diversity and inclusion, this study employs a qualitative research methodology, drawing upon existing literature and empirical data analysis to uncover the nuanced nature of diverse women's contributions within audit committees. Through a systematic examination of case studies and empirical data, the study explores how diverse women's perspectives and leadership styles influence decision-making processes, financial oversight, and overall corporate governance within audit committees.

The findings underscore the substantial influence of diverse women in shaping corporate dynamics, offering specific insights into their contributions to fostering robust and sustainable corporate practices. By advocating for increased recognition and support for diverse women within audit committees, this research emphasizes the broader benefits of inclusivity and diversity in driving organizational success and sustainability on a global scale.

As corporations worldwide strive for greater inclusivity and equity, understanding and acknowledging the pivotal role of diverse women within audit committees emerge as imperative steps towards creating a more equitable and effective corporate landscape. This chapter contributes valuable insights to the ongoing dialogue on gender issues and corporate governance, underscoring the necessity of embracing diversity for the advancement of corporate practices and the realization of organizational goals.

The Importance of Gender Diversity

Gender diversity in the audit committee is essential for promoting effective governance and decision-making within companies. By ensuring that audit committees are composed of members with diverse gender backgrounds, companies can benefit from a wider range of perspectives, experiences, and expertise (Oradi & Izadi, 2020).

One of the primary benefits of gender diversity in the audit committee is the variety of viewpoints it brings to the table. Different genders often have different life experiences and professional backgrounds, which can lead to more thorough discussions and better decision-making processes (Tinkler et al., 2015). When audit committees are diversified, they are better equipped to consider a broader range of factors when making important decisions related to financial reporting and auditing processes (Mwangi, 2018).

Furthermore, diverse audit committees are often more effective at problem-solving and risk assessment. Research has consistently shown that diverse groups are better at identifying and addressing risks than homogeneous groups (Harjoto et al., 2018). By including members of different genders on the audit committee, companies can enhance their ability to identify potential risks and develop effective strategies for mitigating them.

In addition to improving decision-making and risk assessment, gender diversity in the audit committee can also enhance corporate governance. Audit committees play a critical role in overseeing financial reporting processes and ensuring compliance with relevant regulations and standards (Ghafran & Yasmin, 2018). By including members of different genders on the audit committee, companies can ensure that a broader range of skills and experiences are brought to bear on these important governance functions (Pucheta-Martínez et al., 2016).

Moreover, gender diversity in the audit committee can increase stakeholders' confidence in the company's financial reporting processes. When audit committees are gender-diverse, stakeholders are more likely to trust that the committee is providing effective oversight and that the company's financial reports are accurate and reliable (Oradi & Izadi, 2020). This increased confidence can ultimately enhance the company's reputation and contribute to its long-term success.

Finally, ensuring gender diversity in the audit committee is not only beneficial for the company but also essential for compliance with regulations and best practices (Nekhili et al., 2020). Many regulators and governance organizations now emphasize the importance of gender diversity on corporate boards and committees, including audit committees. By ensuring gender diversity, companies can demonstrate their commitment to compliance and best practices, thereby enhancing their overall governance and reputation (Zaid et al., 2020).

Background

The historical perspective on gender diversity in audit committees reflects a gradual evolution shaped by changing societal norms, regulatory frameworks, and corporate governance practices (Uzma, 2018). In the past, audit committees were predominantly composed of male members, reflecting broader gender imbalances within corporate leadership structures. This lack of diversity was often attributed to traditional gender roles and biases that limited women's participation in corporate governance roles (Chijoke-Mgbame et al., 2020). As a result, audit committees were often homogeneous in terms of gender, which may have restricted the range of perspectives and experiences brought to bear on financial oversight and decision-making processes.

However, over the past few decades, there has been a growing recognition of the importance of gender diversity in corporate governance, including audit committees (McLaughlin et al., 2021). This shift has been driven by a variety of factors, including changing societal attitudes towards gender equality, increased awareness of the benefits of diversity, and regulatory reforms aimed at promoting gender diversity within corporate leadership.

Regulators and governance organizations have played a significant role in promoting gender diversity within audit committees by introducing various initiatives and guidelines aimed at increasing the representation of women in corporate leadership roles (Klettner et al., 2016). For example, many countries have introduced requirements or recommendations for companies to have a certain percentage of women on their boards, including audit committees.

As a result of these efforts, there has been a gradual increase in the representation of women in audit committees in recent years (Mnif Sellami & Cherif, 2020). Women are now increasingly being appointed to audit committee positions, bringing a broader range of perspectives, experiences, and skills to these critical governance roles.

While there is still progress to be made, the historical perspective on gender diversity in audit committees reflects a gradual shift towards greater inclusivity and diversity within corporate governance structures (Luh, 2024). As companies continue to recognize the importance of gender diversity in audit committees, it is expected that the representation of women in these roles will continue to increase, leading to more effective financial oversight and decision-making processes (Oradi & Izadi, 2020).

The rest of the paper is structured as such: in section "Existing Research Gaps and the Need for Further Exploration", we briefly review existing research on the impact of diverse women in audit committees. In section "Methodology", we provide an overview of the qualitative research methodology employed in this study. In section "Impact of Diverse Women Representation in Audit Committees", we discuss the impact of diverse women representation in audit committees on decision-making processes, financial oversight, and overall corporate governance. In section "The Significance of Diverse Representation in Audit Committees", we explore the broader implications of diverse representation in audit committees for corporate governance and sustainability. Finally, in section "Conclusion and Recommendations", we provide a conclusion and recommendations based on our findings.

Literature Review

Gender diversity within audit committees has gained increasing attention in recent years due to its significant impact on decision-making processes, financial oversight, and overall corporate governance. Research conducted by Adams and Ferreira highlighted the positive influence of gender-diverse audit committees on decision-making processes, emphasizing the unique perspectives and expertise that women bring to these roles. Similarly, studies by Cheng and Courtenay underscored the importance of gender diversity in enhancing financial oversight and promoting transparency and accountability within organizations. This literature review aims to explore the existing research on the role of diverse women in audit committees, identifying key findings and research gaps, and providing recommendations for future exploration.

Enhanced Decision-Making Processes Research conducted by Adams and Ferreira found that gender-diverse audit committees lead to improved decision-making processes. Women's different perspectives, experiences, and expertise contribute to more comprehensive analyses of financial issues and more robust decision-making within audit committees (Terjesen et al., 2016).

Improved Financial Oversight A study by Cheng and Courtenay showed that gender-diverse audit committees are better equipped to provide effective financial oversight. Diverse women's perspectives and leadership styles, characterized by collaboration, inclusivity, and attention to detail, enhance the effectiveness of audit committees in ensuring the accuracy and reliability of financial reporting processes.

Promotion of Transparency and Accountability Carter et al. found that women leaders within audit committees are strong advocates for transparency, accountability, and ethical behaviour. Their emphasis on these principles helps to establish a culture of integrity and trust within the audit committee and the broader organization.

Innovation and Adaptability Ahern and Dittmar found that diverse women's perspectives and leadership styles enable audit committees to better address emerging issues and challenges in the business environment. Women leaders bring a fresh and innovative approach to problem-solving, helping audit committees navigate complex financial issues and adapt to changing regulatory requirements.

Stakeholder Representation and Engagement Research by Huang Kisgen demonstrated that women leaders within audit committees are more adept at understanding and addressing the needs and concerns of a diverse range of stakeholders. Their deep understanding of stakeholder preferences and their strong communication and relationship-building skills help ensure that audit committee decisions are aligned with the interests of all stakeholders.

Corporate Performance and Sustainability Erhardt et al. found a positive link between gender diversity in audit committees and corporate performance and sustainability. The study found that companies with gender-diverse audit committees are more likely to outperform their peers in terms of financial performance and are better positioned to navigate risks and opportunities in an increasingly complex business environment.

These studies provide updated insights into the crucial role of diverse women in audit committees and their impact on decision-making processes, financial oversight, and overall corporate governance. Embracing gender diversity within audit committees remains essential for promoting integrity, trust, and accountability within organizations.

Existing Research Gaps and the Need for Further Exploration

Despite the growing body of research on the role of diverse women in audit committees, several notable research gaps exist, indicating the need for further exploration.

First, existing research has primarily focused on gender diversity within audit committees, overlooking other dimensions of diversity such as race, ethnicity, and age. Future research should explore how intersectionality impacts the effectiveness of audit committees and whether different dimensions of diversity interact to influence decision-making processes and financial oversight (Rao & Tilt, 2016).

Second, while some studies have examined the short-term impact of gender diversity on audit committee effectiveness, there is a lack of research on the long-term effects. Future research should explore whether gender-diverse audit committees have a sustained impact on corporate governance, financial performance, and sustainability over time (Sultana et al., 2020).

Furthermore, many existing studies have established correlations between gender diversity and audit committee effectiveness but have not explored causal relationships. Future research should use longitudinal and experimental designs to better understand the causal mechanisms through which gender diversity influences decision-making processes, financial oversight, and overall corporate governance (Zattoni et al., 2023).

Moreover, there is limited research on how contextual factors, such as industry type, company size, and national culture, influence the relationship between gender diversity and audit committee effectiveness. Future research should explore how these contextual factors moderate the impact of gender diversity on audit committee effectiveness (Alhababsah & Yekini, 2021).

Additionally, while quantitative studies have dominated the literature on gender diversity in audit committees, there is a need for more qualitative research to provide a deeper understanding of the experiences and perspectives of women in audit committee roles. Qualitative studies can provide insights into the unique challenges and opportunities faced by women in these positions (Khlif & Achek, 2017).

Finally, existing research has primarily focused on the impact of gender diversity on audit committee effectiveness from the perspective of the organization (Chijoke-Mgbame et al., 2020). Future research should also consider the perspectives of other stakeholders, such as investors, regulators, employees, and the broader community, to provide a more comprehensive understanding of the implications of gender diversity in audit committees.

Addressing these research gaps will help to further advance our understanding of the role of diverse women in audit committees and their impact on decision-making processes, financial oversight, and overall corporate governance. By filling these gaps, researchers can provide valuable insights that can inform policies and practices aimed at promoting gender diversity and improving audit committee effectiveness.

Methodology

Qualitative research methodology is a systematic approach used to explore and understand complex phenomena by examining the underlying meanings, patterns, and relationships (Bernard et al., 2016). Unlike quantitative research, which focuses on numerical data and statistical analysis, qualitative research aims to uncover the deeper insights and subjective experiences that shape human behaviour and decision-making (Denzin & Lincoln, 2011).

Dehalwar and Sharma (2023) states at its core, qualitative research is characterized by its emphasis on flexibility, reflexivity, and contextuality. Researchers employ a variety of data collection techniques, including interviews, observations, and document analysis, to gather rich and detailed information about the research topic (Flick, 2018). These data collection methods allow researchers to explore the nuances and complexities of the research subject in-depth, providing a comprehensive understanding of the phenomenon under investigation (Patton, 2015).

Ngulube (2015) argues that one of the key features of qualitative research methodology is its emphasis on interpretation and analysis. Researchers engage in a process of inductive reasoning, using the data collected to identify patterns, themes, and relationships. Through constant comparison and iterative analysis, researchers develop a deeper understanding of the underlying meanings and structures that shape the research topic (Tracy, 2019).

Another important aspect of qualitative research methodology is its focus on reflexivity and researcher subjectivity. Researchers acknowledge their role in shaping the research process and recognize that their own perspectives, biases, and assumptions may influence the research outcomes. By engaging in reflexivity, researchers can critically reflect on their own positionality and its impact on the research process, thereby enhancing the credibility and trustworthiness of the research findings (Bernard et al., 2016).

Overall, qualitative research methodology is a valuable approach for exploring complex phenomena and generating rich and detailed insights into the underlying meanings, patterns, and relationships (Tracy, 2019). By employing a variety of data collection techniques, engaging in interpretive analysis, and embracing reflexivity, qualitative researchers can uncover the deeper complexities of the research topic, providing a comprehensive understanding that goes beyond numerical data and statistical analysis.

Impact of Diverse Women Representation in Audit Committees

Obermire et al. (2021) indicated, diverse women's perspectives play a significant role in shaping decision-making processes within audit committees, offering a unique lens through which to evaluate financial issues and make strategic decisions. They bring a variety of experiences, backgrounds, and viewpoints to the table, enriching the discussions within audit committees. Research has consistently shown that diverse teams are more effective at problem-solving and decision-making, as they consider a broader range of factors and perspectives (Robert Jr et al., 2018). Women often approach problems and situations differently from men, drawing on their diverse backgrounds and experiences to offer new insights and alternative solutions (Orazalin & Baydauletov, 2020). This diversity of perspectives can lead to more comprehensive analyses of financial issues and more robust decision-making within audit committees (Dill & Zambrana, 2020).

Moreover, diverse women's perspectives often prioritize collaboration, inclusivity, and consensus-building, which are critical for effective decision-making within audit committees (Harjoto et al., 2018). Women leaders tend to foster open communication and create an environment where all committee members feel valued and heard. This collaborative approach encourages constructive dialogue and idea-sharing, leading to more informed and well-rounded decisions. By fostering a collaborative environment, diverse women ensure that all committee members' perspectives are considered, resulting in more effective decision-making processes (Poggesi et al., 2016).

Furthermore, diverse women's perspectives bring a strong focus on ethics, integrity, and social responsibility to decision-making processes within audit committees. Women leaders are often strong advocates for transparency, accountability, and ethical behaviour, helping to establish a culture of integrity and trust within the committee and the broader organization (Alhababsah & Yekini, 2021). Their emphasis on ethical decision-making ensures that audit committee decisions are not only financially sound but also aligned with the organization's values and ethical principles.

Overall, diverse women's perspectives have a significant impact on decision-making processes within audit committees, contributing to more comprehensive analyses, more inclusive decision-making, and a stronger focus on ethics and integrity (Alhababsah & Yekini, 2021). By bringing a broader range of experiences, backgrounds, and viewpoints to the table, women enhance the effectiveness of audit committees and contribute to better decision-making outcomes. Embracing gender diversity within audit committees is essential for promoting effective governance and ensuring the long-term success and sustainability of organizations.

Impact of Diverse Women on Overall Corporate Governance Within Audit Committees

Diverse women's impact on overall corporate governance within audit committees extends beyond decision-making processes and financial oversight, influencing various aspects of organizational governance and performance.

- *Enhanced board effectiveness*:
- Diverse women bring a range of perspectives, experiences, and skills to audit committees, enhancing the effectiveness of the board. Their diverse backgrounds and expertise enable audit committees to conduct more thorough analyses of financial issues, identify emerging risks, and make informed decisions. By fostering open communication, collaboration, and consensus-building, diverse women contribute to a more cohesive and effective board (Alqatamin, 2018).
- *Improved stakeholder engagement*:
- Diverse women's perspectives and leadership styles also contribute to improved stakeholder engagement and relationships. Women leaders are more adept at understanding and addressing the needs and concerns of a diverse range of stakeholders, including investors, regulators, employees, and the broader community (Sarwar et al., 2020). Their strong communication and relationship-building skills help ensure that audit committee decisions are aligned with the interests of all stakeholders, promoting transparency, accountability, and trust (Islam et al., 2022).
- *Promotion of ethical leadership*:
- Diverse women within audit committees promote a culture of integrity, transparency, and ethical behaviour within the organization. Women leaders are strong advocates for ethical decision-making and are committed to upholding the highest standards of corporate governance. Their emphasis on ethics and integrity helps to establish a culture of trust and accountability within the audit committee and the broader organization, fostering long-term sustainability and success (Jain & Jamali, 2016).
- *Innovation and adaptability*:
- Diverse women's perspectives also contribute to innovation and adaptability within audit committees. Women leaders bring a fresh and innovative approach to problem-solving, helping audit committees navigate complex financial issues and adapt to changing regulatory requirements (Sarwar et al., 2020). Their ability to think creatively and anticipate emerging trends and challenges helps ensure that the organization remains competitive and resilient in a rapidly changing business environment (Kezar, 2023).

The Significance of Diverse Representation in Audit Committees

The significance of diverse representation in audit committees cannot be overstated, as it directly impacts the effectiveness of corporate governance, financial oversight, and decision-making processes within organizations.

Seierstad (2016) shares a centimetre of diverse representation in audit committees ensures that a wide range of perspectives, experiences, and expertise are brought to the table. Women, along with individuals from different racial, ethnic, and cultural backgrounds, offer unique insights and viewpoints that enrich discussions and lead to more comprehensive analyses of financial issues. This diversity of perspectives helps audit committees identify risks, opportunities, and challenges that may not be apparent from a homogeneous group.

Second, diverse representation in audit committees enhances decision-making processes by promoting open communication, collaboration, and consensus-building. Research has consistently shown that diverse teams are more effective at problem-solving and decision-making because they consider a broader range of factors and perspectives (Jain & Jamali, 2016). Women tend to prioritize collaboration, inclusivity, and attention to detail, which are critical for effective financial oversight and decision-making within audit committees (Robert Jr. et al., 2018).

Moreover, diverse representation in audit committees promotes transparency, accountability, and ethical behaviour within organizations. Women leaders are strong advocates for ethical decision-making and are committed to upholding the highest standards of corporate governance. Their emphasis on ethics and integrity helps establish a culture of trust and accountability within the audit committee and the broader organization, fostering long-term sustainability and success (Byron & Post, 2016; Steckler & Clark, 2019).

Furthermore, Cheung and Lai (2024) expressed that diverse representation in audit committees enhances stakeholder engagement and relationships. Women leaders are more adept at understanding and addressing the needs and concerns of a diverse range of stakeholders, including investors, regulators, employees, and the broader community. Their strong communication and relationship-building skills help ensure that audit committee decisions are aligned with the interests of all stakeholders, promoting transparency, accountability, and trust.

Exploration of the Broader Implications for Corporate Governance and Sustainability

The broader implications of diverse representation in audit committees extend far beyond the immediate scope of financial oversight, influencing corporate governance and sustainability.

Enhanced Corporate Governance

Diverse representation in audit committees contributes to enhanced corporate governance by ensuring a wide range of perspectives, experiences, and expertise are considered in decision-making processes (Kolev et al., 2019). Women and individuals from diverse backgrounds offer unique insights that enrich discussions and lead to more comprehensive analyses of financial issues. This diversity of perspectives helps audit committees identify risks, opportunities, and challenges that may not be apparent from a homogeneous group, thereby strengthening the integrity and effectiveness of corporate governance mechanisms (Robert Jr. et al., 2018).

Strengthened Ethical Leadership

Diverse representation in audit committees promotes transparency, accountability, and ethical behaviour within organizations. Women leaders, in particular, are strong advocates for ethical decision-making and uphold the highest standards of corporate governance. Their emphasis on ethics and integrity helps establish a culture of trust and accountability within the audit committee and the broader organization, fostering long-term sustainability and success (McLaughlin et al., 2021). By prioritizing transparency and accountability, diverse audit committees build trust with stakeholders and enhance the organization's reputation and credibility.

Improved Stakeholder Engagement

Diverse representation in audit committees enhances stakeholder engagement and relationships. Women leaders are more adept at understanding and addressing the needs and concerns of a diverse range of stakeholders, including investors, regulators, employees, and the broader community. Their strong communication and relationship-building skills help ensure that audit committee decisions are aligned with the interests of all stakeholders, promoting transparency, accountability, and trust. This, in turn, strengthens the organization's reputation and enhances its ability to attract investment and talent, contributing to long-term sustainability (Alhababsah & Yekini, 2021).

Long-Term Organizational Performance and Sustainability

Ultimately, diverse representation in audit committees contributes to improved organizational performance and long-term sustainability. Research has shown that companies with gender-diverse audit committees tend to outperform their peers in terms of financial performance and are better positioned to navigate risks and opportunities. By promoting effective governance, transparency, and accountability, diverse audit committees help ensure that the organization remains resilient, competitive, and responsive to the evolving needs of stakeholders and the business environment. This, in turn, contributes to long-term organizational success and sustainability (Islam et al., 2022).

Conclusion and Recommendations

In conclusion, this chapter has underscored the pivotal role of diverse representation, particularly women, within audit committees in shaping corporate governance practices. By examining the evolving discourse on gender diversity and inclusion in corporate governance and employing a qualitative research methodology, this study has provided valuable insights into the nuanced nature of diverse women's contributions within audit committees.

The findings of this research highlight the substantial influence of diverse women in shaping decision-making processes, financial oversight, and overall corporate governance within audit committees. Through a systematic analysis of case studies and empirical data, this chapter has demonstrated how diverse women's perspectives and leadership styles enhance board effectiveness, stakeholder engagement, ethical leadership, and long-term organizational performance and sustainability.

As global corporations strive for greater inclusivity and equity, understanding and acknowledging the pivotal role of diverse women within audit committees become imperative for creating an equitable and effective corporate landscape. By advocating for increased recognition and support for diverse women in audit committees, this research emphasizes the broader benefits of inclusivity and diversity in driving organizational success and sustainability on a global scale.

Moving forward, it is essential for companies to prioritize gender diversity within audit committees and to address existing research gaps to further advance our understanding of the role of diverse women in corporate governance. By filling these gaps and embracing diversity, organizations can promote integrity, trust, and accountability within their audit committees and realize their full potential for long-term success and sustainability.

References

Alhababsah, S., & Yekini, S. (2021). Audit committee and audit quality: An empirical analysis considering industry expertise, legal expertise and gender diversity. *Journal of International Accounting, Auditing and Taxation, 42*, 100377.

Alqatamin, R. M. (2018). Audit committee effectiveness and company performance: Evidence from Jordan. *Accounting and Finance Research, 7*(2), 48.

Al-Shaer, H., & Zaman, M. (2016). Board gender diversity and sustainability reporting quality. *Journal of Contemporary Accounting & Economics, 12*(3), 210–222.

Bernard, H. R., Wutich, A., & Ryan, G. W. (2016). *Analyzing qualitative data: Systematic approaches*. Sage.

Byron, K., & Post, C. (2016). Women on boards of directors and corporate social performance: A meta-analysis. *Corporate Governance: An International Review, 24*(4), 428–442.

Cheung, K. Y., & Lai, C. Y. (2024). Does trust matter in external audits? The role of audit committee chair's trust in external audits. *Managerial Auditing Journal, 39*(1), 1–25.

Chijoke-Mgbame, A. M., Boateng, A., & Mgbame, C. O. (2020, July). Board gender diversity, audit committee and financial performance: evidence from Nigeria. *Accounting Forum, 44*(3), 262–286. Routledge.

Dehalwar, K., & Sharma, S. N. (2023). *Fundamentals of research writing and uses of research methodologies*. Edupedia.

Denzin, N. K., & Lincoln, Y. S. (Eds.). (2011). *The Sage handbook of qualitative research*. Sage.

Dill, B. T., & Zambrana, R. E. (2020). Critical thinking about inequality: An emerging lens. In C. McCann, S.-k. Kim, & E. Ergun (Eds.), *Feminist theory reader* (pp. 108–116). Routledge.

Flick, U. (2018). *An introduction to qualitative research*. Sage.

Ghafran, C., & Yasmin, S. (2018). Audit committee chair and financial reporting timeliness: A focus on financial, experiential and monitoring expertise. *International Journal of Auditing, 22*(1), 13–24.

Harjoto, M. A., Laksmana, I., & Yang, Y. W. (2018). Board diversity and corporate investment oversight. *Journal of Business Research, 90*, 40–47.

Islam, R., French, E., & Ali, M. (2022). Evaluating board diversity and its importance in the environmental and social performance of organizations. *Corporate Social Responsibility and Environmental Management, 29*(5), 1134–1145.

Jain, T., & Jamali, D. (2016). Looking inside the black box: The effect of corporate governance on corporate social responsibility. *Corporate Governance: An International Review, 24*(3), 253–273.

Kezar, A. J. (Ed.). (2023). *Rethinking leadership in a complex, multicultural, and global environment: New concepts and models for higher education*. Taylor & Francis.

Khlif, H., & Achek, I. (2017). Gender in accounting research: a review. *Managerial Auditing Journal, 32*(6), 627–655.

Klettner, A., Clarke, T., & Boersma, M. (2016). Strategic and regulatory approaches to increasing women in leadership: Multilevel targets and mandatory quotas as levers for cultural change. *Journal of Business Ethics, 133*, 395–419.

Kolev, K. D., Wangrow, D. B., Barker, V. L., III, & Schepker, D. J. (2019). Board committees in corporate governance: A cross-disciplinary review and agenda for the future. *Journal of Management Studies, 56*(6), 1138–1193.

Luh, P. K. (2024). Gender of firm leadership, audit committee gender diversity and audit quality through the lens of audit fee: a Ghanaian insight. *Gender in Management: An International Journal, 39*(3), 388–408.

McLaughlin, C., Armstrong, S., Moustafa, M. W., & Elamer, A. A. (2021). Audit committee diversity and corporate scandals: evidence from the UK. *International Journal of Accounting & Information Management, 29*(5), 734–763.

Mnif Sellami, Y., & Cherif, I. (2020). Female audit committee directorship and audit fees. *Managerial Auditing Journal, 35*(3), 398–428.

Mwangi, A. K. (2018). *Effect of audit committee characteristics on quality of financial reporting among non-commercial state corporations in Kenya*. Doctoral dissertation, JKUAT.

Nekhili, M., Gull, A. A., Chtioui, T., & Radhouane, I. (2020). Gender-diverse boards and audit fees: What difference does gender quota legislation make? *Journal of Business Finance & Accounting, 47*(1-2), 52–99.

Ngulube, P. (2015). Qualitative data analysis and interpretation: systematic search for meaning. In E. R. Mathipa & M. T. Gumbo (Eds.), *Addressing research challenges: making headway for developing researchers* (pp. 131–156). Mosala-Masedi.

Obermire, K. M., Cohen, J. R., & Zehms, K. M. (2021). Audit committee members' professional identities: Evidence from the field. *Accounting, Organizations and Society, 93*, 101242.

Oradi, J., & Izadi, J. (2020). Audit committee gender diversity and financial reporting: evidence from restatements. *Managerial Auditing Journal, 35*(1), 67–92.

Orazalin, N., & Baydauletov, M. (2020). Corporate social responsibility strategy and corporate environmental and social performance: The moderating role of board gender diversity. *Corporate Social Responsibility and Environmental Management, 27*(4), 1664–1676.

Patton, M. Q. (2015). *Qualitative research and evaluation methods*. Sage.

Poggesi, S., Mari, M., & De Vita, L. (2016). What's new in female entrepreneurship research? Answers from the literature. *International Entrepreneurship and Management Journal, 12*, 735–764.

Pucheta-Martínez, M. C., Bel-Oms, I., & Olcina-Sempere, G. (2016). Corporate governance, female directors and quality of financial information. *Business Ethics: A European Review, 25*(4), 363–385.

Rao, K., & Tilt, C. (2016). Board composition and corporate social responsibility: The role of diversity, gender, strategy and decision making. *Journal of Business Ethics, 138*, 327–347.

Rezaee, Z., Olibe, K. O., & Minmier, G. (2003). Improving corporate governance: the role of audit committee disclosures. *Managerial Auditing Journal, 18*(6/7), 530–537.

Robert, L. P., Jr., Dennis, A. R., & Ahuja, M. K. (2018). Differences are different: Examining the effects of communication media on the impacts of racial and gender diversity in decision-making teams. *Information Systems Research, 29*(3), 525–545.

Sarwar, H., Ishaq, M. I., Amin, A., & Ahmed, R. (2020). Ethical leadership, work engagement, employees' well-being, and performance: a cross-cultural comparison. *Journal of Sustainable Tourism, 28*(12), 2008–2026.

Seierstad, C. (2016). Beyond the business case: The need for both utility and justice rationales for increasing the share of women on boards. *Corporate Governance: An International Review, 24*(4), 390–405.

Steckler, E., & Clark, C. (2019). Authenticity and corporate governance. *Journal of Business Ethics, 155*, 951–963.

Sultana, N., Cahan, S. F., & Rahman, A. (2020). Do gender diversity recommendations in corporate governance codes matter? Evidence from audit committees. *Auditing: A Journal of Practice & Theory, 39*(1), 173–197.

Terjesen, S., Couto, E. B., & Francisco, P. M. (2016). Does the presence of independent and female directors impact firm performance? A multi-country study of board diversity. *Journal of Management & Governance, 20*, 447–483.

Tinkler, J. E., Whittington, K. B., Ku, M. C., & Davies, A. R. (2015). Gender and venture capital decision-making: The effects of technical background and social capital on entrepreneurial evaluations. *Social Science Research, 51*, 1–16.

Tracy, S. J. (2019). *Qualitative research methods: Collecting evidence, crafting analysis, communicating impact*. Wiley.

Ud Din, N., Cheng, X., Ahmad, B., Sheikh, M. F., Adedigba, O. G., Zhao, Y., & Nazneen, S. (2021). Gender diversity in the audit committee and the efficiency of internal control and financial reporting quality. *Economic Research-Ekonomska istraživanja, 34*(1), 1170–1189.

Uzma, S. H. (2018). Corporate governance practices: global convergence and Indian perspective. *Qualitative Research in Financial Markets, 10*(3), 285–308.

Zaid, M. A. A., Wang, M., Abuhijleh, S. T. F., Issa, A., Saleh, M. W. A., & Ali, F. (2020). Corporate governance practices and capital structure decisions: the moderating effect of gender diversity. *Corporate Governance: The International Journal of Business in Society, 20*(5), 939–964.

Zalata, A., & Roberts, C. (2016). Internal corporate governance and classification shifting practices: An analysis of UK corporate behavior. *Journal of Accounting, Auditing & Finance, 31*(1), 51–78.

Zattoni, A., Leventis, S., Van Ees, H., & De Masi, S. (2023). Board diversity's antecedents and consequences: A review and research agenda. *The Leadership Quarterly, 34*(1), 101659.

Critical Considerations to Attaining and Sustaining Clean Audit Outcomes in the South African Public Sector: A Case of the National School of Government

Izimangaliso Malatjie, Phindile Mkwanazi, and Dino Poonsamy

Abstract A significant objective of the government is to provide democratic and accountable governance through its public sector institutions. Thus, allocating budgets from the national fiscus to public sector institutions means they must manage and utilize it efficiently, effectively, and economically. It also means that public sector institutions must accurately and transparently account for managing and utilizing budgets and how effectively institutions are governed. As such, the audit function is a key methodology used to independently test and evaluate financial and non-financial performance, corporate governance and compliance matters in the public sector. The pinnacle achievement for any institution is obtaining an unqualified audit opinion without material findings, also called a clean audit. It is, therefore, significant that this chapter examines the approach towards attaining a clean audit outcome and shares perspectives and experiences within the public sector. The National School of Government (the NSG) is a government department that provides or facilitates the provision of education, training, and development (ETD) in the public sector. This includes the three spheres of government (national, provincial, and local), state-owned enterprises, and the legislatures. The NSG has sustained a clean audit outcome over the years. Thus, this chapter evaluates the factors contributing to the NSG attaining and sustaining a clean audit outcome over the years. A case study approach is followed to share the experiences and perspectives of the NSG.

Keywords Clean audit · Accountability · Annual reporting · Governance · Public sector

I. Malatjie (✉) · P. Mkwanazi · D. Poonsamy
National School of Government, Pretoria, South Africa
e-mail: Izimangaliso.malatjie@thensg.gov.za; Phindile.mkwanazi@thensg.gov.za; dino.poonsamy@thensg.gov.za

T. Moloi (ed.), *Impacting Society Positively Through Technology in Accounting and Business Processes*, Springer Proceedings in Business and Economics,
https://doi.org/10.1007/978-3-031-84885-8_38

Introduction

The audit function is a key methodology used to independently test and evaluate financial and non-financial performance, corporate governance and compliance matters in the public sector. The pinnacle achievement for any institution is obtaining an unqualified or unmodified audit opinion without material findings, also called a clean audit. Significant emphasis has been placed on attaining clean audits in the South African public sector. From ministers and mayors issuing media statements to the Auditor-General (AG) handing clean audit awards, the attainment has significantly raised the corporate governance bar. Thus, it is clear that having a robust governance function is crucial for overseeing and maintaining transparent administration. Therefore, achieving a clean audit outcome serves as a key indicator of effective or transparent administration within public sector organizations (Department of Cooperative Governance and Traditional Affairs (COGTA), 2009). Various articles (Motubatse et al., 2017) have been written, and interviews with accounting officers have been undertaken to analyse what is required to achieve and sustain a clean audit outcome. It is a common reason that a clean audit may not be guaranteed from one financial year to the next—evidence exists of public sector institutions that have "fallen from grace" down the pecking order to qualified or adverse audit outcomes (AGSA, 2022). It is, therefore, significant that this chapter examines the approach towards attaining a clean audit outcome and shares perspectives and experiences within the public sector.

The National School of Government (NSG) is a government department that provides or facilitates the provision of education, training, and development (ETD) in the public sector. This includes the three spheres of government (national, provincial, and local), state-owned enterprises, and the legislatures (NSG, 2023). The uniqueness in identifying the NSG to gain perspectives and experiences towards a clean audit is based on the fact that it operates two financial accounting systems through its Vote as a national department (Modified Cash Standard) and the Training Trading Account (Generally Recognized Accounting Practice) to generate revenue. In this regard, the NSG has to be audited on both financial statements, which have inter-dependencies and impact the overall audit outcomes. Secondly, the NSG has sustained a clean audit outcome on the Vote account for over 5 years, while the Training Trading Account has attained its first clean audit outcome in as many years.

The chapter further examines factors such as leadership, internal controls, predetermined objectives, effective governance, strategy, and systems contributing to achieving and sustaining a clean audit outcome. The department boasts a well-defined organizational culture characterized by intentional political and administrative leadership, emphasizing transparency, accountability, and sound financial practices. These elements have consistently contributed to achieving clean audit outcomes over several years. The Auditor General (AG) corroborated this in the 2022/23 consolidated audit report, noting that "the number of clean audits continues to increase every year due to significant effort and commitment by the leadership, officials, and governance structures of those institutions" (PMG, 2023). The AG also praised "the 53 auditees (36%) that have maintained their clean audit status throughout the administrative term by institutionalizing and monitoring key controls (including preventative controls) and ensuring that all participants in the accountability ecosystem are dedicated to their monitoring, governance, and oversight responsibilities" (PMG, 2023).

Building a Capable, Ethical, and Developmental State

This year (2024) marks 30 years of freedom and democracy in South Africa. Despite gains made by the democratic government in addressing the socio-economic challenges of poverty, unemployment, and inequality, much needs to be done to emancipate historically disadvantaged South African citizens. The National Development Plan (NDP) points out that "there is an unevenness in capacity that leads to uneven performance in local, provincial, and national government" (RSA, 2012: 408). The problem is that South Africa is not building sufficient capacity and capability at the rate, pace, and scale a dynamic developmental state requires. Poor productivity, corruption, state capture, wastage, and a lack of accountability have all undermined capacity-building efforts (SA, 2022)

The Public Service Commission (PSC), in its 2021 State of the Public Service Report, summarizes the challenges of public service capacity and capability as follows:

- State capacity and capability in South Africa have declined over time and vary significantly, with major deficiencies in many departments and specializations coexisting alongside pockets of strength and excellence.
- Fiscal consolidation has resulted in reduced headcounts and decreased budgets for goods and services, leading to a corresponding loss in state capacity and capability.
- Inefficiencies in resource allocation and poor conversion of resources into outcomes in the public service contribute to and reflect capacity and capability challenges.

There is also "a widespread failure within the government to implement the systems, processes, and controls necessary to standardize constitutional and legislative requirements", resulting in irregularities and losses to the state. According to the AG, there were 327 material irregularities with an estimated total financial loss of R14.7 billion in the three spheres of government. These material irregularities include procurement and payments, resource management, and fraud and compliance.

Mazzucato et al. (2021) contend that an array of institutional weaknesses and governance failures have undermined the state's ability to deliver on its developmental mandate and that "These weaknesses are primarily focused on the organization of the state, the lack of an ethos of accountability and transparency, skill deficiencies, and, in some cases, poorly defined goals". Therefore, it is critical that the public sector has the requisite skills and capacity to plan and monitor performance and achieve the developmental agenda.

Overview of the National School of Government

The NSG (2023) was established as a government training institution with a mandate to provide or arrange for training, and to conduct or arrange for examinations or tests as determined by the Head of the institution or as prescribed for qualifications necessary for the appointment or transfer of individuals within the public service, as outlined in the Public Service Act, 1994 (as amended). The NSG is tasked with ensuring that the basic values and principles in section 195 of the Constitution are integrated into the value system and performance of all public servants and representatives through Education, Training, and Development (ETD) initiatives (NSG, 2023).

The mandate also authorizes the institution to issue diplomas or certificates, or to arrange for their issuance, to individuals who have successfully passed the examinations (NSG, 2018: 7). This mandate is further reinforced by the Public Administration Management Act (PAMA), 2014 (Act No. 11 of 2014), which stipulates that the NSG must promote the progressive realization of the values and principles governing public administration (section 195 of the Constitution of the Republic of South Africa, 1996) through education and training, as well as by enhancing the quality, scope, and impact of human resource capacity development in institutions.

The NSG is also governed by the Public Finance Management Act (PFMA), 1999 (Act No. 1 of 1999) and Section 19 of the Treasury Regulations concerning the establishment and management of the Training Trade Account (TTA). According to the Treasury Regulations, when determining charges for goods or services, the head of the trading entity must aim to recover the full cost of providing those goods or services unless the relevant treasury approves lower charges. Additionally, the head must review user charge rates annually before the budget, with any tariff increases requiring treasury approval. The National School of Government's TTA operates on a cost recovery model with partial funding from transfers received. This approach mandates that the entity recovers all costs associated with designing and developing learning materials and implementing training courses from the course fees (NSG, 2024).

Audit Perspectives

According to Khasodi (2023), within a democratic governance framework like that of South Africa, auditing has emerged as a focal point of governance and a paramount element of effective public sector management. Section 55 of the Public Management Act (PFMA) mandates that the accounting officer of a department must submit financial statements to the Auditor General (AG) for auditing within 2 months after the fiscal year's end. The AG's audit process entails an objective assessment of the stewardship of public funds, the implementation of government policies, and compliance with crucial legislation. The annual audit's scope for each audited entity is specified in the Public Audit Act and the accompanying general notice. It encompasses:

- Ensuring the accuracy of financial statements to benefit their users.
- Evaluating the usefulness and reliability of information in the annual performance report.
- Reporting instances of significant non-compliance with key legislation.
- Identifying critical internal control deficiencies requiring rectification for attaining a clean audit (AGSA, 2024a, 2024b).

Performance audits may also be conducted to ascertain the economical procurement and efficient utilization of resources. The AG subsequently issues an opinion on the department's performance based on the submitted information. The various audit opinions are categorized as follows:

- Clean audit outcome: Financial statements are materially error-free, demonstrating both a financially unqualified audit opinion and no significant findings on performance information and legislative compliance.
- Financially unqualified audit opinion: Financial statements are materially error-free, but there are findings related to reporting on predetermined objectives, legislative non-compliance, or both.
- Qualified audit opinion: Financial statements contain material errors in specific amounts, or there is insufficient evidence to ascertain that specific amounts therein are not materially misstated.
- Adverse audit opinion: Financial statements contain material errors not confined to specific amounts or represent a substantial portion thereof.
- Disclaimer of audit opinion: Insufficient evidence, particularly in documentation, exists to form an audit opinion. This lack of evidence is not limited to specific amounts or comprises a significant portion of the financial statements' information (AGSA, 2024a, 2024b).

The AGSA (2024a, 2024b) emphasized the significance of achieving a clean audit, which signifies that an audited entity's financial statements and performance report provide a transparent and credible overview of its finances and performance vis-à-vis the established targets. Importantly, it also indicates compliance with crucial financial and performance management legislation (PMG, 2023). Additionally, the AG noted that "We have observed that audited entities with established controls and systems for planning, measuring, monitoring, and reporting on their finances and performance, and for adhering to regulations, often possess a strong foundation for delivering services to the citizens of South Africa" (PMG, 2023).

There has been an increase in the number of clean audits for the 2021/22 financial year audit of national and provincial governments; however, the "clean audit status represents only 6% of the R2.58 trillion expenditure budget managed by national and provincial government" (AGSA, 2022).

Conceptual Framework

The Policy Framework for Integrated Planning (2022) identifies the four waves of planning reform in South Africa since 1994 as follows:

(i) From 1994 to 2000—setting the foundations of planning
(ii) From 2001 to 2008—driving coordination and intergovernmental relations
(iii) From 2009 to 2019—planning, monitoring, and evaluation at the centre of government
(iv) From 2019 and beyond—advancing the institutionalization of planning for development

In 2009, the South African government introduced two key policy papers to influence government planning and performance management: the Green Paper on National Strategic Planning and the Improving Government Performance: Our Approach. The former introduced the government to long-term planning and formed the basis for developing the National Development Plan: Vision 2030. The Green Paper noted that "there is little evidence of long-term planning in the public sector, let alone integration of such plans" and the need to "build the capacity of departments and entities to do long-term planning" (The Presidency, 2009). Thus, the planning process in national and provincial governments aligns with the long-term National Development Plan (NDP), the 5-year medium-term plans set by the government, and the development of departmental *5-year strategic plans, annual performance plans, and annual operational plans*.

The policy paper on improving government performance introduced government departments to outcomes-based performance management using the LOGIC model (Inputs-Activities-Outputs-Outcomes-Impact). The four components of the outcomes approach are Problem Analysis, Theory of Change, Intervention Logic, Clear Indicators, Baselines, and Targets. Figure 1 (DPME, 2022) summarizes the planning system in national, provincial, and local government spheres.

The planning processes—strategic, tactical, and operational—are critical to the success (or failure) of organizational and individual performance. If there is no clear strategic vision or direction to plan towards, performance planning will be compromised (DPME, 2022). In the case of the NSG, its vision (build an ethical and capable public sector in service of the people) is directly aligned with priority one of the 2019–2024 Medium-Term Strategic Framework (a capable, ethical, and developmental state). The sixth administration prioritized building state capacity and placed the NSG to lead capacity development interventions. Planning processes are also undertaken twice within the financial year—first a strategic planning workshop focused on strategic analysis and performance review to inform priorities for the new financial year, and a second operational planning workshop focused on implementing plans for the new financial year. The NSG executive management is also encouraged to convene their functional area planning workshops so that all employees are involved in the planning process.

Fig. 1 Government planning system. Source: DPME (2022)

The translation and alignment of plans into performance targets and their monitoring and management thereof is an essential component leading to the determination of audit outcomes. In this regard, Treasury Regulation 5.3.1, read with 36(5) of the PFMA, directs that an "accounting officer of an institution must establish procedures for quarterly reporting to the executive authority to facilitate effective performance monitoring, evaluation and corrective action". To address the challenges of performance monitoring and reporting practices, the DPME (2021) developed an Electronic Quarterly Performance Reporting System (eQPRS) to be used by all national and provincial government institutions. To ensure accountability, the eQPRS makes provision for the following types of users:

- The *Capturer* captures information (targets and actual performance) onto the eQPRS and adds relevant documentation.
- The *Entity Coordinator* has the overall reporting responsibility for the public entity, approves captured information, and configures the budget programme structure and the output indicators.
- The *Accounting Officer* approves and submits quarterly performance information on the eQPRS with a sign-off certificate.
- The *DPME Coordinator, Oversight Department Coordinator, and Treasury Coordinator* provide comments on the quarterly performance information.

In the case of the NSG, quarterly performance reports are discussed at executive and senior management meetings. In cases where quarterly performance targets are not achieved, the relevant programme managers are directed to provide reasons for non-achievement and plans to catch up on the unachieved targets before the following quarterly reporting period.

Governance

Since the new millennium, the focus in the international community has been on good governance, and this, according to the World Bank, emphasizes public sector management, accountability, transparency, and the legal framework for development more than anything else. To summarize the above, Kofi Annan's view on good governance, which many in the academic sphere have agreed with, is relevant; "without good governance, without the rule of law and predictable administration, no amount of charity will set on the path of prosperity" (Kofi Annan, cited in Adejumobi, 2011). Literature reveals that the success of good governance depends largely on sound financial management practices that include accurate financial reporting, openness, and transparency in government finance management (Motubatse et al., 2017).

The AGSA (2024a, 2024b) has devised a monitoring mechanism (inclusive of the widely recognized "key control dashboard") aimed at aiding management and oversight bodies in diligently overseeing the efficiency of their internal controls. These controls, encompassing leadership engagement, financial and performance management, and governance, serve as pivotal catalysts for enhancing audit results (AGSA, n.d.). The subsequent paragraphs will delve into these key controls individually.

Leadership

Leadership is important in any organization as it provides guidance, vision, and support, drives it towards success, and shapes its corporate culture. Effective leadership fosters collaboration and synergy and cultivates a culture of accountability, innovation, and continuous improvement (Taylor, 2023). The AGSA (n.d.) and PWC (2016) highlighted the pivotal role of leadership in driving enhanced audit outcomes, emphasizing the necessity for leadership to cultivate a culture characterized by integrity, ethical business conduct, and effective governance (PWC, 2016). As outlined by the AGSA (2022), leadership is tasked with ensuring the following:

- Appointing competent officials to fill vacancies and fostering stability in key positions to enhance accountability.

- Revitalizing performance planning processes to be comprehensive and aligned with mandates, ensuring that service delivery is meticulously planned and reported on.
- Cultivating a robust financial management ethos, encompassing efficient revenue collection, prudent expenditure, and the prevention and swift recovery of financial losses and wastage.
- Leading by example and enforcing consequences for non-compliance with legislation and accountability lapses to facilitate improved performance and service delivery (AGSA, 2022).

As such, for the NSG to be successful in delivering on its mandate, achieving its objectives, and attaining a clean audit status, it was imperative to hire a qualified Chief Financial Officer (CFO). The appointment of a permanent CFO in October 2010 was a step in the right direction towards working towards a clean audit outcome. According to Mnguni and Subban, working towards good governance requires appointing officials with appropriate qualifications, competencies, and work ethics.

Section 38 of the PFMA (1999) underscores that the accounting officer, who represents leadership, is responsible for ensuring the following:

- Effective, efficient, and transparent financial and risk management systems.
- Implementation of an internal audit system overseen by an audit committee, which must adhere to regulations and instructions outlined in sections 76 and 77 of the PFMA.

Furthermore, the performance management and development system for heads of departments (HODs) is "characterised by four overarching elements, namely employee performance, key government focus areas and Auditor-General's Audit Opinion and Findings and Organisational Performance" (DPSA, 2017). According to the DPSA (2017), the AG findings and opinions contribute 20% to a head of department's final performance assessment score because for the year under review "the Auditor-General report/findings is the most appropriate mechanism to validate the performance outcome of the HOD as well as the departmental performance outcome".

Internal Controls

AGSA (2024a, 2024b) emphasized the pivotal role of leadership concerning the development, execution, and sustenance of efficient internal control mechanisms across governmental departments, municipalities, and entities. Internal controls constitute procedures aimed at preventing inaccuracies and irregularities, detecting issues, and ensuring appropriate remedial actions, thereby upholding the integrity of financial and accounting information. As defined in the 2013 Framework, internal control is "a process, overseen by an entity's board of directors, management, and other staff, designed to provide reasonable assurance regarding the achievement of objectives concerning operations, reporting, and compliance" (COSO, 2023; KPMG, 2013). The Committee of Sponsoring Organizations of the Treadway Commission (COSO) internal control framework (COSO, 2023; KPMG, 2013) comprises five interconnected components: control environment, risk assessment, control activities, information and communication, and monitoring.

Strong internal controls characterize departments that achieve clean audits, and as such, the PFMA (1999) makes it clear that accounting officers must actively ensure that internal controls are appropriate for their specific circumstances and, most importantly, are operating as intended. Therefore, it is imperative that the leadership and executive management are also responsible for constantly monitoring action plans to enhance financial and performance reporting and compliance with laws and regulations (AGSA, 2024a, 2024b). As such, the NSG implemented stringent internal controls to ensure a clean audit outcome and followed the AG guidelines in implementing these internal controls.

Financial and Performance Management Systems

AGSA (2024a, 2024b) recommended the implementation of information technology (IT) tools within organizations to enhance value delivery and performance improvement, emphasizing the importance of managing these tools in alignment with sound IT governance practices. Thus, the NSG had to implement systems to ensure that transactions were verified and correctly captured. This included the introduction of a system that could track invoices and a system that could process all departmental transactions and be able to draw financial reports at any given point in time. The information provided is corroborated by AGSA (2024a, 2024b), which states that for an entity to maintain robust financial controls, management at the appropriate level should consistently scrutinize interim and monthly reports, ensuring the preparation of regular, precise, and comprehensive financial and performance reports supported by credible sources of information. This requirement is also outlined in the PFMA (1999).

Legislative Requirements

The public service is a highly regulated environment that is governed by legislation, policies, rules, and regulations. According to Malatjie et al. (2023), the National Treasury ensures that public sector organizations adhere to these regulations. Moreover, the National Treasury emphasizes the need for accountability and transparency in financial matters. As such, it becomes imperative for departments to adhere to these regulations. Therefore, part of the audit process is to ensure that departments adhere to the various legislative frameworks. As per AGSA (2024a,

2024b), it is imperative for leadership and management to consistently assess and supervise officials' adherence to relevant laws and regulations. The emphasis should be on implementing measures that deter unauthorized and irregular transactions, thus enabling management and senior officials to fulfil their statutory obligations effectively.

Mnguni and Subban elaborate that an effective government administration embodies the principles outlined in the Constitution on a daily basis, actively works to prevent corruption and abuse of power, and remains responsive to the needs of its citizens. To adhere to the legislative requirements in the public sector, the NSG implemented expenditure and supply chain management policies. These were workshopped to all staff to ensure understanding and compliance. Advocacy sessions were held occasionally, and monthly meetings were scheduled with budget managers to ensure compliance and tracking of expenditure.

Conclusion

This paper points out that state capacity and capability are necessary to fulfil the state's role in providing democratic and accountable governance through its public sector institutions. Equally so is the use of public finances to ensure that public service delivery is effective, efficient, and economical to meet citizens' expectations. As such, the audit function remains a key methodology used to independently test and evaluate financial and non-financial performance, corporate governance and compliance matters in the public sector. This all starts with effective planning—from strategic visions and direction to translating these into realistic and achievable plans that can be measured. Planning requires public sector institutions to have the requisite capacity, capability, and leadership commitment to drive these plans. It also requires management commitment to manage performance consistently, the foresight to pre-empt unachievable performance targets, and the determination to arrest poor or non-performance in time. Significant to these processes is to manage accurate reporting back up with relevant and credible data and information. One of the major failures of public sector institutions during the audit of performance objectives is the lack of relevant and credible data and information.

This paper further points out that the NSG has sustained a clean audit outcome, particularly on the Vote Account, over the years. The factors contributing to the sustained clean audit include clear strategic direction (articulated in strategic and annual performance plans), effective quarterly performance monitoring tools and systems, efficient internal controls, and leadership stability and commitment to performance. The NSG also continues to build its internal capacity and capability for effective performance management. Important to note is that an audit is an organization wide responsibility not just finance unit and that management support is required. Most notably lack of proper accounting system does not preclude users from achieving clean audit as such other tools available like excel can be used. Building a culture of compliance is key for the success of the organization and having the right people in finance and supply chain management is a recipe towards a successful audit outcome.

References

Adejumobi, J. (2011). *Introduction: State, economy, and society in a neoliberal regime*. Palgrave McMillan.

Auditor-General South Africa (AGSA). (2022). PFMA 2021/22: Consolidated General Report on National and Provincial Audit Outcomes. Retrieved April 6, 2024, from http://www.agsa.co.za.

Auditor-General South Africa (AGSA). (2024a). Audit information. Retrieved April 6, 2024, from http://www.agsa.co.za.

Auditor-General South Africa (AGSA). (2024b). Importance of ethical leadership in achieving well-functioning municipalities. Retrieved June 11, 2024, from https://www.cogta.gov.za/cgta_2016/wp-content/uploads/2024/03/Importance-of-Ethical-Leadership-in-achieving-well-functioning-municipalities-final.pdf.

Auditor-General South Africa (AGSA). (n.d.). Implementing key internal controls to eliminate undesirable audit outcomes. Retrieved May 2, 2024, from https://www.agsa.co.za/Portals/0/AP/AG/Implementing_key_internal_controls_to_eliminate_undesirable_audit_outcomes.pdf.

COSO. (2023). Applying the COSO ERM framework. Retrieved June 11, 2024, from https://www.coso.org/erm-framework.

Department of Cooperative Governance and Traditional Affairs (COGTA). (2009). *Local government turnaround strategy*. Government Printers.

Department of Planning, Monitoring and Evaluation (DPME). (2021). Electronic quarterly performance reports. Retrieved May 2, 2024, from www.dpme.gov.za.

Department of Planning, Monitoring and Evaluation (DPME). (2022). Policy framework for integrated planning. Retrieved May 2, 2024, from www.dpme.gov.za.

Department of Public Service and Administration (DPSA). (2017). Directive on the Performance Management and Development System for Heads of Department. Retrieved May 4, 2024, from https://www.dpsa.gov.za/dpsa2g/documents/sms/2018/14_4_1_p_11_01_2018.pdf

Khasodi, M. S. (2023). An assessment of clean audit outcomes as an effective determinant of good service delivery: A case study of Midvaal Local Municipality. Master's thesis, North-West University.

KPMG. (2013). COSO internal control—Integrated framework. Retrieved May 2, 2014, from https://assets.kpmg.com/content/dam/kpmg/pdf/2016/05/2750-New-COSO-2013-Framework-WHITEPAPER-V4.pdf.

Malatjie, I., Motubatse, K. N., & Ngcaweni, B. (2023). Financial accountability in the South African public sector: Key roles and responsibilities. In S. Damaray (Ed.), *Responsabilité financière des gestionnaires publics* (pp. 23–38). Mare & Martin.

Mazzucato, M., Qobo, M., & Kattel, R. (2021). Building state capacities and dynamic capabilities to drive social and economic development: The case of South Africa. Retrieved May 4, 2024, from https://www.ucl.ac.uk/bartlett/public-purpose/publications/2021/apr/building-state-capacities-and-dynamic-capabilities-drive-social-change-case.

Motubatse, K. N., Ngwakwe, C. C., & Sebola, M. P. (2017). The effect of governance on clean audits in South African municipalities. *African Journal of Public Affairs, 9*(5), 90–102.

National School of Government (NSG). (2018). Annual performance plan 2018-2019. www.thensg.gov.za

National School of Government (NSG). (2023). Annual performance plan 2023-2024. www.thensg.gov.za

National School of Government (NSG). (2024). Annual performance plan 2024-2025. www.thensg.gov.za

Parliamentary Monitoring Group (PMG). (2023). Auditor-General on 2022/23 National & Provincial Audit Outcomes. Retrieved June 11, 2024, from https://pmg.org.za/committee-meeting/38122/#:~:text=The%20Auditor%2DGeneral%20cited%20poor,provincial%20government%20and%20public%20entities'.

PWC. (2016). King IV An outcomes-based corporate governance code fit for a changing world. Retrieved June 11, 2024, from https://www.pwc.co.za/en/assets/pdf/king-iv-steering-point.pdf.

Republic of South Africa (RSA). (1999). Public Finance Management Act, No. 1 of 1999. Government Gazette, 33059, Apr. 1:1–82.

Republic of South Africa (RSA). (2012). The National Development Plan 2030: Our future—Make it work. Retrieved May 4, 2024, from https://www.gov.za/sites/default/files/gcis_document/201409/ndp-2030-our-future-make-it-workr.pdf.

South Africa (SA). (2022). Review of the National Development Plan 2012-2022. Retrieved June 11, 2024, from https://www.nationalplanningcommission.org.za/assets/Documents/Ten%20Year%20Review%20of%20the%20National%20Development%20Plan_26%20September%202023.pdf.

Taylor, E. (2023). Importance-of-leadership in the workplace. Retrieved May 2, 2024, from https://www.theknowledgeacademy.com/blog/importance-of-leadership.

The Presidency. (2009). Green paper: National strategic planning. Retrieved May 2, 2024, from https://www.gov.za/sites/default/files/gcis_document/201409/greenpapernational-strategic-planning0.pdf.

The Impact of Financial Inclusion on Women Entrepreneurship in South Africa

Amanda F. Mhlongo

Abstract Over the past decade, financial inclusion has gained recognition as one of the main pillars of the developmental goals in South Africa and has been identified as central to sustainable transformation and development of society. Despite this recognition, lack of finance and affordable credit remains one of the biggest hindrances in starting and growing a business in the country. These challenges are exacerbated when it comes to South African women entrepreneurs. Even though women represent more than half of the population, their participation in business is less than 30%. In South Africa, specifically, women entrepreneurs continue to have limited access to finance, which ultimately restricts the growth of their businesses, and they remain largely financially excluded and more specifically, excluded from affordable credit. The purpose of the study was to determine the impact of financial inclusion on women's entrepreneurship and, the extent to which the disparity in women's entrepreneurship can be explained by financial inclusion in South Africa. Through a conceptual framework and in-depth review of literature, we observed that entrepreneurship is positively influenced by financial inclusion, and since women represent more than half the population in South Africa, it is necessary to promote their participation in business. The study further observed that the South African government has made significant progress through various programmes, but this did not always translate into increased participation by women in business. Finally, the study observed that despite the various initiatives that have since been established, there will be no proper direction and measurement of the progress until the country adopts an explicit financial inclusion strategy.

Keywords Financial inclusion · Financial exclusion · Women's entrepreneurship · Sustainable transformation

A. F. Mhlongo (✉)
University of Johannesburg, Johannesburg, South Africa
e-mail: amandam@uj.ac.za

T. Moloi (ed.), *Impacting Society Positively Through Technology in Accounting and Business Processes*, Springer Proceedings in Business and Economics,
https://doi.org/10.1007/978-3-031-84885-8_39

Introduction

One of the biggest hindrances in starting and growing a business in South Africa is the lack of finance and affordable credit. According to Worthington and Xiang (2015) and Zhang et al. (2023), previously disadvantaged business owners and small businesses are the most vulnerable, because capital resources are limited to equity and debt finance. Most small businesses are privately owned and rarely have access to a range of equity funding such as ordinary shares and preference shares, or a range of debt financing such as debentures and bonds. As a result, they rely on internally generated equity like retained earnings and/or owner contributions. Cash flow restrictions and the survivalist nature of small businesses also make it difficult for internally generated equity to be reinvested in the business. Financial institutions, which are the primary providers of debt, need to establish a balance between risk and profit, and tend to restrict access or charge higher interest rates for high-risk borrowers with little or no collateral (Öhman & Yazdanfar, 2015). These adverse conditions make it difficult for South African businesses to operate and grow a business as they are essentially financially excluded.

Even though the South African government has recognised the business sector, and more specifically entrepreneurship, as one of the engines for economic growth, the challenges cited still hinder the success of those who pursue business and access to credit is the primary challenge identified by numerous researchers (Ahmad et al., 2017; Ayandibu & Houghton, 2017; Beck & Demirgüç-Kunt, 2006; Perrin & Weill, 2022). The challenges experienced by entrepreneurs are exacerbated for female entrepreneurs, and according to Giglio (2020) and Ukpere and Witbooi (2011), black women are worse off since they suffer racial and gender discrimination. In South Africa, women make up 51.5% of the population yet account for only 24% of business owners (Stats SA, 2022; Ukpere & Witbooi, 2011), indicating their lack of penetration in the business industry. Over and above the lack of access to economic freedom and opportunity, Ukpere and Witbooi (2011) further state that women are disadvantaged because of other risk dynamics which include financial, social, and personal risks. The potential of female entrepreneurs is not sufficiently utilised because of the challenges they face in South Africa, therefore their contribution to the economic development in this country is limited.

Over the past two decades, financial inclusion has gained recognition as one of the main pillars of the developmental goals in South Africa and has been identified as central to sustainable transformation and development of society. The South African government has positioned financial inclusion at a high level of its national agenda to support economic growth and reduce inequality. Through partnership with the private sector, efforts have been made to give people access to appropriate and affordable financial services. Financial inclusion has also been identified as one of the developmental goals in South Africa (National Development Plan 2030) and has been recognised as central to sustainable transformation and the development of society. It is imperative for developing countries like South Africa to strive continuously to improve financial inclusion to create encouraging environments for entrepreneurship in their economies.

Entrepreneurship is perceived as one of the most significant responses to unemployment, poverty, and deteriorating economic growth (Botha et al., 2015). It is among the essential drivers of economic growth in South Africa, more specifically the value added to gross domestic product (GDP), and this has remained a general trend in some developing countries in Africa. In Ghana, according to Cook and Eyiah (2002), entrepreneurship has played an important role in the delivery of infrastructure facilities essential for better living conditions and lessening the severe unemployment that impends the survival of the disadvantaged. In Kenya, according to Renny (2011), the business sector has become an important source of employment and ground-breaking technologies.

While the South African government is the single largest employer; on its own, it can neither generate sufficient economic growth nor equitable income distribution and requires the participation of the private sector through entrepreneurship in the economy. Stats SA has revealed that capital expenditure by public sector institutions increased by 4.6% in 2022 financial year, with a total expenditure amounting to R209 billion. Through its procurement, the government therefore has the opportunity to develop entrepreneurship by ensuring that a large portion of this expenditure is procured to Small Medium Enterprises (SMEs). The country is in dire need for alternatives to fight poverty and generate adequate economic growth as the unemployment rate has been on the incline while delivery of social services has been undermined by corrupt agencies of the government.

Women entrepreneurs have been designated as the new engines for growth and the rising stars of the economies in developing countries to bring prosperity and welfare (Vossenberg, 2013). According to Fareed et al. (2017) however, although they are essential for growth and development, women still earn less money with their businesses which generally also grow at a slower pace that is if they don't fail all together. These researchers (Fareed et al., 2017) further note that challenges faced by women are commonly faced by all entrepreneurs, however many characteristics of women entrepreneurs and of their enterprises differ from those of men, and therefore require specific policy interventions. Once policies are developed and implemented, research then seeks to observe the effects and analyse the findings.

Entrepreneurs in developing countries face many challenges with financial constraints, at the core of problem more specifically access to financial products and markets as well as the unfavourable environment for doing business. Internationally, numerous studies have been conducted to observe the relationship between women entrepreneurship and financial inclusion (Demirgüç-Kunt et al., 2013; Fareed et al., 2017; Parvin et al., 2012) but in South Africa the focus has been mainly on the progress of financial inclusion and its relationship with various economic factors including SMEs (Finmark Trust, 2015) and Individual Welfare (Nanziri, 2015). There has been limited research on the impact of financial inclusion on women entrepreneurship.

Problem Statement

The post-apartheid transition and transformation of the South African economy has resulted in some dynamics that have had both positive and negative effects on the business environment. For years, transformation was focused on general affirmative action, but this broad focus led to higher levels of inequality. The Human Development Report (2023) stated that South Africa has a Gini coefficient of 0.63, causing it to have one of the highest degrees of inequality worldwide. Although empowering the people through business ownership can lead to addressing inequality, there is no doubt that entrepreneurship is influenced by its environment (Coetsee & Visagie, 1995). Unfortunately, in the South African context, entrepreneurs have been affected by several constraints including lack of access to finance, which is arguably the most critical of these constraints (Cook & Eyiah, 2002). As a result, financial inclusion has emerged as a significant subject on the global agenda for sustainable long-term economic development (Amidžić et al., 2014).

In many Sub-Saharan African countries, women represent more than half of the population yet their participation in business is less than 30%. Although creating decent jobs and promoting entrepreneurship is central to these African countries' agendas, the slow pace of development in the low-income market, which comprises the majority of the population, has made it a challenge (Cull et al., 2017). In this context, the South African government prioritised financial inclusion in the NDP 2030, and identified it as an enabling milestone (Abrahams, 2017), because the inability of the poor to take part in the formal financial sector is one of the reasons for a slow-moving economy. Ardic et al. (2011) argue that there is a strong relationship between financial inclusion and economic growth, which is supported by Demirgüç-Kunt and Klapper (2012), who believe that well-functioning and inclusive financial systems promote entrepreneurship, create greater opportunities for advancement, and benefit the poor.

The challenge for South Africa is that even though female entrepreneurs have been identified as key potential players in developing the economy, they still have limited access to finance, which ultimately restricts the growth of their businesses. Women remain largely excluded from access to finance and more specifically, affordable credit. An inclusive economy with fair access to resources has a better chance of ensuring sustainable economic growth yet the growth rate of women's businesses in emerging countries continues to be unsatisfactory, leading to numerous governments developing initiatives to promote women's entrepreneurship.

Aims and Objectives

In line with the issues raised in the problem statement, the objectives of this article are to:

- *Assess the impact of financial inclusion on women's entrepreneurship.*

- The paper will explore contrasting and supporting views for financial inclusion as catalyst for improving women's entrepreneurship (i.e. assess whether financial inclusion is a key determinant for women's entrepreneurship) in the South African context.
- *Analyse the relationship between women's entrepreneurship and financial inclusion in the South African context.*
- The focus will be on the participation of women in business and their access to financial services.
- *Investigate whether the government's intervention through policy has been effective in improving women's entrepreneurship in South Africa.*
- Despite government's strategic focus on the empowerment of women, gender disparities (i.e. the gender gap) persist in South Africa. This section will review government policies to empower women.

Methodology

This conceptual paper seeks to predict a relationship between women's entrepreneurship and financial inclusion by using a conceptual model. In a study by Jaakkola (2020), a model paper seeks to build a theoretical framework that predicts relationships between concepts. In following this logic, this paper will begin with three propositions which will be further explained through formal reasoning and supported by research from multiple disciplines and real-world applications (Huang & Rust, 2018).

In addition, model papers can identify previously unexplored connections, introduce new constructs, or explain why elements of a process lead to a particular outcome (Cornelissen, 2017). This paper will seek to do the latter by explaining the impact that financial inclusion has on women entrepreneurship in South Africa by summarising arguments from various researchers, depicting the relationship and concluding on three propositions that have been raised.

Proposition 1: Entrepreneurship

Similar to other developing economies in Africa, South Africa has identified entrepreneurship as an essential driver of economic growth.

Proposition 2: Women's entrepreneurship

In South Africa, women make up more than half of the country's population, yet they are less represented in business than men and this is despite having identified women entrepreneurs as new engines for growth and the rising stars in the developing economies.

Proposition 3: Financial inclusion

Financial inclusion is essential to the development of women's entrepreneurship and ultimately the growth of a country's economy yet access to funding is the primary challenge faced by many entrepreneurs.

Overall, the three propositions lay out a foundation that entrepreneurship is perceived as one of the key drivers of economic development and if the South African government can focus on the improvement of financial inclusion incentives for women entrepreneurs, they too can effectively contribute to ensure a sustainable economy for the country.

Proposition 1: Entrepreneurship

Entrepreneurship has been acknowledged as an effective response to a deteriorating economy and includes the eradication of poverty and a reduction in unemployment (Botha et al., 2015; Meyer, 2018). According to the NDP 2030, entrepreneurship is among the critical drivers of economic growth in South Africa, and more specifically, is the value added to the country's GDP. This has remained a general trend in some developing countries in Africa. Further, the NDP 2030 has put greater focus on job creation and identified small and expanding firms as drivers of the 90% of jobs that must be created in South Africa within the next decade. One of the critical actions that will enable this kind of job creation is creating an economy more amenable to business start-ups and development, while also paying attention to credit and access to financial markets (NDP 2030).

In South Africa, the government is the single largest employer in the country, but it cannot generate sufficient economic growth and achieve equitable income distribution at the same time. It requires the participation of the private sector through entrepreneurship in the economy (Luiz, 2002). Through its procurement, the government can develop entrepreneurship by ensuring that a large portion of this expenditure is procured through SMEs. Stats SA has revealed that capital expenditure by South African public sector institutions was R209 billion in 2022, increasing from R199.8 billion in 2021. This increase cements the government as the single biggest provider of capital expenditure (CAPEX). Despite the government's sizeable contribution, preferential procurement on its own is not enough to address the deficiencies of SMEs; South Africa is in severe need of alternatives for fighting poverty while also generating adequate economic growth because the unemployment rate has been on the incline (Adato et al., 2006). These researchers noted that the delivery of social services has been seriously undermined by corrupt government agencies, which further compromises the efforts of the South African government in the fight against poverty, insufficient growth rates, and inequality. The question no longer is whether something should be done, but what must be done. In the view of Adu et al. (2016), there is a dynamic need for South African government to empower entrepreneurs for them to fight against the increasing levels of unemployment and boost formal education. This will result in improving the country's economy.

Proposition 2: Women Entrepreneurship

Women entrepreneurs have been identified as new engines for growth and the rising stars in the economies of developing countries, bringing prosperity and welfare (Vossenberg, 2013). In developed countries like the United States, women are starting and acquiring businesses at a faster rate than in any other segments of the economy (Morrison, 2016), but the concern is that the numbers indicate high volumes of sole proprietors and very small numbers of women in large ventures. This shows that a women's reasons for starting a business are different from those of their male counterparts. According to Morrison (2016), women's reproductive responsibilities and quality-of-life considerations may find them resisting growth as they seek a greater balance between the demands of work (business), family, and personal life. Success among women is defined by their independence and freedom, which factors are more internal than external (Paige & Litterell, 2002), and therefore not driven by profits and wealth. Nguyen (2005) identifies women's need for life balance and flexibility, which drives their entrepreneurial intentions while managing their traditional responsibilities as a wife and a child's primary caregiver. Society is changing though, and these findings may not always hold true.

According to Meyer (2018), access to credit for women entrepreneurs has gained momentum in South Africa, but as a country, our progress has been slow and ineffective in increasing the participation of women in business, and in increasing their access to funding and affordable credit. In the 2022/23 Report on Gender Transformation Public and Private Sectors prepared by the Commission for Gender Equality, it was found that women entrepreneurs in South Africa are more constrained in accessing credit than their male counterparts. In instances where they do obtain funding, they are charged higher interest rates, placing them in the vulnerable state of being over-indebted when cash flows are restricted. Women's involvement in various entrepreneurial activities globally has increased over the years, and as a result they have been empowered both socially and economically, demonstrating that entrepreneurship development and empowerment are complementary. This is further confirmed in a study by Jia et al. (2012), in which women's entrepreneurial development is cited as one of the crucial issues of the contemporary development agenda in many developing countries.

In the South African context where women account for more than half of the population, women's participation in the economy cannot be sidestepped and instead it becomes important for researchers to drive policy recommendations. In fact, the government must realise the importance of women entrepreneurs and endeavour to provide strategies for solidifying the development of women's entrepreneurship in the country. In a study conducted by Das (2000), of women entrepreneurs in the western world, the researcher proposes three factors that influence entrepreneurship:

- Ancestral influences, which include family factors such as genetics that affect personal skills and knowledge

- Incubator organisation, which refers to the type of company where the entrepreneur was previously employed or gained work experience and
- The environment, which includes business conditions, access to finance and support structures, and business mentors

Discrimination based on gender is an environmental challenge that is faced by many African countries, including South Africa. Discrimination has single-handedly infringed upon the development of women entrepreneurs. Llussá (2011) found in her study that women face discrimination both in the workplace and in business. However, she recognises that entrepreneurship may still be the most effective antidote to discrimination based on prejudice and on employers' preferences, as it provides women with an autonomous avenue to circumvent social obstacles to employment, career progress, and fair returns on their efforts. Even though entrepreneurship can be seen as a solution to discrimination, women still face a lot of discrimination compared to their male counterparts, especially in seeking funding for their business ventures. This is supported by the GEM statistics (GEM Report, 2017), which confirm that the percentage of men who are entrepreneurs by opportunity is higher than that of females, who generally tend to pursue careers in business because of need.

The financial inclusion data collected by the World Bank (Global Findex, 2017) prove that an increase in access to mobile money services has rendered sizeable benefits, especially for women, and has helped reduce extreme poverty among women-headed households by 22%. Despite this marginal alleviation of poverty, women entrepreneurs continue to have several bottlenecks and gaps in availability of credit, and although great strides have been made in microfinancing in the past decade, the process in developing countries is slow (Srinivasan, 2009). In a study done in India by Ghosh and Dharmarajan (2017), the findings were similar, where about 8% of women were found to have 8% less access to finance compared to men, and this also translates to the use of financial services, where women utilised 20% less credit than men. This is more severe for women entrepreneurs in the rural areas. According to Sharma et al. (2012), in addition to the financial challenges they face, women entrepreneurs in rural areas receive poor quality information about microfinance, which directly affects their decision-making. It is notable that South Africa is one of the highest gender inequality countries (ranked at number ninety in the world), and yet the country has no significant gender gap in bank account ownership.

It is essential for governments to understand the dynamics of their countries, to devise policies and strategies that are relevant to their own personal traits. Due to apartheid in South Africa, the country has high levels of inequality and gender inequality. Finding effective methods to address these problems could lead to improving the participation of women in the business sector.

Proposition 3: Financial Inclusion

Over the past decade, financial inclusion has appeared as a significant subject on the worldwide agenda for sustainable and long-term economic growth, and many central banks of developed and developing countries have put various initiatives in place to encourage financial inclusion in their countries (Amidžić et al., 2014). South Africa has accepted financial inclusion as one of the drivers of socio-economic development and therefore has committed to focusing on policies that will improve financial access to all citizens of the country (National Development Plan 2030). Despite financial inclusion being identified as central to economic growth, financial constraints remain the biggest challenge entrepreneurs encounter, especially in developing countries (Fareed et al., 2017). Through partnerships with the private sector, the South African government has made efforts that give people access to appropriate and affordable financial services. This is in line with their prioritisation of financial inclusion on its national agenda to support economic growth and reduce inequality.

Financial inclusion can also be viewed as an intervention strategy that seeks to overcome the market friction that hinders markets from operating in favour of the poor and underprivileged. Its objectives include offering incremental and complementary solutions that confront poverty while promoting inclusive development (Oruo, 2013). Simply put, market friction refers to the transaction costs and financial inclusion that promote access to financial services for the poor and disadvantaged while indirectly addressing excessive transaction costs.

Several other studies highlight the transformative power of financial inclusion, which should not be underestimated because improved access to finance by micro enterprises can generate income-earning opportunities and self-reliance for many, thus positively impacting on a country's economic development (Atkinson & Messy, 2013; Han & Melecky, 2014; Oruo, 2013). However, while economic growth must be on the incline to propel financial inclusion, on its own it is not always sufficient to promote equality among the poor and gender equality for the transformation of female entrepreneurs. Financial literacy and transformation are important considerations when attempting to decipher financial inclusion and exclusion in the South African context, where most of the population was previously disadvantaged, resulting in a need to first educate before transformation can be effective.

Discussion: Doing Business as a Woman

South African women have not always been active in business because of the burden of gender discrimination. Black women were worse off because they were both black and female (Witbooi & Ukpere, 2011). Despite these challenges, over the years, women have managed to rise above their challenges in pursuit of equality in general and in business in particular (Minniti & Naudé, 2010). Access to financial services in South Africa remains largely defined by race and gender, which negatively affects the way women do business. These challenges are likely to continue unless efforts are made to address the underlying issues that contribute to constraining the success of women in business (Allahar, 2015). Such constraints include lack of financial skills, lack of training, limited access to markets, and role barriers, to name but a few (Ukpere & Witbooi, 2011).

Empowering Women Through Entrepreneurship

As discussed in the first proposition, entrepreneurship is important for developing countries as it is considered a catalyst for economic growth and to alleviate the pressure on government to support its people through social grants by empowering them through business. Empowerment is defined as a process of increasing the capacity of individuals or groups to make choices and to transform those choices into desired actions and outcomes. Kabeer (2005) describes empowerment as ability to make choices and involve change. In the study, Kabeer (2005) further explains that to be disempowered is to be denied choice, while empowerment refers to processes through which those who have been denied the ability to make choices acquire such an ability.

Empowering women through business must not only seek to address immediate inequalities but also initiate longer-term processes of change (Kabeer, 2005). Fairlie and Robb (2009) argue that institutional transformation is a critical requirement for sustainable gender equality but entails movement along several fronts: from individual to collective agency, from private negotiations to public action, and from the informal sphere to the formal arenas of struggle where power is legitimately exercised.

Women who are empowered through business positively impact economic development and contribute to employment creation and the diversity of entrepreneurship in the economic process (Meyer, 2018). Because women generally engage in survivalist activities, according to Mandipaka (2014), they tend to address poverty eradication and unemployment more immediately and effectively than other government initiatives. The role of women entrepreneurs should not be underestimated, and opportunities must be created to allow women to pursue entrepreneurial ventures (Nxopo, 2014).

Gender Inequalities in Entrepreneurship

South Africa's Gender Inequality Index (GII) is at 0.394, and the country is ranked in the 90th place. If compared to the BRICS countries, China (ranked 37) and Russia (ranked 52) have the lowest levels of gender inequality, while India (ranked 127) has the highest. Brazil and South Africa have relatively similar index values and are ranked 79 and 90, respectively, placing them in the mid-range level of gender inequality. However, South Africa has continued to place great value on developing women entrepreneurs, as observed by several preferential policies that have been integrated into the legislation. According to the 2013 Gender Report of Stats SA, women comprise 23% of South Africa's total employers. In the manufacturing and business sectors they own a marginal 15% and 20%, respectively, in contrast to 85% and 80%, respectively, of firms owned by men. Encouragingly, in the tourism sector, women own 48% of firms compared to men who own 52%, clearly indicating that some sectors are either more attractive or more accessible to women. This is a demonstration that progress in closing the gender gap in developing countries seems more positive when combined with an expansion of women's emancipation (Jia et al., 2012; Kabeer, 2012; Verhoef, 2017).

It is important to note that although access to financial services is central to the development of women entrepreneurs, access to fair credit is equally important (Fareed et al., 2017). As a result, the micro-lending sector in South Africa offers diversity for entrepreneurial development. (Matsebula & Yu, 2017). Although this type of funding gives small businesses access to capital injections, it is excessively expensive because it is unsecured. Busza et al. (2007) argue that microfinance may effectively aid female empowerment, and that the new business skills they acquire may lead to increased self-esteem and self-confidence, conflict resolution, and the ability to network to create larger social circles. However, Busza et al. (2007) also note that the benefits of microfinance in relation to women's entrepreneurship cannot be seen as unlimited, as they are multifaceted.

Although entrepreneurship is critical to economic development, a broad focus on developing entrepreneurs can also lead to higher levels of inequality that widen the gender gap. In South Africa, despite the launch of Broad-based Economic Empowerment (BEE), women's involvement in the business sector is significantly lower than that of their male counterparts. According to the Gender Series Volume IX (2022) of Stats SA, women are more likely than men to be in the lowest income households, comprising 27.1% of this income level opposed to 15.6% for men. The 2022 GEM Report supplements this notion with findings that on average men are 2.3 times more likely to be involved in entrepreneurship than women. Vossenberg (2013) defines the gender gap as the difference between men and women in terms of numbers involved in entrepreneurial activity, motives to start or run a business, industry choice, and business performance and growth.

Despite the evidence that we have explored presenting women's entrepreneurship as essential for growth and development of a country (Fareed et al., 2017), women continue to earn less money through their businesses, which generally also grow at a slower pace, that is, if they do not fail all together. Fareed et al. (2017) further note that the challenges faced by women are generally faced by all entrepreneurs. Yet, many characteristics of women entrepreneurs and of their enterprises differ from those of men, and therefore require specific policy interventions. Some of these differences include attitudes towards risk, differing leadership styles and most importantly, their translated role from their households, which they commonly maintain in their businesses (Minniti & Naudé, 2010).

Little is understood about the gender gap in terms of women's accessibility to finance and/or the specific barriers that restrict access to finance for women relative to men, but it is widely accepted that the role of financial systems that are well-functioning can address income inequality and promote economic growth (Demirgüç-Kunt et al., 2013). Although economies and governments have transformed globally, the different treatment of women under legislation and/or cultural customs constrains them to enter into legal contracts under their own names, including the opening of bank accounts, and these constraints cannot be corrected by a change of legislation. These historic prejudices may not only have created access barriers for women, but also may have produced an involuntary male reservation towards women's entrepreneurship, making it even harder for them to become acquainted with business activities and sustainably integrate into this field.

In many African countries like Ghana, Zimbabwe, and the Democratic Republic of Congo (DRC), women constitute over 50% of the population (as evidenced in the South African context) yet they struggle to achieve parity with the male population in their bid to develop their countries (Cull et al., 2017). A study by McKinsey Global Institute (2016) reveals that in the DRC, the GDP is estimated to increase by 17% or more by 2025 if the country can improve its gender equality at the same rate. According to Cull et al. (2017), the reason for this is that in the DRC, 25% of households are headed by women, due to the recent civil war, while the men are migrant workers. Poverty levels are falling faster in female-headed households in Sub-Saharan Africa than in male-headed homes, indicating the importance of empowering women in the plight of eradicating poverty.

Even though gender inequality is one of the key Millennium Development Goals that are fundamental to human development, violence against women is another factor that upholds gender inequality and is a critical risk factor preventing women's participation in the advancement of the economy (Rodrik, 2008). If women continue to live in fear of their lives, it follows that they will not be free to participate in developing the economy. In addition to the gender-based violence against women, in some rural communities, traditional and cultural customs continue to uphold the assumption that women are inferior, despite the South African government prioritising the improvement of women's status, as stipulated in the Constitution It is to be hoped that this will have a positive impact on women's participation levels.

Women Entrepreneurship as a Solution

While entrepreneurs may generally face similar problems, which are largely centred on access to financial products and markets in addition to the climate for doing business, many characteristics of women entrepreneurs and of their enterprises differ from those of men (Fareed et al., 2017). However, women-owned businesses have the potential to be a key source of job creation and a direct tool to address inequalities, given the current gender gap in both labour participation and entrepreneurship.

Despite all challenges cited, entrepreneurship remains an effective solution for developing an economy and addressing gender-related matters, which must be prioritised to nurture the participation of women in business. This is in line with the second proposition identifying women entrepreneurs as the one of the crucial economic players that can eradicate poverty and contribute positively to a country's economy.

Other Women-Led Initiatives in South Africa

Theoretically, there should not be any differences between initiatives to encourage entrepreneurship among men and women, but because of South Africa's history where in the past men were favoured at the expense of women when it came to entrepreneurial assistance, it is only fitting that the scales should be tipped for a more even distribution of entrepreneurial aid through fast-tracking programmes in favour of female entrepreneurship (Chinomona & Maziriri, 2015).

Furthermore, women have refused to sit on the sidelines when it comes to their development and have established numerous organisations within different sectors that advocate for their development and equality. Botha (2010) identified a few non-profit organisations established to date, namely, the Businesswomen's Association of SA (BWA); the National African Women's Alliance; the National Women in Agribusiness Co-operative; African Women Chartered Accountants; Women in Nuclear; Technology for Women in Business; South African Women Entrepreneurs Network; Women in Research, and so on. There is much controversy on the effectiveness of these organisations in their advocating for women's development. The government has taken an active role in addressing gender inequalities in business by introducing preferential procurement for women entrepreneurs, favourable tax incentives for small businesses, and training and support programmes for women.

Beck et al. (2003) are against preferential treatment in business, whether for purposes of income re-distribution or to address gender equality. They state that business constraints shame the business environment, and that regulation could result in imperfect markets and institutional weaknesses. But for economies built on the injustices of inequality and deliberate upliftment of one race over the other and one gender over the other, these past wrongs cannot be addressed by turning a blind eye and relying on the markets to self-regulate. Effective financial inclusion policies will be required to address historic prejudices.

Conclusion: Financial Inclusion and Women Entrepreneurship

The dynamics that surround women and how they do business depart from those of their male counterparts simply because of cultural and historical aspects that lie outside the scope of this study, but this means that if debt financing is not utilised effectively, it could have detrimental effects on women entrepreneurs. Entrepreneurship can be positively influenced by financial inclusion, and since women represent more than half the population in South Africa, it is necessary to promote their participation in business. Past discrimination against women is motivation for the South African government to introduce relevant policies that will guide the process of fully integrating women into business. Access to financial services and to credit will not solve the financial challenges faced by women entrepreneurs. Strategies must be put in place to ensure that credit is accessible and affordable. The notion that financial inclusion means access to finance is another primary concern because access is limited.

The study was motivated by the lack of women entrepreneurship in South Africa despite the strategic focus by the government to empower women and increase their participation in business. Although several studies (Akisimire et al., 2015; Al-Najjar & Al-Najjar, 2017; Beck & Demirgüç-Kunt, 2006; Botha et al., 2006; Witbooi & Ukpere, 2011) have been conducted to determine the challenges faced by women in business, limited research has been conducted with regard to financial inclusion as a restricting factor. Hence this study intended to add to the pool of knowledge.

As both women entrepreneurship and financial inclusion are social concerns, the study also accessed whether the government's intervention through policy has been effective in improving women's entrepreneurship. Through literature, we observed that the South African government has made significant progress through various programmes, but this did not always translate into increased participation by women in business. The study also observed the challenges facing South Africa in enhancing financial inclusion with a specific focus on gender inequality and although women have higher access to banking services, this too did not translate in to increased participation in business (Meyer, 2018; Mijid, 2014).

In South Africa, the responsibility of improving financial inclusion rests with the National Treasury, which has conducted some research on the topic since 2004. However, until the country adopts an explicit Financial Inclusion Strategy, there will be no proper direction and measurement of the progress (Abrahams, 2017). Despite the various initiatives that have since been established, including the Financial Sector Charter, the Mzanzi Account, the National Credit Act, and mobile banking, there is little central coordination by the National Treasury (Abrahams, 2017). This means that it might be a while longer before strategies that focus directly on reducing gender inequality will be evident.

The first important recommendation is a collaboration between the private and public sectors. Statutory regulations are less effective in addressing inequalities because they end up being a quota exercise that checks boxes and makes little difference in practice. A true collaboration would be driven by the need for economic growth, where government's contribution would yield tangible fiscal benefits in the long run and the role of financial institutions would produce profits and wealth generation for its shareholders. Secondly, policies to address gender inequality in business must be driven and pioneered by women and must focus on initiatives that will promote long-term and sustainable equality in business. Finally, greater structure and focus must lead to research on women's entrepreneurship that will form the basis for relevant policy formulation, while noting that without effective research, there will be a mismatch between what is being addressed and what the problem actually is.

References

Abrahams, R. (2017). Financial inclusion in South Africa: A review of the literature. In *Proceedings of the biennial international conference conducted by the Southern African Accounting Association in 2017*. Champagne Sports Resort, Drakensberg, South Africa.

Adato, M., Carter, M. R., & May, J. (2006). Exploring poverty traps and social exclusion in South Africa using qualitative and quantitative data. *Journal of Development Studies, 42*, 226–247.

Adu, E. O., Ewere, A. D., & Ibrahim, S. I. (2016). Exploring the adequate strategies adopted by women to sustain the growth and development of entrepreneurship in the Nkonkobe Municipality, Eastern Cape. *Journal of Economics, 7*(1), 25–30.

Ahmad, R. A., Ali, A., & Muneer, S. (2017). Impact of financial management practices on SMEs profitability with the moderating role of agency cost. *Information Management and Business Review, 9*(1), 23–30.

Akisimire, R., Kamukama N., Mutaremwa, G., & Tumwine, S. (2015). A borrowing cost model for effective performance of SMEs in Uganda. *World Journal of Entrepreneurship, Management and Sustainable Development, 11*(2), 74–89.

Allahar, H. (2015). The identification and mapping of tourism clusters: An economic development strategy for small countries. *International Journal of Economics, Commerce and Management, 3*(11), 318–335.

Al-Najjar, B., & Al-Najjar, D. (2017). The impact of external financing on firm value and a corporate governance index: SME evidence. *Journal of Small Business and Enterprise Development, 24*(2), 411–423.

Amidžić, G., Massara, A., & Mialou, A. (2014). *Assessing countries' financial inclusion standing—A new composite index* (IMF Working Paper No. WP/14/36). Retrieved January 31, 2024, from https://doi.org/10.5089/9781475569681.001.

Ardic, O. P., Heimann, M., & Mylenko, N. (2011). *Access to financial services and the financial inclusion agenda around the world: A cross-country analysis with a new data set* (Policy Research Working Paper No. WPS 5537). World Bank.

Atkinson, A., & Messy, F. (2013). *Promoting financial inclusion through financial education* (OECD Working Papers on Finance, Insurance and Private Pensions No. 34, pp. 1–53). Retrieved June 20, 2018, from https://doi.org/10.1787/5k3xz6m88smp-en.

Ayandibu, A. O., & Houghton, J. (2017). The role of small and medium scale enterprise in local economic development (LED). *Journal of Business and Retail Management Research, 11*(2), 133–139.

Beck, T., & Demirgüç-Kunt, A. (2006). Small and medium-size enterprises: Access to finance as a growth constraint. *Journal of Banking & Finance, 30*(11), 2931–2943.

Beck, T., Demirgüç-Kunt, A., & Levine, R. (2003). *Small and medium enterprises, growth, and poverty: Cross-country evidence* (Policy Research Working Paper No. 3178). World Bank. Retrieved May 20, 2023, from https://openknowledge.worldbank.org/handle/10986/17742.
Botha, M., Nieman, G., & van Vuuren, J. (2006). Enhancing female entrepreneurship by enabling access to skills. *The International Entrepreneurship and Management Journal, 2*(4), 479–493.
Botha, M., Kunene, T., & Van Vuuren, J. J. (2015). An integrated entrepreneurial performance model focusing on the importance and proficiency of competencies for start-up and established SMEs. *South African Journal of Business Management, 46*(3), 55–66.
Botha, P. (2010). *An analysis of low tax jurisdictions as a means of increasing foreign direct investments from a South Africa point of view.* Doctoral dissertation, University of Pretoria.
Busza, J., Hargreaves, J. R., Kim, J. C., Morison, L. A., Ndhlovu, L. X., Phetla, G. M., Porter, J. D. H., Pronyk, P., & Watts, C. H., (2007). Understanding the impact of a microfinance-based intervention on women's empowerment and the reduction of intimate partner violence in South Africa. *American Journal of Public Health, 97*(10), 1794–1802. Retrieved February 25, 2018, from https://doi.org/10.2105/AJPH.2006.095521.
Chinomona, E., & Maziriri, E. T. (2015). Women in action: Challenges facing women entrepreneurs in the Gauteng Province of South Africa. *The International Business & Economics Research Journal, 14*(6), 835.
Coetsee, J. E., & Visagie, J. C. (1995). SMEs in South Africa: The challenge of change. *Journal of Small Businesses & Entrepreneurship, 12*(1), 64–77.
Cook, P., & Eyiah, A. K. (2002). Financing small and medium-scale contractors in developing countries: a Ghana case study. *Journal of Construction Management and Economics, 21*(4), 357–367.
Cornelissen, J. P. (2017). Preserving theoretical divergence in management research: Why the explanatory potential of qualitative research should be harnessed rather than suppressed. *Journal of Management Studies, 54*(3), 368–383.
Cull, R., Harten, S., Gine, X., Heitman, S., & Rusu, A. B. (2017). Agent banking in a highly under-developed financial sector: Evidence from Democratic Republic of Congo. *World Development, 107*(C), 54–74. Elsevier.
Das, D. J. (2000). Problems faced by women entrepreneurs. In K. Sasikumar (Ed.), *Women entrepreneurship*. Vikas Publishing House.
Demirgüç-Kunt, A., & Klapper, L. (2012, June). *Financial inclusion in Africa: an overview*. World Bank Policy Research (pp. 1–18). Retrieved October 25, 2023, from https://doi.org/10.1596/1813-9450-6088.
Demirgüç-Kunt, A., Klapper, L., & Randall, D. (2013). *Islamic finance and financial inclusion: measuring use of and demand for formal financial services among Muslim adults*. The World Bank.
Fairlie, R. W., & Robb, A. M. (2009). Gender differences in business performance: Evidence from the characteristics of business owners survey. *Small Business Economics, 33*(4), 375–395.
Fareed, F., Gabriel, M., Lenain, P., & Reynaud, J. (2017). *Financial inclusion and women entrepreneurship: Evidence from Mexico* (OECD Economics Department Working Paper No. 1411). Retrieved October 2, 2023, from https://doi.org/10.1787/2fbd0f35-en.
Finmark Trust. (2015). *Financial access and SME size in South Africa*. University of South Africa.
Ghosh, S., & Dharmarajan, V. (2017). What constrains financial inclusion for women? Evidence from Indian micro data. *World Development, 92*(2017), 60–81.
Giglio, F. (2020). Access to credit and women entrepreneurs: A systematic literature review. *European Research Studies Journal, 23*(4), 312–335.
Global Entrepreneurship Monitor—GEM. (2017). The 2017/2018 Global Report.
Global Entrepreneurship Monitor—GEM. (2022). The 2022/2023 Global Report.
Global Findex Database. (2017). Measuring Financial Inclusion and the Fintech Revolution. Washington, DC: World Bank.
Han, R., & Melecky, M. (2014). *Financial inclusion for financial stability: Access to bank deposits and the growth of deposits in the global financial crisis* (Policy Research Working Paper

No. WPS 6577). World Bank. Retrieved May 20, 2018, from https://doi.org/10.1596/1813-9450-6577.
Huang, M. H., & Rust, R. T. (2018). Artificial intelligence in service. *Journal of Service Research, 21*(2), 155–172.
Human Development Report. (2023). United Nations Development Programme (2023-24). The 2023-24 Human Development Report. Available from: https://hdr.undp.org/content/human-development-report-2023-24 (Accessed on 28 March 2024).
Jaakkola, E. (2020). Designing conceptual articles: four approaches. *AMS review, 10*(1), 18–26.
Jia, J., Parvin, L., & Rahman, M. W. (2012). Determinates of women micro-entrepreneurship development: An empirical investigation in rural Bangladesh. *International Journal of Economics and Finance, 4*(5), 254–260. Retrieved February 20, 2024, from https://doi.org/10.5539/ijef.v4n5p254.
Kabeer, N. (2005). Gender equality and women's empowerment: A critical analysis of the third Millennium Development Goal. *Journal of Gender and Development, 13*(1), 13–24.
Kabeer, N. (2012). Women's economic empowerment and inclusive growth: Labour markets and enterprise development. *The Journal of Gender and Development, 44*, 1–65.
Llussá, F. (2011). *Determinants of entrepreneurship: Are women different*? (FEUNL Working Paper 555). Universidade Nova de Lisboa.
Luiz, J. (2002). Small business development, entrepreneurship and expanding the business sector in a developing economy: The case of South Africa. *Journal of Applied Business Research, 18*(2), 53–68.
Mandipaka, F. (2014). An investigation of the challenges faced by women entrepreneurs in developing countries: A case of King Williams' Town, South Africa. *Mediterranean Journal of Social Sciences, 5*(27 P3), 1187.
Matsebula, V., & Yu, D. (2017). *Financial inclusion in South Africa: a NIDS data analysis of household access and the usage of financial services and products*. Department of Economics, University of the Western Cape.
McKinsey Global Institute. (2016). Africa still rising, September 2016. Available https://www.mckinsey.com/mgi/overview/in-the-news/africa-still-rising#/ (Accessed on 25 March 2024).
Meyer, N. (2018). Research on female entrepreneurship: are we doing enough? *Polish Journal of Management Studies, 17*(2), 1–12.
Mijid, N. (2014). Why are female small business owners in the United States less likely to apply for bank loans than their male counterparts? *Journal of Small Business & Entrepreneurship, 27*(2), 229–249.
Minniti, M., & Naudé, W. (2010). What do we know about the patterns and determinants of female entrepreneurship across countries? *The European Journal of Development Research, 22*, 277–293.
Morrison, M. J. (2016). *The global business environment: Challenges and responsibilities*. Palgrave Macmillan.
Nanziri, E. L. (2015). *Financial inclusion and individual welfare: The case of post-apartheid South Africa*. Doctoral dissertation. University of Cape Town.
National Development Plan 2030 (NDP). (2012).
Nguyen, M. (2005). Women entrepreneurs: Turning disadvantages into advantages. Retrieved January 29, 2007, from http://www.preflightventures.com/resources/womenentrepreneursLitSurvey01-2005.htm. Accessed October 20, 2023.
Nxopo, Z. (2014). The role of government in empowering female entrepreneurs in the Western Cape, South African. Doctoral dissertation, Cape Peninsula University of Technology.
Öhman, P., & Yazdanfar, D. (2015). Debt financing and firm performance: an empirical study based on Swedish data. *The Journal of Risk Finance, 16*(1), 102–118. Retrieved May 20, 2024, from https://doi.org/10.1108/JRF-06-2014-0085.
Oruo, J. (2013). The relationship between financial inclusion and GDP growth in Nairobi. MBA Research Project, The University of Nairobi. Retrieved January 31, 2018, from http://www.

eajournals.org/wp-content/uploads/Effects-of-Financial-Inclusion-on-theEconomic-Growth-of-Nigeria-1982-2012.pdf.

Paige, R. C. & Littrell, M. A. (2002). Craft retailers' criteria for success and associated business strategies. *Journal of Small Business Management, 40*(4), pp. 314–331.

Parvin, L., Rahman, M. W., & Jia, J. (2012). Determinates of women micro entrepreneurship development: An empirical investigation in rural Bangladesh. *International journal of Economics and Finance, 4*(5), 254–260.

Perrin, C., & Weill, L. (2022). No man, No cry? Gender equality in access to credit and financial stability. *Finance Research Letters, 47*, 102694.

Renny, M. (2011). Micro and small enterprise sector and existing support system with the emphasis on high-tech orientated entrepreneurship in Kenya. *Journal of Language, Technology & Entrepreneurship in Africa, 3*(1), 99–108.

Rodrik, D. (2008). Understanding South Africa's economic puzzles. *Economics of Transition, 16*(4), 769–797.

Sharma, A., Dua, S., & Hatwal, V. (2012). Micro enterprise development and rural women entrepreneurship: way for economic empowerment. *Arth Prabhand: A Journal of Economics and Management, 1*(6), 114–127.

Statistics South Africa. (2022). Gender Series Volume X: Economic Empowerment, 2016-2022 Report. Available from: https://www.statssa.gov.za/publications/Report-03-10-27/Report-03-10-272022.pdf (Accessed on 26 April 2024).

Srinivasan, N. (2009). Microfinance India, State of the Sector report 2009. Sage India.

Ukpere, W., & Witbooi, M. (2011). Indigenous female entrepreneurship: Analytical study on access to finance for women entrepreneurs in South Africa. *African Journal of Business Management, 5*(14), 646–557.

Verhoef, G. (2017). The rise of financial services in Africa: An historical perspective. In D. T. Redford (Ed.), *Developing Africa's financial services* (pp. 3–42). Emerald.

Vossenberg, S. (2013). *Women entrepreneurship promotion in developing countries: What explains the gender gap in entrepreneurship and how to close it?* (Working Paper No. 2013/08).

Witbooi, M., & Ukpere, W. (2011). Indigenous female entrepreneurship: Analytical study on access to finance for women entrepreneurs in South Africa. *African Journal of Business Management, 5*(14), 5646.

Worthington, A., & Xiang, D. (2015) Finance-seeking behaviour and outcomes for small and medium-sized enterprises. *International Journal of Managerial Finance, 11*(4), 513–530. Retrieved May 4, 2024, from https://doi.org/10.1108/IJMF-01-2013-0005.

Zhang, X., Li, J., Xiang, D., & Worthington, A. C. (2023). Digitalization, financial inclusion, and small and medium-sized enterprise financing: evidence from China. *Economic Modelling, 126*, 106410.

Is the Turnover Tax System Perceived to Be Too Complex for Micro-enterprise Owners/Managers? An Exploratory Study

Astrid Hellberg, Sharon Smulders, and Mphagahlele Ndlovu

Abstract The National Treasury launched the Turnover Tax System (TTS) to alleviate the tax compliance burden of micro-enterprises and negate the need to attain the assistance of a tax practitioner to be tax compliant. Notwithstanding this endeavour instituted to aid micro-enterprises, the uptake remains low. The objective of this study is to examine whether the low adoption rate of the TTS may be attributed to its perceived complexity amongst owners or managers of micro-enterprises. This study was conducted in the Gauteng province (except for a Cape Town and Nelspruit participant), South Africa. A qualitative research approach was implemented. Semi-structured interviews to gather insights from a sample of 19 owners of micro-enterprises were used. The participants were selected through purposive and snowball sampling techniques. The principal finding of this study revealed that participants lacked a comprehension of the TTS; that the participants found the TTS legislation to be too complex and continued to obtain assistance from tax practitioners to comply with their TTS obligations. The TTS concept is viewed as good by micro-enterprise owners although the law and administration thereof are too complex, and the South African Revenue Service (SARS) officials could benefit from refining their understanding of the TTS. For the TTS to be effective and meet its intended objective, it should be simplified from both a legislative and administrative perspective.

Keywords Exploratory qualitative research · Micro-enterprise · SMMEs · Taxation · Tax canons · Turnover tax system

A. Hellberg · S. Smulders · M. Ndlovu (✉)
University of South Africa, Pretoria, South Africa
e-mail: ndlovmo@unisa.ac.za

T. Moloi (ed.), *Impacting Society Positively Through Technology in Accounting and Business Processes*, Springer Proceedings in Business and Economics,
https://doi.org/10.1007/978-3-031-84885-8_40

Introduction

Small, medium, and micro-enterprises (SMMEs) play an important role when it comes to economic growth, employment, and poverty reduction (Ramsuraj, 2023; Saah, 2021; Smulders et al., 2016, 2017). The South African National Development Plan (NDP) directs that SMMEs should generate 90% of the domestic-oriented and services sector employment by 2030 (RSA, 2012).

To address the known high unemployment, hardship, and discrimination present in South Africa, the South African Government implemented various initiatives to support SMMEs (Labuschagne, 2018; Smulders et al., 2016, 2017; Wiese, 2014). However, despite these initiatives and the time and resources invested into the SMMEs sector, the anticipated growth rates of 5.4% and the reduction in unemployment to 14% by 2020 hoped for in the NDP were not achieved (RSA, 2012). Instead, the GDP growth rate is reported at 0.6% for 2023 (Stats SA, 2023) and the unemployment rate at 32.9% in quarter 1: 2024 (Stats SA, 2024).

The Department of Small Business Development (DSBD) identifies five key factors hampering SMMEs' success (The Davis Tax Committee (DTC), 2016). These encompass procurement practices within the public sector, regulatory restrictions, public sector value chain admittance, access to finance difficulties, and provision for unofficial and rural SMMEs (DTC, 2016). Among the regulatory restraints emphasised by the DTC is the burden and associated expenses of adhering to tax regulations, which research suggests disproportionately affect SMMEs with higher costs compared to larger enterprises (Ndlovu, 2015; Smulders et al., 2016, 2017; Smulders & Naidoo, 2013).

Recognising these challenges encountered by SMMEs, the National Treasury and the South African Revenue Services (SARS) launched two incentives, the Small Business Corporation Tax Concession (SBCTC) and the Turnover Tax System (TTS), to assist SMMEs. The SBCTC is accessible to companies with gross income threshold of R20 million or below among other requirements. The TTS, on the other hand, was introduced in 2009 as a "separate tax system" to specifically assist micro-enterprises with a qualifying turnover threshold of R1 million or below among other requirements (SARS, 2024a, 2024b; Stiglingh et al., 2024). The emphasis of this research is the TTS.

The initial implementation of the TTS aimed to incentivise tax registration among the informal sector and small enterprises generating taxable earnings of R1 million or below. This was achieved through the mitigation of compliance expenses and administrative complexities, including recordkeeping, typically associated with standard income tax procedures (NT, 2012). The main objective of the TTS is to facilitate micro-enterprises in fulfilling their tax responsibilities (Lindeque, 2012; SARS, 2024a). The simplification is apparent as micro-enterprises only have to pay one tax, namely the Turnover Tax as opposed to other enterprises paying five other taxes: Income Tax, Provisional Tax, Capital Gains Tax, Value Added Tax, and Dividends Tax (capped at R200,000 annually) (RSA, 1962; SARS, 2024a). The decrease in tax burdens and the ease of calculating the business tax obligations (based on taxable turnover instead on taxable income, thus eliminating the need to keep records of all expense incurred) were introduced with the aim of enabling taxpayers to independently fulfil their tax obligations without the costly aid of a tax consultant, thereby diminishing their tax compliance expenses (NT & SARS, 2010). Consequently, an expectation emerged that micro-enterprises would no longer necessitate the services of tax practitioners, given the perceived ease and straightforwardness of the TTS (NT & SARS, 2010).

For this study, the micro-enterprise definition as contained in the Income Tax Act is adopted. According to Part II of the Sixth Schedule (RSA, 1962), a person qualifies as a micro-enterprise, among other requirements, if that taxpayer is a natural person or enterprise where the "qualifying turnover" of that taxpayer for the year of assessment is R1 million or below.

The TTS tax obligation for a micro-enterprise is calculated by employing the applicable tax rates (refer to Table 1) to a micro-enterprises' "taxable turnover" (RSA, 1962; SARS, 2024a). For this reason, micro-enterprises may be required to pay tax even when they have made losses as the tax liability is not calculated using "taxable profits" but rather "taxable turnover" (RSA, 1962; SARS, 2024a).

For the purposes of this study, complexity refers to the difficulty in understanding how the TTS works from a legislative as well as administrative perspective. Thus, the aim of this study is to explore whether the TTS is perceived to be too complicated for micro-enterprise owners or managers by answering the following research questions:

- Do micro-enterprise owners or managers understand how the TTS works both from a legislative and administrative perspective?
- Do micro-enterprises use tax practitioners to assist them with their TTS compliance obligations, and if so, why?

The presence or the absence of comprehension of how the TTS works from a legislative as well as administrative perspective together with the continued use of tax practitioners will be used as indicators of whether the TTS is perceived by micro-enterprise owners or managers to be complex or not. The continued use of tax practitioners is an important indicator of how complex the TTS is, as oftentimes micro-enterprises outsource tax compliance activities because these tax compliance activities are specialised in nature and too complex for taxpayers to handle on their own (Coolidge et al., 2009).

Table 1 The applicable turnover tax rates for the period 1 March 2024 to 28 February 2025

Taxable turnover (R-amount)	Applicable tax rate
1–335,000	0% of taxable turnover
335,000–500,000	1% of taxable turnover greater than R335,000
500,001–750,000	R1650 plus 2% of taxable turnover greater than R500,000
750,001 and more	R6650 plus 3% of taxable turnover greater than R750,000

Source: RSA (1962); SARS (2024d)

This study is structured as follows: section "Theoretical Framework" provides an overview of the theoretical framework applied, section "Literature Review" highlights the literature review to determine the extent of other academic research that focused on the TTS, and section "Methodology" explains the methodology used in this study followed by the discussion of the demographics of the participants in section "Demographics of Participants" and the results and key findings in sections "Results", "Key Findings", and "Discussions". The final sections (sections "Limitations", "Conclusion", and "Recommendations") provides limitations of the research, conclusion, and recommendations for future studies and practice.

Theoretical Framework

The doctrines of a good tax structure (known as the "tax canons"), originally presented by Smith in "The Wealth of Nations" book, outline the basis of any good tax structure. Smith lays out various rules and doctrines in order to build a good taxation system (AICPA, 2017; Bruwer et al., 2024; Smith, 1776; Soyode & Oyedokun, 2019; Stiglingh et al., 2024). Therefore, this study used Smith's tax canons to aid in outlining the analysis on whether the TTS is perceived to be complex or not for micro-enterprises.

The basic principles of taxation as defined by Smith are the following: equity, certainty, convenience, and economy (Bruwer et al., 2024; Soyode & Oyedokun, 2019; Stiglingh et al., 2024). The foundation of tax policy design even today is still impacted by these four tax principles. Amidst the rapid changes within the modern-day society, subsequent economists have broadened Adam Smith's original four tax principles by incorporating additional doctrines such as transparency and visibility, effective tax administration, productivity, flexibility, and simplicity (AICPA, 2017; Soyode & Oyedokun, 2019; Stiglingh et al., 2024). These supplementary principles are universally acknowledged as essential elements in designing modern-day tax strategies (Stiglingh et al., 2024). Both Smith's (1776) original four tax principles and the aforementioned additional principles were used as the basis in assessing the complexity of the TTS in the context of South Africa. Table 2 elaborates on the meaning of each tax canon that is relevant in the current study, that is: certainty, effective tax administration, simplicity, and transparency and visibility. Although still important in the design of the TTS, the other tax canons (equity, convenience, productivity, and flexibility) are not core to the current study focusing on the perceived complexity of the TTS.

The discussion that follows will focus on previous studies that have considered the TTS.

Table 2 Tax canons and their meanings

Tax canon	Meaning of the tax canon
"Certainty" (Bruwer et al., 2024, p. 3)	The principles of tax certainty anticipates that taxpayers (the micro-enterprise owners) possess the capabilities to calculate the tax liability and know when the tax payments are payable (AICPA, 2017; Bruwer et al., 2024; Stiglingh et al., 2024)
"Effective tax administration" (AICPA, 2017, p. 3)	The tax principle of "effective tax administration" necessitates the design of a tax system to minimise both the administrative burden (encompassing tax collection and compliance costs) for revenue authorities and taxpayers (AICPA, 2017; Sahari et al., 2020; Stiglingh et al., 2024). The effectiveness of tax administration encompasses two facets: firstly, the allocation of the revenue authority resources essential to enforce the tax legislation and secondly, the reduction of the administrative burden placed upon taxpayers to become and remain tax compliant (Stiglingh et al., 2024)
"Simplicity" (AICPA, 2017, p. 3)	The tax principle of "simplicity" necessitates that tax legislation and administrative processes within the tax system should be simple and easy for taxpayers to understand, whilst facilitating compliance in a cost-efficient manner (AICPA, 2017; Arendse, 2017; Sahari et al., 2020; Stiglingh et al., 2024)
"Transparency and visibility" (AICPA, 2017, p. 3)	The tax principle of "transparency and visibility" necessitates taxpayers' awareness of the tax system (visibility) and to comprehend the impact of the tax system on them and others. This entails an understanding of calculating tax, the rationale the tax legislation is based on, and the tax compliance burden resulting from compliance with the legislation (transparency) (AICPA, 2017; Sahari et al., 2020)

Source: Own compilation

Literature Review

The literature was reviewed to ascertain the breadth of former academic studies that focused on the TTS. As will be demonstrated by the literature review below, very little research has been undertaken on the TTS, particularly with a specific focus on its complexity. Most of the studies that tackled the complexity of the tax system focused on a broad range of tax incentives for small business and not only the TTS. Furthermore, most of these studies were conducted more than 8 years ago, there is thus a gap in the literature to establish whether the status quo remains as far as the perceived complexity of the TTS is concerned.

At this point, it is vital to understand that complex tax legislation results in an increased administrative burden to businesses, which in turn leads to high tax compliance costs (Hundsdoerfer et al., 2011; Smulders et al., 2012). Smulders et al. (2012, 2016) found that South African small businesses (in general) have a higher proportional tax compliance burden when it comes to external and internal tax compliance costs and noted that these compliance requirements are often beyond the ability of small business owners or employees, because the tax legislation is complex.

Comparing prior research findings and recommendations on South African small business tax compliance costs with the initiatives introduced by SARS, including the TTS, Smulders and Naidoo (2013) concluded that whilst SARS has addressed most identified tax compliance burdens, challenges remained in areas such as the complexity of tax law, the absence of recordkeeping software tailored for small businesses, and the burden of provisional tax compliance. Aucamp (2010) highlighted the complexity of tax relief measures available to South African SMMEs; characterising the eligibility criteria as narrow and restrictive. Killian et al. (2007) echoed this sentiment, noting the complexity of tax legislation and its adverse impact on small businesses.

Focusing on the effectiveness and uptake of small business tax initiatives introduced by SARS, Naicker and Rajaram (2019) discovered that a significant proportion of respondents were unaware of specific tax initiatives, and only a limited number of small businesses were eligible for small business tax concessions. With specific reference to the TTS and the use of tax practitioners, a proxy for complexity of the legislation (Musimenta & Ntim, 2020); Lindeque (2012) established that only 30% of micro-enterprise owners now complete and submit their tax returns on their own, which implies that the majority of micro-enterprises still make use of tax practitioners.

Other studies that considered the TTS included that of Gluckman and Turner (2018) which investigated the fairness of the TTS by taking into consideration the literature and provisions of the Sixth Schedule to conclude on the fairness. Gluckman and Turner (2018) employed a two open-ended survey questionnaire, to assess participants' comprehension of the TTS, whilst evaluating participants' responses against Adam Smith's tax canons. Gluckman and Turner's (2018) respondents believed that the TTS is unfair.

Another study that looked at the TTS included that of Labuschagne (2018) which investigated whether the Northwest Province SMMEs use the TTS. Labuschagne's study established these SMMEs do not use the TTS and are not benefiting from the tax regime. Labuschagne (2018) describes that the primary factors contributing to the underutilisation of the TTS include participants' lack of awareness, inadequate comprehension of the system, and reluctance to pay tax in the event of incurring losses (which is one of the outcomes of the TTS).

Botha et al. (2020) study highlighted that the size of the SMMEs impacted enterprises' perceptions of the government initiatives, the challenges they face, and the obstacles they need to overcome. The findings showed that government incentives (including TTS) need more work, as the challenges and obstacles were more severe the smaller the enterprise.

The two studies (Gluckman & Turner, 2018; Labuschagne, 2018) on the TTS have, to a limited extent, touched on the complexity of the TTS but this was not the focus of these studies. Furthermore, none of the participants in these studies were registered on the TTS. The current study addressed this shortcoming by including a mix of participants, both registered and not registered on the TTS. Thus, the current study is able to gather perceptions as well as lived experiences from micro-enterprise owners who are registered on the TTS. Furthermore, at the time of conducting this research, studies which looked at the complexity of the TTS were either conducted more than 8 years ago or included a broad range of other small business incentives, such as Smulders and Naidoo (2013); Smulders et al. (2012); Lindeque (2012); Aucamp (2010); and Killian et al. (2007). This study therefore seeks to provide an updated view on whether the concerns raised in prior years with regard to complexity of the TTS have been addressed or have remained the same. The subsequent section explains the research design and methodology adopted to achieve the objective set out in this study.

Methodology

Study Design and Methodology

A qualitative research design was used to establish if micro-enterprises perceive the TTS to be complex or not. As minimal research has been performed on South African micro-enterprises as it pertains to the complexity of the TTS and since no publicly available database of micro-enterprises registered on the TTS is available, an exploratory qualitative research approach was contemplated as the most suitable (Babbie, 2017).

Study Population and Sampling Strategy

As mentioned above, no publicly available database of micro-enterprise owners exists in South Africa. Participants were thus selected using purposive and snowball sample selection techniques (Etikan et al., 2015). In the absence of an SMME database, the researcher used purposive sampling techniques to select an initial cohort of SMMEs to participate in the study. Subsequent to the conclusion of the interviews, participants were requested to recommend additional SMMEs to participate in this study through the application of the snowball sampling method. Creswell (2018) suggests that a sample size of three to ten participants may be sufficient for qualitative research such as this one. This study adopted Creswell's view, and the sample size was increased until responses reached saturation. The eventual participants comprised 19 micro-enterprise owners situated in Gauteng (except for a Cape Town and Nelspruit participant) with an annual taxable turnover below R1 million.

Data Collection

The researcher applied for ethical clearance (refer to the ethical considerations section for the details) with the Ethics Review Committee (ERC) prior to commencing with the interviews. Semi-structured interviews were conducted to solicit observations and perceptions of the respondents on the complexity of the TTS (Walle, 2015). The interviews were conducted in-person in Pretoria and Johannesburg and via video or phone calls for the two participants situated in other provinces during 2019.

Data Analysis

All interviews were transcribed, using the software program SpeechNotes©. Member checks were used to enhance the reliability and credibility of the research data. A second coder was assigned to increase the credibility of the coding in this study. Content analysis was used through holistic and pattern coding with the use of ATLAS.ti™8 QDAS to analyse individual interviews (Bengtsson, 2016; Saldaña, 2016). Emerging themes were then assigned to the two research questions. Finally, the relevant tax canons were applied to each of the key themes to evaluate whether the principles of a good tax system are met.

Ethical Considerations

Prior approval was obtained from the {name taken out to support blind review} Ethics Review Committee. In the application the researcher had to provide details on the sampling method used, the questions to be asked to participants, and the email and documents to accompany the request to participate to be sent to the participants. The ERC approved the ethical clearance application on 9 April 2019 (ERC Reference: 2019_CAS_014). The respondents were allowed to withdraw from the interview at any time.

Demographics of Participants

It is important to first put in context the characteristics of the participants in order to enhance the comprehension and relevance of the results. Table 3 summarises the demographics of the participants.

Table 3 The demographics of the participants of this research study are as follows

Description (1)	Description (2)	No
Participants' academic and professional background	Obtained a degree	15
	Obtained a diploma	3
	Obtained a matric certificate	1
The legal form of the micro-enterprise	Sole proprietors	6
	Close corporations	5
	Private companies	7
	Partnership	1
The trading period of the micro-enterprise	Start-ups (operating fewer than 1 year)	3
	Operated for 1 year but fewer than 3 years	6
	Operated for 3 years but fewer than 5 years	2
	Operated for 5 years but fewer than 10 years	3
	Operated for 10 years or more	5
The main trading activity of the micro-enterprise[a]	Retail Trade (Including Mail Order)	3
	Catering and Accommodation	1
	Transport, Storage and Communication	2
	Financing, Insurance, Real Estate and Business Services	6
	Educational Services	2
	Medical, Dental, Other Health and Veterinary Services	4
	Recreational and Cultural Services	1
	Personal and Household Services	1
The number of individuals employed by micro-enterprises[a]	0	6
	1	5
	2	0
	3	5
	3 and more	4

Source: Own compilation

[a]Some participants who were not registered on the TTS owned more than one business, so the total number is more than 19

Results

The interview data were analysed using the first cycle's holistic code approach (Saldaña, 2016) and the second cycle's pattern code approach (Saldaña, 2016). In order to understand the data collected, inductive and deductive content analysis (Bengtsson, 2016) was used in the above coding patterns. After the first coding cycle, the codes were further compressed during the second coding cycle, linking them to a theme identified during literature review. The second coding cycle was then grouped into emerging themes (Erlingsson & Brysiewicz, 2017). These emerging themes are attributed to the two research questions. The emerging themes are summarised in Table 4.

Table 4 The emerging themes of the study as identified and described

Code group	Meaning of identified emerging theme
Understanding	It refers to the understanding of the participants of the functioning of the TTS from both a legislative and administrative point of view
Assistance	It refers to participants' use of third parties to assist in fulfilling their tax obligations

Source: Own compilation

Key Findings

Most participants primarily focused on the following broad areas of understanding TTS: TTS is a simplified tax system; micro-enterprises' turnover limits are more than R1 million; taxes are calculated on turnover, not profit; or personal service providers are specifically excluded.

Most participants did not understand the following areas of TTS: It replaces the other five taxes; it is required that they submit an annual turnover tax return and make three interim payments each year; that there is a disposal limitation of assets of R1.5 million over 3 years; how to calculate the taxable turnover (including the certain inclusions and exclusions) and tax obligations (including the reduced TTS tax tables); that turnover is taxed only when it is received; an individual's investment income is still taxed under his/her personal income tax return and that an individual/a company cannot have more than one business on the TTS.

The application of the tax canons to these findings may suggest that the lack of understanding on some of the key aspects of the TTS may hinder its effective administration. Additionally, the lack of understanding on some of the key aspects of the TTS suggests that the system lacks transparency.

Most of the participants did not understand the TTS legislation, and this left them uncertain about how it should be applied in their situation. The participants found it difficult to understand TTS legislation due to the use of technical and complex languages. The transparency tax canon appears to be lacking because most of the taxpayers failed to understand how the tax will be imposed on them from the reading of the legislation. Participants stated that the complex and technical language of TTS legislation was insufficiently simple, an important principle of a good tax system. In addition, participants pointed out that SARS officials did not understand the TTS legislation, and the lack of understanding of TTS laws caused unnecessary objections and appeals to taxpayers, and SARS officials appeared to be implementing the tax rules incorrectly according to some participants. This increases the burden of tax administration both for taxpayers and for SARS in their efforts to resolve these issues.

All four taxpayers registered on TTS used third parties. Two (of four) TTS taxpayers use third parties to assist in complying with TTS obligations because they lack the tax knowledge required and have not enough time to obtain this knowledge. The remaining two TTS taxpayers use third parties to assist with general accounting, other legal requirements, and unintended administrative tasks associated with the submission of TTS forms and related questions.

As far as applying tax canons to key theme pertaining to micro-enterprise owners' ability to handle tax compliance matters themselves is concerned, it would seem that the simplicity tax canon has not been adhered to. The continued use of external help suggests that the TTS is not as simple as envisaged. The key findings are discussed in detail below.

Discussions

The findings of this study will be discussed under two headings in line with the research questions, namely: the understanding of the TTS of participants both from a legislative and administrative perspective and whether or not participants obtained assistance with respect to their TTS compliance obligations.

Do Micro-enterprise Owners/Managers Understand How the TTS Works Both from a Legislative and Administrative Perspective?

During the interview, most participants were generally found to have limited understanding of TTS. Two registered TTS participants conducted extensive research to ensure that they deeply understood what TTS means. It is disturbing to note that participant 13 who registered on the TTS was completely dependent on an accountant and had little knowledge of the TTS.

Ten participants argued that the TTS is a simplified tax system. Only three out of ten participants knew that TTS had replaced some taxes. Six participants stated that TTS liability was calculated at a significantly lower tax rate than that of individuals, companies, or trusts.

Participants 13 and 18 rely on accountants for help, and they lack the knowledge or time needed to handle their own taxes. On the contrary, the participants 9 and 17 stated that the calculation of turnover tax was easy, but that they still used accountants for their legislative requirements and administrative ease (by manually submitting returns on behalf of clients and resolving SARS questions). This is contrary to the original intention of the TTS, which aims to enable taxpayers to manage their own tax obligations.

The ten participants explained that the calculation of TTS tax liabilities was based on micro-enterprise revenues rather than business profits. Only participant 9 referred to qualifying turnover and excluded certain sources of income from turnover. Participant 9 explained that income excluded from turnover is shown separately in the personal or corporate income tax returns of taxpayers. This means that the TTS does not replace all income tax principles. Participants 2 confused turnover with profits in their explanations, giving the impression that they did not fully understand the information they had scrutinised. This can emphasise a potential challenge and indicate that tax terminology may be too complex for owners of micro-enterprises.

Nine participants only mentioned the annual turnover of up to R1 million as the only criteria to qualify for TTS. Moreover, the additional criteria referred to frequently by the participants related to personal service providers.

The sixth participant discussed the asset limits affecting their business. Emanating from the deliberations, participants 6 interpreted the law as a measure that does not exceed R1.5 million in assets rather than R1.5 million in assets that cannot be disposed of within 3 years. Participant 9 also stressed that the exemption of investment income was general and that SARS officials used a general approach to refuse applications rather than assess each case on its own merits. In this case, SARS considered its property to be investment income, and its business model to be the same as to that of an asset management company. Participant 9 expressed his frustration with the process of compiling his personal tax returns over and above the turnover tax return, to account for any investment income, thus increasing the burden of tax administration and making the TTS more cumbersome.

Five participants understood that within a tax period they are required to submit returns and payments three times. Participants 8 noted that tax returns and bookkeeping requirements had been reduced to assist micro-enterprises. Participant 5 believed that the frequency of returns submitted by micro-enterprises was lower than that of companies registered in the normal income tax system. Taxpayers enrolled in the TTS system must submit an annual turnover tax return (TT03) and pay three interim payments each year. Another important difference is the level of information to be included in the return. Micro-enterprises must only show the qualifying turnover; companies in the ordinary tax system must show all income earned, including the allowance. When it comes to VAT returns, the statement is correct because the company may have additional administrative burden (return frequency) based on the VAT category of the company. For example, if a business (VAT vendor) is classified as Category A/B (with a turnover of less than R30 million), VAT returns must be submitted every 2 months. However, if a micro-enterprise is classified as Category D, VAT returns must be submitted twice in a year (SARS, 2024c). TTS-registered taxpayers may submit PAYE returns every 6 months, including SDL and UIF, rather than every month.

Participants 5 and 9 also stated that the turnover tax return has been simplified; only the turnover amount should be recorded. However, participant 9 claimed that the tax payment process was challenging because it had to take place in the bank and if the taxpayer had not succeeded, he would have to visit a SARS branch for help. At the time of the study, the participants' statements were partly confirmed by SARS's "Administration for Turnover Tax" (which SARS then removed). The payment of turnover taxes can now be done at a bank or by EFT (SARS, 2024a). In 2024, the SARS amendment identified and explained the information to be captured in a bank or electronic payment (SARS, 2024c).

Four participants expressed dissatisfaction that the returns had to be submitted manually, while all other tax returns could be submitted electronically (e-file).The SARS website then confirmed the participants' statements that electronic filing is not available for TTS. SARS have however implemented some changes since then, as the turnover tax return can be completed online. Taxpayers then had the option to either submit the printed copy at a SARS branch or email it to SARS (SARS, 2024e). Two participants also expressed frustration at unnecessary objections and appeals and associated costs resulting from the lack of knowledge of the TTS by SARS officials who had incorrectly applied the turnover tax rules or later modified their original decisions.

The responses of participants 3 and 12 showed that these taxpayers confused the amount of turnover included in VAT or company income tax returns with the amount of taxable turnover included in turnover tax returns. These participants believe that turnover tax refers to VAT and/or income tax paid on business revenue. This suggests that taxpayers find tax concepts difficult and that different uses of similar terms confuse taxpayers.

However, the sixth participant raised interesting points, stating that SARS did not explain the financial impact of the tax on TTS on micro-enterprises based on low or high profit margins compared to other tax systems. Participant 14 was also concerned that SARS does not allow micro-enterprises to register on the TTS system if they own multiple companies.

The above clearly shows that taxpayers do not fully understand how the TTS affects them, and that transparency canon seems to be violated. SARS has also played a role in this respect, as reflected in the comments of participants on the lack of clear explanation to taxpayers of certain aspects of TTS.

Many of the participants at first affirmed that they had read and comprehended the TTS legislation. As the interviews advanced, more information was obtained during the interviews, which contradicted the first responses of the participants. It was then established that many of the participants had not read the TTS legislation and that in fact they referred to summary information published on the SARS website. This shows potential challenges, as information published on the SARS website is a summary of TTS legislation that does not disclose all relevant details concerning the practical application and impact of TTS. Five of the participants who read the TTS legislation or parts thereof were actually registered TTS members and/or academics with backgrounds in language, law or accounting. In order to determine the functionality of the tax law, the understanding of the participants was considered, as this directly influenced the implementation process at the operational level. Below is an excerpt from some participants' comments on the understanding of tax legislation:

Participant 6:

> ... No, it was not easy to understand. Because all legal jargon is difficult to understand. It is written in an unhelpful and uncooperative English. A number of the words and writings do not make sense...

Participant 14:

> ... It was not that understandable. I had to direct a number of questions about it, to get clarification on it. The information was more technical, and because I didn't have the background behind it, I didn't really grasp what's going on...

Smulders and Naidoo (2013) found that tax laws (including the supposedly simple TTS laws) are still complex, and as noted by the participants of the study, and Killian et al. (2007) found that SMMEs struggled with complex legislation, which increased administrative burden. The findings from the two studies are aligned to what was noted by the participants in the current study, thus, the situation is clearly unchanged for almost 10 years.

Do Micro-enterprises Use Tax Practitioners to Assist Them with Their TTS Compliance Obligations, and If So, Why?

When participants were asked, "Do you receive assistance with the TTS's compliance obligations?" most confirmed that accountants or third parties help them comply with the tax system. Twelve participants specified that they would prefer to transfer their tax compliance obligations to a third party who possess the relevant knowledge and expertise. Over and above the knowledge aspect, 11 participants also argued that they did not have enough time to complete these tasks; they consulted accountants to help them with this and other tax matters required by legislation; they preferred to focus on their niche competences. Two participants registered in TTS used tax experts because they did not have sufficient knowledge and time to ensure compliance with the law. Participant 17 used a third party not for the turnover tax, but rather to help in general accounting matters, legislative requirements (e.g. the submission of CIPC returns), and administrative ease (PAYE and tax calculations and submissions). Participant 9 uses third party services for expediency and to make life easier. Participant 9 explained why he used a third party as follows:

> … at this stage there is a lot of confusion. If you phone SARS helpline number, they are totally confused, if you go to the helpdesk they are totally confused, with some of the requirements and definitions for the TTS. On the TTS … you have to physically fill in the form and take it to a SARS branch … Why do I use the accountant? to make my life easier. The accountant has someone that goes to SARS quite often and then I do not have to sit in the long queues and wait. There is always a query with the TTS, because the people at the SARS office do not understand the rules and forms of the TTS. So, my accountants can go and argue for me at SARS...

It does appear that some of the participants still prefer to utilise the services of a third party to carry out the tax compliance functions, thus negating the aim of the TTS to be a simplified tax system that can be handled internally and is meant to help in alleviating the tax compliance burden. This finding is aligned to that of Musimenta and Ntim (2020) as well as Lindeque (2012) who both established that only a few of micro-enterprise owners complete and submit their tax returns on their own.

Limitations

The level of readability of TTS legislation and additional SARS documents, such as the External Guide on the Administration of the Turnover Tax, was not taken into account because it was outside the scope of this study. Thus, further research is needed on this and the level of education of micro-enterprise owners in relation to the readability and complexity of TTS legislation and SARS additional documents.

Conclusion

It would appear that one of the reasons for the low take-up of the TTS is that it is too complex for micro-enterprise owners. Participants lacked understanding on some of the key tenets of the TTS, such as the eligibility criteria, how to calculate taxable turnover, and the fact that the turnover tax replaced five other taxes. Even more concerning was the finding that most participants were not aware of the TTS legislation. Those that were aware of the TTS legislation lacked an understanding of this legislation. The lack of understanding of the legislation negatively impacts the simplicity and transparency tax canon. Finally, the aim of the TTS to reduce tax compliance costs for micro-enterprises also seems to have fallen by the wayside as many micro-enterprises still utilise tax practitioners to help them with their tax compliance requirements due to the complexity associated with the TTS. In this regard, the TTS lacks simplicity.

The results of this study confirm that the South African government has not done much in the last 10 years to reduce the complexity of the TTS both from a legislative and administrative perspective. More needs to be done by the National Treasury and SARS in making tax compliance easier for entrepreneurs and small business owners, particularly micro-enterprise owners, so that tax compliance does not constitute a hindrance to their growth. To be effective and to meet its intended objective, the TTS must be simplified from both a legislative and administrative perspective.

Recommendations

Participants felt that TTS legislation and the supplementary documents were too complex and technical. Therefore, it is suggested that the legislation and documentation pertaining to the TTS be written on a language level that most entrepreneurs and small business owners can understand. It is suggested that the SARS documents should better explain the TTS (including the advantages and disadvantages thereof) and the practical implications of this tax system on a business. It is also recommended that the Income Tax Act definition for a micro-enterprise must be aligned with other South African legislation, to eliminate any misunderstanding.

References

American Institute of Certified Professional Accountants (AICPA). (2017). *Guiding principles of good tax policy: a framework for evaluating tax proposals* [online]. AICPA. Available from https://us.aicpa.org/content/dam/aicpa/advocacy/tax/downloadabledocuments/tax-policy-concept-statement-no-1-global.pdf [Downloaded on 10 June 2024].

Arendse, J. A. (2017). *An investigation into the introduction of a new wealth tax in South Africa.* Doctoral thesis. Rhodes University.

Aucamp, J. (2010). *A comparative study of tax relief measures for small, medium and micro-enterprises in South Africa and Australia.* Master's thesis. University of Pretoria.

Babbie, E. R. (2017). *The basics of social research* (17th ed.). Cengage Learning.

Bengtsson, M. (2016). How to plan and perform a qualitative study using content analysis. *NursingPlus Open, 2*, 8–14. https://doi.org/10.1016/j.npls.2016.01.001

Botha, A., Smulders, S. A., Combrink, H. A., & Meiring, J. (2020). Challenges, barriers and policy development for South African SMMEs—Does size matter? *Development Southern Africa, 38(2), 153–174.* https://doi.org/10.1080/0376835X.2020.1732872

Bruwer, L., Cass, C., Coetzee, K., Cucciolillo, D., De Hart, K. L., Koekemoer, A., Oosthuizen, A., & Stedall, C. (2024). *A student's approach to taxation in South Africa* (4th ed.). LexisNexis.

Coolidge, J., Ilic, D., & Kisunko, G. (2009, March). *Small businesses in South Africa: who outsources tax compliance work and why*? (Policy Research working paper; no. WPS 4873). World Bank Group. Retrieved June 10, 2024, from http://documents.worldbank.org/curated/en/329051468340273249/Small-businesses-in-south-Africa-who-outsources-tax-compliance-work-and-why.

Creswell, J. W. (2018). *Research design: qualitative, quantitative, and mixed methods approaches* (5th ed.). Sage.

Davis Tax Committee (DTC). (2016). *Second and final report on small and medium business* [online]. Davis Tax Committee. Retrieved June 10, 2024, from https://www.taxcom.org.za/docs/20160414%20DTC%20Final%20SME%20Report.pdf.

Erlingsson, C., & Brysiewicz, P. (2017). A hands-on guide to doing content analysis [online]. *African Journal of Emergency Medicine, 7*(3), 93–99. Retrieved June 10, 2024, from https://doi.org/10.1016/j.afjem.2017.08.001.

Etikan, I., Musa, S. A., & Alkassim, R. (2015). Comparison of convenience sampling and purposive sampling. *American Journal of Theoretical and Applied Statistics, 5*(1), 1–4. https://doi.org/10.11648/j.ajtas.20160501.11

Gluckman, A., & Turner, M. (2018). The perceived fairness of turnover tax. *Journal of Economic and Financial Sciences, 11*(1), 1–10. https://doi.org/10.4102/jef.v11i1.174

Hundsdoerfer, J., Eichfelder, S., & Blaufus, K. (2011). *The hidden burden of the income tax: Compliance costs of German individuals* (Economics Discussion Paper No. 2011/6). Freie Universität Berlin, School of Business. Retrieved June 10, 2024, from https://doi.org/10.2139/ssrn.1980211.

Killian, S., Karlinsky, S. S., Payne, G., & Arendse, J. (2007). Mixed blessing of being designated a small business: a four country comparison. *ATA Journal of Legal Tax Research, 5*(1), 1–34. https://doi.org/10.2308/jltr.2007.5.1.16

Labuschagne, D. (2018). *An analysis of the turnover tax relief available to micro-enterprises in the North-West province.* Master's thesis. North-West University.

Lindeque, B. (2012). *Turnover tax: is it too good to be true for micro businesses in South Africa? An exploratory study.* Master's thesis. University of Pretoria.

Musimenta, D., & Ntim, C.G (2020). Knowledge requirements, tax complexity, compliance costs and tax compliance in Uganda. *Cogent Business & Management, 7*, 1. Retrieved June 10, 2024, from https://doi.org/10.1080/23311975.2020.1812220.

Naicker, Y., & Rajaram, R. (2019). The effectiveness of tax relief initiatives on SMEs in South Africa. *Acta Universitatis Danubius. Œconomica, 15*(4), 125–137.

National Treasury (NT). (2012, January 27). *Explanatory memorandum on the taxation laws amendment bill, 2011* [online]. National Treasury. Retrieved June 10, 2024, from https://www.sars.gov.za/wp-content/uploads/Legal/ExplMemo/LAPD-LPrep-EM-2011-02-Explanatory-Memorandum-Taxation-Laws-Amendment-Bill-2011.pdf.

National Treasury & South African Revenue Services (NT & SARS). (2010). *Explanatory memorandum on the taxation laws amendment bill, 2010* [online]. National Treasury and SARS. Retrieved June 10, 2024, from https://www.sars.gov.za/wp-content/uploads/Legal/ExplMemo/LAPD-LPrep-EM-2010-01-Explanatory-Memorandum-Taxation-Laws-Amendment-Bill-2010.pdf.

Ndlovu, M. (2015). *A comparative study on the tax compliance burden and tax incentives for SMMEs in South Africa*. Master's thesis. University of the Witwatersrand.

Ramsuraj, T. (2023). Assessing the role of entrepreneurship industry and SMEs to economic growth in South Africa. *International Journal of Research in Business and Social Science (2147-4478), 12*(7), 283–291. Retrieved June 8, 2024, from https://doi.org/10.20525/ijrbs.v12i7.2730.

Republic of South Africa (RSA). (1962). *Income Tax Act, No.58 of 1962*. Government Printer.

Republic of South Africa (RSA). (2012). *National Development Plan 2030* [online]. National Planning Commission. Retrieved June 11, 2024, from https://www.gov.za/sites/default/files/gcis_document/201409/ndp-2030-our-future-make-it-workr.pdf.

Saah, P. (2021). The impact of small and medium-sized enterprises on the economic development of South Africa. *Technium Social Sciences Journal, 24*(1), 549–561. Retrieved June 8, 2024, from https://techniumscience.com/index.php/socialsciences/article/view/3734.

Sahari, S. N., Samsudin, S., Bujang, A. A., Suratman, R., Rahman, M. S. A., & Jiram, W. R. A. (2020). General review on Malaysia land taxation. *International Journal of Academic Research in Business and Social Sciences, 10*(3), 554–569. Retrieved June 8, 2024, from https://doi.org/10.6007/IJARBSS/v10-i3/7071.

Saldaña, J. (2016). *The coding manual for qualitative researchers* (3rd ed.). Sage.

Smith, A. (1776). *An inquiry into the nature and causes of the wealth of nations*. Strahan, W. & Cadell, T.

Smulders, S.A. & Naidoo, G. 2013. Addressing the small business tax compliance burden - evidence from South Africa. *Journal of Economic and Financial Sciences, 6*(1):33–54.

Smulders, S. A., Stiglingh, M., Franzsen, R., & Fletcher, L. (2012). Tax compliance costs for the small business sector in South Africa—Establishing a baseline. *eJournal of Tax Research, 10*(2), 184–226. Retrieved June 10, 2024, from https://repository.up.ac.za/bitstream/handle/2263/57401/Smulders_Tax_2012.pdf?sequence=1.

Smulders, S. A., Stiglingh, M., Franzsen, R., & Fletcher, L. (2016). Determinants of internal tax compliance costs: evidence from South Africa. *Journal of Economic and Financial Sciences, 9*(3), 714–729.

Smulders, S. A., Stiglingh, M., Franzsen, R., & Fletcher, L. (2017). Determinants of external tax compliance costs: evidence from South Africa. *South African Journal of Accounting Research, 31(2), 134–150.* https://doi.org/10.1080/10291954.2016.1160175

South African Revenue Services (SARS). (2024a). *Turnover tax* [online]. SARS. Retrieved June 8, 2024, from https://www.sars.gov.za/types-of-tax/turnover-tax/.

South African Revenue Services (SARS). (2024b). *How to register for turnover tax* [online]. SARS. Retrieved June 10, 2024, from https://www.sars.gov.za/types-of-tax/turnover-tax/how-to-register/.

South African Revenue Services (SARS). (2024c). *Tax periods for VAT vendors* [online]. SARS. Retrieved June 10, 2024, from https://www.sars.gov.za/types-of-tax/value-added-tax/tax-periods-for-vat-vendors/.

South African Revenue Services (SARS). (2024d). *Tax rates for turnover tax* [online]. SARS. Retrieved June 10, 2024, from https://www.sars.gov.za/tax-rates/turnover-tax/.

South African Revenue Services (SARS). (2024e). *Annual return* [online]. SARS. Retrieved June 10, 2024, from https://www.sars.gov.za/types-of-tax/turnover-tax/annual-return/.

Soyode, O., & Oyedokun, G. E. (2019). Relevance of Adam Smith canons of taxation to the modern tax system. *Journal of Taxation and Economic Development, 18*(3), 12–34.

Statistics South Africa (Stats SA). (2023). *Economic growth muted as 2023 draws to a close* [online]. Stats SA. Retrieved May 15, 2023, from https://www.statssa.gov.za/?p=17053#:~:text=South%20Africa's%20economy%20grew%20by,quarter%20was%20R1%20158%20billion.

Statistics South Africa (Stats SA). (2024). *Quarterly Labour Force Survey (QLFS)—Q1: 2024* [online]. Stats SA. Retrieved May 15, 2024, from https://www.statssa.gov.za/publications/P0211/Media%20release%20QLFS%20Q1%202024.pdf.

Stiglingh, M., Koekemoer, A. D., Van Heerden, L., Wilcocks, J. S., & Van der Zwan, P. (2024). *SILKE: South African Income Tax 2024*. LexisNexis.

Walle, A. F. (2015). *Qualitative research in business: A practical overview*. Cambridge Scholars Publishing. Retrieved June 10, 2024, from https://www.cambridgescholars.com/resources/pdfs/978-1-4438-6621-7-sample.pdf

Wiese, J. S. (2014). *Factors determining the sustainability of selected small and medium-sized enterprises*. MBA thesis. North-West University.

Impact of Artificial Intelligence in Human Resource Management: A Cross-Sectional Study of Travel Industry in South Africa

Lawrence Ogechukwu Obokoh, Olumide Sunday Adesina, and Mericca Nokuthula Masuku

Abstract Artificial Intelligence is widely used to make work easier and effective in all human endeavors, and Human Resource Management (HRM) is not left out; hence, the need to carry out the study. The study involved sampling 142 travel industry workers in Gauteng, South Africa, to investigate the level of adoption and future direction of AI use in day-to-day activities of human resources (HR). Descriptive statistics, logistic regression, and *t*-test were conducted on the data collected. The findings of this study showed that the HR professionals embraced the use of AI in HR practices and the HR workers believed in the future of AI in HRM. Also, the factors influencing the use of AI for HR practices in South Africa were significant. Therefore, the study recommends that HR professionals in organizations should take advantage of AI. The study aligns with the sustainable development goals (SDGs, 8) about decent work and economic growth. It also aligns with AI for Sustainable Development Goals (AI4SDGs) Think Tank.

Keywords Artificial intelligence · Human resources · Behavioral intention · Logistic regression · South Africa · AI4SDGs

Introduction

The role of human resources is vital in an organization; it is tasked with roles such as recruitment, training, development, performance evaluations, and other key roles. Hence the need to consider a way of making the job easier to achieve optimum

L. O. Obokoh · O. S. Adesina (✉) · M. N. Masuku
University of Johannesburg, Johannesburg, South Africa
e-mail: adesinao@jbs.ac.za

T. Moloi (ed.), *Impacting Society Positively Through Technology in Accounting and Business Processes*, Springer Proceedings in Business and Economics,
https://doi.org/10.1007/978-3-031-84885-8_41

results in the core tasks and the digital platform is one of the provisions available to HR to make their job easier. One major challenge faced by the HR of any organization is in hiring qualified candidates to fit into available jobs (Rozario et al., 2019). The adoption of AI makes the job of an HR personnel easier in shortlisting the candidates whose education and skills match up with the vacant positions in an organization. With the unemployment rate of about 32.7% in South Africa, there are challenges in recruiting the right candidates for a particular job owing to large volume of applications received for every advertised position (Stat SA, 2023). To avoid the Herculean task of getting an applicant who fits into a given job, the use of AI needs to be considered with little or no reservations. Using AI for recruitment purposes requires that once applications are submitted electronically, the AI software scans through the documents and generates the education/skills that match the job requirement (Buzko et al., 2016). Aside from recruitment, HR is also tasked with staff training, and it is important to determine the necessary training and optimal training cost with the help of AI. Having identified the benefits of adopting AI in HR practices, there are challenges associated with the adoption which include factors such as finance, technical know-how, security, personnel resistance to the adoption of AI, biases, and ethical issues, to mention but a few.

The AI has gone beyond the machine and have advanced to Emotional Intelligence (EI) which gravitates toward understanding people's emotions and feelings, thinking, and voice recognition amongst others. The use of smart automation has helped organizations whose staff strength is low in achieving their day-to-day activities. Deloitte is an example of an organization that takes advantage of AI, which helps the employees to give sufficient time for other creative and innovative activities; the report from Deloitte (2023) shows that about thirty-three percent of their employees use AI at the workplace. Berhil et al. (2020) stated that AI will help managers to achieve their daily set goals within the organizations. AI use in an organization repositions the organization for efficient delivery of goods and services, which gives them an economic and competitive advantage over organizations that do not adopt it (Tambe et al., 2019).

Another compelling advantage of Artificial Intelligence adoption in the modern workforce is that it potentially increases employee retention. Studies have shown that AI reduces employee recruitment costs and enhances customer care service, leading to customer satisfaction (Bughin et al., 2018), the use of AI can equally transform business models as mentioned by Duan et al. (2019), and Paschen et al. (2020) also iterated that AI helps in predictive decision-making in an organization. Another related study on the importance of AI adoption within an organization is Faulds and Raju (2021), which emphasized productivity and optimization of business operations. The study by Bankins and Formosa (2020) was based on the use of AI-enabled platforms in the engagement of employees while (Upadhyay & Khandelwal, 2018) focused on talent adoption and prediction; AI-based performance evaluation (Upadhyay & Khandelwal, 2018), other related studies can be found in Votto et al. (2021), and Vrontis et al. (2021), the studies were based on training, talent acquisition, and video interviews.

In recent times, business organizations have thrived on AI-based systems to foster employee–employer relationships and have also enhanced competitive advantage among competing industries (Connelly et al., 2021; Wilson et al., 2017). In the report by Oracle and Future Workplace (2019) reported; adoption of AI in human increased from 32 to 50% as of 2019, and it is expected to increase much more by the end of 2024. Oracle and Future Workplace (2019) iterated that employees seem to trust robots more than human managers because of less complicated procedures.

On the use of AI in HR practices in travel, hospitality, and tourism Bulchand-Gidumal (2022) identified that travel, hospitality, and tourism face diverse challenges. Challenges such as replacing humans with machines, including the ethics and biases in AI use of Artificial Intelligence. The author urged future research to investigate how to tackle the challenges. Bowen and Morosan (2018) shared the same view with Bulchand-Gidumal (2022) stating from experts' prediction that 25% of the workforce in the hospitality industry will be taken over by robots. The authors mentioned that though AI will be of tremendous benefit to the travel and hospitality industry, at the same time, many employees will lose their jobs as machines take over the jobs of humans. The need for customer/client security is of utmost importance in the travel industry, so AI protects client's data, helps to provide rich service, and improves service quality (Jamaluddin & Rahmat, 2023). The author identified future applications of AI in the travel and tourism industry in the form of self-driving vehicles and decision support systems. Ivanov and Webster (2017) conducted a study on customer evaluation of robots, that is, Artificial Intelligence and Service Automation (RAISA) and the result of the study showed that most studies were based on service quality and customer satisfaction. The authors provided a future research direction in the use of AI for HR practices in the travel, hospitality, and tourism industries which is lacking in the existing body of literature (Ivanov et al., 2017).

In the South African context, Chilunjika et al. (2022) conducted a study to identify the opportunities, challenges, and prospects of adopting AI to conduct public sector HR functions in South Africa. The study showed that AI improved public service delivery in the country as it helps to reduce biases in public service recruitment. It also helps HR managers to focus more on strategic operations and reduce routine tasks. The research also showed that the use of AI in the public sector poses a threat to white-collar jobs. On the contrary, King (2024) identified that integrating AI in HR practices provided both opportunities and challenges owing to the rich diversity, complex socio-economic dynamics, and inequality that South Africa's HR ecosystem is characterized by. The adoption of AI must be channelled to tackle the opportunities and challenges the organizations in South Africa are faced with. King (2024) mentioned that employing AI in HR practices would require training of personnel to fill the skill gaps. He also touched on the dispelling fears associated with the adoption of AI, such as loss of job and believe that AI could empower HR professionals, resulting in strategic initiatives that enhance organizational growth and well-being.

Limited studies have delved into the impact of AI on HRM practices in developing countries such as South Africa, such studies can be found in Alam et al. (2020)

and Islam et al. (2022), the studies were based on the adoption of AI in Bangladesh, while Pan et al. (2022) related to China, and Hmoud (2021) related to Europe. The current study seeks to fill the location gap since limited studies have been conducted in South Africa. At the same time fill the methodological gap by conducting categorical data analysis, namely logistic regression. This study will identify the factors that encourage the adoption of AI in HR practices and will use the Unified Theory of Acceptance and Use of Technology theory (UTAUT). The UTAUT was proposed by Venkatesh et al. (2003), and there are four factors associated with UTAUT, namely (1) Performance expectancy, (2) effort expectancy, (3) social influence, and (4) facilitating conditions. The research instrument in this study was developed based on the four aforementioned factors guiding UTAUT theory.

These factors influence the integration of AI into HR practices. Oliveira and Martins (2010) highlighted the moderating factors associated with UTAUT; the factors are age, gender, experience, and voluntariness of use. The UTAUT theory plays a vital role in technology acceptance research as discussed in the study by Wang et al. (2010), Tan and Wang (2010), and Zhou et al. (2010).

Materials and Methods

In this section, the procedure involved in achieving the objective of this study is outlined.

Data Description

The population of the study comprises HR professionals in the travel industry within the Gauteng Province in South Africa. Gauteng is considered the most multicultural and diverse province in South Africa which sufficiently represents the country. This study adopted a cross-section design where respondents answer questions once without having to answer related questions again. The data was collected through online surveys to achieve the research objectives of this study. A purposeful sampling technique was used to determine the participants from the predefined population to solicit responses from the participants who were voluntarily available and were willing to participate in the study (Denscombe, 2014). The sample size for this study was 142. Descriptive analysis was conducted after data collection—statistical methods that described the attributes of the sample (Kotler & Armstrong, 2012, p. 127).

The sampling frame for the HR workers in the South African travel industry does not exist, so the sample size was determined using unlimited population criteria with an 8% margin of error. The computation of sample size was based on the following formula

$$n = \frac{z^2 \times p(1-p)}{e^2}$$
$$n = \frac{1.96^2 \times 0.4(1-0.4)}{0.08^2} \cong 144 \qquad (1)$$

where z is the z score, e is the margin of error, and p is the population proportion. Here we use a population proportion of 40%, a margin of error of 8%, and $z = 1.96$, to arrive at 144 participants. Though 142 participants were involved in this study which is close to the target sample size. The survey was conducted among the 23 HR travel organizations in Gauteng such as Mohlahisi Travel; t Mount Zion Tours and Travels; and MDS VisaPak, to mention but a few.

The questionnaires were in four sections, the first was the demographic characteristics of the respondents. The remaining three sections relate directly to the objective of the study. A three-point Likert scale was used in sessions two to four "Yes," "Maybe," and "No" and administered through Google Form online. The instrument was designed in line with the (UTAUT).

Ethical Consideration

Research ethics are required for research involving human participation (Saunders et al., 2016). Human participation is required in the data collection process in this study; therefore, we ensured that the respondents were not harmed in any way during the data collection process, we also ensured that their responses and private information remained private and confidential and that their integrity and dignity are upheld (Yip et al., 2016).

The following are the ethical steps taken in this study:

(i) The participants of this study were strictly made of HR professionals with two or more years of working experience.
(ii) The questionnaire provided information regarding the expectations and duration of the completion, it also provided confidence in the confidentiality and anonymity of the participants.
(iii) The respondents were aware that no remuneration or compensation was involved in completing the questionnaire. So, it was voluntary participation.
(iv) The contact details of investigators were available for participants should there be the need for any further clarifications or concerns that need to be communicated.

Logistic Regression Model

A logistic regression model was formulated to predict the probability of organizations adopting AI in their HR operations or not based on variables of interest in this study. The model equation is represented as:

The logistic regression uses the logistic function

$$P(X) = \frac{e^{\beta_0 + \beta_i x_i}}{1 + e^{\beta_0 + \beta_i x_i}} \tag{2}$$

Equation (2) would be applied under the result section.

Further workings give

$$\text{In}\left(\frac{P(X)}{1 - P(X)}\right) = \beta_0 + \beta_i x_i \tag{3}$$

The left-hand side is the log odd. Odds are the ratio of the probability of an event happening to the probability of an event not happening.

$$\text{In}\left(\frac{P(X)}{1 - P(X)}\right) = \beta_0 + \beta_1 \times \text{Soph} + \beta_1 \times \text{future} + \beta_3 \times \text{StaffM} \tag{4}$$

where Soph stands for the level of sophistication of AI use, future stands for the future adoption of the use of AI in future, and StaffM stands for staff management.

The method of maximum likelihood estimation would be used to obtain the parameter in Eq. (4).

The dependent variable is a categorical variable that categorizes respondents into whether the organization uses AI or not, coded at (Yes = 1, No = 0). Using a machine learning procedure, the data was split into training and testing sets. 85% of the data was used as a training set, while the remaining 15% was used in the testing phase. Software by the R Core team (2024) was used for the logistic regression analyses, while the SPSS 25 by IBM was used for the descriptive analyses and the *t*-test.

Results

In this session, the results obtained were discussed. The first result is the analysis of the responses by the respondents provided in Table 1.

In Table 1, the values in the bracket are percentages, the table shows that 73 (51.4%) use AI, while 69 (48.6%) don't use AI for HR operations in their various organizations. Also, 39 (27.5%) implement, 47 (33.1%) are not sure, and 56 (39.4%) of the respondents don't implement any AI technologies in HRM practices in their various organizations. The interpretation of the remaining responses follows in that

Table 1 The responses based on the objective of this study

Item	Yes	May be	No
AI adoption in HRM?	73 (51.4)	–	69 (48.6)
Implementation of any AI technologies in HRM practices?	39 (27.5)	47 (33.1)	56 (39.4)
The use of AI for candidate sourcing and screening during recruitment	40 (28.2)	44 (31.0)	58 (40.8)
The use of AI to enhance employee engagement or experience	52 (36.6)	43 30.3)	47 (33.1)
Comfortable with the use of AI	42 (29.6)	57 (40.1)	43 (30.3)
AI adoption in the near future?	51 (25.9)	50 (35.2)	41 (28.9)
Need for training in the use of AI for HR activities?	53 (37.3)	49 (34.5)	40 (28.2)
Has AI improved HRM processes?	42 (29.6)	60 (42.3)	40 (28.2)
The success of AI in recruitment in your organization?	47 (33.1)	52 (36.6)	43 (30.3)
Organization adoption of AI-based tools or systems for any stage of the recruitment process?	35 (24.5)	66 (46.5)	41 (28.9)
Utilization of AI in the onboarding process?	48 (33.8)	47 (33.1)	47 (33.1)
AI improving efficiency and accuracy?	41 (28.9)	46 (32.4)	55 (38.7)
AI in talent retention?	52 (36.6)	32 (22.5)	58 (40.8)
Impact of AI on turnover reduction?	54 (38.0)	43 (30.3)	45 (31.7)
Does AI contribute to higher employee satisfaction?	54 (38.0)	43 (30.3)	45 (31.7)
AI in diversity and inclusion in recruitment?	41 (28.9)	49 (34.5)	52 (36.6)
AI improving the identification of high-potential employees?	38 (26.8)	58 (40.8)	46 (32.4)

manner. Table 2 is the cross-tabulation of the use of AI in organizations versus the future adoption of AI in HRM practices.

Table 2 shows that most of the respondents believe that there is a future in AI adoption for HRM.

The future is significant with estimate 0.8416 which has a positive impact on the log odds of the probability of organizations adopting AI in human resources management. The log odd of users (versus non-users) increases by 0.8416 with respect to the future adoption (Table 3).

Figure 1 shows the coefficient of the logistic regression. The graph duly represents Table 1 sufficiently.

Table 2 Use of AI in organization versus HRM practices in industry in the near future

		Adoption of AI in HRM practices in industry in the near future			
		Yes	May be	No	Total
Use of AI in organization	No	30	24	19	73
	Yes	21	26	22	69
Total		51	50	41	142

Table 3 Binary logistic regression output

	Estimate	SE	*z*-value	Pr(>|*z*|)
(Int)	−2.3181	1.7716	−1.308	0.1907
Soph	−0.4851	0.4271	−1.136	0.2560
Future	0.8416	0.4132	2.037	0.0417*
StaffM	0.8051	0.5945	1.354	0.1757

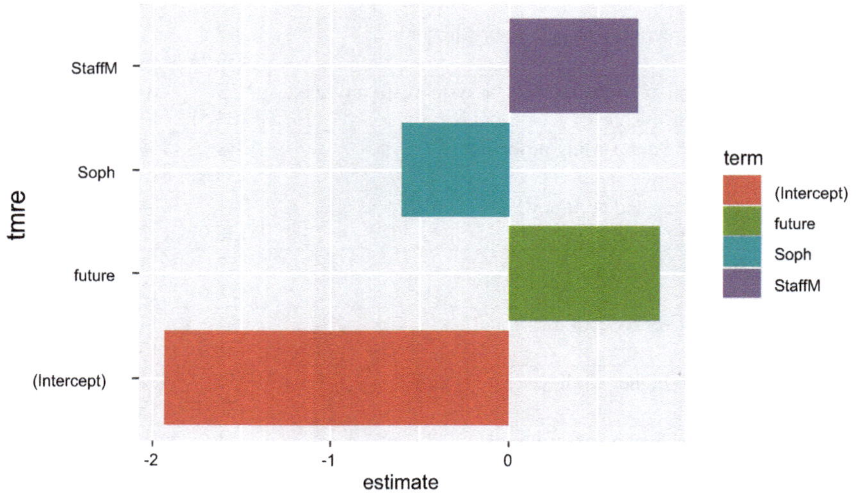

Fig. 1 Coefficient of logistic regression

From Table 4, performance expectancy is significant at *t*-value =−15.240, at 141 degree of freedom, *p*-value =0.000 at 5% level of significance, the test value was 2 (May be). We then concluded that performance expectancy in relation to the factor guiding the use of AI is significant, same with "effort expectancy," "facilitating condition," and "Social influence" at *t*-values of −15.849, −14.620, and −14.608, respectively.

Table 4 Variables on factors associated with UTAUT

	Test value = 2					
					95% confidence interval of the difference	
	t	df	Sig. (2-tailed)	Mean difference	Lower	Upper
Performance expectancy	–15.240	141	0.000	–0.993	–1.12	–0.86
Effort expectancy	–15.849	141	0.000	–1.014	–1.14	–0.89
Facilitating condition	–14.620	141	0.000	–1.007	–1.14	–0.87
Social influence	–14.608	141	0.000	–0.944	–1.07	–0.82

Conclusion

This study investigated the impact of adopting AI on human resource practices in travel industries. The study applied descriptive statistics and categorical data analyses on the data obtained. The study reveals that a reasonable percentage of travel organizations adopt Artificial Intelligence in their HR operations, while some do not due to different reasons some of which was not captured in this study. However, from the survey in this study, it shows that organizations that are not adopting AI could be a result of the cost involved and the technical know-how. The relationship between the response variable shows that the predictor "future" which means that the respondents believed that the future of HRM lies in the use of AI. Therefore, the training of HR personnel to handle AI tools should be a priority. The findings of the study would enlighten the HR professionals; therefore, organizations should pay keen attention to promoting AI in their HR operations and encourage HR personnel to adopt it.

The outcome of this study shows that some South African HR personnel in the travel industry have not yet embraced the use of AI which could be because of fear of job losses to machine, ethical and possible biases, as stated by (Bulchand-Gidumal, 2022; King, 2024). The study conforms with the sustainable development goals (SDDs, 8) on decent work and economic growth. It also aligns with the AI for Sustainable Development Goals (AI4SDGs) Think Tank. Therefore, this study recommends that organizations should employ the necessary AI tools and offer required training to the HR managers to enable them to interact sufficiently with AI tools for optimum outcomes in HR practices such as recruitment, training, appraisals, and retention.

References

Alam, M. S., Khan, T. U. Z., Dhar, S. S., & Munira, K. S. (2020). HR professionals' intention to adopt and use of artificial intelligence in recruiting talents. *Business Perspective Review, 2*(2), 15–30.

Bankins, S., & Formosa, P. (2020). When AI meets PC: Exploring the implications of workplace social robots and a human-robot psychological contract. *European Journal of Work and Organizational Psychology, 29*(2), 215–229. https://doi.org/10.1080/1359432X.2019.1620328.

Berhil, S., Benlahmar, H., & Labani, N. (2020). A review paper on artificial intelligence at the service of human resources management. *Indonesian Journal of Electrical Engineering and Computer Science, 18*(1), 32–40.

Bowen, J., & Morosan, C. (2018). Beware hospitality industry: the robots are coming. *Worldwide Hospitality and Tourism Themes, 10*(6), 726–733.

Bughin, J., Hazan, E., Lund, S., Dahlström, P., Wiesinger, A., & Subramaniam, A. (2018). Skill shift: Automation and the future of the workforce. *McKinsey Global Institute, 1*, 3–84.

Bulchand-Gidumal, J. (2022). Impact of artificial intelligence in travel, tourism, and hospitality, chapter 81. In Z. Xiang, M. Fuchs, U. Gretzel, & W. Höpken (Eds.), *Handbook of e-tourism* (pp. 1943–1962). Springer.

Buzko, I., Dyachenko, Y., Petrova, M., Nenkov, N., Tuleninova, D., & Koeva, K. (2016). Artificial Intelligence technologies in human resource development. *Computer Modelling and New Technologies, 20*(2), 26–29.

Chilunjika, A., Intauno, K., & Chilunjika, S. R. (2022). Artificial intelligence and public sector human resource management in South Africa: Opportunities, challenges and prospects. *SA Journal of Human Resource Management, 20*, a1972. https://doi.org/10.4102/sajhrm.v20i0.1972

Connelly, C. E., Fieseler, C., Černe, M., Giessner, S. R., & Wong, S. I. (2021). Working in the digitized economy: HRM theory & practice. *Human Resource Management Review, 31*(1), 100–112.

Deloitte. (2023). Generative AI and the future of work. Retrieved May 3, 2024, from https://www2.deloitte.com/content/dam/Deloitte/de/Documents/human-capital/Deloitte_GenAI-Future-of-Work.pdf.

Denscombe, M. (2014). *The good research guide for small-scale social research projects* (5th ed.). McGrawHill.

Duan, Y., Edwards, J. S., & Dwivedi, Y. K. (2019). Artificial intelligence for decision making in the era of Big Data—Evolution, challenges and research agenda. *International Journal of Information Management, 48*, 63–71.

Faulds, D. J., & Raju, P. S. (2021). The work-from-home trend: An interview with Brian Kropp. *Business Horizons, 64*(1), 29.

Hmoud, B. (2021). The adoption of artificial intelligence in human resource management and the role of human resources. *Forum Scientiae Oeconomia, 9*(1), 105–118. Wydawnictwo Naukowe Akademii WSB.

Islam, M., Mamun, A. A., Afrin, S., Ali Quaosar, G. A., & Uddin, M. A. (2022). Technology adoption and human resource management practices: The use of artificial intelligence for recruitment in Bangladesh. *South Asian Journal of Human Resources Management, 9*(2), 324–349.

Ivanov, S. H., & Webster, C. (2017). Adoption of robots, artificial intelligence and service automation by travel, tourism and hospitality companies—A cost-benefit analysis. In *Contemporary tourism—Traditions and innovations.*

Ivanov, S. H., Webster, C., & Berezina, K. (2017). Adoption of robots and service automation by tourism and hospitality companies. *Revista Turismo Desenvolvimento, 27*(28), 1501–1517.

Jamaluddin, Z., & Rahmat, A. K. (2023). Artificial intelligence technology in travel, tourism and hospitality: Current and future developments. In A. Hassan & N. A. A. Rahman (Eds.), *Technology application in aviation, tourism and hospitality* (pp. 169–177). Springer.

King, D. (2024). Unlocking the potential of HR AI in the South African context: embracing the human element. Business, Human Resources. Retrieved June 6, 2024, from https://hrtorque.co.za/unlocking-the-potential-of-hr-ai-in-the-south-african-context-embracing-the-human-element/.

Kotler, P., & Armstrong, G. (2012). *Principles of marketing* (14th ed.). Pearson Education.

Oliveira, T., & Martins, M. F. (2010). Understanding e-business adoption across industries in European countries. *Industrial Management & Data Systems, 110*(9), 1337–1354. https://doi.org/10.1108/02635571011087428

Oracle & Future Workplace. (2019). Artificial intelligence is winning more hearts and minds at workplace. Retrieved May 10, 2024, from https://www.orgdch.org/wp-content/uploads/2020/03/FW-EBOOK-InDesign_V3.pdf.

Pan, Y., Froese, F., Liu, N., Hu, Y., & Ye, M. (2022). The adoption of artificial intelligence in employee recruitment: The influence of contextual factors. *The International Journal of Human Resource Management, 33*(6), 125–1147.

Paschen, J., Wilson, M., & Ferreira, J. J. (2020). Collaborative intelligence: How human and artificial intelligence create value along the B2B sales funnel. *Business Horizons, 63*(3), 403–414.

R Core Team. (2024). *R: A language and environment for statistical computing*. R, Foundation for Statistical Computing. https://www.R-project.org/.

Rozario, S. D., Venkatraman, S., & Abbas, A. (2019, August). Challenges in recruitment and selection process: An empirical study. *Challenges, 10*(2), 1–22. MDPI.

Saunders, M., Lewis, P., & Thornhill, A. (2016). *Research methods for business students* (7th ed.). Pearson.

Stat SA. (2023). Statistics South Africa. Retrieved May 14, 2024, from https://www.statssa.gov.za/?m=2023.

Tambe, P., Cappelli, P., & Yakubovich, V. (2019). Artificial intelligence in human resources management: Challenges and a path forward. *California Management Review, 61*(4), 15–42. https://doi.org/10.1177/0008125619867910

Tan, L., & Wang, N. (2010, August). Future internet: The internet of things. In *2010 3rd international conference on advanced computer theory and engineering (ICACTE)* (vol. 5, pp. V5-376–V5-380). IEEE.

Upadhyay, A. K., & Khandelwal, K. (2018). Applying artificial intelligence: implications for recruitment. *Strategic HR Review, 17*(5), 255–258.

Venkatesh, V., Morris, M. G., Davis, G. B., & Davis, F. D. (2003). User acceptance of information technology: Toward a unified view. *MIS Quarterly, 27*(3), 425–478.

Votto, A. M., Valecha, R., Najafirad, P., & Rao, H. R. (2021). Artificial intelligence in tactical human resource management: A systematic literature review. *International Journal of Information Management Data Insights, 1*(2). https://doi.org/10.1016/j.jjimei.2021.100047

Vrontis, D., Makrides, A., Christofi, M., & Thrassou, A. (2021). Social media influencer marketing: A systematic review, integrative framework and future research agenda. *International Journal of Consumer Studies, 45*(4), 617–644.

Wang, C., Wang, Q., Ren, K., & Lou, W. (2010, March). Privacy-preserving public auditing for data storage security in cloud computing. In *2010 proceedings IEEE Infocom* (pp. 1–9). IEEE.

Wilson, H. J., Daugherty, P., & Bianzino, N. (2017). The jobs that artificial intelligence will create. *MIT Sloan Management Review, 58*(4), 14–22.

Yip, C., Han, N. L. R., & Sng, B. L. (2016). Legal and ethical issues in research. *Indian Journal of Anaesthesia, 60*(9), 684.

Zhou, H. B., Liu, Y. L., Jin, S., Zhang, Y., Luo, G. N., & Lu, G. H. (2010). Investigating behaviours of hydrogen in a tungsten grain boundary by first principles: from dissolution and diffusion to a trapping mechanism. *Nuclear Fusion, 50*(2), 025016.

Analysis of Variability in Excess Portfolio Return Using Fama and French Three-Factor Model: Evidence from Nairobi Security Exchange in Kenya

Richard Wamalwa Wanzala and Lawrence Obokoh

Abstract The goal of this study was to use the three-factor model developed by Fama and French to describe excess portfolio return variations. The dependent variables used in this study were the size risk factor, the value risk factor, and the market risk factor. Nine portfolios were created using stocks traded on the Nairobi Securities Exchange in Kenya between January 2001 and December 2022 to serve as independent variables and test the model. The empirical component of the study is based on the monthly excess return for each stock. This study's statistical findings show that large- and medium-sized portfolios outperform small portfolios in terms of realized excess returns. Furthermore, when compared to the other two risk factors, the market risk factor has a more significant and broad impact on portfolio returns. The result of this study revealed that the three-factor model proposed by Fama and French has limited ability to explain variations in portfolio returns. The study's findings are significant because they will assist policymakers in developing measures to encourage both domestic and foreign investors to invest in the NSE, thereby increasing trading volume, which is an important factor in excess return.

Keywords Excess returns · Fama and French three-factor model · Market risk factor · Nairobi Security Exchange · Size risk factor · Value risk factor

Introduction

Over the last six decades, there has been a strong interest in the field of investment analysis and corporate finance in understanding and explaining the interaction between stock and bond risks and returns. Financial researchers have been especially intrigued by modeling the relationship between the expected return on stock

R. W. Wanzala (✉) · L. Obokoh
University of Johannesburg, Johannesburg, South Africa
e-mail: rwanzala@uj.ac.za; rwwanzala@aa.jkuat.ac.ke; lawrence.obokoh@jbs.ac.za

T. Moloi (ed.), *Impacting Society Positively Through Technology in Accounting and Business Processes*, Springer Proceedings in Business and Economics,
https://doi.org/10.1007/978-3-031-84885-8_42

investments and the level of risk associated with those investments. Markowitz's (1952) Modern Portfolio Theory paved the way for a slew of new investment models that link excess portfolio returns to excess market returns. The original Capital Asset Pricing Model (CAPM), proposed concurrently and autonomously by Sharpe (1964), and Lintner (1965), explains asset returns using only one risk factor (the excess market portfolio return). Given its comparatively straightforward and stringent construction, CAPM continues to serve as a blueprint for academics and investment analysts. Nonetheless, the model has proven to be comparatively quantitatively flawed because a single factor cannot capture all risks, prompting the development of more robust asset pricing models such as Fama & French's three-factor model (FF3FM). As a result, this study uses the three-factor model developed by FF3FM (1992, 1993) to describe excess portfolio return variations on the Nairobi Securities Exchange (NSE).

The basic principles of the Fama–French model (FFM) are crucial for shareholders, speculators/brokers, portfolio managers, corporate boards of directors, academics, and policymakers. Using FFM could assist both investors and companies identify viable investment possibilities and maximize their portfolio returns. This allows investors to make informed investment decisions anchored on accurate information and data about optimal diversified portfolios. Furthermore, it can help firms and stock exchange management understand the performance of small- and large-company stocks. Similarly, shareholders and management must understand the performance of high-value stocks (value) and low-value stocks (growth). Besides, investments in portfolios guarantees the firms' long-term financial viability, offers efficient risk management, while contributing to the firms' long-term strategic goals using the risk-return trade-off. Moreover, knowledge of FFM might allow shareholders to assess the performance of the companies in which they have invested, in terms of whether their shares are profitable (robust) or have low operating profits. The performance can also be measured using the company debt-equity ratio to determine whether the company has adopted aggressive or conservative investment policies (Anuno et al., 2023).

The FF3FM was initially created through research in the United States stock markets, but it was subsequently proved to have explanatory power in Europe. However, stock markets in Europe are distinct from those in the USA in that they have smaller market capitalizations. Apart from South Africa, African stock markets have even lower market capitalizations than the United States, Europe, and other developed economies. As a result, findings from FF3FM conducted in developed economies cannot be applied to the Nairobi Securities Exchange (NSE) in Kenya. With limited literature in the Kenyan context, it was prudent to conduct independent research to fill this gap and contribute to the expanding body of literature on FF3FM and excess portfolio returns. As a result, this study used FF3FM to examine the variability in excess portfolio returns in NSE in Kenya. The null hypothesis tested was that FF3FM does not explain the variation in excess return.

The remainder of this study is organized as follows: section "Literature Review" summarizes the theoretical review and previous empirical studies on the Fama and

French three-factor models. Section "Methodology" presents the data source and model specifications. Section "Results and Discussion" presents empirical findings and discussions. The conclusion is provided in section "Conclusion".

Literature Review

Theoretical Review

Markowitz's 1959 publication of the Efficient Market Hypothesis (EMH) provided a forum for discussion of risk minimization, optimal portfolio design, and asset return properties. EMH ushered in a period of extensive study in the direction of the risk-return trade-off continuum, with Sharpe (1964) and Lintner (1965) introducing risk-free assets into the equation via the Capital Asset Pricing Model (CAPM). CAPM offered a distinctive foundation for an efficient portfolio, paving the pathway for the creation of many other efficient portfolios based on this one portfolio and the Risk-Free Asset. According to CAPM, asset returns tend to be a function of market β (covariance between asset and market portfolios). Though empirically robust and straightforward in its application, it failed to adequately clarify the asset return when compared to previous returns. To boost the predictive ability of CAPM, various researchers have attempted to make modifications on this model over the years by identifying alternative explanations for this anomaly, either by modifying methodology, adding additional presumptions, incorporating more variables, or integrating these. These findings have provided valuable understanding into β's predictive power and constraints.

Stock market abnormalities have long raised concerns about the Capital Asset Pricing Model's (CAPM) capability to forecast stock market returns accurately. Banz (1981), Gibbons (1982), Reinganum (1981), Merton (1973), and Ross (1976), all demonstrated anomalies in the market for CAPM. For example, Merton (1973) discovered that expected returns on risky assets may vary from the risk-free rate even though there is no systematic risk and recommended the intertemporal CAPM (ICAPM), whereas Ross (1976) put forward arbitrage pricing theory (APT). Reinganum's 1981 investigation indicates that the straightforward one-period CAPM is mispecified by identifying empirical anomalies. Their research supports the size factor in describing the cross-sectional average return of an asset. They further discovered that the size impact largely incorporates the E/P effect (Reinganum, 1981). Banz (1981) further demonstrated that the CAPM is one of several factors that contribute to an asset's cross-sectional average return. Banz discovered a significant size effect in cross-sectional average returns of US stocks for at least four decades. Gibbons also discovered that if market β is solely utilized to describe cross-sectional mean returns on US stocks from 1926 to 1975, the practical content of the CAPM is not accepted at a significance level of less than 1% (Gibbons, 1982).

Fama and French demonstrate that the covariation in returns associated with book-equity-to-market equity over the covariation described by the market return. The fundamentals (earnings and sales) have a book-equity-to-market equity factor, similar to the common factor in returns. Fernandez claims that the Fama–French factors small-minus-big stocks and high-minus-low stocks have statistically significant explanatory power across nearly all sample return horizons. He contends that small-minus-big stocks and high-minus-low stocks serve as proxies for market risk parameters that the CAPM does not capture, and that the Fama and French factors are more commonly used in practice. FF3FM (1993) incorporates size premium, value premium, and market premium as predictive variables for a portfolio's excess return. The model recommends portfolio construction based on book-to-market, market capitalization, and earnings-to-price because they provide an improved viewpoint on excess portfolio return (Chan et al., 1991; Fama & French, 1992). The model recommends portfolio formation based on market capitalization, book-to-market, and earnings-to-price because they provide a better perspective on excess portfolio return (Chan et al., 1991; Fama & French, 1992; Lakonishok et al., 1994). Thus, FF3FM is used in this study.

Empirical Review

Several studies have empirically examined the Fama and French three-factor model to analyze stock and bond excess returns, yielding varying conclusions. While some studies show that FF3M has limited ability or does not explain excess return (Alaoui & Benfeddoul, 2023; Benali et al., 2023; Zhou, 2023a, 2023b), others show that FF3FM does explain excess return in the stock market (Anuno et al., 2023; Chen et al., 2023; Irejeh & Aninoritse, 2024). Alaoui and Benfeddoul (2023) investigated the performance of the CAPM, the FF3FM, and the Fama and the French five-factor model (FF5FM) on the Casablanca Stock Exchange (CSE) in Morocco. Their study considered monthly data from July 2002 to June 2020. The main findings show that the Gibbons, Ross, and Shanken (GRS) test normally do not accepts all of the tested models. In general, all the tested models were moderately enhanced, but a portion of the variation in Moroccan stock returns remains unclear. Furthermore, Benali et al. (2023) evaluated the pricing effectiveness of the Carhart four-factor (C4FM) and FF3FM for stocks traded on the Moroccan CSE for each month over a 5-year period. The findings of this investigation illustrate that the models in question have only a partial influence on the CSE, limiting their potential to forecast probability of cross-sections of returns. Accordingly, the C4FM model has slightly greater explanatory power than the FF3FM model.

Similarly, Obrimah (2023) investigated whether the FF3FM was robust in pricing of risk preference and discovered that the "market skewness" model or 3-moment CAPM specification surpasses the FFM in terms of pricing all of the risk seeking preferences and risk aversion, as well as the corresponding arbitrary priors. On the other hand, Irejeh and Aninoritse (2024) examined the behavior of 68 stock returns on the Nigerian Stock Exchange from 2013 to 2022 in terms of firm size (market equity), market β, and book-equity-to-market equity. Using FF3FM, the results revealed a significant relationship between book-to-equity-to-market equity variables, firm size, excess stock market returns, and predicted portfolio returns, implying that the FF3FM might explain the variation in stock returns in the Nigerian stock market. Anuno et al. (2023) analyze the effectiveness of the CAPM, FF3FM, and FF5FM on the excess returns of Timor-Leste's equity and bond investments in the international market from 2006 to 2019. Their empirical findings suggest the market factor has a positive and significant relationship with the excess returns of the CAPM, FF3FM, and FF5FM.

Based on FF3FM, Chen et al. (2023) conducted a stock selection strategy study to select a portfolio from the monthly yield of 300 stocks in the CSI 300 Index between January 2012 and December 2021 using size and book market value comparisons. The study discovered that the FF3FM still has some utility in China's capital market, and investors can choose stocks based on the FF3FM. According to the simulation results, the FF3FM's fit has declined significantly since a decade ago, and the FF3FM will become increasingly unsuitable for China's capital market in the future, necessitating continuous optimization and improvement. Furthermore, Khoa and Huynh (2023a, 2023b) conducted a comparison of CAPM and FF3FM on the Hanoi stock market (HNX) between 2010 and 2022 using Machine Learning techniques. Their study results show that the FF3FM model is a better explanation than the CAPM model. Therefore, the conflicting assessments of FF3FM's suitability in examining excess return in various economies call for an independent study in Kenya. Therefore, this study analyzed the variability in excess portfolio return using FF3FM from Nairobi Security Exchange in Kenya.

Methodology

Data Source

This paper focuses on stocks listed on the Nairobi Securities Exchange (NSE) from January 2005 to December 2020. Not all stocks are chosen for model testing, but only those that meet three conditions: the stock issuer is a financial company, the stock is common, and the stock has at least one trading record per month from January to January of the following year (i.e., 13 months of trading in a row). The number of stocks that meet the test conditions varies year to year. Overall, 51 stocks met the defined criteria over the 16-year period. Stock prices were obtained from the NSE. Data on the companies' market capitalization (market value of equity) are derived from the NSE's quarterly and annual trading reports. Data on book values of equity are extracted from annual financial statements (audited and consolidated) that are publicly available on the NSE. Treasury bill returns were obtained from the Central Bank of Kenya.

Model Specification

According to FF3FM, a portfolio's expected excess returns $[E(\psi_M - \psi_f)]$ are explained by the return's sensitivity to three factors. First, consider the excess return on a market portfolio or market premium $(\psi_{it} - \psi_{ft})$. Second, size premium (ΔSB) refers to the difference in returns between small- and large-stock portfolios. Finally, value premium (ΔHL) refers to the difference in returns between high and low book-to-market stock portfolios. According to Fama and French (1992), the excess expected return on a portfolio i is calculated using Eq. (1).

$$E(\psi_i) - \psi_f = \beta_i \left[E(\psi_{Mt} - \psi_f) \right] + \alpha_i E(\Delta SB) + \delta_i E(\Delta HL) \tag{1}$$

where $E(\psi_i)$ is the expected rate of portfolio return; ψ_f is the risk-free rate of return; and $E(\psi_M - \psi_f)$ is the expected rate of excess market portfolio return. $E(\Delta SB)$ represents the expected value of the difference between the excess return on a portfolio of small stocks and a portfolio of large stocks. $E(\Delta HL)$ represents the expected value of the difference in excess return between a portfolio of high book-equity-to-market-equity stocks and a portfolio of low book-equity-to-market-equity stocks. According to Fama and French, regression Eq. (1), can be re-written as Eq. (2).

$$\theta_t^k = \gamma_i + \beta_{it} (\psi_{Mt} - \psi_{ft}) + \alpha_{it} E(\Delta SB) + \delta_{it} E(\Delta HL) + \varepsilon_{it} \tag{2}$$

where ψ_M represents the total market portfolio returns, γ_i is the intercept, $(\psi_{Mt} - \psi_{ft})$ is the excess portfolio return in month t, and ε_{it} is the error term at time t. $(\psi_{Mt} - \psi_{ft})$, ΔSB, and ΔHL indicate expected premiums. β_i, α_i and δ_i represent the asset's sensitivity to each of the three factors at time t. The left-hand side of Eq. (2) is θ_t^k, which represents the test portfolio's returns in month t. k stands for Big/High, Big/Medium, Big/Low, Medium/High, Medium/Medium, Medium/Low, Small/High, Small/Medium, and Small/Low. To test the asset pricing FF3FM, the left-hand-side (LHS) portfolio assets that act as dependent variables and the right-hand-side (RHS) risk factor portfolios that act as independent variables must be delineated.

Delineation of Independent Variables

Consistent with Fama and French, this study considers three risk factors as independent variables: market factor, size factor, and value factor.

Market Factor $(\psi_{Mt} - \psi_{ft})$

The market factor is computed as the discrepancy between the monthly returns of the Kenyan 3-month Treasury bill rate, which is used as a proxy for the risk-free rate, and the NSE-20 share index, which was used as a market portfolio surrogate.

Size Factor (SMB)

The size factor (ΔSB) for each month is the difference between the average returns on three small-stock portfolios (Small/High, Small/Medium, and Small/Low) and the average returns on three large-stock portfolios (Big/High, Big/Medium, and Big/Low) as estimated by Eq. (3).

$$\Delta \text{SB} = \frac{\left[\left(R_t^{\text{S/H}} + R_t^{\text{S/M}} + R_t^{\text{S/L}}\right) - \left(R_t^{\text{B/H}} + R_t^{\text{B/M}} + R_t^{\text{B/L}}\right)\right]}{3} \tag{3}$$

where $R_t^{\text{S/H}}$, $R_t^{\text{S/M}}$, $R_t^{\text{S/L}}$, $R_t^{\text{B/H}}$, $R_t^{\text{B/M}}$, and $R_t^{\text{B/L}}$ represent the monthly returns on the following portfolios S/H, S/M, S/L, B/H, B/M, and B/L at period *t*.

Value Factor (HML)

The value factor (ΔHL) is the difference between the average returns of two high book-equity-to-market equity portfolios (Small/High and Big/High) and two low book-equity-to-market equity portfolios (Small/Low and Big/Low). It is estimated by Eq. (4).

$$\Delta \text{HL} = \frac{\left[\left(R_t^{\text{B/H}} + R_t^{\text{S/H}}\right) - \left(R_t^{\text{B/L}} + R_t^{\text{S/L}}\right)\right]}{2} \tag{4}$$

where $R_t^{\text{B/H}}$, $R_t^{\text{S/H}}$, $R_t^{\text{B/L}}$, and $R_t^{\text{S/L}}$ represent the monthly returns on the stock portfolios B/H, S/H, B/L, and S/L at period *t*.

Delineation of Dependent Variables

After constructing the ΔSB and ΔHL portfolios for the RHS of Eq. (2), nine portfolios are created using a similar procedure to calculate excess portfolio returns for each month. All 51 stocks used in the analysis were sorted by size or market capitalization during each year of the study period and divided into three categories: Big, Medium, and Small. Furthermore, stocks are classified into three groups (high, medium, and low) based on the book-equity-to-market-equity ratio, with high (H) representing the top 30%, moderate (M) representing the middle 40%, and low (L) representing the bottom 30%. As a result, nine portfolios are created by combining the three size groups with the three book-equity-to-market equity groups. According to Tazi et al.'s (2022) methodology, these nine portfolios (Big/High, Big/Medium, Big/Low, Medium/High, Medium/Medium, Medium/Low, Small/High, Small/Medium, and Small/Low) are used as dependent variables in this study. The nine portfolios may be described as:

- The Big/High portfolio includes stocks with a high capitalization (B) and value (H).
- The Big/Medium portfolio combines stocks with high capitalization (B) and medium value (M).
- The Big/Low portfolio includes stocks with high capitalization (B) and low value (L).
- The Medium/High portfolio includes stocks with medium capitalization (M) and high value (H).
- The Medium/Medium portfolio consists of large stocks with medium capitalization (M) and medium value (M).
- The Medium/Low portfolio consists of medium-capitalization (M) and low-valued stocks.
- The Small/High portfolio includes stocks with small capitalization (S) and low value (H).
- The Small/Medium portfolio includes stocks with small capitalization (S) and low value (M).
- The Small/Low portfolio consists of stocks with low capitalization and value.

Results and Discussion

Portfolio return values and their statistical relationships are presented with regression results here.

Preliminary Analysis

Summary Statistics of the Study Variables

Table 1 summarizes descriptive statistics for the dependent variables, while Table 2 does the same for the independent variables.

Table 1 Summary statistics of the dependent variables

Portfolio	Mean	Standard deviation	Minimum	Maximum
Big/High	0.371	0.594	–0.129	3.183
Big/Medium	0.353	0.195	–0.121	0.928
Big/Low	0.391	0.246	–0.209	0.860
Small/High	–0.101	0.471	–0.164	2.371
Small/Medium	–0.138	0.318	–0.085	0.639
Small/Low	0.117	0.519	–0.104	0.990
Medium/High	0.216	0.150	–0.217	2.387
Medium/Medium	0.208	0.193	–0.131	1.563
Medium/Low	0.212	0.135	–0.177	0.591

Observations = 192
Source: Result estimates

Table 2 Summary statistics of the dependent variables

	Market factor ($\psi_{Mt} - \psi_{ft}$)	Size factor (ΔSB)	Value factor (ΔHL)
Mean	–0.0309	–0.8651	–0.0444
Median	0.0399	0.7385	0.0300
Maximum	0.0020	0.1985	0.1050
Minimum	–0.0307	–0.8652	–0.0034
Standard deviation	0.0147	0.0471	0.0967
Skewness	0.0124	0.8695	0.0061
Kurtosis	0.0032	0.9926	0.0117
Observation	0.0436	0.6037	0.0411
JB test stat	7.0262	0.3982	2.0193
p-value	0.10059	0.1627	0.1073

Observations = 192
Source: Result estimates

Table 1 shows the average return rate of stocks with a small market value and a high book-equity-to-market-equity ratio, small market value and a medium book-equity-to-market-equity ratio, and small market value and a book-equity-to-market-equity ratio, indicating that such stocks have poor returns and are more likely to experience financial crises. The Small/Low and Big/High groups have large standard deviations, indicating that the investment risk of these stocks is high. Furthermore, with the exception of stocks with a large market value and a high book-equity-to-market-equity ratio, the average portfolio returns rate declines as the book-equity-to-market-equity ratio increases.

During the study sample period, the market component, value element, and its size all had negative monthly average profits of –0.0309, –0.00139, and –0.00935. Between 2005 and 2020, firms with high market capitalization outperformed those with low capitalization, as indicated by the negative value of the ΔSB. From 2005 to 2020, companies with a low book-equity-to-market-equity ratio outperformed those with a high ratio, as evidenced by the negative ΔHL factor. This result is consistent with Fama and French's theory, which states that value stocks outperform growth stocks and small firms outperform large firms. Table 2 also shows that all three portfolios had negative minimum and positive maximum returns. The market portfolio has the lowest maximum return, so investors can diversify into the value or size portfolios, both of which guarantee higher returns. According to the standard deviation, the market portfolio has the lowest risk, while the value portfolio has the highest. The p-values for each portfolio are insignificant at the 5% level of significance, indicating that the JB statistics of the three portfolio returns are not Gaussian. However, this is not an issue because the normality condition is not required for all study variables, whereas prediction errors must be normally distributed.

Correlation Matrix and Variance Inflation Factor

Table 3 shows a correlation matrix for the nine portfolio returns. According to the table, the stock with a large market value and a high book-to-market ratio has a weak but positive correlation with the remaining eight stocks. Aside from the stock with a small market value and a high book-to-market ratio and the stock with a medium market value and a medium book-to-market ratio, the stock with a large market value and a medium book-to-market ratio has a weak but positive correlation with the remaining six stocks. The stock with a high market value and a low book-to-market ratio has a weak but positive correlation with all other stocks except the one with a small market value and a low book-to-market ratio. Except for the stock with a large market value and a medium book-to-market ratio, the stock with a low market value and a high book-to-market ratio has a weak but positive correlation with the remaining seven stocks. The stock with a large market value and a high book-to-market ratio has a weak but positive correlation with the remaining eight stocks. Aside from the stock with a large market value and a low book-to-market ratio and the stock with a small market value and a medium book-to-market ratio, the stock with a low book-to-market ratio has a weak but positive correlation with the remaining six stocks. Given that all the stocks have either a weak positive or negative pairwise correlation, none of the stocks are removed from the empirical model.

Table 4 displays the correlation and variance inflation factors for three risk factor portfolios. Excess market portfolio return has a weak, negative correlation with ΔSB. Additionally, there is a weak negative correlation between excess market portfolio return and ΔHL. There is a weak but positive correlation between excess market portfolio return and ΔSB. The variance inflation factor for all risk factors exceeds 0.7, indicating that there is no multicollinearity among study variables. Similarly, in Table 5, the variance inflation factor for all nine portfolios is greater than 0.7, indicating that there is no multicollinearity among the study variables.

Table 3 Correlation matrix for dependent variables

Portfolio	Big/High	Big/Medium	Big/Low	Small/High	Small/Medium	Small/Low	Medium/High	Medium/Medium	Medium/Low
Big/High	1								
Big/Medium	0.192	1							
Big/Low	0.268	0.154	1						
Small/High	0.197	–0.291	0.289	1					
Small/Medium	0.304	0.224	0.248	0.259	1				
Small/Low	0.217	0.228	–0.228	0.293	0.152	1			
Medium/High	0.246	0.181	0.182	0.272	0.142	0.301	1		
Medium/Medium	0.161	–0.298	0.285	0.141	0.213	0.164	0.196	1	
Medium/Low	0.298	0.303	0.276	0.139	–0.247	0.219	–0.229	0.161	1

Observations = 192

Source: Result estimates

Table 4 Correlation matrix and variance inflation factor for independent variables

	Market factor ($\psi_{Mt} - \psi_{ft}$)	Size factor (ΔSB)	Value factor (ΔHL)	VIF
Market factor ($\psi_{Mt} - \psi_{ft}$)	1	–0.120	–0.184	0.745
Size factor (ΔSB)	–0.149	1	–0.149	0.839
Value factor (ΔHL)	–0.184	–0.120	1	0.784

Observations = 192
Source: Result estimates

Empirical Results

Fama and French Three-Factor Model

Equation (2) is used to estimate the impact of the three risk factors on excess portfolio returns. The estimation results are summarized in Table 6.

Table 6 demonstrates that the FF3FM is correctly specified, as all intercept values are significantly different from zero at the 5% level of significance. This indicates that the intercept should be close to zero. According to Fama et al. (1993), if the expected excess portfolio return is different from zero, it must compensate for risk. The risk premium is captured by three risk factors: ($\psi_M - \psi_f$), ΔSB and ΔHL. Table 6 shows that all of the market factor coefficients are positive, with small capitalization portfolios having significant market coefficients at the 5% level of significance and large capitalization portfolios having significant market coefficients at the 10% level. The market coefficients of medium-capitalization portfolios are statistically insignificant at the 5 and 10% levels. The smallest size portfolios (Small/High, Small/Medium, and Small/Low) have negative ΔSB coefficients, while the large- and medium-capitalization portfolios have positive coefficients. Similarly, in terms of statistical significance, ΔSB appears significant in all portfolios at the 1% level of significance, with the exception of the big capitalization portfolios, demonstrating the size effect. The size factor (ΔSB) is important for explaining portfolio returns in medium and small portfolios but has no effect on large-scale portfolios.

The ΔHL coefficient is negative in portfolios with lower book-equity-to-market-equity ratios, including Big/Low, Medium/Low, and Small/Low. The ΔHL factor is statistically insignificant for medium-capitalization portfolios at the 5% level. Table 6 shows that, at the significance level of 5%, ΔHL has statistically strong explanatory power only on high book-to-market equity stock portfolios. Low and medium book-to-market equity stock portfolios have statistically insignificant slope coefficients at this level. Given that ΔHL is positive for high book-equity-to-market-equity portfolios, it is expected that (Small/High) > (Medium/High) > (Big/High) on average excess portfolio returns, assuming all else remains constant. In other words, ΔHL value is effective for high book-equity-to-market-equity value portfolios. However, this effect is ambiguous, meaning that book-equity-to-market-equity

Table 5 Variance inflation factor for dependent variables

	Big/High	Big/Medium	Big/Low	Small/ High	Small/ Medium	Small/Low	Medium/High	Medium/Medium	Medium/Low
VIF	0.771	0.851	0.908	0.864	0.829	0.792	0.937	0.748	0.986

Observations = 192

Source: Result estimates

Table 6 Regression results of Fama and French three-factor model

Coefficients	Big/High	Big/Medium	Big/Low	Small/ High	Small/ Medium	Small/Low	Medium/High	Medium/Medium	Medium/Low
Intercept	0.026** (1.128)	0.036** (2.617)	0.061** (1.502)	0.049** (1.789)	0.031** (2.08)	0.052** (2.001)	0.068** (3.416)	0.035** (1.193)	0.029** (2.932)
$(\psi_{Mt} - \psi_{ft})$	0.897* (2.362)	0.571* (2.892)	0.635* (1.591)	0.535** (2.171)	0.586** (2.171)	0.596** (2.163)	0.789 (2.887)	0.872 (3.317)	0.906 (2.472)
ΔSB	0.832 (3.188)	0.563 (2.494)	0.787 (1.794)	–0.661*** (–3.315)	–0.798*** (–2.231)	–0.906*** (–1.929)	0.678*** (1.720)	0.851*** (3.396)	0.781*** (2.968)
ΔHL	1.318** (1.858)	0.798** (3.535)	–0.918** (–3.21)	0.715** (2.502)	0.557 (1.644)	–0.628 (–1.485)	0.852 (2.999)	0.657 (1.552)	–0.672 (–3.266)
Adjusted-R^2	0.832	0.741	0.702	0.671	0.504	0.352	0.513	0.482	0.394
F-statistics	0.000	0.000	0.000	0.000	0.000	0.000	0.000	0.000	0.000

Note: * $p < 0.1$; ** $p < 0.05$; *** $p < 0.01$. Observations = 192. T-statistics are in parenthesis. Sample period = January 2005 to December 2020
Source: Result estimates

ratio affects average excess portfolio returns in an un-systematic and un-explained manner. This finding is consistent with Anuno et al. (2023), who discovered that the two size factors (ΔSB) and value factors (ΔHL) have a negative and significant effect on excess returns in the FF3FM and FF5FM.

Adjusted-R^2 values range from 35.2% for the smallest to 83.2% for the largest portfolios. The FF3FM model has a higher predictive potential for large portfolios (83.2% on average) than it does for small portfolios (35.2% on average). It also shows lower predictive power (39.4% on average) for medium-sized portfolios. The F-statistics obtained using the OLS method have very low *p*-values, indicating that the model fits the data well. The FF3FM assumes significantly greater predictability overall in each of the aforementioned nine portfolios, though to varying degrees. The results show that the FF3FM accounts for a significant portion of the multiple in the dependent variables. The three variables ($\psi_M - \psi_f$), ΔSB and ΔHL yield valid results across all sample portfolios. To summarize, the size impact and value effect appear to be completely intact and partially intact in the NSE from 2005 to 2020. Based on the findings, it was concluded that the FF3FM has limited potential to explain variations in portfolio excess returns.

Conclusion

The aim of this study was to explain the excess portfolio return variations by the FF3FM using stocks operating on NSE during the years from January 2005 to December 2020. The market risk factor, ($\psi_M - \psi_f$), size risk factor (ΔSB), and book-equity-to-market-equity risk factor (ΔHL) were used as the dependent variables while nine portfolios were constructed to form independent variables and to test the FF3FM. Statistical results show that big size and medium size portfolios overwhelm small size portfolios on realized excess returns. Furthermore, high book-equity-to-market equity stock portfolios generate higher excess returns than low book-equity-to-market equity stock portfolios. The market risk factor is found to be effective on all excess portfolio returns. Thus, it is concluded that the FF3FM has a limited ability to explain variations in portfolio excess returns. In terms of limitation, this study is limited geographically because it only focuses on the Nairobi Securities Exchange, leaving out the rest of Africa. However, the findings are interpreted in light of a broader geographical context. The study also did not account for the COVID-19 pandemic, which occurred in 2020, so future research should look into the impact of COVID-19 on excess returns.

References

Alaoui, T. A., & Benfeddoul, S. (2023). The empirical explanatory power of CAPM and the Fama and French three-five factor models in the Moroccan stock exchange. *International Journal of Financial Studies, 11*(1), 47.

Anuno, F., Madaleno, M., & Vieira, E. (2023). Using the capital asset pricing model and the Fama–French three-factor and five-factor models to manage stock and bond portfolios: Evidence from Timor-Leste. *Journal of Risk and Financial Management, 16*(11), 480.

Banz, R. W. (1981). The relationship between return and market value of common stocks. *Journal of Financial Economics, 9*(1), 3–18. North-Holland.

Benali, M., Lahboub, K., & El Bouhadi, A. (2023). Pricing ability of Carhart four-factor and Fama–French three-factor models: Empirical evidence from Morocco. *International Journal of Financial Studies, 11*(1), 20.

Chan, L. K. C., Hamao, Y., & Lakonishok, J. (1991). Fundamentals and stock returns in Japan. *Journal of Finance, 46*, 1739–1789.

Chen, G., Jing, Y., & Zhang, T. (2023, April). Quantitative portfolio selection based on Fama-French 3-factor model: An empirical research. In *FFIT 2022: Proceedings of the international conference on financial innovation, FinTech and information technology, FFIT 2022, October 28–30, 2022, Shenzhen, China* (p. 282). European Alliance for Innovation.

Fama, E. F., & French, K. R. (1992). The cross-section of expected stock returns. *The Journal of Finance, XLVII*(2).

Fama, E. F., & French, K. R. (1995). Size and book-to-market factors in earnings and returns. *The Journal of Finance, 50*(1), 131–155. Wiley.

Fama, E. F., French, K. R., Booth, D. G., & Sinquefield, R. (1993). Differences in the risks and returns of NYSE and NASD stocks. *Financial Analysts Journal, 49*(1), 37–41. CFA Institute.

Gibbons, M. R. (1982). Multivariate tests of financial models: A new approach. *Journal of Financial Economics, 10*(1), 3–27.

Irejeh, E. M., & Aninoritse, L. E. (2024). Fama and French three factor model. *European Journal of Accounting, Auditing and Finance Research, 12*(5), 17–70.

Khoa, B. T., & Huynh, T. T. (2023a). Effectiveness of OLS and SVR in return prediction: Fama-French three-factor model and CAPM framework. *Industrial Engineering & Management Systems, 22*(1), 73–84.

Khoa, B. T., & Huynh, T. T. (2023b). A comparison of CAPM and Fama-French three-factor model under Machine Learning approaching. *Journal of Eastern European and Central Asian Research (JEECAR), 10*(7), 1100–1111.

Lintner, J. (1965). The valuation of risk assets and the selection of risky investments in stock portfolios and capital budgets. *Review of Economics and Statistics, 47*(1), 12–37.

Markowitz, H. (1952). Portfolio selection. *The Journal of Finance, 7*(1), 77–91.

Merton, R. C. (1973). An intertemporal capital asset pricing model. *Econometrica, 41*(5), 867–887. The Econometric Society.

Obrimah, O. A. (2023). Is the Fama and French three factor model robust to the pricing of risk preferences? Available at SSRN 4009123.

Reinganum, M. R. (1981). Misspecification of capital asset pricing: Empirical Anomalies based on earnings' yield and market values. *Journal of Financial Economics, 9*(1), 19–46.

Ross, S. A. (1976). The arbitrage theory of capital asset pricing. *Journal of Economic Theory, 13*(3), 341–360.

Sharpe, W. F. (1964). Capital asset prices: A theory of market equilibrium under conditions of risk. *The Journal of Finance, 19*(3), 425–442.

Tazi, O., Aguenaou, S., & Abrache, J. (2022). A comparative study of the Fama-French three factor and the Carhart four factor models: Empirical evidence from Morocco. *International Journal of Economics and Financial Issues, 12*, 58–66.

Zhou, W. (2023a). A comparative study of Fama-French five factor model and three factor model—A case study of CSI 1000. In *International conference on business and policy studies* (pp. 1546–1554). Springer Nature.

Zhou, Y. (2023b). Evaluation of stock returns of alpha-factor selection strategy based on Fama-French three-factor model. In *3rd international conference on economic development and business culture (ICEDBC 2023)* (pp. 326–335). Atlantis Press.

Competitiveness of Kenyan Coffee: The Price Volatility—Production Perspective

Richard Wamalwa Wanzala, Nyankomo Marwa, Elizabeth Nanziri, and Lawrence Obokoh

Abstract Coffee is Kenya's fourth largest export crop, bringing in about US$0.23 billion in revenue from exports, supporting 700,000 households and providing jobs for over 100,000 people. Despite coffee's significant contribution to Kenya's economic development, the country's production of coffee has been declining over time due to unstable coffee prices in the bifurcated global markets. Thus, the main objective of this study was to answer the following question: "What is the effect of coffee price volatility on Kenyan coffee's competitiveness in the global market?" The coffee data for 21 coffee-producing nations worldwide from 1990 to 2018, which was used in this study to address the research question, was sourced from the International Coffee Organization and World Development Indicators. Price analysis, hedonic regression, and volatility models (GARCH, TARCH, and EGARCH) were used to analyze the data. Out of 18 Arabica coffee-producing nations, Kenya was ranked sixth in the study's results for coffee production. Hedonic regression results show that the production of coffee, exports of coffee, exportable coffee, interest rates, and exchange rates are all negatively impacted by price volatility. Lastly, the study's findings indicate the existence of a leverage effect, which implies that any change in the price of coffee reacts asymmetrically to both good and bad news regarding the volume of coffee traded on the global market. Thus, this study concludes that, to smooth out production, Kenyan policymakers should insulate coffee growers from the effects of price volatility.

Keywords Price volatility · Coffee production · Coffee exports · Exportable coffee · Hedonic regression · Volatility models

R. W. Wanzala (✉) · N. Marwa · L. Obokoh
University of Johannesburg, Johannesburg, South Africa
e-mail: rwanzala@uj.ac.za; nyankomom@uj.ac.za; lawrence.obokoh@jbs.ac.za

E. Nanziri
Stellenbosch University, Stellenbosch, South Africa
e-mail: elizabethn@stellenboschbusiness.ac.za

T. Moloi (ed.), *Impacting Society Positively Through Technology in Accounting and Business Processes*, Springer Proceedings in Business and Economics,
https://doi.org/10.1007/978-3-031-84885-8_43

Introduction

The coffee sector is the fourth largest export crop in Kenya accounting for approximately US$0.23 billion through export earnings, employing 100,000 people, and providing livelihoods for 700,000 households (Wanzala et al., 2022). Despite the significant contributions to the economy, the production of Kenyan coffee has been dwindling over the years. Further, more than 90 percent of Kenya's coffee are for export, which makes the stability of Kenya's coffee economy to be highly dependent on competitive world market conditions that is bifurcated and characterized by highly volatile coffee prices. Among the major competitors of Kenyan coffee exports are Brazil, Colombia, and Vietnam whose coffee suffer lower price volatility to Kenya (ICO, 2019). The coffee prices volatility in the international market affects the domestic coffee prices, Kenya's foreign exchange earnings, exporters' decision, and puts an additional barrier to farmers on their ability to invest and improve the crop (Machuka et al., 2016). Therefore, there is an urgent need for continued improvement of both the production and marketing environment to make Kenya coffee competitive in the international market. This calls for a deliberate effort by the government not only to encourage but also to facilitate more farmers and traders to engage in direct sales and futures market because this brings about increased producer control and accountability in negotiations with international buyers. Therefore, this study examined the effect of coffee price volatility on the competitiveness of Kenya coffee in the global market.

Basically, everyone agrees that volatility in commodity prices is expensive for economies, developing and developed alike. However, because developing economies rely heavily on primary commodities for export earnings, investment growth, employment, income growth, and debt servicing, price volatility tends to be more severe in these regions. Therefore, finding solid information about the effects of reforms is essential for making decisions about international market-sharing agreements, risk management plans, price stabilization programs, and sound development and economic policies. Wanzala et al. (2022) claim that this price volatility led to price risks that created a supply–demand imbalance that almost brought the production of coffee to a complete halt.

In the past, measures to address the longer-term problems of structural and supply–demand imbalances were not taken in response to low coffee prices. The majority of domestic policies concentrated on finding a temporary fix to keep up coffee production by protecting farmers from low prices and taking care of their credit problems. Emergency funds (El Salvador and Costa Rica), price regulations for coffee (Costa Rica), pooling programs (India), put option trading (Brazil), quota-based regulatory and tax regimes (Kenya and Mexico), and the use of stabilization programs (Kenya, Papua New Guinea, and Colombia) are a few examples of these policies. In the past, El Salvador and Costa Rica used money from the emergency kitty to offset the farmers' profits from coffee production during downturns in coffee prices. These funds were recovered from coffee sales between 1994 and 1997 after prices stabilized. Furthermore, Costa Rican coffee law stipulated that coffee producers should receive the average price for the season rather than the price at the time of sale. In India, the pooling program was implemented to more evenly distribute coffee farmers' earnings. Coffee growers in Brazil were able to mitigate risks by trading in the financial and futures markets (put options). While planting restrictions in Kenya kept the supply in line with quotas mostly benefited estate farmers, in Mexico the tax and regulatory regime under quotas benefited smallholder farmers and exporters at the expense of larger farmers.

There are two distinct objectives that drive this investigation. The first objective of this study was to determine how competitive Kenya's prices were with those of other significant coffee producers worldwide in the unstable global market. In doing so, Kenya's well-established price competitiveness on the international coffee market would probably provide insight into marketability metrics for coffee, which would motivate growers to boost output. Second, the long-term relationship between the underlying coffee price and coffee marketability indicators worldwide is ascertained by this study using EGARCH frameworks. Therefore, the size of the estimated long-run relationships between these research variables shows whether price risk needs to be reduced and whether capital needs to be dispersed to farmers to support rural economic growth. Essentially, the estimated empirical results are interpreted to suggest policy enhancements to reduce the risks associated with Kenya's volatile coffee prices.

Literature Review

Theoretical Review

For all producers of commodities, in developed and developing countries, price volatility is a serious issue. Price volatility is an unconditional measure of variability in price caused by the short-term rigidity of supply and demand, which precludes mutual adjustment through slower price movements. Due to various factors such as plant diseases, the gestation period needed for new plants to become productive, droughts and other meteorological events, and other factors, agricultural producers are not always able to fully control the volume of production in the short term, which makes them vulnerable to price volatility. Three variables—state, economic, and market structure variables—have been identified as contributing to the volatility of agricultural commodities' futures or spot prices, including coffee (Aliaga Lordemann et al., 2021). The time-to-maturity impact is the focus of the state variables, which demonstrate that price volatility rises as a contract nears maturity (Samuelson, 1965). Some studies, however, contended that seasonality drives the volatility of daily price changes and that the resolution of uncertainty about underlying supply and demand "state variables" coincides with the passage of time (Milonas, 1986). For instance, price volatility in coffee markets increases during the harvest season and decreases as the year approaches its vegetative phase. The second wave of research on agricultural price volatility focuses on underlying supply and demand factors, such as inventory levels, prices-to-loan ratios, stocks-to-use ratios, and price levels. The price volatility of agricultural commodities is also influenced by other stochastic factors and meteorological factors, such as temperature and rainfall. According to the perspective on economic variables, the decline in coffee market prices worldwide can be primarily attributed to the substantial increase in global supply in contrast to the slow growth in demand, as well as the low-price elasticities of the coffee demand. For example, the rise of productivity in Brazil, the expansion of coffee planting into frost-free areas, and the entry of Vietnam as a major producer and exporter of coffee have all contributed to the overabundance of coffee.

Variables related to market structure, such as trading volumes, market concentration, scalping activity, and regulation, are included in the third wave of research. An international concerted effort has been made to control supply and stimulate demand to affect market fundamentals. The suspension of the quota system administered by the International Coffee Agreement (ICA) in 1989 resulted in a particularly dramatic decline in prices. In the aftermath of the collapse, the average International Coffee Organization composite price dropped by 21% in 1999, 25% in 2000, and 29% in 2001—the lowest annual average since 1971. To regulate supply, the Association of Coffee-Producing Countries (ACPC) was founded even after the collapse of the International Coffee Agreement administered quota. Beginning on October 1, 2000, the association promoted a retention program to hold onto 20% of exports. To keep prices above 95 cents per pound and release supplies onto the market when prices rose above 105 cents per pound, this was done. Only a small number of ACPC members, nevertheless, collaborated and reduced supply. Participating countries would have lost 6.5 percent of their revenue because of the scheme, but nonparticipating countries would have gained 17 percent of their revenue if they had continued to export. The plan was therefore unable to be maintained. It was also discovered that the chances of success were slim, especially since the nations that consume coffee refused to sign the agreement. This would have been required to manage the issue of free riders and cheating. Additionally, market liberalization and devaluation led to supply expansion in certain exporting nations; retailers and roasters exploited their market dominance; and technological advancements in roasting influenced the volatility of coffee prices.

Lowering bid-ask spreads should result in less price volatility because of scaling activities. However, Brorsen (1989) contended that scalping might enhance price variability and enable prices to react to information more quickly. Peck (1981) discovered that scalping increased volatility. The presence of prominent positions relative to total open interest, whether held by speculators or hedgers, can impact price variability through market concentration. Large traders' actions have the potential to decrease liquidity or result in significant price adjustments, which would increase price volatility (Goodwin & Schnepf, 2000). There is inconsistent data regarding how speculation affects price volatility. Speculation has been shown to decrease volatility, according to studies by Ward (1974), Peck (1981), and Brorsen and Irwin (1987). However, the opposite is confirmed by

Cornell (1981), and Chang et al. (1997). Cornell (1981) discovered a positive correlation between variations in daily volume and the degree of volatility. However, fresh research on the effects of the commodity markets' "financialization" process on price volatility was spurred by the 2008 financial crisis, with varying degrees of success. Many specialty coffee traders and organizations view the financialization of coffee as a commodity negatively. It is thought that speculative trades exacerbate price volatility, which has detrimental and destabilizing effects on coffee growers and the industry.

Empirical Review

The impact of fluctuating coffee prices on the welfare and economic manipulation of producers has been the subject of numerous studies (Abebe, 2020; Chaovanapoonphol et al., 2023; Fatih, 2022; Hoai et al., 2023; Singhal & Tarp, 2024; Oko-Isu et al., 2019; Yeshiwas & Berelie, 2020; Zhang et al., 2022). Instead of examining how price volatility affects coffee production or exports, most of these studies have concentrated more on modeling price volatility. Hoai et al. (2023) examined price volatility, linkage, and fluctuation risk among coffee price series from 2004 to 2020 using the Value at Risk (VaR) and DCC-GARCH models. According to the study, Brazil and Colombia are only slightly impacted by the ARCH term at the 1% level, whereas the price of Robusta coffee in two markets and the price of Vietnamese coffee were subject to fluctuations due to two ARCH terms and GARCH terms. Vietnamese coffee has the lowest price volatility risk of any coffee, while Brazilian coffee has the highest price volatility risk. With a clear understanding of the fluctuations and relationships between coffee export price series, policymakers, coffee processing and exporting businesses, and coffee farmers will be able to use the results as a valuable reference to develop appropriate and effective strategies and solutions for managing price volatility risk in the context of sustainable development.

The average daily volatility of Ethiopia's coffee prices from January 1, 2010, to June 30, 2019, was modeled by Abebe (2020). He employed the GARCH-MIDAS component model, which breaks down the conditional variance into two parts: a long-run component that takes into account various frequency macroeconomic indicators using the mixed interval data sampling (MIDAS) specification, and a short-run component that uses a mean-reverting unit GARCH process. According to the estimated model's result, each of the chosen indicators is essential for understanding price volatility. Using a multiple exogenous Bayesian GARCH-X model, Chaovanapoonphol et al. (2023) investigated the impact of exogenous factors on the volatility of coffee prices in Thailand. The multiple exogenous Bayesian GARCH-X model is more fitted to the data than the other models, according to the empirical results of a comparison between the two models. The standard Bayesian GARCH-X model and the first model both estimated the impact of individual exogenous variables separately. The first model's standard error is the smallest when compared to the other models. The findings show that the volatility of raw coffee prices is exacerbated by the growth in demand for coffee bean factories in Thailand and the volume of coffee beans exported from Indonesia. On the other hand, the volatility of raw coffee bean prices will decrease if Brazil's export volume of coffee beans rises.

Using data from 1961 to 2015 from Nigeria, Oko-Isu et al. (2019) investigated how climate change and commodity price volatility affected coffee output. The results demonstrate that the international commodity price of coffee and climate change have an impact on Nigeria's coffee output using fully modified ordinary least square (FMOLS), autoregressive conditional heteroscedasticity (ARCH), and generalized autoregressive conditional heteroscedasticity (GARCH). The study illustrates the possible advantages of raising coffee exports and output through actions to mitigate the effects of climate change and to revive the marketing of agricultural commodities in Nigeria and other developing nations. The impact of volatile coffee prices on Vietnamese farmers' psychological well-being was studied by Singhal & Tarp (2024). The study's conclusion, based on household panel data gathered between 2016 and 2020, indicates that there is a positive correlation between psychological distress among coffee farmers and an increase in the volatility of the global coffee price. Men experience a larger magnitude, and the results hold up well under multiple checks. Corresponding estimates for associated health measures and self-reported happiness provide additional support for these findings. Some of the channels are decreased social capital, increased cognitive load, and alcohol consumption, as well as elevated mental stress brought on by negative expectations for future economic well-being. The findings demonstrate the negative psychological effects of having unpredictable income and lend credence to the idea of social safety nets shielding farmers from regular swings in commodity prices.

It was essential that this study be carried out because there was a dearth of literature in both developed and developing nations connecting the volatility of coffee prices to coffee production. Moreover, there are not many studies, if any, comparing Kenyan coffee's price competitiveness to that of other coffee-producing nations worldwide.

Methodology

Data

The World Bank's World Development Indicators (WDI) and the International Coffee Organization (ICO) provided the secondary data. While information on interest rates and exchange rates came from WDI, information on price, production, exports, and exportable goods came from ICO. There are roughly 56 major coffee-producing nations in the world, of which 22 and 16 are focused on producing Arabica and Robusta coffee, respectively (see Appendix I), according to ICO (2019) statistics. Arabica and Robusta are produced in the remaining 18 nations. However, this study concentrated on 21 countries that were used for comparative analysis to ascertain the price competitiveness of Kenyan coffee because some of the countries lacked consistent data from 1990 to 2018. These nations are Brazil, Colombia, Honduras, Dominican Republic, Guatemala, El Salvador, Mexico, Cuba, Peru, India, Costa Rica, Vietnam; Kenya, Uganda, Tanzania, Rwanda, Burundi, Ethiopia, Togo, Côte d'Ivoire, and Papua New Guinea.

Study Variables

The price, production, exports, exportable, interest rate, and exchange rate are the six variables included in this study. To keep things simple, we will refer to coffee price, production, exports, and exportable coffee variables as coffee marketability indicators. As control variables, the interest rate and exchange rate are employed. The regressor in this case is the price, and the explanatory variables are the interest rate, exchange rate, exports of coffee, production of coffee, and exportable coffee. The price of coffee that is expressed in USD/lb. was converted to USD/kg. In contrast, the production, export, and exportable units of measurement are expressed in 1000 60 kg bags.

Measurement of Price Volatility

One of the reasons behind the recent fluctuations in commodity prices is the growing financialization of commodities, such as coffee, whereby the actions of hedgers enable speculators to influence global benchmark prices for their own financial gain by combining physical and financial prevarication strategies (Struthers, 2019; Tröster & Gunter, 2023). Since coffee is regarded as a financial asset, the price volatility of the study is calculated using annualized volatility, which is estimated using the formula below that is frequently used to calculate stock price volatility:

$$V_{Act} = \sqrt{252} * \sqrt{\left(\overline{P}_{ct} - P_{ict}\right) / n} \quad (1)$$

where V_{Act} is the annualized coffee price volatility for country c in the year t, P_{ict} daily coffee price on an ith day for country c in the year t and $\overline{P}_{ct}$ of the same country in the same year. n is the number of daily coffee prices while 252 is the number of trading days in a year.

Model Specification

Four models—the hedonic regression model: (HRM), the threshold autoregressive conditional heteroscedasticity (TARCH), the generalized autoregressive conditional heteroscedasticity (GARCH), and the exponential generalized autoregressive conditional heteroscedasticity (EGARCH)—were specified to address the study's objective. The relationship between the price of coffee and other marketability indicators was ascertained using HRM. HRM is therefore defined as

$$V_{Act} = \beta_o + \beta_1 \psi_{ct} + \beta_2 \lambda_{ct} + \beta_3 \vartheta_{ct} + + \beta_4 \varpi_{ct} + \beta_5 \pi_{ct} + \varepsilon_t \quad (2)$$

where V_{Act} is the annualized coffee price volatility for country c in the year t; ψ_{ct} is the quantity of coffee produced by country c at time t; λ_{ct} is coffee exported by country c at time t; and ϑ_{ct} is the exportable coffee by country c at time t. ϖ_{ct} and π_{ct} are interest rate and exchange rate of country c at time t, respectively. The interest rate and exchange rate are used as control variables.

The *GARCH* model is a variation of the auto-regressive conditional heteroscedasticity (*ARCH*) model developed by Engle (1982), which presupposes that the error variance might be correlated over time because of the phenomenon of volatility clustering. The *GARCH* model is a function of three terms:

$$\mathcal{K}_t = \varphi + \sum_{i=1}^{q} \delta_i \mu_{t-1}^2 + \sum_{j=1}^{p} \psi_j \mathcal{K}_{t-j} \quad (3)$$

where $\mathcal{K}_t$ is the price of coffee at the year t; φ is the mean; δ_i is the *ARCH* term; and $\psi_j$is the *GARCH* term. *TARCH* is a volatility model that permits the analysis of asymmetric effects. The model was promulgated autonomously by Glosten et al. (1993) and Zakoian (1994). The conditional variance of *TARCH* is written as

$$\mathcal{K}_t = \varphi + \sum_{i=1}^{q} \delta_i \mu_{t-1} + \lambda \mu_{t-1} d_{t-1} + \sum_{j=1}^{p} \psi_j \mathcal{K}_{t-j} \quad (4)$$

where φ, δ, ψ, and λ are the mean, *ARCH* term, *GARCH* term, and asymmetric or leverage effect, respectively. It is assumed that $d_t = 1$ if $\mu_t < 0$ and $d_t = 0$ otherwise. In *Eq*. 4, λ captures the asymmetrical effect of bad or good news. The good news is signified by favorable conditions such as business cycle conditions and demand–supply conditions, while the bad news is signified by conditions such as political instability, climate change, and a high inflation rate. Consequently, bad news ($\mu_t > 0$) and good news ($\mu_t < 0$) have a distinct impact on the conditional variance; that is, the bad news has an impact $\delta + \lambda$ while the good news has an impact on δ. The hypothesis that $\lambda > 0$ is used to test the presence of asymmetric effects. Thus, the impact is said to be asymmetric when $\lambda \neq 0$. Negative λ implies positive price shocks, which generate less volatility, whereas positive λ implies negative price shocks, which generate more volatility.

Finally, *the EGARCH* model is an alternative test used to determine the logarithm of restrictive variance to estimate the extent to which observed volatility reacts asymmetrically to either a favorable or unfavorable state of nature (Maurice & Davis, 2012). Unlike the *GARCH* model, which limits the conditional volatility of coffee prices to respond symmetrically to positive and negative shocks to the coffee market supply process, the *EGARCH* model permits conditional volatility to increase (decrease) when the standardized shocks to the coffee market supply process σ_{t-1}^2, are negative (positive). Consequently, the conditional volatility from the *EGARCH* model may incorporate information on volatilities but is not confined in the conditional volatility estimates emanating from the *GARCH* model (Day & Lewis, 1992). To assess this coffee-restrictive variance, we estimate the following *EGARCH* model:

$$\log \mathcal{K}_t = \varphi + \psi \log \mathcal{K}_{t-j} + \delta \left[\frac{|\mu_{t-1}|}{\sqrt{\mathcal{K}_{t-1}}} \right] + \lambda \left[\frac{|\mu_{t-1}|}{\sqrt{\mathcal{K}_{t-1}}} \right] \quad (5)$$

where δ, ψ, and λ are *ARCH* term, *GARCH* term, and asymmetric or leverage effect, respectively. The $\mathcal{K}_t$ is an asymmetric function of μ_{t-1} and coefficient $\mathcal{K}_t$ is used to estimate the asymmetry. In Eq. 4, ψ denotes the impact of $t - 1$ forecast variance. Thus, volatility clustering is associated with a positive ψ, which suggests that positive coffee price variations are linked to further positive variations and vice versa. δ denotes the effect of price volatility from the earlier period on present period volatility. The hypothesis $\lambda < 0$ is postulated to check the existence of leverage effects. When $\lambda < 0$, it is assumed that the impact is asymmetric, and a negative λ indicates that bad news has a greater impact on volatility than good news of an equal size. The level of tenacity over time of volatility shock is determined by adding the coefficients of δ and ψ. A tenacious volatility shock increases the coffee price volatility. The left-hand side of *Eq.* 5 is the lag of the conditional variance. This suggests that the asymmetric effect is not quadratic but exponential, which indicates that the conditional variance forecasted will be non-negative.

Results

Diagnostic Tests

The diagnostic tests involved examining the time-series properties of the data that included stationarity (unit root test), autocorrelation, multicollinearity, and heteroscedasticity. The Levin, Lin, and Chu t^* unit root test for the panel data for the 21 countries for all the four study variables (coffee price, coffee production, coffee exports, exportable coffee, interest rates, and exchange rate) was highly significant at a 1% level of significance. The Im, Pesaran, and Shin W-stat, Augmented Dickey–Fuller (ADF), Fisher chi-square, and PP–Fisher chi-square unit tests that were

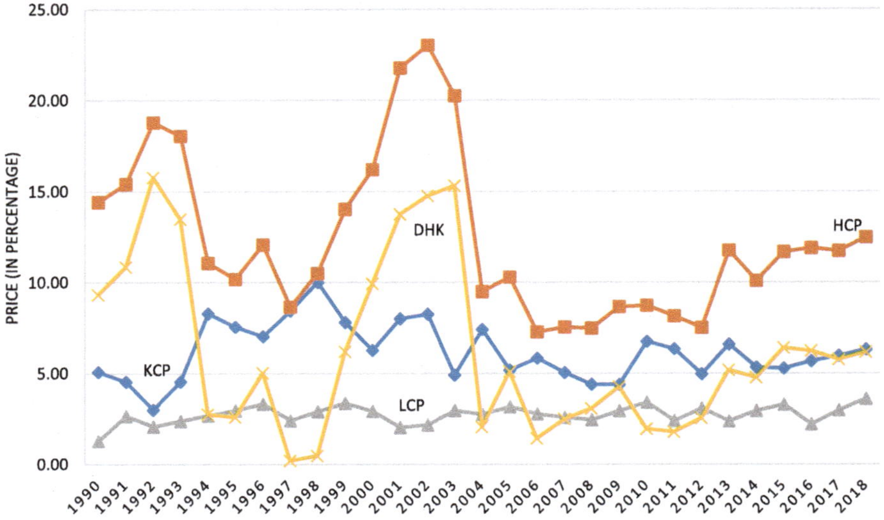

Fig. 1 Trend analysis of Kenyan Coffee in relation to the highest price per year. (Source: Authors' computation)

conducted also indicated that the results to highly significant at a 1% level of significance. This result leads to a conclusion that all the study variables have a unit root or are stationary (see Appendix II). Furthermore, using the variance inflation factor, collinearity was not detected, and results from the Breusch–Godfrey Serial Correlation LM test showed that there was no serial correlation in the data at a 5% level of significance. Finally, the test of the null hypothesis of no heteroskedasticity using the Breusch–Pagan–Godfrey test was accepted at a 5% level of significance. To focus on the objective of the study, neither empirical process nor theoretical underpinnings of this implementation are provided but can be availed on request.

Price Analysis of Kenya Arabica Coffee in Relation to Other Countries

The price analysis involved 18 countries that produce Arabica coffee (Appendix III). The prices of coffee for the 18 countries were ranked from highest to lowest. The difference (DHK) of the highest coffee price (HCP) and Kenyan coffee price (KCP) was obtained to establish whether it was significant. Then the trend for the three prices (HCP, KCP, and DHK) was plotted for the period as shown in Fig. 1.

The highest and the lowest KCP was 10.02% in 1998 and 3.02% in 1992, respectively. The highest HCP was 23.02% in 2002 for Cuba and the lowest was 7.28 in 2006 for India. The highest LCP was 3.61% in 2018 for Uganda and the lowest was 1.29 in 1990 for Uganda. The highest DHK (i.e., the difference between HCP and KCP) was 15.78% in 1992 and the lowest was 0.21% in 1997.

Table 1 Results for hedonic regression for Arabica and Robusta (1990–2018)

Variable	Coefficient	Standard error	*t*-Statistic	Probability
Model 1: Arabica (17 countries including Kenya)				
Production	−0.015	0.002	−6.641	0.000
Exports	−0.014	0.003	−5.246	0.000
Exportable	−0.015	0.004	−4.197	0.000
Interest rate	−0.075	0.155	−2.418	0.017
Exchange rate	−0.029	0.454	−6.668	0.000
Model 2: Robusta (3 countries)				
Production	−0.020	0.018	−1.103	0.273
Exports	−0.084	0.002	−0.179	0.858
Exportable	−0.018	0.019	−0.948	0.345
Interest rate	−0.043	0.042	−8.151	0.017
Exchange rate	−0.019	0.382	−2.928	0.004
Model 2: Kenya				
Production	−1.809	0.407	−4.441	0.000
Exports	−0.055	0.033	−1.655	0.009
Exportable	−1.746	0.426	−4.093	0.000
Interest rate	−0.899	0.434	−2.071	0.040
Exchange rate	−0.407	0.074	−5.439	0.000

Source: Result estimates

Hedonic Regression Model

The result for the hedonic regression is as follows.

Table 1 indicates the results of hedonic regression for 17 Arabica countries producing coffee (Model 1) and 3 countries producing Robusta coffee (Model 2) and Kenya as a producer of coffee (Model 3) for the period of study (1990–2018). These three different analyses were necessitated because of coffee prices of Arabica and Robusta are not the same in the international market. The results for Arabica show that *p*-values for coffee production, coffee exports, exportable coffee, and exchange rate were all highly significant at a 1% level of significance while interest rate was significant at 5% level of significance. The results further show that all five variables had a negative relationship with coffee price volatility. The coefficients in Model 1 in Table 1 c indicate that an increase in coffee price volatility will result in a decrease of coffee production, coffee exports, and exportable coffee by 0.15%, 0.14%, and 0.15%, respectively. Similarly, Model 1 in Table 1 indicates that an increase of price volatility by 1% would result in a corresponding decrease in interest rates and exchange rate by 0.75% and 0.29%, respectively. Although the p-values of coffee production, coffee exports, and exportable coffee for Model 2 in Table 1 are not significant, they are all negatively related to price volatility. However, the p-values of interest rates and exchange rates for Model 2 in Table 1 are statistically significant at 5% level of significance and negatively related to price volatility. For Model 3 in Table 1, coffee production, exportable coffee and exchange rates are statistically significant at 1% level of significance are all negatively related to price volatility. The p-values of coffee exports and interest rates for Model 3 in Table 1 are both statistically significant at 5% level of significance and negatively related to coffee price volatility.

Error Distribution

Table 1 presents values of the Akaike information criterion (AIC) of *GARCH*, *TARCH*, and *EGARCH* analysis. The AIC was used to choose suitable error distribution: normal (Gaussian), Student's *t*, and generalized error distribution (GED). The volatility model with the lowest error distribution was preferred. Hence, normal GED and normal are considered for analysis for Kenya given that Student's *t* has the highest *GARCH*, *TARCH*, and *EGARCH* values. Similarly, GED and normal are considered for analysis for Kenya and 20 coffee-producing countries for *GARCH* and *EGARCH*. However, for *TARCH*, normal and Student's *t* are considered since GED has the highest values (Table 2).

The standardized residual in Fig. 2 showed evidence of excess kurtosis. To model the thick tail in the residuals, we assume that the errors follow a Student's *t*-distribution. Here, we see that the relatively small degrees of freedom parameter for the *t*-distribution suggests that the distribution of the standardized errors departs significantly from normality.

Generalized Autoregressive Conditional Heteroscedasticity (GARCH)

Tables 3 and 4 present summary results for the analysis of the *GARCH* model.

This study examines whether coffee price volatility has explanatory power over regressors (coffee production, coffee exports, exportable coffee, interest rate, and exchange rate) by fitting *GARCH* (1,1) model in the conditional variance Eq. (3). Tables 3 and 4 summarize the results for *GARCH* effects for other coffee-producing countries and Kenya, respectively. In both tables, the coefficient δ is negative (−0.017 for normal and −0.058 for GED, respectively, in Table 3 and −0.014 for

Table 2 Akaike information criterion

Kenya				Twenty coffee-producing countries			
Model	Normal	Student's *t*	GED	Model	Normal	Student's *t*	GED
GARCH	10.1653	10.2417	9.8881	*GARCH*	11.0050	11.0091	10.8876
TARCH	10.1999	10.2728	10.2728	*TARCH*	11.0083	11.0119	11.2275
EGARCH	10.0744	10.1462	9.6969	*EGARCH*	11.0396	11.0445	10.9071

Source: result estimates

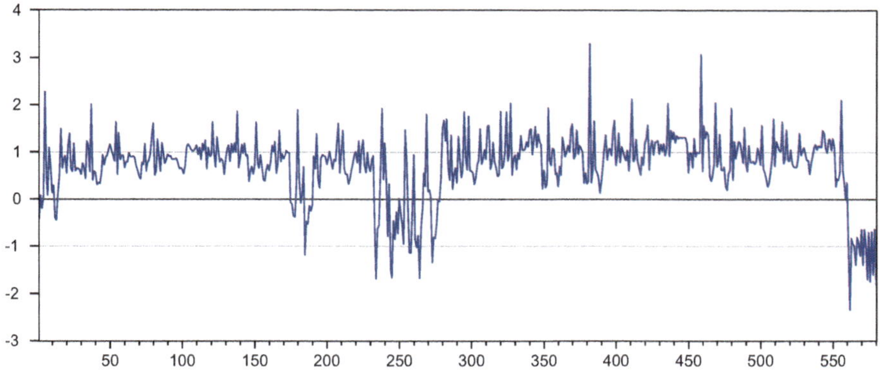

Fig. 2 Standard residual graph for price for 20 countries. (Source: Authors' computation)

Table 3 Results for *GARCH* for twenty countries (1990–2018)

Variable	Coefficient		Standard error		*z*-Statistic		Prob.	
	Normal	GED	Normal	GED	Normal	GED	Normal	GED
Production	−0.012	−0.003	0.001	0.001	−13.587	−4.472	0.000	0.000
Exports	−0.009	−0.004	0.001	0.001	−10.550	−4.755	0.000	0.000
Exportable	−0.014	−0.004	0.001	0.001	−12.106	−3.659	0.000	0.000
Interest rate	−0.034	−0.060	0.045	0.040	−10.021	−0.450	0.000	0.000
Exchange rate	−0.098	−0.092	0.456	0.007	−11.029	−0.875	0.000	0.000
Variance equation								
φ	513.932	605.927	89.826	69.918	5.721	8.666	0.000	0.000
ψ	1.047	0.882	0.151	0.080	6.914	11.038	0.000	0.000
δ	−0.017	−0.059	0.054	0.040	−0.315	−1.460	0.753	0.144

Note: included observations: 580; convergence achieved after 78 iterations; presample variance: backcast (parameter = 0.7)
Source: result estimates

Table 4 Results for *GARCH* for Kenya (1990–2018)

Variable	Coefficient		Standard error		*z*-Statistic		Prob.	
	Normal	GED	Normal	GED	Normal	GED	Normal	GED
Production	−1.882	−1.824	0.171	0.266	−10.979	−6.858	0.000	0.000
Exports	−0.053	−0.064	0.023	0.024	−2.303	−2.699	0.021	0.007
Exportable	−1.838	−1.764	0.190	0.292	−9.701	−6.049	0.000	0.000
Interest rate	−0.066	−0.061	0.317	0.480	−0.868	−0.042	0.000	0.000
Exchange rate	−0.092	−0.084	0.094	0.746	−6.063	−4.080	0.000	0.000
Variance equation								
φ	141.651	239.525	218.593	175.617	0.648	1.364	0.517	0.173
ψ	1.531	1.221	0.918	0.544	1.667	2.245	0.096	0.025
δ	−0.014	−0.031	0.150	0.041	−0.095	−0.766	0.924	0.443

Note: included observations: 29; convergence achieved after 28 iterations; presample variance: backcast (parameter = 0.7)
Source: result estimates

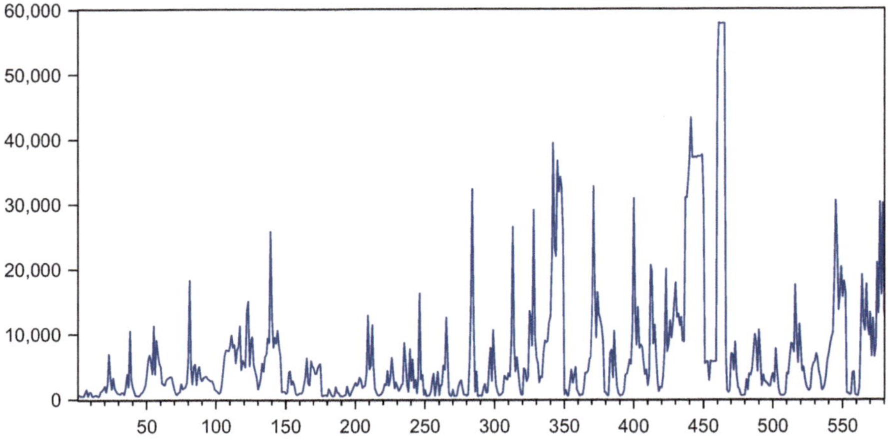

Fig. 3 Conditional variance graph for price for 20 countries

normal and – 0.031 for GED, respectively, in Table 4) and statistically insignificant at 5% level of significance (0.7526 for normal and 0.144 for GED, respectively, in Table 3 and 0.924 for normal and 0.443 for GED, respectively, in Table 4). This result shows that coffee production does not have *a GARCH* effect on the coffee price. Meticulous variations in coffee production are presumed to be triggered only by news of the prevailing changes in coffee prices (Fig. 3).

*Threshold Autoregressive Conditional Heteroscedasticity (*TARCH*)*

Tables 5 and 6 present summary results for the analysis of the *TARCH* model. This model considers the leverage effect.

The presence of leverage effect depicted in both Tables 5 and 6 suggests that each change in coffee price (for Kenya and the other 20 coffee-producing countries) responds asymmetrically to positive and negative news of the quantity of coffee traded in the international market. The parameter ψ of conditional variance equation in Table 5 for other coffee-producing countries is highly significant at the 1% level for both normal and GED, indicating that the current news on coffee production has an impact on the coffee price volatility. This result is reversed for Kenya in Table 6 where ψ is statistically insignificant at the 5% level for normal and GED, indicating that the current news on coffee production does not have an impact on the coffee price volatility.

The coffee production parameter $\delta > 0$ and is positive (0.084 for normal and 0.084 for GED in Table 5 and 1.659 for normal and 1.702 for GED in Table 6). This

Table 5 Results for *TARCH* for 20 countries (1990–2018)

Variable	Coefficient		Standard error		z-Statistic		Prob.	
	Normal	Student *t*	Normal	Student *t*	Normal	Student *t*	Normal	Student *t*
Production	−0.012	−0.012	0.001	0.001	−13.593	−13.584	0.000	0.000
Exports	−0.009	−0.009	0.001	0.001	−10.420	−10.411	0.000	0.000
Exportable	−0.013	−0.013	0.001	0.001	−12.007	−11.999	0.000	0.000
Interest rate	−0.038	−0.037	0.064	0.003	−10.093	−10.082	0.000	0.000
Exchange rate	−0.026	−0.025	0.034	0.041	−18.047	−19.010	0.000	0.000
Variance equation								
φ	513.605	513.949	90.025	98.254	5.705	5.230	0.000	0.000
ψ	1.039	1.039	0.161	0.165	6.431	6.311	0.000	0.000
δ	0.085	0.084	0.394	0.397	0.214	0.213	0.830	0.832
λ	−0.017	−0.017	0.055	0.056	−0.306	−0.299	0.760	0.765

Note: included observations: 580; convergence achieved after 122 iterations; presample variance: backcast (parameter = 0.7)
Source: result estimates

Table 6 Results for *TARCH* for Kenya (1990–2018)

Variable	Coefficient		Standard error		z-Statistic		Prob	
	Normal	GED	Normal	GED	Normal	GED	Normal	GED
Production	−0.059	−0.041	0.101	0.060	−18.412	−30.765	0.000	0.000
Exports	−0.049	−0.050	0.021	0.030	−2.333	−1.657	0.019	0.027
Exportable	−0.020	−0.001	0.087	0.060	−20.806	−29.829	0.000	0.000
Interest rate	−0.041	−0.040	0.030	0.038	−0.093	−3.720	0.000	0.000
Exchange rate	−0.029	−0.026	0.049	0.045	−0.042	−2.491	0.000	0.000
Variance equation								
φ	79.215	82.145	116.421	145.304	0.680	0.565	0.496	0.572
ψ	1.087	1.077	0.698	0.975	1.556	1.105	0.120	0.269
δ	1.660	1.702	1.260	1.600	1.317	1.064	0.188	0.287
λ	−0.003	0.001	0.044	0.142	−0.062	0.007	0.951	0.994

Note: included observations: 29; convergence achieved after 66 iterations; presample variance: backcast (parameter = 0.7)
Source: result estimates

result suggests that the impact is asymmetric, indicating that coffee production is linked with a proliferation in coffee price volatility. Therefore, favorable news on coffee prices heralds an upsurge in coffee production more than unfavorable news. In both Tables 5 and 6, the λ coefficient is not statistically significant at the 5% level, suggesting that past news on coffee production does not influence the coffee price volatility.

Table 7 Results for *EGARCH* for 20 countries (1990–2018)

Variable	Coefficient		Standard error		*z*-Statistic		Prob.	
	Normal	GED	Normal	GED	Normal	GED	Normal	GED
Production	−0.010	−0.003	0.001	0.001	−11.228	−5.026	0.000	0.000
Exports	−0.008	−0.004	0.001	0.000	−9.006	−8.514	0.000	0.000
Exportable	−0.011	−0.004	0.001	0.001	−9.152	−4.702	0.000	0.000
Interest rate	−0.026	−0.030	0.005	0.031	−0.027	−0.056	0.000	0.000
Exchange rate	−0.082	−0.085	0.317	0.045	−0.051	−0.032	0.000	0.000
Variance equation								
φ	1.640	2.089	0.547	0.364	2.999	5.746	0.003	0.000
ψ	1.619	1.349	0.238	0.187	6.815	7.226	0.000	0.000
δ	0.024	0.224	0.159	0.116	0.151	1.923	0.880	0.055
λ	0.620	0.559	0.081	0.054	7.686	10.331	0.000	0.000

Note: included observations: 580; convergence achieved after 35 iterations; presample variance: backcast (parameter = 0.7)
Source: result estimates

Table 8 Results for *EGARCH* for Kenya (1990–2018)

Variable	Coefficient		Standard error		*z*-Statistic		Prob.	
	Normal	GED	Normal	GED	Normal	GED	Normal	GED
Production	−1.829	−1.832	0.352	0.253	−5.193	−7.257	0.000	0.000
Exports	−0.041	−0.026	0.019	0.019	−2.127	−1.405	0.033	0.016
Exportable	−1.793	−1.801	0.368	0.276	−4.877	−6.532	0.000	0.000
Interest rate	−0.406	−0.403	0.942	0.051	−0.085	−0.073	0.000	0.000
Exchange rate	−0.091	−0.095	0.397	0.051	−0.012	−0.423	0.000	0.000
Variance equation								
φ	6.394	6.426	3.679	2.802	1.738	2.294	0.082	0.022
ψ	1.716	1.574	0.848	0.711	2.024	2.214	0.043	0.027
δ	0.287	0.261	0.384	0.235	0.747	1.110	0.455	0.267
λ	−0.183	−0.203	0.499	0.297	−0.366	−0.683	0.714	0.495

Note: included observations: 29; convergence achieved after 28 iterations; presample variance: backcast (parameter = 0.7)
Source: result estimates

*Exponential Generalized Autoregressive Conditional Heteroscedasticity (*EGARCH*)*

The model has been used to test the leverage effect for 20 other countries and Kenya, and the result of the analysis is captured in Tables 7 and 8.

Table 7 shows that cumulatively for 20 countries, there is leverage effect and news impact is asymmetric λ. Thus, the coffee production surges due to good news in the international coffee auction market given that at the 5% level of significance, the coefficients $\lambda > 0$ and positive (0.619 for normal and 0.559 for GED). Further, the *p*-value for coefficients λ for both normal and GED is 0.000, indicating that it is significant at a 5% level of significance. As a result, coefficients λ indicates that coffee price has a positive impact on production and therefore results in less impact on the volatility of production of coffee in the market. However, this result is the opposite of Kenya as summarized in Table 8. The coffee production decreases due to good news in the auction market for the period under evaluation, given that at the 5% level of significance, the coefficients $\lambda < 0$ and negative (−0.183 for normal and −0.203 for GED, respectively) and statistically insignificant (0.714 for normal and 0.495 for GED, respectively). These results show that coffee prices have a negative impact on production, and this leads to more impact on the volatility of production coffee in the market.

Discussion

Globally, research on coffee prices and production has been conducted from different dimensions (Wanzala et al., 2022, 2023, 2024; Novanda et al., 2018). This study deviates from existing ones by taking two approaches: it examines the price competitiveness of Kenya in the global market with other major coffee producers around the world, and it uses volatility models to determine the long-run relationship between price and production of coffee across the world. Nevertheless, the volatility models (GARCH, TARCH, and EGARCH) results of this study are consistent with Rahayu et al. (2015), who analyzed annual producer coffee prices from 1980 to 2011 from both domestic (Indonesia Ministry of Agriculture) and international data (FAO) using the *ARCH/GARCH* model. Rahayu et al. (2015) empirically demonstrated using *EGARCH* that the international coffee price has an asymmetric effect on Indonesia's return coffee price and indicates that the domestic coffee market is not efficient. This study, however, shows that coffee price has a negative impact on production, and this leads to more impact on the volatility of production coffee the market, while Maurice and Davis's (2012) study on the effects of extreme coffee price volatility using *GARCH* type models paint a different picture. Using constant prices of Arabica and Robusta from January 1990 to September 2010 from ICO and ICCO, Maurice and Davis (2012) revealed that coffee price volatility has uneven or varied impacts depending on the nature of the market shock in the Commodity-Dependent Developing Countries (CDDCs).

The results further show that coffee price volatility has statistically insignificant relationship with all five variables under study (i.e., coffee production, coffee exports, exportable coffee, interest rate, and exchange rate). These results are consistent with Oko-Isu et al. (2019), Chaovanapoonphol et al. (2023), Hoai et al. (2023), Singhal and Tarp (2024), and Yeshiwas and Berelie (2020). For instance, examined coffee production reaction to commodity price volatility in Nigeria. Using GARCH ARCH and FMOLS models, they found out that coffee production in Nigeria is influenced by coffee price volatility in the international market. Chaovanapoonphol et al. (2023) analyzed the relationship between and exogenous factors coffee price volatility to Thailand using multiple exogenous Bayesian

GARCH-X. Their results indicate that the increase in demand for exportable coffee and coffee bean export volume in Thailand and Indonesia leads to an increase in coffee price volatility. In contrast, Wanzala et al. (2024) use data from 2001 to 2020 to investigate the impact of exchange rate volatility on Kenyan coffee exports. The study's findings, which make use of the gravity model, show a negative relationship between exchange rate volatility and Kenyan coffee exports.

Implications of Coffee Price Volatility to Kenyan Economy and Policy Direction

Kenya's economy greatly benefits from the coffee industry, which generates a sizable amount of export revenue and supports many people. Price volatility, however, has a ripple effect on other areas of the economy as well, including government net income, inflation, trade balance, lending interest rates, and overall economic growth. For example, the exchange rate is negatively impacted by the volatility of coffee prices, according to the results of the Hedonic regression model:. This is in line with previous research suggesting that fluctuations in commodity prices may be indicative of fluctuations in the real exchange rate and inflation, thereby expanding the original unstable process to the whole economy. Because the burden of adjustment is distributed among more economic agents, who may all be expected to bear lower proportionate costs, this generalization process may be desirable in part. Thus, it is imperative that the Kenyan government find strategies to limit the impact of commodity price volatility on the exchange rate. GoK must diversify its tax bases away from the primary sector, such as coffee, given that the volatility of coffee prices is negatively correlated with lending interest rates. If this does not happen, the nation will continue to face difficulties financing essential public expenditures during periods of low export prices unless countercyclical budgetary assistance is provided on time. As a result, the government must investigate ways to protect its revenue positions in the export commodity futures market and on the financial markets.

The findings demonstrate that the volatility of coffee prices has a statistically significant negative impact on exports, exportable coffee, and coffee production. The long-term supply of coffee is at risk due to the ongoing volatility of coffee prices, as growers start looking for other sources of income. As a result, many Kenyan farmers have uprooted their coffee trees to pursue seemingly profitable crops like tea and horticulture (see Fig. 4), while some have dabbled in real estate investments (Wanzala et al., 2022). This may also have been brought on by concerns about future earnings because of short-term fluctuations in the price of coffee, which can cause anxiety, a sense of hopelessness and lack of self-control, and significant concerns that can lead to mental health issues (Singhal & Tarp, 2024).

So, what can be done to support farmers and increase exports and production of coffee? There are several ways to tackle this. The first way to accomplish this is by using more price risk management tools. While this is typical in major coffee-producing nations, Kenya has not fully embraced it. This could involve, among other things, premium options, long-term pricing, forward contracts, and futures

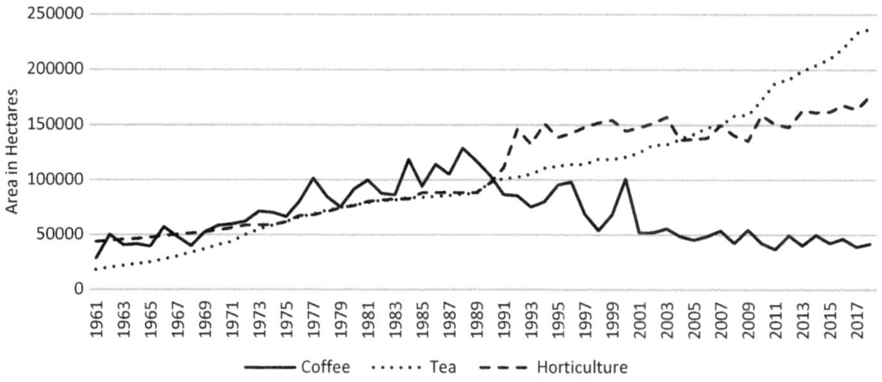

Fig. 4 Coffee production in comparison with tea and horticulture from 1961 to 2018. (*Source: FAOSTAT;* http://www.fao.org/faostat/en/#data/QC)

contracts. These are tools for securing the buyer–farmer relationship and could present chances for farmers (as well as other supply chain participants) to reduce risk. Here is a quick rundown of the advantages these tools can offer farmers. Private agreements known as "forward contracts" allow farmers to know the price they will get for their coffee before it is delivered, which they can use as leverage when applying for credit. By using futures contracts, farmers can effectively hedge their risks associated with speculating about the price of coffee in the future by locking in a future price (set on the exchange) before delivery. For farmers, this trading tool has the potential to lower volatility and limit losses when utilized appropriately. By knowing the price, they will get for their coffee over a longer period, long-term pricing helps farmers better plan and reinvest in their farms. Farmers receive prices that are higher than the market value based on their performance through premiums based on quality, environmental, or social performance. This can help insulate them from some market volatility. Second, farmer insurance products should be expanded to cover loss of returns because of price volatility. Thirdly, promote minimum pricing agreements such as Fair Trade and direct trade, particularly for specialty coffee.

Conclusion

Kenyan coffee's competitiveness with 20 other coffee-producing nations is investigated in this study using price analysis and hedonic regression GARCH, TGARCH, and EGARCH models. Kenya was ranked 6th out of 18 countries that produce Arabica coffee on average. Hedonic regression showed that the regressors (coffee production, exports, exportable coffee, interest rate, and exchange rate) and coffee price volatility have a statistically significant negative relationship. Moreover, the δ coefficient for Kenya and other coffee-producing nations was statistically insignificant and negative, indicating that the price of coffee is not GARCH impacted by coffee production. Lastly, the study's findings indicate the existence of a leverage effect, which implies that any change in the price of coffee reacts asymmetrically to both good and bad news regarding the volume of coffee traded on the global market. This study concludes that minimizing volatile coffee prices is desirable, and that to smoothen production, Kenyan policymakers must provide coffee farmers with protection from the effects of coffee volatility. Due to a lack of data, this study's scope was restricted to just 21 of the major 56 countries that produce coffee worldwide. Consequently, this study recommends that future research concentrates on all 56 countries.

References

Abebe, T. H. (2020). Modeling time-varying coffee price volatility in Ethiopia. *Journal of Applied Economics, 23*(1), 497–518.

Aliaga Lordemann, J., Mora-García, C., & Mulder, N. (2021). *Speculation and price volatility in the coffee market* (*Project Documents*, (LC/TS.2021/59)). Economic Commission for Latin America and the Caribbean (ECLAC).

Brorsen, B. W. (1989). Liquidity costs and scalping returns in the corn futures market. *Journal of Futures Markets, 9*(3), 225–236.

Brorsen, B. W., & Irwin, S. H. (1987). Futures funds and price volatility. *Review of Futures Markets, 6*(2), 118–135.

Chang, E. C., Michael Pinegar, J., & Schachter, B. (1997). Interday variations in volume, variance and participation of large speculators. *Journal of Banking & Finance, 21*(6), 797–810.

Chaovanapoonphol, Y., Singvejsakul, J., & Wiboonpongse, A. (2023). Analysis of exogenous factors to Thailand coffee Price volatility: Using multiple exogenous Bayesian GARCH-X model. *Agriculture, 13*(10), 1973.

Cornell, B. (1981). The relationship between volume and price variability in futures markets. *Journal of Futures Markets, 1*(3), 303–316.

Day, T. E., & Lewis, C. M. (1992). Information content of implied volatilities: Stock market volatility and the information content of stock index options. *Journal of Econometrics, 52*, 267–287.

Engle, R. F. (1982). Auto-regressive conditional heteroscedasticity with estimates of the variance of United Kingdom inflation. *Econometrica, 50*(4), 987–1007.

Fatih, C. (2022). Forecasting models based on fuzzy logic: An application on international coffee prices. *Econometrics, 26*(4), 1–16.

Glosten, L. R., Jagannathan, R., & Runkle, D. (1993). On the relationship between the expected value and the volatility of the nominal excess return on stocks. *Journal of Finance, 48*, 1779–1801.

Goodwin, B. K., & Schnepf, R. (2000). Determinants of endogenous price risk in corn and wheat futures markets. *Journal of Futures Markets: Futures, Options, and Other Derivative Products, 20*(8), 753–774.

Hoai, N., Tuyen, D., Nhien, N., & Hong, N. (2023). The fluctuation linkages and price volatility risk on agricultural commodity market: Evidence from Vietnamese coffee. *Uncertain Supply Chain Management, 11*(4), 1735–1744.

ICO. (2019). *Country Coffee Profile: Kenya.* International Coffee Council, 124th Session, 25–29 March 2019, Nairobi, Kenya.

Machuka, S., Kazungu, K., & Ondieki, C. (2016). Determinants of productivity of small-scale holdings of Arabica coffee in Kenya: A case study of Kiambu County, Kenya. *The International Journal of Humanities & Social Studies, 4*(8), 104–112.

Maurice, N., & Davis, J. (2012). *Unravelling the underlying causes of price volatility in world coffee and cocoa commodity markets* (MPRA Paper No. 43813).

Milonas, N. T. (1986). Liquidity and price variability in futures markets. *Financial Review, 21*(2), 211–238.

Novanda, R. R., Sumartono, E., Asriani, P., Yuliarti, E., Sukiyono, K., Priyono, B., Irnad, R., Suryanty, M., & Octalia, V. (2018). A comparison of various forecasting techniques for coffee prices. *Journal of Physics: Conference Series, 1114*(2018), 012119.

Oko-Isu, A., Chukwu, A. U., Ofoegbu, G. N., Igberi, C. O., Ololo, K. O., Agbanike, T. F., et al. (2019). Coffee output reaction to climate change and commodity price volatility: The Nigeria experience. *Sustainability, 11*(13), 3503.

Peck, A. E. (1981). The adequacy of speculation on the wheat, corn and soybean futures markets. *Research in Domestic and International Agribusiness Management, 2*, 17–29.

Rahayu, M. F., Chang, W., & Anindita, R. (2015). Volatility analysis and volatility spillover analysis of Indonesia's coffee price using ARCH/GARCH, and EGARCH model. *Journal of Agricultural Studies, 3*(2), 37–48.

Samuelson, P. A. (1965, Spring). Proof that properly anticipated prices fluctuate randomly. *Industrial Management Review*, *6*(2), 41.

Singhal, S., & Tarp, F. (2024). Commodity price volatility and the psychological well-being of farmers. *American Journal of Agricultural Economics*.

Struthers, J. J. (2019). Commodity price volatility: Causes, policy options and prospects for African economies. *Logistics and Global Value Chains in Africa: The Impact on Trade and Development*, 133–168.

Tröster, B., & Gunter, U. (2023). The financialization of Coffee, Cocoa and Cotton Value Chains: The role of physical actors. *Development and Change*.

Wanzala, R. W., Marwa, N., & Nanziri, E. (2023). Impact of agricultural credit on technical efficiency and technological gap ratio among coffee farmers in Kenya. In *ICABR conference* (pp. 93–114). Cham, Springer.

Wanzala, R. W., Marwa, N., & Nanziri Lwanga, E. (2024). Impact of exchange rate volatility on coffee export in Kenya. *Cogent Economics & Finance, 12*(1), 2330447.

Wanzala, R. W., Marwa, N. W., & Nanziri, E. L. (2022). Historical analysis of coffee production and associated challenges in Kenya from 1893 to 2018. *Southern Journal for Contemporary History, 47*(2), 51–90.

Ward, R. W. (1974). Market liquidity in the FCOJ futures market. *American Journal of Agricultural Economics, 56*(1), 150–154.

Yeshiwas, D., & Berelie, Y. (2020). Forecasting the covolatility of coffee Arabica and crude oil prices: A multivariate GARCH approach with high-frequency data. *Journal of Probability and Statistics, 2020*(1), 1424020.

Zakoian, J.-M. (1994). Threshold heteroskedastic models. *Journal of Economic Dynamics and Control, 18*(5), 931–995.

Zhang, W., Saghaian, S., & Reed, M. (2022). Influences of power structure evolution on coffee commodity markets: Insights from Price discovery and volatility Spillovers. *Sustainability, 14*(22), 15268.

The Impact of Nigeria's Fuel Subsidy Removal on the Sustainable Development Goals of Selected African Countries: A Cross-Country Impact Assessment

Kola Benson Ajeigbe, Fortune Ganda, and Oji Okpusa Oke

Abstract The objective of this research was to examine the association between fuel subsidies and sustainable development goals in selected African nations covering the period 2010–2022. The study employed the Panel Autoregressive Distributed Lag (PARDL) technique, the fully modified ordinary least squares (FMOLS), and dynamic ordinary least squares (DOLS) techniques. The findings of the techniques affirm that fuel exports, fuel subsidies, energy consumption, and renewable energy exhibit a positive relationship with economic growth, but a negative association with poverty. The estimated coefficients of fuel price and imports reveal negative associations with economic growth and positive connections with poverty in all model specifications. Overall, the outcomes of the FMOLS and DOLS techniques align with the long-term coefficients reported using the PARDL approach. The findings confirmed that the subsidy removal has a long-run positive impact on the selected economies. The outcome suggests a very strong relationship between fuel subsidy, renewable energy, and sustainable economic growth and poverty alleviation. Therefore, if the subsidy is removed, money saved from it must be diverted to developmental projects and renewable energy sources that can boost the economy and alleviate poverty. Based on these findings, it is recommended that nations should divert their resources into renewable energy sources by taking advantage of their seashores, hilly and steep topography areas to mount all their solar gadgets in order to solve energy problems in their countries. Achieving energy efficiency would not only solve electricity supply problem, but would also help grow local industries, attract more foreign investors, change investors' perceptions about Africa, and help transit into the consumption of renewable energy, which is more environmentally friendly. This study provides new insights for nations, policymak-

K. B. Ajeigbe (✉) · F. Ganda
Walter Sisulu University, East London, South Africa
e-mail: bajeigbe@wsu.ac.za; fganda@wsu.ac.za

O. O. Oke
Cape Peninsula University of Technology, Cape Town, South Africa
e-mail: Okeo@cput.ac.za

T. Moloi (ed.), *Impacting Society Positively Through Technology in Accounting and Business Processes*, Springer Proceedings in Business and Economics,
https://doi.org/10.1007/978-3-031-84885-8_44

ers, investors, governments, lending institutions, and other stakeholders on the formulation of efficient policies to boost the achievement of the sustainable development goals (SDGs) in African countries and the entire world at large.

Keywords Economic growth · Energy consumption · Poverty reduction · Renewable energy · Subsidy removal · Sustainable development goals

Introduction

Energy subsidy removal has been a topic of global discussion for more than two decades. Consequently, it has been receiving increasing attention due to the need for policy reform toward achieving SDGs by governments across the globe (McKitrick, 2017). Sustainable development goals have been the major determinants of policy formulation by many countries ever since it was globally articulated. These goals have driven the decisions of nations all over the world in formulating policies that can help in attaining Vision 2030 as the set global targets, and 2050 for African countries (Ekong & Akpan, 2014; United Nations, 2020). In the pursuit to sustainably grow together without leaving anyone behind, eradicate poverty, improve standards of living, and reduce climate change to enhance environmental quality, many nations have embarked on a review of energy subsidies. The most common energy subsidy is fossil fuel subsidies, which significantly contribute to the global rate of climate change (Adekunle & Oseni, 2021). This was corroborated by Gani (2021), who revealed that fossil fuel contributes to over three-quarters of the global emissions. Additionally, Oyedepo (2014) rated energy as the most fundamental issue for sustainable development. Statistically, a global analysis report revealed that fossil fuel has been a global concern accounting for over $7 trillion in 2022 pre-tax amounts, with an equivalent 7.1% of the global real GDP, and with an over 75% increase from 2015's data of $5.3 trillion in subsidies (Black et al., 2023; Van Asselt, 2023). Global amounts projected to achieve clean electricity and cooking gas were estimated by the IMF to be $296 billion. In Nigeria, 2022 expenditure on the fuel subsidy reached ₦4 trillion ($6.088 billion), which accounted for about 23% of the total budget of the nation (₦17.127). Comparing these amounts, the fuel subsidy removal could not be further negotiated in Nigeria or even at the global level (Solarin, 2020). A major concern is the strong link between fossil fuel and environmental degradation, to which the existence of the subsidy significantly contributed. Extant studies revealed that the subsidy removal would reduce fuel consumption rates, thus having a positive impact on environmental quality (Jha & Schmidt, 2021; Wesseh et al., 2016). Apart from the need to achieve the SDGs, many other scholars also linked increasing rates of policy reforms along this line to the recent decline of economic efficiency and effectiveness across the globe (Acharya & Sadath, 2017). Policy reform on subsidies removal has equally been linked by many scholars with indirectly promoting and transiting into renewable energy sources (Shittu et al., 2024; Acharya & Sadath, 2017). The current study examines this area in terms of how Nigeria's subsidy removal has affected countries within the continent, and how it can help governments transiting into the consumption of more renewable energy sources. These and many more factors have motivated various governments to consider removing subsidies in exchange for developmental purposes (Soile & Mu, 2015).

The importance of energy sustainability in relation to economic growth and the alleviation of poverty in every nation cannot be overemphasized. The need to have access to reliable, affordable, and clean energy sources is equally germane for sustainable growth and development (Oyedepo, 2014). Governments all over the world are searching for means of growing sustainably by achieving economic targets, fiscal and environmental performance, and ensuring access to affordable, reliable, and sustainable energy (SDG 7) in a renewable form. Hence, they harness energy resources toward economic efficiency by adopting the policy of subsidy removal (Baz et al., 2021; Jacal et al., 2022). Extant studies have proven that achieving this goal could help achieve other goals, such as a reduction in climate change (SDG 13), no poverty (SDG1), and zero hunger (SDG 2) (Jacal et al., 2022). For instance, the recent removal of the fuel subsidy in Nigeria has sparked many reactions from citizens and other stakeholders who are either directly or indirectly affected by the impact of the decision. Surprisingly, the removal has generated ripple effects in neighboring countries such as Cameroun, Mali, Benin, Niger, Ghana, and other countries on the continent that are heavily dependent on Nigeria for energy consumption or having other related trade relations. This has generated mixed reactions from stakeholders such as policymakers, the public, investors, scholars, governments, companies, and many notable Nigerians all over the world. Understandably, Nigeria, South Africa, and Egypt are the three leading economies on the continent, and Nigeria is heavily connected with many African countries economically, socially, and environmentally, which makes this study important (Aliyu et al., 2018). Energy efficiency and sustainable energy production are critical to every economy in order for the sustainable development goals to be achieved. Hence, the need for sustainable energy sources that can enhance immediate needs (short-run) and future needs (long-run) economic development is inevitable for sustainable development (Emodi & Boo, 2015). Therefore, this study is an insight to countries, policymakers, and other decision-makers to take the subsidy removal policy advantage in transiting into renewable energy sources. Fossil fuel and coal are heavy sources of nonrenewable energy coming from the three leading economies on the continent. Nigeria and Egypt are great sources of fossil fuel whilst South Africa is a major source of coal, which are all nonrenewable sources. As part of the global vision of transiting into renewable energy consumption, it is imperative that these countries diversify into noncarbonated sources of energy in order to improve environmental sustainability and attain a clean environment by reducing emissions and increasing renewable energy consumption (SDG 7). Moreover, other countries on the continent need to also improve on this matter as well in order to achieve these objectives. Another relevance of this study is that Africa has been tagged as having the highest consumption of nonrenewable energy sources, which is a reason to reduce the rate in order to comply with the global vision (International Energy Agency, 2023). Lastly, when there are many energy sources, there will be power stability and the market price of energy consumption will become affordable to every citizen on the continent.

Africa as a continent is blessed with everything that can make this continent the best, as well as to compete with other continents of the world (Mas'ud et al., 2015). The continent is blessed with mineral resources, some of the best weather and environmental conditions, and fertile land for farming, with good and intelligent people that can make things happen and compete with the leaders of the world (Aliyu et al., 2018). The environmental conditions can accommodate diverse energy sources such as solar, gas, hydro, wind, and biomass, which are more renewable and environmentally friendly in nature. Leaders only need to be strategic in terms of decision-making. They need to stop politicizing everything, be futuristic, and use their best hands to turn things around. This study is not advocating that the continent throws away what it has as a nation, but it can improve on the production and make it more renewable in nature and eco-friendly, whilst looking at other alternative sources of energy such as solar, gas, biomass, wind, hydro, etc. Most of the countries on the continent are rich in solar energy sources. For instance, the South African government at the municipal, provincial, and central government levels can take advantage of the seashore, hilly and steep topography areas to mount all their solar gadgets in order to solve the problem of load shedding in the country. This can also be applied to other countries on the continent. Achieving energy efficiency would not only solve electricity supply problems, but also would help attract more foreign investors, change investors' perceptions about Africa, and help transit to the consumption of renewable energy, which is more environmentally friendly than fossil fuel and coal. This would help the continent to be sustainable by employing sustainable energy sources that are eco-friendly. Aliyu et al.'s (2018) study concluded that for African countries to overcome the persistent energy crisis, they need to diversify into renewable energy sources on the continent. Other advantages associated with renewable sources of energy are the reduction of pollution, which can help in the growth of small and medium enterprises.

To narrow this study problem down, this is one of the first empirical studies responding to the possible impact of a total removal of the subsidy. There have been many prior studies before the removal of the subsidy that were mainly based on whether or not the subsidy must be partly or total removed, with a majority of scholars supporting its removal (Iyke, 2015; Nwachukwu et al., 2013; Siddig et al., 2015; Ozgur et al., 2021; Yakubu et al., 2023; Uzonwanne et al., 2015). The objective of this was to examine the possible impact of a total subsidy removal on people, nations, economies, fuel consumption, and renewable energy within the African context. This is the first study in this area that addresses current issues affecting the livelihood of citizens in selected African countries. From the research findings, there is no known study that has related Nigeria's fuel subsidy removal to other African countries as this study does, especially after the subsidy had been removed. Hence, this study adds to the body of knowledge in this regard. This study took this advantage to think outside the box by relating the subsidy removal to renewable energy sources. The reason for this is that fossil fuel contributes more than three-quarters of global emissions (Gani, 2021). This study is part of an insight to achieve the many SDGs as specified by the United Nations come 2030. This objective was structured to solve the above problem. This study that examined the impact of the subsidy removal on the fossil fuel consumption, household income, economic growth, and renewable energy of the selected countries in Africa also addressed the relationship between the subsidy removal and energy consumption and renewable energy. Other parts of this study are arranged as follows: a conceptual and theoretical review, followed by the review of related literature; model specifications; analysis and interpretations; study implications; and conclusion.

Concepts and Literature Review

Achieving the SDGs has been prioritized by many nations and has been the principle directing nations' policymakers globally (Ekong & Akpan, 2014). Factually, all countries in Africa are facing serious challenges that hinder the achievement of the SDGs, to which the energy sectors of various governments contribute a major percentage. The fuel subsidy has been a major energy policy instrument employed by many government leaders for social, economic, and possibly environmental reasons. It is a benefit rendered by the government to its citizens or businesses that could be in the form of cash; a reduction of the cost of goods and services; or tax havens, reductions or exemptions, grants, etc., for corporate organizations. Subsidies help citizens enjoy low prices and acquire goods and services at affordable prices (Yakubu et al., 2023). There are important implications of energy subsidies to the consumer and to the producers, whereby producers sell more, and consumers consume more. However, when the subsidy is removed, consumers consume less, and with excess production the propensity to produce later drops (Ekong & Akpan, 2014).

This research is anchored on the theory of Ecological Modernisation, which opines that policy shifts or reforms are related to sustainable practices. Therefore, this study considers the decision of subsidy removal and how this can help socially, environmentally, politically, and economically impact on sustainably (Van Valkengoed & Van der Werff, 2022; Apeloko & Olajide, 2012; Obasi et al., 2017). Aliyu et al. (2018) concluded that African countries need to diversify into renewable energy sources to overcome the persistent energy crisis. Their review was based on the top three leading economies in Africa (South Africa, Nigeria, and Egypt) and suggested that technology improvement would help to be energy efficient. Mas'ud et al. (2015) evaluated the progress made in renewable energy development in both Nigeria and Cameroon and found that no tangible strategy for renewable implementation has been made by the two nations. Ahenkan and Osei-kojo (2014) assessed the level of achievement of SDGs in Africa using a qualitative approach. Findings revealed that the progress is mixed, as while some countries are making progress in the area of poverty alleviation, strengthening democratic institutions, and building strong economies, many concentrate on climate change control, population control, and unemployment reduction. They suggested that African countries must be more committed to innovativeness in order to tackle climate change for agricultural improvement. Atansah et al. (2017) reviewed and shared the experience of subsidy removal policy from Iran, Nigeria, and India, and suggested that countries must employ public engagement for good communication; a phasing approach; and should be palliative for low-income earners in order to control the crisis.

Wesseh et al. (2016) evaluated the impact of the subsidy removal on imported refined oil in Ghana on prices, carbon dioxide emissions, household demand, firms' production, and real GDP. The results show that the subsidy removal raises all the variables except firms' production. Andor and Voss (2016) determined optimal subsidies for renewable energies in the electricity market between the generation and capacity subsidy, and the result shows that generation subsidies should correspond to the externalities of electricity generation. Acharya and Sadath (2017) employed ARDL and ECM to analyze the welfare impact of energy reform in India, and the findings revealed that the removal of subsidies leads to a generally low demand for fossil fuel. Mundaca (2017) examined the impact of fossil fuel reform on economic growth in MENA countries, revealing that subsidy removal contributes to higher long-run economic growth. Baz et al. (2021) examined the nexus between renewable energy consumption, fossil fuel, and economic growth using the ARDL, time-series, and causality approaches. The results show an asymmetric impact of one variable on the other, with bidirectional relationships confirmed between the variables. Gani (2021) examined the supply-side effect of energy generation from fossil fuels on environmental quality by employing the STIRPAT regression model, and the findings revealed that increasing consumption of fossil fuel adversely impacted environmental quality. Solarin (2020) examined the impact of fossil fuel subsidies on environmental degradation by employing GMM, and the result shows that a 10% increase in fossil fuel subsidies leads to 0.5–1.5% increase in the ecological footprint as a measure of environmental degradation. Wesseh et al. (2016) evaluated the welfare and environmental impact of subsidy removals in Ghana on imported refined oil using a multiregion computable general equilibrium model. The results revealed an improvement of environmental quality due to the removal, with CO_2 increasing at a reduced rate in the short-run, and later reducing in the long-run. Shittu et al. (2024) examined the impact of the fuel subsidy and proposed a compensation and re-investment plan of government to minimize the impact on the citizens. They employed a dynamic computable general equilibrium model, and their results showed that a balanced allocation of resources between compensation and reinvestment would offer better outcomes. Oyedepo (2014) examined the energy efficiency, renewable energy sources, and strategies for implementation in Nigeria. He categorized sustainable energy development strategies into energy savings, efficiency improvement, and replacement of fossil fuel with renewable energy sources available to each country. Vandeninden et al. (2022) assessed the effectiveness of the fossil fuel subsidy in alleviating poverty in Burkina Faso using the price-gap approach, and the results revealed that the energy subsidy is not pro-poor as the subsidy does not have a positive impact on poverty. Gelan (2018) examined the impact of a subsidy reduction in Kuwait by employing a social accounting matrix and a computable general equilibrium model, and the results indicated adverse effects on GDP, as the electricity price significantly rose by 245%. Timilsina and Pargal (2020) investigated the economic impact of the subsidy removal on natural gas and electricity in Bangladesh. The results revealed that the policy is beneficial to the economy. Ofori (2023) accounted for the cross-price substitution effect between gasoline and diesel marketing in Africa using the comprehensive Herberger formula for deadweight loss. Findings suggested that fuel subsidy reforms would be better motivated by other social problems associated with fuel subsidies.

Overview of Energy Distribution in Selected African Countries

In terms of the energy mix and transition to renewable energy sources in Africa, Ghana seems to be on track. Ghana's total energy consumption in the year 2021 for hydroelectricity, fossil fuel, and biomass were 17%, 50%, and 34%, respectively. The country's access to clean fuel and cooking is 30.3%. With the anticipation of South Africa to reduce load shedding by 2.0% in 2023 and 0.8% and 0.4% in 2024 and 2025, respectively, this can only be accelerated by diversifying into renewable energy. The reduction in the impact of load shedding is an indication of improvement in energy supply in South Africa. This can only be sustained with energy reforms. South Africa seems to have taken a positive step by embarking on new energy technologies with energy-efficient appliances that are expected to have significantly lower emissions of greenhouse gases. For instance, Majuba plant, one of the retired ESKOM plants, has transformed the former coal power plant into a renewable energy plant expected to produce about 300MW of energy. The review of carbon tax is another means of enforcing the consumption of renewable energy sources. Energy shortfalls in South Africa are expected to close with the new capacity generation, as well as the Kusile and Koeberg power plants that are under maintenance.

Presently, South Africa's energy supply is dominated by nonrenewable energy sources (coal) of about 65%, followed by 18% of fossil fuel, renewable and waste at 11%, gas at 3%, nuclear at 2%, and geothermal at 1%. Nigeria is blessed with many untapped resources that can make it compete with any nation, but something is fundamentally wrong with the governance. Major sources of energy to the country are from fossil fuel, with the rate of access to clean fuel being 16.8% in 2021. The country is planning to enlarge its renewable sources capacity to be able to end long years of crisis experienced in the energy sector. Presently, the country can divert money saved from the subsidy removal to promote renewable energies in order to cushion the effect on ordinary citizens. In Egypt, energy that comes from fossil fuel is 88.2%; from low carbon, it is 5.7%; while renewable energy stood at 5.65%. In summary, African nations still consume more nonrenewable energy than renewable energies (Statistic review of world Energy, 2023). Figure 1 represents an example of how carbon emissions from fossil fuels that cause environmental degradation.

Fig. 1 Carbon emission

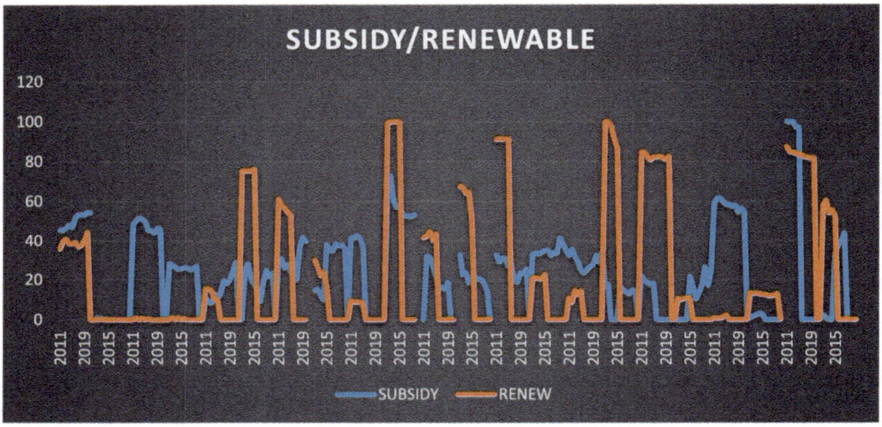

Fig. 2 Subsidy and renewal energy distribution in African countries. (Source: Own research)

Nations are advised to be more innovative in their production in order to consume more renewed products.

Figure 2 depicts the distribution of both the subsidy and renewable energy in African countries. It shows that renewable energy is growing on the continent while subsidies are slowly fading away.

Data and Methodology

Data

This study explores the role of fuel subsidy on sustainable growth using a panel dataset of 22 African economies spanning 2011–2022. The starting and ending periods of the countries considered are dictated by the availability of data. The outcome variable of interest is economic growth measured by GDP per capita growth (annual%) and poverty proxied by the poverty headcount ratio at national poverty

Table 1 Descriptive statistics

Variables	Mean	Maximum	Minimum	Std. dev.
GDP	8.308	1.611	1.445	2.709
POV	6.015	38.700	5.370	8.403
ENG	30.578	27.834	8.602	12.312
FPRI	43.774	3.550	0.270	36.321
FSUB	31.560	29.854	0.395	19.708
FEXP	45.525	99.977	0.036	33.210
FIMP	14.294	30.968	1.079	9.065
RENE	10.826	99.968	6.070	35.118

Note: GDP, economic growth; POV, poverty rate; FSUB, fuel subsidy; ENG, energy consumption; FEXP, fuel export; FIMP, fuel import; FPRI, fuel price; RENE, renewable energy

levels. The independent variable of interest includes energy consumption measured by fossil fuel energy consumption, fuel export proxied by fuel imports (% of merchandise exports), fuel import measured by fuel imports (% of merchandise imports), fuel subsidy proxied by subsidies and other transfers (% of expense), fuel price measured by pump price for gasoline (US$ per liter), and renewable energy proxied by the renewable energy consumption (% of total final energy consumption). The dataset employed for this study is extracted from the World Development Indicators (WDI) database. Table 1 depicts the summary statistics of all the variables under scrutiny. The analysis shows that economic growth and poverty surged by 8.308% and 6.015% during the considered period, with standard deviations of 2.709 and 8.409, respectively, reflecting moderate variability. The average values of other variables such as energy consumption, fuel price, fuel subsidy, fuel export, fuel import, and renewable energy are 30.578%, 43.774%, 31.560%, 45.525%, 14.294%, and 10.826%, respectively. The standard deviation analysis indicates that the data reflect less variability during the considered period.

Empirical Model

This study specifies the dynamic reduced-form equation to explore the linkages between fuel subsidy and sustainable growth in selected African economies as follows:

$$InGDP_{i,t} = \alpha_0 + \beta_1 InFSUB_{i,t} + \vartheta_j InX_{i,t} + \mu_i + v_i + \varepsilon_{it} \tag{1}$$

where $i = 1–N$; $t = 2011–2022$. $InGDP_{i,t}$ represents sustainable economic growth proxied by economic growth and poverty in country i at year t, $InFSUB_{i,t}$ signifies the fuel subsidy of country i at year t, X represents the vector of other explanatory variables including energy consumption, fuel export, fuel import, fuel price, and renewable energy. Additionally, μ_i is the country-specific effect, v_i is the year-specific effect, and ε_{it} represents the unobserved error term. α_0, β_1, and θ_j are the unknown coefficients to be estimated.

Estimation Techniques

This research examined the interconnection between fuel subsidies and sustainable economic growth in selected African countries by employing the panel autoregressive distributed lag model (ARDL) proposed by Pesaran et al. The ARDL model exhibits certain features compared to other panel approaches, such as ordinary least squares (OLS), mean group (MG), and general method of moments (GMM), among others. Specifically, the pooled mean group (PMG) approach simultaneously captures long-run equilibrium and short-run dynamics without sacrificing any information. Secondly, the technique allows intercept, short-run coefficient, and error variance to vary across groups, but mandates that long-run parameters be equal across cross-sections. Thirdly, the approach is applicable regardless of whether the observed variables are stationary at level or first difference. Furthermore, PMG accommodates a short time span and different optimal numbers of lags for each variable, leading to consistent and reliable results. The panel ARDL model can be represented as follows:

$$Y_{it} = \sum_{j=1}^{p} \lambda_{ij} Y_{i,t-j} + \sum_{j=0}^{q} \varphi_{ij}' X_{i,t-j} + \mu_i + \varepsilon_{it} \quad (2)$$

where $i = 1, 2, \ldots, N$ represents the number of countries (cross-sections); $t = 1, 2, \ldots, T$ is the time period, Y_{it} denotes the dependent variables comprising economic growth and poverty , $Y_{i,t-j}$ is the lagged dependent variables; X_{it} is a $kx1$ vector of independent variables; φ_{ij}' are the $kx1$ coefficient vectors, λ_{ij} are scalars, μ_i is the country-specific effects and ε_{it} is the error term, assuming that all the variables in the model are cointegrated and the error term is integrated of order zero [*i. e.* $I(0)$] for all cross-sections. Thus, Eq. (2) is reparametrized into the error correction model as follows:

$$\Delta Y_{it} = \rho_i \left(Y_{i,t-1} - \phi_i' X_{it} \right) + \sum_{j=1}^{p-1} \lambda_{ij}^* \Delta Y_{i,t-1} + \sum_{j=1}^{q-1} \varphi_{ij}' \Delta X_{i,t-j} + \mu_i + \varepsilon_{it} \quad (3)$$

where $\rho_i = -\left(1 - \sum_{j=1}^{p} \lambda_{ij}\right)$ represents the speed of adjustment; $\phi_i = \sum_{j=1}^{p} \lambda_{ij} / \left(1 - \sum_j \lambda_{ij}\right)$ denotes the vector of long-run parameter; and both $\lambda_{ij}^* = -\sum_{m=j+1}^{p} \lambda_{im}$ and $\varphi_{ij}^* = -\sum_{m=j+1}^{q} \varphi_{im}$ represent the short-run parameters, respectively. The parameter is assumed to be negative and statistically significant based on the prior assumption that the variables indicate a return to a long-run equilibrium.

This study further utilizes the fully modified ordinary least squares (FMOLS) and dynamic ordinary least squares (DOLS) developed by Phillips and Hansen and Stock and Watson, respectively, to test the robustness of the PARDL outcomes. The FMOLS and DOLS approaches are notable as consistent and reliable estimators for cointegrated variables, which circumvent issues relating to serial correlations, multicollinearity, and endogeneity among the variables.

Empirical Results

The researchers began the empirical analysis by ascertaining the cross-sectional dependency (CSD) of the variables under scrutiny to circumvent inaccurate outcomes and choose the appropriate techniques. Accordingly, the study employs the Pesaran CSD test to check the CSD of the variables. The outcomes in Table 2 show the existence of cross-sectional dependency among the variables considered, given that the null hypothesis of cross-sectional independence is rejected.

The existence of cross-sectional dependence implies that the use of first-generation panel unit root tests may result in inaccurate outcomes because the correlations between the cross-sectional error components are not disregarded. However, second-generation panel unit root tests account for the cross-sectional dependence of errors. Pesaran (2007) employed the covariate-augmented Dickey (CADF) unit root test to establish the integration order of the series. Table 3 displays the results of the unit root tests, which indicate that fuel imports and renewable energy are stationary at the level, while the other variables become stationary at the first difference. These findings support the joint integration order of the variables.

This study explored the presence of long-run cointegration associations between variables using a second-generation cointegration test: the Westerlund (2008) panel cointegration test. Table 4 presents the results of the Westerlund cointegration test,

Table 2 Cross-sectional dependence results

Variables	Pesaran CD	Prob
GDP	8.920*	0.000
POV	11.271*	0.000
FSUB	10.739*	0.000
ENG	7.259*	0.005
FEXP	15.022*	0.000
FIMP	6.890*	0.009
FPRI	9.107*	0.000
RENE	8.148	0.000

Note: *, **, and *** indicate significance levels for 1%, 5%, and 10%, respectively

Table 3 The results of CADF unit root test

	Constant		Trend	
	Level	First	Level	First
GDP	−0.358	−4.118*	−0.827	−4.218*
POV	−0.850	−3.818*	−0.901	−4.671*
FSUB	−1.439	−4.368*	−1.639	−5.201*
ENG	−0.338	−5.190*	−1.021	−5.729*
FEXP	−1.392	−4.719*	−1.410	−4.853*
FIMP	−3.749**	−5.928*	−3.891**	−6.023*
FPRI	−0.501	−3.722**	−0.619	−4.008*
RENE	−3.592**	−5.128*	−3.792*	−5.248*

Note: *,**, and *** indicate significance levels for 1%, 5%, and 10%, respectively

Table 4 The results of the Westerlund (2008) panel cointegration test

Statistics	1	2
G_t	−4.501*	−4.273*
G_a	−6.122*	−8.015*
P_t	10.389*	−7.288*
P_a	−4.752*	−4.310*

Note: *, **, and *** indicate significance levels for 1%, 5%, and 10%, respectively

which contains two models, with each dependent variable incorporated separately. This finding indicates that the null hypothesis of no cointegration is rejected across the models, providing evidence of long-run cointegration among the series under consideration.

The subsequent stage of this investigation entailed examining the associations between fuel subsidies and sustainable economic growth in selected African nations using the PARDL methodology. In Table 5, the long- and short-run PARDL outcomes are presented, with columns 1 and 2 displaying economic growth and poverty as the dependent variables, respectively. The long-run coefficient results indicate that the estimated coefficients of energy consumption are positively associated with economic growth but have a negative impact on poverty. Specifically, a 1% increase in energy consumption is associated with rise (decrease) in economic growth and poverty by 0.197% and 0.190%, respectively. This finding suggests that increasing energy consumption enhances the productivity of manufacturing and household activities, which bolsters the economic performance and welfare of individuals in African countries. This outcome further emphasizes that securing adequate energy resources is essential for promoting sustainable growth in the selected African economies. This result corroborates the evidence of Aydin (2019), Dai et al. (2022), and Onatunji (2022) but contradicts the findings of Ozturk et al. (2022) and Wang (2022). Moreover, the estimated coefficients of fuel exports exhibit positive and negative values across the various model specifications. More specifically, a 1% surge in fuel export is associated with 0.481% and 0.110% increase (decrease) in economic growth and poverty. This outcome implies that rising fuel exports

Table 5 PARDL results

Variables	GDP – 1	Poverty - 2
C	0.478(0.108)***	0.802(0.201)
ENG	0.197(0. 054)**	−0.190(0.000)*
FEXP	0.481(0.000)*	−0.110 (0.002)*
FIMP	−0.145(0.003)*	0.790(0.000)*
FSUB	0.153(0.000)*	−0.790(0.025)**
FPRI	−0.463(0.000)*	0.283(0.000)*
RENE	0.174(0.000)*	−0.447(0.000)*
Short-run		
ENG	0.892(0.000)*	−0.260(0.040)**
FEXP	0.725(0.000)*	−0.791(0.005)*
FIMP	−0.447(0.000)*	0.103(0.000)*
FSUB	0.150(0.000)	−0.141(0.000)
FPRI	−0.650(0.001)*	0.520(0.034)**
RENE	0.147(0.000)*	−0.183(0.000)*
ECT	−0.781(0.000)*	−0.564(0.000)*
Hausman test	0.393(0.181)	0. 332(0.182)
Log-likelihood	−127.801	−221.474

Note: *, **, and *** indicate significance levels for 1%, 5%, and 10%, respectively

contribute to increased foreign exchange inflows, domestic investment, and import expansion, ultimately promoting economic performance and poverty reduction in the selected African countries. This outcome underscores the significance of expanding fuel exports as a key contributor to the improvement in welfare and economic growth in West African nations. This finding is consistent with those of Sultan and Haque (2018), Mahmood and Murshed (2021), Olayungbo (2019), and Murshed (2022), who reached similar conclusions.

Furthermore, the long-term coefficients of fuel imports are negatively related to economic growth but positively associated with poverty. In particular, this outcome suggests that a 1% increase in fuel import leads to decrease (increase) in economic growth and poverty by 0.145% and 0.790%, respectively. This result indicates that increases in fuel imports exacerbate trade deficits, weaken domestic currencies, and ultimately decrease economic growth and poverty reduction in the African countries analyzed. This finding also emphasizes that relying heavily on fuel imports because of insufficient resources to meet the growing population needs leads to a decline in economic performance and welfare for individuals in the ECOWAS region. This conclusion is consistent with the results of the study by Ihediwa and Adamu (2023), which revealed similar findings. Similarly, the coefficient of fuel price has a negative impact on economic growth, but a positive association with poverty. Specifically, this outcome highlights that a 1% increase in fuel price is associated with rise (decline) in economic growth and poverty by 0.463% and 0.283%, respectively. This outcome suggests that higher fuel prices are linked to increased inflationary pressure and unemployment, which ultimately reduces sustainable economic growth in the selected African economies. This outcome also indicates that a rise in fuel prices dampens firms' manufacturing activities, leading to higher inflation and unemployment rates, thus reducing sustainable economic growth in the analyzed African countries. This conclusion is supported by the empirical results of Zahra and Mahboobeh (2011), Orlu (2017), and Przekota (2022). Moreover, the long-term estimated coefficients of renewable energy are positively related to economic growth, but negatively associated with poverty. This finding implies that 1% increase in renewable energy upsurge (decline) in economic growth and poverty by 0.174% and 0.447%, respectively. This finding indicates that the increased utilization of modern energy resources improves labor productivity and generates more employment opportunities, consequently enhancing sustainable economic performance in the analyzed countries. This finding further highlights that the use of innovative renewable energy resources promotes a greater awareness of energy conservation, reduces the use of fossil energy resources, and ultimately fosters sustainable economic growth in African countries. This outcome is consistent with the empirical results of Jia et al. (2023), Arif et al. (2020), Li et al. (2021), and Arasu et al. (2021), who uncovered similar findings. Furthermore, some scholars also discovered that renewable energy lifts economic development besides economic growth and reduces carbon emissions (Abbasi et al., 2021; Tu et al., 2022; Zhao et al., 2022).

Regarding the main explanatory variables, the long-term estimated coefficients of fuel subsidies show a positive correlation with economic growth, but a negative connection with poverty across all specifications. More specifically, this outcome suggests that a 1% increase in fuel subsidies increase (decrease) economic growth and poverty by 0.153% and 0.790%, respectively. This result indicates that eliminating fuel subsidies leads to the reallocation of government resources from high-income households to low-income ones, thereby promoting sustainable economic growth and poverty reduction. This long-term finding also suggests that removing fuel subsidies will help reduce excessive government borrowing to fund continuous increases in oil imports, appreciate the domestic currency, decrease persistent corruption and decadence, and thus, promote sustainable economic growth in the selected African countries. This result is consistent with the findings of Ozili and Obiora (2023).

The lower panel of Table 5 presents the short-run outcomes derived from the PARDL analysis. The short-run outcomes demonstrate that energy consumption, fuel exports, renewable energy, and fuel subsidies exhibit a positive relationship with economic growth, whereas a negative association is observed with poverty. Conversely, the short-run results reveal that fuel imports and fuel prices exhibit a negative relationship with economic growth yet a positive association with poverty. Overall, short-run outcomes do not exhibit substantial differences from long-run outcomes, particularly in terms of statistical significance. The findings further indicate that the estimated coefficients of ECT are negative and statistically significant across all the models, suggesting that the speed of adjustment from short-run imbalances to long-run equilibrium varies over time.

Table 6 FMOLS and DOLS results

Variables	1	2	3	4
ENG	0.334(0.000)*	−0.463(0.021)**	0.374(0.000)*	−0.281(0.000)*
FEXP	0.179(0.000)*	−0.369(0.000)*	0.351(0.027)**	−0.194(0.000)*
FIMP	−0.721(0.000)*	0.268(0.005)*	−0.626(0.000)*	0.534(0.000)*
FSUB	0.511(0.000)*	−0.149(0.072)***	0.325(0.000)*	−0.240(0.000)*
FPRI	−0.147(0.103)***	0.628(0.000)*	−0.169(0.007)*	0.531(0.000)*
RENE	0.271(0.000)*	−0.103(0.000)*	0.349(0.000)*	−0.105(0.009)*
R^2	0.951	0.755	0.802	0.916

Note: *,**, and *** indicate significance levels for 1%, 5%, and 10%, respectively

This study additionally employed the panel FMOLS and DOLS methods to corroborate the ARDL outcomes. Table 6 displays the FMOLS and DOLS results, with columns 1–2 depicting the FMOLS findings and columns 3–4 presenting the DOLS findings. The findings of the techniques also affirm that fuel exports, fuel subsidies, energy consumption, and renewable energy exhibit a positive relationship with economic growth, but a negative association with poverty. The estimated coefficients of fuel price and imports reveal negative associations with economic growth and positive connections with poverty in all model specifications. Overall, the outcomes of the FMOLS and DOLS techniques align with the long-term coefficients reported using the ARDL approach.

Discussion and Conclusion

This research examined the associations between fuel subsidies and sustainable development goals in selected African nations using the PARDL, FMOLS, and DOLS techniques. It also confirmed the relationship between the subsidy removal and energy consumption and renewable energy. The study focused on SDG 7 and SDG 1, and the relationship between them and fuel subsidy removal. The empirical results from both the short-run and long-run are similar. Generally, the findings revealed that all variables showed significant results. However, while energy consumption, fuel export, fuel subsidy, and renewable energy are positively related to economic growth in both the short-run and long-run, these variables are negatively related to poverty in the both the short- and long-run. On the other hand, in the short- and long-run, while both fuel importation and fuel price revealed a negative relationship with economic growth, the two variables showed positive to poverty. The findings of the techniques also affirm that fuel exports, fuel subsidies, energy consumption, and renewable energy exhibit a positive relationship with economic growth, but a negative association with poverty. The estimated coefficients of fuel price and imports reveal negative associations with economic growth and positive connections with poverty in all model specifications. Overall, the outcomes of the FMOLS and DOLS techniques align with the long-term coefficients reported using the PARDL approach. The long-term estimated coefficients of fuel subsidies and renewable energy show positive correlations with economic growth, but a negative connection with poverty across all specifications. This result is in line with the study of Timilsina and Pargal (2020), who found that subsidy removal on natural gas and electricity in Bangladesh was beneficial to the economy. This result indicates that eliminating fuel subsidies leads to the reallocation of government resources from high-income households to low-income ones, thereby promoting sustainable economic growth and poverty reduction. This long-term finding also suggests that removing fuel subsidies will help reduce excessive government borrowing to fund continuous increases in oil imports, appreciate the domestic currency, decrease persistent corruption and decadence, and thus, promote sustainable economic growth in the selected African countries. Therefore, if the subsidy is removed, it then means that money saved from it must be diverted to developmental projects and renewable energy sources that can boost the economy and alleviate poverty. Conclusively, a very strong relationship between fuel subsidy, renewable energy, and sustainable economic growth and poverty is confirmed. This study would help nations across the globe, policymakers, leaders of nations, and investors. Therefore, it is recommended for nations to divert their resources into renewable energy sources by taking advantage of their seashores, hilly and steep topography areas to mount all their solar gadgets in order to solve the energy problems of their country. This recommendation supports Aliyu et al. (2018), who concluded that African countries should diversify into renewable energy sources to address the perennial energy crisis. Achieving energy efficiency would not only solve electricity supply problems, but also would help to grow local industries, attract more foreign investors, change investors' perceptions about Africa, and help transit to the consumption of renewable energy, which is more environmentally friendly.

References

Abbasi, K. R., Shahbaz, M., Jiao, Z., & Tufail, M. (2021). How energy consumption, industrial growth, urbanization, and CO2 emissions affect economic growth in Pakistan? A novel dynamic ARDL simulations approach. *Energy, 221*, 119793. https://doi.org/10.1016/j.energy.2021.119793

Acharya, R. H., & Sadath, A. C. (2017). Implications of energy subsidy reform in India. *Energy Policy, 102*, 453–462. https://doi.org/10.1016/j.enpol.2016.12.036

Adekunle, I. A., & Oseni, I. O. (2021). Fuel subsidies and carbon emission: Evidence from asymmetric modelling. *Environmental Science and Pollution Research, 28*, 22729–22741. https://doi.org/10.1007/s11356-021-12384-0

Ahenkan, A., & Osei-Kojo, A. (2014). Achieving sustainable development in Africa: Progress, challenges and prospects. *International Journal of Development and Sustainability, 3*(1), 162–176. https://d1wqtxts1xzle7.cloudfront.net/108737693/ijds-v3n1-10-libre.pdf?1702290314

Aliyu, A. K., Modu, B., & Tan, C. W. (2018). A review of renewable energy development in Africa: A focus in South Africa, Egypt and Nigeria. *Renewable and Sustainable Energy Reviews, 81*, 2502–2518. https://doi.org/10.1016/j.rser.2017.06.055

Andor, M., & Voss, A. (2016). Optimal renewable-energy promotion: Capacity subsidies vs. generation subsidies. *Resource and Energy Economics, 45*, 144–158. https://doi.org/10.1016/j.reseneeco.2016.06.002

Apeloko, D. O., & Olajide, O. J. (2012). Chapter eight newspaper coverage of oil subsidy removal remonstration: A thoughtful analysis of 2012 experience in Nigeria. *Environmental Conflicts and Peacebuilding in Africa, 125*. https://lccn.loc.gov/2019037094

Arasu, B. S., Kannaiah, D., Nancy Christina, J., & Shabbir, M. S. (2021). *Selection of variables in data envelopment analysis for evaluation of stock performance*. Management and Labour Studies. https://doi.org/10.1177/0258042X211002511

Arif, A., Sadiq, M., Shabbir, M. S., Yahya, G., Zamir, A., & Bares Lopez, L. (2020). The role of globalization in financial development, trade openness and sustainable environmental -economic growth: Evidence from selected South Asian economies. *Journal of Sustainable Finance & Investment*, 1–18. https://doi.org/10.1080/20430795.2020.1861865

Atansah, P., Khandan, M., Moss, T., Mukherjee, A., & Richmond, J. (2017). When do subsidy reforms stick? Lessons from Iran, Nigeria, and India. *Center for Global Development*. https://www.cgdev.org/publication

Aydin, M. (2019). The effect of biomass energy consumption on economic growth in BRICS countries: A country-specific panel data analysis. *Renewable Energy, 138*, 620–627. https://doi.org/10.1016/j.renene.2019.02.001

Baz, K., Cheng, J., Xu, D., Abbas, K., Ali, I., Ali, H., & Fang, C. (2021). Asymmetric impact of fossil fuel and renewable energy consumption on economic growth: A nonlinear technique. *Energy, 226*, 120357. https://doi.org/10.1016/j.energy.2021.120357

Black, M. S., Liu, A. A., Parry, I. W., & Vernon, N. (2023). *IMF fossil fuel subsidies data: 2023 update*. International Monetary Fund. https://books.google.co.za/books

Dai, L., Jia, R., & Wang, X.. (2022). Relationship between economic growth and energy consumption from the perspective of sustainable development. *Journal of Environmental and Public Health*. 2022 July 20;2022:6884273. https://doi.org/10.1155/2022/6884273

Ekong, C. N., & Akpan, U. F. (2014). On energy subsidy reform and sustainable development in Nigeria. *International Journal of Management and Sustainability, 3*(4), 186–202. https://www.researchgate.net/publication/359803237

Emodi, N. V., & Boo, K. J. (2015). Sustainable energy development in Nigeria: Current status and policy options. *Renewable and Sustainable Energy Reviews, 51*, 356–381. https://doi.org/10.1016/j.rser.2015.06.016

Gani, A. (2021). Fossil fuel energy and environmental performance in an extended STIRPAT model. *Journal of Cleaner Production, 297*, 126526. https://doi.org/10.1016/j.jclepro.2021.126526

Gelan, A. U. (2018). Kuwait's energy subsidy reduction: Examining economic and CO2 emission effects with or without compensation. *Energy Economics, 71*, 186–200. https://doi.org/10.1016/j.eneco.2018.02.014

Ihediwa, C. C., & Adamu, A. (2023). *Effect of imports on economic growth in Nigeria: A sectoral analysis*. Available at SSRN: https://ssrn.com/abstract=4342850 or https://doi.org/10.2139/ssrn.4342850

Iyke, B. N. (2015). Electricity consumption and economic growth in Nigeria: A revisit of the energy-growth debate. *Energy Economics, 51*, 166–176. https://doi.org/10.1016/j.eneco.2015.05.024

Jacal, S., Straubinger, F. B., Benjamin, E. O., & Buchenrieder, G. (2022). Economic costs and environmental impacts of fossil fuel dependency in sub-Saharan Africa: A Nigerian dilemma. *Energy for Sustainable Development, 70*, 45–53. https://doi.org/10.1016/j.esd.2022.07.007

Jha, P., & Schmidt, S. (2021). State of biofuel development in sub-Saharan Africa: How far sustainable? *Renewable and Sustainable Energy Reviews, 150*, 111432. https://doi.org/10.1016/j.rser.2021.111432

Jia, H., Fan, S., & Xia, M. (2023). The impact of renewable energy consumption on economic growth: Evidence from countries along the Belt and Road. *Sustainability, 15*(11), 8644. https://doi.org/10.3390/su15118644

Li, Q., Cherian, J., Shabbir, M. S., Sial, M. S., Li, J., Mester, I., et al. (2021). Exploring the relationship between renewable energy sources and economic growth. The case of SAARC countries. *Energies, 14*(3), 520. https://www.mdpi.com/1996-1073/14/3/520#

Mahmood, H., & Murshed, M. (2021). Oil price and economic growth nexus in Saudi Arabia: Asymmetry analysis. *International Journal of Energy Economics and Policy, 11*(1), 29. https://doi.org/10.32479/ijeep.10382

Mas'ud, A. A., Wirba, A. V., Muhammad-Sukki, F., Mas'ud, I. A., Munir, A. B., & Yunus, N. M. (2015). An assessment of renewable energy readiness in Africa: Case study of Nigeria and Cameroon. *Renewable and Sustainable Energy Reviews, 51*, 775–784. https://doi.org/10.1016/j.rser.2015.06.045

McKitrick, R. (2017). Global energy subsidies: An analytical taxonomy. *Energy Policy, 101*, 379–385. https://doi.org/10.1016/j.enpol.2016.10.035

Mundaca, G. (2017). How much can CO2 emissions be reduced if fossil fuel subsidies are removed? *Energy Economics, 64*, 91–104. https://doi.org/10.1016/j.eneco.2017.03.014

Murshed, M. (2022). The impacts of fuel exports on sustainable economic growth: The importance of controlling environmental pollution in Saudi Arabia. *Energy Report, 8*, 13708–13722. https://doi.org/10.1016/j.egyr.2022.09.186

Nwachukwu, M. U., Mba, H. C., Jiburum, U., & Okosun, A. E. (2013). Empirical analysis of fuel price and subsidy reform in Nigeria. *OPEC Energy Review, 37*(3), 314–326. https://doi.org/10.1111/opec.12003

Obasi, V. U., Ezenkwa, E. C., Onwa, D. O., & Nwogbaga, D. M. (2017). The political economy of fuel subsidy removal In Nigeria. *African Journal of Politics and Administrative Studies, 10*(1), 51–69. https://www.ajol.info/index.php/ajpas/article/view/248685

Ofori, R. O. (2023). The economic cost of fuel subsidies in Ghana. *Socio-Economic Planning Sciences, 87*, 101587. https://doi.org/10.1016/j.seps.2023.101587

Olayungbo, D. O. (2019). Effects of oil export revenue on economic growth in Nigeria: A time varying analysis of resource curse. *Resource Policy, 64*, 101469. https://doi.org/10.1016/j.resourpol.2019.101469

Onatunji, O. G. (2022). Electricity consumption and industrial output: Fresh evidence from economic community of West African states (ECOWAS). *Journal of Economic and Administrative Sciences*, 1026–4116. https://doi.org/10.1108/JEAS-09-2021-0177

Orlu, R. N. (2017). The impact of domestic pricing of petrol on economic growth of Nigeria (1970 – 2013). *Global Journal of Social Sciences, 16*, 1–8. https://www.ajol.info/index.php/gjss/article/view/165589

Oyedepo, S. O. (2014). Towards achieving energy for sustainable development in Nigeria. *Renewable and Sustainable Energy Reviews, 34*, 255–272. https://doi.org/10.1016/j.rser.2014.03.019

Ozgur, O., Aydin, L., Karagol, E. T., & Ozbugday, F. C. (2021). The fuel price pass-through in Turkey: The case study of motor fuel price subsidy system. *Energy, 226*, 120399. https://doi.org/10.1016/j.energy.2021.120399

Ozili, K., & Obiora, K (2023). *Implications of fuel subsidy removal on the Nigerian economy* (August 9, 2023). Public Policy's Role in Achieving Sustainable Development Goals, Available at SSRN: https://ssrn.com/abstract=4535876 or https://doi.org/10.2139/ssrn.4535876

Ozturk, I., Aslan, A., Ozsolak, B., Atay Polat, M., & Turan, Z. (2022). Impact of fossil fuels and renewable energy consumption on economic growth in Paris Club Countries. *Journal of Renewable and Sustainable Energy, 14*(4). https://doi.org/10.1063/5.0086752

Pesaran, M. H. (2007). A simple panel unit root test in the presence of cross-section dependence. *Journal of Applied Econometrics, 22*(2), 265–312. https://doi.org/10.1002/jae.951

Przekota, G. (2022). Do high fuel prices pose an obstacle to economic growth? A study for Poland. *Energies, 15*(18), 6606. https://doi.org/10.3390/en15186606

Shittu, I., Latiff, A. R. A., & Baharudin, S. A. (2024). Assessing the compensation and reinvestment plans for fuel subsidy rationalization in Nigeria: A dynamic computable general equilibrium approach. *Energy, 293*, 130671. https://doi.org/10.1016/j.energy.2024.130671

Siddig, K., Minor, P., Grethe, H., Aguiar, A. & Walmsley, T. (2015). Impacts on poverty of removing fuel import subsidies in Nigeria. *World Bank Policy Research Working Paper*, (7376). https://ssrn.com/abstract=2635707

Soile, I., & Mu, X. (2015). Who benefit most from fuel subsidies? Evidence from Nigeria. *Energy Policy, 87*, 314–324. https://doi.org/10.1016/j.enpol.2015.09.018

Solarin, S. A. (2020). An environmental impact assessment of fossil fuel subsidies in emerging and developing economies. *Environmental Impact Assessment Review, 85*, 106443. https://doi.org/10.1016/j.eiar.2020.106443

Sultan, Z. A., & Haque, M. I. (2018). Oil exports and economic growth: An empirical evidence from Saudi Arabia. *International Journal of Energy Economics and Policy, 8*(5), 281. http://hdl.handle.net/11159/2642

Timilsina, G. R., & Pargal, S. (2020). Economics of energy subsidy reforms in Bangladesh. *Energy Policy, 142*, 111539. https://doi.org/10.1016/j.enpol.2020.111539

Tu, Z., Feng, C., & Zhao, X. (2022). Revisiting energy efficiency and energy related CO2 emissions: Evidence from RCEP economies. *Economic Research-Ekonomska Istraživanja, 35*, 1–21. https://doi.org/10.1080/1331677X.2022.2038651

Uzonwanne, M., Ezenekwe, U., & Iregbenu, P. (2015). Fuel subsidy removal and the Nigerian economy. *Australian Journal of Business and Management Research, 5*(4) https://ssrn.com/abstract=2789897

Van Asselt, H. (2023). The SDGs and fossil fuel subsidy reform. *International Environmental Agreements: Politics, Law and Economics, 23*(2), 191–197. https://doi.org/10.1007/s10784-023-09601-1

Van Valkengoed, A. M., & Van der Werff, E. (2022). Are subsidies for climate action effective? Two case studies in the Netherlands. *Environmental Science & Policy, 127*, 137–145. https://doi.org/10.1016/j.envsci.2021.09.018

Vandeninden, F., Grun, R., & Fecher, F. (2022). Energy subsidies and poverty: The case of fossil fuel subsidies in Burkina Faso. *Energy for Sustainable Development, 70*, 581–591.b. https://doi.org/10.1016/j.esd.2022.08.023

Wang, S. (2022). Differences between energy consumption and regional economic growth under the energy environment. *Energy Reports, 8*, 10017–10024. https://doi.org/10.1016/j.egyr.2022.07.065

Wesseh, P. K., Jr., Lin, B., & Atsagli, P. (2016). Environmental and welfare assessment of fossil-fuels subsidies removal: A computable general equilibrium analysis for Ghana. *Energy, 116*, 1172–1179. https://doi.org/10.1016/j.energy.2016.10.053

Westerlund, J. (2008). Panel cointegration tests of the Fisher effect. *Journal of Applied Econometrics, 23*(2), 193–233. https://doi.org/10.1002/jae.967

Yakubu, M., Abdullahi, M. M., & Maijama'a, R., & Musa, K. S. (2023). Investigating the effect of petroleum subsidy removal on standard of living amidst rising poverty in Nigeria. *Asian Journal of Economics, Finance and Management*, 359–364. https://www.researchgate.net/profile/Kabiru-Saidu-Musa/publication/375085193

Zahra, E., & Mahboobeh, J. (2011). Oil price shocks and economic growth: Evidence from OPEC and OECD. *Australian Journal of Basic and Applied Sciences, 5*(6), 627–635. https://www.sid.ir/paper/192104/en

Zhao, X., Shang, Y., Ma, X., Xia, P., & Shahzad, U. (2022). Does carbon trading lead to green technology innovation: Recent evidence from Chinese companies in resource-based industries. *IEEE Transactions on Engineering Management*, 1–18. https://doi.org/10.1109/TEM.2022.3186905

Expected Credit Loss Provision Practices in South Africa: An Analysis of the Decision Usefulness of the Forward-Looking Disclosures

Ahmed Mohammadali-Haji, Karabo Sihiya, and Kyle Triegaardt

Abstract The 2008 Financial Crisis occurred partially as a result of the delayed credit losses recognised under the incurred loss model in the previous accounting standard, IAS 39, by entities operating in the financial sector. IFRS 9 superseded IAS 39 and with it replaced the incurred loss model with an expected credit loss model. The revised expected credit loss model avoids the 'too little, too late' problem of the incurred loss model. This study analyses the first-time adoption of the expected credit loss model in IFRS 9 and reports on the appropriateness, rigour and decision usefulness of the forward-looking disclosures as it relates to the expected credit loss provision practices on trade receivables in South Africa. The decision usefulness and by implication the appropriateness and rigour of the forward-looking disclosures is assessed by reviewing the nature and extent thereof in financial statements. A disclosure checklist was used for the content analysis and interpretation of a selection of South African listed companies upon the adoption of IFRS 9. The study finds that significant improvements can be made in the disclosure of forward-looking information to improve decision usefulness and thereby contribute positively to the investment in society through responsible use of data in the expected credit loss provision.

Keywords IFRS 9 · Expected credit loss · Credit risk · JSE · Trade receivables · Disclosure · Forward-looking information

A. Mohammadali-Haji (✉) · K. Sihiya
University of Johannesburg, Johannesburg, South Africa
e-mail: ahmedh@uj.ac.za; karabok@uj.ac.za

K. Triegaardt
BDO SA Inc, Johannesburg, South Africa
e-mail: ktriegaardt@bdo.co.za

T. Moloi (ed.), *Impacting Society Positively Through Technology in Accounting and Business Processes*, Springer Proceedings in Business and Economics,
https://doi.org/10.1007/978-3-031-84885-8_45

Background and Research Problem

Trade receivables are amounts due to a firm for goods or services delivered or used but not yet paid for by customers (Kenton, 2019) and these amounts fall within the scope of the International Financial Reporting Standard 9 (IFRS 9) and its predecessor the International Accounting Standard 39 (IAS 39). Essentially, these are amounts due from an entity's core business – and a core source of cash inflows that have not yet been collected.

Trade receivables, along with inventory and cash equivalents, make up the working capital, which can account for up to 70% of a company's total assets (Correia et al., 2013). Changes to either inventories or trade receivables significantly affect cash inflows and cash balances, which in turn affect the entity's ability to generate future revenue (Dan, 2020).

An economy requires financing in order to create leveraged growth, and trade receivables are an important form of financing, especially for businesses (Ukaegbu, 2014). An impairment of trade receivables represents a deterioration in the expected recovery of the trade receivable and therefore, gives vital information about future cash flows and future revenue activities. Responsible financing is vital for a business to keep functioning, and as a result, for the economy as a whole, thereby positively impacting society at large.

An asset is impaired when its carrying amount exceeds its recoverable amount. Usually, an event will have occurred that indicates the value of the asset has decreased (IASB, 2018c). Under International Accounting Standard 39 (IAS 39), financial assets were impaired under the incurred loss model. Objective evidence of an impairment was required, such as the counterparty to the financial asset having defaulted on an instalment, which results in an actual loss for the holder who would in turn impair the financial asset in their financial statements. However, as stated by Cohen and Edwards (2017), this means losses are recognised too late to provide any meaningful warning signs of deteriorating credit to investors.

The 2008 Financial Crisis was one such an event that was partially as a result of the delayed impairment recognition on sub-prime mortgages that led to the United States housing market crash and the collapse of the banking sector, resulting in trillions of dollars of losses and taxpayer-funded bailouts (Chabal, 2013; Valentin & Isa, 2011). The former US president, Barack Obama, classified it as the worst economic crisis since the Great Depression (Milligan, 2009).

Whilst accounting standards did not cause the 2008 Financial Crisis (FCAG, 2009), it did expose certain flaws in the existing accounting standards. As stated by Brooks (2018), IAS 39 required no recognition of impairment losses until a loss was incurred, and as a result there was no disclosure of deteriorating credit, and users were unaware of the deteriorating credit quality of financial assets.

Providing useful financial information that clearly sets out the risk in providing credit allows investors to make informed decisions and mitigates the risk of future crises. In the aftermath of the 2008 Financial Crisis, the International Accounting Standards Board (IASB) issued new standards and modified the existing standards to improve the quality of disclosures in financial statements (Valentin & Isa, 2011), and IFRS 9 with its expected credit loss model seeks to better address exposures to credit risk in the financial statements.

Furthermore, IFRS 9 requires extensive use of forward-looking information in the impairment model. It is the forward-looking information that drives the earlier, and therefore, large impairment allowances to be recorded, and whilst IFRS 9 suggests information to be considered, it is not prescriptive on the information to utilise.

Research Objective and Scope

The objective of this study is to analyse the decision usefulness of forward-looking information disclosed in the financial statements and to report on the appropriateness, rigour and decision usefulness of the forward-looking information. This study focusses on the decision usefulness of the forward-looking information disclosed as part of the application of the expected credit loss model. This information by implication will therefore assist in assessing the decision usefulness of the information provided to the providers of capital in order that they may invest in the entity.

Previous studies have focused on the quality of disclosure or the financial impact for entities operating in the financial sector. Financial institutions are in the business of lending money, whereas the granting of credit by non-financial institutions is a by-product of their core business. Non-financial institutions are less likely to have as strong credit vetting and credit collection processes, as financial institutions do. Whilst the 2008 Financial Crisis centred on the lending by financial institutions, the scope of IFRS 9 also includes other financial instruments and is not limited to one specific industry. For this reason, the focus of this chapter is specifically on the impairment of trade receivables of non-financial entities. The study addresses a gap in the literature by evaluating the forward-looking information disclosed in the various industries other than the financial sector.

Literature Review

Events Leading Up to the Development IFRS 9

IFRS Accounting Standards are developed by the IASB and the application of IFRS is adopted in over 140 jurisdictions (IFRS Foundation, n.d.-a). IAS 39 was issued by the International Accounting Standards Committee (IASC; the predecessor to the IASB) in March 1999 and adopted by the IASB in April 2001 (IFRS Foundation, n.d.-b). A further exposure draft was released in 2002, with the final improved version being issued in 2003 (Camfferman, 2015).

IAS 39 was always an interim standard, but it was not until the 2008 Financial Crisis that stakeholders became more vocal about replacing IAS 39. Clikeman (2020) traced 16 corporate failures over an 80-year period are further identified that the 2008 Financial Crisis was an economic event consisting of not one but several corporate failures. In the United States, the Dow Jones Industrial Average (DIJA) fell by 50%, American households' net worth declined by almost 25%, the unemployment rate doubled to 8.9% and the real gross domestic product fell by 17.9%.

IAS 39 was heavily criticised for exacerbating the 2008 Financial Crisis due to its delayed recognition of credit losses that contributed to overstating the credit quality of mortgage loans (Kim et al., 2021). According to the Financial Crisis Advisory Group (FCAG, 2009), criticisms included that it was difficult to apply this model, particularly the appropriate trigger event that results in the recognition of an impairment. This prevented banks from recording potential future losses even if they could reasonably be predicted (Kim et al., 2021).

FCAG was set up to advise about the accounting standard setting implications of the financial crisis and potential changes in the global regulatory environment in 2009. The FCAG highlighted the delayed recognition of credit losses as a primary weakness in accounting standards and recommended a forward-looking model (FCAG, 2009). Following this report, regulatory bodies, such as the Group of Twenty (G20, 2009) and the Financial Stability Forum (2009), urged for improvements in accounting standards. This finally resulted in a comprehensive review of IAS 39 by the IASB and the subsequent issuing of a new standard, namely IFRS 9.

The Incurred Loss Model

IAS 39 requires objective evidence of impairment of a financial asset to exist before requiring an entity to estimate that financial asset's recoverable amount and comparing the recoverable amount to its carrying amount. It further indicates that impairment losses are only incurred if the impairment is as a result of a loss event (hence, the name incurred loss model). Furthermore, future loss events that may occur are excluded in determining impairment amounts, regardless of how likely they are (IASB, 2004). This makes it clear that the model is in no way forward-looking. As stated by Brooks (2018, p. 125), it '*ignores risks inherent in a business*'.

In its recommendations, the FCAG (2009) recommended an alternative to the incurred loss model, suggesting a model that used more forward-looking information. The alternatives listed were a fair value model and an expected credit loss model. The IASB elected to apply the latter.

Development of IFRS 9

The final, completed version of IFRS 9 was issued in July 2014 and was mandatorily effective on 1 January 2018, with limited exceptions for entities in the insurance industry. This formally introduced the expected credit loss model to IFRS financial statements. There have been subsequent amendments to IFRS 9, but these did not impact the impairment section and are therefore not relevant to this study (IASB, 2018b; IFRS Foundation, n.d.-b).

The Expected Credit Loss Model

Chapter 5.5 of IFRS 9 sets out the expected credit loss model of impairment. The model follows what is referred to in practice as the *'general'*, *'three stage' or 'three step'* approach (BDO, 2019, pp. 50–51). Stage 1 is where the credit risk has not increased significantly since initial recognition, and 12-month expected credit losses are recognised. Stage 2 is where the credit risk has increased significantly subsequent to initial recognition, and lifetime credit losses are recognised. Stage 3 is where a default event has occurred and lifetime expected credit losses are recognised (IASB, 2018b).

IFRS 9 contains a simplification for trade receivables referred to in practice as the *'simplified impairment model'* (BDO, 2019, p. 56). Under this approach an entity is absolved of the requirement to monitor credit risk. In other words, the entity does not need to determine if there has been a significant increase in credit risk. Instead, all trade receivables are accounted for under Stage 2 with lifetime expected credit losses being recognised (IASB, 2018b).

Where the revenue that resulted in the trade receivable does not contain a significant financing component, the simplified impairment model is mandatory. Where a significant financing component does exist, the entity may elect to apply the simplified impairment model or not. This election is set out in the accounting policy (IASB, 2018b).

The measurement of expected credit losses is prescribed by IFRS 9 to include reasonable and supportable information that is available without undue cost or effort at the reporting date about past events, current conditions and forecasts of future economic conditions (IASB, 2018b, pp. A368–A369). IFRS 9 requires the recognition of an impairment loss against financial assets before an actual default event occurs by making use of *'forward-looking information'* (IASB, 2018b, p. A345). This requires the entity to make use of reasonable and supportable information that is readily available to the entity without undue cost or effort. Such information includes information specific to the borrower, general economic conditions and forecasts of both aforementioned items. An example of such observable data is unemployment data (IASB, 2018b, p. A463).

The adoption of the expected loss model is not without consequences as it is considerably more difficult to implement, requiring data and information systems that entities simply do not have. The model is also more susceptible to manipulation, leading to earnings management (Camfferman, 2015).

Forward-Looking Information

The assessment of a significant increase in credit risk and the calculation of expected credit loss both incorporate forward-looking information. The incorporation of forward-looking information into the expected credit loss measurement is one of the most complex aspects of the measurement (PWC, 2017). Further, IFRS 7.35G(b) requires a description of how forward-looking information is incorporated into the expected credit loss calculation (IASB, 2018a). IFRS 9.B.5.5.49 requires an entity to use reasonable and supportable information that is available at the reporting date without undue cost or effort, including information about past events, current conditions and forecasts of future economic conditions (IASB, 2018b).

The standard does not provide an exhaustive list of indicators for the forward-looking information (IASB, 2018b, p. A462). This study will cover five key South African indicators that have been shown in previous studies to be instrumental as inputs to forward-looking information (Adeola & Ikpesu, 2017; Anjom & Karim, 2016; Nkusu, 2011; Rajha, 2016; Stander, 2021). The indicators included in the study are as follows:

- Gross domestic product, arguably the most important factor affecting default of loans, refers to the growth in the performance of the country from 1 year to the next. The gross domestic product is one common economic indicator that has been found to affect the default on loans (Adeola & Ikpesu, 2017).
- Interest rate, as the key driver of the 2008 Financial Crisis that led to many defaults on loans. Interest rate measures the true costs of borrowing and there is empirical evidence that has a found positive correlation between the increased interest rate and the default on loans (Anjom & Karim, 2016; Nkusu, 2011; Rajha, 2016).
- Inflation rate has a similar relationship as interest rate and defaults on loans. A rise in inflation leads to a reduction in purchasing power of consumers, affecting disposable income and thus increases the risk of a default in the loans (Khemraj & Pasha, 2009).
- Unemployment rate, referring to the number of unemployed individuals in a country, is directly correlated with the default rate, being that with no income no payments can be made. Thus, the default rate on loans will increase with an increase in the unemployment rate (Adeola & Ikpesu, 2017).
- Foreign exchange rate, referring to the rate at which the South African currency is exchanged with other currencies. The foreign exchange rate has been proven

to correlate with default on loans in that the weaker the exchange rate the higher the default on the loans (Stander, 2021).

The above factors directly impact the amount of the expected credit loss on provisions and are inputs into the methods used in the measurement of the expected credit loss that is forward-looking. Omitting one of these factors from the measurement of expected credit loss amount could have a direct impact on the ultimate measure of the expected credit loss provision where relevant and material. This means that these factors could be relevant and material in the measurement of expected credit losses if the omission thereof could affect the decisions made by investors and other users. Therefore, where material, it is vital that this information is communicated to investors and users to fully appreciate the credit quality of the trade receivables and the risk of default in making decisions, that is, that the credit information provided is useful in the decision of whether to invest in the entity or not. The next section addresses the disclosures of expected credit loss model, especially around the forward-looking information incorporated.

Disclosures of the Expected Credit Loss Model

The objective of general-purpose financial reporting is to provide financial information about the reporting entity that is useful to existing and potential investors, lenders and other creditors in making decisions relating to providing resources to the entity (IASB, 2023). Extensive disclosure requirements related to the expected credit loss model are contained in IFRS 7 Financial Instruments: Disclosures (IFRS 7) paragraphs 31-38. The objective of the IFRS 7 disclosure requirements is to enable users of the financial statements to evaluate the nature and extent of risks arising from financial instruments to which an entity is exposed to and how the entity manages those risks. The disclosure of forward-looking information in the financial statements is intended to be useful to users in their decision-making (IASB, 2018a).

IFRS 7.35A-38 contains the disclosure specifically for credit risk (IASB, 2018a). These disclosures apply to all financial instruments that subject the entity to credit risk; however, certain disclosures are of particular importance for trade receivables under the expected credit loss model.

IFRS 7.35B(a) requires disclosure of the methods, assumptions and information used to measure expected credit losses. IFRS 7.35B(b) requires quantitative and qualitative information regarding expected credit losses, including reasons for year-on-year changes in such amounts. IFRS 7.35B(c) requires disclosure of credit risk exposure and credit risk concentrations (IASB, 2018a). IFRS 7.35M requires disclosure of the gross carrying amount of trade receivables, as well as its associated expected credit loss allowance amount. IFRS 7.35G(b) requires disclosure of the description of how forward-looking information is incorporated into the expected credit loss calculation (IASB, 2018a).

In 2019, the JSE completed a review specifically focusing on the adoption of IFRS 9 and IFRS 15 in the previous year. The JSE primarily selected entities with December 2018 financial year-ends, covering the various industries listed on the board (JSE, 2019b). IFRS 7.35G disclosures were found to be lacking. In 2021, the JSE found several instances of disclosure omissions, specifically the expected credit loss assessments of 'other receivables', entity-specific inputs and assumptions, how forward-looking information was incorporated into the calculation, and explanations of how changes in the gross carrying amount of trade receivables contributed to the change in the expected credit loss allowance (JSE, 2021).

In 2019, the FRC published the *IFRS 9 Thematic Review: Review of Disclosures in the First Year of Application*. This was the result of a limited-scope desktop review of the financial statements of 20 entities applying IFRS 9 for the first time. Whilst this review focused heavily on banks (50%) and financial services (17%), it did also consider other industries, such as aerospace, mining, telecommunications, oil and gas, and industrial transportation. A key finding was that the disclosure quality was higher for larger banks, but smaller banks needed to improve their disclosures, especially the explanations of how expected credit losses were calculated and the sensitivity of those expected credit losses to changes in future economic conditions (FRC, 2019).

Research Methodology

The objective of this study is to assess the forward-looking information utilised in the impairment provisioning on trade receivables of non-financial entities through an empirical content analysis of annual financial statements.

The research objective is achieved through an empirical study, specifically, a content analysis of the annual financial statements, which considers both quantitative and qualitative data. Content analysis is defined by Saunders et al. (2016, p. 713) as 'an analytical technique that codes and categorises qualitative data in order to analyse them quantitatively' and is a form of documentary research where secondary data (i.e. data prepared for uses other than to achieve the research objective) is evaluated.

Content Analysis of Financial Statements

Content analysis has been widely accepted by researchers, such as Beattie et al. (2004), Kekana (2019), Krippendorff (2019), Kulik (2021), Marx and Mohammadali-Haji (2014) and Mohammadali-Haji et al. (2014) as a suitable strategy in a documentary study. The content analysis is performed through the utilisation of a checklist. The checklist was developed from the literature review and relies on the widely believed economic indicators to be incorporated as part of the forward-looking information. The results were intentionally analysed by assessing the incorporation of the five key economic indicators as part of the forward-looking information in order to conclude the appropriateness, rigour and decision usefulness of the disclosed information.

Study Population

The study population is non-financial institutions listed on the JSE Top 40 as of 1 January 2018. The JSE Top 40 consists of the largest 40 companies by investable market cap in the FTSE/JSE All-Share Index, reflecting an overall performance of various industries. The JSE Top 40 index is selected as the index represents the most significant part of the total market value of the JSE's All-Share Index (Marx & Mohammadali-Haji, 2014) and the results will be a good indication of the overall effect on the greater population of entities that prepare IFRS compliant annual financial statements. The use of the JSE Top 40, as a representative population, is further supported by other studies (Kekana, 2019; Kulik, 2021; Mohammadali-Haji et al., 2014).

As stated by Rossouw (2010), all companies listed on the JSE are required to present financial statements in compliance with IFRS (JSE, 2019a). It is therefore expected that all entities in the population will have adopted IFRS 9 at the latest by the effective date, as stipulated in IFRS 9. IFRS 9 was effective for the financial years beginning on or after 1 January 2018 (IASB, 2018b). The first financial year-end where IFRS 9 was mandatorily required (i.e. excluding entities that elected to early adopt the standard) was therefore 31 December 2018, and the financial year-ends up to but excluding 31 December 2019 are considered. Subsequent financial years are not considered.

The JSE Top 40 consists of 43 securities representing the 40 largest companies by market cap (FTSE, 2023). The list was drawn up effective of the date of the standard being introduced, which was 1 January 2018. There is one additional security which is removed as the entity has two classes of shares.

The entire study population will be tested with the exception of financial institutions. Financial institutions (19 entities) are excluded from the study population as these entities are expected to have had robust credit monitoring practices prior to the adoption of IFRS 9 and the impact of the adoption of IFRS 9 is likely to be more predictable and less significant (Koekemoer, 2022) (Table 1).

The names of the companies making up the population are listed in Annexure 1, and the financial sector entities, included in the JSE Top 40, but excluded from the population, are listed in Annexure 2.

Table 1 Reconciliation of the final population

	Number
Total securities	43
Less financial sector entities	(19)
Less duplication for multiple classes of shares	(1)
Population	23

Source: Authors' own analysis

Source of Documents

The study utilises publicly available financial statements reflecting the adoption of IFRS 9, which are considered secondary sources, as they were not developed with the intention of being used in this study. The financial statements were obtained directly from the respective entities' websites.

Research Findings and Interpretation

This section reports on the findings of the analysis and reports on the appropriateness, rigour and decision usefulness of the forward-looking disclosures. The first part confirms that the entities analysed did apply the expected credit loss model, whilst the remaining discussion is about the nature and extent of the forward-looking information disclosed.

Results from Accounting Policies

As a starting point, the researchers sought to confirm that all entities adopted the expected credit loss model. This is an important starting point as it affirms that the entities being reviewed have indeed applied the expected credit loss model and not the incurred loss model. The expected credit loss model relies on forward-looking information and the remainder of the analysis is on the forward-looking information. Table 2 provides the results for the disclosures on the adoption of the expected credit loss model.

All entities reviewed clearly applied the adoption of IFRS 9 on the effective date. It is noted that no entities adopted IFRS 9 any earlier. All entities disclosed the impact of the adoption of IFRS 9. This is evaluated further below.

Of the 23 entities reviewed, only one had not sufficiently updated its accounting policy to demonstrate compliance with IFRS 9, rather disclosing an accounting policy that was still in line with IAS 39.

Table 2 Frequency of the accounting policies disclosures

Accounting policies	Count yes	Count no	Percentage yes	Percentage no
Does the accounting policy state the application of the expected credit loss model in terms of IFRS 9?	22	1	96%	4%
Has the entity disclosed the effects of the new standard as part of the new effective standards adopted accounting policy note?	23	0	100%	0%

Source: Authors' own analysis

All entities reviewed, complied with the requirements of IFRS by the effective date, with one exception, as noted above. This exception was most likely an oversight in updating the accounting policies rather than non-compliance with the standard. Whilst the accounting policy was lacking in the entity, it was evident that the entity had indeed applied the expected credit loss model in their trade receivables provisioning thereby confirming that this was indeed a disclosure oversight.

Forward-Looking Information

To assess the appropriateness, rigour and decision usefulness of the forward-looking disclosures, the study analysed the five economic indicators identified as part of the literature review and investigated any other additional indicators disclosed as part of the forward-looking information. This was based on the observation of whether the input was explained in the disclosure insofar as it relates to how it was incorporated into the expected credit loss calculation, noting that this is a disclosure requirement of IFRS 7.35G(b).

The Disclosure of the GDP as an Input for the Forward-Looking Information

The gross domestic product is considered a key economic indicator of performance. This study found that only 9% of the population sampled disclosed the GDP as part of the forward-looking information in determining expected credit losses. Whilst the disclosure is lacking, as the disclosure is intended to explain the credit loss model used so that users fully understand the model, it could also highlight that the majority of the population sampled did not incorporate GDP in the forward-looking information despite the findings in most studies that indicate a positive correlation between the performance of the GDP and the default on the loans.

The Disclosure of the Interest Rate as an Input for the Forward-Looking Information

This study found that only 13% of the entities in the sample disclosed the impact of the future interest rate as part of the forward-looking information in determining expected credit losses. The interest rate is directly related to the financial crisis of 2008 and yet 87% of the entities sampled did not consider this an important economic indicator to the forward-looking information disclosed for the expected credit losses. Whilst the disclosure is lacking, it also warrants the question being asked as to whether the impact of interest rates was incorporated into the expected credit loss model.

The Disclosure of the Inflation Rate as an Input for the Forward-Looking Information

The economic indicator with the highest rate of consideration in the sample refers to the inflation rate, with 22% of the sample disclosing the inflation rate as an input in the forward-looking information. Despite this, 78% of the sample still did not disclose the impact of the inflation rate on their expected credit loss calculation. Furthermore, there is an expectation that the inflation rate and the interest rate would be considered in equal measure as they are often seen to work together.

The Disclosure of the Unemployment Rate as an Input for the Forward-Looking Information

The study further found that only 13% of the sample disclosed the unemployment rate as an input for the forward-looking information. This finding is similar to the interest rate inclusion. Whilst the disclosure is lacking, as the disclosure is intended to explain the credit loss model used so that users fully understand the model, it could also highlight that the majority of the population sampled did not incorporate the future expectations of the unemployment rate in the forward-looking information this despite the findings in most studies that indicate a positive correlation between the unemployment rate and the default on the loans.

The Disclosure of the Foreign Exchange Rate as an Input for the Forward-Looking Information

The economic indicator with the lowest consideration rate is the currency with only 4% of the population including this as an indicator in the forward-looking information. Similar to the above, the disclosure compliance is low, with 96% of entities not disclosing foreign exchange as an input.

Table 3 summarises the findings of the five economic indicators above.

Table 3 Forward-looking information

Has the entity disclosed the following forward-looking indicators?	Count yes	Count no	Percentage yes	Percentage no
– GDP	2	21	9%	91%
– Interest rate	3	20	13%	87%
– Inflation rate	5	18	22%	78%
– Unemployment rate	3	20	13%	87%
– Foreign exchange rate	1	22	4%	96%

Source: Authors' own analysis

Table 4 Other forward-looking information

Other forward-looking information
Changes in the political, regulatory and technological environment of the debtor and its business activities
Chemical prices
Food inflation; consumer confidence

Source: Authors' own analysis

The authors find that the disclosure of the above economic indicators is not provided in most companies, despite the IFRS requirements to provide such disclosure and the relevance of the economic indicator to users understanding the behaviour of the expected credit loss model in response to the economic indicator. Further, this also means that there are no disclosures of the behaviour of the expected credit loss model in responses to changes in the indicators, also known as a sensitivity analysis. Lastly, the absence of the disclosure of how the indicator is incorporated in the expected credit loss model also could mean that the input was not taken into account in the expected credit loss calculation.

The authors are aware that these five indicators above are not exhaustive, and the entities may even consider other factors. To provide for this, the authors captured all other factors, whether disclosed quantitatively or only qualitatively mentioned.

These findings are listed below (Table 4).

Only three entities considered the abovementioned forward-looking information, in addition to the indicators discussed above. Whether or not forward-looking information was properly considered or not cannot be determined without assessing the underlying calculations, but the detail of such information is not suitably disclosed.

Conclusion and Recommendations

This study analysed the first-time adoption of the expected credit loss model in IFRS 9 and investigated the appropriateness, rigour and decision usefulness of forward-looking disclosures provided by non-financial entities listed on the JSE as it relates to the expected credit loss provision practices on trade receivables in South

Africa. A content analysis is performed to assess the incorporation of five key economic indicators as inputs in the forward-looking information disclosed in the financial statements.

A positive finding of the study is that all entities in the population applied the expected credit loss model in compliance with IFRS 9. All entities also disclosed the effects of the new standard, as part of the effective standards adopted during the current year. The study further found that there are significant improvements to be made in the disclosure of forward-looking information being considered in trade receivables. This would in turn improve decision usefulness and enable users to make informed credit risk assessments and investment decisions.

The failure to disclose the information also opens the possibility that the impact of the key indicators has not been considered by the entities sampled. This would be a cause for concern given the importance of the indicators and the positive correlation between the indicators and the defaults in the trade receivables. Furthermore, trade receivables are an important financial statement line item and impacts the South African economy. It is therefore important that the information disclosed is appropriate and that IFRS 7 is rigorously applied to ensure that decision-useful information is provided. This in turn contributes to the stability of the economy and positively to the investment in society.

This study has limitations. Firstly, the scope restricts this study to entities that do not operate in the financial sector ('non-financial entities') listed on the Johannesburg Stock Exchange (JSE) Top 40 index at a specific point in time. As such, findings may not necessarily be representative of financial entities listed on the JSE Top 40 index, other listed entities outside of the JSE Top 40 index, and unlisted entities, at later periods in time. Secondly, the study is limited to the financial statements in the year of adoption.

The findings of the study are very relevant today as trade receivables are an important part of the business of an entity and the granting of credit is a key feature of any modern economy. Investors continuously seek more information that is useful to make informed investment decisions. With IFRS 7 being dominant in the banking sector and a lot of focus on research in the banking sector, this study highlights those improvements in the disclosures of forward-looking information in the expected credit losses on trade receivables are warranted. Preparers and auditors of financial statements are also encouraged to take note of the findings.

Acknowledgement This chapter was part of an unpublished dissertation.

Annexure 1: Names of Companies in the Population

Alpha	Instrument	ICB subsector	Gross MCAP
AGL	Anglo American	1775	R 370 115 900 986

Alpha	Instrument	ICB subsector	Gross MCAP
ANG	Anglogold Ashanti	1777	R 52 575 590 187
APN	Aspen Pharmacare Holdings	4577	R 124 734 607 357
BID	BidCorp Ltd	5337	R 100 118 157 282
BIL	BHP Billiton	1775	R 535 473 562 440
BTI	British American Tobacco PLC	3785	R 2 056 696 314 149
BVT	Bidvest Group	2727	R 71 327 059 724
CFR	Compagnie Financiere Richemont AG	3763	R 579 837 600 000
GFI	Gold Fields	1777	R 45 143 222 250
LHC	Life Healthcare Group Holdings	4533	R 38 761 282 611
MEI	Mediclinic International plc	4533	R 80 588 120 871
MNP	Mondi Plc	1737	R 119 059 468 981
MRP	Mr Price Group	5371	R 60 698 455 488
MTN	MTN Group	6575	R 251 983 394 737
NPN	Naspers	5553	R 1 569 384 044 468
REM	Remgro	2727	R 125 165 114 326
SAP	Sappi	1737	R 48 470 643 185
SHP	Shoprite	5337	R 128 320 454 934
SNH	Steinhoff International Holdings N.V.	3726	R 21 614 515 185
SOL	Sasol	1357	R 275 583 362 534
TBS	Tiger Brands	3577	R 87 697 181 030
VOD	Vodacom Group	6575	R 247 831 942 051
WHL	Woolworths Holdings	5373	R 66 977 122 505

Annexure 2: FTSE/JSE Top 40 Financial Sector Companies Excluded from the Study

Alpha	Instrument	ICB subsector	Gross MCAP
BGA	Barclays Africa Group Ltd	8355	R 150 357 060 427
CPI	Capitec Bank Hldgs Ltd	8355	R 124 894 494 329
DSY	Discovery Ltd	8575	R 118 049 211 040
FFA	Fortress REIT Ltd (A)	8674	R 21 972 408 925
FFB	Fortress REIT Ltd (B)	8674	R 44 997 715 200
FSR	Firstrand Limited	8355	R 371 796 864 706
GRT	Growthpoint Prop Ltd	8674	R 79 604 913 065
INL	Investec Ltd	8777	R 27 797 169 061
INP	Investec PLC	8777	R 60 130 099 964
ITU	Intu Properties Plc	8672	R 57 169 147 852
NED	Nedbank Group	8355	R 130 210 402 099
NRP	NEPI Rockcastle PLC	8633	R 122 626 649 777

Alpha	Instrument	ICB subsector	Gross MCAP
OML	Old Mutual	8575	R 188 962 865 806
RDF	Redefine Properties	8674	R 59 495 050 350
RES	Resilient REIT Ltd	8672	R 63 190 659 800
RMH	RMB Holdings	8355	R 110 028 148 811
RNI	Reinet Investments	8985	R 53 358 731 004
SBK	Standard Bank Group	8355	R 314 348 617 083
SLM	Sanlam	8575	R 182 416 926 065

References

Adeola, O., & Ikpesu, F. (2017). Macroeconomic determinants of non-performing loans in Nigeria: An empirical analysis. *The Journal of Developing Areas, 51*(2), 31–43. https://www.jstor.org/stable/10.2307/26415723

Anjom, W., Karim, A.M. (2016). *Relationship between non-performing loans and macroeconomic factors with Bank specific factors: A case study on loan portfolios.*

BDO IFRS Advisory Limited (BDO). (2019). *IFRS in Practice 2019 IFRS 9 Financial Instruments.* Retrieved June 21, 2024, from: https://www.bdo.global/getmedia/367334a4-2a34-446f-8f02-f024c596ec5c/IFRS_IN_PRACTICE_screen.aspx?lang=en-GB

Beattie, V., McInnes, B., & Fearnely, S. (2004). A methodology for analysing and evaluating narratives in annual reports: A comprehensive descriptive profile and metrics for disclosure quality attributes. *Accounting Forum, 28*(3), 205–236.

Brooks, R. (2018). *Bean counters: The triumph of the accountants and how they broke capitalism.* Atlantic Books.

Camfferman, K. (2015). The emergence of the 'Incurred-loss' model for credit losses in IAS 39. *Accounting in Europe, 12*(1), 1–35.

Chabal, P. (2013). The 1997 and 2008 financial crises causes and consequences compared. *Public Administration and Regional Studies, 6th Year*, Galati University Press, 2(12), 5–14.

Clikeman, P. M. (2020). *Called to account: Financial frauds that shaped the accounting profession*. Routledge.

Cohen, B. H. & Edwards, G. A. J. (2017). The new era of expected credit loss provisioning. *BIS Quarterly Review*, (March 2017), 39–56.

Correia, C., Flynn, D., Uliana, E., & Wormald, M. (2013). *Financial management*. Juta.

Dan, P. (2020). Account receivable management and corporate performances: An empirical evidence from quoted manufacturing companies in Nigeria. *Inosr Arts and Management, 6*(1), 116–129.

Financial Crisis Advisory Group (FCAG). (2009). *Report of the Financial Crisis Advisory Group, July 28, 2009.* Retrieved May 31, 2024, from: https://www.ifrs.org/content/dam/ifrs/groups/fcag/report-of-the-fcag.pdf

Financial Reporting Council (FRC). (2019). *IFRS 9 Thematic Review: Review of Disclosures in the First Year of Application*. Retrieved June 21, 2024, from: https://media.frc.org.uk/documents/IFRS_13_Fair_value_measurement.pdf

Financial Stability Forum. (2009). *Report of the Financial Stability Forum on Addressing Procyclicality in the Financial System*.

FTSE. (2023). FTSE/JSE Top 40 Index. *FTSE RUSSEL Factsheet*. Retrieved May 31, 2024, from: https://research.ftserussell.com/Analytics/Factsheets/Home/DownloadSingleIssue?issueName=J200&IsManual=false

Group of Twenty (G20). (2009). *London Summit – Leaders' Statement.* Retrieved May 31, 2024, from: https://www.imf.org/external/np/sec/pr/2009/pdf/g20_040209.pdf

IFRS Foundation. (n.d.-a). *Home – Who we are.* Retrieved May 31, 2024, from: https://www.ifrs.org/about-us/

IFRS Foundation. (n.d.-b). *IFRS 9 Financial Instruments. Home: IFRS Accounting Standards Navigator,* Retrieved May 31, 2024, from: https://www.ifrs.org/issued-standards/list-of-standards/ifrs-9-financial-instruments.html/content/dam/ifrs/publications/html-

International Accounting Standards Board (IASB). (2004). International financial reporting standards (IFRS) part a: IAS 39. In *Financial instruments: Recognition and measurements* (pp. 1635–2003). IASCF Publications Department.

International Accounting Standards Board (IASB). (2018a). *IFRS standards part a IFRS 7 financial instruments: Disclosures* (pp. A267–A327). IFRS Foundation Publications Department.

International Accounting Standards Board (IASB). (2018b). *IFRS standards part a IFRS 9 financial instruments* (pp. A345–A508). IFRS Foundation Publications Department.

International Accounting Standards Board (IASB). (2018c). *IFRS standards part a IFRS 9 financial instruments basis of conclusions* (pp. C515–C867). IFRS Foundation Publications Department.

International Accounting Standards Board (IASB). (2023). *IFRS standards part a conceptual framework for financial reporting* (pp. A11–A98). IFRS Foundation Publications Department.

Johannesburg Stock Exchange (JSE). (2019a). *JSE Limited Listings Requirements Service Issue 26.* Retrieved May 31, 2024, from: https://www.jse.co.za/sites/default/files/media/documents/2019-04/JSE%20Listings%20Requirements.pdf

Johannesburg Stock Exchange (JSE). (2019b). *Final Findings Of Our Thematic Review For Compliance With IFRS 9 And 15, Nov 6, 2019.* Retrieved May 31, 2024, from: https://www.jse.co.za/sites/default/files/jse_document_manager/RW/Internal/Accounting%20Matters/Reports/February%202019%20Report%20Back%20on%20Proactive%20Monitoring%20of%20Financial%20Statements.pdf

Johannesburg Stock Exchange (JSE). (2021). *Report on proactive monitoring of financial statements in 2021.* Retrieved May 31, 2024, from: https://www.jse.co.za/sites/default/files/media/documents/2021-02/Report%20Back%20on%20Proactive%20Monitoring%20of%20Financial%20Statements%20in%202020.pdf

Johannesburg Stock Exchange (JSE). (n.d.). *Industry Classification Benchmark (ICB): New to current ICB code mapping.* Retrieved May 31, 2024, from: https://www.jse.co.za/sites/default/files/media/documents/2021-03/Structural%20conversion%20map%20legacy%20icb%20to%20new%20icb.xlsx

Kekana, K. N. (2019). *A post-implementation review for the identification of subsidiaries in South Africa.* (Masters' Dissertation). University of Johannesburg. Available from: https://johannesburg.summon.serialssolutions.com/?#!/search/document?ho=t&include.ft.matches=f&l=en&q=A%20Post-Implementation%20Review%20for%20the%20Identification%20of%20Subsidiaries%20in%20South%20Africa&id=FETCHMERGED-johannesburg_catalog_b271492013.

Kenton, W. (2019). *Accounts Receivable (AR).* Retrieved October 29, 2019, from: https://www.investopedia.com/terms/a/ accountsreceivable.asp.

Khemraj, T, & Pasha, S. (2009). The determinants of non-performing loans: An econometric case study of Guyana. In *Caribbean Centre for Banking and Finance Bi-annual Conference on Banking and Finance, St. Augustine, Trinidad.*

Kim, J., Ng, J., Wang, C., & Wu, F. (2021). The effect of the shift to an expected credit loss model on loan loss recognition timeliness. *Risk Management & Analysis in Financial Instituitions eJournal, 1*(1), 1–52.

Koekemoer, D. (2022). *Credit risk disclosure practices by the South African banking industry* (Masters' dissertation). University of Johannesburg. Available from: https://ujcontent.uj.ac.za/esploro/outputs/graduate/Credit-risk-disclosure-practices-by-the/9917108607691/filesAndLinks?index=0

Krippendorff, K. (2019). *Content analysis: An introduction to its methodology.* SAGE.

Kulik, Y. (2021). *An analysis of the extensible business reporting language (XBRL) Compliance by South African listed companies,* (Masters' Dissertation). University of Johannesburg. Available from: https://ujcontent.uj.ac.za/esploro/outputs/graduate/An-analysis-of-the-eXtensible-Business/9911640407691

Marx, B., & Mohammadali-Haji, A. (2014). Emerging trends in reporting an analysis of integrated reporting practices by South African top 40 listed companies. *Journal of Economic and Financial Science, 7*(1), 231–250.

Milligan, S. (2009). *A catastrophe looms, Obama tells the nation*. Boston Globe.

Mohammadali-Haji, A. M., Marx, B., & Coetsee, D. (2014). An analysis of the disclosure of financial instruments by selected companies on the JSE limited. *Journal for New Generation Sciences, 12*(1), 65–88.

Nkusu, M., (2011). *Nonperforming loans and macrofinancial vulnerabilities in advanced economies* (IMF Working Paper 11/161). International Monetary Fund.

PWC. (2017). *In depth IFRS 9 impairment: how to include multiple forward-looking scenarios*. Available from: https://www.pwc.com.au/assurance/ifrs/assets/banking-ifrs9-impairment-how-to-include-multiple-forward-looking-scenarios-indepth2017.pdf

Rajha, K. S. (2016). Determinants of non-performing loans: Evidence from the Jordanian Banking Sector. *Journal of Finance and Bank Management, 4*(1), 125–136.

Rossouw, J. (2010). Empirical results of the accounting policies chosen by South African listed companies. *Meditari Accountancy Research, 18*(2), 38–56.

Saunders, M., Lewis, P., & Thornhill, A. (2016). *Research methods for business students* (pp. 122–161). Pearson.

Stander, Y. S. (2021). Quantifying the sources of volatility in the IFRS 9 impairments. *South African Journal of Accounting Research, 35*(3), 191–218.

Ukaegbu, B. (2014). The significance of working capital management in determining firm profitability: Evidence from developing economies in Africa. *Research in International Business and Finance, 31*, 1–16.

Valentin, R. & Isa, T. (2011). Financial crisis' effects on financial reporting. *"Ovidius" University Annals, Economic Sciences Series,* XI(2), 1141–1145.

Artificial Intelligence and Performance of Auditors in the Big Four Audit Firms in Nigeria

Mary Kehinde Salawu and Mariam Gbolasie Elegbede

Abstract The study analysed the effect of artificial intelligence (AI) on the performance of auditors in the audit industry in Nigeria. The study employed descriptive survey research design. The target population for the study were 3240 staff of the Big Four audit firms in Lagos State, Nigeria. This comprised Klynveld Peat Marwick Goerdeler International Limited [KPMG] (1000), Ernst & Young [EY] (640), PricewaterhouseCoopers Corporation [PwC]) (1000) and Deloitte (600). Data were sourced from the websites of the Big Four audit firms. Taro Yamane formula was used to obtain a sample size of 356 respondents, and proportionate sampling technique was used to administer structured questionnaire to the respondents to elicit information on the effect of application of AI on performance in Big Four audit firms. Data were analysed using frequency, mean, percentages and regression analysis. The results revealed that artificial intelligence usage had a positive significant effect on the performance of auditors in the audit industry. The study recommended that audit firms should consider factors such as audit software, gender and professional qualifications in AI integration strategies to maximise its benefits across diverse auditor profiles. Also, management should provide support to auditors to maximise the utilisation of specialised software for various audit tasks most especially to focus on identification of risk and assessment of internal control.

Keywords Artificial intelligence · Big Four · Audit · Performance

M. K. Salawu (✉) · M. G. Elegbede
Obafemi Awolowo University, Osun, Nigeria
e-mail: mksalawu@oauife.edu.ng

T. Moloi (ed.), *Impacting Society Positively Through Technology in Accounting and Business Processes*, Springer Proceedings in Business and Economics,
https://doi.org/10.1007/978-3-031-84885-8_46

Introduction

The modernisation of firms through the application of IT tools has transformed how financial data are recorded and disclosed as evidenced in the audit practice of the Big Four audit firms (Shaikh, 2005; Mansour, 2016; PwC, 2016; Deloitte, 2017a; KPMG, 2021). Less paper documentation is being used for data collection and preservation, which is becoming more widespread (Khemakhe, 2001; Zhao et al., 2004; Arens et al., 2014; Mansour, 2016; EY, 2019; Deloitte, 2021). This boosts the ability of auditing to bring value even when it is very complex (DeFond & Zhang, 2014; PwC, 2019a; Deloitte, 2019).

Recent studies reveal a growing trend among audit firms to incorporate artificial intelligence (AI) into their business processes (Abdulameer et al., 2022; PwC, 2021). These developments pose a problem to organisations' auditors since in such a competitive and technologically advanced business environment it is difficult to keep on top of technology and audit efficiently (Shaikh, 2005; Mansour, 2016). The financial transactions of the organisation and other information collection, documentation and processes must take place in a way that can be explored and understood by auditors, who must be similarly knowledgeable and equipped with cutting-edge technology (Issa et al., 2016; Mansour, 2016). This is to enable adequate planning and timely completion of the audit assignment to produce accurate perspectives on the entity's financial statements (Shaikh, 2005; Messier, 2014; Mansour, 2016). Using artificial intelligence for audits can help auditors tackle this issue by automating the entire auditing procedure (Moffitt et al., 2018).

However, studies on artificial intelligence have underlined that, if we are not careful, mass unemployment and increased income inequality could also lead to job instability. The implementation of AI in the field of auditing poses a potential threat to the employment of entry-level accountant (Rkein et al., 2019; Peng & Chang, 2019). Though AI brings significant advantages to the accounting and auditing field, it is not without risks. The risks encompass various aspects, with a major apprehension being the substitution of human resources with machines and software (PwC, 2019b; Moilanen, 2020). While existing literature suggested that AI may replace routine tasks, it is likely to create new employment opportunities (Deloitte, 2018; Lin & Hazelbaker, 2019; Akinadewo, 2021). It is therefore not clear how auditors perceive the use of AI in view of the potential prospects and problems associated with the deployment of AI by audit firms.

The use of AI in auditing and other accounting functions has the potential to improve efficiency, accuracy and effectiveness in these firms (Omoteso, 2012; Odoh et al., 2018; Hasan, 2022). Despite the increasing adoption of AI by audit firms globally, existing literature shows that there is not enough research that links the application of AI to firm performance (Hasan, 2022; Abdulameer et al., 2022; Dagunduro et al., 2023). This lack of empirical evidence, particularly in developing countries like Nigeria, leaves stakeholders unsure about the efficacy of AI in predicting the performance of audit firms in Nigeria, hence, this study. This study examined the efficacy of artificial intelligence in predicting the performance of the Big Four audit firms in Lagos State, Nigeria.

Literature Review

Artificial Intelligence in Auditing

According to Issa et al. (2016), AI is the ability of computer software to make well-balanced decisions, mimic cognitive functions found in the human mind, make observations of its environments and decisions that will boost its chances of accomplishing a goal. By integrating artificial intelligence throughout the entire audit procedure, repetitive tasks will be eliminated, and it will be simpler for auditors to review enormous amounts of data and obtain a whole picture of the corporate activity (Kokina & Davenport, 2017), making it simple to focus on duties that will benefit clients the most (Luo et al., 2018). As part of the auditing process, it is essential to evaluate the risk of material misstatement.

Financial statements may be materially misstated if financial effects are not sufficiently documented. As a result, transactions should be examined by auditors to ensure there are no errors. Inappropriate transactions and/or other discrepancies may be difficult for auditors to identify later if they are not identified promptly (Shaikh, 2005). High-risk transactions can easily be identified when using auditing techniques based on artificial intelligence. Due to sample population testing, manual auditing may not fully detect this. However, AI technologies allow whole-population testing.

Automation of labour-intensive operations is where most AI capabilities in audits are concentrated (Kokina & Davenport, 2017). Many AI-based technologies have been applied to auditing in the past to perform risk assessment and analytical review procedures, help with categorisation tasks (such as evaluating if a debt is recoverable or a bad debt), assess internal control, perform materiality assessments and make decisions about whether a business should continue to operate (Baldwin et al., 2006). The timing of audits is shifting as a result of analytics, becoming more proactive than reactive and improving their overall efficiency and efficacy similar to how computers changed the scope and methods of audit investigations. Automation now has cognition owing to artificial intelligence facilitating the use of instruments in auditing processes that can perform tasks considerably more swiftly and resembling human movements (Issa et al., 2016). Possibility of helping businesses to achieve predetermined goals of quality and effectiveness in audit assignments in a timely and economical manner (Deloitte, 2015). Cognitive technologies allow users to overcome the usual trade-off between speed, cost and quality, using IT to perform tasks that are still traditionally done by people. These AI technologies can assist in automating duties that auditors have long completed traditionally.

Consequently, auditors will have an increased amount of time to assess advanced analytics, spend more time offering insight and exercise greater professional judgement to concentrate on enhancing quality. For example, document review is one area where AI has proven to be quite helpful; it used to be a time-consuming, laborious process to read through endless pages of contracts to extract crucial terms. This idea has now been technologised using artificial intelligence. The learning technology that is feasible with this type of processing enables the system to be trained on a set of example papers so that it may later learn how to recognise and extract key terms (Raphael, 2015).

Deep learning's capabilities also enable auditors to automate a variety of tasks, including reviewing source documents and emails, analysing conference calls and news, processing paperwork and extracting information from them. These activities could all be used as extra proof in addition to conventional financial qualities. According to Raphael (2015), the auditing process will get efficient, smarter and more perceptive with the successful deployment of cognitive technology. The users of financial statements deserve this since it represents the future of the audit profession.

It has been suggested that these technologies could be utilised for tax auditing and planning (Graham et al., 1991; Bedard & Graham, 1994). O'Leary (1995) carried out a study presenting the numerous AI-related research initiatives being carried out at the time in the fields of management, finance and accounting. Multiple agents, machine learning, neural networks, constraint logic programming, applications of knowledge-based systems, case-based learning, etc., were the most extensively studied subjects there.

Chukwudi et al. (2018) carried out research centred on accounting firms located in the southeastern region of Nigeria to investigate the influence of artificial intelligence on accounting operations within Nigerian accounting companies. Their research, which relied on survey-based descriptive methods, revealed that expert systems played a significant role in shaping the performance of accounting functions in these firms. The authors concluded that AI had a notable impact on the efficiency of accounting activities, indicating a direct correlation between AI and the enhancement of accounting task quality. Furthermore, their findings suggested that artificial intelligence would likely result in the delegation of more decision-making responsibilities to intelligent systems.

Zehong and Li (2018) investigated the use of AI to stop accounting fraud and have a favourable effect on the calibre of accounting information. The article examined the impact of paper intelligence on accounting. According to the study's conclusions, artificial intelligence in accounting has to improve on its seven component skills to function as a fully qualified employee. A study was done by Gusai (2019) to evaluate the state of AI in accounting as well as to ascertain the value of machine learning in the domains of accounting and auditing. Finally, this research on artificial intelligence paves the way for a more hospitable atmosphere in the auditing and accounting industry. Innovations in artificial intelligence can surely greatly aid human endeavours.

Zemánková (2019) carried out research exploring how artificial intelligence affects the efficiency and integrity of the audit process. The primary findings of the research encompassed a comprehensive examination of crucial audit tasks, highlighting the importance of artificial intelligence in the auditing field. Additionally, the study shed light on the key ramifications of implementing blockchain technology in auditing, specifically emphasising enhanced efficiency and reliability, along with a reduced likelihood of errors. Furthermore, it pointed out the emergence of a new era in auditing characterised by continuous assurance. To conclude, the practical outcome of this research involved summarising the latest artificial intelligence tools and innovations developed by the four major accounting firms in Greece.

Luan et al. (2020) discussed big data and AI technology's issues and prospects in educational research, policymaking and industry. These include industry, policy and education in accounting and auditing. They claim that to effectively collaborate and fully realise the promise of AI, professionals and academics from a variety of disciplines must respond to the innovations and challenges brought about by the AI and big data revolution. They also emphasised the fact that the industry, education and policy all share several overlapping areas of interest. Along with lacking the necessary skills and information, many organisations lack vision, which is the main barrier to the collaborative approach that is required to address these shared interests.

Al-Aroud (2020) explored how artificial intelligence technologies impact audit evidence, specifically focusing on the perspectives of certified auditors working in IT companies located in Jordan. The study employed a descriptive research design and involved a sample of 314 auditors. Data for the research was gathered through a structured questionnaire. The study's results revealed a notable and meaningful influence of AI technologies on audit evidence.

Alsoulmi (2020) investigated the factors influencing the digitisation of accounting roles in small- and medium-sized enterprises (SMEs) in Saudi Arabia, along with the challenges posed by digitisation and its impact on financial performance. The study focused on the digitisation process over the past five years, with a sample of 21 Saudi graduates educated abroad. Results revealed significant correlations between the level of digitisation in accounting roles and firm size, sector, and other firm characteristics. Additionally, the study highlighted the correlation between computer-based accounting tasks and improved financial performance, noting significant variations in digitisation levels based on firm size.

In response to the 2020 COVID-19 pandemic in the United States, Rashwan and Alhelou (2020) explored the effects of implementing AI in accounting and auditing organisations. They collected data via a questionnaire from 170 accounting professionals and auditors, analysing 155 valid responses. The study found that artificial intelligence enhances professional performance, efficiency and the ability to handle complex tasks, especially during the pandemic. Results underscored the necessity of AI implementation in accounting and auditing to improve the effectiveness and timely delivery of results.

Rizk (2020) assessed the commitment of Egyptian accounting and auditing firms to enhancing job performance through the use of AI technologies. With a sample of 82 firms, the study aimed to contribute evidence for complying with international accounting standards, particularly regarding quality control needs. Findings revealed a general lack of dedication among Egyptian firms to meet requirements for AI usage in applying international accounting standards. Additionally, firms showed limited awareness of quality control procedures and standards for AI utilisation, indicating a lack of commitment to enhancing skills through AI techniques.

Qhabeel et al. (2022) proposed a model using data mining technologies to predict financial misconduct among Egyptian stock market-listed firms. The authors applied five classification algorithms and found that the naive Bayes algorithm yielded the highest accuracy. The study concluded with a model comprising indicators for performance auditors to predict financial corruption, including liquidity ratios, financial leverage and asset turnover rate, among others. Vărzaru (2022) investigated the adoption of AI technology in Romanian companies' management accounting practices. Findings from 396 managerial accounting experts suggested a likelihood of acceptance of AI techniques. The study revealed that AI techniques in management accounting foster innovation, streamline operations and enhance the usability of accounting information.

Amerahom (2022) explored the perceptions of accountants and auditors regarding their careers amid the advancement of AI technologies. Survey results indicated professionals' awareness of the impact of AI approaches on accounting and auditing methodologies. The study underscored the imperative for integrating AI techniques into these professions and enhancing professionals' awareness to optimise technology utilisation. Rodrigues et al. (2023) explored the impact of artificial intelligence on the audit profession. The research aimed to investigate how the integration of AI could revolutionise the traditional audit framework, leading to enhanced dependability and security when scrutinising financial statements. The research revealed the findings of a survey that utilised a questionnaire to understand the viewpoints of certified auditors from two separate regions in Portugal regarding the possible impact of AI in audits. According to the survey results, the auditors who participated are strongly convinced that the future of their profession relies on the integration of AI, particularly in terms of enhancing the efficiency and effectiveness of audit processes, improving sampling methods, optimising cost-effectiveness and detecting significant anomalies in financial data.

Theoretical Framework

This study was anchored on the Unified Theory of Acceptance and Use of Technology (UTAUT) model. The UTAUT model can be applied to understand the acceptance and use of AI in the Big Four audit firms. Performance expectancy is the extent to which the user perceives that utilising the technology will enhance their effectiveness in their work. In the case of AI in audit firms, performance expectancy can be related to the accuracy and efficiency of AI in detecting errors and anomalies in financial statements. Audit firms can promote the benefits of AI in improving audit quality and reducing the risk of errors.

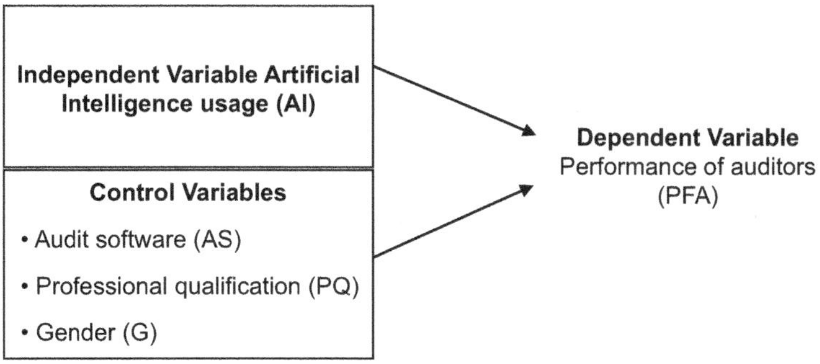

Fig. 1 Conceptual framework. (Source: Aljaaidi et al. 2023)

According to Lee et al. (2021), the UTAUT model can be applied to examine the adoption of AI-based tools in the audit industry. The authors found that performance expectancy, effort expectancy and social influence are significant factors that influence auditors' intentions to use AI-based tools. Additionally, facilitating conditions such as technical support and training also play an important role in the adoption of these tools (Fig. 1).

Methodology

A descriptive survey research design was used in this investigation. The approach has been carefully chosen to gather information and derive conclusions on the effect of AI on the performance of auditors in the Big Four audit firms in Lagos State. The study was conducted using the Big Four audit firms in Lagos State, Nigeria, which are DELOITTE, PwC, EY and KPMG.

The target population of the study which was sourced from the websites of each of the Big Four audit firms comprises over 1000 staff in KPMG, over 1000 staff in PwC, 640 staff in EY and over 600 staff in Deloitte (management staff, accountants and auditors). Random sampling technique was used for selecting the respondents in each of the Big Four audit firms. Taro Yamane formula was used to select a sample size of 356. Primary data was sourced for this study with the aid of a structured questionnaire. The questionnaire elicits responses on artificial intelligence, and these responses are scored using a 5-point Likert scale ranging from not adopted at all to highly adopted.

The instrument was certified as valid in tandem with the expert's opinion. The result of Cronbach alpha $\alpha > 0.7$ shows that Cronbach's coefficients are considered good and are said to have relatively high internal consistency.

Model Specification

This study analysed the effect of AI on the performance of the Big Four audit firms. This study adapted the model specification of Aljaaidi et al. (2023) as it is the latest and it relates to this research. This research also included control variables that previous studies have confirmed to impact auditor performance. These variables encompass the utilisation of audit software (AS), professional qualifications (PQ) and gender (G). The model developed for this study can be represented as follows:

$$\text{PFA} = \text{f}\left(\text{AI}\right)$$

$$\text{PFA} = \text{f}\left(\text{AI,AS,PQ,G}\right)$$

$$PFA_i = \beta_0 + \beta_1 AI_i + \beta_2 AS_i + \beta_3 PQ_i + \beta_4 G_i + e_i$$

where

PFA = performance of auditors
AI = artificial intelligence usage
AS = audit software usage
PQ = professional qualification
G = gender
β_0 = intercept term
β1, + β2.... β4 = the coefficient to be estimated
e = Error term

A Priori Expectation

$$\beta 1, \beta 2, \beta 3, \beta 4 > 0$$

Data were analysed using linear regression technique.

Results and Discussion

Socio-Demographic Characteristics of Respondents

As shown in Table 1, the respondents from Deloitte were 66 (18.5%), 110 (30.9%) were from KPMG, 70 (19.7%) were from EY and 110 (30.9%) were from PwC. The age distribution of the respondents indicated that 71 (19.9%) were less than 26 years. In total, 164 (46.1%) were in the 26–30 age range, 79 (22.2%) were aged

Table 1 The socio-demographic characteristics of respondents

S/N	Variables	Frequency	Percentage
1	Name of audit firm		
	Deloitte	66	18.5
	KPMG	110	30.9
	EY	70	19.7
	PwC	110	30.9
	Total	356	100
2	Age		
	Less than 26 years	71	19.9
	26–30 years	164	46.1
	31–35 years	79	22.2
	36–40 years	22	6.2
	41–45 years	9	2.5
	46–50 years	3	0.8
	51 years and above	8	2.2
	Total	356	100
3	Gender		
	Female	98	27.5
	Male	258	72.5
	Total	356	100
4	Experience		
	Less than 5 years	205	57.6
	5–10 years	122	34.3
	11–15 years	20	5.6
	16–20 years	4	1.1
	21–25 years	2	0.6
	26 years and above	3	0.8
	Total	356	100
5	Academic qualification		
	Diploma	8	2.2
	Bachelors	288	80.7
	Master's	59	16.5
	HND	2	0.6
	Total	356	100
6	Professional qualification		
	NONE	43	12.1
	CISA	4	1.1
	ICAN	264	73.3
	ANAN	2	0.6
	ACCA	28	7.8
	NIM	4	1.1
	CIA	3	0.8

(continued)

Table 1 (continued)

S/N	Variables	Frequency	Percentage
	Others	8	2.4
	Total	356	100
7	Department		
	Audit	198	55.6
	Accounting	21	5.9
	Assurance	42	11.8
	Advisory	20	5.6
	Financial risk management	5	1.4
	Consumer market	9	2.5
	Internal audit	21	5.9
	Finance	6	1.7
	Financial services audit	13	3.7
	Tax	8	2.2
	Others	13	3.7
	Total	356	100
8	Position in current employment		
	Graduate trainee	24	6.7
	Audit trainee	21	5.9
	Junior	23	6.5
	Internal auditor	55	15.4
	External auditor	185	51.8
	Partner	6	1.7
	Analyst	4	1.2
	Manager	8	2.2
	Semi associate	3	0.8
	Senior	14	3.9
	Audit associate	5	1.4
	Assistant manager	5	1.4
	Others	4	1.5
	Total	356	100
9	Level of knowledge about AI		
	Very low	9	2.5
	Low	49	13.8
	Moderate	236	66.3
	High	53	14.9
	Very high	9	2.5
	Total	356	100

Source: Field Survey (2023)

31–35. Also, 22 (6.2%) were between 36 and 40 years old, 9 (2.5%) were aged 41–45, 3 (0.8%) were in the 46–50 age group and 8 (2.2%) were 51 years old or older. The gender classification of respondent's background displayed that 98 (27.5%) of the sampled respondent were female, while 258 (72.5%) were male.

Both male and female respondents participated in the study with a large number of male respondents.

The experience showed that 205 (57.6%) respondents were less than 5 years, 122 (34.3%) had experience for about 5–10 years, 20 (5.6%) were between 11 and 15 years, 4 (1.1%) were between 16 and 20 years, 2 (0.6%) had experience of about 21–25 years and 3 (0.8%) had experience for over 26 years. The academic qualification showed that 8 (2.2%) had a diploma, 2 (0.6%) of the respondents had an HND, 287 (80.6%) had a BSc and 59 (16.6%) had a master's. As regards the professional qualifications of the respondents, 43 (12.1%) had no professional qualification, 4 (1.1%) had CISA, 261 (73.3%) had ICAN, 2 (0.6%) had ANAN, 28 (7.8%) had ACCA, 4 (1.1%) had NIM, 3 (0.8%) had CIA, 3 (0.8%) had ACA and others including CIB, GRC professional, CiPM, COREN, CFA, CIIN, ICAG and CIN were 8 (2.4%).

Furthermore, respondents for audit department were 198 (55.6%), accounting was 21 (5.9%), assurance was 42 (11.8%), advisory 20 (5.6%), financial risk management 5 (1.4%), consumer market 9 (2.5%), internal audit was 21 (5.9%), finance was 6 (1.7%), financial services audit were 13 (3.7%), tax was 8 (2.2%) and others including agricultural economics, ENR, governance, economics, sustainability, administration, GCR, insurance, energy and utilities were 13 (3.7%). The respondent's position in current employment showed that 24 (6.7%) were graduate trainees, 21 (5.9%) were audit trainees, 23 (6.5%) were juniors, 55 (15.4%) were internal auditors, 185 (51.8%) were external auditors, 6 (1.7%) were partners, 3 (0.8%) were analysts, 8 (2.2%) were managers, 3 (0.8%) were semi associates, 14 (3.9%) were seniors, 5 (1.4%) were audit associates, 5 (1.4%) were assistant managers and others including interns, assistants was 4 (1.5%). Respondent's level of knowledge about AI showed that 9 (2.5%) had very low knowledge, 49 (13.8%) had low knowledge, 236 (66.3%) were of moderate knowledge, 53 (14.9%) were high and 9 (2.5%) had very high knowledge.

The Effect of Artificial Intelligence on the Performance of Auditors in the Audit Industry

In Table 2, with a confidence level of 95%, the decision threshold is set at 0.05 ($p = 0.05$). This essentially means that when the p-value (the significance level) is less than or equal to 0.05, we should consider it statistically significant. Conversely, if the p-value is greater than 0.05, we should reject the hypothesis, indicating that it is not statistically significant.

Table 2 Decision rules

Result	Decision
$P \geq 0.05$	Not significant (reject)
$P \leq 0.05$	Significant (accept)

This is dependent on a significant level of 0.05
Source: Author's Computation (2023)

Table 3 Tests of normality

	Kolmogorov–Smirnov			Shapiro–Wilk		
	Statistic	Df	Sig.	Statistic	Df	Sig.
PFA	0.109	356	0.000	0.979	356	0.000

[a]Lilliefors significance correction

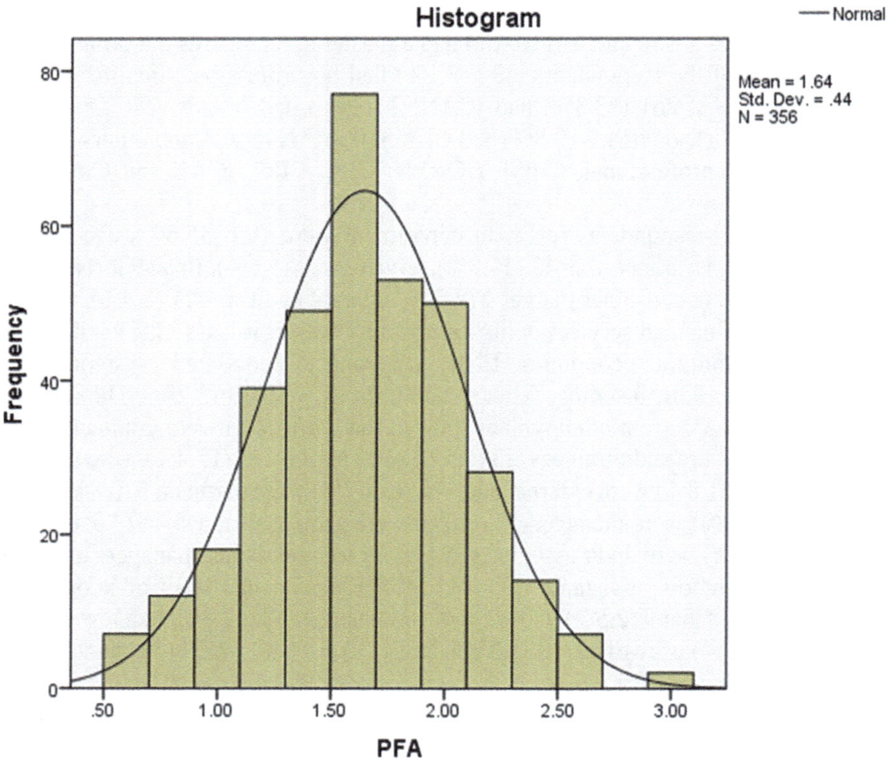

Fig. 2 Histogram showing normality of performance of auditors (PFA) in Big Four. (Source: Chattered by the Author 2023)

Hypothesis
Artificial intelligence has no significant effect on the performance of auditors in the Big Four audit firms.

Normality Test

This study employed Kolmogorov–Smirnov and Shipiro–Wilk test for the normality test of audit firm performance as contained in Table 3. Statistical evidence indicated that the statistic value of 0.109 was shown for Kolmogorov–Smirnov and

Shapiro–Wilk test statistics showed a value of 0.979. Though both tests indicated probability values of 0.000 and 0.000, a histogram presented in Fig. 2 has a relative bell-shaped curve, implying that we should reject the null hypothesis that the data variable is not normally distributed. Hence, we proceeded with further statistical analysis.

Correlation Analysis

Each cell in the correlation table contains a Pearson correlation coefficient, which indicates the strength and direction of the linear relationship between two variables. The values range from −1 (perfect negative correlation) to 1 (perfect positive correlation), with 0 indicating no linear correlation. Table 4 provides a summary analysis to test the relationships among the UTAUT constructs.

AI and P have a weak and a highly significant positive correlation of 0.153, AS and P have a weak and a highly significant positive correlation of 0.155, PQ and P have a very weak and non-significant negative correlation of -0.030, G and P have a weak and a significant positive correlation of 0.114.

There is a positive relationship between artificial intelligence and performance, audit software and performance at the 0.01 level of significance. There is a positive relationship between gender and performance at the 0.05 level of significance. No significant relationship can be found between professional qualification and performance.

Regression Analysis Results

The general form of the equation to predict PFA from AI, AS, PQ and G is predicted PFA = 3.487 + 0.093 (AI) + 0.168 (AS) − 0.022 (PQ) + 0.169 (G). This is obtained from the coefficients table, as shown in Table 5. The *p*-values (Sig.) associated with each coefficient indicate whether the relationship between each independent variable and *P* is statistically significant.

The coefficient for artificial intelligence, AI ($t = 2.286$, $p = 0.023$), is statistically significant, which indicates a *p*-value less than (<) 0.05; for audit software, AS ($t = 2.141$, $p = 0.033$), is statistically significant, which indicates a p-value less than (<) 0.05; and for gender, G ($t = 2.212$, $p = 0.028$), is statistically significant, which indicates a p-value less than (<) 0.05; while the coefficient for a professional qualification, PQ ($t = -1.093$, $p = 0.275$), is not statistically significant, which indicates a *p*-value greater than (>) 0.05. Artificial intelligence usage, AI, has the highest beta value (0.124), indicating it has the strongest standardised effect on P among the variables in the model.

The model summary showed the relationship between the variables, *R* of 0.228 showed the strength and direction of the linear relationship between the

Table 4 Correlations

		AI	AS	PQ	G	P
AI	Pearson correlation	1				
	Sig. (2-tailed)					
	N	356				
AS	Pearson correlation	0.287**	1			
	Sig. (2-tailed)	0.000				
	N	356	356			
PQ	Pearson correlation	0.077	0.041	1		
	Sig. (2-tailed)	0.149	0.437			
	N	356	356	356		
G	Pearson correlation	−0.005	0.045	0.108*	1	
	Sig. (2-tailed)	0.920	0.402	0.042		
	N	356	356	356	356	
P	Pearson correlation	0.153**	0.155**	−0.030	0.114*	1
	Sig. (2-tailed)	0.004	0.003	0.566	0.031	
	N	356	356	356	356	356

*Correlation is significant at the 0.05 level (2-tailed)
**Correlation is significant at the 0.01 level (2-tailed)

Table 5 Effect of artificial intelligence on the performance of auditors

Variables	Unstandardised coefficient		T-statistic	Sig.
	B	Std. error		
Constant	3.487	0.154	22.577	0.000
AI	0.093**	0.041	2.286	0.023
AS	0.168**	0.078	2.141	0.033
PQ	−0.022	0.021	−1.093	0.275
G	0.169**	0.076	2.212	0.028
R	0.228			
R^2	0.052			
Adjusted R^2	0.041			
F-statistic	4.810			
Durbin–Watson stat.	2.248			
Probability	0.001			

Source: Author's computation (2023)
Note: *AI*, artificial intelligence usage; *AS*, audit software usage; *PQ*, professional qualification; *G*, gender
[a]Dependent Variable: PFA *** 1%, ** 5%
[b]Predictors: (Constant), AI, AS, PQ, G

independent variable/predictor (artificial intelligence), the dependent variable (performance of auditors) and the combination of independent variable/ predictor (AI) in decimal or percentage form. In other words, a 22.8% change in performance could be explained by predictor (AI), which indicated a strong positive linear relationship. R square (the coefficient of determination), which showed 0.052, indicated that approximately 5.2% of the variance in the dependent variable (performance of auditors) is explained by the independent variable/predictor (AI), about 94.8% related to other factors not included in the model. This result indicated that embracing artificial intelligence will improve auditor's performance in the Big Four. The Durbin–Watson of 2.248 indicates the absence of autocorrelation (i.e. negative autocorrelation) in the distribution.

The ANOVA table serves as a tool to check for the fitness of data in the model, determining if there exists a statistically significant relationship among the variables. The *F*-statistics is 4.810 and the associated *p*-value is the Sig. column of 0.000 is less than 0.05 as shown in Table 5, $F\,(4, 351) = 4.810$, $p < 0.05$ (the regression model is a good fit of the data). This implies that there is a statistically significant relationship between AI and performance.

The study analysed the effect of AI on the performance of auditors in the audit industry. As shown in Table 5, a coefficient regression value of 0.093 was indicated for artificial intelligence (AI). This value was positive and further proved to be significant at 0.05 level. This indicated that embracing artificial intelligence had the tendency to improve the performance of auditors in the Big Four in Lagos Nigeria. Our finding was in line with the findings of Chen et al. (2018), who found that the audit process, if automated, would primarily improve the quality of the audit. Our finding was further supported by credibility theory as artificial intelligence in auditing could raise quality if the auditing processes were automated.

The regression analysis results indicated that several factors influence auditors' performance expectations regarding AI: artificial intelligence usage, audit software and gender had positive standardised coefficients, indicating that these factors positively influence auditors' performance expectations regarding AI while professional qualifications do not have a significant impact on auditors' performance expectations regarding AI with negative standardised coefficients. The results suggest that auditors in Lagos State generally had a high perception of AI's potential benefits in terms of accuracy, efficiency and quality of work. These findings conformed with the view of Aljaaidi et al. (2023). Artificial intelligence usage had a significant effect on performance as it supported the findings of Odoh et al. (2018), Elegunde and Osagie (2020) and Aljaaidi et al. (2023).

However, there are concerns about job security and the cost of AI implementation; this finding was supported by Rkein et al. (2019), Peng and Chang (2019) and Gopalan et al. (2021). These findings informed audit firms and policymakers about the factors that affected the adoption and acceptance of AI in the audit industry, helping them make informed decisions about AI integration and training programmes for auditors, which supported the view of Rîndașu (2017), Albawwat and Al Frijat (2021) and Dagunduro et al. (2023).

Conclusion and Recommendations

The study revealed that AI had a significant likelihood of influencing the performance of the Big Four audit firms in Lagos State, Nigeria. The utilisation of artificial intelligence in the auditing process positively influenced the performance of auditors in the audit industry, while audit software usage and gender were strong predictors for influencing the use of artificial intelligence in audit firms. The findings concluded that the use of AI has a positive significant effect on the performance of the Big Four audit firms in Lagos State, Nigeria. The study recommended that audit firms should consider factors such as audit software, gender and professional qualifications in AI integration strategies to maximise its benefits across diverse auditor profiles. Also, management should provide support to auditors to maximise the utilisation of specialised software for various audit tasks most especially to focus on identification of risk and assessment of internal control.

References

Abdulameer, M., Mansoor, M., Alchuban, M., Rashed, A., Al-Showaikh, F., & Hamdan, A. (2022). The impact of artificial intelligence (AI) on the development of accounting and auditing profession. In A. Hamdan, A. E. Hassanien, T. Mescon, & B. Alareeni (Eds.), *Technologies, artificial intelligence and the future of learning Post-COVID-19. Studies in computational intelligence* (Vol. 1019). Springer. https://doi.org/10.1007/978-3-030-93921-2_12

Akinadewo, I. S. (2021). Artificial intelligence and accountants' approach to accounting functions. *Covenant Journal of Politics & International Affairs, 9*(1), 40–55.

Al-Aroud, S. F. (2020). The impact of artificial intelligence technologies on audit evidence. *Academy of Accounting and Financial Studies Journal, 24*(2).

Albawwat, I., & Al Frijat, Y. (2021). *An analysis of auditors' perceptions towards artificial intelligence and its contribution to audit quality*. https://doi.org/10.5267/j.ac.2021.2.009.

Aljaaidi, K. S., Alwadani, N. F., & Adow, A. H. (2023). The impact of artificial intelligence applications on the performance of accountants and audit firms in Saudi Arabia. *International Journal of Data and Network Science, 7*(3), 1165–1178.

Alsoulmi, N. (2020). Factors affecting the re-entry experiences of returning Saudi international students after studying abroad. *The Educational journal of the College of Education in Sohag, 69*, 1049–1093.

Amerahom, C. (2022). The impact of using artificial intelligence applications on the future of the accounting and auditing profession. *Journal of Financial and Commercial Research, 23*(2), 244–294.

Arens, A. A., Elder, R. J., & Beasley, M. S. (2014). *Auditing and assurance services*. Pearson Education.

Baldwin, A. A., Brown, C. E., & Trinkle, B. S. (2006). Opportunities for artificial intelligence development in the accounting domain: The case for auditing. *Journal of Intelligent Systems in Accounting, Finance and Management, 14*, 77–86. https://doi.org/10.1002/isaf.277

Bedard, J. C., & Graham, L. E., Jr. (1994). Auditors' knowledge organisation: Observations from audit practice and their implications. *Auditing, 13*(1), 73.

Chen, T., Dong, X., & Yu, Y. (2018). *Audit market competition and audit quality: Evidence from the entry of big 4 into city-level audit markets in the U.S. Audit market competition and audit quality*. Routledge.

Chukwudi, O. L., Echefu, S. C., Boniface, U. U., & Victoria, C. N. (2018). Effect of artificial intelligence on the performance of accounting operations among accounting firms in South East Nigeria. *Asian Journal of Economics, Business and Accounting, 7*(2), 1–11. https://doi.org/10.9734/AJEBA/2018/41641

Dagunduro, M. E., Falana, G. A., Adewara, Y. M., & Busayo, T. O. (2023). Application of artificial intelligence and audit quality in Nigeria. *Humanities, Management, Arts, Education & the Social Sciences Journal, 11*(1), 39–56. www.isteams.net/humanitiesjournal.dx.doi.org/10.22624/AIMS/HUMANITIES/V11N1P4

DeFond, M., & Zhang, J. (2014). A review of archival auditing research. *Journal of Accounting and Economics, 58*(2-3), 275–326.

Deloitte. (2015). Cognitive technologies: The real opportunities for business. *Deloitte Review, 16*, 113–129.

Deloitte. (2018). https://www2.deloitte.com/content/dam/Deloitte/us/Documents/audit/ASC/us-aers-robotic-process-automation-internal-controls-over-financial-reportingconsiderations-for-developing-and-implementing-bots-.pdf

Deloitte. (2019). *Audit 4.0: The future of auditing*. Retrieved from https://www2.deloitte.com/us/en/insights/focus/signals-for-strategists/future-of-auditing.html

Deloitte. (2021). *Artificial intelligence in audit*. Retrieved from https://www2.deloitte.com/global/en/pages/audit/articles/artificial-intelligence-audit.html

Elegunde, A., & Osagie, R. (2020). Artificial intelligence adoption and employee performance in the Nigerian banking industry. *International Journal of Management and Administration, 4*(8), 189–205. https://doi.org/10.29064/ijma.734734

EY. (2019). *The adoption of artificial intelligence in auditing*. Retrieved from https://www.ey.com/en_gl/assurance/the-adoption-of-artificial-intelligence-in-auditing

Gopalan, P., Anitha, R., Ravi, K., & Krishna, M. (2021). Auditors' perception on the impact of artificial intelligence on professional skepticism and judgment in Oman. *Universal Journal of Accounting and Finance, 9*(5), 1184–1190. https://doi.org/10.13189/ujaf.2021.090527

Graham, L., Damens, J., & Vanness, G. (1991). Developing risk and advisorism-An expert system for risk identification Auditing. *A Journal of Practice & Theory, 10*(1), 69–96.

Gusai, O. P. (2019). Robot human interaction: Role of artificial intelligence in accounting and auditing. *Indian Journal of Accounting (IJA), 51*(1), 59–62.

Hasan, A. R. (2022). Artificial intelligence (AI) in accounting & auditing: A literature review. *Open Journal of Business and Management, 10*, 440–465. https://doi.org/10.4236/ojbm.2022.101026

Internal controls over financial reporting considerations for developing and implementing bots (2018).

Introduction to Robotic Process Automation, a Primer. (2015). *Institute for robotic process automation*. Retrieved from http://irpaai.com/introduction-to-robotic-processautomation-a-primer

Issa, H., Sun, T., & Vasarhelyi, M. A. (2016). Research ideas for artificial intelligence in auditing: The formalization of audit and workforce supplementation. *Journal of Emerging Technologies in Accounting, 13*(2), 1–20. https://doi.org/10.2308/jeta-10511

Khemakhe, J. (2001). Integral auditing. *International Journal of Government Auditing, 28*(2), 6–9.

Kokina, J., & Davenport, T. H. (2017). The emergence of artificial intelligence: How automation is changing auditing. *Journal of Emerging Technologies in Accounting, 14*(1), 115–122. https://doi.org/10.2308/jeta-51730

KPMG. (2021). *How KPMG is using artificial intelligence*. Retrieved from https://home.kpmg/xx/en/home/insights/2020/06/how-kpmg-is-using-artificial-intelligence.html

Lee, H. J., Kim, Y., & Yoo, Y. (2021). Understanding the adoption of artificial intelligence in auditing: An application of the UTAUT model. *Journal of Information Systems, 35*(1), 83–101. https://doi.org/10.2308/isys-52445

Lin, T. W., & Hazelbaker, R. (2019). Artificial intelligence in auditing: A research synthesis. *Journal of Information Systems, 33*(2), 1–24.

Luan, H., Geczy, P., Lai, H., Gobert, J., Yang, S. J. H., Ogata, H., Baltes, J., Guerra, R., Li, P., & Tsai, C. C. (2020). Challenges and future directions of big data and artificial intelli-

gence in education. *Frontiers in Psychology, 11*, Article ID: 580820. https://doi.org/10.3389/fpsyg.2020.580820
Luo, J., Meng, Q., & Cai, Y. (2018). Analysis of the impact of artificial intelligence application on the development of accounting industry. *Open Journal of Business and Management, 6*(4), 850–856.
Mansour, E. (2016). Factors affecting the adoption of computer assisted audit techniques in audit process. *Findings from Jordan. Business and Economic Research*, 200–269.
Messier, W. F., Jr. (2014). An approach to learning risk-based auditing. *Journal of Accounting Education, 32*(3), 276–287.
Moffitt, K. C., Rozario, A. M., & Vasarhelyi, M. A. (2018). Robotic process automation for auditing. *Journal of Emerging Technologies in Accounting, 15*(1), 1–10.
Moilanen, K. (2020). *Artificial Intelligence: An analysis of perceptions of the impact of AI on the financial labour market*, 1–40.
O'Leary, D. E. (1995). AI in accounting, finance and management. *Intelligent Systems in Accounting, Finance and Management, 4*, 149–153. https://doi.org/10.1002/j.10991174.1995.tb00088.x
Odoh, L. C., Echefu, S. C., Ugwuanyi, U. B., & Chukwuani, N. V. (2018). Effect of artificial intelligence on the performance of accounting operations among accounting firms in South East Nigeria. *Asian Journal of Economics, Business and Accounting, 7*(2), 1–11.
Omoteso, K. (2012). The application of artificial intelligence in auditing: Looking back to the future. *Expert Systems with Applications, 39*(9), 8490–8495.
Peng, Y., & Chang, J. S. (2019). An exploration on the problems of replacing accounting professions by AI in the future. In *ICIBE 2019*. https://doi.org/10.1145/3364335.3364345.
PricewaterhouseCoopers (PwC). (2016). *Blockchain and smart contract automation: How smart contracts automate digital business*. Available: https://www.PwC.com/us/en/technology-forecast/2016/blockchain/PwCsmart-7
Professional Accountants - the Future: Generation Next. (2016). *Association of Chartered Certified Accountants*. Retrieved from https://www.accaglobal.com/content/dam/ACCA_Global/Technical/Future/generation-next-full-report
PwC. (2019a). *How Tax is leveraging AI —including machine learning —in 2019.*
PwC. (2019b). *Talent trends 2019: Upskilling for a Digital World: Part of PwC's 22nd Annual Global CEO Survey trends series* (p. 10).
PwC. (2021). *How PwC is using artificial intelligence*. Retrieved from https://www.PwC.com/gx/en/issues/data-and-analytics/artificial-intelligence/PwC-how-were-using-ai.html
Qhabeel, S., Hafez, S., & Sadah, E. (2022). A proposed model for reviewing performance to predict financial corruption among listed companies on the Egyptian stock market using data mining technique: Empirical study. *Egyptian Journal of Commercial Studies, 46*(4), 467–530.
Raphael, J. (2015). *How artificial intelligence can boost audit quality*. CFO. www.cfo.com/accounting-tax/2015/06/artificial-intelligence-can-boost-audit-quality/
Rashwan, A. R. M., & Alhelou, E. M. (2020). The impact of using artificial intelligence on the accounting and auditing profession in light of the Corona pandemic. *Journal of Advance Research in Business Management and Accounting.*
Rîndaşu, S. M. (2017). Emerging information technologies in accounting and related security risks – what is the impact on the Romanian accounting profession. *Journal of Accounting and Management Information Systems, 16*, 581–609. https://doi.org/10.24818/jamis.2017.04008
Rizk, A. (2020). The contribution of artificial intelligence technologies in supporting the quality of professional performance of accounting and auditing firms in Egypt: Empirical study on large accounting and auditing firms. *Accounting Thought, 24*(2), 480–563.
Rkein, H., Issa, Z., Awada, F., & Hejase, H. (2019). *Impact of automation on accounting profession and employability: A qualitative assessment from Lebanon* (pp 372–385).
Rodrigues, L., Pereira, J., da Silva, A. F., & Ribeiro, H. (2023). The impact of artificial intelligence on audit profession. *Journal of Information Systems Engineering and Management, 8*(1), 19002. https://doi.org/10.55267/iadt.07.12743

Shaikh, J. M. (2005). E-commerce impact: Emerging technology - electronic auditing. *Managerial Accounting Journal, 20*(4), 408–421.
Vărzaru, A. A. (2022). Assessing artificial intelligence technology acceptance in managerial accounting. *Electronics, 11*(14), 2256.
Zehong, L. & Li, Z. (2018). *The impact of artificial intelligence on accounting*. Advances in Social Science, Education and Humanities Research (ASSEHR), the International Conference on Social Science and Higher Education (ICSSHE), 181
Zemánková, A. (2019). Artificial intelligence and blockchain in audit and accounting: Literature review. *WSEAS Transactions on Business and Economics, 16*, 568–581. www.wseas.org/multimedia/journals/economics/2019/b245107-089.pd
Zhao, N., Yen, D. C., & Chang, I. (2004). Auditing in the e-commerce era. *Information Management & Computer Security, 12*, 389–400. https://doi.org/10.1108/09685220410563360

Funding and Financing Options of Smart City Exemplars: A Model for Upcoming Smart Cities

Dolapo Faith Sule and Tankiso Moloi

Abstract Smart city initiatives are fast becoming popular around the world due to the need to cater for the increasing population in many cities. One of the innovative means of developing smart city is the utilisation of information and communication technology (ICT) to promote inter-operability of systems, better life for the residents, effective transportation, security, sustainability of resources, energy supply services, healthcare and so on. Some countries have been utilising ICT to sustain smart city development initiative, while others are still at proposal stage. The Institute for Management Development (IMD) index reveals in 2023 that Zurich in Switzerland, Oslo in Norway, Canberra in Australia, Copenhagen in Denmark, Lausanne in Switzerland and London in England are the top six smartest cities in the world. Smart city initiatives in these countries were funded and financed from different sources. Despite the advantages of smart city initiatives, the attempts to develop new smart cities across the world have been hampered by financial constraints. This study, therefore, explores the funding and financing paradigm of the top six smart city exemplars in the world in building an adaptable model for upcoming smart cities. The findings reveal that public–private partnerships (PPPs) account for the majority (52%) of funding for smart city projects in the examined top six smart cities. Government funding at various levels makes up 42% of the total funding while private financing contributes only 6% to smart city projects in these exemplary cities. These findings suggest that the success of these cities in becoming global smart city leaders can be attributed to the strong collaboration between the public and private sectors. Therefore, this study recommends that upcoming smart cities should seek more public–private partnership to implement smart city initiatives.

Keywords Smart city development · Financing constraint · Financing and funding model · Project implementation

D. F. Sule (✉) · T. Moloi
College of Business and Economics, University of Johannesburg, Johannesburg, South Africa
e-mail: dsule@uj.ac.za, smoloi@uj.ac.za

T. Moloi (ed.), *Impacting Society Positively Through Technology in Accounting and Business Processes*, Springer Proceedings in Business and Economics,
https://doi.org/10.1007/978-3-031-84885-8_47

Introduction

Smart city, as defined by the Institute for Management Development (IMD), is a city that integrates the use of digital technologies into its networks, services and infrastructure to enhance efficiency, sustainability and liveability for its residents and businesses (IMD, 2023). Smart cities basically utilise information and communication technologies (ICTs) to optimise city functions, enhance government services and improve citizen welfare. The idea of smart city has garnered considerable interest in recent time as a solution to the issues arising from the rapid urbanisation of cities. The global trend towards urban migration has become a major concern for governments and policymakers as more people are relocating from rural areas to cities. In the 1950s, urban populations accounted for 30% (751 million) of the total population of the world, which rapidly rose to 55% (4.2 billion) in 2018 and projected to reach 68% by 2050 (United Nations Department of Economic and Social Affairs, UN DESA, 2018). Due to this increase in urban population, governments across the world have begun to device means to make cities liveable for residents by providing modern infrastructure.

The first-generation smart cities began in the United States as far back as the 1960s and 1970s, with the use of databases aerial photography and cluster analysis to collect data, direct resources, and make reports by the US Community Analysis Bureau aimed at providing effective services, preventing disaster and reducing poverty (The Welding Institute, TWI, 2024). Thereafter, Barack Obama administration implemented some notable smart city projects, thereby triggering the global movement towards urban innovation. The Obama administration committed about $160 million in funding of smart city applications, user interface and communication network, Internet-connected vehicle pilot and Internet of Things (IoT), specifically to reduce urban congestion, protect the environment, improve transportation safety and support economic growth (New et al., 2017). This momentum was further amplified by various initiatives across the globe. For instance, the European Union Digital Agenda was implemented to enhance urban life via integrated software (European Innovation Partnership on Smart Cities and Communities, EIP-SCC, 2020). While Japan's i-Japan strategy and the 2015 Singapore Intelligent Nation plan focused on leveraging technology to improve urban living conditions (Amine, 2024). China also demonstrated its commitment to urban transformation by launching a programme to construct 500 smart city projects in 2018 (Hamilton & Zhu, 2017; Hu, 2020). Similarly, India launched a smart city programme, targeting the development of 100 smart city projects to improve the quality of life of its residents (Bajpai & Biberman, 2021). These initiatives collectively demonstrate the importance of modern urban planning and the development of smart cities to cater for this growing city population.

Based on the numerous benefits that smart city projects can provide; new smart cities are being developed with initiatives that would help them proffer solutions to the challenges brought about by urbanisation. This is because smart city projects foster interoperability among systems, enhance residents' quality of life, improve transportation efficiency, ensure security, promote resource sustainability, provide energy services and enhance healthcare access (Amine, 2024). Furthermore, smart city infrastructures play a crucial role in optimising resource utilisation, enhancing infrastructure management, elevating living standards, supporting environmental initiatives, facilitating efficient waste disposal, attracting investments and stimulating economic development (Aik, 2021).

Despite these numerous benefits that can be derived from smart city projects, many urban areas are struggling to develop and implement such initiatives due to financial limitations (Yorgos et al., 2019; Hu, 2020; Blanck & Ribeiro, 2021). This is because the idea of implementing smart city projects requires substantial financial resources, which can be a significant obstacle for cities seeking to transition to smart cities. For a city to transition to a smart city, it is important to understand the various funding and financing sources that can be explored. According to a report by Hamilton and Zhu (2017), funding and financing are often used interchangeably in the context of project implementation but have distinct meanings. In the context of infrastructure investments, financing involves securing funding from financial institutions to support project execution. In contrast, funding refers to the provision of capital by organisations or governments for the execution of specific projects (Hamilton & Zhu, 2017).

Given this distinction, the funding and financing paradigm of smart cities have evolved over the years as cities are developing various strategies to secure more sources of funding and financing for smart city projects. This shift is driven by the understanding that traditional funding sources, including municipal budgets and grants may not be sufficient to cover the substantial expenses involved in executing smart city projects (Yorgos et al., 2019). As a result, it is crucial to investigate alternative funding and financing options that can provide the necessary resources to support the transformation of cities into intelligent, eco-friendly and resilient urban environments.

Therefore, this study focuses on analysing the funding and financing options used by the six leading smart cities in the world to develop a model that can guide the implementation of upcoming smart city projects. This is because to the best of our knowledge there is no known empirical research on the funding and financing paradigms employed by existing smart cities. Most of the available information is from news sources, reports, rankings, official websites of companies, international organisations and governments, academic search engines and databases. Given this gap, this study analyses the various smart city projects of the top six smart cities and their funding and financing options to develop a comprehensive model that can guide upcoming smart cities in selecting and implementing the most suitable funding and financing strategies based on their specific needs, resources and local context.

Related Literature

Smartest Cities in the World

The IMD has been publishing its annual Smart City Ranking since 2016 (IMD, 2023). This ranking assesses cities based on their performance in various areas such as infrastructure, technology and governance. The smart city ranking index by IMD and Singapore University of Technology in 2023 reveals that Zurich in Switzerland, Oslo in Norway, Canberra in Australia, Copenhagen in Denmark, Lausanne in Switzerland, London in the United Kingdom, Singapore in Asia, Helsinki in Finland, Geneva in Switzerland and Stockholm in Sweden are the 10 smartest cities in the world. These cities have financed and funded different smart city initiatives which has made them the most notable smart city exemplars. Table 1 shows the ranking of these cities in the last 4 years.

Distinguishing Between Funding and Financing Options for Smart City Projects

Financing smart city involves securing funding from financial institutions to support smart city project execution. While there are distinct differences between funding and financing, the primary objective of this study is not to differentiate these concepts. Instead, the study focuses on the funding and financing options used by successful smart city exemplars. This information can serve as a guiding light for emerging smart cities as they navigate their own smart city development paths. Therefore, Table 2 shows the different funding and financing options used by these smart city exemplars.

Table 1 Top 10 smart cities and their ranks in the last 4 years

No	City	Rank 2023	Rank 2021	Rank 2020	Rank 2019
1	Zurich	1	1	1	1
2	Oslo	2	2	2	2
3	Canberra	3	–	–	–
4	Copenhagen	4	5	3	4
5	Lausanne	5	4	–	–
6	London	6	3	10	3
7	Singapore	7	7	7	10
8	Helsinki	8	9	5	6
9	Geneva	9	6	8	7
10	Stockholm	10	11	9	9

Source: IMD (2023) Smart City Index Report

Table 2 Funding and financing sources distinguished

No	Funding sources	Financing sources
1	Property taxes	Commercial banks
2	Business taxes	Development banks
3	Municipal income tax	Project bonds
4	Tolls	Green bonds
5	User charges	Tax increment
6	Pay-for-performance model	Leasing
7	Asset disposal	Vendor financing
8	Federal grants	Credit guarantees

Projects Implemented by Smart City Exemplars and Their Funding and Financing Options

The funding and financing sources for smart cities are diverse because smart city projects are multifaceted, based on the diverse needs of the cities. The private sector, non-governmental organisations and governments at various levels have been involved in executing smart city projects (Younus & Abumandil, 2022). It is also worthy of note that even though cities are smart, they are smart for different reasons. Likewise, smart city initiatives by different cities are funded and financed from different sources. Given these distinctions, the funding and financing sources of each of the top six smart city exemplars have, therefore, been discussed in this study.

Funding and Financing Options of Zurich Smart City

Zurich has a total population of 1,443,000 in 2024 (World Population Review, 2024). According to the Canton of Zurich, the population is expected to increase by 280,000 people in the year 2040, noting that 80% of the anticipated population growth is projected to take place in cities (Schrotter & Hurzeler, 2020). In view of the expected growth in the population of residents in Zurich, the government has implemented a number of projects under its 2030 Smart City Strategy to make the city liveable for residents (Joss et al., 2019). For instance, the digital city project which uses the 3D spatial data to alternate themes of bridges and places in the city was implemented in 2019.

The other implemented projects are Power-to-Heat (P2H) project, which utilises surplus renewable energy to generate heat for residences in the Zurich city. Also, project eZürich was implemented to encourage the use of digital technologies to enhance the efficiency of public services and improve citizen involvement in the City's decision-making (Morningstar, 2021). Implemented project in Zurich includes the Zurich smart parking project that uses real-time data to lead drivers to vacant parking spaces. Also, the Sharing Cities project in Zurich provides smart city solutions that encourage resource sharing, maintainable mobility and citizen participation.

Funding and financing sources of Zurich Smart City are from (i) government budgets in which municipal, regional and national governments allocate funds for smart city initiatives through their annual budgets; (ii) public–private partnerships (PPPs) that involves collaborations between governments and private companies; (iii) grants and subsidies from governments, international organisations and non-profit entities; (iv) venture capital and investment funds; (v) crowdfunding platforms which allow individuals and organisations to raise funds for specific smart city projects; (vi) bonds and loans; (vii) EU Funding from the European Union for smart city projects through programmes like Horizon Europe and the European Regional Development Fund (ERDF); (viii) revenue generation (Zurich City Council, 2018) (Table 3).

Funding and Financing Options of Oslo Smart City in Norway

Oslo Smart City has a population of 1,100,868 residents as of 2024 (World Population Review, 2024). The city has actively engaged in a variety of smart city initiatives aimed at enhancing key areas such as green energy, circular economy, urban mobility and citizen-centric services. To manage these key areas, Oslo employs information and communication technology (ICT) and Internet of Things (IoT) solutions (Nordic Smart City Network, 2023). Over the years, the city has implemented numerous innovative projects to improve the lives of its citizens. These projects include the use of electric buses, zero-emission construction sites, circle-based waste management, water management, city mobility, healthcare, education, industry incentives and green energy systems (Sustainability Report, 2023). Oslo's city development is citizen-oriented, with the government continuously digitalising, based on the needs of its citizens.

The government in Oslo city provides various funding avenues for innovative projects. One such initiative is the regional research fund, offering funding ranging from 200,000 to 350,000 NOK per project (Oslo Business Region, 2020). Additionally, the report also identifies government support for test and development projects with funding ranging from 50,000 to 1,000,000 NOK. Municipalities also collaborate with companies and research communities to develop new solutions, products and services tailored to the needs of the citizens (Nordic Smart City Network, 2023). Furthermore, the City of Oslo offers industry-specific support schemes for city development, volunteering, culture and sustainability (Table 4).

Table 3 Funding and financing options of Zurich Smart City

Some implemented projects	Description	Funding and financing options	Funding and financing sources	Some key references
Power-to-Heat (P2H) System	Utilises surplus renewable energy to generate heat for residences in the Zurich city	Public–private partnerships (PPPs)	Government budget, public–private partnership, grants and subsidies, international organisations, non-profit agencies, venture capital, crowdfunding, European Union	Schrotter and Hurzeler (2020) Morningstar (2021) Joss et al. (2019) Zurich City Council (2018)
e-zurich	Encourage the use of digital technologies to enhance the efficiency of public services and improve citizen involvement in the City's decision-making	Public funding (government budget, European Union)		
Smart parking	Smart parking project that uses real-time data to lead drivers to vacant parking spaces	Public funding		
Sharing cities	It provides smart city solutions that encourage resource sharing, maintainable mobility and citizen participation	Public funding		
e-foresight	A project that focused on developing innovative solutions for energy-efficient urban infrastructure and mobility systems	Private financing		
Smart public transportation	Use of smart technologies such as real-time tracking, predictive maintenance and optimisation algorithms to improve public transportation systems using	Public funding		
Energy management projects	Optimises energy usage in buildings and public spaces through smart grids, renewable energy integration and energy-efficient technologies	Public–private partnerships (PPPs)		
Safety and security	Use of smart surveillance systems, emergency response mechanisms, and crowd management solutions to enhance public safety and security	Public funding		
Smart city lab	An innovative lab created for employees to collaborate with external innovators like companies and universities to test new methods and prototypes	Public–private partnerships (PPPs)		

Table 4 Funding and financing sources of Oslo Smart City

Implemented projects	Description	Funding and financing options	Funding and financing sources	Some key references
Innovation District Hovinbyen	Established to strengthen research-based innovation in green transitioning and circular economy	Public funding	Government budget, public–private partnership, European Union	Sustainability Report (2023) Nordic Smart City Network (2023) Oslo Business Region (2020)
Start-up Service	Created to foster social equity and job creation and to support social and green entrepreneurship	Public funding		
Circular Resource Center	Established to promote recycling of materials in the construction sector in Oslo to reduce the climate footprint from material use	Public–private partnerships (PPPs)		
Oslobygg & Over Easy Solar	This project combines a green roof with a solar system without compromising either, using lightweight solar panels that can be easily installed on top of a sedum roof	Private financing		
Soundsensing	This is a collaboration between the Agency for Water and Wastewater Services and a company developing IoT sound sensors to automatically identify and notify about potential issues with water pumps and valves	Public–private partnerships (PPPs)		

Funding and Financing Options of Canberra Smart City in Australia

Canberra, the capital of Australia, has secured a notable ranking of third in the Smart City Index (IMD, 2023). As of 2024, the population of Canberra city stands at 477,567, according to the World Population Review (2024). At the initial stage, the government of Canberra committed $50 million in infrastructure to the development of smart city initiatives (Hu, 2020). This significant investment was announced by Angus Taylor, the Assistant Minister for Cities and Digital Transformation under Malcom Turnbull government, during the launch of the Smart Cities Plan in 2016. Under this Plan, local councils were eligible to apply for up to $5 million in funding to support local smart technology projects. Canberra's vision for a smart city is centred around fostering a sustainable and competitive economy, laying the groundwork for an integrated programme that will shape the city's future. This involves embracing a digital mindset and delivering integrated smart city initiatives through an open and diversified local economy.

The Australian government continues to support innovative projects that integrate smart technology, data-driven decision-making and people-centred design (Canberra_EU-Delegation-Presentation, 2017). Additionally, the Australia Capital Territory (ACT) Government has taken a proactive part in fostering the development of the renewable energy sector in Canberra through innovation grants (Australia Government, 2016). These grants, part of the ACT Government's renewable energy innovation fund, have provided the energy sector with over $1.2 million in funding for clean energy innovation. So far, the Australian government has already funded 52 smart city projects (Table 5).

Table 5 Funding and financing sources of Canberra Smart City

Some implemented projects	Description	Funding and financing options	Funding and financing sources	Some key references
400 innovation jobs	$100 m was allocated to the ACT economy to sponsor 400 innovation jobs	Public funding	1.Canberra Innovation Network 2. $1b annual international education revenue 3. Public–private partnerships (PPTs) Renewable Energy Innovation Fund (REIF)by the ACT Government Government-based financing options Tax increment financing (TIF) Green bonds Crowdfunding	Canberra EU-Delegation-Presentation (2017) Hu (2020) Australia Government (2016)
Canberra Cyber Hub	Established to strengthen cyber security sector	Public–private partnerships		
Tertiary institutions and industry partnerships	$9.5m invested in 12 research, tertiary and industry partnerships	Public–private partnerships		
Tourism	Pre-pandemic visitors spend $2.5b per annum	Public–private partnerships		
CBRfree Wifi network	Canberra has implemented the CBRfree WiFi network, which provides unlimited Internet service to residents in public spaces	Public funding		
Other projects	ACT powered by 100% renewable electricity, $150m Sustainable Household Scheme rolled out, 20 hydrogen-fuelled vehicles added to the government fleet, electric vehicles incentivised, laptops for every public high school student, 700+ government transactions and services online	Public funding		

Funding and Financing Options of Copenhagen Smart City Project

Copenhagen, with an average population of 1,391,205 residents, is renowned as one of the most liveable cities in the world (World Population Review, 2024). The capital of Denmark is also pursuing smart city initiatives, planning to attain carbon neutrality by 2025 to enhance sustainability. The city upholds high standards in areas such as tap water quality and energy conservation through smart public lighting with LED, positioning itself as a beacon for the green economy (Kirk, 2015). Approximately 250 companies and start-ups are already engaged in driving city development in Copenhagen, with the Danish government engaging in programmes to incentivise more innovators and attract more entrepreneurs (Elsasser, 2023). Leveraging the high level of citizen engagement in Denmark, the city fosters participatory and inclusive projects. Interconnected initiatives in Copenhagen address many smart cities plans simultaneously, including the Strategic Climate Action Plan to reduce CO2 emissions by 20% en route to zero emissions, traffic management enhancements, smart lighting installations at intersections and an intelligent traffic solutions platform utilising Wi-Fi-enabled devices to provide data for transportation monitoring and optimisation (Ulterino et al., 2021). Many of these projects in Copenhagen are classified in Table 6.

Funding and Financing Options of Lausanne Smart City in Switzerland

The population of Lausanne Smart City in 2024 is 465,032 (World Population Review, 2024). The funding and financing strategies employed by Lausanne Smart City in Switzerland encompass a range of approaches to bolster its smart city endeavours. Similar to numerous other smart cities, Lausanne employs innovative financial frameworks to actualise its vision. The funding and financing mechanisms of Lausanne's smart city initiatives are broadly public funding, private financing and public–private partnerships (PPP) (Calzada, 2021; Hamilton & Zhu, 2017; European Commission, 2021). Notable smart city projects in Lausanne include, but not limited to, Eco-Neighbourhoods and the establishment of a Public Wi-Fi Network (Hernandez et al., 2014; Repsol, 2024) (Table 7).

Table 6 Funding and financing sources of Copenhagen Smart City

Implemented projects	Description	Funding and financing options	Funding and financing sources	Some key references
Project Air View	A collaboration between Copenhagen Solutions Laboratory and Google to measure air pollution in the city's streets	Public–private partnerships	1. Energy efficiency loan 2. Public–private 'Green Bank' to seed investment in the cleantech sector 3. Green bond market 4.Public–private partnerships (PPPs) 5. Cities Mission Blending Facility co-financed by Horizon Europe, InvestEU, the EIB Group 6. Investment loans	Merk (2012) Ulterino (2021)
Signature AI	Uses artificial intelligence to reduce and optimise energy consumption in Copenhagen Municipality's buildings, leading to energy and carbon savings	Public–private partnerships		
RAPID	Uses 3D model to assess possible events in public spaces	Public funding		
Copenhagen Connecting plan	It uses data from cell phones, GPS, and sensors to reduce congestion, air pollution and CO_2 emissions. Collaboration between private companies like Rambøll and the tertiary institutions	Public–private partnerships		
Smart lighting system	Enables remote lighting management and control to improve safety for drivers and cyclists	Public–private partnerships		

Table 7 Funding and financing sources of Lausanne Smart City

Implemented projects	Description	Funding and financing options	Some key references
Eco-Neighbourhoods	New neighbourhoods marked as 2000-Watt sites with buildings complying with the environmental regulations	Public–private partnerships (PPP)	European Commission (2021), Hamilton and Zhu (2017), Hernandez et al. (2014), Repsol (2024), Calzada (2021)
Public Wi-Fi Network	Created Quartier du Flon district with reliable and efficient public Wi-Fi network with 44 outdoor and 14 indoor access points	Public funding	
Data collection and analysis	Digital tools used to collect data from mobile phones to study and monitor the behavioural attributes of inhabitants	Public funding	

Funding and Financing Options of London Smart City in the United Kingdom

London, a leading city in the United Kingdom, has a population of 9,748,000 (World Population Review, 2024). In an interview conducted by Susan Hall with the Mayor of London, it was revealed that the city's initiatives are primarily financed from existing budgets (Greater London Authority, 2018). Noteworthy programmes, such as 'Connected London' and the 'Digital Talent Programme', received support from the European Commission until 2021, as well as through collaborative efforts with external partners. Furthermore, specific allocations were made in 2019, including £100,000 per annum for the London Office of Technology and Innovation, £50,000 for the Open Data Institute and £50,000 for cybersecurity support from CIU budgets (Greater London Authority, 2018). In addition, the Smart London team oversees the Sharing Cities Programme, which utilises €24 million in EU funding to pilot smart city technologies in six European cities. Additional funding streams include the Medtech London Funding, with £50,000 allocated between 2016 and 2017, £24,500 in 2017/2018 and £30,000 in 2018/2019 (Buchholz, 2023).

Also, the London Simulator Funding to the tune of £318,816 was received from the Greater London Authority (GLA), £110,000 from the European Union (EU) and £50,000 from Transport for London (TfL) from the period spanning from 2016/2017 to 2019/2020. Recently, London's Mayor Sadiq Khan announced the launch of a £500 million (~US$635 million) fund to support organisations in achieving net zero emission by 2030 (Nexus Integra, 2017; Greater London Authority, 2018) (Table 8).

Methodology

This study employed exploratory research design. Secondary data gathered from published academic articles, academic search engines, reliable news sources, reports, rankings, official websites of companies, international organisations and governments, and other databases were used to analyse the funding and financing model of the selected top-ranked six smart cities in the world. Furthermore, descriptive statistics such as table, graphs and charts were used for this study to analyse the extracted data on the smart city exemplars. A total number of 33 projects were reviewed in Section 2. For ease of analysis and discussion of findings, the funding and financing sources of these identified projects were categorised under public funding, private financing and public–private partnership funding.

Table 8 Funding and financing sources of London Smart City

Projects	Description	Funding and financing options	Funding and financing sources	Some key references
2000 km of cabling across London's Tube network	installed by TfL and BAI Communications, to ensure citizens have uninterrupted 4G Internet access in the London	Public–private partnership (PPTs)	Government funding, public–private partnership (PPTs)	Buchholz (2023), Nexus Integra (2017), Greater London Authority (2018)
Civic Innovation Challenge	Created to help startups develop solutions to tackle city challenges	Public funding		
Connect London programme	responsible for the London city 5G network and fibre-optic coverage	Public–private partnership (PPTs)		
London Development Database (LDD)	A project for managing construction permits and stages in real-time accessible to citizens via the web	Public funding		
Smart Electricity Meters	Implementation of smart electricity meters for sustainable energy management.	Public–private partnership (PPTs)		
Heathrow Pods	Driverless vehicles connecting the city with the airport, enhancing transportation efficiency	Public–private partnership (PPTs)		

Results and Discussion of Findings

The purpose of this study is to provide information on the funding and financing options of the top six smart cities in the world to serve as a guide for upcoming smart cities on how to fund and finance smart city initiatives. The smart city projects implemented in the top six cities were discussed comprehensively in Section 2. The funding and financing sources of these identified projects were further analysed and categorised into three sub-headings, namely public funding, private financing and public–private partnership. This categorisation further provides information on the extent of funding and financing from each of the three categorisations. The results of the funding and financing options of each of the examined smart cities are discussed below.

Funding and Financing Options of Zurich Smart City

In Zurich, a variety of smart city projects have been successfully implemented, including the Power-to-Heat project, e-zurich, smart parking, sharing cities, e-foresight, smart public transportation, energy management projects, safety and security, and the smart city lab. These initiatives have been funded through a diverse range of sources such as the government budget, public–private partnerships, grants and subsidies, international organisations, non-profit agencies, venture capital, crowdfunding and the European Union (Schrotter & Hurzeler 2020; Morninigstar 2021; Joss et al. 2019; Zurich City Council, 2018).

Figure 1 illustrates the funding and financing sources for the smart city projects in Zurich, providing insight into the financial landscape of these endeavours. Public financing, including city funding, national funding and international sources, constitutes 56% of the total funding for Zurich's smart city projects. Private financing accounts for 11%, while public–private partnerships (PPPs) make up 33% of the funding mix. This breakdown highlights the significant role of government funding in supporting smart city initiatives in Zurich, showcasing the dedication of both local and national authorities to the advancement of Zurich as a smart city.

The data suggests that the public sector in Zurich is more willing to bear financial risks compared to the private sector, which may be more cautious about investing in early-stage smart city projects due to the associated risks. Following public sector funding, public–private partnerships contribute 30% of the financing, indicating a growing interest from private entities in smart city projects due to their potential benefits for citizens and businesses. However, there is room for increased private

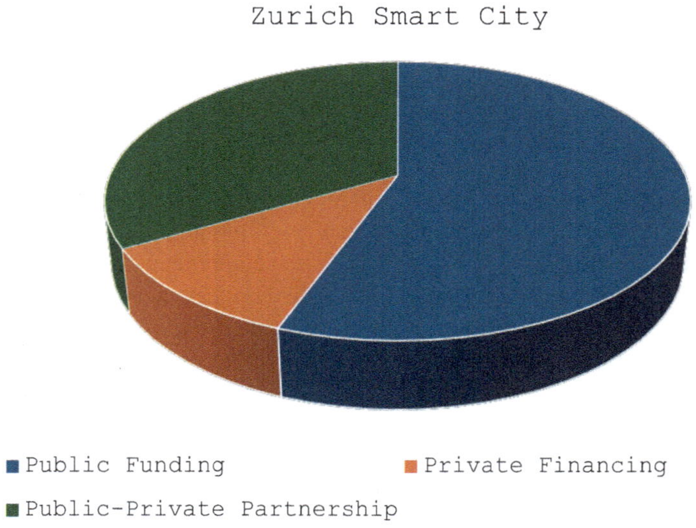

Fig. 1 Percentage of funding and financing options of Zurich Smart City

sector involvement, as the study reveals that private companies have not fully embraced smart city initiatives in Zurich, possibly due to risk aversion and a preference for shared risk with the government rather than assuming full financial responsibility.

Funding and Financing Options of Oslo Smart City

Figure 2 illustrates the funding and financing breakdown for smart city projects implemented in Oslo. The data reveals that public funding accounts for 40% of the total funding for the smart city projects in Oslo. Private financing makes up 20%, while public–private partnerships (PPPs) contribute the remaining 40%. From this information, we can deduce that smart city projects in Oslo are primarily co-funded by the government at various levels and the private sector. This suggests that the private sector in Oslo supports smart city initiatives and is willing to collaborate with the government to achieve this goal. The private sector is ready to take on the same level of financial commitment as the Oslo government. However, sole private financing accounts for 20% of the total funding for smart city initiatives in Oslo. Private investors are still cautious about getting majorly involved in financing smart city projects. This could be due to the large amount of capital required and the level of risk associated with funding new ideas. Therefore, Oslo's smart city projects demonstrate a balanced approach to funding, with significant contributions from both the public and private sectors. While the private sector is supportive and

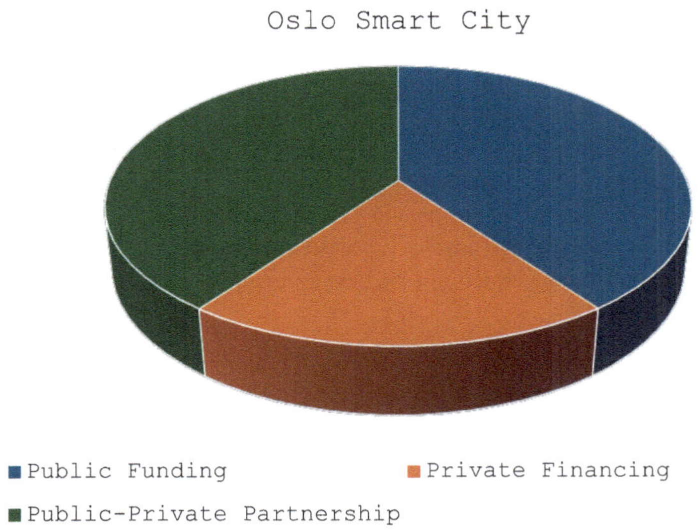

Fig. 2 Percentage of funding and financing options of Oslo Smart City

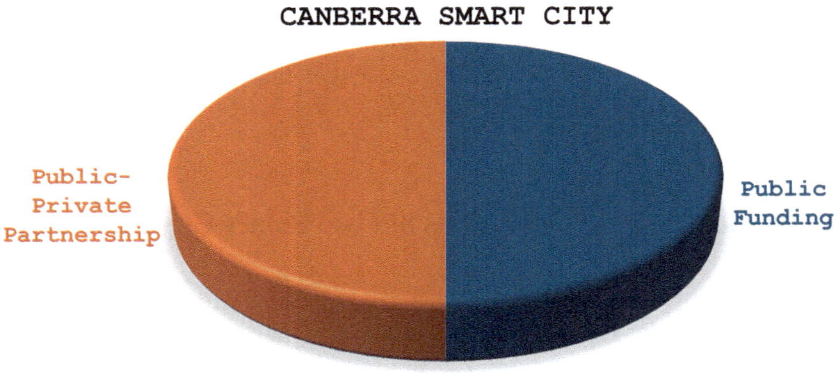

Fig. 3 Percentage of funding and financing options of Canberra Smart City

willing to collaborate, they remain cautious about taking on a larger financial role due to the capital-intensive nature and inherent risks of smart city initiatives.

Funding and Financing Mix for Canberra Smart City

In Fig. 3, the funding and financing options for implemented smart city projects in Canberra show that public financing accounts for 50% of the total fund while public–private partnerships (PPPs) account for 50% of the funding mix. This breakdown suggests that the public sector heavily invested in the development of Canberra's smart city initiatives, providing half of the required funding. The private sector is also actively supporting the growth of Canberra's smart city projects through PPPs, contributing the other half of the funding. From this analysis, it can be inferred that smart city projects in Canberra are jointly funded by the public and private sectors, with an equal split between the two. However, no single smart city project in Canberra was entirely financed by private funding alone. We therefore conclude that the funding and financing option for Canberra's smart city projects demonstrates a collaborative approach between the public and private sectors, with both parties contributing equally to the development of these initiatives.

Funding and Financing Options of Copenhagen Smart City

Figure 4 presents the percentage breakdown of funding and financing options for the implemented projects in Copenhagen Smart City to provide an overview of the funding and financing options of these projects. According to the chart, public financing, which includes city funding, national funding and international sources, accounts for a significant portion of the smart city projects implemented in

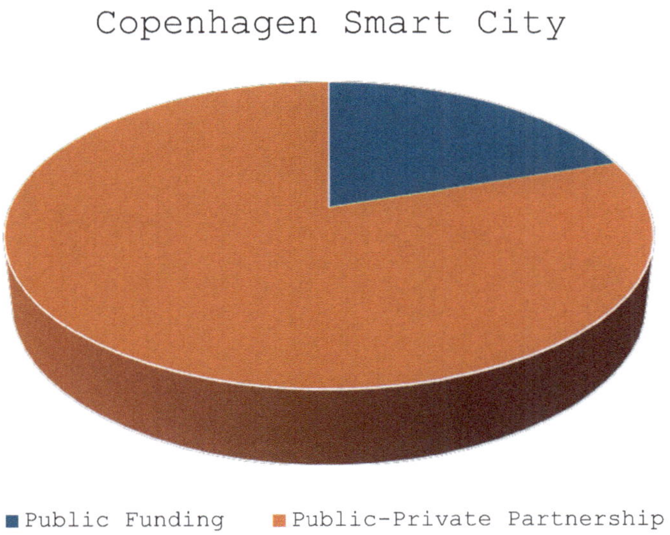

Fig. 4 Percentage of funding and financing options of Copenhagen Smart City

Copenhagen, making up 80% of the total funding. In contrast, public–private partnerships (PPPs) account for only 20% of the funding mix for Copenhagen's smart city projects. The data suggests that smart city projects in Copenhagen are primarily funded by the government at various levels, with a relatively small contribution from the private sector. This information serves as a pointer for the government of Canberra city to consider seeking more industry partnerships to sustain the existing smart city projects and implement new initiatives. By fostering stronger collaboration between the public and private sectors, Canberra city can potentially diversify its funding sources, leverage private sector expertise and resources, and ensure the long-term sustainability of its smart city initiatives.

Funding and Financing Options of Lausanne Smart City

Figure 5 presents the percentage breakdown of funding and financing options for the implemented projects in Lausanne Smart City. This information provides an overview of the funding and financing mix of Lausanne Smart City projects. According to the findings, public funding accounts for 67% of the smart city projects implemented in Lausanne while public–private partnerships (PPPs) account for the remaining 33% of the funding. This data suggests that smart city projects in Lausanne are primarily funded by the government at various levels, with a significant portion of the projects being financed through public funds. The private sector also plays a role in supporting smart city initiatives through partnerships with the government. However, it is important to note that there are no projects that are

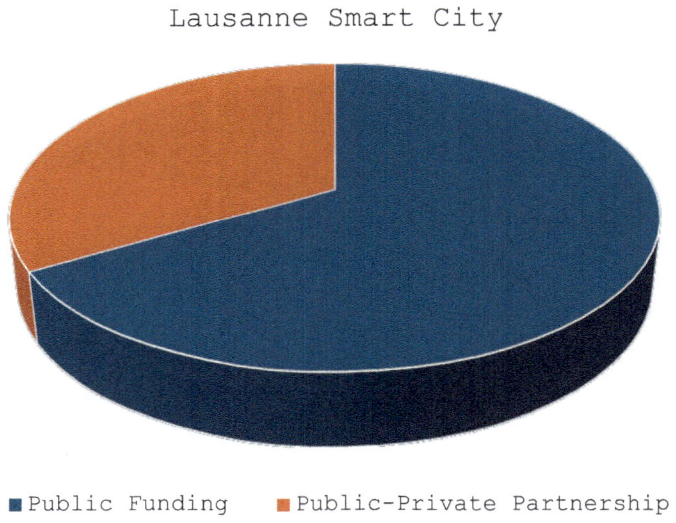

Fig. 5 Percentage of funding and financing options of Lausanne Smart City

solely financed by the private sector. This observation highlights the need for the government of Lausanne city to seek more industry partnerships to sustain the existing smart city projects and implement new initiatives. By diversifying the funding sources and increasing private sector involvement, the city can ensure the long-term sustainability and growth of its smart city projects. This approach can also lead to more innovative solutions and a more efficient use of resources.

Funding and Financing Options of London Smart City

Figure 6 illustrates the diverse sources of funding and financing utilised for the implementation of projects in London Smart City. Notably, the funding and financing structure of these projects is characterised by a significant reliance on public funding, which accounts for 80% of the total. In contrast, a combination of public and private funding makes up the remaining 20%. This distribution suggests that the London government has adopted a funding strategy that is largely self-sufficient, with minimal reliance on private financing for the implementation of its smart city projects.

Funding and Financing Options of Smart City Exemplars

Figure 7 displays the funding and financing options of the top six smart city exemplars. The analysis reveals that public–private partnerships (PPPs) account for the majority (52%) of funding for smart city projects in these leading cities. Government

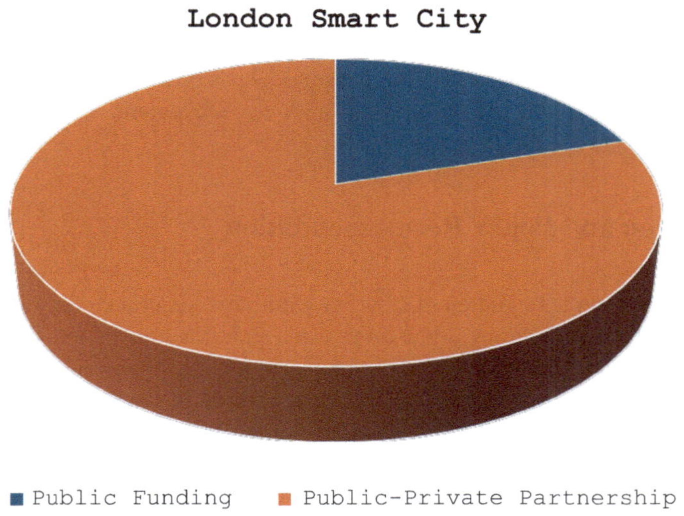

Fig. 6 Percentage of funding and financing options of London Smart City

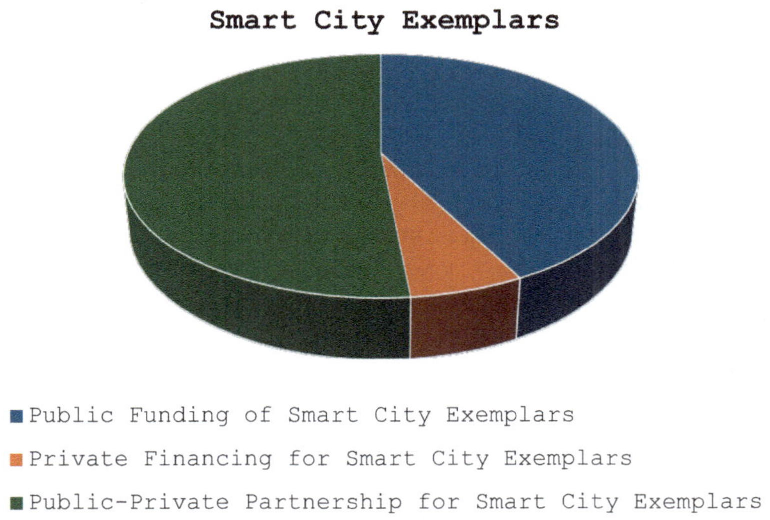

Fig. 7 Percentage of funding and financing options of all the smart city exemplars

funding at various levels makes up 42% of the total funding while private financing contributes only 6% to smart city projects in these exemplary cities. These findings suggest that the success of these cities in becoming global smart city leaders can be attributed to the strong collaboration between the public and private sectors. The significant involvement of industry partners through PPPs has enabled these cities to implement ambitious smart city initiatives and secure their top rankings. The relatively low percentage of private financing (6%) indicates that these cities have been able to leverage government resources and public–private collaborations to drive their smart city transformations. This model has proven effective in propelling these cities to the forefront of the global smart city movement.

Conclusion and Policy Recommendation

The successful implementation of smart city initiatives is crucial for addressing the pressing challenges faced by urban areas, such as traffic congestion, resource scarcity, environmental degradation and social inequalities. Due to this, this study explored the innovative funding and financing options of the top six smart cities in the world to provide a model for upcoming smart cities. The analysis reveals that public–private partnerships (PPPs) account for the majority (52%) of funding for smart city projects in these leading cities. Government funding at various levels makes up 42% of the total funding while private financing contributes only 6% to smart city projects in these exemplary cities. These findings suggest that the success of these cities in becoming global smart city leaders can be attributed to the strong collaboration between the public and private sectors. The significant involvement of industry partners through PPPs has enabled these cities to implement ambitious smart city initiatives and secure their top rankings. The relatively low percentage of private financing (6%) indicates that these cities have been able to leverage government resources and public–private collaborations to drive their smart city transformations. This model has proven effective in propelling these cities to the forefront of the global smart city movement. The findings of this study can, thus, serve as a valuable resource for policymakers, urban planners and city leaders of upcoming smart cities in their efforts to transform their cities into sustainable, resilient and technologically advanced urban centres.

Limitation of the Study

This study only focused on the funding and financing options of the top six smart cities in the world. Future research can expand the scope of investigation to include a wider range of smart cities, beyond just the top six. Analysing the funding and financing models across a more diverse set of established smart cities would provide a more comprehensive understanding of the strategies being employed.

References

Aik, W. (2021). Evaluation of economic benefits of smart city initiatives. *Scentia International Economic Review*. https://doi.org/10.52514/sier.v1i1.4

Amine, R. (2024). Smart cities: Development and benefits. In F. Belaïd & A. Arora (Eds.), *Smart cities: Social and environmental challenges and opportunities for local authorities* (pp. 1–15). Springer. https://doi.org/10.1007/978-3-031-35664-3

Australia Government. (2016). *Smart Cities Plan*. Retrieved from https://cites.infrastructure.gov.a

Bajpai, N., & Biberman, J. (2021). *India's Smart City Program: Challenges and Opportunities*. CSD Working Paper Series Towards a New Indian Model of Information and Communications Technology-Led Growth and Development. Center for Sustainable Development, Earth Institute, Columbia University.

Blanck, M. Ribeiro, J. L. D. (2021). Smart cities financing system: An empirical modelling from the European context. Cities (116) ISSN 0264-2751. https://doi.org/10.1016/j.cities.2021.103268.

Buchholz, L. (2023). Top 10: Most sustainable smart cities. *Sustainability Magazine.*. Retrieved from https://sustainabilitymag.com/articles/top-10-smart-cities-in-the-world-in-2023

Calzada, I. (2021). Book review: Smart city citizenship. *Journal of Contemporary Urban Affair, 5*(1), 145–150. https://scholar.google.com/scholar?hl=en&as_sdt=0%2C5&q=igor+calzada+%282021%29+Smart+city+citizenship&btnG=

Canberra_EU-Delegation-Presentation. (2017). https://www.eeas.europa.eu/delegations/australia/press-release-joint-press-statement-eu-australia-energy-relations_en?s=163

Elsasser, M. (2023). 11 Copenhagen-based startups you should know! *Startup Valley*. Retrieved from https://startupvalley.news/copenhagen-based-startups/

European Commission. (2021). *100 climate-neutral and smart cities by 2030: Implementation Plan*. Retrieved from https://research-and-innovation.ec.europa.eu/system/files/2021-09/cities_mission_implementation_plan.pdf

Greater London Authority. (2018). *Smarter London Together*. Retrieved from https://www.london.gov.uk/sites/default/files/smarter_london_together_v1.66-_published.pdf

Hamilton, S. & Zhu, X. (2017). Funding and financing smart cities. *Deloitte Centre for Government Insights*. Retrieved from https://www2.deloitte.com/content/dam/Deloitte/us/Documents/public-sector/us-ps-funding-and-financing-smart-cities.pdf

Hernandez, D. V. Isabel, R. & Albor Pallares, R. A. (2014). *Financing instruments for Smart City projects based on Internet of Things*. Retrieved from https://www.politesi.polimi.it/bitstre

Hu, R. (2020). Australia's national urban policy: The smart cities agenda in perspective. *Australia Journal of Social Issues*, 1–17. https://doi.org/10.1002/ajs4.104

IMD (2023) IMD Smart City Index Report (2023). Retrieved from https://imd.cld.bz/IMD-Smart-City-Index-Report-20231/2/

Joss, S., Sengers, F., Schraven, D., Caprotti, F., & Dayot, Y. (2019). The smart city as global discourse: Storylines and critical junctures across 27 cities. *Journal of Urban Technology, 26*(1), 3–34.

Kirk, M. (2015 October 19). Copenhagen's "smart" new street lamps shine brighter for cyclists. *Bloomberg*. Retrieved from https://www.bloomberg.com/news/articles/2015-10-19/copenhagen-s-new-smart-street-lamps-can-shine-brighter-for-cyclists-or-dim-to-save-energy

Merk, O., Saussier, S., Staropoli, C., Slack, E., & Kim, J-H. (2012). Financing green urban infrastructure. *OECD Regional Development Working Papers* 2012/10. Retrieved from https://www.oecd.org/cfe/regionaldevelopment/WP_Financing_Green_Urban_Infrastructure.pdf

Morningstar, M. (2021, November 8). Zurich smart city. *Lanast.*. https://www.aboutsmartcities.co.

New, J., Castro, D., & Beckwith, M. (2017). How national governments can help smart cities succeed. *Centre for Data Innovation*

Nexus Integra. (2017) *Top 10 smart cities in the world*. Retrieved from https://nexusintegra.io/top-10-smart-cities/

Nordic Smart City Network. (2023). *Smart Oslo and Baerum*. https://nscn.eu/Oslo

Oslo Business Region. (2020). Retrieved from https://oslobusinessregion.no/

Repsol. (2024). *What are smart cities? Smart cities are already a reality*. Retrieved from https://www.repsol.com/en/energy-and-the-future/technology-and-innovation/smart-cities/index.cshtml

Schrotter, G., & Hurzeler, C. (2020). The digital twin of the city of Zurich for urban planning. *Journal of Photogrammetry, Remote Sensing and Geoinformation Science, 88*, 99–112.

Sustainability Report. (2023). Retrieved from. https://sustainability.fb.com/2023-sustainability-report/

The Welding Institute. (TWI, 2024). *What is a smart city? Definition and examples*. Retrieved from https://www.twi-global.com/technical-knowledge/faqs/what-is-a-smart-cityu/19047/documents/

Ulterino, M., Smith, D., Baker, K., Heeckt, C., & Gavron, N. (2021). *Green Economy Leader Report - Copenhagen*. Retrieved from https://international.kk.dk/sites/default/files/2021-09/Green%20Economy%20Leader%20Report%20-%20Copenhagen.pdf

United Nation Department of Economic and Social Affairs. (UN DESA, 2018). *68% of the world population projected to live in urban areas by 2050, says UN*.

World Population Review. (2024). *Zurich Population 2024*. Retrieved from https://worldpopulationreview.com/world-cities/zurich-population

Yorgos, Y. J. S., Golias, M., Dedes, G., Douligeris, C., & Mishra, S. (2019). Challenges, risks and opportunities for connected vehicle services in smart cities and communities. *IFAC-PapersOnLine, 51*(34), 139–144. https://doi.org/10.1016/j.ifacol.2019.01.056

Younus, A. M., & Abumandil, M. (2022). *AI-centric smart city ecosystem technologies, design, and implementation*. Taylor and Francis. Retrieved from https://www.researchgate.net/

Zurich Council. (2018). *Strategy smart city Zurich*. Retrieved from https://www.stadt-zuerich.ch//content/dam/stzh/portal/Deutsch/politik-der-stadt-zuerich/grafik-und-foto/smartcity/Smart_City_Zurich_Strategy.pdf

Conceptualising Performance Measurement Systems in the Energy Sector: A Systematic Literature Review

Marilyn Sithole

Abstract The research highlights the need for continuous performance measurement systems (PMSs) conceptualisation in the energy sector necessitated by dynamic complexities (i.e. regulatory frameworks, multiple energy sources, and environmental issues). The main aim of this study is to conceptualise PMS in the energy sector through a systematic literature review (SLR). The qualitative study consists of the SLR and PMS audit guided by both the Preferred Reporting Items for Systematic Reviews and Meta-Analyses (PRISMA) 2020 framework and the Shareholders' Power and Interest Matrix. The study includes 33 academic journals from 2010 to 2024, cutting across the World Bank income classifications for developed and developing countries. Stakeholder influence in PMS design remains dominant for government institutions with stakeholders in developed countries having more power and influence than those in developing countries. Amongst other findings and contributions, the study concludes that there is a need for an integrated performance measurement system (IPMS) that holistically aligns strategic, tactical, and operational objectives, technology, management control, and responsiveness to external stimuli. This would be expected to create a viable and agile energy sector with practical administrative successes, energy security, and independence in energy servitisation, a widespread problem across all countries. The research recommends a systems approach in PMS conceptualisation over a cause-and-effect, fragmented, or bureaucratic approach. This research makes a novel contribution to the management accounting discipline which serves as a valuable resource for researchers, practitioners, and policymakers to conceptualise PMS effectively.

Keywords Performance measurement systems · Integrity audit · Deployment audit · The energy sector

M. Sithole (✉)
University of Free State, Bloemfontein, South Africa

T. Moloi (ed.), *Impacting Society Positively Through Technology in Accounting and Business Processes*, Springer Proceedings in Business and Economics,
https://doi.org/10.1007/978-3-031-84885-8_48

Introduction

Recently, more scholars began to advocate for a systems' thinking approach in PMS development and deployment to resolve the gap between expected and actual performance in the dynamic energy sector (Tannir et al., 2023; Kowal, 2019). The dynamic and complex changes in the energy sector required continuous conceptualisation of performance measurement systems (PMSs) to ensure sectorial viability, effective monitoring and control. Scholars García-Moreno and López-Ruiz (2023) through case study and Lyu and Liu's (2021) mixed method study affirm the dynamism and complexities in the energy sector as well as the need for viable and relevant PMSs.

Various scholars characterised these energy sector changes as either evolutionary (Hrga et al., 2020), revolutionary (Kowal, 2019), adaptative (Trzeciak & Jonek-Kowalska, 2021), or reconstructive (Granger, 2023) in nature. Evolution is deemed incremental and encompasses transformation, while revolutionary changes are sudden and transformative. Adaptation is incremental and consists of realignment (Andriuškevičius et al., 2022) juxtapositioned with reconstruction, which comprised of sudden and rapid changes made in alignment with existing strategies (Gitelman & Kozhevnikov, 2023).

The changes in the energy sector included new energy mixes and production processes (Gitelman & Kozhevnikov, 2023), increasing environmental sustainability issues requirements (Rabe et al., 2020), technologies (Andriuškevičius et al., 2022), international and industrial diversification (Westerman et al., 2020) and globalisation (Gitelman & Kozhevnikov, 2023). External and internal factors influenced the strategic, tactical, and operations in the energy sector (Andriuškevičius et al., 2022; Hrga et al., 2020). These complexities were in part caused by diverse regulatory frameworks (Rabe et al., 2020), energy sources (Granger, 2023), and domestic legal issues (Weigel & Fischedick, 2019).

The changes affected management control systems leading to the subsequent redesign and redeployment of performance measurement systems (PMSs). Various models and frameworks, including the International Standards Organisation (ISO), influenced the continuous process of PMS conceptualisation. Kowal (2019) advocated for a multi-dimensional and cross-cutting PMS.

Sivill (2011) conceptualised a comprehensive and effective PMS that ensured monitoring and controlling at systems level, organisational level, and the time frame. The organisational level consists of several stakeholders (shareholders, directors, managers, and operations), and the system level is the supply chain, company, departments, equipment, sites, and subsystems. The time element refers to historical records, forecasts, and reports on quality assurance (fault detection). Figure 1 illustrates the dimensions of energy performance measurement systems.

Scholars agreed that PMSs that measured the complete system would create a sustainable and viable business organisation (Da Silva et al., 2019; Andrés et al., 2018; Giret et al., 2018).

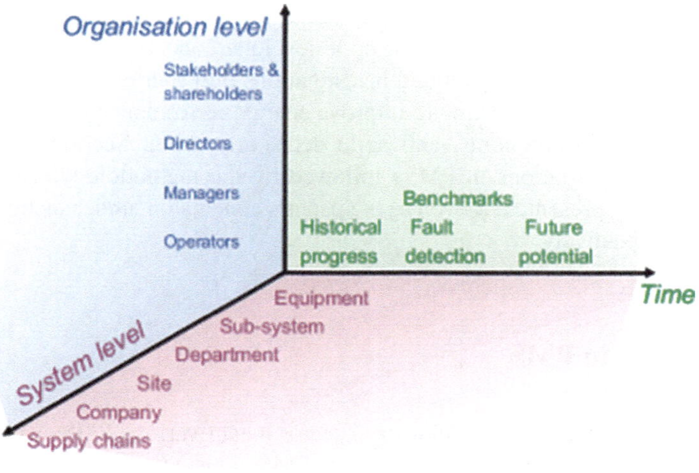

Fig. 1 Dimensions of energy performance measurement systems. Source: Sivill (2011)

The energy sector experienced dynamic changes that required viable and sustainable changes in PMSs (Andriuškevičius et al., 2022; Hrga et al., 2020; Lyu & Liu, 2021; Westerman et al., 2020). However, the reality was that the PMSs were stagnant and heavily regulated by the government (Čeryová et al., 2020). Bureaucracy and low autonomy in decision-making and PMS design remained common themes in the energy sector (Westerman et al., 2020). Moreover, the literature on PMS conceptualisation in the energy sector mainly focused on a cause-and-effect, fragmented, and bureaucratic approach rather than a systems approach (Andriuškevičius et al., 2022; Hrga et al., 2020; Lyu & Liu, 2021). Asikainen's (2016) qualitative study discusses the lack of appropriate PMS in the energy sector.

Scholars Bin-Nashwan et al. (2017); Henri & Journeault, (2010); Shafiq (2014); and Journeault (2010) agreed that minimal studies on energy sector PMS conceptualisation were published in developing countries. Loftsgarden (2020) conceded to this notion and expressed that while limited studies on PMS were evident in developing countries, several studies were prevalent in developed countries. Despite various studies on PMS development in developed countries, there still had been no significant change in PMS for eight years within nations of the Organisation for Economic Cooperation and Development (OECD) specifically Finland, France, Ireland, Germany, Austria, and Spain (Sulich & Sołoducho-Pelc, 2022; Schlör et al., 2013; Kowal 2019; Schlör et al., 2013).

Operating the energy sector based on the And Then a Miracle Occurs (ATAMO) approach was widespread in developed countries and was not practical and feasible (Quinn, 2017). ATAMO is a principle where management would complacently hope for "a miracle" in this case, in the form of improved performance without having corrected the design and deployment of PMSs (Quinn, 2017). The reform, the conceptualisation of PMSs, is relevant to resolve performance issues across various dimensions and, address the current and emerging complexities in the energy sector.

This research uses a SLR to conceptualise a PMS that ensures viability and sustainability in the energy sector for both developed and developing countries. The study addresses the gap of limited investigations into energy sector PMSs in developing countries while seeking to improve energy performance by reducing bureaucracy, increasing autonomy, and agile decision-making. Section two presents a discussion on variations in PMSs followed by the methodology. The results and discussion are presented, as well as the paper's conclusion, under sections four, five, and six, respectively.

Variations in PMS

The complexities across the industrial sector meant various PMSs were developed to fit the diverse demands. Variations of PMSs existed across different industrial sectors (Kowal, 2019; Kovačević, 2023; Moisan et al., 2023), within companies in the same industry (Sangwa & Sangwan, 2018), and within the organisation itself (Alves & Lourenço, 2023). The ISO created a standardised framework that ensured that despite the diversity in the PMSs, their viability and reliability would allow benchmarking (Granger, 2023).

The synergistic approaches to PMS deployment were in response to the global influence, the general instability, and the dynamism of the external environment (Tannir et al., 2023). PMS development became the solution as they responded to the transformation of globalisation and digital disruption (Borkovcova et al., 2022). External drivers of change in the energy sector sought to replace non-renewable energy sources with renewable energy, thus altering the energy mix. A shift in stakeholders' power and interest meant the energy sector adapted to their growing and emerging environmental and social concerns (García-Moreno & López-Ruiz, 2023). A highly adaptive and flexible integrated measurement system was required to address domestic and global concerns emanating from the fragmented application of PMS (Granger, 2023; Asikainen, 2016; Jasiukevicius & Christauskas, 2011).

An in-depth analysis would show that deficient performance was linked to the phenomenon of poor deployment and integrity issues (Bititci et al., 1997, 2018). Continuous review of PMS over time led to improved integrity and deployment procedures (Gitelman & Kozhevnikov, 2023). Deployment issues led to failure to monitor, evaluate, and control emerging issues (Lin et al., 2023; Hiesterman et al., 2020). Kowal (2019), in a mixed method case study, further ascribed failures in performance to poor PMS deployment. Kovačević (2023) questioned the described poor deployment as occurring within poor governance, incompetence, and negligence. Kovačević (2023) focused on PMS integrity. PMSs that lack integrity would be devoid of the rigour needed for adequate montoring and controlling (Hiesterman et al., 2020). This lack of rigour became evident since PMS were misaligned with strategic goals, had ill-defined KPIs, and measured output instead of outcomes (Gouvea da Costa, 2023; Moisan et al., 2023).

As Sivill (2011) pointed out, auditing PMS is important since it affects organisational success. Negative consequences of PMSs included sub-optimisation, rigging, repressing innovation, misstatement, poor decision-making, myopia, fixation, sub-optimisation, and gaming the system (Lehtonen, 2012; Micheli & Manzoni, 2010; Goddard et al., 2000; Smith, 1995). PMSs of low integrity essentially offer a closed, authoritative manner of representation, discouraging responsibility and engendering resistance and risk; avert innovation, creativity, and achievement; lead to dissimulation and distortion of data and/or ignore the plurality of values and points of view.

PMS conceptualisation is envisaged as a deterrent to the spiralling adverse effects caused by mismanagement and incorrect PMS deployment. The "Hicksian complementarity" is a term that describes how uncontrolled costs in the production process can lead to cascading ripple effects in energy generation, transmission, and distribution (Lyu & Liu, 2021). Therefore, the integrity and deployment of PMS need to be audited to ensure improved performance.

Methodology

In this paper, the SLR of the PMS in the energy sector uses the PRISMA checklist. The SLR minimises errors and bias. The PRISMA flow diagram explains the steps in identifying source material, screening, and registering articles used in the study protocol. The SLR approach is scientific and follows an evidence-based approach from searching, selecting, and analysing literature (Wahh et al., 2020; Khandelwal et al., 2019).

Information Sources Google Scholar, Web of Science, and Scopus are the websites used to source the literature. The research used both theoretical and empirical papers /case studies.

Search Strategy A comprehensive strategy using key search words was used. The search focuses on the keywords appearing in the research title. Keywords used ("performance measurement system*"OR viable systems model*") AND ("energy sector*" OR electricity OR energy industry* energy sector" OR performance measurement systems" "performance measurement systems" "monitoring performance measurement") from Google Scholar, Scopus, and Web of Science from 2010 to 2024.

Eligibility Criteria The first step involved the identification of peer-reviewed journals published between 2010 and 2024. The study was conducted on the energy sector for both developing and developed countries based on the World Bank classifications of Low-Income countries (LICs), Lower Middle-Income Countries (LMIC), Upper Middle-Income Countries (UMICs), and High-Income Countries (HICs). The focus, therefore, is on the energy sector administration and conceptualisation of PMS. Empirical studies on PMSs and their indicators, deployment, integrity, and outcomes were included in the study.

Identification Papers identified as duplicates from the three search engines were removed. So were papers that are ineligible, but have no translation to English. The study includes papers detailing different energy mixes (renewable and non-renewable). It also includes energy generation, transmission, and distribution. Studies on energy servitisation are included.

Selection Process The selection process included screening criteria to exclude documents that are not associated with the research questions. Search results to which the researcher had no access to were regarded as unrelated to the research questions and were filtered by automation involving multiple screening stages and included only the most relevant studies. Full-text screening was then conducted to assess the eligibility of studies further.

Data Charting Data extracted from each included study were organised according to the author, information related to PMS, World Bank classification, publication year, and country. This criterion was used for data extraction purposes. Colour coding was then used to assist in classifying information and extracting meaning. Findings and literature concerning PMS are used to conceptualise PMS in this study. Content analysis was also used, which enabled the systematic charting of data for purposes of facilitating comparison, synthesis, and identification of themes across studies.

Availability of Data Code and Other Materials All data extraction is cited, and a table of the 33 articles and their respective authors is referenced to promote transparency and reproducibility. The 33 articles are tabulated, and their significant contributions to PMS conceptualisation are disclosed. This ensures the replicability of the study and provides an audit trail.

Critical Appraisal of Individual Sources of Evidence To assess the quality and reliability of each source, a critical appraisal using the following criteria is done: the risk of bias, methodological rigour, and relevance to the research question.

Risk of Bias The bias is minimised by analysing literature across the World Bank income classifications such as the Low-Income Countries (LICs), Lower Middle-Income Countries (LMIC), Upper Middle-Income Countries (UMICs), and High-Income Countries (HICs) (World Bank, 2024). Analysis of PMS is not restricted to a single geographical area. Figure 2 below uses Page et al., (2021) PRISMA to show the procedures followed for data collection and analysis in this study.

Data Items Search strategies yielded 815 records, then reduced to 75 using Harzing publish or perish (2016). This is because duplicates and ineligible and inaccessible articles were removed. Having narrowed the search to include articles from 2010 to

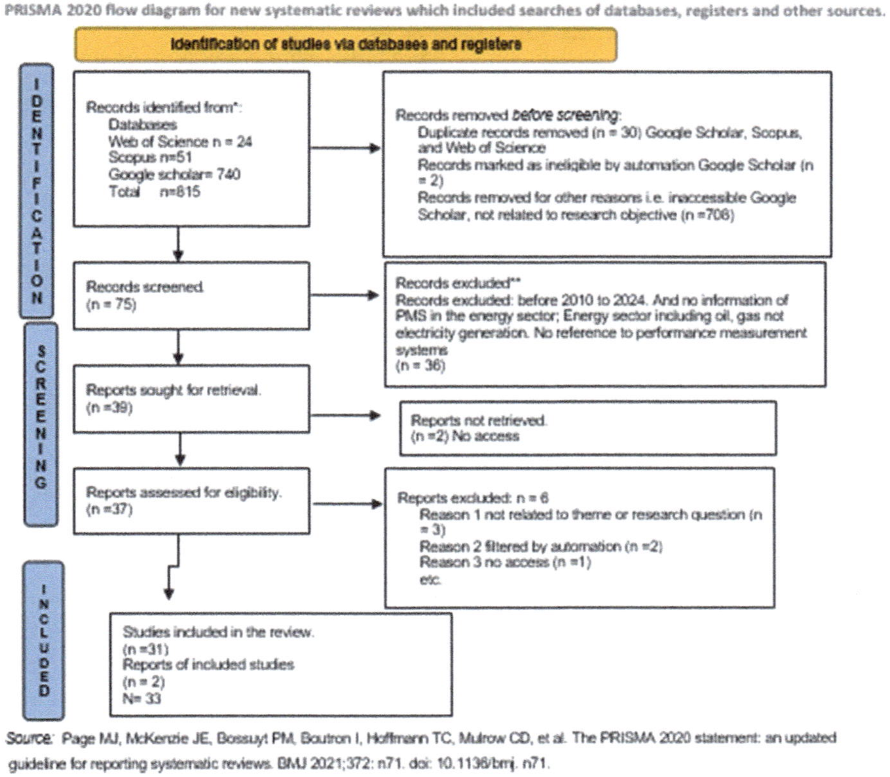

Fig. 2 The PRISMA 2020 framework applied to this study

2024, only 39 remain. Automatic filtration reduced them to 33. Data extraction is based on the 33 articles listed in the methodology. The sample size consists of 33 articles, which ensures data saturation.

The main findings are synthesised to provide critical success factors. Theoretic models such as the stakeholders power and interest matrix and the World Bank income classifications are applied to the case study of 33 searched documents relating to energy sector organisations. A graphical presentation shows data from the World Bank regarding the countries included in the 33 articles reviewed.

The overall PMS conceptualisation process for this study is depicted in the flow chart below:

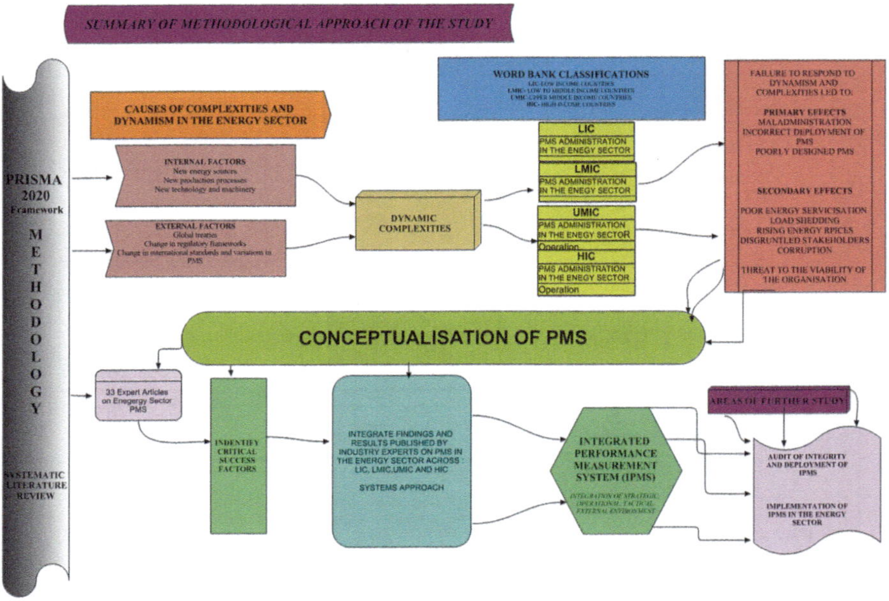

Source: (Researchers Own, 2024)

Results and Findings

The World Bank clusters the global countries into four strata: the Low-Income Countries (LICs), the Lower Middle-Income Countries (LMICs), the Upper Middle-Income Countries (UMICs), and the High-Income Countries (HICs). To reduce bias, the studied literature sources covered these country clusters as colour-coded below to find out the recommendations by various energy experts on PMS improvement. These colour codes shall be used for further analysis.

Table 1 provides a list of countries discussed in the 33 articles. The World Bank Income Classifications places countries into classification based on their income, i.e. LIC (3), LMIC (7), UMIC (7), and HIC (9). In total, the energy sector PMS is discussed in 26 countries. Given the SLR, it was interesting to see scholars identify common and uncommon features in the energy sector across the 26 countries (Kowal, 2019; Singh et al., 2022; Rahman et al., 2022).

The study in Table 2 synthesises findings and recommendations from the 33 articles to determine the authors, and methodologies suggest ways to improve PMS using colour coding based on the World Bank classification.

Table 2 depicts the articles selected in the PRISMA framework across LIC, LMIC, UMIC, and HIC clusters. The information is further distilled to produce critical areas of improvement in PMS in the energy sector. Table 2 illustrates the findings and recommendations of the 33 articles concerning the gaps and

Table 1 Countries, World Bank income classification, and designated colour codes

Counties mentioned in the 33 Articles from the SLR with	World Bank Income classification	Colour code
1. Bangladesh 2. Pakistan 3. Ethiopia	Low-Income Countries (LICs)	
1. South Africa 2. Nigeria 3. Kenya 4. India 5. Malaysia 6. Vietnam 7. Philippines	Lower Middle-Income Countries (LMICs)	
1. Greece 2. Croatia 3. Russia 4. China 5. Poland 6. Türkiye 7. Azerbaijan	Upper Middle-Income Countries (UMICs)	
1. Germany 2. United Kingdom (UK) 3. Saudi Arabia 4. Italy 5. Australia 6. Belgium 7. Czech Republic 8. Finland 9. France	High-Income Countries (HICs)	

Source: Researchers Own (2024)

improvements needed in PMS applied in the energy sector. The findings and recommendations are classified across the World Bank classifications. The findings illustrate that PMS conceptualisation requires flexibility. This substantiates the literature which highlighted that new energy mixes and production processes (Gitelman & Kozhevnikov, 2023), environmental sustainability (Rabe et al., 2020), technologies (Andriuškevičius et al., 2022), international and industrial diversification (Westerman et al., 2020), and globalisation (Gitelman & Kozhevnikov, 2023) required measurement systems. PMS would be required to measure the external and internal factors (strategic, tactical, and operations) (Andriuškevičius et al., 2022; Hrga et al., 2020). Table 3 depicts the nominal scale showing the frequency of PMS-related articles per World Bank classification from the 33 identified articles discussed in Table 2.

The nominal scale in Table 3 confirms that studies on PMS conceptualisation are more commonly done in developed countries than in developing countries. The table shows that 18.18% of research was done in LICs; 15.15% in LMICs; and 39.39% in UMICs and HICs. These results confirm findings from various scholars

Table 2 Identified areas of PMS improvement by author and World Bank cluster

Author 2010 -2014	Methodology	Suggested improvements to PMS design	Colour Code
Kowal, B. (2019).	Qualitative	• Improve integration. • Revise performance indicators. • Must be multidimensional.	UMIC
Rahman, M. M., Hasan, M. A., Shafiullah, M., Rahman, M. S., Arifuzzaman, M., Islam, M. K., & Rahman, S. M. (2022)	Quantitative	• The indicator is based on three policy outcomes: decarbonising energy, improving energy efficiency and managing energy demand. • Must apply to multiple sectors. • Effectiveness of technological, investment, and social welfare considerations.	HIC
Trzeciak, M., & Jonek-Kowalska, I. (2021).	Qualitative	• Include measurement of 'soft' management areas, such as work, communication, or quality implemented quality management system, e.g., ISO. • Audit the implementation of corrective actions and reports on PMS. • Systemic PMS management. • The scope of PMS includes global program management standards and technological, technical, and economic issues.	UMIC
Khan, A. N., Yahya, F., & Waqas, M. (2022).	Quantitative	• PMS to prevent the Agency problem and promote gender diversity and the interests of multiple shareholders. • Balancing conservative and aggressive Working Capital Management strategies (conservative, moderate, and aggressive)	
Singh, M.; Jiao, J.; Klobasa, M.; Frietsch, R. (2022)	Qualitative	• PMS must consider customers, economies, and new actors with innovation, digitalisation, and sustainability. • PMS must bridge the gap between technological advancement and business model practices. • PMS in Energy Software must measure Comfort and Heating, Flexibility and Trading, Energy Efficiency and Management, Solar and Microgrid, Charging and Battery, and Energy Software solutions. • PMS must be customer-centric, outcomes-based and lead to service innovations.	LMIC
Dobrova, K. B., Danilochkina, N. G., Cherner, N. V., Dobrov, V. P., Dobrov, P. P., & Sepiashvili, E. N. (2018)	Qualitative	• PMS aligned to energy policy. • PMS must consist of technologies and lower costs. • Integrates organisational, technical, analytical, and regulatory measures. • Must facilitate structural and substantive analysis. • Promote energy benchmarking, energy outsourcing, and energy monitoring. • Aligned to EN 16001 and ISO 50001.	UMIC
Volkova, I. O., Filinov, N. B., Kuskova, V. V., & Titova, N. L. (2012)	Quantitative	• PMS must show a causal relationship between management and firm performance at all levels. • Must establish a causal relationship of complex cause-effect relationships.	UMIC

Source: Researchers Own (2024)

Table 3 Nominal scale showing the frequency of PMS-related articles per World Bank classification from the 33 identified articles

World Bank classification	Frequency of occurrence	Percentage
LIC	6/33	**18.18%**
LMIC	5/33	**15.15%**
UMIC	13/33	**39.39%**
HIC	13/33	**39.39%**

Source: Researchers Own (2024)

Table 4 Nominal scale showing the frequency of occurrence of each methodology across the 33 articles

Methodology	Frequency of occurrence	Percentage
Quantitative	7/33	**21.21%**
Qualitative	15/33	**45.45%**
Mixed	11/33	**33.33%**

Source: Researcher's own (2024)

highlighted in the literature (Henri & Journeault, 2010; LopezValeiras et al., 2016; Shafiq, 2014; Bin-Nashwan et al., 2017; Kowal, 2019; Schlör et al., 2013; Sulich & Sołoducho-Pelc, 2022). This also explains the lag in performance in the energy sector in developing countries with minimal adaptation, evolution, revolution, and reconstruction of PMS despite the complexities and dynamism of the energy sector (Nwaiwu, 2021; Lee & Gerner, 2020; Mendoza & Initiative, 2022; Drago & Gatto, 2022).

Table 2 cited the methodology used in PMS conceptualisations, and these methodologies are discussed in detail in Table 4. Table 4 presents a nominal scale showing the methodology commonly used in 33 PMS studies selected using PRISMA.

Table 4 shows that 45.45% are qualitative; mixed studies make up 33.33% and quantitative studies make up 21.21% of the selected articles. The gaps in PMS integrity and deployment in this research are discussed according to the various methodologies in Table 5, firstly with the qualitative, secondly the quantitative and thirdly mixed methods.

Results from the qualitative studies illustrate gaps in deployment and integrity that compromised performance in the energy sector. The scholars identified a lack of integration, insufficient targets and metrics for the social and environmental aspects (Lee & Gerner, 2020); gaps in data collection (Hrga et al., 2020; Lehtonen, 2012); limited use of technology and analytics such as artificial intelligence and machine learning (Wanday & Ajour El Zein, 2022); inadequate focus on non-financial metrics (Višković & Franki, 2015); incomplete alignment with organisational goals (Trzeciak & Jonek-Kowalska, 2021; Novruzova, 2020) as compromising to energy sector performance. PMS design dictated by government and legislation remained inflexible to the environment (external and internal) (Gitelman & Kozhevnikov, 2023; Lyu & Liu, 2021; Birech, 2011). Scholars found that PMS conceptualisation that was politically motivated neglected financial management

Table 5 Qualifying the colour code for the shareholder matrix

POWER (P)	COLOUR CODE & QUALIFICATION
High	Stakeholders that influence PMS designs and are actively involved in deployment policy. They possess decision-making authority and resource control. These are critical vital investors.
Middle	Stakeholders can make contributions that are implemented. They have moderate authority and power to influence specific areas.
Low	Contributions towards PMS are based on minimal or no consideration. Peripheral involvement with limited decision-making and engagement.
INTEREST (I)	
High	Stakeholders benefit from PMS deployment and design. They are investors and stand to directly benefit, have strong advocacy, and have created long-term relationships. Engage these stakeholders closely, keep them informed, and involve them in decision-making processes.
Middle	Stakeholders follow performance and have minimal benefits. Moderate interest and involvement. Possess high variability in engagements.
Low	Stakeholders have access to evaluations online or in newspapers and make no meaningful comments, contributions, or benefits. Passive observers with limited interest.

Source: Researchers Own (2024)

principles (Nwaiwu, 2021; Trzeciak & Jonek-Kowalska, 2021; Loftsgarden, 2020; Novruzova, 2020).

The quantitative studies highlighted gaps existing in PMS. These included data quality issues during data collection. Data quality is compromised as the energy sector provides inaccurate, incomplete, and untraceable data over decades (Makridou et al., 2024). The energy sector also failed to adapt PMSs to effectively measure renewable energy (Drago & Gatto, 2022). PMSs were inundated with complexity and overcomplications that denied their users' simplicity and practicality (Njenga & Olweny, 2016; Volkova, 2012). KPIs had a limited scope focusing on financial issues and lacked key sustainability issues (Makridou et al., 2024). The qualitative studies emphasised the failed alignment of PMS with stakeholder expectations leading to failed service delivery. The performance targets continuously lead to dissatisfaction and conflict (Wanday et al., 2022; Huseyin et al., 2016).

Mixed method studies identified limited integration of PMS into decision-making (Chan, 2018); bureaucracy and lack of continuous development (Andriuškevičius et al., 2022) as a deterrent to effective performance. PMS integrity was compromised through non-responsiveness (May et al., 2015); output management instead of outcomes-based management (Rabe et al., 2020); over-emphasis on short-term results (Mendoza & Initiative, 2022); poorly defined metrics for socio-environmental issues (Chan, 2018). ESG metrics remained vague, irrelevant, and difficult to understand, especially those relating to carbon emissions (Makki & Alqahtani, 2023; Andriuškevičius et al., 2022; Rabe et al., 2020; May et al., 2015).

Having analysed the development of various PMSs across literature, a distinct link between PMS development and strategy is evident (Lin et al., 2023; Westerman et al., 2020; Lu et al., 2018; Figge et al., 2002; Kaplan & Norton, 1992; Lynch &

Cross, 1991). According to the literature, PMS is linked to strategy in a cyclic flow of continuous feedback and feedforward processes described in the four points: (i) Strategy informing PMS development; (ii) PMS informing strategic changes or renewals; (iii) PMS evolving to match new strategies; and (iv) PMS and emergent strategies.

All four of these points are not adequately visible in the energy sector. PMS does not inform strategy, and vice versa, as political interference exists (Loftsgarden, 2020; Novruzova, 2020). The disruption of these feedforward and feedback processes with political innuendo and price capping has minimised the advantages of the cyclic and symbiotic relationship expected between the components. Strategic renewal and emergent strategies were deterred by the bureaucratic nature of the energy sector (Gitelman & Kozhevnikov, 2023).

This study found that PMS influences process flow and activity. The feedforward and feedback from PMS results inform management processes (Mattoni et al., 2019; Da Silva et al., 2019). PMS in the energy sector does not inform business processes and activities as these are already stipulated in policy documents and legislation (Gitelman & Kozhevnikov, 2023). This lengthy process slows down decision-making.

Based on the systematic literature review, the following stakeholder power and interest matrix was created to determine the influence (interest and power) stakeholders have on the energy sector PMS. Energy servitisation and consumer satisfaction should have an appropriate PMS. The shareholder matrix in this is expanded beyond the quadrants (which have high and low evaluations for stakeholder power and interest) to have a six-box analysis (with high, medium, and low assessments for stakeholder power and interest). Table 5 explains the shareholder influence divided into power and interest, followed by a qualified colour code.

The conventional stakeholder matrix is modified in Table 6 to reflect information from the 33 articles derived from the PRISMA 2020 framework. The table discusses the different stakeholders and their power and influence across LIC, LMIC, UMIC, and HIC countries in the SLR. The qualified colour codes from Table 6 are applied to this table.

The 33 articles referred to various stakeholders, including government agencies, citizens, business entities, management, private and public power producers, and policymakers. These stakeholders have different powers and influence over PMS conceptualisation. Table 6 in this study illustrates the varying degrees of influence (low, medium, and high) exerted by each stakeholder across the World Bank income classifications.

Table 6 highlights that UMICs and HICs generally grant more power and influence over PMS design to its stakeholders compared to the more bureaucratic LICs and LMICs (Mendoza & Initiative, 2022; Singh et al., 2022: Lee & Gerner, 2020). Citizen satisfaction and energy servicification were highly regarded in UMIC and HIC (Makki & Alqahtani, 2023; Andriuškevičius et al., 2022; Drago & Gatto, 2022).

The metasystem comprises management and their ability to coordinate, synthesise, and integrate PMS results. An evaluation of management competency determined the proficiency of PMS deployment (Novruzova, 2020). PMS selection and

Table 6 Adapted stakeholder power and interest matrix

Stakeholder Matrix	LIC		LMIC		UMIC		HIC	
Stakeholders	**Power**	**Interest**	**Power**	**Interest**	**Power**	**interest**	**Power**	**Interest**
International Bodies and Treaties e.g. • United Nations Sustainability Goals • Just Transition Bill • World Bank • Geo-Political Tensions	L	L	M	H	H	H	H	H
Domestic Stakeholders e.g. • Government Bodies-SCOPA; COGTA etc. • Legislation PFMA; MFA etc. • Parliament • National Treasury	H	H	H	H	M	H	M	H
Citizens/Consumers	L	H	L	H	H	H	H	H
Business Entities	L	M	L		H	H	H	H
Energy Sector Management	L	M	L	M	H	H	H	H
Energy Sector Employees	L	L	L	L	L	M	M	M
Private And Public Power Producers	L	M	L	M	M	M	L	H
Investors	L	L	L	M	M		M	M
Policymakers	H	H	H	H	H	H	H	H

Source: Researchers Own (2024)

continuous improvement are processes that require experienced management (Gitelman & Kozhevnikov, 2023). Management determined the culture of continuous development of PMS and identified suitable KPIs and critical success areas (Andriuškevičius et al., 2022). Results from PMS are correctly interpreted and reviewed for decision-making, improvement, and strategic alignment. The managers are, therefore, required to continuously develop PMS that is responsive to a organisation's needs (Lyu & Liu, 2021; Davis & Albright, 2004; De Toni & Tonchia, 2001).

Management's role is to synthesise information from PMS applied to the internal and external environment to solve problems, lead innovation, and improve business processes and strategies (Alves et al., 2023). The rational bounded theory presents a limitation for management (Wasiuzzaman, Ibrahim & Kawi, 2022). The use of technology can, however, combat the access to information and the limited time available to apply it to make decisions (Westerman et al., 2020; Višković & Franki, 2015). The management roles have now shifted to the identification of relevant software systems, artificial intelligence, and machine learning to ensure assistance in decision-making and charting the way in the energy sector (Cagno, Negri, Neri & Giambone, 2023; Genta, Sanyé-Mengual, Sala & Lombardi, 2022). Cyber security is also essential as the information produced and interpreted from PMS needs to be secured against hackers. Management needs to ensure the security of the information.

Moreover, PMS assists in quantifying and qualifying the effectiveness of management processes, activities, and outcomes (Khan et al., 2022). This relationship is symbiotic as management and PMS reinforce each other. However, this symbiotic relationship between management and PMS should be managed in a manner that ensures that the agency problem (self-interest by management at the expense of the organisation) is curbed (Rahman et al., 2022). Management experience, competency, and qualifications are important as they would ensure that PMS deployment is suitably done. Moreover, the integrity of newly developed PMS is ascertained (Cagno, Negri, Neri & Giambone, 2023; Davis & Albright, 2004). The paper found that greater autonomy is required for management to ensure flexibility and agility in decision-making, PMS deployment and design.

The results from the systematic review of the literature ascertain that a PMS used in the energy sector is linked to the public management theories used by the energy sector. This is true for OECD countries that use the post new public management model (NPM) (Njenga, 2016). This allows managers greater autonomy, systems thinking approach, agility, and freelance to develop and deploy PMS at their discretion. Innovation, problem-solving, and creativity are encouraged to resolve energy problems (Chan, 2018). Several African and Asian countries lean more on a spectrum that runs from traditional public management and new public management theory which results in a hybrid version where PMS development and deployment are frustrated by red tape measures (Habib & Mourad, 2023). Bureaucracy hinders agility and quick response needed by the energy sector (Lee & Gerner, 2020). Russia (Novruzova, 2020), Arabs (Habib & Mourad, 2023; Rahman et al., 2022), and China (Lyu & Liu, 2021; Chan, 2018) also weaved their way with a combination of the two and gradually adopted the post-NPM model (Lyu & Liu, 2021; Chan, 2018).

Having reviewed various papers with divergent methodologies and findings, the following recurring themes were noted about the elements required for a PMS of good integrity. Critical success factors for PMSs of good integrity have the following attributes identified across the 33 articles. These PMSs should be aligned with the vision, mission, values, and strategy of the entity (Granger, 2023; Makridou et al., 2024) and must possess relevant KPIs that are modifiable (Lyu & Liu, 2021; Huseyin et al., 2016). Furthermore, they are expected to ensure reliable data collection (Gitelman & Kozhevnikov, 2023), ensure data-driven decisions (Chan, 2018) and transparent reporting (Capece et al., 2013). PMSs in the energy sector should encompass stakeholder engagement (Loftsgarden, 2020) and allow flexibility, and agility in decision-making, problem-solving, and innovation (Nwaiwu, 2021; Rabe et al., 2020). PMSs should promote regular monitoring and evaluation (Wanday et al., 2022), produce relevant information (Khan et al., 2022; Fichera et al., 2020; Volkova, 2012), and promote continuous improvement (Makki & Alqahtani, 2023;

Lehtonen, 2012). The PMS should ideally integrate governance and risk management (Mendoza & Initiative, 2022; Schlör et al., 2013).

The study found that PMS should be contingent in nature (Novruzova, 2020) and establish accountability and responsibility centres (Drago & Gatto, 2022; Dobrova et al., 2018; Birech, 2011) that would lead to improved energy sector performance. Benchmarking and comparability with international standards in PMS were also crucial (Westerman et al., 2020; May et al., 2015). A PMS of integrity would generally be associated with generalisability and transferability (Njenga, 2016). Trzeciak et al. (2021) recommended the ideal PMS to be multi-dimensional, multilevel, and scalable.

Recommendations

The results and findings from this study identify the critical success factors and attributes required for PMS integrity and efficient deployment of the tool. To determine the integrity and viability of the tool, the study recommends the viable system model (VSM) (Tannir et al., 2023; Bititci et al., 1997, 2018). The VSM allows for the conceptualisation of PMS that possesses critical success areas which allows for the integration and evolution of the PMS. The VSM states that for a system to produce viable performance results and remain sustainable in a dynamic, complex, and turbulent environment, a systems approach needs to be applied—the strategic, operational, and tactical need to be integrated with the external environment and management (Tannir et al., 2023; Bititci, 1999, Bititci et al., 2018).

The gaps presented from the audit of PMS in the energy sector faced various upheavals, internally and externally, that affected measurement systems. PMSs did not change at the same speed as existing changes. Energy sector PMSs needed frequent audits of integrity and deployment because of the turbulent and dynamic environment (Adamkaite et al., 2023). PMSs were regarded as indispensable as they assisted managers with prioritisation, quick decision-making, and responsiveness to changes (Alves & Lourenço, 2023; Bititci et al., 2012). Disruptions from the external environment and strategic renewal have affected the energy sector. Business processes have evolved with the coming decentralisation of transmission, generation, and distribution functions, and private providers of electricity have been introduced (Herath, Herath, & Cullum, 2023; Andriuškevičius et al., 2022). Moreover, the call to shut down coal plants and adopt renewable energy was underway. Droughts had impacted hydroelectric power while the growing energy demand increased with urbanisation, immigration, and the Fourth Industrial Revolution (4IR) (Korhonen, Jääskeläinen, Laine & Saukkonen, 2023; Ruan & Liu, 2021). Expected outcomes had great variances from actual outcomes. When the energy sector continuously fails to meet stakeholder needs, this leads to increased strikes and politicisation of energy by political opposition (Da Silva et al., 2019; Mattoni et al., 2019). Given the turbulences mentioned above, it is, therefore, necessary to continuously monitor and audit the integrity and deployment of PMS (Aziza et al., 2019; Bititci et al., 1997).

The researcher recommends the development of IPMS which is the next evolutionary stage. The evolution and adaptation of PMS to include multi-dimensional measures and a systems approach was inevitable to ensure viable monitoring, controlling, and evaluation processes. This is inevitable due to the dynamic nature of the energy sector (Sardi, Sorano, Cantino & Garengo, 2023; Sauermann, 2023; Tayler, 2010). This meant both internal and external systems were considered in designing PMS. IPMS can have a significant impact on policies and societies because they are often viewed as reliable, factual data. However, studies show that it is important to look at indicators in the context of the larger policymaking process they are part of.

IPMS became a viable means to ensure sustainability in the energy sector. IPMS ensured that strategic, operational, and tactical objectives synchronised with external environmental changes affecting the energy landscape (Tannir et al., 2023; Bititci et al., 1997, 2018). In other words, understanding how indicators fit into the bigger picture of decision-making helps us see their true influence (Lehtonen, 2012). The result of this feedforward and feedback process between strategy and PMS was integral to the formulation and evolution of integrated performance measurement systems (IPMS) (Laine & Saukkonen, 2023; Ruan & Liu, 2021; Sanchez & Gomez-Conde, 2016).

Conclusions

In conclusion, this SLR assists in conceptualising PMS across the energy sector in various geographical locations. Findings and results from 33 scholarly documents display strategies and outcomes associated with PMS adoption and utilisation. It includes an analysis of developed and developing countries. The limitations of the study are that it does not include private producers and small-scale energy producers. These are suggested areas of further study.

The critical success factors of PMS application in the energy sector are synthesised to include leadership approach, organisational change, technology, and stakeholder engagement. The integrity and deployment of the tools are also important as they facilitate decision-making processes, impact performance, and drive continuous improvement. It is worth noting that PMS may have unintended outcomes that must be managed to enhance operational efficiency, improve service quality, and for greater strategic alignment.

The researcher advocates for continued research efforts aimed at advancing the conceptualisation of PMS for effectiveness and efficiency in the energy sector. The study recommends a multifaceted, integrated, and systems approach to PMS, i.e. an Integrated Performance Measurement System (IPMS). By understanding these determinants, the energy sector is better able to design, deploy, audit, and optimise PMS benefits.

The study underscores the need to consider limitations and pitfalls in PMS, e.g. data validity, reliability, and measurement bias. Leveraging the insights from this energy sector review, a compelling case for more robust, data-driven approaches to PMS can be developed to foster viability and sustainable growth.

References

Adamkaite, J., Streimikiene, D., & Rudzioniene, K. (2023). The impact of social responsibility on corporate financial performance in the energy sector: Evidence from Lithuania. *Corporate Social Responsibility and Environmental Management, 30*(1), 91–104.

Alves, C. L., Skorych, V., De Noni Jr, A., Hotza, D., González, S. Y. G., & Heinrich, S. (2023). Optimizing the energy consumption of the porcelain tile manufacturing process using flowsheet simulations. *Preprints Machines, 11*(2), 137–137. https://doi.org/10.3390/machines11020137

Alves, I., & Lourenço, S. M. (2023). Subjective performance evaluation and managerial work outcomes. *Accounting and Business Research, 53*(2), 127–157.

Andrés, N., Sahraoui, F., Galtier, S., Hadid, L. Z., Dmitruk, P., & Mininni, P. D. (2018). Energy cascade rate in isothermal compressible magnetohydrodynamic turbulence. *Journal of Plasma Physics, 84*(4).

Andriuškevičius, K., Štreimikienė, D., & Alebaitė, I. (2022). Convergence between indicators for measuring sustainable development and M&A performance in the energy sector. *Sustainability, 14*(16), 10360. https://doi.org/10.3390/su141610360

Asikainen, M. (2016). *Challenges to the development of energy performance measurement: A systems thinking approach* (Master's thesis).

Bin-Nashwan, S. A., Abdullah, N. S., & Obaid, M. M. (2017). A review of literature in management control system (MCS) business strategy, and firm performance. *International Journal of Management Research and Reviews, 7*(2), 99.

Birech, K. W. (2011). The effect of performance contracting strategy on the Performance of state corporations in the Energy sector in Kenya (Doctoral dissertation).

Bititci, U. S. (1999). Performance measurement systems in manufacturing. *International Journal of Operations & Production Management, 19*(4), 349–367.

Bititci, U., Garengo, P., Dörfler, V., & Nudurupati, S. (2012). Performance measurement: Challenges for tomorrow. *International Journal of Management Reviews, 14*(3), 305–327. Blackwell Publishing Ltd.

Bititci, U. S., Carrie, A. S., & McDevitt, L. (1997). Integrated performance measurement systems: A development guide. *International Journal of Operations & Production Management, 17*(5), 522–534. MCB UP Ltd. https://doi.org/10.1108/01443579710167230

Bititci, U. S., Ojha, R., Ghadge, A., & Tiwari, M. K. (2018). Bayesian network modelling for supply chain risk propagation. *International Journal of Production Research, 56*(17), 5795–5819. Taylor & Francis.

Borkovcova, A., Černá, M., & Sokolova, M. (2022). Blockchain in the energy sector—systematic review. *Sustainability Journal, 14*(22), 14793.

Cagno, E., Negri, M., Neri, A., & Giambone, M. (2023). One framework to rule them all: An integrated, multi-level and scalable performance measurement framework of sustainability, circular economy, and industrial symbiosis. *Sustainable Production and Consumption, 35*, 55–71.

Capece, G., Di Pillo, F., & Levialdi, N. (2013). The performance assessment of energy companies. *APCBEE Procedia, 5*, 265–270.

Čeryová, D., Bullová, T., Turčeková, N., Adamičková, I., Moravčíková, D., & Bielik, P. (2020). Assessment of the Renewable Energy Sector Performance Using Selected Indicators in European Union Countries. *Resources, 9*(9), 102. https://doi.org/10.3390/resources9090102

Chan, W. L. (2018). Big data analytics in supply chain management: Implications for performance optimization. *International Journal of Production Economics, 195*, 1–12.

Davis, S., & Albright, T. (2004). An investigation of the effect of balanced scorecard implementation on financial performance. *Management Accounting Research, 15*(2), 135–153.

Da Silva, L., Domingos, P., & Pavan, E. (2019). Sustainability indicators for urban solid waste management in large and medium-sized worldwide cities. *Journal of Cleaner Production, 237*, 117802. DGNB system. https://www.dgnb-system.de/en/system/version-2020-international/index.php

De Toni, A., & Tonchia, S. (2001). Performance measurement systems, characteristics, and measures. *International Journal of Operations & Production Management, 21*(1/2), 46–71.

Dobrova, K. B., Danilochkina, N. G., Cherner, N. V., Dobrov, V. P., Dobrov, P. P., & Sepiashvili, E. N. (2018). Innovational management of industrial enterprises in the energy sector.

Drago, C., & Gatto, A. (2022). Policy, regulation effectiveness, and sustainability in the energy sector: A worldwide interval-based composite indicator. *Energy Policy, 167*, 112889.

Figge, F., Hahn, T., Schaltegger, S., & Wagner, M. (2002). The sustainability balanced scorecard – Linking sustainability management to business strategy. *Business Strategy and the Environment, 11*(5), 269–284.

Franco-Santos, M., Lucianetti, L., & Bourne, M. (2012). Contemporary performance measurement systems: A review of their consequences and a framework for research. *Management Accounting Research, 23*(2), 79–119.

García-Moreno, S., & López-Ruiz, V. R. (2023). A Review of the energy sector as a key factor in industry 4.0: The case of Spain. *Energies, 16*(11), 4446.

Genta, C., Sanyé-Mengual, E., Sala, S., & Lombardi, P. (2022). The Consumption Footprint as possible indicator for environmental impact evaluation at the city level. The case study of Turin (Italy). *Sustainable Cities and Society, 79*, 103679.

Giret, S., Hu, Y., Masoumifard, N., Boulanger, J. F., Juère, E., Kleitz, F., & Larivière, D. (2018). Selective separation and preconcentration of scandium with mesoporous silica. *ACS Applied Materials & Interfaces, 10*(1), 448–457.

Giret, A., Julián, V., Corchado, J. M., Fernández, A., Salido, M. A., & Tang, D. (2018). How to choose the greenest delivery plan: A framework to measure key performance indicators for sustainable urban logistics. In *Advances in production management systems. Smart manufacturing for industry 4.0: IFIP WG 5.7 International conference, APMS 2018, Seoul, Korea, August 26-30, 2018, Proceedings, Part II* (pp. 181–189). Springer International Publishing.

Gitelman, L. D., & Kozhevnikov, M. V. (2023). New approaches to the concept of energy transition in the times of energy crisis. *Sustainability, 15*(6), 5167.

Goddard, A., Mellett, H., & Richards, S. (2000). Multidimensional performance assessment in the public sector: The case of the National Health Service. *Financial Accountability & Management, 16*(3), 211–228. https://doi.org/10.1111/1468-0408.00111

Gouvea da Costa, S. E. (2023). Industrial rescheduling approaches: Where are we and what is missing? In *Proceedings of the 11th international conference on production research – Americas (ICPR 2022)* (pp. 738–750). Springer. https://doi.org/10.1007/978-3-031-36121-0_58

Granger, M. (2023). Measuring business performance through financial metrics. *Journal of Financial Economics, 151*(1), 98–112.

Griffith, R., & Neely, A. (2009). Performance pays and managerial experience in multitask teams: Evidence from within a firm. *Journal of Labor Economics, 27*(1), 49–82.

Habib, A. M., & Mourad, N. (2023). The influence of environmental, social, and governance (ESG) practices on US firms' performance: Evidence from the coronavirus crisis. *Journal of the Knowledge Economy*, 1–22.

Harzing, A. W. (2016). Publish or Perish. [online] Harzing.com. Available at: https://harzing.com/resources/publish-or-perish/. Accessed 24 June 2024.

Henri, J.-F., & Journeault, M. (2010). Eco-control: The influence of management control systems on environmental and economic performance. *Accounting, Organizations and Society, 35*(1), 63–80.
Herath, Herath, & Cullum. (2023). simultaneously used qualitative and quantifiable economic indicators. *Economcs, 41*(1).
Hiesterman, A., Meyer, C., & O'Sullivan, P. (2020). The influence of corporate governance on performance outcomes in public companies. *Journal of Corporate Governance, 28*(6), 79–94.
Hrga, A., Capuder, T., & Žarko, I. P. (2020). Demystifying distributed ledger technologies: Limits, challenges, and potentials in the energy sector. *IEEE Access, 8*, 126149–126163.
Jasiukevicius, L., & Christauskas, C. (2011). The application of performance measurement systems at the electricity sector of Lithuania. *Engineering Economics, 22*(3), 283–291.
Journeault, M. (2010). The influence of eco-control on environmental and economic performance: A natural resource based approach. In Crises et nouvelles problématiques de la valeur (pp. CD-ROM).
Kaplan, R. S., & Norton, D. P. (1992). The balanced scorecard: Measures that drive performance. *Management Accounting Journal*, 71–79.
Kovačević, B. (2023). The development of a new SOFI model for performance management of medium-sized and large companies. *Decision Making: Applications in Management and Engineering, 6*(2), 95–125.
Korhonen, T., Jääskeläinen, A., Laine, T., & Saukkonen, N. (2023). How performance measurement can support achieving success in project-based operations. *International Journal of Project Management, 41*(1).
Kowal, B. (2019). Key performance indicators in a multi-dimensional performance card in the energy sector. *IOP Conference Series: Earth and Environmental Science, 214*(1), 012093. IOP Publishing.
Lee, A. D., & Gerner, F. (2020). Learning from power sector reform experiences: The case of Vietnam. *World Bank Policy Research Working Paper,* (9169).
Lehtonen, H. (2012). The relationship between corporate social responsibility and performance: A systematic review. *Journal of Business Ethics, 107*(2), 265–285.
Lin, G., Zhao, Y., Fu, J., & Jiang, D. (2023). Renewable energy in China's abandoned mines. *Science, 380*(6646), 699–700.
Loftsgarden, C. (2020). *How ESG performance affects the corporate financial performance*. An empirical study of the energy sector (Master's thesis, OsloMet–Oslo Metropolitan University).
Lopez-Valeiras, E., Gonzalez-Sanchez, M. B., & Gomez-Conde, J. (2016). The effects of the interactive use of management control systems on process and organizational innovation. *Review of Managerial Science, 10*(3), 487–510. https://doi.org/10.1007/s11846-015-0165-9
Lynch, R. L., & Cross, K. F. (1991). *Measure up! The 7 drivers of business performance*. The Free Press.
Makki, A. A., & Alqahtani, A. Y. (2023). Capturing the effect of the COVID-19 pandemic outbreak on the financial performance disparities in the energy sector: A hybrid MCDM-based evaluation approach. *Economies, 11*(2), 61.
Makridou, G., Doumpos, M., & Lemonakis, C. (2024). Relationship between ESG and corporate financial performance in the energy sector: Empirical evidence from European companies. *International Journal of Energy Sector Management, 18*(4), 873–895.
Mattoni, B., Mangione, A., Pompei, L., Bisegna, F., Iatauro, D., Spinelli, F., & Zinzi, M. (2019). An alternative method for the assessment of the typical lighting energy numeric indicator for different outdoor illuminance conditions. *In Building Simulation IBPSA, 16*, 1224–1230.
May, G., Barletta, I., Stahl, B., & Taisch, M. (2015). Energy management in production: A novel method to develop key performance indicators for improving energy efficiency. *Applied Energy, 149*, 46–61.
Mendoza, M. N., & Initiative, S. (2022). *Lessons learned: Fossil fuel subsidies and energy sector reform in the Philippines*. International Institute for Sustainable Development (IISD).

Micheli, P., & Manzoni, J. F. (2010). Strategic performance measurement: Benefits, limitations and paradoxes. *Long Range Planning, 43*(4), 465–476.
Njenga, E. N. (2016). *The relationship between stock market performance and economic growth in the East Africa community* (Doctoral dissertation, University of Nairobi).
Novruzova, A. H. E. (2020). New technologies in energy sector and automated energy accounting systems and their main factors of influence on ecology. *International Journal on Technical and Physical Problems of Engineering (IJTPE), 42*, 53–57.
Nwaiwu, F. (2021). Digitalisation and sustainable energy transitions in Africa: Assessing the impact of policy and regulatory environments on the energy sector in Nigeria and South Africa. *Energy, Sustainability and Society, 11*(1), 48.
Page, M. J., McKenzie, J. E., Bossuyt, P. M., Boutron, I., Hoffmann, T. C., Mulrow, C. D., et al. (2021). The PRISMA 2020 statement: An updated guideline for reporting systematic reviews. *PLoS Medicine, 18*(3), e1003583. https://doi.org/10.1371/journal.pmed.1003583
Quinn, R. E. (2017). The competing values framework: Understanding performance through organizational culture. *Organizational Dynamics, 46*(2), 55–67.
Rabe, W., Kostka, G., & Habich-Sobiegalla, S. (2020). Socio-economic development and infrastructure cost performance in China: Comparing transport and energy sectors. *Journal of Current Chinese Affairs, 49*(2), 185–206.
Rahman, M. M., Hasan, M. A., Shafiullah, M., Rahman, M. S., Arifuzzaman, M., Islam, M. K., & Rahman, S. M. (2022). A critical, temporal analysis of Saudi Arabia's initiatives for greenhouse gas emissions reduction in the energy sector. *Sustainability, 14*(19), 12651.
Ruan, L., & Liu, H. (2021). Environmental, social, governance activities and firm performance: Evidence from China. *Sustainability, 13*(2), 767.
Sanchez, M. B., & Gomez-Conde, J. (2016). The interactive use of management control systems affects the process and organisational innovation. *Organizations and Society, 35*(1), 63–80.
Sangwa, N. R., & Sangwan, K. S. (2018). Development of an integrated performance measurement framework for lean organizations. *Journal of Manufacturing Technology Management, 29*(1), 41–84.
Sardi, A., Sorano, E., Cantino, V., & Garengo, P. (2023). Big data and performance measurement research: Trends, evolution, and future opportunities. *Measuring Business Excellence, 27*(4), 531–548.
Sauermann, J. (2023). Performance measures and worker productivity. *IZA World of Labor*, 17–94.
Schlör, H., Fischer, W., & Hake, J. F. (2013). Methods of measuring sustainable development of the German energy sector. *Applied Energy, 101*, 172–181.
Shafiq, M. (2014). Emerging trends in geo-politics of Asia Pacific Region. *Islamabad Policy Research Institute (IPRI) Journal, 14*(1), 81–101.
Sivill, L. (2011). Success factors of energy management in energy-intensive industries: Energy performance measurement. *Review of Managerial Science, 10*(3), 487–510.
Sulich, A., & Sołoducho-Pelc, L. (2022). Changes in energy sector strategies: A literature review. *Energies, 15*(19), 7068.
Tannir, A. K., Al-Rousan, H. M., & Al-Hamami, N. A. (2023). Performance management in healthcare organizations: Insights into key performance indicators (KPIs). *Journal of Healthcare Management, 68*(2), 104–120.
Tayler, W. B. (2010). The balanced scorecard as a strategy-evaluation tool: The effects of implementation involvement and a causal-chain focus. *The Accounting Review, 85*(3), 1095–1117.
Trzeciak, M., & Jonek-Kowalska, I. (2021). Monitoring and control in program management as effectiveness drivers in polish energy sector. *Diagnosis and directions of improvement. Energies, 14*(15), 46–61.

Višković, A., & Franki, V. (2015). Status of Croatia's energy sector framework: Progress, potential, challenges and recommendations. *Thermal Science, 19*(3), 751–770.
Volkova, T. (2012). The academic salary system: Conditions and trends in Latvia. In *Paying the professoriate* (pp. 205–214). Routledge.
Wahh, S., Ali, H., & Hassan, R. (2020). Digital transformation and organizational performance: A study of the ICT sector. *Information & Management, 57*(7), 103274.
Wanday, J., & Ajour El Zein, S. (2022). Higher expected returns for investors in the energy sector in Europe using an ESG strategy. *Frontiers in Environmental Science, 10*, 1031827.
Wasiuzzaman, S., Ibrahim, S. A., & Kawi, F. (2022). Environmental, social and governance (ESG) disclosure and firm performance: Does national culture matter? *Meditari Accountancy Research*. https://doi.org/10.1108/MEDAR-06-2021-1356
Weigel, P., & Fischedick, M. (2019). Review and categorization of digital applications in the energy sector. *Applied Sciences, 9*(24), 5350.
Westerman, B., Bonnet, D., & Ferraris, C. (2020). The digital transformation of organizations: Performance implications for traditional industries. *Management Decision, 58*(6), 1290–1307.
World Bank. (2024). *World Bank country and lending groups*. Accessed August 11, 2024, from https://datahelpdesk.worldbank.org/knowledgebase/articles/906519-world-bank-country-and-lending-groups

Managerial Ability, Audit Firm Industry Specialisation, and Audit Pricing in Commercial Banks: A Mediation Analysis

Tajudeen John Ayoola, Eghosa Godwin Inneh, and Lawrence Ogechukwu Obokoh

Abstract The association between managerial ability and audit pricing is limited and mixed in the literature. The mixed results may be due to the non-consideration of the plausibility of a mediating variable influencing the association. Therefore, this study, conducted in the context of the Nigerian banking industry, assesses the mediating role of audit firm industry specialisation on the association between managerial ability and audit pricing. Managerial ability is proxied using the Data Envelopment Analysis (DEA)–Tobit regression model, audit firm industry specialisation is proxied using an indicator variable that is equal to one if the audit firm has at least a market share of 30%, while audit pricing is proxied using audit fees. Secondary data obtained from the audited annual financial statements of 11 listed deposit money banks (commercial banks) between 2011 and 2022 are used for this study. The causal mediation analysis framework in an instrumental-variable regression model is adopted to empirically achieve the study's objective. The findings show that audit firm industry specialisation mediated the association between managerial ability and audit pricing in the Nigerian banking industry. Our findings have implications for bank management, audit firms, and regulatory agencies.

Keywords Nigerian banks · Managerial ability · Audit pricing · Audit firm industry specialisation · Data envelopment analysis · Causal mediation analysis

---

T. J. Ayoola (✉)
University of Johannesburg, South Africa and Obafemi Awolowo University, Ile-Ife, Nigeria
e-mail: alabiayoolaaca@oauife.edu.ng; tjayoola@uj.ac.za

E. G. Inneh · L. O. Obokoh
University of Johannesburg, Johannesburg, South Africa
e-mail: einneh@uj.ac.za; eghinneh@oauife.edu.ng; lawrence.obokoh@jbs.ac.za

T. Moloi (ed.), *Impacting Society Positively Through Technology in Accounting and Business Processes*, Springer Proceedings in Business and Economics,
https://doi.org/10.1007/978-3-031-84885-8_49

Introduction

The empirical literature on the effect of managerial ability on audit pricing is scant but growing. The reason for the scarcity of the literature can be traced to the earlier assumption of the neo-classical economic theory, which assumes management's homogeneity in decision-making (Andreou et al., 2016). Though the agency theory recognises the role of agents in owner–manager relationships with some consideration for rationality (Ben Abdesslem et al., 2022), the neo-classical economic theory relegated the role of soft skills to an irrelevant level. However, the advent of some theories, like the upper echelon (Hambrick & Mason, 1984) and the resource-based theories (Barney, 1986; Lippman & Rumelt, 1982; Wernerfelt, 1984), brought the role of management to the limelight and recognised it as a critical element for positive organisational outcomes (Bamber et al., 2010; Bertrand & Schoar, 2003). This position crystallises many studies on managerial ability, defined as the 'ability to transform corporate resources into revenue, profit or some other value relative to its industry peers' (Demerjian et al., 2012, p. 149).

One decision management has to make is the payment of commensurate audit fees to audit firms for the audit engagement. Studies have shown that management is enormously interested in audit decision-making (Duellman et al., 2015), necessitating studies on the association between managerial ability and audit pricing. However, the empirical literature on the effect of managerial ability on audit pricing can be divided into two strands. The first strand examines the direct association between managerial ability and audit fees, and the results show that audit firms grant audit fee discounts to firms with high-ability managers (Krishnan & Wang, 2015; Mitra et al., 2019; Salehi et al., 2020). All the studies, except Salehi et al. (2020), use firms in the United States of America (USA) to examine the effect of managerial ability on audit fees, and the results show a negative association, indicating that high-ability managers extract lower audit fees for their firms. The studies also adopt the Demerjian et al. (2012) measures of managerial ability using the data envelopment analysis (DEA)–Tobit regression. The second strand of the literature investigates the moderating role of contextual variables such as financial distress (Gul et al., 2018), auditor litigation risk, regulation, and auditor's familiarity with the client (Li & Luo, 2017) on the association between managerial ability and audit fees. Their results show that the relationship between managerial ability and audit pricing depends on some contextual factors acting as moderators.

An analysis of the current empirical literature shows four gaps. First, except for Salehi et al. (2020), all the other studies are domiciled in the USA. Second, most studies excluded the banking industry because of its peculiar financial statement structure. Third, studies have neglected the indirect effect of managerial ability on audit pricing, which may be transmitted through a third variable called the mediator. Fourth, prior studies have been underpinned by the agency, upper echelon, and signalling theories. Consequently, we contribute to the empirical literature on the association between managerial ability and audit pricing in four ways. First, we situate our study in Nigeria, a sub-Saharan African country. The results from prior studies in the USA and Iran may not apply to developing economies like Nigeria, which are characterised by different institutional arrangements and corporate governance structures. Second, the study is carried out within the banking industry to address the gap identified in the study of Ben Abdesslem et al. (2022, p. 2) that studies on managerial ability in the banking sector are needed. Third, we extend the body of knowledge by examining the mediating effect of audit firm industry specialisation on the association between managerial ability and audit pricing in the Nigerian banking industry. Moderation and mediation are third-variable models (Caemmerer et al., 2024) but differ substantially. On the one hand, mediators are intermediate or intervening variables that partially or fully explain how and why the explanatory variable is related to the response variable (Holland et al., 2017). On the other hand, moderators are intervening variables that influence the magnitude and direction of the effect of an explanatory variable on the response variable; they explain when and for whom an association between the response and explanatory variables applies (Fairchild & McQuillin, 2010).

Finally, we adopt the audit demand/supply theories to complement existing theories in explaining the indirect association between management ability and audit pricing. We conjecture that high-ability managers for legitimacy/signalling strategy may demand the service of an audit firm industry specialist to demonstrate the effectiveness of the financial reporting process. However, the role of the auditor specialist in the association between managerial ability and audit pricing needs to be clarified. On the one hand, an auditor specialist may earn an audit fee premium to compensate for specialisation, reputation, and litigation risk, resulting in higher audit fees. This aligns with the audit supply, reputational, and risk effort theories. On the other hand, employing an industry specialist may result in economies of scale and lower audit fees. Despite the importance of auditor industry specialisation, empirical research on its relationship with audit fees and managerial ability still needs to be explored. Therefore, investigating the mediating role of audit industry specialisation in the association between managerial ability and audit pricing serves as a point of departure from prior studies and extends the body of knowledge on ability-pricing studies.

The motivation for this study derives from the non-consideration of the indirect association between managerial ability and audit pricing via a mediator and the need to bridge that gap. The study is conducted within Nigerian commercial banks (deposit money banks). Nigeria is reputed as the second largest economy in Africa, with growth potential. The statutory regulatory agencies for the banking industry include the Financial Reporting Council of Nigeria (CBN), the Central Bank of Nigeria (CBN), the Security and Exchange Commission (SEC), the Nigerian Deposit Insurance Corporation (NDIC), and the Nigerian Exchange Group (NGX). These regulatory agencies provide oversight to the banking industry because of the sector's importance to the country's development. The Nigerian banking industry is exclusively audited by the four international auditing firms (Big4) who parade themselves as auditor specialists. Thus, the Nigerian banking sector presents a compelling context for investigating the mediating role of audit firm industry specialisation on the association between managerial ability and audit pricing. Though studies on audit pricing have been conducted in the banking industry, its association with managerial ability has been underexplored. To the authors' knowledge, this is one of the studies on the indirect association between managerial ability and audit pricing through audit firm industry specialisation as a mediating variable.

The remainder of the study is structured as follows: Section "Review of Literature and Hypotheses Development" covers the literature review, while Section "Methodology" details the methodological design. Sections "Results and Discussion" and "Conclusion" detail the discussion of findings and conclusion, respectively.

Review of Literature and Hypotheses Development

Conceptualisation of Audit Pricing, Managerial Ability, and Audit Firm Industry Specialisation

Audit pricing: Audit pricing is the remuneration paid to audit firms for audit engagements. It is usually proxied by the natural logarithm of audit fees.

Managerial ability: Managerial ability has been conceptualised as a multidimensional concept with various definitions (Curi & Lozano-Vivas, 2020). Managerial ability (also referred to as a high-ability manager, able manager, managerial talent, managerial efficiency, or managerial capability) is the ability to transform corporate resources to achieve value for the firm (Demerjian et al., 2012). Prior to the seminal treatise of Demerjian et al. (2012) measure of managerial ability derived from data envelopment analysis (DEA), some proxies that have been used to measure the concept of managerial ability include returns on assets and chief executive officer (CEO) characteristics (Baik et al., 2012). However, these proxies depict variables outside management's control (Chen & Lin, 2018).

Demerjian et al. (2012) introduced a two-stage process of determining managerial ability using DEA. The first stage consists of determining the firm efficiency through a non-parametric methodology known as data envelopment analysis. The second step involves the determination of the managerial ability score, where the efficiency scores in the first stage are regressed on some contextual variables in a model. The residual from the model is captured as the managerial ability of the firm, distinct from the impact of the firm. The managerial ability score of Demerjian et al. (2012) has been adjudged as a better proxy because of its ability to accommodate multiple input and output variables, and its robustness in efficiency and flexibility. The proxy is adopted because of its wide acceptability sequel to the numerous empirical validations of its robustness and reliability by other studies (e.g., Chen & Lin, 2018; Curi & Lozano-Vivas, 2020).

Audit firm industry specialisation: Audit firm industry specialisation (also known as specialist auditor, industry specialist auditor, or auditor industry specialisation) is a differentiation strategy created for sustainable competitive advantage

(Casterella et al., 2004). Specialisation can be at the partner, office/city, national/ firm, or global level (Carson, 2009; Dao & Pham, 2014). Audit firm industry specialisation has two broad metrics: market versus portfolio shares (Audousset-Coulier et al., 2016). The market metric is determined as the proportion of audit fees (or client sales revenue or assets) over the total audit fees (or total clients' sales or assets) in the same industry (Balsam et al., 2003). The portfolio metric is determined as the proportion of audit fees earned by an audit firm in one industry over the audit fees earned across all the industries served by the audit firm (Dunn & Mayhew, 2004; Owhoso et al., 2002). The basis for calculating the specialist status can be sales revenue (Zhang et al., 2017), number of clients (Zhang et al., 2017), total assets (Krishnan, 2003; Rusmin & Evans, 2017), or audit fees (Cassell et al., 2019). DeFond et al. (2000) argue that using audit fees aligns with the industrial organisation theory and is preferred to other indices. An audit specialist status is recognised where an audit firm has the largest market share in the industry or where an audit firm has a market share above a particular threshold, usually 30% or both (Dao & Pham, 2014; Habib & Bhuiyan, 2011).

Managerial Ability and Audit Firm Industry Specialisation

The association between managerial ability and audit firm industry specialisation is scant in the literature. We adopt the legitimacy and signalling theories to explain the relationship between managerial ability and audit firm industry specialisation. According to the legitimacy theory, managers may employ a specialist auditor to convey the quality of their stewardship responsibilities to the business owners. High-ability managers endeavour to legitimise their stewardship by managing the owners' perceptions and reducing the information asymmetry between them by employing specialist auditors (Caramanis & Lennox, 2008; Lobo & Zhao, 2013). This perspective also aligns with the audit demand theory, which places responsibility on managers to demand the services of a specialist audit firm. According to the signalling theory, managers may employ specialist auditors as a signalling mechanism for a robust and reliable financial reporting system (Mali & Lim, 2021). Therefore, we hypothesise as follows:

H1: Managerial ability significantly accounts for variability in audit firm industry specialisation.

Audit Firm Industry Specialisation and Audit Pricing

The literature on the relationship between audit firm industry specialisation and audit fees is mixed and inconclusive (Scott & Gist, 2013). The association can be positive, negative, or insignificant. A positive association between auditor industry specialisation and audit fees reflects an audit fee premium to recoup the investment in acquiring technical skills, knowledge, and expertise, to provide for litigation risks, or as a premium for a firm reputation (Craswell et al., 1995). This position aligns with the product differentiation, reputational, audit supply, and litigation risk theories. The product differentiation theory posits that specialist auditors offer differentiated services for higher audit fees (Mayhew & Wilkins, 2003; Casterella et al., 2004; Cahen et al., 2008). The reputational theory posits that specialist auditors expend enormous money to acquire high skills, industry-specific technical knowledge, and expertise to earn a reputation for high-quality service. This reputation is compensated by high audit fees (Craswell et al., 1995; Mohd Kharuddin & Basioudis, 2022). The audit supply theory posits that an audit firm may charge a fee premium to cater for its investment in industry-specific skills, knowledge, and expertise, recoup the initial investment, compensate for its reputation, and provide for the risk of litigation (Skinner & Srinivasan, 2012). The litigation risk theory posits that specialist auditors charge a fee premium to cater to the litigation risks of an audit engagement.

A negative association between auditor industry specialisation and audit fees implies an audit fee discount (Casterella et al., 2004). This position aligns with the production efficiency theory and bargaining theory. The production efficiency theory opines that audit fee discounts occur when a specialist auditor achieves economies of scale due to specialisation (Fung et al., 2012; Cahan et al., 2008). The bargaining theory opines that specialist auditors may offer an audit fee discount by succumbing to the greater bargaining power of clients with high-ability managers. An insignificant association between audit firm industry specialisation and audit fees may result from a set-off between differentiation and productive economies hypotheses (Scott & Gist, 2013). Therefore, we hypothesise as follows:

H2: Audit firm industry specialisation significantly accounts for variability in audit pricing.

Managerial Ability and Audit Pricing

The empirical and theoretical literature on the association between managerial ability and audit fees is limited and inconclusive. Most empirical literature posits a negative association (Krishnan & Wang, 2015; Mitra et al. 2019; Salehi et al., 2020), indicating that auditors grant audit fees discount to firms with high-ability managers. This position aligns with some theories, including bargaining theory, production efficiency theory, and managerial ability hypothesis, which aligns with the audit demand/supply theory. According to the bargaining theory, high-ability managers use their bargaining abilities to convince the auditors to discount fees to their firms. The production efficiency theory argues that economies of scale achieved by specialist auditors are passed to their clients in the form of lower audit fees (Cahan et al., 2008). Therefore, we hypothesise as follows:

H3: Managerial ability significantly accounts for variability in audit pricing.

Mediating Role of the Audit firm Industry Specialisation on the Association Between Managerial Ability and Audit Pricing

One gap in the literature is the non-consideration of the causal pathway through which managerial ability affects audit pricing. A mediator variable 'lies along the causal pathway between an independent and dependent variable, explaining all or part of the effect of the independent variable on the dependent variable' (Nitzl et al. 2016). The intervening variable in the association between managerial ability and audit pricing is audit firm industry specialisation. High-ability managers attempting to legitimise their position and signal their effectiveness can employ an auditor industry specialist to audit their financial statements. This aligns with the audit demand theory, which places a responsibility on high-ability managers to demonstrate their effectiveness to the owners (principals) and reduce the information asymmetry.

However, industry specialist auditors can offer a fee discount or earn a fee premium. On the one hand, the industry specialists will earn a fee premium to compensate for their reputation, industry-specific skills, and knowledge or provide for litigation risks. On the other hand, industry specialist auditors will offer fee discounts to firms with high-ability managers because of the bargaining power of the managers because of the low audit risk as a result of financial reporting quality achieved by the high-ability manager, or because of the economies of scales due to production efficiency of the specialist auditor. This position aligns with both the audit demand-supply theory. Audit demand theory requires the high-ability managers to request the services of specialist auditors but bargain for fee discounts. In contrast, audit supply theory requires the specialist auditor to either earn a fee premium for reputation, technical knowledge, and litigation risk or give a fee discount because of cost savings due to specialisation or bargaining power of the high-ability managers.

We argue that audit firm industry specialisation is a critical intermediate variable, among other variables that partially explain the indirect association between managerial ability and audit pricing. Thus, we propose as follows:

H3: Audit firm industry specialisation partially mediates the association between managerial ability and audit pricing.

Methodology

Data Source, Sample, and Variables

There are 23 deposit banks in Nigeria, comprising 14 publicly listed banks and nine privately owned banks whose financial statements are inaccessible. We, therefore, expunge all nine privately listed banks. Out of the 14 publicly listed banks, we expunge the banks acquired during the period under consideration and those reporting in currencies other than the Nigerian currency (Naira). Therefore, these conditions limit the sample to 11 banks. The study is carried out between 2011 and 2022. The base year, 2011, is considered the starting year because the financial reporting landscape changed in 2011 due to the adoption of the International Financial Reporting Standards (IFRS) in the Nigerian banking industry.

Statements of banks, Central Bank of Nigeria reports, Nigerian Stock Exchange (NSE) publications and SecuriThe description of the response, explanatory, mediator, instrumental, and control variables are as follows:

Response variable—Audit pricing (Y): In line with prior studies (e.g. Griffin & Lont, 2011***), the study adopts the natural logarithm of audit fees as the dependent variable. Audit fees are the remuneration paid to an audit firm for an*** audit engagement.

Explanatory variable—Managerial ability (X): The study adopts Demerjian et al.'s 2-stage DEA–Tobit regression model. The first stage involves the determination of firm efficiency using two input variables (customer deposits and net interest income) and two output variables (property, plant, and equipment; *V* and staff cost). Therefore, the model for the banks' efficiency analysis is as follows:

$$MAX\theta = \frac{\mu 1\text{DEP} + \mu 2\text{NETINC}}{v1\text{PPE} + v2\text{LABOUR} +} \quad (1)$$

DEP represents customer deposits; NETINC represents net interest income; PPE represents property, plant, and equipment; LABOUR represents staff costs.

Regarding DEA orientation, the input-based orientation model is adopted with a variable return to scale (VRS) assumption because of its suitable finite sample property and convergence properties (Banker & Park, 2021; Banker et al., 2022). In the second stage, we apply the firm efficiency scores generated in the first stage to estimate efficiency attributable to management only by regressing the efficiency scores derived in the first stage on some firm characteristics (Demerjian et al., 2012). Therefore, managerial ability is extracted as the residual of the following model:

$$\text{DEASC} = \beta_1\text{SIZ} + \beta_2\text{MkT} + \beta_3\text{FLOW} + \beta_4\text{AGE} + \beta_5\text{SUB} + \beta_7\text{YEAR} + e_{\text{it}} \quad (2)$$

SIZ represents banks' total assets; MKT represents market share; FLOW represents free cash flow; AGE represents the number of years the bank has existed; SUB represents the number of subsidiaries; and YEAR represents year dummies.

Following prior studies (e.g. Garcia-Meca & Garcia-Sanchez, 2018), we adopt the DEA–Tobit regression model of Demerjian et al. (2012) to extract the managerial ability score.

Mediator variable—Audit firm industry specialisation (M): The study adopts market share (based on audit fees) as the basis for the industry specialisation. According to Mayhew and Wilkins (2003, p. 33), market share allows 'audit firms with large market shares to develop more industry-specific knowledge and expertise, spread industry-specific training costs over more clients to produce quality services at a cost-effective rate'. Statements of banks, Central Bank of Nigeria reports, Nigerian Stock Exchange (NSE) publications and Securi.

Instrumental variable—Size (Z): Firm size, measured as the logarithm of total assets, often accounts for over 70% of the variation in audit fees (Hay et al., 2006). Studies have shown the importance of the size effect as a critical driver in audit pricing decisions (Kohlbeck et al., 2008; Scott & Gist, 2013).

Control variables: The study adopts two control variables: financial risk measured by an indicator variable equal to one if the bank records a net loss for a particular year and zero otherwise. The second control variable is audit tenure, which is determined as the logarithm of the number of years an audit firm has been engaged.

Model Specification and Analytical Techniques

Following the technique of prior studies (e.g. Dippel et al., 2020; Frölich & Huber, 2017), the models for the achievement of the objective are as follows:

$$\text{SPEC}_{it} = \beta_0 + \beta_1\text{MGR}_{it} + \beta_2\text{SIZE}_{it} + \beta_3\text{LOSS}_{it} + \beta_4\text{TEN}_{it} + e_{it} \quad (3)$$

$$\text{FEE}_{it} = \beta_0 + \beta_1\text{MGR}_{it} + \beta_2\text{SPEC}_{it} + \beta_3\text{SIZE}_{it} + \beta_4\text{LOSS}_{it} + \beta_5\text{TEN}_{it} + e_{it} \quad (4)$$

Where 'SPEC' represents audit firm industry specialisation, 'MGR' represents managerial ability, and 'SIZE' represents firm size. 'LOSS' represents firms with negative returns on assets, 'TEN' represents auditor tenure, and 'FEE' represents audit fees. In model 1, the mediator (SPEC) is regressed on the independent variable (MGR), the instrument (SIZE), and two control variables (LOSS and TEN). In model 2, the response variable (FEE) is regressed on the explanatory variable (MGR), the mediator (SPEC), the instrument (SIZE), and two control variables (LOSS and TEN).

We adopt the Dippel et al. (2020) causal mediation analysis framework in an instrumental-variable regression model because prior studies have expressed endogeneity on managerial ability and other bank characteristics arising from reverse causality (Andreou et al., 2016). We also consider Baron and Kenny (1986) and Zhao et al. (2010) models as robustness tests or alternative techniques for determining mediation. Baron and Kenny (1986) are pioneers of mediation analysis. The authors posit that the determination of mediation follows a four-way approach. The steps and equations for achieving Baron and Kenny's (1986) technique are shown in Fig. 1. According to Baron and Kenny (1986), the following conditions must hold for mediation to occur:

'First, the independent variable must affect the mediator in Step 2 of Fig. 1. Second, the independent variable must be shown to affect the dependent variable in

Fig. 1 Mediation analysis. Source: Adapted from Barron and Kenny's (1986) four-step approach for mediation analysis

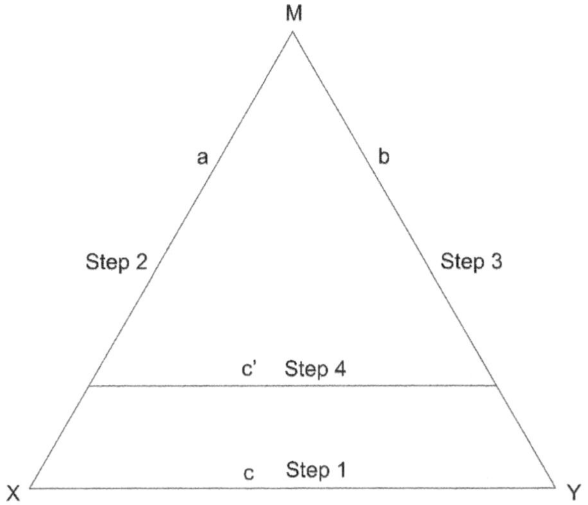

Step 1 of Fig. 1. Third, the mediator must affect the dependent variable in Step 3 of Fig. 1'.

Furthermore, the Sobel test (Sobel, 1982) is recommended to test the validity of the results. There have been many arguments against Baron and Kenny's model. First, some studies (e.g. Shrout & Bolger, 2002) argue that Step 1 of Baron and Kenny's model is unnecessary in determining mediation, which has been supported in other studies. Second, the Sobel test may not reveal mediation in a large sample, resulting in Type II errors. Therefore, the bootstrapping technique is recommended as an alternative to the Sobel test in determining mediation. The bootstrapping procedure generates confidential intervals that suggest mediation when the intervals do not contain zero (Hayes, 2009; Preacher & Hayes, 2004, 2008). We also adopt the one-step approach of Zhao et al. (2010), which posits that a significant indirect effect is sufficient to establish mediation. They further argued that a bootstrap method should be adopted to test the significance of the indirect step.

Step 1: Use a simple regression model of Y on X to show that the exposure is associated with the outcome.

$$Y = i_3 + c'X + bM \tag{5}$$

Step 2: Use a simple regression model of M on X to show that the exposure is associated with the mediator.

$$M = i2 + aX \tag{6}$$

Step 3: Use a multiple regression model of Y on X and M to show that the mediator (after controlling for the exposure) is associated with the outcome.

$$Y = i3 + c^{'}X + bM \tag{7}$$

Step 4: Use the same model in Step 3 to quantify the direct effect (c') of the exposure (after controlling for the mediator) on the outcome.

Results and Discussion

Pre-estimation Analyses

The study conducts pre-estimation tests to ensure the model fits the data. To this end, we compute the descriptive statistics and correlation matrix to gain an initial understanding of the data. We also conduct two diagnostic tests comprising multicollinearity using variance inflation factor (VIF) and an outlier test. Finally, we determine the appropriateness of the sample size and statistical power analysis to assess the reliability of the results. The results are shown in Table 1. From the descriptive statistics, the audit fee (FEES) has a mean of 12.57, skewness is mildly greater than zero, while kurtosis is less than three, indicating that the audit fee is roughly symmetrical with normal distribution, lighter tails, and a flat peak. The managerial ability (MGR) has a mean of 0.02, skewness is less than zero, while kurtosis is less than three, indicating that the variable has an approximately normal distribution, roughly symmetrical, with lighter tails and a flat peak. Audit firm industry specialisation (SPEC) has an average of 0.33, which suggests that about 33% of the sample is audited by an industry specialist. The variable is mildly normal, with skewness above zero and a kurtosis of less than three. Firm size (SIZE)

Table 1 Correlation matrix and descriptive statistics of the variables

	FEES	MGR	SPEC	SIZE	LOSS	TEN
Correlation matrix						
LNFEES	1.00					
MGR	−0.65*	1.00				
SPEC	0.46*	−0.35*	1.00			
SIZE	0.91*	−0.67*	0.40*	1.00		
LOSS	−0.24*	0.05	−0.02	−0.31*	1.00	
TEN	0.16	−0.00*	0.07	0.04	−0.15	1.00
Descriptive statistics						
Obs	144	144	144	144	144	144
Mean	12.57	0.02	0.33	21.30	0.05	1.40
Std. Dev	0.82	0.01	0.47	0.98	0.22	0.72
Min	11.08	−0.00	0.00	18.87	0.00	0.00
Median	12.58	0.02	0.00	21.31	0.00	1.61
Max	14.33	0.05	1.00	23.43	1.00	2.30
Skew	0.11	−0.27	0.71	−0.09	4.20	−0.56
Kurtosis	2.08	2.72	1.50	2.42	18.62	2.21
VIF		1.95	1.23	2.30	1.21	1.03

has a mean of 21.3 and ranges from 21.3 to 23.4. The results also show that about 5% of the sample recorded negative returns on assets (LOSS) for the period under consideration, while the average tenure is 1.4 and ranges from 1.6 to 2.3.

The correlation matrix shows that audit fees are significantly and positively related to audit firm industry specialisation and size. At the same time, they are significantly and negatively associated with managerial ability and financial risk. However, audit fees are insignificantly related to audit tenure. Multicollinearity through variance inflation factor is conducted, and the results show that multicollinearity is not a problem, as no variable has a VIF above the threshold of 5. We also conduct an outlier test using Cook's distance, and the result shows that no variable is above the cutoff of 1. Finally, following prior studies (e.g. Muthén & Muthén, 2002; Ayoola, 2022), we apply the Monte Carlo application platform of Schoemann et al. (2017) to assess sample size and statistical power. The analysis is run twice with double replications of 1000 and 5000 to ensure stable convergence of values. The benchmark is a statistical power of about 0.8 and above at a 5% significance level (Cohen, 1988; Fritz & MacKinnon, 2007). The results show a statistical power of 98%, which indicates that the sample size will reject a false null hypothesis for the mediation effect 98% of the time. The results exceed the benchmark of 70%.

Regression Results and Discussion of Findings

The study examines the role of audit firm industry specialisation as a mediator between managerial ability and audit pricing in the Nigerian banking industry. The study disentangles the effect of managerial ability on audit pricing into a direct component and an indirect component via audit firm industry specialisation. The study applies the Dippel et al. (2020) technique of causal mediation in an instrumental-variable setting, where we instrument managerial ability by firm size.

To achieve our objective, we make four hypotheses. The first hypothesis (H1) states that managerial ability is significantly related to audit firm industry specialisation (MGR → SPEC). The results validate this hypothesis with evidence that managerial ability is significantly and negatively associated with audit firm industry specialisation (coef = −27.25, p = 0.000). These results align with audit demand, legitimacy, and signalling theories. This result shows high-ability managers demand specialist auditors' services for legitimacy and signalling. The Dippel et al. (2020) method does not test the second hypothesis (H2) because it is insignificant in determining mediation. The third hypothesis (H3) states that managerial ability significantly accounts for variability in audit pricing (MGR → FEE). The results validate this hypothesis with evidence that managerial ability significantly negatively affects audit fees (coef = −99.54, p = 0.000), indicating that high-ability managers extract audit fee discounts for their firms. This position aligns with the findings of prior results (e.g. Krishnan & Wang, 2015; Mitra et al. 2019; Salehi et al., 2020), which suggest that lower audit fees are procured from firms with high-ability managers.

The fourth hypothesis (H4) states that audit firm industry specialisation partially mediates the association between managerial ability and audit pricing. Audit firm industry specialisation exerted a significantly positive effect on audit fees (coef = 4.29, $p = 0.001$), while managerial ability paled into insignificance after the introduction of audit firm industry specialisation into Eq. (4), indicating complete mediation. The results show that audit firm industry specialisation explains 117% of the total effect. In sum, the results show evidence of a complete mediation because the direct effect between managerial ability and audit pricing is no longer statistically significant upon the introduction of audit firm industry specialisation in Eq. (4).

The study makes additional analyses using Baron and Kenny's (1986) and Zhao et al.'s (2010) techniques to determine the robustness of the results. Using Baron and Kenny's (1986) methodology shown in Panel D of Table 2, the results show the presence of partial mediation as Steps 1, 2, and 3, as well as Sobel's test, is significant. Using the Zhao et al. (2010) method, as shown in Panel E of Table 2, the results show the presence of complementary partial mediation as Steps 1 and 3 and the bootstrapped test are significant.

Theoretical and Managerial/Practical Contributions

The study makes a theoretical contribution to ability-pricing studies. It applies the audit demand/supply theories to explain the indirect association between managerial ability and audit pricing through audit firm industry specialisation. The results show that audit firm industry specialisation mediates the association between managerial ability and audit pricing. The study's results show the relevance of industry specialisation in the audit process regarding practical contribution. Therefore, regulatory authorities should incentivise audit firms to invest in and continuously develop bank-specific skills, knowledge, and expertise for cost-effective pricing. The banks should also motivate high-ability managers to achieve high financial reporting quality with fewer risks, enabling the audit firms to discount audit fees.

Conclusion

The study examines the mediating role of audit firm industry specialisation in the association between managerial ability and audit pricing in the Nigerian banking industry. Managerial ability is proxied using the Data Envelopment Analysis (DEA)–Tobit regression model, audit firm industry specialisation is proxied using an indicator variable that is equal to one if the audit firm has at least a market share of 30%, while audit pricing is proxied using audit fees. The Dippel et al. (2020) technique of causal mediation in an instrumental-variable setting is adopted to achieve the objective, while Baron and Kenny's (1986) causal mediation model and

Table 2 Results for the mediating role of audit firm industry specialisation on the association between managerial ability and audit pricing in the Nigerian banking industry

H	Paths	Dippel et al. (2020) method	Baron and Kenny (1986) method	Zhao et al. (2010) method	Decision on hypothesis
A	B	C	D	E	F
	Direct path				
H1	MGR → SPEC	−27.25*** (−5.68)	−15.64*** (−4.43)	−15.64*** (−4.43)	Accept H1
H2	SPEC → FEES		0.45*** (4.29)		Accept H2
H3	MGR → FEES	−99.54*** (−13.24)	−42.73*** (−9.06)	−42.73*** (−9.06)	Accept H3
	Indirect path				
H4	MGR → SPEC → FEES				Accept H4
	MGR → FEES	17.39 (0.70)			
	SPEC → FEES	4.29*** (3.33)			
	Control variables				
	LOSS → FEES		−0.73*** (−3.38)		
	TEN → FEES		0.13** (1.98)		
	First stage	181.833			
	Second stage	10.243			
	Total effect	−99.54			
	Direct effect	17.39			
	Indirect effect	−116.93			
	Other tests:				
	Sobel test		−7.00*** (−3.08)		
	Bootstrapped test			−7.00*** (−3.10)	
	Confidence interval		−11.46; −2.55	−11.72; −3.01	

Zhao et al.'s (2010) technique are applied as robustness tests. While Sobel's (1982) z-test complemented Baron and Kenny's (1986) results, the bootstrapping technique complemented Zhao et al.'s (2010) methodology. The findings suggest that audit firm industry specialisation mediated the association between managerial ability and audit pricing. The results show high-ability managers extract audit fee discounts from industry specialist auditors. This study extends knowledge on the indirect effect of managerial ability on audit pricing through audit firm industry specialisation. While previous studies have focused substantially on the direct effect of managerial ability on audit pricing and the moderating effect of contextual factors on the association, the novel focus of the current research is on the mediating role of audit firm industry specialisation on the association between managerial ability and audit pricing.

The study has some limitations, which future studies can explore. First, future studies can explore other indices and techniques for measuring managerial ability. We use the DEA approach of Demerjian et al. (2012); other studies can explore the Stochastic Frontier Analysis (SFA) perspective. Two, the study focuses on the Nigerian banking industry; therefore, the results of this study may not apply to other industries and developing economies because of different institutional structures and governance frameworks. Finally, other studies can examine variables that can act as moderators and mediators in the ability-pricing study.

References

Andreou, P. C., Philip, D., & Robejsek, P. (2016). Bank liquidity creation and risk-taking: Does managerial ability matter? *Journal of Business Finance and Accounting, 43*(1–2), 226–259. https://doi.org/10.1111/jbfa.12169

Audousset-Coulier, S., Jeny, A., & Jiang, L. (2016). The validity of auditor industry specialisation measures. *Auditing, 35*(1), 139–161. https://doi.org/10.2308/ajpt-51176

Ayoola, T. J. (2022). Audit fees, audit seasonality and audit quality in Nigeria: A mediation analysis. *Journal of Financial Reporting and Accounting*. https://doi.org/10.1108/JFRA-01-2022-0010

Baik, B., Choi, S., Farber, D. B., & Zhang, J. (2012). Managerial ability and earnings quality: An international analysis. *עלון הנוטע, 66*(September), 37–39.

Balsam, S., Krishnan, J., & Yang, J. S. (2003). Auditor industry specialization and earnings quality. *Auditing, 22*(2), 71–97. https://doi.org/10.2308/aud.2003.22.2.71

Bamber, L. S., Jiang, J., & Wang, I. Y. (2010). What's my style? The influence of top managers on voluntary corporate financial disclosure. *Accounting Review, 85*(4), 1131–1162. https://doi.org/10.2308/accr.2010.85.4.1131

Barney, J. B. (1986). Strategic factor markets: Expectations, luck, and business strategy. *Management Science, 32*(10), 1231–1241. https://doi.org/10.1287/mnsc.32.10.1231

Baron, R. M., & Kenny, D. A. (1986). The moderator-mediator variable distinction in social psychological research: Conceptual, strategic, and statistical considerations. *Journal of Personality and Social Psychology, 51*(6), 1173–1182. https://doi.org/10.1037/0022-3514.51.6.1173

Ben Abdesslem, R., Chkir, I., & Dabbou, H. (2022). Is managerial ability a moderator? The effect of credit risk and liquidity risk on the likelihood of bank default. *International Review of Financial Analysis, 80*. https://doi.org/10.1016/j.irfa.2022.102044

Bertrand, M., & Schoar, A. (2003). Managing with style: The effect of managers on firm policies. *Quarterly Journal of Economics, 118*(4), 1169–1208. https://doi.org/10.1162/003355303322552775

Caemmerer, J. M., Hennessy, B., & Niileksela, C. R. (2024). Third variables in longitudinal research: Application of longitudinal mediation and moderation in school psychology. *Journal of School Psychology, 103*. https://doi.org/10.1016/j.jsp.2024.101283

Cahan, S. F., Godfrey, J. M., Hamilton, J., & Jeter, D. C. (2008). Auditor specialization, auditor dominance, and audit fees: The role of investment opportunities. *Accounting Review, 83*(6), 1393–1423. https://doi.org/10.2308/accr.2008.83.6.1393

Caramanis, C., & Lennox, C. (2008). Audit effort and earnings management. *Journal of Accounting and Economics, 45*(1), 116–138. https://doi.org/10.1016/j.jacceco.2007.05.002

Carson, E. (2009). Industry specialization by global audit firm networks. *Accounting Review, 84*, 355–382. https://doi.org/10.2308/accr.2009.84.2.355

Cassell, C., Hunt, E., Narayanamoorthy, G., & Rowe, S. P. (2019). A hidden risk of auditor industry specialization: Evidence from the financial crisis. *Review of Accounting Studies, 24*(3), 891–926. https://doi.org/10.1007/s11142-019-09508-w

Casterella, J. R., Francis, J. R., Lewis, B. L., & Walker, P. L. (2004). Auditor industry specialization, client bargaining power, and audit pricing. *Auditing, 23*(1), 123–140. https://doi.org/10.2308/aud.2004.23.1.123

Chen, S. S., & Lin, C. Y. (2018). Managerial ability and acquirer returns. *Quarterly Review of Economics and Finance, 68*, 171–182. https://doi.org/10.1016/j.qref.2017.09.004

Cohen, J. (1988). *Statistical power analysis for the behavioural sciences*. Lawrence Earlbaum Associates. Retrieved from http://scholar.google.nl/scholar?q=Cohen%2C+J+%281988%29+Statistical+power+analysis+for+the+behavioral+sciences&btnG=&hl=nl&as_sdt=0%2C5#0

Craswell, A. T., Francis, J. R., & Taylor, S. L. (1995). Auditor brand name reputations and industry specializations. *Journal of Accounting and Economics, 20*(3), 297–322. https://doi.org/10.1016/0165-4101(95)00403-3

Curi, C., & Lozano-Vivas, A. (2020). Managerial ability as a tool for prudential regulation. *Journal of Economic Behavior and Organization, 174*, 87–107. https://doi.org/10.1016/j.jebo.2020.03.023

Dao, M., & Pham, T. (2014). Audit tenure, auditor specialization and audit report lag. *Managerial Auditing Journal, 29*(6), 490–512. https://doi.org/10.1108/MAJ-07-2013-0906

DeFond, M. L., Francis, J. R., & Wong, T. J. (2000). Auditor industry specialization and market segmentation: Evidence from Hong Kong. *Auditing, 19*(1), 49–66. https://doi.org/10.2308/aud.2000.19.1.49

Demerjian, P., Lev, B., & McVay, S. (2012). Quantifying managerial ability: A new measure and validity tests. *Management Science, 58*(7), 1229–1248. https://doi.org/10.1287/mnsc.1110.1487

Dippel, C., Ferrara, A., & Heblich, S. (2020). Causal mediation analysis in instrumental-variables regressions. *Stata Journal, 20*(3), 613–626. https://doi.org/10.1177/1536867X20953572

Duellman, S., Hurwitz, H., & Sun, Y. (2015). Managerial overconfidence and audit fees. *Journal of Contemporary Accounting and Economics, 11*(2), 148–165. https://doi.org/10.1016/j.jcae.2015.05.001

Dunn, K. A., & Mayhew, B. W. (2004). Audit firm industry specialization and client disclosure quality. *Review of Accounting Studies, 9*(1), 35–58.

Fairchild, A. J., & McQuillin, S. D. (2010). Evaluating mediation and moderation effects in school psychology: A presentation of methods and review of current practice. *Journal of School Psychology, 48*(1), 53–84. https://doi.org/10.1016/j.jsp.2009.09.001

Fritz, M. S., & MacKinnon, D. P. (2007). Required sample size to detect the mediated effect. *Psychological Science, 18*(3), 233–239. https://doi.org/10.1111/j.1467-9280.2007.01882.x

Fung, S. Y. K., Gul, F. A., & Krishnan, J. (2012). City-level auditor industry specialization, economies of scale, and audit pricing. *Accounting Review, 87*(4), 1281–1307. https://doi.org/10.2308/accr-10275

Griffin, P. A., & Lont, D. H. (2011). Audit fees around dismissals and resignations: Additional evidence. *Journal of Contemporary Accounting and Economics, 7*(2), 65–81. https://doi.org/10.1016/j.jcae.2011.10.001

Gul, F. A., Khedmati, M., Lim, E. K. Y., & Navissi, F. (2018). Managerial ability, financial distress, and audit fees. *Accounting Horizons, 32*(1), 29–51. https://doi.org/10.2308/acch-51888

Habib, A., & Bhuiyan, M. B. U. (2011). Audit firm industry specialization and the audit report lag. *Journal of International Accounting, Auditing and Taxation, 20*(1), 32–44. https://doi.org/10.1016/j.intaccaudtax.2010.12.004

Hambrick, D. C., & Mason, P. A. (1984). Upper echelons: The organization as a reflection of its top managers. *Academy of Management Review, 9*(2), 193–206. https://doi.org/10.5465/amr.1984.4277628

Hayes, A. F. (2009). Beyond Baron and Kenny: Statistical mediation analysis in the new millennium. *Communication Monographs, 76*(4), 408–420. https://doi.org/10.1080/03637750903310360

Holland, S. J., Shore, D. B., & Cortina, J. M. (2017). Review and recommendations for integrating mediation and moderation. *Organizational Research Methods, 20*(4), 686–720. https://doi.org/10.1177/1094428116658958

Krishnan, G. V. (2003). *Does big 6 auditor industry expertise constrain earnings management? Accounting Horizons*. American Accounting Association. https://doi.org/10.2308/acch.2003.17.s-1.1

Krishnan, G. V., & Wang, C. (2015). The relation between managerial ability and audit fees and going concern opinions. *Auditing, 34*(3), 139–160. https://doi.org/10.2308/ajpt-50985

Li, Y., & Luo, Y. (2017). The contextual nature of the association between managerial ability and audit fees. *Review of Accounting and Finance, 16*(1), 2–20. https://doi.org/10.1108/RAF-01-2016-0012

Lippman, S. A., & Rumelt, R. P. (1982). Uncertain imitability: An analysis of interfirm differences in efficiency under competition. *The Bell Journal of Economics, 13*(2), 418. https://doi.org/10.2307/3003464

Lobo, G. J., & Zhao, Y. (2013). Relation between audit effort and financial report misstatements: Evidence from quarterly and annual restatements. *Accounting Review, 88*(4), 1385–1412. https://doi.org/10.2308/accr-50440

Mali, D., & Lim, H.-J. (2021). Can audit effort (hours) reduce a firm's cost of capital? Evidence from South Korea. *Accounting Forum, 45*(2), 171–199.

Mayhew, B. W., & Wilkins, M. S. (2003). *Audit firm industry specialization as a differentiation strategy: Evidence from fees charged to firms going public*. American Accounting Association. https://doi.org/10.2308/aud.2003.22.2.33

Mitra, S., Jaggi, B., & Al-Hayale, T. (2019). Managerial overconfidence, ability, firm-governance and audit fees. *Review of Quantitative Finance and Accounting, 52*(3), 841–870. https://doi.org/10.1007/s11156-018-0728-3

Mohd Kharuddin, K. A., & Basioudis, I. G. (2022). A Review of Theories on Auditor Industry Specialisation. *International Journal of Academic Research in Business and Social Sciences, 12*(9). https://doi.org/10.6007/ijarbss/v12-i9/14723

Muthén, L. K., & Muthén, B. O. (2002). How to use a Monte Carlo study to decide on sample size and determine power. *Structural Equation Modeling, 9*(4), 599–620. https://doi.org/10.1207/S15328007SEM0904_8

Nitzl, C., Roldan, J. L., & Cepeda, G. (2016). Mediation analysis in partial least squares path modelling, Helping researchers discuss more sophisticated models. *Industrial Management and Data Systems, 116*(9), 1849–1864. https://doi.org/10.1108/IMDS-07-2015-0302

Owhoso, V. E., Messier, W. F., & Lynch, J. G. (2002). Error detection by industry-specialized teams during sequential audit review. *Journal of Accounting Research. Blackwell Publishing Inc.* https://doi.org/10.1111/1475-679X.00075

Preacher, K. J., & Hayes, A. F. (2004). SPSS and SAS procedures for estimating indirect effects in simple mediation models. *Behavior Research Methods, Instruments, and Computers, 36*(4), 717–731. https://doi.org/10.3758/BF03206553

Preacher, K. J., & Hayes, A. F. (2008). Asymptotic and resampling strategies for assessing and comparing indirect effects in multiple mediator models. *Behavior Research Methods, 40*, 879–891. https://doi.org/10.3758/BRM.40.3.879

Rusmin, R., & Evans, J. (2017). Audit quality and audit report lag: Case of Indonesian listed companies. *Asian Review of Accounting, 25*(2), 191–210. https://doi.org/10.1108/ARA-06-2015-0062

Salehi, M., Mousavi Shiri, M., & Hossini, S. Z. (2020). The relationship between managerial ability, earnings management and internal control quality on audit fees in Iran. *International Journal of Productivity and Performance Management, 69*(4), 685–703. https://doi.org/10.1108/IJPPM-07-2018-0261

Scott, W. D., & Gist, W. E. (2013). Forced auditor change, industry specialization and audit fees. *Managerial Auditing Journal, 28*(8), 708–734. https://doi.org/10.1108/MAJ-11-2012-0779

Schoemann, A. M., Boulton, A. J., & Short, S. D. (2017). Determining power and sample size for simple and complex mediation models. *Social Psychological and Personality Science, 8*(4), 379–386. https://doi.org/10.1177/1948550617715068

Shrout, P. E., & Bolger, N. (2002). Mediation in experimental and nonexperimental studies: New procedures and recommendations. *Psychological Methods, 7*(4), 422–445. https://doi.org/10.1037/1082-989X.7.4.422

Skinner, D. J., & Srinivasan, S. (2012). Audit quality and auditor reputation: Evidence from Japan. *Accounting Review, 87*(5), 1737–1765. https://doi.org/10.2308/accr-50198

Sobel, M. E. (1982). Asymptotic confidence intervals for indirect effects in structural equation models. *Sociological Methodology, 13*, 290. https://doi.org/10.2307/270723

Wernerfelt, B. (1984). A resource-based view of the firm. *Strategic Management Journal, 5*(2), 171–180. https://doi.org/10.1002/smj.4250050207

Zhao, X., Lynch, J. G., & Chen, Q. (2010). Reconsidering Baron and Kenny: Myths and truths about mediation analysis. *Journal of Consumer Research, 37*(2), 197–206. https://doi.org/10.1086/651257

Assessing Nigeria's Fourth Industrial Revolution Policy Alignment with Sustainable Development Goals: An In-Depth Exploration

Olawale Olufemi Akinrinde

Abstract Fourth Industrial Revolution (4IR) policies are the frameworks for the attainment of sustainable development. This is because there is no aspect of the Sustainable Development Goals that is not driven by the 4IR. The synergy between Fourth Industrial Revolution (4IR) policies and Sustainable Development Goals (SDGs) is gaining increasing attention, as nations seek to leverage technological advancements for sustainable development. However, little understanding exists as to the extent to which Nigeria's policies on 4IR align with the quest for the SDGs. This study critically examines the nexus between 4IR policies and the SDGs, especially SDGs 1, 2, 8, and 9, in Nigeria. Relying on qualitative method, data are elicited through semi-structured interviews and focus group discussions with policymakers, academics, and industry. This is aided by desktop and document reviews. Elicited data are analysed thematically with a view to ascertaining recurring patterns, themes, and categories within the collected data. Findings, therefore, reveal that whilst considerable Nigeria's 4IR policies exist, the current 4IR policies in Nigeria have been inadequate in comprehensively propelling the drive for the attainment of SDGs in Nigeria ahead of 2030. This study, therefore, suggests the initiation, formulation, and implementation of 4IR policies that are geared towards achieving the SDGs.

Keywords 4IR · Technology · Policy · SDGs · Nigeria

O. O. Akinrinde (✉)
University of Johannesburg, Johannesburg, South Africa
e-mail: oakinrinde@uj.ac.za

T. Moloi (ed.), *Impacting Society Positively Through Technology in Accounting and Business Processes*, Springer Proceedings in Business and Economics,
https://doi.org/10.1007/978-3-031-84885-8_50

Introduction

Industrial revolutions are not new in human evolution. To understand the fourth industrial revolution, it is as tantamount as perusing a series of impressive technological achievements that are making a big impact on our economy. Of a fact, fitting into the stages of the industrial revolution that have shaped our history, it indirectly reflects the first technological revolution that happened between 1760 and 1840 (Bikse et al., 2022). No doubts, the industrial revolution kicked off with game-changing innovations like the steam engine, machines taking over textile production, swapping out charcoal for coke, mass-producing steel, and introducing railways. This whole transformative era completely turned things around and shifted from a lifestyle centred around farming and craftsmanship to one where industry and machines took the lead, totally changing the way we live and how our economy is structured. Yet, during the second industrial revolution spanning from 1870 to 1914, there was a shift towards using electric power to massively produce steel, electrify, improve telecommunications, and eventually bring about the development of the motor car and the production line (Faissal Bassis & Armellini, 2018; Ladimeji, 2020). As for the third industrial revolution, it kicked off in the middle of the last century. This time around, we saw the rise of digital systems, communication breakthroughs, and rapid advancements in computing power, ushering in new methods of generating, processing, and sharing information. This led to the automation of production through the application of electronics and information technology. We are already beginning the fourth industrial revolution, which will build on the achievements of the third. The convergence of technology defines this new phase, dissolving differences between the physical, digital, and biological realms. Computational design, additive manufacturing, materials engineering, and synthetic biology are being integrated by engineers, designers, and architects. Their goal is to pave the path for a healthy interaction between microbes, our bodies, everyday products, and even the structures we live in (Bikse et al., 2022, p. 5).

From the first industrial revolution in Europe to the fourth revolution in recent times, the essence of the industrial revolution has always been the drive to advance human development. Indeed, technology has always been the fulcrum around which all industrial revolutions have revolved. The Fourth Industrial Revolution (4IR) is no exception. Recent technological advancements in terms of sophisticated technologies employment in aspects of human existence underscore the 4IR's global phenomenon. Countries across the globe have been quite deliberate in their attempts to initiate and implement policies that could advance the 4IR. This is because 4IR and its associated technologies, such as artificial intelligence (AI), robotics, machine learning (ML), and the Internet of Things (IOT), have become critical to the advancement of all aspects of human development (Bikse et al., 2022). In their attempts to key into the demands of the present world of 4IR, countries have begun to delve into policy formulations and implementations believed to be capable of entrenching the trajectories of the 4IR in the developmental aspirations. There is, however, no disputing of the attendant positive trajectories that have accompanied the emergence of the 4IR in virtually all countries across the globe.

In the United States, for instance, there are corroborating trajectories highlighting the positives of 4IR policies on SDG, especially in the area of SDG 2—Zero Hunger. Precision agriculture, for instance, was introduced by the United States' authority to optimise crop production and minimise food waste (Laar et al., 2017, 2020). The farmers have embraced this 4IR-backed technology, among many others that include sensors, drones, and data analytics geared towards fine-tuning the crop production processes to a sustainable, efficient, and systematic approach. These modern tools have assisted farmers to improve their crop yields, use resources more efficiently, and cut down on food losses and waste, hence bringing about a boost in food production efficiency, less harm to the environment, and significant progress towards achieving SDG 2.

The trajectories from Germany's 4IR path have not been different. Germany has launched the Industry 4.0 Initiative, with emphasis set on the SDG 8—Decent Work and Economic Growth. The core objective is straightforward: to foster economic growth by embracing the digital revolution and automating manufacturing processes. The means to this end are impressive, with the integration of the Internet of Things (IoT), Artificial Intelligence (AI), and robotics into its manufacturing processes. This initiative has spurred job creation, boosted exports, and spurred economic growth. It is thus a clear testament to the power of 4IR in supporting decent work and economic development.

China and its Belt and Road Initiative (BRI) is another example. The BRI, without any quantum of doubts, intersects with SDG 9: Industry, Innovation, and Infrastructure. The BRI leverages the strengths of 4IR technologies to build infrastructure and foster economic cooperation along the historical Silk Road routes. The mechanism of action further involves hefty investments in 5G, AI, and transportation infrastructure. This has resulted in tangible improvements in infrastructure across the countries involved and in partnership with China, further boosting innovation and facilitation of international trade. In essence, the 4IR-compliant BRI has played a substantial role in realising SDG 9 by driving forward industry, innovation, and robust infrastructure development.

In Africa, Kenya has taken a significant step towards addressing SDG 1 through 4IR, with a view to eliminating poverty. Specifically, the M-Pesa Mobile Payment System in Kenya, a 4IR-compliant payment system with the clear objective of increasing financial inclusion and reducing poverty, was launched and implemented in Kenya. The 4IR intelligence behind the M-Pesa system is quite fascinating. The Fourth Industrial Revolution technologies such as mobile phones and digital payments were leveraged to extend financial services to people who were hitherto without any access to conventional banking systems and unbanked. M-Pesa has thus become a lifeline for many. The positive impact of the 4IR-backed M-Pesa has shown that it was not just about making and facilitating payments but equally about enabling small-scale businesses to thrive and giving people access to financial services within the context of relevant technologies they had never had (Birkel et al.,

2019). In practical terms, the M-Pesa payment innovation system is without a doubt facilitating the reduction of extreme poverty, albeit SDG 1.

Rwanda is another country on an inspiring journey of technological transformation, and at the heart of this endeavour are several noteworthy projects and initiatives. These projects collectively represent Rwanda's commitment to harnessing the power of technology and innovation to enhance the well-being of its citizens and achieve the SDGs, especially SDGs 1, 2, 8, and 9. Specifically, Rwanda initiated the Smart Kigali project, which imagines a city where technology seamlessly integrates into daily life, making public services more efficient, transportation more accessible, and utilities more reliable. This comprehensive initiative is on a mission to transform the capital city into a smart city. It is about bringing innovative solutions to the forefront, ensuring that Kigali thrives in the digital age. Coupled with this is the Zipline's drone delivery services. The Zipline's drone delivery network, known as "Zipline Rwanda", epitomises this idea of unmanned aerial vehicles that crisscross the Rwandan skies to deliver critical medical supplies to remote and underserved areas. They bridge the gap between life-saving resources and those who need them the most. The Zipline Rwanda is a 4IR initiative that exemplifies the incredible potential of technology for the greater good. The "One Laptop Per Child (OLPC)" is another step that has been undertaken in the direction of 4IR in Rwanda. Since education is the cornerstone of progress and all goals of the SDGs, Rwanda is keen on ensuring that its youth have access to digital resources and knowledge. OLPC is an educational programme that is making a difference by providing students with laptops and online educational materials. It is about breaking down barriers to learning, making education accessible to all, and preparing the next generation for a tech-driven world. Similarly, at the intersection of 4IR, policy, and the SDGs lies the Irembo project. The Irembo is an e-government platform committed to simplifying interactions between the citizens and the Rwandan government. It offers a wide array of government services online, making it easier and more convenient for citizens to access essential services. It is about reducing bureaucracy and enhancing the relationship between the Rwandan state and its people.

In a similar manner, the Rwandan TASAFI digital financial platform is Rwanda's 4IR answer to a cashless future. The TASAFI is a digital payment platform that facilitates transactions for various government services and taxes. TASAFI has been a step towards a more efficient, transparent, and cashless economy, making financial interactions smoother and more accessible. The blockchain-based land registration committed to reducing land disputes, ensuring property rights, and creating a trustworthy land registry, the e-Soko that connects farmers and traders through a digital platform, and the KLab and Innovation Spaces that nurture tech startups and innovation are a few of the policy directions in the area of 4IR in Rwanda. These projects collectively embody Rwanda's unwavering commitment to leveraging technology and innovation to advance its economy and improve the lives of its citizens. They further underscore the transformative potential of Fourth Industrial Revolution policies and technologies in making a positive impact across various Sustainable Development Goals. Whether it is poverty reduction, hunger eradication, economic growth, or infrastructure development, the 4IR has shown itself to be a powerful ally in the pursuit of these vital global objectives.

At the risk of overemphasis, the Fourth Industrial Revolution (4IR) now stands as a dynamic global force reshaping economies, societies, and governance structures. Nigeria, as the most populous African nation, finds itself at the heart of this transformative journey. With rapid technological advancements and ambitious development objectives, the alignment of Nigeria's 4IR policies with the Sustainable Development Goals (SDGs) has become an imperative task. Nigeria's pivotal role in shaping the trajectory of the African continent within the 4IR era cannot be overstated. The integration of cutting-edge technologies such as artificial intelligence, big data, and the Internet of Things promises to revolutionise industries, enhance service delivery, and drive economic growth. In parallel, the SDGs offer a holistic roadmap for addressing global challenges, spanning from poverty eradication and health and well-being to quality education, gender equality, and sustainable economic development. Nigeria, like many other countries, has recognised the importance of embracing the Fourth Industrial Revolution (4IR) to foster economic growth and development. The government has initiated policies and strategies aimed at harnessing the potential of emerging technologies and digital transformation (Awofala et al., 2017).

For instance, among several others, Nigeria has initiated, within the scope of the 4IR, a digital national economic policy known as the National Digital Economy Policy and Strategy (NDEPS). This national 4IR strategy outlines Nigeria's approach to leveraging digital technologies for economic growth (Ukwandu et al., 2023). It has facilitated several trainings of the youth in the area of tech, digital business, and employment. Similarly, a social investment programme, N-Power, that includes various projects relating to skills development and job opportunities, including in the area of digital skills and literacy for Nigerian youth, continues to be implemented in Nigeria. The National Identification Number (NIN) is another policy direction that is currently being taken within the context of the 4IR in Nigeria. This government-owned National Identity Management Commission has been championing the digital identity management, which includes the National Identification Number (NIN) project.

Another 4IR-compliant policy framework Nigeria has, particularly e-Naira. As the Central Bank of Nigeria's digital currency project, which is part of broader efforts to modernise the financial system, the e-Naira is a legal tender within the Nigerian business and economic space. The e-Naira therefore allows the digital use of the Nigerian legal tender without the hassles of possessing and tendering cash for transaction. Similarly, the National Broadband Plan (2020–2025), a 4IR-compliant policy and plan, remains on course to expand broadband access and connectivity across Nigeria.

The Nigerian Communications Satellite (NigComSat), a state-owned satellite communication company that focuses on expanding broadband access and satellite-based Internet services, the Nigerian Digital Innovation and Entrepreneurship Skills Training Programme, which seeks to provide digital skills training to young Nigerians, and the National Information Technology Development Agency (NITDA)

Initiatives, which organise and support various digital innovation hubs and skills development programmes among Nigerians, are among the notable policy frameworks within the context of promoting and leveraging the 4IR for sustainable development.

While 4IR holds enormous promises in terms of increased productivity, innovation, and global competitiveness, its implications for sustainable development remain a topic of concern. Since its adoption in 2015, several countries across the globe began to domesticate the SDGs blueprint. In this context, the 4IR and its associated technological trajectories were therefore seen as a veritable panacea towards achieving and complementing the actualisation of the SDGs. With the year 2030 halfway, it is increasingly becoming clear that the global desire to have achieved each of all the SDGs may remain a wishful desire (Ukwandu et al., 2023). Like many other African countries, Nigeria's match towards the attainment of the SDGs by 2030 has been fraught with increasing poverty, unemployment, food insecurity, and hunger, as well as inadequate infrastructural facilities, among others. Despite Nigeria's adoption of the global SDGs framework and several 4IR policies put in place, SDG-related challenges continue to abound. This study is therefore an attempt to empirically query the extent to which Nigeria's 4IR policies have influenced its SDGs drive. Specifically, the study will attempt to explain: how well has Nigeria's Fourth Industrial Revolution Policy aligned with the Sustainable Development Goals? And what are the challenges towards Nigeria's 4IR policies alignment with and positive impact on SDGs 1, 2, 8, and 9?

Empirical Review and Theoretical Matters

Scholarly and empirical attempts to understand and explore the nature of the relationship between 4IR and SDGs have not been in short supply in the literature. Studies have sought to unravel how and ways 4IR contributes to the drive generally to the attainment of the SDGs. The querying of scholarly databases such as SCOPUS, Web of Science, EBSCO, and ScienceDirect, with a view to ascertaining the state of knowledge in the extant body of knowledge, clearly reveals a subsisting gap in the extant body of knowledge, especially with regard to the Nigerian context and experience of how 4IR has shaped and affected the quest for SDGs. Amid the intense scrutiny of the technical intricacies surrounding the Fourth Industrial Revolution (4IR) in scholarly circles, there is a notable omission of vital aspects like poverty eradication, eradication of hunger, environmental considerations, and the social repercussions of the employment of 4IR policies in development projects, especially within the context of developing and underdeveloped countries. Scholars such as Birkel et al. (2019) have underscored the scarcity of comprehensive research that embraces the economic, ecological, social, and sustainable development facets within the realm of 4IR in developing countries like Nigeria.

The complexities woven into the fabric of 4IR stretch far beyond economic calculations, sparking concerns about job losses and the widening gap of inequality that underlines the SDGs, specifically SDGs 1, 2, 8, and 9. Interestingly, the immediate positive outcome of 4IR manifests in the sustainability of manufacturing economies and smart and cost-effective approaches to labour, among others (Prisecaru, 2016). The digital transformation of the manufacturing sector, for instance, ripples through efficiency, supply chains, energy efficiency, innovative business models, cost-effectiveness, skill development, and the bottom line of corporations, among others (Ejsmont et al., 2020). This intricate impact significantly contributes to specific SDGs, notably SDGs 1 (No Poverty), 2 (Zero Hunger), 8 (Decent Work and Economic Growth), and 9 (Industry, Innovation, and Infrastructure), thereby recognising and proactively addressing the broader implications of 4IR becomes imperative, ensuring that technological progress aligns harmoniously with the overarching goals of sustainable development. Although Siekmann et al. (2023), Bikse et al. (2022), Sajitha et al. (2021), Buryak (2018), Xu et al. (2018), and Schwab (2017) have also reinforced the significant level of relationship between the 4IR and the SDGs, their studies did not account for how the 4IR is shaping the drive for the SDGs, particularly SDGs I, 2, 8, and 9 at the microcosm levels.

Similarly, Telukdarie et al. (2018) have also attempted an interrogation of how best to tackle the problem of inter-site issues, the global standardisation need, and inter-functional integration through Industry 4.0. Their study further opined a global system strategy for major multinational corporations that combine tasks such as research and development (R&D), asset optimisation, corporate planning, and supply chain. This strategy for Telukdarie et al. (2018) addresses inter-site issues, global standardisation needs, and inter-functional integration capable of resulting in strategic and operational advantages. This extends the frontiers of knowledge in the 4IR; however, their study remains restricted to the area of global business' integration and standardisation.

In another context, Berawi's "the role of industry 4.0 in achieving sustainable development goals" offers a closely related context to how 4IR shapes the global drive for SDGs (Berawi, 2019). For Berawi (2019), the Sustainable Development Goals (SDGs) are like a global blueprint for making the world a better place. They are not just about ending poverty; they are also about boosting health and education, creating prosperity, and ensuring the environment stays healthy too. It is basically about working together on a global scale with a view to making lives better. The idea is to bring in everything—environment, society, economy, and governance—into the mix when trying to make things better. Berawi further argued that to make this happen in terms of achieving the SDGs, we need the 4IR and its associated smart technologies that are kind to the environment and eco-technologically friendly. These are tools and approaches that not only get the job done efficiently but also fit in with what each community needs (Berawi, 2019). For him, in the age of Industry 4.0, we must imagine technology as a key player in shaping a future where our communities are not only thriving socially and economically but are also in harmony with the environment.

Technologies like the Internet of Things, artificial intelligence, data analytics, machine learning, and 3D printing are tools we can use to make sustainable development and environmental responsibility a reality on a global scale. It is like having a super toolbox to create, expand, and keep an eye on how well we are doing with our global efforts. As 4IR continues to shape the way we live, it is not just about convenience; it is about making a positive, long-lasting impact on how we take care of our environment through sustainable practices (Berawi, 2019).

While Berawi's "the role of industry 4.0 in achieving sustainable development goals" provides adequate empirical pretext to understanding how the 4IR or industry 4.0 shapes sustainable development goals, it is quite limited in scope and too generic. The scope of Berawi's thesis did not take into cognisance the significance of local context and dynamisms to the nexus between 4IR and the SDGs.

Similarly, analysing the current body of literature further, Bikse et al. (2022) emphasise the diverse and intricate opportunities ushered in by the fourth industrial revolution. Spanning various fields like artificial intelligence (AI), cloud computing, advanced robotics, the Internet of Things (IoT), autonomous vehicles, 3D printing, nanotechnology, biotechnology, materials science, energy storage, quantum computing, and other emerging technologies, these prospects resonate on a deeper level when contrasted with earlier transformative shifts, such as the paradigm initiated by the microprocessor revolution in the 1970s.

Historical trends have further revealed that consumers have been the primary beneficiaries of industrial revolutions, with numerous tasks now achievable remotely. From organising transport to booking restaurants, buying groceries, making payments, and enjoying various forms of entertainment, activities can be executed instantly, anytime, and virtually anywhere. Looking ahead, technological innovation promises a supply-side miracle, bringing long-term gains in efficiency and productivity (Schwab, 2016). Transportation and communication costs will decrease, global supply chains will become more effective, and trade costs will diminish, unlocking new markets and fostering economic growth. While technological advancements have traditionally boosted labour productivity, the fourth industrial revolution poses challenges. Automation and robotics threaten routine tasks, impacting professions such as accounting, taxi driving, and paralegal work. However, studies indicate that the net effect will likely be positive, with more jobs created than lost (Ladimeji, 2020; Bikse et al., 2022). A study in Austria found a positive correlation between digitalisation and job growth, emphasising the importance of upgrading skills (Coulter, 2018). Zahidi's predictions align with this perspective, foreseeing accelerated automation, the creation of new jobs, the emphasis on analytical thinking and creativity, and the competitiveness of businesses tied to skill upgrading (Zahidi, 2016).

Nonetheless, while there has been a plethora of studies on the 4IR phenomenon and its connection to the global quest for the SDGs, studies remain scantily available on the assessment of this nexus within the context of local realities. The point here is that the closest study on the implication of 4IR and its associated policies and technologies for the SDGs was the study carried out by Ladimeji (2020). In the study undertaken by Ladimeji (2020), the focus is on the flourishing of ICT activity in Nigeria in the early decades of this century, despite a lack of significant government policy support. For him, a central cultural conflict emerges between individuals viewing the national surplus as readily available funds for immediate consumption and those acknowledging it as prospective capital for strategic investments in the nation's future. However, the introduction of meticulously crafted policies holds the potential to bring about remarkable and rapid transformations in this scenario (Ladimeji, 2020). This study, while acknowledging the existing gap, seeks to understand, from the context of Nigerian experience, how the 4IR policies in Nigeria have affected its drive for SDGs.

Theorising 4IR and the SDGs: The Innovation Systems Approach

Applying the Innovation Systems Theory to explore the Fourth Industrial Revolution (4IR) and Sustainable Development Goals (SDGs) in Nigeria involves delving deeply into the intricate web of connections, the diverse array of participants, and the inner workings ingrained in the innovation system. The Innovation Systems Theory, also known as the National Systems of Innovation and often associated with scholars like Christopher Freeman and Bengt-Åke Lundvall, focuses on understanding how innovation occurs within a system of interconnected actors, institutions, and processes. Although Lundvall was the first to introduce the concept of an "innovation system" back in 1985, the roots of this idea stretch back to Friedrich List's 1841 notion of "The National System of Political Economy". It is interesting to think that List could have just as well called it "The National System of Innovation". Then, in 1988, Christopher Freeman played a key role in popularising the term "National Innovation System" while studying the success of the Japanese economy. Every now and then, people use the term "innovation ecosystem" to highlight the lively interactions among a diverse group of participants. The theory of innovation systems functions as a structured framework crafted to understand the intricate web of relationships among diverse entities within a system, including enterprises, universities, and research institutes. This idea underscores the crucial role played by the exchange of technology and information among individuals, businesses, and institutions in propelling the innovation process forward (McGunagle & Zizka, 2020). The innovation systems theory is a framework that helps understand and analyse the process of innovation within an economy or a specific industry. The theory consists of four essential elements: a reevaluation of national production systems through a neo-Schumpeterian lens, empirical investigations rooted in the home-market theory of international trade, a microeconomic view of innovation as a collaborative process, and valuable observations regarding how institutions contribute to shaping innovative activities (Faissal Bassis & Armellini, 2018). It goes beyond a traditional linear model of innovation and recognises that innovation is a complex and interactive process involving various actors, institutions, and factors (Canco et al., 2021; Gavriluka et al., 2022). It goes beyond a narrow view of innovation solely as technological advancements and emphasises the broader socio-economic context. In breaking it down, innovation systems come in various forms like national, regional, local, technological, and sectoral. Pinpointing exactly what makes up an innovation system is an ongoing topic where people are still hashing out the details. However, some folks describe it as a kind of framework that brings together different parts and how they are all connected, shaping how new ideas start, gain acceptance, and prove effective.

Within the Nigerian context, the strategic foundation for Nigeria's Fourth Industrial Revolution (4IR) entails a complex web of relationships among diverse stakeholders, encompassing government agencies, businesses, educational institutions, research centres, and the broader public. The effectiveness of each element and the strength of their interactions play a pivotal role in shaping the extent of wealth creation, economic development, and global competitiveness for individual nations.

As emphasised in a study featured in the IEEE Conference Publication, entities, both human and non-human, such as government bodies, universities, and research institutes, remain integral components of the 4IR (Isola et al., 2010). They play a crucial role in generating economic opportunities and wealth that can propel progress towards Sustainable Development Goals (SDGs), notably SDGs 1, 2, 8, and 9. Despite a substantial 730% increase in budgetary allocation to Science and Technology (S&T) in Nigeria, rising from N 1.5 billion (US 0.11 billion) in 2006 over 8 years, these figures represented only 0.11% of the GDP (Isola et al., 2010). Nigeria's contribution to global Research and Development (R&D) expenditure is a mere 0.01%, reflecting a Global Competitiveness Index (GCI) ranking of 94 out of 134 nations, with no representation in the world's top 500 universities (Isola et al., 2010).

It is abundantly clear that Nigeria's vision for the Fourth Industrial Revolution (4IR) holds great promise in unleashing economic opportunities and prosperity within the country. However, realising this promise calls for substantial investments in Science & Technology Research & Development (R&D) over the next decades. These investments should be thoughtfully directed to open doors for researchers, particularly in cutting-edge fields like AI, robotics, and machine learning, with a keen eye on both research and the development of new innovative products. The success of this initiative hinges on how seamlessly the 4IR policies work together, playing a pivotal role in shaping the landscape of wealth creation, economic progress, global competitiveness, and the SDGs. In view of this, it is the cardinal objective of this study to contribute to the policy efforts geared towards achieving the SDGs, particularly SDGs 1, 2, 8, and 9 by 2030 in Nigeria, sub-Saharan Africa, and the globe by critically examining the level of policy alignment within the context of Nigeria's 4IR policies and its quest for the SDGs, particularly SDGs 1, 2, 8, and 9, adhering to the research guide below.

Methodology

The research methodology for this study is qualitative in nature. The study uses a case study approach to explore the alignment of Nigeria's Fourth Industrial Revolution (4IR) policy with the United Nations' Sustainable Development Goals (SDGs). The focal points for data collection are the Nigerian Ministry of Communications and Digital Economy, Ministry of Science and Technology, Ministry of Education, Ministry of Works, National Information Technology Development Agency (NITDA), National Office for Technology Acquisition and Promotion (NOTAP), and National Space Research and Development Agency (NASRDA).

The study uses purposive sampling to select participants who have knowledge and experience in the implementation of 4IR policies and SDGs in Nigeria. The sample includes policymakers, academics, industry experts, and civil society organisations. Data are collected through semi-structured interviews, focus group discussions, and document analysis. Semi-structured interviews are undertaken with policymakers, academics, and industry experts to acquire a deeper understanding of the execution of Fourth Industrial Revolution (4IR) policies and Sustainable Development Goals (SDGs) in Nigeria. Additionally, focus group discussions are held with civil society organisations to grasp their viewpoints regarding the congruence of 4IR policies with SDGs. Furthermore, document analysis is employed to scrutinise policy documents, reports, and other pertinent materials. The data collected are therefore analysed using thematic and content analysis. The analysis involves identifying patterns, themes, and categories in the data. The findings of the study are thus presented in a narrative form, supported by quotes from the participants and relevant literature.

1. **Presentation of Data**

Here, we present the data elicited from the field arising from the unstructured interviews conducted with the participants within the study's sites.

Demographic Information

In order to ensure strict adherence to ethical standards, only participants above the age of 18 were interviewed. Equally, they freely consented to be interviewed. However, due the confidentiality of their responses and identities, the names of the participants were clearly left out in this data presentation.

What is your age range?

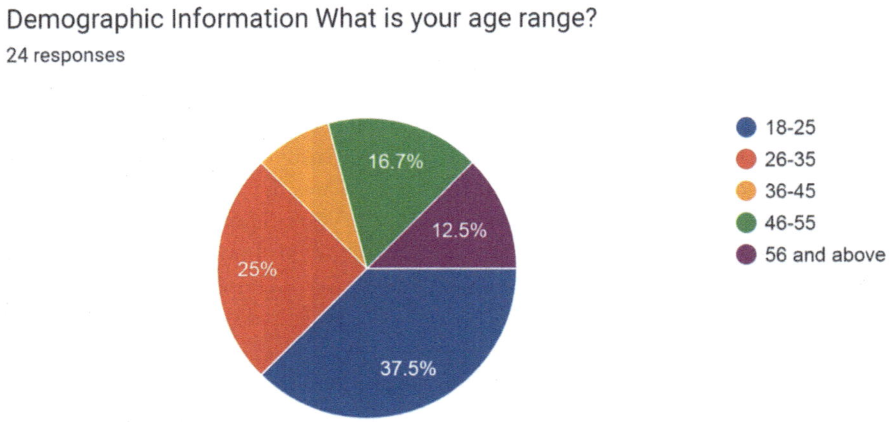

Sources: Author's compilation

What is your gender

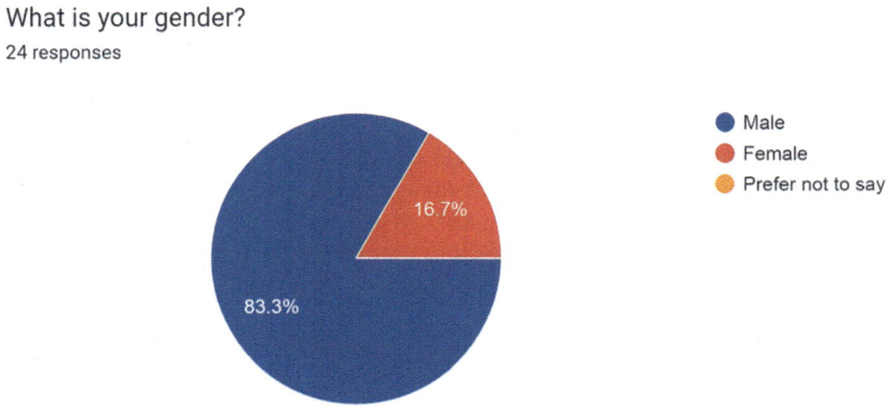

Author's compilation

What is your educational background?

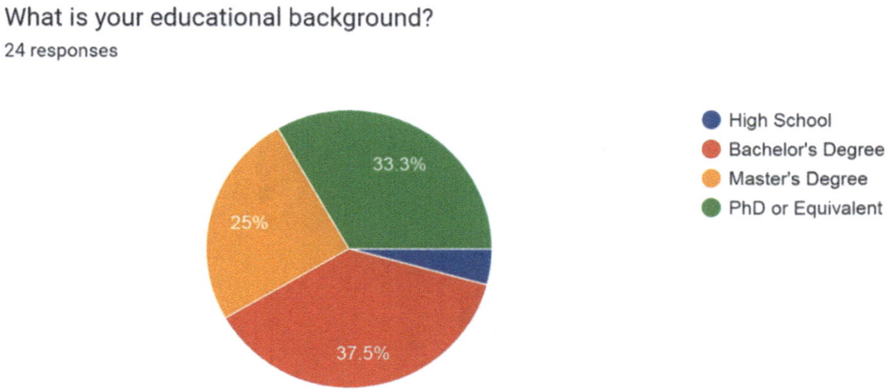

Author's compilation

In which sector do you currently work?

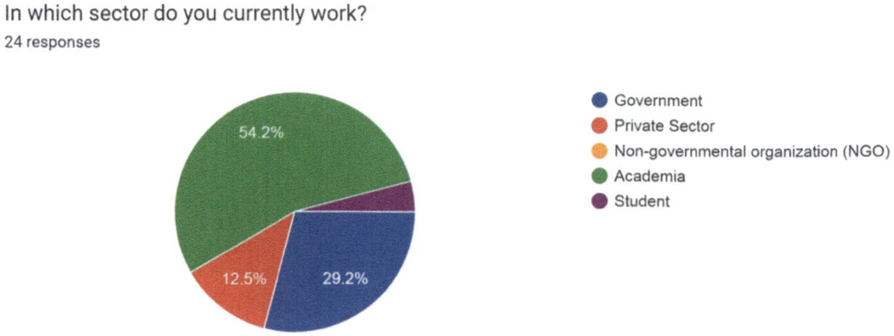

Author's compilation

How familiar are you with Nigeria's Fourth Industrial Revolution Policy?

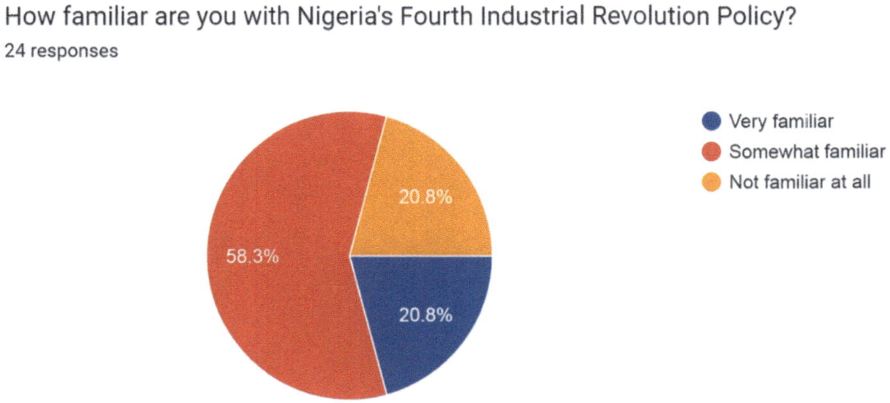

Author's compilation

Have you read or received information about the Sustainable Development Goals (SDGs)?

Have you read or received information about the Sustainable Development Goals (SDGs)?
24 responses

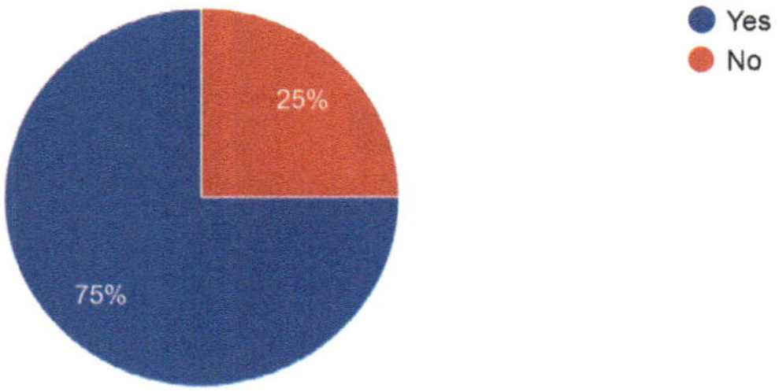

Author's compilation

In your opinion, how well is Nigeria's Fourth Industrial Revolution Policy aligned with the Sustainable Development Goals, especially SDGs 1, 2, 8, & 9?

In your opinion, how well is Nigeria's Fourth Industrial Revolution Policy aligned with the Sustainable Development Goals, especially SDGs 1,2,8 & 9?
24 responses

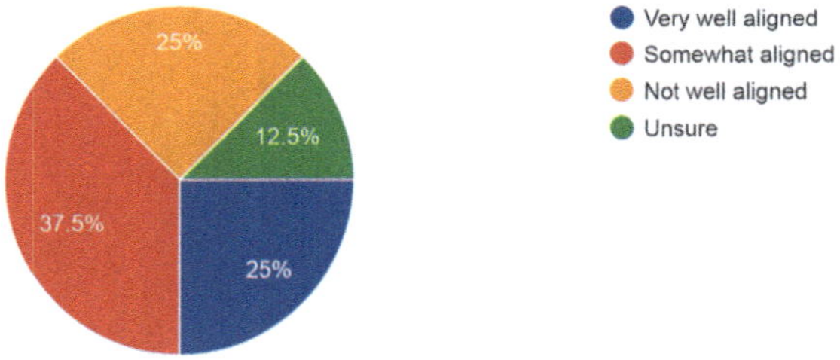

Author's compilation

Which specific areas of the Fourth Industrial Revolution policy do you think contribute most to the achievement of the SDGs 1, 2, 8, & 9?

Which specific areas of the Fourth Industrial Revolution policy do you think contribute most to the achievement of the SDGs 1,2,8 & 9?
24 responses

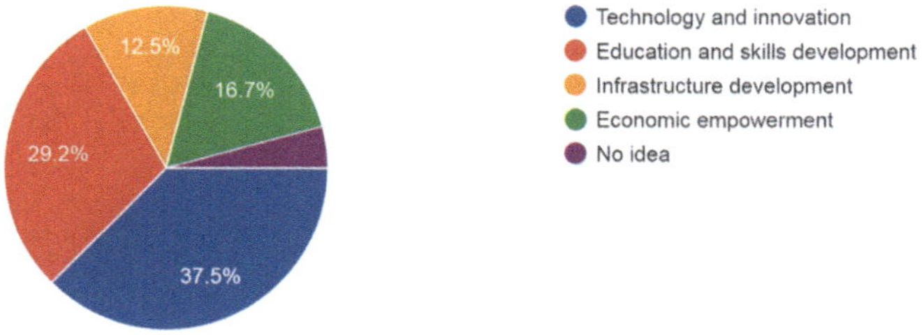

Author's compilation

How effectively do you think the Nigerian government is implementing the Fourth Industrial Revolution Policy to support sustainable development especially SDGs 1, 2, 8, & 9?

How effectively do you think the Nigerian government is implementing the Fourth Industrial Revolution Policy to support sustainable development especially SDGs 1,2,8 & 9?
24 responses

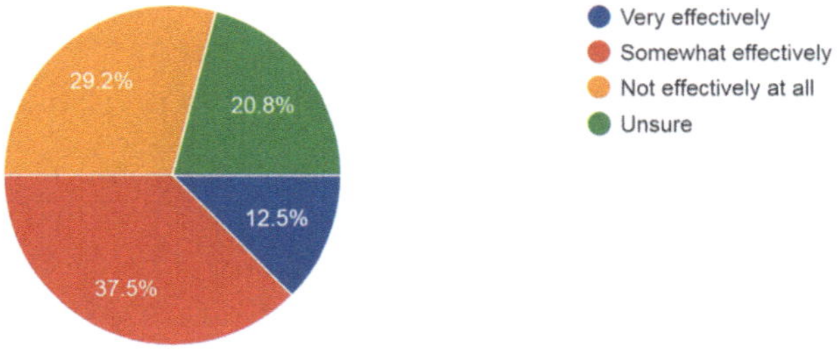

Author's compilation

Do you believe there is adequate involvement of various stakeholders (government, private sector, and civil society) in shaping and implementing the Fourth Industrial Revolution Policy?

Do you believe there is adequate involvement of various stakeholders (government, private sector, civil society) in shaping and implementing the Fourth Industrial Revolution Policy?
24 responses

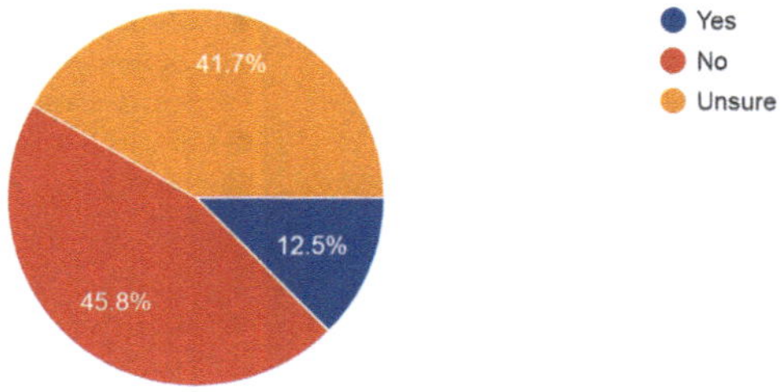

Author's compilation

To what extent do you think the Fourth Industrial Revolution Policy addresses environmental sustainability and climate change concerns?

To what extent do you think the Fourth Industrial Revolution Policy addresses environmental sustainability and climate change concerns?
24 responses

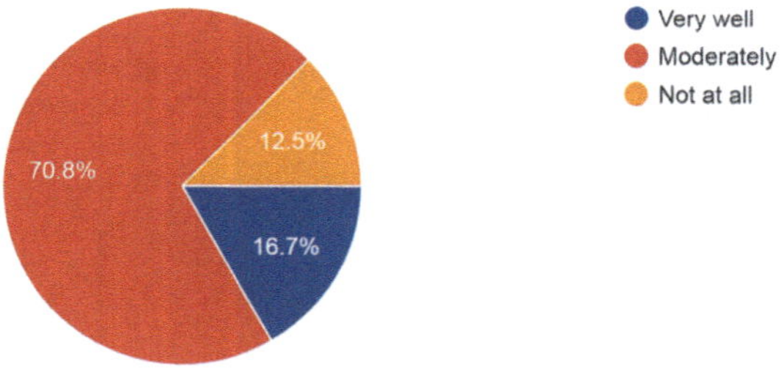

Author's compilation

Do you believe there is sufficient awareness and education among the general public about the Fourth Industrial Revolution and its potential impact on sustainable development?

Do you believe there is sufficient awareness and education among the general public about the Fourth Industrial Revolution and its potential impact on sustainable development?
24 responses

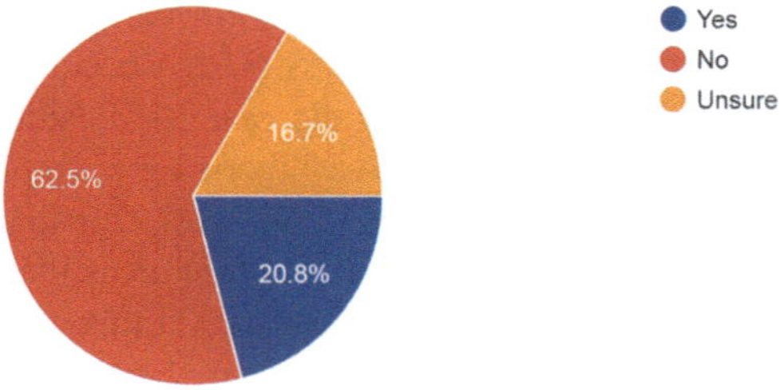

Author's compilation

How effectively do you think the Nigerian government is implementing the Fourth Industrial Revolution Policy to support sustainable development, especially SDGs 1, 2, 8, & 9?

How effectively do you think the Nigerian government is implementing the Fourth Industrial Revolution Policy to support sustainable development, especially SDGs 1,2,8 & 9?
24 responses

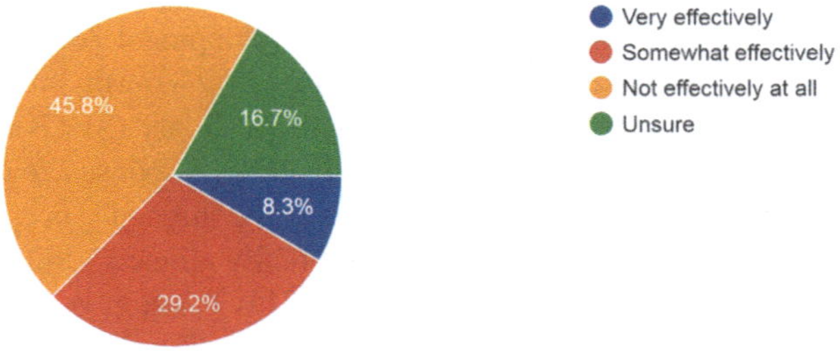

Author's compilation

Thematic and Content Analysis of Findings

In this section, we explicate on the elicited date. Data earlier presented are analysed here using thematic and content analytical tool.

Nigeria's Fourth Industrial Revolution Policy and Sustainable Development Goals

Nigeria, as expected of every third-world country, is currently struggling to keep up to speed with the current trajectories of the SDGs, especially given the fast-approaching expiration of the deadline set for the year 2030. Although, in recognition of the need to pursue the SDGs, successive Nigerian governments had initiated and implemented various policies geared towards actualising the SDGs. Acknowledging that there is policy emphasis on certain areas like youth inclusiveness in STEM and infrastructure development, however, it raises concerns about the effectiveness of these efforts, suggesting that they may be more symbolic ("shock value") than producing tangible and sustainable impacts.

Similarly, the advances in technology coupled with the realities of the current fourth industrial revolution imply that countries must begin to align their SDGs policy with the trajectories of the fourth industrial revolution, where primacy of technology, artificial intelligence, robotics, financial technology, and scientific breakthroughs, among others, hold sway on the research question about "How well has Nigeria's Fourth Industrial Revolution Policy aligned with the Sustainable Development Goals?" the majority of the responses elicited from participants from the study sites through Key Informant Interviews identified the primacy of lack of policy alignment in Nigeria's 4IR and SDG policies. Participants 1, 3, 4, 5, and 6 from the National Information Technology Development Agency (NITDA) highlighted concerns about the alignment between the Fourth Industrial Revolution (4IR) policy and the Sustainable Development Goals (SDGs) in Nigeria (KII/NITDA/Abuja, 2023). A common theme in their responses revolves around the "need for Nigeria's 4IR and SDGs policies to be aligned", given that the current level of policy alignment is "poor" and "not really aligned", thus suggesting a perceived lack of synchronisation in the policy. This position is further buttressed by the current state of lack of consistency in the pursuit of specifically SDGs 1, 2, 8, and 9.

Similarly, a participant from the Communications and Digital Economy expresses scepticism about the impact of policy efforts, using terms like "shock value" and "no feasible concrete impact". This theme suggests a perception that policy initiatives have lacked tangible outcomes. This is irrefutable given the current state of adaptation to the 4IR global dictates in Nigeria. For instance, while 4IR emphasises innovation and technological advancement, Nigeria still grapples with infrastructural deficiencies that impede its ability to fully harness the benefits of the digital era. Inadequate access to reliable electricity and poor Internet connectivity continue to hinder the progress towards achieving SDG 9 in Nigeria. Till date, Nigeria has yet to put in place a functional and comprehensive policy that guarantees uninterrupted electricity supply. The lack of a comprehensive national strategy for technology adoption and infrastructure development exacerbates the disparities in industrialisation and innovation across regions. This position further corroborates Ukwandu et al. (2023). According to their conducted survey, 60% of participants in their study believe that governmental entities at various levels in Nigeria are not providing sufficient proof to showcase their readiness to harness the promised potentials of the 4IR digital ecosystem (Ukwandu et al., 2023). Additionally, there is a perceived lack of substantial efforts in developing the necessary capacity to address risks associated with the 4IR.

One of the participants from the academia perceives that the current inherent nexus introduces a metaphorical representation, thus judging them to be paralleled (KII/NOTAP, Abuja, 2023). This suggests a conceptualisation of the 4IR Policy and the SDGs as running parallel without intersecting, implying a lack of convergence.

Barriers to Nigeria's 4IR Policies and their Alignments with SDGs

In the wealth of research exploring the barriers and effects of the fourth industrial revolution, otherwise known as 4IR, much attention has been dedicated to understanding its impact on the workplace and the environment. Yet, amidst these discussions, it is worth noting that the diverse technologies under the 4IR umbrella have the potential to shake up various Sustainable Development Goals (SDGs), influencing their targets. Within the tapestry of contemporary challenges, issues like poverty (SDG 1) and global hunger (SDG 2) take centre stage. The Fourth Industrial Revolution leaves its distinct mark on these two crucial goals. While it may not offer immediate remedies for poverty, for instance, the 4IR opens up a range of possibilities to tackle global hunger. Unmanned Aerial Vehicles (UAVs), which are currently in use for tech-assisted farming in certain regions, hold promise for elevating agricultural practices (Tripicchio et al., 2015). As Artificial Intelligence (AI) and Autonomous Vehicles (AV) continue to advance, farmers could gain the tools to use resources more efficiently, potentially boosting future agricultural outputs (Schwab, 2016; Li et al., 2017). Furthermore, Genetic Engineering, a component of the 4IR, emerges as a potential tool to address global hunger. Cultivating genetically modified crops, for instance, including plants and animals in agriculture has the potential to enhance resilience, increase yields, and even introduce healing properties into their genetic makeup.

The ongoing discussion in the scientific community revolves around how the Fourth Industrial Revolution is shaping economic growth (SDG 8). On one side, some experts, like Li et al. (2017), emphasise its profound impact on the Global Economy, while others argue that there is a noticeable slowdown happening worldwide. The latter perspective gains strength from concrete evidence, especially when we compare the Global Economy's growth rate of 5% annually before the 2008 crisis to the current rate, hovering around 3%. Supporters of the slowdown theory highlight the expected deflationary consequences stemming from 4IR, primarily due to structural unemployment resulting from the displacement of existing jobs (Schwab, 2016).

The collaborative influence of the Internet of Things and big data analytics is playing a significant role in shaping Sustainable Industrialisation (SDG 9). The marriage of these technologies gives rise to smart factories, paving the way for a reduction in CO2 emissions. In tandem, the advent of New Materials, paired with advancements in 3D printing and innovative business models, guides us towards unlocking the full potential of recycling and renewable resources. This journey seamlessly integrates these advancements into the circular economy, marking a pivotal step towards a more sustainable future.

Surprisingly, despite the few positive dividends of the 4IR in Nigeria like in most developing countries, almost all developing countries continue to grapple with varying degrees of obstacles towards their drive for SDGs, most especially SDGs 1, 2, 8, and 9. Similarly, Nigeria's case has not been different. With the 2030 deadline fast approaching, it will take an unlikely miracle, if any does exist, for the SDGs to be achieved. In Nigeria, for instance, businesses overwhelmingly point to access to finance as their primary challenge, with 23.6% identifying it as the key constraint. This is followed by electricity at 13.6%, competition from the informal sector at 11.3%, and political instability at 10.3%. Across the African continent, in 18 out of 47 surveyed countries, access to finance stands out as the most substantial obstacle to both business operations and the achievement of the Sustainable Development Goals (SDGs). Political instability is the primary concern in eight countries, while electricity is highlighted in seven countries (Bughin et al., 2018).

In addition to the aforesaid, infrastructure challenge remains one of the core obstacles towards achieving SDGs 1, 2, 8, and 9 through the instrumentality of the 4IR. In simple terms, Nigeria is dealing with a shortage of essential infrastructure, including unreliable power supply and insufficient Internet connectivity. These limitations pose a barrier to the widespread adoption of 4IR technologies, which heavily rely on a robust and dependable infrastructure. This position was clearly captured in the narrative of one of the participants of the study. For the mid-level executive worker in the National Space Research and Development Agency (NASRDA), "Nigeria is going nowhere as long as the issue of lack of electricity persists" (IDI/NASRDA/Abuja, 2023). Buttressing this claim, Nigeria, as of now, remains one of the several developing countries in Africa and other third worlds yet to have a constant uninterrupted power supply. The implication of this on the SDGs drive, specifically SDGS 1, 2, 8, and 9, is the rampaging level of poverty, hunger, and unemployment, among others.

Another barrier unanimously alluded to by the participants is the issue of digital divide and inequality among different groups in the population of the Nigerian state. What this implies is that the divide makes it challenging for 4IR technologies to be adopted equitably, leading to certain groups benefiting more and widening existing inequalities. Nigerians resident in slums like the Makoko area of Lagos are not only disadvantaged in comparison to those living in urban areas such as Lekki and Asokoro, among others, in terms of accessing 4IR technologies capable of bringing about SDGs 1, 2, 8, and 9.

Another recurring theme in the finding is the issue of skills gaps. Nigeria continues to grapple with the task of preparing its workforce to meet the demands of these emerging technologies, as there often exists a gap between the skills possessed by the workforce and those sought after by the job market. Till date, Nigeria faces a severe challenge in providing education and training programmes to equip its workforce with the skills needed for jobs in fields like data science, artificial intelligence, and cybersecurity. According to Business Day (2022), over 50% of Nigeria's population lacks digital skills. This corroborates the general consensus among this study's participants. A participant, in this line of view, remarked that while countries like India, China, Japan, and South Korea are training their kids in the realm of artificial intelligence and coding, we are busy erecting religious centres (IDI/Academia/Osogbo, 2023).

Finally, the most fundamental barrier hampering the effective alignment of Nigeria's 4IR policies to the quest for SDG attainment is weak policy enforcement mechanisms. Despite having numerous policies pertaining to 4IR and its consolidation in place to regulate emerging technologies, the enforcement and implementation mechanisms have been severely weak. For instance, despite the fact that there are policies against the use of technologies for cybercrimes, Nigeria remains one of the hubs of high cyber and Internet.

Conclusion

In summary, a cursory assessment of Nigeria's alignment of policies related to the Fourth Industrial Revolution (4IR) with Sustainable Development Goals (SDGs) has revealed a complex and challenging landscape. Similar to many developing nations, Nigeria is grappling with difficulties in navigating the paths of SDGs, particularly as the 2030 deadline approaches. Despite the various initiatives and policies implemented by successive governments towards SDGs, concerns have emerged about the effectiveness of these efforts, indicating a gap between policy emphasis and tangible impact. Findings have underscored a significant lack of alignment between Nigeria's 4IR policy and SDGs, as highlighted by the study's participants. The perceived poor synchronisation between Nigeria's 4IR and SDGs policies raises questions about the effectiveness of the current approach towards attaining SDGs 1, 2, 8, and 9. A number of barriers implicated include infrastructure deficiencies hindering the adoption of 4IR technologies, a digital divide exacerbating societal inequalities, a skills gap in the workforce, and weak policy enforcement mechanisms. However, while acknowledging the positive impacts of 4IR on specific SDGs, such as addressing global hunger and shaping sustainable industrialisation, the overall narrative suggests a considerable gap in policy alignment and implementation. The ongoing challenges, including inadequate infrastructure and a lack of digital skills, present formidable obstacles to achieving SDGs 1, 2, 8, and 9. Essentially, findings have underscored the urgency for Nigeria to address these barriers systematically while aligning its policies with the transformative potential of 4IR, and strengthen enforcement mechanisms to bridge the existing gap between policy rhetoric and impactful outcomes. Without addressing these challenges, the race to achieving SDGs by the year 2030 may remain daunting and challenging for Nigeria.

References

Awofala, O. A., Olabiyi, O. S., Ogunleye, A., & Uchenna, N. (2017). School administrators' perceptions of the employability of preservice science, technology, and mathematics teachers through teaching practice in Nigeria. *International Journal of Research in Education and Science, 3*, 42–55.

Berawi, M. A. (2019). The role of Industry 4.0 in achieving sustainable development goals. *International Journal of Technology, 10*(4), 644–647.

Bikse, V., Grinevica, L., Rivza, B., & Rivza, P. (2022). Consequences and challenges of the fourth industrial revolution and the impact on the development of employability skills. *Sustainability, 14*(12). https://doi.org/10.3390/su14126970

Birkel, H. S., Veile, J. W., Müller, J. M., Hartmann, E., & Voigt, K. (2019). Development of a risk framework for Industry 4.0 in the context of sustainability for established manufacturers. *Sustainability, 11*(384). https://doi.org/10.3390/su11020384

Bughin, J., Seong, J., Manyika, J., Chui, M., & Joshi, R. (2018). *Notes from the AI frontier: Modeling the impact of AI on the world economy*. McKinsey.

Buryak, V. V. (2018). Digital economy: Breakthrough technologies in education. *Innovative Science*, 55–59.

Business Day. (2022, May 19). *Over 50% of Nigeria's population lack digital skills*. Retrieved from https://businessday.ng/technology/article/over-50-of-nigerias-population-lack-digital-skills-world-bank/

Canco, I., Kruja, D., & Iancu, T. (2021). AHP, a reliable method for quality decision making: A case study in business. *Sustainability, 13*.

Coulter, S. (2018, June 26). The impact of digitalisation on the quantity and quality of work: An Austrian perspective. *London School of Economics and Political Science*. Retrieved from https://blogsdev.lse.ac.uk/netuf/2018/06/26/the-impact-of-digitalisation-on-the-quantity-and-quality-of-work-an-austrian-perspective/

Ejsmont, K., Gladysz, B., & Kluczek, A. (2020). Impact of Industry 4.0 on sustainability: Bibliometric literature review. *Sustainability, 12*(5650). https://doi.org/10.3390/su12145650

Faissal Bassis, N., & Armellini, F. (2018). Systems of innovation and innovation ecosystems: A literature review in search of complementarities. *Journal of Evolutionary Economics, 28*, 1053–1080. https://doi.org/10.1007/s00191-018-0600-6

Gavriluka, N., Grecu, S. P., & Chiriac, H. C. (2022). Sustainability and employability in the time of COVID-19: Youth, education and entrepreneurship in EU countries. *Sustainability, 14*.

Isola, O. O., Ogundari, I. O., and Siyanbola, W. O. (2010). The Nigerian National Innovation System: A critical look at research & development (R&D) and innovation capabilities in selected universities. Paper presented at the PICMET 2010 Technology Management for Global Economic Growth Conference, 12 September 2016 at http://ieeexplore.ieee.org/xpls/abs_all.jsp?arnumber55603446.

Laar, E. V., Deursen, A. J. A. M. V., Dijk, J. A. G. M. V., & Haan, J. D. (2017). The relation between 21st-century skills and digital skills: A systematic literature review. *Computers in Human Behavior, 72*, 577–588.

Laar, E. V., Deursen, A. J. A. M. V., & Dijk, J. A. G. M. V. (2020). *Determinants of 21st century skills and 21st-century digital skills for workers: A systematic literature*. Sage Open.

Ladimeji, O. A. (2020). The fourth industrial revolution and Nigeria: A policy conundrum and high stakes for the future of the African continent. *The Thinker, 8*.

Li, G., Hou, Y., & Wu, A. (2017). Fourth industrial revolution: Technological drivers, impacts, and coping methods. *Chinese Geographical Science, 27*(4), 626–637.

McGunagle, D., & Zizka, L. (2020). Employability skills for 21st-century STEM students: The employers' perspective. *Higher Education Skills and Work-Based Learning, 10*, 1–22.

Prisecaru, P. (2016). Challenges of the fourth industrial revolution. *Knowledge Horizons Economics, 8*, 57–62.

Sajitha, B., Dahlman, C. J., Kanehira, N., & Tilmes, K. (2021). *The converging technology revolution and human capital: Potential and implications for South Asia*. World Bank.

Schwab, K. (2016, January). The fourth industrial revolution: What it means and how to respond. *World Economic Forum*. Retrieved from https://www.weforum.org/agenda/2016/01/the-fourth-industrial-revolution-what-it-means-and-how-to-respond/#.

Schwab, K. (2017). *The fourth industrial revolution*. Penguin Books.

Siekmann, F., Schlör, H., & Venghaus, S. (2023). Linking sustainability and the fourth industrial revolution: A monitoring framework accounting for technological development. *Energy, Sustainability and Society, 13*(26). https://doi.org/10.1186/s13705-023-00405-4

Telukdarie, A., Buhulaiga, E., Bag, S., Gupta, S., & Luo, Z. (2018). Industry 4.0 implementation for multinationals. *Process Safety and Environmental Protection, 118*, 316–329.

Tripicchio, P., Satler, M., Dabisias, G., Ruffaldi, E., & Avizzano, C. A. (2015). Towards smart farming and sustainable agriculture with drones. In *2015 International Conference on Intelligent Environments* (pp. 140–143). IEEE.

Ukwandu, E., Okafor, E. N., Ikerionwu, C., Olebara, C., & Ugwu, C. (2023). Assessing cybersecurity readiness of Nigeria to Industry 4.0. In *International Conference on Cybersecurity, Situational Awareness, and Social Media, Cyber Science* (pp. 355–374). Springer Proceedings in Complexity.

Xu, M., David, J. M., & Kim, S. H. (2018). The fourth industrial revolution: Opportunities and challenges. *International Journal of Financial Research, 9*, 90–95.

Zahidi, S. (2016). Recession and automation changes our future of work, but there are jobs coming, report says. *World Economic Forum*. Retrieved from https://www.weforum.org/press/2020/10/recession-and-automation-changes-our-future-of-work-but-there-are-jobs-coming-report-says-52c5162fce/

Designing Research and Development Tax Incentives: Lessons for South Africa

Nolukhanyo Mkala and Roshelle Ramfol

Abstract Remaining relevant in a fast-paced competitive, solution-driven business environment requires substantial investments toward innovation. Section 11D of the Income Tax Act 58 of 1962, as amended promotes private sector investment in scientific and technological research and development activities in South Africa. This incentive encourages economic innovations that hold the potential to transform the economy and benefit society by supporting novel ideas, methods, and technologies. This paper applies a qualitative lens toward exploring fiscal design considerations that optimize research and development activities in South Africa. Based on these insights, the paper proposes a framework for designing research and development tax incentives. Recommendations include the role of collaboration between government, industry, and research institutions in fostering a vibrant innovation ecosystem. Overall, this paper contributes to the ongoing fiscal policy dialogue on promoting innovation and research and development investment in South Africa.

Keywords Research and development · Tax incentives · Fiscal design

Introduction

Government support for Research and Development (R&D) activities through funding, incentives, and infrastructure is vital for encouraging innovation and driving economic development in South Africa (Olaoye et al. 2021). Prioritizing R&D investment can yield diverse and varied benefits essential for strengthening South Africa's economy and enhancing its global competitiveness (Kahn et al., 2024). Increased R&D investment can spur competitiveness, encourage job creation, facilitate the development of cutting-edge technologies, and drive the commercialization

N. Mkala · R. Ramfol (✉)
University of South Africa, Pretoria, South Africa
e-mail: mkalan@unisa.ac.za; ramfor@unisa.ac.za

T. Moloi (ed.), *Impacting Society Positively Through Technology in Accounting and Business Processes*, Springer Proceedings in Business and Economics,
https://doi.org/10.1007/978-3-031-84885-8_51

of new products (Kahn et al., 2024). This investment also contributes to the development of new industries, the improvement of existing ones, and overall economic development in South Africa (Kahn et al., 2024). Additionally, R&D investment is crucial for achieving sustainable development goals, ensuring global competitiveness, diversifying the economy, attracting foreign investment, and building a knowledge-based society (Caesar et al., 2018; Kahn et al., 2024). The study investigates the adequacy of the South African research and design tax incentive toward supporting innovation.

A comprehensive strategy that integrates fiscal, monetary, quality, and economic optimization considerations is indispensable for enhancing R&D activities in South Africa (Wenjuan & Zhao, 2023; Yue et al., 2023). Optimizing R&D activities entails addressing various fiscal design considerations (National Treasury, 2021; World Bank, 2019). The optimal design of corporate taxation and R&D policies must account for firms' heterogeneous research productivity and technological spillovers across firms (Akcigit et al., 2022). A qualitative approach was employed to explore secondary sources of publicly available data sourced from journal articles and government reports.

This paper is structured as follows: the following section discusses the "principles of a good tax system" and the requisites to design R&D tax incentives. Second, a review is conducted of the key provisions in Section 11D of the Income Tax Act. Third, limitations in South Africa's R&D policy are identified. Fourth, policy lessons are drawn from the comparative countries. Fifth, presents the recommendations and conclusions.

Principles of a Good Tax System

Principles of a good tax system provide a robust framework for evaluating the fairness and efficiency of tax systems, guiding policymakers in creating equitable and effective tax policies. An efficient tax should minimize distortions in economic behavior, not discourage productive activities, and avoid unnecessary market distortions (Association of International Certified Professional Accountants, 2017). This often involves balancing generating government revenue and promoting a healthy, productive economy (Smith, 1776). To achieve these goals, tax systems often strive for simplicity, neutrality, and transparency (Mirrlees & Stuart, 2010). A simple tax system reduces compliance costs and makes it easier for taxpayers to understand and adhere to the rules (Association of International Certified Professional Accountants, 2017). A tax system is considered neutral when it does not influence individuals or businesses to make economic decisions based on tax considerations rather than market forces. Transparency promotes accountability, ensuring trust between the government and taxpayers (Mirrlees & Stuart, 2010). Good tax design principles for R&D tax incentives include neutrality, efficiency, certainty, simplicity, effectiveness, fairness, and flexibility in promoting innovation and technological advancements (Fischer et al., 2021; OECD, 2015; Jamel et al., 2021). Neutrality ensures that tax incentives do not distort business decisions, efficiency ensures that the incentives achieve their intended goal at the lowest cost, certainty provides predictability for businesses, simplicity makes it easier for businesses to claim the incentives, effectiveness measures the impact of the incentives on innovation and technological advancements, fairness ensures that all eligible businesses can benefit equally, and flexibility allows for adjustments in response to changing economic conditions (Fischer et al., 2021; OECD, 2015; Jamel et al., 2021).Good tax design principles involve creating a tax credit system that encourages businesses to invest in R&D activities (OECD, 2015). This can be achieved by offering a generous tax credit that rewards innovative companies for their efforts in developing new technologies and products (OECD, 2015). Additionally, the tax credit should be easily accessible to businesses of all sizes, not just large corporations (OECD, 2015). By creating a tax incentive that is both substantial and inclusive, governments can effectively stimulate R&D investment and drive economic growth through innovation (OECD, 2015).

Overview and Key Provisions in Section 11D of the Income Tax Act

Section 11D of the Income Tax Act 58 of 1962, as amended ("Section 11D"), aims to promote and incentivize private sector investment in scientific and technological research and development (R&D) activities within South Africa (De Gouveia, 2013; National Treasury, 2021; Rakgotho, 2018). By providing tax incentives to companies engaged in qualifying R&D projects, the legislation seeks to stimulate innovation, promote technological advancement, enhance competitiveness, and contribute to the country's economic growth and development (De Gouveia, 2013; National Treasury, 2021; Rakgotho, 2018).

Section 11D provides a framework for incentivizing private sector investment in R&D activities in South Africa by allowing companies to deduct qualifying R&D expenditure from their taxable income (De Gouveia, 2013; National Treasury, 2021; Rakgotho, 2018). To qualify for the benefits under Section 11D, companies must meet certain eligibility criteria (De Gouveia, 2013; National Treasury, 2021; Rakgotho, 2018). The company must be engaged in trade, meaning it must be actively involved in the regular conduct of business operations (De Gouveia, 2013; National Treasury, 2021; Rakgotho, 2018). Section 11D was implemented with the overarching objective of driving the country toward achieving a targeted R&D expenditure equivalent to 1% of the Gross Domestic Product (GDP) (De Gouveia, 2013; National Treasury, 2021; Rakgotho, 2018).

The R&D tax incentive was introduced on 2 November 2006 and has several amendments to enhance its effectiveness in achieving its objectives (National Treasury, 2021). One of the most notable changes occurred in 2012 with the introduction of a pre-approval process (National Treasury, 2021). This process is overseen by the Department of Science and Innovation ("DSI"), with support from an adjudication committee responsible for evaluating applications and providing recommendations to the Minister of Higher Education, Science and Innovation (National Treasury, 2021).

The introduction of this pre-approval process signified a shift toward a more structured and rigorous approach to administering the R&D tax incentive, likely aimed at ensuring that funds are allocated to projects with the highest potential for innovation and economic impact (National Treasury, 2021).

The existing tax incentive encompasses two key components, as outlined by the National Treasury: firstly, an automatic 100% deduction for tax purposes on R&D expenditure; and secondly, an additional 50% allowance for tax purposes contingent upon the approval of a specific research and development project permitting the deduction of operating expenses incurred exclusively for the purpose of conducting R&D at a rate of 150%, subject to approval by the Minister of Higher Education, Science, and Innovation (De Gouveia, 2013; National Treasury, 2021; Rakgotho, 2018). This applies regardless of whether these expenses could be classified as capital expenditures (De Gouveia, 2013; National Treasury, 2021; Rakgotho, 2018).

On 15 December 2021, the R&D tax incentive duration period was reviewed and was extended for another 10 years, effective from 1 January 2024 until 31 December 2033 (KPMG, 2023; National Treasury, 2024). This extension incorporates amendments aimed at improving by simplifying the definition of R&D, fostering improved administrative efficiency and clarity (National Treasury, 2024). The restriction on R&D related to internal business processes has also been removed (KPMG, 2023; National Treasury, 2024).

This decision reflects the government's commitment to supporting R&D activities within South Africa while also ensuring that public funds are utilized efficiently and effectively to drive innovation and economic development (KPMG 2023; National Treasury, 2024). The definition of R&D is aimed at ensuring that the incentive encourages activities that genuinely contribute to innovation and technological advancement within the country (National Treasury, 2024; KPMG, 2023).

Section 11D provides key provisions to incentivize R&D investment (De Gouveia, 2013; National Treasury, 2021; Rakgotho, 2018). Companies that meet the eligibility criteria under Section 11D are entitled to deduct a portion of their qualifying R&D expenditure from their taxable income (De Gouveia, 2013; National Treasury, 2021; Rakgotho, 2018). The deduction allows companies to reduce their tax liability, thereby providing a financial incentive to invest in R&D activities. The legislation specifies the types of expenditure that qualify for the tax deduction, including expenses incurred on scientific or technological research, experimental development, and related activities. Qualifying expenditure may be deducted in the year it is incurred or carried forward to future years if not fully utilized in the current year.

The amount of the tax deduction allowable under Section 11D is typically calculated as a percentage of the qualifying R&D expenditure incurred by the company (De Gouveia, 2013; National Treasury, 2021; Rakgotho, 2018). The specific percentage may vary depending on the nature of the R&D activities and other factors prescribed by the legislation. Companies claiming tax incentives under Section 11D are required to comply with certain reporting and documentation requirements to substantiate their eligibility for the deduction (De Gouveia, 2013; National Treasury,

2021; Rakgotho, 2018). This may include maintaining detailed records of R&D expenditure, obtaining certification from the DSI where applicable, and providing supporting documentation to the tax authorities upon request.

The company must undertake scientific or technological research and development activities aimed at achieving scientific or technological advancement in its field (De Gouveia, 2013; National Treasury, 2021; Rakgotho, 2018). These activities typically involve systematic investigation or experimentation directed toward the development of new products, processes, or services, or the improvement of existing ones (De Gouveia, 2013; Ernst & Young, 2022; National Treasury, 2021; Rakgotho, 2018). The company must incur expenditure directly related to the qualifying R&D activities (De Gouveia, 2013; National Treasury, 2021; Rakgotho, 2018). This expenditure includes costs associated with personnel, materials, equipment, and overhead expenses directly attributable to R&D projects (De Gouveia, 2013; Ernst & Young, 2022; De Gouveia, 2013; National Treasury, 2021; Rakgotho, 2018). In some cases, companies may be required to obtain certification from the DSI to verify the eligibility of their R&D activities for tax incentives under Section 11D (De Gouveia, 2013; Ernst & Young, 2022; National Treasury, 2021; Rakgotho, 2018). The certification process typically involves the submission of detailed information about the R&D projects and their potential scientific or technological benefits.

Shortcomings in the R&D Tax Incentives in South Africa

The tax incentive for R&D in South Africa is expected to be effective in encouraging companies to invest in scientific and technological research and development (Dippenaar, 2018; Ndlovu & Inglesi-Lotz, 2020), as the incentive offers a 150% tax deduction on qualifying expenses (Calitz et al., 2021; National Treasury, 2021; Rakgotho, 2018). However, studies evaluating the effectiveness and efficiency of existing R&D tax incentives in South Africa have highlighted various shortcomings in this country's fiscal policy (National Treasury, 2021). In comparison to countries in the Organisation for Economic Co-operation and Development (OECD), South Africa's R&D tax incentives were found to be insufficient in promoting research and development activities (National Treasury, 2021).

Governments worldwide increasingly rely on tax incentives to promote business R&D and encourage innovation and economic growth. The OECD has developed guidelines and recommendations for effective R&D tax incentives, with South Africa falling short in comparison to these standards. Studies have shown that South Africa's current R&D tax incentives are not sufficient in promoting research and development activities when compared to other OECD countries (National Treasury, 2021; Neubig et al., 2016; World Bank, 2019). This highlights a need for the country to re-evaluate and potentially improve its fiscal policies to better support innovation and drive economic growth through increased R&D investments (Tau, 2019). This is especially important in a global economy where competition in R&D is increasingly fierce among not just OECD countries but also emerging economies like Brazil, China, and India (Tau, 2019).

The shortcomings in the R&D tax incentives in South Africa include limited accessibility for small- and medium-sized enterprises, high administrative burden and complex application processes, unequal benefits for companies in different sectors, unclear eligibility criteria, lack of clear policy studies and empirical research to evaluate effectiveness, and insufficient data for comprehensive impact evaluation (Lombaard & Mosoma, 2023; Maseko, 2017; National Treasury, 2021; World Bank, 2019).

Additionally, the current incentive may not be effectively encouraging innovation and technological advancement in certain key industries, such as renewable energy and healthcare (Hausmann et al., 2023; Maseko, 2017). There is a persistent need to find innovative ways of unlocking government and industry funding to effectively promote innovation and technological advancement in these key industries (Atalla et al., 2022).

By incentivizing R&D investment in these critical sectors, South Africa can drive transformative change and accelerate progress toward a more sustainable and healthy future. Collaborations with academic institutions and international partners could be one of the ways South Africa could enhance innovation and technological advancements in its renewable energy and healthcare industries (Hausmann et al., 2023). The inadequate support for collaboration between industry and research institutions creates challenges in measuring the effectiveness and impact of the incentives on innovation and economic growth, and a lack of transparency in the administration and monitoring of these incentives (Hausmann et al., 2023).

Comparative Analysis

The shortcomings in the South African R&D sector include high administrative burden and complex application processes, unequal benefits for companies in different sectors, unclear eligibility criteria, lack of clear policy studies and empirical research to evaluate effectiveness, and insufficient data for comprehensive impact evaluation (Lombaard & Mosoma, 2023; Maseko, 2017; National Treasury, 2021; World Bank, 2019). The OECD and South Africa have fostered a reciprocal collaboration to share good policy practices (OECD, 2023). The comparative countries Germany, Singapore, and the United Kingdom are OECD countries that have harnessed significant investments in R&D activities.

The comparative analysis benchmarks best practices highlighting several areas where South Africa could enhance its incentive structure to encourage increased R&D investment more effectively by firms (National Treasury, 2021). Countries such as Germany, United States, and Singapore have implemented successful R&D tax incentive programs that could serve as models for South Africa (Ernst & Young, 2022; United Nations Trade & Development, 2023).

Germany provides a simplified and efficient application process for small- and medium-sized enterprises (“**SMEs**”) interested in research and development. This is achieved through a program named, Zentrales Innovationsprogramm Mittelstand

(“**ZIM**”) (Federal Government, 2024). ZIM is a Central Innovation Program for SMEs, a funding initiative by the Federal Ministry for Economic Affairs and Climate Action (Federal Government, 2024). A key feature of ZIM is its focus on the needs of SMEs, offering an easy application process and quick decision-making. The aim is to enhance the innovative capabilities of SMEs. It is the largest innovation program in Germany for SMEs (Federal Government, 2024). It funds numerous new projects each year across Germany, making it the largest innovation program in the country for SMEs (Federal Government, 2024). In order to be eligible for ZIM funding, companies must have operations in Germany and must be looking to develop new products, improve existing ones, or enhance technical services (Federal Government, 2024). Research and technology organizations, both public and private, can also receive funding if they are collaborating with an SME. The program is open to all industries and areas of technology, but projects must be highly innovative, market-driven, and carry a significant technological risk (Federal Government, 2024).

In the United States, the tax credit has been a key driver of innovation and technological advancement for decades (Ernst & Young, 2022). The U.S. tax credit allows companies to claim a percentage of their qualified research expenses as a credit against their federal tax liability, thereby reducing the after-tax cost of R&D activities (Ernst & Young, 2022). The R&D tax credit is calculated by applying the relevant credit rate to qualified R&D expenses. These eligible expenses include salaries paid to employees directly involved in R&D projects, costs of materials used in R&D work, and fees for contract research services.

The credit rate is 6% for small companies and 14% for large companies. This tax credit can be used to reduce your business’ income tax liability on a dollar-for-dollar basis. If a company does not owe any income taxes, it may carry forward the credit to apply to future tax obligations. In some cases, certain states offer refunds to businesses that claim the R&D tax credit (Ernst & Young, 2022). The U.S. tax credit provides simplicity, stability, and generous benefits, which have incentivized firms across various industries to invest heavily in R&D (Ernst & Young, 2022).

Singapore’s Refundable Investment Credit (“**RIC**”) is another noteworthy example of a successful R&D tax incentive program (Inland Revenue Authority of Singapore, 2024; Ernst & Young, 2024; PricewaterhouseCoopers, 2024; Bake et al., 2024). Singapore introduced a new tax credit in 2024, a Global Anti-Base Erosion (GloBE) rules-compliant qualified tax credit aimed at promoting substantive, high-value economic activities in the country (Inland Revenue Authority of Singapore, 2024; Ernst & Young, 2024; PricewaterhouseCoopers, 2024; Bake et al., 2024). The RIC, designed to attract investments from global companies with expertise, incentivizes significant investments in key economic sectors and new areas of growth (Ernst & Young, 2024; Inland Revenue Authority of Singapore, 2024; PricewaterhouseCoopers, 2024; Baker et al., 2024). Eligible activities include investing in new productive capacity, expanding digital services, establishing headquarters, commodity trading, innovation, research and development, and green technologies (Ernst & Young, 2024; Inland Revenue Authority of Singapore, 2024; PricewaterhouseCoopers, 2024; Baker et al., 2024).

Qualifying expenditures may include various costs such as capital, manpower, training, professional fees, and intangible assets (Baker et al., 2024; Ernst & Young, 2024; Inland Revenue Authority of Singapore, 2024; PricewaterhouseCoopers, 2024). The credit can offset corporate income tax payments, and any unused credits will be refunded to the company in cash within 4 years (Baker et al., 2024; Ernst & Young, 2024; Inland Revenue Authority of Singapore, 2024; PricewaterhouseCoopers, 2024). The RIC aims to make Singapore competitive and attract investments that bring meaningful economic activities to the country (Bake et al., 2024; Ernst & Young, 2024; Inland Revenue Authority of Singapore, 2024; PricewaterhouseCoopers, 2024).

In the case of the U.K., specific features have been identified that can help evaluate the impact of tax incentives in a simpler institutional setting. These characteristics include the scope and generosity of the incentives, the ease of access and application process for firms, the stability and predictability of the incentive scheme, and the alignment of these incentives with broader innovation policy goals. For example, a broad scope and generous tax incentives can encourage firms to invest more in R&D activities, leading to increased innovation and technological advancement (Dechezleprêtre et al., 2016). This simple and straightforward application process makes it easier for firms to take advantage of the incentives, thus reducing administrative burden and promoting uptake among eligible businesses (Dechezleprêtre et al., 2016). Moreover, the stable and predictable incentive scheme provides firms with the confidence to undertake long-term R&D projects and make strategic investments in innovation (Dechezleprêtre et al., 2016).

South Africa can benchmark best practice policies from the comparative countries by adopting key features such as simplicity, stability, generosity, and strategic alignment with national innovation priorities. Simplifying eligibility criteria, increasing incentives, providing more flexibility, improving monitoring and evaluation, and considering additional measures such as grants or direct funding could help enhance the effectiveness of South Africa's R&D tax incentive program (National Treasury, 2021; OECD, 2015; Tau, 2019; World Bank, 2019). Overall, the current incentive structure may not effectively encourage increased R&D investment by firms, leading to lower-than-expected levels of R&D spending and innovation outputs (OECD, 2015; IMF, 2015). Expanding the comparative analysis to include more countries with successful R&D tax incentive programs can provide valuable insights and benchmarks for South Africa as it seeks to enhance its own incentive structure and promote greater investment in research and development activities.

Recommendations and Conclusion

Some suggested reforms to enhance the overall impact and benefits of the R&D tax incentive for South Africa include increasing the rate of the tax credit to encourage more investment in research and development activities, expanding the scope of eligible R&D activities beyond just scientific and technological R&D to include other innovative industries could attract a wider range of businesses to take advantage of the incentive, simplifying the application process for claiming the incentive, providing more support and guidance to companies on how to properly claim the incentive, along with conducting regular reviews and evaluations of the program's effectiveness, could help ensure that it continues to promote research and development activities in the country and providing more guidance on the tax regulations related to R&D to ensure compliance with regulations and prevent abuse (Lombaard & Mosoma, 2023; National Treasury, 2021; World Bank, 2019).

According to Section 11D of the Income Tax Act, businesses can claim a tax credit of up to 150% of their qualifying R&D expenditure but increasing this rate could further incentivize investment in R&D (World Bank, 2019). Additionally, including more types of R&D activities as eligible for the incentive, as outlined in Section 11D (1), could attract a wider range of industries to participate. Simplifying the administrative requirements for claiming the incentive, as detailed in Section 11D (4), would make it more accessible to small and medium enterprises (World Bank, 2019). Lastly, providing clearer guidelines on the tax regulations related to R&D, such as Sections 11D (2) and 11D (5), could help businesses better understand and take advantage of the incentive (World Bank, 2019).

Enhancing the effectiveness of R&D tax incentives includes setting appropriate tax credit rates, ensuring simplicity and certainty in the eligibility criteria, providing sufficient flexibility for different types of research activities, and implementing mechanisms to monitor and evaluate the outcomes. Additionally, coordination with other innovation policies and programs, such as grants and loans, has proven to further enhance the impact of R&D tax incentives. Aligning R&D tax incentives with broader innovation policy goals, such as increasing collaboration between firms and research institutions or promoting the commercialization of innovations, can help to maximize the overall impact of these incentives on the economy. By considering these specific features of the policy, policymakers can better design and implement R&D tax incentives that effectively support and stimulate innovation in the South African economy.

References

Akcigit, U., Hanley, D., & Stantcheva, S. (2022). Optimal taxation and R&D policies. *Econometrica, 90*(2), 645–684.

Association of International Certified Professional Accountants. (2017). *Guiding principles of good tax policy: A framework for evaluating tax proposals* [online]. Available from: https://us.aicpa.org/content/dam/aicpa/advocacy/tax/downloadabledocuments/tax-policy-concept-statement-no-1-global.pdf [Accessed: 9 May 2024].

Atalla, G., Mills, M., & McQueen, J. (2022). *Six ways that governments can drive the green transition [online]*. Available from: https://www.ey.com/en_gl/government-public-sector/six-ways-that-governments-candrive-the-green-transition (Accessed: 15 April 2024).

Bake, McKenzie, Wong, & Leow. (2024). *Singapore Budget 2024 — key tax updates* [online]. Available from: https://insightplus.bakermckenzie.com/bm/attachment_dw.action?attkey=FRbANEucS95NMLRN47z%2BeeOgEFCt8EGQJsWJiCH2WAWuU9AaVDeFgk23EcE077cM&nav=FRbANEucS95NMLRN47z%2BeeOgEFCt8EGQbuwypnpZjc4%3D&attdocparam=pB7HEsg%2FZ312Bk8OIuOIH1c%2BY4beLEAe4WDZNI853wo%3D&fromContentView=1 [Accessed: 9 May 2024].

Caesar, A. E., Chen, H., Udimal, T. B., & Osei-Agyemang, A. (2018). The influence of R&D on economic development in the West African Sub-Region. *Open Journal of Social Sciences, 6*(3), 215–228.

Calitz, E., Muwanga-Zake, E., Sithole, A., & Steyn, W. (2021). Depreciation allowances in South Africa. *Studies in Economics and Econometrics, 45*(1), 1–22.

De Gouveia, K. N. (2013). *Income tax incentives for renewable energy research and development and implementation: A comparison between South Africa and China.*

Dechezleprêtre, A., Einiö, E., Martin, R., Nguyen, K. T., & Van Reenen, J. (2016). *Do tax incentives for research increase firm innovation? An RD design for R&D.* National Bureau of Economic Research.

Dippenaar, M. (2018). The role of tax incentives in encouraging energy efficiency in the largest listed South African businesses. *South African Journal of Economic and Management Sciences, 21*(1), 1–12.

Ernst & Young. (2022). *Worldwide R&D Incentives* [online]. Available from: https://assets.ey.com/content/dam/ey-sites/ey-com/en_gl/topics/tax/tax-guides/2022/ey-worldwide-r-and-d-incentives-guide-2022.pdf [Accessed: 9 May 2024].

Ernst & Young. (2024). *Introduction of refundable investment credit and additional concessionary tax rate tier on various incentives* [online]. Available from: https://www.ey.com/en_gl/tax-alerts/singapore-budget-2024%2D%2D-introduction-of-refundable-investment-cr [Accessed: 9 May 2024].

Federal Government. (2024). *Funding for SMEs.* [online]. Available from: https://www.foerder-info.bund.de/foerderinfo/en/funding-for-smes/funding-for-smes_node.html [Accessed: 9 May 2024].

Fischer, S., Riley, T., & Sanger, T. (2021). *Five common misconceptions about the R&D tax credit—and whether you qualify* [online]. Available from: https://www.mossadams.com/articles/2021/03/company-qualifications-for-the-r-d-tax-credit [Accessed: 9 May 2024].

Hausmann, R., O'Brien, T., Fortunato, A., Lochmann, A., Shah, K., Venturi, L., Enciso-Valdivia, S., Vashkinskaya, E., Ahuja, K., Klinger, B., Sturzenegger, F., & Tokman, M. (2023). *Growth through inclusion in South Africa [online].* CID Faculty Working Paper Series. Available from: https://growthlab.hks.harvard.edu/sites/projects.iq.harvard.edu/files/growthlab/files/2023-11-cid-wp-434-south-africa-growth-throughinclusion.pdf [Accessed: 26 April 2024].

Inland Revenue Authority of Singapore. (2024). *Refundable Investment Credit (RIC)* [online]. Available from: https://www.iras.gov.sg/schemes/disbursement-schemes/refundable-investment-credit-(ric) [Accessed: 9 May 2024].

International Monetary Fund. (2015). *Fiscal policy and long-term growth.* IMF Policy Paper [online]. International Monetary Fund. Available from: [Accessed:8 May 2024].

Jamel, N. E. S. M., Hamid, N. A., & Zawawi, S. N. (2021). Analysing SST 2.0 burden using the guiding principles of good tax policy. *GATR Accounting and Finance Review, 6*(3), 167–177. https://doi.org/10.35609/afr.2021.6.3(5)

Kahn, A., Kasongo, A., Sithole, M. M. & Ramoroka, K.H. (2024). An analysis of the micro-and macro-economic determinants of firm R&D intensity in the South African business sector. *African Journal of Science, Technology, Innovation and Development*, 1–12.

KPMG. (2023). *South Africa: Proposed amendments to section 11D R&D tax incentive* [online]. Available from: https://kpmg.com/us/en/home/insights/2023/08/tnf-south-africa-proposed-amendments-to-section-11d-r-d-tax-incentive.html [Accessed: 9 May 2024].

Lombaard, E. & Mosoma, I. (2023). *The refinement of South Africa's R&D tax incentive* [online]. KPMG. Available from: The refinement of South Africa's R&D tax incentive (kpmg.com) [Accessed: 6 May 2024].

Maseko, L. (2017). *Research and Development (R&D) Tax Incentives; Indigenous Knowledge Systems Bill: briefing* [online] https://pmg.org.za/committee-meeting/24550/ [Accessed: 6 May 2024].

Mirrlees, J.A., & Stuart, A. (2010). *Dimensions of tax design: The Mirrlees review.* Oxford University Press.

National Treasury. (2021). *Discussion document: Reviewing the design, implementation and impact of South Africa's Research and Development Tax Incentive [online]*. National Treasury of South Africa. Available from: https://www.treasury.gov.za/comm_media/press/2021/TaxPolicyDiscussion/2021121501%20Discussion%20Document%20-%20Research%20and%20Development%20Tax%20Incentive.pdf [Accessed 6 May 2024].

National Treasury. (2024). *Changes to R&D tax incentive as of 1 January 2024* [online]. National Treasury of South Africa. Available from: https://www.dst.gov.za/rdtax/index.php/changes-to-r-d-tax-incentive-as-of-1-january-2024 [Accessed 10 May 2024].

Ndlovu, V., & Inglesi-Lotz, R. (2020). The causal relationship between energy and economic growth through research and development (R&D): The case of BRICS and lessons for South Africa. *Energy, 199*, 117428.

Neubig, T., Galindo-Rueda, F., Appelt, S., Criscuolo, C. & Bajgar, M. 2016. *Fiscal incentives for R&D and innovation in a diverse world* [online]. Available from: https://www.oecd-ilibrary.org/sites/9789264257573-8-en/index.html?itemId=/content/component/9789264257573-8-en [Accessed 6 May 2024].

OECD. (2015). *Addressing the Tax Challenges of the Digital Economy [online]. OECD Publishing.* Available from: https://www.oecd-ilibrary.org/addressing-the-tax-challenges-of-the-digital-economy-action-1-2015-final-report_5jrw8x0hdl42.pdf [Accessed 10 May 2024].

OECD. (2023). *Tax incentives play a key role in the business R&D support policy mix in the OECD area and beyond [online]*. OECD Publishing. Available from: https://www.oecd.org/innovation/tax-incentives-RD-innovation/ [Accessed 6 May 2024].

Olaoye, I. J., Ayinde, O. E., Ajewole, O. O., & Adebisi, L. O. (2021). The role of research and development expenditure and governance on economic growth in selected African countries. *African Journal of Science, Technology, Innovation and Development, 13*(6), 663–670.

PricewaterhouseCoopers. (2024). *Worldwide R&D Incentives* [online]. Available from: https://www.pwc.com/sg/en/publications/singapore-budget/commentary/refundable-investment-credit.html [Accessed: 9 May 2024].

Rakgotho, C. M. (2018). *South African tax incentives as a motivation for the private sector to invest in research and development* (Doctoral dissertation, North-West University).

Smith, A. (1776). *An Inquiry into the Nature and Causes of the Wealth of Nations [online]*. Available from: https://www.ibiblio.org/ml/libri/s/SmithA_WealthNations_p.pdf [Accessed: 14 May 2024].

Tau, T. (2019). *A critical analysis of the relevance of the South African research and development tax incentive to small and medium-sized enterprises (SMEs) and start-ups* (Doctoral dissertation).

United Nations Trade and Development. (2023). *World Investment Report: Investing in sustainable energy for all.* [online]. United Nations. Available from: https://unctad.org/publication/world-investment-report-2023 [Accessed 9 May 2024].

Wenjuan, S., & Zhao, K. (2023). Balancing fiscal expenditure competition and long-term innovation investment: Exploring trade-offs and policy implications for local governments. *PLoS One, 18*(11), 0293158.

World Bank Group. (2019). *Impact evaluation of the R&D tax incentive in South Africa* [online]. World Bank. Available from: https://www.treasury.gov.za/comm_media/press/2021/TaxPolicyDiscussion/2021121501%20RefDocA%20-%20Impact%20Evaluation%20of%20the%20R&D%20Tax%20Incentive%20in%20South%20Africa%20-%20World%20Bank%-20-%20Sept%202019.pdf [Accessed 6 May 2024].

Yue, Z., Yang, G., & Wang, H. (2023). How do tax reductions motivate technological innovation? *Humanities and Social Sciences Communications, 10*, 775. https://doi.org/10.1057/s41599-02302305-6

Auditor Independence: Does Audit Engagement Lead Partner Rotation Matter?

Eghosa Godwin Inneh

Abstract Following the Enron financial scandal, several mechanisms were introduced, including audit rotation, to improve audit independence and financial reporting quality. Audit rotation is based on two perspectives: audit firm and partner rotation. Most countries have adopted one of the two audit rotations to improve audit quality. However, few countries have adopted both audit mechanisms, including Nigeria. In Nigeria, several studies subsisted on audit firm rotation, neglecting the audit partner rotation, even though humans may be responsible for the impairment of audit quality rather than the firm. Our study filled the gap by examining the effect of audit partner tenure on financial reporting quality to determine whether audit partner rotation matters. In answering the study's objective, data was collected from the financial report of Nigerian Deposit Money Banks using a census study and estimated using the Ordinary Least Square (OLS). The result showed that auditors' independence is compromised with an elongated audit tenure and invariably results in a lower audit quality. The study aligned with the fresh eye hypothesis and supported the mandatory audit partner regulation to minimise the familiarity threat from a close auditor–client association arising from a long audit partner's tenure.

Keywords Audit partner rotation · Audit firm rotation · Audit independence · Financial reporting quality · Ordinary least square

Introduction

The most effective means to guarantee the quality of financial reporting is through the external auditor (Fan & Wong, 2005; Mouselli et al., 2014). Following the demise of Arthur Anderson in the Enron corporate scandal, the demand for credible financial reports increased as other external stakeholders were sceptical of the

E. G. Inneh (✉)
University of Johannesburg, Johannesburg, South Africa
e-mail: einneh@uj.ac.za; eghinneh@oauife.edu.ng

T. Moloi (ed.), *Impacting Society Positively Through Technology in Accounting and Business Processes*, Springer Proceedings in Business and Economics,
https://doi.org/10.1007/978-3-031-84885-8_52

quality of the financial reporting. To restore the faith of the other external stakeholders, the legal and institutional frameworks across the globe instituted corporate governance mechanisms, including auditing guidelines and regulations, to improve audit independence. Auditor independence is one of the essential media for ensuring the integrity of financial reports, and among these is audit rotation. According to Florio (2024), the discourse of audit rotation is fierce globally at present, and there are two perspectives on this: audit firm rotation and audit partner rotation.

In comparison, both audit rotation regulations intend to minimise familiarity threats by introducing a fresh eye examination. The audit firm rotation assumes auditor independence is enhanced by mandatorily changing the audit firm within regular intervals, which invariably changes the audit partner. In contrast, the audit partner rotation assumes the lead partner's actions influence the audit quality and independence; therefore, financial reporting quality is guaranteed by rotating the audit engagement lead partner.

Globally, countries use audit rotation to improve financial reporting quality (Tessema & Abou-El-Sood, 2023). However, most countries adopt one of the two audit rotation mechanisms, but more countries favour audit partner rotation (Lennox, 2014). For example, Lennox et al. (2014) indicated that most European countries, China, and the United States of America, adopted the audit partner rotation, neglecting the firm rotation. Furthermore, Lennox et al. (2014) claim that examining whether audit partner rotation strengthens financial reporting quality is a Hercules task, as limited or no information exists, in many of these jurisdictions, on the tenure and change of the audit engagement lead partner's hence, resulting into limited empirical evidence on the subject matter.

Contrary to those above, unlike in most jurisdictions, the Nigerian institution framework mandated audit firm and partner rotation (FRCN, 2011, 2016). In the Nigerian banking sector, the audit clients must disclose the statutory audit firm name, lead engagement partner name, signature, and professional certification numbers in their financial report. The disclosure of this audit rotation contents should enable numerous empirical evidence to subsist in Nigeria. Although there is sufficient evidence on audit firm rotation in Nigeria (Agbi et al., 2023; Bassey et al., 2020; Onwuchekwa et al., 2012; Temitope et al., 2023), scarce literature (Mgbame et al., 2012) exists on the audit partner audit rotational policies, even though the institutional framework created an enabling environment for this type of research.

Hence, the study provided the research question: Does this audit partner rotation matter? The study intends to answer the research question by examining the effect of audit partner rotation on financial reporting quality. The study fills the gap in knowledge by contributing to the scanty literature on audit partner tenure and financial reporting quality. The study measures the financial reporting quality using the inverse of discretionary accrual and earnings persistence, which are rarely employed by Nigerian audit-related studies but are considered most appropriate as almost all financial statements in Nigeria have a clean report. The study considers the audit firm rotation as an integral part of the study but not the primary variable of interest. The scope of the study is limited to the banking industry, which is justified because the legal framework instituted the auditing regulations relating to audit partner and audit firm rotation.

In achieving the study's objective, other parts of the paper are subdivided into groups. Section "Literature Review and Hypothesis Development" addresses the literature review and hypothesis development; section "Methodology" provides a methodology. Section "Results and Discussion" discusses the results obtained, and, finally, section "Conclusion" presents a conclusion from the study.

Literature Review and Hypothesis Development

The Nigerian Institutional Environment

Empirical studies (Azoro et al., 2021; Lawan, 2011; Ogunkan, 2022; Salihu et al., 2015) regarded the Nigerian institutional framework as weak. The rule of law index, an integral part of the corporate governance indexes, supported the assertion that the Nigerian legal framework is weak (WGI, 2023). There is less adherence to instituted laws and policies in Nigeria. However, the Nigerian banking industry is fairly regulated, and most banks operating in Nigeria usually adhere to institutional policies. Regulatory bodies such as the Companies Allied Matters Act (CAMA), Banking and Other Financial Institutions Act (BOFIA), and the Financial Reporting Council of Nigeria (FRCN) enact regulations to ensure financial reporting quality at all times. Audit regulations are enacted on audit firms' and audit partners' tenure. FRCN (2011) Section 9 (1) stipulates a mandatory audit firm and partner rotation; FRCN (2011) Section 9 (2) states that the audit firm should spend a maximum of 10 years on a particular audit assignment; and Section 9 (4) indicates that the audit firm must observe a cooling-off period of 7 years before returning to the same audit engagement. Furthermore, Section 9 (6) for audit partners stipulates a maximum audit period of 5 years on the same audit engagement and the cooling-off period at the audit firm's discretion.

Theoretical Frameworks and Hypothesis Development

The quality of the financial report is a tri-party affair: the management, the shareholders, and the auditors (Inneh et al., 2022). In agreement with the stewardship theory, the management should report the performance and state of the firm's financial position regularly, usually yearly, to the shareholders. The agency theory assumes that the management embarks on opportunistic behaviour due to information asymmetry (Jian et al., 2024); hence, there is a need for an auditor to examine and form an opinion on the financial statement. Financial reporting is deemed quality when it lacks material misstatement (DeAngelo, 1981). Following the corporate financial scandals in the twenty-first century's first decade, the need for auditor independence increases. Audit independence is of the mind but guarantees several mechanisms, including the audit rotation.

Audit rotation is the change in the audit firm or partner to improve auditor independence and quality. There are two types of audit rotation: the audit firm and the lead engagement partner. Mandatory audit firm rotation is the change of audit firm upon working for an audit client for the maximum of years stipulated by law, while mandatory audit partner rotation is the change of lead engagement. Irrespective of the form of audit rotation, the learning effect and fresh eye hypothesis subsist, and the intention is to improve the audit quality (Chen et al., 2024). The learning effect hypothesis posits that auditors acquire experience and knowledge on audit engagement as their tenure increases (Bleibtreu & Stefani, 2018). The hypothesis's proponents believe that audit firms or partners struggle and learn in the early years of a new engagement, but in subsequent years, the audit quality improves (Harber et al., 2024; Lee et al., 2009; Van Deventer, 2023). Hence, the proponents of the learning effect hypothesis are against the mandatory audit rotation policy.

Conversely, the opponents of the learning effect hypothesis refuted the postulation of the learning hypothesis on the account that a long audit tenure results in a close association between the auditor and the clients (Lennox & Wu, 2018; Lennox et al., 2014). They argued that long audit tenure increases the familiarity threat (Bell et al., 2015; Gipper et al., 2021; Lennox & Wu, 2018; Qin & Xiao, 2024), compromises audit independence, and invariably impairs audit quality. The opponents of the learning effect hypothesis supported the fresh eye hypothesis. The fresh eye hypothesis posits the need for audit rotation and examination of the financial statement by the new incoming auditors. The proponents of the fresh eye hypothesis argued that audit rotation improves audit quality as the new incoming auditors introduce new perspectives into the audit engagements from the early year of engagement, contrary to the argument of the proponents of the learning effect hypothesis.

Furthermore, the proponents of the fresh eye hypothesis argued that familiarity threat, resulting in long audit tenure, is reduced when auditors are rotated. Finally, the proponents of this hypothesis claim that outgoing auditors will increase their audit efforts in the latter years of their engagement, which will also improve adult quality (Qin & Xiao, 2024). The fresh eye hypothesis supported the audit partner audit rotation, claiming that the knowledge and experience of the outgoing auditor will be retained when both the outgoing and incoming audit partners are from the same audit firms. The fresh eye hypothesis assumes the audit quality process is preserved as the audit team on the assignment will remain the same, and the incoming lead partners will have access to the outgoing lead engagement auditors and their working papers.

Anchoring on the fresh eye hypothesis, empirical studies (Garcia-Blandon et al., 2020; Jadiyappa et al., 2021; Tepalagul & Lin, 2015) showed that audit partner tenure in rotation is positively related to audit quality; this invariable connoted that long audit partner tenure compromises audit quality. Conversely, studies (Chen et al., 2008; Johnson et al., 2002) also showed that audit partner tenure positively relates to financial reporting quality, premised on the learning effect theory. Based on the extant related literature, the study assumes that there is a relationship between audit partner rotation and audit quality, which is stated in alternative form:

H1: There is a relationship between audit partner rotation and financial reporting quality.

Methodology

Research Design

The study employed a longitudinal research design. The panel data comprised 12 Deposit Money Banks (DMBs) over 12 years (2011–2022), resulting in 144 firm-year observations. A census study was adopted, and all the DMBs listed on the floor of the Nigerian Exchange Group were considered, subject to the existence and operation of these DMBs and the availability of data on all the variables of interest over the period. The non-financial institutions were not considered for the study based on the distinction in the measurement metrics of financial reporting in the two sectors. The base year was 2011, which was justified by the FRCN 2011 regulations regarding audit rotation in Nigeria.

Model Specification and Variables Definition

A hypothesis was developed to answer the audit partner–financial reporting quality association proposition. The audit partner tenure (APT) was measured using the successive years of the leading partner in an audit assignment, while the inverse of the discretionary accrual measures the Financial Reporting Quality (FRQ) (Inneh et al., 2024; Krauß et al., 2015) and earning persistence (García-Meca & García-Sánchez, 2018). Based on the learning effect theory, the study assumes a positive association between the APT and FRQ, which is consistent with studies (Chen et al., 2008; Johnson et al., 2002). Conversely, the familiarity threat evidenced decreased FRQ with elongated audit partner tenure (APT) (Garcia-Blandon et al., 2020; Jadiyappa et al., 2021; Tepalagul & Lin, 2015). Based on the theories and extant literature, the study assumes a directional association between the primary variable of interest in the model.

$$\text{FRQ}_{it} = \beta_0 + \beta_1 \text{APT}_{it} + \varepsilon_{it} \tag{1}$$

The model was expanded by adding the audit firm tenure (AFT) and bank-specific attributes such as firm size, complexity, profitability, and liquidity/capital structure. The natural logarithm of the total assets (LNTA) depicts the firm size, and the number of employees (EMPLOY) represents the model's bank complexity. Studies (Dechow & Dichev, 2002; Johnson et al., 2002) indicate that firm size is directly related to FRQ; larger firms have the resources to engage a reputable audit firm to maintain their investors and attract potential investors. The complexity of the banks can be measured using proxies like the number of segments, volume of transactions, and number of employees, among others. However, the study elected to measure banks' complexity using the number of employees by each DMB. Return on assets (ROA) and Loss (LOSS) are consistent profitability metrics (Krauß et al., 2015). The ROA is measured using profit after tax deflated by total assets, while the LOSS is a dichotomous variable of one provided the bank makes a loss and zero otherwise.

The capital structure is represented using leverage (LEV). The LEV is measured using debt capital, which consists of the summation of the long and short debts scaled down by total assets. The study assumed a positive association between LEV and FRQ, consistent with studies (Asthana & Boone 2012; Choi et al. 2010). The cash flow from operation is divided by total assets and represented by (CFO); the study assumed a positive relationship of the variable with FRQ (Chung & Kallapur, 2003). Financial distress (FIN) was measured using the Zmijewski's (1984) financial condition index. The study assumed a positive association with FRQ.

The expanded model

$$\begin{aligned}\mathrm{FRQ}_{it} &= \beta_0 + \beta_1\mathrm{APT}_{it} + \beta_2\mathrm{AFT}_{it} + \beta_3\mathrm{LNTA}_{it} + +\beta_4\mathrm{LOSS}_{it} + \beta_5\mathrm{CFO}_{it} \\ &\quad +\beta_6\mathrm{LEV}_{it} + \beta_7\mathrm{EMPLOY}_{it} + \beta_8\mathrm{FIN}_{it} + \beta_9\mathrm{ROA}_{it} + \varepsilon_{it}\end{aligned} \tag{2}$$

The discretionary accrual is measured consistent with the study (McNichols 2002; McNichols & Stubben, 2008) stated:

$$\frac{\mathrm{TA}_{it}}{A_{it-1}} = \beta_0 + \beta_1\frac{\mathrm{OCF}_{it-1}}{A_{it-1}} + \beta_2\frac{\mathrm{OCF}_{it}}{A_{it-1}} + \beta_3\frac{\mathrm{OCF}_{it+1}}{A_{it-1}} + \varepsilon_{it} \tag{3}$$

TA = Total accrual measured as net income minus operating cash flow of firm i in year t

A = Total asset

OCF = Operating cash flow

$it-1$ = One period lag for all the panel data

ε_{it} = The residual and its inverse represents the financial reporting quality

Results and Discussion

Descriptive Statistics

Table 1 describes the variables of interest in model 2. The result indicated that the mean of the APT is 2.42, indicating that the lead partners of DMBs audit engagement are rotated every 2.42 years. The rationale for the change could be to reduce the close association between the audit lead partner and the bank's management and comply with the mandatory audit rotation of 5 years. However, the result could

Table 1 Descriptive statistics

Variables	Mean	Median	Maximum	Minimum	Std. Dev.	Prob
AFT	5.06	5.00	10.00	1.00	2.95	0.00
APT	2.42	2.00	7.00	1.00	1.49	0.00
LNTA	2.78	1.79	1.50	1.57	2.76	0.00
Loss	0.05	0.00	1.00	0.00	0.26	0.00
CFO/TA	0.03	0.03	0.49	−0.19	0.09	0.00
LEV	0. 91	0.87	0.96	0.23	0.57	0.00
Employee	4725.62	3452.00	1327.00	1011.00	3184.46	0.00
FIN	0.04	0.02	0.32	0.00	0.04	0.00
ROA	0.09	0.01	0.16	−0.09	0.02	0.00
FRQ	0.00	−0.00	0.04	−0.07	0.01	0.00

Source: Author's computation (2024)

Where AFT denotes audit firm tenure; APT is the audit partner tenure; assets represent total assets; CFO/TA represents the ratio of cash from operations to total assets; LEV represents leverage; Employee represents a total number of employees; FIN represents the ratio of cash from equity and debt issuances to total assets. ROA denotes return on assets. FRQ represents financial reporting quality

influence the FRQ due to the frequency change of the auditor, which may affect learning, especially if the lead partner does not have prerequisite knowledge in the industry. However, the proponents of audit partner rotation believe that lead partners are more experienced and would still perform even in a new audit engagement. The maximum value of APT of seven exceeded the 5-year mandatory period audit partner rotation. The AFT has a mean value of 5.05 years with a maximum of 10 years and a minimum of 1 year. The median value for this variable is 5. The statistics of AFT indicate that the Nigerian DMBs, on average, changed audit firms before the 10-year mandatory period. The change in investors' motivation might be to strengthen the FRQ, but when the management of the DMBs calls for the change in the audit firm, it might signal opinion shopping.

The descriptive statistics of the bank size (LNTA) has a mean of 21.74, median of 21.33, maximum of 23.43, and minimum of 18.87. The descriptive statistics of the LNTA are not of economic importance except that they are delogged through exponential power. The average bank had a total asset of N 2,777,275,815 during the years of observation and a median value of N 1,790,321,689. The maximum value of assets owned by any of the banks was N 14,972,309,000, while the minimum value was N 156,506,504. The range, the difference between the banks with the highest total assets and minimum total assets amounting to N 14,815,802,496, indicates the classification of banks in Nigeria.

The loss (LOSS) has a mean value of 0.05, which indicates that approximately 5% of the banks made a loss during the year of study. The maximum and the minimum of the LOSS are one and zero, respectively; the rationale for this is that the variable metric was dichotomous. CFO representing cash from operations to total assets had an average of 3.42% for the banks during the years of observation. It had a maximum value of 49.31% and a minimum value of −19.62%. The median for

Table 2 Correlation analysis and VIF analysis

	Variable	1	2	3	4	5	6	7	8	9	10	VIF
1	AFT	1.00										1.26
		0.00										
2	APT	0.34	1.00									1.09
		0.00	0.00									
3	LnTA	0.01	−0.15	1.00								1.94
		0.90	0.06	0.00								
4	LOSS	0.00	0.05	−0.31	1.00							3.39
		0.98	0.50	0.00	0.00							
5	CFO/TA	0.10	−0.18	0.25	−0.19	1.00						1.34
		0.22	0.03	0.00	0.82	0.00						
6	Leverage	−0.01	0.12	−0.26	0.12	−0.20	1.00					1.31
		0.90	0.13	0.00	0.16	0.20	0.00					
7	Employ	0.06	−0.14	0.78	−0.17	0.06	−0.39	1.00				3.24
		0.47	0.09	0.00	0.03	0.43	0.00	0.00				
8	FIN	−0.10	−0.04	−0.14	−0.10	−0.30	0.07	−0.11	1.00			1.17
		0.20	0.63	0.09	0.24	0.00	0.39	0.20	0.00			
9	ROA	−0.01	−0.14	0.42	−0.66	0.08	−0.27	0.32	−0.04	1.00		2.13
		0.82	0.08	0.00	0.00	0.32	0.00	0.00	0.60	0.00		
10	FRQ	−0.11	−0.08	−0.41	−0.58	0.03	0.17	−0.29	−0.00	−0.90	1.00	
		0.16	0.34	0.00	0.00	0.71	0.04	0.00	0.96	0.00	0.00	

Source: Author's computation (2024)

Where AFT denotes audit firm tenure; APT is the audit partner tenure; assets represent total assets; CFO/TA represents the ratio of cash from operations to total assets; LEV represents leverage; Employee represents a total number of employees; FIN represents the ratio of cash from equity and debt issuances to total assets. ROA denotes return on assets. FRQ represents financial reporting quality

this variable was 3.5%. During the years of observation, the banks had an average leverage of 0.91, indicating that Nigerian banks are highly geared, with an average debt finance of 91%. The banks had an average employee size of 4726 during the years, with a maximum value of 13,237 and a minimum value of 1011. The medium value for this variable was 3452.

Furthermore, Table 2 also showed that ROA has an average of 0.09, indicating that the Nigerian banks have a return of 9% of total assets as profit. Finally, Table 1 shows that the FRQ has a mean and median of 0.00. The result is expected as the variable is derived from the residual of Eq. (3).

Correlation Analysis and Variance Inflation Factor

Table 2 displayed the degree of the multicollinearity among the regressors in a pair-wise method using the correlation matrix and Variance Inflation Factor (VIF) of the explanatory variables used in the study. Based on extant literature, a multicollinearity problem is possible when two regressors have a correlation association of at least

0.8, and the problem is affirmed when the VIF surpasses the threshold of 5. Based on the results in Table 2, the highest pairwise association between the regressors (LNTA and EMPLOY) is 0.78 between total assets and number of employees. However, the result of the correlation association is closer to the threshold of 0.8, which indicates the possibility of multicollinearity. However, the VIF results of these two variables, LNTA =1.98 and EMPLOY = 3.24, indicate that there are fewer problems of multicollinearity on the account that the VIF of these two stimuli variables were less than the threshold of 5. Hence, the study employs the Ordinary Least Square (OLS) to estimate the model without resulting in a spurious regression.

Furthermore, the correlation analysis result possesses economic importance other than the multicollinearity problem. For instance, a positive relationship between APT and AFT at (Pc = 0.341, Prob < 0.05) indicates that when an audit firm has an elongated audit tenure, the leading partner tenure also increases, which might increase the familiarity threat. There is a negative correlation between leverage (LEV) and firm size (LNTA) (Pc = −0.267, Prob < 0.05), evidencing a negative relationship between the financial leverage of a company and its size. The LEV_LNTA association connote that larger companies tend to employ equity finance. The correlation analysis of Employ and LnTA has a strong, statistically significant positive relationship (Pc = 0.786, Prob < 0.05). The results of EMPLOY_LNTA indicate that large firms are associated with increased complexity.

Regression Estimation and Discussion of Results

The unit root test was performed to determine the level of stationarity and prevent a spurious regression, but the result was not displayed for brevity. The unit root test result indicated that all variables of interest were stationary at level. The study employed the OLS to estimate Eq. (2) to solve the hypothesis. The fixed effect, random effect, and Pooled effect form of OLS was carried out. Moreover, the Hausman and Breusch–Pagan tests were carried out to ascertain the appropriate analysis method; the result in Table 3 showed that the FEM (Column II result) is the appropriate method of analysis. The adjusted R-square is 0.8422, indicating that the explanatory variables accounted for 84.22% of the change FRQ. Also, the F statistics is 44.17 at a $P < 0.05$, indicating that the model is fit.

The result showed that audit partner tenure and financial reporting quality association is negative and significant, as evidenced in the result presented in Table 3 (coff = −0.040, $t = -3.345$). The result is supported by studies (Bell et al., 2015; Gipper et al., 2021; Lennox & Wu, 2018; Qin & Xiao, 2024) indicating the likelihood of the lead engagement partners compromising audit quality due to close association with clients. The result aligns with the agency theory and fresh eye hypothesis, supporting the mandatory audit partner rotation policy. However, there could be fear of loss of engagement experience and knowledge loss when the lead engagement partners are rotated, but this will have minimal effect on the audit quality as the incoming lead partner still has at his disposal the same audit team member

Table 3 Regression analysis using OLS

Dependent Variable	Pool Audit quality	FEM Audit quality	REM Audit quality
Independent variable	Coef (t-stat)	Coef (t-stat)	Coef (t-stat)
Audit firm tenure	−0.031 (−1.010)	0.032 (−1.271)	0.023 (−1.461)
Audit partner tenure	−0.038*** (−4.789)	−0.040*** (−3.345)	−0.0388*** (−3.318)
LnTA	0.010*** (−2.700)	0.011*** (1.969)	0.010* (1.891)
Loss	0.0149*** (−2.311)	−0.016*** (−1.973)	−0.014*** (−2.027)
CFO/TA	0.0240*** (3.992)	0.022*** (4.445)	0.024*** (4.190)
Leverage	0.018*** (2.3925)	0.019*** (2.3822)	0.018* (1.881)
FIN	0.015 (0.111)	0.05 (0.0401)	0.015 (0.142)
ROA	0.8999*** (10.7158)	0.8970*** (9.5577)	0.8999*** (11.4623)
C	0.021 (1.2890)	0.035 (1.0446)	0.031 (0.318)
R-squared	0.8518	0.8631	0.8518
Adjusted R-squared	0.8430	0.8422	0.8430
F-stat	97.0328	44.1769	97.0327
Hausman		73.08 ($p < 0.05$)	
Breusch–Pagan		65.45 ($P < 0.05$)	
Observations	144	144	144

Source: Author's computation (2024)

Where AFT denotes audit firm tenure; APT is the audit partner tenure; assets represent total assets; CFO/TA represents the ratio of cash from operations to total assets; LEV represents leverage; Employee represents a total number of employees; FIN represents the ratio of cash from equity and debt issuances to total assets. ROA denotes return on assets. FRQ represents financial reporting quality

on the same audit assignment, the audit working papers, audit plan and audit procedure and access to the outgoing partner if need be since both are with the same audit firm.

The result showed that audit firm tenure is insignificant and negatively related to audit quality. The consequence indicated that the audit firms' tenure does not necessarily improve audit quality. The result contradicts the postulation that audit firms acquire client knowledge and experience on the same audit engagement as their tenure increases and invariably improves quality.

Table 4 Robustness Check of Audit Partner Rotation and Audit Quality

Method DEP. VAR	Pool Audit quality	FEM Audit quality	REM Audit quality
Independent variable	Coef (t-stat)	Coef (t-stat)	Coef (t-stat)
Audit firm tenure	−0.063 (−0.920)	−0.022 (−0.217)	−0.063 (−0.646)
Audit partner tenure	−0.531*** (−2.123)	−0.852*** (−3.839)	−0.531 *** (−3.105)
LnTA	1.490*** (3.993)	1.860 (1.363)	1.490*** (5.726)
Loss	0.335 (0.175)	−0.598 (−0.361)	0.335 (0.247)
CFO/TA	1.082 (0.310)	1.553 (0.559)	1.082** (0.424)
Leverage	1.343*** (3.443)	0.1336 (0.108)	1.343*** (3.6987)
FIN	5.462* (−1.850)	−0.4831 (−0.093)	−5.4621 (−1.140)
ROA	35.914*** (4.608)	7.783 (0.330)	35.914*** (2.215)
C	−1.052 (−0.131)	0.812 (0.892)	−0.535 (−0.105)
R-squared	0.847	0.871	0.847
Adjusted R-squared	0.823	0.837	0.823
F-stat	36.129	25.491	36.129
Hausman		34.041 ($p < 0.05$)	
Breusch–Pagan		63.032 ($p < 0.05$)	
Observations	144	144	144

Source: Author's computation (2024)
Where AFT denotes audit firm tenure; APT is the audit partner tenure; assets represent total assets; CFO/TA represents the ratio of cash from operations to total assets; LEV represents leverage; Employee represents a total number of employees; FIN represents the ratio of cash from equity and debt issuances to total assets. ROA denotes return on assets. FRQ represents financial reporting quality

Robustness Check

The study used the variable substitution method to check the analysis's robustness. The dependent variable of the inverse of discretionary accrual was substituted for earnings persistence as an alternative proxy to measure audit quality. The fixed effect method (FEM) was also used as the method of analysis, based on the result of the Hausman and Breusch–Pagan Test as displayed in Table 4. Based on the result presented in Table 4 using FEM, the model is fit with an F statistic of 25.4911, significant at $P(0.05)$. Furthermore, the Adjusted R square value is 0.837, alluding to the regressors in the model, which accounted for an 83.7% change in audit quality.

The results showed that the audit firm tenure is negative but insignificantly related to audit quality, as evidenced by statistics of ($t = 0.0225, 0.2171$) consistent with the earlier regression. Furthermore, the association audit partner tenure and audit quality indicated a negative and significant relationship with statistics of ($t = 0.852, -3.839$). The result confirms the earlier assertion of audit partner rotation using discretionary accrual as the audit quality metrics.

Conclusion

The study examined the effect of audit partners' tenure on audit quality to ascertain whether there is a need for a mandatory audit rotation policy in the Nigerian banking environment. Longitudinal data was collected from the 12 Nigerian-listed DMBs from 2011 to 2022 using a census study to provide answers to the study hypothesis. The OLS estimation technique was used in the analysis, and a robustness check was carried out by substituting the discretionary financial report quality metric with earnings persistence. The results showed that the audit independence and quality are compromised due to the lead engagement partner's long tenure, though it contradicts the learning effect theory. The result aligns with agency theory and is consistent with the fresh eye hypothesis, as audit quality is compromised due to the close association between audit and client. The study supports the mandatory audit partner rotation.

References

Agbi, A. I., Okoye, E. I., & Nwoye, U. J. (2023). Audit quality disclosures of public non-financial firms in Nigeria: A focus on predictive factors. *Journal of Global Accounting, 9*(2), 304–320. https://journals.unizik.edu.ng/joga/article/view/220

Asthana, S. C., & Boone, J. P. (2012). Abnormal audit fee and audit quality. *Auditing: A Journal of Practice and Theory, 31*(3), 1–22. https://doi.org/10.2308/ajpt-10294

Azoro, C. J., Onah, C. A., & Agulefo, Q. O. (2021). Weak institutions and poor governance in Nigeria: A socio-legal perspective. *African Journal of Law, Political Research and Administration, 4*(2), 61–70. https://doi.org/10.52589/AJLPRA-5IUFPPRU

Bassey, B. E., Omini, E. U., Olatunbosun, A., Asi, E. U., & Emmanuel, A. S. (2020). Auditors independence and audit quality in Nigeria. *Journal of Critical Reviews, 7*(17), 624–635. https://www.researchgate.net/profile/Bassey-Bassey-5/publication/344446383_Auditors_Independence_and_Audit_Quality_in_Nigeria/links/5f765dbea6fdcc00865010 4e/Auditors-Independence-and-Audit-Quality-in-Nigeria.pdf

Bell, T. B., Causholli, M., & Knechel, W. R. (2015). Audit firm tenure, non-audit services, and internal assessments of audit quality. *Journal of Accounting Research, 53*(3), 461–509. https://doi.org/10.1111/1475-679X.12078

Bleibtreu, C., & Stefani, U. (2018). The effects of mandatory audit firm rotation on client importance and audit industry concentration. *The Accounting Review, 93*(1), 1–27. https://doi.org/10.2308/accr-51728

Chen, C. Y., Lin, C. J., & Lin, Y. C. (2008). Audit partner tenure, audit firm tenure, and discretionary accruals: Does long auditor tenure impair earnings quality? *Contemporary Accounting Research, 25*(2), 415–445. https://doi.org/10.1506/car.25.2.5

Chen, C., Liu, Z., Tang, W., & Tuo, L. (2024). Accounting reporting complexity, audit engagement partner mandatory rotation, and audit quality. *Journal of Corporate Accounting and Finance, 35*(2), 157–170. https://doi.org/10.1002/jcaf.22679

Choi, J.-H., Kim, J.-B., & Zang, Y. (2010). Do abnormally high audit fees impair audit quality? *Auditing: A Journal of Practice and Theory, 29*(2), 73–97. https://doi.org/10.2308/aud.2010.29.2.115

Chung, H., & Kallapur, S. (2003). Client importance, non-audit services, and abnormal accruals. *The Accounting Review, 78*(4), 931–955. https://doi.org/10.2308/accr.2003.78.4.931

Deangelo, L. E. (1981). Auditor size and audit quality. *Journal of Accounting and Economics, 3*(3), 183–199. https://doi.org/10.1016/0165-4101(81)90002-1

Dechow, P. M., & Dichev, I. D. (2002). The quality of accruals and earnings: The role of accrual estimation errors. *The Accounting Review, 77*(S-1), 35–59. https://doi.org/10.2308/accr.2002.77.s-1.35

Fan, J. P., & Wong, T. J. (2005). Do external auditors perform a corporate governance role in emerging markets? Evidence from East Asia. *Journal of Accounting Research, 43*(1), 35–72. https://doi.org/10.1111/j.1475-679x.2004.00162.x

Financial Reporting Council of Nigeria. (2011). https://frcnigeria.gov.ng/

Financial Reporting Council of Nigeria. (2016). https://frcnigeria.gov.ng/

Florio, C. (2024). A structured literature review of empirical research on mandatory auditor rotation. *Journal of International Accounting, Auditing and Taxation*, 100623. https://doi.org/10.1016/j.intaccaudtax.2024.100623

Garcia-Blandon, J., Argilés-Bosch, J. M., & Ravenda, D. (2020). Audit firm tenure and audit quality: A cross-European study. *Journal of International Financial Management and Accounting, 31*(1), 35–64. https://doi.org/10.1111/jifm.12098

García-Meca, E., & García-Sánchez, I. M. (2018). Does managerial ability influence the quality of financial reporting? *European Management Journal, 36*(4), 544–557. https://doi.org/10.1016/j.emj.2017.07.010

Gipper, B., Hail, L., & Leuz, C. (2021). On the economics of mandatory audit partner rotation and tenure: Evidence from PCAOB data. *The Accounting Review, 96*(2), 303–331. https://doi.org/10.2308/tar-2018-0347

Harber, M., Duboisée De Ricquebourg, A., & Maroun, W. (2024). Costs and benefits of mandatory audit firm rotation: Initial engagement experience of audit committee chairs and engagement partners. *In Accounting Forum, 48*(1), 63–89. https://doi.org/10.1080/01559982.2022.2130812

Inneh, E., Fakunle, I. O., Busari, R. R., & Olatunji, I. G. (2022). Audit characteristics and financial reporting timeliness of Nigerian listed non-financial institution. *Journal of Economics and Behavioral Studies, 14*(2 (J)), 13–25. https://doi.org/10.22610/jebs.v14i2(J).3277

Inneh, E. G., Ayoola, T. J., Olasanmi, O. O., Fakunle, I. O., & Ologunde, O. A. (2024). Does the strength of women in the upper echelon influence earnings quality? The application of critical mass theory. *International Journal of Applied Economics, Finance and Accounting, 18*(2), 270–281. https://doi.org/10.33094/ijaefa.v18i2.1387

Jadiyappa, N., Hickman, L. E., Kakani, R. K., & Abidi, Q. (2021). Auditor tenure and audit quality: An investigation of moderating factors prior to the commencement of mandatory rotations in India. *Managerial Auditing Journal, 36*(5), 724–743. https://doi.org/10.1108/MAJ-12-2020-2957

Jian, J., He, K., Liu, Y., & Sun, Y. (2024). Corporate social responsibility: Opportunistic behavior under earnings management? *Asia-Pacific Journal of Accounting and Economics, 31*(2), 247–268. https://doi.org/10.1080/16081625.2023.2170891

Johnson, V. E., Khurana, I. K., & Reynolds, J. K. (2002). Audit-firm tenure and the quality of financial reports. *Contemporary Accounting Research, 19*(4), 637–660. https://doi.org/10.1506/LLTH-JXQV-8CEW-8MXD

Krauß, P., Pronobis, P., & Zülch, H. (2015). Abnormal audit fees and audit quality: Initial evidence from the German audit market. *Journal of Business Economics, 85*, 45–84. https://link.springer.com/article/10.1007/s11573-014-0709-5

Lawan, M. (2011). Law and development in Nigeria: A need for activism. *Journal of African Law, 55*(1), 59–85. https://doi.org/10.1017/S0021855311000039

Lee, H. Y., Mande, V., & Son, M. (2009). Do lengthy auditor tenure and the provision of non-audit services by the external auditor reduce audit report lags? *International Journal of Auditing, 13*(2), 87–104. https://doi.org/10.1111/j.1099-1123.2008.00406.x

Lennox, C. (2014). Auditor tenure and rotation. In *The Routledge companion to auditing* (pp. 89–106). Routledge. https://www.taylorfrancis.com/chapters/edit/10.4324/9780203094921-9/auditor-tenure-rotation-clive-lennox

Lennox, C., & Wu, X. (2018). A review of the archival literature on audit partners. *Accounting Horizons, 32*(2), 1–35. https://doi.org/10.2308/acch-51942

Lennox, C. S., Wu, X., & Zhang, T. (2014). Does mandatory rotation of audit partners improve audit quality? *The Accounting Review, 89*(5), 1775–1803. https://doi.org/10.2308/accr-50800

McNichols, M. F. (2002). Discussion of the quality of accruals and earnings: The role of accrual estimation errors. *The Accounting Review, 77*(s-1), 61–69. https://doi.org/10.2308/accr.2002.77.s-1.61

McNichols, M. F., & Stubben, S. R. (2008). Does earnings management affect firms' investment decisions? *The Accounting Review, 83*(6), 1571–1603. https://doi.org/10.2308/accr.2008.83.6.1571

Mgbame, C. O., Eragbhe, E., & Osazuwa, N. P. (2012). Audit partner tenure and audit quality: An empirical analysis. *European Journal of Business and Management, 4*(7), 154–162. https://www.academia.edu/download/29441144/Partner-Tenure-and-Audit-Quality-An-Empirical-Analysis.pdf

Mouselli, S., Abdulraouf, R., & Jaafar, A. (2014). Corporate governance, accruals quality and stock returns: Evidence from the UK. *Corporate Governance, 14*(1), 32–44. https://doi.org/10.1108/CG-12-2012-0093

Ogunkan, D. V. (2022). Achieving sustainable environmental governance in Nigeria: A review for policy consideration. *Urban Governance, 2*(1), 212–220. https://doi.org/10.1016/j.ugj.2022.04.004

Onwuchekwa, J. C., Erah, D. O., & Izedonmi, F. (2012). Mandatory audit rotation and audit quality: Survey of Southern Nigeria. *Research Journal of Finance And Accounting, 3*(8), 70–77. https://core.ac.uk/download/pdf/234629343.pdf

Qin, Y., & Xiao, H. (2024). The mandatory audit partner rotation policy and cost of debt. *Journal of Accounting and Public Policy, 44*, 107182. https://doi.org/10.1016/j.jaccpubpol.2024.107182

Salihu, S. I., Yusof, Y., & Halim, R. (2015). Tracing the weaknesses of the regulatory framework for clinical trial in Nigeria. *Journal of Business and Social Review in Emerging Economies, 1*(2), 77–86. https://doi.org/10.26710/jbsee.v1i2.10

Temitope, A. O., Anichebe, A. S., & Ifeoma, O. H. (2023). Effects of audit tenure and fee on audit quality of selected food production companies in Nigeria. *Trinitarian: International Journal of Arts and Humanities, 1*(2), 1–21. https://journals.ezenwaohaetorc.org/index.php/TIJAH/article/viewFile/2191/2237

Tepalagul, N., & Lin, L. (2015). Auditor independence and audit quality: A literature review. *Journal of Accounting, Auditing and Finance, 30*(1), 101–121. https://doi.org/10.1177/0148558X14544505

Tessema, A., & Abou-El-Sood, H. (2023). Audit rotation, information asymmetry and the role of political connections: International evidence. *Meditari Accountancy Research, 31*(5), 1352–1385. https://doi.org/10.1108/MEDAR-03-2021-1226

Van Deventer, L. (2023). *Mandatory audit firm rotation in South Africa: Suggested solutions to prospective problems* (Doctoral Dissertation, North-West University (South Africa)). https://orcid.org/0000-0002-4863-071X

World Governance Indicator. (2023). https://www.worldbank.org/content/dam/sites/govindicators/doc/wgisourcedatarevisions.pdf

Zmijewski, M. E. (1984). Methodological issues related to the estimation of financial distress prediction models. *Journal of Accounting Research, 22*, 59–82. https://doi.org/10.2307/2490859

Integrating Artificial Intelligence, Blockchain, and Business Data Analytics into the University of Johannesburg Commercial Accounting Diploma Curriculum

Rachel Tholakele Khoza

Abstract Industry 4.0 and digital technological innovations have facilitated faster, flexible, and efficient production, consumption, and transmission of information. Consequently, technological advancements such as Artificial Intelligence (AI), Blockchain Technologies (BT), and Business Data Analytics (BDA) are reshaping the daily tasks of accountants worldwide and the accounting field can capitalize and benefit from new opportunities. Notably, the accounting profession is rapidly evolving, as are the skills and careers of accounting professionals. In response to these changes, the accounting profession has developed competency frameworks and career path publications to assist its members in adapting, addressing challenges, and seizing new opportunities. However, the university curriculum often introduces these technological advancements as separate modules rather than embedding them into the existing course content. Technology is reshaping accounting and educational institutions must equip students with the necessary skills to succeed in digital environments. By integrating digital technologies into the curriculum, students can acquire knowledge about modern accounting practices to meet the evolving needs of the industry. This study follows a qualitative research method that utilizes desktop research since it is theoretical in nature. It builds on existing research studies to explore the integration of AI, BT, and BDA into the University of Johannesburg's (UJ) Commercial Accounting Diploma Curriculum. It also expands on the educational framework by proposing learning outcomes to be covered in the curriculum and providing teaching guidelines to support the new insertions. The study concludes that, the current curriculum does not integrate digital technologies and suggests the adoption of a new curriculum that addresses this gap.

Keywords Industry 4.0 · Technological Innovation · Artificial Intelligence · Blockchain · Business Data Analytics · Accounting Curriculum

R. T. Khoza (✉)
University of Johannesburg, Johannesburg, South Africa
e-mail: rkhoza@uj.ac.za

T. Moloi (ed.), *Impacting Society Positively Through Technology in Accounting and Business Processes*, Springer Proceedings in Business and Economics,
https://doi.org/10.1007/978-3-031-84885-8_53

Introduction

Industry 4.0 is a term that is mostly used in the business world and Erboz (2017, p. 2) defines it as "a collective term for technologies of value chain organization." Erboz (2017, p. 3) further states that "industry 4.0 deals with more digitized systems and network integration via smart systems." Industry 4.0 is also referred to as the Fourth Industrial Revolution (4IR) and is characterized by a fusion of technologies that blurs the lines between the physical, digital, and biological spheres (Mhlanga & Moloi, 2020). Radziwill (2018) notes that 4IR is distinct due to its scope, velocity, and systemic impact, all of which have no historical precedent. Rapid technological advancements are the hallmark of 4IR (Bayode et al., 2019), which includes the integration of technologies such as big data analytical tools, cloud computing, and other emerging technologies into global manufacturing supply chains. Other key technologies of the fourth industrial revolution include AI, robotics, the Internet of Things (IoT), 3D printing, genetic engineering, and quantum computing (Moloi & Marwala, 2020). Inevitably, 4IR is introducing new technologies that pose a threat to traditional employment and certain industries (Hattingh, 2018; Moloi & Marwala, 2020).

The 4IR era requires new sets of skills which encompass complex problem-solving, critical thinking, and social and cognitive skills (Maisiri et al., 2019). Notably, technological innovation is the defining characteristic of 4IR, and it is bringing significant changes to different aspects of life, including business and education (Moloi & Mhlanga, 2021). The current and future students will operate in the 4IR environment to cultivate a digital economy and thus, create new job opportunities that demand digital skills and capabilities from workers (Grenčíková et al., 2021).

Digital technologies have transformed the accounting profession, supplementing traditional methods of work with AI, blockchain, and data analytics (Qasim & Kharbat, 2020; Igou et al., 2023). AI automates tasks, provides insights through predictive analytics, and handles large volumes of data, freeing accountants to focus on strategic and advisory roles. Meanwhile, blockchain technology is revolutionizing transparency and security in financial transactions (Cazazian, 2022). It enhances financial reporting and compliance by maintaining data integrity and reducing the risk of fraud (Roszkowska, 2021). Its applications in audits, smart contracts, and real-time financial monitoring require accountants to understand its mechanics and benefits (Han et al., 2023). In tandem, Business Data Analytics (BDA) utilizes data to derive insights and make informed decisions. Accounting helps identify trends, anticipate financial consequences, and optimize operational efficiencies. Accountants need to understand data analytics tools and processes to provide value-added services (Bose et al., 2023).

Thus, it is critical for the University of Johannesburg (UJ) to consider updating its Commercial Accounting Diploma curriculum to include AI, blockchain, and BDA. This would form part of UJ's commitment to align its programs with industry needs and technological advancements and produce graduates that are proficient in both traditional accounting principles and modern technology. This would enhance their competitiveness in the global job market. Including these technologies in the curriculum reinforces UJ's commitment to creating an innovative and relevant learning environment. The foregoing sets the stage for examining the prospect of adding AI, blockchain, and BDA to UJ's Commercial Accounting Diploma program. The study notes the paucity of literature that discusses the impact of these digital technologies and seeks to explore how new technologies are being used in accounting and auditing professions and to suggest ways to incorporate these technologies into accounting courses.

The question of "how can AI, blockchain, and data analytics be integrated into the UJ's Commercial Accounting Diploma curriculum that will allow students to acquire modern accounting practices to meet the evolving needs of the industry?" can then be asked.

Literature Review

This section of the paper briefly discusses the literature on emerging technologies and an overview of UJ's Diploma in Commercial Accounting current curriculum.

Overview of Emerging Technologies

Emerging technologies are referred to as innovations in the process of development, acceptance, or societal integration (Oke & Fernandes, 2020). These technologies have the potential to have a big impact on a lot of different parts of human existence, like entertainment and transportation as well as communication and healthcare (Alam, 2022; Agarwal et al., 2020). Fomunyam (2019) argues that they have the power to change markets, reorganize industries, and fundamentally alter how we live and work. They represent advances in science, engineering, and design. Numerous ground-breaking inventions have emerged because of the recent decades' fast rate of technological advancement. These include, among other things, biotechnology, nanotechnology, renewable energy, AI, BT, BDA, augmented reality (AR), virtual reality (VR), Internet of Things (IoT), and quantum computing (Erboz, 2017; Moloi & Marwala, 2020). Each of these technologies has the potential to transform several industries and provide solutions for difficult problems that humanity faces.

For example, AI is a technology that has the potential to surpass human skills and can perform complicated activities that call for human intelligence (Agarwal et al., 2020; Pandl et al., 2020). The Chartered Institute of Management Accountants [CIMA] (2022) notes that robotization is changing work processes, human–human interaction, and identifying jobs that can be automated quickly. AI encourages the integration of emerging technologies in the 4IR (Goodell et al., 2021; Zhang et al., 2021) and it is one of the primary forces behind industrial development. In fact, the vast volumes of data produced by social media, web apps, and Internet of Things devices have proliferated artificial intelligence (AI), with the data being used to train machine learning algorithms (Kumar et al., 2023).

Similarly, blockchain technology is becoming increasingly well-known as a tool with numerous uses across different fields (Xie et al., 2020; Wang et al., 2022). After bitcoin emerged in 2008 (Nakamoto, 2008), blockchain has gained popularity and it continues to be a disruptive technology that changes how people connect, track transactions, and automate payments, among other things (Roszkowska, 2021). Indeed, blockchain has opened opportunities that enable the direct transference of value between its users in a secure and trusted manner. Moreover, with the execution of smart contracts, the checking of approvals and compliances can become simpler, as blockchain is a shared database that is synchronized across multiple sites, and thus, such activities can be agreed on by each participant in a distributed network (Soleymani & Paquet, 2020). The data in blockchain is stored in blocks with hash values and timestamps, wherein the blocks are created based on a consensus protocol such as a proof of work or a proof of stake (Xie et al., 2020; Wang et al., 2022)—proof of stake is less expensive than proof of work due to higher energy efficiency (Nguyen et al., 2019). Adding "blocks" of data to a ledger known as the blockchain, which is kept up to date by a network of peer-to-peer computers, is how blockchain technology stores and verifies transactional records (Coyne & McMickle, 2017). This technology can drastically alter market structures and business models across a wide range of industries, including accounting (Zhang et al., 2020).

Overview of UJ Commercial Accounting Diploma Current Curriculum

Globally, accounting is essential to the operation of companies, organizations, and economies (Mosteanu & Faccia, 2020). To give decision-makers accurate and timely information, it entails the methodical recording, analysis, and reporting of financial activities (Shair, 2021). The need for qualified accountants who can successfully traverse this complexity and contribute to organizational success is rising as the corporate landscape changes and gets more complex (Jejeniwa et al., 2024). To address this need, the UJ Diploma in Commercial Accounting curriculum offers students a strong foundation in financial management, auditing, taxation, and accounting principles. Table 1 shows the core modules of the current UJ Diploma in Commercial Accounting.

By stating the current typical undergraduate course sequence in the accounting program (as shown in Table 1), this study can identify the weaknesses and opportunities for the curriculum. The current tendency has been to include any IT related topics in only one course (generally, in auditing). Thus, the current study engages seminal research highlighting the use of new technologies in the accounting

Table 1 UJ diploma in commercial accounting curriculum core modules

Level of study	Subjects
First Year	Cost and Financial Management 1
	Financial Accounting 1
	Financial Services Computing 1
Second Year	Auditing and Internal Controls 2
	Financial Accounting 2
	Cost and Financial Management 2
Third Year	Financial Accounting 3
	Cost and Financial Management 3
	Auditing and Internal Controls 3
	Taxation 3

Source: Authors' own work

profession, maps prior research concerning emerging themes and related areas in the accounting profession and accounting educational program (see Table 3). It further suggests a new curriculum (Table 4) that incorporates emerging technologies.

Research Methodology

This section covers the theoretical framework and research approach followed in this study.

Theoretical Framework

This section discusses the theoretical perspective and highlights the significance of updating the accounting curriculum's contents to consider the most recent developments in technology and business practices.

Accounting graduates need to be prepared by their universities to take on important roles, advance good managerial decision-making, support efficient capital markets, and serve the public interest (Igou et al., 2023; Qasim et al., 2022). Adapting university curricula to meet the demands of the business environment can be viewed from the perspective of the university's role in modern societies as the disseminator of formal knowledge, especially when discussing the significance of including an e-business module in undergraduate business programs (Maali & Al-Attar, 2020; Qasim et al., 2022). Curriculum design serves as the foundation of educational systems, which provides the structures and direction for teaching and learning activities (Qasim & Kharbat, 2020).

Within the sphere of curriculum design, there are various theoretical frameworks which provide guidance and perspectives that inform the development, implementation, and evaluation of educational programs (Kong & Lai, 2022). These frameworks influence not only the content and structure of curriculum but also the pedagogical practices, assessment strategies, and overall learning outcomes. The development of curriculum theory has been facilitated by academics and educators throughout history, who have drawn from fields including anthropology, psychology, sociology, and philosophy (Yackel et al., 1991; Qasim & Kharbat, 2020). Downey et al. (2019) provides a blueprint for the process of curriculum redesign. Their goal was to outline the necessary modifications and their implementation. They began by outlining each course by identifying the needs of the students, considering the abilities of the current teachers, and creating the curricula priority. The faculty had to be gathered and the governance and leadership style decided upon to guarantee a smooth process that included documenting and prioritizing the hiring of new teachers.

Fowler et al. (2015) conducted a thorough investigation into the curriculum reform process and provided a checklist to help other educational institutions replicate it. Three curriculum design frameworks served as the foundation for their checklist: (1) Wolf's (2007) approach, which was characterized as "faculty-driven, data-informed, and educational-developer supported"; (2) Lattuca and Stark's (2009) approach, which viewed curriculum design as a crucial decision-making process involving several levels (i.e., purposes, content, sequence, learners, instructional processes, instructional resources, evaluation, and adjustment); and (3) Diamond (2008) outlines the five main features of system theory as follows: "(a) forces those using it to think in ideal terms; (b) encourages the use of diagrams to show structure and content; (c) relies heavily on the use of data; (d) encourages a team approach; and (e) is politically sensitive."

The well-known Tyler (2013) modernist model, which follows a logical and sequential process dependent on planning and market demands, is one of the most instructive curriculum designs. It classifies the four primary curriculum components—methods, evaluation, experiences, and purposes. Numerous curriculum redesign strategies have relied on this model since it was first presented in 1949 and revised in 2013. This is because of its simplicity and efficacy. Lau (2011) however, criticized the model for being unaccountable and for having an imprecise decision-making process overall. The framework used in this study to redesign the accounting curriculum is Tyler's (2013) model. The technique incorporates the work of Downey et al. (2019) and Fowler et al. (2015) to address some of the problems brought out by Lau (2011).

Research Approach

This study follows a qualitative research method that utilizes desktop research since it is theoretical in nature. Desk research is described as the process of gathering information available in published form, rather than obtaining the data directly (Zegeye et al., 2009). According to Maciejewska et al. (2022), desk research is a quick process as data is already available as there are many sources from which relevant data can be collected and used. It aims at gaining a broader understanding of the subject matter, and since it is based on tried and tested data, which has been previously analyzed and filtered, it is less time consuming and cost effective. While desk research may seem straightforward, it still requires the meticulous selection of information and secondary data that is relevant for the study. Thus, the researcher focused on the data sources that offered the most pertinent information for the study. To avoid any repetition, and to ensure that the study questions are addressed, the gathered data was integrated, compared, put together, and analyzed.

The study focused the search on various databases from 2014 to 2024 and used the keywords, "artificial intelligence, blockchain, business data analytics, and accounting curriculum." The database selection was limited to Academic Search Complete, EBSCOhost, and Google Scholar due to access restrictions and requirements for paid subscriptions to access other databases. This step involved creating a database of AI, BCT, and BDA articles associated with the accounting curriculum. Developing such a database was required to identify prominent AI, BCT, and BDA topics. Database exclusion and inclusion criteria were developed based on topic coverage, year of publication, search words, and article type. The researcher selected scholarly articles on AI, BCT, BDA and accounting curricula from multiple reliable sources.

The researcher collected peer-reviewed journal articles that contained the terms "AI, BCT, BDA and accounting curriculum" in their titles, abstracts, content, and keywords. In the initial search, 100 articles relating to AI, BCT, and BDA were found. The author reviewed the abstracts and scopes to determine which articles were suitable and selected those focused on AI, BCT, BDA, and accounting. After applying the selection criterion, the author identified 17 out of 100 relevant publications published in academic journals between 2019 and 2024. This data is available online and can be used in the research process.

Digitalized UJ Commercial Accounting Diploma Curriculum

This section gives an overview of the UJ Diploma in Commercial Accounting Curriculum in the context of emerging technologies and discusses the skills needed in the emerging technologies era skills. It further highlights the need to adapt and redesign the UJ Diploma in Commercial Accounting Curriculum and discusses the proposed learning outcomes and guidelines.

Emerging Technologies and UJ Diploma in Commercial Accounting Curriculum

According to Moloi and Mhlanga (2021), 4IR is characterized by an extraordinary rate of technological innovation and has brought numerous changes in various areas of life, including business and education. Although education has tried to adapt to these developments, the effectiveness of technology and its challenges is not documented in this sector. Every culture, region, or nation's strengths and shortcomings are greatly influenced by its educational system (Fomunyam, 2019). Further, Fomunyam (2019) suggests that, considering the rapid advancements in economics, technology, and industrial knowledge, education is a critical factor in determining a society's ability to succeed globally. Thus, education is a vital and necessary component that supports the idea that an economy needs education to compete in the global market. New technologies have emerged in recent years, changing how businesses operate. Recent technology developments that have had a significant impact on the accounting profession have been documented by accounting scholars (Qasim et al., 2022).

An increasing number of institutions have fast-tracked the pace at which technology is incorporated into the curriculum in response to the growing usage of digital technologies in businesses and societies, as well as a commitment to meeting twenty-first century students' technological needs through digital learning (Kay et al., 2021). They have realized the need to transform learning experiences to reflect current and emerging technologies and global trends in business (Sousa & Rocha, 2019). Previous studies have indicated the gap between the applied technologies used in the industry and the accounting curriculum (Rezaee et al., 2018; Qasim & Kharbat, 2020). This disparity causes two primary issues: (1) graduates with significantly less expertise of market technologies than predicted and (2) the continued slow and difficult adoption of these technologies (Janvrin & Watson, 2017). However, limited research studies have been done to fast track the integration of new technologies into the accounting curriculum. The accounting and auditing industry is seeing a drastic increase in the use of blockchain technology (BT), business data analytics (BDA), and artificial intelligence (AI).

Global data production, capture, reproduction, and consumption are expected to increase significantly. This essay makes the case that, given the accounting and auditing industries' present rapid adoption of emerging technologies, these tools ought to be included into accounting curricula to promote quick adoption and better equip students to handle the rapid technological changes in the market. "Technological developments represent an important area that should be covered across accounting curricula, to expose changes in the marketplace and to enhance the employability of graduates" (Kotb et al., 2019).

Emerging Technologies Era Skills Needed

The following studies were reviewed, and the types of digital skills that can be incorporated in the curriculum were identified and are discussed in the Table 2 (WEF, 2020; Sousa & Rocha, 2019; Kay et al., 2021; Igou et al., 2023; UNESCO, 2018, March 15; ACCA, 2016, June; Thomson Reuters, 2018; Sage, 2019; Bughin et al., 2018; Rumbens et al., 2019; Capita, 2019; Accenture, 2017). Three general types of digital skills were identified, as Table 2 illustrates. First, the common digital competencies connect to fundamental legacy technology that accountants have already embraced and employed extensively. As an illustration, consider cloud-based accounting programs, commonplace business intelligence (BI) tools, and the automation of tax return processing. The second set of advanced digital skills pertains to accountants' experience with disruptive technologies like advanced BI apps, blockchain, and artificial intelligence. Additionally, although programming was designated as a distinct talent, it falls under the more general heading of advanced digital skills. Third, the evaluation noted data skills as an additional subset of digital abilities that are required in addition to these two other skill categories.

A successful undergraduate curriculum should be designed and constructed with the technical expertise, knowledge, and proficiency of the industry in mind, and it must include the skills above as discussed in Table 2. This has the potential to improve graduates' employability and adapt quickly to technological advancements of the industry. The accounting curriculum has come under critique for being unadaptable to change and for emphasizing technical accounting knowledge above the technological know-how and competency required in the workforce (Qasim et al., 2022).

Table 2 Digital skills for future accountants

Basic digital skills	Develop and master digital skills with core technologies already adopted at scale (e.g., cloud, standard BI, and digitization of tax returns).
Advanced digital skills	Become familiar with newer and more advanced technologies (e.g. AI, Blockchain, and advanced BI).
	Programming (e.g., from a user perspective, contextualized, and broad).
Data skills	Data management skills (e.g., accuracy, consistency, and relevance).
	Data analysis (e.g., synthesis of diverse data types and effective presentation).

Adapted: Qasim and Kharbat (2020)

Table 3 Mapping prior literature themes and areas of accounting

Author(s) (Year)	Themes emerging from prior studies examining AI, BT, and BDA in the accounting and auditing fields	Focus area
Zhang, Y., Xiong, F., Xie, Y., Fan, X. and Gu, H., (2020).	The impact of artificial intelligence and blockchain on the accounting profession	Accounting and Auditing
Han, H., Shiwakoti, R. K., Jarvis, R., Mordi, C., & Botchie, D. (2023).	Accounting and auditing with blockchain technology and artificial Intelligence: A literature review. *International Journal of Accounting Information Systems*	Accounting and Auditing
Bose, S., Dey, S. K., & Bhattacharjee, S. (2023).	Big data, data analytics and artificial intelligence in accounting: An overview. *Handbook of big data research methods*	Accounting
Kumar, S., Lim, W. M., Sivarajah, U., & Kaur, J. (2023).	Artificial intelligence and blockchain integration in business: trends from a bibliometric-content analysis	
Cazazian, R. (2022).	Blockchain technology adoption in artificial intelligence-based digital financial services, accounting information systems, and audit quality control	Auditing, Financial Accounting, and Taxation and Cost and Financial Management 1
Wang, Z., Li, M., Lu, J., & Cheng, X. (2022).	Business Innovation based on artificial intelligence and Blockchain technology	Auditing, Financial Accounting, and Taxation and Cost and Financial Management 1
Abu Huson, Y., Sierra-García, L., & Garcia-Benau, M. A. (2024).	A bibliometric review of information technology, artificial intelligence, and blockchain on auditing.	Auditing
Qasim, A., El Refae, G. A., & Eletter, S. (2022).	Embracing emerging technologies and artificial intelligence into the undergraduate accounting curriculum: Reflections from the UAE	Auditing, Financial Accounting, and Taxation and Cost and Financial Management
Farayola, O. A. (2024)	Revolutionizing banking security: integrating artificial intelligence, blockchain, and business intelligence for enhanced cybersecurity	Cost and Financial Management
Mosteanu, N. R., & Faccia, A. (2020)	Digital systems and new challenges of financial management–FinTech, XBRL, blockchain and cryptocurrencies	Auditing, Financial Accounting, and Taxation and Cost and Financial Management

(continued)

Table 3 (continued)

Author(s) (Year)	Themes emerging from prior studies examining AI, BT, and BDA in the accounting and auditing fields	Focus area
Faccia, A., Al Naqbi, M. Y. K., & Lootah, S. A. (2019, August).	Integrated cloud financial accounting cycle: how artificial intelligence, blockchain, and XBRL will change the accounting, fiscal and auditing practices.	Financial Accounting
Adelekan, O. A., Adisa, O., Ilugbusi, B. S., Obi, O. C., Awonuga, K. F., Asuzu, O. F., & Ndubuisi, N. L. (2024).	Evolving tax compliance in the digital era: a comparative analysis of AI-driven models and blockchain technology in US tax administration	Taxation
Shakil, M. H., & Tasnia, M. (2022).	Artificial intelligence and tax administration in Asia and the Pacific	Taxation
Atayah, O. F., & Alshater, M. M. (2021).	Audit and tax in the context of emerging technologies: A retrospective analysis, current trends, and future opportunities	Auditing and Taxation
Faccia, A., & Mosteanu, N. R. (2019).	Tax evasion, information systems and blockchain	Taxation
Federico, C., & Thompson, T. (2019).	Do IRS computers dream about tax cheats: Artificial intelligence and big data in tax enforcement and compliance	Taxation
Belahouaoui, R., & Attak, E. H. (2024).	Digital taxation, artificial intelligence, and Tax Administration 3.0: improving tax compliance behavior–a systematic literature review using textometry (2016–2023)	Taxation

Source: Authors' own work

The Need to Adapt UJ Diploma in Commercial Accounting Curriculum

This section discusses the necessity of incorporating BT, BDA, and AI within the accounting curriculum. The integration's rationale is based on the technologies' intrinsic expanding significance in the accounting and auditing fields and the skills needed. Many requests have been made recently for the accounting curriculum to be revitalized by incorporating technology advancements that are occurring in business operations (Handoyo & Anas, 2019; Qasim et al., 2022; Rao et al., 2023). Mapping of previous research is done to the areas in the accounting profession and accounting educational program that includes emerging technologies. The examination of seminal research highlighting the application of new technologies in the accounting profession is shown in Table 3.

Redesigning UJ Diploma in Commercial Accounting Curriculum

This section covers the suggested new UJ Diploma in Commercial Accounting Curriculum following Tyler's (2013) approach, with the integration of Downey et al. (2019) and Fowler et al. (2015). This paper suggests integrating new technologies at different course levels across the accounting curriculum. The following studies have suggested the importance and how the AI, BT, and BDA be included in the accounting curriculum (Clayton & Clopton, 2019; Qasim & Kharbat, 2020; Qasim et al., 2022; Zhang et al., 2020; Kumar et al., 2023; Bose et al., 2023).

The suggested UJ Diploma in Commercial Accounting is shown in Table 4. This study proposes that the "methods" for such redesign should include AI, BT, and BDA in courses at three different levels (First Year, Second Year, and Third Year). Table 2 discussed the skills needed for accountants; first year is suggested to include basic digital skills, second year should include advanced digital skills, and third year to include data skills. The literature agrees on a few basic truths, one of which

Table 4 Proposed Commercial Diploma in Accounting Curriculum

Level of study	Subjects
First Year	Cost and Financial Management 1
	Financial Accounting 1
	Financial Services Computing 1 (Includes digital concepts)
	Digital Technology 1 (Covers basic digital skills)
Second Year	Auditing and Internal Controls 2
	Financial Accounting 2
	Cost and Financial Management 2
	Digital Accounting 2 (Covers advanced digital skills)
Third Year	Financial Accounting 3
	Cost and Financial Management 3
	Auditing and Internal Controls 3
	Taxation 3
	Digital Accounting 3 (Covers data skills)

Source: Authors' own work

Table 5 Proposed learning outcomes and assignments

Course title	Assignment	Learning outcome
• Cost and Financial Management 1 • Cost and Financial Management 2 • Cost and Financial Management 3	Cases, Lectures, Readings Debates, Presentations	• Understand the main concepts of financial management and how to use AI, BT, and BDA to implement them. • Understand BDA techniques useful for the decision-making process. • Understand the use of BT in performance measures and accountability.
• Financial Accounting 1 • Financial Accounting 2 • Financial Accounting 3	Cases, Lectures, Readings Debates, Presentations	• Understand the main concepts of financial accounting and how to use AI, BT, and BDA to implement them. • Gain understanding of using BT in the accounting cycle. • Use BDA in analyzing financial statements. • Use XBRL in financial reporting.
Financial Services Computing 1A	Cases, Readings	• Gain an overview of the fundamental concepts of AI, BT, and BDA and their applications in business.
• Digital Accounting 1 (Covers basic digital skills) • Digital Accounting 2 (Covers advanced digital skills) • Digital Accounting 3 (Covers data skills)	Cases, Readings	• Develop and master digital skills with core technologies already adopted at scale (e.g. cloud, standard BI, and digitization of tax returns). • Become familiar with newer and more advanced technologies (e.g., AI, Blockchain, and advanced BI). • Understand how BT and other technologies can improve a company's processes and operations. • Programming (e.g., from a user perspective, contextualized, and broad). • Data management skills (e.g., accuracy, consistency, and relevance). • Data analysis (e.g., synthesis of diverse data types and effective presentation).
• Auditing and Internal Control 2 • Auditing and Internal Control 3	Examples from Industry Cases, Debates	• Understand analytical techniques useful for audit engagements. • Link audit analytics to corporate continuous monitoring and business process support. • Gain an overview of contemporary applications of AI in auditing and assurance.
Taxation 3	Cases, Lectures, Readings Debates, Presentations	• Digitalization of tax returns and other tax functions.

Source: Authors' own work

is that undergraduates should not be taught abstract notions without supporting evidence from experience (Clayton & Clopton, 2019).

A new suggested course on "Digital Accounting" that covers the fundamentals, intermediate and advanced AI, BT, and BDA, and other related technologies is suggested. The plan is to include these technologies into current accounting curricula and explain the "purpose" to students so they may comprehend why this knowledge is necessary. Since new concepts and trends in technology are always emerging, accounting information systems have been transformed into "digital accounting" to adopt a more comprehensive viewpoint. According to Deshmukh (2006), "digital accounting" refers to the modifications made to accounting because of new technology. This course will fulfill this curriculum goal. These are the primary accounting and auditing domains that are presently utilizing the technologies under review, according to the literature. As previous research has shown, the use of AI, BT, and BDA in the accounting and auditing fields is still in its infancy. Therefore, this study recommends that incorporating these technologies into the accounting curriculum be a component of already-existing courses, or a component of the curriculum's "experiences."

Proposed Learning Outcomes and Guidelines for UJ Diploma in Commercial Accounting Curriculum

When designing a curriculum, it is not only the content that is important, but also the methods of teaching are critical. Table 5 outlines a potential learning outcome that emphasizes the key competencies that need to be prioritized to establish a strong foundation for this kind of program. Flexibility is important in deciding the technologies to be used and the system must be open to experimentation and continual adoption of emerging technologies. That ensures a simple process to incorporate new technology that emerges into the curriculum or to replace any outdated technology with a new one.

Table 6 presents an "evaluation" criterion that should be adhered to during the teaching process of the suggested curriculum. Creating guidelines is beneficial when implementing such a program, particularly when the teacher lacks experience with the technology. Since students are not expected to be technical people, many educators may emphasize the technical elements, which will make studying more difficult for them overall. One of the crucial resources for improving students' abilities to evaluate and comprehend data to increase their competency is the case study. It is important to remember that any curriculum modification should consider the likelihood of resistance or acceptance from teachers and students about the introduction of new course topics and the use of technology. Kim and Kankanhalli (2009) combined the technological acceptance model, resistance literature, and status quo bias theory to provide a more comprehensive explanation of user resistance to the adoption of new enterprise technologies. They proposed that organizational support and self-efficacy for change, on the other hand, directly and indirectly decrease user resistance, and that transfer costs play a significant role in both processes.

Table 6 Course teaching guidance

Course title	What to teach/What to learn	Learning outcome
• Cost and Financial Management 1 • Cost and Financial Management 2 & • Cost and Financial Management 3	• Use of Big Data and data analytics in performance measures and balanced scorecard.	• Do not go in depth, students are required to have a general understanding about using these technologies in the accounting profession. • Do not use outdated materials or case studies. • Do not go into technical details since students are required to have a general understanding about using these technologies in the accounting profession. • Do not focus on the technical/ technological aspects. The idea here is to use technology rather than the creation of the technology. • Do not focus on only producing the data, but how to interpret the data and understand the meaning behind the numbers. • Do not focus on details and technical technology, but make sure that the decision-making process is well understood and implemented with the used decision support system. • Do not ignore the different scenarios that may be applicable to such topics.
• Financial Accounting 1 Financial Accounting 2 Financial Accounting 3	• General case studies from the industry. • Use up-to-date materials. • Invite experts from the industry to present their experience of using such technologies in the profession. • Introduce students to XBRL for business reporting. • Big Data and fair value reporting, off balance sheet information. • Introduce students to data analytics tools for corporate financial statement analysis.	
Financial Services Computing 1A	• Giving students a general overview of the use of new technologies in business operations and how the accounting profession is utilizing these technologies.	
• Business Technology 1 (Covers basic digital skills) • Business Technology 2 (Covers advanced digital skills) • Business Technology 3 (Covers Data Skills))	• Use the different technologies to enhance decision-making processes and choices.	
• Auditing and Internal Control 2 • Auditing and Internal Control 3	• Start to relate existing auditing processes performed by auditors to AI and machine learning. • Introduce students to Big Data and data analytics techniques to detect anomalies and fraud. • Introduce students to continuous auditing using AI.	
Taxation 3		

Adapted: Qasim and Kharbat (2020)

Conclusion, Limitations, and Recommendations

Due to the enormous development of technological platforms and interactions between local and global businesses, technology integration is unavoidable in business. As a result, companies across all industries are currently revamping their processes and assignments to provide themselves a competitive edge in both short- and long-term plans, and they are searching for qualified workers to help them build these practices (Clayton & Clopton, 2019). Higher education institutions that strive to generate graduates who are employable face ongoing and changing obstacles because of this ever-changing corporate climate. The accounting curriculum has come under fire in the literature for being change-resistant. Nonetheless, the accounting industry is adapting quickly to technological developments in corporate operations. The quality of accounting graduates and, consequently, their employability will suffer because of this uneven response from academics and the industry. The danger is that if this conundrum persists in the future, recruiting IT graduates with technical expertise in blockchain, data analytics, and AI may replace hiring accounting graduates in the accounting field. The incorporation of contemporary technologies into accounting curricula should be given careful thought by academics creating the curriculum. Hence, to remain competitive, the curriculum of the UJ Diploma in Commercial Accounting must be redesigned. This will give the diploma graduates an advantage since they normally compete with degree graduates for employment.

The limitation of the study is that it only focuses on the UJ Diploma in Commercial Accounting without considering accounting diplomas from other institutions. It also only focuses on the diploma and not on accounting degree programs. Future studies should consider diplomas from other institutions and over and above that, each course's specific themes should be covered from the viewpoints of the lecturers, students, and other stakeholders. The degree in accounting should also be considered for future research since most organizations employ students with a degree rather than one with a diploma. A comparative study with other institutions who are offering accounting programs should also be considered for further research studies. Different structures may be proposed in response to the ongoing demands from the workplace for increased accountability and efficiency (Fowler et al., 2015), particularly in cases when some courses may be split or combined to meet the needs of the market. To find the ideal combination, this inquiry is a work in progress that requires the cooperation of all parties involved.

References

Abu Huson, Y., Sierra-García, L., & Garcia-Benau, M. A. (2024). A bibliometric review of information technology, artificial intelligence, and blockchain on auditing. *Total Quality Management and Business Excellence, 35*(1–2), 91–113.

ACCA. (2016, June). *Professional accountants – The future: Drivers of change and future skills*, 1–88.

Accenture. (2017). *New skills now: Inclusion in the digital economy* (p. 46). Retrieved from https://www.accenture.com/t20171012t025413z__w__/in-en/_acnmedia/pdf-62/accenture-new-skills-now-report.pdf (Accessed on 13 May 2024).

Adelekan, O. A., Adisa, O., Ilugbusi, B. S., Obi, O. C., Awonuga, K. F., Asuzu, O. F., & Ndubuisi, N. L. (2024). Evolving tax compliance in the digital era: A comparative analysis of AI-driven models and blockchain technology in US tax administration. *Computer Science and IT Research Journal, 5*(2), 311–335.

Agarwal, Y., Jain, M., Sinha, S., & Dhir, S. (2020). Delivering high-tech, AI-based health care at Apollo hospitals. *Global Business and Organizational Excellence, 39*(2), 20–30.

Alam, T. (2022). Blockchain cities: The futuristic cities driven by Blockchain, big data and Internet of Things. *GeoJournal, 87*(6), 5383–5412.

Atayah, O. F., & Alshater, M. M. (2021). Audit and tax in the context of emerging technologies: A retrospective analysis, current trends, and future opportunities. *International Journal of Digital Accounting Research, 21*.

Bayode, A., van der Poll, J. A., & Ramphal, R. R. (2019, November). 4th industrial revolution: Challenges and opportunities in the South African context. In *Proceedings of the 17th Johannesburg international conference on science, engineering, technology and waste management*, Johannesburg (pp. 18–19).

Belahouaoui, R., & Attak, E. H. (2024). Digital taxation, artificial intelligence and Tax Administration 3.0: Improving tax compliance behavior–a systematic literature review using textometry (2016–2023). *Accounting Research Journal, 37*(2), 172–191.

Bose, S., Dey, S. K., & Bhattacharjee, S. (2023). Big data, data analytics and artificial intelligence in accounting: An overview. *Handbook of Big Data Research Methods*, 32–51.

Bughin, J., Hazan, E., Lund, S., Dahlström, P., Wiesinger, A., & Subramaniam, A. (2018). Skill shift: Automation and the future of the workforce. *McKinsey Global Institute, 1*, 3–84.

Capita. (2019). *Robot wars or automation alliances? People, technology and the future of work* (p. 17). Retrieved from https://www.capita.com/sites/g/files/nginej146/files/2019-11/capita-future-of-workreport.pdf (Accessed on 13 May 2024).

Cazazian, R. (2022). Blockchain technology adoption in artificial intelligence-based digital financial services, accounting information systems, and audit quality control. *Review of Contemporary Philosophy, 21*, 55–71.

Chartered Institute of Management Accountants [CIMA]. (2022). *What Big Data and AI mean for the Finance Professional*. Retrieved from https://www.cimaglobal.com/CGMA-Store/Finance-Futurist-Blogs/Blog-What-Big-Data-and-AI-mean-for-the-Finance-Professional/ (Accessed on 13 May 2024)

Clayton, P. R., & Clopton, J. (2019). Business curriculum redesign: Integrating data analytics. *Journal of Education for Business, 94*(1), 57–63.

Coyne, J. G., & McMickle, P. L. (2017). Can blockchains serve an accounting purpose? *Journal of Emerging Technologies in Accounting, 14*(2), 101–111.

Deshmukh, A. (2006). A framework for digital accounting. In *Digital accounting: The effects of the Internet and ERP on accounting* (pp. 1–14). IGI Global.

Diamond, R. M. (2008). *Designing and assessing courses and curricula: A practical guide* (3rd ed.). Jossey-Bass.

Downey, D. J., O'Connor, L. T., Abell, L., Armanino, D., Jepson, M., Kadakal, R., et al. (2019). Navigating the process of curriculum redesign in sociology: Challenges and lessons from one program. *Teaching Sociology, 47*(2), 87–101.

Erboz, G. (2017). How to define industry 4.0: Main pillars of industry 4.0. *Managerial Trends in the Development of Enterprises in Globalization Era, 761*, 767.

Faccia, A., & Mosteanu, N. R. (2019). Tax evasion, information systems and blockchain. *Journal of Information Systems and Operations Management, 13*(1), 65–74.

Faccia, A., Al Naqbi, M. Y. K., & Lootah, S. A. (2019, August). Integrated cloud financial accounting cycle: How artificial intelligence, blockchain, and XBRL will change accounting, fiscal and

auditing practices. In *Proceedings of the 2019 3rd International Conference on Cloud and Big Data Computing* (pp. 31–37).
Farayola, O. A. (2024). Revolutionizing banking security: Integrating artificial intelligence, blockchain, and business intelligence for enhanced cybersecurity. *Finance and Accounting Research Journal, 6*(4), 501–514.
Federico, C., & Thompson, T. (2019). Do IRS computers dream about tax cheats: Artificial intelligence and big data in tax enforcement and compliance. *Journal of Tax Practice and Procedure, 21*, 35.
Fomunyam, K. G. (2019). Education and the Fourth Industrial Revolution: Challenges and possibilities for engineering education. *International Journal of Mechanical Engineering and Technology, 10*(8), 271–284.
Fowler, D., Lazo, M., Turner, J., & Hohenstein, J. (2015). Facilitating program, faculty, and student transformation: A framework for curriculum redesign. *Journal of Transformative Learning, 3*(1), 59–73.
Goodell, J. W., Kumar, S., Lim, W. M., & Pattnaik, D. (2021). Artificial intelligence and machine learning in finance: Identifying foundations, themes, and research clusters from bibliometric analysis. *Journal of Behavioral and Experimental Finance, 32*, 100577.
Grenčíková, A., Kordoš, M., & Navickas, V. (2021). The impact of Industry 4.0 on education contents. *Business: Theory and Practice, 22*(1), 29–38.
Han, H., Shiwakoti, R. K., Jarvis, R., Mordi, C., & Botchie, D. (2023). Accounting and auditing with blockchain technology and artificial Intelligence: A literature review. *International Journal of Accounting Information Systems, 48*, 100598.
Handoyo, S., & Anas, S. (2019). Accounting education challenges in the new millennium era. *Journal of Accounting Auditing and Business, 2*(1).
Hattingh, S. (2018). Preparing the workforce for the Fourth Industrial Revolution. *Skills at Work, Theory and Practice Journal, 9*(1), 6–18.
Igou, A., Power, D. J., Brosnan, S., & Heavin, C. (2023). Digital futures for accountants. *Journal of Emerging Technologies in Accounting, 20*(1), 39–57.
Janvrin, D. J., & Watson, M. W. (2017). "Big Data": A new twist to accounting. *Journal of Accounting Education, 38*, 3–8.
Jejeniwa, T. O., Mhlongo, N. Z., & Jejeniwa, T. O. (2024). The role of ethical practices in accounting: A review of corporate governance and compliance trends. *Finance and Accounting Research Journal, 6*(4), 707–720.
Kay, J., Ferns, S. J., Russell, L., Smith, J., & Younger, A. (2021). Innovation in work-integrated learning. In *Advances in research, theory and practice in work-integrated learning* (pp. 133–144). Routledge.
Kim, H. W., & Kankanhalli, A. (2009). Investigating user resistance to information systems implementation: A status quo bias perspective. *MIS Quarterly*, 567–582.
Kong, S. C., & Lai, M. (2022). A proposed computational thinking teacher development framework for K-12 guided by the TPACK model. *Journal of Computers in Education, 9*(3), 379–402.
Kotb, A., Abdel-Kader, M., Allam, A., Halabi, H., & Franklin, E. (2019). Information technology in the British and Irish undergraduate accounting degrees. *Accounting Education, 28*(5), 445–464.
Kumar, S., Lim, W. M., Sivarajah, U., & Kaur, J. (2023). Artificial intelligence and blockchain integration in business: Trends from a bibliometric-content analysis. *Information Systems Frontiers, 25*(2), 871–896.
Lattuca, L. R., & Stark, J. S. (2009). *Shaping the college curriculum: Academic plans in context* (2nd ed.). Jossey-Bass.
Lau, J. Y. (2011). *An introduction to critical thinking and creativity: Think more, think better*. Wiley.
Maali, B., & Al-Attar, A. M. (2020). Accounting curricula in universities and market needs: The Jordanian case. *Sage Open, 10*(1), 2158244019899463.

Maciejewska, A., Kuzak, Ł., Sobieraj, J., & Metelski, D. (2022). The impact of opencast lignite mining on rural development: A literature review and selected case studies using desk research, panel data and GIS-based analysis. *Energies, 15*(15), 5402.

Maisiri, W., Darwish, H., & Van Dyk, L. (2019). An investigation of industry 4.0 skills requirements. *South African Journal of Industrial Engineering, 30*(3), 90–105.

Mhlanga, D., & Moloi, T. (2020). COVID-19 and the digital transformation of education: What are we learning on 4IR in South Africa? *Education Sciences, 10*(7), 180.

Moloi, T., & Marwala, T. (2020). *Artificial intelligence in economics and finance theories*. Springer.

Moloi, T., & Mhlanga, D. (2021). *Key features of the fourth industrial revolution in South Africa's basic education system*.

Mosteanu, N. R., & Faccia, A. (2020). Digital systems and new challenges of financial management–FinTech, XBRL, blockchain and cryptocurrencies. *Quality–Access to Success, 21*(174), 159–166.

Nakamoto, S. (2008). A peer-to-peer electronic cash system. *Bitcoin, 4*(2), 15.

Nguyen, C. T., Hoang, D. T., Nguyen, D. N., Niyato, D., Nguyen, H. T., & Dutkiewicz, E. (2019). Proof-of-stake consensus mechanisms for future blockchain networks: Fundamentals, applications, and opportunities. *IEEE Access, 7*, 85727–85745.

Oke, A., & Fernandes, F. A. P. (2020). Innovations in teaching and learning: Exploring the perceptions of the education sector on the 4th industrial revolution (4IR). *Journal of Open Innovation: Technology, Market, and Complexity, 6*(2), 31.

Pandl, K. D., Thiebes, S., Schmidt-Kraepelin, M., & Sunyaev, A. (2020). On the convergence of artificial intelligence and distributed ledger technology: A scoping review and future research agenda. *IEEE Access, 8*, 57075–57095.

Qasim, A., & Kharbat, F. F. (2020). Blockchain technology, business data analytics, and artificial intelligence: Use in the accounting profession and ideas for inclusion into the accounting curriculum. *Journal of Emerging Technologies in Accounting, 17*(1), 107–117.

Qasim, A., El Refae, G. A., & Eletter, S. (2022). Embracing emerging technologies and artificial intelligence into the undergraduate accounting curriculum: Reflections from the UAE. *Journal of Emerging Technologies in Accounting, 19*(2), 155–169.

Radziwill, N. M. (2018). *Quality 4.0: Let's Get Digital-The many ways the fourth industrial revolution is reshaping the way we think about quality*. arXiv preprint arXiv:1810.07829.

Rao, K. V., Murala, D. K., & Panda, S. K. (2023). Blockchain: A study of new business model. In *Recent advances in blockchain technology: Real-world applications* (pp. 187–214). Springer International Publishing.

Rezaee, Z., Dorestani, A., & Aliabadi, S. (2018). Application of time series analyses in Big Data: Practical, research, and education implications. *Social Science Research Network, 15*(1), 183–197.

Roszkowska, P. (2021). Fintech in financial reporting and audit for fraud prevention and safeguarding equity investments. *Journal of Accounting and Organizational Change, 17*(2), 164–196.

Rumbens, D., Richardson, C., Lee, C., Mizrahi, J., & Roche, C. (2019). *The path to prosperity: Why the future of work is human*. Deloitte.

Sage. (2019). *CFO 3.0—Digital transformation beyond financial management* (p. 19).

Shair, H. S. (2021). The role of lean thinking practices in enhancing the quality of financial reports-An analytical study of the views of a sample of employees at Bank of Baghdad. *International Journal of Economics, Business and Management Research*. doi: 10.51505.

Shakil, M. H., & Tasnia, M. (2022). Artificial intelligence and tax administration in Asia and the Pacific. In *Taxation in the digital economy* (pp. 45–55). Routledge.

Soleymani, F., & Paquet, E. (2020). Financial portfolio optimization with online deep reinforcement learning and restricted stacked autoencoder—Deep Breath. *Expert Systems with Applications, 156*, 113456.

Sousa, M. J., & Rocha, Á. (2019). Digital learning: Developing skills for digital transformation of organizations. *Future Generation Computer Systems, 91*, 327–334.

Thomson Reuters. (2018). *The accountant of tomorrow. Accountancy in 2028 Survey*. Retrieved from https://tax.thomsonreuters.co.uk/wp-content/private/pdf/uk/report/Thomson-Reuters-Accountant-of-Tomorrow-Report.pdf (Accessed on 13 May 2024).

UNESCO. (2018). *Digital skills critical for jobs and social inclusion*. UNESCO. Retrieved from https://en.unesco.org/news/digital-skills-critical-jobs-and-social-inclusion (Accessed on 13 May 2024).

Wang, Z., Li, M., Lu, J., & Cheng, X. (2022). Business Innovation based on artificial intelligence and Blockchain technology. *Information Processing and Management, 59*(1), 102759.

WEF. (2020). The future of jobs report: 2020–1–163. *World Economic Forum*. http://www3.weforum.org/docs/WEF_Future_of_Jobs_2020.pdf (Accessed on 13 May 2024).

Wolf, P. (2007). A model for facilitating curriculum development in higher education: A faculty-driven, data-informed, and educational developer–supported approach. *New Directions for Teaching and Learning, 112*, 15–20.

Xie, Y., Fan, X., & Gu, H. (2020). The impact of artificial intelligence and blockchain on the accounting profession. *IEEE Access, 8*, 110461–110477.

Yackel, E., Cobb, P., & Wood, T. (1991). Small-group interactions as a source of learning opportunities in second-grade mathematics. *Journal for Research in Mathematics Education, 22*(5), 390–340.

Zegeye, A., Worku, A., Tefera, D., Getu, M., & Sileshi, Y. (2009). *Introduction to research methods*. Graduate studies and research office Addis Ababa University.

Zhang, Y., Xiong, F., Xie, Y., Fan, X., & Gu, H. (2020). The impact of artificial intelligence and blockchain on the accounting profession. *IEEE Access, 8*, 110461–110477.

Zhang, C., Bengio, S., Hardt, M., Recht, B., & Vinyals, O. (2021). Understanding deep learning (still) requires rethinking generalization. *Communications of the ACM, 64*(3), 107–115.

Towards a Future-Ready Accounting Education: Opportunities and Challenges of Integrating Artificial Intelligence into Contemporary Accounting Curricula

Omolola Ayobamidele Arise and Tankiso Moloi

Abstract The accounting profession is undergoing a profound transformation due to the rapid advancement of Artificial Intelligence (AI) technologies. As AI systems automate routine tasks and augment decision-making processes, accounting curricula must evolve to equip students with necessary skills and knowledge. This study explores the opportunities and challenges of integrating AI into contemporary accounting education. Through a comprehensive literature review, the study identifies essential AI competencies for accounting students, such as digital literacy, critical thinking, and problem-solving. It proposes the AI Competency Adaptation Framework (AICAF) to guide curriculum development. The results highlight benefits like enhanced decision-making, increased efficiency, and personalised learning. However, challenges such as curriculum redesign, faculty development, and ethical issues, including bias risk and job displacement, are also addressed. The study concludes with recommendations for educational institutions, accreditation bodies, and professional organisations to create future-ready graduates. This study highlights the necessity for accounting education to evolve with technological advancements, offering a framework for integrating AI into the curriculum. By addressing these issues, the study contributes to the ongoing discourse on the future of accounting education and provides actionable insights for stakeholders involved in shaping the next generation of accounting professionals.

Keywords Artificial intelligence integration · Accounting education reform · Digital literacy enhancement · Ethical AI use · Interdisciplinary collaboration · Future-ready curriculum

O. A. Arise (✉) · T. Moloi
University of Johannesburg, Johannesburg, South Africa
e-mail: smoloi@uj.ac.za

T. Moloi (ed.), *Impacting Society Positively Through Technology in Accounting and Business Processes*, Springer Proceedings in Business and Economics,
https://doi.org/10.1007/978-3-031-84885-8_54

Introduction

The rapid advancement of Artificial Intelligence (AI) and big data has brought significant changes to the accounting industry, transforming the role of accountants from mere record-keepers to strategic managers. This shift, driven by globalisation and technological advancements, has made conventional accounting duties less critical, placing greater emphasis on strong analytical and decision-making abilities (Agbo, 2023; Gusai, 2019). AI technologies, such as robotic process automation and expert systems, enhance the accuracy and efficiency of tasks like auditing and financial reporting (Kommunuri, 2022; Tandiono, 2023). These advancements are not only revolutionising the professional landscape for accountants but also altering the educational prerequisites as the discipline evolves (Tiwari, 2020).

Despite the growing integration of AI into the accounting profession, many accounting curricula have yet to fully incorporate AI-related competencies and pedagogical approaches (Kwafo, 2019; Abbas, 2023). This paradigm shift necessitates a re-evaluation of traditional curricula to ensure graduates are equipped with the skills and knowledge to thrive in an AI-driven landscape (Agbo, 2023). The traditional curriculum, primarily focused on manual data management, now faces challenges in meeting the demands for analytical competencies facilitated by new AI-driven tools (Liu, 2020). The gap between educational programmes and industry demands risks producing graduates who lack the essential skills to adapt to the AI-driven revolution in accounting (Agbo, 2023; Odonkor et al., 2024).

This study aims to explore the opportunities and challenges associated with integrating AI into contemporary accounting curricula. Through a comprehensive literature review, it identifies the essential AI competencies that accounting students must acquire to remain relevant and competitive. Additionally, the study examines the benefits and challenges of incorporating AI into accounting education and provides insights and recommendations for educational institutions, accreditation bodies, and professional organisations.

Integrating AI into accounting curricula is crucial for various stakeholders. For educational institutions, this study offers a roadmap for curricular redesign and faculty development, enabling the production of future-ready graduates capable of leveraging AI technologies effectively. For students, acquiring AI-related competencies will enhance their employability and career prospects in an AI-driven job market. The accounting profession will benefit from a pool of skilled professionals proficient in using AI tools and techniques, enhancing efficiency, accuracy, and value-added services. By addressing the opportunities and challenges of integrating AI into accounting education, this study contributes to the discourse on the future of accounting education and provides a framework for collaboration between educational institutions and professional bodies to create a robust, adaptive workforce ready for the AI-driven transformation of the accounting profession.

Structure of the Paper

To provide a guide through the content, this paper is structured as follows: Section "Theoretical Framework" discusses key theories and relevant literature in the Theoretical Framework and Literature Review section. Section "Research Methodology" describes the criteria and process for selecting and reviewing the literature in the Methodology section. The potential benefits of AI integration are explored in Section "Opportunities of AI in Accounting Education". Section "Challenges of AI Integration" examines the obstacles and complexities associated with AI integration. The Proposed Framework for AI Integration is introduced and explained in Section "Proposed Framework for AI Integration". Section "Discussion" analyses the findings and links them to the objectives. Finally, Section "Conclusion" summarises the key points and offers actionable suggestions in the Conclusion and Recommendations section.

Theoretical Framework

The integration of Artificial Intelligence (AI) into accounting education requires a solid theoretical framework. The three key theories that underpin this study are Constructivism, which emphasises active, experiential learning; the Technological Pedagogical Content Knowledge (TPACK) framework, which focuses on the interplay between technology, pedagogy, and content; and the Diffusion of Innovations (DoI) theory, which explains how new technologies are adopted. Additionally, the study introduces "AI-Driven Competency Evolution Framework" (AICEF) which provides a framework for understanding the impact of AI on professional competencies in accounting.

Constructivism

Constructivism, deeply rooted in the works of Piaget (1980) and Vygotsky (1962), revolutionises education by emphasising that knowledge is actively constructed by learners through experiences and social interactions (Bada & Olusegun, 2015). This learner-centred approach contrasts with traditional views of knowledge transmission from teacher to student. Instead, constructivist learning environments encourage students to engage in problem-solving, experimentation, and real-world tasks (Tsai et al., 2023), thereby fostering independent problem-solving, creativity, and critical thinking. The principles of constructivism include active knowledge construction, continuous knowledge reconstruction, and the teacher's role as a facilitator (Minishi-Majanja & Kiplang'at, 2005).

Technological Pedagogical Content Knowledge (TPACK)

The integration of AI into accounting education could be supported by several theoretical frameworks and models. One prominent framework is the (TPACK) model developed by Koehler & Mishra (2009). TPACK emphasises the intersection of technological knowledge, pedagogical knowledge, and content knowledge as essential for effective technology integration in education. It posits that effective teaching with technology requires an understanding of the complex interactions between technology, pedagogy, and content. A study by Schmidt et al. (2009) developed and validated an assessment instrument to measure pre-service teachers' TPACK. This instrument was designed to evaluate teachers' self-assessment of their technological, pedagogical, and content knowledge. The TPACK framework and its assessment instrument provides valuable insights into the knowledge teachers need to integrate AI technologies into accounting education effectively. The TPACK framework highlighted the importance of a balanced approach, ensuring that educators possess deep technological knowledge (TK), effective pedagogical strategies (PK), and a robust understanding of accounting content (CK). Figure 1 visually represents

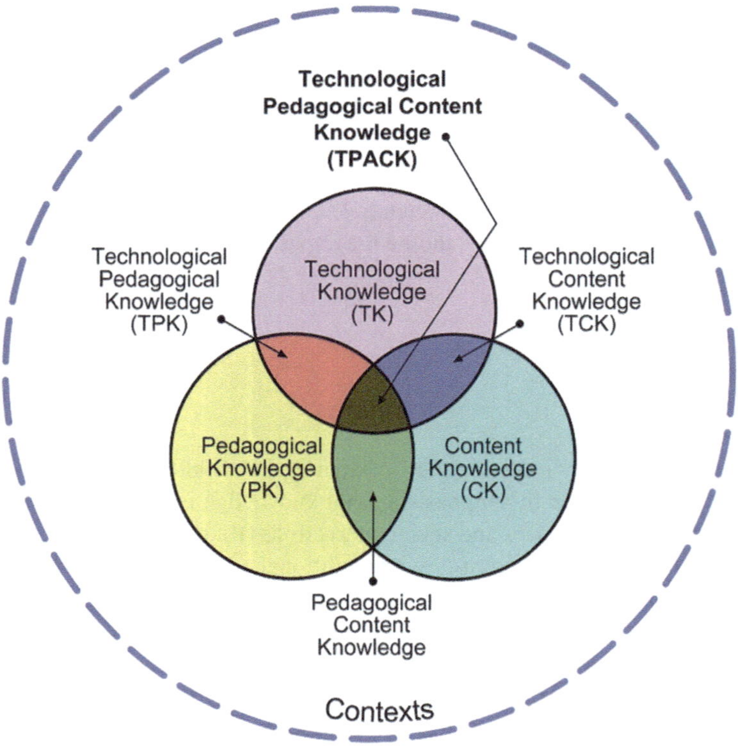

Fig. 1 Graphic representation of technological pedagogical content knowledge (TPACK) (Archambault & Barnett, 2010)

the components of the TPACK framework and their intersections. At the intersection of CK, PK, and TK lies Technological Pedagogical Content Knowledge (TPACK), representing an intuitive understanding of teaching content with appropriate pedagogical methods and technologies. This integrated knowledge base is crucial for preparing students to navigate the complexities of AI-driven accounting practices (Schmidt et al., 2009).

Diffusion of Innovations (DoI)

Another relevant theoretical framework is the DoI Theory (Rogers, 1995), which explores the process by which new technologies or ideas are adopted within a social system. The (DoI) theory, developed by Rogers (2014), offers a comprehensive framework for understanding how new ideas and technologies spread within a social system. Key principles of the theory, such as relative advantage, compatibility, complexity, trialability, and observability, are crucial for influencing the adoption rate of innovations. These principles have been successfully applied in fields like Library and Information Science (LIS) (Minishi-Majanja & Kiplang'at, 2005), and healthcare (Dearing & Cox, 2018) to promote the adoption of Information and Communication Technologies (ICTs) and other innovations. For instance, Minishi-Majanja & Kiplang'at (2005) illustrated the significance of information literacy programmes and change agents in promoting ICT adoption among agricultural researchers and LIS students. Likewise, in healthcare, Dearing and Cox (2018) showed that the adoption of innovations, such as telemedicine, has been supported by policies and infrastructure tailored to meet the specific needs of the target audience.

Applying DoI theory to accounting education could enhance the integration of AI technologies. Educators can leverage the theory's principles by highlighting the efficiency and accuracy improvements AI brings to accounting tasks (relative advantage) ensuring AI tools align with existing accounting curricula (compatibility), simplifying AI tools and providing comprehensive training (reducing complexity), allowing students to experiment with AI tools through hands-on projects (trialability), and demonstrating the tangible benefits of AI through real-world case studies (observability) (Almaiah et al., 2022).

Educational institutions can create a conducive environment for AI integration, preparing students for future demands in the accounting profession. Figure 2 outlines the integration of Constructivism, TPACK, and DoI, showing their individual components (**AI Competency Adaptation Framework (AICAF)**), while Fig. 3 presents the theoretical lens of how they collectively enhance accounting education with AI. By drawing upon these theoretical frameworks, educational institutions can develop effective strategies for integrating AI into accounting curricula, ensuring that students acquire the necessary competencies to thrive in the AI-driven accounting profession.

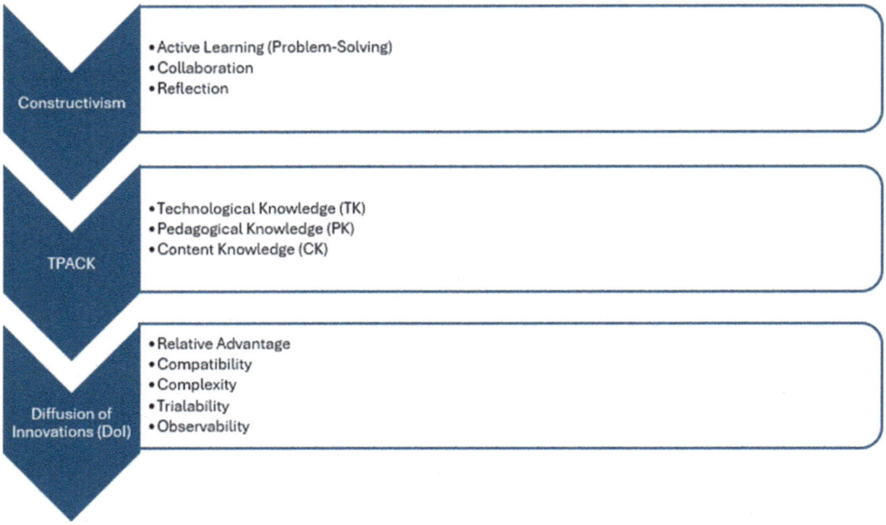

Fig. 2 AI Competency Adaptation Framework (AICAF). Source: Author's compilation deduced from the literature

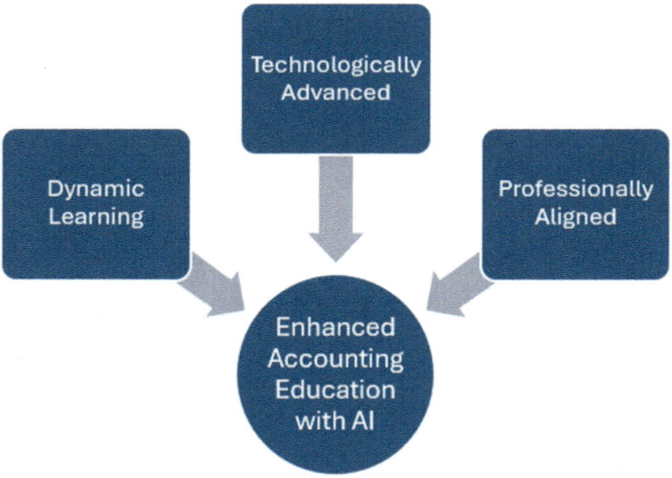

Fig. 3 Theoretical lens. Source: Author's compilation deduced from the literature

Figure 3 demonstrates the intersection and complementarity of various theoretical frameworks to provide a comprehensive approach to integrating AI into accounting education. By combining Constructivism, Technological Pedagogical Content Knowledge (TPACK), and Diffusion of Innovations (DoI), the AI Competency Adaptation Framework (AICAF) was developed. The study proposes a robust and multifaceted framework that addresses multiple dimensions of AI integration, including pedagogy, technology adoption, and ethical considerations. This integrated approach ensures that AI adoption in accounting education is holistic and effective.

The visual representation in Fig. 3 serves as a roadmap for educational institutions, guiding them to align AI integration with educational goals and industry needs. It offers a comprehensive lens through which the study's findings and recommendations can be understood and applied, illustrating the synergy between the different theoretical foundations. This summary highlights how these frameworks work together to support the successful incorporation of AI into accounting curricula, ultimately preparing students for the evolving demands of the accounting profession.

AI Competency Adaptation Framework (AICAF)

AICAF provides a framework for understanding how AI impacts professional competencies in accounting. This framework suggests that the integration of AI into professional practices necessitates a shift in the required skill set for accountants. It emphasises the need for continuous learning and adaptation to new technological tools and processes. AICAF highlights the importance of developing AI literacy, ethical considerations in AI use, and the ability to critically evaluate AI outputs. This framework addresses the strengths and weaknesses of existing models by incorporating a focus on ethical AI practices and continuous professional development, ensuring accountants are well-equipped to handle AI-driven transformations in their field. By drawing upon these theoretical frameworks, educational institutions can develop effective strategies for integrating AI into accounting curricula, ensuring that students acquire the necessary competencies to thrive in the AI-driven accounting profession.

Research Methodology

To ensure a comprehensive and systematic review of the literature on integrating Artificial Intelligence (AI) into accounting education, a structured methodology was adopted. This section outlines the criteria and methodology followed in the literature review process, including how the selected papers were sourced.

Search Process

The literature search was conducted using several academic databases, including Google Scholar, JSTOR, and ScienceDirect, as well as professional accounting and educational journals. Keywords used in the search included artificial intelligence, digital literacy, accounting education, accounting curriculum, higher education, technological pedagogy, opportunities, and challenges.

The initial search yielded many sources, which were then filtered based on specific inclusion and exclusion criteria. The inclusion criteria were:

- Peer-reviewed journal articles, conference proceedings, and scholarly books.
- Publications focusing on the integration of AI into accounting education or related fields.
- Sources published within the last 10 years to ensure relevance and timeliness; and
- Publications in English.

Sources that did not meet these criteria were excluded from further analysis.

Data Extraction and Synthesis

The data extraction process in this study involved several meticulous steps to ensure a comprehensive review of the literature. Initially, all potential literature was gathered based on the defined search strategy. This was followed by a screening phase, where titles and abstracts were reviewed to assess their relevance to the study's objectives. Subsequently, the eligibility of the selected articles was confirmed by reading the full texts to ensure they met the inclusion criteria. Relevant information such as study objectives, methodologies, key findings, and recommendations were then extracted from the eligible articles. This rigorous process ensured that only pertinent literature was included in the review.

Following data extraction, the collected information was synthesised to identify common themes, trends, and gaps in the literature. This synthesis was instrumental in informing the discussion on the opportunities and challenges of integrating AI into accounting education. By identifying these patterns, the study was able to provide a comprehensive overview of how AI can enhance accounting education and the potential obstacles that may arise. This thematic analysis also highlighted the areas where further research is needed, thereby contributing to the ongoing discourse on the subject.

To ensure the reliability and validity of the selected literature, a quality assessment was conducted using specific criteria. Methodological rigour was evaluated by examining the research design, data collection, and analysis methods of each study. The relevance and contribution of each study were assessed based on the significance of their findings to the field of accounting education. Additionally, the citation impact of each study was considered by looking at the number of citations and the impact factor of the publishing journal. Despite the comprehensive approach to the literature review process, inherent limitations associated with the selection and interpretation of sources might affect the generalisability of the findings.

Limitations

The review has certain limitations, including potential publication bias, the exclusion of non-English studies, and reliance on available databases that may not cover all relevant literature. Nevertheless, by adopting this structured methodology, the literature review provides a robust framework for understanding the integration of AI into accounting education, enhancing the validity of the findings and offering clear insights into the opportunities and challenges in this evolving field.

Literature Review

The last decade has seen a considerable influx of AI technologies in the accounting profession, from the automation of regular processes, such as data input, reconciliations, and compliance checks, to increasing efficiency and lowering the risk of human error (Rožman et al., 2023). The integration of AI has shifted accounting from manual, error-prone processes to more efficient, AI-driven methodologies, which significantly enhances the accuracy and speed of financial operations (Odonkor et al., 2024). Furthermore, AI-based analytics and predictive modelling tools such as machine learning algorithms and data analytics are being leveraged to provide insights into financial performance, risk management, and decision-making processes (Odonkor et al., 2024). Leading accounting firms and organisations have invested heavily in AI technologies, recognising their potential to streamline operations, improve accuracy, and deliver value-added services to clients (Faggella, 2020). For example, Faggella (2020) notes that the Big Four accounting firms; Deloitte Touche Tohmatsu Limited (Deloitte), Ernst & Young Global Limited (EY), PricewaterhouseCoopers (PwC), and Klynveld Peat Marwick Goerdeler (KPMG), which are major players in the accounting industry have high investments in AI technologies to enhance their services. Faggella (2020) reported that Deloitte has developed various AI-driven tools and partnered with AI firms through their Deloitte Catalyst programme to enhance financial services with AI solutions. They focused on improving audit accuracy and streamlining processes with machine learning and natural language processing technologies. In the same vein, PwC has made a significant investment in AI technologies, including GL.ai, which leverages machine learning to analyse audit data. The firm also utilised natural language processing for complex document analysis and digital twin technology for strategic planning in industries like automotive. While EY integrated AI into its auditing processes with tools like computer vision and drones. The firm's AI-enabled systems are designed to enhance data processing efficiency and accuracy, enabling accountants to focus on higher-level strategic tasks. EY, however, focuses on augmenting human auditors with advanced AI tools to improve audit quality. Similarly, KPMG's KPMG Clara platform incorporates AI to enhance audit quality by analysing complete data sets, identifying risks, and generating audit evidence. They have also partnered with

Microsoft to expand their AI capabilities, focusing on both co-piloting and auto-piloting AI functions in audits. However, the extent of AI integration varies across firms and industries, with some sectors being early adopters while others lag.

AI in Accounting Education

While the accounting profession has embraced AI technologies, the integration of AI components into accounting curricula has been relatively slower (Liu, 2020). One of the primary concerns highlighted by Liu (2020) is the outdated nature of teaching methods that still focuses heavily on theoretical knowledge without sufficient practical application. The author argues that the traditional teaching approach does not align well with the dynamic and technologically driven landscape of what is required for modern accounting education.

Consequently, this results in practical teaching that often does not extend beyond the classroom, limiting students' exposure to real-world scenarios and up-to-date practices crucial for their professional development in the age of AI. Additional research supported the finding of a discrepancy between the current educational programmes and the technological skills demanded by the industry (Agbo, 2023). This gap highlights the urgent need for academic institutions to update their curricula to include relevant technological training that prepares students for the challenges of modern accounting roles. For instance, Guşe and Mangiuc (2022) conducted a study on the integration of digital technologies in accounting functions, highlighting how the advancements were transforming both the scope of accounting practices and the educational needs of accountants. The analysis focused on the digital skills taught in Romanian universities, particularly within the curricula of business bachelor's programmes in the country's major university cities. The findings revealed a significant potential for the institutions to produce specialists who are well-equipped to navigate and lead the digital transformation in accounting. Although, some institutions have commenced the incorporation of AI-related courses or modules within their accounting programmes, covering topics such as data analytics, machine learning, and AI applications in accounting (Stine et al., 2019; Abitoye et al., 2023). However, the depth and breadth of these offerings vary considerably, with some institutions offering comprehensive AI-focused tracks while others provide only a cursory introduction to the subject (Shiohira, 2021; Wadsworth et al., 2024). Also, the pedagogical approaches employed in these AI-related courses often differ, ranging from traditional lecture-based methods to hands-on experiential learning and project-based assignments (Zawacki-Richter et al., 2019). It is however imperative to emphasise the benefits of AI in the accounting curriculum because it equips future accountants with the skills necessary to navigate and leverage advanced technologies that are transforming the industry. It also fosters a more dynamic and forward-thinking accounting profession.

Opportunities of AI in Accounting Education

AI presents transformative opportunities in accounting education by enhancing learning experiences through personalised and adaptive learning tools, facilitating a deeper understanding of complex financial concepts. Also, AI-driven analytics might help educators track student progress and identify areas needing improvement, ultimately fostering a more efficient and effective learning environment.

- **Enhancing educational outcomes**

- The integration of AI into accounting curricula presents a significant opportunity to enhance educational outcomes and develop critical competencies among students (Guşe & Mangiuc, 2022). Enhancing educational outcomes is a systematic endeavour that involves the integration of innovative teaching methods, technology, and personalised learning strategies to improve student performance and engagement (Ajayi-Nifise et al., 2024). Research has shown that active learning, which includes collaborative projects, problem-solving activities, and interactive discussions, significantly enhances student understanding and retention of material compared to traditional lecture-based instruction (Freeman et al., 2014; Tsai et al., 2023). AI technologies could foster digital literacy, enabling students to navigate and leverage digital tools and platforms effectively (Niemi, 2021). Furthermore, AI-based applications and case studies can stimulate critical thinking and analytical skills, as students grapple with complex data sets, pattern recognition, and decision-making scenarios (Bates et al., 2020).

- For instance, incorporating AI-driven data analytics tools into coursework can help students develop proficiency in extracting insights from large data sets, identifying trends, and making data-driven decisions (Bates et al., 2020). Additionally, AI-powered simulations and virtual environments can provide students with opportunities to apply accounting principles and practices in realistic scenarios, honing their problem-solving abilities and decision-making skills (Stütz et al., 2022; Abitoye et al., 2023).
- **Improving decision-making and efficiency**
- AI tools and systems can significantly enhance decision-making processes and operational efficiency within educational settings (Pedro et al., 2019; de Souza Zanirato Maia et al., 2023). AI-driven analytics can provide insights into student performance, learning patterns, and curricular effectiveness, enabling educators and administrators to make informed decisions regarding instructional strategies, resource allocation, and programme improvements (Zawacki-Richter et al., 2019). Moreover, AI-powered chatbots and virtual assistants can streamline administrative tasks, such as answering common queries, scheduling appointments, and providing personalised guidance to students (Winkler & Söllner, 2018). These AI-enabled solutions not only improve efficiency but also enhance the overall student experience by providing timely and accessible support.
- **Predictive roles and personalisation**

- Powerful capabilities are offered by AI technologies in predicting student performance and personalising educational experiences (Tapalova & Zhiyenbayeva, 2022). Through machine learning algorithms and predictive analytics, AI systems can analyse student data, such as academic records, learning patterns, and engagement levels, to identify potential areas of struggle or excellence (Akçapinar et al., 2020). Based on these predictions, educational institutions can implement targeted interventions, such as personalised tutoring, adaptive learning materials, or tailored support services, to address individual student needs and enhance their learning outcomes (Kurilovas, 2020). In addition, AI-powered recommender systems can suggest personalised study resources, course selections, or extracurricular activities based on students' interests, strengths, and career aspirations (Bodily & Verbert, 2017).
- By leveraging the predictive capabilities of AI, educational institutions can move towards a more proactive and personalised approach to education, optimising student success and fostering a learner-centric environment.

Challenges of AI Integration

Integrating AI into various industries poses significant challenges, including data privacy concerns, ethical considerations, and the potential displacement of jobs (Whittlestone et al., 2019; Dwivedi et al., 2021; Mohamed & Frank, 2023). Moreover, the complexity of AI technologies necessitates substantial investment in infrastructure and training, which can be a barrier for many organisations (Alsheiabni et al., 2019; Singh et al., 2020).

- **Curriculum redesign**
- Integrating AI into accounting curricula necessitates a comprehensive overhaul of existing programmes and course offerings. This process requires a thorough review and revision of learning outcomes, course content, and pedagogical approaches to effectively incorporate AI-related competencies (Tavares et al., 2023; Agbo, 2023). For example, Liu (2020) contends that, one of the primary concerns is the outdated nature of teaching methods that still focus heavily on theoretical knowledge without sufficient practical application. This traditional approach does not align well with the dynamic and technologically driven landscape of modern accounting. The practical teaching often does not extend beyond the classroom, limiting students' exposure to real-world scenarios and up-to-date practices, which is crucial for their professional development in the age of AI (Moloi & Mhlanga, 2021). Hence, developing new courses or modules focused on AI applications in accounting, data analytics, and machine learning may be necessary, which might be a time-consuming and resource-intensive endeavour. Furthermore, the accounting curricula must strike a balance between traditional accounting knowledge and emerging AI-related skills, to ensure that students

receive a well-rounded education that prepares them for both traditional and AI-driven roles within the profession (Richins et al., 2017).

- **Faculty development**
- Effective integration of AI into accounting education hinges on the availability of qualified and knowledgeable faculty members. Many current faculty members may lack the necessary expertise in AI technologies, data analytics, and machine learning, as these disciplines were not part of their formal training or education (Sangster et al., 2020). Bridging this knowledge gap requires substantial investment in professional development programmes, workshops, and training opportunities to equip faculty with the skills and competencies needed to teach AI-related content effectively (Abitoye et al., 2023). Additionally, faculty members may need to adapt their teaching methodologies to incorporate active learning strategies, project-based assignments, and hands-on experiences that align with the practical application of AI in accounting contexts (Pathways Commission, 2022). This shift in pedagogical approaches may require significant effort and support to ensure successful implementation.
- **Infrastructure and investment**
- Integrating AI into accounting curricula often necessitates substantial investments in technology infrastructure and resources. Educational institutions may need to acquire specialised software, computing power, and data storage solutions to support AI-driven applications, simulations, and analytics (Sangster et al., 2020). Ensuring seamless access to these resources for students and faculty, as well as maintaining and updating the infrastructure, can be a significant financial burden, particularly for institutions with limited budgets. Furthermore, securing funding for ongoing professional development, curriculum redesign initiatives, and faculty support may pose challenges, as institutions grapple with competing priorities and resource constraints (Frey & Osborne, 2017).
- **Ethical considerations and bias**
- The use of AI in accounting education and practice raises important ethical concerns and the potential for biased outcomes. AI systems can perpetuate and amplify existing biases present in the data used for training, leading to discriminatory or unfair decisions (Lloyd, 2018; Ferrara, 2023). For instance, AI-driven credit scoring models or fraud detection algorithms may exhibit biases against certain demographic groups, which could have far-reaching implications for accounting and financial decision-making processes. Additionally, the reliance on AI systems raises questions about accountability, transparency, and explainability, particularly in situations where AI-driven decisions or recommendations have significant consequences (Martin, 2019). Accounting educators must ensure that students receive comprehensive training on ethical AI practices, including recognising and mitigating biases, ensuring data privacy and security, and maintaining human oversight and accountability.

Proposed Framework for AI Integration

Explanation of the AI Competency Adaptation Framework (AICAF)

The AI Competency Adaptation Framework (AICAF) is designed to address the evolving needs of accounting professionals in the age of AI. This framework emphasises continuous learning and adaptation to new technological tools and processes. It consists of several key components:

- **AI Literacy**: Developing a fundamental understanding of AI technologies and their applications in accounting. This involves teaching students the basics of AI, including how it works and its potential uses in the accounting field.
- **Ethical AI Use**: Training students to recognise and mitigate biases in AI systems and to ensure transparency and accountability. This component emphasises the importance of ethical considerations in the use of AI.
- **Critical Evaluation**: Equipping students with the skills to critically assess AI outputs and make informed decisions. This involves teaching students how to interpret AI-generated insights and apply them in a practical accounting context.
- **Interdisciplinary Collaboration**: Encouraging collaboration between accounting professionals and experts in AI, data science, and related fields. This component highlights the need for accountants to work with other professionals to effectively leverage AI technologies.

Incorporating AI into AICAF for Accounting Education

Incorporating AI into AICAF for accounting education involves several key steps that align with the core components of the framework.

- **AI Literacy**

- Incorporating AI literacy into accounting education involves integrating fundamental AI concepts into existing and new courses, providing learning resources like textbooks and case studies on AI applications in accounting, to prepare students to understand and leverage AI technologies in their careers.
- **Ethical AI Use**
- To ensure ethical AI use, accounting programmes should include modules on AI ethics, covering topics like bias, transparency, and accountability, using real-world case studies and discussions on regulations to help students navigate the ethical landscape of AI in accounting.
- **Critical Evaluation**
- Developing students' critical evaluation skills for effectively using AI in accounting involves training them to critically assess AI-generated data and insights,

teaching methods for validating AI outputs, and including practical exercises for analysing and interpreting AI-generated reports, enabling informed decision-making.

- **Technological Proficiency**
- Enhancing technological proficiency requires providing hands-on training in AI software and tools commonly used in accounting, offering workshops and labs for practical experience, integrating AI tools in courses, and collaborating with software providers to keep students updated on the latest AI advancements.
- **Interdisciplinary Collaboration**
- Promoting interdisciplinary collaboration involves creating courses that combine accounting, computer science, and data science, encouraging projects and teamwork to integrate different expertise, and partnering with AI and technology companies to provide practical insights and internship opportunities.
- **Faculty Development**
- Faculty development is essential for integrating AI into accounting education, involving professional development programmes and workshops to keep educators updated on AI advancements, encouraging participation in AI research, and fostering a culture of continuous learning.
- **Curriculum Redesign**
- A comprehensive curriculum redesign is necessary to incorporate AI-related content into accounting programmes, including reviewing and updating existing courses, developing new AI-focused modules, and continuously collecting feedback from students and industry professionals to ensure the curriculum remains relevant and effective.
- **Infrastructure and Investment**
- Investing in necessary technology infrastructure is critical for supporting AI-driven education, involving allocating funds for AI tools, software, hardware, setting up data labs and cloud-based platforms, and ensuring ongoing maintenance and technical support, while seeking grants and funding opportunities to further support these initiatives.
- **Implementation Strategy**

- Developing a structured implementation strategy with clear goals, timelines, and milestones is crucial for successful AI integration, involving assigning responsibilities, creating a roadmap, and regularly monitoring and evaluating progress to make necessary adjustments for effective and sustainable incorporation of AI into the accounting curriculum.

Strengths and Weaknesses

- **Strengths**

- The strengths of the outlined approach include an emphasis on continuous professional development, ensuring that professionals remain updated with the

latest advancements and practices in their field. Additionally, it prioritises ethical considerations in the use of AI, fostering a responsible and conscientious application of technology. This approach also promotes interdisciplinary collaboration, encouraging the integration of diverse perspectives and expertise, which can lead to more innovative and comprehensive solutions.
- **Weaknesses**
- However, the approach also has its weaknesses. It requires significant investment in faculty development and infrastructure, which can be a considerable financial burden for educational institutions. Furthermore, there may be resistance from traditional educational institutions that are hesitant to embrace change and adopt new methodologies. This resistance can hinder the effective implementation and integration of AI and other emerging technologies in the educational landscape.

Implementation Strategy

To implement the AICAF effectively, institutions should:

- Incorporate AI-related courses and modules into existing accounting programmes.
- Provide ongoing professional development for faculty members.
- Invest in the necessary technology infrastructure.
- Foster partnerships with industry and technology experts to stay updated on the latest AI advancements.

By following the AICAF, educational institutions can ensure that their accounting programmes are aligned with the latest industry trends and technological advancements. This alignment is crucial for producing graduates who are not only proficient in traditional accounting practices but also adept at using AI tools and techniques to enhance their professional capabilities.

In summary, the study's results provide a comprehensive overview of the essential AI competencies for accounting students and the benefits and challenges of integrating AI into accounting education. The AI Competency Adaptation Framework (AICAF) offers a structured approach for educational institutions to develop curricula that prepare students for the AI-driven future of the accounting profession.

Discussion

This section highlights the profound impact that AI technologies are having on the accounting profession and the consequent need for accounting education to adapt and evolve. The integration of AI into accounting curricula presents both significant opportunities and challenges that must be carefully navigated. On the opportunities side, the findings align with broader trends in education where AI is increasingly being recognised as a powerful tool to enhance learning outcomes, improve decision-making processes, and personalise educational experiences (Zawacki-Richter et al., 2019).

The capacity of AI to cultivate essential proficiencies, including digital literacy, critical thinking, and analytical abilities, in accounting students is notably remarkable, given the critical nature of these competencies in the AI-dominated accounting environment (Agbo, 2023). Furthermore, the findings related to the potential of AI for improving operational efficiency and predictive capabilities in educational settings resonate with the wider adoption of AI in various industries for streamlining processes and leveraging data-driven insights (Winkler & Söllner, 2018; Akçapinar et al., 2020). However, the challenges identified in this study, such as curriculum redesign, faculty development, infrastructure investment, and ethical considerations, are not unique to the accounting discipline. These challenges are reflective of the broader difficulties faced by educational institutions and educators in integrating emerging technologies into their curricula and teaching practices (Ruggiero & Mong, 2015; Sangster et al., 2020; De Vera et al., 2021).

The ethical concerns and potential biases associated with AI applications echo the growing discourse around responsible AI and the need for robust governance frameworks to mitigate potential risks and ensure fairness, transparency, and accountability (Martin, 2019).

Linking Results to Objectives

The study's results are directly linked to its objectives by identifying the essential AI competencies for accounting students and exploring the potential benefits and challenges of integrating AI into accounting education. The AI Competency Adaptation Framework (AICAF) provides a practical roadmap for institutions to develop future-ready graduates equipped to navigate the AI-driven transformation of the accounting profession.

Implications for Stakeholders

The findings of this study have significant implications for various stakeholders involved in accounting education and the accounting profession. The study emphasises the necessity for proactive measures by policymakers and accreditation bodies to facilitate the incorporation of AI into accounting curricula. This may entail the modification of accreditation criteria, the provision of resources and direction for the development of curricula, and the promotion of cooperation among academic establishments, industry counterparts, and professional organisations.

The creation of thorough AI integration techniques will need to be given top priority by educational institutions and instructors. This includes initiatives to revamp the curriculum, programmes for the faculty training and development, and expenditures for the required infrastructure of technology. In this process, interdisciplinary collaboration with specialists in domains like computer science, data analytics, and educational technology can be quite beneficial.

Professional accounting bodies and industry associations are crucial in establishing the required AI skills for accounting professionals and contributing to curriculum development. In addition, they can enhance the professional growth of accounting practitioners in the field of AI by providing continuing education opportunities, certifications, and tools. Finally, the successful integration of AI into accounting education requires a synchronised effort among all stakeholders, with a shared commitment to preparing future-ready graduates equipped with the knowledge and skills to navigate the AI-driven transformation of the accounting profession.

Conclusion

The future of accounting education is closely linked to the AI revolution, requiring educational institutions to proactively modify their curricula to provide graduates with the necessary abilities for the changing scenario. The incorporation of artificial intelligence (AI) into accounting education poses both obstacles and prospects, allowing institutions to improve the significance and excellence of their programmes. By adopting AI technologies, they may develop a new cohort of professionals who are skilled in traditional accounting and proficient in utilising AI tools to foster creativity, enhance decision-making, and deliver value-added services.

Going forward, collaboration and a future-oriented mindset among stakeholders are crucial. Educational institutions should prioritise curriculum redesign, faculty development, and infrastructure investments to create AI-infused learning experiences. Policymakers and accreditation bodies need to provide support and guidance, while professional organisations and industry partners should contribute expertise and resources to shape AI-focused curricula. By addressing challenges and seizing AI opportunities, the accounting education community can prepare a future-ready workforce that will advance the profession into a new era of excellence, innovation, and value creation.

Recommendations

Based on the findings of this study, several strategies and best practices are recommended for the effective integration of AI into accounting curricula. Educational institutions should collaborate with industry partners, professional bodies, and technology experts to develop a comprehensive AI integration framework outlining essential AI competencies, learning outcomes, and curricular components. A modular and flexible approach, incorporating AI-related courses or specialisations within existing accounting programmes, allows for gradual adaptation as AI technologies evolve. Prioritising experiential learning through hands-on, project-based experiences, such as case studies, simulations, and industry internships, enables students to apply AI tools in real-world scenarios. In addition, fostering interdisciplinary collaborations among accounting faculty, computer science experts, data analysts, and educational technologists ensures the development of relevant and cutting-edge AI-infused curricula.

Institutions should invest in comprehensive faculty development programmes, including workshops, professional certifications, and industry exposure opportunities, to equip educators with the necessary skills to teach AI-related content effectively. Leveraging online and blended learning platforms can provide accessible and scalable AI-related resources, allowing students to engage with AI tools and simulations at their own pace. It is also crucial to address ethical considerations in AI, incorporating modules on bias mitigation, data privacy, transparency, and accountability in AI-driven decision-making processes. Finally, given the rapid pace of AI advancements, institutions should establish mechanisms for regular curriculum review and updates to ensure that the content remains relevant and aligned with industry needs and technological developments.

While this study provides valuable insights into the opportunities and challenges of integrating AI into accounting education, several areas warrant further exploration to enhance understanding and implementation. Conducting empirical research to evaluate the effectiveness of various AI integration strategies on student learning outcomes, skill development, and employability would provide crucial data-driven insights. Comparative studies across different disciplines could identify unique challenges and best practices, fostering interdisciplinary knowledge sharing and collaboration. Longitudinal studies tracking the long-term impacts of AI-infused accounting curricula on career trajectories, industry preparedness, and professional competencies would offer a comprehensive understanding of lasting effects. Additionally, research into developing robust ethical guidelines and regulatory frameworks is essential for ensuring the responsible use of AI in accounting education, promoting fairness, transparency, and accountability.

Exploring the integration of AI into accounting curricula from an international perspective, considering cultural, regulatory, and technological variations across regions, would enrich the understanding and inform more inclusive strategies. As AI technologies continue to evolve, research is needed to examine the implications of emerging AI paradigms such as explainable AI, multi-agent systems, and quantum computing on accounting education and practice. By addressing these future research directions, the accounting education community can refine and enhance its strategies for integrating AI, ensuring that accounting curricula remain relevant, forward-looking, and responsive to the rapidly evolving technological landscape.

Future Research Directions

Further research is needed to:

- Evaluate the effectiveness of various AI integration strategies on student learning outcomes and employability.
- Conduct comparative studies across different disciplines to identify unique challenges and best practices.
- Explore the long-term impacts of AI-infused accounting curricula on career trajectories and industry preparedness.
- Develop robust ethical guidelines and regulatory frameworks for AI use in accounting education.

By addressing these recommendations and research directions, the accounting education community can refine and enhance its strategies for integrating AI, ensuring that accounting curricula remain relevant, forward-looking, and responsive to the rapidly evolving technological landscape.

References

Abbas, K. (2023). *Essays on digitalization and artificial intelligence technologies in the accounting profession* [Doctoral dissertation], University of Pisa.

Abitoye, O., Abdul, A. A., Babalola, F. I., Daraojimba, C., & Oriji, O. (2023). The role of technology in modernizing accounting education for Nigerian students – A review. *International Journal of Management and Entrepreneurship Research, 5*(12), 892–906.

Agbo, E. I. (2023). Future of accounting education practices: Leveraging on emerging technologies. *European Review in Accounting and Finance, 7*(3), 15–24.

Ajayi-Nifise, A. O., Odeyemi, O., Mhlongo, N. Z., Ibeh, C. V., Elufioye, O. A., & Awonuga, K. F. (2024). The future of accounting: Predictions on automation and AI integration. *World Journal of Advanced Research and Reviews, 21*(2), 399–407.

Akçapinar, G., Chen, M. R. A., Majumdar, R., Flanagan, B., & Ogata, H. (2020, March). Exploring student approaches to learning through sequence analysis of reading logs. In *Proceedings of the tenth international conference on learning analytics and knowledge* (pp. 106–111).

Almaiah, M. A., Alfaisal, R., Salloum, S. A., Hajjej, F., Shishakly, R., Lutfi, A., Alwarad, M., Mulhem, A. A., Alkhdour, T., & Al-Maroof, R. S. (2022). Measuring institutions' adoption of artificial intelligence applications in online learning environments: Integrating the innovation diffusion theory with technology adoption rate. *Electronics, 11*(20), 3291.

Alsheiabni, S., Cheung, Y., & Messom, C. (2019). Factors inhibiting the adoption of artificial intelligence at organizational level: A preliminary investigation. In *Americas conference on information systems 2019* (p. 2). Association for Information Systems.

Archambault, L. M., & Barnett, J. H. (2010). Revisiting technological pedagogical content knowledge: Exploring the TPACK framework. *Computers and Education, 55*(4), 1656–1662.

Bada, S. O., & Olusegun, S. (2015). Constructivism learning theory: A paradigm for teaching and learning. *Journal of Research and Method in Education, 5*(6), 66–70.

Bates, T., Cobo, C., Mariño, O., & Wheeler, S. (2020). Can artificial intelligence transform higher education? *International Journal of Educational Technology in Higher Education, 17*(1), 1–12.

Bodily, R., & Verbert, K. (2017). Review of research on student-facing learning analytics dashboards and educational recommender systems. *IEEE Transactions on Learning Technologies, 10*(4), 405–418.
de Souza Zanirato Maia, J., Bueno, A. P. A., & Sato, J. R. (2023). Applications of artificial intelligence models in educational analytics and decision making: A systematic review. *World, 4*(2), 288–313.
De Vera, J. L., Andrada, M. D., Bello, A., & De Vera, M. G. (2021). Teachers' competencies in educational technology integration on instructional methodologies in the new normal. *Lukad: An Online Journal of Pedagogy, 1*(1), 61–80.
Dearing, J. W., & Cox, J. G. (2018). Diffusion of innovations theory, principles, and practice. *Health Affairs, 37*(2), 183–190.
Dwivedi, Y. K., Hughes, L., Ismagilova, E., Aarts, G., Coombs, C., Crick, T., et al. (2021). Artificial intelligence (AI): Multidisciplinary perspectives on emerging challenges, opportunities, and agenda for research, practice and policy. *International Journal of Information Management, 57*, 101994.
Faggella, D. (2020). *AI in the accounting big four – Comparing Deloitte, PwC, KPMG, and EY.* WWW Document, Emerj, The AI Research and Advisory Company. Retrieved from https://emerj.com/ai-sector-overviews/ai-in-theaccounting-big-four-comparing-deloitte-pwc-kpmg-and-ey/
Ferrara, E. (2023). Fairness and bias in artificial intelligence: A brief survey of sources, impacts, and mitigation strategies. *Science, 6*(1), 3.
Freeman, S., Eddy, S. L., McDonough, M., Smith, M. K., Okoroafor, N., Jordt, H., & Wenderoth, M. P. (2014). Active learning increases student performance in science, engineering, and mathematics. *Proceedings of the National Academy of Sciences, 111*(23), 8410–8415.
Frey, C. B., & Osborne, M. A. (2017). The future of employment: How susceptible are jobs to computerisation? *Technological Forecasting and Social Change, 114*, 254–280.
Gusai, O. P. (2019). Robot human interaction: Role of artificial intelligence in accounting and auditing. *Indian Journal of Accounting, 51*(1), 59–62.
Guşe, G. R., & Mangiuc, M. D. (2022). Digital transformation in Romanian accounting practice and education: Impact and perspectives. *Amfiteatru Economic, 24*(59), 252–267.
Koehler, M., & Mishra, P. (2009). What is technological pedagogical content knowledge (TPACK)? *Contemporary Issues in Technology and Teacher Education, 9*(1), 60–70.
Kommunuri, J. (2022). Artificial intelligence and the changing landscape of accounting: A viewpoint. *Pacific Accounting Review, 34*(4), 585–594.
Kurilovas, E. (2020). On data-driven decision-making for quality education. *Computers in Human Behavior, 107*, 105774.
Kwafo, D. (2019). *The impacts of artificial intelligence on management accounting students: A case study* at Oulu Business School, University of Oulu (Master's thesis, D. Kwafo).
Liu, C. (2020). The reform and practice of the practical teaching of higher vocational accounting in the background of artificial intelligence. In *2019 International Conference on Education Science and Economic Development (ICESED 2019)* (pp. 98–100). Atlantis Press.
Lloyd, K. (2018). *Bias amplification in artificial intelligence systems.* arXiv preprint arXiv:1809.07842.
Martin, K. (2019). Ethical implications and accountability of algorithms. *Journal of Business Ethics, 160*(4), 835–850.
Minishi-Majanja, M. K., & Kiplang'at, J. (2005). The diffusion of innovations theory as a theoretical framework in library and information science research. *SA Journal of Libraries and Information Science, 71*(3), 211–224.
Mohamed, S., & Frank, L. (2023). *Challenges and the path forward: Security concerns, robust data sets, and job displacement.*
Moloi, T., & Mhlanga, D. (2021). *Key features of the fourth industrial revolution in South Africa's basic education system.*

Niemi, H. (2021). AI in learning: Preparing grounds for future learning. *Journal of Pacific Rim Psychology, 15*, 18344909211038105.

Odonkor, B., Kaggwa, S., Uwaoma, P. U., Hassan, A. O., & Farayola, O. A. (2024). The impact of AI on accounting practices: A review: Exploring how artificial intelligence is transforming traditional accounting methods and financial reporting. *World Journal of Advanced Research and Reviews, 21*(1), 172–188.

Pathways Commission. (2022). *The Pathways Commission: Charting a national strategy for the next generation of accountants*. Retrieved from https://pathwayscommission.com/

Pedro, F., Subosa, M., Rivas, A., & Valverde, P. (2019). *Artificial intelligence in education: Challenges and opportunities for sustainable development*.

Richins, G., Stapleton, A., Stratopoulos, T. C., & Wong, C. (2017). Big data analytics: Opportunity or threat for the accounting profession? *Journal of Information Systems, 31*(3), 63–79.

Rogers, E. M. (1995). Diffusion of innovations: Modifications of a model for telecommunications. *Die Diffusion von Innovationen in der Telekommunikation*, 25–38.

Rogers, E. M., Singhal, A., & Quinlan, M. M. (2014). Diffusion of innovations. In *An integrated approach to communication theory and research* (pp. 432–448). Routledge.

Rožman, M., Tominc, P., & Vrečko, I. (2023). Building skills for the future of work: Students' perspectives on emerging jobs in the data and AI cluster through artificial intelligence in education. *Environment and Social Psychology, 8*(2), 1–24.

Ruggiero, D., & Mong, C. J. (2015). The teacher technology integration experience: Practice and reflection in the classroom. *Journal of Information Technology Education: Research, 14*.

Sangster, A., Stoner, G., & Flood, B. (2020). Insights into accounting education in a COVID-19 world. *Accounting Education, 29*(5), 431–562.

Schmidt, D. A., Baran, E., Thompson, A. D., Mishra, P., Koehler, M. J., & Shin, T. S. (2009). Technological pedagogical content knowledge (TPACK): The development and validation of an assessment instrument for preservice teachers. *Journal of Research on Technology in Education, 42*(2), 123–149.

Shiohira, K. (2021). *Understanding the impact of artificial intelligence on skills development. Education 2030*. UNESCO-UNEVOC International Centre for Technical and Vocational Education and Training.

Singh, R. P., Hom, G. L., Abramoff, M. D., Campbell, J. P., & Chiang, M. F. (2020). Current challenges and barriers to real-world artificial intelligence adoption for the healthcare system, provider, and the patient. *Translational Vision Science and Technology, 9*(2), 45–45.

Stine, J., Trumbore, A., Woll, T., & Sambucetti, H. (2019). *Implications of artificial intelligence on business schools and lifelong learning*. Final report at Academic Leadership Group.

Stütz, S., Berding, F., Reincke, S., & Scheper, L. (2022). Characteristics of learning tasks in accounting textbooks: An AI assisted analysis. *Empirical Research in Vocational Education and Training, 14*(1), 10.

Tandiono, R. (2023). The impact of artificial intelligence on accounting education: A review of literature. In *E3S Web of Conferences* (Vol. 426, p. 02016). EDP Sciences.

Tapalova, O., & Zhiyenbayeva, N. (2022). Artificial intelligence in education: AIEd for personalised learning pathways. *Electronic Journal of e-Learning, 20*(5), 639–653.

Tavares, M. C., Azevedo, G., Marques, R. P., & Bastos, M. A. (2023). Challenges of education in the accounting profession in the Era 5.0: A systematic review. *Cogent Business and Management, 10*(2), 2220198. 1–30.

Tiwari, D. (2020). *Are the accounting curricula enough to equip the students to be the future accountants? An examination of the accounting modules of universities* (Doctoral dissertation, Dublin, National College of Ireland).

Tsai, C. A., Song, M. Y. W., Lo, Y. F., & Lo, C. C. (2023). Design thinking with constructivist learning increases the learning motivation and wicked problem-solving capability—Empirical research in Taiwan. *Thinking Skills and Creativity, 50*, 101385.

Wadsworth, F., Blaney, J., Springsteen, M., Coburn, B., Khanal, N., Rodgers, T., Livingston, C., & Muknahallipatna, S. (2024). Frameworks and challenges for implementing machine learning curriculum in secondary education. *International Journal of Technology in Education and Science, 8*(1), 164–181.

Whittlestone, J., Nyrup, R., Alexandrova, A., Dihal, K., & Cave, S. (2019). *Ethical and societal implications of algorithms, data, and artificial intelligence: A roadmap for research.* Nuffield Foundation.

Winkler, R., & Söllner, M. (2018, July). Unleashing the potential of chatbots in education: A state-of-the-art analysis. In *Academy of management proceedings* (Vol. 2018, No. 1, p. 15903). Briarcliff Manor, NY: Academy of Management.

Zawacki-Richter, O., Marín, V. I., Bond, M., & Gouverneur, F. (2019). Systematic review of research on artificial intelligence applications in higher education – Where are the educators? *International Journal of Educational Technology in Higher Education, 16*(1), 1–27.

Going Green: The Impact of Green Dynamic Capability and Development Behavior on Competitive Advantage of Nigerian Agro-Allied Firms

Banji Rildwan Olaleye

Abstract As a result of intensifying competition, growing environmental attitudes are attracting the attention of corporate stakeholders. This trend is driving efforts to achieve a green competitive advantage and consider the potential impact of green development practices on businesses. Despite their high relevance to the agro-based industry and recent emergence, the elements motivating green development behavior and green competitive advantage remain largely unexplored. This study's goals are to create a theoretical model of green development behavior, test it against other models using data from Nigerian agro-allied industries, and then look at how green dynamic capability affects the results. The researchers used descriptive statistics and the partial least squares structural equation modeling (PLS-SEM) method to analyze data from 351 respondents from 12 listed agro-allied firms in Nigeria. The empirical results show that all dimensions of green development behavior—including company tangible resources, corporate intangible resources, market environment, public supervision and policy, and institutional environment—have a significant positive effect on determining green development behavior. Beyond that, it became clear that businesses with environmentally conscious practices can gain a long-term market advantage by embracing green development behavior and green dynamic capability, as evidenced by the Natural Resource-Based View (NRBV) theory, which posits a company's competitive advantage in relation to its natural environment, hence, contributing to the fields of green behavior, green development theory, and business development theory.

Keywords Agro-allied industries · Green development behavior · Green dynamic capability · Green competitive advantage · Partial least squares structural equation modeling (PLS-SEM)

B. R. Olaleye (✉)
North-West University, Business School, Potchefstroom, South Africa

T. Moloi (ed.), *Impacting Society Positively Through Technology in Accounting and Business Processes*, Springer Proceedings in Business and Economics,
https://doi.org/10.1007/978-3-031-84885-8_55

Introduction

As competition in the marketplace heats up, more and more organizations are under pressure to deliver customers something fresh, different, and valuable. Environmental management reflects a company's efforts to enhance its standing and productivity. Research on environmental sustainability has emerged (May et al., 2021). Similarly, corporations should take responsibility for protecting the environment to deal with climate change and other environmental crises (Davies et al., 2019). For their company operations to have long-term, beneficial effects on the environment, they need to implement environmental control measures and become more sustainable. How easily can corporations maintain their green development behavior for long-term competitive advantage? That is the remaining question.

A lot of people talk about globalization and greening, which is great for businesses since it encourages them to do their part for the environment and gives consumers more for their money (Norton et al., 2017; Unsworth et al., 2020). Businesses have been able to embrace resource-intensive and high-turnover manufacturing methods since the beginning of the industrial revolution (Li et al., 2020a, 2022). As a result of this situation, the idea of green development emerged with the goal of coordinating the relationship between economic development and ecological environmental protection (Li et al., 2020b; Ilyas et al., 2020). According to research (Oyebanji et al., 2017; Anabaraonye et al., 2019), the government of Nigeria has been actively working to promote green development to accomplish a holistic change in the country's sustainable economic, environmental, and social development.

In Nigerian context, green economic opportunities are associated with the vast potential for environmentally friendly agricultural production, renewable energies, ecotourism, and coastal revitalization. Nigeria can lead the way in green economic growth if it fully commits to utilizing its natural resource potential. Scholars and industry stakeholders have been increasingly focused on this area to gain a better grasp of the notion of green development (Olaleye, 2023; Wang et al., 2021). Li et al. (2019, 2020a) argued that businesses must adopt green and low-carbon development practices to achieve green transformation because of these factors.

Based on the research of Li et al. (2019, 2020a, 2020b), this study defines "green development behavior" (GDB) as actions taken by businesses to promote a development objective that is good for the environment and the company's growth. All parties involved, aware of the growing importance of GDB, are thinking about how they might help alleviate the environmental crisis.

Based on the research conducted by Habib et al. (2020), and Somjai and Jermsittiparsert (2019), it was concluded that several internal and external factors are likely to influence GBD as an organizational behavior. In the context of developing nations like Nigeria, however, there is a dearth of empirical research that examines these aspects. There is a wealth of theoretical literature on green business development, as it relates to green competitive advantage in industries like hospitality (Fatoki, 2021; Li et al., 2020a, 2022; Wang et al., 2021), but none had considered agro-based industry.

Numerous studies have examined environmentally conscious company practices, ranging from the individual level to the strategy level. Studies have focused on human resources (Abubakar et al., 2022; Freitas et al., 2020), green behavior (May et al., 2021; Unsworth et al., 2020; Peng et al., 2020; Dumont et al., 2017), and employee well-being (Kim et al., 2018). When it comes to creating environmentally friendly business practices, the people who work for a firm have a significant impact because they are the ones who put policies and strategies into action. Consequently, being environmentally conscious at work is crucial.

Prior research has discovered some characteristics that could potentially impact corporate green development across industries, but most of these studies have struggled to accurately measure these factors. For example, it is possible that the studies conducted by Aslam et al. (2018), Shahzad et al. (2020), and Somjai and Jermsittiparsert (2019) did not go far enough in explaining the generally accepted factors that determine GDB because they only looked at one side of the issue, such as how government environmental regulations affect business green development.

This study utilized green development behavior also called enterprise green development behavior (EDGB) and a previously designed scale to evaluate the determining factors in the context of Nigerian agro-allied firms. This research seeks to address the following questions: Does the market environment, public supervision, and enterprise green development behavior in Nigeria depend on determinant factors such as corporate tangible and intangible resources, public policies and institutions, and public supervision? Does the green dynamic capability have the potential to mitigate the determining variables?

To the best of the researcher knowledge, this is the first study to empirically analyze the drivers of green development behavior in the context of Nigeria. Further, it contributes to the boundaries of knowledge on enterprise green development behavior and overall sustainable development. Additionally, the researcher investigates the impact of determining factors on enterprise green development behavior (EDGB), focusing on the potential moderating function of dynamic capability. Our research also offers an empirical model of green development behavior, which might serve as a springboard for additional investigations. Also, make a good recommendation for businesses and the government to follow when formulating legislation to promote green development practices, which would boost businesses' green competitiveness.

Literature Review

Natural Resource-Based View (NRBV)

Expanding on the RBV by Hart (1995), the NRBV posits that a company's competitive advantage stems from its connection to the natural environment. The natural resource-based view (NRBV) also provides an explanation for the connection between green development behavior (GDB) and green competitive advantage. The idea asserts benefits through three interrelated pillars: product stewardship, pollution avoidance, and sustainable development.

Olaleye et al. (2023) mentioned that integrating operations with a sustainability perspective is the goal of the natural resource-based view (NRBV), which emphasizes on the organization's resources and capabilities. Hence, NRBV can be used as a foundation to figure out company's long-term viability. Multiple connections to competitiveness attest to the importance of the "natural resource-based view" (NRBV) and its continued relevance in contemporary business (Aribaba et al., 2019; Olaleye, 2023). Several pertinent concerns emerge, one of which is the need to examine the current state of NRBV resource availability. Menguc and Ozanne (2005) found that when it comes to NRBV resources and their importance for sustainability and long-term competitive advantage, very few individuals really understand. When it comes to maintaining an advantage over others over time, few recognize the value of NRBV resources (Menguc & Ozanne, 2005). The most important part of understanding the NRBV theory, according to, are conceptualizations.

When it comes to competing company operations that aim to contribute to ecological and societal development, the Natural Resource-Based View (NRBV) philosophy provides a solid theoretical foundation. The natural resource-based paradigm has been the dominant academic framework for explaining sustainable, competitive operations up until recently. NRBV advocates (Hart & Dowell, 2011; Olajide et al., 2019) assert that an organization's competitiveness stems from its interactions with its natural environment. Using their NRBV framework, which emphasizes the competencies that contribute to sustainable development, companies can gain a competitive edge in the market.

Green Development Behavior (GDB)

Incorporating green behaviors is a key component of achieving sustainability. Multiple studies have used the ideas of ecological worry and environmental concern to try to understand green behaviors. The "Green business" has emerged as an important debate among scholars and managers of businesses worldwide (González-Rodríguez et al., 2021; Yusliza et al., 2020). According to Merli et al. (2019), "green business" means that a company is actively working to lessen or eliminate its negative effects on either society or the environment.

Green Dynamic Capability (GDC)

A company's capacity to adapt to a changing market depends on its green dynamic capabilities, which focus on the ways in which the company may reuse and recycle its current assets and information. This study refers to Chen et al.'s (2015) definition of green dynamic capability and defined green dynamic capability as "the ability of a company to exploit its existing resources and knowledge to renew and develop its green organizational capabilities to react to the dynamic market." Regarding the measurement perspectives for dynamic capability, Teece et al. (1997) outlined it as follows: Dynamic capabilities denote the ability of the firm to integrate, build, and reconfigure internal and external competences to address rapid environmental changes. Green dynamic capabilities are concerned with a firm's ability to exploit existing resources and knowledge to renew and develop green organizational capabilities to react to the dynamic market.

The growth of environmentally friendly businesses and their long-term viability go hand in hand. Research on sustainable business development has a strong theoretical basis, thanks to the work of a few scholars around green business. Policy circles have increasingly embraced sustainable development in recent decades, but current global production and consumption patterns cannot continue (Naidoo & Gasparatos, 2018). All things considered; sustainable business development is largely responsible for the current state of research on environmentally friendly company growth. Research on industrial companies' green development is also lacking in depth and systematicity, making it unable to identify the reasons that motivate industrial firms to engage in green development or evaluate their own performance in this area.

Green Competitive Advantage (GCA)

When a company has a competitive advantage, it is in a position of strength in the market. Because of this, the company can have better results than its rivals (Porter, 1985a, 1985b). Based on Banerjee's analysis, the RBV (Barney, 1991) tries to explain sustainability from an economic perspective rather than a social or environmental one, and a firm's resource base determines its sustained competitive advantage. Gaining and keeping customers is the key to success for any agro-allied business, and one way to stand out from the competition is to be portrayed as an ethical and conscientious leader in one's industry. Hence, to gain a competitive edge, companies that produce agricultural products must incorporate environmental concerns into their strategies. Chen and Chang (2013) stated that GCA occurs when a company takes a stand on environmental management issues that its rivals find difficult to replicate. When environmental techniques are successful, enterprises experience GCA, which means they continue to reap the benefits of such methods over time (Chen et al., 2006). Astuti and Datrini (2021) define GCA as a scenario where a company takes a stand on environmental preservation that its competitors find difficult to match. Apart from agro-based enterprises achieving a competitive advantage through environmental innovation, enhancing performance, increasing market share, improving customer retention and acquisition, and improving the company's environmental image can all contribute to this advantage.

Green Development Behavior and Green Competitive Advantage

Employees engage in "green behavior" when they do their jobs in an eco-conscious way (De Roeck & Farooq, 2018). This includes things like recycling, conserving resources, taking part in environmental projects, and enacting greener regulations. The term "green behavior" can refer to a wide range of employee activities that either help or hurt efforts to keep the environment habitable, as stated by Ones and Dilchert (2012). Environmentally conscious activity can also provide a lasting competitive advantage. People are more likely to show their support for green projects when they work for companies that they see as renowned (May et al., 2021).

The growth of environmentally friendly businesses and their long-term viability go hand in hand. Research on sustainable business development has a strong theoretical basis, thanks to the work of a few scholars in green business. Policy circles have increasingly embraced sustainable development in recent decades, but current global production and consumption patterns cannot continue (Naidoo & Gasparatos, 2018). All things considered; sustainable business development is largely responsible for the current state of research on environmentally friendly company growth. Research on industrial companies' green development is also lacking in depth and systematicity, making it unable to identify the reasons that motivate industrial firms to engage in green development or evaluate their own performance in this area. These assumptions lead us to hypothesize a relationship between green development behavior and green competitive advantage.

H1: Green development behavior has a positive and significant influence on green competitive advantage.

Green Dynamic Capability, Green Development Behavior, and Green Competitive Advantage

Competitive advantage is the responsive ability when enterprises face diverse needs in an external dynamic competitive environment. Therefore, a firm's relative position within an industry is given by its sustainable competitive advantage. From a resource-based view, the more firm-specific resources a firm has, the more valuable it is. Besides, Porter (1985a, 1985b) proposed generic competitive strategy and the value chain to describe how a firm uses activities to build competitive advantage. Thus, sustainable competitive advantage includes a unique activity or product valued by customers that competitors cannot easily imitate. How is competitive advantage created and implemented? Porter (1985a, 1985b) believed that a firm gains competitive advantage by performing these strategically important activities more cheaply or better than its competitors. Competitive advantage is viewed as a function of how resources (including knowledge) are combined with other resources to develop new competencies and knowledge. In summary, resources, strategies, and activities are the assets that an organization has for creating competitive advantage.

Green dynamic capabilities, according to Chen and Chang (2013), are the abilities of a company to exploit its existing resources and knowledge to renew and develop its green organizational capabilities to react to the dynamic market. Firms act and react in the pursuit of market opportunities and thus green dynamic capability rapidly develops into a flourishing issue. Addressing environmental issues dealing with consumer, firms can deeply make a commitment to environmental practices. With resource and knowledge, firms can exploit their capabilities to design products/services to reflect customers' green philosophy. The green market shows no signs of slowing and firms must adapt to the ever-changing marketplace today to achieve green competitive advantage in business. Based on these assumptions, the researcher hypothesizes a relationship between green dynamic capability, green development behavior, and green competitive advantage

H2: Green dynamic capability has a positive influence on green competitive advantage.

H3: Green dynamic capability moderates the relationship between green development behavior and green competitive advantage.

To sum up, after delving into a wealth of theoretical insights and empirical findings, the hypothesis development was completed. See Fig. 1.

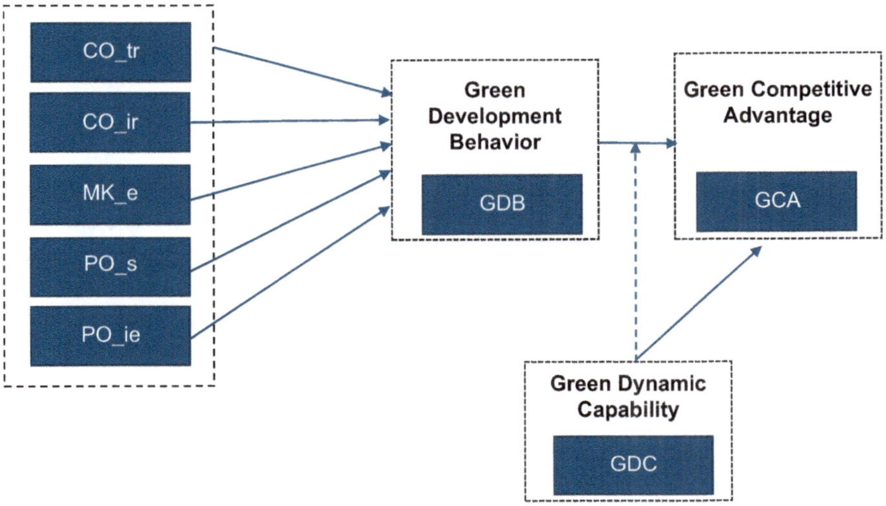

Fig. 1 Research model

Methodology

Population and Sampling

Procedure

The focus of the study is on quoted agro-allied companies.

The National Bureau of Statistics (NBS) divides the agro-allied business into four groups: food, beverages, and tobacco; textiles, clothing, and footwear; wood and wood products; and pulp, paper, and paper goods. The researcher used the cross-sectional survey method to collect data from the respondents in a quantitative study. The survey focused on managers and employees, who were expected to understand environmental strategy, competitive advantage, and dynamic capability in the context of the green economy. The researcher created a list of agro-based firms, as well as a list of quoted companies on the Nigeria Stock Exchange (NSE). The researcher adopted the simple random sampling method to select firms that operate using agricultural-related products.

The researcher selected five employees, including managers, from 12 companies spread across three major states in each region of the country, representing a population of 600. The initial data collection took place in September 2023, with a focus on gathering respondent demographics as well as information about the independent variables (green development behavior and green dynamic capability). Second, in December 2023, the researcher collected information on the moderating variable (green dynamic capability) and the dependent variable. The researcher collected 376 surveys in total, of which 351 proved to be valid, as 24 were treated as outliers and deleted permanently from the data set. Therefore, the estimated response rate stands to be 58.5%. Table 1 depicts the basic information about the sample data.

Measure

Chen and Chang (2013) and Lin and Chen (2017) propose a scale for evaluating green dynamic capability. Included in GDC were five items, such as "The company has the ability to quickly monitor the environment to identify new green opportunities" and "The company has the ability to assimilate, learn, generate, combine, share, transform, and apply new green knowledge." In contrast, Chen and Chang's (2013) research employs four items to assess green competitive advantage. Lastly, green development behavior was measured on the dimension of internal factors and external factors with 31 items as cited in the study of Li and Long (2020a, 2020b). Meanwhile, the questions were based on a five-point Likert scale, where 1 represents "strongly disagree" and 5 represents "strongly agree."

Analysis and Results

To analyze the research model, the study employed a partial least squares analysis using SmartPLS 3.3.2. According to Kock and Lynn (2012), the researcher conducted a full collinearity test using the variance inflation factor (VIF) for values above 3 to guarantee bias-free results. The results were indeed free from bias, as the VIF range was 1.771 to 2.445.

Table 1 depicts the demographic profile of the respondent. Table 1 shows that there are 259 male respondents (73.8%) and 92 female respondents (26.2%) when it comes to the gender mix. The study included participants of various ages, and the age distribution of those who responded was also evenly dispersed. There were 27 responses (or 7.7% of the total) in the 18–30 age bracket, 108 in the 31–40 age bracket, 153 in the 41–50 age bracket, and 63 (or 17.9%) in the over-50 age bracket. With 247 (or 70.4%) of the total respondents holding a bachelor's or first-degree qualification, descriptive statistics for participants' educational attainment reveal that this is the most common level of education, followed by those with a diploma certificate. Of the total respondents, 25 (7.1) held a postgraduate degree, while 38 (10.8) had a high school certificate. Table 1 reveals that out of the total number of respondents, almost average (39.6% of the total) had work experience falling between 4–6 years, while 89 (25.4%) have worked for more than 6 years, and 26.2% have 1–3 years of experience, of the remaining 8.8% working below a year.

Table 1 Demographics

Measures	Items	Frequency ($n = 351$)	%
Gender	Male	259	73.8
	Female	92	26.2
Age	18–30	27	7.7
	31–40	108	30.8
	41–50	153	43.6
	50 and above	63	17.9
Education	High school	38	10.8
	Diploma	41	11.7
	University degree	247	70.4
	Postgraduate degree	25	7.1
Job Tenure	Less than a year	31	8.8
	1–3 years	92	26.2
	4–6 years	139	39.6
	Over 6 years	89	25.4

Source: Own work

Measurement Model

To ensure that the variables were convergently valid, we used a confirmatory factor analysis together with the "Average Variance Extracted" (AVE). For this study, we relied on composite reliability and Cronbach's alpha. If the item's factor loading is greater than 0.55, it is considered legitimate, according to Wallace et al. (2023). According to Awang (2015), for an item to be considered for inclusion, its AVE must be at least 0.50, and an alpha value higher than 0.70 is necessary for evaluating the items' internal consistenc. Composite reliability, Cronbach's alpha, factor loading, and AVE all fulfilled the requirements, as shown in Table 2. According to Ab Hamid et al. (2017), discriminant validity ensures the reliability of capturing events that none of the other measures in the model can reliably measure. By comparing the AVE and CR values, we may ascertain if the validity is discriminant or convergent.

Several studies have confirmed convergent validity when the AVE and CR values surpass 0.50 and 0.70, respectively (Fornell & Larcker, 1981; Vetbuje & Olaleye, 2022). In the meantime, all AVEs surpass 0.5, except for GDB (AVE = 0.457). However, since the indicators of all sisters (CA, rho_A, and CR) surpass 0.7, we affirm the convergent validity (Iyer, 2017; Olaleye et al., 2021, 2023). Anderson and Gerbing (1988) achieved discriminant validity when the square root of the AVE values exceeded the correlation values of the constructs; however, in the present study, the AVE for GDB is below the correlation of the construct. Furthermore, the "Fornell and Larcker approach" (Henseler et al., 2015) suggested replacing the Fornell and Larcker (1981) criterion with the "heterotrait-monotrait" (HTMT) correlation ratio. Kline (2005) deemed the model constructs to have excellent discriminant validity when their HTMT values were less than 0.9 and immediately greater than the square roots of the AVEs (see Tables 3 and 4). Hence, this shows that there is definite discriminant validity between variables.

Once all the tests from the measurement model assessment were complete, we executed the PLS-SEM estimation. Figures 2 and 3 summarize the results of the PLS-SEM hypothesis testing. The p-value supports the hypothesis's relevance. In behavioral science, the p-value must be less than 0.05 to reject the null hypothesis (Andres, 2012; Charoensukmongkol, 2023). Chin et al. (2003), and Hossain et al. (2023) also use this criterion in PLS-SEM analysis to reject the null hypothesis.

We measured the model's predictive power using R^2. Falk and Miller (1992) suggested R^2 meet 0.10. Figure 2 shows our R^2 estimate of 0.533. To understand the structural model, one must study the measurement model. R^2 indicates a structure's ability to explain the dependent variable and its independent components. Like prior investigations (Bahadir et al., 2024; Qing et al., 2023), the researcher utilized one-tailed bootstrapping with 5000 subsamples to determine path coefficient weights and significance. According to Table 5, green development behavior may account for 44.7% of green dynamic capability and 53.3% of green competitive advantage.

According to Hypothesis 1, green development behavior is positively associated with green competitive advantage. The positive association between the variables

Table 2 Factor loading, AVE, and reliability of variables

Latent variables	Loadings (λ)	CA (>0.7)	rho_A (>0.7)	CR (>0.7)	AVE (>0.5)
Green development behavior	**IBM**	**0.960**	**0.961**	**0.963**	**0.457**
Corporate intangible resources	*CO_ir*	0.845	0.846	0.890	0.617
CO_ir1	0.836***				
CO_ir2	0.833***				
CO_ir3	0.811***				
CO_ir4	0.798***				
Corporate tangible resources	CO_tr	0.871	0.873	0.912	0.721
CO_tr1	0.754***				
CO_tr2	0.860***				
CO_tr3	0.810***				
CO_tr4	0.840***				
CO_tr5	0.786***				
CO_tr6	0.743***				
CO_tr7	0.780***				
CO_tr8	0.758***				
CO_tr9	0.604***				
Market environment	**MK_e**	0.903	0.904	0.924	0.636
MK_e1	0.799***				
MK_e2	0.803***				
MK_e3	0.825***				
MK_e4	0.831***				
MK_e5	0.842***				
MK_e6	0.811***				
MK_e7	0.654***				
Policy & institutional environment	**PO_ie**	0.768	0.777	0.851	0.589
PO_ie1	0.765***				
PO_ie2	0.712***				
PO_ie3	0.824***				
PO_ie4	0.763***				
Public supervision	**PO_s**	0.910	0.918	0.930	0.657
PO_s1	0.829***				
PO_s2	0.880***				
PO_s3	0.889***				
PO_s4	0.856***				
PO_s5	0.861***				
PO_s6	0.672***				
PO_s7	0.649***				
Green dynamic capability	**GDC**	**0.843**	**0.846**	**0.889**	**0.616**
GDC1	0.759***				

(continued)

Table 2 (continued)

Latent variables	Loadings (λ)	CA (>0.7)	rho_A (>0.7)	CR (>0.7)	AVE (>0.5)
GDC2	0.800***				
GDC3	0.847***				
GDC4	0.791***				
GDC5	0.721***				
Green competitive advantage	**GCA**	**0.805**	**0.809**	**0.873**	**0.634**
GCA1	0.816***				
GCA2	0.819***				
GCA3	0.841***				
GCA4	0.701***				

Source: Author's computation, 2023
*** denotes significant loadings above

Table 3 Discriminant validity of variables (Fornell-Larcker criterion)

Constructs	GCA	GDB	GDC
Green competitive advantage (GCA)	**0.796**		
Green development behavior (GDB)	0.713	**0.676**	
Green dynamic capability (GDC)	0.609	0.714	**0.785**

Table 4 Discriminant validity of variables (HTMT ratio)

Constructs	GCA	GDB	GDC
Green competitive advantage (GCA)			
Green development behavior (GDB)	0.807		
Green dynamic capability (GDC)	0.738	0.795	–

was shown in the model estimation ($\beta = 0.595$, $t = 8.827$, $p < 0.05$). The association's statistical significance supports Hypothesis 1.

The second hypothesis asserts a positive correlation between green dynamic capability and green competitive advantage. The positive association between the variables is shown in the model estimation ($\beta = 0.249$; $t = 3.054$, $p < 0.05$). The association's statistical significance supports Hypothesis 2.

Hypothesis 3 states that green dynamic capability moderates the relationship between green and development behavior and green competitive advantage. The positive association between the variables, as shown in the model estimation ($\beta = 0.152$; $t = 2.581$, $p < 0.05$), remains significant. The association's statistical significance supports Hypothesis 3.

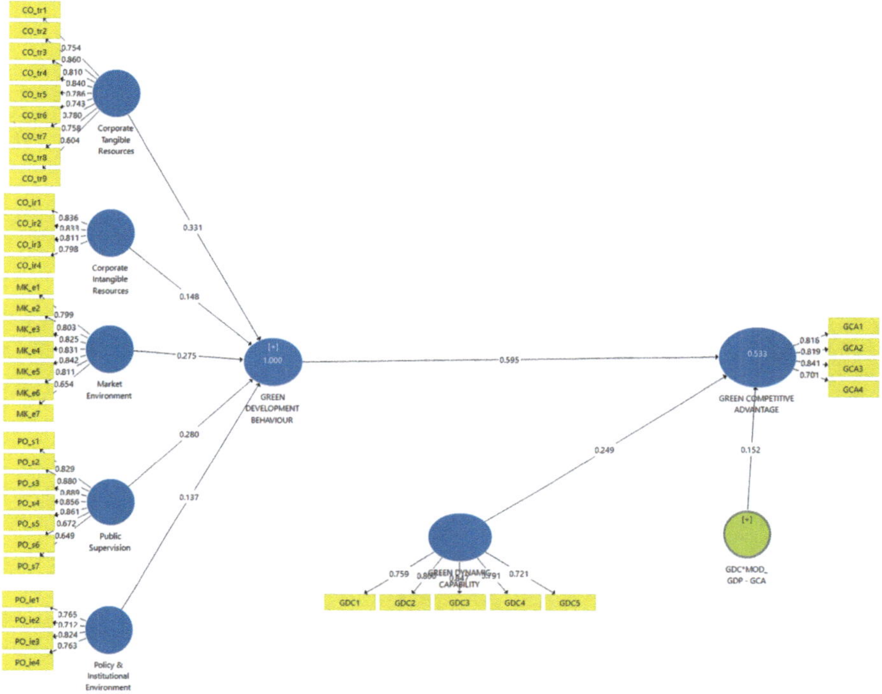

Fig. 2 Assessment of structural model. Note: ** $p < 0.05$. *Source*: Author's computation

Discussion and Conclusion

This study analyzes the effect of both green development behavior and competitive advantage by considering the moderating role of green dynamic capability. The author used 351 valid questionnaires from Nigerian agro-based manufacturing enterprises to demonstrate support for both direct and indirect paths. The following aspects of this research reflect its key findings:

First, H1, which posits that green development, also referred to as enterprise development behavior, has a significant impact on green competitive advantage, was supported. This result is consistent with the view that academics and practitioners have recently encouraged firms to exhibit GDB. Porter and van der Linde (1995), for instance, argue that considering environmental sustainability as an additional cost of doing business is a false perspective; instead, we should view it as a win-win strategy to boost competitiveness. Lee and Kim (2011) point out that the fundamental idea of suppliers' participation in green product development is to provide a competitive advantage and support the win-win logic of green and competition.

Relevant literature supports the second hypothesis by showing that dynamic capabilities help firms gain an advantage even in the green economy (Ambrosini & Bowman, 2009; Eisenhardt & Martin, 2000; Khan et al., 2019; Salunke et al., 2019; Teece, 2018; Zahra et al., 2006). Meanwhile, the reason for this may be that

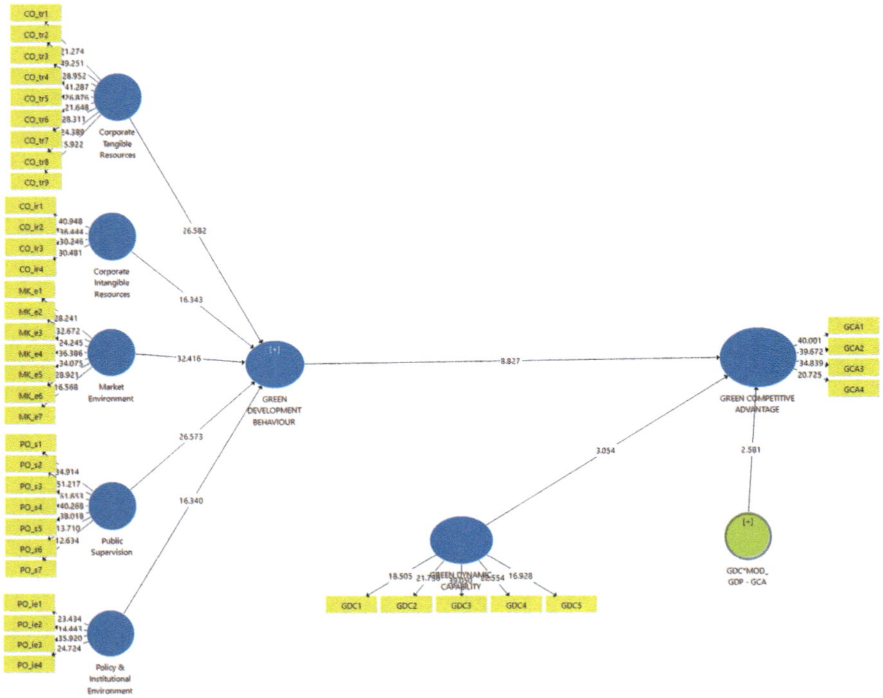

Fig. 3 *t*-statistics

Table 5 Hypotheses testing

Hypothesis	Parameters	β	SE	t-value	R^2	p-value	F	
	Direct effects							
H1	GDB → GCA	0.595	0.067	8.827	0.533	0.000	0.342	Significant
H2	GDC → GCA	0.249	0.083	3.054	0.533	0.002	0.054	Significant
	Indirect effect							
H3	GDC*MOD_ GDB → GCA	0.152	0.073	2.581	–	0.001	0.106	Significant

Source: Own work

Notes. *GDB* Green development behavior, *GCA* Green competitive advantage, *GDC* Green dynamic capability

agro-based enterprises establish contacts with different kinds of external actors (such as suppliers, wholesalers, and retailers) in the process of green production, enhancing their internal and external resource integration capabilities to compete and gain an edge over rivalries.

Achieving a competitive edge and producing ecologically sustainable products are both within the capabilities of organizations with strong GDC (Dangelico et al., 2017). Companies with GDC are better able to meet customer demand for environmentally friendly products and comply with strict environmental requirements, according to previous research (Demirel & Kesidou, 2019). Meanwhile, adopting GDC and presenting a positive image of environmental responsibility and behavior can help businesses gain a competitive edge and attract consumers who are environmentally sensitive (Sarwar et al., 2023; Li et al., 2022).

Companies have presented the concept of green dynamic capability to further the cause of sustainable development and environmental protection in response to the worldwide need for such measures. The enterprise's green dynamic capability is an important asset that focuses on eco-friendly development policies, technological advancements, consumer demand, and internal and external resources for environmental protection. It also includes the ability to integrate, build, and reconfigure these resources. According to Kleinbaum and Stuart (2014) and Li and Liu (2014), businesses that can adapt quickly to changes in their environment are better able to meet the demands of their customers and the market, as well as gain an advantage over their competitors.

Finally, green dynamic capability positively moderates the relationship between green development behavior and green competitive advantage. This result of the third hypothesis affirms the fact that the higher the dynamic capability developed in the green economy, the better agro-based firms compete, considering the careful consideration of green development behavior. Hence, the dimension of GDB, if keenly considered by managers of agro-based firms, would result in gaining a competitive edge.

Since dynamic capabilities emerge as a critical factor in maintaining a company's competitive advantage (Teece, 2007; Nguyen et al., 2023), their moderating role remains a valuable support through the relevance of green development behavior. Companies equipped with green dynamic capabilities possess the ability to integrate knowledge from diverse sectors and channel it into innovation, effectively converting potential opportunities into business advantages. By being attuned to environmental changes, businesses can collect and utilize market information, promptly identifying opportunities and threats.

Implications in Theory and Practice

An environmental strategy can improve the competitive advantage of agro-based manufacturing enterprises, even though environmental activities are not without their risks and costs. Establishing an environmental strategy to achieve GCA should be a top priority for agro-allied firm management. Executives and staff at agro-allied businesses would do well to attend seminars and classes focused on environmental strategy. Achieving environmental goals should be a metric for management and staff advancement in agro-based manufacturing companies.

Secondly, the research provides data gathered from a real-world context, specifically the manufacturing sector in a developing nation like Nigeria. Sustainable development, which seeks to balance economic, environmental, and social goals, has replaced economic growth as the primary emphasis of manufacturing (agro-based) business in developing nations (Higgins-Desbiolles et al., 2019). Past literature has sadly failed to investigate how the agricultural production industry in developing nations might gain a competitive edge through environmentally conscious business practices (Ahmed Mustafi et al., 2024; Amir & Dhyani, 2018; Martínez-Falcó et al., 2023). This study, the first of its kind in agro-based management, explains green development behavior and green dynamic capacities for the sector in an emerging country like Nigeria. Because there is still a lack of research on the topic, this study fills a significant knowledge gap by providing abundant evidence that agro-allied enterprises in developing nations can gain a competitive edge through green business. As a result, our research model provides valuable insights for scholars in developing nations who wish to investigate how green development behavior and green dynamic capability contribute to the rise of the manufacturing (agro-based) sector in these countries.

Furthermore, the results show that green dynamic capability significantly promotes green development behavior to gain a green competitive advantage. Therefore, Nigerian agro-based firms should focus on improving their green dynamic capability to arrive at a green edge. Specifically, it is necessary for business managers to establish professional environmental protection agencies and establish close collaboration with product design, manufacturing, marketing, and other departments to facilitate efficient and quick access to customers' environmental requirements for products and to understand the industry's green innovation and green development trends in a timely manner to improve environmental information insight capability. Finally, the researcher also argues that agro-allied company managers should use green dynamic capabilities to their advantage from a resource-based standpoint. An agro-based manufacturing company can achieve and maintain GDC by conducting operations in accordance with a strategy that prioritizes green dynamic capability.

Limitations and Future Research

While planning future studies, it is important to keep in mind the study's limitations. The rapid collection of sample data via the survey questionnaire was one step. When determining the outcome of a causal relationship between variables, this cross-sectional data could be misleading. As a result, to further investigate the factors' relationships, future studies should gather longitudinal data and apply time-series approaches. Furthermore, due to the ineffective management of several exogenous variables, the survey questionnaire is not ideal for evaluating causal linkages. Future studies should use alternative research strategies, such as experiments, to verify the findings of this study's research model. Thirdly, this study tested hypotheses using data sampled from Nigeria's agro-allied industry. Any conclusions drawn from data collected in one country may not be applicable to other situations. The research framework must understand the significant role of various social, cultural, political, and economic factors in shaping the green business challenges of the agro-allied industry. Importantly, researchers must compare these contextual impacts. In future studies, it is important for researchers to consider how factors such as top management roles, organizational culture, CSR initiatives, green innovation, and green service innovation affect the competitive advantage of agro-based manufacturing companies. We need to conduct more studies and introduce control variables to identify these factors.

Conclusion

Corporations, such as agro-allied firms, must optimally distribute their resources across solutions to adapt to the complex and ever-changing world, all while facing resource pressures and turbulent conditions. Organizations need to be nimble if they want to stay afloat in today's cutthroat business environment. A company needs to think about who its stakeholders are and what they want. How a company interacts with its natural surroundings is one factor that an environmental orientation plan considers. Desirably, the NRBV states that a company's environmental strategy and its connection to nature might help it gain a competitive edge. To explain how GDB influences GCA, the researcher theorized that GDC acts as a moderator. The study contributes empirically to the existing understanding of how green development behavior and green dynamic capability being an environmental strategy impacts the competitive advantage of agro-allied enterprises.

References

Ab Hamid, M. R., Sami, W., & Sidek, M. M. (2017, September). Discriminant validity assessment: Use of Fornell & Larcker criterion versus HTMT criterion. In Journal of physics: Conference series (Vol. 890, No. 1, p. 012163). IOP Publishing.

Abubakar, A., Belwal, S., Mohammed, N., & Mohammed, U. D. (2022). Sustainable competitive advantage through corporate social responsibility (CSR) and green behavior strategies. *Discrete Dynamics in Nature and Society, 2022*, 1–8.

Ahmed Mustafi, M. A., Dong, Y. J., & Hosain, M. S. (2024). The mediating role of perceived competitive advantage on the relationships between green supply chain management practices and operational performance: Evidence from Bangladeshi manufacturing firms. *Benchmarking: An International Journal.*

Ambrosini, V., & Bowman, C. (2009). What are dynamic capabilities and are they a useful construct in strategic management? *International Journal of Management Reviews, 11*(1), 29–49.

Amir, M., & Dhyani, A. (2018). Measuring the influence of green-marketing practices on firms' competitive advantage: A study of selected food and beverage companies. *NICE Journal of Business, 13*(2), 57–72.

Anabaraonye, B., Okafor, J. C., & Eriobu, C. M. (2019). Green entrepreneurial opportunities in climate change adaptation and mitigation for sustainable development in Nigeria. *Journal of Environmental Pollution Management, 2*(2), 102.

Anderson, J. C., & Gerbing, D. W. (1988). Structural equation modeling in practice: A review and recommended two-step approach. *Psychological Bulletin, 103*(3), 411–423.

Andres, L. (2012). *Designing and doing survey research.* Sage.

Aribaba, F. O., Ahmodu, O. A., Olaleye, B. R., & Yusuff, S. A. (2019). Ownership structure and organizational performance in selected listed manufacturing companies, Nigeria. *Journal of business Studies and Management Review, 3*(1), 9–14.
Aslam, H., Rashid, K., Wahla, A. R., & Tahira, U. (2018). Drivers of green supply chain management practices and their impact on firm performance: A developing country perspective. *Journal of Quantitative Methods, 2*(1), 87–113.
Astuti, D. A., & Datrini, L. K. (2021). Green competitive advantage: Examining the role of environmental consciousness and green intellectual capital. *Management Science. Letters, 11*, 1141–1415.
Awang, Z. (2015). SEM Made Simple: A Gentle Approach to Learning Structural Equation Modelling. SEM Made Simple: A Gentle Approach to Learn Structural Equation Modelling. Bandar Baru Bangi, Malaysia: MPWS Rich Publ.
Bahadır, F., Yeşiltaş, M., Sesen, H., & Olaleye, B. R. (2024). The relation between perceived organizational support and employee satisfaction: The role of relational psychological contract and reciprocity ideology. *Kybernetes, 53*(1), 102–122.
Barney, J. (1991). Firm resources and sustained competitive advantage. *Journal of Management, 17*(1), 99–120.
Charoensukmongkol, P. (2023). The interaction of organizational politics and political skill on employees' exposure to workplace cyberbullying: The conservation of resources theory perspective. *Asia-Pacific Journal of Business Administration.* https://doi.org/10.1108/APJBA-08-2022-0364
Chen, Y. S., & Chang, C. H. (2013). The determinants of green product development performance: Green dynamic capabilities, green transformational leadership, and green creativity. *Journal of Business Ethics, 116*, 107–119.
Chen, Y. S., Lai, S. B., & Wen, C. T. (2006). The influence of green innovation performance on corporate advantage in Taiwan. *Journal of Business Ethics, 67*, 331–339.
Chen, Y. S., Lin, Y. H., Lin, C. Y., & Chang, C. W. (2015). Enhancing green absorptive capacity, green dynamic capacities and green service innovation to improve firm performance: An analysis of structural equation modeling (SEM). *Sustainability, 7*(11), 15674–15692.
Chin, W. W., Marcolin, B. L., & Newsted, P. R. (2003). A partial least squares latent variable modeling approach for measuring interaction effects: Results from a Monte Carlo simulation study and an electronic-mail emotion/adoption study. *Information Systems Research, 14*(2), 189–217.
Dangelico, R. M., Pujari, D., & Pontrandolfo, P. (2017). Green product innovation in manufacturing firms: A sustainability-oriented dynamic capability perspective. *Business Strategy and the Environment, 26*(4), 490–506.
Davies, P., Hernandez, M. P., & Wyatt, T. (2019). Economy versus environment: How corporate actors harm both. *Critical Criminology, 27*(1), 85–99.
De Roeck, K., & Farooq, O. (2018). Corporate social responsibility and ethical leadership: Investigating their interactive effect on employees' socially responsible behaviors. *Journal of Business Ethics, 151*(4), 923–939.
Demirel, P., & Kesidou, E. (2019). Sustainability-oriented capabilities for eco-innovation: Meeting the regulatory, technology, and market demands. *Business Strategy and the Environment, 28*(5), 847–857.
Dumont, J., Shen, J., & Deng, X. (2017). Effects of green HRM practices on employee workplace green behavior: The role of psychological green climate and employee green values. *Human Resource Management, 56*(4), 613–627.
Eisenhardt, K. M., & Martin, J. A. (2000). Dynamic capabilities: What are they? *Strategic Management Journal, 21*(1011), 1105–1121.
Falk, R. F., & Miller, N. B. (1992). *A primer for soft modeling*. University of Akron Press.
Fatoki, O. (2021). Environmental orientation and green competitive advantage of hospitality firms in South Africa: Mediating effect of green innovation. *Journal of Open Innovation: Technology, Market, and Complexity, 7*(4), 223.
Fornell, C., & Larcker, D. F. (1981). Evaluating structural equation models with unobservable variables and measurement error. *Journal of Marketing Research, 18*(1), 39–50.

Freitas, W. R. D. S. J. H., Caldeira-Oliveira, A. A., Teixeira, N. O. S., & Teixeira, T. B. (2020). Green human resource management and corporate social responsibility. *Bench marking: An International Journal, 27*(4), 1551–1569.

González-Rodríguez, M. R., Díaz-Fernández, M. C., Shi, F., & Okumus, F. (2021). Exploring the links among corporate social responsibility, reputation, and performance from a multi-dimensional perspective. *International Journal of Hospitality Management, 99*, 103079.

Habib, M. A., Bao, Y., Ilmudeen, A., & Soobaroyen, T. (2020). The impact of green entrepreneurial orientation, market orientation and green supply chain management practices on sustainable firm performance. *Cogent Business & Management, 7*(1), 1743616.

Hart, S. L. (1995). A natural-resource-based view of the firm. *Academy of Management Review, 20*(4), 986–1014.

Hart, S. L., & Dowell, G. (2011). Invited editorial: A natural-resource-based view of the firm: Fifteen years after. *Journal of Management, 37*(5), 1464–1479.

Henseler, J., Ringle, C. M., & Sarstedt, M. (2015). A new criterion for assessing discriminant validity in variance-based structural equation modeling. *Journal of the Academy of Marketing Science, 43*, 115–135.

Higgins-Desbiolles, F., Moskwa, E., & Wijesinghe, G. (2019). How sustainable is sustainable hospitality research? A review of sustainable restaurant literature from 1991 to 2015. *Current Issues in Tourism, 22*(13), 1551–1580.

Hossain, M. A., Amin, R., Masud, A. A., Hossain, M. I., Hossen, M. A., & Hossain, M. K. (2023). What drives people's behavioral intention toward telemedicine? An emerging economy perspective. *SAGE Open, 13*(3), 21582440231181394.

Ilyas, S., Hu, Z., & Wiwattanakornwong, K. (2020). Unleashing the role of top management and government support in green supply chain management and sustainable development goals. *Environmental Science and Pollution Research, 27*(8), 8210–8223. https://doi.org/10.1007/s11356-019-07268-3

Iyer, R. D. (2017). Developing and validating a questionnaire to measure some factors of school culture: A psychometric process. *Prabandhan: Indian Journal of Management, 10*(11), 7–18.

Khan, S. Z., Yang, Q., & Waheed, A. (2019). Investment in intangible resources and capabilities spurs sustainable competitive advantage and firm performance. *Corporate Social Responsibility and Environmental Management, 26*(2), 285–295.

Kim, H., Woo, E., Uysal, M., & Kwon, N. (2018). Effects of corporate social responsibility (CSR) on employee well-being in the hospitality industry. *International Journal of Con temporary Hospitality Management, 30*(3), 1584–1600.

Kleinbaum, A. M., & Stuart, T. (2014). Network responsiveness: The social structural micro foundations of dynamic capabilities. *Academy of Management Perspectives, 28*(4), 353–367.

Kline, T. J. (2005). *Psychological testing: A practical approach to design and evaluation*. Sage Publications.

Kock, N., & Lynn, G. (2012). Lateral collinearity and misleading results in variance-based SEM: An illustration and recommendations. *Journal of the Association for Information Systems, 13*(7), 5436–5580.

Lee, K., & Kim, J. (2011). Integrating suppliers into green product innovation development: An empirical case study in the semiconductor industry. *Business Strategy and the Environment, 20*(8), 527–538.

Li, X., Du, J., & Long, H. (2019). Theoretical framework and formation mechanism of the green development system model in China. *Environment and Development, 2019*(32), 100465.

Li, X., Du, J., & Long, H. (2020a). Understanding the green development behavior and performance of industrial enterprises (GDBP-IE): Scale development and validation. *International Journal of Environmental Research and Public Health, 17*(5), 1716.

Li, X., Du, J., & Long, H. (2020b). Mechanism for green development behavior and performance of industrial enterprises (GDBP-IE) using partial least squares structural equation modeling (PLS-SEM). *International Journal of Environmental Research and Public Health, 17*(22), 8450.

Li, D., & Liu, J. (2014). Dynamic capabilities, environmental dynamism, and competitive advantage: Evidence from China. *Journal of Business Research, 67*(1), 2793–2799.

Li, D., Tang, F., & Zhang, L. (2020). Differential effects of voluntary environmental programs and mandatory regulations on corporate green innovation. *Natural Hazards, 103*(3), 3437–3456.
Li, W., Waris, I., Sun, C., Hameed, I., Bhutto, M., & Ali, R. (2022). Understanding the role of corporate social responsibility and sustainable supply chain management in shaping the consumers' intention to use sharing platforms. *Frontiers in Psychology, 13*, 970444.
Lin, Y. H., & Chen, Y. S. (2017). Determinants of green competitive advantage: The roles of green knowledge sharing, green dynamic capabilities, and green service innovation. *Quality and Quantity, 51*, 1663–1685.
Martínez-Falcó, J., Sánchez-García, E., Millan-Tudela, L. A., & Marco-Lajara, B. (2023). The role of green agriculture and green supply chain management in the green intellectual capital–sustainable performance relationship: A structural equation modeling analysis applied to the Spanish wine industry. *Agriculture, 13*(2), 425.
May, A. Y. C., Hao, G. S., & Carter, S. (2021). Intertwining corporate social responsibility, employee green behavior, and environmental sustainability: The mediation effect of organizational trust and organizational identity. *Economics, Management & Financial Markets, 16*(2), 32–61.
Menguc, B., & Ozanne, L. K. (2005). Challenges of the 'green imperative': A natural resource-based approach to the environmental orientation-business performance relationship. *Journal of Business Research, 58*(4), 440–438.
Merli, R., Preziosi, M., Acampora, A., & Ali, F. (2019). Why should hotels go green? Insights from guests experience in green hotels. *International Journal of Hospitality Management, 81*, 169–179.
Naidoo, M., & Gasparatos, A. (2018). Corporate environmental sustainability in the retail sector: Drivers, strategies and performance measurement. *Journal of Cleaner Production, 203*, 125–142.
Nguyen, X. H., Nguyen, K. L., Nguyen, T. V. H., Nguyen, T. T. H., & Ta, V. L. (2023). The impact of green organizational capabilities on competitive advantage of construction enterprises in Vietnam: The mediating role of green innovation. *Sustainability, 15*(16), 12371.
Norton, T. A., Zacher, H., Parker, S. L., & Ashkanasy, N. M. (2017). Bridging the gap between green behavioral intentions and employee green behavior: The role of green psychological climate. *Journal of Organizational Behavior, 38*(7), 996–1015.
Olajide, O. A., Kwak, D. W., He, Q., & Lim, M. (2019). A conceptual framework of environmental sustainability in the oil and gas supply chains: Natural resource-based view (NRBV) and institutional theory approaches. In Proceedings of the 24th international symposium on logistics (ISL 2019) (pp. 95–103). Centre for Concurrent Enterprise, Nottingham University.
Olaleye, B. R. (2023). Influence of eco-product innovation and firm reputation on corporate social responsibility and competitive advantage: A mediation-moderation analysis. *Journal of Public Affairs, 23*(4), e2878.
Olaleye, B. R., Abdurrashid, I., & Mustapha, B. (2023). Organizational sustainability and TQM practices in hospitality industry: Employee-employer perception. *The TQM Journal.*
Olaleye, B. R., Ali-Momoh, B. O., Herzallah, A., Sibanda, N., & Aminat, F. A. (2021). Dimensional context of total quality management practices and organizational performance of SMEs in Nigeria: Evidence from mediating role of entrepreneurial orientation. *International Journal of Operations and Quantitative Management, 21*(4), 399–415.
Ones, D. S., & Dilchert, S. (2012). Employee green behaviors. *Managing Human Resources for Environmental Sustainability, 32*, 85–116.
Oyebanji, I. J., Bamidele, A., Khobai, H., & Le Roux, P. (2017). Green growth and environmental sustainability in Nigeria. *International Journal of Energy Economics and Policy, 7*(4), 216–223.
Peng, J., Yin, K., Hou, N., Zou, Y., & Nie, Q. (2020). How to facilitate employee green behavior: The joint role of green transformational leadership and green human resource management practice. *Acta Psychologica Sinica, 52*(9), 1105.
Porter, M. E. (1985a). *Competitive strategy*. The Free Press.
Porter, M. E. (1985b). *Creating and sustaining superior performance*. The Free Press.

Porter, M. E., & Van der Linde, C. (1995). Toward a new conception of the environment competitiveness relationship. *The Journal of Economic Perspectives, 9*(4), 97–118.

Qing, W., Amin, M. B., Gazi, M. A. I., Khan, W., Al Masud, A., & Alam, M. N. (2023). Mediation effect of technology adaptation capabilities between the relationship of service quality attributes and customer satisfaction: An investigation on young customers perceptions toward e-commerce in China. *IEEE Access, 11*, 123904–123923.

Salunke, S., Weerawardena, J., & McColl-Kennedy, J. R. (2019). The central role of knowledge integration capability in service innovation-based competitive strategy. *Industrial Marketing Management, 76*, 144–156.

Sarwar, H., Aftab, J., Ishaq, M. I., & Atif, M. (2023). Achieving business competitiveness through corporate social responsibility and dynamic capabilities: An empirical evidence from emerging economy. *Journal of Cleaner Production, 386*, 135820.

Shahzad, M., Qu, Y., Javed, S. A., Zafar, A. U., & Rehman, S. U. (2020). Relation of environment sustainability to CSR and green innovation: A case of Pakistani manufacturing industry. *Journal of Cleaner Production, 253*, 119938.

Somjai, S., & Jermsittiparsert, K. (2019). Role of pressures and green supply chain management practices in enhancing the operational efficiency of firms: Evidence from Thailand. *International Journal of Supply Chain Management, 8*(4), 437–445.

Teece, D. J. (2007). Explicating dynamic capabilities: The nature and micro foundations of (sustainable) enterprise performance. *Strategic Management Journal, 28*, 1319–1350.

Teece, D. J. (2018). Business models and dynamic capabilities. *Long Range Planning, 51*(1), 40–49.

Teece, D. J., Pisano, G., & Shuen, A. (1997). Dynamic capabilities and strategic management. *Strategic Management Journal, 18*(7), 509–533.

Unsworth, K. L., Davis, M. C., Russell, S. V., & Bretter, C. (2020). Employee green behavior: HOW organizations can help the environment. *Current Opinion in Psychology, 42*, 1–6.

Vetbuje, B. G., & Olaleye, B. R. (2022). Relationship between emotional intelligence, emotional labour, job stress, and burnout: Does coping strategy work? *Journal of Intelligence Studies in Business, 12*(1), 6–19.

Wallace, G. T., Barrett, K. C., Henry, K. L. et al. (2023). Examining underlying structures of cognitive emotion regulation strategies using exploratory structural equation modeling. *Qual Quant 57*, 4171–4192. https://doi.org/10.1007/s11135-022-01531-5

Wang, H., Khan, M. A. S., Anwar, F., Shahzad, F., Adu, D., & Murad, M. (2021). Green innovation practices and its impacts on environmental and organizational performance. *Frontiers in Psychology, 11*, 553625.

Yusliza, M. Y., Yong, J. Y., Tanveer, M. I., Ramayah, T., Faezah, J. N., & Muhammad, Z. (2020). A structural model of the impact of green intellectual capital on sustainable performance. *Journal of Cleaner Production, 249*, 119334.

Zahra, S. A., Sapienza, H. J., & Davidsson, P. (2006). Entrepreneurship and dynamic capabilities: A review, model and research agenda. *Journal of Management Studies, 43*(4), 917–955.

The Nexus Between Corporate Cash Holdings and Corporate Financialisation in Listed South African Non-financial Firms

Trust Chireka and Abor Yeboah

Abstract South Africa continues to experience symptoms of premature deindustrialisation and a stagnant economy wherein non-financial corporations have increased the proportions of the cash holdings and financialisation. This study investigates whether the gains from corporate financialisation, driven by the growth of shareholder value ideology, influence the cash holding behaviour of non-financial firms. There have been observable patterns of increasing cash holdings, reduced real investment, and increased participation in financial activities by traditionally non-financial corporations. There remains a dearth of empirical studies that investigate whether corporate cash holdings are driven by the financialisation of non-financial firms. We analyse panel data of NCFs listed on the South African, Johannesburg Stock Exchange (JSE) covering a period from 2000 to 2020. This study finds that the financialisation of investments and operations of non-financial firms positively drives corporate cash holdings. Cash holdings provide firms with the flexibility to invest in profitable but short-term financial investments. By showing the confluence between corporate financialisation and corporate cash holdings, this study can assist policymakers in understanding how shareholder value maximisation ideology has transformed corporate strategy from the traditional 'retain and reinvest' to 'dominate and distribute' and to 'downsize and distribute'. This study provides a new way of understanding the drivers of cash holdings of NCFs listed on the JSE. The increasing financialisation of South African NCFs is enabled by high corporate cash holdings.

Keywords Corporate cash holdings · Corporate financialisation · Non-financial corporations · Johannesburg stock exchange

---

T. Chireka (✉) · A. Yeboah
Walter Sisulu University, Mthatha, South Africa
e-mail: tchireka@wsu.ac.za; ayeboah@wsu.ac.za

T. Moloi (ed.), *Impacting Society Positively Through Technology in Accounting and Business Processes*, Springer Proceedings in Business and Economics,
https://doi.org/10.1007/978-3-031-84885-8_56

Introduction

Since the 1980s, the global economy has witnessed a growing trend towards financialisation. This shift has gathered pace with non-financial corporations (NCFs) increasing their share of financial assets in what has been viewed as a race to financialise (Wang, 2019). The study averred that NFCs have, in pursuit of higher returns from financial assets, forsaken their traditional role in the real economy for the virtual economy leaving some dire social and economic consequences in their trail. Financialisation, especially of NCFs, hampers sustained productive investments that are critical in enhancing industrialisation and physical-capital formation. This, in turn, derails the efforts to achieve inclusive and sustainable structural transformation, especially in emerging economies (Andreoni et al., 2021).

Large, dominant businesses that, in the past, expanded by keeping and reinvesting sizable portions of their profits (retain and reinvest) have shifted, since the emergence of shareholder value maximisation (SVM) ideology, first towards a 'dominate and distribute' system and then towards a 'downsize and distribute' one (Andreoni et al., 2023). Businesses that follow the 'retain and reinvest' policy can expand greatly in terms of size, productivity, and market share. Consequently, they can produce goods that are innovative, high-quality, and reasonably priced. The distribution of this value among the different 'stakeholders' in the company will be determined by how much each one can appropriate in terms of gains and how much the regulatory framework governing corporate governance permits. With stock markets serving as the primary institutional mechanism for removing capital from businesses, power has shifted from regulators to shareholders in increasingly unregulated markets, making highly profitable innovative firms more vulnerable to 'predatory value extraction' (Lazonick & Shin, 2019). As such, NCFs have increasingly shifted towards the 'downsize and distribute' strategy by financialising their investments and operations.

Alvarez (2015a, 2015b) further found that financialisation of non-financial firms (defined as the growing dependence on earnings generated from financial activities) significantly undercut the bargaining power of many social actors especially labour, while placing more power and wealth in the hands of shareholders and managers. In South Africa, various studies have chastised NCFs for sabotaging the structural transformation agenda by withholding investments to accentuate production, consumption, and technological transfer (Andreoni et al., 2021; Zalk, 2017). These firms have tended to cut back on real investments, increased cash holdings, and financial investments.

Davis (2018) found evidence supporting the hypothesis that one of the factors driving the growing cash holdings by non-financial corporates is the growing proclivity for these firms to engage in activities that generate financial income. This is consistent with the observations in financialisation literature that non-financial firms are increasingly providing financial services, which have traditionally been the domain of banks and other financial institutions (Krippner, 2011). A typical example is automobile companies that no longer limit their activities to manufacturing and selling automobiles, but now offer financing to their potential customers.

Despite the coincidence of rising corporate cash holdings and corporate financialisation of NCFs in emerging market economies, there is a dearth of empirical studies that examine the relationship between corporate cash holdings and financialisation of NCFs (Rabinovich & Pérez Artica, 2022). Davis (2018) found that United States of America (US) NFCs were conforming to the shareholder value ideology by increasing their cash holdings and growing their financial assets. The ideology of maximising shareholder value not only manifests itself in increasing shareholder payouts—in the form of dividends, share buybacks, and capital gains—but also in shifts in institutional and regulatory frameworks to enable growing transfers of profits to financial markets (Andreoni et al., 2021). Davis (2018) averred that US NFCs were increasingly motivated to hold more cash due to the growing opportunities to make huge profits from borrowing and lending money. Rabinovich and Pérez Artica (2022) reported similar findings for NCFs in Latin American economies.

While most corporate cash holdings studies in South Africa have viewed cash holdings as idle resources that inflict opportunity costs on shareholders, Karwowski et al. (2022) argued that corporate cash holdings are increasingly being held as interest-bearing financial assets. As such South African NFCs have become major lenders in the domestic economy. Despite these observations, studies are yet to empirically link corporate cash holdings and the financialisation of South African NFCs. This study thus investigates whether cash holdings of South African NFCs are influenced by corporate financialisation. We find a significantly positive relationship between corporate cash holdings and financialisation. This finding indicates that increasing financialisation leads to a higher preference, by South African NCFs, to hold more cash.

Literature Review

NCFs and Financialisation

Different motives have been cited for the shift, by non-financial firms, from traditional investments and sources of profits towards financial investments. First, there is a general acceptance that the global economy has stagnated since the 1970s, leaving little opportunities for profit generation from traditional activities such as consumption and investment (Magdoff & Sweezy, 1987; Davis, 2016). With demand slowing down, competition increasing due to globalisation, and the impasse between corporate and labour, the financial sector has been welcomed as a worthy and noiseless alternative for generating income (Orhangazi 2008; Davis, 2016).

The post-Keynesian theory of the firm posits that although managers have a long-term preference for corporate expansion, either organically or by acquisitions, shareholders, on the other hand, prefer profits (Rabinovich, 2019). With shareholders gaining more power through hostile take-over and share-based remuneration, Rabinovich and Pérez Artica (2022) explained that non-financial firms have increasingly neglected real investments in favour of financial investments. Indeed, literature documents that shareholder ideology has shifted towards promoting managerial short-termism where 'value' is viewed to be synonymous with share price, which in turn results in higher corporate cash holdings. For instance, the proliferation of stock-based compensation provides an explicit motivation for managers to prioritise the short-term share price increases over longer-term performance. Cash holdings afford managers the flexibility to redirect funds towards share price-based indicators of firm performance when the firm's share price falls or when the firm misses the financial market-based performance targets (Davis, 2018).

Corporate Financialisation and Corporate Cash Holdings in South Africa

In the past three decades, South Africa has witnessed a surge in corporate cash holdings (Chireka & Moloi, 2023) complemented with low investment rates (Karwowski et al., 2022). Against this backdrop, it is no surprise that several academics have investigated the drivers of the observed cash hoarding (Chireka & Fakoya, 2017: Keeton, 2018). At one end, NCFs have been accused of being unpatriotic and holding the country to ransom by simply not investing (Mbindwane, 2015). A number of empirical studies have however found some justifications for corporate cash holdings. For instance, Keeton (2018) and Nyamgero (2015) argued that corporate cash holdings by South African firms were consistent with global trends. NCFs were also found to be, justifiably, holding cash for precautionary and transactional motives (Chireka & Fakoya, 2017; Thompson, 2021). However, most of these studies have not implicitly tested the speculative motive of holding cash.

A nascent strand of literature has observed that non-financial firms in South Africa are increasingly curtailing long-term investments, such as expanding productive capacities and infrastructural investments, in favour of short-term and often speculative financial instruments (Ashman et al. 2011). Karwowski (2018) also highlighted the growing importance of the speculative motive in explaining the accumulative growth of NCFs' financial investments. Karwowski (2018) identified this phenomenon as the financialisation of NCFs and measured it as the expansion of financial assets relative to real activity. The primary role of NCFs is the development of productive capabilities and infrastructure. When NCFs abandon their role as drivers of real investment for financial investments, as seen in the accumulation of financial assets and other liquid assets, there are sufficient grounds to suspect that the financialisation of NFCs is well underway.

Donnelley (2017) recorded that, as of February 2017, South African NCFs were sitting on cash piles equating to 17% of the national GDP (approximately R719 billion). Karwowski (2018) argued that the estimation by Donnelley (2017) underestimated the real extent of the corporate liquidity holdings as corporates held liquid assets in different forms. For instance, corporates can keep time deposits with domestic banks, allowing them to earn interest on their deposits. Firms can also invest in various financial instruments such as low risk (and low yielding) government bonds or more innovative, high risk and high-yielding instruments such as financial derivatives. Karwowski (2018) postulated that such instruments can generate more income than the traditional firms' productive operations.

Nascent literature documents evidence of NCFs, South Africa not an exception, cutting back on real investment in favour of more speculative short-term and financial investments to generate shareholder value (Karwowski, 2018; Ashman et al., 2021). Several empirical studies find evidence to the effect that financialisation has an adverse impact on physical investment of NCFs (Barradas & Lagoa, 2017). However, there remains a dearth of studies that investigate whether the lures of financialisation can explain the corporate cash holdings. Davis (2018) found a positive relationship between the cash holdings of US NCFs and net interest income earned from financial assets. This finding gives credence to the hypothesis that US NCFs hold more cash to engage in financial activities. In their study domiciled in Latin American economies of Argentina, Brazil, Chile, Mexico, and Peru, Rabinovich and Pérez Artica (2022) found that interest income from financialisation was a significant determinant of NCFs' cash holdings in Brazil and Chile.

In the South African context, Karwowski et al. (2022) investigated the impact of financialisation on the cash holdings of South African NCFs. However, this study did not focus on Johannesburg Stock Exchange (JSE) listed firms. The study also made use of a database that limited the study period between 2010 and 2017. These limitations make the findings of Karwowski et al. (2022) incomparable to other studies that analysed at least two decades' worth of data from listed firms. This study fills this gap by investigating financialisation as a determinant of corporate cash holdings in listed South African NCFs. Our study period stretches from year 2000 to 2022 and hypothesises the following:

Ho: Corporate financialisation is significantly and positively related to corporate cash holdings.

Methodology

Research Design

This study follows a non-experimental approach as there is no planned treatment and no random assignment in the current investigation (Welman et al., 2005). In non-experimental research, the observed changes in the independent variable may be attributed to one or more dependent variables. The research employs a quantitative single-method approach, utilising archived data to gather pertinent financial, institutional, and macro-level characteristics. In particular, the correlational form of this study allows for the simultaneous analysis of cross-sectional and longitudinal trends in company cash holdings.

Research Sample and Data

We obtain firm specific financial data for JSE-listed NFCs from the IRESS database from the year 2000 to 2020. The sample consists of 149 NFCs equating to 2 392 firm observations. Data relating to institutional and macroeconomic conditions are sourced from the World Bank, Federal Reserve Economic Data (FRED), and Bureau for Economic Research (BER).

Measuring Corporate Financialisation

To measure corporate financialisation, this study follows the approach of Demir (2009) and Zhao and Su (2022) in using the ratio of financial assets to total assets. While other studies measure corporate financialisation using profit return, this measure is susceptible to movements on the financial markets. Financial assets include financial investments and loans.

Model Specifications

To estimate the relationship between corporate cash holdings and corporate financialisation, we adopt the methodology of Rabinovich and Pérez Artica (2022)

$$\text{Cash}_{i,t} = \alpha_0 + \alpha_1 \text{Cash}_{i,t-1} + \alpha_2 \text{Fin}_{i,t} + \sum_{k=0}^{n} \beta_l X_{i,t}^{f} + \sum_{k=0}^{n} \beta_l X_{i,t}^{l} + \sum_{k=0}^{n} \beta_l X_{i,t}^{m} + \varepsilon_{i,t} \quad (1)$$

where α is the constant term, $\alpha_0 \ldots \alpha_3$ are coefficients of the independent variables, and the i,t subscripts denote the ith firm at time period t. $\text{Fin}_{i,t}$ refers to the level of financialisation of firm I at time t. $X_{i,t}^{f}$ represent firm-specific factors, $X_{i,t}^{l}$ represent prevailing institutional conditions at time t, and X_{t}^{m} represent the obtaining macroeconomic factors at time t. β_l represent the parameters on the firm-specific, macroeconomic, and institutional control factors, from the kth factor to the nth.

The dependent variable, $\text{Cash}_{i,t}$ is defined as cash and cash equivalents, normalised by total assets. Cash includes any instruments or financial assets that can be converted to cash at short notice. On the independent variables, we modify the equation used by Davis (2018) by including the lagged value of Cash to factor in the dynamism of corporate cash holdings.

This study predicts that if NCFs are actively financialising, then the relationship between corporate cash holdings and financial assets will be statistically significant and positive.

This study is closest to Rabinovich and Pérez Artica (2022) who use a different proxy for financialisation of Latin American NCFs. However, the former do not

Table 1 Data description

Code	Description	Measurement
Dependent variable		
$Cash_{i,t}$	Corporate cash holdings	Cash and cash equivalents plus short-term investments over total assets
Independent variables		
Fin	Financial assets	Interest and dividends from investment securities over total assets
Control variables		
Firm-specific factors		
$SIZE_{i,t}$	Firm size	The natural logarithm of the book value of firm *i*'s total assets at time *t*
$LEV_{i,t}$	Leverage	The short-term debt, plus the long-term debt divide by the total assets of firm *i* at time *t*
$MTB_{i,t}$	Growth opportunity	The ratio of the market value of firm i at time *t*
$DIV_{i,t}$	Dividends	Dividends per share divided by earnings per share
$LIQ_{i,t}$	Liquid asset substitutes	Net working capital less cash divided by the total assets of firm *i* at time *t*
$CF_{i,t}$	Cash flow	Earnings after interest, dividends, and taxes, but before depreciation, deflated by total assets
$CAPEX_{i,t}$	Capital expenditure	Capital investment, deflated by total assets
Institutional factors		
FD	Financial development	Measured as an average of four proxy variables that describe the financial institutions and financial markets—depth, access, efficiency, and stability. (Available from the World Competitiveness Report, World Bank)
COR	Corruption	A publicly available measure that indicates the extent of the abuse of public power used for personal benefit, considering both small and large forms of corruption
Macro factors		
EPU	Economic policy uncertainty	The average of 12-monthly BBD indices within a fiscal year (developed by Baker et al., 2016)
BC	Business confidence	Business confidence is quantified by assessing the confidence that manufacturers, wholesalers, retailers, building contractors, and new vehicle sales dealers have about prevailing conditions
MP	Monetary policy	If the annual average interest rate increases, the monetary policy that year is contractionary (takes the value of 1); otherwise, it is expansionary (takes the value 0)
EG	Economic growth	The rate of change in gross domestic product (GDP)

control for institutional and macroeconomic factors that can influence corporate cash holdings decisions. This study, thus, extends Rabinovich and Pérez Artica (2022) study by investigating the role of financialisation in determining cash holdings by listed South African NCFs. Table 1 describes all the variables used in this investigation.

Summary Statistics

In Table 2 we show the summary statistics for the variables used in this study. The mean for CASH in the study sample is 0.164, showing that the average NCF on the JSE has 16% of its assets in cash. The mean for the main independent variable, corporate financialisation (Fin) is 0.077, greater than the median (0.006) suggesting that more than 50% of the firms have lower than average financial assets to total assets ratio. Table 3 presents the Pearson correlation matrix which shows that there is no high correlation (greater than 0.8) among the independent variables indicating no multicollinearity issues. This is also supported by the Variance Inflation Factor (VIF) test (Table 4), which shows that all variables have very low VIFs.

Ethical Considerations

The ethical clearance (SAREC20221124/04) for this study was granted by the e School of Accounting Research Ethics Committee (SAREC) at the University of Johannesburg.

Results

Table 4 presents the random effects (RE) and fixed effects (FE) estimation results from Eq. 1. The R-squared measure, for both RE and FE, is above 0.5 indicating the goodness of fit for the model used in this study. Our results show that financialisation (Fin) is positively related to Cash at the 1% significance level, and this is consistent in both RE and FE estimations. This shows that an increase in the proportion of financial assets held by NCFs is related to an increase in corporate cash holdings. We argue that NCFs might be increasing cash holdings for the speculative purposes of generating income from financial assets. This is consistent with Davis' (2018) findings that traditional US-based NCFs are increasing their participation in financial services, such as borrowing and lending, to generate financial income.

Relating to the firm specific control variables, we find that Size and Liq have negative impact of corporate cash holdings, while Lev, Capex, C_Flow, MTB, and Div exert positive influence on cash holdings. While these findings are consistent with previous South African studies (Chireka & Moloi, 2023), the negative impact of Lev and Capex on Cash is a departure from previous findings. We argue that when corporates actually borrow to increase cash holdings driven by the speculative motive. We further posit that South African NCFs increase capital expenditure when they have sufficiently high cash holdings.

With regard to institutional factors controlled for, this study finds that FD and Cor exert negative influence on cash holdings. The results indicate that better

Table 2 Descriptive statistics

	Cash	Fin	Size	Lev	Liq	Capex	C_Flow	Div	MTB	FD	BC	Corr	EPU	MP	EG
Mean	0,164	0,077	14,923	0,638	0,045	0,075	0,066	0,666	2,552	121,905	43,703	0,090	0,545	0,450	0,705
standard error	0,022	0,008	0,044	0,041	0,035	0,007	0,016	0,010	0,177	0,186	0,320	0,004	0,008	0,010	0,056
Median	0,069	0,006	15,147	0,466	0,048	0,035	0,043	1,000	1,510	124,094	40,500	0,020	0,495	0,000	1,044
Mode	0,000	0,000	15,820	0,610	-0,072	0,000	0,055	1,000	0,000	117,881	40,500	0,020	1,024	0,000	-0,987
Std Dev	1,093	0,389	2,154	2,002	1,729	0,339	0,781	0,472	8,634	9,176	15,768	0,210	0,375	0,498	2,762
Range	47,065	9,587	23,198	66,484	105,533	13,733	47,154	1,000	340,690	45,105	58,750	0,734	1,284	1,000	12,072
Min	0,000	0,000	6,342	0,000	-70,970	0,000	-32,174	0,000	-5,990	97,317	21,750	-0,184	0,059	0,000	-7,481
Max	47,065	9,587	29,540	66,484	34,562	13,733	14,980	1,000	334,700	142,422	80,500	0,550	1,343	1,000	4,591
Count	2425	2425	2425	2425	2425	2425	2425	2425	2392	2425	2425	2425	2425	2425	2425
Con. Lvl (95,0%)	0,044	0,015	0,086	0,080	0,069	0,013	0,031	0,019	0,346	0,365	0,628	0,008	0,015	0,020	0,110

Note: Table 2 shows the descriptive statistics for the variables used in this study. All variables are defined in full in Table 1

Table 3 Pearson correlation

	Fin	Size	Lev	Liq	Capex	C_Flow	Div	MTB	FD	BC	Corr	EPU	MP	EG
Fin	1													
Size	−0,126	1												
Lev	0,189	−0,191	1											
Liq	−0,127	0,027	−0,216	1										
Capex	0,418	−0,167	0,452	−0,026	1									
C_Flow	0,126	−0,017	0,346	−0,347	0,199	1								
Div	−0,060	0,198	−0,003	0,007	−0,036	0,026	1							
MTB	0,011	−0,041	0,041	−0,037	0,000	−0,669	0,071	1						
FD	−0,024	0,057	−0,036	−0,020	−0,014	−0,047	0,052	0,079	1					
BC	−0,012	−0,127	0,019	0,020	0,014	−0,021	0,081	0,098	0,244	1				
Corr	−0,010	−0,207	0,052	0,032	0,037	−0,002	0,022	0,036	−0,200	0,514	1			
EPU	−0,018	0,183	−0,047	−0,013	−0,043	−0,015	0,002	−0,031	0,277	−0,469	−0,622	1		
MP	0,005	0,078	−0,026	0,022	−0,036	−0,040	0,029	0,024	0,368	0,076	−0,105	0,532	1	
EG	−0,040	−0,142	0,008	0,017	−0,008	−0,014	0,088	0,076	0,278	0,768	0,496	−0,262	0,100	1

Note: This table presents the Pearson correlation matrix for the independent variables used in our analysis

Table 4 Variance inflation factors

Variable	VIF	1/VIF
BC	3.59	0,278
EPU	3.43	0,292
C_Flow	3.22	0,311
EG	2.99	0,334
MTB	2.60	0,385
Cor	2.40	0,416
MP	1.94	0,515
Lev	1.61	0,621
Capex	1.52	0,657
FD	1.50	0,666
Liq	1.39	0,719
Fin	1.25	0,799
Size	1.17	0,858
Div	1.09	0,921
Mean VIF	**2.12**	

Note: This table shows the VIFs calculated for the independent variables used in this study. All VIFs are less than 10 indicating that there is no multicollinearity among the independent variables

financial development and control of corruption reduces the need for corporate cash holdings. The other macroeconomic factors, EPU, MP, and EG are found to have no significant impact on the level of cash holdings (Table 5).

Robustness Test

We test whether our results are robust to an alternative measure of corporate financialisation. We use interest income and non-operating income net of interest income deflated by total assets (Fin 2) to proxy corporate financialisation. Interest income measures the interest and dividends derived from financial assets. This measure is different from the net interest income used by Davis (2018). Consistent with Rabinovich and Pérez Artica (2022), we do not subtract interest expenses from interest income as they include costs of financing productive activities. However, interest income does not capture other financial gains such as income generated from exchange rate movements and capital gains (Rabinovich & Pérez Artica, 2022). To capture these gains, we add another variable, non-operating income net of interest income and standardise it with total assets.

We find that the relationship between corporate cash holdings and financialisation still remains positive and significant at 1% level. Our main findings are thus robust to alternative measures of corporate financialisation (Table 6).

Other diagnostic tests, such as tests for normality, panel data unit root tests, test for serial correlation, and the Sargan test for overidentifying restrictions, were also

Table 5 Estimation results based on Eq. 1 for period 2000 to 2020

	Random Effects	Fixed Effects
Fin	0,2136***	0,2164***
	(0,0368)	(0,0395)
Size	−0,0375***	−0,0359***
	(0,0065)	0,0137
Lev	0,2041***	0,2125***
	(0,0081)	(0,0084)
Liq	−0,3288***	−0,3342***
	(0,0087)	(0,0089)
Capex	0,2343***	0,2178
	(0,0463)	(0,0479)
C_Flow	0,1711***	0,1592***
	(0,0292)	(0,0309)
Div	0,0950***	0,0574
	(0,0284)	(0,0357)
FD	−0,0029*	−0,0029*
	(0,0017)	(0,0017)
PTB	0,0049**	0,0049*
	(0,0024)	(0,0026)
Cor	−0,1629*	−0,1884*
	(0,0946)	(0,0962)
EPU	−0,0285	−0,0199
	(0,0547)	(0,0545)
MP	0,0425	0,0419
	(0,0340)	(0,0335)
EG	0,0023	0,0020
	(0,0060)	(0,0061)
Number of Obs	2392	2392
Number of groups	149	149
R-sq	0.5409	0.5304

Note: This table presents the estimations obtained by the random effects and fixed effects regression analysis. Standard errors are shown in parentheses. ***, **, and * represent statistical significance at 1%, 5%, and 10% respectively

conducted to ensure the reliability of the study's inferences. The results of these tests are available from the author on request.

Conclusion

Corporate financialisation and corporate cash holdings are two themes that have gained prominence in finance literature. Both result in the growth of the shareholder value conception and a growing preference, by NCFs, for financial investment over

Table 6 Estimation results using an alternative measure for financialisation

	RE	FE
Fin2	11,773***	12,166***
	(0,181)	(0,185)
Size	−0,017***	−0,046***
	(0,005)	(0,008)
Lev	−0,029***	−0,038***
	(0,006)	(0,006)
Liq	−0,112***	−0,106***
	(0,006)	(0,006)
Capex	−0,395***	−0,435***
	(0,028)	(0,028)
C_Flow	0,067***	0,057***
	(0,018)	(0,018)
MTB	0,003***	0,002
	(0,001)	(0,002)
Div	0,052***	0,053**
	(0,019)	(0,021)
FD	−0,001	−0,001
	(0,001)	(0,001)
BC	0,003***	0,003***
	(0,001)	(0,001)
Cor	−0,159***	−0,202***
	(0,056)	(0,057)
EPU	0,002	0,021
	(0,037)	(0,037)
MP	0,017	0,016
	(0,021)	(0,021)
EG	−0,005	−0,008*
	(0,005)	(0,005)
Number of observations	2390	2390
Number of groups	149	149
R-squared	0.651	0.628

Note: This table presents the estimations obtained by the random effects and fixed effects regression analysis when financialisation is measured as total of financial investment income and interest income deflated by total assets. Standard errors are shown in parentheses. ***, **, and * represent statistical significance at 1%, 5%, and 10%, respectively physical investment. The excessive pursuit of shareholder value incentivises short-term goals for managers and increases the need for cash holdings. Given the socio-economic ills that derive from a lack of physical investment, this study investigated the relationship between corporate cash holdings and financialisation.

We use data of JSE-listed NCFs from 2000 to 2020, measuring financialisation as the ratio of financial assets to total assets and investigating its impact of cash holdings. Our results show that corporate financialisation positively impacts corporate cash holdings. This is consistent with Davis (2018) who found that NCFs would increase cash holdings to distribute cash to shareholders as well as increase interest income from financial assets. Rabinovich and Pérez Artica (2022) explain that firms from developing economies were benefitting from arbitrage gains from differences in interest rates and exchange rate fluctuations. As such, these firms will increase both cash holdings and financial assets. Our results are contrary to Karwowski et al. (2022) who found no significant relationship between corporate cash holdings and financialisation in South African NCFs. However, their study focussed on unlisted firms which do not benefit from stock market mechanism to extract wealth (Lazonick & Shin, 2019). Andreoni et al. (2023) show that financialisation is associated with the allocative efficiency of the stock markets.

This study has important practical implications for policy makers who seek to drive real investment by NCFs. Regulators need to understand why financial investment has overtaken real investment as the preferred investment destination for NCFs. Social, institutional, and macroeconomic factors that might hamstring real investment need to be addressed if corporates are to have confidence to increase physical investment. For academics, this study adds to the burgeoning corporate financialisation literature by providing empirical evidence of its effect on cash holdings in South African NCFs. Future studies can focus on how financialisation affects other corporate fundamentals such as investment efficiency and capital structure. Studies could also investigate how institutional and macroeconomic environments impact on corporate financialisation.

References

Alvarez, I. (2015a). Financialization, non-financial corporations and income inequality: The case of France. *Socio-Economic Review, 13*(3), 449–475.

Alvarez, I. (2015b). Financialization, non-financial corporations and income inequality: The case of France. *Socio-Economic Review, 13*(3), 449–475. https://doi.org/10.1093/ser/mwv007

Andreoni, A., Robb, N. & Van Huellen, S. (2021). Profitability without investment: How financialization undermines structural transformation in South Africa. https://eprints.soas.ac.uk/35446/1/Pages%20from%209780192894311.pdf.

Andreoni, A., van Huellen, S. & Robb, N. (2023). Financialisation of non-financial corporations in South Africa: An integrated framework to study variations across sectors, value chains and firms. https://eprints.soas.ac.uk/id/eprint/39439.

Ashman, S., Fine, B., & Karwowski, E. (2021). The relevance of financialization for African economies: Lessons from South Africa. https://eprints.soas.ac.uk/id/eprint/36164

Ashman, S., Fine, B., & Newman, S. (2011). The crisis in South Africa: Neoliberalism, financialization and uneven and combined development. *Socialist Register, 47.*

Baker, S. R., Bloom, N., & Davis, S. J. (2016). Measuring economic policy uncertainty. *The Quarterly Journal of Economics, 131*(4), 1593–1636. https://doi.org/10.1093/qje/qjw024

Barradas, R., & Lagoa, S. (2017). Financialization and Portuguese real investment: A supportive or disruptive relationship? *Journal of Post Keynesian Economics, 40*(3), 413–439. https://doi.org/10.1080/01603477.2017.1286940

Chireka, T., & Fakoya, M. B. (2017). The determinants of corporate cash holdings levels: Evidence from selected South African retail firms. *Investment Management and Financial Innovations, 14*(2), 79–93. https://doi.org/10.21511/imfi.14(2).2017.08

Chireka, T., & Moloi, T. (2023). Managerial ability and corporate cash holdings adjustment speed in South African listed firms. *Acta Commercii, 23*(1), 10. https://doi.org/10.4102/ac.v23i1.1180

Davis, L. E. (2016). Identifying the "financialization" of the nonfinancial corporation in the US economy: A decomposition of firm-level balance sheets. *Journal of Post Keynesian Economics, 39*(1), 115–141. https://doi.org/10.1080/01603477.2015.1116370

Davis, L. (2018). Financialization, shareholder orientation and the cash holdings of US corporations. *Review of Political Economy, 30*(1), 1–27. https://doi.org/10.1080/09538259.2018.1429147

Demir, F. (2009). Financial liberalization, private investment and portfolio choice: Financialization of real sectors in emerging markets. *Journal of Development Economics, 88*(2), 314–324. https://doi.org/10.1016/j.jdeveco.2008.04.002

Donnelley, L. (2017). No investment strike–Kganyago. Mail & Guardian, viewed 24 February 2024, from No 'investment strike'—Kganyago—The Mail & Guardian (mg.co.za).

Karwowski, E. (2018). Corporate financialization in South Africa: From investment strike to housing bubble. *Competition & Change, 22*(4), 413–436. https://doi.org/10.1177/1024529418774924

Karwowski, E., Szymborska, H., Lesame, K., & Thoka, T. (2022). Determinants of corporate cash holdings in South Africa (No. 2022/85). *WIDER working paper*. http://hdl.handle.net/10419/267834.

Krippner, G. R. (2011). *Capitalizing on crisis: The political origins of the rise of finance*. Harvard University Press.

Keeton, G. (2018). "Post-Truth," "Alternative Facts" and "Fakenomics". *South African Journal of Economics, 86*(1), 113–124. https://doi.org/10.1111/saje.12181

Lazonick, W., & Shin, J. S. (2019). *Predatory value extraction: How the looting of the business corporation became the US norm and how sustainable prosperity can be restored.* Oxford University Press.

Magdoff, H., & Sweezy, P. M. (1987). *Stagnation and the financial explosion*. NYU Press.

Mbindwane, B. (2015). Investment strike: Unpatriotic corporate citizens are taxing South Africa. *The daily maverick*, viewed 24 February 2024, from Investment strike: Unpatriotic corporate citizens are taxing South Africa (dailymaverick.co.za).

Nyamgero, F. (2015). Are South African firms holding more cash than before? PhD Thesis, Gordon Institute of Business Science, University of Pretoria (South Africa).

Orhangazi, Ö. (2008). Financialisation and capital accumulation in the non-financial corporate sector: A theoretical and empirical investigation on the US economy: 1973–2003. *Cambridge Journal of Economics, 32*(6), 863–886. https://doi.org/10.1093/cje/ben009

Rabinovich, J. (2019). The financialization of the non-financial corporation. A critique to the financial turn of accumulation hypothesis. *Metroeconomica, 70*(4), 738–775. https://doi.org/10.1111/meca.12251

Rabinovich, J., & Pérez Artica, R. (2022). Cash holdings and corporate financialization: Evidence from listed Latin American firms. *Competition & Change*, 10245294221117275. https://doi.org/10.1177/10245294221117275

Thompson, C. B. (2021). A South African perspective on the corporate cash holding conundrum. PhD Thesis, School of Accounting, College of Business and Economics, University of Johannesburg.

Wang, C. (2019). A literature review on corporate financialization. *American Journal of Industrial and Business Management, 9*(3), 647–657. https://doi.org/10.4236/ajibm.2019.93044

Welman, C., Kruger, F., & Mitchell, B. (2005). *Research methodology*. Oxford University Press.

Zalk, N. E. (2017). The things we lost in the fire: The political economy of post-apartheid restructuring of the South African steel and engineering sectors. PhD Thesis, Department of Economics, SOAS University of London.

Zhao, Y., & Su, K. (2022). Economic policy uncertainty and corporate financialization: Evidence from China. *International Review of Financial Analysis, 82*, 102182. https://doi.org/10.1016/j.irfa.2022.102182

Digital Trust in Banking: Post Graduate Students Perspective

Pulane Modiha

Abstract Digital innovations have transformed the way in which customers interact with their banks and manage their finances. An increasing number of banks are receiving instructions and providing services to their clients via the internet and other digital platforms. Channels like the internet and mobile applications have lowered costs, increased efficiencies, and broken down time barriers in the provision of bank services. The banking sector still relies heavily on trust, which motivates customers to adopt digital banking services in the face of a world that has become more digitally connected. Therefore, for customers to truly use banks' digital channels, it is critical that they are trusted. This study aims to investigate the dynamics of digital trust from the perspective of bank customers. A descriptive quantitative research methodology was employed, using a questionnaire to gather information from 407 participants across four prestigious business schools: Wits Business School, Gordon Institute of Business Science, Management College of Southern Africa, and Johannesburg Business School. Additionally, a smaller cohort from other universities was included. The key findings indicate that a significant majority (65%) of participants use digital banking services for most or all their banking needs, with mobile banking applications being the preferred channel. Trust in digital banking was generally high, with 315 (77%) participants expressing high to very high trust levels. However, security concerns were prevalent, with 50% extremely concerned about the security of their personal and financial information. Participants suggested several improvements to enhance their trust and satisfaction, including advanced security measures, better protection against coercion, improved customer support, and user-friendly interfaces. Specific recommendations included biometric authentication, real-time fraud detection, and consistent engagement on security updates. The findings emphasise the importance of robust security measures and responsive customer support to foster greater trust and satisfaction. By addressing these areas, banks can enhance their digital offerings, leading to increased adoption and customer retention.

P. Modiha (✉)
University of Johannesburg, Johannesburg, South Africa

T. Moloi (ed.), *Impacting Society Positively Through Technology in Accounting and Business Processes*, Springer Proceedings in Business and Economics,
https://doi.org/10.1007/978-3-031-84885-8_57

Keywords Digital trust · Digital channels · Customer experience · Security · Privacy · Reliability · Transparency · Banking · Regulatory compliance · Ethical standard

Introduction

The way customers interact with their banks and handle their accounts has changed considerably as a result of digital innovations (Scott et al., 2017). In the past, banking was mostly done through in-person interactions (Brevoort & Wolken, 2009). However, nowadays, it is done through a number of channels, the most recent of which are the Internet and mobile banking applications (Alonso et al., 2022). Customers want greater convenience in their busy schedules, and they do not want their bank's location to limit them. However, customers will be less likely to use digital channels and complete transactions digitally if they lack confidence in the bank digital services (Pavithra, 2021). As a result, trust is a critical success factor for digital banking (Kiefer, 2000). This poses the question; what level of trust do bank customers have in digital banking? This study aims to examine the topic of digital trust in banking from the perspective of South African postgraduate students, mainly top four business schools' postgraduates in Gauteng province.

Perspective from postgraduate students was sort given the following reasons:

- Fresh Perspectives: Postgraduate students frequently approach research subjects from fresh angles. Their varied experiences inspire original ideas and perspectives.
- Current Knowledge: A large number of postgraduate students are knowledgeable about the most recent developments and patterns in digital technology as well as banking procedures. Studying a constantly developing topic like digital trust in banking requires having a thorough understanding of current developments.

The inspiration for this paper arose from current focus and continued initiatives towards digital transformation and adoptions in the banking sector. According to the World Economic Forum (2023) Africa leads the world in terms of mobile banking transactions, account holders, and services. In places where traditional banking networks are not present, the rise of mobile and digital banking has made money more accessible to millions of Africans. The World Economic Forum (2023) further reports that the continent of Africa is often referred to as a banking industry leader as millions of Africans have acquired access to banking services during the past 20 years without ever setting foot in a traditional bank branch, since many countries have jumped straight to mobile banking to provide better access to the unbanked. Furthermore, as new companies and services disrupt the industry, Africa seems destined to continue setting the standard for digital banking.

Globally, a large number of studies on digital trust have been conducted. A study on the "Multi-dimensional role of trust in Internet banking adoption" was carried out by Yousafzai et al. (2009). Their research revealed that purpose is a direct antecedent of perceived danger as well as trust, which is a multifaceted construct with three antecedents: perceived security, perceived privacy, and perceived trustworthiness. However, only clients of Halifax Bank of Scotland who use online banking were eligible to participate in this study.

Similarly, Pikkarainen et al.'s (2004) study on online banking adoption in Zimbabwe outlined the elements banks must consider to boost the use of their digital channels. The findings of the study indicate that perceived usefulness and information on online banking on the web site were the main factors influencing online banking acceptance. However, bank charges and the lack of formal accounts are preventing customers from using online banking. Lastly, the study by Sun et al. (2017) emphasises the knock-on effects brought about by digital trust, including perceptions of usability and structure quality. Even if South African banks are leading the way in digital transformation and online banking, there is still a gap in the context of determining confidence in digital channels.

Theoretical Framework

By highlighting the importance of a bank's perceived ability, goodness, and integrity in fostering trust with clients, Mayer, Davis, and Schoorman's Model of Trust offers a fundamental framework for analysing digital trust in banking (Mayer et al., 1995). This model helps pinpoint the essential characteristics that impact trust in digital banking settings. In addition, customers' perceptions of the dangers associated with digital banking, such as security and privacy issues, are clarified by the Perceived Risk Theory. Social Exchange Theory adds even more depth to our knowledge by emphasising how trust is developed reciprocally through good interactions and the perceived advantages of digitised banking services (Blau, 1964). By considering both the pragmatic and psychological aspects of customer–bank interactions, integrating these theories offers a thorough method for comprehending and improving digital trust in banking.

Literature Review

An Overview of Digital Trust in Banking

The digital environment is required for the majority of financial services; however, the adoption and utilisation of banking services are significantly impacted by digital trust (Pi et al., 2012). According to Pi et al. (2012) today's world revolves around mobile phones. The proliferation of mobile phones is changing people's lives, relationships, and social interactions. The increasing use of mobile devices has a severe impact on bank services offering (Tiwari et al., 2006). The financial industry needs to decide how to react in a proactive manner. Therefore, investments in building digital trust are now absolutely necessary (Donner & Tellez, 2008). Whilst the adoption of technology offers many opportunities, it has also created risks which impact on digital trust (Maria, 2016). Trust in banking and financial institutions is a crucial phenomenon that is thought to result in customer loyalty and retention, which in turn leads to the creation of a long-term, sustainable customer base (Bhat et al., 2018).

Definition of Digital Trust

Trust is the willingness of a customer to engage with a bank's operations, independent of its ability to oversee or manage them, on the premise that the bank will take a substantial action on the trustor's behalf (Suh & Han, 2002). This broad definition makes it clear that trust is an essential principle in creating and preserving connections between businesses and their customers. In the context of e-commerce, trust is even more crucial because it is recognised as an important reason for customers to communicate with businesses online (Lewicki & Brinsfield, 2012).

According to McKnight et al. (2002), the term "digital trust" describes a person's belief in the morality and goodness of an unknown party serving as the trustee, based on the knowledge that the party would fulfil a significant obligation for the trustor independent of the trustor's ability to supervise or manage the trustee. Kim et al. (2008) indicate that trust can be seen as an example of taking a risk; in certain circumstances, trust is not necessary if there is no perceived risk.

Why Digital Trust in Banking Is Important

Since banks are regarded as reliable financial mediators, trust is crucial in the banking industry (Madjid, 2013). Customers will continue to be encouraged to save and do other business with the bank if they have faith in their financial institutions (Lin, 2011). Providing outstanding customer service, guaranteeing customer deposits, and upholding customers' rights to high-quality goods and services are all necessary to earn their trust (Aumma, 2023). Digital trust can be established by strict customer oversight and ongoing community involvement in banking (Bose et al., 2013),

The ability to attract and keep loyal customers, promote word-of-mouth advertising, lower communication expenses are just a few examples that depend on trust (Zalloum et al., 2019). For financial services, especially those that use ICT, privacy, and security issues are crucial, and concerns about these aspects of services' security and privacy are only going to increase (Pearson & Benameur, 2010). Lean digital entrants are currently posing an increasing threat to the traditional banking industry (Vives, 2019). Neobanks have been further stimulated by the emergence of numerous mobile banks delivering modern services across the world. Furthermore, massive technology companies, or "Big Tech", are utilising platform tactics to support a steady financial sector that generates data together and serves customers with larger firms (Stulz, 2022). In the financial sector, trust is intimately correlated with success (Becerra et al., 2008).

Factors Influencing Digital Trust in Banking

Digital trust is shaped and influenced by a multitude of elements, from technological factors to human behaviour and society dynamics (Shah & Shah, 2024). It is imperative that people, businesses, and policymakers comprehend these characteristics in order to effectively navigate the digital landscape (Belanche et al., 2014). Some of the major variables affecting digital trust are security, transparency and accountability, user experience, data privacy and consent, reputation, cyber threats, culture, and regulation (Chew Han Ei et al., 2023).

Security

Digital trust is greatly impacted by how well online platforms, websites, and service providers adopt security procedures (Alghazo et al., 2017). Users are more likely to communicate and engage freely in digital areas when they have confidence that their transactions and data are secure (Belanger et al., 2002). Online banking services have been linked to an increase in card fraud, according to a recent study by Beju and Făt (2023). The steps of credit card fraud are depicted in Fig. 1 below, which suggests that the quantity of card scams has increased in recent years due to the rising use of cards.

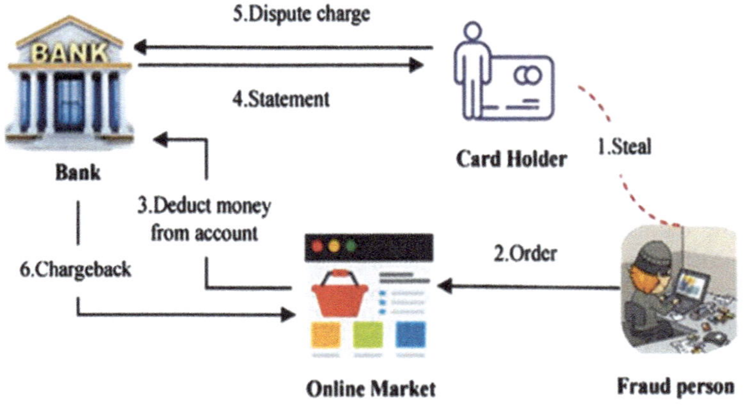

Fig. 1 Systemic fraud in banking. Steps of credit card fraud (Source: Rtayli & Enneya, 2020, p. 2)

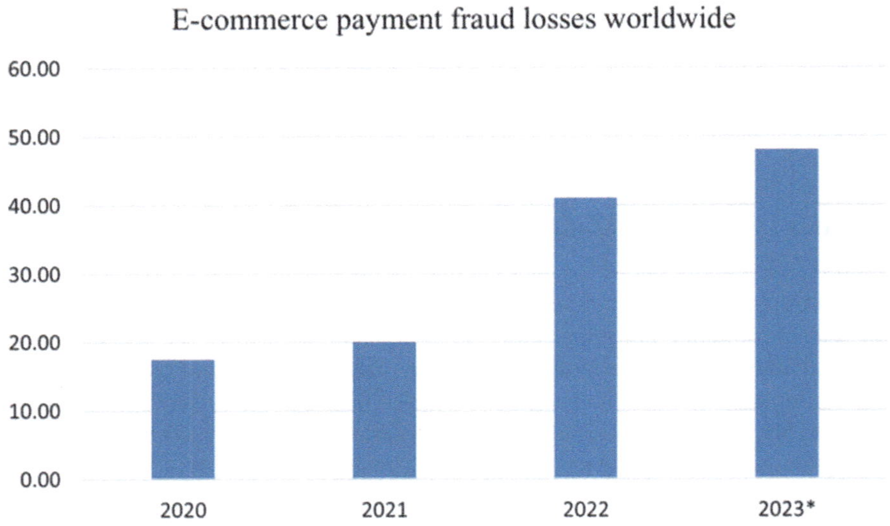

Fig. 2 E-commerce payment fraud losses worldwide. E-commerce payment fraud losses worldwide (Source: Beju, & Făt, 2023, p. 58)

The card issuer, the cardholder, and the store are all impacted by card fraud, which is classified as a white-collar crime (Rtayli & Enneya, 2020). The bank, who issues the card, is typically the party most impacted because it will bear the loss and reimburse the customer for the money they have lost. Since card owners are the least impacted parties in this circuit, they are legally protected. The area of the business that takes card payments bears the most responsibility.

Banks are attempting to increase security in order to combat the threat of card theft by constructing sophisticated systems that can detect fraudulent activity and by coming up with new ways to identify previous fraud attempts (Lynch, 2005). The prevalence of Internet payments has led to an increase in card fraud tactics and a corresponding rise in financial criminality worldwide as depicted by the below Fig. 2 (Beju & Făt, 2023).

Transparency and Accountability

Trust is developed by openness about data collection, storage, and usage procedures (Adjei, 2015). Customers anticipate terms of service agreements, privacy policies, and disclosures of data sharing practices to be brief and easy to understand. Furthermore, standards of accountability that show a dedication to protecting user interests—like breach notifications and prompt customer support—build trust over time (Hartzog & Richards, 2021).

According to Kumar (2023) cyberattacks affect the banking industry more frequently than other industries. Banks worldwide have been compromised by hackers and data breach incidents are on the rise (Gulyás & Kiss, 2023). The average yearly cost of cybercrime for the banking industry was estimated to be $18.3 million per organisation, according to the Accenture 2020 Cost of Cybercrime Study (Raghavendra, 2023). Cyberattack-related financial losses can have serious consequences for banks, undermining client trust and jeopardising their stability. In addition, the Accenture study found that it took an average of 56 days to resolve a cyberattack in the banking industry, which led to extensive downtime and recovery efforts.

User Experience

Digital trust is enhanced by a smooth and simple user interface (Kaasinen, 2005). Positive impressions are evoked by user-friendly, responsive, and visually appealing websites and applications. On the other hand, bad interface design, slow loading speeds, and a high rate of mistake can undermine user confidence and drive them away. Trust in digital interactions is further strengthened by a consistent user experience across platforms and devices (Sasisuriyaphoom & Choompolsathien, 2021).

Data Privacy and Consent

Establishing digital trust requires upholding data protection laws and respecting user privacy (Wright et al., 2009). Users are empowered and trust is fostered when they have control over their personal data through permission methods. Users are reassured when they receive clear information about how their data will be used and have the option to opt out of data collection business processes, which shows respect for their right to privacy (Karjoth et al., 2002).

In the digital age, client behaviour data is a crucial asset for any bank trying to understand its clients' present and future requirements, making data protection even more important than ever (Mantelero, 2016). The security of personal data is a topic that requires careful consideration in light of the rise of new services (such as big data, cloud computing, Internet of Things, and geolocation) that rely on the transport and processing of personal data (Tene & Polonetsky, 2012).

Reputation

Digital trust is influenced by user reviews and reputation (Zloteanu et al., 2018). Online platforms and services gain credibility through social validation, positive ratings, and endorsements from reliable sources. On the other hand, unfavourable comments or allegations of unethical activity can damage reputations and erode confidence (Ryu & Han, 2021). Consistency, integrity, and responsiveness to customer comments are necessary for establishing and preserving a positive online reputation.

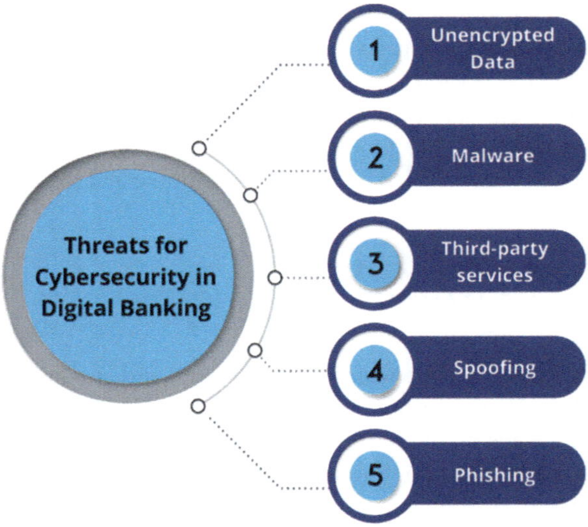

Fig. 3 Threats for cyber security in digital banking. An overview of cyber security in digital banking sector (Source: Kumar, 2023)

Cyber Threats in Banks

Digital trust is at risk from the constantly changing cyber threat events. Strong cybersecurity measures are essential, as seen by the rise of identity theft incidents, data breaches, and cyberattacks (Kumar, 2023). The primary goal of cyber security in digital banking is to offer protection for user accounts that contain digital currency, such as credit and debit cards, during transactions (Kumar, 2023). Figure 3 below highlights threats for cyber security in digital banking.

Data Encryption

One common concern to all digital banking is that data that is left unencrypted (or hidden) can be readily exploited by hackers or cybercriminals, leading to serious problems for the industry.

Malware

Digital transactions are made using peer-to-peer user devices; hence, security is required. This malware program compromises sensitive data that is transferred over the network to carry out significant attacks on digital banking.

Third-Party Services

In an effort to provide better service to their bank holders, several banks and financial institutions make use of third-party services. There is a risk of bank data hacking if the user gives third parties access to their bank information, including ATM pins, CVVs, and OTPs.

Spoofing

It is the most recent type of cyberthreat that digital banks must deal with. Cybercriminals will mimic the URL of the banking website, making it appear and even function like it is real. Criminals steal bank credentials from users when they access their login window and use them at a later time.

Phishing

It is the most well-known and oldest cyberthreat that aims to obtain private data via SMS, phone call, email, or other means, including ATM PIN, CVV, OTP, and credit card or debit card details.

Maintaining digital trust in the face of rising cyber risks requires proactive risk mitigation techniques, quick incident response processes, and awareness of possible threats (Muhammad et al., 2022). As cyberattacks are becoming more common and carry serious legal consequences, cybersecurity risks are still at the top of the list of global risks, according to Agrafiotis et al., 2018. The dangers that banks confront are more numerous and sophisticated as AI and automation grow more intelligent (Jakšič & Marinč, 2019).

Culture

Perceptions of digital trust are influenced by cultural norms and social norms (Hwang, 2005). People's online trust behaviours are influenced by a variety of factors, including their technology literacy, privacy beliefs, and past experiences with data breaches. It is imperative for global firms and organisations that operate in multiple marketplaces to comprehend differences in culture and adjust their trust-building methods accordingly (Khan et al., 2017).

Fig. 4 The Trial of Trust. Source: Miller and Hoffman (2011)

Regulations

Due to the technology-driven nature of digital banking, strong legal and regulatory frameworks are required to guarantee security, privacy, and dependability—all of which are essential for fostering customer trust (Gupta & Shukla, 2024). Globally, policymakers are coming to understand that the current state of privacy and information security law and regulation does not offer sufficient levels of confidence to support the Global Data Infrastructure (GDI). It can be difficult to identify characteristics universal to many cultures from the increasingly fragmented and disjointed patchwork of international privacy and security laws (Miller & Hoffman, 2011). Establishing confidence in the GDI is obviously a shared task, and it cannot be accomplished by a single organisation. Establishing a "Triangle of Trust" that unites government, business, and non-governmental organisations (NGOs) is advantageous to all parties. The trial of trust is demonstrated in Fig. 4 below.

The "base" of the Triangle should be established by the government through the development of high-level compliance guidelines and regulations as well as by consistent, reliable, and coordinated enforcement. Industry is one of the "sides" that collaborates with the government to suggest best practices that enable businesses to abide by rules and laws. The last "side" is made up of NGOs, which include advocacy groups, academia, think tanks, and civil society. They support the government and business in codifying industry best practices, resolving disputes to free up limited government enforcement resources for more urgent problems, and assisting with professional education for privacy and information security. The "length" of this side of the triangle will change depending on a number of factors, such as the particular country, economy, or problem at hand.

Research Methodology

A systematic method for gathering and analysing numerical data to characterise the features of a particular population is descriptive quantitative research methodology, which makes use of a questionnaire (Rahi, 2017). A structured questionnaire was used in this study to collect information from 407 participants. The survey was structured into five primary sections: demographic information, digital banking service usage, a perception of trust, security concerns, and customer experience.

Demographic Information: In this section, the respondents' age, gender, and highest level of education were gathered as baseline demographic information. These variables are essential for comprehending the participants' backgrounds and for relating the data analysis to demographic characteristics.

Usage of Digital Banking Services: Data on participants' usage of digital channels (e.g., mobile apps, online banking portals) and frequency of use were gathered. The purpose of this part was to comprehend the respondents' adoption and usage patterns of digital banking.

Perception of Trust: Participants rated their own levels of trust and noted the elements that support their trust in order to determine the degree of confidence in digital banking services. Understanding the trust dynamics in the context of digital banking is essential, since it can affect user adoption and behaviour.

Security concerns: Questions in this section were centred around the respondents' experiences with fraud and their concerns about the security of digital banking services. Identification of potential challenges to adoption and effective use of digital financial services requires a thorough understanding of security concerns.

Customer Experience: In this section, respondents' overall satisfaction with digital banking services was examined, along with their recommendations for enhancements and likelihood of continuing with the services in future. This section's insights can improve customer experience and retention strategies.

The data were presented in a comprehensible manner using descriptive statistics including frequency distributions and percentages. Likert scales were used to evaluate respondents' concerns about trust and security, giving a quantifiable indication of their views. Additionally, the customer experience was quantified to provide information on satisfaction levels and possible areas for improvements. The results of this descriptive quantitative analysis offer a comprehensive overview of user demographics, usage trends, degrees of trust, security issues, and general user satisfaction with digital banking services.

Research Results and Discussion

Introduction to the Research Findings

The following section presents the findings and discussion of the study on postgraduate students in Gauteng, focusing on four prominent institutions: Wits Business School (WBS), Gordon Institute of Business Science (GIBS), Johannesburg

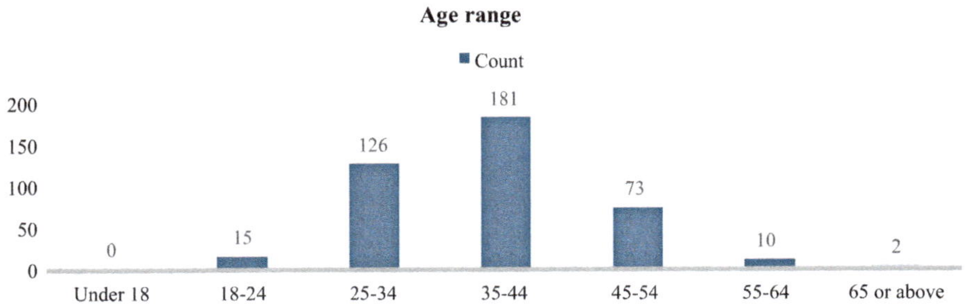

Fig. 5 The age of participants

Business School (JBS), and Management College of Southern Africa (MANCOSA). These institutions were selected due to their significant representation and influence in the province's business education landscape.

This study aimed to explore various aspects of the student experience as customers of the bank, including use of banks digital channels, their trust in the channels, concerns and perceived security offered by digital channels. To achieve a comprehensive understanding, the study employed a stratified random sampling method to ensure that postgraduate students within these schools were represented in our sample.

Results and Discussions

A sample of 407 was examined, comprising a diverse group of students from WBS, GIBS, JBS, and MANCOSA, alongside a smaller cohort of graduates from other universities in Gauteng. The demographic breakdown included age, gender, and level of study. These attributes are presented below in Figs. 5, 6, and 7.

Regarding the **age distribution**, the majority 181 (44%) of the participants were in the age category 35–44 years, this was followed by 121 (31%) aged 24–34 years. Only 73 (18%) of participants were aged 45–54, with 15 (4%) and 10 (2.5%) in the age categories 18–24 years and 55–64 years, respectively. Only 2 (<1%) participants were in age category 65 or above and there were no under 18s. The age distribution of participants indicates a predominant presence of mid-career professionals (35–44) and younger adults (24–34). The mid-career age is likely to have more financial responsibilities and higher stakes in secure digital banking, whilst the younger adults are likely more tech-savvy and familiar with digital services, potentially influencing higher trust in digital banking. Figure 5 below provides an illustration of age range of participants:

In terms of **gender distribution**, the sample included 252 (62%) female students and 153 (38%) male students, with 1 participant who preferred not to say and 1 non-binary. The gender distribution of the sample indicates a significant majority of female participants. The male participants, though in the minority, still constitute a

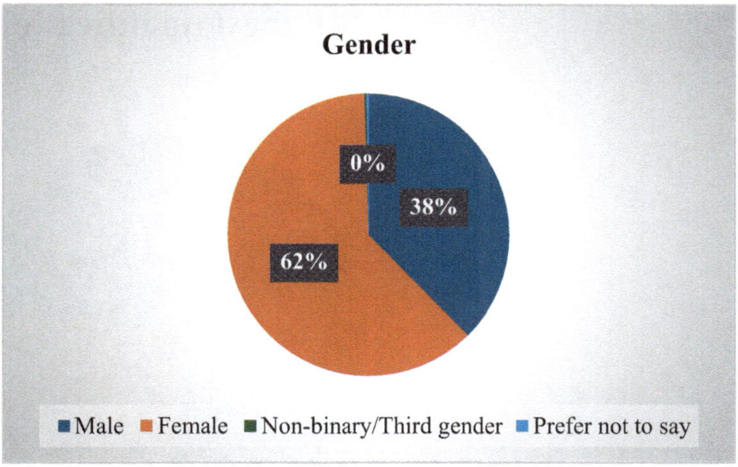

Fig. 6 Participants gender

substantial proportion. Their perspectives on digital banking trust contribute to a balanced understanding of gender-based differences in trust levels and security concerns. The inclusion of non-binary and undisclosed gender participants, although minimal, reflects an attempt to be inclusive (Fig. 6).

Concerning **qualifications**, a large number of participants—116 (28%)— had a bachelor's degree as their highest qualification, followed by honours degrees 102 (25%), diplomas 92 (23%), master's degrees 85 (21%), and doctoral qualifications 12 (3%). The distribution of qualifications among the participants provides insight into how educational attainment influences digital trust. The varied levels of educational attainment suggest that trust in digital banking services may correlate with the participants' knowledge and experience. Higher educational qualifications could correspond with a better understanding of the use of digital channels, trust, security, and customer experience (Fig. 7).

Regarding the **usage of digital banking services,** a large number 266 (65%) of participants always use digital banking services for most (if not all of their banking needs). This suggests a strong reliance on digital channels for financial transactions and management. It indicates that digital banking has become an integral part of their daily financial routines, offering convenience and accessibility, followed by 65 (18%) who use digital banking services multiple times a day. This frequent usage pattern reflects the ease of access and efficiency offered by digital platforms. These users likely prefer the convenience of managing their finances in real time, such as checking balances, making payments, and transferring funds, all with the click of a button. Very few of the participants (less than 20%) use digital banking services only a few times a week or in a month, with only 2 participants who mentioned that they rarely use digital banking services. This suggests that while digital banking is prevalent among postgraduate students, there is still a segment of users who rely on traditional banking methods or prefer less frequent interaction with digital

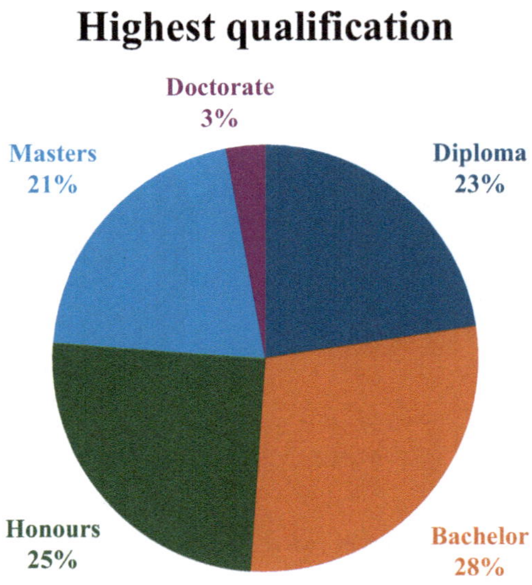

Fig. 7 Highest qualification

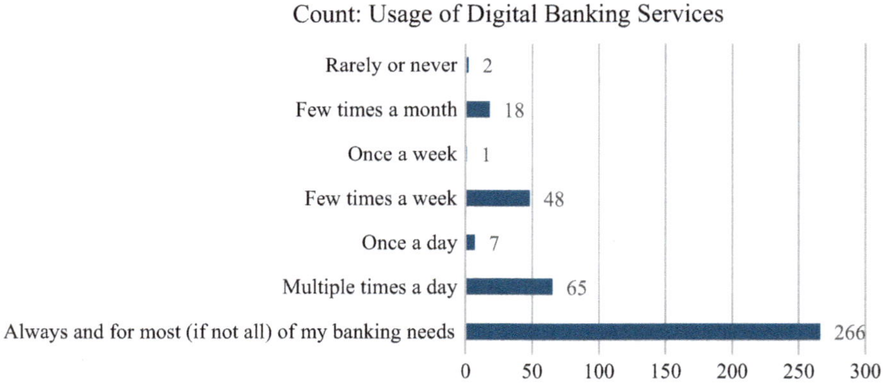

Fig. 8 Usage of digital banking services

platforms. Only a negligible number of participants mentioned that they rarely use digital banking services. This indicates a very small minority who may have reservations or limitations regarding digital banking, such as concerns about security, lack of access to technology, or preference for in-person banking services (Fig. 8).

Digital Channel Used The findings regarding the usage of digital banking channels provide valuable insights into the preferences and trends of the bank customers. More than 88% (360) of participants use mobile banking applications. 219 of the participants (54%) utilised online banking, which comes in second. 117 (42%) participants utilise digital wallets like Google Wallet and Apple Pay, while 131 (32%) participants use alternative digital platforms like PayPal, Snap Scan, and PayU. The

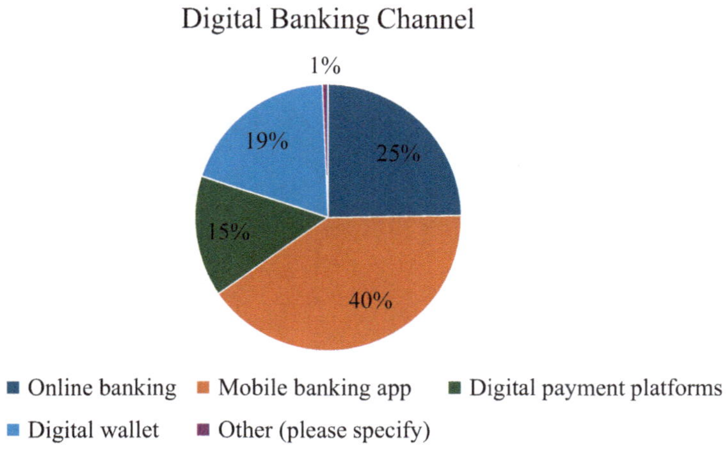

Fig. 9 Digital channel used

overwhelming majority of participants (88%) prefer using mobile banking applications over other digital channels. This indicates a strong preference for the convenience and accessibility offered by mobile apps, allowing users to manage their finances on-the-go using smartphones or tablets. Online banking, while slightly lower in usage compared to mobile apps, still commands a significant portion of participants (54%). Online banking platforms provide similar functionalities as mobile apps but are accessed through web browsers on computers or laptops, offering flexibility for users who prefer larger screens or specific features not available on mobile devices. This suggests that while mobile apps are favoured for their mobility, online banking remains essential for users requiring more comprehensive banking functionalities or those who prefer accessing services through desktop devices.

Digital wallets like Google Wallet and Apple Pay, along with alternative digital payment platforms such as PayPal, Snap Scan, and PayU, also demonstrate notable usage among participants, with 42% and 32%, respectively. These findings suggest a growing trend towards adopting digital wallets and alternative payment platforms, reflecting evolving consumer preferences for convenient, secure, and versatile payment solutions beyond traditional banking methods.

Majority Utilise Multiple Channels It is noteworthy that the majority of participants utilise multiple digital channels for various banking services. This indicates a diversified approach towards banking, with users leveraging different platforms based on their specific needs, preferences, and the functionalities offered by each channel (Fig. 9).

When considering Trust, a very large number (173) of participants have high to very high (142) trust in digital banking services. Only 90 participants had moderate

Fig. 10 Trust rating

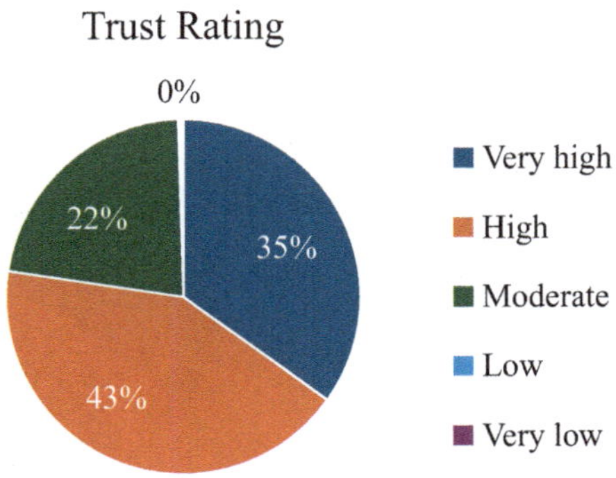

trust with only 1 who showed low and very low trust. These findings indicate a generally positive perception of digital banking among the sampled students, with a notable 315 (77%) participants expressing high to very high trust. This is a strong endorsement of the digital banking infrastructure's current state, highlighting the success of banks in building a secure and reliable digital environment. Only two participants indicated low or very low trust in digital banking services. This minuscule number suggests that extreme distrust is rare among the surveyed group (Fig. 10).

Top 3 Factors Contributing to High Trust

1. **Security Measures**: The high levels of trust are influenced by the robust security measures implemented by banks. The focus on securing personal and financial information reassures users about the safety of their transactions.
2. **Bank Reputation**: Established banks with strong reputations in the industry likely instil greater confidence among users.
3. **User-Friendliness**: The ease of use and intuitive design of digital banking platforms also play a crucial role.

Other factors considered were transparency of policies and terms of service, prompt and efficient customer support, and previous positive experiences with digital banking services (Fig. 11).

Additionally, participants shared other factors impacting on trust:

- Banks' willingness to take responsibility for breaches resulting from weaknesses in its systems.
- The turnaround times when fraud happens.
- Third parties' ability to create debit orders especially those less than R100.

The findings from the study indicate that security concerns remain a significant issue among participants. 198 (49%) are extremely concerned, with 108 (26%) moderately concerned: 62 (15%) are slightly concerned and 39 (10%) indicated not concerned. This high level (75%) of concern suggests that despite the trust in digital banking platforms, security remains a critical issue for users (Fig. 12).

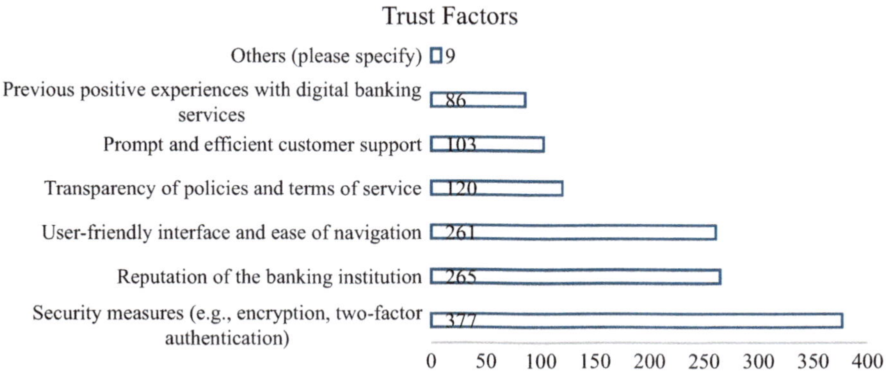

Fig. 11 Trust factors

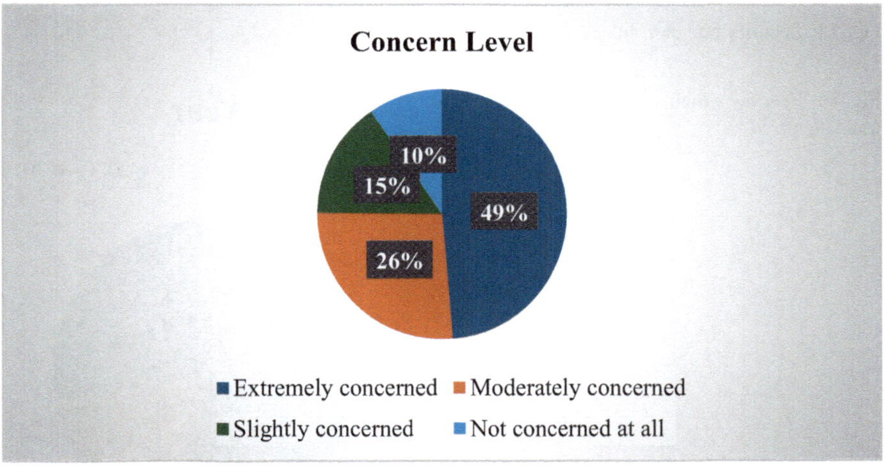

Fig. 12 Concern level

The majority of participants (80%) have not experienced fraud or security breaches on digital platforms. This indicates that while security concerns are high, actual incidents of fraud or breaches are relatively low. The 19% of participants who have experienced fraud or security breaches represent a significant minority; however, their experience highlights potential vulnerabilities and areas for improvement (Fig. 13).

Of the 19% participants who experienced fraud, most fraudulent activities happened in the years 2019 and 2023. The clustering of fraud incidents in 2019 and 2023 suggests that these years may have seen specific vulnerabilities or spikes in fraudulent activities targeting digital banking services.

It is essential to investigate whether these years correspond with major changes in digital banking platforms, regulatory changes, or broader cyber threats. **2019**: This year may have seen the introduction of new technologies or banking services

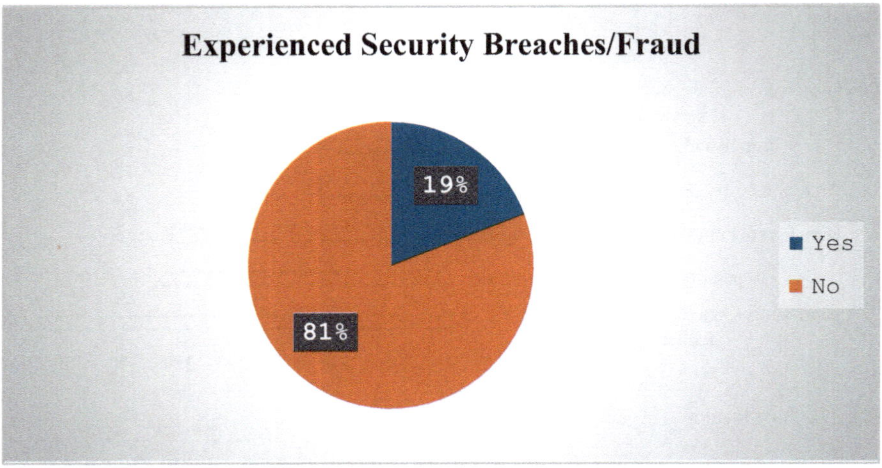

Fig. 13 Security breach/fraud

Fig. 14 Year for which fraud occurred

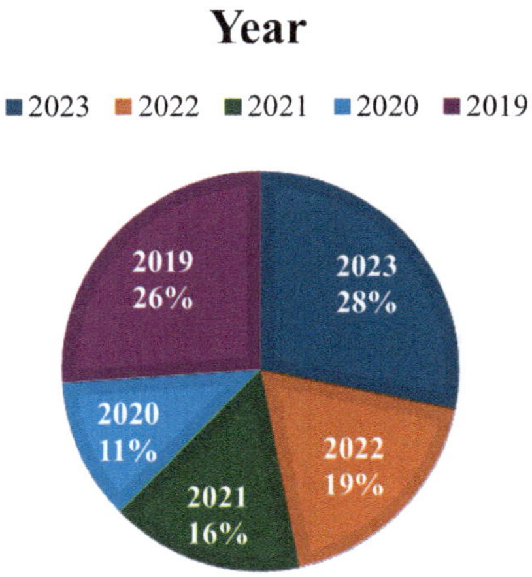

that, initially, had security vulnerabilities that were exploited by fraudsters. **2023**: Similarly, this year might reflect new patterns of cyberattacks, possibly due to advancements in hacking techniques or lapses in updating security protocols (Fig. 14).

Lastly the study observed **customer experience**, with participants being asked about their satisfaction levels in using digital banking services. A substantial number of participants indicated "satisfied" (56%) and "very satisfied" (34%). With a marginal number being neutral (9%) and only 2 (less than 1%) participants dissatisfied. The combined 90% of participants who reported being satisfied or very satisfied indicates a strong overall positive reception towards digital banking services among postgraduate students. This high satisfaction rate suggests that the digital banking services currently offered are meeting the expectations and needs of most users effectively.

Fig. 15 Satisfaction level

The 9% of participants who reported a neutral experience may indicate areas where the digital banking services are adequate but not exceptional. This group presents an opportunity for banks to delve deeper into specific aspects of their services that could be enhanced to convert neutral users into satisfied ones. The very low dissatisfaction rate (less than 1%) is a positive outcome, suggesting that major issues or negative experiences with digital banking are rare (Fig. 15).

Furthermore, a large number of participants have expressed a high likelihood of using digital services with 338 (85%) expressing "very likely", 60 (15%) "likely", and only 8 participants remaining neutral. One participant indicated "unlikely" with no response is for "very unlikely". The overwhelming majority (85%) of participants indicating they are very likely to continue using digital banking services reflects a strong commitment and positive experience with these platforms. This high likelihood suggests that the current digital banking services meet or exceed user expectations, leading to continued use and reliance on these services. The neutral stance of 8 participants may indicate areas of mild concern or ambivalence that could be addressed to enhance their likelihood of continued use (Fig. 16).

In closing, participants were invited to share improvements they would like to see in digital banking services to enhance their trust and satisfaction.

Recommendations for Digital Banking Improvements Based on User Feedback: Key Areas of Improvements

1. Security Enhancements:
    - Credit Card Security: Enhance measures for credit card transactions to prevent fraud.
    - Kidnap Protection: Implement security protocols such as emergency passwords that can immediately lock accounts if users are coerced to transfer money.
    - Increased Authentication: Use biometric authentication and robust encryption to protect personal and financial information.
    - Proactive Fraud Detection: Develop machine learning algorithms to detect and decline suspicious transactions. Tools to block known fraudulent entities from accessing accounts.

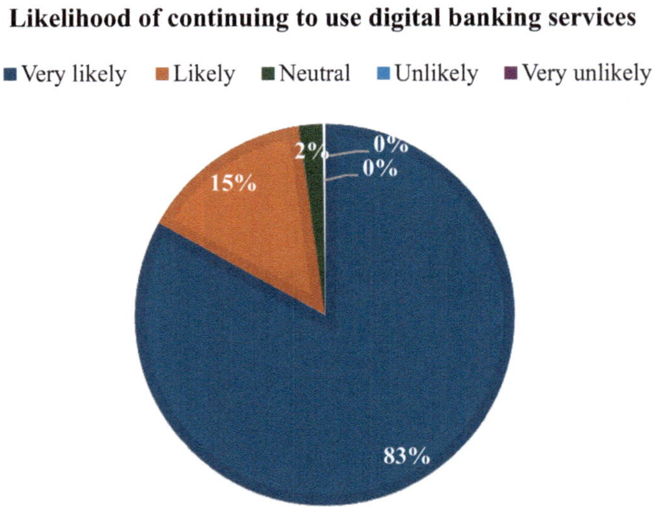

Fig. 16 Likelihood of continuing to use digital banking services

- Real-Time Transaction Monitoring: Provide peace of mind through proactive monitoring and immediate fraud alerts.

2. User Experience and Interface Improvements:
   - Mobile and Online Banking Integration: Improve the transition between mobile apps and online versions to ensure consistency and usability across platforms.
   - User-Friendly Interfaces: Streamline user interfaces for better navigation and overall user experience.
   - Paperless Transactions: Move towards fully paperless processes to enhance efficiency and user convenience.
3. Customer Support Enhancements:
   - Human Interaction Prioritisation: Ensure quick transition to human support when BOTS cannot resolve issues.
   - Improved Telecommunication Audio: Enhance the quality of customer service calls to reduce frustration and improve communication.
   - Quick Response for Errors: Provide swift resolutions for issues like unauthorised transactions or transfers to incorrect accounts.
4. Educational and Interactive Sessions:
   - Fraud Prevention Education: Regularly engage with customers, especially the elderly, to educate them on fraud prevention and risk mitigation.
   - Ongoing Customer Engagement: Maintain frequent communication with customers about updates and new security measures in digital banking services.

5. Transaction and Payment Improvements:
    - Real-Time Payments: Enable all transactions, including those on non-business days and holidays, to be processed in real time without extra charges.
    - Forex Rate Confirmation: Provide real-time confirmation of foreign exchange rates during transactions.
    - Enhanced Payment Authentication: Use selfies or other biometric methods for all payments to add an extra layer of security.
6. Additional Features and Services:
    - Home Loan Application Updates: Integrate home loan application status updates into the banking app for convenience.
    - Youth Banking App: Develop a dedicated app for younger users to encourage early adoption of digital banking.
    - Point of Sale Integration: Extend the tapping/scanning facility to local vendors, including those in townships and rural areas.
    - Reduced Banking Charges: Lower transaction fees to make digital banking more affordable.
7. Operational Reliability:
    - Reduced Downtime and Errors: Ensure high availability of services and minimise system outages.
    - Improved Internet Connectivity: Address connectivity issues to ensure uninterrupted access to digital banking services.
    - Faster Weekend Support: Provide robust customer support during weekends and holidays to address any urgent issues.

Recommendations for Banks

1. Security Protocols:
    - Implement layered security measures, including biometric authentication, encryption, and real-time monitoring.
    - Develop emergency response features, such as special passwords or pins, which can instantly lock accounts in high-risk situations.
2. User Interface Design:
    - Continuously refine mobile and online interfaces to ensure a seamless and intuitive user experience.
    - Communicate interface changes clearly and provide guidance to help users navigate new features.
3. Customer Support Optimisation:
    - Enhance the efficiency of transitioning from automated systems to human support, especially for complex issues.

- Improve the audio quality of customer service calls and ensure reliable communication channels.

4. Educational Initiatives:
   - Regularly update customers on new fraud tactics and preventive measures.
   - Provide targeted educational sessions for vulnerable groups, such as the elderly, to empower them with knowledge and confidence.
5. Service Accessibility:
   - Ensure that banking services are accessible and functional at all times, including weekends and holidays.
   - Address technical issues promptly to maintain user trust and satisfaction.
6. Feedback Implementation:
   - Actively solicit and incorporate customer feedback into service improvements.
   - Demonstrate responsiveness to user concerns by implementing suggested enhancements and communicating these updates effectively.

Conclusion

The usage of digital banking services was notably high, with a substantial portion of respondents utilising mobile banking applications frequently. Trust in digital banking was generally high, influenced significantly by security measures, bank reputation, and user-friendliness. However, security concerns remained prevalent, with almost half of the participants expressing extreme concern over the security of their personal and financial information.

The study also highlighted that a minority of respondents had experienced fraud or security breaches, emphasising the need for robust security measures. Customer satisfaction with digital banking services was high, with a majority indicating satisfaction and a strong likelihood of continued use. The participants also provided valuable suggestions for improvements, focusing on enhanced security measures, better user interfaces, and more responsive customer support.

In conclusion, the findings from this study provide a comprehensive overview of postgraduate students' demographics, usage patterns, trust levels, security concerns, and overall satisfaction with digital banking services. This information is crucial for banks and financial service providers aiming to enhance their digital offerings and address customer concerns effectively. By implementing the suggested improvements, banks can foster greater trust and satisfaction among their digital banking users, ultimately leading to higher adoption rates and customer retention.

The current study revealed that while trust in digital banking is generally high among postgraduate students in Gauteng, significant security concerns persist. These concerns highlight the need for robust security measures to enhance trust and ensure user satisfaction. Given the critical role of security in influencing trust and the prevalence of security concerns among users, further research is needed to explore the impact of specific enhanced security measures on digital trust.

References

Adjei, J. K. (2015). Explaining the role of trust in cloud computing services. *Info, 17*(1), 54–67.

Agrafiotis, I., Nurse, J. R., Goldsmith, M., Creese, S., & Upton, D. (2018). A taxonomy of cyber-harms: Defining the impacts of cyber-attacks and understanding how they propagate. *Journal of Cybersecurity, 4*(1), tyy006.

Alghazo, J. M., Kazmi, Z., & Latif, G. (2017, November). Cyber security analysis of internet banking in emerging countries: User and bank perspectives. In *2017 4th IEEE international conference on engineering technologies and applied sciences (ICETAS)* (pp. 1–6). IEEE.

Alonso, M., Gutiérrez, E., Moral-Benito, E., Posada, D., Tello-Casas, P., & Trucharte, C. (2022). In-person access to banking services in Spain: A comparison with other countries and other types of services. *Documentos Ocasionales/Banco de España, 2215.*

Aumma, H. (2023). Customer satisfaction and service quality in mobile financial services. Thesis Centria university of applied sciences Bachelor of Business Administration, International Business September 2023.

Becerra, M., Lunnan, R., & Huemer, L. (2008). Trustworthiness, risk, and the transfer of tacit and explicit knowledge between alliance partners. *Journal of Management Studies, 45*(4), 691–713.

Beju, D. G., & Făt, C. M. (2023). Frauds in banking system: Frauds with cards and their associated services. In *Economic and financial crime, sustainability and good governance* (pp. 31–52). Springer.

Belanche, D., Casaló, L. V., Flavián, C., & Schepers, J. (2014). Trust transfer in the continued usage of public e-services. *Information & Management, 51*(6), 627–640.

Belanger, F., Hiller, J. S., & Smith, W. J. (2002). Trustworthiness in electronic commerce: The role of privacy, security, and site attributes. *The Journal of Strategic Information Systems, 11*(3–4), 245–270.

Bhat, S. A., Darzi, M. A., & Parrey, S. H. (2018). Antecedents of customer loyalty in banking sector: A mediational study. *Vikalpa, 43*(2), 92–105.

Blau, P. M. (1964). *Exchange and power in social life*. Wiley.

Bose, R., Luo, X. R., & Liu, Y. (2013). The roles of security and trust: Comparing cloud computing and banking. *Procedia-Social and Behavioral Sciences, 73*, 30–34.

Brevoort, K. P., & Wolken, J. D. (2009). *Does distance matter in banking?* (pp. 27–56). Springer US.

Ei, C. H., Tan, J., & Soon, C. (2023). *Digital trust and why it matters*. Institute of Policy.

Donner, J., & Tellez, C. A. (2008). Mobile banking and economic development: Linking adoption, impact, and use. *Asian Journal of Communication, 18*(4), 318–332.

Gulyás, O., & Kiss, G. (2023). Impact of cyber-attacks on the financial institutions. *Procedia Computer Science, 219*, 84–90.

Gupta, V., & Shukla, S. (2024). Consumer trust in digital banking: A qualitative study of legal and regulatory impacts. *Interdisciplinary Studies in Society, Law, and Politics, 3*(2), 18–24.

Hartzog, W., & Richards, N. (2021). The surprising virtues of data loyalty. *Emory LJ, 71*, 985.

Hwang, Y. (2005). An empirical study of online trust and consumer behavior: Cultural orientation, social norms, and personal innovativeness in information technology.

Jakšič, M., & Marinč, M. (2019). Relationship banking and information technology: The role of artificial intelligence and FinTech. *Risk Management, 21*, 1–18.

Kaasinen, E. (2005). User acceptance of mobile services: Value, ease of use, trust and ease of adoption.

Karjoth, G., Schunter, M., & Waidner, M. (2002, April). Platform for enterprise privacy practices: Privacy-enabled management of customer data. In *International workshop on privacy enhancing technologies* (pp. 69–84). Springer.

Khan, I. U., Hameed, Z., & Khan, S. U. (2017). Understanding online banking adoption in a developing country: UTAUT2 with cultural moderators. *Journal of Global Information Management (JGIM), 25*(1), 43–65.

Kiefer, T. (2000). The future role of banks in electronic commerce-trust as the crucial factor of success in "Business Enabling"

Kim, D. J., Ferrin, D. L., & Rao, H. R. (2008). A trust-based consumer decision-making model in electronic commerce: The role of trust, perceived risk, and their antecedents. *Decision Support Systems, 44*(2), 544–564.

Kumar, M. (2023). An overview of cyber security in digital banking sector. *East Asian Journal of Multidisciplinary Research, 2*(1), 43–52.

Lewicki, R. J., & Brinsfield, C. (2012). *Measuring trust beliefs and behaviours. Handbook of research methods on trust* (Vol. 29).

Lin, H. F. (2011). An empirical investigation of mobile banking adoption: The effect of innovation attributes and knowledge-based trust. *International Journal of Information Management, 31*(3), 252–260.

Lynch, J. (2005). Identity theft in cyberspace: Crime control methods and their effectiveness in combating phishing attacks. *Berkeley Technology Law Journal, 20*, 259.

Madjid, R. (2013). Customer trust as relationship mediation between customer satisfaction and loyalty at Bank Rakyat Indonesia (BRI) Southeast Sulawesi. *The International Journal of Engineering and Science, 2*(5), 48–60.

Mantelero, A. (2016). Personal data for decisional purposes in the age of analytics: From an individual to a collective dimension of data protection. *Computer Law & Security Review, 32*(2), 238–255.

Maria, A. R. (2016). Digital trust: A case study of enterprise content management (Doctoral dissertation, Asia e University).

Mayer, R. C., Davis, J. H., & Schoorman, F. D. (1995). An integrative model of organizational trust. *Academy of Management Review, 20*(3), 709–734.

McKnight, D. H., Choudhury, V., & Kacmar, C. (2002). The impact of initial consumer trust on intentions to transact with a web site: A trust building model. *The Journal of Strategic Information Systems, 11*(3–4), 297–323.

Miller, J., & Hoffman, D. (2011). Sponsoring trust in tomorrow's technology: Towards a global digital infrastructure policy. *International Data Privacy Law, 1*(2), 83–91.

Muhammad, T., Munir, M. T., Munir, M. Z., & Zafar, M. W. (2022). Integrative cybersecurity: Merging zero trust, layered defense, and global standards for a resilient digital future. *International Journal of Computer Science and Technology, 6*(4), 99–135.

Pavithra, C. B. (2021). Factors affecting customers' perception towards digital banking services. *Turkish Journal of Computer and Mathematics Education (TURCOMAT), 12*(11), 1608–1614.

Pearson, S., & Benameur, A. (2010, November). Privacy, security and trust issues arising from cloud computing. In *2010 IEEE second international conference on cloud computing technology and science* (pp. 693–702). IEEE.

Pi, S. M., Liao, H. L., & Chen, H. M. (2012). Factors that affect consumers' trust and continuous adoption of online financial services. *International Journal of Business and Management, 7*(9), 108.

Pikkarainen, T., Pikkarainen, K., Karjaluoto, H., & Pahnila, S. (2004). Consumer acceptance of online banking: An extension of the technology acceptance model. *Internet Research, 14*(3), 224–235.

Raghavendra, K. (2023). Challenges in securing banking systems: emerging trends, risks, and defensive strategies.

Rahi, S. (2017). Research design and methods: A systematic review of research paradigms, sampling issues and instruments development. *International Journal of Economics & Management Sciences, 6*(2), 1–5.

Rtayli, N., & Enneya, N. (2020). Enhanced credit card fraud detection based on SVM-recursive feature elimination and hyper-parameters optimization. *Journal of Information Security and Applications, 55*, 102596.

Ryu, E. A., & Han, E. (2021). Social media influencer's reputation: Developing and validating a multidimensional scale. *Sustainability, 13*(2), 631.

Sasisuriyaphoom, M. P., & Choompolsathien, A. (2021). *Marketing 5.0: How to improve user experience with digital solutions (No. 306535)*. Thammasat University. Faculty of Journalism and Mass Communication.

Scott, S. V., Van Reenen, J., & Zachariadis, M. (2017). The long-term effect of digital innovation on bank performance: An empirical study of SWIFT adoption in financial services. *Research Policy, 46*(5), 984–1004.

Shah, S. S., & Shah, S. A. H. (2024). Trust as a determinant of social welfare in the digital economy. *Social Network Analysis and Mining, 14*(1), 1–27.

Stulz, R. M. (2022). Fintech, bigtech, and the future of banks. *Journal of Applied Corporate Finance, 34*(1), 106–117.

Suh, B., & Han, I. (2002). Effect of trust on customer acceptance of internet banking. *Electronic Commerce Research and Applications, 1*(3–4), 247–263.

Sun, B., Sun, C., Liu, C., & Gui, C. (2017). Research on initial trust model of mobile banking users. *Journal of Risk Analysis and Crisis Response, 7*(1).

Tene, O., & Polonetsky, J. (2012). Big data for all: Privacy and user control in the age of analytics. *Northwestern Journal of Technology and Intellectual Property, 11*, 239.

Tiwari, R., Buse, S., & Herstatt, C. (2006, July). Mobile banking as business strategy: Impact of mobile technologies on customer behaviour and its implications for banks. In *2006 technology management for the global future-PICMET 2006 conference* (Vol. 4, pp. 1935–1946). IEEE.

Vives, X. (2019). Digital disruption in banking. *Annual Review of Financial Economics, 11*, 243–272.

World Economic Forum. (2023, November). Here's why Africa is the world leader in digital and mobile banking. https://www.weforum.org/agenda/2023/11/africa-digital-mobile-banking-financial-inclusion/.

Wright, D., Gutwirth, S., Friedewald, M., De Hert, P., Langheinrich, M., & Moscibroda, A. (2009). Privacy, trust and policy making: Challenges and responses. *Computer Law & Security Review, 25*(1), 69–83.

Yousafzai, S., Pallister, J., & Foxall, G. (2009). Multi-dimensional role of trust in Internet banking adoption. *The Service Industries Journal, 29*(5), 591–605.

Zalloum, L., Alghadeer, H., & Nusairat, N. (2019). The effect of using mobile banking services applications on electronic word of mouth: The mediating role of perceived trust. *International Business Research, 12*(9), 62–80.

Zloteanu, M., Harvey, N., Tuckett, D., & Livan, G. (2018). Digital identity: The effect of trust and reputation information on user judgement in the sharing economy. *PLoS One, 13*(12), e0209071.

Risk and Challenges in Experiential Learning in Accounting Education: The Use of Riipen.com for Team Projects Assigned by Industry Partners

Zlatinka Blaber, Barry Palatnik, Shree Nanguneri, and Ashok Naraian

Abstract This paper discusses two accounting instructors' and two industry partners' experiences with experiential learning in accounting classes from 2021 to 2024. Experiential learning and hands-on class projects have been praised for their positive impact on learning; however, there are also risks and challenges to adopting such projects in the classroom. The platform used was Riipen.com, the largest online experiential learning platform in North America that helps connect instructors and their classes with industry partners from around the world. The students from various classes were given the opportunity to work individually or in teams toward the completion of a short project for an industry partner selected by the instructor on Riipen's open marketplace. On Riipen, learners may receive feedback from the industry partner. The instructors graded the learners on their Riipen work. The four research questions (RQs) in this study are empirical. RQ1 is: "What kind of Riipen projects did the industry partners provide to the accounting students?" RQ2 is: "How did the students perform on the Riipen projects with respect to regular attendance of and timely contributions to project meetings (industry partners' and faculty feedback)?" RQ3 is: "What are the industry partners' and instructors' impressions of student engagement with the Riipen projects?" RQ4 is: "What are the industry partners' and instructors' impressions of students' quality of work with respect to completion of project objectives?" To answer these questions, the authors use experiential learning theory, the theory that assumes that learners learn the best by doing. The findings are the following. Answer to RQ1: The projects were from a variety of industries, both from startups and from more established companies.

Z. Blaber (✉)
Salem State University, Salem, MA, USA
e-mail: zblaber@salemstate.edu

B. Palatnik
Stockton University, Galloway, NJ, USA
e-mail: barry.palatnik@stockton.edu

S. Nanguneri · A. Naraian
Millennium Global Business Solutions, Westlake Village, CA, USA

T. Moloi (ed.), *Impacting Society Positively Through Technology in Accounting and Business Processes*, Springer Proceedings in Business and Economics,
https://doi.org/10.1007/978-3-031-84885-8_58

These projects required the completion of various tasks, such as creating a business plan, creating a product pricing model, doing statistical analysis, etc. Answer to RQ2: The students' performance was determined by the industry partners and instructors to vary from non-engagement to regular attendance of meetings and timely contributions to projects. Answer to RQ3: Student engagement was generally good (although this varied from class to class and from team to team) according to the industry partners and instructors. The instructors observed that some students opted out of the Riipen project and decided to do an alternative assignment instead, or decided to switch teams or work individually. Answer to RQ4: According to industry partners and instructors, the students' quality of work varied from lack of contribution to the Riipen project to excellent work that met or exceeded the projects' objectives.

Keywords Accounting education · Experiential learning · Industry partnerships · Riipen.com

Introduction

Experiential learning and hands-on classroom projects have been praised for their positive impact on learning and students' professional development (Bin Babador, 2024; Butler et al., 2019; Chisholm et al., 2009; Eckhaus et al., 2017; Rossetti, 2023; Sinha, 2023; Spanjaard et al., 2018). By participating in internships or getting involved in hands-on projects for actual business entities or not-for-profits, students tend to improve their communication and time management skills, build confidence, and enhance their employability prospects. This is particularly true for business and accounting students, many of whom will become tomorrow's business leaders. However, given the myriad of benefits of experiential learning, specifically in accounting, there are also multiple risks and challenges to adopting real-life business and accounting projects in the classroom (Ford et al., 2023; Van den Beemt et al., 2023), such as the risk of low student engagement, the risk of student apprehension or fear of participation in a real business project, risks of low quality of work, client acquisition and management challenges, student challenges, faculty challenges, and challenge-based learning issues. The research gap that this paper addresses is the link between risks and challenges of experiential learning in accounting education and student engagement and quality of work in experiential learning projects.

This paper's research objective is to discuss instructors' and industry partners' experiences with experiential learning in accounting classes. In particular, two industry partners from one American business entity from the open marketplace of Riipen.com and two instructors from two public universities in the United States discuss their experiences with student engagement and performance on Riipen projects from 2021 to 2024. Student performance is important to study both from the perspective of industry partners and instructors since such a study provides a holistic view of the workings of actual academia-industry partnerships, including the hurdles encountered. The four research questions (RQs) of this pedagogical accounting study are empirical:

RQ1: "What kind of Riipen projects did the industry partners provide to the accounting students?"
RQ2: "How did the students perform on the Riipen projects with respect to regular attendance of and timely contributions to project meetings (industry partners' and faculty feedback)?"
RQ3: "What are the industry partners' and instructors' impressions of student engagement with the Riipen projects?" and
RQ4: "What are the industry partners' and instructors' impressions of students' quality of work with respect to completion of project objectives?"

Method and Theoretical Framework

To answer the above research questions, the authors use auto-ethnography (Zicari & Perera-Aldama, 2020; Zou, 2021) as a method of research. Auto-ethnography relies on an actor's recollections of events and note keeping, often in a journal, as sources of data. The theoretical framework used is experiential learning theory, the theory that assumes that learners learn the best by doing. This theory involves learning from experience or engaging in "active learning" (Lavoie & Rosman, 2007) where learners are expected to do something practical. Experiential learning (Kolb, 1984) has been the focus of much accounting pedagogy research (see, for example, Barua & Gujarathi, 2022; Butler et al., 2021; Young & Warren, 2011).

Review of the Literature

Experiential Learning in Accounting

For Butler et al. (2019), experiential learning is about doing, reflecting, thinking, and applying knowledge to real-life situations. Experiential learning is a type of "service-learning." Still and Clayton (2004, p. 470) summarize Waterman's (1997) definition of "service-learning" as a method via which students learn and develop through their active participation in well-organized service experiences that meet the needs of the local community and that are coordinated by the learning institution. Besides, experiential learning is integrated into the learners' academic curriculum. Further, experiential learning provides students with opportunities to use their newly acquired skills, capabilities, and knowledge in real life. What is taught at school is enhanced by extending student learning beyond the classroom and into the local community.

A variety of accounting classes have been studied from the lens of experiential learning theory. For example, an accounting principles class has learned accounting concepts, while playing the Accounting Marathon board game (López-Hernández et al., 2023). These authors propose self-efficacy and learning motivation as mediating variables in the relationship between experiential learning and self-perceived academic performance among students. Van Akkeren and Tarr (2022) and Alshurafat et al. (2020) find that experiential learning is particularly relevant to forensic accounting students and auditing students (English & Koeppen, 1993; Hart et al., 2017; Siegel et al., 1997). Experiential learning, especially when done in teams and in and out of the classroom, has been found to be particularly effective in accounting education in general (Carland et al., 1994; Dellaportas, 2015).

Traditional internships have also been the focus of accounting research. These are usually paid or for-credit and they tend to last for more than 100 h (Beard, 2007; Beck & Halim, 2008). Renschler et al. (2023) demonstrate how a university developed a winter internship program to help its diverse accounting student population gain better access to the public accounting profession. Non-traditional, i.e. micro-internships (for example, internships with fewer than 100 h) have not been examined much in the literature.

Based on such accounting pedagogical studies, the benefits of experiential learning in accounting are clear—increased self-efficacy, enhanced academic performance and employability, better confidence, and improved communication skills among learners. Yet, experiential learning has not been studied much from the perspective of its risks and challenges and from industry partners' perspectives. The literature abounds of instructors' perspectives on experiential learning. Academia-industry experiential learning partnerships encounter their own successes, difficulties, risks, and challenges that deserve to be examined in more detail.

Riipen.com as an Experiential Learning Platform

Riipen is a Canadian company that has created an experiential learning platform, Riipen.com. Riipen bridges the gap between educators, learners, and employers. It facilitates employers' projects with interested educators from a plethora of disciplines—accounting, arts, business, engineering, humanities, social sciences, etc. Educators from institutions with Riipen subscriptions can choose which project(s) from Riipen's open marketplace best fit(s) the course content and students' skill level. Projects can be done either in person or online and either individually or in teams. Riipen is known for fostering equity and inclusion since *all* students in a class, not just a few, are offered to do a Riipen project as part of the semester grade/term mark. Quibrantar and Ezezika (2023), for instance, explain how Riipen's Level UP Remote Internship Program helps marginalized communities overcome geographic barriers. This program helps students better transition from school to work.

Besides Riipen, there are other experiential learning platforms, such as the Austral Group (Austral Group, n.d.), which has been providing experiential learning to help students with real-world challenges outside of the classroom since 2005. This company's network of industry partners is from Europe, Latin America, and the United States. Their projects can also be either in person or online. Forage, another experiential learning platform, started in 2017. Its mission is to create scalable project-based learning to bridge the gap between practice and classroom learning. Their experiential learning platform is free to students (Forage, n.d.). Parker Dewey offers paid micro-internships for both college students and recent graduates from the United States. Through their micro-internships, students obtain knowledge and skills for eventual full-time employment (Parker, n.d.).

Data Presentation, Analysis, and Findings

The two instructors engaged some of their classes in several Riipen projects from 2021 to 2024. Table 1 presents information on some of the two instructors' Riipen industry partners and classes working with them.

As observed from Table 1, there was a variety of industry partners from a variety of industries. Some industry partners were from the United States, while others from Canada. The two instructors used Riipen projects during and after the COVID-19 pandemic when the use of long-distance, interactive technologies, such as Microsoft Teams and Zoom, facilitated virtual communication and project execution. Per Table 1, the accounting students involved mostly communicated with business entities' owners and top management. The majority of companies were composed of startups.

Table 2 gives more information on the student teams and industry partners' feedback provided on teams' or individual students' performance on Riipen.com. Riipen projects that did not receive feedback on the Riipen platform are not included in Table 1 and Table 2.

The following observations come from the two instructors' auto-ethnography recollections and written notes on how the Riipen projects went. The Riipen projects' titles, based on Table 2, differed from project to project. Usually, the titles of the projects reflected closely the business entity's specific business needs at the time of posting the project on Riipen. Based on student enrollment, there was a different number of teams and a different number of student members per team. Some students switched teams later in the semester/term if their teammates were not contributing to the collaborative work. Other students preferred to work alone. The Riipen.com feedback from industry partners to students in the form of 1 to 5 stars also varied from team to team and sometimes from student to student (see Table 2). Some students were more involved in the project than others. The instructors observed that, generally, students from in-person classes tended to be more involved in the Riipen project than students from online, asynchronous classes. This is to be expected since in all the in-person classes of one of the instructors, attendance and participation counted as 25% of the semester grade/term mark. Moreover, students who did not hold full-time jobs while studying full time tended to do better on the

Table 1 Industry partners, classes, timing of the Riipen projects, industry, and job titles of industry partners

Number) Industry partner (website)	Class name (undergraduate /graduate)	Semester	Location of the industry partner	Industry of the industry partner	Industry partner's contact person's job title
1) Honey Sweetie Acres (https://honeysweetieacres.com/)	Accounting analysis for decision making (graduate)	Spring 2021	Ohio, USA	Cosmetics and beauty	Owner
2) RHST Industries (https://www.rhstindustries.com/)	Management accounting (undergraduate)	Spring 2021	Québec, Canada	Technology, environment	President
3) Pillir (pillir.io)	Cost accounting (undergraduate)	Spring 2021	Arizona, USA	Technology, IT & computing	Chief Revenue Officer (CRO)
4) Hybrid Helix (https://HybridHELIX.consulting)	Accounting analysis for decision making (graduate)	Fall 2021	New Mexico, USA	Retail, Marketing & Advertising	Executive Strategy Consultant & Co-Founder
5) MentaMorph (https://www.mentamorph.com)	Cost accounting (undergraduate)	Spring 2024	Texas, USA	Education, Consumer Goods & Services, Banking & Finance, IT & computing	Founder
6) Grey-Box (https://www.grey-box.ca/)	Cost accounting (undergraduate)	Spring 2024	Québec, Canada	Education, non-profit, Philanthropic & Civil Society, IT & computing, technology, telecommunications	Chief Executive Officer (CEO)

Riipen project than those who worked full time and studied full time. Thus, working full while studying full time was found to be a major risk and challenge to doing well on the Riipen projects. A success story: one student shared with his instructor that the Riipen project helped him obtain his first full-time job after college since the student talked about the Riipen project during the interview and the employer seemed to be very impressed with what the student shared.

The two industry partners, co-authors of this paper, from Millennium Global Business Solutions (MGBS) facilitated a Riipen project in Spring 2024, a project that is not part of Tables 1 and 2. The project covered the following topics: debt versus income ratio trends of families from rural, urban, and suburban areas of the

Table 2 Riipen project titles, teams' details, feedback received, and class modality

Number of industry partners from Table 1) Riipen project title	Number of student teams (total number of students) (teams' details)	Feedback from industry partner (1–5 stars)	Class modality
1. Managerial Accounting Project	Six (25 students) (Team 1: 4 members, Team 2: 5 members, Team 3: 5 members, Team 4: 4 members, Team 5: 3 members, Team 6: 4 members)	One team received 4.5/5 stars, while the other teams did not receive any feedback	Online, synchronous, i.e. on Zoom
2. Pricing Model Development	Nine (34 students) (Team 1: 4 members, Team 2: 2 members, Team 3: 3 members, Team 4: 5 members, Team 5: 5 members, Team 6: 3 members, Team 7: 3 members, Team 8: 3 members, Team 9: 6 members)	One team received 5 stars. One team received 4 stars. One team received 3.5 stars. One team received 3 stars. Two teams received 2.5 stars. Two teams received 2 stars. One team received no feedback	Online, asynchronous
3. Cost- Benefits of Software Development Transformation	Five (17 students) (Team 1: 6 members, Team 2: 2 members, Team 3: 4 members, Team 4: 4 members, Team 5: 1 member)	Team 1 received 1 star. Team 2 received 4 stars. One member of Team 3 received 5 stars, the other members of the team—no feedback. Team 4 received 3 stars. Team 5 received no feedback	Online, synchronous
4. Bookkeeping and Accounting for Small Startup	Four (16 students) (Team 1: 5 members, Team 2: 3 members, Team 3: 4 members, Team 4: 4 members)	The members of all teams received 5 stars	Online, synchronous
5. Develop Price and Cost Models for Financial Game and Workshops Product	Two (7 students) (Team 1: 4 members, Team 2: 3 members)	The members of both teams received 2.5 stars	Online, asynchronous
6. Commercialization—Social Impact Project	Five (21 students) (Team 1: 4 members, Team 2: 5 members, Team 3: 3 members, Team 4: 5 members, Team 5: 4 members)	The members of all teams received 5 stars	Online, asynchronous

United States, causal analysis of spending versus saving habits, and modeling causes and effects related to spending and savings habits. Team 1 of the MGBS project focused on a detailed statistical analysis on rural, urban, and suburban families' fiscal habits, while Team 2 devised a mathematical model displaying variables that influenced family fiscal habits. The learners were expected to know or learn some statistics to achieve the project's objectives. According to the two industry partners' autoethnography reflections, students gained a unique experience in having a practical application of their academic knowledge and tended to be actively engaged in the project. Most learners worked hard with respect to the MGBS project and communicated regularly with MGBS's representatives. Some students did not communicate with the industry partners at all or chose to communicate with them in the last moment before the project was due. Most students had a strong commitment to successfully complete the project, given a tight schedule—the students were responsible for managing academic requirements, professional responsibilities, and the Riipen project all in parallel. This concludes the auto-ethnography presentation of the two industry partners. Let us now answer the four research questions posed at the beginning of this paper.

Answer to RQ1: The Riipen projects were from a variety of industries (consumer goods, IT, telecommunications, etc., per Table 1), both from startups and from more established companies, but mostly from startups. The projects required the completion of various tasks, such as creating a business plan, creating a product pricing model, doing statistical analysis, and so on, per Table 2. Accounting classes were thus introduced to a large variety of projects that were either closely linked to the material studied in class or not so linked to the material covered, but that required additional research on the part of the students.

Answer to RQ2: The students' performance was determined by the industry partners and instructors to vary from student non-engagement to regular student attendance of team meetings with the industry partners and teammates and to timely contributions to projects. Overall, the students performed well on the Riipen projects with respect to regular attendance of and timely contributions to project meetings, according to the industry partners and faculty members involved.

Answer to RQ3: Impressions of student engagement was generally good, although this varied from class to class and from team to team, according to industry partners and instructors. The instructors observed that some students opted out of the Riipen project and decided to do an alternative assignment or decided to switch teams or work individually. The reason for this that many students provided to their instructors was that students worked full time and studied full time and that a Riipen project would add a heavy time commitment to their schedules. Some industry partners expected the student teams to meet them once a week for 12 weeks during the semester. The fact that most students received 25% of the semester grade/term mark on this project weakened students' arguments that the project was too time consuming.

Answer to RQ4: According to industry partners, the students' quality of work varied from lack of contribution to the Riipen project to excellent work that met or exceeded the projects' objectives (please see the star rankings in the third column of

Table 2). For example, many students received 5 star rankings from the industry partners, while others received only 1–2 stars. How students performed depended on their level of involvement, professionalism, communication skills, punctuality, teamwork, analytical thinking, innovation, and desire to research the topic assigned. The two instructors noted that some students consulted with the university business librarian to find relevant resources for the Riipen project, and that this consultation contributed to good quality work on the projects. Some students also sought the instructors' help and advice during office hours or via email. These students tended to receive positive feedback from the industry partners. Students who did not work on the project or who worked on it in the last moment either received no feedback from the industry partners or received poor feedback (1 or 2 stars).

Discussion and Conclusion

The auto-ethnography data provided above by the two instructors and the two industry partners, all co-authors of this paper, are evidence to the fact that every Riipen project experience is unique in terms of student engagement and student quality of work. The instructors and industry partners shared data in the form of tables and in the form of narrative journal notes and recollections of student work. Most students did a good faith effort to address the tasks expected from them by the industry partners. The instructors also did their best to facilitate the academia-industry partnerships, a task that may be time-consuming and that requires attention to detail and regular communication. The industry partners were very generous with their time facilitating the Riipen projects. They met regularly with the student teams during the semester/term and answered any student questions.

The Forbes Coaches Council (FCC, 2022) provides examples of experiential learning best practices, such as carefully choose the experiential project, require learners to make decisions and be accountable for these decisions, and nurture the relationships established. Moreover, the FCC contends that educators and learners should be willing to accept both success and failure, educators and learners need to self-reflect, educators need to be open-minded, and experiential learning should be designed to learn from mistakes. These are good points to consider when evaluating the effectiveness of Riipen projects and student performance, such as in this paper.

Experiential learning in accounting education (Alshurafat et al., 2020; Barua & Gujarathi, 2022; Butler et al., 2021; English & Koeppen, 1993; Hart et al., 2017; Marriott et al., 2015; Renschler et al., 2023; Siegel et al., 1997; Still & Clayton, 2004), in theory, is beneficial to students, industry partners, educators, and academic institutions alike. In practice, these partnerships are not without their risks and challenges. The risks and challenges do affect student engagement and student quality of work. For example, one of the two instructors noticed that due to the high cost of living in the Boston, Massachusetts area, many students felt compelled to study and work full time. This weaned such students away from the Riipen project and these students opted to write an essay or do the Bloomberg Environmental,

Social, Governance (ESG) certificate instead, after obtaining permission for this switch of assignments from the instructor. It is unfortunate that adverse financial circumstances detract students from experiential learning opportunities. Another hurdle was the online, asynchronous class modality in some of the classes. In some of these classes, the instructor could only communicate with learners via email and video posted on the learning management system, not in person, nor via video conferencing. Not checking emails on time contributed to some students' procrastination until a few days before the Riipen project was due and this led to the disappointment of some industry partners and the instructors.

The limitation of this study includes the fact that only six Riipen projects were included in the two tables and accompanied by the auto-ethnography reflections by the two instructors. This is because only six Riipen projects received feedback from industry partners on the Riipen platform. About 10 more Riipen projects were conducted by the two instructors, but they received no feedback from the industry partners on the Riipen platform. Only one Riipen project accompanied the auto-ethnography reflections of the two industry partners in this paper. This Riipen project was not one from the tables since it did not receive feedback from the industry partners. In the future, if more Riipen projects are added to the two tables (and consequently, more auto-ethnography data), the conclusions of this study will be, perhaps, different.

No matter what the risks and challenges are, experiential learning such as Riipen projects should be undertaken by colleges and universities as much as possible. Accreditation bodies, such as the Association to Advance Colleges and Schools of Business (AACSB), value active learning very highly. Parents of prospective students regularly inquire about internship opportunities at university open houses. Besides, employers tend to ask about prior work experience during job interviews with recent college and university graduates. Experiential learning is well positioned to be an important part of the future of education since it prepares learners for the many demands of the real world of business and employment. Active learning should be embraced, not feared or put aside, no matter the risks and challenges it brings.

References

Alshurafat, H., Beattie, C., Jones, G., & Sands, J. (2020). Perceptions of the usefulness of various teaching methods in forensic accounting education. *Accounting Education, 29*(2), 177–204. https://doi-org.corvette.salemstate.edu. https://doi.org/10.1080/09639284.2020.1719425

Austral Group. (n.d.). Connecting universities and companies to solve real-world business challenges. Retrieved May 14, 2024, from https://learning.theaustralgroup.com/.

Barua, S. K., & Gujarathi, M. R. (2022). Prestige Projects Limited: Challenges in transitioning to new accounting policy. *Issues in Accounting Education, 37*(1), 109. https://doi.org/10.2308/ISSUES-2020-074

Beard, D. (2007). Assessment of internship experiences and accounting core competencies. *Accounting Education, 16*(2), 207–220. https://doi-org.corvette.salemstate.edu. https://doi.org/10.1080/09639280701234625

Beck, J. E., & Halim, H. (2008). Undergraduate internships in accounting: What and how do Singapore interns learn from experience? *Accounting Education, 17*(2), 151–172. https://doi-org.corvette.salemstate.edu. https://doi.org/10.1080/09639280701220277

Bin Babador, M. H. (2024). FEXES3.0: Enhancing business management skills via experiential learning for foundation students. *Global Business and Management Research, 16*(2), 409–417. Suppl. Special Issue: South East Asia International Islamic Philanthropy Conference. https://corvette.salemstate.edu/login?qurl=https%3A%2F%2Fwww.proquest.com%2Fscholarly-journals%2Ffexes3-0-enhancing-business-management-skills-via%2Fdocview%2F3055537043%2Fse-2%3Faccountid%3D13661.

Butler, M. G., Church, K. S., King, G. H., & Spencer, A. W. (2021). Do your students know what they don't know? An accounting competencies strategy. *Issues in Accounting Education, 36*(4), 207. https://doi.org/10.2308/ISSUES-19-083

Butler, M. G., Church, K. S., & Spencer, A. W. (2019). Do, reflect, think, apply: Experiential education in accounting. *Journal of Accounting Education, 48*, 12–21. https://doi.org/10.1016/j.jaccedu.2019.05.001

Carland, J. W., Carland, J. C., & Dye, J. L. (1994). Accounting education: A cooperative learning strategy. *Accounting Education, 3*(3), 223. https://doi-org.corvette.salemstate.edu. https://doi.org/10.1080/09639289400000021

Chisholm, C. U., Harris, M. S. G., Northwood, D. O., & Johrendt, J. L. (2009). The characterisation of work-based learning by consideration of the theories of experiential learning. *European Journal of Education, 44*(3), 319–337. http://www.jstor.org/stable/27743176.

Dellaportas, S. (2015). Reclaiming 'sense' from 'cents' in accounting education. *Accounting Education, 24*(6), 445–460. https://doi-org.corvette.salemstate.edu. https://doi.org/10.1080/09639284.2015.1114456

Eckhaus, E., Klein, G., & Kantor, J. (2017). Experiential learning in management education. *Business, Management & Education/Verslas, Vadyba Ir Studijos, 15*(1), 42–56. https://doi-org.corvette.salemstate.edu. https://doi.org/10.3846/bme.2017.345

English, D. M., & Koeppen, D. R. (1993). The relationship of accounting internships and subsequent academic performance. *Issues in Accounting Education, 8*(2), 292–299. https://corvette.salemstate.edu/login?qurl=https%3A%2F%2Fwww.proquest.com%2Fscholarly-journals%2Frelationship-accounting-internships-subsequent%2Fdocview%2F210910075%2Fse-2%3Faccountid%3D13661.

Forage. (n.d.). Enable students, from any background, the ability to upskill & land amazing careers. Retrieved May 14, 2024, from https://www.theforage.com/.

Forbes Coaches Council. (2022, June 10). 14 great examples of experiential learning in the workplace. Retrieved May 10, 2024, from https://www.forbes.com/sites/forbescoachescouncil/2022/06/10/14-great-examples-of-experiential-learning-in-the-workplace/?sh=7994a71947a7.

Ford, S. J., Goana, T. H., & Gill, A. K. (2023). Extracurricular student-run consulting projects: Experiential learning, benefits and challenges at Axis Consulting. *The International Journal of Management Education, 21*(3). https://doi.org/10.1016/j.ijme.2023.100851

Hart, M., Kremin, J., & Pasewark, W. R. (2017). Growing up: How audit internships affect students' commitment and long-term intentions to work in public accounting. *Issues in Accounting Education, 32*(2), 47–63. https://doi-org.corvette.salemstate.edu. https://doi.org/10.2308/iace-51431

Kolb, D. (1984). *Experiential learning: Experience as a source of learning and development.* Pearson Education.

Lavoie, D., & Rosman, A. J. (2007). Using active student-centered learning-based instructional design to develop faculty and improve course design, delivery, and evaluation. *Issues in Accounting Education, 22*(1), 105–118. https://corvette.salemstate.edu/

login?qurl=https%3A%2F%2Fwww.proquest.com%2Fscholarly-journals%2Fusing-active-student-centered-learning-based%2Fdocview%2F210906456%2Fse-2%3Faccountid%3D13661.

López-Hernández, C., Lizarraga-Álvarez, G. I., & Soto-Pérez, M. (2023). Enhancing learning of accounting principles through experiential learning in a board game. *Accounting Education, 32*(3), 300–331. https://doi-org.corvette.salemstate.edu. https://doi.org/10.1080/09639284.2022.2059770

Marriott, P., Tan, S. M., & Marriott, N. (2015). Experiential learning—a case study of the use of computerised stock market trading simulation in finance education. *Accounting Education, 24*(6), 480–497. https://doi-org.corvette.salemstate.edu. https://doi.org/10.1080/09639284.2015.1072728

Parker, D. (n.d.). About us. Retrieved May 14, 2024, from https://www.parkerdewey.com/about.

Quibrantar, S. M., & Ezezika, O. (2023). Evaluating student engagement and experiential learning in global classrooms: A qualitative case study. *Studies in Educational Evaluation, 78*, 101290. https://doi.org/10.1016/j.stueduc.2023.101290

Renschler, M. E., Riley, T. J., & Stuart, A. C. (2023). From equal to equitable: Developing an inclusive winter internship program. *Issues in Accounting Education, 38*(1), 163–183. https://doi-org.corvette.salemstate.edu. https://doi.org/10.2308/ISSUES-2021-101

Rossetti, G. (2023). Applying Kolb's experiential learning theory to an event management course: Practical guidelines for educators. *Event Management, 27*(7), 1025–1040. https://doi.org/10.3727/152599523X16896548396752

Siegel, P. H., Omer, K., & Agrawal, S. P. (1997). Video simulation of an audit: An experiment in experiential learning theory. *Accounting Education, 6*(3), 217–230. https://doi-org.corvette.salemstate.edu. https://doi.org/10.1080/096392897331451

Sinha, E. (2023). 'Co-creating' experiential learning in the metaverse—extending the Kolb's learning cycle and identifying potential challenges. *The International Journal of Management Education, 21*(3), 100875. https://doi.org/10.1016/j.ijme.2023.100875

Spanjaard, D., Hall, T., & Stegemann, N. (2018). Experiential learning: Helping students to become 'career-ready'. *Australasian Marketing Journal, 26*(2), 163–171. https://doi.org/10.1016/j.ausmj.2018.04.003

Still, K., & Clayton, P. R. (2004). Utilizing service-learning in accounting programs. *Issues in Accounting Education, 19*(4), 469–486. https://corvette.salemstate.edu/login?qurl=https%3A%2F%2Fwww.proquest.com%2Fscholarly-journals%2Futilizing-service-learning-accounting-programs%2Fdocview%2F210903201%2Fse-2%3Faccountid%3D13661.

Van Akkeren, J. K., & Tarr, J.-A. (2022). The application of experiential learning for forensic accounting students: The mock trial. *Accounting Education, 31*(1), 39–66. https://doi-org.corvette.salemstate.edu. https://doi.org/10.1080/09639284.2021.1960573

Van den Beemt, A., Vázquez-Villegas, P., Gómez Puente, S., O'Riordan, F., Gormley, C., Chiang, F.-K., Leng, C., Caratozzolo, P., Zavala, G., & Membrillo-Hernández, J. (2023). Taking the challenge: An exploratory study of the challenge-based learning context in higher education institutions across three different continents. *Education Sciences, 13*(3), 1–23. https://doi.org/10.3390/educsci13030234

Waterman, A. S. (1997). *Service-learning: Applications from the research.* Lawrence Erlbaum Associates.

Young, M., & Warren, D. L. (2011). Encouraging the development of critical thinking skills in the introductory accounting courses using the challenge problem approach. *Issues in Accounting Education Suppl. Special Issue on the First Course in Accounting, 26*(4), 859–881. https://corvette.salemstate.edu/login?qurl=https%3A%2F%2Fwww.proquest.com%2Fscholarly-journals%2Fencouraging-development-critical-thinking-skills%2Fdocview%2F1013839001%2Fse-2%3Faccountid%3D13661.

Zicari, A., & Perera-Aldama, L. (2020). Building from scratch: An auto-ethnographic approach for the development of a social reporting model. *Social and Environmental Accountability Journal, 40*(2), 101–115. https://doi.org/10.1080/0969160X.2020.1765825

Zou, Y. (2021). Methodological insights experiencing and knowing in the field: An autoethnographic account of conducting audit fieldwork in China. *Accounting, Auditing & Accountability Journal, 34*(3), 680–698. https://doi.org/10.1108/AAAJ-07-2020-4706

A Case of Business Strategies for Positioning and Competitiveness in South Africa

Zoé Julie Bosch, Dirk Rossouw, and Maria Bounds

Abstract Literature and world news provide evidence of the need for strategy adjustments in the search for excellence, thus allowing manufacturers to achieve a strong marketing position on a continuous basis. This research investigated business strategies, brand trust, brand awareness and brand positioning in the case of a motorcycle manufacturer in South Africa. A case study strategy was selected, allowing an exhaustive and in-depth study of the perceptions of the motorcycle manufacturer and its employees regarding the direction the motorcycle manufacturer would take in terms of strategic brand awareness and positioning in order to gain maximum competitive advantage. The population was the motorcycle manufacturer in South Africa with its numerous dealerships across the country. However, for the sample, the head office and a few dealerships spread across Gauteng were selected, as most dealerships were situated in this province. Both methods of convenience sampling and purposive sampling were used for the initial contact with the head office and the individual dealerships. Assessing the interpretive paradigm allowed for semi-structured interviews to be held, thus allowing for an in-depth understanding of interviewee perceptions, opinions, and experiences to be derived. Once the data had been collected, a process of transcribing followed, which allowed for the coding of multiple emerging themes from the interviews. These themes were coded using the software, Atlas.ti, which serves as a qualitative analysis tool. It was found that collaboration was lacking among the several dealerships situated across the Gauteng region. The importance of resolving this matter is critical to ensure factors such as customer satisfaction, while attaining more market share. Additionally, it is crucial for the manufacturer to modify and incorporate the necessary strategies to target and acquire new markets.

Keywords Strategy · Brand awareness · New markets · Consumers

---

Z. J. Bosch · D. Rossouw · M. Bounds (✉)
University of Johannesburg, Johannesburg, South Africa
e-mail: drossouw@uj.ac.za; mariab@uj.ac.za

T. Moloi (ed.), *Impacting Society Positively Through Technology in Accounting and Business Processes*, Springer Proceedings in Business and Economics,
https://doi.org/10.1007/978-3-031-84885-8_59

Introduction

Manufacturers should constantly identify current consumer preferences and new segments within the market which the manufacturer could potentially target (Mtanga & McCamel, 2019). New mobility is receiving increased attention globally, including South Africa. This would require motorcycle manufacturers to implement new strategies as well as change their strategic decision-making and strategic positioning in order to keep up with the consumer demands and gain an increasingly more competitive advantage (Martin, 2019).

At the same time, manufacturers need to consider the weakened market conditions across the country, despite the automotive industry revealing considerable potential through the increasing middle-income class of consumers (Barnes et al., 2018). Decreased business activities led to the loss of employment, the reduction in national content of all vehicles within the automotive sector, and the loss of any localisation benefits gained in the 2 years prior to the pandemic (West, 2020).

South Africa is recognised as the market leader on the African continent when it comes to vehicle production. Since motorcycles are used mainly for recreation, the majority of those sold have an engine capacity over 150 cc. This is especially relevant in the small motorcycles and scooters category (Business Wire, 2020). Manufacturing capabilities, recognised in South Africa as resources to assemble motorcycles, are available and the production of various parts is possible, but this remains unexploited. Additionally, there is the potential for growth in the demand for low-cost motorcycles in the lower income market, allowing for a less expensive, more time-efficient mode of transport (Mtanga & McCamel, 2019). It is therefore necessary to supply motorcycles in alignment with market needs, making lives easier and more affordable.

Problem Statement and Objectives

The change in consumer demands is affecting the market within the motorcycle industry. The market is increasingly moving towards the digitalisation of vehicles, which is having a big impact on the motorcycle industry. With the start of a new era, new mobility is receiving increased attention globally, including South Africa. This would require motorcycle manufacturers to implement a new strategy, to change their strategic decision-making and strategic positioning to keep up with the consumer demands, and to gain an increasingly more competitive advantage. Motorcycle manufacturers want to remain on top of the new trending technology, which necessitates continuous updates and improvement of processes in order to change the strategic market positioning.

The following research question was derived: How should the motorcycle manufacturer in South Africa view and adapt its brand trust and awareness to gain a competitive advantage?

Primary Objective

The primary research objective was to determine the motorcycle manufacturer's current brand positioning in South Africa, thus ensuring a competitive advantage within the South African motorcycle industry.

Review of Literature

Although motorcycle manufacturers are based worldwide, specific attention is given to South Africa.

Business Strategies to Determine Market Positioning

The fast-paced transformation of industrial revolutions requires the motorcycle manufacturer to re-evaluate its strategic model in order to generate and exploit newfound opportunities. These strategic choices will involve the change in resources as well as the organisation's process. Through this, organisations gain a newfound understanding of the changes in the market (Deloitte & McKinsey & Company, 2019).

When an organisation defines its business strategy, it is critical for it to determine its strategic positioning, meaning how customers are served in the market in terms of competitive advantage. To build a long-lasting customer relationship, three elements are important, namely attracting customers, customer satisfaction, and customer retention, which are described to be at the core of customer bonding (Dean & Company, 2018).

Dean and Company (2018) describe customer bonding as the driving force in shaping the organisational strategy. Creating a strategy revolves around a framework whereby the product orientation is researched, meaning that the product and its sales and how it appeals to the public are investigated. Furthermore, it involves determining the product's positioning compared to competitors' products and ways to exceed customer expectations. Organisations tend to standardise their product offerings for customers, which are offered using mass channels of distribution.

Baines et al. (2005) describe strategic positioning as a concept to guide the organisation when achieving goals and objectives set according to the value chain. Strategic positioning involves the decisions made by managers to determine which activities will occur and be operated internally and which will be operated externally in terms of being monitored and controlled by suppliers, organisational partners, and distributors, as well as the end-customers. Torok (2019) specifies that "business strategy often takes its lessons from battle", which means that strategies are amended, modified, and strengthened every time they face intense competition on the market.

This creates the goal to improve the organisation, which needs to be done through the strategy. It calls for the brand to be located as best as possible in the hearts and minds of the marketplace. This will create a competitive advantage, which is particularly important owing to the continuously changing environment; it allows the organisation to create a firm and set image within the marketplace. Porter (1980) developed three generic competitive strategies. These strategies have an influential position in the field of strategic management. They enable organisations at the business level to establish and categorise several strategies to determine the overall competitive direction and the segment they are looking to target in order to achieve a competitive advantage. Porter stresses that each of the three generic competitive strategies represents varying options to an organisation looking to demonstrate competitive advantage.

The competitive strategies have been grouped into cost leadership, focus, and differentiation strategies, all of which represent different strategic alternatives. These concepts are used to assist managers in developing key operation procedures, as well as gaining an increased advantage over competitors. Achieving competitive advantage within an industry requires the organisation to give their complete support and commitment to implementing the generic strategy effectively. The implementation of the generic strategy permits an increased return, as well as gaining increased competitive advantage over rivals (Porter, 1980).

Strategic positioning prompts management to analyse the variety of divergent strategies that they can implement. Therefore, it is crucial for managers to investigate and thoroughly examine the market segment that they are looking to target in order to achieve a competitive advantage with the strategy that they have chosen to pursue (Prabhakar Rajkumar & Abraham, 2018). Figure 1 below illustrates the generic (competitive) strategies with potential advantages they could create.

Fig. 1 Potential advantages of generic (competitive) strategies. *Source:* Prabhakar Rajkumar and Abraham (2018)

The South African Motorcycle Industry

The local automotive industry has been through a prominent transformation since the emergence of the South African democracy. The industry is dominated mainly by globally recognised organisations, with increased volumes of importing as well as exporting. Subsequently, these organisations have demonstrated the competency to manufacture vehicles both effectively and efficiently, as measured against the highest global standards. Many South African organisations involved in the assembly and manufacturing of vehicles have secured global recognition through the precision and quality of manufactured products (Barnes et al., 2018).

Favoured motorcycles used for commuting purposes range from cruisers to adventure motorcycles. In South Africa specifically, the latter allow for much more comfort in terms of handling rougher roads and potholes. Nevertheless, the costs of a high-end motorcycle along with the gear, parts, and accessories that are required are high (Le Roux, 2018). A cheaper and more convenient mode of transport in South Africa would be low-end motorcycles. However, these have not been brought into the country on a large scale. Instead, more expensive motorcycles that are heavier, newer in model and incorporated with the latest technology are owned by the wealthier 10% of the South African population (Mtanga & McCamel, 2019).

In 2020, businesses were forced to take on an unavoidable challenge, namely the COVID-19 pandemic. They were obligated to look into a crisis response as a method of survival, as most countries globally were faced with lockdown regulations, strict laws and, for some, the decline of business. Based on the direction of the market, organisations were required to follow health and safety protocols, perhaps even providing more for the community, as a way of setting a favourable image for customers (Butler & Rivera, 2020).

When an organisation defines the business strategy, it is critical for it to determine the strategic positioning, meaning how customers are served in the market and in terms of the competitive advantage. To build a long-lasting customer relationship, three elements are important, namely attracting customers, customer satisfaction, and customer retention, which are described to be at the core of customer bonding (Dean & Company, 2018).

Furthermore, according to Dean and Company (2018) it involves determining the product's positioning compared to competitors' products and ways to exceed customer expectations. Organisations tend to standardise their product offerings for customers, which are offered using mass channels of distribution. A type of confidence then becomes apparent, more specifically among the end-customers of the products. In combining these various aspects with the creation of long-term customer relationships, an indestructible link between the customer and the organisation is created which is referred to as the customer bonding effect. This can also be described as a long-term relationship that involves trust, transparency, and a valuable engagement for all parties concerned.

Key Factors to Maintain a Competitive Advantage

Various studies refer to managing competitive advantage and discuss factors to consider, to gain, as well as to maintain competitive advantage. Some of these key factors are innovation, quality, service, speed, cost competitiveness, and sustainability (Bateman et al., 2019).

To secure and increase competitive advantage, an organisation must ensure the execution of continuous innovation, which is to create, modify, or invent a new good or service. This requires flexibility in strategy to adapt to the changing needs of customers and new competitors entering the market (Bateman et al., 2019). To compete successfully, organisations need to introduce new products and services faster than rivals, at a very high quality and at extremely competitive prices. Concurrent increases in service and product quality, assortment, and personalisation have led customers to become more attentive to the relation between quality and price. Through an increased level of difficulty in competing in the markets, an organisation's ultimate survival is dependent on the ability to ensure that sufficient profits are gained through accurate forecasting of future economic circumstances, along with the impact created by competitive and technological advancements (Pistoni & Songini, 2017).

Quality is defined as the assurance of excellence in the product that the organisation manufactures. For an organisation to remain competitive, customer expectations of high-quality products and services need to be met at a consistent level. Deming states that long-term relationships result in increased quality and decreased costs (quoted by Bateman et al., 2019). Enhancing the quality of a product or service is regarded as one of the best ways to increase customer satisfaction. Especially with the increase and continuous improvement in technology, expectations rise for the manufacturing and provision of a product to the market or a service at speed, allowing for executions, response rates, and the delivery of products and/or services to be done in a fast and timely manner. Today, speed has become, as organisations call it, a "strategic imperative" (Bateman et al., 2019).

The term "service" refers to providing the customer with a level of service, taking the speed of service and dependability into account, that they expect or demand at the specific moment and time that they want it. This allows an organisation to create and build on long-term relationships, thereby enabling it to either gain more or sustain competitive advantage (Bateman et al., 2019). Customers often compare prices when purchasing a product; therefore, it is important for an organisation to provide both quality and affordable products, to allow for an increased brand image leading to competitive advantage (Bateman et al., 2019).

The emergence of technology has transformed the labour markets, resulting in the automation of many processes. Therefore, knowledge and skills have become increasingly popular and hunted by various organisations. By making use of skills as a powerful tool, labourers can assist strategists in preparing for the future by acquiring skills and knowledge required. In addition, rather than newly acquiring these skills from the labour market, these can be developed for upcoming innovations and changes (Lu, 2019). Researchers and developers are therefore constantly under pressure to identify and determine customer preferences, as well as newly available emerging market segments (Mtanga & McCamel, 2019).

Research Methodology

The research design consists of a process of planning how the research will be carried out and what methods will be used. Several definitions of variables, as well as those of cases, are determined, leading to the articulation of either a research hypothesis or the research question, which in turn will be tested against collected data (Cardano, 2020). An interpretivist research paradigm was followed, making it possible to understand the world according to the insights and experiences of the interviewees. In other words, an understanding was constructed of the various insights and experiences provided (Thanh & Thanh, 2015). A qualitative research approach was used, a process that can be thought of as the phrasing of an argument to convince the community of the credibility of the conclusions reached (Cardano, 2020).

A case study strategy enables the collection of rich data that is detailed in content within the social context, thus allowing for a better understanding of the environment in question (Willis, 2007). Therefore, a case study strategy was selected, allowing an exhaustive and in-depth study of the perceptions of the motorcycle manufacturer and its employees regarding the direction that the motorcycle manufacturer would take in terms of strategic positioning in order to gain maximum competitive advantage.

The population was the motorcycle manufacturer in South Africa with its numerous dealerships across the country. However, for the sample, the head office and a few dealerships spread across Gauteng were selected, as most dealerships were situated in this province. Both methods of convenience sampling and purposive sampling were used for the initial contact with the head office and the individual dealerships. Sampling methods have been divided into two different categories, namely probability sampling and non-probability sampling (Bryman & Bell, 2014). Owing to the qualitative approach, non-probability sampling methods were used.

Therefore, the appropriate sample size, which will echo the purpose of a specific study in qualitative research, consists of 16 to 24 interviews to develop a rich understanding of the issues at hand. Code saturation refers to the moment when similar answers are heard, covering a wide variety of possibilities. However, meaning saturation refers to the moment when the data from the interviews are fully understood and rich in content (Hennink et al., 2016). For this research, however, the sample consisted of 29 interviewees (see biographical data).

The data collection process involved semi-structured interviews conducted with various interviewees within the head office and the individual dealerships. An interview guide was used to assist in pre-determining topics or questions, ensuring consistency among interviews. Interviews took approximately half an hour to ensure the collection of rich data. The data were analysed by means of content analysis. This followed a specific process, using Atlas.ti, while following the steps set out by Du Plooy-Cilliers et al. (2014) to conduct the content analysis. The process included coding various phrases and words that were deemed important in the realisation of the research objectives and the research question of the study. This led to the creation of numerous categories and varying themes. Through this, a pattern emerged from the collected data, which was used when drawing final conclusions.

Ethics

In applying ethics, the interests and rights of the research participants, as well as the general public are protected, safeguarding their well-being and dignity throughout the course of the study (Silverman, 2013). Ensuring that the research met moral standards, primary ethics included strategies to obtain informed consent from interviewees, thus establishing a sense of trust and a relationship between the two parties, to stipulate the risks of the research in comparison with the benefits, to ensure the confidentiality level of the research carried out, and lastly to explain the part played by the researcher and her reflections (Haines, 2017).

Findings

Biographical Data

This section contains some personal information on the research interviewees. A total of 29 interviews were held. Since all individual dealerships were owned separately, they faced different challenges within the organisation, placing themselves differently from the rest of the dealerships.

Interviewees' Role in the Brand

To achieve the intent of purposive sampling, research interviewees were employed under the following positions (Fig. 2):

The role of the dealer principal was explained as one that takes on the general operations of the individual dealership, ensuring "that the business is economically viable, and that it is actually worth investing in, as well as giving a return back to the individuals who have invested into this business".

The managing director of the brand within South Africa took on a similar role to the dealer principals, only over a broader spectrum, namely overseeing "the entire

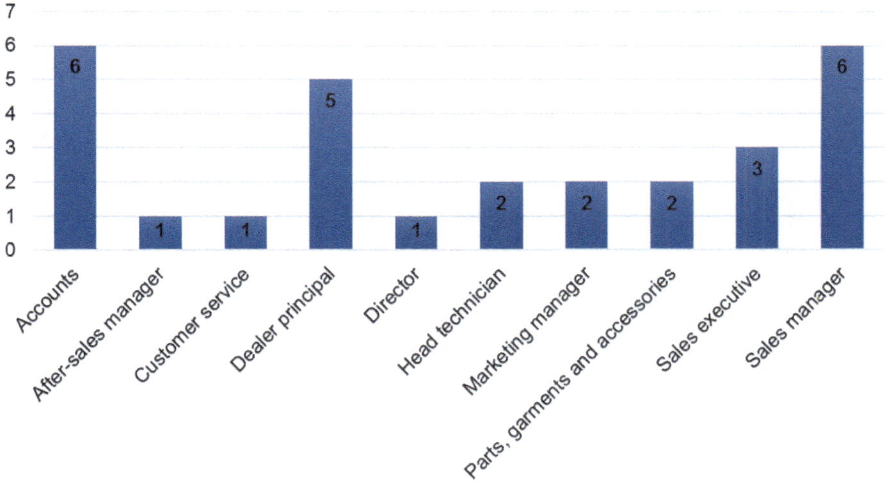

Fig. 2 Interviewee roles within the brand

scope of the business". This included regular interactions with the various dealerships, ensuring that all principles were implemented correctly and that the philosophy and core values were represented appropriately.

The after-sales manager elaborated more on the role in question. Following their main goal of always keeping the customer riding, the customer service manager oversaw "all the technical issues, warranties, training for the dealers", taking on a big role, ensuring that the satisfaction and expectations of consumers were always met.

At head office level, the marketing manager was required to be involved in the racing scene as a team manager, ensuring that the team racers produced the right marketing for the sponsors and interaction. This took the marketing manager towards the tasks of brand development, brand launching, and brand positioning. In addition, assistance was provided to the sales executives, ensuring that the right marketing was conducted for an increased flow in motorcycle sales.

The PGA side of the business refers to the "related parts to the brand's motorcycles", covering a broad range of spare parts, clothing, and accessories. This role required the employees to ensure that all the products demanded by consumers were in stock or were placed on order accordingly. The sales executives provided sales assistance to customers. Here, the customer was dealt with first-hand. The sales executive was required to have adequate knowledge of the evaluation of motorcycles, as well as selling an upgraded package to the customer.

The role of the sales manager differed between head office level and dealership level. At head office, the sales manager was required to order the relevant motorcycles from headquarters situated in Europe. This included the stock control, importing, and distribution of the motorcycles to the individual dealerships. The sales managers at dealership level were responsible for "all the sales driven issues and looking over all the responsibilities" of the individual sales executives.

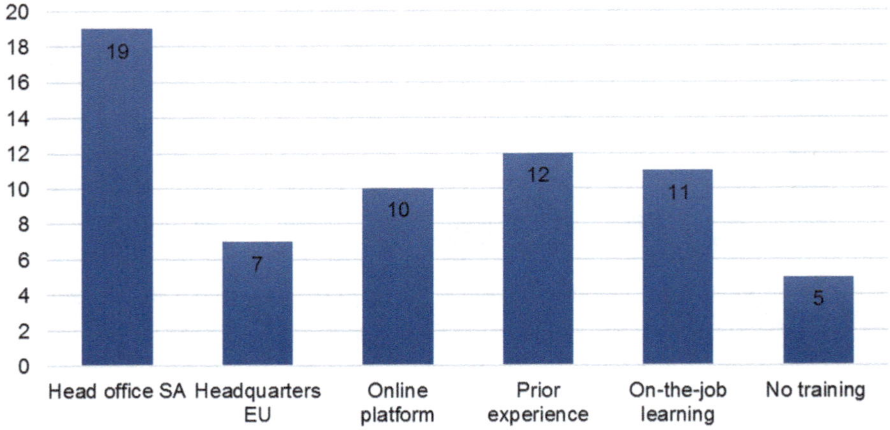

Fig. 3 Training completed by interviewees

Additionally, one sales manager was specifically contracted to "rebuild the sales team", described as the "basis of any retail business".

Training Completed by Interviewees

This question in the demographics section dealt with the training that the various interviewees had undergone. This provided a better understanding of the knowledge they had acquired and how this had been achieved. This would also provide a better examination of the complete responses received and why the individuals had responded the way they had (Fig. 3).

The majority of the interviewees had undergone training through head office, specifically 19 of the 29 interviewees. For further and more in-depth training, some employees had been sent to headquarters, located in Europe. This training was specifically for those working at head office level and the head technicians to ensure product knowledge.

As described by 17 interviewees, the courses had consisted of training on specific job positions. For instance, six of the sales representatives listed the following training courses: "product training systems", "upgrades from model to model", "sales related issues", "new motorcycle development", and "sales training", and further detail was provided, namely: "customer satisfaction, upsell, cross-selling, and the year before that, we did an accessories shop layout training".

Section 2

This section consists of the main interview questions on the research objective of the study.

Competences for a Competitive Advantage

Figure 4 below illustrates the recurrence of the five different themes. These were based on repetitions found throughout the interviews, highlighting the importance of these strategic competences.

Most interviewees (12) referred to the technological advancements, and how these had improved the motorcycles over the years to be "better than all the rest". Over the years, a competitive advantage had been achieved through implemented improvements. According to six interviewees, these implementations had led to "improvements with the motor" and others. Moreover, they explained that the brand ensured that improvements were made on an annual basis, safeguarding the newly released motorcycles as "a better version of the one the year before". Customer satisfaction was another recurring strategic competency. It was mentioned that "South Africans like to talk" and therefore would share their experience with fellow riders and fanatic.

Parallel to the definitions provided by Porter (2001) and Wickham (2001), strategic positioning was defined as gaining an understanding of the manufacturer's competitors and how they set themselves apart from these rivals. It was additionally confirmed by interviewees that a guideline was followed in terms of delivering value to customers. Utilising organisational resources and capabilities provided the

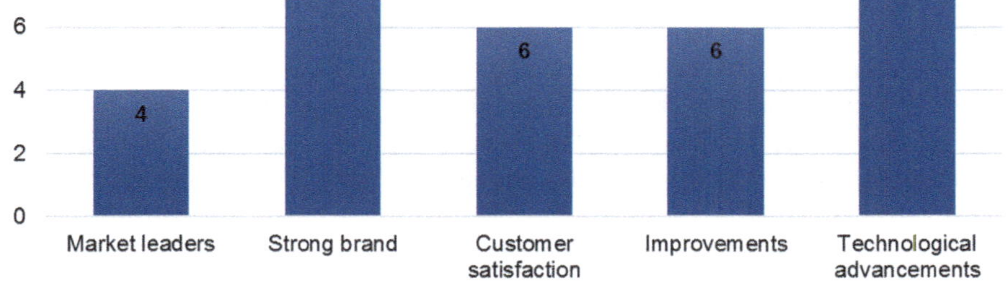

Fig. 4 Competences for a competitive advantage

possibility for offers to be packaged specifically for clients, ensuring the achievement of a competitive advantage, as was further noted by Gamble et al. (2017).

Bateman et al. (2019) refer to factors that need to be considered when managing competitive advantage. Some of these factors for success were also mentioned by interviewees, proving their importance within the manufacturer. Sustainability, service, and speed were noted on multiple occasions. Based on the explanations provided that specifically apply to the manufacturer, sustainability is required for continuous business and growth within the country.

Based on data analysed from the interviews, it is evident that the key factors for success as identified by Bateman et al. (2019) have a significant impact on organisational success. Some of the factors were mentioned by the interviewees when defining their understanding of the term "strategic positioning", and evidently these were some of the few keys that resulted in the organisation gaining and maintaining a competitive advantage within the market, allowing them to have the majority of the market share in the industry. In addition, it was established that the brand needs to develop according to the competitors in the market. This is in line with Low (2019) who stresses the importance of accurate management of information, to ensure survival over and above a strong strategic positioning.

Following the discussions, it was confirmed that the listed strategic capabilities provide for a competitive advantage for the manufacturer, which will be elaborated on. This is in line with Favaro, who states that strategies are based on the decisions made by higher management to both increase the value of the organisation in the long term and to maintain and/or gain competitive advantage.

Additionally, the manufacturer's technological advancements ensure that the safety features of the motorcycles are continuously upgraded and added to. Especially in South Africa, the safety aspect is a major contributor to people's decisions to purchase a motorcycle (Droppa, 2018).

Current Strategies Implemented for a Competitive Advantage

Following the findings shown in Fig. 5, it is evident that the majority of the interviewees highlighted the importance of customer satisfaction. This was achieved by means of implementing the other strategies highlighted above to "understand the needs of the customers and how they want to communicate, because it's all changing".

The motorcycle manufacturer incorporated the core values in every operation, including the production of PGA. They remained "true to those core values" with every strategic decision made. To "innovate" was listed as a strategy. This is where the core values were followed while continuously "bringing something fresh to the customers".

The strategy of continuously adapting to the changes of the market was mentioned by interviewees on two separate occasions. Interviewees considered that in

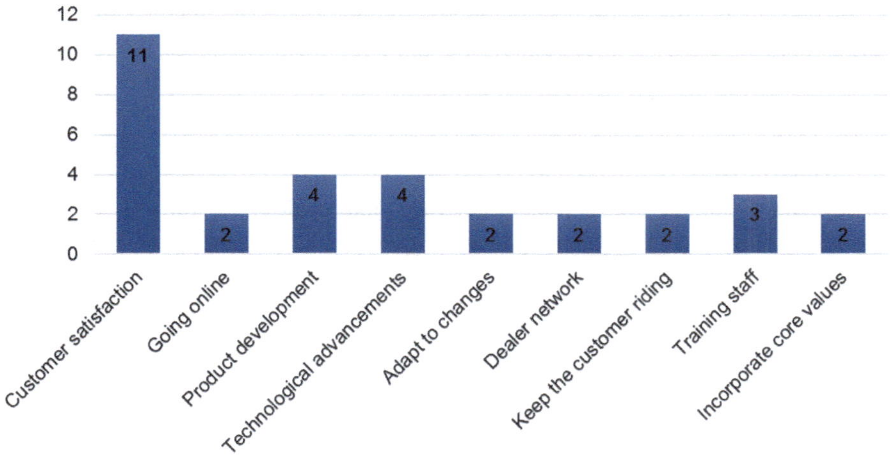

Fig. 5 Current strategies implemented

South Africa, it was vital for the motorcycle manufacturer to "understand their market, to understand where the country is going".

With a declining market in South Africa, it was pointed out that the market's way of thinking and spending had changed, providing the solution that "the spending of their money needs to be in such a way that it's a win-win situation". Consequently, the brand was continuously adapting to the changes to remain "attractive to people" and to "improve the sales". Emphasising that further growth targets were implemented by headquarters in Europe, managers were said to strategise to achieve "a 25% growth on a negative market for the next year to follow".

Adapting to the changes provides an introduction for the next strategy. As the industry was described by interviewees as becoming more digitalised, the importance of continuous technological advancements was stressed to ensure that customer satisfaction was achieved throughout various innovations. Finally, the role of increased social media and online marketing was mentioned by two interviewees. As the industry was becoming more digitalised, the motorcycle manufacturer focused "on the social aspect in marketing", as this allowed information to reach customers faster, while "getting people to side with" the brand.

In summary, it was agreed that all the strategic themes led to achieving customer satisfaction. According to interviewees, this was accomplished by providing the best possible service, which was achieved through training, allowing the brand to keep the "customer riding at all times". This led to the use of increased technology in product development.

It must be noted that the younger generation did not grow up with motorcycles that had the bare minimum when it came to technology and are therefore unaware how to operate such machines. This is also observed by Doepker who states that the advancements brought on by the Fourth Industrial Revolution require increased creativity. A change in skills and knowledge is required for future innovations and fast-approaching changes, which is in line with Low (2019).

Gamble et al. (2017:2) also state that the strategy acts as a guideline on how the target market should be served valuably and, more importantly, how this value will be created through organisational capabilities and resources. Furthermore, this broadening of the range of motorcycles has further supported the diversification theory of Frenken (quoted by Kublina, 2015), defining the knowledge spill-over that is created through the incorporation of various industries, or in the case of the motorcycle manufacturer, a broad range of motorcycles providing for different types of riding, such as off-road racing, adventure riding, or even hard-core weekend road riding trips.

Further Market Improvements

Interviewees were asked to provide suggestions for improving brand trust and awareness of the motorcycle manufacturer, as seen in Fig. 6.

The majority (23 out of 29) of the interviewees were able to provide a variety of possible suggestions. This was particularly helpful, as their daily exposure to the brand provided interesting insights that would otherwise possibly not have been recognised. They were able to identify potential problems that could be eliminated.

It was noted by four interviewees that the motorcycle manufacturer should spend more time with customers. The next suggestion, made by four interviewees, was that processes and systems should be updated, to allow for an increased flow of communication between the dealerships—"systems to better control and to make it easier for all of us to communicate". Interviewees suggested that "whatever technology is available to make that process faster will be beneficial", allowing for work tasks to be completed at a faster pace.

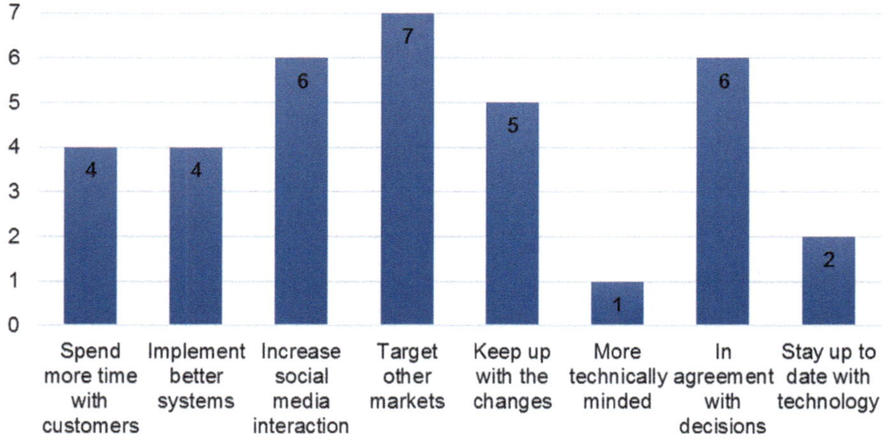

Fig. 6 Future strategic positioning

The next suggestion, mentioned by seven interviewees, dealt with the targeting of different or new markets. This took on a broad spectrum of meanings. For one, the need for increased commuting was expressed by one of the interviewees. They believed that it was vital to enter into the mobility market by communicating to customers "that to sit in traffic for three hours on a day versus a half an hour on a motorbike, will [make] their lives easier".

However, the motorcycles imported into South Africa are still different from those favoured in Europe. This is owing to the nature of the riders preferring to commute, whereas South Africa is a non-commuting country. The law is also applied differently, and the legislation around the consumption of CO_2 emissions is increasing, which promotes the increased manufacturing of electric-powered engines (Mitterreiter, 2018).

In summary, the motorcycle manufacturer appears to have a strong strategic positioning within South Africa. This is reflected in customer satisfaction, which is deemed a sustainable competitive advantage if value creation for customers is continuously achieved and increased (Kruger, 2010). By ensuring that technological advancements are implemented, the motorcycles imitate the technology that is regarded as a norm in Europe, proving advancements into the Fourth Industrial Revolution as a brand.

Managerial Implications

These recommendations are based on potential problems that were observed throughout the data collection and analysis process.

It is evident that strategies need to be adapted according to the changing environments. Overall, the changing environment consists of various factors, thus further shifting the environment into a newer and more advanced era. This requires organisations to remain flexible and to adapt readily and modify the strategic plan required to remain competitive and ensure further growth with the changing demands of the market. Ensuring readiness to adapt according to these changes will promote the organisation's strategic positioning.

The declining market—Problems mentioned revolved around the difficulty of operating in current markets. Thus, it was made clear that further product introductions became challenging, as new product introductions remained a concern. Therefore, it is suggested that the brand is required to "look at new markets".

The brand's image—The next problem that was raised throughout an interview was the brand's image. Often customers compared prices when purchasing a product; therefore, it is important for an organisation to provide both quality and affordable products to allow for an increased brand image leading to competitive advantage.

A point of saturation—Another issue mentioned during an interview was the saturated market. It is recommended that, since the "biggest growth opportunity" remained in the road market, increased focus should be placed on this segment.

Although the brand had a variety of offerings to promote to the new markets, awareness had not been achieved, and interviewees believed that the problem remained in advertising, as it was not carried out “in their spaces”.

People have been described as becoming lazier, and the ease of carrying out business through technology while saving time and costs is adding to this trend. Customers can make their purchases over the Internet without having to take the time to drive out to a dealership and finding what is most suitable for them. This app allows sales staff to make a “video feed” on the motorcycle a customer is looking to purchase. This is to ensure that the customer’s demands and needs are met. Financing of the motorcycle is finally arranged online. This concept is gaining increased traction.

Another suggestion is that a brand ambassador would be required to get involved in various events, with the explanation that the involvement of influential people would allow others to “consider the product and the brand”, which would especially include targeting children “to get kids out and active again”. An interviewee stated that parents often walked into the dealerships looking for a way to get their children off electronics such as tablets and computers. Therefore, the brand was believed to provide the “ideal family sport”.

Spending more time with customers could ensure that the voice of the customer would be heard, making it an easier task to target them in an appropriate way in the future.

Many dealerships needed to be renewed and upgraded, furnished with new equipment, including the organising and planning of additional training. This would enable the dealership to “go the extra mile to meet the customer’s expectation” .

To ensure that the manufacturer maintains this strong strategic positioning, a further corporate-level growth strategy is advised. Corporate-level strategies ensure that the correct foundation is provided, strengthening survival and sustainability. At this level, the diversified strategy or growth strategy should be followed as the manufacturer is already recognised for constantly increasing its market share and profit margin although the industry is currently facing a decline in South Africa and a broad product offering should be available, catering for a variety of riding types.

Conclusion

Relevant to the objective to suggest strategies for the stronger positioning of the brand, the dynamic environment that the motorcycle manufacturer finds itself in, especially in South Africa, calls for continuous adjustments to be made to the organisation’s strategy and goals. This is achieved by constantly investigating the markets and identifying the changing demands. If the demands can be met on a continuous basis, success and growth become constant in the motorcycle industry, despite the declining market in South Africa.

Therefore, as our times change, with increased means of technology and competition, it is critical for organisations' managers to be aware of the changes that occur around them. These changes need to be analysed, and management needs to be ready to implement modifications to their strategy at any time. An organisation is required to constantly update their strategy according to the changing environment to keep up with the competition in the industry. Consequently, to allow for increased competitive advantage, a change in strategy entails informing employees to enable them to produce beneficial input. Simultaneously, decision-makers and strategists must analyse the situation and the speed at which a change in strategy is required, in order to address those critical calls for change.

Limitations

The scope of the study was limited to staff only, and the target market and acquired customers were not involved. This study thus focused solely on the perceptions, opinions, and understandings internal to the manufacturer's operations. Also, the population was limited to Gauteng for the sake of convenience. However, these create opportunities for potential future and further research.

Future Research

As the study was focused on the Gauteng region, opportunities for further research are presented. These possibilities could include further samples on customers, as well as other regions. Additionally, this study could be carried out across Africa, to establish the overall strategic positioning relative to the Fourth Industrial Revolution.

References

Baines, T., Kay, G., Adesola, S., & Higson, M. (2005). Strategic positioning: An integrated decision process for manufacturers. *International Journal of Operations and Production Management, 25*(2), 180–201.

Barnes, J., Black, A., Comrie, D., & Hartogh, T. (2018). *Geared for growthSouth Africa's automotive industry masterplan to 2035*. Department of Trade and Industry.

Bateman, T. S., Snell, S. A., & Konopaske, R. (2019). *Management: Leading & collaborating in a competitive world* (13th ed.). McGraw-Hill Education.

Bryman, A., & Bell, E. (2014). *Research methodology*. Cape Town.

Business Wire. (2020). *South African two-wheeler market forecast, 2020–2025—assesses the impact of COVID-19 on the industry*. Available from: https://www.businesswire.com/news/home/20200623005551/en/South-African-Two-Wheeler-Market-Forecast-2020-2025.

Butler, M., & Rivera, K. (2020). How to respond when a crisis becomes the new normal. Available from: https://www.strategy-business.com/blog/How-to-respond-when-a-crisis-becomes-the-new-normal?gko=ff6a3.

Cardano, M. (2020). *Defending qualitative research: Design, analysis, and textualization*. Routledge.

Dean and Company. (2018). *Strategic positioning*. Available from: https://dean.com/delta-model/strategic-positioning.

Deloitte, & McKinsey & Company. (2019). Technology: Company news South Africa. Forum: Strategies for the fourth industrial revolution. Available from: https://www.bizcommunity.com/Article/196/706/191392.html.

Droppa, D. (2018). *Where to now for SA motorcycle industry?* Available from: https://www.iol.co.za/motoring/bikes/where-to-now-for-sa-motorcycle-industry-15246872.

Du Plooy-Cilliers, F., Davis, C., & Bezuidenhout, R. (2014). *Research matters*. Juta.

Gamble, J. E., Peteraf, M. A., & Thompson, A. A., Jr. (2017). *Essentials of strategic management: The quest for competitive advantage* (5th ed.). McGraw-Hill Education.

Haines, D. (2017). Ethical considerations in qualitative case study research recruiting participants with profound intellectual disabilities. *Research Ethics, 13*(3–4), 219–232.

Hennink, M. M., Kaiser, B. N., & Marconi, V. C. (2016). Code saturation versus meaning saturation: How many interviews are enough? *Qualitative Health Research, 27*(4), 591–608.

Kublina, S. (2015). Related variety, unrelated variety and regional growth: Development patterns and role of absorptive capacity. *Regional Studies, 20*(1), 2–5.

Kruger, S. (2010). In H. De Bruyn (Ed.), *Strategic management: A southern African perspective* (6th ed.). Entrepro.

Le Roux, J. (2018). *I was so fed up with traffic that I bought a motorbike—and the results were surprising*. Available from: https://www.businessinsider.co.za/by-switching-to-a-motorbike-this-journalist-is-beating-cape-towns-traffic-and-reducing-his-travel-costs-in-half-2018-6.

Low, A. (2019). Technical standards for smart manufacturing: Evolution and strategic positioning. In *Smart factories: Issues of information governance*. Indiana University.

Lu, J. (2019). *Skills, not job titles, are the new metric for the labour market*. Available from: https://www.weforum.org/agenda/2019/07/skills-not-job-titles-are-the-new-metric-for-the-labour-market/.

Martin, L. (2019). *How motorcycle giant XXX is making its mark on the Asian market*. Available from: https://www.manufacturingglobal.com/company/how-motorcycle-giant-XXX-group-making-its-mark-asian-market#.

Mitterreiter, S. (2018). XXX and XXX: An XXX partnership in the motorcycle industry. In S. Schmid (Ed.), *Internationalization of business* (pp. 99–123). Springer.

Mtanga, S., & McCamel, R. (2019). Motorcycle parts and aftermarket industry regional value chain in southern Africa. *UNU-WIDER Working Paper, 38*, 1.

Pistoni, A., & Songini, L. (Eds.). (2017). *Strategic managerial control for the servitization strategy*. Emerald.

Porter, M. E. (1980). *Competitive strategy: Techniques for analyzing industries and competitors*. The Free Press.

Porter, M. E. (2001). Strategy and the internet. Available from: https://hbr.org/2001/03/strategy-and-the-internet.

Prabhakar Rajkumar, D. K., & Abraham, M. (2018). Strategic positioning and sustainable competitive advantage for growth of industry. *Shanlax International Journal of Management, 5*(2), 160–167.

Silverman, D. (2013). *Doing qualitative research: A practical handbook* (4th ed.). Sage.

Thanh, N. C., & Thanh, T. T. L. (2015). The interconnection between interpretivist paradigm and qualitative methods in education. *American Journal of Educational Science, 1*(2), 24–27.

Torok, G. (2019). *Strategic positioning: The battle for market dominance*. Available from: https://www.powermarketing.ca/strategic_positioning.html60-571.

West, E. (2020). SA motor industry set to get hit hard by COVID-19 lockdown, the DTI warns. Available from: https://www.iol.co.za/business-report/economy/sa-motor-industry-set-to-get-hit-hard-by-covid-19-lockdown-the-dti-warns-46713799

Wickham, P. A. (2001). *Strategic entrepreneurship: A decision making approach to new venture creation and management* (2nd ed.). Pearson Education.

Willis, J. W. (2007). Foundations of qualitative research: Interpretive and critical approaches. In M. Jost & R. Nilakanta (Eds.). Sage.

The Impact of Emerging Technologies on Internal Audit Functions

Rozanne Janet Smith, Evelinah Maredi, and Phumzi Mthimunye

Abstract Emerging technologies offer significant benefits to internal auditing, however internal audit functions (IAFs) face challenges in keeping up with rapid digital transformation. This study investigated the barriers that impede IAF's adoption of emerging technologies. This aided considerably in determining how the barriers affected the IAF's overall effectiveness. A qualitative research method is applied with a questionnaire design, selecting respondents from South African public research councils with an in-house IAF. Data was collected through a structured questionnaire directed at Chief Audit Executives (CAEs), responsible for IAF performance. The findings of the study indicate that although councils have embraced emerging technologies, their IAFs lack technological innovation because of inadequate support from the audit committee, a lack of support from top management, and an unproductive IAF. Technological expertise, financial constraints, modifications to the internal environment, training, knowledge, change management, and the age of the technology infrastructure are some of the barriers contributing towards a lack of adoption. By addressing these barriers, IAFs will be better equipped to integrate emerging technology and function more effectively. This study fills the gap in the existing body of knowledge pertaining to the South African public sector by highlighting the essential organizational components that are necessary for IAFs to effectively incorporate digitalization into their internal auditing process. The findings derived from empirical research offer insightful discussions for IAF leaders to initiate the process of digitizing internal audits with the objective of generating value for various stakeholders.

Keywords Internal audit function · Effectiveness · Technology · Emerging technology · Senior management · Audit committee · Barriers

---

R. J. Smith (✉) · E. Maredi · P. Mthimunye
University of Johannesburg, Johannesburg, South Africa
e-mail: rozannes@uj.ac.za; emaredi@uj.ac.za

T. Moloi (ed.), *Impacting Society Positively Through Technology in Accounting and Business Processes*, Springer Proceedings in Business and Economics,
https://doi.org/10.1007/978-3-031-84885-8_60

Introduction

Technology is commonly known as a significant enabler and catalyst of business strategy, as well as the primary mechanism through which organizations accomplish their goals (Ramamoorti & Weidenmier, 2004). Technology has had a profound impact on the internal auditing profession and how Internal Audit Functions (IAF) provide value to stakeholders. Emerging technologies have the potential to transform the internal auditing process and will continue to impact the design and implementation of business controls (KPMG, 2020). Examples of these technologies are those outlined by the 4th Industrial Revolution (4IR), which include artificial intelligence (AI), robotics, genetic engineering, quantum computing, the Internet of Things, 3D printing, machine learning (ML), blockchain, and sophisticated analytics. To stay up with these developments, internal auditing methods need to change as well (Moorthy et al., 2011).

Emerging Technology and the Internal Audit Function

The transformation of internal audit into a versatile, highly skilled, and technologically enabled function is crucial in meeting stakeholder needs and expectations (Information Systems and Audit Association (ISACA) & Protiviti, 2019; Deloitte, 2018a). The integration of emerging technologies can enhance the effectiveness and success of internal auditors in assisting organizations in managing issues and achieving their objectives (Chambers, 2017). To prioritize emerging technologies in its processes, internal audit must embrace technology to improve audit quality and uncover new insights (KPMG, 2017). Collaboration among auditors, oversight bodies, standard developers, and stakeholders is necessary to explore how technological advancements can improve audit quality (International Auditing and Assurance Standards Board [IAASB] 2017). However, the lack of support from senior management and audit committees, limited resources, inadequate technology management skills, insufficient awareness of technology among internal auditors, organizational lag in digital transformation, and challenges in change management make it difficult to adapt to emerging technologies (Vasarhelyi et al., 2008; Kim et al., 2009; Lotto, 2014; Ahmi et al., 2014; PwC, 2015, Cangemi, 2016; DFSA, 2017; PwC, 2018, 2019; Muneer et al., 2019; Mokhitli & Kyobe, 2019; Kovanen, 2020; Damanik et al., 2020). Understanding the capabilities and limitations of emerging technology can encourage its implementation and full utilization by IAFs (Deloitte, 2019).

Organizational Barriers to Emerging Technology Adaptation

The framework known as the Technological, Organizational, and Environmental (TOE) framework delineates the trio of factors that exert influence on an organization's decision to adopt and implement technology (Baker, 2012). Within the confines of this research, emphasis is placed on the "organizational" facet of the TOE framework, with the aim of deliberating on the obstacles encountered by organizations in their endeavour to embrace emerging technologies. According to the definition provided by Ahmi et al. (2014), the internal components of an organization that hold sway over the adoption and implementation of digital innovations encompass the dimensions of scope, size, and managerial structure. The outcome of this study reveals that the barriers to the integration of emerging technologies within the IAF are represented by the existence of senior management support, the role played by the audit committee, and the IAF itself.

Senior Management Support

Singh et al. (2021) assert that senior management's support and commitment establish the organizational climate surrounding the IAF and guarantee the independent execution of the audit process. Insufficient financial support and inadequate resources contribute to the inefficiency of the IAF. The Asian Confederation of Institutes of Internal Auditors (ACIIA, 2021) posits that senior management ought to endorse the IAF's transformation plans, presenting a compelling business case for innovation and emphasizing the role of emerging technology.

Audit Committee Role

The optimal functioning of the IAF hinges on the support of both the audit committee and management (Public Sector Audit Committee Forum [PSACF] n.d.-b). An efficient IAF assists the audit committee in fulfilling its responsibilities, thereby enhancing its effectiveness (PSACF n.d.-b). The involvement of the audit committee in internal audit activities elevates the efficacy of internal audit efforts. Familiarity with the staffing requirements, resource allocation, funding, and succession planning of the internal audit function enable the audit committee to better comprehend how best to support the IAF (Deloitte, 2018d).

Internal Audit Function

According to the Institute of Internal Auditors (IIA), the IAF oversees providing senior management, audit committees, and the board of directors with assurances regarding the efficacy of governance, risk management, and control activities (IIA, 2017). IAFs support the accounting officer in the public sector of South Africa in maintaining strong controls, which include the information system environment, operational and financial information dependability, operational efficacy, asset protection, and legal and regulatory compliance (Treasury Regulation, 2005). Sawyer (2014) asserts that by promoting the value-added contributions of internal audit, the CAE is essential in supporting the efficacy of the IAF. For the audit plan to be properly carried out, the CAE must guarantee the proper, sufficient, and effective deployment of internal audit resources (IIA, 2017). As organizations use advanced technology, the internal audit approach and methodology should develop, get better, and add value, ensuring the IAF's success (Axt et al., 2022).

Internal Audit Function Effectiveness

Musah et al. (2018) emphasize the importance of management support in determining the effectiveness of internal audits. The quality of internal auditing and management support have a significant impact on the effectiveness of internal audits (Mihret & Yismaw, 2007). The size of the IAF, the quality of professionals, and the independence of the IAF are also crucial factors for the effectiveness of internal audit, as Musah et al. (2018) states. IAFs face difficulties with staffing, shortage of critical skills as well as expertise on technology use (iKutu, 2014; Deribe & Regasa, 2014; Deloitte, 2018c). Flexible co-sourcing agreements, according to Feizizadeh (2012), can deal with these problems.

Research Statement, Aims, and Objectives

The aim of this research is to discuss the organizational barriers to the adoption of emerging technologies by in-house IAFs and this will aid in identifying the impact of the barriers on the overall effectiveness of the IAF. Key research objectives include: (i) establishing technology as a key enabler for an effective IAF; (ii) determine the level of emerging technologies usage by the IAF; (iii) determine the organizational barriers preventing IAF from adopting emerging technologies; and (iv) determine the impact of these barriers on IAF effectiveness. The research combines empirical research with existing literature to achieve the research objectives.

Literature Review

Research Councils in South Africa

State Research Councils are established by the South African Government through Acts of Parliament and as stated by Late (2018) to advance research and innovation and support the development of a knowledge-based economy. They play a crucial role in the national innovation system, promoting research and development in science, engineering, technology, and social sciences (Late, 2018). According to the Organization for Economic Cooperation and Development (OECD, 2011), government research councils provide services such as basic and applied research, policy support, training, knowledge and technology transfer, service provision, research funding, technological facilities, and standardization and certification. South Africa has five government research councils, including Agricultural Research Council (ARC); Council for Geoscience (CGS); Council for Scientific and Industrial Research (CSIR); Human Sciences Research Council (HSRC) and South African Medical Research Council (SAMRC). The primary mandate of these councils includes the provision, production, and transfer of knowledge for decision-making and societal development, the maintenance of high-quality applied research, and the management of organization-specific functions and tasks assigned to them by a parliamentary act (Late, 2018). According to Marx and Ravjee (2015), research councils play a crucial role in the socio-economic system and the development of technology within these organizations influences the role of the IAF that supports them. To effectively audit these councils, the IAF needs to use advanced techniques and technology. However, Lotto (2014) and Garven and Scarlata (2020) argue that internal audit lags in the effective use of technology. Effective IAFs rely on technology, data mining, predictive modelling, and continuous audit techniques to improve the quality of the audit process (Feizizadeh, 2012).

Technology as a Key Driver of an Effective Internal Audit Function

Turetken et al. (2020) identified several key indicators that contribute to the effectiveness of an IAF. These indicators include the fulfilment of audit plans, the rate of implementation, the quality of reporting, and the analysis of audit results. Mubarrok (2018) suggests that the 4IR is set to revolutionize the auditing profession by automating audit methods, reducing the need for sampling, and shortening the overall audit time. The digitalization of workflows in internal auditing is bringing about significant changes, with new technologies offering the potential to reduce human dependency, lower costs, and enhance efficiency (Betti & Sarens, 2020). While traditional audits still provide retrospective security measures, advanced technologies enable real-time monitoring of current economic events, thereby enhancing security

(IIA Netherlands & EY, 2021). The adoption of more frequent and real-time testing can further improve the efficiency and effectiveness of IAFs (Mokhitli & Kyobe, 2019). Integrating technology into the audit process is crucial for the IAF to achieve high levels of effectiveness (Mustapha & Lai, 2017). Ahmi et al. (2014) emphasizes that the effectiveness and productivity of IAFs depend on the technological tools utilized. Technology serves as a bridge between the positive contributions of the IAF and management support (Muneer et al., 2019). According to IIA Netherlands and EY (2021), the main criteria for automating the audit process include gaining insights into existing internal controls, identifying risk indicators, and detecting potential fraud tendencies.

IAFs are increasingly integrating technology into their activities, for example using automated tools such as Generalized Audit Software (GAS), test data generators, computer-assisted audit programs and computer-assisted audit tools and techniques (CAATTs) (Ramamoorti & Weidenmier, 2004; Moorthy et al., 2011; Motubatse et al., 2015a, 2015b; Mokhitli & Kyobe, 2019). These tools improve the efficiency and effectiveness of the audit and have been proven to be effective in achieving audit objectives, as suggested by Rakipi et al. (2021). According to Braun and Davis (2003), IAFs frequently deploy CAATTs to increase efficacy and efficiency. However, Al-Hiyari et al. (2019) observed inadequate use of CAATTs. To meet the challenges of rapid technological advances, auditing standards require auditors to use CAATTs (Janvrin et al., 2009). In the era of big data, IAFs need to evolve their techniques to add value to their organizations (Rakipi et al., 2021), and data analysis tools such as data mining can help IAFs improve their assurance and advisory services (Rakipi et al., 2021). These tools have been found to increase the effectiveness of internal audits (Huang et al., 2022), and their use has also influenced the CAE's ability to build strong relationships with senior management and report to the audit committee (Rakipi et al., 2021).

To enhance audit efficiency and effectiveness, the integration of technology within the internal audit profession is of utmost importance. Nowadays, numerous large IAFs are incorporating technology throughout the entire audit process, not solely limited to the fieldwork and execution stages (Alqaraleh et al., 2022). Nevertheless, there is still room for improvement, as IAFs need to embrace advanced techniques to remain at the forefront of strategic and technological advancements, fulfil stakeholder expectations, and address emerging risks (Deloitte, 2018c).

Level of Emerging Technology Usage by Internal Auditors

Cangemi (2016) and the Dubai Financial Services Authority (DFSA) (2017) claim that most IAFs are falling behind in technological innovation. Additionally, the ACIIA (2021) and Protiviti (2020) suggest that auditors have limited access to emerging technology. In fact, over half of CAEs are concerned that lack of technology adoption may result in a loss of value for their organization, as found by a PwC (2018) survey titled "State of the Internal Audit Profession". Protiviti (2020) has highlighted the necessity to build skills and competencies in emerging technologies to prepare the future generation of IAF.

To meet evolving stakeholder needs, the IAF needs to adapt to digital transformation, as emphasized by ACIIA (2021). This requires learning new technological skills, developing new audit procedures, and using advanced technologies to control emerging technology deployments, as suggested by PwC (2018). Investing in advanced tools and methodologies can provide significant benefits, as noted by Cangemi (2016). The advent of technology has changed the scope and procedures of auditing, leading to improved resource utilization, increased efficiency, cost savings, higher quality output, and increased shareholder value, as highlighted by Deloitte (2018e). Therefore, the IAF should be a digital leader, adopting technologies like data analytics, robotics, AI, agile, and drone technology ahead of the rest of the organization, as recommended by Christ et al. (2019).

The choice and implementation of emerging technologies are significantly influenced by the corporate context, and the internal audit adoption is linked to organizational deployment, as pointed out by PwC (2018). However, the IAF is rarely consulted on the decision to implement emerging technology, as noted by Christ et al. (2019). Auditors are hesitant to apply technologies that are far ahead of their organizations, as asserted by Gepp et al. (2018). Nonetheless, the IAF plays a crucial role in improving business operations and managing risks and must act.

The 4IR has led to the rapid automation of various tasks (Moffitt et al., 2018). This automation has the potential to streamline the entire internal audit process, including risk assessments, audit planning, fieldwork, and reporting (Deloitte, 2018e). By incorporating robot process automation (RPA) during fieldwork, internal auditors can now audit the entire population instead of relying on sampling techniques (Deloitte, 2018e). Furthermore, the integration of natural language processing (NLP) and machine learning (ML) with RPA allows for the scanning and summarization of various sources such as annual reports, regulatory filings, phone transcripts, websites, articles of association, and meeting minutes, thereby providing a comprehensive overview of the business (Chartered Professional Accountants of Canada & the American Institute of Certified Public Accountants, 2020).

Prominent audit firms are actively leveraging emerging technologies to enhance their internal audit practices (Lenz & Hahn, 2015). For instance, Deloitte has successfully utilized AI tools like Auditmap.ai and Argus to automate risk assessment processes, utilizing machine learning to identify potential threats (Shapiro, 2020). Similarly, KPMG's Content Abstraction Tool (KCAT) employs machine learning to examine contracts and ensure compliance with the new International Financial Reporting Standards (IFRS) standards (Kifer, 2021). PwC's Halo, on the other hand, utilizes data analysis techniques to identify problematic areas within journal entries, such as questionable keywords, unauthorized sources, or high postings exceeding authorized limits (Kokina & Davenport, 2017). Overall, these audit firms are at the forefront of implementing these technologies to enhance their internal audit capabilities (Kokina & Davenport, 2017).

Research has demonstrated that various organizational factors, including management support, technology competency, and standards, play a crucial role in the adoption of technology by internal auditors (Li et al., 2018). The Unified Theory of Acceptance and Use of Technology (UTAUT) has been found to be effective in influencing the adoption of GAS (Mahzan & Lymer, 2014), while performance and effort expectancy are also significant factors in the adoption of CAATTs (Al-Hiyari et al., 2019). According to Shamsuddin et al. (2015), internal auditors prefer CAATTs due to their ease of use and capabilities. The adoption of technology by audit firms is influenced by factors such as size, readiness, and top management commitment (Rosli et al., 2013), and technologically competent staff and appropriate training are essential for efficient utilization of audit technologies (Thottoli, 2021).

Although studies have shown that the internal audit process can be digitalized (Protiviti, 2019; PwC, 2018, 2019; IIA Netherlands & EY, 2021), IAFs face challenges in adopting advanced technologies due to organizational delays and lack of investment (Lois et al., 2020). Digital skills are identified as the primary barrier to adopting technologies (Betti & Sarens, 2020; KPMG, 2021; Atayah & Alshater, 2021; IIA Netherlands & EY, 2021), with internal auditors citing lack of training as a major reason (Lois et al., 2020). Additionally, Sethibe and Naidoo (2022) cited poor data quality, insufficient technological investment, and talent management as key impediments to the use of robotics in auditing. To remain relevant, the audit profession must incorporate new digital-technology-based metrics, capabilities, skills, and business models (Fotoh & Lorentzon, 2021).

Organizational Barriers to Technology Adoption

The TOE framework, developed by Baker (2012), identifies various organizational factors that play a role in influencing the adoption of technology. These factors include characteristics and resources such as employee linking structures, intra-organizational communication processes, organization size, and slack resources. Similarly, Lenz and Hahn (2015) conducted a study that echoes the importance of organizational factors in influencing the effectiveness of the IAF. They identified factors such as the organization itself, IAF resources, IAF processes, and IAF relationships as crucial determinants of effectiveness.

When it comes to integrating emerging technologies into audit techniques, Axt et al. (2022) highlight three critical areas for the IAF to focus on: positioning, people, and process. These areas are essential for successfully incorporating new technologies into the audit function. Additionally, the decision to adopt technology is influenced by perceived advantages and the organization's technological readiness, as discussed by David et al. (2010).

It is important to recognize that organizational factors play a significant role in determining the effectiveness of internal audit. Lenz et al. (2017) emphasize the crucial nature of these factors in ensuring the success of the internal audit function. To achieve this, the CAE, board, and senior management should engage in discussions and reach agreements regarding the responsibilities, authority, and expectations of the internal audit function. Furthermore, they should consider the appropriate organizational placement of internal audit and establish clear reporting relationships between the CAE and other stakeholders, as recommended by the Institute of Internal Auditors (IIA, 2016).

Senior Management Support

The lack of management support is a significant issue faced by the IAF in the South African public sector (Motubatse et al., 2015a, 2015b). The role of senior management is crucial in providing support to the IAF by ensuring the availability of adequate and relevant resources and funding (PSACF, n.d.-a). A two-way relationship between internal audit and senior management is essential for achieving organizational objectives and fulfilling internal audit mandates (Sarens & De Beelde, 2006). Numerous studies have demonstrated that support from senior management significantly contributes to the effectiveness of internal audit (Mihret & Yismaw, 2007; Hailemariam, 2014; Lenz & Hahn, 2015; Dellai & Omri, 2016; Noraini et al., 2018). Senior management support is critical for the overall recognition and appreciation of internal audits within the organization (Sarens & De Beelde, 2006). This support greatly enhances the integrity, objectivity, and moral courage of internal auditors, thereby leading to higher effectiveness in their work (Sari & Sirajuddin, 2019).

The assessment of senior management support for internal audits involves factors such as their involvement, allocation of internal audit resources, and responsiveness to audit findings (Abdullah & Mustafa, 2020). Sarens and de Beelde (2006) have also identified other indicators, including the monitoring of action plans, changes in the organization's risk and internal control profile, and significant alterations to policies and processes. To ensure effectiveness, management should provide the IAF with the necessary resources and demonstrate a commitment to implementing internal audit recommendations (Mihret & Yismaw, 2007). However, Motubatse et al. (2015a, 2015b) argue that the recurrence of audit findings and the slow implementation of IAF recommendations indicate a lack of management support. To ensure effective management in the public sector, it is crucial to implement the findings and suggestions put forth by the IAF (Baharud-din et al., 2014). Internal auditors rely on senior management for funding and evaluation, and maintaining a positive relationship with them is of utmost importance (Sarens & De Beelde, 2006).

The absence of management support can be attributed to various factors, one of which is the perceived expectation of the internal audit role. According to the Chartered Professional Accountants (CPA) and American Institute of Certified Public Accountants (AICPA) (2020), the emergence of new technologies has further widened this expectation gap. Betti and Sarens (2020) also suggest that senior management anticipates the IAF to engage in more consulting activities related to emerging technological challenges. To bridge this gap and enhance the effectiveness of internal audit, it is crucial for CAEs to have frequent interactions with senior management (PwC, 2017).

Audit Committee Role

Mamaile (2020) and Dzomira (2020) discovered that public sector audit committees lack effectiveness, while iKutu (2014) concluded that senior management in many organizations do not provide adequate protection to IAFs. Mubako (2019) further emphasized that the absence of a strong relationship between the audit committee and IAF results in insufficient support for the latter. To address these issues, IIA South Africa (2021) suggests that audit committees and oversight bodies should prioritize the protection and assistance of internal auditors and the internal auditing profession.

The effectiveness of the IAF heavily relies on a strong working relationship with senior management and the audit committee (Deloitte, 2018b). The audit committee's support is crucial in enabling the IAF to perform its duties effectively (Lenz & Hahn, 2015; Deloitte, 2018d), as it oversees the internal audit programme and processes (Oussii and Boulila Taktak, 2018) and reviews the effectiveness of the IAF (Treasury Regulation, 2005). The audit committee must ensure that senior management actively supports the IAF (Deloitte, 2018d), and that the CAE is aware of organizational strategic initiatives (IIARF, 2013). To build an internal audit brand, the audit committee should meet privately with CAEs outside scheduled meetings, provide resources, set a strong tone at the top, emphasize adequate control, encourage open communication, and ensure that the CAE attends all audit committee meetings (Deloitte, 2018b). Maintaining open communication with management and the audit committee is crucial for the IAF to ensure alignment with stakeholders' priorities (Feizizadeh, 2012).

The IAF plays a crucial role in facilitating the governance oversight responsibilities of the audit committee (Tušek & Pokrovac, 2012, Ackermann, 2016; Noraini et al., 2018). According to Jaggi (2023), the IAF assists the audit committee by assessing the charter, keeping them informed about new regulations, and serving as a trainer. The audit committee should participate in determining the allocation of internal audit resources (Ruppel, 2006) and support the IAF's investment in and use of audit technology (Garven & Scarlata, 2020). Regularly evaluating the organizational structure ensures that the IAF has the necessary resources and expertise to carry out its mission effectively (IIA, 2006).

The Internal Audit Function

As highlighted by Idema and Weel (2018) and Noraini et al. (2018), the IAF plays an important role in evaluating the efficiency and effectiveness of internal control as well as in enhancing stakeholders' value. According to Roussy et al. (2020), fulfilling stakeholder expectations is essential to the IAF's organizational importance. Several attributes of an effective IAF have been identified by prior research (Coetzee & Erasmus, 2017; Singh et al., 2021; Muneer et al., 2019). These attributes include competence, adequate positioning and resourcing, quality, continuous improvement, insight, proactiveness, future-focus, efficiency, and senior management support.

The CAE plays a crucial role in managing the IAF to ensure it adds value to the organization (IIA, 2017). The CAE must ensure that the IAF operates with adequate resources, qualified personnel, continuous professional education, and appropriate tools (IIA Netherlands, 2016). The leadership style of the CAE also influences the effectiveness of the IAF (Dal Mas & Barac, 2018). Furthermore, the CAE's influence may be a significant factor in technology investment decisions (Garven & Scarlata, 2020).

To ensure the success of the IAF, the CAE must develop relationships with all stakeholders and the members of the IAF team (Sawyer, 2014). Regular evaluation of the CAE's performance as the head of the IAF is necessary (Sawyer, 2014). The competency of internal auditors is crucial for the efficiency of the IAF (Singh et al., 2021). Continuous improvement in competency, effectiveness, and service quality is essential for the IAF's reputation (IIA, 2009). Moreover, the presence of qualified individuals is a prerequisite for the IAF to fulfil its obligations (Arena & Azzone, 2009). The CAE must also adapt to the evolving demands of the industry (Sawyer, 2014) and ensure the presence of qualified professionals with diverse experience across various business process domains (Stanciu, 2012).

The rapid evolution of the IAF necessitates a collective intelligence that is both flexible and forward-thinking, as noted by ACIIA (2021). To address the skills gap, Stanciu (2012) suggests that the CAE should develop a training programme for staff development, allocate sufficient funding, and consider alternative staffing plans. Technology can aid IAFs in developing recruitment strategies and talent acquisition plans that align with their organizational structure, goals, and long-term strategy, as highlighted by Axt et al. (2022). Deloitte (2018c) proposes alternative resourcing models, such as co-sourcing, occasional use of external resources, quest auditors, and outsourcing. Relying on third parties, such as temporary workers, tool vendors, audit/consulting companies, or internal IT resources, is a common strategy for meeting initial, intermittent, or urgent audit needs, as noted by Axt et al. (2022). Given the shifting labour market, retention issues, and skill shortages, alternative sourcing plans are crucial for IAFs to fill and retain critical skills, as emphasized by KPMG (2021).

Methodology

Method

The research study utilized a qualitative research method to identify the characteristics of the population sample and gain insights into the factors that contribute to the limited utilization of emerging technologies. According to Shiburi et al. (2022), qualitative research is beneficial as it allows the researcher to be closer to the text and provides more insight into complex language. Data was collected through a questionnaire, which aimed to identify the factors that discourage the adoption and implementation of emerging technologies by the IAFs. This research method was informed by two prior studies: Ahmi et al. (2014) conducted a questionnaire-based investigation on IT adoption among internal auditors in the Malaysian public sector, while Damanik et al. (2020) employed a questionnaire to analyse the factors that impede IT usage in the audit process within the Indonesian State Audit Agency. A questionnaire, as described by Roopa and Rani (2012), is a reliable tool for gathering consistent and coherent information for analysis. By building upon previous research, the chosen research methodology offers valuable insights into the barriers to adopting emerging technologies.

Research Design

The research objectives shaped the literature review, methodology, and data collection techniques. This study specifically focused on identifying the barriers faced by in-house IAFs in adopting emerging technologies and the subsequent impact on the effectiveness of the IAF. The population for this study consisted of the five state research councils, namely ARC, CGS, CSIR, HSRC, and SAMRC. From this population, only three of the research councils have in-house IAF, and, therefore, the sample is three. The CAE of each of the research councils were asked to complete the questionnaire. Due to the small sample, a qualitative approach was taken in the study, as no statistical analysis was necessary to describe the findings. The study can be replicated in any public sector institution with an in-house IAF.

Data Collection

The primary data was collect using a questionnaire specifically targeted at the heads of IAFs referred to as CAEs in state research councils who are responsible for managing the IAF. The questionnaire itself consisted primarily of closed-ended questions, which included Yes/No questions, multiple choice questions, and scaled questions that were anchored on a five-point Likert scale. Additionally, open-ended questions were included to address the dependent variable and obtain a more comprehensive understanding of the impact that the lack of adoption of emerging technologies has on the effectiveness of the IAF. The design of the questionnaire was informed by the insightful literature review that was undertaken. The participants answered questions regarding their relationship with senior management and the audit committee, resource allocation, and the level of use of emerging technologies by both the IAF and the organization.

Ethical Considerations

Ethical clearance was obtained from the Universities Research and Ethics Committee. The ethical clearance number is SAREC20221124/01. The authors applied the Harvard referencing method to ensure that all sources used are cited and given the relevant credit.

The questionnaire itself was divided into four sections: Demographics, Technology Landscape (IAF and the Organization), Organizational factors related to the adoption of emerging technologies, and IAF effectiveness. Its purpose was to provide background knowledge on the IAF and the organization, gain insight into the digitalization of the IAF and the organization, understand the organizational factors that hinder the IAF from adapting to emerging technologies, and determine whether these factors have an impact on the effectiveness of the IAF. The questionnaire was designed using Google Forms and distributed to participants via email.

Data Analysis and Interpretation

The primary objective of the study was to identify the obstacles within an organization that hinder the implementation of emerging technologies by the IAF, and to assess their impact on the effectiveness of the IAF. To gain a comprehensive understanding, the collected data was organized based on respondents' demographics, shedding light on their perspectives and the current state of technology adoption and utilization. The data gathered from the questionnaire is discussed below and categorized according to the research objectives.

Finding

Summary of the Key Findings

The study aimed to accomplish its research objectives by conducting a literature review and an empirical study. The findings obtained from the questionnaire were supported by the existing literature. The research commenced with a research statement that highlighted the lack of realization of benefits brought about by emerging technologies in most in-house IAFs. To address this statement, the study was designed to achieve four research objectives. Firstly, it aimed to establish technology as a crucial driver of an effective IAF. Secondly, it sought to determine the extent to which emerging technologies were being utilized by IAFs. Thirdly, it aimed to identify the organizational barriers that hindered the implementation of these technologies by IAFs. Lastly, it aimed to determine the impact of these barriers on the effectiveness of IAFs. To address the research statement and objectives, the research combined the empirical research with the existing literature.

Research Objective (i): Establish Technology as a Key Driver of an Effective IAF

The literature review emphasizes that traditional audits do not provide real-time assurance, whereas advanced technology tools enable real-time assurance on current events. The digitalization of the IAF has brought benefits to the profession, as technology is necessary for expediting processes and improving performance. An IAF that is technologically advanced is viewed as a strategic partner, and investing in emerging technologies expands the scope of audits and allows for ongoing audits. The adoption of emerging technologies reduces reliance on human work, enhances audit efficiency, and improves data analytics. Many large IAFs utilize technology throughout the entire internal audit lifecycle.

Research Objective (ii): Determine the Level of Emerging Technologies Usage by IAF

The examination of existing literature has brought to light the fact that internal audit has refrained from utilizing enabling technology, resulting in a negative impact on stakeholder expectations and a decrease in value. However, emerging technologies such as AI, RPA, NLP, and ML have the capability to automate the internal auditing process. Unfortunately, the IAFs are not involved in the decision-making process regarding investments in these developing technologies. The implementation of advanced auditing systems is a costly endeavour, and the lack of digital skills serves as the primary obstacle. Audit firms, on the other hand, are at the forefront of adopting these technologies, influenced by factors such as management support, technological competence, the Unified Theory of Acceptance and Use of Technology (UTAUT), performance expectancy, and effort expectancy.

Based on an empirical study, it was discovered that research councils exhibit varying levels of technology maturity, with senior management showing dedication towards aligning with emerging technologies. Approximately 67% of these councils have already implemented 4IR enabling technologies. While internal audits have automated their processes, they have not yet embraced emerging technologies. A significant portion (67%) of CAEs believe that the profession is lagging in technological innovation due to a lack of skills, capital investment, organizational support, technology knowledge, and training. The level of digital transformation within an organization is the most influential factor when it comes to the adoption of technology.

Research Objective (iii): Discuss the Organizational Barriers that Deter IAF from Implementing Emerging Technologies

Senior Management Support

According to existing literature, the majority of IAFs encounter a significant obstacle in their ability to be effective, primarily due to a lack of support from senior management. This absence of support is evident in the insufficient allocation of resources, the lack of commitment to implementing internal audit recommendations, and the failure to keep internal audits informed about organizational plans. The perceived disparity in expectations regarding the role of internal audit further contributes to this lack of support. Nevertheless, the support of senior management is vital for the effectiveness of internal audit.

Empirical findings demonstrate that the relationship between CAEs and senior management is a crucial factor in determining the effectiveness of internal audit. The involvement of senior management in internal audit plans and their response to audit reports serve as indicators of management support. Furthermore, a significant 67% of CAEs report that senior management displays interest in the IAF's intentions to incorporate innovative technology and actively supports its endeavours to acquire and develop relevant talent and capabilities.

Role of the Audit Committee

Literature highlights that the effectiveness of the IAF is enhanced by the support of the audit committee. However, in the South African public sector, both the IAFs and audit committees are found to be ineffective. To ensure the IAF's efficiency, the audit committee plays a crucial role in approving the budget allocation and resource plan of the IAF. Additionally, it is responsible for evaluating the IAF's capacity to execute the audit plan, ensuring the smooth functioning of the IAF, and supporting its initiatives to invest in and utilize audit technology.

Based on an empirical study, CAEs believe that audit committee support is instrumental in enabling the IAF to achieve effectiveness. However, when there are ineffective interactions between the IAF and the audit committee, it results in insufficient support. To address this issue, the audit committee should undertake the review and approval of the IAF's resource plan and budget. Furthermore, it should provide support to the IAF in acquiring or developing the necessary talent and capabilities. Lastly, the audit committee must ensure that the IAF has adequate resources and competency to fulfil its mandate effectively.

Internal Audit Function

Literature reveals that a successful IAF necessitates certain factors, including organizational autonomy, adequate financial resources, competent personnel, and sufficient support. However, IAFs encounter organizational challenges such as insufficient budget allocation, difficulty in retaining skilled staff, and inadequate backing from senior executives. While an in-house IAF proves effective, an outsourced IAF adds further value. The effectiveness of an IAF is contingent upon the competency and leadership of the CAE. The proficiency of internal auditors is a crucial characteristic of a successful IAF.

Empirical research findings indicate that most CAEs disagree with the notion that internal auditors lack motivation to embrace emerging technologies. They believe that internal auditors are comfortable with the current state of technological innovation and exhibit reluctance towards change. To successfully implement emerging technologies, proper training and skills are imperative. To address gaps in technology skills, it is recommended to provide training to existing staff, hire internal auditors with technological expertise, and consider co-sourcing.

Research Objective (iv): Determine the Impact the Barriers Have on IAF Effectiveness

According to the research, technology plays a crucial role in facilitating an efficient IAF, and the process of digital transformation has a significant impact on enhancing the effectiveness of IAF. The effectiveness of IAF is influenced by various factors such as organizational autonomy, formal authorization, accessibility, financial resources, workforce, support from stakeholders, and adherence to professional standards. The efficiency of IAF is evaluated based on the completion of audit plans, timely submission of reports, feedback from stakeholders, and consulting activities.

Conclusion

The objective of this study was to investigate the obstacles that prevent in-house IAFs in state research councils from adopting emerging technologies. The research revealed that most IAFs are not taking full advantage of digital innovations, which could lead to increased efficiency, improved accuracy, and better utilization of scarce resources. The adoption of advanced technologies could significantly enhance the overall effectiveness of the IAF. The literature review indicated that senior executives do not provide sufficient support to IAFs, resulting in perceived ineffectiveness and a lack of value. Although the audit committee supports IAF's efforts to incorporate technological innovations, it falls short in determining whether the IAF has the necessary resources and expertise to execute the audit plan. The IAF faces several challenges in fulfilling its mandate and adding value to the business, including a lack of skills, inadequate budget, insufficient resources, and inadequate support from senior management. The empirical findings suggest that IAFs have not yet embraced emerging technology and have not yet identified the ideal role for it in their processes.

The study concluded that the barriers to adopting emerging technology have a significant impact on IAF effectiveness. Without the support of senior management and the audit committee, implementing emerging technology would be challenging for the IAF. Internal auditors must be committed to driving and embracing technological change, and IAF effectiveness is dependent on several factors, including organizational support, resources, budget, competency, and technology. Support from senior management and the audit committee is critical in providing a suitable budget, resources, and participation in IAF operations.

Limitations, Recommendations, and Future Research

The present study encountered certain limitations that should be acknowledged. Firstly, the available literature on the utilization of emerging technology by IAFs in South Africa was limited, which may have restricted the depth of analysis. Additionally, the study focused solely on in-house IAFs within state research councils, thereby excluding outsourced or co-sourced IAFs. Furthermore, the study specifically concentrated on the South African context, which may limit the generalizability of the findings to other regions or countries.

Moreover, it is important to note that the questionnaire responses were restricted to CAEs of the research councils, thereby excluding valuable insights from internal audit staff, senior executives, and audit committee members. This exclusion may have limited the comprehensiveness of the data collected and the overall understanding of the barriers to emerging technology adoption within the IAFs.

Nevertheless, this study made significant contributions to the existing literature by examining the barriers to emerging technology adoption within in-house IAFs in state research councils in South Africa and assessing their impact on effectiveness. The findings of this research address a gap in the literature and shed light on the organizational components necessary for IAFs to successfully integrate innovation into their internal auditing processes.

Based on the empirical findings, this study provides valuable areas of discussion for heads of IAFs to initiate the journey towards digitalization of internal audit practices. However, it is recommended that future research should focus on developing an internal audit technology strategy roadmap, with a particular emphasis on organizational factors that influence technology adoption. Additionally, exploring other elements of the TOE framework, such as technological and environmental factors, would further enhance the understanding of the barriers and facilitators of emerging technology adoption within IAFs.

References

Abdullah, A., & Mustafa, A. (2020). Factors impact on internal audit effectiveness: The case of Duhok University in Kurdistan-Iraq. *International Business and Accounting Research Journal, 4*(2), 89–94. https://doi.org/10.15294/ibarj.v4i2.128

ACIIA. (2021). *Internal Audit transformed: Future of work, emerging risks, and trends*. Retrieved February 08, 2022, from https://www.aciia.asia/wp-content/uploads/2021/06/2020-IA-Survey-Report_June-2021.pdf.

Ackermann, C. (2016). Using triangulation to view internal audit's governance functioning. *Corporate Ownership and Control, 13*(4), 287–296. https://doi.org/10.22495/cocv13i4c2p2

Ahmi, A., Saidin, S., & Abdullah, A. (2014). IT adoption by internal auditors in the public sector: A conceptual study. *Procedia Social and Behavioural Sciences, 164*, 591–599. https://doi.org/10.1016/j.sbspro.2014.11.151

Al-Hiyari, A., Al Said, N., & Hattab, E. (2019). Factors that influence the use of computer assisted audit techniques (CAATs) by internal auditors in Jordan. *Academy of Accounting and Financial Studies Journal, 23*(3), 1–15.

Alqaraleh, M. H., Almari, M. O. S., Ali, B. J., & Oudat, M. S. (2022). The mediating role of organizational culture on the relationship between information technology and internal audit effectiveness. *Corporate Governance and Organisational Behavior Review, 6*(1), 8–18. https://doi.org/10.22495/cgobrv6i1p1

Arena, M., & Azzone, G. (2009). Identifying organisational drivers of internal audit effectiveness. *International Journal of Auditing, 13*(1), 43–60. https://doi.org/10.1111/j.1099-1123.2008.00392.x

Atayah, O. F., & Alshater, M. M. (2021). Audit and tax in the context of emerging technologies: A retrospective analysis, current trends, and future opportunities. *International Journal of Digital Accounting Research, 21*, 95–128. https://doi.org/10.4192/1577-8517-v21_4

Axt, P., Koorn, R., Raven, P., Chuah, H & Solomons, K. (2022). *Leveraging technology within internal audit functions: Technology-enabled internal audit.* Retrieved April 17, 2023, from https://www.compact.nl/en/articles/leveraging-technology-within-internal-audit-functions/.

Baharud-din, Z., Shokiyah, A., & Ibrahim, M. S. (2014). Factors that contribute to the effectiveness of internal audit in public sector. *International Proceedings of Economics Development and Research, 70*, 126–132. https://doi.org/10.7763/IPEDR

Baker, J. (2012). *The technology organisation environment framework, information systems theory* (pp. 231–245). University of Hamburg. https://doi.org/10.1007/978-1-4419-6108-2_12

Betti, N., & Sarens, G. (2020). Understanding the internal audit function in a digitalised business environment. *Journal of Accounting & Organisational Change, 17*(2), 197–216. https://doi.org/10.1108/JAOC-11-2019-0114

Braun, R. L., & Davis, H. E. (2003). Computer-assisted audit tools and techniques: Analysis and perspectives. *Managerial Auditing Journal, 18*(9), 725–731. https://doi.org/10.1108/02686900310500488

Cangemi, P. (2016). Views on internal audit, internal controls, and internal audit's use of technology. *The EDP Audit, Control, and Security Newsletter, 53*(1), 1–9. https://doi.org/10.1080/07366981.2015.112818

Chambers, R. (2017). *Internal auditing and the fourth industrial revolution.* Retrieved October 20, 2021, from https://www.richardchambers.com/internal-auditing-and-the-fourth-industrial-revolution/.

Chartered Professional Accountants of Canada & The American Institute of Certified Public Accountants. (2020). *The data-driven audit: How automation and AI are changing the audit and the role of the auditor.* Retrieved October 20, 2021, from https://us.aicpa.org/content/dam/aicpa/interestareas/frc/assuranceadvisoryservices/downloadabledocuments/the-data-driven-audit.pdf.

Christ, M. H., Eulerich, M., & Wood, D. A. (2019). *Internal auditors' response to disruptive innovation.* Internal Audit Foundation.

Coetzee, P., & Erasmus, L. (2017). What drives and measures public sector internal audit effectiveness? Dependent and independent variables. *International Journal of Auditing, 21*(3), 237–248. https://doi.org/10.1111/ijau.12097

Dal Mas, L. O., & Barac, K. (2018). The influence of the chief audit executive's leadership style on factors related to internal audit effectiveness. *Managerial Auditing Journal, 33*(8/9), 807–835. https://doi.org/10.1108/MAJ-12-2017-1741

Damanik, A., Handayani, P., & Pinem, A. (2020). The barriers of IT utilization: A case study of Indonesian audit organisation. In *3rd international conference on computer and informatics engineering. Yogyakarta, Indonesia, 15-16 September* (pp. 280–285). Institute of Electrical and Electronics Engineer. https://doi.org/10.1109/IC2IE50715.2020.9274664

David, D., Agboh, D., & Radhakrishnan, A. (2010). Factor influencing the adoption of technologies in developing countries: An empirical study. *Journal of Academy of Business and Economics, 10*(4), 1–15.

Dellai, H., & Omri, M. A. B. (2016). Factors affecting the internal audit effectiveness in Tunisian organisations. *Research Journal of Finance and Accounting, 7*(16).

Deloitte. (2018a). *Internal Audit 3.0: The future of Internal Audit is now.* Retrieved April 13, 2022, from https://www2.deloitte.com/content/dam/Deloitte/global/Documents/Audit/gx-internal-audit-3.0-the-future-of-internal-audit-is-now.pdf.

Deloitte. (2018b). *Audit Committee Resource Guide.* Retrieved February 15, 2022, from https://www2.deloitte.com/za/en/pages/audit/articles/audit-committee-resource-guide.html.

Deloitte. (2018c). *Global Chief Audit Survey.* Retrieved February 08, 2022, from https://www2.deloitte.com/bg/en/pages/audit/articles/global-chief-audit-executive-research-survey.html.

Deloitte. (2018d). *The role of the audit committee.* Retrieved February 15, 2022, from https://deloitte.wsj.com/articles/overseeing-internal-audit-the-role-of-the-audit-committee-1542765732.

Deloitte. (2018e). *Adopting automation in internal audit Using robotic process automation and cognitive intelligence to fortify the third line of defense.* Retrieved April 06, 2022, from https://www2.deloitte.com/content/dam/Deloitte/us/Documents/risk/adopting-robotic-process-automation-in-internal-audit.pdf.

Deloitte. (2019). *Moving Internal Audit Deeper into the Digital Age: Part 1.* Retrieved February 14, 2022, from https://www.theiia.org/en/products/bookstore/moving-internal-audit-deeper-into-the-digital-age-part-1-a-structured-methodology-for-leveraging-automation-to-modernize-the-internal-audit-function/.

Deribe, W., & Regasa, D. (2014). Factors determining internal audit quality: Empirical evidence from Ethiopian commercial banks. *Research Journal of Finance and Accounting, 5*(23), 86–94.

Dubai Financial Services Authority. (2017). *Understanding the impact of technology in audit and finance.* Retrieved October 15, 2021, from https://www.icaew.com/-/media/corporate/files/middle-east-hub/understanding-the-impact-of-technology-in-audit-and-finance.ashx.

Dzomira, S. (2020). Corporate governance and performance of audit committee and internal audit functions in an emerging economy's public sector. *Indian Journal of Corporate Governance, 13*(1), 85–98. https://doi.org/10.1177/0974686220923789

Feizizadeh, A. (2012). Strengthening internal audit effectiveness. *Indian Journal of Science and Technology, 5*(5), 2777–2778. https://doi.org/10.17485/ijst/2012/v5i5.18

Fotoh, L. E., & Lorentzon, J. I. (2021). The impact of digitalization on future audits. *Journal of Emerging Technologies in Accounting, 18*(2), 77–97. https://doi.org/10.2308/JETA-2020-063

Garven, S., & Scarlata, A. (2020). An examination of factors associated with investment in internal auditing technology. *Managerial Auditing Journal, 35*(7), 955–978. https://doi.org/10.1108/MAJ-06-2019-2321

Gepp, A., Linnenluecke, M. K., O'Neill, T. J., & Smith, T. (2018). Big data techniques in auditing research and practice: Current trends and future opportunities. *Journal of Accounting Literature, 40*(1), 102–115. https://doi.org/10.1016/j.acclit.2017.05.003

Hailemariam, S. (2014). Determinants of internal audit effectiveness in the public sector, case study in selected Ethiopian public sector offices, Ph.D. Thesis. Jimma University, Ethiopia. Retrieved April 20, 2022, from https://opendocs.ids.ac.uk/opendocs/handle/20.500.12413/5418.

Huang, F., No, W. G., Vasarhelyi, M. A., & Yan, Z. (2022). Audit data analytics, machine learning, and full population testing. *The Journal of Finance and Data Science, 8*, 138–144. https://doi.org/10.1016/j.jfds.2022.05.002
iKutu. (2014). *The status of and demand for internal auditing in South African National Government Departments*. Retrieved October 20, 2021, from https://www.iiasa.org.za/page/Ikutu_Report_on_Internal_Audit.
Idema, S., & Weel, P. (2018). Audit Analytics. Compact 2018/4. From, https://www.compact.nl/en/articles/audit-analytics.
Institute of Internal Auditing. (2006). The Audit Committee: Purpose, process, professionalism., From, https://www.theiia.org/globalassets/documents/about110us/about-internal-audit/the-audit-committee-internal-audit-oversight.pdf.
Institute of Internal Auditors Research Foundation (IIARF). (2013). The IIARF white paper: The Audit Committee and the CAE: Sustaining a Strategic Partnership, From, https://www.iia.nl/the-audit-committee-and-the-cae-sustaining-a-strategic-partnership.
Institute of Internal Auditing. (2016). Data Analytics: Elevating Internal Audit's Value. https://www.theiia.org/en/standards/international-professionalpracticesframework/.
Institute of Internal Auditors Netherlands. (2016). Measuring the Effectiveness of the Internal Audit Function Practical tools for internal auditors. From, https://www.iia.nl/SiteFiles/vakpub/IIA_Bro%20A4%20Effectiviteitsmeting%20IAF%20ENG%20DIGITAL.pdf.
Institute of Internal Auditors and Global Technology Audit Guide. (2017). *GTAG 16: Data analysis technologies*. Retrieved April 12, 2023, from https://na.theiia.org/standards-guidance/recommended-guidance/technology/Pages/GTAG-16-Data-Analysis-Technologies.aspx.
Institute of Internal Auditors Netherlands & Ernst and Young. (2021). *How does digitalization change the role and way of working of internal audit: an exploratory overview?* Retrieved April 06, 2022, from https://www.iia.nl/SiteFiles/Rapport_Digitalization_2021_LR(1).pdf.
Institute of Internal Auditors Practice Advisory. (2009). Retrieved April 13, 2022, from https://www.theiia.org/globalassets/documents/resources/internal-auditings-role-in-corporate-governance-may-2018/internal-auditings-role-in-corporate-governance.pdf.
Institute of Internal Auditors South Africa. (2021). *Plight of internal auditor's report 2021*. Retrieved April 21, 2023, from www.iiasa.co.za.
Institute of Internal Auditors. (2017). *International Professional Practices Framework (IPPF)*. Retrieved April 06, 2022, from https://www.theiia.org/en/standards/international-professional-practices-framework/.
International Auditing and Assurance Standards Board. (2017). Exploring the growing use of technology in the audit, with a focus on data analytics. Retrieved October 20, 2021, from https://www.iaasb.org/publications/exploring-growing-use-technology-audit-focus-data-analytics.
Jaggi, J. (2023). When does the internal audit function enhance audit committee effectiveness? *The Accounting Review, 98*(2), 329–359. https://doi.org/10.2308/TAR-2021-0089
Janvrin, D., Bierstaker, J., & Lowe, D. J. (2009). Investigation of factors influencing the use of computer-related audit procedures. *Journal of Information Systems, 23*(1), 97–118. https://doi.org/10.2308/jis.2009.23.1.97
Kifer, C. (2021). *A stable, robust and scalable AI solution*. Retrieved April 6, 2022, from https://www.ibm.com/downloads/cas/10N9MNKJ.
Kim, H., Mannino, M., & Nieschwietz, R. (2009). Information technology acceptance in the internal audit profession: Impact of technology features and complexity. *International Journal of Accounting Information Systems, 10*(4), 214–228. https://doi.org/10.1016/j.accinf.2009.09.001
Kokina, J., & Davenport, T. H. (2017). The emergence of artificial intelligence: How automation is changing auditing. *Emerging Technologies in accounting, 14*, 117–122. https://doi.org/10.2308/jeta-51730
Kovanen, A. (2020). Risks of intelligent automation and their impact on internal audit, M.Com Thesis. Tampere University, Finland. Retrieved April 6, 2022, from https://trepo.tuni.fi/bitstream/handle/10024/121440/KovanenAnni.pdf?sequence=2.

KPMG. (2017). *Enhancing the strategic value of internal audit*. Retrieved April 06, 2022, from https://assets.kpmg/content/dam/kpmg/be/pdf/2017/Enhancing-the-strategic-value-of-internal-audit.pdf.

KPMG. (2020). *20 key risks to consider by internal Audit before 2020*. Retrieved Septewmber 12, 2021, from https://assets.kpmg/content/dam/kpmg/ch/pdf/key-risks-internal-audit-2018.pdf.

KPMG. (2021). *Technology internal audit: 2022 and beyond: Aligning to heightened expectations*. Retrieved April 06, 2022, from https://advisory.kpmg.us/articles/2021/technology-internal-audit.html.

Late, E. (2018). Reading orientations in state research institutes. *Information Research, 23*(2) http://InformationR.net/ir/23-2/paper795.html.

Lenz, R., & Hahn, U. (2015). Synthesis of empirical internal audit effectiveness literature pointing to new research opportunities. *Managerial Auditing Journal, 30*(1), 5–33. https://doi.org/10.1108/MAJ-08-2014-1072

Lenz, R., Sarens, G., & Hoos, F. (2017). Internal audit effectiveness: Multiple case study research involving chief audit executives and senior management. *The EDP Audit, Control, and Security Newsletter, 55*(1), 1–17. https://doi.org/10.1080/07366981.2017.1278980

Li, H., Dai, J., Gershberg, T., & Vasarhelyi, M. A. (2018). Understanding usage and value of audit analytics for internal auditors: An organisational approach. *International Journal of Accounting Information Systems, 28*, 59–76. https://doi.org/10.1016/j.accinf.2017.12.005

Lois, P., Drogalas, G., Karagiorgos, A., & Tsikalakis, K. (2020). Internal audits in the digital era: Opportunities, risks and challenges. *EuroMed Journal of Business, 15*(2), 205–217. https://doi.org/10.1108/EMJB-07-2019-0097

Lotto, J. (2014). Examining the impact of information technology on internal auditing effectiveness in Tanzanian organisations. *Time Journals of Social Sciences, 2*(3), 13–23. www.timejournals.org/tjss

Mahzan, N., & Lymer, A. (2014). Examining the adoption of computer-assisted audit tools and techniques: Cases of generalized audit software use by internal auditors. *Managerial Auditing Journal, 29*(4), 327–349. https://doi.org/10.1108/MAJ-05-2013-0877

Mamaile, L. J. (2020). The role of internal audit functions at State Owned Enterprises in South Africa. *International conference on public administration and development alternatives, virtual conference, 07–09 October.* (pp. 160–168). http://hdl.handle.net/10386/3256.

Marx, B., & Ravjee, H. (2015). An analysis of the evolving role of information technology with respect to selected standard and its impact on internal audit. *Journal for New Generation Sciences, 13*(3), 101–119.

Mihret, D., & Yismaw, A. (2007). Internal audit effectiveness: An Ethiopian public sector case study. *Managerial Auditing Journal, 22*(5), 470–484. https://doi.org/10.1108/02686900710750757

Moffitt, K. C., Rozario, A. M., & Vasarhelyi, M. A. (2018). Robotic process automation for auditing. *Journal of emerging technologies in accounting, 15*(1), 1–10.

Mokhitli, M., & Kyobe, M. (2019). Examining factors that impede internal auditors from leveraging information technology for continuous auditing. *International conference on computing, control and industrial engineering, Durban, South Africa, 6–8 March*. Institute of Electrical and Electronics Engineers, (pp. 1–6). https://doi.org/10.1109/ICTAS.2019.8703610.

Moorthy, K., Seetharaman, A., Mohamed, Z., Gopalan, M., & San, L. (2011). The impact of information technology on internal auditing. *African Journal of Business Management, 5*(9), 3523–3539. https://doi.org/10.5897/AJBM10.1047

Motubatse, K., van Staden, M., Steyn, B., & Erasmus, L. (2015a). Audit tools and techniques: Crucial dimensions of internal audit engagements in South Africa. *Journal of Economics, 6*(3), 269–279. https://doi.org/10.1080/09765239.2015.11917616

Motubatse, N., Barac, K., & Odendaal, E. (2015b). Perceived challenges faced by the internal audit function in the South African public sector: A case study of The National Treasury. *African Journal of Science, 7*(6), 401–407. https://hdl.handle.net/10520/EJC183310.

Mubako, G. (2019). Internal audit outsourcing: A literature synthesis and future directions. *Australian Accounting Review, 29*(3), 532–545. https://doi.org/10.1111/auar.12272

Mubarrok, A. Z. (2018). *Auditing in 4.0 ERA*. Retrieved May 25, 2022, from https://iaijabar.or.id/wp-content/uploads/2018/07/Auditing-in-4.0-Era-Ahmad-Zakie-Mubarrok-SE-M.Acc-CACP-CPA.pdf.

Muneer, S., Basheer, M., Shabbir, R., & Zeb, A. (2019). Does information technology (IT) expedite the internal audit system? Determinants of internal audit effectives: Evidence from Pakistani Banking Industry. *The Dialogue, 14*(2), 145–157.

Musah, A., Gapketor, E., & Anokye, F. (2018). Determinants of internal audit effectiveness in state-owned enterprises (SOEs) in Ghana. *Journal of Accounting and Management, 8*(1), 52–68. http://hdl.handle.net/11159/3068.

Mustapha, M., & Lai, S. J. (2017). Information technology in audit processes: An empirical evidence from Malaysian audit firms. *International Review of Management and Marketing, 7*(2), 53–59. https://www.econjournals.com/index.php/irmm/article/view/4077.

Noraini, S., Zaini, J. A., Mustaffha, N., & Norhanizah, J. (2018). Internal audit effectiveness in Zakat institutions from the perspective of the Auditee. *Management and Accounting Review, 17*(3), 17–36. https://doi.org/10.24191/mar.v17i3.786

Organisation for Economic Co-operation and Development. (2011). *Actor brief on public research organisations*. Retrieved May 25, 2022, from https://silo.tips/download/actor-brief-on-public-research-organisations-pros.

Oussii, A. A., & Boulila Taktak, N. (2018). The impact of internal audit function characteristics on internal control quality. *Managerial Auditing Journal, 33*(5), 450–469. https://doi.org/10.1108/MAJ-06-2017-1579

Protiviti. (2020). Achieving audit relevance, From, https://www.protiviti.com/us-en/surve

Public Sector Audit Committee Forum. (n.d.-a). *Overseeing and evaluating an internal audit function's effectiveness*. Retrieved March 15, 2022, from https://www.psacf.co.za/resource/collection/FDA73195-0CB8-46C8-8B58-6EDBEA3A4055/PSACF_IAF._Effectiveness_PaperEmail.pdf.

Public Sector Audit Committee Forum. (n.d.-b). *The role of audit committees in relation to the external and internal audit process*. Retrieved April 15, 2023, from https://saicawebprstorage.blob.core.windows.net/uploads/resources/The_role_of_audit_committees_in_relation_to_the_external_and_internal_audit_process.pdf.

PwC. (2015). *State of the internal audit profession study*. Retrieved February 14, 2022, from www.pwc.com.

PwC. (2017). *Transforming internal audit to drive digital value meeting technology disruption with strategically aligned solutions*. Retrieved April 6, 2022, from https://www.pwc.com/sg/en/risk-assurance/assets/internal-audit-transform-ia-to-drive-digital-value.pdf.

PwC. (2018). *State of the internal audit profession study*. Retrieved February 14, 2022, from https://www.pwc.com/sg/en/publications/state-of-internal-audit-profession-study-2018.html.

PwC. (2019). State of the internal audit profession study. Elevating internal audit's role: The digitally fit function. Retrieved February 14, 2022, from http://pwc.com/us/internalauditstudy.

Rakipi, R., De Santis, F., & D'Onza, G. (2021). Correlates of the internal audit function's use of data analytics in the big data era: Global evidence. *Journal of International Accounting, Auditing and Taxation, 42*(c). https://doi.org/10.1016/j.intaccaudtax.2020.100357

Ramamoorti, S., & Weidenmier, M. (2004). *Chapter 9: The pervasive impact of information technology on internal auditing*. The Institute of Internal Auditors Research Foundation.

Roopa, S., & Rani, M. S. (2012). Questionnaire designing for a survey. *Journal of Indian Orthodontic Society, 46*(4), 273–277.

Rosli, K., Yeow, P & Eu-Gene, S. (2013). Adoption of audit technology in audit firms. *ACIS 2013: Information systems: Transforming the future: Proceedings of the 24th Australasian conference on information systems. Melbourne, Australia, 4–6 December.* RMIT Research Repository, (pp. 1–12). http://researchbank.rmit.edu.au/view/rmit:160987.

Roussy, M., Barbe, O. & Raimbault, S. (2020). Internal audit: from effectiveness to organisational significance. *Managerial Auditing Journal, 35*(2), 322–342. https://doi.org/10.1108/MAJ-01-2019-2162

Ruppel, W. (2006). *Not-for-profit audit committee best practices*. Wiley.

Sarens, G., & De Beelde, I. (2006). The relationship between internal audit and senior management: A qualitative analysis of expectations and perceptions. *International Journal of Auditing, 10*, 219–241.

Sari, I. A., & Sirajuddin, B. (2019). Influence integrity, objectivity and moral courage by the effectiveness of internal audit senior management support for variable moderation. *KnE Social Sciences, 3*(26), 42–52. https://doi.org/10.18502/kss.v3i26.5357

Sawyer, E. (2014). *The chief audit executive: Understanding the role and professional obligations of a CAE*. Institute of Internal Auditors Research Foundation.

Sethibe, T., & Naidoo, E. (2022). The adoption of robotics in the auditing profession. *South African Journal of Information Management, 24*(1), 1–7. https://doi.org/10.4102/sajim.v24i1.1441

Shamsuddin, A., Rajasharen, L., Maran, D., Ameer, M. F. M., & Muthu, P. (2015). Factors influencing usage level of computer assisted audit techniques (CAATs) by internal auditors in Malaysia. *Proceeding-Kuala Lumpur International Business, Economics and Law Conference, 6*(1), 123–131.

Shapiro, D. (2020). *Artificial intelligence for internal audit and risk management*. Retrieved October 13, 2021, from https://towardsdatascience.com/artificial-intelligence-for-internal-audit-and-risk-management-94e509129d49.

Shiburi, K. S., Marx, B., & Smith, R. J. (2022). Internal audit disclosure practices by schedule 2-listed South African Stateowned entities. *Southern African Journal of Accountability and Auditing Research, 24*, 81–95.

Singh, P. K., Ravindran, S., Ganesan, Y., Abbasi, G., & Haron. (2021). Antecedents and internal audit quality implications of internal audit effectiveness. *International Journal of Business Science and Applied Management, 16*(2), 1–21.

Stanciu, V. (2012). *Proceedings of the 7th international conference accounting and management information systems, 7th international conference on intelligent information processing, Bucharest Romania, 29–30 September*. Association for Computing Machinery.

Thottoli, M. M. (2021). Impact of information communication technology competency among auditing professionals. *Accounting Analysis Auditing, 8*(2), 38–47. https://doi.org/10.26794/2408-9303-2021-8-2-38-47

Treasury Regulation. (2005). Retrieved October 13, 2021, from https://www.treasury.gov.za/legislation/pfma/regulations/gazette_27388.pdf.

Turetken, O., Jethefer, S., & Ozkan, B. (2020). Internal audit effectiveness: Operationalization and influencing factors. *Managerial Auditing Journal, 35*(2), 238–271. https://doi.org/10.1108/MAJ-08-2018-1980

Tušek, B., & Pokrovac, I. (2012). Interdependence between audit committee and internal audit. Corporate Board: Role, duties, and composition. *International Scientific Journal, 8*(2), 6–14. https://doi.org/10.22495/cbv8i2art1

Vasarhelyi, M., Kuenkaikaew, S., Littley, J. & Williams, K. (2008). Continuous auditing technology adoption in leading internal audit organisations. Research gate. Retrieved April 23, 2023, from https://www.researchgate.net/publication/229004600_Continuous_Auditing_technology_adoption_in_leading_internal_audit_organisations.

Cost Implications of Fringe Benefits on the Profitability of SMEs in the Cape Metropole

Nasiphi Wendy Mphoswa, Oji Okpusa Oke, and Jimmy Makoni

Abstract Small- and medium-sized businesses are encountering more difficulties in paying their staff as a result of insufficient capital funding. Therefore, the unequal distribution of fringe benefits among employees has a negative impact on the profitability of Small and Medium Enterprises in the Cape Metropole. Finding out how fringe benefits affected SMEs in the Cape Metropole was the purpose of this study. Data was gathered from ten small- and medium-sized businesses in the Cape Metropole, representing a sample of one hundred participants. The instrument for collecting data from respondents was a self-administered questionnaire, and a descriptive survey design was chosen. The paradigm used in the study was positivistic. Purposive sampling is the method used to choose study participants. Tables and graphs were created from the collected data after it was analysed using descriptive statistics in SPSS. The study's findings showed that fringe benefits significantly impact a company's profitability since they raise incentives and compensation, which lowers corporate profits. Employee benefits are therefore seen as an equal responsibility for the employer. Consequently, the performance of the organization may suffer if there are no fringe benefits offered. The study's goal was to provide Small- and Medium-Sized Businesses with an understanding of how fringe benefits support improved work environments and the overall accomplishment of goals.

Keywords COVID-19 · Gender · Fringe benefits · Profitability · Small and medium enterprises

N. W. Mphoswa (✉) · O. O. Oke · J. Makoni
Cape Peninsula University of Technology, Cape Town, South Africa
e-mail: 212275992@mycput.ac.za; Okeo@cput.ac.za; MAKONIJ@cput.ac.za

T. Moloi (ed.), *Impacting Society Positively Through Technology in Accounting and Business Processes*, Springer Proceedings in Business and Economics,
https://doi.org/10.1007/978-3-031-84885-8_61

Introduction

This study aimed to ascertain the impact of fringe benefits on the profitability of Small and Medium Enterprises (SMEs) operating in the Cape Metropole. This chapter provides a general background to the study, including the research problem, the purpose of the research, the objectives and the research design, as well as the methodology adopted in this study. The chapter further provides information on data collection and the ethical considerations observed.

Background to the Study

Recently, it has become clear that organisations around the world face challenges and obstacles when it comes to making their employees more productive and competitive. This led Olatunji et al. (2021, p. 55) to suggest that an organisation's management can positively influence employee to increase productivity by offering fringe benefits. Furthermore, it delineated the extent to which a worker feels a sense of belonging to the company and desires to maintain active participation (Olatunji et al., 2021, p. 55).

To lessen the negative consequences of a fast-paced, cutthroat business environment, Ndichu (2017, p. 23) argues that organisations must plan for a skilled workforce. Mabaso (2017, p. 24) adds that in such a dynamic and changing business climate, incentives are the only way that successful organisations can keep a competent, qualified workforce and maintain a highly motivated workforce. Moreover, a company's compensation programme influences employee attitude and engagement. Offering perks can create a sense of belonging, boost morale, and increase productivity (Zirra et al., 2019, p. 12).

Fringe benefits are benefits that an employer offers to a worker as payment for services rendered, therefore these benefits supplement employees' salaries and wages (Vashistha & Khan 2020, p. 7). In essence, these benefits primarily serve to improve the standard of living for employees and their families and to improve their quality of life; such benefits include retirement benefits and pensions, paid time off, medical assistance or health insurance, use of company vehicles, and training allowances for employees (Zirra et al., 2019, p. 13). Further supporting the aforementioned claims, Werner and Balkin (2021, p. 11) argue that benefits enhance candidate pool, increase employee retention, lower costs, and boost company output by attracting and retaining workers with specific attitudes, values, knowledge, skills, and abilities. However, offering these benefits can be expensive for certain companies, which leads to low employee morale and high staff turnover (Kamau, 2013, p. 27). The Australian Human Rights Commission states that gender-based discrimination in compensation and perks cannot be used to deny opportunities for training, overtime, or higher positions (Australian Human Rights Commission, 1984, p. 17). In South Africa (SA), the gender pay gap, or the difference in compensation between men and women for doing the same or similar labour remains a major stumbling block to achieving gender equality (Bosch & Barit, 2020, p. 5). Tan et al. (2016, p. 3) note that most SMEs, especially small businesses, cannot afford to give benefits to their employees due to the high cost of providing them. This argument cannot be separated from the fact that SMEs are small with limited resources, even though they are adaptable to shifting market conditions (Obokoh & Goldman, 2016, p. 339).

SMEs are widely acknowledged for growing the economy by creating job opportunities and functioning as production engines and are recognised globally for their distinctive influence on economic development (Dhanah, 2016, p. 14). Vuba (2019, p. 1) asserts that SMEs have the potential to boost the SA Gross Domestic Product (GDP) and generate jobs. SMEs represent 90% of businesses and account for between 50 and 60% of employment in developing countries, making them the engine of many economies in the developing world. SMEs also play a significant role in supporting economies globally (Painter & Dobie, 2014, p. 17).

In developing nations, SMEs foster economic growth and tackle severe poverty issues; as a result, they account for more than 60% of GDP (Dhanah, 2016, p. 11). According to Rungani and Potgieter (2018, p. 7), SMEs in SA comprise 91% of formal business entities and contribute between 52 and 57% to the country's GDP, as well as 61% of job opportunities. Maduekwe and Kamala (2016, p. 67) report that SMEs contribute to economic growth and job creation, but often fail due to improper use of performance indicators, lack of employee benefits, and cost impact on profitability. Widespread COVID-19 in SA has caused significant employment losses, decreased company profitability, and business terminations (Small Business Development, 2021, p. 34). Hence, the pandemic has significantly impacted the nation's daily life causing unprecedented circumstances and affecting people's lifestyles globally (Small Business Development, 2021, p. 35).

Given the significance of SMEs in creating employment opportunities and because these are some of the sectors still seeing significant growth rates, it is essential to evaluate and investigate the cost implications of fringe benefits on the profitability of SMEs.

Statement of Research Problem

The majority of SMEs globally spend significant amounts of money on reward programmes designed to inspire, retain, and recruit new staff (Ndichu, 2017, p. 11). The profitability of SMEs is severely negatively impacted by the rising expense of fringe benefits. To support these assertions, Anele et al. (2017, p. 98) note that although organisations have a variety of reward systems in place that consider both intrinsic and extrinsic factors and are meant to promote and advance employee welfare, yet SMEs encounter difficulties when it comes to paying staff fairly and developing an incentive system. The main issue that is becoming increasingly prevalent in many SMEs is the management's incapacity to fairly reward all personnel due to inadequate funding standards and capital (Anele et al., 2017, p. 99). Moreover, in many SMEs, underpaying workers also causes unhappiness, which further reduces output and raises staff turnover. This is evidenced by the excessive staff turnover rate being experienced by many SMEs in SA. As a result, this leads to a struggle for enterprises to become sustainable, which eventually has a negative effect on their total profitability.

The research problem can be briefly stated as follows: "The profitability of SMEs in the Cape Metropole is adversely influenced due to the unequal distribution of fringe benefits amongst employees".

Aim of the Study

The aim of this study is to ascertain the impact of fringe benefits on SMEs operating in the Cape Metropole.

Research Questions and Sub-questions

Research Questions

The primary research question is:

How to ascertain the impact of fringe benefits on SMEs operating in the Cape Metropole?

The sub-questions in support of the main research question are:

(a) What are the implications of fringe benefits on SMEs?
(b) What are the types of fringe benefits offered by SMEs in the Cape Metropole?
(c) Does gender affect the provision of fringe benefits?
(d) What is the impact of COVID-19 on SME fringe benefits?
(e) What is the relationship between fringe benefits and SME performance?

Research Objectives

The **primary objective is:** To ascertain the impact of fringe benefits on SMEs operating in the Cape Metropole.

The **secondary objectives** are:

(a) Understanding the implications of fringe benefits on SMEs.
(b) Exploring the types of fringe benefits offered by SMEs in the Cape Metropole.

(c) Determining the impact of gender on the provision of fringe benefits.
(d) Assessing the impact of COVID-19 on SME fringe benefits.
(e) Establishing the relationship between fringe benefits and SMEs' performance.

This inquiry's remaining sections are organized as follows: The second section provides a thorough literature review; the third section provides a detailed overview of methodology; the fourth section shows the main findings and discussions; and the fifth section illustrates the summary of the study, recommendations, limitations, and future research on the study.

Literature Review

Theoretical Framework

The previous section gave an overview of the research, outlining the problem statement, research objectives and questions, research design and methodology, contribution, and dissertation structure. This section provides a thorough literature review that was undertaken to provide a theoretical grasp of the field of research. The chapter focuses on the inability of management to provide fringe benefits equally to employees. It also explores the current support offered to SMEs in the Cape Metropole.

Agency Theory This theory suggests that there might be conflicts of interest between the owners (shareholders) and managers of SMEs regarding the allocation of resources, including fringe benefits. It can be used to explore how fringe benefits affect managerial behaviour and decision-making in SMEs, potentially impacting profitability.

Human Capital Theory This theory posits that investments in employee benefits, such as training and development programmes included in fringe benefits, can enhance the skills and productivity of employees. Understanding how these investments translate into increased profitability for SMEs could be explored within this framework.

Transaction Cost Economics This theory focuses on the costs associated with conducting transactions within organisations. Fringe benefits could be seen as a mechanism to reduce transaction costs by incentivising employees to stay with the company longer, reducing turnover costs and maintaining organisational knowledge and stability.

Stakeholder Theory

SMEs have various stakeholders, including employees, owners, customers, and the community. Fringe benefits can be seen as a way to balance the interests of these stakeholders. This theory can help in understanding how different types of fringe benefits impact the relationships between SMEs and their stakeholders and, consequently, their profitability.

Resource-Based View (RBV) RBV suggests that a firm's unique resources and capabilities contribute to its competitive advantage and, ultimately, its profitability. Fringe benefits, such as a positive organisational culture or employee loyalty fostered through benefits programmes, can be considered as valuable resources that contribute to SMEs' profitability within this framework.

Expectancy Theory This psychological theory proposes that individuals are motivated to perform when they believe that their efforts will lead to desired outcomes. Fringe benefits, such as performance-based bonuses or healthcare coverage, can influence employees' perceptions of the relationship between effort and reward, thus affecting their motivation and, potentially, SMEs' profitability.

Empirical Discussion

Small and Medium Enterprises

SMEs are well-defined in a variety of senses and are recognised in numerous ways by various people and organisations but a company that is considered a small business in one country may be classified differently in another country. Total assets, the size of the workforce employed, and yearly turnover are some of the variables that are commonly used in various definitions (Bouazza et al., 2015, p. 111).

Importance of SMEs to the Economy

In SA, SMEs are recognised as a key factor in promoting inclusive growth and development and as such, the government emphasises the significance of these entities in job creation, innovation, and competitiveness, with a target of 90% of new jobs created (Bhorat et al., 2018, p. 3). However, the entry and expansion of these businesses might result in a durable mechanism through which the wages of those at the bottom of the wage distribution can be raised and the level of inequality can be decreased (Bhorat et al., 2018, p. 4).

Understanding the Implications of Fringe Benefits on SMEs

Fringe Benefits

Fringe benefits are rewards given to workers to increase productivity and efficiency; they are non-wage forms of compensation provided in addition to regular salaries or bonuses as part of corporate membership to employees or a group (Mugaa et al., 2018, p. 15).

Fringe Benefits Discussion

Fringe benefits are other types of remuneration besides salary which form an important part of an employee's remuneration package (Mabaso, 2017, p. 32). Fringe benefits complement other forms of cash payments, such as wages and salaries, and are intended to improve the quality of an employee's work life and increase collaboration and productivity (Mabaso, 2017, p. 33).

Reasons Why Fringe Benefits Should Be Offered

Sharma and Jaiswal (2018, p. 176) assert that people are driven by more than just money and very few people claim that money has no motivational power at all.

Below are the six main justifications for structuring compensation packages rather than eliminating fringe benefits:

It is the law: Legislation requires fringe benefits such as social protection, medicare, and family and medical leave, and, in the USA, these benefits are federally mandated (Sharma & Jaiswal, 2018, p. 177).

Duty to bargain with unions: Almost all employee benefits are suitable for compulsory U.S. negotiations because, during collective bargaining, businesses are unable to disregard union demands and refuse benefits separately (Sharma & Jaiswal, 2018, p. 177).

Competition: Most small businesses now give their employees some incentive programmes, if only paid time-off and employees' pay-off coverage (Sharma & Jaiswal, 2018, p. 179).

Benefits are tax advantageous: Unlike federal and state taxable compensation, most benefits are either tax-free or non-taxable, allowing employers to deduct expenses for the year without actually increasing the employee's taxable income (Sharma & Jaiswal, 2018, p. 176).

Employees want benefits: Employees know that it is more favourable for their employers to receive benefits due to tax incentives and economies of scale and agree to receive benefits as part of their total compensation (Sharma & Jaiswal, 2018, p. 176).

Benefits support employer strategies: Employers find that certain benefits are even more competitive than compensation in helping to achieve employee recruiting, retention, productivity goals, cost management, and social responsibility (Sharma & Jaiswal, 2018, p. 178).

Exploring the Types of Fringe Benefits Offered by SMEs in the Cape Metropole

According to Oguejiofor and Umeano (2018, p. 3), Fringe benefits are crucial for organisational success, as they fulfil employees' needs and improving performance, however, leadership should prioritise creating a long-term success environment by offering benefits beyond employment contracts. Providing fringe benefits can lead to enhanced individual and organisational outcomes (Oguejiofor & Umeano, 2018, p. 3).

Types of Fringe Benefits

Health Protection Benefits

This is a form of benefits earned by workers for accidents and injuries associated with employment (Oguejiofor & Umeano, 2018, p. 7). In addition, Sharma and Jaiswal (2018, p. 176) assert that sickness benefits are approximately 50% of the average monthly salary and are payable for two consecutive insurance periods of 91 days. As a result, maternity benefits are payable to and cover women subject to contributory conditions like incarceration, miscarriage, surgical termination of pregnancy, or any pregnancy-related disease.

Old Age and Retirement

Benefits under old age and retirement include pension, gratuity, provident fund, therapy for old age, old age support, retired employees' medical benefits, retired employees' travel concessions, work for the deceased employee's sons/daughters and the like (Poonam, 2016, p. 20).

Employee Security

Employees should also be provided with physical and occupational protection to ensure the employee and his family members are covered. A minimum and constant wage or salary gives employees a sense of protection (Sharma & Jaiswal, 2018,

p. 178). In SA, employers are required under the Occupational Health and Safety Act 85 of 1993 to establish a safe workplace free from materials that pose a risk of harm and microbes that might infect people (South Africa, Department of Health, 2006, p. 18).

Educational and Housing Allowance

Educational and tuition assistance incentives are widely sought-after by staff. These systems were found to help the retention of employees and hiring. The service covers any or all expenditures, including formal education courses and degree programmes (Oguejiofor & Umeano, 2018, p. 6). In SA, a permanent, fixed-term, or full-time employee that fulfils the criteria for a housing allowance may be eligible to receive one (South African Heritage Resources Agency [SAHRA], 2006, p. 3).

Payment for Time Not Worked

According to Sharma and Jaiswal (2018, p. 180), the Factory Act, Act No. 63 of 1948, prohibits adult employees from working more than 48 h a week in factories. Certain organisations may have legal criteria for working hours; however, adult workers must have a weekly paid holiday, usually Sunday, in compliance with the Act (Sharma & Jaiswal, 2018, p. 180). In South Africa, Department of Labour (2002, p. 8) reveals that employers are required to provide a minimum of one continuous hour of lunch breaks to workers who put in more than 5 h of labour every day. However, only tasks that cannot be left unattended or completed by another employee may be expected of the employee during a lunch break (South Africa, Department of Labour, 2002, p. 8).

The Importance of Offering Fringe Benefits

According to Nguyen (2017, p. 15), staff who are highly motivated perform better and are more productive and effective. Motivation is central to success because motivated people put in more effort to accomplish a task than the expected good result. As a result, employee satisfaction and joy create a positive attitude in the workplace and goals are achieved (Nguyen, 2017, p. 15). Kose et al. (2015, p. 29) add that satisfaction contributes to inspiring employees, growing their performance and commitment, thereby helping them balance work and life, as well as decreasing labour turnover. Consequently, some of the fringe benefits are deemed to be part of the taxable income (Zirra et al., 2019, p. 14). According to Poonam (2016, p. 23), to minimise employee turnover rates, organisations should offer fringe benefits that encourage employees to stay, invest in a strong team of professionals, and focus on improving employee morale. Therefore, understanding and catering to employee needs can boost morale, job dedication, and productivity, leading to increased profitability and overall success (Poonam, 2016, p. 23). However, highly motivated employees are less likely to leave, improving organisation performance by reducing turnover and increasing profitability (Wiklund & Jansson, 2019, p. 33). As a result, by offering these kinds of benefits it indicates that you believe in your organisation enough to invest in your workers (Poonam, 2016, p. 24).

Determining the Impact of Gender on the Provision of Fringe Benefits

The Provision of Gender in the Workplace

Paying men and women disproportionate salaries for equal labour is against the law but the law against sex discrimination in the form of uneven employee fringe benefits is less clear (William & Mary Law Review, 1976, p. 5). Discriminatory fringe benefit distribution has lately been raised by Congress, the courts, and a variety of administrative bodies; hence, fringe benefits have grown significantly in recent years, averaging 25% of total payroll expenditures for businesses (William & Mary Law Review, 1976, p. 5). In terms of pay and benefits, SA has a history of discriminating against employees based on their gender, colour, and other characteristics (CCMA, 2018, p. 117). As a result, by guaranteeing that any variation in terms and circumstances of employment between employees performing similar or nearly identical job is deemed unfair discrimination, the Employment Equity Act (EEA) and Employment Equity Regulations seek to safeguard workers (CCMA, 2018, p. 116).

Equal Pay for Equal Work

In the areas of compensation, employment benefits, working conditions, and job classification and grading, unfair discrimination is prohibited. It is on this premise that litigants who have complained about unequal pay practices have sought redress in the Labour Court (Laubscher, 2016, p. 815). Hlongwane (2004, p. 14) reports that to promote workplace equity, the government of SA has passed the Labour Relations Act (LRA) and the EEA, meaning that benefits such as maternity benefits that workers receive as part of their package should be subject to substantive equality.

Labour Relations Act (LRA)

An unfair labour practice is defined under the LRA, Act 28 of 1956 as any act or omission that has or may have adversely harmed any employee or class of employees (Maharaj, 2019, p. 15).

Employment Equity Act (EEA)

The Employment Equity Act, No. 55 of 1998, was adopted by the South African parliament on October 12, 1998, with its main goal to "promote workplace equality through fostering equal opportunity and fair treatment in the workplace by eliminating unjust discrimination", thereby giving effect to the Constitution's Section 9 provisions (Mabathoana, 2019, p. 22).

Employment Equity Amendment Act (EEAA)

According to Cliffe Dekker Hofmeyr (2015, p. 10), on August 1, 2014, the Employment Equity Amendment Act, No. 47 of 2013 (EEAA) and new regulations published by Government Gazette Notice 37873, came into force. To better achieve the EEA's goal of establishing workplace equity through the pursuit of equal opportunity and fair treatment, the EEA was modified by the EEAA regulations (Cliffe Dekker Hofmeyr, 2015, p. 17).

Assessing the Impact of COVID-19 on SME Fringe Benefits

COVID-19 Pandemic

COVID-19 is a global emergency with death, and economic and business destruction, affecting the health system, environment, business, social movements, workers, and job opportunities. Governments globally have put restrictions in place to stop the spread of COVID-19 (Warsame, 2020, p. 22).

Effect of the COVID-19 on SMEs

According to Zeidy (2020, p. 10), SMEs are crucial in the growth of the economy of African countries. They are a vital driver of the African economy, creating jobs and enhancing growth, especially among young people. They supply vital goods and services to companies and households, but the growth of SMEs in Africa is limited by poor support, lack of financial support, corruption, lack of training and experience, inadequate income and poor infrastructure and as a result, they are very vulnerable to the harmful effects of COVID-19 (Zeidy, 2020, p. 10).

Establishing the Relationship Between Fringe Benefits and SME Performance

Principal Measure of Fiscal, Business, and Company Performance

According to Mijić et al. (2018, p. 100), profitability is the principal measure of fiscal, business, and company performance, and is a key performance metric as a measure of a business's ability to make a profit in relation to investments.

Profitability for SMEs

A small business's success or failure depends on its financial stability (Nketsiah, 2018). However, one of the most common issues that these firms face is their inability to maintain sufficient cash flow and working capital to be successful. The more effectively a business manages its finances the more it can improve its profitability (Nketsiah, 2018, p. 9). Popa and Ciobanu (2014, p. 17) argue that it is well established that there are increasingly more funding constraints facing small- and medium-sized companies, which impacts their profitability and thus presents a major challenge for SMEs to attract investments and or access loans that slows growth. In additional to the above, Prijadi and Desiana (2017, p. 37) affirm that optimal working capital boosts profitability and profits for SMEs in foreign trade, while loans to banks boost sales but can impede growth due to collateral.

Profitability Indicator for SMEs

Performance indicators may include standard indices of accounting like market share, profitability, and revenue growth (Nketsiah, 2018, p. 10). Additionally, non-financial goals and owners overall satisfaction are very important too, especially when evaluating SME performance (Nketsiah, 2018, p. 11). Consequently, organisational performance can be analysed using both financial and non-financial metrics (Nketsiah, 2018, p. 12). However, sales volumes are examined as one of the elements used to evaluate a company's performance, as SMEs often do not maintain records of their assets and liabilities to employ other success measures, including ROA and/or Return on Equity (ROE) (Nketsiah, 2018, p. 14). Toma (2013, p. 5) argues that measuring a business' profits in terms of bank balances does not say much about profitability. Profitability indicators like break-even analysis and margin are used to measure business profitability and return on investment (ROI).

Research Methodology

Methodology is the "strategy, plan of action, process, or design" that guides one's selection of research methods, as it helps the researcher decide which types of data are needed for a study and which data collection methods are best suited for the study's objectives (Rehman & Alharthi, 2016, p. 51). An in-depth closed-ended questionnaire was used to collect data from SME employees. This research falls within the positivistic research paradigm as it is typical quantitative and uses a description survey design. However, positivism is treated as a combination of substantive concepts, variables, and problems related to appropriate methodological approaches and tools (Kivunja & Kuyini, 2017, p. 26). As a result, descriptive research seeks to quantify the frequency with which a relationship between variables manifests (Kamau, 2013, p. 35). Moreover, this study used a purposive and snowballing sampling technique as this research focuses on small samples. However, the purposive sampling method is a type of non-probability sampling that works best when conducted with knowledgeable experts in a particular cultural field (Tongco, 2007, p. 149). Hence, data from a sample of 100 participants, including 10 SMEs operating in the Cape Metropole, was purposively collected. This equates to 10 participants for each chosen SME entity.

In this study, a structured questionnaire is employed as a research tool. This survey tool is appropriate for this study because it is less expensive, more convenient for respondents and researchers, and is simpler when collecting data from a large number of participants (Kibangou, 2019, p. 10). Structured surveys have prepopulated responses, requiring respondents to select the one that best suits their situation. Most questionnaires have an "any other response, specify" section but there is limited room for additions except in extremely unusual circumstances as answers are predetermined (McGrath, 2022, p. 21). The survey is organised and planned using five distinct objectives, five sub-questions, and one main survey question. The closed-ended questionnaire format was chosen for its rapid completion.

A self-administered survey and information gathered from primary sources was used to support this study. However, door-to-door surveys were conducted in SMEs in the Cape Metropole to gather information from managers and lower-level employees. Within 14 days, participants who were reachable and eager to respond had their questionnaires completed and collected. In this study, primary data was collected quantitatively and analysed with descriptive statistics using the Statistical Package for Social Science Statistics (SPSS) software. In this study, charts and percentages were utilised to rank the answers to the 5-point Likert scale questions as well as to summarise and characterise the data responses. Reliability and validity were examined in this study to make sure that identical results would be obtained even if the questionnaire was sent to a different population at a different time and with a similar technique.

Table 1 Descriptive statistics of questions 4.1.1 to 4.1.6

Statement	N Valid	Missing	Mean	Std. Dev	Sum
4.1.1 We offer/receive either of the following: (medical benefits; leave; retirement benefits; housing allowance; educational funding).	46	0	3.80	1.310	175
4.1.2 Organisations find it difficult to offer benefits due to COVID-19 pandemic.	46	0	3.35	1.418	154
4.1.3 Productivity increases when there are rewards or cost offered.	46	0	3.70	1.314	170
4.1.4 Health protection benefits are more imperative than any other benefits.	46	0	3.83	1.081	176
4.1.5 Organisations can witness a positive impact on employee job satisfaction when employees work adaptable hours.	46	0	3.89	1059	179
4.1.6 The lack of fringe benefits affects organisation's performance.	46	0	3.72	1.344	171

Findings

The study results from the questionnaire given to the respondents were examined in this chapter.

In Section A of the questionnaire, respondents were requested to provide information on their personal profiles as well as the profiles of their respective enterprises. Their age, gender, position in the company, occupation in the current position, and highest level of education were among the personal profile details sought. The length of time of the company's existence, the number of employees, and the size of the organisation were all asked as part of the business profile information.

Section B of Questionnaire: General Factors of Fringe Benefits to Employees and the Organisation

Table 1 contains the descriptive statistics relevant to questions 4.1.1 to 4.1.6 in Section B of the questionnaire.

Summary Statistics

- **N Valid**: Number of valid responses
- **Missing**: Number of missing responses
- **Mean**: Average rating
- **Std. Dev**: Standard deviation
- **Sum**: Total of ratings

Table 2 Frequency distribution of responses on benefits offered: medical benefits; leave; retirement benefits; housing allowance; and educational funding

Response	Frequency	%	Valid %	Cumulative %
Strongly disagree	5	10.9	10.9	10.9
Disagree	4	8.7	8.7	19.6
Unknown	2	4.3	4.3	23.9
Agree	19	41.3	41.3	65.2
Strongly agree	16	34.8	34.8	100.0
Total	46	100.0	100.0	

Table 3 Challenges in offering benefits due to COVID-19 pandemic

Response	Frequency	%	Valid %	Cumulative %
Strongly disagree	7	15.2	15.2	15.2
Disagree	6	13.0	13.0	28.3
Unknown	10	21.7	21.7	50.0
Agree	10	21.7	21.7	71.7
Strongly agree	13	28.3	28.3	100.0
Total	46	100.0	100.0	

Table 2 presents the findings on employee benefits and their impacts on organisations, reflecting the means, standard deviations, and sums of responses for each statement.

The majority of employees totalling to 76.1% (34.8 + 41.3) strongly agree and agree that they receive these benefits, with 19.6% not agreeing and 4.4% unknown. However, employee benefits are crucial for attracting and retaining skilled, driven, and productive employees, therefore, they are part of the employees' compensation package that is supplied by the employer, providing security and time spent money (Ahmad et al., 2013, p. 3). As a result, in Table 1, the mean value of 3.80 with a Std Dev of 1.310 confirms these results.

Table 3 demonstrates that 28.3% of respondents strongly agreed and 21.7% agreed. Unknown is 21.7%, 15.2% strongly disagreed, and 13% disagreed. The majority of respondents strongly agreed that the COVID-19 pandemic made it difficult for businesses to provide benefits. These results confirm the proposition that the COVID-19 pandemic has had a significant impact on the survival of SMEs. The mean value of 3.35 with a Std Dev of 1.418, as seen in Table 1, confirms these results. According to Islam et al. (2020, p. 592), the global business community has been rocked by the COVID-19 outbreak. However, small- and medium-sized businesses in particular had many difficulties managing their operations, earnings, and budgets.

As shown in Table 4, 58.7% (39.1 + 19.6) of respondents fully agreed that productivity increases when there are rewards or costs offered, 21.7% disagree, while 19.6% are unknown. The mean value as illustrated in Table 1 is 3.70 with a Std Dev of 1.314. Gbande (2016, p. 207) supports the above results by stating that for any

Table 4 Impact of rewards on productivity

Response	Frequency	%	Valid %	Cumulative %
Strongly disagree	3	6.5	6.5	6.5
Disagree	7	15.2	15.2	21.7
Unknown	9	19.6	19.6	41.3
Agree	9	19.6	19.6	60.9
Strongly agree	18	39.1	39.1	100.0
Total	46	100.0	100.0	

Table 5 Importance of health protection benefits

Response	Frequency	%	Valid %	Cumulative %
Disagree	7	15.2	15.2	15.2
Unknown	10	21.7	21.7	37.0
Agree	13	28.3	28.3	65.2
Strongly agree	16	34.8	34.8	100.0
Total	46	100.0	100.0	

public or private organisation, employees want to feel valued and appreciated to work more productively. However, reward systems are initiatives put in place by an organisation to recognise employees' achievements and spur them on to greater productivity.

As shown in Table 5, 63.1% (34.8 + 28.3) agree that health benefits are more important than any other benefits, while 21.7% are unknown, meaning that they were not sure if health care protection benefits are more important to them, while 15.2% disagree with the statement. There is clear evidence that workforce health is closely linked to workforce productivity and national economic health, however, it also indicates that employers are increasingly aware of this relevance and are interested in improving worker health by expanding worker health protection and wellness programmes (Kamau, 2013, p. 35).

According to Table 1, the mean value is 3.89 with a Std Dev of 1.059. As reflected in Table 6, 76.1% (28.3 + 47.8) of respondents stated that an organisation can witness a positive impact on employee job satisfaction when employees work adaptive hours, while 15.2% of respondents were unsure about the statement, and a further 8.7% do not agree. However, productivity is significantly impacted by absenteeism and ineffective time management. Maintaining a healthy balance between work and personal duties increases workplace productivity and efficiency. Because of this, workers and employers from many organisations have realised the necessity of workplace flexibility (Govender, 2018, p. 270).

Table 7 and Fig. 1, shows that 69.6% (34.8 + 34.8) of respondents believe that a lack of fringe benefits can significantly impact an organisation's performance. This is supported by the mean value of 3.72 and a Std Dev of 1.344 in Table 1. Mismanaged reward systems can lead to ineffective performance, high turnover rates, and low moral (Mugaa et al., 2018, p. 11).

Table 6 Impact of adaptable working hours on employee job satisfaction

Response	Frequency	%	Valid %	Cumulative %
Strongly disagree	3	6.5	6.5	6.5
Disagree	1	2.2	2.2	8.7
Unknown	7	15.2	15.2	23.9
Agree	22	47.8	47.8	71.7
Strongly agree	13	28.3	28.3	100.0
Total	46	100.0	100.0	

Table 7 Impact of lack of fringe benefits on organisational performance

Response	Frequency	%	Valid %	Cumulative %
Strongly disagree	5	10.9	10.9	10.9
Disagree	5	10.9	10.9	21.7
Unknown	4	8.7	8.7	30.4
Agree	16	34.8	34.8	65.2
Strongly agree	16	34.8	34.8	100.0
Total	46	100.0	100.0	

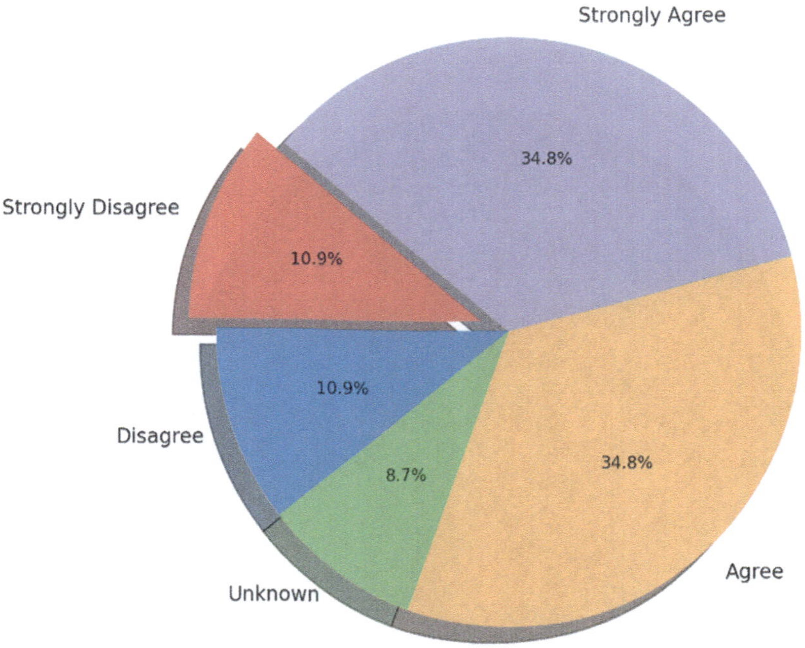

Fig. 1 A lack of fringe benefits affects an organisation's performance

Section C of Questionnaire

Implications of Fringe Benefits on the Organisation

As seen in Table 8 and Fig. 2, 52.2% of the respondents agree that fringe benefits do affect the profits of the business because they believe that perks reduce company profits due to higher incentives and remuneration. A further 37% of respondents disagree that benefits affect profitability. Tan et al. (2016, p. 4) point out that the issue of increasing costs is the first difficulty in offering employee perks.

Throughout many enterprises, both the employer and the employee bear the risk of paying the fringe benefits tax within the organisation. As seen in Table 9 and Fig. 3, 58.7% of participants believe that both employees and employers bear the risk, whereas 26.1% opine only the employer and 15.2% believe only the employee bears the risk. According to SARS (2021), any benefit given to an employee by an

Table 8 Impact of fringe benefits on business profits

Response	Frequency	%	Valid %	Cumulative %
True	24	52.2	52.2	52.2
False	17	37.0	37.0	89.1
3	5	10.9	10.9	100.0
Total	46	100.0	100.0	

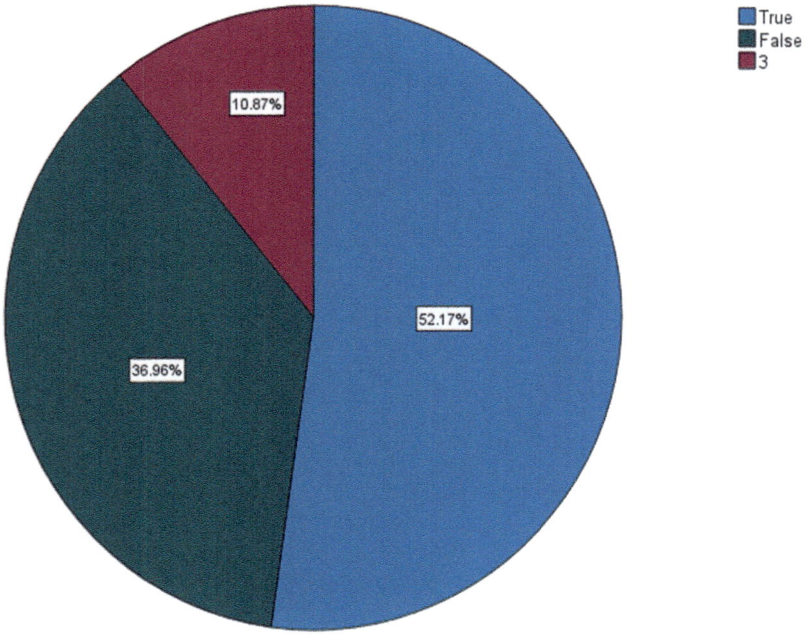

Fig. 2 Do fringe benefits affect the profits of the business

Table 9 Responsibility for paying fringe benefits tax within the organisation

Response	Frequency	%	Valid %	Cumulative %
The employer	12	26.1	26.1	26.1
The employee	7	15.2	15.2	41.3
Both employee and employer	27	58.7	58.7	100.0
Total	46	100.0	100.0	

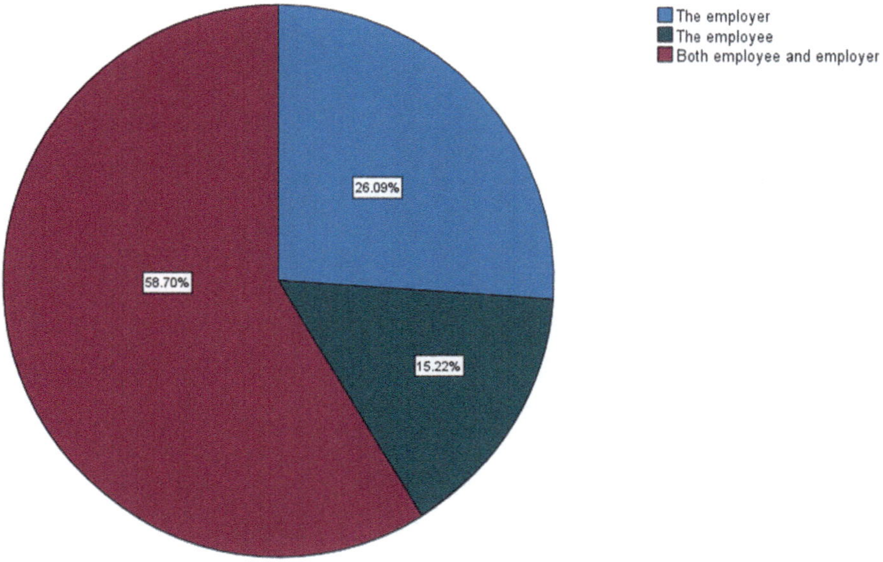

Fig. 3 Who bears the risk of paying fringe benefits tax in the organisation

institution connected to an employer in exchange for services is considered to be a taxable benefit given by the employer to the employee.

Table 10 and Figure 4 show that up to 26.1% of respondents receive less than R5000 and between R20,001 and R25,000 in fringe benefits per year, while 23.9% receive between R5000 and R10,000 per year, and 13% receive between R10,001 and R15,000 per year, with those in the R15,001–R20,000 bracket accounting for 10.9% of annual fringe benefits. Modisane (2019, p. 57) buttresses that fringe benefits rates depend on how much a company pays the employee and how much an employee receives in benefits. However, according to the South African Income Tax Act (1962, p. 10), fringe benefits are considered a part of gross income but some of them also have allowable deductions that could lower the amount of tax that employees owe.

Table 10 Distribution of total annual fringe benefits and expenditure rated on a 5-point Likert scale

Response	Frequency	%	Valid %	Cumulative %
1 > R5000	12	26.1	26.1	26.1
2 is between R5001 and R10,000	11	23.9	23.9	50.0
3 is between R10,001 and R15,000	6	13.0	13.0	63.0
4 is between R15,001 and R20,000	5	10.9	10.9	73.9
5 is between R20,001 and R25,000	12	26.1	26.1	100.0
Total	46	100.0	100.0	

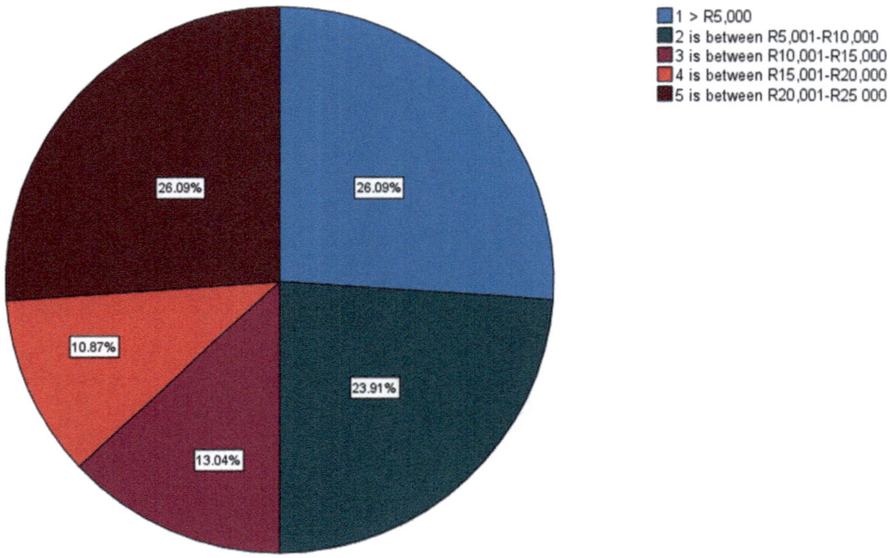

Fig. 4 Total annual fringe benefits and expenditure when rated using a 5-point Likert scale

Conclusion

The primary objective of the study was to ascertain the impact of fringe benefits on SMEs in the Cape Metropole.

The introduction of the study, background, problem statement, aim, objectives, and research questions were addressed in this chapter. An overview of the research approach and study design was stated, as well as the formulation of the study's theoretical and empirical objectives. The study also outlined the structure of the study.

The study reviewed existing literature on various types of fringe benefits common in small businesses, and the profitability of SMEs in the Cape Metropole. In addition, literature on gender in the workplace and the challenges experienced by SMEs in the wake of the COVID-19 pandemic were reviewed.

The methodology applied in this study, including the research design and data collection instrument was discussed. The statistical procedures and data analysis methodology were also described.

The results obtained from the data collected were presented and discussed. The analysis of descriptive statistics in SPSS and variables under consideration is provided in tables and pie charts, along with inferential analysis.

Recommendations

The research recommends that SMEs should continue to provide healthcare benefits to their employees since it would help them develop a feeling of loyalty and increase their productivity. Moreover, SMEs to improve employee recognition systems for good work, since this will encourage them and increase their productivity. In conclusion, the study suggests that SMEs should continue to provide security benefits to their employees, as this will boost staff productivity and overall organisational performance.

Management should examine their fringe benefit packages regularly to inspire people to be more devoted to their jobs. In addition, management should make sure that employee benefits are tailored to their requirements, and that incentive programmes are clearly and transparently connected to performance.

Limitations of the Study

The scope of this study was to analyse how the costs of fringe benefits affected the total profitability of SMEs operating in the Cape Metropole. According to Chakabva (2015, p. 44) and Eltahir (2018, p. 22), frequent limitation is slanted to the possible issue. As a result, the value of benefits to other employees may be diminished by actual variations in benefit schemes; however, common limitation is biased to the potential issue. A sample of 100 participants from 10 SMEs that operate in the Cape Metropole was included in the study. This equates to 10 participants for each chosen SME entity. However, due to the COVID-19 pandemic, companies were closed, and people were working from home. Only a few SMEs were open and those who were open were operating on a staff rotating schedule. Consequently, the questionnaires were delivered by hand and companies asked the researcher to leave the questionnaires and collect them once they were completed. As a result, only 46 questionnaires were returned, 20 were not returned because some companies were closed when the researcher went to collect them, and 21 were misplaced due to the staff rotating schedule. A further 13 questionnaires were declined by the respondents even though they agreed to participate initially.

Suggestions for Future Research

Further research on fringe benefits might be undertaken in the Western Cape as a whole, given that this study was limited to SMEs operating only in the Cape Metropole. The results of this study were based on a sample of 100 respondents, and future research may employ a bigger sample size. This study was quantitative but qualitative research may be performed through interviews to gain a better knowledge of how fringe benefits impact a company's profitability.

References

Ahmad, R., Yei, E. T. P., & Bujan, S. (2013). Relationship between types of benefit (leave, loan and retirement plan) and employees' retention. *International Journal of Education Research, 1*(8), 1–13.

Anele, C., Jasmine, T.-A., & Amakiri, D.-S. (2017). Reward system and employee work attitude among small and medium scale enterprises in Port-Harcourt, Rivers State, Nigeria. *European Journal of Business Management, 9*(36), 94–102.

Australian Human Rights Commission. (1984). *Sex Discrimination Act 1984. Sex discrimination and sexual harassment.*

Bhorat, H., Asmal, Z., Lilenstein, K. & van der Zee, K. (2018). *SMMEs in South Africa: Understanding the constraints on growth and performance.* Development Policy Research Unit, working paper 201802.

Bosch, A., & Barit, S. (2020). Gender pay transparency mechanisms: Future directions for South Africa. *South African Journal of Science, 116*(4–4), 1–6.

Bouazza, A. B., Ardjouman, D., & Abada, O. (2015). Establishing the factors affecting the growth of small and medium-sized enterprises in Algeria. *American International Journal of Social Science, 4*(2), 101–115.

Chakabva, O. (2015). *The effectiveness of risk management practices of small, medium and micro enterprises (SMMEs) which provide microfinance in the Cape Metropole, South Africa.* Masters thesis. Cape Peninsula University of Technology.

Cliffe Dekker Hofmeyr (CDH). (2015). *Equal pay.*

Commission for Conciliation, Mediation and Arbitration (CCMA). (2018). *Equal pay for work of equal value.*

Dhanah, D. (2016). *Small businesses and job creation in South Africa* [Unpublished Master's thesis, University of Cape Town].

Eltahir, O. A. B. (2018). Factors affecting the performance & business success of small & medium enterprises in Sudan (Case study: Omdurman). *International Journal of Small Business and Entrepreneurship Research, 6*(6), 14–22.

Gbande, R. (2016). Effects of reward system on productivity in the local government system in Benue State. *Journal of Economics and Sustainable Development, 7*(22), 202–210.

Govender, L. (2018). Flexible work arrangements, job satisfaction and performance. *Journal of Economics and Behavioral Studies, 10*(3), 268–277.

Hlongwane, N. (2004). *Commentary on South Africa's position regarding equal pay for work of equal value: A comparative perspective.* [Unpublished Master's thesis, University of the Western Cape].

Islam, D. M. Z., Khalid, N., Rayeva, E., & Ahmed, U. (2020). COVID-19 and financial performance of SMEs: Examining the nexus of entrepreneurial self-efficacy, entrepreneurial resilience and innovative work behavior. *Revista Argentina de Clínica Psicológica, 29*(3), 587–593.

Kamau, H. (2013). *Fringe benefits effects on employee productivity in the public sector (a case of State Department of Water, Nairobi County, Kenya).* [Masters thesis, Kenyatta University].

Kibangou, S. R. (2019). *The use of management accounting tools to improve the business performance of small and medium manufacturing enterprises in Cape Town.* [Unpublished Masters thesis, Cape Peninsula University of Technology].

Kivunja, C., & Kuyini, A. B. (2017). Understanding and applying research paradigms in educational contexts. *International Journal of Higher Education, 6*(5), 26.

Kose, S., Tetik, H. T., & Atac, L. O. (2015). A general evaluation of fringe benefits provided in Turkey: The case of IC 100. *Business Economics, 4*(9), 26–33.

Laubscher, T. (2016). Equal pay for work of equal value—A South African perspective. *Industrial Law Journal, 37*(2), 804–830.

Mabaso, M. C. (2017). *The influence of rewards on job satisfaction and organisational commitment among academic staff at selected universities of technology in South Africa.* [PhD thesis, Durban University of Technology].

Mabathoana, M. (2019). *A comparative study on the principles of equal pay for equal work in South Africa in the context of gender discrimination.* [Unpublished Masters' thesis, University of the North-West].

Maduekwe, C. C., & Kamala, P. (2016). Performance measurement by small and medium enterprises in Cape Metropolis, South Africa. *Problems and Perspectives in Management, 14*(2), 65–55.

Maharaj, P. (2019). A critical analysis of section 6(4) of the Employment Equity Act: Is it likely to achieve its stated objectives? Masters thesis, University of Cape Town. http://hdl.handle.net/11427/30794

McGrath, M. J. (2022). *A primer of pastoral Spanish.* Catholic University of America Press.

Mijić, K., Nuševa, D., & Jakšić, D. (2018). The determinants of SMEs' profitability in the wholesale and retail sector in Serbia. *Faculty of Economics Subotica, 1*, 97–112.

Modisane, Y. M. (2019). *The role of fringe benefits on the tax planning of employees in Rustenburg's metropolitan area.* [Unpublished Masters' thesis, North-West University].

Mugaa, L. G., Guyo, D. W., & Odhiambo, P. R. (2018). Influence of career progression on employee performance in large commercial banks in Nairobi City County in Kenya. *Journal of Entrepreneurship and Project Management, 2*(2), 1–19.

Ndichu, J. N. (2017). *Effects of incentives and rewards on employee productivity in small banks in Kenya: A case study of First Community Bank.* Master's thesis, United States International University Africa.

Nguyen, L. (2017). *The impact of employee motivation on organizational effectiveness.* Thesis. Vaasan Ammattikorkeakoulu University of Applied Sciences.

Nketsiah, I. (2018). Financial management practices and performance of SMEs in Ghana: The moderating role of firm age. *Open Journal of Economics and Commerce, 1*(4), 8–18.

Obokoh, L., & Goldman, G. (2016). Infrastructure deficiency and the performance of small- and medium-sized enterprises in Nigeria's liberalised economy. *Acta Commercii, 16*(1), a339.

Oguejiofor, C. J., & Umeano, N. E. (2018). Fringe benefits and employees' performance in selected brewery firms in Anambra State. *Journal of Sciences and Multidisciplinary Research, 10*(1), 1–14.

Olatunji, K. A., Olufemi, L. M., & Omotayo, R. S. (2021). Effects of fringe benefits on employee's productivity in selected food and beverages production companies in Ogun State, Nigeria. *Annals of Spiru Haret University. Economic Series, 21*(2), 55–72.

Painter, M., & Dobie, K. (2014). Ethics and sustainability within SMEs in sub-Saharan Africa: Enabling, constraining and contaminating relationships. *African Journal of Business Ethics, 4*(4), 7–19.

Poonam. (2016). Impact of fringe benefits in current competitive scenario. *International Research Journal of Commerce Arts and Science, 7*(6), 19–27.

Popa, A.-E., & Ciobanu, R. (2014). The financial factors that influence the profitability of SMEs. *International Journal of Academic Research in Economics and Management Sciences, 3*(4).

Prijadi, R., & Desiana, P. M. (2017). Factors affecting the profitability and growth of Small & Medium Enterprises (SMEs) in Indonesia. *International Journal of Economics and Management, 11*(Special Issue 1), 35–44.

Rehman, A. A., & Alharthi, K. (2016). An introduction to research paradigms in distance education. *International Journal of Educational Investigations, 3*(8), 51–59.

Rungani, E. C., & Potgieter, M. (2018). The impact of financial support on the success of small, medium and micro enterprises in the Eastern Cape province. *Acta Commercii, 18*(1), 1–12.

Sharma, K., & Jaiswal, N. (2018). A study on employees' attitude towards fringe benefits. *International Journal of Engineering and Management Research, 8*(02), 176–180.

Small Business Development. (2021). *The impact of COVID 19 on micro and informal businesses in South Africa.*

South Africa, Department of Health. (2006). *Occupational Health and Safety Policy for the National Department of Health.*

South Africa, Department of Labour. (2002). *Basic Conditions of Employment Amendment, Act No. 11 of 2002.*

South African Heritage Resources Agency (SAHRA). (2006). *Amended Housing Allowance Policy and Guarantee Scheme*, 1–7.

South African Income Tax Act. (1962). *Income Tax Act, no. 58 of 1962.*

South African Revenue Service (SARS). (2021). *External guide for employers in respect of employment tax incentive.*

Tan, S. C., Tolos, H., & Manab, N. (2016). Employee benefits in small medium enterprises (SMEs): Practice and challenges. *SSRN Electronic Journal.*

Toma, C. (2013). *How to analyze profitability* (pp. 1–16). Zions Business Resource Center, Business Builder.

Tongco, M. D. C. (2007). Purposive sampling as a tool for informant selection. *Ethnobotany Research and Applications, 5*, 147–158.

Vashistha, N., & Khan, A. (2020). A study on the effects of fringe benefits on job satisfaction. *International Journal of Research and Analytical Reviews, 7*, 6–1.

Vuba, S. (2019). *The missed opportunity: SMMEs in the South African economy.* Sponsored supplement to the Mail & Guardian.

Warsame, A. A. (2020). The impacts of COVID-19 on small and medium enterprises. *European Journal of Business and Management, 12*(25).

Werner, S., & Balkin, D. B. (2021). Strategic benefits: How employee benefits can create a sustainable competitive edge. *The Journal of Total Rewards, 30*(1), 8–22.

Wiklund, F., & Jansson, S. (2019). *Employee loyalty and the factors affecting it a qualitative study comparing people with different working experiences on their view of employee loyalty* [Masters' thesis, Umeå University], Sweden. Zone Publications.

William & Mary Law Review. (1976). 17(1). Sex discrimination in employee fringe benefits. https://scholarship.law.wm.edu/wmlr/vol17/

Zeidy, I. A. (2020). *Economic impact of Covid-19 on micro, small and medium enterprises (MSMEs) in Africa and policy options for mitigation.* Common Market for Eastern and Southern Africa.

Zirra, C. T. O., Mambula, C. J., & Anyatonwu, P. (2019). *Impact of fringe benefits on employee performance: A study of Nasco Group.* Jos Plateau State, Bukidnon State University.

Semi-Skilled and Skilled Employment Tax Incentives: A Comparative Analysis of South Africa, Australia, and Canada

Ivan Beumer and Herman Albertus Viviers

Abstract One of the primary reasons contributing to the high unemployment rate in South Africa is the substantial portion of the South African population lacking sufficient education and training. Employers' endeavour to generate new employment opportunities during challenging economic times is compounded by the urgent demand for a skilled South African workforce equipped with the specific skills desired by employers. These adverse conditions elucidate the pivotal importance of mechanisms, such as tax incentives, in encouraging employers to create new employment opportunities and to upskill employees through on-the-job training. The purpose of this chapter is to evaluate the design variables of prevailing South African employment tax incentives in terms of their support and encouragement for employers to create semi-skilled and skilled employment opportunities through on-the-job training in South Africa. To achieve this, an inductive research approach is employed, utilising both a literature review and comparative analyses as research methods to qualitatively analyse various design variables of employment tax incentives in South Africa. Subsequently, these design variables are compared with employment tax incentives of Australia and Canada by examining their tax legislative requirements and practical applications. This chapter contributes by highlighting specific design variables embedded within employment-related tax incentives that may discourage employers from utilising them. Finally, this chapter makes recommendations to inform the South African tax regulator on potential amendments that could enhance the attractiveness of the prevailing South African employment-related tax incentives for creating semi-skilled and skilled employment opportunities through on-the-job training.

Keywords Employer · Employment · On-the-job training · Semi-skilled and skilled employees · South Africa · Tax incentive

I. Beumer · H. A. Viviers (✉)
North-West University, Potchefstroom, South Africa
e-mail: ivan.beumer@pwc.com; herman.viviers@nwu.ac.za

T. Moloi (ed.), *Impacting Society Positively Through Technology in Accounting and Business Processes*, Springer Proceedings in Business and Economics,
https://doi.org/10.1007/978-3-031-84885-8_62

Introduction

During February 2024, it was reported that 32.1 per cent (%) of the South African labour force were unemployed (Stats SA, 2024). This unemployment rate is 27% higher than the world average (The World Bank, 2024). One of the main reasons for the high South African unemployment rate is the significant proportion of South Africans who are not adequately educated and trained (Ranchhod, 2019). Employers, particularly small, medium, and micro-sized enterprises (SMMEs), are cautious about employing individuals due to strict South African labour laws and the high labour cost associated with employment, such as the cost of training employees and annual increases in the minimum wage (Bertrand & Crépon, 2020). Furthermore, employers are reluctant to employ individuals who lack the required skills and work experience, as the need for further training necessitates additional training expenditure (Coad et al., 2014; Elnaga & Imran, 2013).

In South Africa, the employee cohort is generally characterised by low productivity, which results in a "skills gap" between what employers seek and what the labour market can supply (Department of Employment and Labour, 2020). Levesque (2019) describes the "skills gap" as the fundamental mismatch between the skills employers require and the skills that job seekers or employees possess. To combat poverty and stimulate economic growth in South Africa, it is essential to address this skills gap by creating new employment opportunities for semi-skilled and skilled employees.

The Department of Employment and Labour describes various occupational levels in terms of Annexure EEA9 to the *Employment Equity Act* 55 of 1998, whereby an individual could hold a skilled, semi-skilled, or unskilled employment position (Republic of South Africa, 1998). An individual holding a *skilled employment* position possesses the ability to apply a broad range of knowledge with respect to products, techniques, and/or processes. Such an individual can evaluate procedures and effectively apply past experiences to find appropriate solutions for various work-related problems. Skilled employees are expected to determine primarily their own priorities, as the tasks or work assigned to them are not always stipulated. Furthermore, these tasks may require some initiative from the skilled employee in terms of how such tasks need to be performed or conducted (Republic of South Africa, 1998).

In comparison, an individual holding a *semi-skilled employment* position is characterised as being accountable for the direct product, process, service, or quality, and consequently plays an incremental role in the improvement of existing procedures or processes. Semi-skilled employees need to be able to make decisions regarding the appropriate course of action based on pre-set standards, past experiences, and/or training (Republic of South Africa, 1998). The employability needs of South African employers to obtain semi-skilled and skilled employees require individuals capable of practical application and dealing with real-world problems in meaningful ways (Martensen & Grønholdt, 2009).

To address the skills gap, governments utilise mechanisms, such as tax incentives, to encourage employers to educate and train employees in the formal workplace, while simultaneously creating new employment opportunities (Polackova et al., 2004). A tax incentive can be described as a mechanism that results in a reduction in the overall tax liability of a taxpayer and a loss of government revenue due to the reduction of the tax base or specific taxes owed (Bratić, 2006). Therefore, a tax incentive serves to encourage a taxpayer to act in a specific way that supports, assists in achieving, or aligns with specific objectives set by a regulating public authority (Cedefop, 2009).

The existence of tax legislation aimed at incentivising and promoting the creation of semi-skilled and skilled employment opportunities through on-the-job training is futile if its design, in terms of administrative burdens, technical complexities, and ease of application, discourages *bona fide* employers from utilising such incentives (SAICA, 2020). Nevertheless, employers are inclined to employ inexperienced individuals for semi-skilled and skilled employment positions who lack specific skills and/or knowledge or possess only technical knowledge if they can benefit financially from doing so. From a tax perspective, these financial benefits are provided through tax incentives, which may include tax deductions available to employers under the *Income Tax Act* 58 of 1962 (Republic of South Africa, 1962), as well as indirect employment tax incentives provided under the *Employment Tax Incentives Act* 26 of 2013 (ETIA) (Republic of South Africa, 2013).

This highlights the need to evaluate the design variables of the current employment tax incentives in South Africa to determine if their design successfully encourages employers to create semi-skilled and skilled employment opportunities through on-the-job training. The main purpose of this chapter is to evaluate and compare the design variables of the prevailing tax incentives in South Africa, aimed at encouraging employers to create semi-skilled and skilled employment opportunities through on-the-job training, with the design variables of the tax incentives in Australia and Canada.

This chapter aims to contribute by making recommendations, where possible, on how the prevailing South African employment tax incentives could be amended and improved to support the encouragement of employers, from a tax perspective, in creating semi-skilled and skilled employment opportunities in South Africa through on-the-job training.

The remainder of this chapter is structured as follows: Firstly, the research methodology applied within this chapter is outlined and justified. This is followed by a review and conceptualisation of the prevailing tax incentives available to employers in South Africa aimed at encouraging the creation of semi-skilled and skilled employment opportunities. Next, these employment tax incentives are evaluated to identify design variables that might discourage employers from utilising these tax incentives. Finally, the chapter compares these identified design variables of the South African tax incentives with those in Australia and Canada to evaluate how these design variables can be amended by the South African tax regulator to encourage employers to use them and better support the creation of employment opportunities in South Africa by upskilling employees through on-the-job training. The chapter concludes with recommendations and an acknowledgment of the research limitations.

Methodology

The research conducted in this study is positioned within the interpretivist paradigm (Aliyu et al., 2014) to gain better insights into the socially constructed phenomena (Bahari, 2010; Saunders et al., 2007) concerning how employers are encouraged or discouraged by the prevailing South African tax incentives to create semi-skilled and skilled employment opportunities through on-the-job training. An inductive research approach (Rocco et al., 2003) was followed to identify and conceptualise the various design variables of employment tax incentives in South Africa, Australia, and Canada. These design variables were qualitatively evaluated (Creswell, 2003) through a review of the prevailing literature (Fink, 2014) and a comparative analysis (Esser & Vliegenthart, 2016).

A literature review was conducted to conceptualise the tax incentives of each country by unpacking them in terms of their tax legislative requirements and practical application. Reviews in the literature highlighted the various design variables associated with each type of tax incentive that might discourage employers from using the employment tax incentives. These design variables were compared with one another to draw conclusions and make recommendations.

Literature Review: Employment Tax Incentives in South Africa

To encourage the creation of semi-skilled and skilled employment opportunities through on-the-job training in South Africa, the South African government has introduced various incentives for employers from a tax perspective. These include the following:

The Learnership Agreement Allowance

The learnership tax incentive in terms of section 12H of the Act (Republic of South Africa, 1962) was originally introduced in 2002 to incentivise employers to invest in training and to encourage skills development and job creation (National Treasury, 2002). This incentive affords employers a tax deduction in the form of an annual allowance for employing and directly or indirectly educating or training semi-skilled and skilled employees. Additionally, a once-off completion allowance is allowed per employee (learner) if this employee successfully completes the learnership agreement. Table 1 summarises the quantum of the annual and/or completion allowance granted to an employer in terms of section 12H of the Act (Republic of South Africa, 1962) for each full month that it employed an employee in possession of a qualification on a specific National Qualifications Framework (NQF) level (SAQA, 2014) in terms of a learnership agreement registered with the Sector Education and Training Authority (SETA). To encourage employers to employ individuals with a disability, the scope of the provision was broadened (effective from 1 July 2006) to allow an employer who educates and trains individuals with a disability to claim an additional allowance in terms of a registered learnership agreement (National Treasury, 2016). To avoid tax abuse of the learnership allowances, Interpretation Note 20 (Issue 8) (SARS, 2021a) determines that where more than one employer is a party to the registered learnership agreement, only the lead employer (usually the employer responsible for paying the learner's remuneration) will be eligible to deduct section 12H allowances for a specific learner.

However, this incentive had a sunset clause, applying only to registered learnership agreements entered into before 1 April 2024. The reason behind the limited window period was to allow the government the opportunity to reassess the country's employment and skills development situation and to remove the additional allowances granted by the Act, subject to satisfactory employment targets and skills development levels being reached. Nevertheless, according to the 2024 National Budget Speech (National Treasury, 2024), it was indicated that this tax incentive will be extended and will continue to apply to registered learnership agreements

Table 1 Quantifying the current annual and completion allowance under section 12H

Annual allowance (available per year of assessment)		
Current NQF level (before completion)	**Learner without a disability**	**Learner with a disability**
NQF level 1 to 6	R40,000	R60,000
NQF level 7 to 10	R20,000	R40,000
Completion allowance (Learnership agreement <u>shorter</u> than 24 months) only available upon completion		
NQF level when completed	**Learner without a disability**	**Learner with a disability**
NQF level 1 to 6	R40,000	R60,000
NQF level 7 to 10	R20,000	R50,000
Completion allowance (Learnership agreement <u>longer</u> than 24 months) only available upon completion		
NQF level when completed	**Learner without a disability**	**Learner with a disability**
NQF level 1 to 6	R40,000 per year	R60,000 per year
NQF level 7 to 10	R20,000 per year	R40,000 per year

(R = South African Rand (currency))
Source: Authors' compilation deduced from the Republic of South Africa (1962)

entered into between employers and employees on or before 31 March 2027 (Visser, 2024).

Employment Tax Incentive Act (ETIA)

The ETIA (Republic of South Africa, 2013) was introduced in response to the high rate of youth unemployment in South Africa. The South African government legislated this act mainly to encourage employers to hire young and less experienced employees (National Treasury, 2013). The ETIA was enacted in 2013 and is currently set to end effectively on 28 February 2029 (Republic of South Africa, 2016). However, there is little evidence suggesting that the ETIA is indeed effective (Ebrahim et al., 2017). The ETIA has been amended numerous times, including changes to the minimum wage amount, penalties imposed for misplaced employees, the maximum allowed monthly remuneration, and the amount the employer can claim under this act (SARS, 2021b).

The ETIA serves as a tax incentive available to eligible employers in the form of a saving that accrues to the employer based on the quantum of the monthly remuneration of its qualifying employees for the first 36 months of employment. This period aligns with the time employers need to internalise, train, and educate newly appointed individuals through on-the-job training within created semi-skilled and skilled employment positions. In practice, this "saving amount" is not physically received from SARS; rather, it represents the amount of employees' tax in the form of Pay-As-You-Earn (PAYE) withheld by the employer from the salaries of its qualifying employees, which it is not required to be paid to SARS.

Table 2 shows how the employment tax incentive available to employers is quantified by considering the monthly remuneration paid to the qualifying employee, the period for which the qualifying employee is employed, and the amount or percentage that may be claimed.

An "eligible employer" is an employer who is registered for the purposes of withholding employees' tax (PAYE), as required in terms of paragraph 15 of the Fourth Schedule to the Income Tax Act (Republic of South Africa, 1962). "Qualifying employees" are mainly individuals between the ages of 18 and 29 who

Table 2 Quantifying the tax incentive for eligible employers in terms of the ETIA

Monthly remuneration	Employment tax incentive per month of the first 12 months	Employment tax incentive per month of the second and third 12 months
R0–R1999	75% of the monthly remuneration	37.5% of the monthly remuneration
R2000–R4499	R1500 per month	R750 per month
R4500–R6499	R1500 − (75% × (monthly remuneration − R4500))	R750 − (37.5% × (monthly remuneration − R4500))
R6500 or more	None	None

(R = South African Rand (currency))
Source: Republic of South Africa (2013)

are not connected persons, as defined in section 1(1) of the Income Tax Act (Republic of South Africa, 1962), in relation to their employers.

Evaluation of the Design Variables of the South African Tax Incentives

Based on the findings deduced from the review and conceptualisation of the South African employment tax incentives introduced to encourage and promote the creation of employment opportunities, the following design variables were identified that might discourage employers from utilising these employment tax incentives:

The Learnership Agreement Allowance

Mismatch Between Employees in Need of Employment and Employees Targeted by Employers

During 2016, the National Treasury conducted a review of its Learnership Tax Incentive. This review indicated that the utilisation of these tax incentives is predominantly concentrated in industries and sectors that are more specialised in nature (National Treasury, 2016). It has been noted that employers are more inclined to hire and train individuals with higher NQF level qualifications (highly skilled individuals), compared to those with lower NQF level qualifications (individuals with basic skills), as the benefits employers derive from employees with higher NQF level qualifications are greater than those from training employees with lower NQF level qualifications. However, the majority of the unemployed possess qualifications at NQF levels of 1 to 4 (National Treasury, 2016). Therefore, it is argued that the learnership incentive is not effective in improving the employment prospects of those most vulnerable to unemployment (National Treasury, 2016). Consequently, it is concluded that the learnership agreement tax incentive does not fully achieve its aim of promoting overall job creation, which was one of the reasons for its introduction into the South African Income Tax Act.

Mismatch Between the Skills Provided and Required

The National Treasury's (2016) review highlighted the fact that employers raised concerns about the inconsistencies between the requirements of various SETAs and the misalignment of these requirements with those of employers. This mismatch poses a significant challenge, as not all learners who complete their learnership agreements possess the necessary skills to fulfil their roles and responsibilities, as expected by their employers. Consequently, there appears to be a gap between the skills provided by training providers and those required in practice by employers. Studies conducted by McGrath et al. (2006), Kraak (2008), and Reddy et al. (2010) attribute this gap to the fact that the requirements and performance targets set by the respective SETAs do not sufficiently consider the quality of the skills being developed. The National Treasury's Learnership Tax Incentive Review (2016) confirmed that this issue persisted in 2016, highlighting the prevailing gap between the skills provided by training providers and those required by employers. Although SETAs conduct research to understand market skill requirements, this research is often considered poor quality and largely unreliable (National Treasury, 2016). Therefore, it is concluded that the SETAs' inability to manage and align the skills development needs of employers adequately with the skills provided by training providers is a crucial factor discouraging employers from utilising the learnership agreement tax incentive.

Administration Issues

To qualify for the tax incentive, section 12H(1) mandates that a signed learnership agreement must be registered with a SETA in the prescribed manner (Republic of South Africa, 1962). A SETA can establish and register a learnership agreement provided that the agreement: (i) includes a structured learning component; (ii) includes a structured work experience component; (iii) leads to a qualification registered by the South African Qualifications Authority (SAQA) associated with a trade, occupation, or profession; and (iv) is registered with the Director General in the prescribed manner (Republic of South Africa, 1998).

However, employers who participated in the National Treasury (2016) survey and perceived the tax incentive negatively tended to be those who experienced significant administrative difficulties in managing and benefitting from the qualifying learnership agreements. Although SETAs play an important role in the administrative efficiency of the learnership agreement tax incentive, some SETAs are considered barriers to the effectiveness of this allowance. Survey respondents indicated that the respective SETAs were unable to provide them with the correct information to successfully register a qualifying learnership agreement. Furthermore, this issue is worsened by the fact that different SETAs require different steps and procedures for the registration process of various learnership agreements (National Treasury, 2016).

Employers also indicated that not all SETAs have sufficient learnership agreements available. Tax administration data reveals a high utilisation of learnership agreement allowances in certain sectors, while the use of this tax incentive is very limited in others (National Treasury, 2016). Therefore, it is evident that measures must be implemented to ensure that the design of learnership agreements leads to the acquisition of skills across all sectors. This would address the dire need for and shortage of skills in the South African economy (Kerrin et al., 2017). Hence, it is concluded that the administrative issues experienced with the SETAs are a significant stumbling block that discourages employers from entering into learnership agreements and utilising this tax incentives provided by the South African Income Tax Act.

The Employment Tax Incentive Act

Abuse of the ETIA Causing Harm to the Fiscus

Rohhamlal (2018) indicated that abuse of this employment tax incentive occurs when employers claim the incentive in situations where actual employment relationships do not exist. In the case of *State Information Technology Agency (SITA) (Pty) Ltd v CCMA* (2008), which evaluated the nature of an employment contract, it was held that the following criteria should be considered to determine whether an employment relationship exists: (i) the employer's right to control and supervise the employee; (ii) whether the employee's role is an integral part of the operations of the employer; and (iii) the extent to which the employee is economically dependent on the employer.

To comply with the requirements of the definition of an "employee" in terms of the ETIA, an individual must receive remuneration that constitutes "income", as defined for normal tax purposes, be documented in the employer's records, and work for the employer (Republic of South Africa, 2013). The risk with this definition is that while it is easy for an employer to document an individual in its records (thus complying with one of the requirements), it is challenging for SARS to determine whether the individual in fact works for the employer and whether the individual directly or indirectly assists in carrying on or conducting the business of the employer. This effectively allows an individual to comply with all the requirements of an employee in terms of the ETIA without genuinely fulfilling the role. Consequently, it is possible for an employer to claim the employment tax incentive, while only funding the individual's studies without really hiring the individual as an employee. The abuse of the employment tax incentive is a critical issue in the practical application of the ETIA, as it might encourage employers to claim this tax incentive without having employed a *bona fide* employee, thereby defeating the purpose of the ETIA.

Employing Persons with a Disability

The ETIA is only available to employers who employ individuals earning less than R6500 per month, commonly referred to as the "wage ceiling" (National Treasury, 2016). Since the cost of employing and training persons with disabilities is higher, it seems that the wage ceiling related to the ETIA does not promote the employability of employees with disabilities. Additionally, to meet the Black Economic Empowerment (BEE) requirements and qualify for BEE benefits, a specific percentage of wage expenditure must be spent on persons with disabilities. According to the BEE point system, an employer can obtain two points if 2% of all its employees are black persons with disabilities (SAIPA, 2017). Therefore, it seems that achieving this BEE target is hindered by the ETIA wage ceiling, as the requirements for qualifying for BEE benefits and the ETIA tax incentive seem contradictory (Van der Merwe, 2019). This contradiction might discourage employers from utilising the tax incentive under the ETIA and from employing persons with disabilities.

Comparative Analysis

Motivation for Selecting Australia and Canada for Comparison to South Africa

Australia and Canada both have lower unemployment rates compared to South Africa. In Australia, the unemployment rate has decreased from 11% in 1995 to 3.9% in 2024 (Australian Bureau of Statistics, 2024), while in Canada it has dropped from 11.4% in 1994 to 6.1% in 2024 (Statistics Canada, 2024). These figures are significantly lower than South Africa's unemployment rate. Despite Australia's low unemployment rate of 3.7% in 2022 (The World Bank, 2023), the country implemented a skills training incentives programme in July 2022 aimed at developing a skilled Australian workforce. This programme offers special tax treatment to employers who provide on-the-job training to their employees, subject to specific requirements (Australian Government, 2023). Similarly, Canada has a broad range of incentives focused on education and training, particularly through on-the-job training via apprenticeships. In 2022, Canada had more than 60 apprenticeship trades (on-the-job training opportunities) in place, designed to supply the necessary skills for the Canadian labour market (Red Seal, 2023).

Therefore, both Australia and Canada utilise tax incentives to encourage and promote the training of individuals from the employer's perspective. The focus of this chapter on comparing South Africa to Australia and Canada is motivated by the fact that these countries are actively promoting skills development among their employees, including on-the-job training opportunities for semi-skilled and skilled employees. This focus on skill development is also a critical area for improvement in a South African context.

Furthermore, both Australia and Canada are members of the Organisation for Economic Co-Operation and Development (OECD), which is an international organisation established with the aim of making governments work together to develop global standards and establish improved policies to increase the livelihood of its citizens (Bainbridge, 2000). Although South Africa is not a formal member of the OECD, it is one of the OECD's five key partners, which means that South Africa also shares and contributes to the goals and objectives of the OECD (OECD, 2018). Therefore, because Australia, Canada, and South Africa are working together to improve policies on an international platform such as the OECD, this serves as further motivation why these three countries are considered comparable to one another within the scope of this chapter. It is advocated that lessons could be learned by the South African legislator when South Africa's employment tax incentives are compared to that of Australia and Canada.

Conceptualising Employment Tax Incentives in Australia and Canada

Australia introduced a "skills and training boost allowance" in 2022 to support small businesses in building a better-trained and more productive workforce (Treasury, 2022). The reason for the late introduction of this Australian employment tax incentive, compared to South Africa's learnership agreement allowance introduced in 2002, is that prior to 2022, the Australian government preferred government subsidies over direct tax incentives to promote on-the-job training (Parliament of Australia, 2022). The "skills and training boost tax allowance" for upskilling employees is only available to entities classified as "small business entities", defined as those with an annual turnover of less than 10 million Australian dollars. This allowance is regulated under section 328-445 of the *Income Tax Assessment Act* 38 of 1997 (ITAA) (Australia, 1997a) and section 328-450 of the *Income Tax (Transitional Provisions) Act* 40 of 1997 (ITTPA) (Australia, 1997b).

Section 328-445 of the ITTPA (Australia, 1997b) permits small business entities to deduct 20% of their "eligible expenditure" incurred against their assessable income. Eligible expenditure includes costs that an employer must incur for providing either in-person training for one or more of its employees present in Australia, or online training for at least one of its employees. This allowance specifically aims to support small business in their growth, which can involve employing less skilled employees who will need subsequent training to develop their skills and enhance their productivity (Treasury, 2022). The training allowed under section 328-445 of the ITTPA encompasses a broad range of training across all industry sectors (Australia, 2011).

In Canada, the "Apprenticeship Job Creation Tax Credit" (AJCTC) is provided as a tax incentive under the *Canadian Income Tax Act* (R.S.C, 1985, c. 1 (5th Supp.)) (CITA) (Canada, 1985). The AJCTC aims to equip employees with the required skills through education and training, while in formal employment. Introduced in 2006 (Government of Canada, 2023) and regulated under section 127 of the CITA (Canada, 1985), the AJCTC assists employers to offset the cost of hiring and training employees who have entered into an apprenticeship agreement. This is achieved through a tax credit against the employer's income tax liability (Canada, 1985), equal to the lesser of the following:

- 2000 Canadian dollars per employee; or
- 10% of the eligible salary or wage payable by the employer in the taxation year to the eligible apprentice in respect of the eligible apprentice's employment at

the employer in a business carried on in Canada by the employer during the same taxation year.

The eligible salaries and wages payable under section 127(9) of the ITA (Canada, 1985) include only those salaries and wages paid by the employer to eligible apprentices during the first 24 months of each apprenticeship (Canada, 1985). Any unused portion of the credits can be carried forward to subsequent taxation years for up to a maximum of 20 years, according to section 127(9) of the ITA (Canada, 1985). This provision allows Canadian employers to defer the use of the tax incentive, ensuring they are not obligated to utilise the entire AJCTC in the year they become eligible to claim it.

Comparative Analysis Between South Africa, Australia, and Canada

The comparative analysis between these three countries aims to highlight differences in prevailing employment tax incentive design variables. These differences can inform recommendations to improve prevailing tax incentives in South Africa, thereby encouraging the creation of semi-skilled and skilled employment opportunities. The analysis focuses on the employment tax incentives in South Africa, Australia, and Canada, examining seven types of design variables: (i) format; (ii) taxpayer status of employers; (iii) registration requirements; (iv) quantum; (v) targeted employee type; (vi) skills obtained by employees; and (vii) mode of training.

Format of the Tax Incentive

The AJCTC tax incentive in Canada is granted to employers as a tax credit, contrasting with the allowance deducted from taxable income in South Africa and assessable income in Australia. Although both the learnership agreement allowance in South Africa and the skills and training boost allowance in Australia can create an assessed loss position, a tax incentive in the form of a tax credit has been found to be more beneficial to taxpayers in South Africa. This is because an assessed loss might be ringfenced or limited under section 20A and section 20 of the *Income Tax Act* (Republic of South Africa, 1962). A tax credit is considered more beneficial from a tax perspective, as it directly offsets a taxpayer's tax liability, whereas a tax allowance is less beneficial. The latter only reduces a taxpayer's taxable income (or assessable income in an Australian context), after which the tax rate must still be applied.

Taxpayer Status of the Employer Qualifying for the Tax Incentive

The South African learnership agreement allowance is considered more inclusive than those in Australia and Canada, as it allows any type of employer to qualify, regardless of the employer's tax status. This inclusivity means that any entity, whether a natural person or a company, can qualify for the section 12H allowance. In addition, if the employer is a company, there are no restrictions or limitations based on its classification for normal tax purposes. This means that a company can qualify for the section 12H tax incentive whether or not it meets the requirements of a "small business corporation", as defined in section 12E(4)(*a*) of the *Income Tax Act* (Republic of South Africa, 1962), provided the other conditions of section 12H are met.

In contrast, only employers classified as "small business entities", as defined by the ITTP (Australia, 1997b) qualify for the skills and training boost allowance tax incentive in Australia. This makes the Australian tax incentive more restricted and limited. Furthermore, unlike in Canada, where an employer's eligibility for the AJCTC tax incentive is denied if the employer itself is a public company, non-resident, or a listed company, these controls and classifications do not affect a South African employer's eligibility for the section 12H learnership agreement allowance. Hence, the South African learnership agreement allowance is more inclusive than both the skills and training boost allowance in Australia and the AJCTC tax incentive in Canada. The tax status (i.e. taxpayer type and classification) of a South African employer does not impact or exclude them from using this tax incentive.

Registration Requirements

The administration of the section 12H learnership agreements, heavily influenced by the SETAs, presents a major obstacle. Employers face challenges in getting learnership agreements registered with the respective SETAs and obtaining confirmation that the agreements have been successfully completed. South African employers must provide proof of these steps to qualify for the section 12H annual and completion allowances. These administrative hurdles might discourage employers from utilising the section 12H tax incentive. In contrast, the South African ETIA does not have registration requirements.

The Australian tax incentive does not require registration with a specific body; instead, it permits training providers and/or regulating bodies to determine if registration is necessary. This approach offers greater flexibility for employers, allowing them to decide whether to enter an agreement and/or register it with a specific body based on the requirements set by the training providers or regulating bodies.

Quantum of Tax Incentives

The quantum of the section 12H allowance in South Africa is the same, irrespective of the industry in which the employer's business operates. However, some industries might require more funds than others to train employees. In contrast, the quantum of the skills and training boost allowance for Australian employers and the AJCTC for Canadian employers varies based on the size of the eligible salary or wage payable.

Targeted Employee Type by the Tax Incentive

The tax incentives promoting on-the-job training in South Africa support and encourage employers to create semi-skilled and skilled employment opportunities for all types of employees. The section 12H learnership agreement allowance is aimed at all employees, including those with disabilities, who are required to undergo on-the-job training. In contrast, the tax incentive under the ETIA focuses specifically on encouraging the training of individuals between the ages of 18 and 29. However, the ETIA does not provide an increased tax benefit for training persons with disabilities. In Australia, the skills and training boost allowance is available to any employer who ensures that his/her employees receive on-the-job training. The AJCTC in Canada is exclusively targeted at employees entering an apprenticeship.

Skills Obtained by Employees

Employers' dissatisfaction with the type and quality of skills required by learners upon completing their learnership agreements contributes to their reluctance to engage in new qualifying agreements and create additional semi-skilled and skilled employment opportunities through on-the-job training. This reluctance stems from concerns that SETAs prioritise meeting performance targets over ensuring the development of high-quality and relevant skills. Consequently, mismatches between the skills sought by employers and those acquired by learners after completing their learnerships persist. Additionally, SETAs' inability to understand the skill needs and requirements of employers further discourages the utilisation of the section 12H tax incentive.

The skills and training boost allowance implemented in Australia offers an allowance to any employer whose employees undergo training from a training provider authorised by an authorised body. Unlike South African learnership programmes, the skills and training boost allowance provides greater flexibility, as it is not limited solely to learnership agreements. This allowance extends to various

Employment-Based Training (EBT) models, including internships, cadetships, apprenticeships, and pure on-the-job training. The flexibility of these EBT models enables employers to choose a specific model that best suits their individual requirements. This flexibility ensures that the skills acquired through EBT models in Australia are generally aligned with the skills sought by Australian employers.

Mode of Training

The Australian skills and training boost allowance permits training to be conducted in person for one or more employees located in Australia, or as remote online training, without the requirement that employees participating remotely be present in Australia. In comparison, neither the South African learnership agreement allowance nor the Canadian AJCTC specify or require any specific modes of training. However, due to the traditional nature of learnership agreements and apprenticeships, this training is usually conducted in person. Similarly, the tax incentive under the ETIA does not mandate or specify any particular training mode.

Some employers might mistakenly believe that the section 12H allowance can only be utilised if education and training are provided in person. This misconception can prevent or discourage employers from using and applying the section 12H tax incentive, especially in instances where in-person working practices have shifted to remote or hybrid approaches of work and training due to the COVID-19 pandemic.

Conclusion and Recommendations

The purpose of this study was to evaluate whether the design of the prevailing South African tax incentives effectively supports and encourages employers, from a tax perspective, to create semi-skilled and skilled employment opportunities through on-the-job training in South Africa.

Based on the findings from evaluating the design variables of the tax incentives and the comparative analysis, it became evident that there is room for improvement in the design and administration of South Africa's current employment tax incentives. Some of the design variables, tax practices, and tax treatments of Australian and Canadian tax incentives serve as valuable guidance for proposed amendments. These improvements can increase employers' willingness to use South African employment tax incentives to create semi-skilled and skilled employment opportunities through on-the-job training.

Recommendations (where relevant) per design variable evaluated are as follows:

Format of the Tax Incentive
It is recommended that the South African tax regulator considers replacing the section 12H learnership agreement allowance with a tax credit similar to the AJCTC in Canada. This change will likely make the incentive more attractive to employers.

Registration Requirements
It is recommended that the requirement of registering a learnership agreement with a specific SETA in South Africa be reconsidered. However, it is important to maintain the requirement that the training provided should be accredited by a regulating body governing training programmes in South Africa. This adjustment could improve the flexibility and efficiency of how training is provided.

Quantum of Tax Incentives
It is recommended that the South African tax regulator considers adopting a more flexible system regarding the quantum of the allowance for on-the-job training opportunities across different industries with varying training expenditure needs. The Australian skills and training boost allowance provides valuable guidance for this recommendation. The Australian allowance is determined based on the eligible expenditure charged by the training provider, allowing the amount to vary according to the employer's needs. To prevent abuse of the tax incentive, it is also recommended that the quantum of the allowance granted be governed by mandating the training provider, rather than the employer, to determine the amount of eligible expenditure.

Employee Type Targeted by the Tax Incentive
It is recommended that the tax regulator increases the savings benefit granted to employers regarding the employees' tax (PAYE) they must withhold from the remuneration of qualifying employees if the employee has a "disability", as defined for normal tax purposes. This change will encourage employers to create semi-skilled and skilled job opportunities for disabled young people by providing additional savings benefits when paying monthly PAYE for such employees to SARS. Furthermore, it is recommended that South Africa incorporates a tax incentive measure specifically aimed at encouraging employers to create employment opportunities for individuals with an NQF level of 1 to 6, as this is where the demand in the labour market is highest.

Skills Obtained by Employees
Mechanisms or procedures are recommended to align the skills set needs of employers with the skills learners acquire through various learnership agreements. It is further suggested that the SETAs involve key stakeholders within specific sectors (i.e. the major role-players within each sector) to help them understand the current skill set needs of employers and plan for the future skill set needs of these sectors.

Skills Obtained by Employees
It is also recommended that the scope of trades, sectors, and industries in which education and training qualify for the section 12H tax incentive be expanded beyond the current SETAs. This expansion will allow for a broader range of skills to be

obtained via learnership agreements, as part of on-the-job training. Broadening the scope will help create more job opportunities and address the high unemployment rate in South Africa.

Mode of Training

It is recommended that the South African learnership agreement regulations be amended to clarify that the allowance is available regardless of the mode of training provided. Hence, all modes of education and training—whether in person, remotely (i.e. online), or through a hybrid approach (i.e. a combination of in-person and online training)—should qualify for the section 12H learnership agreement allowance. Clarifying this in section 12H's legislative regulations might encourage more employers to utilise this tax incentive.

Limitations of the Research

The scope and focus of this chapter were limited to examining the prevailing tax incentives available exclusively to employers and did not include the tax incentives accessible to employees. Furthermore, the chapter's context considered only semi-skilled and skilled employees, with unskilled employees being excluded from the analysis.

References

Aliyu, A. A., Bello, M. U., Kassim, R., & Martin, D. (2014). Positivist and non-positivist paradigm in social science research: Conflicting paradigms or perfect partners? *Journal of Management and Sustainability, 4*(3), 79–95.

Australia. (1997a). *Income Tax Assessment Act 38 of 1997*.

Australia. (1997b). *Income Tax (Transitional Provisions) Act 40 of 1997*.

Australia. (2011). *Tertiary Education Quality and Standards Agency Act 73 of 2011*.

Australian Bureau of Statistics. (2024). *Headline estimates of employment, unemployment, underemployment, participation, and hours worked from the monthly labour force survey*. Retrieved from: https://www.abs.gov.au/statistics/labour/employment-and-unemployment/labour-force-australia/latest-release

Australian Government. (2023). *Australian apprenticeships: Employer incentive fact sheet*. Retrieved from https://www.australianapprenticeships.gov.au/aus-employer-incentives#:~:text=Employers%20can%20claim%2010%25%20of,all%20primary%20eligibility%20requirements

Bahari, S. F. (2010). Qualitative versus quantitative research strategies: Contrasting epistemological and ontological assumptions. *Sains Humanika, 52*(1), 17–28.

Bainbridge, T. (2000). A brief history of the OECD. *OECD Observer, 2000*(2), 1–124.

Bertrand, M., & Crépon, B. (2020). Teaching labor laws: Evidence from a randomized control trial in South Africa. *J-PAL, 2020*, 1–47.

Bratić, V. (2006). Tax expenditures: A theoretical review. *Financial Theory and Practice, 30*(2), 113–127.

Canada. (1985). *Income Tax Act (R.S.C, 1985, c. 1 (5th Supp.))*.

Cedefop. (2009). *Using tax incentives to promote education and training*. Retrieved from https://www.cedefop. europa.eu/files/5180_en.pdf

Coad, A., Daunfeldt, S., Johansson, D., & Wennberg, K. (2014). Whom do high-growth firms hire? *Industrial and Corporate Change, 23*(1), 293–327.

Creswell, J. W. (2003). *Research design: Qualitative, quantitative, and mixed methods approaches*. Sage.

Department of Employment and Labour. (2020). *Plan for research to promote South Africa's productivity*. Retrieved from http://www.labour.gov.za/plan-for-research-to-promote-south-africa's-productivity

Ebrahim, A., Leibbrandt, M., & Ranchhod, V. (2017). *The effects of the employment tax incentive on South African employment*. UNI-WIDER.

Elnaga, A., & Imran, A. (2013). The effect of training on employee performance. *European Journal of Business and Management, 5*(4), 137–147.

Esser, F., & Vliegenthart, R. (2016). Comparative research methods. In J. Matthes, R. Potter, & C. S. Davis (Eds.), *International Encyclopedia of communication research methods*. Wiley-Blackwell.

Fink, A. (2014). *Conducting research literature reviews: From the internet to paper* (4th ed.). Sage.

Government of Canada. (2023). *Apprenticeship job creation tax credit*. Retrieved from https://www.canada.ca/en/revenue-agency/services/tax/individuals/topics/about-your-tax-return/tax-return/completing-a-tax-return/deductions-credits-expenses/line-41200-investment-tax-credit/apprenticeship-job-creation-tax-credit.html

Kerrin, M., Mamabolo, M. A., & Kele, T. (2017). Entrepreneurship management skills requirements in an emerging economy: A South African outlook. *The Southern African Journal of Entrepreneurship and Small Business Management, 9*(1), 1–10.

Kraak, A. (2008). A critical review of the National Skills Development Strategy in South Africa. *Journal of Vocational Education & Training, 60*(1), 1–18.

Levesque, E. M. (2019). *Understanding the skills gap and what employers can do about it*. Brookings Institution.

Martensen, A., & Grønholdt, L. (2009). Quality in higher education: Linking graduates' competencies and employers' needs. *International Journal of Quality and Service Sciences, 1*(1), 67–77.

McGrath, S., Akoojee, S., Gewer, A., Mabizela, M., Mbele, N., & Roberts, J. (2006). An examination of the vocational education and training reform debate in Southern Africa. *Compare: A Journal of Comparative Education, 36*(1), 85–103.

National Treasury. (2002). *Explanatory memorandum on the Taxation Laws Amendment Bill, 2002*.

National Treasury. (2013). *Draft explanatory memorandum on the Employment Tax Incentive Bill, 2013*. National Treasury. Retrieved from https://www.sars.gov.za/wp-content/uploads/Legal/ExplMemo/Employment-Tax-Incentive-Bill-EM-31-October-2013.pdf

National Treasury. (2016). *Learnership Tax Incentive Review*. National Treasury. Retrieved from https://www.treasury.gov.za/public%20comments/TLAB%20and%20TALAB%202016%20Draft/2016%20Draft%202nd%20Batch%20%20Learnership%20Tax%20Incentive%20Review%20-%20public.pdf

National Treasury. (2024, February 21). *Budget speech*.

OECD (Organisation for Economic Cooperation and Development). (2018). *South Africa and the OECD*. Retrieved from https://www.oecd.org/southafrica/south-africa-and-oecd.htm

Parliament of Australia. (2022). *Apprenticeship incentives*. Retrieved from https://www.aph.gov.au/About_Parliament/Parliamentary_Departments/Parliamentary_Library/pubs/rp/BudgetReview202223/ApprenticeshipIncentives

Polackova, H. B., Valenduc, C. M. A., & Swift, Z. L. (2004). *Tax expenditures: Shedding light on government spending through the tax system: Lessons from developed and transition economies*. World Bank.

Ranchhod, V. (2019). *Why is South Africa's unemployment rate so high?* Southern Africa Labour and Development Research Unit (SALDRU). Retrieved from https://www.saldru.uct.ac.za/2019/02/28/why-is-south-africas-unemployment-rate-so-high/

Red Seal. (2023). *Red seal trades*. Retrieved from https://www.red-seal.ca/eng/trades/tr.1d.2s_l.3st.shtml

Reddy, R., Bhorat, H., Powell, M., Visser, M., & Arends, F. (2010). *Skills supply and demand in South Africa*. Department of Higher Education and Training. Retrieved from https://hsrc.ac.za/uploads/pageContent/7429/LMIP_SkillsSupplyandDemand_Sept2016.pdf

Republic of South Africa. (1962). *Income Tax Act 58 of 1962*. Government Printer.

Republic of South Africa. (1998). *Employment Equity Act 55 of 1998*. Government Printer.

Republic of South Africa. (2013). *Employment Tax Incentive Act 26 of 2013*. Government Printer.

Republic of South Africa. (2016). *Taxation Laws Amendment Act 15 of 2016*. Government Printer.

Rocco, T. S., Bliss, L. A., Gallagher, S., & Perez-Prado, A. (2003). Taking the next step: Mixed methods research organizational systems. *Information Technology, Learning, and Performance Journal, 21*(1), 19–26.

Rohhamlal, N. (2018). *A critical analysis of the employment tax incentive* (Master's dissertation). University of Witwatersrand, Johannesburg.

SAICA (South African Institute of Chartered Accountants). (2020). *Employment tax incentive abuse scheme*. Retrieved from https://www.saica.co.za/News/NewsArticlesandPressmediareleases/tabid/695/itemid/6361/language/en-ZA/language/en-ZA/Default.aspx

SAIPA (South African Institute of Professional Accountants). (2017). *Understanding BEE: Bringing accounting to life*. Retrieved from https://www.saipa.co.za/wp-content/uploads/2017/07/BEE-webinar-July-2017-for-link-to-be-created.pdf

SAQA (South African Qualification Authority). (2014). *Assessment of the impact of the South African National Qualifications Framework*.

SARS (South African Revenue Service). (2021a). *Interpretation Note 20 (Issue 8). Additional deductions for learnership agreements*.

SARS (South African Revenue Service). (2021b). *Guide to the employment tax incentive*.

Saunders, M., Lewis, P., & Thornhill, A. (2007). *Research methods for business students*. Prentice Hall.

State Information Technology Agency (SITA) (Pty) Ltd v CCMA, 2008 29 ILJ 2234 (LAC).

Statistics Canada. (2024). *Unemployment rate by province and territory, April 2024*. Retrieved from https://www150.statcan.gc.ca/n1/daily-quotidien/240510/mc-a001-eng.htm

Stats SA (Statistics South Africa). (2024). *Quarterly Labour Force Survey (QLFS) Q4:2023*. Retrieved from https://www.statssa.gov.za/publications/P0211/Media%20release%20QLFS%20Q4%202023.pdf

The World Bank. (2023). *Unemployment, total (% of total labor force) (Modelled ILO estimate) - Australia, Canada*. Retrieved from https://data.worldbank.org/indicator/SL.UEM.TOTL.ZS?locations=AU-CA

The World Bank. (2024). *Unemployment, total (% of total labor force) (Modeled ILO estimate)*. Retrieved from https://data.worldbank.org/indicator/SL.UEM.TOTL.ZS

Treasury. (2022). *Treasury Laws Amendment (measures for consultation) Bill 2022: Skills and training boost*. Retrieved from https://treasury.gov.au/sites/default/files/2022-08/c2022-305552-em.pdf

Van der Merwe, D. (2019). *How to enable the disabled - Complying with the BEE Act*. Retrieved from https://serr.co.za/how-to-enable-the-disabled-complying-with-the-b-bbee-act

Visser, B. (2024). *Budget 2024: Tax incentives summarised*. Retrieved from https://www.bdo.co.za/en-za/insights/featured-insights/budget-2024-tax-incentives-summarised

A Comparative Analysis of the South African Public Sector Procurement Process with Recognised Practices: A Case of Fraud Prevention Controls

Tshimangadzo Caroline Tshikhovhokhovho

Abstract Fraud is a worldwide concern and has spread throughout different divisions of the government, including the procurement division. The purpose of the study is to address fraud prevention controls available in fighting fraud in the government procurement process. The research objectives are (1) to determine the ideal public procurement process, (2) to identify weaknesses in the South African (SA) public procurement process, and (3) enhancements (controls) that can be further implemented to fight fraud in the South African public procurement process. This chapter used a thematic content analysis of extant literature on fraud prevention controls, from which an ideal public procurement process was derived, and shortcomings and enhancements identified. The articles were sorted into themes to be able to perform a comparative analysis between the normative themes from the literature and the normative requirements in South African treasury legislation. Findings revealed that the National Treasury has sufficiently implemented the available fraud prevention controls to prevent fraud in the public sector procurement process. Findings also revealed shortcomings and enhancements that the treasury legislation can take into consideration for implementation as a continuous collective effort to prevent fraud in the procurement process. The study addressed currently available controls to prevent fraud in the procurement process of the government of South Africa. It is significant to policymakers for consideration during the review and update of the procurement-related policies. Future research can focus on how corporate governance can be used to prevent fraud in the government's procurement process.

Keywords Public sector procurement process · Procurement process · Fraud · Fraud prevention controls · Enhancements

T. C. Tshikhovhokhovho (✉)
University of Venda, Thohoyandou, South Africa
e-mail: caroline.shavhani@univen.ac.za

T. Moloi (ed.), *Impacting Society Positively Through Technology in Accounting and Business Processes*, Springer Proceedings in Business and Economics,
https://doi.org/10.1007/978-3-031-84885-8_63

Background and Introduction

Fraud is a challenge to all organisations and happens irrespective of the size, profitability, or industry (Mangala & Kumari, 2017; Peiris & Aruppala, 2021). It has a chance to occur in any organisation where employees are given access to spend money (Gunawan, 2019). At a global level, fraud is routinely becoming a million-dollar business and is causing damage into the billions (Dzomira, 2015; Venter, 2007). PWC's Global Economic Crime and Fraud Survey in 2022 revealed that 52% of organisations around the globe had experienced fraud (PWC, 2022). The ACFE's Report to the Nations on Occupational Fraud 2022 found that more than $3.6 billion is lost during acts of fraud per year (ACFE, 2022). On a positive note, the PWC's (2022) survey revealed an overall decrease in fraud by 2% from 2020 to 2022, resulting from improved controls implemented in organisations (PWC, 2022).

Dr. Aaron Motsoaledi, the South African Minister of Home Affairs, in his speech, on the 24th of May 2022 at the Department of Home Affairs, while addressing the Department of Home affairs personnel, the Independent Electoral Commission, the National Assembly, Government Printing Works, Border Management Authority, and the media stated that "our people are tired of corruption" (Department of Home Affairs, 2022). It is for this reason that South Africa has started to impose heavier punishment for fraud, for example, a fraudster was given a 20-year jail sentence for stealing R4.9 trillion (Cape Business News, 2019). This indicates that the public's procurement system is willing to fight fraud.

Amongst others, fraud and corruption is a serious phenomenon affecting public institutions of developing countries (Nurmandi & Kim, 2015). The impact of fraud has been found to be tremendous and detrimental to the country's economy (Macailao, 2020). Fraud consequences become harmful to the public finances, reputation, confidence, and structure (Handayani & Kawedar, 2021; Tan, 2013; Weingärtner et al., 2021).

Understanding Fraud in the Public Procurement Process

In relation to this study, this section defines various types of fraud. Fraud can be defined as an intentional deception through concealing or misrepresenting information that endangers other people's financial interests and benefits the perpetrator's financial interests (Handayani & Kawedar, 2021). Cressey (1950), cited in Dorminey et al. (2012), found that fraud occurs when the perpetrator has the opportunity to do so, can rationalise his/her acts, and in such cases that there is pressure to commit fraud.

Procurement fraud refers to a type of fraud that occurs in any stage of the procurement process, such as the initiation, delivery, or payment phase (Ramamoorti & Curtis, 2003). Public procurement refers to the government acquiring goods/services through public money (Modrušan et al., 2021). In the public sector, expenditure management is a fundamental aspect of the sustainable delivery of quality services, and its purpose is to achieve three interconnected objectives, which are to improve fiscal discipline, optimising allocation of resources in line with budgetary policy priorities, and ensure good operational management (Kinuthia et al., 2018). However, procurement fraud disturbs this objective, and it is increasing every year, but, more in the government sector than in the private sector (Rustiarini et al. 2019). This is because the government plans a large sum of amount in procurement expenditures (Gichio, 2014; Venter, 2007). In support of the latter, South African government spends about 12% of the GDP on public procurement (The Organisation for Economic Co-operation and Development (OECD)).

Fraud in the Public Procurement Process in South Africa

A study conducted by Dewata et al. (2022) found that fraud in procurement occurs when there is a deviation within the procurement process. The traditional government procurement system has weaknesses that a perpetrator can exploit to commit fraud (Arcangeli, 2020). Sometimes the procurement system allows the perpetrator to physically meet with the government officer to bribe him/her to award the tender to the perpetrator (Wicaksono et al., 2017). Examples to the procurement system weaknesses resulting in fraud in the South African context are as follows: fraud was committed through the procurement of personal protective equipment during the Covid-19 pandemic (Public Service Commission, 2022), the Special Investigation Unit (SIU) (Special Investigation Unit (SIU), 2022) reported that three Mpumalanga government officials were arrested for fraud amounting to R5.9 million, which was committed through collusion over the purchase of personal protective equipment, the Auditor General South Africa (AGSA) report revealed that about 88 auditees have been suspected of fraud within the supply chain processes (AGSA, 2021) in the 2020/2021 financial year, and the Northwest Department of Health was found to have been charged an amount of R3.3 million for the maintenance of medical equipment instead of R144 562 market-related price (AGSA, 2021).

Fraud Prevention Controls in the Public Sector Procurement Process

Fraud prevention controls in the procurement process refer to measures that aim to stop fraudulent procurement of goods/services while improving transparency, accountability, efficiency, etc. (Wardani et al., 2021). These controls are meant to limit procurement abuse resulting in fraud (Passas, 2007). Fraud prevention controls can be successfully implemented if there are effective internal management strategies (Wardani et al., 2021). One of the effective management strategies is the monitoring of the procurement process and internal control system (Matthew et al., 2013).

Numerous studies have been conducted on fraud prevention in the public procurement process. For example, Rendon and Rendon (2015) conducted a study where, through a survey, they assessed the knowledge of the workforce of the Department of Defense (DoD) (a public entity) on procurement internal controls and their perceptions. From this study, they found that they lacked knowledge and recommended that the DoD improves its procurement internal controls to help reduce fraud risks while ensuring auditability (Rendon & Rendon, 2015). Modrušan et al. (2021) conducted a review of the available detection techniques and models used to detect suspicious sources in the public procurement process. The results of this study revealed that the models available are based on the quality of historical data and can only provide early warning signs. Wardani et al. (2021) research on the effect of fraud prevention in Yogyakarta City found a positive effect on fraud prevention in the procurement process. Dewata et al. (2022) researched the effect of good governance and internal controls on preventing fraud in the government's (South Sumatra Province) procurement process. The study found a partial positive and significant effect of good governance and internal controls on the government's procurement process. From the research above, there seems to be little done on how fraud prevention controls can be effectively implemented. For this reason, this study is intended to address this gap in research, which is to understand the ideal procurement process, its weaknesses (in the SA context), and enhancements that can be implemented to improve these controls.

In the context of the South African government, fraud prevention controls that have been implemented in effort to fight and mitigate fraud are various laws like the Prevention and Combating Corrupt Activities Act (12/2004), the Constitution of the Republic of South Africa (108/1996), the Public Finance Management Act (1/1999) (hereafter referred to as the PFMA), the Municipal Finance Management Act (56/2003), Prevention of Organised Crimes Act (121/1998), and the Financial Intelligence Act (38/2001). "The National Treasury has further implemented various legislation which guide the procurement process and are intended to control and prevent fraud that may occur. Examples include: Updated Guideline on Irregular Expenditure (2015b) which provides guidance on the identification and application of irregular expenditure; Guideline on Fruitless and Wasteful Expenditure (2015a) clarifies the interpretation of issues related to fruitful and wasteful expenditure; Guideline on Unauthorised Expenditure (2015c) which provides clarity on the interpretation of unauthorised expenditure; Preferential Procurement Policy Framework Act (PPPFA) (2000) guides the implementation of PPP policy; Preferential Procurement Regulations (2001) guides the application of preferential procurement; Treasury Practice Notes (Supply Chain Management Practice Notes—National Treasury Instruction on Note on enhancing compliance monitoring and improving transparency and accountability in Supply Chain Management (2011) emphasises the need to apply fundamental principles in the procurement process; Practice Note 4 (2008/2009) Irregular Expenditure (2009) clarifies procedures to follow when dealing with irregular expenditure; Practice Note SCM 5 of 2004:

Training SCM Officials (2004a) provides minimum training that procurement authorities require; Practice Note SCM 4 of 2003: Code of Conduct for Supply Chain Management Practitioners (2003) provides the code that SCM practitioners should adhere to".

The above-mentioned legislation serves to ensure that the public institution's funds are spent effectively and economically (Tan, 2013). However, despite the available laws, fraud persists. This provides evidence that mechanisms that the public sector has currently put in place are not yielding the results needed to achieve its prevention (Public Service Commission, 2022). As a result, this warrants further investigation on what is the ideal public procurement system, the weaknesses in the South African government procurement process, and the enhancements that can be implemented to further prevent fraud.

Research Methodology

To achieve the research objectives, which are to determine the ideal public procurement process, to identify weaknesses in the South African government procurement process and its enhancements, the study considered the following research questions: (1) what is the ideal public procurement process? (2) what are the weaknesses in the SA public procurement process? and (3) what are the enhancements that can be implemented in the SA government procurement process? The first research step was to use a thematic content analysis of the literature on fraud prevention controls to derive an ideal procurement process (refer to Diagram 1: The ideal public procurement process). Clarke and Braun (2017) describe a thematic content analysis as "a method for identifying, analysing, and interpreting patterns of meaning ('themes') within qualitative data". Thematic analysis is flexible, useful, provides rich, detailed information, and is also suitable to answer the questions to identify concerns people may have on a certain event (Vaismoradi et al., 2013). It is also flexible in terms of data collection and sample size (Clarke & Braun, 2017). In line with the above, I used the following search criterion and key terms: "fraud prevention tools"; "fraud prevention methods"; "preventing fraud in the public sector"; and "preventing fraud

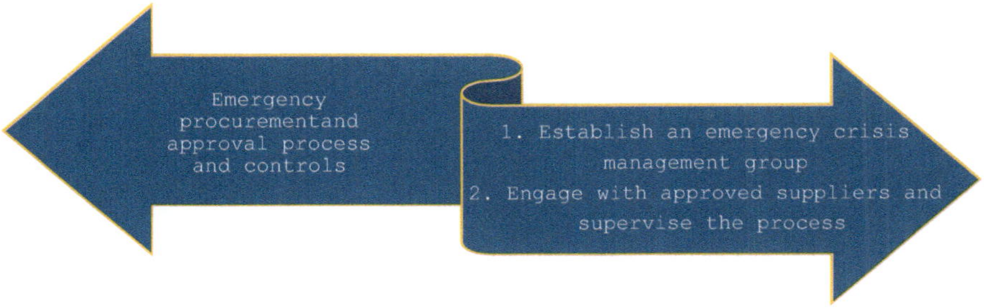

Diagram 1 A schematic illustration of the ideal public sector procurement process

in the procurement process". The search was done on the University of Pretoria Google Scholar, which provides access to various databases such as Proquest, Ebscohost, Emerald, Science Direct, etc. Therefore, all the results used were from these various databases. The focus of the search covered the period 2003 to 2022. Earlier results were excluded as they became irrelevant for the discussion, and the study was done in 2022, hence the exclusion of 2023 data. Additionally, in line with Clarke and Braun (2017), all results were analysed, critiqued, and synthesised for relevancy and narrowed down by determining whether they are fit for the theme, had an abstract, were written in English, relevant for the government procurement process, published and publicly accessible. As a result, a total of 67 articles were usable and critically referenced.

The aim of thematic analysis is to analyse information by breaking texts into smaller groups (Vaismoradi et al., 2013). In line with the latter authors, and Clarke and Braun (2017), these articles were grouped into three themes of the ideal procurement process, which are demand, acquisition, and logistics management. Furthermore, the discussion separately discussed the emergency procurement process and controls in addition to the normal procurement process (refer to Fig. 1 A schematic illustration of the emergency procurement process). This was done so that the chapter can focus on a normative discussion (by comparing the ideal procurement process and the treasury legislation normative requirements) to be able to identify weaknesses in the South African public procurement process while identifying enhancements from recognised practices (Broome, 1999; Siena, 2007). Therefore, these themes were used to form a discussion that separates the research content gathered and to provide clarity as to whether the treasury legislation was in line with the literature. Where the treasury legislation did not provide sufficient controls, this was then identified as a shortcoming/weakness for the treasury to consider for implementation (enhancement).

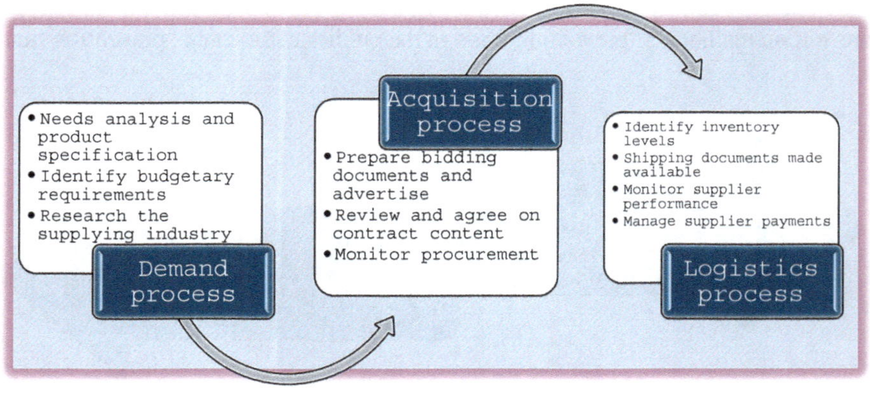

Fig. 1 A schematic illustration of the emergency procurement process

South African National Treasury Legislation (or Treasury Legislation)

For comparison with the ideal literature procurement process, the researcher identified, inspected, and used procurement procedure-related legislation (Guidelines, Regulations, and Practice Notes) obtained from the National Treasury website, Legislations, PFMA which the below discussion was based, and these are: Treasury Regulations related to Strategic Planning as published in Government Gazette No. 29644 also known as Treasury Regulation 2005 Gazette No. 27388 (2005a, 2005b); Supply Chain Management documents (General Procurement Guidelines (n.d.), Policy to guide uniformity in procurement reform processes in government, (2003a)), Practice Note 6 (2007/2008) Procurement of goods/services by means other than through the invitation of competitive bids (2008).

This chapter also elaborated on enhancements identified during the search for an ideal procurement process. Some articles revealed various other prevention controls, which the South African public sector can implement to fight fraud within the procurement process. I then classified these controls as enhancements. These enhancements can be modified and improve the current way of doing things (Siena, 2007). To form a detailed argument of these enhancements, in addition to the search done above, I conducted a further search on the University of Pretoria Google Scholar. In line with Clarke and Braun on thematic analysis (2017), the search was done on various key words as shown in Table 1—Enhancements search criterion, key words, and results used. All results were analysed, critiqued, and synthesised

Table 1 Enhancements search criterion, key words, and results used

No	Identified enhancement	Search criterion and keywords used	First search results used (from main search criterion)	Additional search results used
1.	E-procurement	e-procurement to prevent fraud in the public sector	6	11
2.	Corporate governance	Corporate governance in preventing fraud; corporate governance and fraud prevention	7	0
3.	Data analytics	Data analytics and fraud prevention in the public procurement	4	8
4.	Contract modifications	Procurement contract modification; and contract modifications	4	5
5.	Audit function	Audit to prevent fraud in the public procurement	5	13
Total search results used			26	37
Total used articles for enhancements identified (first and second search results combined)			63	

for relevancy by determining whether they were fit for the identified enhancement; had an abstract; only used articles written in English; published and were accessible. I only reviewed the first 20 articles, as articles beyond that were no longer fit to substantiate the discussion related to the identified enhancement. A total of the additional searches revealed 37 usable results. Consequently, a total of 63 articles were identified as usable for the enhancement discussion and were critically read and used to form an argument (refer to below Table 1 for the breakdown of results).

Results and Discussions

Results obtained are discussed below, and a summary has been provided in Appendix 1 entitled *A comparison between literature and the National Treasury Legislation procurement process, and the identification of weaknesses.*

The literature collected was reviewed and synthesised to develop an ideal procurement process for the public sector. The process was developed by grouping the data into three phases: demand, acquisition, and logistics management (*Refer to* Diagram 1*: The ideal public procurement process*). The discussion compared the ideal process to what is in the National Treasury legislation and identified weaknesses/shortcomings. In addition, the discussion further continued to compare the ideal emergency procurement process in the literature to that in the National Treasury legislation. The discussion was grouped into two phases, namely establish an emergency crisis management team and engage with approved suppliers and supervise the process (*Refer to* Fig. 1 A schematic illustration of the emergency procurement process). Both the discussions discussed shortcomings identified from the current National Treasury process compared to the ideal process.

A comparison between literature and the National Treasury Legislation procurement process, and the identification of weaknesses.

Demand Management

Needs Analysis and Product Specification

The first step to obtaining goods/services is to perform a needs analysis and identify the product/services specifications (Lanclos & Phillips, 2014). This can be done by inspecting and observing whether there is sufficient inventory levels and documenting what levels of the goods/services are required (Malle et al., 2022; Rendon & Rendon, 2016). The next step is to have all acquisition needs approved at the prescribed level of approval (Dzomira, 2015). Lastly, the public institutions ought to decide on the type of contract, statement of work, terms, and conditions, and the bid awarding strategy that would be suitable to meet the identified goods/services (Lanclos & Phillips, 2014; Murti & Kurniawan, 2020). The treasury legislation is in line with this ideal process as they perform a needs assessment, and precisely determine the goods/services required before an actual acquisition (National Treasury SCM, 2004a; Policy to guide Uniformity in Procurement Reform Processes in government, 2003a).

Identify Budgetary Requirements

Once the desired goods/services are clearly defined, the procurement official must develop a cost estimation to link to the approved budget (Murti & Kurniawan, 2020). The cost estimation of the goods/services needs to be evaluated for reasonability by surveying the prices (Lanclos & Phillips, 2014; Maulidi, 2017; Peiris & Aruppala, 2021; Rendon & Rendon, 2016). The treasury legislation is in line with this process as it links all purchasing requirements to the budget (National Treasury SCM Guideline, 2004b; Policy to guide Uniformity in Procurement Reform Processes in Government, 2003a).

Research the Supplying Industry

Studies revealed that it is vital to survey the industry from which the desired goods/services are supplied (Maulidi, 2017; Murti & Kurniawan, 2020). Maulidi (2017) adds that the surveys help with keeping abreast of the most recent prices charged. Several authors are of the same view where their study revealed that market research ought to be used as an opportunity to investigate the industry suppliers' capabilities and business practices at large (Lanclos & Phillips, 2014; Rendon & Rendon, 2016). In line with the literature, the treasury legislation indicates the importance of analysing the supplying industry (National Treasury SCM Guideline, 2004b; Policy to guide Uniformity in Procurement Reform Processes in government, 2003a).

Acquisition Management

Prepare Bidding Documents and Advertise

The public institution ought to approach the market to advertise the bid to purchase goods/services (Rendon & Rendon, 2016). This can be done by sending a request for a proposal (Lanclos & Phillips, 2014). Furthermore, bids/requests for proposals ought to be advertised for at least 15–30 days on various platforms, such as the agency's electronic procurement portal, notices, and announcements (Lanclos & Phillips, 2014; Rendon & Rendon, 2016). The next step is to prepare and review bid documents to determine whether they clearly define how the supplier will deliver the projected goods/services (Maulidi, 2017; Rendon & Rendon, 2016; Weingärtner et al., 2021). The treasury legislation is in line with the literature, as it requires that the market be approached for all bids (National Treasury SCM Guideline, 2004b; Policy to guide Uniformity in Procurement Reform Processes in government, 2003a).

Review and Agree on Contract Content

Several studies revealed that it is ideal for a procurement officer to select and award the bid to the cheapest supplier (Maulidi, 2017; Weingärtner et al., 2021). The qualifying selected supplier and the procurement officer ought to review bidding documents and contract content, such as compliance requirements, completeness, costs, working schedule, reasonability, etc., and have a mutual agreement on the contract terms and conditions (Lanclos & Phillips, 2014; Maulidi, 2017; Peiris & Aruppala, 2021). Rendon and Rendon (2016) agree with the latter authors by adding that the review process helps with providing assurance on how the organisation's needs will be provided. In line with literature, the treasury legislation ensures that proper contract documents are negotiated and signed (National Treasury SCM Guideline, 2004b).

Monitor Procurement

Another important aspect of this process is to monitor and supervise the procurement of goods/services to ensure that it is not breached (Kamaliah et al., 2018; Maulidi, 2017; Wardani et al., 2021). One of the ways to monitor and supervise the procurement process is by implementing a code of conduct, by which all procurement personnel will abide (Wright, 2007). This code of conduct ought to be developed and clearly defined by the Chief Accounting Officer (Dewata et al., 2022; Mangala & Kumari, 2017; Rashid et al., 2022; Zager et al., 2016). As a result, transparency will be encouraged, thereby curbing any undesirable outcomes in the public procurement (Gallego et al., 2021; Sow et al., 2018). The National treasury monitoring process takes place to determine whether the proper procurement process is followed and whether planned goals are met by reviewing issues such as compliance with standards, policy, efficiency, contract breach, etc. (SCM, 2004a). This is in line with the literature.

In addition to developing a code of conduct, and to ensure effective supervision of the procurement process, a study conducted by Rustiarini et al. (2019) revealed that procurement personnel ought to be provided with training in order to reduce unwanted non-compliance to the procurement process, including fraud awareness training, anti-fraud training, ethics training, and training to overcome fraud, and which have been found to be important to prevent the risk of fraud or breach occurring in the procurement process (Handayani & Kawedar, 2021; Malle et al., 2022; Maulidi, 2017; Omar & Abu Bakar, 2012; Sow et al., 2018). All these trainings should be continuously revised through posters, group meetings, newsletters, or awareness on the internal website (Dzomira, 2015). Treasury legislation does provide sufficient controls to avoid abuse of the supply management system, such as disclosure of conflict of interest, not accepting gifts, etc. (National Treasury, 2003a,

2003b, 2003c). However, the only training provided is that which relates to the supply chain management process (National Treasury, 2003a, 2003b, 2003c). This fraud-related training aspect of supervision is not clearly addressed in the National Treasury, therefore, identified as a shortcoming.

Logistics Management

Monitor Supplier Performance

Research has revealed that it is important to monitor supplier performance to ensure that they deliver in compliance with the contract specifications (Lanclos & Phillips, 2014). In support of the latter, the supplier and procurement personnel ought to file all delivery documents for received goods/services (Maulidi, 2017). In this way, the procurement personnel will inspect and be able to measure and monitor items delivered and determine whether the supplier is still delivering in compliance with the agreed terms and conditions (Rendon & Rendon, 2016). As a result, should it be apparent that the supplier is not delivering in accordance with the contract, not meeting the provisions specified, or endangering the contract, then the contract ought to be terminated (Lanclos & Phillips, 2014). The treasury legislation is in line with the literature, as they review and monitor vendor performance to ensure compliance throughout the contract period, and where expectations are not met, they reconsider the arrangement (National Treasury SCM Guideline, 2004b; General Procurement Guidelines, n.d.).

Supplier performance can be monitored through the fraud hotline systems and policies (Dzomira, 2015). Many authors are of the same view, as their studies emphasise that is it important for the public sector to provide confidential and effective reporting platforms to the public for reporting any breach of the supply chain management system (Mangala & Kumari 2017; Maulidi, 2017; Othman et al., 2015; Peiris & Aruppala, 2021; Rashid et al., 2022; Wardani et al., 2021). To ensure effective use, procurement personnel ought to communicate the availability of these systems to employees and monitor them continuously (Bănărescu, 2015). Not only will these platforms assist in monitoring the performance of the supplier, but they will also assist in preventing fraud (Bierstaker et al., 2006; Sow et al., 2018). To further strengthen the effectiveness of these platforms, the public sector ought to invite internal auditors to assess these platforms on a continuous basis (Motubatse, 2014). Treasury legislation appears to be in line with the literature as it formally requires the procurement officers to establish mechanisms to receive and consider complaints regarding non-compliance and breaches of the supply chain management system (National Treasury, 2003a, 2003b, 2003c); National Treasury (2003a, 2003b, 2003c). Furthermore, treasury legislation requires public institutions to take reasonable steps to prevent abuse; investigate any allegations reported; take steps against the official who is guilty of abusing the procurement system; report the official to the National Treasury; and to report improper conduct to the South African Police Services (National Treasury, 2003a, 2003b, 2003c). The literature did not dwell further on the action steps that ought to be taken should an official or supplier be found not complying with the principles of the procurement of the public sector. Thus, the National Treasury seems to have sufficient action plans to deal with the employees involved.

Manage Supplier Payments

Before payment is made, all supporting documents and information must be obtained (Maulidi, 2017). Lanclos and Phillips (2014) add that supplier payments ought at least to be supported by the following: name of contractor and invoice date; contract number; description, price, and quantity of goods/services delivered; shipping and payment terms; other substantiating documentation required by the contract; and where and to whom the payment is to be sent. This supporting information ought to be checked as part of the logistics management and for use in invoicing and payment (Weingärtner et al., 2021). As a result, this process will ensure that the acquired goods/services were within the prescribed budget (Maulidi, 2017). After payment has been completed, and all administrative issues have been attended to, the government can close out the contract by not allowing any further work or payment on the contract (Lanclos & Phillips, 2014; Maulidi, 2017; Rendon & Rendon, 2016). In line with the literature, the treasury legislation obtains supporting documents before payment, but there is no clarification on whether the contract is close-out. Therefore, the latter is identified as a shortcoming.

The Emergency Procurement Process and Controls

Establish an Emergency Crisis Management team

Guang and Yi (2012) argue that public institutions ought to establish an emergency crisis management team, which should be responsible for responding to a crisis procurement quickly and effectively. An emergency crisis management team reduces induced emergency procurement and corruption (Kinuthia et al., 2018). Several authors argue that all emergency procurement needs ought to be supported with valid reasons and be approved accordingly (Dzomira, 2015; Schultz & Søreide, 2008). Although it may be acceptable to document reasons for emergency purchases, Schultz and Søreide (2008) believe that the fraud risk can be minimised by reducing the need for urgent purchases and enforcing procurement procedures. The emergency crisis management team must perform checks and balances with the intent to prevent abuse through emergency procurement (Sian & Smyth, 2022). In addition, checks and the approval process ought to be improved by strengthening the supervision, audit, and examination of government procurement (Guang & Yi, 2012). Additionally, the emergency crisis management team should continuously review and improve disaster management strategies (Buor, 2019). Treasury legislation is in line with the literature as it requires reasons and approval at the prescribed level for all emergency procurement (National Treasury SCM, 2004a; Practice Note 6: Procurement of goods/services by means other than through the invitation of competitive bids, 2008). However, the treasury legislation is silent on the formal formation of a crisis management team, which will be responsible for managing all emergency procurement as described above, therefore, identified as a shortcoming.

Engage with Approved Suppliers and Supervise the Process

Schultz and Søreide (2008) are of the view that emergency procurement ought to be engaged with suppliers on which the government already has a history. Furthermore, only standard goods/services should be acquired (Schultz & Søreide, 2008). This too should be supervised by the emergency crisis management team, who will ensure that the purchase is done effectively (Guang & Yi, 2012). Treasury legislation is in line with literature as they use a database of prospective suppliers for emergency procurement (National Treasury SCM, 2004a).

Overall, from the ideal public procurement process, the treasury legislation seems to contain sufficient controls to prevent fraud in the procurement process. However, the shortcomings identified above and summarised below, if implemented, can further improve the current prevention controls, thereby improving the fraud prevention status of the procurement process in South Africa. These are: The treasury legislation does not provide fraud-related training to supervisors of the procurement process; no close-out report is prepared; and does not formally address whether there should be a crisis management team for emergency procurement.

Enhancements Identified

During the literature search of an ideal procurement process, and weaknesses on the public sector procurement process, results also revealed certain controls and measures that do not appear in the Treasury legislation and are deemed to be of importance in reducing fraud in the procurement process of the public sector. This section will discuss these enhancements in the section below.

E-procurement

Electronic System to Acquire Goods/Services According to Set Rules

E-procurement is a designed electronic system (with specified rules) that can be used to acquire goods/services by electronic means (Azmi & Rahman, 2015; Basheka et al., 2012; Neupane et al., 2014a). At the demand management phase, the public's buying of goods/services decisions can be registered in this system (Gallego et al., 2021). Examples of types of e-procurement systems are e-informing, e-sourcing, e-tendering, e-ordering, e-contract management, etc. (Neupane et al., 2012b). The system is transparent on the procurement cycle and related activities, such as the selection of suppliers, ordering process applied, receiving of goods, payment, contracts, etc., and can be used in all phases of the procurement process (Azmi & Rahman, 2015; Peiris & Aruppala, 2021; Zahra et al., 2021). The system can keep record of all supplier contracts and the related supporting documentation (Weingärtner et al., 2021).

Benefits of Using the e-Procurement System

The e-procurement system avoids unnecessary projects or tender documents being registered, as all acquisition decisions are logged and monitored (Gallego et al., 2021; Neupane et al., 2012a, 2012b; Weingärtner et al., 2021). This is possible as the system can trace users who log and record information, thus making it easy to review and trace for the purposes of accountability (Gallego et al., 2021; Neupane et al., 2012a, 2012b). The tender process is automated while allowing an easy bidding process, increasing competition, logging real-time information, etc. (Neupane et al., 2012a, 2012b). Furthermore, the transparency level of the system allows it to keep an audit trail, and keep all information centralised, thereby making it possible for the system to be auditable (Moon, 2005; Neupane et al., 2012a, 2012b).

E-procurement avoids human interference, while ensuring effectiveness and efficiency (Weingärtner et al., 2021). As a result, personal preferences for purchasing decisions are reduced, while competition among suppliers and bidders is enhanced (Neupane et al., 2014a, 2014b; Wicaksono et al., 2017). This means that a public official and a vendor will not be able to collude while using an e-procurement system (Wicaksono et al., 2017). The system accepts or rejects a supplier based on set rules (Azmi & Rahman, 2015). It is proven to allow better management of awarding government contracts without any manipulation (Azmi & Rahman, 2015).

Several authors found that the e-procurement system has a positive relationship with fraud prevention in public sector procurement (Azmi & Rahman, 2015; Neupane et al., 2014a, 2014b; Wardani et al., 2021). Corroborating this, Gallego et al. (2021) found that the system can be used to identify concerning transactions, which ultimately prevent corruption and inefficiency within the procurement process. Consequently, the system can reduce fraud opportunities in the public sector procurement process (Neupane et al., 2014a, 2014b).

Corporate Governance

The National Treasury is silent on the application of corporate governance at the management level as a measure to prevent fraud within the procurement process. Effectiveness in the procurement process can be experienced if the management of the public sector enforces the following principles: transparency, accountability, responsibility, independence, fairness, and equality (Dewata et al., 2022). Other authors added that public officials ought to be encouraged to practice and improve these principles strongly to achieve an effective procurement process (Hamdani & Albar, 2016; Widilestariningtyas & Karo, 2016). This was further substantiated by other authors, who found that good corporate governance is capable to fight fraud and is considered as a prevention tool (Gunawan, 2019:100; Kamaliah et al., 2018). Lastly, a study conducted by Bierstaker et al. (2006) found that 94% of organisations that adopt corporate governance are operationally effective. Therefore, for the above benefits, it is important to improve corporate governance in the public sector (Rashid et al., 2022).

Data Analytics

Data Analytics Is a Testing and Analytical System

Data analytics is used to test data and maintain its quality (Alencar, 2021; Eilifsen et al., 2020). The system is most useful when there is information recorded in large databases (Baldomir et al., 2018). There are various types of data analytics programs that can be adopted by the Government, such as payable software, statistical software, and data visualisation (Bănărescu, 2015). There are also text mining and cluster analysis data analytics tools that can be used to improve the visibility of procurement patterns (Tan & Lee, 2015). A study conducted by Tan and Lee (2015) revealed that the government ought to consider the approach of developing data analytics, as it prevents and detects fraud in the procurement process. This can be implemented at the acquisition management and logistics management phases to prevent fraud (Elgendy & Elragal, 2014). By so doing, they will be able to predict the probability of corruption in the procurement process and further find suitable controls (Põlluste, 2019).

Benefits of Data Analytics

By adopting any of the data analytics models, the government will be able to make efficient decisions in terms of acquiring goods/services at a cost-effective price (Tan & Lee, 2015). It is, however, important to note that data analytics models can be efficiently used on the existing, quality, and integral procurement data (Ramamoorti & Curtis, 2003). Also, data analytics can identify hidden insights and suspicious behaviour within the procurement process (Alencar, 2021; Elgendy & Elragal, 2014). This is why some authors argue that the system can be used as an early warning system to detect and prevent unwanted cases of fraud in the procurement system (Modrušan et al., 2021). As a result, fraud is prevented before it occurs (Lanclos & Phillips, 2014).

Contract Modifications

The National Treasury supply chain management legislation does not explicitly provide clear guidance for the contract modifications process. Changes of contract terms of Government procurement usually occur during the production/service delivery phase (at logistics management—monitoring performance) (Chan et al., 2010). Unfortunately, contract modifications are argued to result in delays and increase the risk of fraud due to manipulation (Brodec & Janeček, 2015; Kaliba et al., 2009). Fazekas et al. (2013) are also of the same view, who in their study, found that one of the risks of corruption was due to contracts that were modified.

To reduce or prevent the risk of fraud in the procurement process, bidders ought to incorporate the likelihood of modifications during the scope definition, mainly for that which may impact the contract cost (De Silva et al., 2017). Furthermore, Government ought to manage and at least provide the following limitations to reduce any unwanted outcomes during contract modifications: allow modifications for strictly necessary changes, a given modification ought not to be on any condition that affects the awarding procedure, price modifications should not be allowed, and the contract must still meet the agreed contractual requirements (García-Andrade, 2016; Murti & Kurniawan, 2020:18; Rendon & Rendon, 2016; Weingärtner et al., 2021). When contract modifications are properly managed, contracts are most likely to be fulfilled within the budget, and the contractor deprived an opportunity to fraudulently increase prices (De Silva et al., 2017).

Audit Function

To Make Use of Audit Function to Prevent Fraud

There are various types of audits which Government can adopt to prevent fraud and to get assurance that the procurement of goods/services aligns with the principles of integrity, truthfulness, honesty, transparency, fairly, and accountability (Arifin & Hartadi, 2020). Government can consider implementing a probity audit, which is a real-time audit on the public sector procurement of goods/services to defeat fraudulent issues (Arifin & Hartadi, 2020; McCue et al., 2015). The probity audit can be substantiated with a public sector procurement audit, which involves the gathering and evaluation of procurement information to determine whether the procurement process principles are complied with or not (Etse & Asenso-Boakye, 2014). This type of audit ensures accountability, transparency, and prevents any improper conduct, such as fraud that may arise within the procurement process (Etse & Asenso-Boakye, 2014).

Another type of audit is the internal audit function (Widilestariningtyas & Karo, 2016). Internal audit generally involves obtaining assurance on operations of an organisation (Etse & Asenso-Boakye, 2014). A study conducted by Widilestariningtyas and Karo (2016) and Othman et al. (2015) found that internal auditors can prevent fraud in any operational process, as they are involved on a day-to-day business operation. However, for internal auditors to be efficient within the procurement process, there needs to be a fraud red flag in the process that triggers the audit (Rustiarini et al., 2019). The internal auditor can bring the following value to add within the procurement process: ascertaining whether there are weaknesses in the procurement controls, investigating the history of past fraud events, identifying any illegal procurement transactions processed, analysing complaints received, etc., and providing recommendation for the procurement process to be effective (Baltos et al., 2018; Giriūnas & Mackevičius, 2014; Zager et al., 2016). Therefore, it is imperative that internal auditors are involved as part of the tender process from the beginning to the end, to allow them, at minimum, to evaluate whether the tender has been awarded fairly without discrimination, favour, or manipulation (Mantzaris, 2014). Not only does internal audit prevent fraud but can also recommend ways in which the procurement process can be improved (Baltos et al., 2018; Omar & Abu Bakar, 2012). Therefore, internal audit is necessary and helps Government to prevent fraud in the procurement process (Wicaksono et al., 2017). The treasury legislation do not formally enforce the internal or any audit function. Though the government has internal audit functions across various divisions, it is therefore advised that the function is formally added to Treasury legislation.

On the other hand, there is an external audit, which plays an important part in preventing fraud in the public sector procurement process (Mangala & Kumari, 2017). External audit is generally known to focus on the financial aspects of an organisation (Etse & Asenso-Boakye, 2014). External audit has the capability to determine methods for preventing fraud when auditing the public sector procurement (Isroilov et al., 2020). One of the ways to prevent fraud is by closing loopholes of the procurement function through recommendations (Gichio, 2014). However, to ensure that an external audit is effective, Government should ensure auditability of procurement information, by having competent staff, processes, ensure transparency, and accountability (Rendon & Rendon, 2016). Yearly external audits on procurement fraud have been proven to reduce the likelihood of fraud occurring (Giriūnas & Mackevičius, 2014).

Lastly, all the above-mentioned types of audits can work efficiently and effectively when they are continuously conducted (Baltos et al., 2018). Continuous audit is in any case, regarded as a fraud procedure to prevent fraud (Bierstaker et al., 2006; Isroilov et al., 2020). Of course, audits can be efficient and effective in preventing fraud in public sector institution procurement, but Gallego et al. (2021) found that conducting audits can be both expensive and time-consuming for an organisation. Therefore, the Government ought to take the above into account when deciding on audit-related measures to further improve the fight against fraud in the public sector.

Conclusion

Prevention of fraud in the public procurement process has become one of the major discussions around the world. This is because the government plans large amounts of public procurement, which attracts fraudsters. There are numerous research studies that focus on fraud prevention in the public procurement process. There is however, limited research done on how the South African government procurement process can be improved following the persisting fraud incidents. For this reason, the researcher believes that if the government can identify weaknesses in the procurement process, it can easily place sufficient control measures to prevent fraud. As a result, goods/services will be procured in a fair, equitable, transparent, competitive, and cost-effective manner. The purpose of this study was to address fraud prevention controls that are available for implementation by the public sector in fighting fraud in the procurement process. The chapter's research objectives were to determine the ideal procurement process, identify weaknesses in the current procurement process compared to recognised practices, and identify the enhancements that can be implemented to continuously fight fraud in the South African government procurement process. The study adopted a thematic content analysis of literature to achieve the research questions which are: (1) what is the ideal public procurement process? (2) what are the weaknesses in the South African public procurement process? and (3) what are the enhancements that can be implemented to fight fraud in the South African government procurement process?

Findings showed that the currently implemented fraud prevention controls by the South African treasury legislation in the procurement process seem to be sufficiently rolled out but has shortcomings. The following shortcomings were identified: The treasury legislation does not provide fraud-related training to supervisors of the procurement process; no close-out report is prepared; and does not formally address whether there should be a crisis management team for emergency procurement. Even though Treasury legislation have sufficient controls, they are not preventing fraud in its entirety. Therefore, the chapter further revealed enhancements that can be implemented over and above the current prevention controls of the treasury legislation, which are deemed to be of importance to prevent fraud in the procurement process. The identified enhancements are as follows: e-procurement, corporate governance, data analytics, contract modifications, and audit function. These enhancements ought to be able to prevent fraud in the public sector procurement should they be implemented per the literature. It is then important to note that a single prevention control will not prevent fraud, and therefore, other controls ought to continuously be researched and adopted into the public institution's culture to prevent fraud. As a result, these collective efforts can prevent fraud in the public sector procurement process. This study is significant to policymakers of the procurement process for consideration during the review and update of the procurement-related policies. They should take cognisant of the ideal procurement process, use it to develop necessary improved controls that address the weakness/shortcomings identified above, and consider the enhancements continuously. Such consideration will further positively respond to the United Nations Sustainable Development Goals number 8 (Decent work and economic growth) and 12 (Responsible consumption and production).

Future Studies

From the research done, it was noted that most of the research has been done on the controls guiding the procurement process of the public sector or government. However, there is limited research done on corporate governance and how it can be used effectively to prevent fraud in the public sector procurement process. Consequently, researchers may consider conducting surveys on how corporate governance can be used in the public sector to prevent fraud in the procurement process.

Appendix 1. A Comparison between Literature and the National Treasury Legislation Procurement Process, and the Identification of Weaknesses

No	Theme	Literature ideal public procurement process	National Treasury Legislation procurement process
1	1.1 **Demand management**	***1. Need analysis and product specification*** • Selecting contract type, contract awarding strategy, and product/service specification needed (Lanclos & Phillips, 2014; Murti & Kurniawan, 2020; Rendon & Rendon, 2016). (a) Inventory observation and inspection to determine the required inventory (Dzomira, 2015; Malle et al., 2022). ***2. Identify budget requirements*** • Developing preliminary budgets and cost estimates (Lanclos & Phillips, 2014; Maulidi, 2017; Murti & Kurniawan, 2020; Peiris & Aruppala, 2021; Rendon & Rendon, 2016). ***3. Research the supplying industry*** • Conducting market research and capabilities for potential suppliers (Lanclos & Phillips, 2014; Murti & Kurniawan, 2020; Rendon & Rendon, 2016) (a) The government should conduct surveys to keep abreast of suppliers, products, and prices for goods/services (Maulidi, 2017)	1. A needs assessment to ensure that goods/services are acquired, and specifications are precisely determined (SCM, 2004a): (a) Inventory levels are set and determination of required stock is done (SCM, 2004a, Policy to guide Uniformity in Procurement Reform Processes in government, 2003a) 2. Requirements are linked to the budget (SCM, 2004a; Policy to guide Uniformity in Procurement Reform Processes in government, 2003a) 3. The supplying industry must be analysed and assessed (SCM, 2004a; Policy to guide Uniformity in Procurement Reform Processes in government, 2003a).

No	Theme	Literature ideal public procurement process	National Treasury Legislation procurement process
2	**2.1 Acquisition management**	***1. Prepare biding documents, advertise*** • Advertise bids to the public and obtain quotations (Maulidi, 2017; Lanclos & Phillips, 2014; Rendon & Rendon, 2016; Weingärtner et al., 2021). ***2. Review and agree on contract content*** • Review terms of reference, compliance, completeness, costs, working schedules, technical requirements, terms and conditions, reasonability, and content of the agreements (Lanclos & Phillips, 2014; Maulidi, 2017; Peiris & Aruppala, 2021; Rendon & Rendon, 2016; Weingärtner et al., 2021). ***3. Monitor procurement*** • The procurement of goods/services should be monitored and supervised by authorities (Wardani et al., 2021) (a) Code of conduct, fraud plan, awareness, and training (Dewata et al., 2022; Dzomira, 2015; Gallego et al., 2021; Handayani & Kawedar, 2021; Kamaliah et al., 2018; Malle et al., 2022; Mangala and Kumari 2017; Maulidi, 2017; Omar & Abu Bakar, 2012; Rashid et al., 2022; Rustiarini et al., 2019; Sow et al., 2018; Wright, 2007; Zager et al., 2016).	1. To decide on the way the market will be approached (advertising) (SCM, 2004a; Policy to guide Uniformity in Procurement Reform Processes in government, 2003a). Different approval levels for specified thresholds (Practice Note SCM, 2003b). 2. Review contract documents for signing (SCM, 2004a) • Monitoring process takes place to determine whether the proper procurement process is followed against planned goals, standards, compliance, policy, costs, etc. (SCM, 2004a). (a) Procurement personnel encouraged to comply with ethical standards, avoiding abuse of the supply chain management system; SCM training offered to procurement personnel; (Practice Note SCM, 2003b; Treasury Regulation, 2005a, 2005b; General Procurement Guidelines, n.d.). The offering of fraud-related training is not clearly addressed in the National Treasury Legislation, and, therefore, will be discussed as a shortcoming.

No	Theme	Literature ideal public procurement process	National Treasury Legislation procurement process
3	**3.1. Logistics management**	*1. **Monitor supplier performance*** • Monitor and measure the contractor performance to ensure that it is delivered in compliance to the contract (Lanclos & Phillips, 2014; Maulidi, 2017; Rendon & Rendon, 2016). (a) Develop fraud hotline systems and policies (Bănărescu, 2015; Bierstaker et al., 2006; Dzomira, 2015; Mangala & Kumari 2017; Maulidi, 2017; Motubatse, 2014; Othman et al., 2015; Peiris & Aruppala, 2021; Rashid et al., 2022; Sow et al., 2018; Wardani et al., 2021; Wright, 2007). *2. **Manage supplier payments*** • Manage supplier payments, through obtaining supporting information, and close out the supplier (Lanclos & Phillips, 2014; Maulidi, 2017; Rendon & Rendon, 2016; Weingärtner et al., 2021).	(1) The review of vendor performance is done against the delivery periods, quality, quantity, challenges, compliance, goals, efficiency, contract breach, etc. (SCM, 2004a; Policy to guide Uniformity in Procurement Reform Processes in government, 2003a). – Monitor the supplier against agreed terms and reconsider for cession if not complying (General Procurement Guidelines, n.d.). (a) Establish a mechanism to receive and consider complaints regarding non-compliance in the SCM National Treasury (Practice Note SCM, 2003b) • Payment is done after supporting documentation is provided, and according to contract spec (SCM, 2004a). • However, it is not clear whether the close out is done, therefore, will be discussed as a shortcoming.

1	The procurement and approval process of emergency procurement	***(1) Establish an emergency crisis management team*** • Establishment of the emergency leadership group responsible for emergency procurement, and to reduce the need for emergency purchases (Buor, 2019; Dzomira, 2015; Guang & Yi, 2012; Kinuthia et al., 2018; Schultz & Søreide, 2008; Sian & Smyth, 2022). ***(2) Engage with approved suppliers and supervise the process*** • Emergency procurement should be engaged with approved suppliers in the system (Guang & Yi, 2012; Schultz & Søreide, 2008).	Document reasons for the emergency procurement, approved by the Accounting Officer (for transactions less than R1 million) and reported by the Accounting Officer to the Auditor General within 10 working days for transactions above R1 million (National Treasury Practice Note 8, 2007; Practice Note 6: Procurement of goods/services by means other than through the invitation of competitive bids, 2008). Some aspects (leadership group) not addressed in the National Treasury and will be discussed under shortcoming • Emergency procurement is done by use of database of prospective suppliers or in any manner at the best interest of the government (SCM, 2004a).

References

ACFE. (2022). *Occupational fraud 2022: A report to the nations*. [Online]. Accessed August 03, 2020, from 2022+Report+to+the+Nations.pdf (amazonaws.com)

Alencar, E. C. N. (2021). *Assessing the potential for detecting fraud in the Brazilian public procurement using Latent Class Analysis* (pp. 1–69). University of California, Irvine.

Arcangeli, J. (2020). *Transnet warns public of procurement scam*. [Online]. Accessed June 23, 2022, from https://www.sanews.gov.za/south-africa/transnet-warns-public-procurement-scam

Arifin, J., & Hartadi, T. (2020). The implementation of probity audit to prevent fraud in public procurement of goods and services for government agencies. *Jurnal Akuntansi dan Auditing Indonesia*, 11–21.

Auditor General South Africa. (2021). *Consolidated general report on national and provincial audit outcomes*. [Online]. Accessed August 03, 2022, from *Consolidated PFMA General Report 2020-21 - FINAL 8 December.pdf (agsa.co.za)

Azmi, K. S. A., & Rahman, A. A. L. A. (2015, June). E-Procurement: A tool to mitigate public procurement fraud in Malaysia? In *European conference on digital government* (p. 361). Academic Conferences International Limited.

Baldomir, R. A., Van Erven, G. C., & Ralha, C. G. (2018, October). Brazilian government procurements: An approach to find fraud traces in companies relationships. In *Anais do XV Encontro Nacional de Inteligência Artificial e Computacional* (pp. 752–762). SBC.

Baltos, G., Doni, L., & Balodis, J. (2018). The international public procurement evolution: New strategic challenges met in collaboration with internal audit advisory services. *Academic Journal of Interdisciplinary Studies, 7*, 193–205.

Bănărescu, A. (2015). Detecting and preventing fraud with data analytics. *Procedia Economics and Finance, 32*, 1827–1836.

Basheka, B. C., Oluka, P. N., & Mugurusi, G. (2012). Adopting new approaches for public procurement efficiency: Critical success factors (CSFs) for the implementation of e-procurement in Uganda's public sector. *International Journal of Procurement Management, 5*(6), 712–732.

Bierstaker, J. L., Brody, R. G., & Pacini, C. (2006). Accountants' perceptions regarding fraud detection and prevention methods. *Managerial Auditing Journal, 21*(5), 520–535.

Brodec, J., & Janeček, V. (2015). How does the substantial modification of a public contract affect its legal regime? *Thomson Reuters (Professional) UK Limited and Contributors, 24*(3), 90–105.

Broome, J. (1999). Normative requirements. *Ratio, 12*(4), 398–419.

Buor, J. K. (2019). Appraising the interactions between public-sector procurement policy and disaster preparedness. *International Journal of Disaster Risk Reduction, 36*, 101–120.

Cape Business News. (2019). *South Africa: Fraud considered more serious than murder heavier punishment imposed.* [Online]. Accessed September 20, 2022, from South Africa: fraud considered more serious than murder Heavier punishment imposed - Cape Business News (cbn.co.za).

Chan, D. W., Lam, P. T., Chan, A. P., & Wong, J. M. (2010). Achieving better performance through target cost contracts: The tale of an underground railway station modification project. *Facilities, 28*(5/6), 261–277.

Clarke, V., & Braun, V. (2017). Thematic analysis. *The Journal of Positive Psychology, 12*(3), 297–298.

Cressey, D. R. (1950). The criminal violation of financial trust. *American Sociological Review 15*(6), 738–743.

De Silva, D. G., Dunne, T., Kosmopoulou, G., & Lamarche, C. (2017). Contract modification and bidding in highway procurement auctions. *Mimeo, 2017*, 1–43.

Department of Home Affairs. (2022). *Speech by Minister of Home Affairs, Dr Aaron Motsoaledi, (MP), on the occasion of the* 2022/23 *Department of Home Affairs Budget Vote*. [Online]. Accessed September 20, 2022, from Department of Home Affairs - Speech by Minister of Home Affairs, Dr Aaron Motsoaledi, (MP), on the occasion of the 2022/23 Department of Home Affairs Budget Vote (dha.gov.za)

Dewata, E., Farah, E. H., Jauhari, H., & Sari, Y. (2022). Good governance and internal control on the prevention of fraud in the procurement of goods and Services for government agencies. In *5th FIRST T3 2021 international conference (FIRST-T3 2021)* (pp. 150–154).

Dorminey, J., Fleming, A. S., Kranacher, M. J., & Riley, R. A., Jr. (2012). The evolution of fraud theory. *Issues in Accounting Education, 27*(2), 555–579.

Dzomira, S. (2015). Fraud prevention and detection. *Prevention, 6*(14), 37–42.

Eilifsen, A., Kinserdal, F., Messier, W. F., Jr., & McKee, T. E. (2020). An exploratory study into the use of audit data analytics on audit engagements. *Accounting Horizons, 34*(4), 75–103.

Elgendy, N., & Elragal, A. (2014). Big data analytics: A literature review paper. In *Advances in data mining. Applications and theoretical aspects: 14th industrial conference, ICDM 2014, St. Petersburg, Russia, July 16–20, 2014. Proceedings 14* (pp. 214–227). Springer.

Etse, D., & Asenso-Boakye, M. (2014). Public procurement audit process in practice a case study of the public procurement Authority Office in Kumasi and the Procurement Unit of the Kumasi Polytechnic. *International Journal of Economics, Commerce and Management, 2*(2), 1–12.

Fazekas, M., Chvalkovska, J., Skuhrovec, J., Tóth, I. J., & King, L. P. (2013). Are EU funds a corruption risk? The impact of EU funds on grand corruption in Central and Eastern Europe. In *The anticorruption frontline. The ANTICORRP project* (Vol. 2, pp. 68–89). Barbara Budrich.

Gallego, J., Rivero, G., & Martínez, J. (2021). Preventing rather than punishing: An early warning model of malfeasance in public procurement. *International Journal of Forecasting, 37*(1), 360–377.

García-Andrade, X. C. (2016). Modification of public contracts and its regulatory models. *Proceedings Paper, 46*, 1000–1017.

Gichio, D. (2014). Public procurement in Kenya. *Adili, 145*, 1–11.

Giriūnas, L., & Mackevičius, J. (2014). Evaluation of frauds in public sector. *Entrepreneurship and Sustainability Issues, 1*(3), 143–150.

Guang, Y., & Yi, W. (2012, August). The improvement of governmental emergency procurement on resolving public crisis. In *2012 International Conference on Public Management (ICPM-2012)* (pp. 423–428). Atlantis Press.

Gunawan, I. (2019). Effective corporate governance to prevent fraud in public sector in Indonesia. *Asia Pacific Fraud Journal, 4*(1), 96–100.

Hamdani, R., & Albar, A. R. (2016). Internal controls in fraud prevention effort: A case study. *Jurnal Akuntansi dan Auditing Indonesia, 20*(2), 127.

Handayani, S., & Kawedar, W. (2021). Could the minimization of opportunity prevent fraud? An empirical study in the auditors' perspective. *Accounting, 7*(5), 1157–1166.

Isroilov, B. I., Abduganiyev, U. K., & Ibragimov, B. B. (2020, May). Financial control of public procurement to prevent corruption in the development of digital economy. In *2nd international scientific and practical conference "modern management trends and the digital economy: From regional development to global economic growth" (MTDE 2020)* (pp. 546–552). Atlantis Press.

Kaliba, C., Muya, M., & Mumba, K. (2009). Cost escalation and schedule delays in road construction projects in Zambia. *International Journal of Project Management, 27*(5), 522–531.

Kamaliah, K., Marjuni, N. S., Mohamed, N., Mohd-Sanusi, Z., & Anugerah, R. (2018). Effectiveness of monitoring mechanisms and mitigation of fraud incidents in the public sector. *Administratie Si Management Public, 30*, 82–95.

Kinuthia, E. K., Odundo, P. A., & Nyagah, G. (2018). Aspects of procurement reforms that influence expenditure management in Public Secondary Schools in Kenya: A focus on emergency procurement. *International Journal of Business and Management, 13*(6), 129–143.

Lanclos, J., & Phillips, T. (2014). *Data analytics in procurement fraud prevention*, pp. 1–64.

Macailao, M. C. (2020). Raising the red flags: The concept and indicators of occupational fraud. *Journal of Critical Reviews, 7*(11), 26–29.

Malle, G. G., Mwonge, L. A., & Naho, A. (2022). Effectiveness of fraud prevention and detection methods in the public sector in Tanzania. *Journal of Accounting and Taxation, 14*(1), 30–36.

Mangala, D., & Kumari, P. (2017). Auditors' perceptions of the effectiveness of fraud prevention and detection methods. *Indian Journal of Corporate Governance, 10*(2), 118–142.

Mantzaris, E. A. (2014). Public procurement, tendering and corruption: Realities, challenges and tangible solutions. *African Journal of Public Affairs, 7*(2), 67–79.

Matthew, K., Patrick, K., & Denise, K. (2013). The effects of fraudulent procurement practices on public procurement performance. *International Journal of Business and Behavioural Sciences, 3*(1), 17–27.

Maulidi, A. (2017). The investigation and elimination of public procurement fraud in government sectors (A case study in Indonesia's procurement system: Cases from 2006 to 2012). *International Journal of Economics and Financial Issues, 7*(2), 145–154.

McCue, C. P., Prier, E., & Swanson, D. (2015). Five dilemmas in public procurement. *Journal of Public Procurement, 15*(2), 177–207.

Modrušan, N., Rabuzin, K., & Mršic, L. (2021). Review of public procurement fraud detection techniques powered by emerging technologies. *International Journal of Advanced Computer Science and Applications, 12*(2), 1–9.

Moon, M. J. (2005). E-procurement management in state governments: Diffusion of e-procurement practices and its determinants. *Journal of Public Procurement, 5*(1), 54–72.

Motubatse, K. N. (2014). Perceived role of internal auditing in fraud prevention and detection in South African public sector national departments. *African Journal of Public Affairs, 7*(3), 61–71.

Murti, A., & Kurniawan, T. (2020, August). Implementation and impact of internal control in preventing fraud in the public sector. In *Proceedings of the 3rd International Conference on Administrative Science, Policy, and Governance Studies, ICAS-PGS* 2019, *October 30–31*. Universitas Indonesia.

National Treasury. (2000). *Preferential procurement policy framework act (PPPFA)*. [Online]. Accessed June 12, 2024, from PPPFA.pdf (treasury.gov.za)

National Treasury. (2001). *Preferential procurement regulations*. [Online]. Accessed June 12, 2024, from gazette_22549.pdf (treasury.gov.za)

National Treasury. (2003a). *Policy to guide uniformity in procurement reform process in government*. [Online]. Accessed June 14, 2024, from Policy to Guide Uniformity in Procurement Reform Processes in Government.pdf (treasury.gov.za)

National Treasury. (2003b). *Practice note SCM 4 of 2003: Code of conduct for supply chain management practitioners*. [Online]. Accessed June 14, 2024, from SCM-PracNote 03 4.pdf (treasury.gov.za)

National Treasury. (2003c). *Regulations in terms of the public finance management act, 1999: Framework for supply chain management*. [Online]. Accessed August 03, 2022, from Supply Chain Management Framework Gazette 25767 dated 0512… (treasury.gov.za)

National Treasury. (2004a). *Practice note SCM 5 of 2004: Training of SCM Officials*. [Online]. Accessed June 24, 2024, from SCM-PracNote 04 5.pdf (treasury.gov.za)

National Treasury. (2004b). *Supply chain management—A guide for accounting officer/authorities*. [Online]. Accessed June 27, 2022, from Microsoft Word - SCM Jan900-Guidelines.doc (treasury.gov.za)

National Treasury. (2005a). *Schedule Treasury Regulations for departments, trading entities, constitutional institutions and public entities issued in terms of the Public Finance Management Act of 1999*. [Online]. Accessed August 03, 2022, from gazette_27388.pdf (treasury.gov.za)

National Treasury. (2005b). *Treasury Regulation 2005 Gazette No. 27388 dated 15 March 2005*. [Online]. Accessed June 12, 2024, from gazette_27388.pdf (treasury.gov.za)

National Treasury. (2011). *National Treasury instruction note on enhancing compliance monitoring and improving transparency and accountability in supply chain management*. [Online]. Accessed June 14, 2024, from 20110531 Instruction Note on Enhancing Compliance Monitoring SCM.pdf (treasury.gov.za)

National Treasury. (2015a). *Guideline on fruitless and wasteful expenditure*. [Online]. Accessed June 10, 2024, from Guideline on Fruitless and Wasteful Expenditure 27 May 2014.pdf (treasury.gov.za)

National Treasury. (2015b). *Updated guideline on irregular expenditure*. [Online]. Accessed June 12, 2024, from Updated Guideline on Irregular Expenditure.pdf (treasury.gov.za)

National Treasury. (2015c). *Guideline on unauthorised expenditure*. [Online]. Accessed June 10, 2024, from Guideline on Unauthorised Expenditure 27 May 2014.pdf (treasury.gov.za)

National Treasury. (n.d.). *General procurement guidelines*. [Online]. Accessed June 12, 2024, from General Procurement Guidelines.pdf (treasury.gov.za)

National Treasury Practice Note 8. (2007). *Supply chain management: Threshold values for the procurement of goods, works and services by means of petty cash, verbal/written price quotation or competitive bids*. [Online]. Accessed May 02, 2022, from Reference: (treasury.gov.za)

Neupane, A., Soar, J., & Vaidya, K. (2012a). Evaluating the anti-corruption capabilities of public e-procurement in a developing country. *The Electronic Journal of Information Systems in Developing Countries, 55*(1), 1–17.

Neupane, A., Soar, J., Vaidya, K., & Yong, J. (2012b, January). Role of public e-procurement technology to reduce corruption in government procurement. In *Proceedings of the 5th international public procurement conference (IPPC5)*. University of Southern Queensland.

Neupane, A., Soar, J., & Vaidya, K. (2014a). An empirical evaluation of the potential of public e-procurement to reduce corruption. *Australasian Journal of Information Systems, 18*(2), 21–44.

Neupane, A., Soar, J., Vaidya, K., & Yong, J. (2014b). Willingness to adopt e-procurement to reduce corruption: Results of the PLS path modelling. *Transforming Government: People, Process and Policy, 8*(4), 500–520.

Nurmandi, A., & Kim, S. (2015). Making e-procurement work in a decentralized procurement system: A comparison of three Indonesian cities. *International Journal of Public Sector Management, 28*(3), 198–220.

Omar, N., & Abu Bakar, K. M. (2012). Fraud prevention mechanisms of Malaysian government-linked companies: An assessment of existence and effectiveness. *Journal of Modern Accounting and Auditing, 8*(1), 15–31.

Organisation for Economic Co-operation and Development (OECD). Public procurement. [Online]. Accessed August 19, 2022, from Public procurement - OECD.

Othman, R., Aris, N. A., Mardziyah, A., Zainan, N., & Amin, N. M. (2015). Fraud detection and prevention methods in the Malaysian public sector: Accountants' and internal auditors' perceptions. *Procedia Economics and Finance, 28*, 59–67.

Passas, N. (2007). *Corruption in the procurement process/outsourcing government functions: Issues, case studies, implications. Report to Institute for Fraud Prevention*. Northeastern University.

Peiris, G. K. H., & Aruppala, W. D. N. (2021). A study on fraud prevention and detection methods in Sri Lanka. *Kelaniya Journal of Management, 10*(2), 37–56.

Põlluste, M. K. (2019). Detecting corruption in public procurement through open data analysis. *D Space at Tartu University Library*, 1–81.

Public Service Commission (PSC). (2022). *Annual performance plan for the 2021/2022 financial year*. [Online]. Accessed September 15, 2022, from *Final_2021-22_APP_dated_9_March_2021.pdf (pmg.org.za)

PWC. (2022). *PWC's global economic crime and fraud survey 2022*. [Online]. Accessed August 19, 2022, from Protecting the perimeter: The rise of external fraud (PwC's Global Economic Crime and Fraud Survey 2022)

Ramamoorti, S., & Curtis, S. (2003). Procurement fraud & data analytics. *Journal of Government Financial Management, 52*(4), 1–8.

Rashid, M. A., Al-Mamun, A., Roudaki, H., & Yasser, Q. R. (2022). An overview of corporate fraud and its prevention approach. *Australasian Accounting, Business and Finance Journal, 16*(1), 101–118.

Rendon, R. G., & Rendon, J. M. (2015). Auditability in public procurement: An analysis of internal controls and fraud vulnerability. *International Journal of Procurement Management, 8*(6), 710–730.

Rendon, J. M., & Rendon, R. G. (2016). Procurement fraud in the US Department of Defense: Implications for contracting processes and internal controls. *Managerial Auditing Journal, 31*(6/7), 748–767.
Rustiarini, N. W., Nurkholis, N., & Andayani, W. (2019). Why people commit public procurement fraud? The fraud diamond view. *Journal of Public Procurement, 19*(4), 345–362.
Schultz, J., & Søreide, T. (2008). Corruption in emergency procurement. *Disasters, 32*(4), 516–536.
Sian, S., & Smyth, S. (2022). Supreme emergencies and public accountability: The case of procurement in the UK during the Covid-19 pandemic. *Accounting, Auditing & Accountability Journal, 35*(1), 146–157.
Siena, A. (2007, April). Engineering normative requirements. In *RCIS* (pp. 439–444).
South Africa. (1996). *Constitution of the Republic of South Africa, no. 108 of 1996*. [Online]. Accessed May 12, 2020, from https://www.gov.za/sites/default/files/images/a108-96.pdf
South Africa. (1998). *Prevention of organised crimes act, no. 121 of 1998*. [Online]. Accessed August 03, 2022, from Prevention of Organised Crime Act 121 of 1998 | South African Government (www.gov.za)
South Africa. (1999). *Public finance management act, no. 1 of 1999*. [Online]. Accessed May 12, 2020, from https://www.gov.za/sites/default/files/gcis_document/201409/a1-99.pdf
South Africa. (2001). Financial intelligence Centre *act, no. 38 of 2001*. [Online]. Accessed August 03, 2022, from Financial Intelligence Centre Act 38 of 2001 | South African Government (www.gov.za)
South Africa. (2003). *Local Government: Municipal Finance Management Act, No. 56 of 2003*. [Online]. Accessed August 03, 2022, from Local Government: Municipal Finance Management Act 56 of 2003 | South African Government (www.gov.za)
South Africa. (2004). *Prevention and combating of corrupt activities act, no. 12 of 2004*. [Online]. Accessed August 03, 2022, from Prevention and Combating of Corrupt Activities Act 12 of 2004 | South African Government (www.gov.za)
Sow, A. N. G., Basiruddin, R., Mohammad, J., & Rasid, S. Z. A. (2018). Fraud prevention in Malaysian small and medium enterprises (SMEs). *Journal of Financial Crime, 25*(2), 499–517.
Special Investigation Unit. (2022). *SIU welcomes arrest of Mpumalanga official and businessman over PPE corruption*. [Online]. Accessed August 03, 2022, from SIU welcomes arrest of Mpumalanga official and businessman over PPE corruption | South African Government (www.gov.za)
Tan, L. H. (2013). *An analysis of internal controls and procurement fraud deterrence* (pp. 1–125). Naval Postgraduate School Monterey CA.
Tan, M. H., & Lee, W. L. (2015). Evaluation and improvement of procurement process with data analytics. *International Journal of Advanced Computer Science and Applications, 6*(8), 70.
Vaismoradi, M., Turunen, H., & Bondas, T. (2013). Content analysis and thematic analysis: Implications for conducting a qualitative descriptive study. *Nursing & Health Sciences, 15*(3), 398–405.
Venter, A. C. (2007). A procurement fraud risk management model. *Meditari Accountancy Research, 15*(2), 77–93.
Wardani, D. K., Primastiwi, A., & Hanisah, H. (2021). Fraud prevention of government procurement of goods and services in local government. *Jurnal Akuntansi, 25*(2), 256–275.
Weingärtner, T., Batista, D., Köchli, S., & Voutat, G. (2021). Prototyping a smart contract based public procurement to fight corruption. *Computers, 10*(7), 85.
Wicaksono, A. P., Urumsah, D., & Asmui, F. (2017). The implementation of E-procurement system: Indonesia evidence. In *SHS web of conferences* (Vol. 34, p. 10004). EDP Sciences.
Widilestariningtyas, O., & Karo, R. S. K. (2016). The influence of internal audit and internal control on fraud prevention in Bandung regency government. *Journal of Administrative and Business Studies, 2*(3), 143–150.
Wright, R. (2007). Developing effective tools to manage the risk of damage caused by economically motivated crime fraud. *Journal of Financial Crime, 14*(1), 17–27.

Zager, L., Malis, S. S., & Novak, A. (2016). The role and responsibility of auditors in prevention and detection of fraudulent financial reporting. *Procedia Economics and Finance, 39*, 693–700.

Zahra, F., Abdullah, M. I., Kahar, A., Din, M., & Nurfalah, N. (2021). Preventing procurement fraud in e-purchasing for Indonesian local governments. *The Journal of Asian Finance, Economics and Business, 8*(2), 505–511.

An Assessment of the VAT Exemption for Education Services in South Africa and the Treatment in Comparative Countries

Mariam Mia and Tsireledzo Ambani Mulaudzi

Abstract This study assesses whether the exemption of educational services from VAT in South Africa aligns with the initial intention behind its enactment. The research focuses on tertiary education in South Africa and considers alternative VAT approaches taken by countries with comparable VAT systems and internationally highly ranked universities. In particular, the VAT treatment of educational services in Ghana is analysed. A qualitative study was performed through a doctrinal analysis of relevant legislative provisions of South African and Ghanaian legislation. A reform-oriented research approach was adopted, involving a review of articles, publications from revenue administrations, and industry experts in relation to the research objectives. A significant reason behind the VAT exemption of educational services was to prevent an administrative burden on educational institutions. The study found that many institutions provide taxable supplies alongside education, necessitating registration for VAT. This requires complex apportionment calculations for claiming input taxes, creating an administrative burden that is at odds with the intention behind the exemption. Where educational institutions are unable to claim input tax, a cost of the 'trapped' VAT arises, which is borne by institutions and recoverable only through raising fees and the cost of education. Previous studies have considered zero-rating education or subjecting it to VAT. An alternative approach is adopted by Ghana wherein educational services are VAT exempt but a portion of 2.5 percent of the VAT collected is earmarked for spending on education. Implementing strategies based on the Ghanaian treatment may address the needs of government and universities in South Africa.

Keywords Value-added taxation · Exemption · Educational services

M. Mia (✉) · T. A. Mulaudzi
University of the Witwatersrand, Johannesburg, South Africa
e-mail: mariam.mia@wits.ac.za; tsireledzo.mulaudzi@wits.ac.za

T. Moloi (ed.), *Impacting Society Positively Through Technology in Accounting and Business Processes*, Springer Proceedings in Business and Economics,
https://doi.org/10.1007/978-3-031-84885-8_64

Introduction and Background to the Study

Value-added taxation (VAT) was introduced in South Africa in 1991. According to a report published by the VAT Committee (1991) appointed by the Minister of Finance in South Africa at the time, educational services were classified as exempt supplies primarily because the cost of providing education was heavily financed by government. Policy makers were reluctant to place an administrative burden and compliance costs on educational institutions, including universities, to keep records or account for VAT. Educational services were seen as merit goods with great importance in South Africa. Relating to the approach of zero-rating educational services, the VAT Committee (1991) asserted that this would place an obligation on the institutions to register as VAT vendors and have the responsibility of record keeping and submitting returns. Zero-rating would require institutions to charge VAT at a rate of zero percent on tuition, boarding, and lodging fees, while being entitled to claim input tax for VAT paid on the acquisition by these institutions, of supplies used to provide educational services.

In the interest of administrative efficiency and simplicity, the supply of educational services was exempted from VAT. Educational services is not defined in the legislation; however, section 12(h) of the Value-Added Taxation Act No. 89 of 1991 (the 'VAT Act') lists the services that are exempt. Essentially, educational services from a pre-primary level to a tertiary level fall within the ambit of the exemption. In the context of universities, this encompasses goods and services for which tuition or boarding and lodging fees are changed, and which are wholly or mainly provided for the benefit of students and necessary or incidental to providing educational services (Eagar, 2024).

In recent years, there are significantly fewer institutions that are wholly subsidised by government (Grant Thornton, 2022). Numerous public educational institutions are partially subsidised by government grants, and within these institutions, there has been a shift in activities, from primarily providing education to increasingly supplementing subsidy income through the provision of taxable supplies which are subject to VAT at a standard rate. Moreover, privately owned providers of educational services bear their own costs without support from the state (Grant Thornton, 2022) and also conduct enterprises in conjunction with their VAT exempt educational offerings.

Educational institutions which provide both exempt educational services and taxable goods and services in the course of furtherance of an enterprise for South Africa VAT purposes quickly reach the compulsory VAT registration threshold of R1 million of taxable supplies made within a 12-month period. This is set out in section 23 of the VAT Act. Resultantly, an administrative responsibility to register, submit VAT returns, and retain certain documentation arises.

VAT vendors who incur VAT on acquiring taxable goods and services may claim input tax in accordance with the provisions of section 17(1) of the VAT Act. The legislation allows a taxpayer to claim input tax to the extent of making taxable supplies. Institutions are prevented from claiming input tax on supplies used exclusively in providing educational services and limited in the amount of input tax claimable from SARS for expenses incurred in producing both taxable and exempt supplies. Mixed-use supplies require institutions to perform complex apportionment calculations for input tax purposes (Jugdhaw, 2018). These compliance obligations render the initial intention behind the VAT exemption moot. The administrative obligations and challenges under the exemption are more onerous for educational institutions compared to the responsibilities that would have arisen if educational services were subject to VAT at the standard rate (National Treasury, 2005).

Regarding acquisitions of supplies used exclusively to provide educational services and for which input tax is not claimable, a cost of 'trapped' VAT arises because the educational institutions incur VAT on the purchase of goods and services including software, learning management systems, books, stationery, and informational technology hardware. There is no corresponding input tax recovery of these costs by the already resource-constrained institutions. This results in the cost being borne by the educational institutions or effectively passed on to students though increased fees. This is incongruous with the political and economic objectives of government in making education more affordable and accessible (Jugdhaw, 2018).

It is apparent that the VAT exemption of educational services no longer accords with the initial intention behind the exemption and appears to fall foul of the equity, convenience, and simplicity principles of a good tax system. This requires reassessing the current VAT treatment and recommending amendments which cater to the needs of both the fiscus and the institutions.

Literature Review

The Landscape of Higher Learning Institutions in South Africa

According to Branson and Whitelaw (2023), universities in South Africa are primarily funded by government subsidies related to student enrolments, graduations, and research outputs as well as student fees for tuition and accommodation. Many students are supported by government through the National Student Financial Aid Scheme (NSFAS) which was expanded in 2018. Following the expansion, universities experienced a decline in total funding. This is explained by decreases in direct subsidies to universities and more funding allocated to the NSFAS. Approximately 25 percent of this funding takes the form of allowances paid to students, instead of the institutions themselves. The result is budgetary and resource constraints which impact on the sustainability of these institutions (Branson & Whitelaw, 2023).

To supplement government-related funding and donations from non-governmental benefactors, many public higher education institutions in South Africa have turned to market sources of income including investment income, contract or commercial research, and sales of goods and services (Wangenge-Ouma & Cloete, 2008). Universities let out commercial real estate, sell educational books and materials, engage in small business development ventures, develop patents for business use, and provide consulting services (Eagar, 2024). While the receipt of interest and dividend income from investments would be exempt as financial services in terms of the VAT Act, the supply of goods and services unrelated to student accommodation and tuition would fall within the ambit of vatable supplies and be subject to VAT in the hands of institutions that meet the compulsory registration threshold.

Many universities generate both exempt and taxable supplies. No input tax may be claimed on supplies for exclusive use in providing educational service as this relates wholly to non-taxable supplies and educational institutions are required to perform apportionment calculations to determine the amount of input tax that can be claimed on mixed-use acquisitions for taxable and exempt supplies (Eagar, 2024).

VAT Provisions Specific to Higher Learning Institutions in South Africa

Section 17(1) of the VAT Act states that the method to determine the extent of input tax claimable in respect of supplies acquired to provide taxable and exempt supplies is determined using a ratio set out by the Commissioner in a ruling. Rulings are published under Chapter 7 of the Tax Administration Act No. 28 of 2011 (the 'Tax Admin Act'), and in certain instances, a group of taxpayers may apply for a class ruling in terms of section 41B of the VAT Act.

Regarding the VAT input apportionment calculation, SARS issued the revised Binding General Ruling 16 Issue 3 (BGR16) on 27 March 2023 (Van der Zwan, 2024). BGR16 provides the default standard turnover-based method of apportionment which applies in the absence of any other specific method applicable to a taxpayer. BGR16 stipulates that where a VAT class ruling (VCR) has been issued by SARS to a taxpayer or class of taxpayers, the VCR must be used to calculate the ratio for input tax apportionment (SARS, 2023).

BGR16 provides that taxpayers should consider the appropriateness of the apportionment methods applied and consider requesting the withdrawal of rulings if applicable. An evaluation on the appropriateness of the VCR applicable to institutions of higher learning in South Africa is out of the scope of this chapter.

Universities South Africa (Universities SA) is an umbrella body that represents the interests of 26 public universities in South Africa (Universities SA, 2024). This body applied for a VCR from SARS which was issued on 31 July 2012. The ruling provides a tailored formula which considers the research activities of universities and allows claiming input tax at different rates depending on the type of research conducted by the institution. Moreover, the ruling stipulates a 12.5 percent ceiling on input tax relating to university overheads (Grant Thornton, 2022). The ruling applies to universities falling under Universities SA. It has been periodically renewed and its provisions remain in force at the time of writing this chapter (Eagar, 2024).

Challenges Arising from the VAT Exemption of Educational Services in South Africa

In addition to the general tax compliance obligations of levying VAT, submitting returns to SARS, and retaining requisite documentation, universities cannot avoid processing complex input tax apportionment calculations for supplies acquired and used to provide both exempt educational services and other vatable supplies (Grant Thornton, 2022).

Universities falling under Universities SA must use the apportionment method set out in the VCR. Other institutions falling outside this body would typically use BGR16 if the resultant apportionment ratio obtained is 'fair and reasonable' (SARS, 2023). According to Eagar (2024), determining whether an apportionment method is fair and reasonable is subject to interpretation and this opens a taxpayer up to the risk of disputes with SARS.

The VCR provides different percentages for the extent of claiming input tax on contract research projects. These percentages depend on the type of research conducted and the VCR provides for, inter alia, the following (Grant Thornton, 2022):

- Basic research conducted by students does not entitle the institution to any input tax on acquisitions of supplies used in conducting this type of research;
- Certain applied and contract research which involves some student involvement entitles the institutions to claim a credit of 50 percent of the VAT incurred in respect of these studies as input tax.
- Certain research containing no student involvement entitles the institution to claim the full input tax cost incurred on acquisitions of supplies used in conducting this type of research.

The classification and accompanying determination of the extent of claiming input tax must be determined per contract. Universities engage in hundreds of projects. This creates the onerous task of considering the terms and details of each research contract to classify the type of research, followed by applying the apportionment percentage in respect of acquisitions of supplies used for each of those projects (Eagar, 2024).

The VCR imposes a limitation of claiming no more than 12.5 percent of input tax on university overheads. Eagar (2024) argues that this limitation oversimplifies the reality of the use of university overheads and is prejudicial to universities. For example, in instances where universities supply accommodation, typically exempt boarding and lodging is provided exclusively to students for periods falling within the academic terms and taxable commercial accommodation is exclusively provided to consumers during certain university holiday periods. Restricting the extent of input tax claimable on overheads incurred in this context is not indicative of the extent of use of the supplies by the university and results in a portion of 'trapped' VAT costs where the taxable use exceeds this ceiling (Eagar, 2024).

Application of the VCR was tested in courts in TUUP v Commissioner for the South African Revenue Service (VAT 22402) [2024] ZATC 1 (17 January 2024).

SARS disallowed the taxpayer from claiming input tax above the 12.5 percent cap, despite the taxpayer indicating that the extent of use of the supplies acquired exceeded this percentage. The court ruled in favour of SARS. In general, South African courts have displayed a restrictive interpretation of the VAT exemption, providing little leeway for universities to justify claiming input tax outside the limitations under the VAT Act and rulings (Eagar, 2024).

Regarding supplies acquired for use solely in providing exempt educational services, universities are not entitled to claim any input tax. The resultant 'trapped' VAT is a cost that must be suffered by the university itself which exacerbates the existing challenges of rising operational costs coupled with diminishing government funding. This requires providing more taxable supplies and continuing the cycle (Grant Thornton, 2022). Alternatively, the trapped VAT cost could be passed on to students though increased fees. This stands in conflict with government's objectives of affordable and accessible education in South Africa.

Further to the challenges outlined above, many educational institutions do not have the technical expertise or knowledge to perform the VAT calculations, and which require an understanding of the VCR and application of nuanced change in use adjustments (Grant Thornton, 2022). Resultantly, universities need professional tax experts to advise on and aid in their VAT compliance.

Zero-Rating Educational Services

The Australian Approach

In accordance with the objective of identifying international approaches that may aid in improving and reforming the South African treatment of educational services, previous studies have considered whether zero-rating the supply would be suitable in a South African context. Australian tax law contains a General Sales Tax (GST) which is a VAT equivalent tax type. Under the GST, various listed education and related supplies carry no tax charge on making these supplies but still entitle the supplier of education to claim input tax credits on acquisitions used in carrying on the enterprise. The law does not provide a blanket tax-free provision but rather specifies the supplies that carry no GST charge, with reference to definitions in various Australian Education Acts. Providers of education are required to apply the legislation on a case-by-case basis to determine the tax treatment and cannot take it for granted that a supply will be zero-rated if provided by a school or university (Jugdhaw, 2018).

Applicability in South Africa

The zero-rating of educational services would be most beneficial to financially strained institutions as this treatment would allow for the recovery of VAT paid on acquisitions of taxable supplies and there would be no trapped VAT costs.

According to National Treasury (2005), zero-rating educational services would adversely affect the cash flow of the fiscus, making it challenging to justify this approach. The Davis Tax Committee (2018) has described the approach of zero-rating as a 'blunt' tool or a runner-up approach to achieving equity objectives of government, in part because this approach shrinks the tax base of a country and may demand a higher standard rate to address the shortfall in revenue that would result from an introduction of more zero-rated items (DTC, 2018).
A simple VAT design with minimal zero-ratings and exemptions results in the efficiency of the tax system. SARS was found to have a high collections efficiency ratio compared to other countries (DTC, 2018). Zero-rating educational services would reduce the VAT base and introduce the burden to keep VAT records for institutions that only supply educational services.

Subjecting Educational Services to VAT

Single Standard Rate

The approach of taxing educational services at the standard rate is taken by New Zealand, a country with a modern VAT design wherein there is a single, low VAT rate and no merit-based VAT exemptions. Education is subject to VAT at the standard rate of 15 percent in New Zealand (Jugdhaw, 2018).

Subjecting educational services to VAT at 15 percent in South Africa may be viewed as a tax on knowledge (National Treasury, 2005) and therefore challenging to politically justify. Additionally, because VAT is designed to place the obligation for the tax on the final consumer, this would raise the cost of fees and would not align with governments' objectives to keep the cost of education low and therefore accessible to all in South Africa (Grant Thornton, 2022).

Differentiated Rates

In China, the VAT system provides for several different tax rates ranging from 0 percent to 13 percent. Educational services are subject to VAT at a rate of 6 percent (EY, 2024). Research has consistently shown that the use of multiple rates in the design of a VAT system is economically and administratively inefficient (DTC, 2018). Differentiated VAT rates raise compliance costs and distort consumer and supplier choices. Differentiated rates introduce complexity in developing tax policy which delineates the supplies falling within the ambit of each band of the different rates. Evidence and experience have indicated that the benefits of a simple tax design with a single rate vastly outweigh any possible benefits of subjecting merit goods to lower rates of VAT (DTC, 2018). It is recommended that South Africa does not consider changes which would subject educational services to VAT at a rate different to 15 percent.

The Need for an Alternative Approach

Despite the extensive use of exemptions, zero-rated supplies, and differentiated rates within VAT systems globally, research indicates that an ideal VAT system limits the use of these approaches and, in the interest of efficiency and simplicity, addresses objectives through expenditure-related fiscal policy (National Treasure, 2005). This is supported by the Davis Tax Committee (2018), which states that expenditure-related policies in relation to education and health may be more effective in addressing equity objectives in these areas as opposed to measures which amend the imposition of VAT.

Research Problem

Due to the increasing range of taxable supplies provided by universities in recent years, VAT registration and compliance requirements need to be met by these institutions.

Input tax can only be recovered to the extent that a supply acquired is used in the making of taxable supplies. This requires complex apportionment calculations for universities, based on an understanding of the VCR applicable to these vendors, as well as technical expertise in performing change in use adjustments.

The cost of trapped VAT arises as a result of the 12.5 percent cap on the rate of recovery of university overheads and in respect of supplies acquired to solely use in providing exempt educational services.

In light of the above-mentioned challenges faced by universities, the following research problem arises: Meeting the VAT compliance obligations has become onerous and expensive for public and private universities that provide taxable and exempt supplies in South Africa and the restrictions on claiming input tax increase the operational costs of universities.

Research Objective

The salient objective of this study is to determine whether the VAT treatment of educational services in Ghana may find application in South Africa and aid in reforming the current legislative provisions contained in the VAT Act in South Africa. Although other countries take different approaches to the VAT treatment of education services, these have been explored in previous studies and publications. Accordingly, this chapter centres on the Ghanaian approach.

Research Methodology

Qualitative research is a type of methodology that explores and provides deeper insights into real-world problems (Tenny et al., 2017). The aim of this chapter is to assess whether the exemption of educational services from VAT in South Africa aligns with the initial intention behind its enactment and consider, inter alia, whether approach taken by Ghana, a country with a similar VAT system and universities ranked in the top 500 universities internationally, may be fitting in a South African context. In this pursuit, a qualitative study was performed which involved a doctrinal analysis of legislation and case law. Doctrinal research is the core method for legal research and is an investigation into the law, legal concepts, and the relationship between rules. This study adopted a reform-oriented approach, which evaluates whether existing provisions within the law are adequate and provides recommendations for changes and improvements (Hutchinson, 2012).

This study involved a review of additional relevant publications available in the public domain and which were appropriately referenced in this chapter.

Importance of the Study

Scholarly research should be engaged in solving challenges and concerns in society (Brew, 2001). An issue faced by educational institutions in South Africa is a lack of funding to support their operations (Jugdhaw, 2018). The current VAT exempt status of educational institutions in South Africa adversely affects the financial sustainability of institutions which provide higher education. The aim of this study is to propose recommendations to alleviate VAT-related financial burdens on these institutions and ensure that the overall VAT treatment aligns with good tax principles of efficiency and equality.

The Treatment of Educational Services for VAT Purposes in South Africa

Imposition of VAT in South Africa

In South Africa, the legislative provisions pertaining to VAT are housed in the VAT Act. Section 1 sets out the definitions for interpretation of the law, and section 7 sets out the requirements for imposing VAT. Section 7(1)(a) provides:

> **Imposition of value-added tax**—(1) Subject to the exemptions, exceptions, deductions and adjustments provided for in this Act, there shall be levied and paid for the benefit of the National Revenue Fund a tax, to be known as the value-added tax—
>
> (a) on the supply by any vendor of goods or services supplied by him on or after the commencement date in the course or furtherance of any enterprise carried on by him

The subsequent sub-paragraphs of section 7 address the imposition of VAT on the importation of goods and services by any person. These sections are out of the scope of this study.

Section 7 sets out several requirements for imposing VAT. These requirements are listed and analysed in the context of this study below. Firstly, there must be a supply of goods or services. 'Supply' is a defined term which includes the

> performance in terms of a sale, rental agreement, instalment credit agreement and all other forms of supply, whether voluntary, compulsory or by operation of law, irrespective of where the supply is effected, and any derivative of **"supply"** shall be construed accordingly

Educational institutions sell education in exchange for student fees. The fees are subsidised by government grants, but this still falls within the ambit of a supply for VAT purposes.

The focus of this study is on universities in South Africa and the educational services supplied by these institutions; therefore, an analysis of the term 'goods' is not included in this chapter. The term 'services' is defined in the VAT Act as

> anything done or to be done, including the granting, assignment, cession or surrender of any right or the making available of any facility or advantage

The definition excludes the supply of certain items including goods and money. In this context of this study, providing education is a service as it is something done or to be done by universities in South Africa.

The VAT Act requires that the supply is made in the course of furtherance of an enterprise. The law contains an extensive definition of an 'enterprise'. Only the portion relevant to this study is included in this chapter. An enterprise includes

> (a) in the case of any vendor, any enterprise or activity which is carried on continuously or regularly by any person in the Republic or partly in the Republic and in the course or furtherance of which goods or services are supplied to any other person for a consideration, whether or not for profit, including any enterprise or activity carried on in the form of a commercial, financial, industrial, mining, farming, fishing, municipal or professional concern or any other concern of a continuing nature or in the form of an association or club;

The definition explicitly excludes an activity

> to the extent to which it involves the making of exempt supplies are not deemed to be the carrying on of an enterprise

Section 12(h) exempts educational services from VAT, and therefore, the provision or supply of educational services is not considered to be the carrying on of an enterprise.

In continuing with the requirements to levy output tax, in instances where goods or services are provided in the course of furtherance of an enterprise, the supply must be made by a vendor. The VAT Act defines a **'vendor'** as

> any person who is or is required to be registered under this Act

The registration requirements are set out in section 23 of the VAT Act and provide for both compulsory and voluntary registration requirements. This chapter does not include an analysis of the voluntary requirements because the challenges for universities arise in respect of compliance obligations caused by the need to compulsorily register for VAT. The definition of a vendor also addresses when a person is deemed to be a vendor. These listed provisions are not relevant to this study and excluded from this analysis.

With regard to compulsory registration, section 23(1) provides

> Every person who, on or after the commencement date, carries on any enterprise and is not registered, becomes liable to be registered—
>
> (a) at the end of any month where the total value of taxable supplies made by that person in the period of 12 months ending at the end of that month in the course of carrying on all enterprises has exceeded R1 million;
>
> (b) at the commencement of any month where the total value of the taxable supplies in terms of a contractual obligation in writing to be made by that person in the period of 12 months reckoned from the commencement of the said month will exceed the above-mentioned amount:

The obligation to register only applies in respect of meeting the R1 million threshold in respect of taxable supplies. A university would not have to register for VAT in respect of providing educational services, irrespective of the amount of fee income generated because this pertains to exempt supplies which are non-taxable supplies. Many universities do not only supply educational services and instead supply various taxable goods and services. Once a university reaches the R1 million threshold, it must register as a VAT vendor.

Exemption from the Imposition of VAT

The VAT Act Defines an 'Exempt Supply' in Section 1 as

> a supply that is exempt from tax under section 12

Section 12 of the VAT Act lists various types of exempt supplies, but this study only analyses educational services listed in subsection (h), which fall within the ambit of the study. As set out in paragraph (i), educational services include:

> the supply of educational services—
>
> (aa) provided by the State or a school registered under the South African Schools Act, 1996 (Act No. 84 of 1996), or a public college or private college established, declared or registered as such under the Further Education and Training Colleges Act, 2006 (Act No. 16 of 2006;
>
> (bb) by an institution that provides higher education on a full time, part-time or distance basis and which is established or deemed to be established as a public higher education institution under the Higher Education Act, 1997 (Act No. 101 of 1997), or is declared as a public higher education institution under that Act, or is registered or conditionally registered as a private higher education institution under that Act; or ...
>
> ...(ii) the supply by a school, university, technikon or college solely or mainly for the benefit of its learners or students of goods or services (including domestic goods and services) necessary for and subordinate and incidental to the supply of services referred to in subparagraph (i) of this paragraph, if such goods or services are supplied for a consideration in the form of school fees, tuition fees or payment for lodging or board and lodging; or

(iii) the supply of services to learners or students or intended learners or students by the Joint Matriculation Board referred to in section 15 of the Universities Act, 1955 (Act No. 61 of 1955):

Provided that vocational or technical training provided by an employer to his employees and employees of an employer who is a connected person in relation to that employer does not constitute the supply of an educational service for the purposes of this paragraph;

Essentially, the supply by a university in South Africa of education and other related goods and services that are for the benefit of students for which tuition or boarding and lodging fees are charged by the institution is exempt from VAT. An institution levies output tax on these fees charged to students and cannot claim input tax on the costs incurred to provide these educational services to students.

In addition to listing the supplies of goods and services that are exempt from VAT, section 12 stipulates that any VAT incurred to make exempt supplies will not be allowed as input tax claimable in the hands of the vendor.

Entitlement to Claim Input Tax

Input tax in the context of this study is defined in section 1 of the VAT Act as

in relation to a vendor, means—

(a) tax charged under section 7 and payable in terms of that section by—

(i) a supplier on the supply of goods or services made by that supplier to the vendor;

Section 17(1) provides the requirements which must be met before a vendor is entitled to claim input tax. The law provides that:

Where goods or services are acquired … by a vendor partly for consumption, use or supply (hereinafter referred to as the intended use) in the course of making taxable supplies and partly for another intended use, the extent to which any tax which has become payable in respect of the supply to the vendor or the importation by the vendor, as the case may be, of such goods or services … may be, the same ratio (as determined by the Commissioner in accordance with a ruling as contemplated in Chapter 7 of the Tax Administration Act or section 41B) as the intended use of such goods or services in the course of making taxable supplies bears to the total intended use of such goods or services …

This provision indicates that input tax can only be claimed by a VAT vendor for VAT actually charged to them when acquiring taxable supplies and only to the extent that the particular acquisition is used in making taxable supplies. With respect to goods and services acquired for use solely in making exempt supplies, no input tax may be claimed.

Where goods and services are acquired by a university to make mixed supplies, the input tax must be apportioned in accordance with rules contained in the VCR for universities falling under Universities SA or in the case of other higher leaning institutions, in line with the ratio contemplated in BGR16.

The Treatment of Educational Services for VAT Purposes in Ghana

Table 1 sets out the various VAT rates in Ghana since 1995.

Presently, there are several Acts that govern VAT in Ghana. The VAT Act 870 of 2013 (the 'VAT Act 870') sets out levying provisions in relation to VAT charged at 15% and details on the timing and calculation rules. The Exemptions Act 1083 of 2022 (the 'Exemption Act') defines and lists the exemptions from VAT. The Ghana Education Trust Fund Act 881 of 2000 (the 'GETFund Act') read together with the Five Hundred and Eighty-First Act details the levy of the Ghana Education Trust Fund (GETFund) and the rules pertaining to administration of the fund and what the funding may be used for. Several other Acts provide details of the other levies imposed in Ghana in a VAT context, but the details of these laws are out of the scope of this study.

The 2.5 percent increase in the VAT rate, introduced in 2000, was allocated to the GETFund which is intended to support education in Ghana. The 2.5 percent increase in January 2014 was allocated to the National Health Insurance (NHI) levy. In 2021 a COVID-19 Health Recovery (CHR) levy was introduced at a rate of 1% of taxable goods supplied and services rendered in Ghana as part of VAT. This brought the effective VAT rate to 21.9 percent (Ofori et al., 2020). The decision by revenue authorities to exempt certain items from VAT is informed by administrative and compliance cost considerations and perceived difficulty in identifying the appropriate VAT output to be levied (Ebrill et al., 2001). The decision to exempt educational services was influenced by external benefits in relation to education. In the public sector, education is commonly offered at a subsidised price or at no fee; therefore, imposing VAT at a standard rate may intensify competition between the private and public sector (Ebrill et al., 2001). The Exemptions Act of 2022 of the Republic of Ghana (Exemptions Act) defines an exemption as:

> ... a wavier or variation of a tax, levy, rate, duty, fee or charge provided for under an enactment or a variation of the timing of the payment of a tax, levy rate, duty, fee or charge which results in a reduction in the effective liability of the payer.

Educational services are listed in the VAT Amendment Act 948 which was promulgated in 2017 (VAT Amendment Act) as part of items that are exempt from VAT. The VAT Act 870 defines educations services as the services supplied to students as:

Table 1 VAT rates in Ghana since 1995

Year	VAT rate
1995	Introduced at 17.5% and repealed soon after introduction
1998	Reintroduced at 10%
2000	12.5%
2013	15%

Adapted from Ofori et al. (2020)

… part of the education program provided by any one of the following establishments that is duly registered or licensed by the Minister for Education:

a. a day care, including adult day care, provider;
b. a pre-primary, primary, or secondary school;
c. a technical college, community college or university;
d. an educational institution established for the promotion of adult education, vocational training, or technical education; or
e. an institution established for the education or training of physically or mentally challenged persons;

The VAT Act 870 also regards the supply of certain educational materials as exempt. These include textbooks and supplementary readers as listed on the Ministry of Education approved list, newspapers, atlases, charts, maps and music. This exemption excludes imported newspapers, architectural and similar drawings, scientific and technical works, periodicals, magazines, trade catalogues, price lists, greeting cards, almanacs, calendars, diaries, and stationery.

The supply of laboratory and library equipment for use in rendering educational services is also exempt from VAT.

The GETFund is fed by the 2.5 percent levy charged within the scope of the wider VAT system in Ghana. This fund was introduced to finance education at all levels by the Ghanaian government. The GETFund levy is not charged on educational services themselves as these are exempt from VAT. Instead, the 2.5 percent is levied on regular taxable goods and services falling within the scope of VAT in Ghana and this funding is reserved for use in the GETFund (PWC, 2023).

Section 2(2) of the Five Hundred and Eighty-First Act outlines the various educational services that are funded by the GETFund as listed below:

(a) to provide financial support to the agencies and institutions under the Ministry of Education, through the Ministry, for the development and maintenance of essential academic facilities and infrastructure in public educational institutions particularly, in tertiary institutions,
(b) to provide supplementary funding to the Scholarship Secretariat for the grant of scholarships to gifted but needy student for studies in second cycle and accredited tertiary institutions in Ghana,
(c) to contribute monies from the Fund towards the operation of student loans schemes for students in accredited tertiary institutions through loan scheme mechanisms and agencies, approved by the Minister,
(d) to provide, through the National Council on/tertiary Education, grants to tertiary institutions,
    (i) to train brilliant students as members of facilities,
    (ii) to undertake research and other academic programmes of relevance to national development, and
(e) to provide monies to support such 7 other educational activities and programmes for the promotion of education as the Minister in consultation with the Board may determine.

The GETFund Act provides the following in respect of the levy:

(a) an amount of money, equivalent to two- and one-half percent out of the prevailing rate of the Value Added Tax to be paid by the Value Added Tax Service to the Fund or …

VAT applies to the supply of goods and services that are not exempt from VAT and not classified as zero-rated or VAT Flat Rate Scheme (VFRS) supplies in Ghana

(PWC, 2023). The output VAT to be levied on the supply of taxable goods and services rendered in Ghana is calculated in the following manner:

The VAT exclusive amount of a supply is first subjected to the 2.5 percent NHI levy, followed by applying the 2.5 percent GETFund levy and then applying the 1 percent CHR levy. This is followed by applying the 15 percent VAT rate to the amount inclusive of the NHI, GETFund, and CHR levies. Based on this calculation the effective VAT rate amounts to 21.9 percent (Ghana Revenue Authority, 2021).

To illustrate the application of the VAT and levy provisions, an example is included below:

Example: A registered supplier/vendor for Ghanaian VAT purposes makes the taxable supply through the sale of an asset that costs a VAT exclusive amount of 100,000 Ghanaian Cedi (GHC).

Result

Step 1: Application of the various levies

GHC 100000 × 2.5% GETFund levy = GHC 2500
GHC 100000 × 2.5% NHI levy = GHC 2500
GHC100 000 × 1% CHR levy = GHC 1000

Step 2: Determination of the amount subject to VAT at 15%

The sum of C = GHC 100000 + GHC 2500 + GHC 2500 + GHC 1000 = GHC 106000.

Step 3: Calculation of the VAT output

GHC 106000 × 15% = GHC15 900
Total tax levied under the VAT system in Ghana on the supply of the taxable good
GHC 2500 + GHC 2500 + GHC 1000 + GHC 15900 = GHC 21900

The result is an effective tax rate under the collective VAT system of 21.9 percent.

Input VAT is claimed on goods supplied and services rendered in Ghana; this includes imported goods and services which are used by the taxpayer wholly, exclusively, and necessary for trade purposes to the extent of making taxable supplies; it is important to note that no VAT input deduction can be claimed on the NHI, GETFund, and CHR levies (PWC, 2023).

Taxpayers making both taxable and exempt supplies can only claim a portion of input tax on goods and services that is attributable to making taxable supplies; this means that for institutions of higher learning or institutions offering education services as defined in the VAT Act 870 will claim a portion of input VAT which is attributable to making taxable supplies and not the educational services as those are exempt (PWC, 2023). However, the VAT cost or burden suffered is alleviated by the support provided through the GETFund levy.

The levies are not considered to be VAT itself and therefore do not entitle a taxpayer to claim input tax on the cost of the levies incurred.

Findings and Recommendations

According to National Treasury (2005), globalisation has led to the convergence of tax policies as different jurisdictions seek guidance from other countries to improve and enhance their domestic legislation. Tax reform should however be economically and practically fitting for the country considering change. Public finance theory postulates that it is more pragmatic and efficient to address equity objectives of a State through expenditure measures such as subsidies and grants in place of tax levying amendments. An expenditure-related approach has also been described as the most ideal approach from a VAT policy and design perspective (DTC, 2018).

Based on the analysis of the Ghanaian approach to education in the VAT context, it is evident that the VAT system has both a VAT imposition and an expenditure-focused approach to addressing the objectives of providing affordable education to students in Ghana and reducing the financial burden on universities and other institutions of learning in the country.

Ghana is comparable to South Africa in respect of the following:

- Both tax jurisdictions are developing countries in Africa.
- Both countries have a standard VAT rate of 15 percent.
- Both countries have universities ranked within the top 50 universities in Africa and a significant number of international students attending the universities (Unirank, 2024).
- Educational services are exempt from VAT in both Ghana and South Africa.

Ghana and South Africa differ in respect of the following:

- In addition to the educational services exemption, Ghana provides a further exemption of textbooks and other educational materials as detailed in the study.
- In addition to the standard VAT rate of 15 percent, charged on Ghanaian taxable supplies under their VAT system, there are additional levies of 2.5 percent, 2.5 percent, and 1 percent which result in an effective tax rate of 21.9 percent.
- Educational services are defined in Ghanaian tax legislation.
- Revenues collected in the form of levies are earmarked for various governmental projects and initiatives.

Recommendations

It is recommended that South Africa provides a definition for educational services in the VAT Act as this accords with the principles of a good tax system through providing additional certainty to taxpayers (SILKE, 2024).

It is recommended that South Africa does not adopt the Ghanaian approach of charging additional levies on taxable supplies, but instead considers earmarking a portion of the 15 percent standard rate of VAT charged on taxable supplies for spending exclusively on education in South Africa. The reason for this is because the introduction of additional levies would not be favourable from a political standpoint as this would increase taxes in South Africa. This would result in an increased tax compliance burden for all VAT vendors in South Africa. Furthermore, this approach would create a layer of complexity in calculating the VAT amount each period and does not accord with principles of a good tax system. This study does not make a recommendation on the proportion of VAT that should be allocated to spending on education, and this consideration is out of the scope of this chapter.

- It is recommended that the portion of funding that will be allocated to supporting universities in South Africa is paid directly to the universities in the form of subsidies or grants to provide relief to these institutions in respect of VAT compliance and trapped VAT costs. The proposed treatment would not create complexity or additional compliance burdens on vendors. The issue of complex input tax apportionment calculations for educational institutions is not remedied by these recommendations; however, this would be an area for further study in future.

Conclusion

This chapter aimed to determine whether the VAT treatment of educational services in Ghana may find application in South Africa and aid in reforming the current legislative provisions contained in the South African VAT Act.

Taking cognisance of the challenges experienced by educational institutions which arise from the VAT exemption of educational services in South Africa, this study addressed the research objective through identifying features and provisions contained in the Ghanaian VAT system and providing recommendations to reform the South African approach.

The recommendation to include a definition of educational services in the South African legislation seeks to provide certainty to taxpayers. Guidance can be taken from the Ghanaian definition and adapted to the needs of South Africa.

The recommendation to designate a portion of VAT levied at 15% on taxable supplies made in South Africa seeks to alleviate the financial burden on universities that experience trapped VAT costs in instances where they are prevented or limited from claiming input tax in terms of the VAT Act or the VCR. In this regard, and as done by Ghana, South Africa should legislate the education-related projects that the funding can be used for.

Areas for future research include identifying a suitable percentage from the current 15% VAT rate that can be allocated to funding educational services, whether the VCR should be amended, and whether additional amendments could be beneficial in addressing the needs of universities and government.

References

Branson, N., & Whitelaw E. (2023). *South Africa's higher education funding conundrum: Could the current funding system hamper social mobility and university performance?* Retrieved June 15, 2024, from https://globaldev.blog/south-africas-higher-education-funding-conundrum-could-the-current-funding-system-hamper-social-mobility-and-university-performance/#:~:text=How%20is%20higher%20education%20funded,enrolment%20and%20student%20graduation%20rates

Brew, A. (2001). *The nature of research: Inquiry in academic contexts* (1st ed.). Routledge. https://doi.org/10.4324/9780203461549

DTC (Davis Tax Committee). (2018). *Final report on VAT for the Minister of Finance*. Retrieved June 15, 2024, from https://www.taxcom.org.za/docs/20180329%20Final%20DTC%20VAT%20Report%20to%20the%20Minister.pdf

Eagar, C. (2024). *VAT apportionment at tertiary education institutions - TUUP v SARS Case No.: VAT 22402*. Retrieved June 15, 2024, from https://www.linkedin.com/pulse/vat-apportionment-tertiary-education-institutions-tuup-chris-eagar-vbr5f/

Ebrill, L. P., Keen, M., & Perry, V. J. (2001). The modern VAT. In L. P. Ebrill, M. Keen, & V. J. Perry (Eds.), *The modern VAT* (pp. 84–100). International Monetary Fund. https://doi.org/10.5089/9781589060265.071

EY. (2024). *Worldwide VAT, GST and sales tax guide*. Retrieved June 15, 2024, from https://www.ey.com/en_gl/tax-guides/worldwide-vat-gst-and-sales-tax-guide

Ghana Revenue Authority. (2021). *Ghana revenue authority*. Retrieved June 15, 2024, from Ghana Revenue Authority https://gra.gov.gh/domestic-tax/tax-types/vat-standard/

Grant Thornton. (2022). *Tax in the Education Sector (South Africa)*. Retrieved June 15, 2024, from https://www.grantthornton.co.za/Newsroom/tax-in-the-education-sector-south-africa/

Hutchinson, T. (2012). Defining and describing what we do: Doctrinal legal research. *Deakin Law Review, 17*(1), 1321–3660. https://doi.org/10.21153/dlr2012vol17no1art70

Jugdhaw, D. (2018). Is *the value-added-tax treatment for educational services still valid? Is zero-rating a better alternative to the current VAT treatment? Are there any other alternative VAT treatments available?* (Master's Dissertation). University of Cape Town. Retrieved June 15, 2024, from http://hdl.handle.net/11427/29413

National Treasury (National Treasury, Republic of South Africa). (2005). *The VAT treatment of merit goods and services T16/05*. Retrieved June 15, 2024, from https://www.treasury.gov.za/publications/other/vat%20merit%20goods%20final%20report%20%20-%2015%20oct%202007.pdf

Ofori, M. S., Fumey, A., & Nketiah-Amponsah. (2020). Forecasting value added tax revenue in Ghana. *Journal of Economics and Financial Analysis, 4*(2), 63–99. https://doi.org/10.1991/jefa.v4i2.a37. Retrieved: June 15, 2024.

PWC. (2023). *PWC. Vat in Africa Ghana overview*. Retrieved June 15, 2024, from https://www.pwc.co.za/en/publications/vat-in-africa/ghana-overview.html

SARS (South African Revenue Service). (2023). *Binding general ruling (VAT) 16 (Issue 3) Standard turnover-based method of apportionment*. Retrieved June 15, 2024, from https://www.sars.gov.za/wp-content/uploads/Legal/Rulings/BGR/Legal-IntR-R-BGR-16-Standard-turnover-based-method-of-apportionment.pdf

South Africa. National Treasury. (2011). *Value-added tax Act No. 89 of 1991*. Government Printer.

Stiglingh, M., Koekemoer, A. D., van Heerden, L., Wilcocks, J. S., & van der Zwan, P. (2024). *SILKE: South African Income Tax 2024*. South Africa: Lexis Nexis.

Tenny, S., Brannan, J. M., & Brannan, G. D. (2017). *Qualitative study*. Retrieved June 15, 2024, from https://www.ncbi.nlm.nih.gov/books/NBK470395/

Unirank. (2024). *Top 200 universities in Africa 2024 African University ranking*. Retrieved June 15, 2024, from https://www.4icu.org/top-universities-africa/

Value-Added-Tax-Committee. (1991). *Report of the value-added-tax committee*. University of Cape Town.

Van der Zwan, P. (2024). *VAT apportionment: Revised ruling*. Retrieved June 15, 2024, from https://tax.pvdz.co.za/vat-apportionment/

Wangenge-Ouma, G., & Cloete, N. (2008). Financing higher education in South Africa: Public funding, non-government revenue and tuition fees. *South African Journal of Higher Education, 22*(4), 906–919. https://doi.org/10.4314/sajhe.v22i4.25824

Data-Driven Innovation: Leveraging Big Data for Business Growth—A Bibliometric Review and Meta-Analysis

Ephias Munangi and Athenia Bongani Sibindi

Abstract Technological advancements combined with big data have disrupted the traditional approach of conducting and growing businesses. To survive and maintain a competitive edge in the digital era, it is vital to generate new business models. This chapter applied a bibliometric review and meta-analysis by utilizing the SCOPUS database to explore the academic research that has been conducted on big data innovation and its impact on business growth. The VOSviewer software was utilized to construct and visualize the bibliometric networks from the extracted data. The findings show an increase in the number of documents published on the topic from 2021 to 2023. Entrepreneurship, integration, innovation, data analytics, and technological advancements were dominant issues in leveraging big data for business growth. The significance of the study is that the study identified the research gaps from the previous studies and explored how organizations can leverage big data for business growth.

Keywords Artificial intelligence · Big data · Big data-driven innovation · Business growth · Data analytics

Introduction

Big data has been defined in three scales of volume (data from various sources), variety (structured and unstructured), and velocity (speed data is collected, administered, and analyzed in real time) (Helfert, n.d.). The volume, variety, and velocity of data impact the data quality which influences the value of the data. An additional attribute of veracity is essential such as the degree of confidence in the data collected that it is accurate and credible (Mikalef et al., 2020). It is massive data

E. Munangi · A. B. Sibindi (✉)
University of South Africa, Pretoria, South Africa
e-mail: 49018019@mylife.unisa.ac.za; sibinab@unisa.ac.za

T. Moloi (ed.), *Impacting Society Positively Through Technology in Accounting and Business Processes*, Springer Proceedings in Business and Economics,
https://doi.org/10.1007/978-3-031-84885-8_65

combined with technology that help reveal useful information that improves decision making; therefore, value is an additional distinct feature. The innovation around functional, operational, strategic, and new business models using data is what is referred to as data-driven innovation (Akter et al., 2021). Market orientation is an integral aspect in the development of data-driven innovation that ameliorates firm performance. Furthermore, open knowledge search strategy that provides access to a greater number of information sources that can bring forth ideas and resources leads to better innovators (Jetzek et al., 2014). It is the right data that is correctly analyzed that ultimately produces richer, deeper, and valuable insights.

Big data can be useful to interact with customers in real time based on experience, reducing time for service delivery, cost reductions, and analytics in risk management (customer retention and new customers) or pricing (how to price products) (Davenport & Dyché, 2013). When data is integrated through the use of complex advanced technologies of machine learning and artificial intelligence, it is equally important to prioritize the type of analytics we do. Social factors have been found to be just as important as technical factors in determining big data analytics business value (Oesterreich et al., 2022). Social value even extends to corporate social responsibility. In addition, the organizational structure of the process with a data-driven culture or a data-driven mindset of who leads the initiative, where it fits within the organization, and how to manage the projects plays a pivotal role. Executive management support, skilled talent (quantitative analysts, data science capabilities, programmers with ability to code) with thorough market orientation applied to available data, and infrastructure are essential elements for success.

The most cited paper from the sample suggests a seven-step standardized process for data-driven innovation. This involves product conceptualization (conceptualize the market needs), data acquisition (from structured and unstructured sources), data refinement (converts abstract data into implementable data structure), data storage and retrieval (infrastructure for data management), distribution (sharing and updating data on a near real-time basis), presentation (unified data platform with proper data sharing across silos), and market feedback (to gain customer insights) as the final step (Sultana et al., 2021). The authors propose an innovation model that involves defining and understanding the problem, planning and task clarification, defining target customers, identifying competitive advantage, fine-tuning product design, and pricing among other things. Changes to business models to include advanced information and communication technologies that substantially improve the efficiency and effectiveness of operations (Netflix applies personalized movie recommendations for clients, self-driving cars through application of machine learning, Google, LinkedIn, etc.).

A strategic actionable plan that realizes opportunities to integrate and turn data into tasks that can be implemented contributes toward gaining a competitive advantage (Mikalef et al., 2020). Pro-active data analytics after data warehousing produce desired results if quality of data is good, that is, being reliable and trustworthy, data is managed well, and the necessary investments are made in big data that is applied to artificial intelligence (AI) initiatives. Privacy and security regarding the usage of data, however, remains a challenge with issues such as Protection of Personal

Information Act (POPIA) legislative requirements (Thomas et al., 2022). Security vulnerabilities have become inevitable considering cyber threats that target cloud storage and cloud computing, and this has necessitated stricter data governance processes and data management strategies.

A bibliometric literature review is employed to illustrate the productive trends and identify the most influential authors, most influential documents, and the most influential sources around the study. Network analysis and visualization of citation analysis of documents, co-citation analysis of authors, and analysis of co-occurrence are provided for better interpretation of the data. Thereafter, meta-analysis is conducted to assist with focus areas that require attention to obtain more information that is beneficial to the study.

The rest of the chapter is organized as follows: Section 2 reviews the related literature. Section 3 presents the research methodology of the study. The results of the study are presented and analyzed in Sect. 4. The research findings are discussed in Sect. 5. Section 7 concludes the article.

Literature Review

Technology Adoption

Previous studies reveal a significant impact of information technology on firm productivity (Oliveira & Fraga Martins, 2011). This necessitated discussion of the some of the prominent technology adoption models and theories relevant to the study.

The Theory of Diffusion of Innovations (DIT) advanced by Rogers in 1995 states that adoption is acceptance of an innovation deciding it is the best (Rogers, 2003). Adoption of newness is through certain channels among the members of a social system on the structure and function. Innovation and adoption happen after understanding, persuasion, decision, implementation, and confirmation (Sahin, 2006). This explains technology readiness with age, gender, and income level being determinants to adoption of technology. Innovation adoption is based on perceived advantages, compatibility, user friendliness, observability, social system, and organization readiness for change (Bakkabulindi, 2014).

Fishbein and Ajzen's Theory of Reasonable Action (RA) was proposed in 1975, and it revealed that attitudes are dependent on perceptions which affect attitude and behavior (Mishra et al., 2014). What determines behavioral intentions is attitude toward the behavior and subjective norms.

Technology Acceptance Model (TAM) introduced by Fred Davis in 1986 perceived usefulness and ease of use to impact attitude and determine intention and eventually actual usage of technology (Lai, 2017). Furthermore, the model influences designs and technology adoption strategies.

The accelerated pace of technological advancement has helped immensely for companies in pursuit of entrepreneurial activities to innovate and have sustained growth (Vrontis et al., 2022). Internet of Things (IoT) technology that includes machine learning, robotics, artificial intelligence, big data analytics, and network technologies with interconnected smart devices has facilitated exchange of data in real time and improved the upscaling process. New business values are created through technology applied on big data to stimulate new modes of interactions and functions with potential customers. Digital technologies improve productivity, reduce costs, promote innovation, and help organizations remain competitive and grow (Wang, 2023).

The lack of skilled staff who provide specialized labor has been highlighted as a hindrance to technology adoption (Carroni et al., 2023). Furthermore, retention of employees with the right skills is costly even if companies recruit personnel with the demanded expertise. Similarly, development of the required skills is also an expensive exercise with efficiency gains only enjoyed later when the value added is realized. Technology adoption is also based on company strategy with some opting to take a gradual approach toward the transformation decision prioritizing other focus areas (Cirillo et al., 2023). However, previous studies reveal a direct nexus between economic growth and digital technology adoption (Elfaki & Ahmed, 2024). Technological transformation has an effect on economy as it impacts inflation, labor markets, and production innovations and lowers transaction costs by improving operational effectiveness and efficiency.

Innovation

Innovation allows organizations to obtain a competitive advantage in a constantly changing business environment (Gupta, 2021). It is through innovative business models combined with the use of emerging technologies that helps organizations grow and perform better.

Innovation management can be viewed as a form of organizational capability that contributes toward wealth creation (Lawson & Samson, 2001). This involves seven elements of vision and strategy (providing clarity of purpose), harnessing the competence base, organizational intelligence (learning about customers and competitors), creativity and idea management, organizational structures and systems (governance matters), culture and climate (tone from the top providing employees with the "license to fail" over a specified duration of time), and management of technology.

Innovation capability is the ability to realize opportunities in the market and draw advantages through new product, service offerings, and processes that add value (Hanchi & Kerzazi, 2020). Dynamic capabilities have been defined as a "firm's ability to integrate, build, and reconfigure internal and external competences to address rapidly changing environments." It is the data-driven culture and innovative capabilities within an organization applying technology that influences and improves firm performance (Chaudhuri et al., 2024).

Innovation means new ideas, processes, services, and products and requires change. Objective is to develop new products and offer services from big data that enables fact-based decision making. The big data phenomenon requires a clear strategy of all possible uses of data to capitalize on digital innovation for sustainable business growth (Acciarini et al., 2023). Appropriate analytical algorithms and code to process and manipulate the data for better descriptive, diagnostic, predictive, prescriptive, augmented, and cognitive models are essential. Strategic market agility with dynamism and creativity to address the ever-changing customer needs drives growth (Sultana et al., 2022).

It is the market through acceptance and measure of relevance that determines categorization of creation either as an invention or innovation (Kusiak, 2009). It is the accurate, complete, and consistent data used on complex technology tools, analyzed with appropriate algorithms, that leads to superior innovations. In the innovation process, any use of data that creates value is referred to as data-driven innovation (Cavanillas et al., n.d.). Successful results are attained when the big data services and products are aligned with business objectives. Awareness of algorithmic biases such as data bias, method bias, and societal bias and the ability to address them helps to produce better data-driven innovations (Akter et al., 2021). Artificial intelligence innovation when it provides valuable insights combining big data and advanced analytics produces unmatched results (Yablonsky, n.d.).

Big Data

Data is considered the new currency and oil, and like oil, it needs to be refined, processed, and turned into something useful (Krotov & Johnson, 2023). Vast amounts of data through use of technology in the digital era are increasingly becoming readily available at an alarming rate (Jetzek et al., 2014). How you use the data you have to identify opportunities is very important. Data is one of the most important strategic assets that help understand customer behaviors to establish their product needs and service preferences. Existing processes do however need to be automated for efficiency as the generation and utilization of digital data has become ubiquitous. Development of new products entails novelty (latitude highlighting uniqueness in comparison to competition) and meaningfulness illustrating the degree of appropriateness and usefulness of the product (Amabile, 2012).

Organizations learn more and quicker about the market through data sharing, and can intelligently allocate resources, exchange advanced knowledge, and contribute toward economic development (Wei et al., 2024). This is enabled as the infrastructure coupled by the vast amount of data collected facilitates entry of new companies in the market. Big data is valuable when it addresses the needs of an enterprise and if it is accurate, consistent, timely, and complete and complies with legislative requirements (Ridzuan & Zainon, 2024). The raw data must first be accessed and then utilized correctly to produce desirable output. The challenges however extend to heterogeneity, latency, scalability, processing, and use of effective visualization tools in handling big data (Al-Ali et al., 2024).

Data Analytics

Many Big Tech companies have diversified and expanded their operations to financial services leveraging big data in their possession extrapolated to valuable insights (Selmy et al., 2024). Emerging big data open-source solutions co-exist with data warehouses for analysis of data from multiple sources to turn unrelated sources of data into coherent insights and help make agile decisions in real time. Furthermore, the good big data manipulation provides good data visualizations for reporting. Designing and developing improved data-driven innovations maintains a business's competitive advantage that drives value in a highly competitive business environment.

To help with the implementation of big data analytics in processes and operations, a big data analytics strategy is important, and capabilities which include resourcing the data and the ability to access, integrate, and deliver the data are necessary (Alsghaier, 2017). Systems effectiveness is dependent on the quality of information employed (Haque Sazu & Akter Jahan, 2022). It is important to do data analytics on good data as that drives business development.

The use of advanced technologies that includes artificial intelligence and machine learning, cloud-based solutions, and edge computing helps automate data analysis processes and realize the full potential of the data (Ochuba et al., 2024). Data analytics is pivotal to establish trends in the market and provide insights to maximize on opportunities and make good strategic decisions that support business growth. However, data analytics has its own challenges that include risks, growth of data, variety of tools, management quality, variety of users, heterogeneous data, fraud, scalability, complexity, data storage, data integration, security, and privacy (Garg et al., 2021).

Business Growth

There must be return on investment to improve business performance that reduces costs or ameliorate revenue for the big data efforts. It is not necessarily the volume of data that matters, but instead diverse data sources and new data types, combining both structured and unstructured (customer attitude, behavior, preferences, and satisfaction) data that yields the best results from data-driven innovations. Identify customer product needs and service preference and business models that focus on the impact of digital innovations knowing how and where the company creates value in industry (Teece, 2010).

Business analysis requires business intelligence to query and report on acquired information and be in a position to map a way forward after a thorough assessment of current data (Ajah & Nweke, 2019). Therefore, increased big data utilization and implementation of the big data solutions are just as important, as they are now regarded an essential element of a growing economy functioning properly (Schroeder, 2016).

Methodology

Bibliometric Review and Meta-analysis

A bibliometric review and meta-analysis were applied in this study. The bibliometric review relates to the use of quantitative studies on research publications to assess scientific research. The application uses both statistical and mathematical methods to evaluate the quality and quantity of published documents to establish trends or pattern of a specific research area. The bibliometric review method measures impact of published articles and citations after statistical analysis thereof that show linkages between articles (Fetscherin & Heinrich, 2015). Meta-analysis, on the other hand, combines the results of multiple scientific studies. Performance of articles is illustrated through matrices such as the number of citations and total h-index. VOSviewer software has been used to conduct citation analysis of documents, co-citation analysis of authors, and analysis of co-occurrence bibliometric techniques.

Data and Methods

The data was retrieved from the SCOPUS database using an appropriate Boolean mix of keywords with query string as "Data-driven innovation" AND "Business Growth." These keywords were entered into the SCOPUS advanced search TITLE-ABS-KEY interface as a part of a title or words mentioned in the abstract. The focus on the title and abstract narrows our search to achieve the objective of the study and obtain relevant topic that is significant to our research area. This step returned a total of 22 documents to conduct the bibliometric analysis.

The bibliometric methodological approach reviews the past and assesses the current situation to map beneficial strategy on data-driven innovation that can grow the business if the relevant link is established and various elements of work established that can add value.

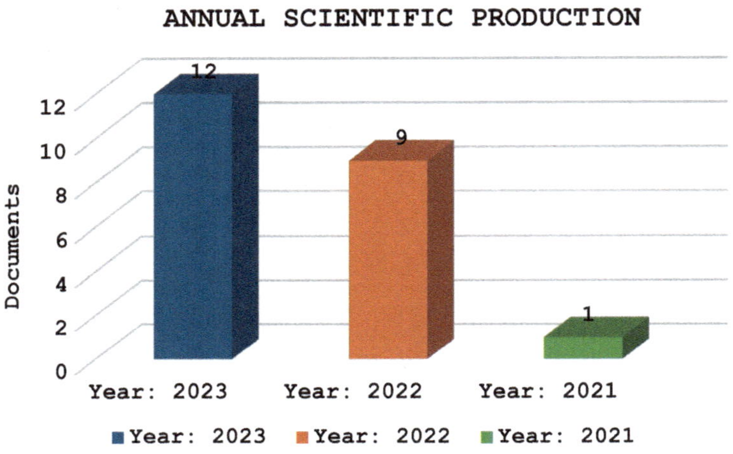

Fig. 1 Number of documents and year of publishing. Source: Author's own compilation (Data sourced from SCOPUS)

Research Findings

Main Information About Data

The sample data for this study was collected for the period 2021–2023 and found 22 documents that consist of 18 articles, 2 books, 1 book chapter, and 1 review. The top subject area of the results was Business, Management, and Accounting.

Production Trends from the Sample of the Study

Figure 1 shows the state of publishing on data-driven innovation and business growth. The chart illustrates an exponential increase from 2021 to 2023 being the timeframe data was analyzed. This provides evidence of more focus on the relationship between data-driven innovation and business growth lately.

Most Influential Authors from Sample of the Study

Table 1 shows a list of the 10 most prolific authors with a respected reputable voice based on the sample of the research area. Details of first year of publishing, total published papers, total citations, current affiliation, and country are presented. In addition, the author's h-index is provided as a metric that evaluates author's research performance based on quantity and quality of work.

Table 1 Influential authors from sample of the study

Author	SCOPUS ID	Year of 1st publication	TP	h-index	TC	Current Affiliation	Country
Chatterjee Sheshadri	56857082100	2015	172	41	3548	Indian Institute of Technology Kharagpur	India
Chaudhuri Ranjan	24544416000	2006	136	23	1623	Indian Institute of Management Ranchi	India
Vrontis Demetris	57195339008	1998	394	50	8381	University of Nicosia	Cyprus
Agag G. Mohamed	56332822900	2014	44	21	1656	Nottingham Business School	United Kingdom
Palacios-Marques Daniel	36739545300	2003	116	30	3579	Universitat Politecnica de Valencia	Spain
Ribeiro-Soriano Domingo	56862259400	1997	212	43	6605	Universitat Politecnica de Valencia	Spain
Saura Jose Ramon	57200338646	2017	84	27	2351	Universidad Rey Juan Carlos, Madrid	Spain
Abdullah Haim Hilman	38661234200	2011	74	11	478	Universiti Utara Malaysia, Sintok	Malaysia
Akter Shariar	36058277700	2007	119	38	8570	University of Wollongong	Australia
Alghamdi Omar A	57218760749	2022	14	3	53	Najran University, Najran	Saudi Arabia

List of 10 most prolific authors in research area
TP, total publication; *TC*, total citation
Note: h-index is based upon number of documents and number of citations
Source: Author's own compilation (Data sourced from SCOPUS)

Most Influential Documents from Sample of the Study

Table 2 presents connections that are relevant to the research topic and helps identify areas for future studies. Scope for future research can be guided by the most influential documents, the ones with the highest Field-Weighted Citation Impact (FWCI) figures.

Table 2 Most cited authors and the article title

Author	Title	Source	Year	Citations	FWCI
Sultana, S., Akter, S., Kyriazia, E., Wamba, S.F.	Architecting and developing big data-driven innovation (ddi) in the digital economy	Journal of Global Information Management 29(3), pp. 165–187	2021	49	3.14
Alzaidi, M. S., Agag, G.	The role of trust and privacy concerns in using social media for e-retail services: The moderating role of COVID-19	Journal of Retailing and Consumer Services, 68, 103042	2022	31	4.47
Vrontis, D., Chaudhuri, R., Chatterjee, S.	Adoption of digital technologies by SMEs for sustainability and value creation: Moderating role of entrepreneurial orientation	Sustainability (Switzerland), 14(13), 7949	2022	21	4.63
Saura, J. R., Palacios-Marques, D., Ribeiro-Soriano, D.	Digital marketing in SMEs via data-driven strategies: Reviewing the current state of research	Journal of Small Business Management, 61(3), pp. 1278–1313	2023	15	11.88
Pham, C. T. A., Magistretti, S., Dell'Era, C.	The role of design thinking in Big Data innovations	Innovation: Organization and Management, 24(2), pp. 290–314	2022	12	2.71
Zastempowski, M.	What shapes innovation capability in micro-enterprises? New-to-the-market product and process perspective	Journal of Open Innovation: Technology Market, and Complexity, 8(1), 59	2022	10	5.18
Mokbel Al Koliby, I. S., Abdulla, H. H., Mohd Suki, N.	Linking entrepreneurial competencies, innovation and sustainable performance of manufacturing SMEs	Asia-Pacific Journal of Business Administration	2022	5	2.18
Saura, J. R., Palacios-Marques, D., Ribeiro-Soriano, D.	Data-driven strategies in operation management: mining user-generated content in Twitter	Annals of Operations Research	2022	5	0.93

(continued)

Table 2 (continued)

Author	Title	Source	Year	Citations	FWCI
Chatterjee, S., Chaudhuri, R., Vrontis, D., Galati, A.	Digital transformation using industry 4.0 technology by food and beverage companies in post COVID-19 period: from DCV and IDT perspective	European Journal of Innovation Management	2022	4	0.24
Zhang, M., Jedin, M. H.	Firm innovation and technical capabilities for enhanced export performance: The moderating role of competitive intensity	Review of International Business and Strategy	2022	4	1.06

FWCI: Field-Weighted Citation Impact (How well the cited document is in comparison to similar documents)

Table 3 The highly published journals and their most cited article

Journal	TP	TC	Cite Score Oct 2023	The most cited article	Times cited	Publisher
Sustainability Switzerland	53,399	319,126	6.0	Impacts of the COVID-19 pandemic on life of higher education students: A global perspective	889	MDPI
Journal of Retailing And Consumer Services	1444	25,401	17.6	Predicting green product consumption using theory of planned behaviour and reasoned action	1045	Elsevier Ltd
Annals of Operations Research	1674	11,855	7.1	A tutorial on the cross-entropy method	1858	Elsevier Ltd
Asia-Pacific Journal of Business Administration	104	631	6.1	Critical success factors of public private partnership (PPP) implementation in Malaysia	119	Elsevier Ltd
Corporate And Business Strategy Review	129	110	0.9	Age and prior working experience effect on entrepreneurial intention	11	Virtus Interpress

The 5 most productive journals with their most cited article
TP, total publications; *TC*, total citations

Most Influential Sources from Sample of the Study

Table 3 illustrates the 5 most productive journals from the sample of the study showing details of total publications, total citations, and the most cited article and the publisher. The cite score changes and has been provided based on October 2023 SCOPUS update figures.

Network Analysis and Visualization

The following section is based on network analysis and visualization. Citation analysis of documents, co-citation analysis of authors, and occurrence analysis of keywords are conducted using VOSviewer application to visualize the research trends in data-driven innovation and business growth.

Citation Analysis of Documents

Figure 2 Cluster 1—Sultana S.; Akter S.; Kyriazis E.; Wamba S.F. (2021), Cluster 2—Alzaidi M. S.; Agag G. (2022), Cluster 3—Vrontis D.; Chaudhuri R.; Chatterjee S. (2023), Cluster 4—Saura J. R.; Palacios-marques D.; Ribiero-soriano D. (2023), Cluster 5: Pham C. T. A.; Magistrelli S.; Dell'era C. (2022), and Cluster 6—Zastempowski M. (2022). The rest have below double-digit citations. The closer the documents are to each other shows the level of relatedness. Size of the blocks illustrates the number of citations of documents

Fig. 2 Citation analysis of documents

Table 4 Co-citation of authors and the clusters

Cluster	Number of items	Authors
1 (Red)	9	Gunasekaran A., Akter S., Wamba S.F., Childe S. J., Dubey R., Davenport T.H., Liu Y., Saura J. R., Kraus S.
2 (Green)	6	Agag G., Eid R., Wang. Y., Ringle C. M., Sarstedt M., Hair J. F.
3 (Blue)	4	Dwivedi Y.K., Rana N. P., Mogaji E., Nguyen N. P.
4 (Yellow)	4	Chaudhuri R., Vrontis D., Chatterjee S., Treece D. J.

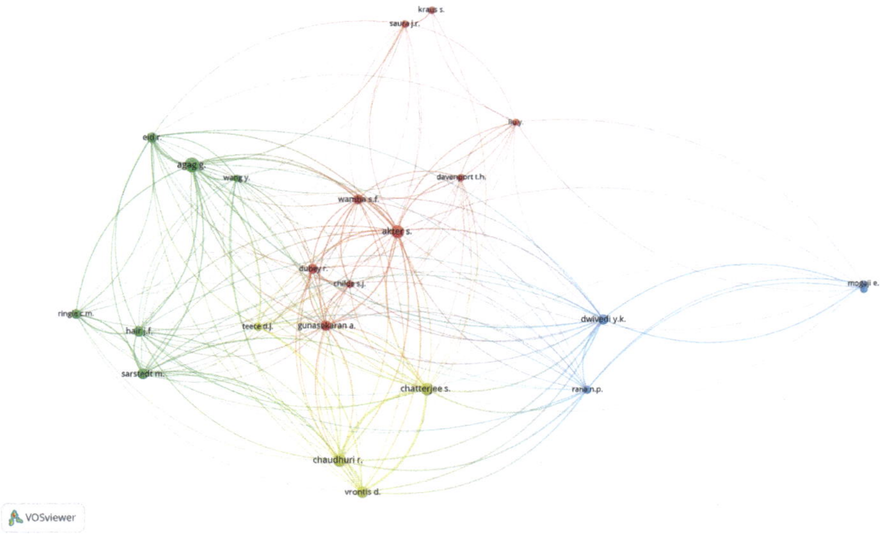

Fig. 3 Co-citation analysis of co-authors

Co-citation Analysis of Authors

Table 4 groups authors into the 4 different clusters based on contents of the documents and citation's relationship.

Figure 3 shows measurement of the similarity of the contents of the documents based on the citation's relationship. Bibliometric data was used as the source and the analysis wasconducted using the VOSviewer software for network visualization. The minimum number of citations selected of an author is 10. Out of 4768 authors, 23 met the threshold.

Table 5 Occurrence of keywords and their clusters

Cluster	Number of items	Occurrence
1 (Red)	4	Entrepreneurship, entrepreneur, COVID-19, theoretical study
2 (Green)	4	digital transformation, big data, big data analytics, entrepreneurial orientation
3 (Blue)	3	Sustainability, Business, Technology Adoption
4 (Yellow)	3	Competitive Advantage, Uncertainty Analysis, Competitiveness
5 (Purple)	2	Innovation, SMEs

Analysis of Co-occurrence

Table 5 shows further analysis using VOSviewer software to construct and visualize bibliometric networks.

Figure 4 illustrates the network visualization of the author's keywords produced by VOSviewer, showing color, circle size, font size, and thickness of connecting lines as the nexus of the relationship among key words. Out of the 153 keywords, 17 met the threshold when the minimum number of occurrences of a keyword is 2. One item was removed as it was less relevant and remained with 16 items in 5 clusters.

Discussion of Findings

Data was collected from the SCOPUS database and thereafter we conducted a bibliometric meta-analysis. The method was used to gain more insight on the progress that has been made on data-driven innovation and its impact on business growth from 2021 to 2023. Furthermore, the analysis illustrates the most cited articles together with the most influential authors giving awareness of the relevant journals.

The results of the study reveal that the use of data combined with technological advancements has been on the rise in recent years. The results of the study further documented that to remain competitive in this highly volatile business environment across any industry, it has become highly imperative to invest in technology and use big data and apply appropriate analytics to develop new products and design new services that can grant the business growth prospects. Moreover, having personnel with the expertise for proper analysis is just as important as the quality of data acquired.

The results of the study are significant because they highlight key areas to focus on that are relevant to have success in endeavors to attain business growth through data-driven innovation. The bibliometric review and meta-analysis of the study support the notion that businesses can indeed grow and improve as a result of embracing data-driven innovation.

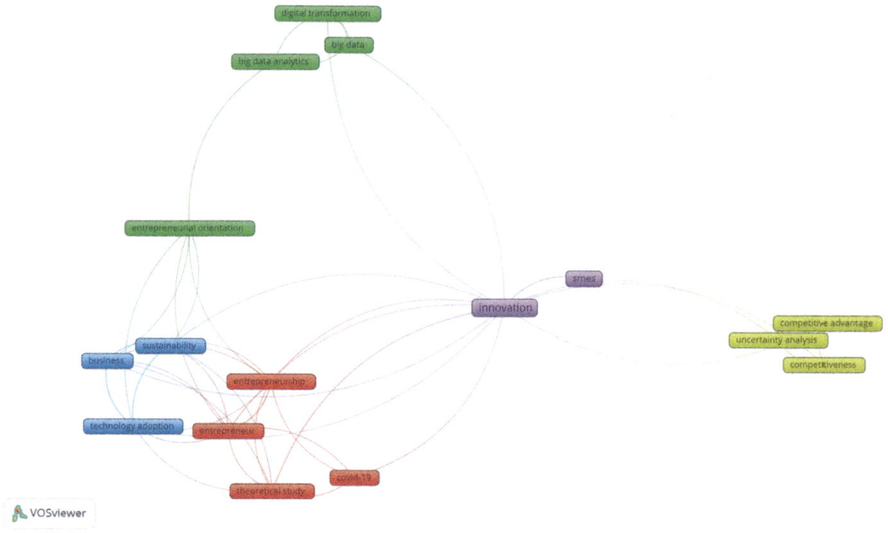

Fig. 4 Occurrence analysis of keywords

Conclusion

The primary goal was to establish trends and identify research gaps in data-driven innovation and business growth. The study adopted a bibliometric review and meta-analysis by utilizing studies that were extracted from the SCOPUS database over the period 2021–2023.

The study reports the trend of the previous studies using the Boolean mix of "Data-driven innovation" AND "Business Growth" as bibliometric indicators obtained from the SCOPUS database. Bibliometric details of a total of 22 documents were extracted from the SCOPUS database. The data acquired was thereafter exported onto VOSviewer software and used to provide network analysis and visualization.

The results of the study showed an increase in the number of documents relevant to the topic from 2021 to 2023. It is interesting to note that data analytics has received so much attention in previous studies as it should since it determines output. It is also documented that even though the focus is on data and technology, being innovative, it is important that emphasis is placed on the sustainability of the business proposals.

Notwithstanding that bibliometric and meta-analysis is a sound scientific statistical analysis method, it remains subjective. Limitations include the variations as a result of time periods applied that may alter results as well as possibility of various terms to search for the data. As such, the results of the study are based on what this research obtained from the SCOPUS database, and it is important to note that other authors may have their articles not indexed in SCOPUS and therefore excluded from analysis. This study, however, provides a holistic overview based on our sample of current research on global scale of data-driven innovation and business growth.

The scope of future research is establishing how best to collect, store, and analyze unstructured data to improve productivity, cut costs, and grow businesses. This is taking into consideration the value we can derive from readily available data even accessible on open source. Therefore, the recommendation is vigilance in addressing governance matters when using data to grow businesses ethically.

References

Acciarini, C., Cappa, F., Boccardelli, P., & Oriani, R. (2023). How can organizations leverage big data to innovate their business models? A systematic literature review. *Technovation, 123*. https://doi.org/10.1016/j.technovation.2023.102713

Ajah, I. A., & Nweke, H. F. (2019). Big data and business analytics: Trends, platforms, success factors and applications. *Big Data and Cognitive Computing, 3*(2), 1–30. https://doi.org/10.3390/bdcc3020032

Akter, S., McCarthy, G., Sajib, S., Michael, K., Dwivedi, Y. K., D'Ambra, J., & Shen, K. N. (2021). Algorithmic bias in data-driven innovation in the age of AI. *International Journal of Information Management, 60*. https://doi.org/10.1016/j.ijinfomgt.2021.102387

Al-Ali, A. R., Gupta, R., Zualkernan, I., & Das, S. K. (2024). Role of IoT technologies in big data management systems: A review and smart grid case study. *Pervasive and Mobile Computing, 100*. https://doi.org/10.1016/j.pmcj.2024.101905

Alsghaier, H. (2017). The importance of big data analytics in business: A case study. *American Journal of Software Engineering and Applications, 6*(4), 111. https://doi.org/10.11648/j.ajsea.20170604.12

Amabile, T. M. (2012). *Componential theory of creativity*.

Bakkabulindi, F. (2014). A call for return to Rogers' innovation diffusion theory. *Makerere Journal of Higher Education, 6*(1), 55. https://doi.org/10.4314/majohe.v6i1.4

Carroni, E., Delogu, M., & Pulina, G. (2023). Technology adoption and specialized labor. *International Economics, 173*, 249–259. https://doi.org/10.1016/j.inteco.2023.01.003

Cavanillas, J. M., Curry, E., & Wahlster, W. (n.d.). *New horizons for a data-driven economy: A roadmap for usage and exploitation of big data in Europe*.

Chaudhuri, R., Chatterjee, S., Mariani, M. M., & Wamba, S. F. (2024). Assessing the influence of emerging technologies on organizational data driven culture and innovation capabilities: A sustainability performance perspective. *Technological Forecasting and Social Change, 200*. https://doi.org/10.1016/j.techfore.2023.123165

Cirillo, V., Fanti, L., Mina, A., & Ricci, A. (2023). The adoption of digital technologies: Investment, skills, work organisation. *Structural Change and Economic Dynamics, 66*, 89–105. https://doi.org/10.1016/j.strueco.2023.04.011

Davenport, T. H., & Dyché, J. (2013). *Big data in big companies*.

Elfaki, K. E., & Ahmed, E. M. (2024). Digital technology adoption and globalization innovation implications on Asian Pacific green sustainable economic growth. *Journal of Open Innovation: Technology, Market, and Complexity, 10*(1). https://doi.org/10.1016/j.joitmc.2024.100221

Fetscherin, M., & Heinrich, D. (2015). Consumer brand relationships research: A bibliometric citation meta-analysis. *Journal of Business Research, 68*(2), 380–390. https://doi.org/10.1016/j.jbusres.2014.06.010

Garg, A., Popli, R., & Sarao, B. S. (2021). Growth of digitization and its impact on big data analytics. *IOP Conference Series: Materials Science and Engineering, 1022*(1). https://doi.org/10.1088/1757-899X/1022/1/012083

Gupta, A. K. (2021). Innovation dimensions and firm performance synergy in the emerging market: A perspective from dynamic capability theory & signaling theory. *Technology in Society, 64*. https://doi.org/10.1016/j.techsoc.2020.101512

Hanchi, S., & Kerzazi, L. (2020). Startup innovation capability from a dynamic capability-based view: A literature review and conceptual framework. *Journal of Small Business Strategy*.

Haque Sazu, M., & Akter Jahan, S. (2022). Impact of big data analytics on business performance. *International Research Journal of Modernization in Engineering Technology and Science*. Retrieved from www.irjmets.com

Helfert, M. (n.d.). *Big data quality-towards an explanation model in a smart city context.*

Jetzek, T., Avital, M., & Bjorn-Andersen, N. (2014). Data-driven innovation through open government data. *Journal of Theoretical and Applied Electronic Commerce Research, 9*(2), 100–120. https://doi.org/10.4067/S0718-18762014000200008

Krotov, V., & Johnson, L. (2023). Big web data: Challenges related to data, technology, legality, and ethics. *Business Horizons, 66*(4), 481–491. https://doi.org/10.1016/j.bushor.2022.10.001

Kusiak, A. (2009). Innovation: A data-driven approach. *International Journal of Production Economics, 122*(1), 440–448. https://doi.org/10.1016/j.ijpe.2009.06.025

Lai, P. (2017). The literature review of technology adoption models and theories for the novelty technology. *Journal of Information Systems and Technology Management, 14*(1), 21–38. https://doi.org/10.4301/S1807-17752017000100002

Lawson, B., & Samson, D. (2001). Developing innovation capability in organisations: A dynamic capabilities approach. *International Journal of Innovation Management, 05*(03), 377–400. https://doi.org/10.1142/s1363919601000427

Mikalef, P., Pappas, I. O., Krogstie, J., & Pavlou, P. A. (2020). Big data and business analytics: A research agenda for realizing business value. *Information and Management, 57*(1). https://doi.org/10.1016/j.im.2019.103237

Mishra, D., Akman, I., & Mishra, A. (2014). Theory of reasoned action application for green information technology acceptance. *Computers in Human Behavior, 36*, 29–40. https://doi.org/10.1016/j.chb.2014.03.030

Ochuba, N. A., Amoo, O. O., Okafor, E. S., Akinrinola, O., & Usman, F. O. (2024). Strategies for leveraging big data and analytics for business development: A comprehensive review across sectors. *Computer Science & IT Research Journal, 5*(3), 562–575. https://doi.org/10.51594/csitrj.v5i3.861

Oesterreich, T. D., Anton, E., Teuteberg, F., & Dwivedi, Y. K. (2022). The role of the social and technical factors in creating business value from big data analytics: A meta-analysis. *Journal of Business Research, 153*, 128–149. https://doi.org/10.1016/j.jbusres.2022.08.028

Oliveira, T., & Fraga Martins, M. (2011). Literature review of information technology adoption models at firm level. *The Electronic Journal Information Systems Evaluation, 14*, 110.

Ridzuan, F., & Zainon, W. M. N. W. (2024). A review on data quality dimensions for big data. *Procedia Computer Science, 234*, 341–348. https://doi.org/10.1016/j.procs.2024.03.008

Rogers. (2003). *Diffusion of innovations by Everett Rogers (1995).*

Sahin, I. (2006). Detailed review of Rogers' diffusion of innovations theory and educational technology-related studies based on Rogers' theory. *The Turkish Online Journal of Educational Technology, 5.*

Schroeder, R. (2016). Big data business models: Challenges and opportunities. *Cogent Social Sciences, 2*(1). https://doi.org/10.1080/23311886.2016.1166924

Selmy, H. A., Mohamed, H. K., & Medhat, W. (2024). Big data analytics deep learning techniques and applications: A survey. *Information Systems, 120*, 102318. https://doi.org/10.1016/j.is.2023.102318

Sultana, S., Akter, S., Kyriazis, E., & Wamba, S. F. (2021). Architecting and developing big data-driven innovation (DDI) in the digital economy. *Journal of Global Information Management, 29*(3), 165–187. https://doi.org/10.4018/JGIM.2021050107

Sultana, S., Akter, S., & Kyriazis, E. (2022). How data-driven innovation capability is shaping the future of market agility and competitive performance? *Technological Forecasting and Social Change, 174*. https://doi.org/10.1016/j.techfore.2021.121260

Teece, D. J. (2010). Business models, business strategy and innovation. *Long Range Planning, 43*(2–3), 172–194. https://doi.org/10.1016/j.lrp.2009.07.003

Thomas, L., Gondal, I., Oseni, T., & Firmin, S. (2022). A framework for data privacy and security accountability in data breach communications. *Computers and Security, 116*. https://doi.org/10.1016/j.cose.2022.102657

Vrontis, D., Chaudhuri, R., & Chatterjee, S. (2022). Adoption of digital technologies by SMEs for sustainability and value creation: Moderating role of entrepreneurial orientation. *Sustainability (Switzerland), 14*(13). https://doi.org/10.3390/su14137949

Wang, L. (2023). Digital transformation and total factor productivity. *Finance Research Letters, 58*. https://doi.org/10.1016/j.frl.2023.104338

Wei, X., Li, H., & Wang, Y. (2024). Does big data infrastructure development promote new enterprises entry: Evidence from China. *Finance Research Letters, 60*. https://doi.org/10.1016/j.frl.2023.104828

Yablonsky, S. A. (n.d.). *Multidimensional data-driven artificial intelligence innovation*. Retrieved from https://asi.ru/eng/nti/

The Impact of ERP Upgrades on Employee Productivity: An Empirical Study in South African Higher Education Institution

Lethiwe Nzama-Sithole

Abstract This study aims to explore the productivity impact of ERP upgrades, focusing on the service quality of the updated system during a specific pivotal time. Data was collected through a questionnaire distributed among ERP system users across departments such as Expenditure, Revenue, Payroll, HR, and ICS. Respondents were selected from the study population using a purposive sampling technique. The collected data was analysed using descriptive statistics and structural equation modelling techniques facilitated by SPSS software. The results indicated that while most respondents acknowledged improvements in the Oracle system's user-friendliness and reporting capabilities, there were significant concerns regarding the adequacy of training provided, the ease of completing year-end reporting tasks, and the overall impact on productivity during the upgrade period. Specifically, 60% of respondents found it challenging to submit work reports on time, and 73.3% were dissatisfied with the upgraded system's impact on productivity. Furthermore, 53.3% felt highly inconvenienced due to the disruptions caused by the upgrade. Based on these findings, the study recommends that future ERP upgrades involve more comprehensive planning and communication, adequate training sessions before and after the upgrade, and better timing of upgrades to avoid critical reporting periods. Additionally, involving end users in the testing phase and providing ongoing support can enhance system acceptance and minimise productivity losses. These steps can help HEIs and other organisations optimise their ERP upgrade processes, ensuring smoother transitions and improved outcomes.

Keywords Enterprise resource planning · Productivity · Employee satisfaction · HEI

L. Nzama-Sithole (✉)
University of Johannesburg, Johannesburg, South Africa
e-mail: lethiwen@uj.ac.za

T. Moloi (ed.), *Impacting Society Positively Through Technology in Accounting and Business Processes*, Springer Proceedings in Business and Economics,
https://doi.org/10.1007/978-3-031-84885-8_66

Introduction

In today's rapidly evolving business landscape, organisations encounter many challenges. These include navigating intense competition, asserting market influence, and keeping pace with ongoing advancements in information technology (IT) (Ramadhani et al., 2023; Nzama, 2021; AlMuhayfith & Shaiti, 2020). Moreover, leveraging IT innovations strategically becomes pivotal for gaining a competitive edge (Aljarrah, 2021; Domagała et al., 2021; Nzama, 2021). As a result, these challenges significantly reshape the landscape of organisational management. In today's competitive business landscape, the rapid evolution of information technology plays a pivotal role. This dynamic has intensified competition among organisations (Ramadhani et al., 2023). Managers must leverage technology to benefit their organisations and stay successful and competitive. Doing so enhances information flow, cut costs, streamlines operations, diversifies products, fosters supplier connections, and promptly meets customer demands (Aroba et al., 2023; Qutaishat et al., 2012).

IT has equipped businesses with many tools to streamline their management functions. Nonetheless, there is a growing demand for empirical evidence, including research studies validating that investing in IT yields favourable outcomes for firms (Aljarrah, 2021; Nzama, 2021). Melville et al. (2004) and AlMuhayfith and Shaiti (2020) assert that IT holds significant benefits, presenting various potential advantages such as increased productivity, enhanced flexibility, reduced costs, and improved quality. Furthermore, Chopra et al. (2022) argues that ERP systems in commercial businesses are widely recognised and commonly employed for integrating and automating processes, improving performance, and reducing costs.

Several studies have been conducted in different parts of the world. Qutaishat et al. (2012) conducted one in the telecommunication sector in Jordan. Qutaishat et al. (2012) found that organisational impact significantly affects employee productivity, service quality, and innovation. Satisfaction only influences service quality and innovation, not productivity, possibly due to inadequate training.

The recommendation is to create a training programme that educates employees about the changes resulting from ERP implementation. At the same time, AlMuhayfith and Shaiti (2020) conducted an exploratory study to identify the factors contributing to an ERP system's practical and successful use. However, their study was limited to small and medium enterprises in Saudi. Their study found that management support, user satisfaction, and training significantly impact ERP usage and that ERP enhances SMEs' performance. Chopra et al. (2022) conducted a study investigating utilising ERP systems in the manufacturing industry for productivity improvement. They suggest that post-implementation activities like software updates and maintenance are crucial in the lifecycle of an ERP system to maximise its economic benefits.

Another study in Turkey explored the factors that influence the ERP systems' readiness stage on project success immediately after going live from the project management perspective (Kirmizi & Kocaoglu, 2022). The study was limited to the project managers' perspective in Turkey and highlighted critical success factors that project managers need to consider when implementing ERP systems. Domagała et al. (2021) conducted a study that investigated the post-implementation process of ERP system development and weighted the options of upgrade or reimplementation of the ERP system. They found proper decision-making is crucial even if the organisation upgrades its system instead of implementing it post-implementation. Domagała et al. (2021) concluded that identifying the optimal time for a technical upgrade is essential for minimising ERP system maintenance costs.

The ERP system implementation and upgrade research is not limited to international technology and information systems researchers. However, it has grown in attraction from researchers in accounting and management (AlMuhayfith & Shaiti, 2020). Another study conducted in Peru focused on ERP users in a Peruvian education enterprise. It examined the impact of implementing an ERP system on process management, which in turn enhances the performance of employees (Cruz-Torres et al., 2021). The study's findings were that ERP systems can improve the organisation's performance; however, this might depend on improving process management. Cruz-Torres et al. (2021) further caution that there should be change management in place to assist in dealing with resistance that the users may encounter at the beginning of the implementation process, and there should be a training process in place to improve the competencies of staff for the better use of the ERP systems. A study conducted in Indonesia by Ramadhani et al. (2023) identified 12 critical success factors to consider when implementing an ERP system.

Most studies also investigate ERP systems' influence on large organisations (AlMuhayfith & Shaiti, 2020). In the South African context, studies have been conducted to assess the effect of enterprise resource planning systems on the financial statement audit of a higher education institution (Nzama, 2015, 2021); however, these studies did not focus on users' productivity. Another study conducted in HEI was by Aroba et al. (2023), who outlined the impact of the ERP system's digital transformation on the supply chain management process in HEI. They found that ERP systems only partially cover all business operations involved in the supply chain process.

The scope of this study is limited to the HEI in South Africa, which had recently undergone a significant upgrade of its Oracle EBS System, which required extended system downtime of over seven working days. These were critical days for the HEI as they were the period in which the HEI finalised its annual financial statement reporting, which should be ready for an external audit. Therefore, one must understand the impact of the timing of these significant ERP upgrades and the downtime on the employees' productivity, satisfaction, and acceptance of the newly upgraded system.

The rest of the chapter is structured as follows: Section 2 offers a critical review and discussion of related previous studies. Section 3 elaborates on the fundamental concepts and notations utilised in the chapter. Section 4 discusses and illustrates the research approach employed. Data analysis and results are presented and discussed in Sect. 5. Section 6 presents the discussion and conclusion. Finally, Section 7 delves into the implementation of the study and outlines directions for future research.

Literature Review

The main objective of this study is to determine the impact of ERP system upgrades on employee productivity. The secondary objectives linked to these broader objectives are

- To determine whether the ERP upgrades significantly affected the HEI financial year-end reporting and employee productivity.
- To determine whether ERP users' satisfaction significantly affects service quality.

The Enterprise Resource Planning (ERP) System

The excerpt discusses the increasing significance of Enterprise Resource Planning (ERP) systems in modern business operations. Initially adopted primarily by the manufacturing sector, ERP systems are widely utilised across various sectors, including non-profit organisations and government agencies (AlMuhayfith & Shaiti, 2020). They integrate various software units with a central database to efficiently manage resources like assets and human resources (Aljarrah, 2021; Nzama, 2015, 2021).

Implementing ERP systems promises numerous benefits for organisations, including enhanced productivity, streamlined business processes, and improved information sharing. In comparison, large enterprises have traditionally been the primary adopters (Aljarrah, 2021; AlMuhayfith & Shaiti, 2020).

There are four main types of enterprise applications: enterprise systems, supply chain management systems, customer relationship management systems, and knowledge management systems. This chapter focuses on enterprise systems, also known as enterprise resource planning (ERP) systems. ERP systems help organisations integrate their various functional business processes—such as manufacturing, finance, sales, and human resources—previously managed separately into a unified software system. A central data repository facilitates this integration, enabling efficient information utilisation across different departments within the organisation (Qutaishat et al., 2012).

Qutaishat et al. (2012) state that organisational impact and user satisfaction are the primary metrics for evaluating ERP implementation. User satisfaction encompasses attitudes towards factors like information accuracy and completeness. Organisational impact gauges how ERP usage enhances organisational performance, including achieving business goals and improving operational efficiency.

This measure encompasses both effectiveness and efficiency-based improvements to capture the full benefits of ERP systems (Qutaishat et al., 2012).

The Impact of the ERP Systems Upgrade on Employee Productivity

The literature highlights various factors influencing the usage of ERP systems, with implications for human capital. Studies by Ruivo et al. (2012), Nwankpa and Roumani (2014), Chang et al. (2008), Lin (2010), and Bokhari (2005) collectively reveal vital determinants such as complexity, compatibility, training, user satisfaction, and top management support. Aroba et al. (2023) also caution on the complexity of adopting a new ERP system and suggest factors that need to be considered by the organisation when planning to adopt ERP systems. These factors have consistent associations with ERP system usage. For instance, management support and training are crucial in facilitating successful ERP adoption. Companies that prioritise training initiatives and provide adequate support from top management will likely see higher levels of ERP system usage among their employees. Additionally, factors like user satisfaction and compatibility significantly impact the adoption and utilisation of ERP systems (Aljarrah, 2021).

Aljarrah's (2021) findings underscore the importance of investing in human capital development to maximise the benefits of ERP implementation. By ensuring employees are adequately trained and supported, organisations can enhance system usage, improving efficiency and effectiveness in business operations. Moreover, understanding these factors can inform strategies for successful ERP implementation and utilisation, ultimately contributing to organisational success and competitiveness.

Enhancing employee productivity is paramount in today's fiercely competitive business environment. Providing timely information empowers employees, a feature achievable through integrated technologies like ERP. Qutaishat et al. (2012) support this view by highlighting that investing in ICT solutions bolsters labour productivity, with ERP systems playing a particularly positive role in this endeavour.

Theoretical Framework

For a study examining the impact of ERP system upgrades on employee productivity and related factors, the following theoretical frameworks can provide a comprehensive understanding of the dynamics involved:

Technology Acceptance Model (TAM)

The TAM, developed by Davis (1989), focuses on individuals' acceptance and adoption of new technologies. It posits that perceived usefulness and perceived ease of use are critical determinants of users' attitudes and intentions towards using technology. Studies such as Aljarrah (2021) and Nzama (2021) have applied TAM to analyse users' perceptions and behaviours towards ERP systems.

Unified Theory of Acceptance and Use of Technology (UTAUT)

UTAUT, proposed by Venkatesh et al. (2003), extends TAM by incorporating additional factors such as social influence, facilitating conditions, and behavioural intention. This framework has been widely used to examine technology adoption and usage in various contexts, including ERP systems (Aljarrah, 2021).

Social Cognitive Theory (SCT)

SCT, developed by Bandura (1999), emphasises the role of observational learning, self-efficacy, and outcome expectations in shaping individuals' behaviour. In the context of ERP system upgrades, SCT can help understand how employees' beliefs about their capabilities to use the upgraded system (self-efficacy) and their expectations of the system's outcomes (outcome expectations) influence their adoption and usage behaviours.

Organisational Change Theories

Theories of organisational change, such as Lewin's Change Management Model, Kotter's Eight-Step Change Model, or the Satir Change Model, provide insights into implementing ERP system upgrades within organisations. These frameworks focus on understanding the stages of change, resistance to change, and strategies for managing organisational transitions effectively. They have been applied in various studies examining ERP implementations (Aljarrah, 2021).

Integrating these theoretical frameworks into the study design can provide a robust theoretical foundation for analysing the impact of ERP system upgrades on employee productivity and related outcomes, drawing from established principles in technology adoption, organisational behaviour, and change management.

Research Methodology

This study aims to identify the impact of ERP upgrades on employees' productivity, especially during the critical time of finalising the year-end financial reporting, the updated system's service quality, and the satisfaction and acceptance of employees with the upgraded system. Data was collected through a questionnaire distributed to ERP System (Oracle) users working in a higher education institution. A purposive sampling technique was implemented to select respondents from the study population. The population emanated from the Finance Expenditure, Revenue, and Payroll divisions. The data collected from the questionnaire was analysed using the descriptive statistics and structural equation model to test the study hypotheses using SPSS.

An exploratory study is imperative to comprehend the research context, mirroring previous studies (Aljarrah, 2021) and formulating research hypotheses grounded in the three primary relationships. To accomplish this, individuals utilising ERP systems across various roles (e.g. IT managers and ERP section heads) have been invited to participate, irrespective of whether their organisations have implemented ERP systems. A mixed-method approach was followed.

Research Hypotheses

- ERP system upgrades have a significant effect on year-end financial reporting.
- ERP users' satisfaction has a significant effect on employees' productivity.
- ERP users' satisfaction has a significant effect on service quality.

Sample

The study was limited to an HEI where an upgrade of the ERP system was conducted in January 2022, and the data was collected. A questionnaire was distributed to ERP System (Oracle) users working in an HEI. A purposive sampling technique was used for respondents from the study population. The same was drawn from the population within the Finance Divisions of the Finance Expenditure Division of Procurement, Supply Management, Assets Management, Stores, Accounts Payable and Payroll Departments, and the Student Finance Division.

The data collected from the questionnaire was analysed using SPSS for descriptive analysis and thematic analysis of the two long questions included. All information from the data collection was treated as confidential and only used to produce aggregate results. Fifteen respondents completed the questionnaire with a positive representative rate for all divisions selected. Table 1 shows the same characteristics.

Table 1 The main characteristics of the study's sample

	Category	Frequency	Percentage
Education			
	High school certificate—matric or less	1	6.7
	Diploma	5	33.3
	Bachelor's degree	7	46.7
	Postgraduate degree (hons, master's, or PhD)	2	13.3
Roles			
	Oracle production frequent user	7	46.7
	Department supervisor	4	26.7
	Department manager	3	20.0
	Department system specialist	1	6.7
Experience			
	Below 5 years	5	33.3
	5–10 years	3	20.0
	11–15 years	2	13.3
	16 years and above	5	33.3

Measures

The questionnaires collected information from the selected sample, including demographic characteristics, ERP implementation, employees' productivity, and service quality. Two qualitative questions were also included in the questionnaire to ascertain ERP users' views on the impact of upgrades on their productivity. The measurement of the collected information is further explained below.

Measures of the ERP Successful Upgrade

ERP upgrade was measured via two dimensions, user satisfaction and organisational impact, using a five-point Likert-type scale ranging from 1 (strongly disagree) to 5 (strongly agree). The respondents assessed seven items: degree of ERP upgrade satisfaction (e.g. the ERP provides output and reports I need).

Employees' Productivity

Job productivity was assessed by asking participants, "On your most recent performance appraisal for your current job this year, what rating did you receive from your supervisor?" Responses were rated on a scale of 1 (poor) to 5 (excellent). Bright (2007) and Qutaishat et al. (2012) note that this question is widely used to gauge employee productivity.

Results

Descriptive statistics, including means, standard deviations, and zero-order correlations between study variables, were computed using IBM SPSS Statistics 29.

Table 2 represents the results of a survey about whether proper planning and communication occurred during an Oracle upgrade.

Most respondents (73.3%) believed there was proper planning and communication during the Oracle upgrade. In comparison, a smaller portion (26.6% combined from the last two rows) had a differing view, with 13% being neutral and 13.3 disagreeing.

Table 3 represents responses to the statement, "There was sufficient training provided during and after the Oracle upgrade."

The data suggests that while a significant portion of respondents felt the training was insufficient (rating 2), a notable group found it more adequate (ratings 4 and 5). The majority view leans towards the training needing to be more sufficient.

Table 4 represents responses to the statement, "I was able to perform and complete my year-end reporting tasks easily."

Table 2 Planning and communication

There was proper planning and communication during the Oracle upgrade					
		Frequency	Per cent	Valid per cent	Cumulative per cent
Valid	2	11	73.3	73.3	73.3
	3	2	13.3	13.3	86.7
	4	2	13.3	13.3	100.0
	Total	15	100.0	100.0	

Table 3 Training

Sufficient training was provided during and after the Oracle upgrade					
		Frequency	Per cent	Valid per cent	Cumulative per cent
Valid	2	7	46.7	46.7	46.7
	3	3	20.0	20.0	66.7
	4	4	26.7	26.7	93.3
	5	1	6.7	6.7	100.0
	Total	15	100.0	100.0	

Table 4 Productivity

I was able to perform and complete my year-end reporting tasks with ease					
		Frequency	Per cent	Valid per cent	Cumulative per cent
Valid	1	2	13.3	13.3	13.3
	2	10	66.7	66.7	80.0
	3	3	20.0	20.0	100.0
	Total	15	100.0	100.0	

Table 5 Productivity and efficiency

I have submitted my work reports on time during the Oracle System upgrade					
		Frequency	Per cent	Valid per cent	Cumulative per cent
Valid	1	1	6.7	6.7	6.7
	2	9	60.0	60.0	66.7
	3	3	20.0	20.0	86.7
	4	2	13.3	13.3	100.0
	Total	15	100.0	100.0	

Table 6 Employee satisfaction with updated system

I am satisfied with the updated Oracle system					
		Frequency	Per cent	Valid per cent	Cumulative per cent
Valid	1	1	6.7	6.7	6.7
	2	11	73.3	73.3	80.0
	3	3	20.0	20.0	100.0
	Total	15	100.0	100.0	

The data indicates that most respondents (66.7%) found it challenging to perform and complete their year-end reporting tasks, with a notable portion finding it difficult (13.3%). Only a small percentage felt neutral about completing these tasks, and none found it easy.

Table 5 represents responses to the statement, "I have managed to submit my work reports on time during the Oracle System upgrade."

The data indicates that most respondents (60.0%) found submitting their work reports on time challenging during the Oracle System upgrade, with a small portion (6.7%) finding it very difficult. A smaller group (13.3%) managed to submit on time, while 20.0% were neutral.

Table 6 represents responses to the statement, "I am satisfied with the updated Oracle system."

The data indicates that most respondents (73.3%) were dissatisfied with the updated Oracle system, with a small portion (6.7%) being very dissatisfied. A smaller group (20.0%) had a neutral stance on satisfaction.

Table 7 represents responses to the statement, "I am satisfied with my level of productivity during the Oracle system upgrade."

The data indicates that most respondents (60.0%) were dissatisfied with their productivity levels during the Oracle system upgrade, with a smaller portion (13.3%) being very dissatisfied. A smaller group (26.7%) had a neutral stance on their productivity levels.

Table 8 represents responses to the statement, "I felt inconvenienced during the Oracle upgrade as my work mode was distracted."

Table 7 Employee satisfaction with productivity levels

I am satisfied with my level of productivity during the Oracle system upgrade					
		Frequency	Per cent	Valid per cent	Cumulative per cent
Valid	1	2	13.3	13.3	13.3
	2	9	60.0	60.0	73.3
	3	4	26.7	26.7	100.0
	Total	15	100.0	100.0	

Table 8 System upgrade distractions

I felt inconvenienced during the Oracle upgrade as my work mode was distracted					
		Frequency	Per cent	Valid per cent	Cumulative per cent
Valid	2	4	26.7	26.7	26.7
	3	3	20.0	20.0	46.7
	4	8	53.3	53.3	100.0
	Total	15	100.0	100.0	

The data indicates that most respondents (53.3%) felt highly inconvenienced during the Oracle upgrade due to distractions in their work mode. A significant portion (26.7%) felt moderately inconvenienced, while a smaller group (20.0%) experienced moderate inconvenience. This suggests that the upgrade had a notable disruptive impact on the employees' work modes.

Table 9 presents responses to the statement, "The report drawn from the latest version of the Oracle system has improved compared to the previous versions."

The data suggests that most respondents (60.0%) perceived an improvement in reports drawn from the latest version of the Oracle system compared to previous versions. A notable portion (26.7%) expressed moderate agreement, while a smaller minority (13.3%) strongly agreed with the statement.

Table 10 represents responses to the statement, "It is now easier to navigate the Oracle System than the previous versions."

The data indicates that a significant portion of respondents (80.0%) perceived an improvement in the ease of navigating the Oracle System compared to previous versions. While a majority agreed with this statement, a minority (20.0%) strongly agreed, suggesting that some users found the improvement especially notable.

Table 11 represents responses to the statement, "The latest Oracle System is easy to understand."

The data indicates that most respondents (73.3%) found the latest Oracle System easy to understand, while a smaller portion (26.7%) agreed to a lesser extent. Overall, the majority view leans heavily towards ease of understanding.

Table 9 Reporting

The report drawn from the latest version of the Oracle system has improved compared to the previous versions					
		Frequency	Per cent	Valid per cent	Cumulative per cent
Valid	2	4	26.7	26.7	26.7
	3	9	60.0	60.0	86.7
	4	2	13.3	13.3	100.0
	Total	15	100.0	100.0	

Table 10 User-friendly

Navigating the Oracle System is now easier than the previous versions					
		Frequency	Per cent	Valid per cent	Cumulative per cent
Valid	2	6	40.0	40.0	40.0
	3	6	40.0	40.0	80.0
	4	3	20.0	20.0	100.0
	Total	15	100.0	100.0	

Table 11 Easy to understand

The latest Oracle System is easy to understand					
		Frequency	Per cent	Valid per cent	Cumulative per cent
Valid	2	11	73.3	73.3	73.3
	3	4	26.7	26.7	100.0
	Total	15	100.0	100.0	

Exploratory Analysis

Two questions were asked of the respondents to get their views on the impact of the ERP upgrade on their productivity, and the answers were analysed using themes.

The first question was, "Does using the newly upgraded system enhance productivity? Please explain." Seven out of the fifteen respondents indicated that the upgrade had no significant changes as they could not notice any changes to the new upgraded system compared to the old version. Others indicated that there was a material improvement by indicating, "We are now able to store our contracts with alerts." From this comment, it is visible that this respondent sees a benefit and improvement in having alerts when recording contracts. There was also a mixture of views by respondents on how the upgrade affected them, and some of the responses are quoted below:

Positive:

- User-friendly and effective
- Makes life easier
- Faster compared to the previous Oracle system

Negative:

- The latest upgrade is insignificant, but we expect more remarkable improvements with Oracle Cloud.
- Transition taking longer than desired.

A mixture of positive and negative:

- Some aspects have a positive impact, such as accessing new functionality. However, impossible upgrade timelines led to inadequate testing and inaccurate data, negatively impacting productivity.

The second question was, "Does the use of the newly upgraded system enhance the quality of services you provide to your client/customers? Please explain." For this question, ten respondents indicated that the upgraded ERP system did not enhance the quality of work they offer their clients.

Upgrades are often done on a "like-to-like" basis, not testing or implementing new functionality. One respondent quoted the following as issues that they picked up relating to the upgrade.

- Services remain the same after upgrades.
- Long timelines for implementation lead to last-minute crises.
- Need more time for testing and deployment.
- Timelines for the project needed to be more consistent and adequately communicated.
- Proper implementation and upgrade handling are essential for service delivery and functionality.

While the other six respondents responded with a yes with the following themes when justifying their responses.

- A few errors picked up.
- User-friendly and effective.
- The new system makes reporting quick and easy.
- Can enhance service quality.

Discussions

This study explored the impact of ERP system upgrades on employee productivity, focusing on service quality and user satisfaction during a critical financial reporting period. The findings indicate that while there were perceived improvements in the system's user-friendliness and reporting capabilities, significant challenges were experienced in training adequacy, ease of completing year-end tasks, and overall productivity.

Most respondents acknowledged improvements in the Oracle system's user-friendliness and reporting capabilities, aligning with previous literature highlighting the benefits of ERP systems in enhancing operational efficiency and information accuracy (Qutaishat et al., 2012; Aljarrah, 2021). Specifically, 73.3% of respondents found the updated system easier to navigate, and 60% noticed an improvement in the quality of reports. These findings are consistent with studies by Nzama (2021) and AlMuhayfith and Shaiti (2020), which emphasise the potential of ERP systems to streamline processes and improve data quality.

However, significant concerns were raised regarding the adequacy of training during the upgrade. A majority of respondents (46.7%) felt that the training was insufficient, which aligns with the findings of Qutaishat et al. (2012) and AlMuhayfith and Shaiti (2020), who found that inadequate training can hinder the successful adoption and usage of ERP systems. The lack of comprehensive training likely contributed to the challenges faced in completing year-end reporting tasks, with 66.7% of respondents reporting difficulties in this area. This underscores the importance of proper training and support during ERP implementations, as Ramadhani et al. (2023) and Aroba et al. (2023) highlighted.

The disruptions caused by the upgrade significantly impacted productivity, with 60% of respondents reporting challenges in submitting work reports on time and 73.3% expressing dissatisfaction with their productivity levels during the upgrade. These disruptions align with findings from Domagała et al. (2021), who stress the importance of careful planning and timing in ERP system upgrades to minimise operational disruptions. Additionally, 53.3% of respondents felt highly inconvenienced due to the upgrade, further highlighting the negative impact on their work modes.

In terms of user satisfaction, a substantial portion of respondents (73.3%) expressed dissatisfaction with the updated Oracle system, suggesting that the benefits of the new features still needed to be fully realised due to the challenges above. This finding aligns with the Technology Acceptance Model (TAM) and Unified Theory of Acceptance and Use of Technology (UTAUT), which emphasise that perceived ease of use and usefulness are critical determinants of user satisfaction and acceptance (Davis, 1989; Venkatesh et al., 2003).

Recommendations

Based on the study's findings, several recommendations are proposed to enhance the effectiveness of future ERP upgrades and mitigate the challenges identified:

Comprehensive Training Programmes:

- *Pre-Upgrade Training*: Develop and implement comprehensive training sessions before the ERP upgrade to familiarise users with the new system features and functionalities. This can improve user confidence and ease the transition.
- *Post-Upgrade Support*: Provide ongoing training and support post-upgrade to address any issues and reinforce learning. This aligns with the recommendations by Qutaishat et al. (2012) and Ramadhani et al. (2023).

Effective Planning and Communication

- Ensure detailed planning of the upgrade process, considering critical business periods to minimise disruptions. As suggested by Domagała et al. (2021), aligning upgrade schedules with non-critical times can prevent significant productivity losses.

Clear Communication

- Maintain clear and consistent communication with all stakeholders throughout the upgrade process. This includes informing users about the upgrade timeline, potential impacts, and support available, which is crucial for managing expectations and reducing resistance to change (Lewin's Change Management Model).

User Involvement in Testing:

- Involve end users in the testing phase of the ERP upgrade to gather feedback and identify potential issues early. This participatory approach can enhance system acceptance and ensure the system meets user needs, supporting the findings of Cruz-Torres et al. (2021).

Enhanced System Support:

- Establish dedicated support teams to provide immediate assistance during and after the upgrade. This can help resolve issues quickly and maintain productivity levels.
- Feedback mechanisms:

Continuous Feedback Loop

- Implement mechanisms for continuous user feedback to monitor the system's performance and address any emerging issues promptly. This ongoing engagement can improve user satisfaction and system effectiveness.

HEIs and other organisations can optimise their ERP upgrade processes by implementing these recommendations, ensuring smoother transitions and improved outcomes. These steps can help mitigate the challenges identified in this study, ultimately enhancing employee productivity and satisfaction with the ERP system.

Conclusion

In conclusion, this study aims to assess the impact of ERP system upgrades on employee productivity within a higher education institution (HEI). The primary objective was to determine how these upgrades influenced employee productivity, with secondary objectives focusing on their effects on financial year-end reporting and service quality and the relationship between ERP users' satisfaction and service quality. The findings shed light on several key aspects of ERP system upgrades within the HEI context. While most respondents perceived proper planning and communication during the upgrade process, there were mixed views regarding the sufficiency of training provided. Challenges in productivity and timely reporting were evident during the upgrade period, underscoring the importance of effective change management strategies. Employee dissatisfaction with the upgraded system and productivity levels highlights the need to address user concerns to enhance overall satisfaction and productivity. Despite these challenges, reporting and user-friendly navigation improvements were positively perceived, suggesting potential benefits in enhancing operational efficiency and user experience.

The study's findings emphasise the critical role of comprehensive planning, transparent communication, and training investment to optimise ERP system upgrade outcomes. Furthermore, ongoing evaluation and employee involvement are essential for continuous improvements and successful ERP implementation. Moving forward, organisations should prioritise addressing user concerns, minimising disruptions during upgrades, and fostering a positive work environment conducive to productivity and satisfaction. By addressing these aspects, HEIs can maximise the benefits of ERP system upgrades and enhance their effectiveness in supporting organisational goals and objectives.

Limitations and Future Research

This research is limited to ERP key users' perspectives on an HEI. Thus, the study is limited to only one HEI out of 26 HEIs in the country. For future studies in this area, several recommendations can be made to explore further the impact of ERP system upgrades on employee productivity and related factors within different organisational contexts:

Longitudinal studies: Conduct longitudinal studies to track the long-term effects of ERP system upgrades on employee productivity, satisfaction, and organisational performance. Longitudinal research can provide insights into how these factors evolve over time and whether initial challenges persist or diminish over the long term.

Comparative analysis: Compare the impact of ERP system upgrades across different industries, organisational sizes, and geographical locations. Comparative studies can reveal potential differences in the effects of upgrades based on contextual factors, helping to identify best practices and tailor strategies to specific organisational needs.

Qualitative research: Supplement quantitative data with qualitative insights to better understand employees' experiences with ERP system upgrades. Qualitative research methods such as interviews, focus groups, or case studies can provide rich, nuanced perspectives on the challenges, benefits, and overall impact of upgrades on employees and organisational processes.

Employee training interventions: Explore the effectiveness of different training interventions in preparing employees for ERP system upgrades. Comparative studies can assess the impact of various training methods (e.g. in-person training, e-learning modules, hands-on workshops) on user proficiency, confidence, and performance post-upgrade.

Change management strategies: Investigate the role of change management strategies in facilitating successful ERP system upgrades. Research could focus on identifying effective change management practices, communication strategies, and leadership approaches to minimise resistance to change and promote user acceptance.

By addressing these areas in future research endeavours, scholars can contribute to a more comprehensive understanding of the implications of ERP system upgrades for organisations and their employees, ultimately informing evidence-based practices for successful implementation and optimisation.

References

Aljarrah, M. (2021). The impact of enterprise resource planning system of human resources on the employees' performance appraisal in Jordan. *WSEAS Transactions on Environment and Development, 17*(35), 351–359.

AlMuhayfith, S., & Shaiti, H. (2020). The impact of enterprise resource planning on business performance: With the discussion on its relationship with open innovation. *Journal of Open Innovation: Technology, Market, and Complexity, 6*(3), 87.

Aroba, O. J., Chisita, C. T., Buthelezi, N., & Mthethwa, N. (2023, February). Higher education enterprise resource planning system transformation of supply chain management processes. In *International congress on information and communication technology* (pp. 415–424). Springer Nature Singapore.

Bandura, A. (1999). Social cognitive theory: An agentic perspective. Asian journal of social psychology, 2(1), 21–41.

Bokhari, R. H. (2005). The relationship between system usage and user satisfaction: A meta-analysis. *Journal of Enterprise Information Management, 18*(2), 211–234.

Bright, L. (2007). Does person-organization fit mediate the relationship between public service motivation and the job performance of public employees?. Review of public personnel administration, 27(4), 361–379.

Chang, M. K., Cheung, W., Cheng, C. H., & Yeung, J. H. (2008). Understanding ERP system adoption from the user's perspective. *International Journal of Production Economics, 113*(2), 928–942.

Chopra, R., Sawant, L., Kodi, D., & Terkar, R. (2022). Utilisation of ERP systems in the manufacturing industry for productivity improvement. *Materials Today: Proceedings, 62*, 1238–1245.

Cruz-Torres, W., Alvarez-Risco, A., & Del-Aguila-Arcentales, S. (2021). Impact of enterprise resource planning (ERP) implementation on performance of an education enterprise: Structural equation Modeling (SEM). *Studies in Business and Economics, 16*(2), 37–52.

Davis, F. D. (1989). Technology acceptance model: TAM. Al-Suqri, MN, Al-Aufi, AS: Information Seeking Behavior and Technology Adoption, 205(219): 5.

Domagała, A., Grobler-Dębska, K., Wąs, J., & Kucharska, E. (2021). Post-implementation ERP software development: Upgrade or reimplementation. *Applied Sciences, 11*(11), 4937.

Kirmizi, M., & Kocaoglu, B. (2022). The influencing factors of enterprise resource planning (ERP) readiness stage on enterprise resource planning project success: A project manager's perspective. *Kybernetes, 51*(3), 1089–1113.

Lin, H. F. (2010). An investigation into the effects of IS quality and top management support on ERP system usage. *Total Quality Management, 21*(3), 335–349.

Melville, N., Kraemer, K., & Gurbaxani, V. (2004). Information technology and organisational performance: An integrative model of IT business value. *MIS Quarterly*, 283–322.

Nwankpa, J., & Roumani, Y. (2014). Understanding the link between organisational learning capability and ERP system usage: An empirical examination. *Computers in Human Behavior, 33*, 224–234.

Nzama, L. L. (2015). *The effect of enterprise resource planning systems on the financial statement audit of a higher education institution*. University of Johannesburg.

Nzama, L. (2021). Enterprise resource planning (ERP) upgrades in South African higher education institutions: Pros, cons and financial efficacy. *Journal of Global Business and Technology, 17*(1), 98–109.

Qutaishat, F. T., Khattab, S. A., Zaid, M. K. S. A., & Al-Manasra, E. A. (2012). The effect of ERP successful implementation on employees' productivity, service quality, and innovation: An empirical study in the telecommunication sector in Jordan. *International Journal of Business and Management, 7*(19), 45.

Ramadhani, P., Indrijawati, A., & Ferdiansyah, M. I. (2023). Studi Literatur Sistematis: Faktor Penentu Keberhasilan Penerapan ERP Dalam Organisasi. *ISAFIR: Islamic Accounting and Finance Review, 4*(1), 58–71.

Ruivo, P., Johansson, B., Oliveira, T., & Neto, M. (2012). Determinants that influence ERP use and value: Cross-country evidence on Scandinavian and Iberian SMEs. *Procedia Technology, 5*, 354–362.

Venkatesh, Viswanath, Michael G. Morris, Gordon B. Davis, and Fred D. Davis. (2003). "User acceptance of information technology: Toward a unified view." MIS quarterly: 425–478.

GPSR Compliance

The European Union's (EU) General Product Safety Regulation (GPSR) is a set of rules that requires consumer products to be safe and our obligations to ensure this.

If you have any concerns about our products, you can contact us on ProductSafety@springernature.com

In case Publisher is established outside the EU, the EU authorized representative is:

Springer Nature Customer Service Center GmbH
Europaplatz 3
69115 Heidelberg, Germany

Batch number: 10761593

Printed by Printforce, the Netherlands